ADVERTISING AND PROMOTION

AN INTEGRATED MARKETING COMMUNICATIONS PERSPECTIVE

ADVERTISING AND PROMOTION

AN INTEGRATED MARKETING COMMUNICATIONS PERSPECTIVE

11e

George E. Belch & Michael A. Belch

Both of San Diego State University

McGraw Hill Education

ADVERTISING & PROMOTION

1 2 3 4 5 6 7 8 9 LWI 21 20 19 18 17

ISBN 978-1-259-92169-8
MHID 1-259-92169-7

To Jessica and Milos—thanks for making me so proud! (MAB)

To Gayle and all those who S↑2C—Keep up the fight! (GEB)

ABOUT THE AUTHORS

Dr. George E. Belch

George E. Belch is professor of marketing and chair of the marketing department at San Diego State University, where he teaches integrated marketing communications and strategic marketing. Prior to joining San Diego State, he was a member of the faculty in the Graduate School of Management, University of California, Irvine. He received his PhD in marketing from the University of California, Los Angeles. Before entering academia, Dr. Belch was a marketing representative for the DuPont Company. He also worked as a research analyst for the DDB Worldwide advertising agency.

Dr. Belch's research interests are in the area of consumer processing of advertising information as well as managerial aspects of integrated marketing communications. He has authored or coauthored more than 30 articles in leading academic journals and proceedings, including the *Journal of Marketing Research, Journal of Consumer Research, International Journal of Advertising, Journal of Promotion Management, Journal of Advertising,* and *Journal of Business Research.* In 2000, he was selected as Marketing Educator of the Year by the Marketing Educators' Association for his career achievements in teaching and research. He also received the Distinguished Faculty Member Award for the College of Business Administration at San Diego State University in 1994 and 2003.

Dr. Belch has taught in executive education and development programs for various universities around the world. He has also conducted seminars on integrated marketing communications as well as marketing planning and strategy for a number of multinational companies including Sprint, Microsoft, Qualcomm, Arbitron, Square D Corporation, Armstrong World Industries, and Texas Industries.

Dr. Michael A. Belch

Michael (Mickey) A. Belch is a professor of marketing at San Diego State University and is also director of the Centre for Integrated Marketing Communications at San Diego State. He received his undergraduate degree from Penn State University, his MBA from Drexel University, and his PhD from the University of Pittsburgh.

Before entering academia he was employed by the General Foods Corporation as a marketing representative, and has served as a consultant to numerous companies including McDonald's, Whirlpool Corporation, Senco Products, GTI Corporation, IVAC, May Companies, Phillips-Ramsey Advertising and Public Relations, and Daily & Associates Advertising. He has conducted seminars on integrated marketing and marketing management for a number of multinational companies and has also taught in executive education programs in France, Amsterdam, Spain, Chile, Peru, Argentina, Colombia, China, Slovenia, and Greece. He is the author or coauthor of more than 50 articles in academic journals and proceedings in the areas of advertising, consumer behavior, and international marketing including the *Journal of Advertising, Journal of Advertising Research, Journal of Business Research, Journal of Promotion Management,* and *International Journal of Advertising.* Dr. Belch is also a member of the editorial review board of the *Journal of Advertising* and the *International Journal of Advertising.* He received outstanding teaching awards from undergraduate and graduate students numerous times. He also received the Distinguished Faculty Member Award for the College of Business Administration at San Diego State University in 2007. He was recently awarded the Giep Franzen Fellowship from the University of Amsterdam.

PREFACE

THE CHANGING WORLD OF ADVERTISING AND PROMOTION

Nearly everyone in the modern world is influenced to some degree by advertising and other forms of promotion. Organizations in both the private and public sectors have learned that the ability to communicate effectively and efficiently with their target audiences is critical to their success. Advertising and other types of promotional messages are used to sell products and services as well as to promote causes, market political candidates, and deal with societal problems such as alcohol and drug abuse. Consumers are finding it increasingly difficult to avoid the efforts of marketers, who are constantly searching for new ways to communicate with them.

Most of the people involved in advertising and promotion will tell you that there is no more dynamic and fascinating field to either practice or study. However, they will also tell you that the field is undergoing dramatic transformations that are changing the ways marketers communicate with consumers forever. The changes are coming from all sides—clients demanding better results from their advertising and promotional dollars; lean but highly creative smaller ad agencies; sales promotion and direct-marketing firms, as well as interactive agencies, that want a larger share of the billions of dollars companies spend each year promoting their products and services; consumers who have changed the ways they respond to traditional forms of advertising; new media and new technologies that are reshaping the ways marketers communicate with consumers. We are experiencing perhaps the most dynamic and revolutionary changes of any era in the history of marketing, as well as advertising and promotion. These changes are being driven by advances in technology and developments that have led to the rapid growth of communications through digital media, particularly the Internet, social media, and mobile devices.

Companies from outside the traditional advertising industry are rapidly changing the process of making and delivering advertising messages to consumers. Marketers are looking beyond traditional mass-media advertising to find new and more effective ways to communicate with their target audiences. They recognize there are numerous ways to reach their current and prospective customers and bring them into contact with their products and services. Many marketers view digital ads as a more cost-effective way to reach specific target markets and measure the results of their marketing efforts. Major changes are taking place in the way marketers are using the Internet for marketing communications, including new applications that facilitate interactive information sharing and collaboration and bilateral, as opposed to unilateral, communication. Web 2.0 developments mean that digital users are no longer limited to the passive viewing of information and can interact with one another as well as companies and/or organizations. These applications have led to the development of social networking sites, video sharing sites, blogs, and online communities which have all experienced explosive growth. A little more than a decade ago Facebook, Twitter, YouTube, Instagram, and LinkedIn did not even exist. Facebook now has more than 1.6 billion users around the world, Twitter boasts over 300 million, and nearly 5 billion videos are viewed each day on YouTube, including many of the TV commercials and other promotional videos created by marketers. Nearly all companies or organizations have a Facebook, Instagram, and Twitter page that they use to keep in constant contact with their customers while many marketers are also beginning to use Snapchat to reach younger consumers. These tools, along with other types of social media, have become an integral part of most marketers' marketing communications programs. However, the increased use of the Internet and social media is only the latest in a number of fundamental changes that have been occurring in the way companies plan, develop, and execute their marketing communications programs.

For decades the advertising business was dominated by large, full-service Madison Avenue–type agencies. The advertising strategy for a national brand involved creating one or two commercials that could be run on network television, a few print ads that would run in general-interest magazines, and some sales promotion support such as coupons or premium offers. However, in today's world there are a myriad of media outlets—print, radio, cable and satellite TV, and mobile to mention a few—competing for consumers' attention. Marketers are looking beyond traditional media to find new and better ways to communicate with their customers because they no longer accept on faith the value of conventional advertising placed in traditional media. Major marketers have moved away from a reliance just on mass-media advertising and are spending more of their marketing communications budgets in specialized media that target specific markets. Companies are also spending more of their monies in other ways such as event marketing, sponsorships, cause-related promotions, and viral marketing. Advertising agencies are recognizing that they must change the way they do business.

In addition to redefining the role and nature of their advertising agencies, marketers are changing the way they communicate with consumers. They know they are operating in an environment where advertising messages are everywhere, consumers channel-surf past most TV commercials, and brands promoted in traditional ways often fail. New-age advertisers are redefining the notion of what an ad is and where it runs. Stealth messages are being woven into the culture and embedded into movies and TV shows or made into their own form of entertainment. Many experts argue that "branded content" is the wave of the future, and there is a growing movement to reinvent advertising and other forms of marketing communication to be more akin to entertainment. Companies are using branded entertainment as a way of reaching consumers by creating short films that can be viewed online, arranging product placements, and integrating their brands into movies and television shows to promote their products and services.

A number of factors are impacting the way marketers communicate with consumers. The audiences that marketers seek, along with the media and methods for reaching them, have become increasingly fragmented. Advertising and promotional efforts have become more targeted and are often retargeted to specific audiences over the Internet. Retailers have become larger and more powerful, forcing marketers to shift money from advertising budgets to sales promotion. Marketers often expect their promotional dollars to generate immediate sales and are demanding more accountability from their agencies. The digital revolution is in full force, and new ways to communicate with consumers are constantly being developed. Many companies are coordinating all their communications efforts so that they can send cohesive messages to their customers. Some companies are building brands with little or no use of traditional media advertising, relying instead on digital and social media. Many advertising agencies have acquired, started, or become affiliated with sales promotion, direct-marketing, interactive agencies, and public relations companies to better serve their clients' marketing communications needs. Their clients have become "media-neutral" and are asking that they consider whatever form of marketing communication works best to target market segments and build long-term reputations and short-term sales.

This text introduces students to this fast-changing field of marketing communications. While advertising is its primary focus, it is more than just an introductory advertising text because there is more to most organizations' promotional programs than just advertising. As marketers now have changed the mix of traditional media and new media in their communications strategies, the focus of this text has changed as well, placing additional emphasis on new media. The changes discussed previously are leading marketers and their agencies to approach advertising and promotion from an integrated marketing communications

(IMC) perspective, which calls for a "big picture" approach to planning marketing and promotion programs and coordinating the various communication functions. To understand the role of advertising and promotion in today's business world, one must recognize how a firm can use all the promotional tools to communicate with its customers. The eleventh edition of this text has addressed this issue, and more than any previous edition now offers a much broader IMC perspective.

TO THE STUDENT: PREPARING YOU FOR THE NEW WORLD OF ADVERTISING AND PROMOTION

Some of you are taking this course to learn more about this fascinating field; many of you hope to work in advertising, digital/social media, or some other promotional area. The changes in the industry have profound implications for the way today's student is trained and educated. You will not be working for the same kind of marketing communication agencies that existed a few years ago. If you work on the client side of the business, you will find that the way clients approach advertising and promotion is changing dramatically.

Today's student is expected to understand all the major marketing communication tools: advertising, direct marketing, sales promotion, public relations, personal selling, and of course the Internet and the rapidly growing areas of social media and mobile marketing. You will also be expected to know how to research and evaluate a company's marketing and promotional situation and how to use various tools to develop effective communication strategies and programs. Marketers are also giving more attention to the determination of return on investment (ROI) of various IMC tools as well as the challenges they face in making this evaluation. This book will help prepare you for these challenges.

As professors we were, of course, once students ourselves. In many ways we are perpetual students as we are constantly striving to learn more about the constantly changing field of IMC. We share many of your interests and concerns and are often excited (and bored) by the same things. Having taught in the advertising and promotion area for a combined 80-plus years, we have developed an understanding of what makes a book in this field interesting to students. In writing this book, we have tried to remember how we felt about the various texts we used throughout the years and to incorporate the good things and minimize those we felt were of little use. We have tried not to overburden you with definitions, although we do call out those that are especially important to your understanding of the material.

We also remember that as students we were not always excited about theory. But to fully understand how integrated marketing communications works, it is necessary to establish some theoretical basis. The more you understand about how things are supposed to work, the easier it will be for you to understand why they do or do not turn out as planned.

Perhaps the question students ask most often is, How do I use this in the real world? In response we provide numerous examples of how the various theories and concepts in the text can be used in practice. A particular strength of this text is the integration of theory with practical application. Nearly every day an example of advertising and promotion in practice is reported in the media. We have used many sources, such as *Advertising Age, Adweek, The Wall Street Journal, Bloomberg Businessweek, The Economist, Fortune, Forbes, Sales & Marketing Management, Fast Company,* and numerous online sites such as eMarketer, Mashable, MediaPost.com, ClickZ News, and many, many more to find practical examples that are discussed throughout the text. We have spoken with marketing and agency personnel about the strategies and rationale behind the ads and other types of promotions we use as examples. Each chapter begins with a vignette that presents an example of an advertising or promotional campaign or other interesting insights. Every chapter also contains several **IMC Perspectives** that present in-depth discussions of particular issues related to the chapter material and show how companies are using integrated marketing communications. **Global Perspectives** are presented throughout the text in recognition of the increasing importance of international marketing and the challenges of advertising and promotion and the role they play in the marketing programs of multinational marketers. **Ethical Perspectives** focus attention on important social issues and show how advertisers must take ethical considerations into account when planning and implementing advertising and promotional programs. **Digital and Social Media Perspectives** focus on how changes and/or advances in the use of social media are impacting the field of integrated marketing communications.

Each chapter features beautiful four-color illustrations showing examples from many of the most current and best-integrated marketing communication campaigns being used around the world. We have included more than 350 advertisements and examples of numerous other types of promotion, all of which were carefully chosen to illustrate a particular concept, theory, or practical application. Please take time to read the opening vignettes to each chapter, the IMC, Global, Ethical, and Digital and Social Media Perspectives, and study the diverse ads and illustrations. We think they will stimulate your interest and relate to your daily life as a consumer and a target of advertising and promotion.

TO THE INSTRUCTOR: A TEXT THAT REFLECTS THE CHANGES IN THE WORLD OF ADVERTISING AND PROMOTION

Our major goal in writing the eleventh edition of *Advertising and Promotion* was to continue to provide you with the most comprehensive and current text on the market for teaching advertising and promotion from an IMC perspective. This new edition focuses on the many changes that are occurring in areas of marketing communications and how they influence advertising and promotional strategies and tactics. We have done this by continuing with the *integrated marketing communications perspective.* Most companies now approach advertising and promotion from an IMC perspective, coordinating the various promotional-mix elements with other marketing activities that communicate with a firm's customers. Many advertising agencies are also developing expertise in direct marketing, sales promotion, event sponsorship, the Internet, social media, and mobile and other areas so that they can meet all their clients' integrated marketing communications needs— and, of course, survive.

The book is built around an integrated marketing communications planning model and recognizes the importance of coordinating all of the promotional-mix elements to develop an effective communications program. Although traditional and new media advertising is often the most visible part of a firm's promotional program, attention must also be given to direct marketing, sales promotion, public relations, support media, and personal selling. The text also integrates theory with practice. To effectively plan, implement, and evaluate IMC programs, one must understand the overall marketing process, consumer behavior, and communications theory. We draw from the extensive research in advertising, consumer behavior, communications, marketing, sales promotion, and other fields to give students a basis for understanding the marketing communications process, how it influences consumer decision making, and how to develop promotional strategies.

While this is an introductory text, we do treat each topic in some depth. We believe the marketing and advertising student of today needs a text that provides more than just an introduction to terms and topics. The book is positioned primarily for the introductory advertising, marketing communications, or promotions course as taught in the business/marketing curriculum. It can also be used in journalism/communications courses that take an integrated marketing communications perspective. Many schools also use the text at the graduate level. In addition to its thorough coverage of advertising, this text has chapters on sales promotion, direct marketing, the Internet including social media and mobile marketing, support media such as outdoor advertising, product placement and integration, and publicity/public relations. These chapters stress the integration of advertising with other promotional-mix elements and the need to understand their role and the contribution they make to the overall marketing program.

ORGANIZATION OF THIS TEXT

This book is divided into seven major parts. In Part One we examine the role of advertising and promotion in marketing and introduce the concept of integrated marketing communications. Chapter 1 provides an overview of advertising and promotion and its role in modern marketing. The concept of IMC and the factors that have led to its growth are discussed. Each of the promotional-mix elements is defined, and an IMC planning model shows the various steps in the promotional planning process. This model provides a framework for developing the integrated marketing communications program and is followed throughout the text. Chapter 2 examines the role of advertising and promotion in the overall marketing program, with attention to the various elements of the marketing mix and how they interact with advertising and promotional strategy. We have also included coverage of market segmentation, target marketing, and positioning in this chapter so that students can understand how these concepts fit into the overall marketing programs as well as their role in the development of an advertising and promotional program.

In Part Two we cover the promotional program situation analysis. Chapter 3 describes how firms organize for advertising and promotion and examines the role of ad agencies and other firms that provide marketing and promotional services. We discuss how ad agencies are selected, evaluated, and compensated as well as the changes occurring in the agency business. Attention is also given to other types of marketing communication organizations such as direct marketing, sales promotion, and digital interactive agencies as well as public relations firms. We also consider whether responsibility for integrating the various communication functions lies with the client or the agency. Chapter 4 covers the stages of the consumer decision-making process and both the internal psychological factors and the external factors that influence consumer behavior. The focus of this chapter is on how advertisers can use an understanding of buyer behavior to develop effective advertising and other forms of promotion.

Part Three analyzes the communication process. Chapter 5 examines various communication theories and models of how consumers respond to advertising messages and other forms of marketing communications. Chapter 6 provides a detailed discussion of source, message, and channel factors.

In Part Four we consider how firms develop goals and objectives for their integrated marketing communications programs and determine how much money to spend and where to spend it in trying to achieve them. Chapter 7 stresses the importance of knowing what to expect from advertising and promotion, the differences between advertising and communication objectives, characteristics of good objectives, and problems in setting objectives. We have also integrated the discussion of various methods for determining and allocating the promotional budget into this chapter. These first four sections of the text provide students with a solid background in the areas of marketing, consumer behavior, communications, planning, objective setting, and budgeting. This background lays the foundation for the next section, where we discuss the development of the integrated marketing communications program.

Part Five examines the various promotional-mix elements that form the basis of the integrated marketing communications program. Chapter 8 discusses the planning and development of the creative strategy and advertising campaign and examines the creative process. In Chapter 9 we turn our attention to ways to execute the creative strategy and some criteria for evaluating creative work. Chapters 10 through 13 cover media strategy and planning and the various advertising media. Chapter 10 introduces the key principles of media planning and strategy and examines how a media plan is developed. Chapter 11 discusses the advantages and disadvantages of the broadcast media (TV and radio) as well as issues regarding the purchase of radio and TV time and audience measurement. Chapter 12 considers the same issues for the print media (magazines and newspapers). Chapter 13 examines the role of traditional support media such as outdoor and transit advertising, advertising in movie theaters, as well as the tremendous increase in the use of nontraditional branded entertainment strategies such as product placements, product integration, and in-game advertising.

In Chapters 14 through 17 we continue the IMC emphasis by examining other promotional tools that are used in the integrated marketing communications process. Chapter 14 explores the role of direct marketing. This chapter examines the ways companies communicate directly with target customers through various direct-response media, including direct mail, infomercials, direct-response TV commercials, and e-commerce. Chapter 15 provides a detailed discussion of marketers' use of the Internet and digital and social media. We examine the increasing use of display ads, blogs, mobile, paid search, and social media. We also give more attention to how the Internet is used to implement various IMC activities including both Web 1.0 and 2.0 strategies, as well as mobile marketing. Chapter 16 examines the area of sales promotion, including both consumer-oriented promotions and programs targeted to the trade (retailers, wholesalers, and other intermediaries). Chapter 17 covers the role of publicity and public relations in IMC as well as corporate advertising and cause-related marketing. Basic issues regarding personal selling and its role in promotion strategy are presented in Chapter 22, which is available online in this edition.

Part Six of the text consists of Chapter 18, where we discuss ways to measure the effectiveness of various elements of the integrated marketing communications program, including methods for pretesting and post-testing advertising messages and campaigns, in both traditional and new media. In Part Seven we turn our attention to special markets, topics, and perspectives that are becoming increasingly important in contemporary marketing. In Chapter 19 we examine the global marketplace and the role of advertising and other promotional-mix variables such as sales promotion, public relations, and the Internet in international marketing.

The text concludes with a discussion of the regulatory, social, and economic environments in which advertising and promotion operate. Chapter 20 examines industry self-regulation and regulation of advertising by governmental agencies such as the Federal Trade Commission, as well as rules and regulations governing sales promotion, direct marketing, and marketing on the Internet. Because advertising's role in society is constantly changing, our discussion would not be complete without a look at the criticisms frequently levied, so in Chapter 21 we consider the social, ethical, and economic aspects of advertising and promotion.

CHAPTER FEATURES

The following features in each chapter enhance students' understanding of the material as well as their reading enjoyment.

Learning Objectives

Learning objectives are provided at the beginning of each chapter to identify the major areas and points covered in the chapter and guide the learning effort. We also indicate where specific learning objectives are covered within the chapter and how the discussion questions are keyed to the objectives.

Chapter Opening Vignettes

Each chapter begins with a vignette that shows the effective use of integrated marketing communications by a company or ad agency or discusses an interesting issue that is relevant to the chapter. These opening vignettes are designed to draw the students into the chapter by presenting an interesting example, development, or issue that relates to the material covered in the chapter. Companies, brands, and/or campaigns featured in

the opening vignettes include Charmin, Under Armour, Buick, Always, TurboTax, Dasani, Hershey, and Coca-Cola. Some of the chapter openers discuss current topics and issues impacting integrated marketing communications such as the rapid growth and popularity of programmatic media buying; the impact of the digital revolution on advertising agencies, measurement of the effectiveness of advertising and promotional messaging and media; changes occurring in traditional media including television, magazines, and newspapers and how they are impacting their use by advertisers; programs supported by marketers such as World Water Day; and public relations problems and opportunities faced by companies as well as movements such as the empowerment of women.

IMC Perspectives

These boxed items feature in-depth discussions of interesting issues related to the chapter material and the practical application of integrated marketing communications. Each chapter contains several of these insights into the world of integrated marketing communications. Some of the companies/brands discussed in the IMC Perspectives include Abercrombie & Fitch, American Apparel, 7UP, Taco Bell, GEICO, MTV, Playboy, and the Detroit Pistons. Issues discussed in The IMC Perspectives include the increasing use of in-house advertising agencies; the role of neuroscience in studying the processing of advertising messages; changes in the measurement of viewing audiences for television commercials; the increasing use of attack ads in political campaigns; how companies use the purchase funnel to manage and guide their IMC programs; the growing popularity of college sports and how they are impacted by television; theories on why infomercials are effective; and sports teams' use of direct marketing to market their teams.

Global Perspectives

These boxed items provide information similar to that in the IMC Perspectives, with a focus on international aspects of advertising and promotion. Some of the companies/brands whose international advertising programs are covered in the Global Perspectives include Procter & Gamble, PepsiCo, and Facebook. The Global Perspectives also discuss topics such as the challenges of developing marketing communication programs in China; celebrities who appear in commercials abroad while protecting their image in the United States; and communication problems in international advertising.

Ethical Perspectives

These boxed items discuss the moral and/or ethical issues regarding practices engaged in by marketers and are also tied to the material presented in the particular chapter. Issues covered in the Ethical Perspectives include subliminal advertising; programs designed to empower women; the debate over the advertising practices in the depiction of women; issues related to native advertising; unethical practices by Internet marketers; and whether direct-to-consumer advertising of pharmaceutical products should be permitted.

Digital and Social Media Perspectives

These boxed items provide a detailed discussion of how changes and advances in digital and social media are impacting the practice of integrated marketing communications. Some of the topics and issues covered in the Digital and Social Media Perspectives include the various ways the digital revolution and developments in technology are impacting the practice of IMC; the increasing use of digital billboards; the measurement of advertising effectiveness using digital techniques; various ways marketers are using virtual reality to communicate with consumers; the role of social media in dealing with publicity; how digital media are impacting traditional print media such as newspapers and magazines; how many marketers are developing creative campaigns for their brands that can go viral through social media; the impact of social media on television viewing behavior; and how marketers are increasingly using digital and social media as part of their IMC programs, often at the expense of traditional media.

Key Terms

Important terms are highlighted in boldface throughout the text and listed at the end of each chapter with a page reference. These terms help call students' attention to important ideas, concepts, and definitions and help them review their learning progress.

Chapter Summaries

These synopses serve as a quick review of important topics covered and a very helpful study guide.

Discussion Questions

Questions at the end of each chapter give students an opportunity to test their understanding of the material and to apply it. The questions can also serve as a basis for class discussion or assignments. The discussion questions are also keyed to the learning objectives for the chapter.

Four-Color Visuals

Print ads, display ads, billboards, and other examples appear throughout the book. More than 400 ads, charts, graphs, and other types of illustrations are included in the text.

Changes in the Eleventh Edition

We have made a number of changes in the eleventh edition to make it as relevant and current as possible, as well as more interesting to students:

- **Updated Coverage of the Emerging Field of Integrated Marketing Communications** The eleventh edition continues to place a strong emphasis on studying advertising and promotion from an integrated marketing communications perspective. We examine contemporary perspectives of integrated marketing communications that have been developed by those doing research and theory development in the area. We also consider developments that are impacting the way marketers communicate with consumers, particularly through the use of digital and social media. Innovative social media–based campaigns for a variety of brands that rely heavily on user-generated content are featured, and attention is given throughout this edition to ways marketers are utilizing Facebook, Twitter, Instagram, Snapchat, and other social media tools. Technologies such as the convergence of television, computers, and mobile devices with the Internet are changing the way companies are using advertising along with other marketing tools to communicate with their customers. In this new edition we examine how these cutting-edge developments are impacting the IMC program of marketers.

- **Expanded Emphasis on Digital and Social Media** The eleventh edition includes up-to-date information on the Internet and other forms of interactive media and how they are being used by marketers. As the business world has expanded its use of digital and social media, and decreased its emphasis on traditional media, we have made significant changes to reflect this movement. The Internet chapter has been revised to reflect the impact of developments related to Web 2.0 while updating information regarding Web 1.0 from the last edition; the title has been changed to "The Internet: Digital and Social Media" to better reflect the content therein. We discuss the use of various Web 2.0 tools that facilitate interactive information sharing and collaboration, including social media and user-generated content such as videos (YouTube), blogs, and podcasts. The discussion on the use of mobile has been expanded to reflect this important development. Specific examples of how companies are using these tools in their IMC programs are provided. We discuss a number of digital-based tools and strategies used by marketers, including display advertising, paid search, behavioral targeting, retargeting, and the use of mobile media. This chapter discusses the latest developments in areas such as audience measurement and methods for determining the effectiveness of digital advertising as well as social media. Discussion of the role of digital and social media as important integrated marketing communications tools and of the ways they are being used by marketers is integrated throughout the eleventh edition.

- **Digital and Social Media Perspectives** In this edition we continue the feature called *Digital and Social Media Perspectives*. These boxed items are designed to focus attention on changes and advances in digital and social media and how they are impacting the practice of integrated marketing communications. There have been significant advances in technology over the past decade and most consumers now have a third screen in their lives either in the form of some type of mobile device such as a smartphone or a tablet. Mobile devices have become an integral part of the lives of many consumers, and traditional media such as magazines and newspapers have developed digital versions of their publications to retain readers as well as to survive. For most marketers, social media tools such as Facebook, Instagram and Twitter have become a basic part of their IMC programs. The various digital and social media perspectives provide students with insight into how advances in digital technology are impacting marketing.

- **New Chapter Opening Vignettes** *All* of the chapter opening vignettes in the eleventh edition are new and were chosen for their currency and relevance to students. They demonstrate how various companies and advertising agencies use advertising and other IMC tools. They also provide interesting insights into some of the current trends and developments that are taking place in the advertising world.

- **New and Updated IMC Perspectives** All of the boxed items focusing on specific examples of how companies and their communications agencies are using integrated marketing communications are new or have been updated, and they provide insight into many of the most current and popular advertising and promotional campaigns being used by marketers. The IMC Perspectives also address interesting issues related to advertising, sales promotion, direct marketing, marketing on the Internet, and personal selling.

- **New and Updated Global and Ethical Perspectives** Nearly all of the boxed items focusing on global and ethical issues of advertising and promotion are new; those retained from the tenth edition have been updated. The Global Perspectives boxes examine the role of advertising and other promotional areas in international markets. The Ethical Perspectives features discuss specific issues, developments, and problems that call into question the ethics of marketers and their decisions as they develop and implement their advertising and promotional programs.

- **Contemporary Examples** The field of advertising and promotion changes very rapidly, and we

continue to keep pace with it. Wherever possible we updated the statistical information presented in tables, charts, and figures throughout the text. We reviewed the most current academic and trade literature to ensure that this text reflects the most current perspectives and theories on advertising, promotion, and the rapidly evolving area of integrated marketing communications. We also updated most of the examples and ads throughout the book. *Advertising and Promotion* continues to be the most contemporary text on the market, offering students as timely a perspective as possible.

Chapter-by-Chapter Changes

Chapter 1: New chapter opener focuses Charmin toilet tissue and how Procter & Gamble has added social media to traditional media to the IMC program for the brand. Also discusses how Charmin is one of the most creative brands on social media. **Charmin is one of the brands being featured in the new video cases being produced for 11e.**

- New Digital and Social Media Perspective: "A World without Digital Advertising: Be Careful What You Wish For" discusses how consumers are using technology to avoid traditional as well as digital ads, and the long-run implications of this for the advertising industry
- Updated Digital and Social Media Perspective on how the digital revolution is impacting IMC
- Updated figures on top advertisers
- Added discussion on concept of Paid, Owned, and Earned Media
- New ads throughout the chapter

Chapter 2: New chapter opener focuses on "Creating a New Image for Buick" and discusses Buick's attempt to reposition the 100+-year-old auto to appeal to a younger market.

- Updated IMC Perspective on targeting Millennials
- Updated discussion of marketers' attempts to reach the Hispanic market
- Updated charts and graphs
- New ads throughout the chapter

Chapter 3: New chapter opener focuses on "Can Advertising Agencies Survive the Digital Revolution?"

- New Digital and Social Media Perspective on how many companies are bringing advertising in-house rather than relying on outside agencies.
- New IMC Perspective on Droga5 agency, which has been widely recognized for its outstanding creative work and has been recognized as Agency of the Year by *Advertising Age* and *Adweek* in recent years
- Updated IMC Perspective on agency compensation issues and the ongoing controversy over agencies receiving rebates from the media

- Emphasis on the changing role of advertising agencies and how they must adapt to survive these changes
- Updated figures on top agencies
- Update ads throughout the chapter

Chapter 4: New chapter opener focuses on "Is Successful Branding Just about Emotions, Color, and Emojis?"

- New IMC Perspective "Subliminal Advertising—Maybe It Does Work After All!"
- Additional new IMC Perspective "Neuromarketing: Gaining Valuable Insights into the Consumer's Brain, or Overstepping the Bounds?"
- Updated charts and graphs
- New ads throughout the chapter

Chapter 5: New chapter opener focuses on award-winning "Like a Girl" viral campaign for Procter & Gamble's Always feminine protection product.

- Updated Digital and Social Media Perspective "Consumer Packaged-Goods Marketers Turn to Digital Media" discusses role of digital and social media for low-involvement products
- Updated perspective on Elaboration Likelihood Model and research challenging its findings
- New ads throughout chapter

Chapter 6: New chapter opener on how Under Armour has been able to compete against larger competitors such as Nike and Adidas in the battle to sign athletes to endorsement deals. Discusses UA endorsers such as NBA basketball star Stephen Curry, golfer Jordan Spieth, MLB baseball star Bryce Harper, and ballerina Misty Copeland. Under Armour was featured in a video case study for the 10e that focused on its IMC program for targeting women as well as its entry into the market for basketball shoes; this video is available for use with the 11e as well.

- New IMC Perspective "Marketers Run into Problems with Athlete Endorsers" discusses problems Nike has had with some of its high-profile endorsers such as Maria Sharapova, Tiger Woods, Lance Armstrong, and others
- New Digital and Social Media Perspective "YouTube Stars Are the New Celebrities to Teens" discusses implications for marketers
- Updated ads throughout the chapter

Chapter 7: New chapter opener reviews "Changing Media Habits Means Changing Budget Allocations. Is Digital the New King?" and discusses whether the rush to digital media is the best strategy using examples of how traditional companies like Hershey are changing their media strategies.

- New Digital and Social Media Perspective "Are Social, Digital, and Mobile Media Changing the Ways Marketers Use Consumer Funnels—Or Are These Funnels Even Relevant?" examines how some companies no longer feel consumer funnels are relevant
- New IMC Perspective "Companies Like Coca-Cola, Kraft, P&G, and 7UP Believe That Advertising Works" discusses how during periods of decreasing sales or economic downturns many successful companies increase, rather than decrease, media expenditures
- Updated figure on advertising to sales ratios by industry sector
- Updated charts and graphs
- New ads throughout the chapter

Chapter 8: New chapter opener focuses on IMC program used by Intuit's TurboTax tax preparation software and creative advertising developed for the brands such as the "It Doesn't Take a Genius to Do Your Taxes" campaign. **TurboTax is one of the companies/brands being featured in the new video cases for 11e.**

- New Digital and Social Media Perspective that discusses the top ad campaigns of the 21st century and how they are moving beyond traditional media and using social media
- Additional new Digital and Social Media Perspective that focuses on how the move toward digital advertising is creating a need for speed and challenging the pretesting of creative work
- Updated ads throughout the chapter

Chapter 9: New chapter opener focuses on the Coca-Cola Company's DASANI brand of bottled water, and how creative advertising has helped the brand become the market leader and led to several new line extensions, such as DASANI Drops® and DASANI Sparkling water. **DASANI is one of the companies/brands being featured in the new video cases for 11e.**

- New Digital and Social Media perspective "Marketers Use Virtual Reality to Create Immersive Experiences for Consumers" focuses on how AT&T has used VR to help deter texting and driving, and how retailers and professional sports teams are using the technology for creative experiences for customers and fans
- Updated IMC Perspective on IMC program for fast-food chain Taco Bell and its "Live Más" campaign which led to company being selected as Marketer of the Year by *Advertising Age* in 2013. Taco Bell was featured in a video case study for the 10e and this video is available for use with the 11e as well.
- New section added to the 11e on Creative Tactics for Online Advertising that includes discussion of tactics for online display advertising as well as online video
- New Digital and Social Media Perspective on award-winning "Unstoppable" campaign created by the

Martin Agency for GEICO insurance; this campaign won all of the major creative awards in 2016
- New ads throughout the chapter

Chapter 10: New chapter opener "Programmatic: Advertising's Newer, Better Mousetrap—Is Buying Better with Robots?" describes and examines the hottest new means of purchasing media today and the pros and cons of programmatic media buying

- Updated figure on leading national advertisers
- New explanation of how to read an MRI+ report, written and provided by GfK-MRI
- New figure on media usage by snowboarders reflecting more digital media usage
- New IMC Perspective "Being Social, Cosmopolitan, and Other Factors May Determine Which Media You Use"
- Updated charts and graphs
- New ads throughout the chapter

Chapter 11: New chapter opener discusses "The Future of Television and How It Will Impact Advertising."

- Emphasis throughout the chapter on the changing role of television and how it is being impacted by factors such as cord-cutting, multitasking, growth of online viewing, and other factors
- Updated IMC Perspective on how television rights play a major role in funding college sports
- New IMC Perspective discusses MTV and how the cable channel is trying to return to its roots of music and entertainment to connect with young viewers
- Updated discussion of radio advertising
- Updated photos throughout the chapter

Chapter 12: New chapter opener discusses challenges facing the magazine industry and the goal of a program developed by the Association of Magazine Media to guarantee advertisers that print ads work.

- New IMC Perspective "*Playboy* Magazine Tries to Rebrand Itself"
- New Digital and Social Media Perspective "Can Newspapers Survive the Digital Revolution?"
- Updated discussion of how both magazines and newspapers are being impacted by the Internet and digital media
- Updated images throughout the chapter

Chapter 13: New chapter opener reviews "The Brandchannel Product Placement Awards: Product Placements, Integrations, and Branded Entertainment Remain Popular."

- Extended discussion of out of home (OOH) advertising
- New Digital and Social Media Perspective "Billboards Come into the Digital Age" discusses the new technologies being employed by digital

OOH advertisers and some of the issues involving privacy, etc.
- Discussion on the declining state of usage of the Yellow Pages
- Updated charts and graphs
- New ads throughout the the chapter

Chapter 14: New chapter opener focuses on "SkyMall—Will Flying Ever Be the Same?" SkyMall, once a fixture on airlines, has gone out of business so far as hard copies on planes but is hoping to make a comeback.

- Updated examples of how sports teams use direct marketing to increase fan attendance and enjoyment
- New IMC Perspective "Infomercials: Shopping at 3 a.m.?" discusses the continued success of infomercials
- Updated charts and graphs
- New ads throughout the chapter

Chapter 15: A more in-depth perspective of digital and social media and the pros and cons of using these media. New chapter opener reviews "The Mad Rush to Digital: Smart Management or Lemmings?" and examines how media budgets are being shifted from traditional media to digital, and whether this is a result of sound marketing decisions or "me too" strategies.

- New Ethical Perspective "Native Advertising: Are We Giving Customers What They Want or Deceiving Them?" explains and examines the role of native advertising, and also examines the ethical and legal issues regarding the use of native ads
- The most current discussion of digital and social media of any text on the market
- New section IMC: Using Social and Other Media—Web 2.0 is updated discussion of social media (such as Facebook, Twitter, and Instagram) and how Instagram is increasing its share of the advertising buy
- Additional new Ethical Perspective "Influencer Marketing: Using Social Media Celebrities to Market Brands" discusses the use of "influencers" or opinion leaders, including celebrities, to market products
- Expanded discussion of augmented and virtual reality by advertisers
- Updated discussion of measuring digital effectiveness
- Updated charts and graphs
- Increased and updated discussion of the use of mobile
- New ads throughout the chapter

Chapter 16: New chapter opener discusses how marketers are falling into the discounting trap and how there may be no way out.

- New IMC Perspective on retailer JCPenney and how a new strategy to wean its customers off discounts and coupons failed

- New Digital and Social Media Perspective discusses how mobile coupons are becoming very popular
- Updated discussion of changes impacting the sales promotion industry and ways marketers use promotions including both consumer and trade promotions
- Updated examples of promotions throughout the chapter

Chapter 17: New chapter opener focuses on "Marketers Find That Doing Good Has Its Rewards" and discusses that advertisers who support causes often reap both financial and emotional rewards.

- New Digital and Social Media Perspective "Using Social Media Often Leads to Good Results—for Someone!" discusses the use of social and digital media to improve and/or repair the effects of publicity through digital and social media
- New IMC Perspective "Holding on to a Good Reputation Is Not as Easy as It Seems" explains how achieving a good reputation requires a high degree of effort by marketers and public relations practitioners and examines the causes and results that occur when a company suffers from negative publicity
- Updated charts and graphs
- New ads throughout the chapter

Chapter 18: Much more integration of measuring the effectiveness of digital and social media. New chapter opener "The 2016 Ogilvy Award Winners" discusses the Ogilvy Award winners for 2016 and examines how the awards have shifted from a focus on creativity to an IMC perspective.

- New Digital and Social Media "The Advertising Effectiveness Metrics of the Future—Testing Emotions?" examines how advertisers are measuring the effectiveness of their ads using new metrics including impact on emotions, facial expressions, physiological measures, etc.
- Additional new Digital and Social Media Perspective "Physiological Methods, Eye Tracking, and Mouse Hovering Lead to More Effective Testing"
- Expanded discussion of measurement in the digital and social arena
- Updated charts and graphs
- New ads throughout the chapter

Chapter 19: New chapter opener focuses on global advertising campaign developed for Coca-Cola using the "Taste the Feeling" tagline. Discusses reasons for the global campaign as well.

- New Global Perspective focusing on how marketers are looking to China for growth and the challenges they face in developing IMC programs for the world's largest consumer market
- New Global Perspective that focuses on the IMC program used by the country of Qatar to help win the rights to host the 2022 FIFA World Cup; two video cases were developed on Qatar's efforts to win the FIFA World Cup for 10e and are also available for use with 11e
- Updated Digital and Social Media Perspective on how Facebook wants to dominate social media in countries around the world and what it is doing to achieve this goal
- Updated discussion of global advertising campaigns used by marketers
- New photos throughout the chapter

Chapter 20: New chapter opener discusses new rules and regulations developed by the Federal Trade Commission for online endorsers.

- New Ethical Perspective discussing whether direct-to-consumer drug advertising should be banned
- Updated discussion of changes in rules and regulations impacting all forms of IMC including advertising, sales promotion, and digital media
- New and revised photos throughout the chapter

Chapter 21: New chapter opener discusses the empowerment of women in advertising.

- Ethical Perspective "Abercrombie and American Apparel (NSFW) Shock Consumers into Their Ads—but Apparently Not into Their Stores" discusses the effectiveness (or lack thereof) of using shock advertising and how it has not worked for some companies that have employed this form of advertising
- New Digital and Social Media Perspective "How Far Have We Come on Racial Equality?" examines the use of minorities in advertising and the increasing use of interracial couples and families in ads; also examines whether these ads have become more acceptable to viewers
- Updated charts and graphs
- New ads throughout the chapter

Chapter 22: Online chapter.

- New Digital and Social Media Perspective "Is Technology Disrupting the CRM Process?"
- Additional new Digital and Social Media Perspective "How the Internet Revolutionized Personal Selling"
- Updated charts and graphs
- New ads throughout the chapter

SUPPORT MATERIAL

A high-quality package of instructional supplements supports the eleventh edition. Nearly all of the supplements have been developed by the authors to ensure their coordination with the text. We offer instructors a support package that facilitates the use of our text and enhances the learning experience of the student.

Instructor's Manual

The instructor's manual is a valuable teaching resource that includes learning objectives, chapter and lecture outlines, answers to all end-of-chapter discussion questions, and further insights and teaching suggestions. Additional discussion questions are also presented for each chapter. These questions can be used for class discussion or as short-answer essay questions for exams.

Manual of Tests

A test bank of more than 1,500 multiple-choice questions has been developed to accompany the text. The questions provide thorough coverage of the chapter material, including opening vignettes and IMC, Global, Ethical, and Digital and Social Media Perspectives.

Computerized Test Bank

A computerized version of the test bank is available to adopters of the text.

Video Supplements

A video supplement package has been developed specifically for classroom use with this text. It includes 10 video cases that provide a detailed examination of the IMC strategies and programs for various companies and brands. All of the videos include interviews with key executives from the various companies and/or their advertising agencies and were produced in cooperation with each company.

Three new video cases have been produced for the eleventh edition. The first new video focuses on Charmin, and shows how the iconic brand from Procter & Gamble has continued to adapt with the times and integrates traditional media with digital/social media and mobile marketing. The video covers the history of the brand, including a long-running and successful campaign featuring the popular Mr. Whipple character—an icon in the advertising world—to the current day. It shows how P&G and its advertising agency Publicis continue to develop creative marketing campaigns using digital and social media for a consumer staple product like toilet tissue. The second video examines the integrated marketing program for TurboTax which is the leading brand of tax preparation software and a division of Intuit. The video focuses on the company's introduction of TurboTax Absolute Zero® which disrupted the tax preparation category by offering federal and state tax preparation free of charge. It examines a big idea–led campaign titled "It doesn't take a genius to do your taxes" developed by the Wieden+Kennedy agency. The campaign includes TV spots featuring some of the world's greatest minds appearing in amusing commercials showing that TurboTax is so simple and intuitive that even real-life geniuses can't make it any easier to use or understand. The video also discusses how TurboTax leveraged its Super Bowl commercial featuring legendary actor Sir Anthony Hopkins through the use of social media. The third new video case is on DASANI, which is owned by the Coca-Cola Company, and examines how the Lambesis agency used creative advertising and digital marketing to make DASANI the leading brand of bottled water. It also focuses on the IMC strategy used to launch two line extensions for the brand, DASANI Drops® and Dasani Sparkling water.

In addition, four videos have been kept from the last edition as they are still very relevant and interesting. The first video focuses on Taco Bell's "Live Más" IMC campaign that is designed to make the brand attractive and relevant to young, hip, and cross-cultural consumers by focusing on food as an experience and lifestyle. This video also examines Taco Bell's introduction of the Doritos Locos Tacos (DLT) which emerged as a co-branding initiative with snack food giant Frito-Lay and has been one of the most successful new product introductions in the history of the fast-food industry. The IMC program used for the launch of the Nacho Cheese and Cool Ranch versions of the DLT is covered in the video. The second video focuses on Under Armour which has become the fastest-growing brand in the athletic shoe and apparel market and is now second only to Nike in most product/market segments. The video focuses on the IMC program used by Under Armour including the role of athletes as endorsers and digital/social media. It also covers two major strategic initiatives for Under Armour—its efforts to increase its share of the female market and its launch of a line of basketball shoes. The video examines the campaign developed by Under Armour to target women, which relies heavily on social media as well as traditional media. It also focuses on the "Are You From Here?" campaign that was used to market its line of new basketball shoes.

The third video focuses on the IMC efforts used by the Middle Eastern country of Qatar to support its bid to become the host nation for the 2022 FIFA World Cup football (soccer) tournament. The video examines the strategy used by the Qatar Supreme Committee to compete against other countries for the rights to host the World Cup and the IMC program that was used in support of this effort. A second shorter Qatar video is also included which focuses on the legacy that the country hopes to achieve by hosting the World Cup including the diversification of its economy, improvements in infrastructure and to create a better understanding of the Middle East region.

The video supplement package also includes three videos produced for previous editions of the book, two of which focus on innovative social media campaigns. These include a video on a social media campaign called the "Fiesta Movement" which was used by the Ford Motor Co. to introduce the new Fiesta subcompact automobile to the U.S. market in 2010. The "Fiesta Movement" was very successful and a second generation of the social media campaign was used again in 2013. Another video is for PepsiCo's Mountain Dew soft-drink brand and examines the "Dewmocracy" campaign which is another social media–driven initiative that the company used to add a new flavor of the product line for the popular soft drink. The video focuses on how collective intelligence and user-generated content from loyal Mountain Dew drinkers was used to develop the flavor, packaging, and name as well as the advertising to launch the latest addition to the brand franchise. A new Dewmocracy campaign is currently running. A second Under Armour video is also included in the supplement package that was produced in 2008 and focuses on the advertising, digital media, sponsorships, and other IMC tools used to build the brand during its first decade. This video can be used along with the more recent Under Armour video to show how far the company has come in less than two decades and the role IMC has played in its tremendous success.

MCGRAW-HILL
CONNECT® MARKETING

Less Managing. More Teaching.
Greater Learning.

McGraw-Hill *Connect Marketing* is an online assignment and assessment solution that connects students with the tools and resources they'll need to achieve success. *Connect Marketing* helps prepare students for their future by enabling faster learning, more efficient studying, and higher retention of knowledge.

McGraw-Hill *Connect Marketing* Features

Connect Marketing offers a number of powerful tools and features to make managing assignments easier,

so faculty can spend more time teaching. With *Connect Marketing* students can engage with their coursework anytime and anywhere, making the learning process more accessible and efficient. *Connect Marketing* offers you the features described below.

Online Interactives

Online Interactives are engaging tools that teach students to apply key concepts in practice. These Interactives provide students with immersive, experiential learning opportunities. Students will engage in a variety of interactive scenarios to deepen critical knowledge on key course topics. They receive immediate feedback at intermediate steps throughout each exercise, as well as comprehensive feedback at the end of the assignment. All Interactives are automatically scored and entered into the instructor's gradebook.

Student Progress Tracking

Connect Marketing keeps instructors informed about how each student, section, and class is performing, allowing for more productive use of lecture and office hours. The progress-tracking function enables you to:

- View scored work immediately and track individual or group performances with assignment and grade reports.
- Access an instant view of student or class performances relative to learning objectives.
- Collect data and generate reports required by many accreditation organizations, such as AACSB.

Smart Grading

When it comes to studying, time is precious. *Connect Marketing* helps students learn more efficiently by providing feedback and practice material when they need it, where they need it. When it comes to teaching, your time is also precious. The grading function enables you to:

- Have assignments scored automatically, giving students immediate feedback on their work and side-by-side comparisons with correct answers.
- Access and review each response; manually change grades or leave comments for students to review.
- Reinforce classroom concepts with practice tests and instant quizzes.

Simple Assignment Management

With *Connect Marketing* creating assignments is easier than ever, so you can spend more time teaching and less time managing. The assignment management function enables you to:

- Create and deliver assignments easily with selectable end-of-chapter questions and test bank items.
- Streamline lesson planning, student progress reporting, and assignment grading to make classroom management more efficient than ever.
- Go paperless with eBooks and online submission and grading of student assignments.

Instructor Library

The *Connect Marketing* Instructor Library is your repository for additional resources to improve student engagement in and out of class. You can select and use any asset that enhances your lecture. The *Connect Marketing* Instructor Library includes:

- Instructor's Manual
- PowerPoint files
- TestBank
- Videos
- eBook

ASSURANCE OF LEARNING READY

Many educational institutions today are focused on the notion of *assurance of learning,* an important element of some accreditation standards. *Advertising and Promotion: An Integrated Marketing Communications Perspective* is designed specifically to support your assurance of learning initiatives with a simple, yet powerful solution.

Each test bank question for *Advertising and Promotion: An Integrated Marketing Communications Perspective* maps to a specific chapter learning outcome/objective listed in the text. You can use our test bank software, or *Connect Marketing* to easily query for the learning outcomes/objectives that directly relate to the learning objectives for your course. Connect's AACSB-tagged quiz and test banks provide an easy testing solution, with reports like the Category Analysis Report, saving time by providing a one-click solution for displaying mastery of objectives at the individual, section, and course levels.

AACSB Statement

The McGraw-Hill Companies is a proud corporate member of AACSB International. Understanding the importance and value of AACSB accreditation, *Advertising and Promotion: An Integrated Marketing Communications Perspective,* 11e, recognizes the curricula guidelines detailed in the AACSB standards for business accreditation by connecting selected questions (in the text and/or the test bank) to the six general knowledge and skill guidelines in the AACSB standards.

The statements contained in *Advertising and Promotion: An Integrated Marketing Communications Perspective,* 11e, are provided only as a guide for the users of this textbook. The AACSB leaves content coverage and assessment within the purview of individual schools, the mission of the school, and the faculty. While *Advertising and Promotion: An Integrated Marketing Communications Perspective,* 11e, and the teaching package make no claim of any specific AACSB qualification or evaluation, we have within *Advertising and Promotion: An Integrated Marketing Communications Perspective,* 11e, labeled selected questions according to the six general knowledge and skills areas.

MCGRAW-HILL CUSTOMER CARE CONTACT INFORMATION

At McGraw-Hill, we understand that getting the most from new technology can be challenging. That's why our services don't stop after you purchase our products. You can e-mail our Product Specialists 24 hours a day to get product-training online. Or you can search our knowledge bank of Frequently Asked Questions on our support website. For Customer Support, call 800-331-5094 or visit mpss.mhhe.com. One of our Technical Support Analysts will be able to assist you in a timely fashion.

Create

Craft your teaching resources to match the way you teach! With McGraw-Hill Create, www.create.mheducation.com, you can easily rearrange chapters, combine material from other content sources, and quickly upload content you have written like your course syllabus or teaching notes. Find the content you need in Create by searching through thousands of leading McGraw-Hill Education textbooks. Arrange your book to fit your teaching style. Create even allows you to personalize your book's appearance by selecting the cover and adding your name, school, and course information. Order a Create book and you'll receive a complimentary print review copy in three to five business days or a complimentary electronic review copy (eComp) via e-mail in about one hour. Go to www.create.mheducation.com today and register. Experience how McGraw-Hill Create empowers you to teach *your* students *your* way.

MCGRAW-HILL HIGHER EDUCATION AND BLACKBOARD HAVE TEAMED UP. WHAT DOES THIS MEAN FOR YOU?

- **Your life, simplified.** Now you and your students can access McGraw-Hill Education's *Connect* and Create right from within your Blackboard course—all with one single sign-on. Say goodbye to the days of logging in to multiple applications.

- **Deep integration of content and tools.** Not only do you get single sign-on with *Connect* and Create, you also get deep integration of McGraw-Hill Education content and content engines right in Blackboard. Whether you're choosing a book for your course or building *Connect* assignments, all the tools you need are right where you want them—inside of Blackboard.

- **Seamless gradebooks.** Are you tired of keeping multiple gradebooks and manually synchronizing grades into Blackboard? We thought so. When a student completes an integrated *Connect* assignment, the grade for that assignment automatically (and instantly) feeds your Blackboard grade center.

- **A solution for everyone.** Whether your institution is already using Blackboard or you just want to try Blackboard on your own, we have a solution for you. McGraw-Hill Education and Blackboard can now offer you easy access to industry leading technology and content, whether your campus hosts it, or we do. Be sure to ask your local McGraw-Hill Education representative for details.

ACKNOWLEDGMENTS

While this eleventh edition represents a tremendous amount of work on our part, it would not have become a reality without the assistance and support of many other people. Authors tend to think they have the best ideas, approach, examples, and organization for writing a great book. But we quickly learned that there is always room for our ideas to be improved on by others. A number of colleagues provided detailed, thoughtful reviews that were immensely helpful in making this a better book. We are very grateful to the following individuals who worked with us on earlier editions. They include

Lisa Abendroth, *University of Saint Thomas*
Natalie Adkins, *Creighton University–Omaha*
Bruce Alford, *Louisiana Tech University*
David Allen, *St. Joseph's University*
Neil Alperstein, *Loyola University Maryland*
Craig Andrews, *Marquette University*
Sheila Baiers, *Kalamazoo Valley Community College*
Subir Bandyopadhyay, *University of Ottawa*
Allen Bargfrede, *Berklee College of Music*
Michael Barone, *Iowa State University*
Jerri Beggs, *Illinois State University*
Mike Behan, *Western Technical College and Viterbo University*
John Bennet, *University of Missouri*
Elizabeth Blair, *Ohio University–Athens*
Janice Blankenburg, *University of Wisconsin–Milwaukee*
Karen Bowman, *University of California–Riverside*
Kathy Boyle, *University of Maryland*
Terry Bristol, *Oklahoma State University*
Beverly Brockman, *University of Alabama*
Kendrick Brunson, *Liberty University*
Lauranne Buchanan, *University of Illinois*
Jeffrey Buchman, *Fashion Institute of Technology*
Roy Busby, *University of North Texas*
Victoria Bush, *University of Mississippi*
Christopher Cakebread, *Boston University*
Nathaniel Calloway, *University of Maryland–University College*
Margaret C. Campbell, *University of Colorado–Boulder*
Les Carlson, *Clemson University*
Lindell Chew, *University of Missouri–St. Louis*
Oscar Chilabato, *Johnson & Wales University*
Bob Cline, *University of Iowa–Iowa City*
Catherine Cole, *University of Iowa*
Mary Conran, *Temple University–Philadelphia*
Sherry Cook, *Missouri State University*

Kevin Cumiskey, *Oklahoma State University–Stillwater*
Robert Cutter, *Cleveland State University*
Andrew Czaplewski, *University of Colorado–Colorado Springs*
Richard M. Daily, *University of Texas–Arlington*
Don Dickinson, *Portland State University*
Robert H. Ducoffe, *Baruch College*
Roberta Elins, *Fashion Institute of Technology*
Nancy Ellis, *Suffolk Community College*
Robert Erffmeyer, *University of Wisconsin–Eau Claire*
John Faier, *Miami University*
Terri Faraone, *Mt. San Antonio College*
Raymond Fisk, *Oklahoma State University*
Theresa Flaherty, *James Madison University*
Alan Fletcher, *Louisiana State University*
Marty Flynn, *Suffolk Community College*
Judy Foxman, *Southern Methodist University*
Amy Frank, *Wingate University*
Jon B. Freiden, *Florida State University*
Stefanie Garcia, *University of Central Florida*
Geoff Gordon, *University of Kentucky*
Norman Govoni, *Babson College*
Donald Grambois, *Indiana University*
Debora Grossman, *State University of New York–Buffalo*
Stephen Grove, *Clemson University*
Charles Gulas, *Wright State University–Dayton*
Robert Gulonsen, *Washington University*
Holly Hapke, *University of Kentucky–Lexington*
Bill Hauser, *University of Akron*
Diana Haytko, *Florida Gulf Coast University*
Yi He, *California State University–East Bay*
Amanda Helm, *University of Wisconsin–Whitewater*
Ron Hill, *Villanova University*
JoAnn Hopper, *Western Carolina University*
Paul Jackson, *Ferris State College*
Karen James, *Louisiana State University–Shreveport*
Christopher Joiner, *George Mason University*
Leslie Kendrick, *Johns Hopkins University*
Robert Kent, *University of Delaware*
Don Kirchner, *California State University–Northridge*
Paul Klein, *St. Thomas University*
Susan Kleine, *Arizona State University*
Patricia Knowles, *Clemson University*
David Koehler, *University of Illinois–Chicago*
Gary Kritz, *Seton Hall University*
Ivy Kutlu, *Old Dominion University*
Dr. Barbara Lafferty, *University of South Florida–Tampa*

Dana Lanham, *University of North Carolina–Charlotte*

Clark Leavitt, *Ohio State University*

Ron Lennon, *Barry University*

Lauren Lev, *Fashion Institute of Technology*

Aron Levin, *Northern Kentucky University*

Tina Lowry, *Rider University*

Karen Machleit, *University of Cincinnati*

Scott Mackenzie, *Indiana University*

Stacey Massey, *Texas A&M University*

Elizabeth Moore, *Notre Dame*

Joe Msylivec, *Central Michigan University*

Darrel Muehling, *Washington State University–Pullman*

Barbara Mueller, *San Diego State University*

John H. Murphy II, *University of Texas–Austin*

Mark Neckes, *Johnson & Wales University*

Peter Noble, *Southern Methodist University*

Kathy O'Donnell, *San Francisco State University*

Mandy H. Ortiz, *University of Alabama–Tuscaloosa*

Carol Osborne, *USF Tampa*

Charles Overstreet, *Oklahoma State University*

Notis Pagiavlas, *University of Texas–Arlington*

Paul Prabhaker, *DePaul University, Chicago*

William Pride, *Texas A&M University*

Astrid Proboll, *San Francisco State University*

Sanjay Putrevu, *SUNY University at Albany*

Sekar Raju, *University at Buffalo*

Joel Reedy, *University of South Florida*

Kristen Regine, *Johnson & Wales University*

Glen Reicken, *East Tennessee State University*

Herb Ritchell, *DePaul University*

Scott Roberts, *Old Dominion University*

Michelle Rodriques, *University of Central Florida*

Herbert Jack Rotfield, *Auburn University–Auburn*

Judith Sayre, *University of North Florida*

Allen D. Schaefer, *Missouri State University*

Hope Schau, *University of Arizona*

Carol Schibi, *State Fair Community College*

Denise D. Schoenbachler, *Northern Illinois University*

Lisa Sciulli, *Indiana University of Pennsylvania*

Andrea Scott, *Pepperdine University*

Elaine Scott, *Bluefield State College*

Eugene Secunda, *New York University*

Tanuja Singh, *Northern Illinois University*

Lois Smith, *University of Wisconsin*

Harlan Spotts, *Northeastern University*

Monique Stampleman, *Fashion Institute of Technology*

Mary Ann Stutts, *Southwest Texas State University*

James Swartz, *California State Polytechnic University–Pomona*

Ric Sweeney, *University of Cincinnati*

Janice Taylor, *Miami University*

Robert Taylor, *Radford University*

Brian Tietje, *Cal State Polytechnic*

Frank Tobolski, *DePaul University*

Kevin Toomb, *University North Carolina–Charlotte*

Mindy Treftz, *Columbia College–Christian County*

Lisa Troy, *Texas A&M University*

Deb Utter, *Boston University*

Jim Walker, *Northwest Missouri State University*

Mike Weigold, *University of Florida–Gainesville*

John Weitzel, *Western Michigan University*

Donna Wertalik, *Virginia Polytechnic Institute*

Kenneth C. Wilbur, *University of Southern California*

Roy Winegar, *Grand Valley State University*

Richard Wingerson, *Florida Atlantic University*

Terrence Witkowski, *California State University–Long Beach*

Merv H. Yeagle, *University of Maryland–College Park*

Elaine Young, *Champlain College*

Robert Young, *Northeastern University*

We are particularly grateful to the individuals who provided constructive comments on how to make this edition better:

Aysen Bakir, *Illinois State University*

Hulda Black, *Illinois State University*

Carolyn Bonifield, *University of Vermont*

Jungsil Choi, *Cleveland State University*

Christina Chung, *Ramapo College of New Jersey*

Theresa Clarke, *James Madison University*

Robert Daniel Dahlen, *Ohio University*

Sara Dommer, *Georgia Institute of Technology*

Mary Edrington, *Drake University*

Mark Elton, *Western Oregon University*

Bruce Freeman, *Kean University*

Keith Alan Gosselin, *California State University–Northridge*

Kimberly Goudy, *Central Ohio Technical College*

Nancy Gray, *Arizona State University*

Aditi Grover, *Oklahoma State University*

Charles Gulas, *Wright State University*

Diana Haytko, *Florida Gulf Coast University*

Eileen Kearney, *Maricopa County Community College*

Linda LaMarca, *Tarleton State University*

Rachel Lundbohm, *University of Minnesota–Crookston*

Jessica Matias, *University of Minnesota–Crookston*

Catherine Mezera, *West Virginia University*

Paula Morris, *Salisbury University*

Richard Murphy, *Jacksonville University*

Jay Page, *University of Cincinnati–Clermont College*

Cara Peters, *Winthrop University*

Gregory Rapp, *Portland Community College*

Christopher Ross, *Trident Technical College*

Trina Sego, *Boise State University*

Stacy Smulowitz, *University of Scranton*

Melissa St. James, *California State University–Dominguez Hills*

LaTonya Steele, *Durham Technical Community College*

Michelle Steven, *St. Francis College*

Lisa Troy, *Texas A&M University*

Ramaprasad Unni, *Tennessee State University*

Deborah Utter, *Boston University*

Ying Wang, *Youngstown State University*

Judith Washburn, *University of Tampa*

Rick Wilson, *Texas State University*

We would also like to acknowledge the cooperation we received from many people in the business, advertising, and media communities. This book contains several hundred ads, illustrations, charts, and tables that have been provided by advertisers and/or their agencies, various publications, and other advertising and industry organizations. Many individuals took time from their busy schedules to provide us with requested materials and gave us permission to use them. A special thanks to all of you.

A manuscript does not become a book without a great deal of work on the part of the publisher. Various individuals at McGraw-Hill Education have been involved with this project over the past several years. Our Product Development Manager on the eleventh edition, Katie Eddy, along with Brand Manager Meredith Fossel, provided valuable guidance and have been instrumental in making sure we continue to write the best IMC book on the market. A special thanks goes to Claire Hunter, our developmental editor, for all of her efforts and for being so great to work with. Thanks also to Susan Trentacosti for doing a superb job of managing the production process and DeAnna Dausener for coordinating the permissions and licensing process. We also want to once again acknowledge the outstanding work of Jennifer Blankenship for obtaining permissions for most of the ads that appear throughout the book. Thanks to the other members of the product team—Susan Gouijnstook, Kelly Delso, Kristy Dekat, Kerry Shanahan, Kelly Sheehan, Robin Lucas, Elizabeth Schonagen, Mary Conzachi, Danielle Clement, Karen Jozefowicz, Susan K. Culbertson, Egzon Shaqiri, Ann Marie Jannette—for all their hard work on this edition. Also, special thanks to Sharon From at Intuit, Chad Farmer and Brian Munce at The Lambesis Agency, and Dan Cohen at Publicis New York, as well as the Charmin brand team at Procter & Gamble, for their help in coordinating the production of the new videos for this edition. We also want to acknowledge the great work of Rick Armstrong in filming and editing all of the videos for the past three editions of the book. If we missed anyone, please accept our apologies.

We would like to acknowledge the support we have received from the Fowler College of Business at San Diego State University. As always, a great deal of thanks goes to our families for putting up with us while we were revising this book. Once again we look forward to returning to what we think is normal. Finally, we would like to acknowledge each other for making it through this ordeal for the eleventh time! Our families and friends will be happy to know that we still get along after all this—though we are beginning to think we are just numb. Our parents would be proud!

George E. Belch
Michael A. Belch

Your guide through the exciting world

Why It's a Powerful Learning Tool

The eleventh edition continues to provide you with the most comprehensive and current text on the market in the area of advertising and promotion from an integrated marketing communications perspective. The following features in each chapter enhance students' understanding of the material as well as their reading enjoyment.

CHAPTER OPENERS

Learning Objectives are provided at the beginning of each chapter to identify the major areas and points covered in the chapter and guide the learning effort. Each chapter also begins with a **Chapter Opening Vignette** that shows the effective use of integrated marketing communications by a company or ad agency or discusses an interesting issue that is relevant to the chapter. Some of the companies and brands profiled in the opening vignettes include Procter and Gamble, Buick, Under Armour, TurboTax (Intuit), and the Coca-Cola Company.

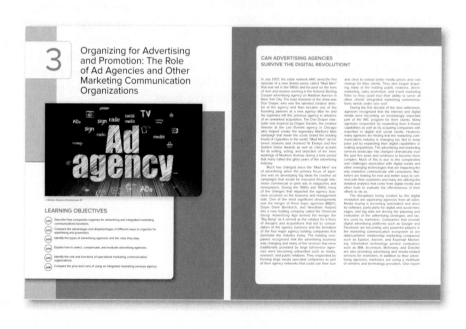

# of advertising and promotion.

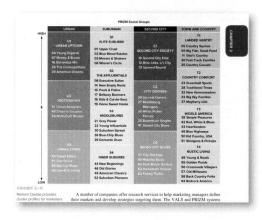

EXHIBIT 2–11
Nielsen Claritas provides cluster profiles for marketers

A number of companies offer research services to help marketing managers define their markets and develop strategies targeting them. The VALS and PRIZM systems

CHAPTER PEDAGOGY

Four-Color Visuals throughout the book consist of photoboards, commercial shots, charts, graphs, and over 400 print ads. **Key Terms** are highlighted in boldface throughout the text and listed at the end of each chapter with a page reference. **Chapter Summaries** serve as a quick review of important topics covered and as a study guide. **Discussion Questions** tagged to learning objectives at the end of each chapter give students an opportunity to test their understanding of the material and to apply it. These questions can also serve as a basis for class discussion or assignments.

REAL-LIFE EXAMPLES

The authors have used many sources to find practical examples to use throughout the text. In addition to the integration of the strategy and rationale behind the ads and other types of promotion that are used for current examples of industry practice, there are special in-depth discussions highlighted in boxed sections. **IMC Perspectives** present in-depth discussion of particular issues related to the chapter material and show how companies are using integrated marketing communications. **Global Perspectives** are presented throughout the text in recognition of the increasing importance of international marketing and the challenges of advertising and promotion and the roles they play in the marketing programs of multinational marketers. **Ethical Perspectives** focus attention on important social issues and show how advertisers must take ethical considerations into account when planning and implementing advertising and promotional programs. **Digital and Social Media Perspectives** provide a detailed discussion of how changes and advances in technology the use of digital media are impacting the practice of integrated marketing communications.

INSTRUCTOR RESOURCES

The resources available online for instructors include downloadable versions of the Instructor's Manual, Video Instructor's Manual, PowerPoint Presentations, Cases and case teaching notes. Instructors can access Advertising Target Practice, and the video clips through

www.connect.mheducation.com.

McGraw-Hill Connect®
Learn Without Limits

Connect is a teaching and learning platform that is proven to deliver better results for students and instructors.

Connect empowers students by continually adapting to deliver precisely what they need, when they need it, and how they need it, so your class time is more engaging and effective.

73% of instructors who use **Connect** require it; instructor satisfaction **increases** by 28% when **Connect** is required.

Analytics

Connect Insight®

Connect Insight is Connect's new one-of-a-kind visual analytics dashboard—now available for both instructors and students—that provides at-a-glance information regarding student performance, which is immediately actionable. By presenting assignment, assessment, and topical performance results together with a time metric that is easily visible for aggregate or individual results, Connect Insight gives the user the ability to take a just-in-time approach to teaching and learning, which was never before available. Connect Insight presents data that empowers students and helps instructors improve class performance in a way that is efficient and effective.

Mobile

Connect's new, intuitive mobile interface gives students and instructors flexible and convenient, anytime–anywhere access to all components of the Connect platform.

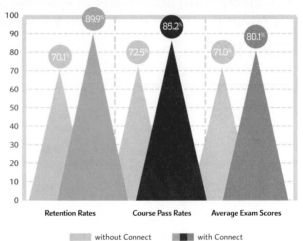

Connect's Impact on Retention Rates, Pass Rates, and Average Exam Scores

- Retention Rates: without Connect 70.1%, with Connect 89.9%
- Course Pass Rates: without Connect 72.5%, with Connect 85.2%
- Average Exam Scores: without Connect 71.0%, with Connect 80.1%

without Connect / with Connect

Using **Connect** improves retention rates by **19.8%**, passing rates by **12.7%**, and exam scores by **9.1%**.

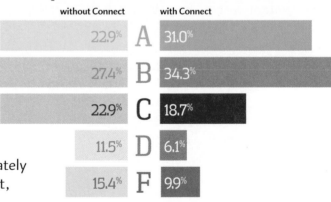

Impact on Final Course Grade Distribution

	without Connect	with Connect
A	22.9%	31.0%
B	27.4%	34.3%
C	22.9%	18.7%
D	11.5%	6.1%
F	15.4%	9.9%

Students can view their results for any **Connect** course.

Adaptive

THE **ADAPTIVE**
READING EXPERIENCE
DESIGNED TO TRANSFORM
THE WAY STUDENTS READ

More students earn **A's** and **B's** when they use McGraw-Hill Education **Adaptive** products.

SmartBook®

Proven to help students improve grades and study more efficiently, SmartBook contains the same content within the print book, but actively tailors that content to the needs of the individual. SmartBook's adaptive technology provides precise, personalized instruction on what the student should do next, guiding the student to master and remember key concepts, targeting gaps in knowledge and offering customized feedback, and driving the student toward comprehension and retention of the subject matter. Available on tablets, SmartBook puts learning at the student's fingertips—anywhere, anytime.

Over **8 billion questions** have been answered, making McGraw-Hill Education products more intelligent, reliable, and precise.

www.mheducation.com

STUDENTS WANT

SMARTBOOK®

95% of students reported **SmartBook** to be a more effective way of reading material.

100% of students want to use the Practice Quiz feature available within **SmartBook** to help them study.

100% of students reported having reliable access to off-campus wifi.

90% of students say they would purchase **SmartBook** over print alone.

95% of students reported that **SmartBook** would impact their study skills in a positive way.

McGraw Hill Education

*Findings based on 2015 focus group results administered by McGraw-Hill Education

BRIEF CONTENTS

DETAILED CONTENTS

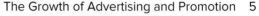

Part Two

Integrated Marketing Communications Program Situation Analysis

Part Three — Analyzing the Communication Process

Part Four

Objectives and Budgeting for Integrated Marketing Communications Programs

7. ESTABLISHING OBJECTIVES AND BUDGETING FOR THE PROMOTIONAL PROGRAM   220

Part Five

Developing the Integrated Marketing Communications Program

8. CREATIVE STRATEGY: PLANNING AND DEVELOPMENT   264

Part Six   Monitoring, Evaluation, and Control

Part Seven   Special Topics and Perspectives

19. INTERNATIONAL ADVERTISING AND PROMOTION   650

20. REGULATION OF ADVERTISING AND PROMOTION   688

ADVERTISING AND PROMOTION

AN INTEGRATED MARKETING COMMUNICATIONS PERSPECTIVE

1

An Introduction to Integrated Marketing Communications

Source: Charmin by Procter & Gamble and Publicis Worldwide

LEARNING OBJECTIVES

LO1 Describe the role of advertising and other promotional elements in marketing.

LO2 Discuss the evolution of the integrated marketing communications (IMC) concept.

LO3 Explain the increasing value of the IMC perspective in advertising and promotional programs.

LO4 Identify the elements of the promotional mix.

LO5 Identify the contact points between marketers and their target audiences.

LO6 Describe the steps in the IMC planning process.

CHARMIN: THE SASSIEST BRAND ON SOCIAL MEDIA

If you were to ask consumers to name one of the most creative and engaging brands on social media, it is unlikely they would name Charmin toilet tissue. Many consumers might still associate Charmin with the iconic Mr. Whipple and the "Please don't squeeze the Charmin" advertising campaign that ran for more than two decades and has been recognized as one of best ads campaign of the 20th century. Creating interest and excitement is very challenging for marketers when they are selling a product that is not exactly glamorous and is associated with one of life's less savory necessities, not to mention one that is often joked about and/or is not at the top of the list of most social conversations. Nonetheless, consumers spend more than $9 billion a year on toilet paper and Charmin has become the market leader in product category by using an IMC strategy that is anything but seat-of-the-pants, so to speak.

The story of Charmin goes back nearly a hundred years when the toilet tissue was first manufactured in 1928 at the Hoberg Paper Company in Wisconsin. The product was designed to reflect feminine fashions of the day and was described as "charming" by an employee and from there the name "Charmin" was born. The company changed its name to the Charmin Paper Company in 1950 and a few years later added a baby graphic to its packaging to symbolize gentle softness and quality. Procter & Gamble (P&G) acquired the company in 1957 as it saw Charmin as a great opportunity to compete against Scott Paper, Kimberly-Clark, and other companies that were dominating the paper products markets.

While gentleness and softness have always been key product attributes for toilet tissue, P&G's advertising agency, Benton and Bowles, initially struggled to find a way to convince consumers that Charmin was gentler and softer than competing brands that were making similar claims. However, in 1964 the agency came up with the creative idea of developing an advertising campaign around a prissy supermarket manager who would become upset at his customers for squeezing packages of Charmin so they could feel the softness. A character named Mr. Whipple was created to promote Charmin's "squeezable softness" and the TV commercials featured him scolding shoppers for squeezing packages of Charmin, but then sneaking a pleasure-filled squeeze himself. The "Please Don't Squeeze the Charmin" campaign ran for more than 20 years and Mr. Whipple appeared in more than 500 TV commercials as well as magazine and newspaper ads. Mr. Whipple became one of the most successful icons in advertising history and during the 1970s was named the third best-known American, trailing only then-President Richard Nixon and the Reverend Billy Graham. None of the leading brands had ever come up with a better way to communicate the "softness" of toilet paper, and the campaign helped make Charmin the market leader and sell a lot of toilet paper.

P&G has continued to innovate around the Charmin brand, introducing line extensions such as unscented Charmin and Charmin Free products which are free of inks, dyes, and perfumes. In 1999, after a 14-year hiatus, P&G brought back Mr. Whipple for a campaign promoting a major improvement in the brand. However, at the beginning of the new millennium P&G and its advertising agency, Publicis New York, took the advertising for Charmin in a new direction by launching a new animated campaign called "Call of Nature" featuring a bear in the woods experiencing the comfortable feeling of Charmin. The campaign originated in the United Kingdom but was brought to the United States; a year later the Charmin animated bears welcomed three cubs to the family.

While the cute and clumsy animated bears have been the advertising symbol for Charmin for the past two decades, the IMC campaign for the brand has evolved in new directions that might make anyone raised in the Mr. Whipple era a little uncomfortable. Publicis New York created an integrated campaign using the tagline "Enjoy the go" that included ads featuring the animated bears as well as a microsite, mobile apps, social media, branded bathroom breaks, and charitable/cause marketing components. As part of the campaign, P&G brought Charmin-branded public bathrooms to Times Square in New York City for the holiday season. The website included a countdown to New Year's and let consumers interact with the "Charmin Go Team," a group of actors who entertained people at the restrooms, which featured a giant toilet for photo opportunities, a digital graffiti wall, a video "can-fessional" booth, as well as themed toilet seat covers ranging from boxing to disco.

The charity component of the campaign let consumers "Go for Good" as Charmin donated $1 for every visitor to the toilets to select charities such as Boys & Girls Club of America, The Harlem Children's Zone, and Angels in Waiting. P&G has also created a cause marketing program called the Charmin Relief Project which has supported causes such as asking consumers to nominate and help select 100 firehouses across the country that received a year's supply of toilet paper.

Charmin has become one of the most active brands on social media with more than 1 million fans on Facebook and over 70,000 Twitter followers; it also has a presence on video platforms such as YouTube and Vine. The Charmin social media team, which includes five members from the P&G brand management team as well as eight from the agency side, continually monitors fan feedback across the various platforms to assess consumer sentiment and fine-tune its messaging. The social media strategy for Charmin has evolved along with the social media landscape and has created one of the most engaged brand communities by using content that is both relevant and entertaining and relies on humor as its key ingredient. Charmin engages consumers on social media by not just focusing on toilet paper, but rather on the human experience of everything bathroom related. A key component of Charmin's "Enjoy the Go" campaign is the popular hashtag #tweetfromtheseat where followers can contribute potty protocol thoughts. With regard to Charmin's move into social media, Dan Cohen, senior vice president and creative director at Publicis, notes: "We believed that Charmin had a right to start a bigger more public conversation about going to the bathroom . . . and the timing was right with brands becoming active in social media."

Another example of how Charmin has pushed the envelope in its use of social media and beyond is a series of Charmin Intermissions created by Publicis New York. The Charmin Intermissions are 60- and 30-second television commercials that invite consumers to use the bathroom and "enjoy the go"

instead of watching a traditional commercial. Each Charmin Intermission is tagged and boosted in social to the surprise and delight of millions of relieved consumers throughout the country. To date, the brand has run these cheeky branded units during specific events including the Olympics, on Christmas Eve and New Year's Eve, and on Saturday Movie Night.

Charmin has also moved into mobile marketing by sponsoring and then acquiring the SitOrSquat app that helps consumers find the cleanest public restrooms worldwide and also provides user-generated listings of bathroom locations, ratings, hours of operation, and other details. Nearly a million consumers have downloaded the app and it has generated a tremendous amount of earned media from bloggers on social media and news stories in traditional media.

Charmin's brand team and Publicis New York understand the importance of having entertaining as well as relevant content to connect with consumers on social media. They continue to utilize a variety of channels to develop an IMC program that creates interest in the Charmin brand and helps differentiate what could easily be a highly commoditized product. Their work has not gone without notice; *Time* magazine selected Charmin as "the sassiest brand on Twitter" in 2014 based on recommendations from a panel of social media and marketing experts who rated brands that tweet the best quips, digs, and smackdowns. Developing creative campaigns to sell toilet paper may not be one of the most coveted jobs in marketing for many people. However, don't tell that to those who market Charmin and continue to find creative ways to get consumers to "enjoy the go."

Sources: Charmin Story, www.charmin.com/en-us/about-us/charmin-history; Chris Syme, "How Charmin Became the Sassiest Brand on Twitter," *SocialMediaToday*, March 4, 2014, www.socialmediatoday.com/content/how-charmin-became-sassiest-brand-twitter; Allan Ripp, "Charmin 'Rolls Out' Bold New Native Ad Campaign," *Adweek*, February 28, 2014, www.adweek.com/news/advertising-branding/charmin-rolls-out-bold-new-native-ad-campaign-156016.

The opening vignette illustrates how Procter & Gamble (P&G) has adapted its marketing strategy for Charmin to respond to changes taking place in the way marketers communicate with consumers. It provides an excellent example of how the roles of advertising and other forms of marketing communication are changing in the modern world of marketing. In the past, advertising was a relatively simple process as most companies relied primarily on ads run in the mass media to deliver their marketing messages to large numbers of consumers who watched television, listened to radio, and read magazines and newspapers. However, today's marketers recognize that the rapidly changing media environment is making it increasingly difficult to reach their target audiences and communicate effectively with them.

EXHIBIT 1–1

Mobile marketing is part of the integrated marketing communications program for Charmin

Source: Charmin by Procter & Gamble and Publicis Worldwide

The mass media are losing their viewers, listeners, and readers to the highly fragmented but more narrowly targeted digital media that allow consumers to be more actively engaged in the communication process. Consumers are no longer passive message recipients who will sit back and receive unfiltered advertising messages dictated by marketers. They want to be in more control of the content they receive from the media, and they are seeking out information, as well as entertainment, from a myriad of sources.

The various marketing communication tools used by Procter & Gamble for the Charmin brand show how companies are using *integrated marketing communications (IMC)* to reach their target audiences. P&G still uses traditional mass-media advertising through TV, magazines, and newspapers as well as out-of-home media to drive awareness, communicate information, and drive sales for the Charmin product line. P&G also uses these offline channels to influence online behavior by driving consumers to its website (www.charmin.com), which provides information about the various Charmin products, coupons, and other promotional offers, tips, and articles, and information on various causes supported by the brand through the Charmin Relief Project. Charmin is also promoted by through various social media platforms that have become an increasingly important part of the digital marketing campaigns of many companies. Consumers are encouraged to connect with Charmin through Facebook and Twitter while commercials and other entertaining videos for the brand are available on YouTube as well as Vine. Charmin is also using mobile marketing to connect with consumers on their smartphones by sponsoring the SitOrSquat app (Exhibit 1–1). Publicity for Charmin and its various marketing communication campaigns is generated through social media as well as public relations activities. Promotional efforts for Charmin are extended to retail stores where point-of-purchase displays and other tactics are used to encourage retailers to stock and promote the various brands in the product line.

Procter & Gamble, along with thousands of other companies, recognizes that the way it communicates with consumers and other relevant audiences to promote its products and services is changing rapidly and it must keep pace by integrating a variety of communication tools into its marketing programs.

The fragmentation of mass markets, the rapid growth of the Internet and other new digital media, the emergence of global markets, economic uncertainties, and changing lifestyles and media consumption habits of consumers are all changing the way companies develop their marketing programs—particularly advertising and promotion.[1] Developing marketing communication programs that are responsive to these changes is critical to the success of every company.

THE GROWTH OF ADVERTISING AND PROMOTION

Advertising and promotion are an integral part of our social and economic systems. In our complex society, advertising has evolved into a vital communications system for both consumers and businesses. The ability of advertising and other promotional methods to deliver carefully prepared messages to target audiences has given them a major role in the marketing programs of most organizations. Companies ranging from large multinational corporations to small retailers increasingly rely on advertising and promotion to help them market products and services. In market-based economies, consumers have learned to rely on advertising and other forms of promotion for information they can use in making purchase decisions.

In 1980, advertising and sales promotion were the dominant forms of marketing communication used by most companies, and total expenditures in the United

States across the two were just over $100 billion. Media advertising accounted for $53 billion, while $49 billion was spent on sales promotion techniques such as product samples, coupons, contests, sweepstakes, premiums, and rebates as well as trade allowances and discounts to retailers. By 2016, total marketing communications expenditures in the United States were estimated to be nearly $571 billion, with $127 billion being spent on traditional media advertising (television, radio, magazines, newspapers outdoor, cinema), $68 billion going to digital/online advertising, $51 billion going to direct mail and other forms of direct marketing such as e-mail marketing, $25 billion spent on sponsorships and experiential/event marketing, and the remaining $300 billion being spent on consumer and trade promotion.[2]

It is particularly interesting to note the amount of advertising spending being shifted from traditional media such as broadcast and print to online digital advertising formats including search, display, and video ads as well as social media. Total spending on digital advertising by U.S. marketers is expected to reach $100 billion by 2020 and represent 45 percent of all media advertising spending.[3] The largest category of Internet advertising is paid search on search engines such as Google, Yahoo!, and Bing, which accounts for nearly half of all online ad expenditures. Online display advertising follows close behind and is being driven by the growth in video ads being shown online. Spending on social media platforms such as Facebook, Twitter, Instagram, and Snapchat will be the fastest-growing digital channel over the next several years. Much of the growth in digital advertising is being driven by mobile marketing whereby ads, text messages, and promotional offers are sent directly to mobile devices such as smartphones and tablets. The shift to mobile marketing is occurring as consumers spend more time on their mobile devices and less time with traditional media. It is estimated that adults in the United States spend nearly three hours a day on mobile devices, with more than half of that time spent on smartphones.[4] Thus, while the traditional media and sales promotion still account for the majority of companies' marketing communications expenditures, more monies are being allocated to nontraditional media and the amount is expected to continue to increase rapidly, particularly for digital-originated advertising. Much of the growth in marketing communications investments will come from the shift of traditional "below-the-line" promotional spending in areas such as coupons, contests and sweepstakes, loyalty programs, and trade-directed marketing to digital solutions that provide marketers with more efficiency and measurable results.

Global marketing communications expenditures have grown as well over the past several decades. Advertising expenditures outside North America increased from $55 billion in 1980 to an estimated $382 billion in 2017.[5] While the United States still accounts for nearly a third of the world's advertising expenditures, nearly half of global ad expenditures are now occurring in Western Europe and the Asia-Pacific region followed by Latin America. After the United States, the top countries in advertising spending are China, Japan, the United Kingdom, Germany, and Brazil. Both foreign and domestic companies spend billions more on sales promotion, direct marketing, event sponsorship, and public relations as well as various forms of nontraditional media, all of which have become important components of their marketing communication programs. As is the case in the United States, Internet ad spending—which includes mobile, social, display, and search ads—is growing rapidly around the globe and is expected to increase its share of the total ad market to 41 percent by 2019.[6]

Advertising and promotion spending is expected to continue to increase as marketers around the world recognize the value and importance of advertising and other forms of marketing communication. Integrated marketing communications play an important role in the marketing programs of companies in their efforts to communicate with and sell their products and services to consumers. To understand the role integrated marketing communications play in the marketing process, let us first examine the marketing function.

THE ROLE OF MARKETING

Marketing has never been more important or more pervasive than it is today. Organizations ranging from large multinational corporations to small entrepreneurial companies and local businesses recognize that marketing is an important business function and plays a critical role in their ability to compete in the marketplace. For nearly two decades, the American Marketing Association (AMA), the organization that represents marketing professionals in the United States and Canada, defined marketing as *the process of planning and executing the conception, pricing, promotion, and distribution of ideas, goods, and services to create exchanges that satisfy individual and organizational objectives.*[7] This definition of marketing focused on **exchange** as a central concept in marketing and the use of the basic marketing activities to create and sustain relationships with customers.[8] For exchange to occur there must be two or more parties with something of value to one another, a desire and ability to give up that something to the other party, and a way to communicate with each other. Advertising and promotion play an important role in the exchange process by informing customers of an organization's product or service and convincing them of its ability to satisfy their needs or wants.

Not all marketing transactions involve the exchange of money for a product or service. Nonprofit organizations such as various causes, charities, religious groups, the arts, and colleges and universities (probably including the one you are attending) receive millions of dollars in donations every year. Many nonprofit organizations use ads to solicit contributions from the public such as the one shown in Exhibit 1–2 for the American Red Cross which responds to approximately 70,000 disasters in the United States every year including floods, fires, tornadoes, hurricanes, and earthquakes that affect tens of thousands. Donors generally do not receive any material benefits for their contributions; they donate in exchange for intangible social and psychological satisfactions such as feelings of goodwill and altruism.

While many still view exchange as the core phenomenon or domain for study in marketing, there is also agreement among most academicians and practitioners that the discipline is rapidly changing. To reflect these changes, the AMA adopted a revised definition of **marketing** in 2007, which is as follows:

> Marketing is the activity, set of institutions, and processes for creating, communicating, delivering and exchanging offerings that have value for customers, clients, partners, and society at large.[9]

EXHIBIT 1–2

Nonprofit organizations use advertising to solicit contributions and support

Source: American Red Cross

Not all heroes wear capes.

Every nine minutes, volunteers help the American Red Cross bring help and hope to people in need. Join us and make a difference in your community.

Be a hero. Volunteer today.

American Red Cross

Sign up at redcross.org
#BeAHero

This revised definition is viewed as being more reflective of the role of nonmarketers to the marketing process. It also recognizes the important role marketing plays in the process of creating, communicating, and delivering value to customers, as well as society at large. Today, most markets are seeking more than just a one-time exchange or transaction with customers. The focus of market-driven companies is on developing and sustaining *relationships* with their customers. Successful companies recognize that creating, communicating, and delivering *value* to their customers is extremely important. **Value** is the customer's perception of all the benefits of a product or service weighed against all the costs of acquiring and consuming it.[10] Benefits can be functional (the performance of the product), experiential (what it feels like to use the product), and/or psychological (feelings such as self-esteem or status that result from owning a particular brand). Costs include the money paid for the product or service as well as other factors such as acquiring information about the product/service, making the purchase, learning how to use it, maintaining the product, and disposing of it.

The Marketing Mix

Marketing facilitates the exchange process and the development of relationships by carefully examining the needs and wants of consumers, developing a product or service that satisfies these needs, offering it at a certain price, making it available through a particular place or channel of distribution, and developing a program of promotion or communication to create awareness and interest. These four Ps—product, price, place (distribution), and promotion—are elements of the **marketing mix**. The basic task of marketing is combining these four elements into a marketing program to facilitate the potential for exchange with consumers in the marketplace.

The proper marketing mix does not just happen. Marketers must be knowledgeable about the issues and options involved in each element of the mix. They must also be aware of how these elements can be combined to form an effective marketing program that delivers value to consumers. The market must be analyzed through consumer research, and the resulting information must be used to develop an overall marketing strategy and mix.

The primary focus of this book is on one element of the marketing mix: the promotional variable. However, the promotional program must be part of a viable marketing strategy and be coordinated with other marketing activities. A firm can spend large sums on advertising, sales promotion, or other forms of marketing communication, but it stands little chance of success if the product is of poor quality, is priced improperly, or does not have adequate distribution to consumers. Marketers have long recognized the importance of combining the elements of the marketing mix into a cohesive marketing strategy. Many companies also recognize the need to integrate their various marketing communications efforts, such as media advertising, direct marketing, sales promotion, Internet marketing, social media, event sponsorships, and public relations, to achieve more effective marketing communications.

INTEGRATED MARKETING COMMUNICATIONS

For many years, the promotional function in most companies was dominated by mass-media advertising. Companies relied primarily on their advertising agencies for guidance in nearly all areas of marketing communication. Most marketers did use additional promotional and marketing communication tools, but sales promotion and direct-marketing agencies as well as package design firms were generally viewed as auxiliary services and often used on a per-project basis. Public relations agencies were used to manage the organization's publicity, image, and affairs with relevant publics on an ongoing basis but were not viewed as integral participants in the marketing communications process.

Many marketers built strong barriers around the various marketing and promotional functions and planned and managed them as separate practices, with different budgets, different views of the market, and different goals and objectives. These companies failed to recognize that the wide range of marketing and promotional tools must be coordinated to communicate effectively and present a consistent image to target markets.

The Evolution of IMC

During the 1980s, many companies began taking a broader perspective of marketing communication and recognizing the need for a more strategic integration of their promotional tools. The decade was characterized by the rapid development of areas such as sales promotion, direct marketing, and public relations, which began challenging advertising's role as the dominant form of marketing communication. These firms began moving toward the process of **integrated marketing communications (IMC)**, which involves coordinating the various promotional elements and other marketing activities that communicate with a firm's customers.[11] As marketers embraced the concept of integrated marketing communications, they began asking their ad agencies to coordinate the use of a variety of promotional tools rather than relying primarily on media advertising. A number of companies also began to look beyond traditional advertising agencies and use other types of promotional specialists to develop and implement various components of their promotional plans.

Many agencies responded to the call for synergy among the promotional tools by acquiring PR, sales promotion, and direct-marketing companies and touting themselves as IMC agencies that offer one-stop shopping for all their clients' promotional needs.[12] Some agencies became involved in these nonadvertising areas to gain control over their clients' promotional programs and budgets and struggled to offer any real value beyond creating advertising. However, the advertising industry soon recognized that IMC was more than just a fad. Terms such as *new advertising, orchestration*, and *seamless communication* were used to describe the concept of integration.[13] A task force from the American Association of Advertising Agencies (the "4As") developed one of the first definitions of integrated marketing communications:

> a concept of marketing communications planning that recognizes the added value of a comprehensive plan that evaluates the strategic roles of a variety of communication disciplines—for example, general advertising, direct response, sales promotion, and public relations—and combines these disciplines to provide clarity, consistency, and maximum communications impact.[14]

EXHIBIT 1–3

Montblanc uses a variety of marketing-mix elements, including price, product design, brand name, and distribution strategy, to create a high-quality, upscale image for its watches. Does incorporating a well-known celebrity into this ad help reinforce Montblanc's image?

Source: Montblanc

The 4As' definition focused on the process of using all forms of promotion to achieve maximum communication impact. However, advocates of the IMC concept argued for an even broader perspective that considers *all sources of brand or company contact* that a customer or prospect has with a product or service.[15] They noted that the process of integrated marketing communications calls for a "big-picture" approach to planning marketing and promotion programs and coordinating the various communication functions. It requires that firms develop a total marketing communications strategy that recognizes how all of a firm's marketing activities, not just promotion, communicate with its customers.

Consumers' perceptions of a company and/or its various brands are a synthesis of the bundle of messages they receive or contacts they have, such as media advertisements, price, package design, direct-marketing efforts, publicity, sales promotions, websites, point-of-purchase displays, and even the type of store where a product or service is sold. The integrated marketing communications approach seeks to have all of a company's marketing and promotional activities project a consistent, unified image to the marketplace. It recognizes that every customer interaction with a company or brand across a host of contact points represents an opportunity to deliver on the brand promise, strengthen customer relationships and deepen loyalty. It calls for a centralized messaging function so that everything a company says and does communicates a common theme and positioning. For example, Montblanc uses classic design and a distinctive brand name as well as high price to position its watches as high-quality, high-status products. This upscale image is enhanced by the company's strategy of distributing its products only through boutiques, jewelry stores, and other exclusive shops, including its own stores. Montblanc also occasionally uses celebrities such as actor Hugh Jackman in its advertising as shown in the ad in Exhibit 1–3.

Many companies have adopted this broader perspective of IMC. They see it as a way to coordinate and manage their marketing communication programs to ensure that they send customers a consistent message about the company and/or its brands. For these companies, integration represents an improvement over the traditional method of treating the various marketing and promotion elements as virtually separate activities. However, this perspective of IMC has been challenged on the basis that it focuses primarily on the tactical coordination of various communication tools with the goal of making them look and sound alike.[16] It has been criticized as an "inside-out marketing" approach that is a relatively simple matter of bundling promotional-mix elements together so they have one look and speak with one voice.[17] As IMC continued to evolve, both academicians as well as practitioners recognized that a broader perspective was needed that would view the discipline from a more strategic perspective.

A Contemporary Perspective of IMC

As marketers become more sophisticated and develop a better understanding of IMC, they are recognizing that it involves more than just coordinating the various elements of their marketing and communications programs into a "one look, one voice" approach. IMC is now recognized as a business process that helps companies identify the most appropriate and effective methods for communicating and building relationships with customers and other stakeholders. Don Schultz of Northwestern University has developed what many think is a more appropriate definition of IMC:

> Integrated marketing communication is a strategic business process used to plan, develop, execute and evaluate coordinated, measurable, persuasive brand communications programs over time with consumers, customers, prospects, employees, associates and other targeted relevant external and internal audiences. The goal is to generate both short-term financial returns and build long-term brand and shareholder value.[18]

There are several important aspects of this definition of IMC. First, it views IMC as an ongoing strategic business process rather than just tactical integration of various communication activities. It also recognizes that there are a number of relevant audiences that are an important part of the process. Externally these include customers, prospects, suppliers, investors, interest groups, and the general public. It also views internal audiences such as employees as an important part of the IMC process. Schultz also notes that this definition reflects the increasing emphasis that is being placed on the demand for accountability and measurement of the *outcomes* of marketing communication programs as well as marketing in general.

Many companies are realizing that communicating effectively with customers and other stakeholders involves more than just the tactical use of the traditional marketing communication tools. These firms, along with many advertising agencies, are embracing IMC and incorporating it into their marketing and business practices. It is true, however, that not all companies have moved beyond the stage of simply bundling promotional-mix elements together and made the organization changes and investment that are needed for true integration. Moreover, some academics and practitioners have questioned whether IMC is just another "management fashion" whose influence will be transitory.[19] Critics of IMC argue that it merely reinvents and renames existing ideas and concepts and question its significance for marketing and advertising thought and practice.[20]

While the debate over the value and relevance of IMC is likely to continue, proponents of the concept far outnumber the critics. IMC is proving to be a permanent change that offers significant value to marketers in the rapidly changing communications environment they are facing in the new millennium. IMC has been described as one of the "new-generation" marketing approaches being used by companies to better focus their efforts in acquiring, retaining, and developing relationships with customers and other stakeholders.[21] We will now discuss some of the reasons for the growing importance of IMC.

Reasons for the Growing Importance of IMC

The IMC approach to marketing communications planning and strategy is being adopted by both large and small companies and has become popular among firms marketing consumer products and services as well as business-to-business marketers. There are a number of reasons why marketers are adopting the IMC approach. A fundamental reason is that they understand the value of strategically integrating the various communications functions rather than having them operate autonomously. By coordinating their marketing communication efforts, companies can avoid duplication, take advantage of synergy among promotional tools, and develop more efficient and effective marketing communication programs. Advocates of IMC argue that it is one of the easiest ways for a company to maximize the return on its investment in marketing and promotion.[22]

The move to integrated marketing also reflects an adaptation by marketers to a changing environment, particularly with respect to consumers, technology, and media consumption behavior. For decades, reaching consumers was relatively easy as marketers could run their ads in mass media (so named because they reach mass audiences) such as television, radio, magazines, and newspapers. The formula was really very simple as the mass media had a symbiotic relationship with mass marketers such as automotive firms, consumer packaged-goods companies, and many others. The media companies would develop and deliver expensive, but high-quality content that would in turn attract large audiences. The marketers would pay large amounts of money to the television and radio networks and stations and/or magazine and newspaper publishers for access to the mass audiences who would receive the advertising messages that encouraged them to purchase the marketers' products and services. The advertising revenue that the media companies received would be used to produce the high-quality content which in turn would allow the media to continue to deliver the viewers, listeners, and readers that the marketers coveted.

Over the past decade, however, there have been major changes in the media landscape that are impacting the traditional mass media and the economic model that has supported them. There has been an evolution to *micromarketing* as the mass audience assembled by network television and augmented by other mass media is fragmenting at an accelerating rate.[23] Viewing audiences are moving from the traditional broadcast networks (ABC, CBS, NBC, and Fox) to more narrowly targeted programs on cable networks such as ESPN, USA, CNN, and MTV, as well as to other forms of entertainment such as Netflix, Hulu, Amazon Prime, and video on demand (VOD). Many younger consumers spend just as much time watching videos on YouTube or Vimeo as they do watching television. The Internet has become an important advertising medium with online versions of nearly every television station, newspaper, and magazine. The crude banners and pop-up ads that initially defined Internet advertising are giving way to more refined formats such as paid search, which is the fastest-growing form of online advertising, as well as video and other forms of engaging content.

EXHIBIT 1–4

What makes Google AdWords the most popular platform for online search advertising?

Source: Google Inc.

Advertisers can use the Internet in a more targeted way than traditional media. They can run their ads on websites or social media sites that are narrowly targeted to consumer interests or have their ads appear on search engines such as Google, Yahoo!, and Bing which are seen when people are seeking information about a product or service. For example, Google dominates as the online search advertising marketer with its keyword-targeted advertising program called AdWords (Exhibit 1–4). Social networking sites such as Facebook, Snapchat, Twitter, LinkedIn, Instagram, and YouTube have become pervasive on the Internet and make it possible for people to share content, opinions, insights, and experiences as well as educate one another about companies, brands, and various issues.[24]

Digital and Social Media Perspective 1–1 > > >

A WORLD WITHOUT DIGITAL ADVERTISING: BE CAREFUL WHAT YOU WISH FOR

Consumers are often annoyed by advertising and many, if not most, would welcome the opportunity to avoid ads altogether. In fact, consumers have been routinely avoiding advertising messages for years by using a remote control to change channels during the commercial break of a television show or switching radio stations in cars when the music ends and the ads begin. Digital video recorders (DVRs), which were first introduced by TiVO in 1999 and are now in nearly 50 percent of U.S. homes, have given consumers yet another way to avoid advertising by making it possible for viewers to fast-forward through content (including the commercials) when watching a recorded show. Studies have shown that 55 percent of television viewing is now done on a delayed or on-demand basis through DVRs, video streaming subscriptions, and other options, and the number rises to 72 percent among millennials. It is estimated that half of the viewers watching a recorded television show routinely skip the commercial. The number would be higher if it were not for the fact that many of them are too busy on their smartphones and tablets to fast-forward through the ads given that two-thirds of viewers watch TV while also engaged with a second screen. Some consumers avoid television ads altogether by paying for subscriptions to Netflix, Showtime, or HBO, which are commercial free, or purchasing the *No Commercials* plan on Hulu.

Marketers recognize that it has become more difficult to get consumers to watch and/or pay attention to their television commercials. They also know that people are spending more time online than with traditional media and thus are shifting more of their media spending to various forms of digital advertising. Spending on digital advertising by marketers has already surpassed traditional media of newspapers and magazines and is expected to overtake television by 2019 and account for nearly 40 percent of all ad spending. However, as marketers shift their ads online, they are dealing with yet another weapon being used by consumers to avoid advertising—ad blockers. While most consumers have installed ad-blocking software on their desktop and laptop computers, many are now doing so on their mobile devices (smartphones and tablets), filtering out most ads. The battle to avoid being bombarded with ads on mobile devices shifted in favor of consumers in the fall of 2015 when Apple revealed that it was adding "content blocking" extensions in the new iOS 9 operating system for its Safari mobile browser. A few months later ad-blocking capabilities became available on mobile devices using the Android operating system such as the popular Samsung Galaxy phones and tablets.

If you are like many people and spend a great amount of time online, ad blocking probably sounds like a good idea because it allows you to avoid being exposed to a myriad of annoying ads, most of which are of little or no interest to you. However, the advertising industry, as well as online publishers such as newspapers, magazines, blogs, and the multitude of websites available on the Internet, are concerned over the impact ad blockers are having on their digital advertising business. The reason for their concern is that ad blocking has the potential to undermine the central business model for much of the Internet. This model is really quite simple as the companies that offer content online make money by selling advertising space on the websites, apps, and social media sites that we all visit, and they get

To respond to the media fragmentation, marketers are increasing their spending on media that are more targeted and can reach specific market segments. Many marketers are shifting more of their advertising budgets to the Internet as digital ad spending is expected to increase from 32 percent of total U.S. advertising expenditures in 2016 to 45 percent by 2020. Meanwhile, traditional print advertising is expected to decline by 2 percent annually. Internet advertising has already surpassed newspaper and magazine advertising and is expected to overtake TV advertising by 2018.[25] There appears to be no stopping the fragmentation of the consumer market as well as the proliferation of media. The success of marketing communication programs will depend on how well companies make the transition from the fading age of mass marketing to the new era of micromarketing. Most marketers are learning that it no longer makes economic sense to send an advertising message to the many in hopes of persuading the few.

In addition to the proliferation of media and fragmentation of audiences, marketers are also facing the challenge of consumers being less responsive to traditional advertising. Many consumers are turned off by advertising and other forms of marketing communication as they are tired of being bombarded with

Browse fast, safe and free of annoying ads with Adblock Browser

Email me the download link

The most popular ad blocker for desktop browsers is now available for your Android* and iOS** devices.

* Adblock Browser is compatible with devices running Android 2.3 and above. Installation requires about 24 MB of internal storage, 384 MB of RAM and a display that is at least 320 pixels high and 240 pixels wide.
** Only available on iPhone and iPad with iOS 8 and above installed.

Source: Adblock Browser by Eyeo GmbH

paid based on the number of people who see or click on the ads. For most sites, it is estimated that between 10 to 50 percent of their visitors use an ad blocker, which means that a significant percentage of the audience the company could be profiting from has disappeared. Adding to the problem is the fact that millennials, who are one of the most coveted target markets for many advertisers, are most likely to use ad blockers; surveys have found that 41 percent of this age group have installed the software.

Most consumers are glad that they do not have advertising messages cluttering the content on their smartphones and tablets and enjoy being able to fast-forward through television commercials. However, those who see ads as something to avoid might want to take a moment to think about what would happen if we lived in an ad-free world. Without advertising television networks and local stations would have to rely entirely on viewers for revenue and the average household, which is already paying well over $100 a month for subscription TV service, would see their monthly bills increase by 50 percent and they would get a lot fewer channels. Nearly all of the social media sites where younger consumers in particular spend much of

their time—such as Facebook, Instagram, and Snapchat—generate nearly all of their income from advertising. You might ask yourself how much you would be willing to pay per year for an ad-free Facebook and whether you would be willing to pay to subsidize the 450 million users who reside in what Facebook calls the rest of the world (everywhere but the United States, Canada, Europe, and Asia-Pacific) and could not pay even modest subscription fees.

In addition to the television industry and social media sites, web publishers as well as the magazine and newspaper industry would be devastated if they lost all of their advertising revenue. Many people are already reading content from magazines and newspapers for free online as most publications have been unsuccessful in getting people to pay for subscriptions to their digital versions or consumers find a way to get around their firewalls. Thus, digital advertising is critical to their survival. The next time you do a Google search for a class assignment or just for some information on a specific topic, product, or service, remember that Google is basically an ad-serving company that generates nearly 90 percent of its revenue from advertising.

So if you are like most consumers and do not like advertising because your find it irritating, annoying, and intrusive, you might want to think twice about what the world would be like without it. Perhaps *Advertising Age* writer Simon Dumenco described it best: "To all the ad haters and ad blockers out there, well, keep this in mind: As famed copywriter Oscar Wilde once wrote, 'When the Gods wish to punish us, they answer our prayers.'"

Sources: Jack Neff, "The Big Agenda: What Lies Ahead for Marketing in an Increasingly Ad-Free Future," *Advertising Age*, January 11, 2016, http://adage.com/article/print-edition/big-agenda-ad-industry-2016/302067/; Simon Dumenco, "Imagine a World without Ads," *Advertising Age*, September 28, 2015, pp. 28–32; Maureen Morrison and Tim Peterson, "The War on Advertising," *Advertising Age*, pp. 10–12; Adam Satariano, "If You Blocked This Ad, We Wouldn't Get Paid," *Bloomberg Businessweek*, September 27, 2015.

sales messages.[26] Many consumers in the millennial generation age cohort (which includes most college students) are skeptical of traditional advertising. Having grown up in an even more media-saturated and brand-conscious world than their parents did, they respond to advertising differently and prefer to encounter marketing messages in different places and from different sources. Marketers recognize that to penetrate the skepticism and capture the attention of the millennials, as well as other age cohorts, they have to bring their messages to them in different ways such as integrating their brands into TV shows and movies. For example, Pepsi developed a creative tie-in to the movie *Back to the Future Part II* by creating 6,500 bottles of a limited-edition soft drink called "Pepsi Perfect" that was featured in the movie[27] (Exhibit 1–5). Many marketers are also shifting their ad spending to television programming that consumers are more likely to watch live, such as college and NFL football games, rather than watching on a delayed basis on a DVR and fast-forwarding through the commercials.[28] Consumers are actively seeking ways to avoid advertising messages, not only on television but online as well by installing ad blockers on their computers, tablets, and smartphones. Digital and Social Media Perspective 1–1 discusses the impact ad-blocking software is

having on digital advertising, which is at the core of the business model for online publishers, websites, and social media.

The integrated marketing communications movement is also being driven by fundamental changes in the way companies market their products and services and an ongoing marketing revolution that is changing the rules of marketing.[29] These changes and developments are affecting everyone involved in the marketing and promotional process. Marketers can no longer be tied to a specific communication tool (such as media advertising); rather, they should use whatever contact methods offer the best way of delivering the message to their target audiences. Ad agencies continue to reposition themselves as offering more than just advertising expertise; they strive to convince their clients that they can manage all or any part of clients' integrated marketing communications needs. Most agencies recognize that their future success depends on their ability to understand how to develop and place advertising messages not just for traditional media but also for the rapidly evolving areas of digital marketing, including social media and mobile.

The Role of IMC in Branding

One of the major reasons for the growing importance of integrated marketing communications over the past decade is that it plays a major role in the process of developing and sustaining brand identity and equity. As branding expert Kevin Keller notes, "Building and properly managing brand equity has become a priority for companies of all sizes, in all types of industries, in all types of markets."[30] With more and more products and services competing for consideration by customers who have less and less time to make choices, well-known brands have a major competitive advantage in today's marketplace. Building and maintaining brand identity and equity require the creation of well-known brands that have favorable, strong, and unique associations in the mind of the consumer.[31] Companies recognize that brand equity is as important an asset as factories, patents, and cash because strong brands have the power to command a premium price from consumers as well as investors. While competitors may be able to duplicate their product designs and manufacturing processes, it is very difficult to duplicate the beliefs, images, and impressions that are ingrained in the mind of consumers as well as the emotions brands evoke. Figure 1–1 shows the world's most valuable brands, as measured by Interbrand, a leading brand consultancy company.

Brand identity is a combination of many factors, including the name, logo, symbols, design, packaging, and performance of a product or service as well as the image or type of associations that come to mind when consumers think about a brand. It encompasses the entire spectrum of consumers' awareness, knowledge, and image of the brand as well as the company behind it. It is the sum of all points of encounter or contact that consumers have with the brand, and it extends beyond the experience or outcome of using it. These contacts can also result from various forms of integrated marketing communications activities used by a company, including mass-media advertising, sales promotion offers, sponsorship activities at sporting or entertainment events, websites on the Internet, social media, and direct-mail pieces such as e-mails, brochures, catalogs, or DVDs. Consumers can also have contact with or receive information about a brand in stores at the point of sale; through articles or stories they see, hear, or read in the media; or through interactions with a company representative, such as a salesperson. For many companies, mass-media advertising has long been the cornerstone of their brand-building efforts. However, astute marketers recognize that the way consumers relate to brands is changing and they can no longer build and maintain brand equity merely by spending large sums of money on media advertising and other forms of marketing communication. Brands

FIGURE 1–1

Best Global Brands 2015
Report

Rank	Brand	Brand Value (billions)
1	Apple	$170,276
2	Google	120,314
3	Coca-Cola	78,423
4	Microsoft	67,670
5	IBM	69,095
6	Toyota	49,048
7	Samsung	45,297
8	General Electric	42,267
9	McDonald's	39,809
10	amazon	37,948

Source: "Interbrand's Best Global Brands 2015" is a look at financial performance of the brand, role of brand in the purchase decision process, and the brand strength. Go to http://interbrand.com/best-brands/best-global-brands/2015/ for more information.

are becoming less about the actual product or service and more about how people relate to them. Consumers today demand more than just product/service quality or performance as many view brands as a form of self-expression. It is also widely recognized that marketing is now in the relationship era and companies must connect with consumers based on trust, transparency, engagement, and authenticity. As one chief marketing officer notes: "the future of marketing isn't about getting people to buy your brand, but to buy *into* your brand."[32]

The relationship between brands and their customers has become much more complex. One reason for this is that today's consumer knows much more about brands and the companies that make them than ever before. The value chain of companies has become increasingly visible, and consumers often select brands based on the social, economic, and environmental records and policies of the companies that make them. **Sustainability**, which refers to development that meets the needs of the current generation without compromising the ability of future generations to meet their needs, has become a very important issue for both consumers and corporation.[33] Companies are addressing sustainability by carefully examining the social and environmental impacts of their marketing strategies. This means reevaluating their product and service portfolios, as well as the way these products and services are created, produced, and marketed. Exhibit 1–6 shows an ad from the campaign for the General Electric Company's ecomagination sustainability initiative, which is a companywide commitment to address global challenges such as the need for cleaner, more efficient sources of energy, reduced emissions, and abundant sources of clean water.

Cynicism about corporations remains high following the Great Recession, and many companies must continue to work hard to gain consumer trust and confidence. Companies are also finding it more difficult to control their brand image because the Internet provides consumers with a wealth of information about their products and services that can be easily accessed and shared. They can use the Internet to make price and quality comparisons or to learn what others think about various brands as well as learn about their experiences or satisfaction with them. The pervasiveness of social media has transformed traditional word-of-mouth into viral "word-of-mouse" messages that fly around Facebook, Twitter, YouTube, or Yelp at the speed of send. Consumers' passion for brands shows no sign of waning

EXHIBIT 1–6

This ad, part of the
General Electric's
ecomagination
initiative, shows its
commitment to clean
water

Source: General Electric

There are oceans of clean water out there.

Water purification technology from GE turns seawater into fresh, usable water. So no matter where you are on earth, the well will never run dry. To learn more, visit ecomagination.com.

GE imagination at work

and in fact may be getting stronger. However, the ways that companies connect consumers to their companies and brands are changing.

Marketers recognize that in the modern world of marketing, there are many different opportunities and methods for *contacting* current and prospective customers to provide them with information about a company and/or brands. The challenge is to understand how to use the various IMC tools to make such contacts and deliver the branding message effectively and efficiently. A successful IMC program requires that marketers find the right combination of communication tools and techniques, define their role and the extent to which they can or should be used, and coordinate their use. To accomplish this, the persons responsible for the company's communication efforts must have an understanding of the IMC tools that are available and the ways they can be used.

THE PROMOTIONAL MIX: THE TOOLS FOR IMC

Promotion has been defined as the coordination of all seller-initiated efforts to set up channels of information and persuasion in order to sell goods and services or promote an idea.[34] While implicit communication occurs through the various elements of the marketing mix, most of an organization's communications with the marketplace take place as part of a carefully planned and controlled promotional program. The basic tools used to accomplish an organization's communication objectives are often referred to as the **promotional mix** (Figure 1–2).

FIGURE 1–2

Elements of the Promotional
Mix

The Promotional Mix

| Advertising | Direct marketing | Digital/ Internet marketing | Sales promotion | Publicity/ public relations | Personal selling |

Traditionally the promotional mix has included four elements: advertising, sales promotion, publicity/public relations, and personal selling. However, in this text we view direct marketing as well as digital/Internet marketing that takes place online as major promotional-mix elements that marketers use to communicate with their target markets. Each element of the promotional mix is viewed as an integrated marketing communications tool that plays a distinctive role in an IMC program. Each may take on a variety of forms. And each has certain advantages.

Advertising

Advertising is defined as any paid form of nonpersonal communication about an organization, product, service, or idea by an identified sponsor.[35] The *paid* aspect of this definition reflects the fact that the space or time for an advertising message generally must be bought. An occasional exception to this is the public service announcement (PSA), whose advertising space or time is donated by the media, usually to a nonprofit organization or cause.

The *nonpersonal* component means that advertising involves mass media (e.g., TV, radio, magazines, newspapers) that can transmit a message to large groups of individuals, often at the same time. The nonpersonal nature of advertising means that there is generally no opportunity for immediate feedback from the message recipient (except in direct-response advertising). Therefore, before the message is sent, the advertiser must consider how the audience will interpret and respond to it.

Advertising is the best-known and most widely discussed form of promotion, probably because of its pervasiveness. It is also a very important promotional tool, particularly for companies whose products and services are targeted at mass consumer markets such as automobile manufacturers and packaged-goods and drug companies. Nearly 200 companies spend over $200 million on advertising in the United States each year including spending in measured media (television, radio, newspapers, magazines, outdoor, and Internet display advertising) as well as unmeasured media (direct marketing, promotion, online search, social media, and other forms). Figure 1–3 shows the advertising and promotion expenditures of the 25 leading national advertisers.

There are several reasons why advertising is such an important part of many marketers' IMC programs. First, media advertising is still the most cost-effective way to reach large numbers of consumers with an advertising message. Television in particular is an excellent way for marketers to reach mass markets. The average television program on the four major television networks during prime time (8:00 p.m. to 11:00 p.m.) reaches nearly 5 million households. The cost per thousand households reached on network TV during prime time in 2015 was $23.81.[36] Popular shows such as *NCIS, The Big Bang Theory*, and *The Voice* can reach between 15 and 20 million viewers each week. And while the viewing audiences for cable networks such as ESPN, CNN, and MTV are smaller than those for the major networks, their programming appeals to more specific audiences that many marketers are trying to reach. Magazines such as *Time, Sports Illustrated*, and *People* have a weekly circulation of more than 3 million and can reach more than 10 million people since there are multiple readers of each issue. Thus, for marketers who want to build or maintain brand awareness and reach mass markets with their advertising message, media advertising remains an excellent way to do so.[37]

Advertising is also a valuable tool for building company or brand equity because it is a powerful way to provide consumers with information as well as to influence their perceptions. Advertising can be used to create favorable and unique images and associations for a brand, which can be very important for companies selling products or services that are difficult to differentiate on the basis of functional attributes. Brand image plays an important role in the purchase of many products

FIGURE 1–3

25 Leading Advertisers in the United States, 2015

Rank	Advertiser	Ad Spending (millions)
1	Procter & Gamble	4,265
2	AT&T	3,866
3	General Motors Co.	3,495
4	Comcast Corp.	3,436
5	Verizon Communications	2,749
6	Ford Motor Co.	2,678
7	American Express Co.	2,349
8	Fiat Chrysler Automobiles	2,250
9	Amazon	2,198
10	Samsung Electronics Co.	2,123
11	Walmart Stores	2,090
12	JPMorgan Chase & Co.	2,063
13	Johnson & Johnson	2,009
14	L'Oreal	1,994
15	Pfizer	1,926
16	Toyota Motor Corp.	1,802
17	Walt Disney Co.	1,798
18	Time Warner	1,690
19	Berkshire Hathaway	1,683
20	Anheuser-Busch InBev	1,682
21	Capital One Financial Corp.	1,651
22	21st Century Fox	1,633
23	Deutsche Telekom (T-Mobile)	1,600
24	Macy's	1,587
25	Bank of America Corp.	1,573

Source: "200 Leading National Advertisers," *Advertising Age*, June 27, 2016, p. 16. Copyright © Crain Communications 2016.

and services, and advertising is still recognized as one of the best ways to build a brand. Exhibit 1–7 shows an ad from a campaign run by the American Advertising Federation promoting the value of advertising.

The nature and purpose of advertising differ from one industry to another and/or across situations. Companies selling products and services to the consumer market generally rely heavily on advertising to communicate with their target audiences, as do retailers and other local merchants. However, advertising can also be done by an industry to stimulate demand for a product category such as beef or milk. Advertising is also used extensively by companies who compete in the business and professional markets to reach current and potential customers. For example,

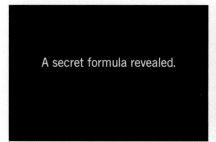

EXHIBIT 1–7

The American Advertising Federation promotes the value of advertising

© *American Advertising Federation*

business-to-business (B2B) marketers use advertising to perform important functions such as building awareness of the company and its products, generating leads for the sales force, reassuring customers about the purchase they have made, or helping create a favorable image of the company. B2B marketers generally target their advertising to reach key decision makers in other companies and often run their ads in business publications such as magazines and newspapers, although television and the Internet are the largest categories for B2B ad spending. Many products such as personal computers, tablets, smartphones, and printers along with services such as finance and banking, telecommunications, and insurance are marketed to both business customers and consumers. Thus, marketers sometimes develop ad campaigns that serve both markets.[38] The leading B2B advertisers include major corporations such as Microsoft, AT&T, IBM, and General Electric.[39] Exhibit 1–8 shows an ad from an integrated campaign for Microsoft's Surface Pro 4 tablet that targets both the consumer and business markets and positions it as "the tablet that can replace your laptop." Figure 1–4 describes the most common types of advertising.

Direct Marketing

One of the fastest-growing sectors of the U.S. economy is **direct marketing**, in which organizations communicate directly with target customers to generate a response and/or a transaction. Traditionally, direct marketing has not been considered an element of the promotional mix. However, because it has become such an integral part of the IMC program of many organizations and often involves separate objectives, budgets, and strategies, we view direct marketing as a component of the promotional mix.

Direct marketing is much more than direct mail and mail-order catalogs. It involves a variety of activities, including database management, direct selling, telemarketing, and direct-response advertising through direct mail, online, and various broadcast and print media. Some companies, such as Tupperware, Avon, Mary Kay, Herbalife, and Amway, do not use any other distribution channels, relying on independent contractors to sell their products directly to consumers. Companies such as L.L.Bean, Lands' End, and J.Crew have been very successful in using direct marketing to sell their clothing products. The FTD Companies has a diversified portfolio of brands sold primarily through direct marketing including ProFlowers, Personal Creations, Cherry Moon Farms, Flying Flowers, Flowers Direct, Sincerely, and Gifts.com. Dell became a market leader in the computer industry by selling a full line of personal computers through direct marketing.

EXHIBIT 1–8

Business-to-business advertisers such as Microsoft use advertising to promote their products and services

Source: Microsoft

One of the major tools of direct marketing is **direct-response advertising**, whereby a product is promoted through an ad that encourages the consumer to purchase directly from the manufacturer. Traditionally, direct mail has been the primary medium for direct-response advertising, although television and the Internet have become increasingly important media. Direct-response advertising and other forms of direct marketing have become very popular over the past two decades, owing primarily to changing lifestyles, particularly the increase in two-income households.

FIGURE 1–4

Classifications of Advertising

ADVERTISING TO CONSUMER MARKETS

National Advertising
Advertising done by large companies on a nationwide basis or in most regions of the country. Most of the ads for well-known companies and brands that are seen on prime-time TV or in other major national or regional media are examples of national advertising. The goals of national advertisers are to inform or remind consumers of the company or brand and its features, benefits, advantages, or uses and to create or reinforce its image so that consumers will be predisposed to purchase it.

Retail/Local Advertising
Advertising done by retailers or local merchants to encourage consumers to shop at a specific store, use a local service, or patronize a particular establishment. Retail or local advertising tends to emphasize specific patronage motives such as price, hours of operation, service, atmosphere, image, or merchandise assortment. Retailers are concerned with building store traffic, so their promotions often take the form of direct-action advertising designed to produce immediate store traffic and sales.

Primary- versus Selective-Demand Advertising
Primary-demand advertising is designed to stimulate demand for the general product class or entire industry. Selective-demand advertising focuses on creating demand for a specific company's brands. Most advertising for products and services is concerned with stimulating selective demand and emphasizes reasons for purchasing a particular brand.
    An advertiser might concentrate on stimulating primary demand when, for example, its brand dominates a market and will benefit the most from overall market growth. Primary-demand advertising is often used as part of a promotional strategy to help a new product gain market acceptance, since the challenge is to sell customers on the product concept as much as to sell a particular brand. Industry trade associations also try to stimulate primary demand for their members' products, among them cotton, milk, orange juice, pork, and beef.

ADVERTISING TO BUSINESS AND PROFESSIONAL MARKETS

Business-to-Business Advertising
Advertising targeted at individuals who buy or influence the purchase of industrial goods or services for their companies. Industrial goods are products that either become a physical part of another product (raw material or component parts), are used in manufacturing other goods (machinery), or are used to help a company conduct its business (e.g., office supplies, computers). Business services such as insurance, travel services, and health care are also included in this category.

Professional Advertising
Advertising targeted to professionals such as doctors, lawyers, dentists, engineers, or professors to encourage them to use a company's product in their business operations. It might also be used to encourage professionals to recommend or specify the use of a company's product by end-users.

Trade Advertising
Advertising targeted to marketing channel members such as wholesalers, distributors, and retailers. The goal is to encourage channel members to stock, promote, and resell the manufacturer's branded products to their customers.

NEW ARRIVALS
We'll keep building the gear. You'll keep getting better.

EXHIBIT 1–9

Under Armour is an example of a company that successfully sells its products online as well as through retail channels

Source: Under Armour, Inc.

This has meant more discretionary income but less time for in-store shopping. The availability of credit cards and toll-free phone numbers has also facilitated the purchase of products from direct-response ads. More recently, the rapid growth of mobile devices to access the Internet is fueling the growth of direct marketing. Many consumers go straight to their smartphones or tablets to search for information about a product or service and they are very comfortable with making purchases through a mobile device. The convenience of shopping through catalogs or on a company's website and placing orders online has become very appealing to many consumers, and marketers recognize that this can be an effective way to augment their sales through traditional retail channels. For example, Under Armour, the leading company in the performance apparel market, generates a significant amount of sales through its website in addition to selling its products through sports retail stores (Exhibit 1–9).

Direct-marketing tools and techniques are also being used by companies that distribute their products through traditional distribution channels or have their own sales force. One of the major trends in marketing that has emerged over the past decade is that of **omnichannel retailing** whereby companies sell their products through multiple distribution channels including retail stores, online, catalogs, and mobile apps. However, it is about more than just offering a product or service through multiple channels. An omnichannel strategy involves using a combination of physical or offline channels as well as digital or online channels to influence a customer's shopping experience including research before a purchase and service after a sale.[40] Direct marketing plays a big role in the integrated marketing communications programs of consumer-product companies and business-to-business marketers. They use telemarketing to call customers directly and attempt to sell them products and services or qualify them as sales leads. Marketers also send out e-mails, direct-mail pieces ranging from simple letters and flyers to detailed brochures, catalogs, and DVDs to give potential customers information about their products or services. Direct-marketing techniques are also used to distribute product samples.

Many companies now have extensive databases containing customer names; mail and e-mail addresses; geographic, demographic, and psychographic profiles; purchase patterns, media preferences, credit, and other financial information; and other relevant customer characteristics. Marketers use this information to target their current and prospective customers through a variety of direct-marketing methods such as direct mail, e-mail marketing, telemarketing, and others. These databases are an integral part of companies' customer relationship management (CRM) programs, which involve the systematic tracking of customer preferences and behaviors and modifying a product or service to meet individual needs and wants.[41]

Digital/Internet Marketing

Over the past decade or so we have been experiencing perhaps the most dynamic and revolutionary changes of an era in the history of marketing and integrated marketing communications in particular. These changes are being driven by advances in technology and developments that have led to the dramatic growth of communication through interactive, digital media, particularly via the Internet. **Interactive media** allow for a two-way flow of communication whereby users can participate in and modify the form and content of the information they receive in real time. Unlike other forms of marketing communication—such as traditional media advertising—that are one-way in nature, the new interactive media allow users to perform a variety of activities such as receive, alter, and share information and images; make inquiries;

respond to questions; and even make purchases online. The rapid growth of the Internet and, more recently, social media is changing the nature of how companies do business and the ways they communicate and interact with consumers. Every day more consumers around the world are gaining access to the Internet's World Wide Web of information available to users. There are now more than 3.6 billion Internet users around the world, including 281 million in the United States, where 78 percent of the households are connected to the Internet, 87 percent of which have broadband access.[42] Nearly all marketers are making the Internet an integral part of their marketing communications, as well as overall business strategy.

The Internet is actually a multifaceted marketing communication tool. On one hand, it is an advertising medium as many marketers pay to run display or banner ads promoting their products and services on the websites of other companies, organizations, and web publishers. Advertisers also pay Internet search engines such as Google, Bing, and Yahoo! to place ads in or near relevant search results based on keywords. Paid search has become the most widely used form of Internet advertising. The Internet can also be used as a marketing communication tool in its own right because it is a medium that can be used to execute all of the elements of the promotional mix. In addition to advertising on the Web, marketers offer sales promotion incentives such as coupons, contests, and sweepstakes online, and they use the Internet to conduct direct marketing, personal selling, and public relations activities more effectively and efficiently.

We are well into the second phase of the Internet revolution (often referred to as "Web 2.0," where the focus is on collaboration and sharing among Internet users. This has given rise to the development and growth of **social media**, which refers to online means of communication and interactions among people that are used to create, share, and exchange content such as information, insights, experiences, perspectives, and even media themselves. It is estimated that nearly three-quarters of Americans have a social network profile and are using one or more social media platforms such as Facebook, Twitter, Google+, LinkedIn, Instagram, YouTube, and Pinterest. Usage of social media among teens and young adults (18 to 29) is particularly high with 90 percent of this age group using social networking sites.[43] Social media have revolutionized how companies communicate with, listen to, and learn from their customers and have become a major marketing tool for most companies. Companies and organizations are using social media as well by creating Facebook and Instagram pages, YouTube channels or Twitter accounts, or by posting advertisements and videos on YouTube, Vimeo, and other sites.[44]

For many years consumers accessed the Internet and social media primarily through their personal computers (PCs) including desktops and laptops. However, with the growth of smartphones and tablets there has been a dramatic shift in the way people go online; the majority of those who own these mobile devices prefer to access the Internet on them. The growing popularity of smartphones and tablets along with the decisions of wireless carriers such as Sprint, Verizon Wireless, AT&T, and T-Mobile to open their mobile phone services to advertising and other forms of promotion has opened up a new way for marketers to connect with consumers.[45] Advertising is already pervasive on the first two screens in most consumers' lives—televisions and personal computers—and more and more ads and promotional messages are appearing on the "third screen" of mobile phones and tablets. This has led to the explosive growth of **mobile marketing** which is promotional activity designed for delivery to cell phones, smartphones, tablets, and other handheld devices including apps, messaging, commerce, and customer relationship management. Although mobile marketing and advertising is still in its nascent stage, spending in the medium is expected to reach $61 billion by 2018 and to increase from 10 percent of U.S. media ad spending in 2014 to nearly 30 percent over this period.[46]

Marketers are extremely interested in mobile marketing since messages can be delivered that are specific to a consumer's location or consumption situation.[47] One of the major factors driving the growth of this medium is the development of mobile

EXHIBIT 1–10

The ShopSavvy app allows shoppers to make price comparisons before making a purchase

Source: ShopSavvy, Inc.

shopping services and apps that consumers can use to make shopping more economical, efficient, productive, and fun. Services are now available that provide consumers with mobile coupons sent directly to their cell phones that can be redeemed at the point of purchase. Other mobile apps that are now available include price comparison apps such as ShopSavvy, Purchx, or RedLaser that allow consumers to scan a barcode and compare prices at a given location against nearby competitors, or online retailers and social sourcing apps such as Fashim or Bazaarvoice that provide consumers with outside opinions and feedback on their mobile devices while making a purchase (Exhibit 1–10). Marketers are finding a number of creative ways to connect with consumers through their mobile devices by developing their own brand-specific applications as well as games, videos, and ads. For example, Starbucks has developed apps for iPhones and Android mobile devices that allow customers to find Starbucks locations, look up nutritional information, order ahead and pick up drinks to avoid waiting in line, and manage their Starbucks Rewards accounts.

The interactive nature of the Internet and social media is one of their major advantages. This capability enables marketers to gather valuable personal information from customers and prospects and to adjust their offers accordingly, in some cases in real time. For example, a number of companies adjust prices and display different product offers to consumers based on a variety of characteristics such as their web browsing history and location, which includes proximity to rival stores.[48] Another advantage of the Internet is that it provides marketers with the capability to more closely and precisely measure the effects of their advertising and other forms of promotion. There a number of metrics that can be generated when consumers visit websites or spend time on social media, which allow marketers to determine how consumers are responding to their campaigns, how well they are engaging them, and the return on investment they are receiving from their promotional dollars.

Companies recognize the advantages of the Internet, and many are increasing the role various forms of digital and social media play in their IMC programs. They are developing campaigns that integrate their websites, social media, and mobile marketing with other aspects of their IMC programs such as media advertising. Digital and Social Media Perspective 1–2 discusses how the digital revolution has impacted integrated marketing communications since the beginning of the new millennium and given rise to the growth of social media and mobile marketing.

Sales Promotion

The next variable in the promotional mix is **sales promotion**, which is generally defined as those marketing activities that provide extra value or incentives to the sales force, the distributors, or the ultimate consumer and can stimulate immediate sales. Sales promotion is generally broken into two major categories: consumer-oriented and trade-oriented activities.

Consumer-oriented sales promotion is targeted to the ultimate user of a product or service and includes couponing, sampling, premiums, rebates, contests, sweepstakes, and various point-of-purchase materials (Exhibit 1–11). These promotional tools encourage consumers to make an immediate purchase and thus can stimulate short-term sales. *Trade-oriented sales promotion* is targeted toward marketing intermediaries such as wholesalers, distributors, and retailers. Promotional and merchandising allowances, price deals, sales contests, and trade shows are some of the promotional tools used to encourage the trade to stock and promote a company's products.

EXHIBIT 1–11

Coupons, like this one for Bumble Bee Sensations, are a popular consumer-oriented sales promotion tool

Source: Bumble Bee Foods, LLC

Digital and Social Media Perspective 1–2 > > >

THE DIGITAL REVOLUTION HITS IMC

When the new millennium began, technology was just beginning to impact the practice of integrated marketing communications. The Internet was still constrained by technological limitations such as bandwidth problems, and most consumers were accessing the Web via dial-up telephone services such as AOL, NetZero, and EarthLink. Search engines such as Google, Yahoo!, and MSN were in their infancy and products such as the BlackBerry and the iPod were just being launched. In 2000 the average consumer spent less than 30 minutes online each day versus more than four hours today. When planning a new IMC campaign for a client, advertising agencies would conceive and develop advertising primarily for mass-media channels such as television, radio, and/or print. The online component would be an add-on such as a website that played a supportive role by providing information about a company or brand, promotional offers, or a place to watch commercials or view print ads or brochures. Many experts were still pointing to the bursting of the dot-com bubble and failure of online companies as evidence that the Web was overhyped, and it would be many years before its potential would be realized.

However, by the middle of the first decade of the new millennium, the transformation of the Internet was well under way as a new version of the World Wide Web was taking shape. The term *Web 2.0* is often used to describe the changes that have taken place with the Internet which include applications that facilitate interactive information sharing and collaboration and bilateral, as opposed to unilateral, communication. On Web 2.0 sites users are not limited to the passive viewing of information and can interact with one another as well as change website content. These applications gave rise to social networking sites, video sharing sites, wikis, blogs, review sites, and online communities that have experienced explosive growth.

Prior to 2004, Facebook, Twitter, YouTube, and LinkedIn did not even exist and MySpace was only a year old. Facebook was launched by Mark Zuckerberg at Harvard University in early 2004, but its membership was initially limited to Harvard students before quickly expanding to other colleges in the United States and Canada. By late 2006 the social networking site was available to everyone 13 years and older. By 2010 Facebook had more than 500 million members and just two years later in September 2012, it reached the milestone of 1 billion monthly active members. By 2016 Facebook had 1.6 billion active users worldwide and was operating in nearly every major country in the world except China. In 2012 Facebook purchased Instagram, which now has over 400 million users, nearly three-quarters of whom are outside the United States with half of them living in Europe and Asia. Two years later the company acquired WhatsApp which is the world's most popular messaging platforms with more than 700 million users. Twitter was launched in July 2006 and by the end of 2015 the microblogging service had more than 500 million registered users, more than 300 million of whom are active and send nearly 500 million tweets each day.

YouTube was launched in 2005 by three former PayPal employees and just a year later the video sharing website was purchased by Google for $1.6 billion and quickly became the world's largest video sharing website. More than 4 billion videos are viewed on YouTube every day, making it one of the most visited sites on the Internet. Companies of all sizes recognize the value of YouTube as a marketing tool and have developed YouTube brand channels as a way of engaging consumers and delivering content to them. Snapchat was founded in 2012 by Evan Spiegel and several classmates at Stanford as an ephemeral photo and video sharing app and now has 100 million active users. A year after it was launched, Snapchat turned down a $3 billion offer from Facebook to buy the company and it is now worth an estimated $15 to $20 billion as marketers are finding it to be an effective way to reach younger consumers with short videos and other content.

Mobile phones have also become an important part of our lives as 90 percent of American adults now own a cell phone and most of us find them indispensable. More than half of U.S. adults now own a smartphone, with ownership being particularly high among millennials (18 to 34) at 90 percent. Apple introduced its first iPhone in 2007; a

---

Among many consumer packaged-goods companies, sales promotion is often 60 to 70 percent of the promotional budget.[49] Many companies have shifted the emphasis of their promotional strategy from advertising to sales promotion. Reasons for the increased emphasis on sales promotion include declining brand loyalty and increased consumer sensitivity to promotional deals. Another major reason is that retailers have become larger and more powerful and are demanding more trade promotion support from their vendors.

Promotion and *sales promotion* are two terms that often create confusion in the advertising and marketing fields. As noted, promotion is an element of marketing by which firms communicate with their customers; it includes all the promotional-mix

Source: © tanuha2001/Shutterstock RF

and tablets has given rise to an entirely new type of marketing that is commonly referred to as mobile marketing, which involves promotional activities designed for delivery to these devices. Many media including television networks and stations, magazines, and newspapers have developed digital platforms to deliver their content that include full-screen and full-color interactive ads as well as the capability to watch commercials and other videos. A number of mobile apps are designed to facilitate the purchase process and include applications for comparison shopping, product and service reviews, or coupon delivery directly to phones. Many marketers are delivering digital advertising messages and promotion offers directly to consumers' mobile devices that can be targeted to specific locations and consumption situations. This has resulted in marketers focusing their efforts on responsive web design which involves creating websites that are easy to view, read, and navigate across various types of devices such as desktops, laptops, tablets, and mobile phones.

The rapid pace of technological change impacting the daily lives of consumers presents a major challenge to marketers who must adapt their IMC strategies and tactics or risk becoming irrelevant. Marketing consultant Avi Dan has described the challenge very well by noting that "Ten years ago a marketer needed to know maybe 100 things to be effective: some aspects of positioning, some aspects of media, some media research, some pricing and some distribution. However, now that number is in the thousands. And whereas technology used to advance incrementally, it now evolves exponentially." It is likely that the advances in technology that occurred during the first two decades of the new millennium will pale in comparison to those that will occur over the next 10 years. However, marketers will have little choice but to embrace these changes and view them as an opportunity rather than a threat.

Sources: Max Chafkin and Sarah Frier, "If You Don't Know It by Now, You'll Never Make Millions on Snapchat," *Bloomberg Businessweek*, March 7–13, 2016, pp. 50–55; Aaron Smith, "U.S. Smartphone Use in 2015," Pew Research Center, April 1, 2015, www.pewinternet.org/2015/04/01/us-smartphone-use-in-2015/; Giselle Abramovich, "15 Mind-Blowing Stats about Mobile Marketing," *Advertising Age*, July 30, 2015, http://adage.com/article/adobe-marketing-cloud/15-mind-blowing-stats-mobile-marketing/299574/; Avi Dan, "Why Brands Should Embrace Technological Change," *Advertising Age*, January 10, 2010, http://adage.com/article/cmo-strategy/marketing-brands-embrace-technological-change/141478/.

year later smartphones using Google's Android operating system, which is now the most popular by market share, became available. Two years later another type of mobile device became available when Apple introduced the iPad tablet PC which uses the same proprietary operating system (OS) as the iPhone. Major competitors quickly launched tablets based on Google's Android OS, such as the Samsung Galaxy, Amazon Kindle Fire, and Microsoft Surface. While there were very few software applications (apps) available for the first iPhone, there are now nearly 1.6 million apps available for smartphones and tablets using the Apple OS as well as Android mobile devices.

People around the world are using their smartphones and tablets to access the Internet and are spending more than half of their time online using smartphone applications. Millennials are spending nearly 70 percent of their connected time on smartphones while older consumers spend about 30 percent of their digital time with smartphones and 18 percent with tablets. The rapid growth of smartphones

elements we have just discussed. However, many marketing and advertising practitioners use the term more narrowly to refer to sales promotion activities to either consumers or the trade (retailers, wholesalers). In this book, *promotion* is used in the broader sense to refer to the various marketing communications activities of an organization.

Publicity/Public Relations

Another important component of an organization's promotional mix is publicity/public relations.

Publicity   **Publicity** refers to nonpersonal communications regarding an organization, product, service, or idea not directly paid for or run under identified sponsorship. It usually comes in the form of a news story, editorial, or announcement about an organization and/or its products and services. Like advertising, publicity involves nonpersonal communication to a mass audience, but unlike advertising, publicity is not directly paid for by the company. The company or organization attempts to get the media to cover or run a favorable story on a product, service, cause, or event to affect awareness, knowledge, opinions, and/or behavior. Techniques used to gain publicity include press releases, press conferences, feature articles, photographs, films, and video news releases.

An advantage of publicity over other forms of promotion is its credibility. Consumers generally tend to be less skeptical toward favorable information about a product or service when it comes from a source they perceive as unbiased. For example, the success (or failure) of a new movie is often determined by the reviews it receives from film critics, who are viewed by many moviegoers as objective evaluators. Another advantage of publicity is its low cost, since the company is not paying for time or space in a mass medium such as TV, radio, or newspapers. While an organization may incur some costs in developing publicity items or maintaining a staff to do so, these expenses will be far less than those for the other promotional programs.

Publicity is not always under the control of an organization and is sometimes unfavorable. Negative stories about a company and/or its products can be very damaging. For example, recently the food and beverage industry has received a great deal of negative publicity regarding the nutritional value of their products as well as their marketing practices, particularly to young people. Companies such as Kraft Foods, General Mills, PepsiCo, Coca-Cola, and others have been the target of criticism by consumer activists who have argued that these companies contribute to the obesity problem in the United States by advertising unhealthy foods to children.[50] Chipotle Mexican Grill received a tremendous amount of negative publicity in late 2015 when scores of people across nine states were sickened with a strain of *E. coli* after eating at its restaurants.[51] The health concerns were covered widely in the media and led to a 15 percent decline in sales over a several-month period. In addition to making major changes in its food safety practices, Chipotle responded to the crisis by using social media to explain the problem to loyal customers and offering rainchecks for free meals and discount coupons to bring customers back to its stores.[52]

Public Relations   It is important to recognize the distinction between publicity and public relations. When an organization systematically plans and distributes information in an attempt to control and manage its image and the nature of the publicity it receives, it is really engaging in a function known as public relations. **Public relations** is defined as "a strategic communication process that builds mutually beneficial relationships between organizations and their publics."[53] Public relations generally has a broader objective than publicity, as its purpose is to establish and maintain a positive image of the company among its various publics. Thus, it involves managing relationships with a number of important audiences, including investors, employees, suppliers, communities, and governments (federal, state, and local) as well as consumers.

Public relations uses publicity and a variety of other tools—including special publications, participation in community activities, fund-raising, sponsorship of special events, and various public affairs activities—to enhance an organization's image. Companies also use advertising as a public relations tool. For example, the ad shown in Exhibit 1–12 is part of the American Honda Motor Co.'s corporate social responsibility campaign which communicates the company's stance on important issues such as social values, business ethics, diversity, environmental stewardship, and community involvement. The ad promotes Honda's commitment to building fuel efficient products, such as the Honda Jet, and innovating and creating jobs in America.

Building more than just cars.

Honda's commitment to building fuel-efficient products, creating jobs and innovating here in America continues with the new HondaJet. With the Over-The-Wing Engine Mount, the HondaJet is the fastest, highest-flying, most fuel-efficient, and most spacious jet in its class.

HONDA

Advancing America on the ground and in the sky.
HondaInAmerica.com/HondaJet

HONDA
The Power of Dreams

EXHIBIT 1–12

Honda uses advertising to enhance its corporate image by showing its commitment to building products and creating jobs in America

Source: American Honda Motor Co., Inc. and Rubin Postaer and Associates

Traditionally, publicity and public relations have been considered more supportive than primary to the marketing and promotional process. However, many firms have begun making PR an integral part of their predetermined marketing and promotional strategies. PR firms are increasingly touting public relations as a communications tool that can take over many of the functions of conventional advertising and marketing.[54]

Personal Selling

The final element of an organization's promotional mix is **personal selling**, a form of person-to-person communication in which a seller attempts to assist and/or persuade prospective buyers to purchase the company's product or service or to act on an idea. Unlike advertising, personal selling involves direct contact between buyer and seller, either face-to-face or through some form of telecommunications such as telephone sales. This interaction gives the marketer communication flexibility; the seller can see or hear the potential buyer's reactions and modify the message accordingly. The personal, individualized communication in personal selling allows the seller to tailor the message to the customer's specific needs or situation.

Personal selling also involves more immediate and precise feedback because the impact of the sales presentation can generally be assessed from the customer's reactions. If the feedback is unfavorable, the salesperson can modify the message. Personal-selling efforts can also be targeted to specific markets and customer types that are the best prospects for the company's product or service.

While personal selling is an important part of the promotional mix, it will not be covered in this text because it is not a direct part of the IMC program in most companies. Also, personal selling is managed separately in most organizations and is not under the control of the advertising or marketing communications manager. However, throughout the text we will address the many ways and situations in which various IMC tools such as media advertising, digital marketing, and sales promotion must be coordinated with the personal-selling program.

IMC INVOLVES AUDIENCE CONTACTS

The various promotional-mix elements are the major tools that marketers use to communicate with current and/or prospective customers as well as other relevant audiences. However, each of these tools is multifaceted since there are various types of media advertising (print, broadcast, outdoor) and sales promotion as well as ways by which marketers use the Internet (websites, social media, online advertising). Moreover, there are additional ways companies communicate with current and prospective customers that extend beyond the traditional promotional mix. Figure 1–5 provides a more extensive list of the ways by which marketers can communicate with their target audiences.

Many companies are taking an *audience contact* or *touch point* perspective in developing their IMC programs whereby they consider all of the potential ways of reaching their target audience and presenting the company or brand in a favorable manner. A **touch point** refers to each and every opportunity the customer has to see or hear about the company and/or its brands or have an encounter or experience

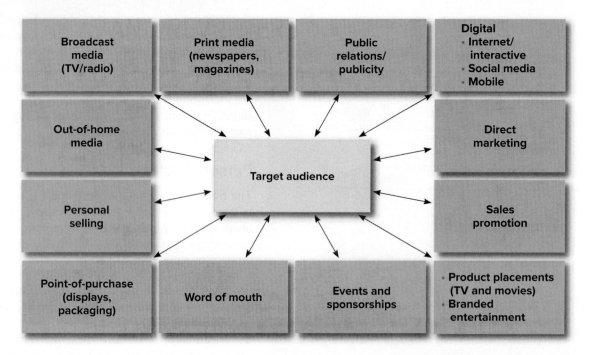

FIGURE 1–5

IMC Audience Contact Tools

with it. These contacts can range from simply seeing or hearing an ad for a brand to actually having the opportunity to use or experience a brand in a retail store or interacting with the company during a sales transaction or service encounter. Tom Duncan notes that there are four basic categories of contact or touch points.[55] These are as follows:

- *Company-created touch points* are planned marketing communication messages created by the company such as advertisements, websites and social media sites, news/press releases, packaging, brochures and collateral material, sale promotions, and point-of-purchase displays along with other types of in-store décor. Company-created touch points account for a large part of an IMC program and have the advantage of being under the control of the marketer.
- *Intrinsic touch points* are interactions that occur with a company or brand during the process of buying or using the product or service such as discussions with retail sales personnel or customer service representatives. Intrinsic touch points are often not under the direct control of the marketing department or IMC program. However, Duncan notes that marketers should make suggestions regarding ways to manage and improve these interactions with customers in order to send a positive message about the company or brand. There are also various types of intrinsic touch points that are controlled, or at least may be influenced, by the marketing or IMC manager. These include the design and functioning of the company and/or brand website or social media pages, as well as the packaging, which can contain product information and impact the customers' experience of using a product. Marketers are also finding ways to communicate with consumers during the process of making a purchase by using some of the mobile marketing techniques discussed earlier.
- *Unexpected touch points* are unanticipated references or information about a company or brand that a customer or prospect receives that is beyond the control of the organization. Probably the most influential type of unexpected contact is a word-of-mouth message which refers to a personal communication that

EXHIBIT 1–13

Reviews on Yelp are a very important touch point and source of information for consumers in selecting restaurants

Source: Yelp Inc.

comes from friends, associates, neighbors, co-workers, or family members. Unexpected messages may also come from other sources such as the media which may print or broadcast stories about a company and/or its brands, as well as experts who write about products and services. Another type of unexpected touch point that has become very influential is websites that provide reviews of products and services. Some of these sites provide expert reviews while others give reviews from other customers. For example, CNET is widely used by consumers looking for reviews of specific brands of consumer electronic products. TripAdvisor provides nearly 2 million travel-related reviews and opinions each year from travelers around the world. It is important to note that information received from unexpected touch points can be either positive or negative. Most of you have probably relied on reviews from Yelp for a variety of local businesses such as restaurants, bars, retail stores, and professional services. Yelp averages 142 million unique visitors each month, and the reviews provided on its website are a very important source of information for many consumers (Exhibit 1–13).

- *Customer-initiated touch points* are interactions that occur whenever a customer or prospect contacts a company. Most of these contacts involve inquiries or complaints consumers might have regarding the use of a product or service and occur through calls made directly to the company, via e-mails, or through specific sections of websites to which customers are directed. Many of the customer-initiated contacts are handled through customer service departments, although a number of companies have in-bound telemarketing departments as part of their direct sales efforts. The manner in which marketers handle customer-initiated contacts has a major impact on their ability to attract and retain customers. Moreover, many companies try to differentiate themselves on the basis of customer service and promote their customer orientation in their advertising and other aspects of their IMC programs. They also encourage current or prospective customers to contact them by calling toll-free numbers or by putting their website addresses on packages, in ads, and in various promotional materials.

Marketers who take a contact or touch point perspective recognize that consumers' perceptions and opinions of a brand, as well as their purchase behavior, result from the information they receive and experiences and interactions they have with the company and its products or services. They also recognize that not all touch points are equally effective and they differ in regard to a company's ability to control or influence them. Figure 1–6 plots the four categories of touch points in terms of their relative impact and the marketer's ability to control them.

As can be seen in this figure, company-planned touch points are the easiest to control but are lowest in terms of impact. Marketers can control the nature and type of advertising and other forms of promotion that they send to their target audiences, but consumers often discount these messages since they receive so many of them and they recognize the persuasive intent that underlies them. At the other extreme, unexpected messages are often the most impactful

FIGURE 1–6

IMC Touch Points: Control vs. Impact

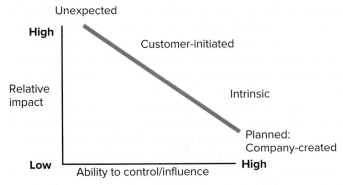

FIGURE 1–7

Paid, Owned, and Earned
Media

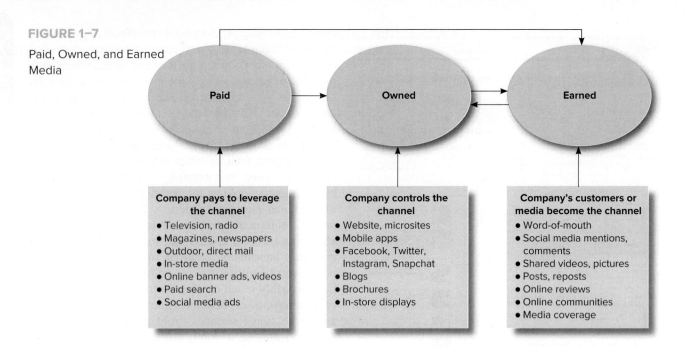

but are the most difficult to control. Duncan notes than an unexpected message can be very powerful because it has the power of third-party credibility since the people who provide the information are often perceived as more believable than company sources because they have no vested interest in the success or failure of the company or brand.[56] Customer-initiated and intrinsic messages fall in between unexpected and company-created messages with respect to impact as well as the ability of the marketer to control them.

Paid, Owned, and Earned Media

Another categorization of the various types of customer touch points that has become very popular is that of paid, owned, and earned media as shown in Figure 1–7[57] **Paid media** refers to channels a marketer pays to leverage and includes traditional advertising media such as television, radio, print, outdoor, and direct mail as well as various forms of digital advertising such as paid search and online display and video ads. **Owned media** refers to channels of marketing communication that a company controls, such as its websites, blogs, and mobile apps as well as social media channels such as Facebook, Twitter, Instagram, and YouTube. **Earned media** is exposure for a company or brand that it did not have to pay for and is generated by outside entities such as the media or the general public. Earned media has traditionally been viewed as exposure for a company or brand generated by its public relations/publicity efforts or through favorable word of mouth. However, with the growth of digital and social media, earned media exposure is taking place online through social media and as a result of the viral marketing efforts of marketers which focus on getting consumers, as well as the media, to share information about their company and/or brands. This can occur through tweets and re-tweets on Twitter, social media posts on Facebook or Instagram, product reviews, blogs, video sharing, and discussions within online communities.

Marketers making effective use of integrated marketing communications today will use a combination of all three forms of media. For example, advertising through paid media is still an efficient way to generate awareness of and interest in a company or brand, particularly among mass markets. Media advertising can also be used to drive consumers to various forms of owned media such as a Facebook or Instagram page for a company or brand and/or its website where more content can be provided to encourage greater involvement and engagement. Well-executed and coordinated paid and owned media efforts can also serve as a catalyst for generating earned media when the media and/or consumers find information or content about a company or brand to be interesting or valuable enough that they want to write about it or share it others. An important aspect of earned media is that information about a company or brand that comes from stories in the media or is shared through social media is often perceived as more credible and authentic than paid advertising messages and thus can have a greater influence on consumers.

Marketers must determine how valuable each of the various forms of media and contact tools are for communicating with their current and prospective customers and how they can be combined to form an effective IMC program. This is generally done by starting with the target audience and determining which IMC tools will be most effective in reaching, informing, and persuading them and ultimately influencing their behavior. It is the responsibility of those involved in the marketing communications process to determine how the various contact tools will be used to reach the target audience and help achieve the company's marketing objectives. The IMC program is generally developed with specific goals and objectives in mind and is the end product of a detailed marketing and promotional planning process. We will now look at a model of the process that companies follow in developing and executing their IMC programs.

THE IMC PLANNING PROCESS

In developing an integrated marketing communications strategy, a company combines the various promotional-mix elements, balancing the strengths and weaknesses of each to produce an effective communication program. **Integrated marketing communications management** involves the process of planning, executing, evaluating, and controlling the use of the various promotional-mix elements to effectively communicate with target audiences. The marketer must consider which promotional tools to use and how to integrate them to achieve marketing and communication objectives. Companies also must decide how to distribute the total marketing communications budget across the various promotional-mix elements. What percentage of the budget should be allocated to advertising, sales promotion, the Internet, sponsorships, and personal selling?

As with any business function, planning plays an important role in the development and implementation of an effective integrated marketing communications program. This process is guided by an **integrated marketing communications plan** that provides the framework for developing, implementing, and controlling the organization's IMC program. Those involved with the IMC program must decide on the role and function of the specific elements of the promotional mix, develop strategies for each element, determine how they will be integrated, plan for their implementation, and consider how to evaluate the results achieved and make any necessary adjustments. Marketing communications is but one part of, and must be integrated into, the overall marketing plan and program.

A model of the IMC planning process is shown in Figure 1–8. The remainder of this chapter presents a brief overview of the various steps involved in this process.

Review of the Marketing Plan

The first step in the IMC planning process is to review the marketing plan and objectives. Before developing a promotional plan, marketers must understand where the company (or the brand) has been, its current position in the market, where it intends to go, and how it plans to get there. Most of this information should be contained in the **marketing plan**, a written document that describes the overall marketing strategy

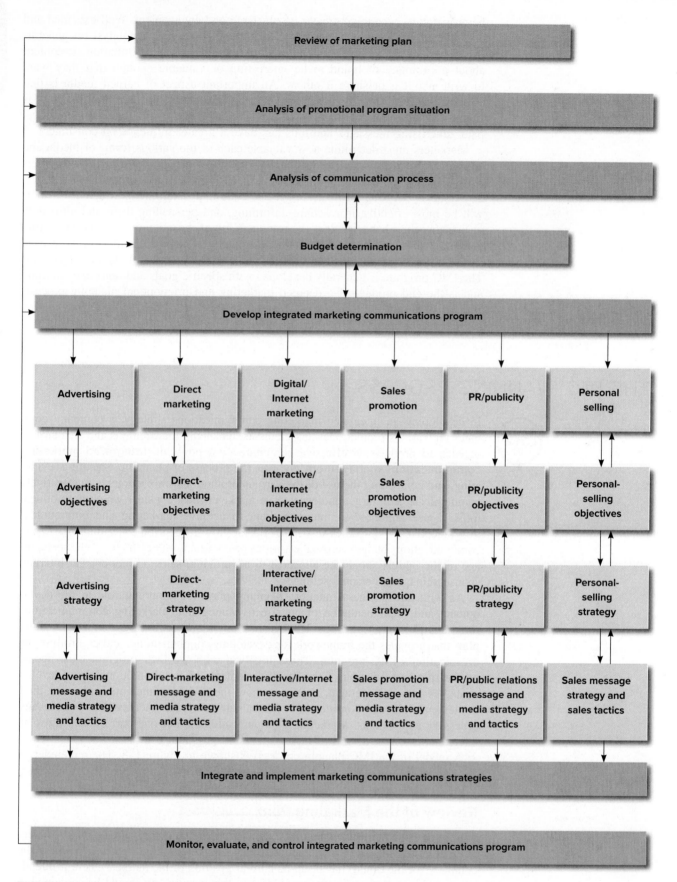

FIGURE 1–8 An Integrated Marketing Communications Planning Model

FIGURE 1–8

(Concluded)

Review of Marketing Plan
Examine overall marketing plan and objectives
Role of advertising and promotion
Competitive analysis
Assess environmental influences

Analysis of Promotional Program Situation

Internal analysis
  Promotional department
    organization
  Firm's ability to implement
    promotional program
  Agency evaluation and selection
  Review of previous program
    results

External analysis
  Consumer behavior analysis
  Market segmentation and target
    marketing
  Market positioning

Analysis of Communication Process
Analyze receiver's response processes
Analyze source, message, channel factors
Establish communication goals and objectives

Budget Determination
Set tentative marketing communications budget
Allocate tentative budget

Develop Integrated Marketing Communications Program

Advertising
  Set advertising objectives
  Determine advertising budget
  Develop advertising message
  Develop advertising media strategy
Direct marketing
  Set direct-marketing objectives
  Determine direct-marketing budget
  Develop direct-marketing message
  Develop direct-marketing media
    strategy
Digital/Internet marketing
  Set interactive/Internet marketing
    objectives
  Determine interactive/Internet
    marketing budget
  Develop interactive/Internet message
  Develop interactive/Internet media
    strategy

Sales promotion
  Set sales promotion objectives
  Determine sales promotion budget
  Determine sales promotion tools
    and develop messages
  Develop sales promotion media
    strategy
Public relations/publicity
  Set PR/publicity objectives
  Determine PR/publicity budget
  Develop PR/publicity messages
  Develop PR/publicity media strategy
Personal selling
  Set personal-selling and sales
    objectives
  Determine personal-selling/sales
    budget
  Develop sales message
  Develop selling roles and
    responsibilities

Integrate and Implement Marketing Communications Strategies
Integrate promotional-mix strategies
Create and produce ads
Purchase media time and space
Design and implement direct-marketing programs
Design and distribute sales promotion materials
Design and implement public relations/publicity programs
Design and implement digital/Internet marketing programs

Monitor, Evaluate, and Control Integrated Marketing Communications Program
Evaluate promotional program results/effectiveness
Take measures to control and adjust promotional strategies

and programs developed for an organization, a particular product line, or a brand. Marketing plans can take several forms but generally include five basic elements:

1. A detailed situation analysis that consists of an internal marketing audit and review and an external analysis of the market competition and environmental factors.
2. Specific marketing objectives that provide direction, a time frame for marketing activities, and a mechanism for measuring performance.
3. A marketing strategy and program that include selection of target market(s) and decisions and plans for the four elements of the marketing mix.
4. A program for implementing the marketing strategy, including determining specific tasks to be performed and responsibilities.
5. A process for monitoring and evaluating performance and providing feedback so that proper control can be maintained and any necessary changes can be made in the overall marketing strategy or tactics.

For most firms, the integrated marketing communications plan is an integral part of its marketing strategy and plan. Thus, those involved with the IMC process must know the roles advertising and other promotional-mix elements will play in the overall marketing program. The IMC plan is developed similarly to the marketing plan and often uses its detailed information. Promotional planners focus on information in the marketing plan that is relevant to the promotional strategy.

Promotional Program Situation Analysis

After the overall marketing plan is reviewed, the next step in developing a promotional plan is to conduct the situation analysis. For the IMC program, the situation analysis focuses on the factors that influence or are relevant to the development of a promotional strategy. Like the overall marketing situation analysis, the promotional program situation analysis includes both an internal and an external analysis.

Internal Analysis   The **internal analysis** assesses relevant areas involving the product/service offering and the firm itself. The capabilities of the firm and its ability to develop and implement a successful IMC program, the organization of the marketing communications department, and the successes and failures of past programs should be reviewed. The analysis should study the relative advantages and disadvantages of performing the promotional functions in-house as opposed to hiring an external agency (or agencies). For example, the internal analysis may indicate the firm is not capable of planning, implementing, and managing certain areas of the IMC program. If this is the case, it would be wise to look for assistance from an advertising or digital agency or some other promotional facilitator. If the organization is already using an external agency, the focus will be on the quality of the agency's work and the results achieved by past and/or current campaigns.

In this text we will examine the functions advertising agencies perform for their clients, the agency selection process, compensation, and considerations in evaluating agency performance. We will also discuss the role and function of other promotional facilitators such as digital/interactive agencies, sales promotion firms, direct-marketing companies, public relations agencies, and media specialists as well as marketing and media research firms.

Another aspect of the internal analysis is assessing the strengths and weaknesses of the firm or the brand from an image perspective. Often the brand equity and image a firm brings to the market will have a significant impact on the way the firm can advertise and promote itself as well as its various products and services. Companies or brands that are new to the market or those for whom perceptions are negative may have to concentrate on their images, not just the benefits or attributes of the specific product or service. On the other hand, a firm with a strong reputation and/or brand image is already a step ahead when it comes to marketing its products or services. For example, Starbucks has an outstanding image that is a result of the quality of its

EXHIBIT 1–14

Starbucks has a very strong brand image and reputation as a socially responsible company

Source: Starbucks

coffee and other products as well as its reputation as a socially responsible company. The company is recognized as a good citizen in its dealings with communities, employees, suppliers, and the environment. Starbucks recognizes that being recognized as a socially responsible company is an important part of its tremendous growth and success. The company publishes a Global Responsibility Annual Report each year that focuses on sustainability issues as well as its social, environmental, and economic impact on the communities where Starbucks does business (Exhibit 1–14).

The internal analysis also assesses the relative strengths and weaknesses of the product or service; its advantages and disadvantages; any unique selling points or benefits it may have; its packaging, price, and design; and so on. This information is particularly important to the creative personnel who must develop the advertising message for the brand.

Figure 1–9 is a checklist of some of the areas one might consider when performing analyses for promotional planning purposes. Addressing internal areas may require information the company does not have available internally and must gather as part of the external analysis.

External Analysis The **external analysis** focuses on factors such as characteristics of the firm's customers, market segments, positioning strategies, and competitors, as shown in Figure 1–9. An important part of the external analysis is a detailed consideration of customers' characteristics and buying patterns, their decision processes, and factors influencing their purchase decisions. Attention must also be given to consumers' perceptions and attitudes, lifestyles, and criteria for making purchase decisions. Often, marketing research studies are needed to answer some of these questions.

A key element of the external analysis is an assessment of the market. The attractiveness and growth potential of various market segments must be evaluated and the segments to target must be identified. Once the target markets are chosen, the emphasis will be on determining how the company or brand should be positioned. What image or place should it have in consumers' minds?

This part of the promotional program situation analysis also includes an in-depth examination of both direct and indirect competitors. While competitors were analyzed in the overall marketing situation analysis, even more attention is devoted to promotional aspects at this phase. Focus is on the firm's primary competitors: their specific strengths and weaknesses; their segmentation, targeting, and positioning strategies; and the promotional strategies they employ. The size and allocation of their promotional budgets, their media strategies, and the messages they are sending to the marketplace should all be considered.

The external phase also includes an analysis of the marketing environment and current trends or developments that might affect the promotional program. Marketers must consider relevant demographic, economic, and sociocultural factors and how they are impacting their markets. For example, consumers have become more focused on health and nutrition, which has had a major impact on the soft-drink industry. Sales of carbonated soft drinks have been declining for more than a decade as a result of consumer concerns over their nutritional value and the high number of calories from added sugar as well as the artificial sweetener used in diet sodas. These concerns have led many consumers to turn to alternative beverages

Internal Factors	External Factors
Assessment of Firm's Promotional Organization and Capabilities	*Customer Analysis*
Organization of promotional department	Who buys our product or service?
Capability of firm to develop and execute promotional programs	Who makes the decision to buy the product?
	Who influences the decision to buy the product?
Determination of role and function of ad agency and other promotional facilitators	How is the purchase decision made? Who assumes what role?
Review of Firm's Previous Promotional Programs and Results	What does the customer buy? What needs must be satisfied?
	Why do customers buy a particular brand?
Review previous promotional objectives	Where do they go or look to buy the product or service?
Review previous promotional budgets and locations	When do they buy? Any seasonality factors?
Review previous promotional-mix strategies and programs	What are customers' attitudes toward our product or service?
	What social factors might influence the purchase decision?
Review results of previous promotional programs	Do the customers' lifestyles influence their decisions?
Assessment of Firm or Brand Image and Implications for Promotion	How is our product or service perceived by customers?
	How do demographic factors influence the purchase decision?
Assessment of Relative Strengths and Weaknesses of Product or Service	*Competitive Analysis*
	Who are our direct and indirect competitors?
What are the strengths and weaknesses of product or service?	What key benefits and positioning are used by our competitors?
What are its key benefits?	What is our position relative to the competition?
Does it have any unique selling points?	How big are competitors' ad budgets?
Assessment of packaging, labeling, and brand image	What message and media strategies are competitors using?
	Environmental Analysis
How does our product or service compare with competition?	Are there any current trends or developments that might affect the promotional program?

FIGURE 1–9

Areas Covered in the Situation Analysis

such as teas, juices, bottled water, flavored waters, and sports drinks. This has created a market opportunity for marketers who have launched new beverage products that are positioned as being healthier and having more nutritional value. Exhibit 1–15 shows an ad for BodyArmor, which is a new sports drink that competes with Gatorade and Powerade by focusing on its nutritional attributes and using a number of high-profile athletes as endorsers.

EXHIBIT 1–15

BodyArmor is a new brand that competes in the sports beverage market. What external factors create a market opportunity for BodyArmor?

Source: BA Sports Nutrition, LLC

Analysis of the Communication Process

This stage of the promotional planning process examines how the company can effectively communicate with consumers in its target markets. The promotional planner must think about the process consumers will go through in responding to marketing communications. The response process for products or services for which consumer decision making is characterized by a high level of interest is often different from that for low-involvement or routine purchase decisions. These differences will influence the promotional strategy.

Communication decisions regarding the use of various source, message, and channel factors must also be considered. The promotional planner should recognize the different effects various types of advertising messages might have on consumers and whether they are appropriate for the product or brand. Issues such as whether a celebrity spokesperson should be used and at what cost may also be studied.

Preliminary discussion of media-mix options (print, TV, radio, digital, direct marketing), including how they they can be used to reach the target market and their cost implications, might also occur at this stage.

An important part of this stage of the promotional planning process is establishing communication goals and objectives. In this text, we stress the importance of distinguishing between communication and marketing objectives. **Marketing objectives** refer to what is to be accomplished by the overall marketing program. They are often stated in terms of sales, market share, or profitability.

Communication objectives refer to what the firm seeks to accomplish with its promotional program. They are often stated in terms of the nature of the message to be communicated or what specific communication effects are to be achieved. Communication objectives may include creating awareness or knowledge about a product and its attributes or benefits; creating an image; or developing favorable attitudes, preferences, or purchase intentions. Communication objectives should be the guiding force for development of the overall marketing communications strategy and of objectives for each promotional-mix area.

Budget Determination

After the communication objectives are determined, attention turns to the promotional budget. Two basic questions are asked at this point: How much will the IMC program cost? How will the money be allocated across different media, geographic markets, and time periods? Ideally, the amount a firm needs to spend on advertising and promotion should be determined by what must be done to accomplish its communication objectives. In reality, promotional budgets are often determined using a more simplistic approach, such as how much money is available or a percentage of a company's or brand's sales revenue. At this stage, the budget is often tentative. It may not be finalized until specific promotional-mix strategies are developed.

Developing the Integrated Marketing Communications Program

Developing the IMC program is generally the most involved and detailed step of the promotional planning process. As discussed earlier, each promotional-mix element has certain advantages and limitations. At this stage of the planning process, decisions have to be made regarding the role and importance of each element and their coordination with one another. As Figure 1–8 shows, each promotional-mix element has its own set of objectives and a budget and strategy for meeting them. Decisions must be made and activities performed to implement the promotional programs. Procedures must be developed for evaluating performance and making any necessary changes.

For example, the advertising program will have its own set of objectives, usually involving the communication of some message or appeal to a target audience. A budget will be determined, providing the advertising manager and the agency with some idea of how much money is available for developing the ad campaign and purchasing media to disseminate the ad message.

Two important aspects of the advertising program are development of the message and the media strategy. Message development, often referred to as *creative strategy*, involves determining the basic appeal and message the advertiser wishes to convey to the target audience. This process, along with the ads that result, to many students is the most fascinating aspect of promotion. *Media strategy* involves determining which communication channels will be used to deliver the advertising message to the target audience. Decisions must be made regarding which types of media will be used (e.g., newspapers, magazines, radio, TV, outdoor, digital) as well as specific media selections (e.g., a particular magazine or TV program). This task requires careful evaluation of the media options' advantages and limitations, costs, and ability to deliver the message effectively to the target market.

Once the message and media strategies have been determined, steps must be taken to implement them. Most large companies hire advertising agencies to plan and produce their messages and to evaluate and purchase the media that will carry their ads. However, most agencies work very closely with their clients as they develop the ads and select media, because it is the advertiser that ultimately approves (and pays for) the creative work and media plan.

A similar process takes place for the other elements of the IMC program as objectives are set, an overall strategy is developed, message and media strategies are determined, and steps are taken to implement them. While the marketer's advertising agencies may be used to perform some of the other IMC functions, they may also hire other communication specialists such as direct-marketing and interactive and/or sales promotion agencies, as well as public relations firms.

Monitoring, Evaluation, and Control

The final stage of the IMC planning process is monitoring, evaluating, and controlling the promotional program. It is important to determine how well the IMC program is meeting communication objectives and helping the firm accomplish its overall marketing goals and objectives. The IMC planner wants to know not only how well the promotional program is doing but also why. For example, problems with the advertising program may lie in the nature of the message or in a media plan that does not reach the target market effectively. The manager must know the reasons for the results in order to take the right steps to correct the program.

This final stage of the process is designed to provide managers with continual feedback concerning the effectiveness of the IMC program, which in turn can be used as input into the planning process. As Figure 1–8 shows, information on the results achieved by the IMC program is used in subsequent promotional planning and strategy development.

PERSPECTIVE AND ORGANIZATION OF THIS TEXT

Traditional approaches to teaching advertising, promotional strategy, or marketing communications courses have often treated the various elements of the promotional mix as separate functions. As a result, many people who work in advertising, sales promotion, direct marketing, digital/Internet, or public relations tend to approach marketing communications problems from the perspective of their particular specialty. An advertising person may believe marketing communications objectives are best met through the use of media advertising; a promotional specialist argues for a sales promotion program to motivate consumer response; a public relations person advocates a PR campaign to tackle the problem. These orientations are not surprising, since each person has been trained to view marketing communications problems primarily from one perspective.

In the contemporary business world, however, individuals working in marketing, advertising, and other promotional areas are expected to understand and use a variety of marketing communication tools, not just the one in which they specialize. Ad agencies no longer confine their services to the advertising area. Many are involved in sales promotion, public relations, direct marketing, event sponsorship, digital/interactive, and other marketing communication areas. Individuals working on the client or advertiser side of the business, such as brand, product, or promotional managers, are developing marketing programs that use a variety of marketing communication methods.

This text views advertising and promotion from an integrated marketing communications perspective. We will examine the promotional-mix elements and their roles in an organization's integrated marketing communications efforts. Although media advertising may be the most visible part of the communications program, understanding its role in contemporary marketing requires attention to other promotional areas such as the Internet and digital marketing, direct marketing, sales promotion, and public relations. Not all the promotional-mix areas are under the direct control of the advertising or marketing communications manager. For example, as noted earlier, personal selling is typically a specialized marketing function outside the control of the advertising or promotional department. Likewise, publicity/public relations is often assigned to a separate department. All these departments should, however, communicate to coordinate all the organization's marketing communication tools.

The purpose of this book is to provide you with a thorough understanding of the field of advertising and other elements of a firm's promotional mix and show how they are combined to form an integrated marketing communications program. To plan, develop, and implement an effective IMC program, those involved must understand marketing, consumer behavior, and the communication process. The first part of this book is designed to provide this foundation by examining the roles of advertising and other forms of promotion in the marketing process. We examine the process of market segmentation and positioning and consider their part in developing an IMC strategy. We also discuss how firms organize for IMC and make decisions regarding ad agencies and other firms that provide marketing and promotional services.

We then focus on consumer behavior considerations and analyze the communication process. We discuss various communication models of value to promotional planners in developing strategies and establishing goals and objectives for advertising and other forms of promotion. We also consider how firms determine and allocate their marketing communications budget.

After laying the foundation for the development of a promotional program, this text will follow the integrated marketing communications planning model presented in Figure 1–8. We examine each of the promotional-mix variables, beginning with advertising. Our detailed examination of advertising includes a discussion of creative strategy and the process of developing the advertising message, an overview of media strategy, and an evaluation of the various media (print, broadcast, and support media). The discussion then turns to the other areas of the promotional mix: direct marketing, digital/Internet marketing, sales promotion, and public relations/publicity. Our examination of the IMC planning process concludes with a discussion of how the program is monitored, evaluated, and controlled. Particular attention is given to measuring the effectiveness of advertising and other forms of promotion.

The final part of the text examines special topic areas and perspectives that have become increasingly important in contemporary marketing. We will examine the area of international advertising and promotion and the challenges companies face in developing IMC programs for global markets as well as various countries around the world. The text concludes with an examination of the environment in which integrated marketing communications operates, including the regulatory, social, and economic factors that influence, and in turn are influenced by, an organization's advertising and promotional program.

Summary

Advertising and other forms of promotion are an integral part of the marketing process in most organizations. Over the past decade, the amount of money spent on advertising, sales promotion, direct marketing, and other forms of marketing communication has increased tremendously, both in the United States and in foreign markets. There has been a very large increase in the amount of monies spent on digital advertising done through the Internet as well as various forms of nontraditional media, some of which did not exist at the beginning of the new millennium, such as social media. To understand the role of advertising and promotion in a marketing program, one must understand the role and function of marketing in an organization. The basic task of marketing is to combine the four controllable elements, known as the marketing mix, into a comprehensive program that facilitates exchange with a target market. The elements of the marketing mix are the product or service, price, place (distribution), and promotion.

For many years, the promotional function in most companies was dominated by mass-media advertising. However, more and more companies are recognizing the importance of integrated marketing communications, coordinating the various marketing and promotional elements to achieve more efficient and effective communication programs. A number of factors underlie the move toward IMC by marketers as well as ad agencies and other promotional facilitators. Reasons for the growing importance of the integrated marketing communications perspective include a rapidly changing environment with respect to consumers, technology, and media. The IMC movement is also being driven by changes in the ways companies market their products and services. A shifting of marketing expenditures from traditional media advertising to other forms of promotion as well as nontraditional media, the rapid growth of the Internet and social media, a shift in marketplace power from manufacturers to retailers, the growth and development of database marketing, the demand for greater accountability from advertising agencies and other marketing communication firms, and the fragmentation of media markets, as well as changing media consumption patterns, are among the key changes taking place.

Promotion is best viewed as the communication function of marketing. It is accomplished through a promotional mix that includes advertising, personal selling, publicity/public relations, sales promotion, direct marketing, and digital/Internet marketing. The inherent advantages and disadvantages of each of these promotional-mix elements influence the roles they play in the overall marketing program. In developing the IMC program, the marketer must decide which tools to use and how to combine them to achieve the organization's marketing and communication objectives. Many companies are taking an audience contact or touch point perspective in developing their IMC programs whereby they consider all of the potential ways of reaching their target audience and presenting the company or brand in a favorable manner. The four primary categories of contact points include company planned, intrinsic, unexpected, and customer initiated. These contact points vary with respect to the impact they have on the customer and marketers' ability to control them. Another categorization of the various types of customer contact points that has become very popular is that of paid, owned, and earned media.

Promotional management involves coordinating the promotional-mix elements to develop an integrated program of effective marketing communication. The model of the IMC planning process in Figure 1–8 contains a number of steps: a review of the marketing plan; promotional program situation analysis; analysis of the communication process; budget determination; development of an integrated marketing communications program; integration and implementation of marketing communications strategies; and monitoring, evaluation, and control of the promotional program.

Key Terms

exchange 7	direct-response advertising 19	owned media 30
marketing 7	omnichannel retailing 21	earned media 30
value 7	interactive media 21	integrated marketing communications
marketing mix 8	social media 22	management 31
integrated marketing	mobile marketing 22	integrated marketing communications
communications (IMC) 8	sales promotion 23	plan 31
sustainability 15	publicity 26	marketing plan 31
promotion 16	public relations 26	internal analysis 34
promotional mix 16	personal selling 27	external analysis 35
advertising 17	Touch point 27	marketing objectives 37
direct marketing 19	paid media 30	communication objectives 37

Discussion Questions

1. Discuss the role of integrated marketing communications in the marketing program for a brand such as Charmin. Discuss how Procter & Gamble uses various IMC tools to market Charmin and maintain its position as the leading brand of toilet tissue? (LO 1-2, 1-5)

2. Evaluate Procter & Gamble's decision to make digital and social media such an important part of the IMC program for Charmin. Why do you think P&G has been successful in using social media in the IMC program for Charmin? (LO 1-2, 1-5)

3. Discuss the role integrated marketing communications plays in the marketing program of companies and organizations. Discuss some of the ways the use of the various promotional mix tools has changed over the past decade and factors driving these changes. (LO 1-1)

4. Discuss some of the ways technology is making it possible for consumers to avoid advertising messages and the impact this is having on the advertising and media industries. (LO 1-2, 1-3)

5. Discuss how the digital revolution is impacting the ways marketers plan and implement their integrated marketing communications programs. Identify three specific technological developments and discuss how each is impacting the IMC program of companies. (LO 1-3, 1-4)

6. Discuss the opportunities and challenges facing marketers with regard to the use of mobile marketing. What are some of the ways marketers can use mobile marketing as part of their IMC program? (LO 1-4, 1-5)

7. What is meant by a consumer contact or touch point? Choose a specific company or brand and discuss how it is using the four categories of touch points discussed in the chapter. (LO 1-5)

8. What is meant by the categorization of touch points into paid, owned, and earned media? Choose a specific company or brand and discuss how it is using these three categories of media. (LO 1-5)

9. Find an example of company or brand that has reduced its spending on traditional mass-media advertising and is allocating more of its IMC budget to digital media. Do you agree with this decision or do you think this company or brand should be maintaining its spending on traditional media advertising? (LO 1-5, 1-6)

10. Why is it important for those who work in marketing to understand and appreciate all the various integrated marketing communications tools and how they can be used effectively? (LO 1-6)

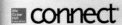

Digital users can access their personalized and adaptive SmartBook, Ad Forum Video Cases, and interactive exercises to review chapter concepts.

2

The Role of IMC in the Marketing Process

© Buick

LEARNING OBJECTIVES

LO1 Describe the role of advertising and promotion in an organization's integrated marketing program.

LO2 Define target marketing.

LO3 Discuss the role of market segmentation in an IMC program.

LO4 Describe positioning and repositioning strategies.

LO5 Identify the marketing-mix decisions that influence advertising and promotional strategy.

CREATING A NEW IMAGE FOR BUICK

Would you consider buying a Buick? Probably not. The first thing that usually comes to mind when someone mentions a Buick is "old"—old-fashioned, owned by older people, a car you would expect your grandfather to drive. Certainly not something you would think about buying just after you graduated college. Well, Buick is out to change that image. The 116-year-old car company wants to appeal to a younger audience and to sell them more cars. To accomplish this, Buick has engaged in a major repositioning effort to change its image and become more appealing to a younger audience including millennials.

In 2014, approximately 53 percent of Buick buyers were over the age of 55. Like its GM partner, Oldsmobile, Buick was concerned about extinction (Oldsmobile also had an older demographic buyer and went out of business in 2004 after a 107-year history). But rather than go away quietly, Buick is making a comeback.

It started with the introduction of badly needed new car models. Considering the fact that 80 percent of the approximately 500,000 Buicks on the road in 2015 were no longer being built—including the lumbering Buick Century and LeSabre models—or (as noted by GM's marketing VP) were piled in a scrap yard or in front of a bingo parlor, the image they projected was clearly not attractive to the younger crowd. It was time for a change. The redesigned new models include an attractive Enclave sport-utility vehicle (SUV), a smaller cross-over Encore, a BMW 3 Series–sized Regal, and the Cascada—the first Buick convertible introduced in the last 25 years. All were designed to appeal to the millennial market. Showrooms were redesigned, customer service was improved, and a new mantra exuding "happiness" became pervasive. Sales were up and continuing to climb.

But what perhaps has led to most of the success was a powerful and effective IMC program centered around the "That's a Buick?" ad campaign that poked a little fun at the automobile's image. The commercials featured older people and millennials seeing a new Buick for the first time, and not believing that the car is really a Buick. In one spot a grandmother doesn't believe her grandson's new car is a Buick. In another, a valet attendee can't find a Buick because he apparently is looking for a less stylish car. (He finds it when he pushes the button on the key chain and the lights blink.) Once he finds it he is also incredulous. Other ads feature the same theme of surprising people that a Buick could be so attractive. The wide variety of commercials and then a montage of snippets caught and held viewers' attention. After two years running, the spots show no signs of wearing out.

A second campaign targeted even more specifically at millennials and titled "#BuickHappiness," emphasizes the happiness and the "zen of driving." While offering a "24 Hours of Happiness Test Drive," the campaign attempts to convey a sense of well-being in everything the car company does. In addition to traditional ads, the campaign was promoted through a series of online videos, podcasts, digital images, and numerous press releases as well as other touch points that included a video of an Israeli supermodel and yogi Bar Refaeli posing outside a Buick Encore and advice from "happiness researcher" Shawn Anchor. Dr. Dot, a Hollywood masseuse, is also included demonstrating self-relaxation techniques to help drivers battle driver's stress. The goal of the campaign was to reach out to even more millennials, and also baby boomers, in an attempt to create an overall good feeling for the new GM models as well as to expand beyond the "That's a Buick?" campaign while again showing the repositioned brand.

For the first time in its history, Buick ran its first Super Bowl commercial on Super Bowl 50 (2016) to introduce the newest entry and its first convertible in 25 years, the Cascada. The commercial featured New York Giants wide receiver Odell Beckham making the call on actor Emily Ratajkowski's contortionist move to catch a wedding bouquet. The catch is similar to, and a reminder of, his "catch heard around the world," in which Odell catches a touchdown pass that defies imagination. Ellie Kemper is used in a digital-media-only campaign, while all of the celebrities are heavily involved in online chatter. The Super Bowl has long been known as an excellent place to have your commercial noticed, but it is also a haven for online chatter. As many as 25 million tweets were posted about the 2015 game, at the rate of 395,000 a minute, while Facebook reported that 65 million users talked about the 2015 game, creating 265 million posts, comments, and likes. Beckham's 3.6 million Instagram followers and Ratajkowski's 4.7 million offer the opportunity for huge social media buzz. And these consumers are not your "grandfathers." Buick is clearly honing in on a younger audience through its media strategy.

While Buick is expected to continue these efforts for a while, additional strategies are being designed as well. Most of them are targeted to millennials and/or boomers, and all of them are designed to change the image of the product line—or create a new image among those who don't yet have one. Is it possible that the repositioned "old" car can become hip? Buick certainly hopes so.

Sources: Michelle Castillo, "Odell Beckham Jr. Helps Buick Catch Super Bowl Glory in New Ad," February 7, 2016, www.cnbc.com; Dale Buss, "Buick Touts Happiness and Zen to Engage Chilled Out Car Buyers," August 25, 2015, www.brandchannel.com; Drew Singer, "Buick to Extend Run of Successful 'That's a Buick?' Ad Campaign, but Focus Will Shift," May 25, 2015, www.gmauthority.com; "Global Powers of Luxury Goods 2016: Engaging the Future Luxury Consumer," 2015, www.deloitte.com.

Marketers know that to be successful they must understand their buyers and potential buyers and develop specific strategies to best reach them. These include the identification of market opportunities, market segmentation, target marketing and positioning, and marketing program development. As can be seen in the lead-in to this chapter, this is often a challenging task.

In this chapter, we take a closer look at how marketing strategies influence the role of promotion and how promotional decisions must be coordinated with other areas of the marketing mix. In turn, all elements of the marketing mix must be consistent in a strategic plan that results in an integrated marketing communications program. We use the model in Figure 2–1 as a framework for analyzing how promotion fits into an organization's marketing strategy and programs.

This model consists of four major components: the organization's marketing strategy and analysis, the target marketing process, the marketing planning program development (which includes the promotional mix), and the target market. As the model shows, the marketing process begins with the development of a marketing strategy and analysis in which the company decides the product or service areas and

FIGURE 2–1

Marketing and Promotions Process Model

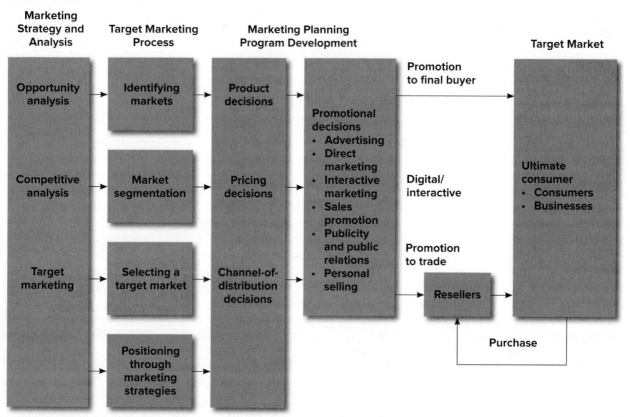

particular markets where it wants to compete. The company must then coordinate the various elements of the marketing mix into a cohesive marketing program that will reach the target market effectively. Note that a firm's promotion program is directed not only to the final buyer but also to the channel or "trade" members that distribute its products to the ultimate consumer. These channel members must be convinced there is a demand for the company's products so they will carry them and will aggressively merchandise and promote them to consumers. Promotions play an important role in the marketing program for building and maintaining demand not only among final consumers but among the trade as well.

As noted in Chapter 1, all elements of the marketing mix—product, price, place (distribution), and promotion—must be integrated to provide consistency and maximum communications impact. Development of a marketing plan is instrumental in achieving this goal.

As Figure 2–1 shows, development of a marketing program requires an in-depth analysis of the market. This analysis may make extensive use of marketing research as an input into the planning process. This input, in turn, provides the basis for the development of marketing strategies in regard to product, pricing, distribution, and promotion decisions. Each of these steps requires a detailed analysis, since this plan serves as the road map to follow in achieving marketing goals. Once the detailed market analysis has been completed and marketing objectives have been established, each element in the marketing mix must contribute to a comprehensive integrated marketing program. Of course, the promotional program element (the focus of this text) must be combined with all other program elements in such a way as to achieve maximum impact.

MARKETING STRATEGY AND ANALYSIS

Any organization that wants to exchange its products or services in the marketplace successfully should have a **strategic marketing plan** to guide the allocation of its resources. A strategic marketing plan usually evolves from an organization's overall corporate strategy and serves as a guide for specific marketing programs and policies. As we noted earlier, marketing strategy is based on a situation analysis—a detailed assessment of the current marketing conditions facing the company, its product lines, or its individual brands. From this situation analysis, a firm develops an understanding of the market and the various opportunities it offers, the competition, and the **market segments** or target markets the company wishes to pursue. We examine each step of the marketing strategy and *planning* in this chapter.

Opportunity Analysis

A careful analysis of the marketplace should lead to alternative market opportunities for existing product lines in current or new markets, new products for current markets, or new products for new markets. **Market opportunities** are areas where there are favorable demand trends, where the company believes customer needs and opportunities are not being satisfied, and where it can compete effectively. The Manischewitz company—you may have heard the ad slogan "Man-O-Manischewitz! What a wine!"—a marketer of kosher foods, has revived its decades-old slogan to take advantage of a new marketing opportunity. Based on research that showed that four out of five buyers of kosher foods are not traditional Jewish consumers, Manischewitz has increased its marketing efforts in an attempt to capture more of the mainstream market. Knowing that there has been an increase in interest in ethnic foods and health consciousness and that, as a result of the recession, more consumers are eating meals at home, the company hopes to reach more

EXHIBIT 2–1

Manischewitz sees the mainstream market as an opportunity

© Manischewitz

consumers (Exhibit 2–1). The company's new IMC program includes a multimillion-dollar advertising budget, web programs, in-store promotions, a "Cook Off," and public relations activities designed to promote its kosher food line.[1]

A company usually identifies market opportunities by carefully examining the marketplace and noting demand trends and competition in various market segments. A market can rarely be viewed as one large homogeneous group of customers; rather, it consists of many heterogeneous groups, or segments. In recent years, many companies have recognized the importance of tailoring their marketing to meet the needs and demand trends of different market segments.

For example, different market segments in the personal computer (PC) industry include the home, government, education, science, and business markets. These segments can be even further divided. The business market consists of both small companies and large corporations; the education market can range from elementary schools to colleges and universities. A company that is marketing its products in the auto industry must decide in which particular market segment or segments it wishes to compete. This decision depends on the amount and nature of competition the brand will face in a particular market. Many auto companies are now competing in the hybrid car market, offering a variety of models (Exhibit 2–2). Mercedes is now competing in the light-duty truck market. IMC Perspective 2–1 discusses one of the most sought-after segments by marketers—millennials.

A competitive analysis is an important part of marketing strategy development and warrants further consideration.

Competitive Analysis

In developing the firm's marketing strategies and plans for its products and services, the manager must carefully analyze the competition to be faced in the marketplace. This may range from direct brand competition (which can also include its own brands) to more indirect forms of competition, such as product substitutes.

EXHIBIT 2–2

Many car companies, as shown in this ad for Mercedes-Benz, now compete in the hybrid market. In addition to the hybrid market, what are some other ways that car companies can target automotive consumers?

Source: Mercedes-Benz USA

EXHIBIT 2–3

SoBe, which is owned by Pepsi, offers a variety of enhanced waters and is an example of direct brand competition

Source: SoBe by PepsiCo

EXHIBIT 2–4

V8 revitalizes its image and extends its line

Source: V8 by Campbell Soup Company

EXHIBIT 2–5

In this ad, Samsung compares itself to Apple but does not actually display the Apple name or logo, allowing Samsung to keep the focus on its brand

Source: Samsung

For example, growth in the bottled water market has led numerous companies to compete in this area and offer different product varieties (Exhibit 2–3).

At a more general level, marketers must recognize they are competing for the consumer's discretionary income, so they must understand the various ways potential customers choose to spend their money. The impact of the worldwide economic downturn has made manufacturers of luxury goods brands rethink their marketing strategies. Sales of luxury products fell during the recession in 2008 and again in 2009. However, by 2013 the top 100 luxury brands rebounded with an 8.2 percent growth rate.[2]

An important aspect of marketing strategy development is the search for a **competitive advantage**, something special a firm does or has that gives it an edge over competitors. Ways to achieve a competitive advantage include having quality products that command a premium price, providing superior customer service, having the lowest production costs and lower prices, and dominating channels of distribution. Competitive advantage can also be achieved through advertising that creates and maintains product differentiation and brand equity, an example of which was the long-running advertising campaign for Michelin tires, which stressed security as well as performance. The strong brand images of Apple, Samsung, Nike, BMW, and McDonald's give them a competitive advantage in their respective markets.

Recently, there has been concern that some marketers have not been spending enough money on advertising to allow leading brands to sustain their competitive edge. Advertising proponents have been calling for companies to protect their brand equity and franchises by investing more money in advertising instead of costly trade promotions. Some companies, recognizing the important competitive advantage strong brands provide, have been increasing their investments in them. Campbell Soup Company introduced a new advertising campaign in an attempt to revitalize its 80-year-old V8 vegetable juice brand. Replicating the highly successful campaign of the 1970s in which people got bopped on the head with the catchphrase "I could've had a V8," and stressing the brand's health aspects while extending the product line, Campbell's saw double-digit sales gains[3] (Exhibit 2–4).

Competitors' marketing programs have a major impact on a firm's marketing strategy, so they must be analyzed and monitored. The reactions of competitors to a company's marketing and promotional strategy are also very important. Competitors may cut price, increase promotional spending, develop new brands, or attack one another through comparative advertising (Exhibit 2–5). One of the more intense competitive rivalries is

IMC Perspective 2-1 > > >

Reaching Millennials—A True Marketing Challenge

One would think that a cohort that consists of 80 million persons with a spending power of $172 billion would be the ideal target market for American companies. Yet the millennials generation—those born between 1982 and 2000 and also known as gen Y—is proving to be one of the most difficult of any segment for marketers to reach in decades. Marketers have referred to this group as "the cheapest ever," "stingy," and/or "disinterested"—among other not so endearing terms—when describing their buying behaviors. It seems they just don't want to buy. At the same time, the cohort is just too large in size and has too much buying power to ignore: They are expected to spend over $10 trillion in their lifetimes. As a result, a number of companies, rather than ignoring them, are attempting to better understand them in an attempt to develop marketing programs that might attract their interest.

Unfortunately, millennials are not that easily understood. Maybe they don't buy because much of their life has been spent in a bad economy. Jobs have been hard to come by, salaries are not increasing, and housing is expensive. As a result, many (even after graduating from college) live at home with their parents, take mass transit, carpool, or walk to work and don't have a lot of disposable income. Many are saddled with college loan debts. Perhaps they suffer from information overload, as almost all of them are socially connected, the vast majority multitask frequently, and they are the most educated, mobile, and tech-savvy generation in history. Or maybe what they are interested in purchasing is different from previous generations—travel spending has increased over recent years, while new car purchases have been less than expected. Many would prefer to pay for enhanced cell phone services rather than make a car payment. There is no doubt that their media habits are more complex, making it easier to reach them but harder to get their attention. Or maybe the media contribute to their consumer behaviors by making it easier to communicate with others, sharing many things such as product evaluations in their discussions.

Since World War II, the U.S. economy has been driven by automobile and home sales. Now it seems that millennials are not interested in either—at least when it comes to buying. Rather, they have become a "sharing economy" in which everything from clothing to homes to automobiles is shared rather than purchased. Companies like car2go and Zipcar—the world's largest car-sharing company with over 700,000 members—are growing at a rapid pace. So fast, in fact, that Avis (the car rental conglomerate) purchased Zipcar for $500 million in 2013. Also expanding is Airbnb, a place for travelers to share bedrooms and other household accommodations, and both Uber and Lyft (the alternatives to taxis) continue to grow and expand to new markets.

One company trying to understand millennials is General Motors (GM). GM's research has shown that new vehicle purchases in the 21- to 34-year-old age group are down 35 percent from 1985. The percentage of teens and 20-somethings with driver's licenses has also decreased. While some of this can be attributed to the economy, all of it cannot. Because of their high connectivity and educational status (higher-educated persons tend to have greater buying power) GM believes that millennials still provide strong market potential, but automakers just haven't figured them out yet. Rather than impose the values of the older generations, GM is trying to adapt by reaching them on their own terms. Chevrolet has partnered with RelayRides, a company that allows members to rent out their vehicles to other users. As seen in the lead-in to this chapter GM's Buick division has redesigned and repositioned its cars to be more attractive to this segment. The key to capturing millennials, according to 31-year-old John McFarland, GM's "youth emissary," is to "give

the battle between Coca-Cola and Pepsi. A number of other intense competitive rivalries exist in the marketplace, including Hertz and Avis, Verizon and AT&T, and Apple and Samsung.

A final aspect of competition is the growing number of foreign companies penetrating the U.S. market and taking business from domestic firms. In products ranging from beer to cars to electronics, imports are becoming an increasingly strong form of competition with which U.S. firms must contend. As we now compete in a global economy, U.S. companies must not only defend their domestic markets but also learn how to compete effectively in the international marketplace.

Target Market Selection

After evaluating the opportunities presented by various market segments, including a detailed competitive analysis, the company may select one, or more, as a target market. This target market becomes the focus of the firm's marketing effort, and

© Car2go N.A., LLC

on U.S. and international millennials suggests there are at least four subsegments that must be approached differently by marketers. An article at emarketer.com, for example, reports on studies that demonstrate that younger and older millennials often differ in their shopping habits. No doubt tied to income, older millennials (those 25–34) spend more on furniture, health care, pets, and entertainment. Those under 25 report being more concerned about their personal debt and more likely to buy brands associated with a good cause. As noted by Erin Mulligan Nelson in *Advertising Age* magazine, if companies think all they have to do to reach this cohort is to employ social media, they are going to miss the mark. Nelson contends that to reach millennials, marketers must employ media that provide content about the brand—blogs, websites, and applications—even strangers providing testimonials. Millennials want to be informed, and want to be heard, often valuing their mobile phones over other tangible good items. Emma Bazilian, reporting on a study of 1,000 consumers between the ages of 18 and 34, agrees that social media may be the best way to reach millennials, but also believes that traditional media are still important. The study conducted by MPA and GfK MRI found that while Facebook is the most used social site, 93 percent of those surveyed said they read magazines and that contests and coupons are also a big influence on their purchase decisions, as is word of mouth—particularly from their friends.

So while millennials may be seen as the next great frontier for marketers, reaching them may not be as easy or as lucrative as it seems. Nevertheless, at least in the short run, companies continue to focus their lens at this segment as advertisers reported that they expect to spend 500 percent more dollars targeting millennials than on all other age groups *combined* in the next few years!

Sources: "How Younger and Older Millennial Shoppers Differ," January 18, 2016, www.emarketer.com; "The Millennial Lens Needs Focus," November 19, 2015, www.warc.com; Andrew Martin, "Car Sharing Catches on as Zipcar Sells to Avis," January 2, 2013, www.nytimes.com; Emma Bazilian, "Study: Millennials Engage with Magazines via Social Media," August 23, 2012, www.adweek.com; Jordan Weissmann, "How Do You Sell a Car to a Millennial?" April 4, 2012, www.theatlantic.com.

them exactly what they want and nothing more." So far, GM appears to be having success.

Another company seeking to do business with gen Y is Wawanesa, an insurance company that has been around since 1896 but is far less known than competitors like State Farm, Allstate, and GEICO. Wawanesa recently discovered that millennials don't want to take the time to complete insurance forms the traditional way—on paper. (Allstate apparently found this out earlier, which led to the founding of Esurance.) To respond to this threat, Wawanesa increased its web presence, offering online quotes and allowing customers to pay bills and even file claims online. In addition, the company increased its marketing efforts targeted to this cohort. Other insurance companies now offer a mobile app to allow access to one's insurance account.

While many companies are increasing their use of online offerings, social media, and digital apps to appeal to this generation, offering a strong online presence is not the only strategy that must be undertaken to reach millennials. A number of studies have shown that all millennials are not the same, and that there are segments within the segment. One report

goals and objectives are set according to where the company wants to be and what it hopes to accomplish in this market. As noted in Chapter 1, these goals and objectives are set in terms of specific performance variables such as sales, market share, and profitability. The selection of the target market (or markets) in which the firm will compete is an important part of its marketing strategy and has direct implications for its advertising and promotional efforts.

Recall from our discussion of the integrated marketing communications planning program that the situation analysis is conducted at the beginning of the promotional planning process. Specific objectives—both marketing and communications—are derived from the situation analysis, and the promotional-mix strategies are developed to achieve these objectives. Marketers rarely go after the entire market with one product, brand, or service offering. Rather, they pursue a number of different strategies, breaking the market into segments and targeting one or more of these segments for marketing and promotional efforts. This means different objectives may be established, different budgets may be used, and the promotional-mix strategies may vary, depending on the market approach used.

THE TARGET MARKETING PROCESS

FIGURE 2–2

The Target Marketing
Process

LO2-2

Because few, if any, products can satisfy the needs of all consumers, companies often develop different marketing strategies to satisfy different consumer needs. The process by which marketers do this (presented in Figure 2–2) is referred to as **target marketing** and involves four basic steps: identifying markets with unfulfilled needs, segmenting the market, targeting specific segments, and positioning one's product or service through marketing strategies.

Identifying Markets

When employing a target marketing strategy, the marketer identifies the specific needs of groups of people (or segments), selects one or more of these segments as a target, and develops marketing programs directed to each. This approach has found increased applicability in marketing for a number of reasons, including changes in the market (consumers are becoming much more diverse in their needs, attitudes, and lifestyles); increased use of segmentation by competitors; and the fact that more managers are trained in segmentation and realize the advantages associated with this strategy. Perhaps the best explanation, however, comes back to the basic premise that you must understand as much as possible about consumers to design marketing programs that meet their needs most effectively.

Target market identification isolates consumers with similar lifestyles, needs, and the like and increases our knowledge of their specific requirements. The more marketers can establish this common ground with consumers, the more effective they will be in addressing these requirements in their communications programs and informing and/or persuading potential consumers that the product or service offering will meet their needs.

Let's use the beer industry as an example. Years ago, beer was just beer, with little differentiation, many local distributors, and few truly national brands. The industry began consolidating; many brands were assumed by the larger brewers or ceased to exist. As the number of competitors decreased, competition among the major brewers increased. To compete more effectively, brewers began to look at different tastes, lifestyles, and so on of beer drinkers and used this information to design their marketing strategies. This process resulted in the identification of many market segments, each of which corresponds to different customers' needs, lifestyles, and other characteristics.

The beer market has changed dramatically over the past few years, with domestic brands and imports increasing their consolidation efforts. One of the faster-growing segments—craft breweries—itself now consists of four segments with numerous offerings available in each (Figure 2–3). Most of the large traditional

FIGURE 2–3

The U.S. Craft Beer Market

| Microbrewery |
| Brewpub |
| Contract brewing company |
| Regional craft brewery |

Source: Craft Beer Industry Market Segments, Brewers Association, 2016.

brewers also have product offerings in each segment, competing with each other as well as smaller craft microbreweries (Exhibit 2–6). Each appeals to a different set of needs. Taste is certainly one; others include image, cost, and social appeal. A variety of other reasons for purchasing are also operating, including the consumer's social class, lifestyle, and economic status.

Marketers competing in nearly all product and service categories are constantly searching for ways to segment their markets in an attempt to better satisfy customers' needs. The remainder of this section discusses ways to approach this task.

Market Segmentation

It is not possible to develop marketing strategies for every consumer. Rather, the marketer attempts to identify broad classes of buyers who have the same needs and will respond similarly to marketing actions. **Market segmentation** is dividing a market into distinct groups that (1) have common needs and (2) will respond similarly to a marketing action.

The more marketers segment the market, the more precise is their understanding of it. But the more the market becomes divided, the fewer consumers there are in each segment. Thus, a key decision is, How far should one go in the segmentation process? Where does the process stop? As you can see by the strategy taken in the beer industry, it can go far!

In planning the promotional effort, managers consider whether the target segment is substantial enough to support individualized strategies. More specifically, they consider whether this group is accessible. Can it be reached with a communications program? For example, you will see in Chapter 10 that in some instances there are no media that can efficiently be used to reach some targeted groups. Or the promotions manager may identify a number of segments but be unable to develop the required programs to reach them. The firm may have insufficient funds to develop the required advertising campaign, inadequate sales staff to cover all areas, or other promotional deficiencies. After determining that a segmentation strategy is in order, the marketer must establish the basis on which it will address the market. The following section discusses some of the bases for segmenting markets and demonstrates examples of advertising and promotions applications.

EXHIBIT 2–6

Traditional breweries are now offering craft beers. MillerCoors recently purchased craft brewery Saint Archer Brewing Co. of San Diego to help it compete more effectively in different market segments.

Source: Saint Archer Brewing Co.

Bases for Segmentation As shown in Figure 2–4, several methods are available for segmenting markets. Marketers may use one of the segmentation variables or a combination of approaches. Consider the market segmentation strategy that might be employed to market snow skis. The consumer's lifestyle—active, fun-loving, enjoys outdoor sports—is certainly important. But so are other factors, such as age (participation in downhill skiing drops off significantly at about age 30) and income (have you seen the price of a lift ticket lately?), as well as marital status. Let us review the bases for segmentation and examine some promotional strategies employed in each.

Geographic Segmentation In the **geographic segmentation** approach, markets are divided into different geographic units. These units may include nations, states, counties, or even neighborhoods. Consumers often have different buying habits depending on where they reside. Regional differences may exist in regard to food, drinks,

FIGURE 2-4 Some Bases for Market Segmentation

Main Dimension	Segmentation Variables	Typical Breakdowns
Customer Characteristics		
Geographic	Region	Northeast; Midwest; South; West; etc.
	City size	Under 10,000; 10,000–24,999; 25,000–49,999; 50,000–99,999; 100,000–249,999; 250,000–499,999; 500,000–999,999; 1,000,000 or more
	Metropolitan area	Metropolitan statistical area (MSA)
	Density	Urban; suburban; small town; rural
Demographic	Gender	Male; female
	Age	Under 6 yrs; 6–11 yrs; 12–17 yrs; 18–24 yrs; 25–34 yrs; 35–44 yrs; 45–54 yrs; 55–64 yrs; 65–74 yrs; 75 yrs plus
	Race	African American; Asian; Hispanic; White/Caucasian; etc.
	Life stage	Infant; preschool; child; youth; collegiate; adult; senior
	Birth era	Baby boomer (1946–1964); generation X (1965–1976); baby boomlet/generation Y (1977–present)
	Household size	1; 2; 3–4; 5 or more
	Residence tenure	Own home; rent home
	Marital status	Never married; married; separated; divorced; widowed
Socioeconomic	Income	<$15,000; $15,000–$24,999; $25,000–$34,999; $35,000–$49,999; $50,000–$74,999; $75,000–$99,999; $100,000+
	Education	Some high school or less; high school graduate (or GED); etc.
	Occupation	Managerial and professional specialty; technical, sales and administrative support; service; farming, forestry, and fishing
Psychographic	Personality	Gregarious; compulsive; introverted; aggressive; ambitious
	Values (VALS)	Actualizers; fulfilleds; achievers; experiencers; believers; strivers; makers; strugglers
	Lifestyle (Claritas)	Settled in; white picket fence; and 46 other household segments
Buying Situations		
Outlet type	In-store	Department; specialty; outlet; convenience; supermarket; superstore/mass merchandiser; catalog
	Direct	Mail order/catalog; door-to-door; direct response; Internet
Benefits sought	Product features	Situation specific; general
	Needs	Quality; service; price/value; financing; warranty; etc.
Usage	Usage rate	Light user; medium user; heavy user
	User status	Nonuser; ex-user; prospect; first-time user; regular user
Awareness and intentions	Product knowledge	Unaware; aware; informed; interested; intending to buy; purchaser; rejection
Behavior	Involvement	Minimum effort; comparison; special effort

facebook.com/cheerwine

DRINK Cheerwine SOFT DRINK LEGEND SINCE 1917

LEGEND

BORN IN THE SOUTH. RAISED IN A GLASS.™

attitudes toward foreign products, and the like. For example, many companies consider California a very different market from the rest of the United States and have developed specific marketing programs targeted to the consumers in that state. Other companies have developed programs targeted at specific regions. Exhibit 2–7 shows an ad for Cheerwine, just one of the regional soft-drink "cult brands"—along with Jackson Hole Huckleberry (Wyoming), Vernors (Michigan), and Moxie (New England)—that have found success by marketing in regional areas (in this case, the South). One company—Olde Brooklyn Beverage Company—even went so far as to promote a brand based on a specific section of New York City, differentiating it from bigger brands by promoting the product's "Brooklyn Attitude."

Demographic Segmentation Dividing the market on the basis of demographic variables such as age, sex, family size, education, income, and social class is called **demographic segmentation**. Secret deodorant and the Lady Schick shaver are products that have met with a great deal of success by using the demographic variable of sex as a basis for segmentation. WomensHealth.com, a website targeting women, may be one of the most successful websites on the Internet (Exhibit 2–8). It is interesting to note that the top 10 websites for women are further segmented by age, lifestyle, and so forth.

Although market segmentation on the basis of demographics may seem obvious, companies discover that they need to focus more attention on a specific demographic group. For example, IKEA—noting that more than 70 percent of its shoppers are women—has enhanced its store environment to be more "women friendly," as have Home Depot and Walmart. Dell Computers and Verizon (among others) have discovered that this may not be as easy as it seems, since recent efforts by both companies have achieved less than favorable results.[4,5] As seen in IMC Perspective 2–1, companies are also finding it difficult to reach the millennial age segment. As a result, a number of companies have begun to focus more attention on the baby boomer market—those 76 million Americans born between 1946 and 1964. Given their huge spending power, this age segment has become more attractive to a number of companies including travel agencies and pharmaceutical companies among others.

EXHIBIT 2-8

WomensHealth.com has successfully targeted women and is an excellent example of using gender as a basis for successful demographic segmentation. What are the pros and cons to using gender as a basis for demographic segmentation?

Source: WomensHealth.com

WomensHealth.com Health/Wellness Website

Timeline About Likes Photos Videos

Health/Wellness Website

Search for posts on this Page

PEOPLE

WomensHealth.com
June 10 at 6:27am

Women living with endometriosis and polycystic ovary syndrome have another celebrity ally. Actress Daisy Ridley opens up about her journey to diagnosis and the day-to-day stresses of PCOS.

As the Hispanic Market Grows, So Do Challenges for Marketers

Source: Target Brands, Inc.

How important is the U.S. Hispanic market to marketers? Consider these facts: (1) Hispanics constitute 17 percent of the U.S. population, numbering over 50 million; (2) they control well over $1.5 trillion in buying power annually; (3) the Hispanic food market more than doubled between 2005 and 2010 and constituted an estimated 25 percent of the total retail food market in 2015; (4) by 2020 Hispanics will constitute 20 percent of the total U.S. population and 28.6 percent by 2060; and (5) they are younger than the rest of the U.S. general population. That's the good news. There is no doubt that Hispanics constitute an attractive market segment, and will for years to come.

Now for the bad news. Due to the diversity of this group, marketers are finding it extremely difficult to market to them.

Their shopping behaviors differ markedly from the general population as they tend to be more careful, deliberate, and knowledgeable about products, spending more time considering the options. Latinos differ in other ways as well. Hispanics have a higher than average poverty level, are more likely to be bilingual, and are more likely to live in urban areas. At the same time they are considered to be more "tech savvy" than the general population, and are more likely to compare prices via mobile devices—but less likely to download coupons or apps or use QR codes. Unlike their general market counterparts, Latinos rarely do one-stop shopping for convenience and to save time, preferring to shop until they feel they get the best deal. They also like to shop close to home, preferring to deal with friends, family, and peers when they buy. While they were once considered to be fiercely brand loyal, this is no longer the case. Most importantly, the value to the family is first and foremost in the Latino purchase decision.

There are also differences within the Latino culture. A study reported in the *Journal of Cultural Marketing Strategy* examined media behaviors across three generational levels of the U.S. Latino population, concluding that to be successful, marketers had to go beyond just language to truly understand and reach this market. For example, the findings showed that while Spanish-language TV stations Univision and Telemundo ranked first and second for most-watched networks among first-generation Hispanics, Univision ranked only fifth among the third generation. The top five networks watched by this group were all in English. In addition, the

Recognizing their need for retirement planning, Wachovia has increased its marketing efforts to this segment.[6] *AARP, The Magazine,* is targeted to the 34 percent of the population who are 50+, and has over 47 million readers[7] (Exhibit 2–9). IMC Perspective 2–2 describes some companies' efforts to attempt to reach another popular and growing segment, the Hispanic market.

Other products that have successfully employed demographic segmentation include Dove (sex); Doan's Pills (age); Coca-Cola (race); Mercedes-Benz, Lexus, and BMW cars (income); and Banquet prepackaged dinners (family size).

While demographics may still be the most common method of segmenting markets, it is important to recognize that other factors may be the underlying basis for homogeneity and/or consumer behavior. The astute marketer will identify additional bases for segmenting and will recognize the limitations of demographics. As noted by media strategist Jamie Beckland, many marketers are relying less on demographics and more on psychographic profiling.[8]

Psychographic Segmentation Dividing the market on the basis of personality, lifecycles, and/or lifestyles is referred to as **psychographic segmentation**. While there is some disagreement as to whether personality is a useful basis for segmentation, lifestyle factors have been used effectively. Many consider lifestyle the most effective criterion for segmentation.

The determination of lifestyles is usually based on an analysis of the activities, interests, and opinions (AIOs) of consumers. These lifestyles are then correlated longer the first generationers were in the United States, the more their English network watching increased by as much as 20 to 30 percent. Dr. Jake Beniflah, executive director at the Center for Multicultural Science, characterized it as a "paradigm shift" with major implications for marketers hoping to reach Latinos through television. Beniflah noted that the use of generational levels and age is an effective predictor of what TV programs U.S. Latinos are watching.

Given this diversity (and there are more differences than discussed here), what does the marketer need to do to reach this lucrative segment of the population? Many of the top 50 spending advertisers have substantially increased their spending into Latino advertising allocating over $3.4 billion to this segment, with Procter & Gamble spending the most followed by AT&T. For the first time, Target has introduced a new television campaign called "#SinTraduccion," or "without translation"—the company's first Latino-focused effort to rely on cultural differences rather than merely translate English-speaking ads into Spanish. The new campaign is part of an overall effort to attract more of the Latino market by using language that has no English translation. The ads will appear on prime-time shows including "Jane the Virgin" on the CW, "Modern Family" on USA, and "The Big Bang Theory" on TBS. Target is also targeting Latino millennials; research showed that 54 percent of this segment said that Target was their favorite brand. To reach this group, the retailer is adding social media into the mix, using Twitter and Facebook to court the millennial shopper.

Another department store chain, JCPenney, has also targeted this segment launching a high-profile campaign tied to the 2014 World Cup. The ads focused exclusively on female sports fans and were entirely in Spanish with English subtitles. Nestlé has found success by reaching out to Latina moms with an integrated bilingual strategy. The campaign "Echale Agua a Tu Vida" ("Put Water in Your Life") for its Pure Life brand of water underscores the importance of healthy hydration and active lifestyles for the moms and their families. Among other tactics, Nestlé has teamed up with the U.S. Soccer Foundation, offering free soccer instruction and interactive and educational clinics for kids 5 to 12 in a number of cities in the United States. (Soccer is clearly the sport of choice for Hispanics.) Nestlé has employed TV personality Cristina Saralegui to be its spokesperson and has devoted a website to inspire moms to be healthier by incorporating water into their daily routines.

Dunkin' Donuts has also launched a campaign targeted specifically to this segment. The theme of this campaign "Que estas tomando?" ("What are you drinking?") also uses an integrated strategy employing Hispanic television, radio, social media, public relations, and in-store promotions as well as a Spanish-language website. The primary goal of the campaign, says John Castello, chief global marketing and innovation officer at Dunkin' Brands, is to "reflect the importance and the loyalty of our Hispanic consumers." For the first time ever the longtime tagline "America Moves with Dunkin'" will also appear in Spanish ("America se Mueve con Dunkin'").

Companies have clearly discovered the value and importance of the Hispanic market. The companies here seem to have developed strategies to reach this market as well.

Sources: Samantha Masunaga, "Target Takes Aim at Latinos in New Marketing Campaign," *Los Angeles Times,* April 18, 2015, pp. C1, C5; "Look beyond Language to Reach Hispanics," October 20, 2015, www.warc.com; Laura Wood, "Marketing to US Hispanics—Social, Demographic, Economic and Cultural Intricacies," *Business Wire,* July 19, 2012; Terry Mangano, "As Hispanic Population Grows, So Too Do Challenges for Marketers—5 Insights," *Promo* (online), January 23, 2012; Karlene Lukovitz, "Dunkin' Launches Multi-Platform Hispanic Campaign," *Marketing Daily,* March 29, 2012; Allison Cerra, "Nestlé Pure Life Centers 'Echale Agua a Tu Vida' Campaign around Latina Moms," August 16, 2011, www.drugstorenews.com.

EXHIBIT 2–9

AARP, The Magazine targets the 50+ segment

© The McGraw-Hill Companies, Inc./ Mark Dierker, photographer

with the consumers' product, brand, and/or media usage. For many products and/or services, lifestyles may be the best discriminator between use and nonuse, accounting for differences in food, clothing, and car selections, among numerous other consumer behaviors.[9]

Psychographic segmentation has been increasingly more popular with the advent of the values and lifestyles (VALS) program. Although marketers employed lifestyle segmentation long before VALS and although a number of alternatives—for example, PRIZM—are available, VALS remains one of the more popular options. VALS 2 divides Americans into eight lifestyle segments that exhibit distinctive attitudes, behaviors, and decision-making patterns. VALS is also available for the Japan and UK markets (both have six lifestyle segments).[10] The VALS 2 system is an excellent predictor of consumer behaviors, and a number of companies now employ lifestyle segmentation to position brands, determine value propositions, and select media.

Another form of psychographic analysis relies on the use of multiple databases including social profile data (available through almost all social networks), behavioral data (tracking users through their online behaviors), and lifecycle data (stage of the consumer's lifecycle, e.g., buying diapers, graduating high school, etc.). Amazon.com has successfully used this strategy for some time, and others are now starting to see the advantages offered over traditional demographic profiling.[11]

Behavioristic Segmentation Dividing consumers into groups according to their usage, loyalties, or buying responses to a product is **behavioristic segmentation**. For example, product or brand usage, degree of use (heavy vs. light), and/or brand loyalty are combined with demographic and/or psychographic criteria to develop profiles of market segments. In the case of usage, the marketer assumes that nonpurchasers of a brand or product who have the same characteristics as purchasers hold greater potential for adoption than nonusers with different characteristics. As you will see in Chapter 15, many companies target consumers through social media like Facebook based on behavioristic segmentation.

Degree of use relates to the fact that a few consumers may buy a disproportionate amount of many products or brands. Industrial marketers refer to the **80–20 rule**, meaning 20 percent of their buyers account for 80 percent of their sales volume. Again, when the characteristics of these users are identified, targeting them allows for a much greater concentration of efforts and less wasted time and money. The same heavy-half strategy is possible in the consumer market as well. The majority of purchases of many products (e.g., soaps and detergents, shampoos, cake mixes, beer, dog food, colas, bourbon, and toilet tissue—yes, toilet tissue!) are accounted for by a small proportion of the population. Perhaps you can think of some additional examples.

Benefit Segmentation In purchasing products, consumers are generally trying to satisfy specific needs and/or wants. They are looking for products that provide specific benefits to satisfy these needs. The grouping of consumers on the basis of attributes sought in a product is known as **benefit segmentation** and is widely used (Exhibit 2–10).

Consider the purchase of a wristwatch. While you might buy a watch for particular benefits such as accuracy, water resistance, or stylishness, others may seek a different set of benefits. Watches are commonly given as gifts for birthdays, Christmas, and graduation. Certainly some of the same benefits are considered in the purchase of a gift, but the benefits the purchaser derives are different from those the user will obtain. Ads that portray watches as good gifts stress different criteria to consider in the purchase decision. The next time you see an ad or commercial for a watch, think about the basic appeal and the benefits it offers.

The Process of Segmenting a Market The segmentation process develops over time and is an integral part of the situation analysis. It is in this stage that marketers attempt to determine as much as they can about the market: What needs are not being fulfilled? What benefits are being sought? What characteristics distinguish among the various groups seeking these products and services?

A number of alternative segmentation strategies may be used. Each time a specific segment is identified, additional information is gathered to help the marketer understand this group.

For example, once a specific segment is identified on the basis of benefits sought, the marketer will examine psychographic characteristics and demographics to help characterize this group and to further its understanding of this market. Behavioristic segmentation criteria will also be examined. In the purchase of ski boots, for example, specific benefits may be sought—flexibility or stiffness—depending on the type of skiing the buyer does. All this information will be combined to provide a complete profile of the skier.

	URBAN	SUBURBAN	SECOND CITY	TOWN AND COUNTRY

HIGH

U1
URBAN UPTOWN

04 Young Digerati
07 Money & Brains
16 Bohemian Mix
26 The Cosmopolitans
29 American Dreams

S1
ELITE SUBURBS

01 Upper Crust
02 Blue Blood Estates
03 Movers & Shakers
06 Winner's Circle

C1
SECOND CITY SOCIETY

10 Second City Elite
12 Brite Lites, Li'l City
13 Upward Bound

T1
LANDED GENTRY

05 Country Squires
09 Big Fish, Small Pond
11 God's Country
20 Fast-Track Families
25 Country Casuals

S2
THE AFFLUENTIALS

08 Executive Suites
14 New Empty Nests
15 Pools & Patios
17 Beltway Boomers
18 Kids & Cul-de-Sacs
19 Home Sweet Home

T2
COUNTRY COMFORT

23 Greenbelt Sports
28 Traditional Times
32 New Homesteaders
33 Big Sky Families
37 Mayberry-ville

$

U2
MIDTOWN MIX

31 Urban Achievers
40 Close-In Couples
54 Multi-Culti Mosaic

C2
CITY CENTERS

24 Up-and-Comers
27 Middleburg Managers
34 White Picket Fences
35 Boomtown Singles
41 Sunset City Blues

S3
MIDDLEBURBS

21 Gray Power
22 Young Influentials
30 Suburban Sprawl
36 Blue-Chip Blues
39 Domestic Duos

T3
MIDDLE AMERICA

38 Simple Pleasures
42 Red, White & Blues
43 Heartlanders
45 Blue Highways
50 Kid Country, USA
51 Shotguns & Pickups

U3
URBAN CORES

59 Urban Elders
61 City Roots
65 Big City Blues
66 Low-Rise Living

S4
INNER SUBURBS

44 New Beginnings
46 Old Glories
49 American Classics
52 Suburban Pioneers

C3
MICRO-CITY BLUES

47 City Startups
53 Mobility Blues
60 Park Bench Seniors
62 Hometown Retired
63 Family Thrifts

T4
RUSTIC LIVING

48 Young & Rustic
55 Golden Ponds
56 Crossroads Villagers
57 Old Milltowns
58 Back Country Folks
64 Bedrock America

LOW

EXHIBIT 2–11

Nielsen Claritas provides cluster profiles for marketers

A number of companies offer research services to help marketing managers define their markets and develop strategies targeting them. The VALS and PRIZM systems discussed earlier are just a few of the services offered; others use demographic, socioeconomic, and geographic data to cluster consumer households into distinct "microgeographic" segments. One of these companies, Nielsen Claritas, provides demographic and psychographic profiles of geographic areas as small as census track, block group, or zip code +4. Users of the system include Ace Hardware, Walmart, and numerous others. (See Exhibit 2–11.)

Selecting a Target Market

The outcome of the segmentation analysis will reveal the market opportunities available. The next phase in the target marketing process involves two steps: (1) determining how many segments to enter and (2) determining which segments offer the most potential.

Determining How Many Segments to Enter Three market coverage alternatives are available. **Undifferentiated marketing** involves ignoring segment differences and offering just one product or service to the entire market. For example, when Henry Ford brought out the first assembly-line automobile, all potential consumers were offered the same basic product: a black Ford. For many years, Coca-Cola offered only one product version. While this standardized strategy saves the company money, it does not allow the opportunity to offer different versions of the product to different markets.

EXHIBIT 2-12

Hilton uses positioning that focuses on the consumer

© Hilton Worldwide, Inc.

Differentiated marketing involves marketing in a number of segments, developing separate marketing strategies for each. For example, the Marriott hotel chain offers a variety of customer services for different travelers, including vacation, business, long or short stay, and so forth.

The third alternative, **concentrated marketing**, is used when the firm selects one segment and attempts to capture a large share of this market. Volkswagen used this strategy in the 1950s when it was the only major automobile company competing in the economy-car segment in the United States. While Volkswagen has now assumed a more differentiated strategy, other companies have found the concentrated strategy effective. For example, Rolls-Royce has focused its automobile business exclusively on the high-income segment, while L'Oréal competes in the cosmetics and beauty segment.

Determining Which Segments Offer Potential The second step in selecting a market involves determining the most attractive segment. The firm must examine the sales potential of the segment, the opportunities for growth, the competition, and its own ability to compete. Then it must decide whether it can market to this group. Stories abound of companies that have entered new markets only to find their lack of resources or expertise would not allow them to compete successfully. After selecting the segments to target and determining that it can compete, the firm proceeds to the final step in Figure 2–2: the market positioning phase.

Market Positioning

LO2-4

EXHIBIT 2-13

In this advertisement, Burt's Bees uses a benefit positioning strategy by comparing the ingredients in its lip balm to that of its competitors

Source: Burt's Bees

Approaches to Positioning Positioning strategies generally focus on either the consumer or the competition. While both approaches involve the association of product benefits with consumer needs, the former does so by linking the product with the benefits the consumer will derive or creating a favorable brand image, as shown in Exhibit 2–12. The latter approach positions the product by comparing it and the benefit it offers versus the competition. Products like Scope Outlast mouthwash (positioning itself as five times longer lasting than competitors) and Burt's Bees (positioned as a better value than its competitors) have employed this strategy successfully (Exhibit 2–13).

Many advertising practitioners consider market positioning the most important factor in establishing a brand in the marketplace. David Aaker and John Myers note that the term *position* has been used to indicate the brand's or product's image in the marketplace.[12] Jack Trout and Al Ries suggest that this brand image must contrast with those of competitors. They say, "In today's marketplace, the competitors' image is just as important as your own. Sometimes more important."[13] Trout notes that a good branding strategy cannot exist without positioning. He further states that branding is about the process of building a brand, while positioning is about putting that brand in the mind of the consumer.[14] Thus, *positioning,* as used in this text, relates to the image of the product and/or brand relative to competing products or brands. The position of the product or brand is the key factor in communicating the benefits it offers and differentiating it from the competition. Let us now turn to strategies marketers use to position a product.

Positioning has been defined as "the art and science of fitting the product or service to one or more segments of the broad market in such a way as to set it meaningfully apart from competition."[15] As you can see, the position of the product, service, or even store is the image that comes to mind and the attributes consumers perceive as related to it. This communication occurs through the message itself, which explains the benefits, as well as the media strategy employed

EXHIBIT 2–14

5-hour ENERGY positions itself as an energy shot; by promoting its vitamins, nutrients, zero sugar, and low-calories it sets itself apart from its competitors

Source: 5-hour ENERGY

to reach the target group. Take a few moments to think about how some products are positioned and how their positions are conveyed to you. For example, what comes to mind when you hear the name Mercedes, Dr Pepper, or Apple? What about department stores such as Neiman Marcus, Sears, and JCPenney? Now think of the ads for each of these products and companies. Are their approaches different from their competitors'? When and where are these ads shown? What is the message they are trying to communicate?

DEVELOPING A POSITIONING STRATEGY

A number of positioning strategies might be employed in developing a promotional program. David Aaker and J. Gary Shansby discuss six such strategies: positioning by product attributes, price/quality, use, product class, users, and competitor.[16] Aaker and Myers add one more approach, positioning by cultural symbols.[17]

Positioning by Product Attributes and Benefits

A common approach to positioning is setting the brand apart from competitors on the basis of the specific characteristics or benefits offered. Sometimes a product may be positioned on more than one product benefit. Marketers attempt to identify **salient attributes** (those that are important to consumers and are the basis for making a purchase decision). For example, when Apple first introduced its computers, the key benefit stressed was ease of use—an effective strategy, given the complexity of computers in the market at that time. While Apple still maintains this position, it is innovative products that comes to mind as well. More recently, there have been a number of new water products that enhance hydration, help the body to exert physical power, increase immunities, and so on. 5-hour ENERGY positions itself as a sugar-free energy shot that comes in a variety of flavors (Exhibit 2–14).

Positioning by Price/Quality

EXHIBIT 2–15

Kohl's positions its brand as having good value for the right price

© NetPhotos/Alamy

Marketers often use price/quality characteristics to position their brands. One way they do this is with ads that reflect the image of a high-quality brand where cost, while not irrelevant, is considered secondary to the quality benefits derived from using the brand. Premium brands positioned at the high end of the market use this approach to positioning.

Another way to use price/quality characteristics for positioning is to focus on the quality or value offered by the brand at a very competitive price. For example, Kohl's takes the position of a family-oriented specialty store offering good value (Exhibit 2–15). Remember that although price is an important consideration, the product quality must be comparable to, or even better than, competing brands for the positioning strategy to be effective.

Positioning by Use or Application

Another way to communicate a specific image or position for a brand is to associate it with a specific use or application. The Intuit ad shown in Exhibit 2–16 is specifically targeted to small business owners and/or entrepreneurs.

Payroll doesn't have to be so frustrating.
Unless you like the extra fiber in your diet.

intuit.
Payroll

Payroll stressing you out? Start using Intuit® Payroll and make it easy on yourself. With a few clicks you can pay employees and file tax forms. Just enter employee hours and Intuit Payroll automatically calculates everything else. And, if you need it, there's live expert support. Saving you time and pencils every month.

| From the maker of QuickBooks® | Learn more at IntuitPayroll.com |

| Online Demo | 30-Day FREE Trial | Live Support |

EXHIBIT 2–16

Intuit offers products specifically useful to small business owners

EXHIBIT 2–17

Arm & Hammer baking soda demonstrates numerous product uses

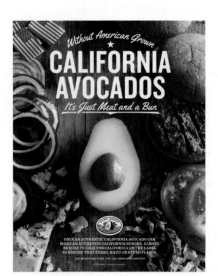

EXHIBIT 2–18

In this ad, how does the California Avocado Commission use positioning to effectively market California Avocados?

Source: California Avocado Commission

While this strategy is often used to enter a market on the basis of a particular use or application, it is also an effective way to expand the usage of a product. For example, Arm & Hammer baking soda has been promoted for everything from baking to relieving heartburn to eliminating odors in carpets and refrigerators (Exhibit 2–17).

Positioning by Product Class

Often the competition for a product comes from outside the product class. For example, airlines know that while they compete with other airlines, trains and buses are also viable alternatives. Amtrak has positioned itself as an alternative to airplanes, citing cost savings, enjoyment, and other advantages. Dole fruit juices encourage consumers to "drink their fruits," claiming that 8 ounces of juice is the equivalent of two fruits. V8 promotes drinking one's vegetables. Rather than positioning against another brand, an alternative strategy is to position oneself against another product category. The California Avocado Commission launched a major IMC campaign to more strongly position itself as a fruit (as opposed to a vegetable). The print, radio, outdoor, and online campaign took a humorous approach, positioning the avocado as a "fun fruit," while at the same time demonstrating the healthy advantages relative to other fruits and vegetables, and providing numerous products for which it might become an alternative, including cream cheese, butter, and dips. Copy points for the ads were provided by the commission to retailers (Exhibit 2–18). A Mountain High yogurt ad positions the product as a substitute for other baking ingredients.

Positioning by Product User

Positioning a product by associating it with a particular user or group of users is yet another approach. An example would be the Globe Shoes ad shown in Exhibit 2–19. This ad emphasizes identification or association with a specific group, in this case, skateboarders.

Positioning by Competitor

Competitors may be as important to positioning strategy as a firm's own product or services. Advertisers used to think it was a cardinal sin to mention a competitor in their advertising. However, in today's market, an effective positioning strategy for a product or brand may focus on specific competitors. This approach is similar to positioning by product class, although in this case the competition is within the same product category. Perhaps the best-known example of this strategy was Avis, which positioned itself against the car-rental leader, Hertz, by stating, "We're number two, so we try harder." The Samsung ad shown earlier (Exhibit 2–5) is an example of positioning a brand against the competition. When positioning by competitor, a marketer must often employ another positioning strategy as well to differentiate the brand.

Positioning by Cultural Symbols

Aaker and Myers include an additional positioning strategy in which cultural symbols are used to differentiate brands. When it is associated with a meaningful symbol, the brand is easily identifiable and differentiated from others. Examples are the Jolly Green Giant, the Keebler elves, Speedy Alka-Seltzer, the Pillsbury Doughboy, the Wells Fargo stagecoach, Ronald McDonald, Chiquita Banana, and Mr. Peanut. Tony the Tiger (who has been used by Kellogg's for over 60 years—with a few minor facelifts) clearly qualifies as a cultural symbol (Exhibit 2–20). Each of these symbols has successfully differentiated the product it represents from competitors'.

Repositioning

One final positioning strategy involves altering or changing a product's or brand's position. **Repositioning** a product usually occurs because of declining or stagnant sales or because of anticipated opportunities in other market positions. Repositioning is often difficult to accomplish because of entrenched perceptions about and attitudes toward the product or brand. The lead-in to this chapter discusses an interesting example of a long-established brand—Buick—taking a new direction. Others who have attempted to change their position include JCPenney, La-Z-Boy, and MTV, with varying degrees of success.

Before leaving this section, you might stop to think for a moment about the positioning (and repositioning) strategies pursued by different companies. Any successful product that comes to mind probably occupies a distinct market position.

DEVELOPING THE MARKETING PLANNING PROGRAM

The development of the marketing strategy and selection of a target market(s) tell the marketing department which customers to focus on and what needs to attempt to satisfy. The next stage of the marketing process involves combining the various elements of the marketing mix into a cohesive, effective marketing program. Each marketing-mix element is multidimensional and includes a number of decision areas. Likewise, each must consider and contribute to the overall IMC program. We now examine product, price, and distribution channels and how each influences and interacts with the promotional program.

Product Decisions

An organization exists because it has some product, service, or idea to offer consumers, generally in exchange for money. This offering may come in the form of a physical product (such as a soft drink, pair of jeans, or car), a service (banking, airlines, or legal assistance), a cause (Special Olympics, American Cancer Society), or even a person (a political candidate). The product is anything that can be marketed and that, when used or supported, gives satisfaction to the individual.

A *product* is more than just a physical object; it is a bundle of benefits or values that satisfies the needs of consumers. The needs may be purely functional, or they may include social and psychological benefits. For example, the campaign for Michelin tires stresses the quality built into Michelin tires (value) as well as their performance and durability (function). The term **product symbolism** refers to what a product or brand means to consumers and what they experience in purchasing and using it.[18] For many products, strong symbolic features and social and psychological meaning may be more important than functional utility.[19] For example, designer clothing such as Versace, Gucci, and Prada is often purchased on the basis of its symbolic meaning and image, particularly by teenagers and young adults. Advertising plays an important role in developing and maintaining the image of these brands.

Product planning involves decisions not only about the item itself, such as design and quality, but also about aspects such as service and warranties as well as brand name and package design. Consumers look beyond the reality of the product and its ingredients. The product's quality, branding, packaging, and even the company standing behind it all contribute to consumers' perceptions.[20] In an effective IMC program, advertising, branding, and packaging are all designed to portray the product as more than just a bundle of attributes. All are coordinated to present an image or positioning of the product that extends well beyond its physical attributes.

EXHIBIT 2–21

Rolex creates strong brand equity through advertising

Source: Rolex Watch U.S.A., Inc.

EXHIBIT 2–22

This ad for WD-40 successfully uses its packaging to show a few of the many uses for the product

Source: WD-40 Company

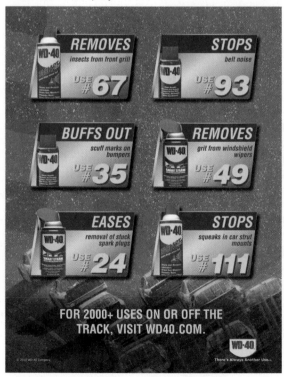

Branding Branding is about building and maintaining a favorable identity and image of the company and/or its products or services in the mind of the consumer. The goal of branding is to (1) build and maintain brand awareness and interest; (2) develop and enhance attitudes toward the company, product, or service; and (3) build and foster relationships between the consumer and the brand. The **brand identity** consists of the combination of the name, logo, symbols, design, packaging, and image of associations held by consumers. Think for a minute about the ads for Nike; the product benefits and attributes are usually not even mentioned—yet information about the brand is communicated effectively.

One important role of advertising in respect to branding strategies is creating and maintaining **brand equity**, which can be thought of as an intangible asset of added value or goodwill that results from the favorable image, impressions of differentiation, and/or the strength of consumer attachment to a company name, brand name, or trademark. Brand equity allows a brand to earn greater sales volume and/or higher margins than it could without the name, providing the company with a competitive advantage. The strong equity position a company and/or its brand enjoys is often reinforced through advertising. For example, Rolex watches command a premium price because of their high quality as well as the strong brand equity they have developed through advertising (Exhibit 2–21).

Packaging Packaging is another aspect of product strategy that has become increasingly important. Traditionally, the package provided functional benefits such as economy, protection, and storage. However, the role and function of the package have changed because of the self-service emphasis of many stores and the fact that more and more buying decisions are made at the point of purchase. Wrigley's gum, recognizing that as many as two-thirds of all purchases made in the supermarket are unplanned, has increased its efforts to attract attention at the checkout counter. The Chicago company is taking a closer look at how and why consumers buy impulse items at the checkout as well as how Wrigley's can be more effective in gaining their attention to increase sales.[21] The package is often the consumer's first exposure to the product, so it must make a favorable first impression. A typical supermarket has more than 30,000 items competing for attention. Not only must a package attract and hold the consumer's attention, but it must also communicate information on how to use the product, divulge its composition and content, and satisfy any legal requirements regarding disclosure. Moreover, many firms design the package to carry a sales promotion message such as a contest, sweepstakes, or premium offer.

Many companies view the package as an important way to communicate with consumers and create an impression of the brand in their minds. In other instances packages can extend the brand by offering new uses (Exhibit 2–22). Design factors such as size, shape, color, and lettering all contribute to the appeal of a package and can be as important as a commercial in determining what goes from the store shelf to the consumer's shopping cart. Many companies use packaging to create a distinctive brand image and identity. The next time you walk by a perfume counter, stop to look at the many unique package designs (see Exhibit 2–23).

EXHIBIT 2–23

This Dior perfume packaging creates product image

© Keith Jackson/Alamy

Price Decisions

The *price variable* refers to what the consumer must give up to purchase a product or service. While price is discussed in terms of the dollar amount exchanged for an item, the cost of a product to the consumer includes time, mental activity, and behavioral effort.[22] The marketing manager is usually concerned with establishing a price level, developing pricing policies, and monitoring competitors' and consumers' reactions to prices in the marketplace. A firm must consider a number of factors in determining the price it charges for its product or service, including costs, demand factors, competition, and perceived value. From an IMC perspective, the price must be consistent with the perceptions of the product, as well as the communications strategy. Higher prices, of course, will communicate a higher product quality, while lower prices reflect bargain or "value" perceptions. A product positioned as highest quality but carrying a lower price than competitors would only confuse consumers. In other words, the price, the advertising, and the distribution channels must present one unified voice speaking to the product's positioning.

Relating Price to Advertising and Promotion Factors such as product quality, competition, and advertising all interact in determining what price a firm can and should charge. Studies have shown that pricing and advertising strategies go together. High relative ad expenditures should accompany premium prices, and low relative ad expenditures should be tailored to low prices. These results obviously support the IMC perspective that one voice must be conveyed. In a recent and comprehensive study, it was shown that exposure to television ads reduces consumers' tendencies to react to price changes. The study further showed that heavy users of the product category were most likely to have their sensitivities reduced.[23]

Distribution Channel Decisions

As consumers, we generally take for granted the role of marketing intermediaries or channel members. If we want a six-pack of soda or a box of detergent, we can buy it at a supermarket, a convenience store, or even a drugstore. Manufacturers understand the value and importance of these intermediaries.

One of a marketer's most important marketing decisions involves the way it makes its products and services available for purchase. A firm can have an excellent product at a great price, but it will be of little value unless it is available where the customer wants it, when the customer wants it, and with the proper support and service. **Marketing channels**, the place element of the marketing mix, are "sets of interdependent organizations involved in the process of making a product or service available for use or consumption."[24]

The distribution strategy should take into consideration the communication objectives and the impact that the channel strategy will have on the IMC program. Stewart and colleagues discuss the need for "integrated channel management," which "reflects the blurring of the boundaries of the communications and distribution functions."[25] Consistent with the product and pricing decisions, where the product is distributed will send a communications message. Does the fact that a product is sold at Neiman Marcus or Saks convey a different message regarding its image than if it were distributed at Kmart or Walmart? If you think about it for a moment, the mere fact that the product is distributed in these channels communicates an image about it in your mind. Stewart gives examples of how channel elements contribute to communication—for example, grocery store displays, point-of-purchase merchandising, and shelf footage. The distribution channel in a well-integrated marketing program serves as a form of reminder advertising. The consumer sees the brand name and recalls the advertising. (Think about the last time you passed a McDonald's. Did it remind you of any of McDonald's ads?)

A company can choose not to use any channel intermediaries but, rather, to sell to its customers through **direct channels**. This type of channel arrangement is sometimes used in the consumer market by firms using direct-selling programs, such as Advocare, Tupperware, and Mary Kay, or firms that use direct-response advertising, telemarketing, or the Internet to sell their products. Direct channels are also frequently used by manufacturers of industrial products and services, which are often selling expensive and complex products that require extensive negotiations and sales efforts, as well as service and follow-up calls after the sale.

Chapter 15 provides a discussion of the role of the Internet and digital media in an IMC program. As will be seen, the Internet is relied on by many companies as a direct channel of distribution, since they offer products and services for sale on their websites. Amazon.com and Barnesandnoble.com are just two of the many examples of such efforts.

Most consumer-product companies distribute through **indirect channels**, usually using a network of wholesalers (institutions that sell to other resellers) and/or retailers (which sell primarily to the final consumer).

Developing Promotional Strategies: Push or Pull?

Most of you are aware of advertising and other forms of promotion directed toward ultimate consumers or business customers. We see these ads in the media and are often part of the target audience for the promotions. In addition to developing a consumer marketing mix, a company must have a program to motivate the channel members. Programs designed to persuade the trade to stock, merchandise, and promote a manufacturer's products are part of a **promotional push strategy**. The goal of this strategy is to push the product through the channels of distribution by aggressively selling and promoting the item to the resellers, or trade.

Promotion to the trade includes all the elements of the promotional mix. Company sales representatives call on resellers to explain the product, discuss the firm's plans for building demand among ultimate consumers, and describe special programs being offered to the trade, such as introductory discounts, promotional allowances, and cooperative ad programs. The company may use **trade advertising** to interest wholesalers and retailers and motivate them to purchase its products for resale to their customers. Trade advertising usually appears in publications that serve the particular industry.

A push strategy tries to convince resellers they can make a profit on a manufacturer's product and to encourage them to order the merchandise and push it through to their customers. An alternative strategy is a **promotional pull strategy**, spending money on advertising and sales promotion efforts directed toward the ultimate consumer. The goal of a pull strategy is to create demand among consumers and encourage them to request the product from the retailer. Seeing the consumer demand, retailers will order the product from wholesalers (if they are used), which in turn will request it from the manufacturer. Thus, stimulating demand at the end-user level pulls the product through the channels of distribution.

Whether to emphasize a push or a pull strategy depends on a number of factors, including the company's relations with the trade, its promotional budget, and demand for the firm's products. Companies that have favorable channel relationships may prefer to use a push strategy and work closely with channel members to encourage them to stock and promote their products. A firm with a limited promotional budget may not have the funds for advertising and sales promotion that a pull strategy requires and may find it more cost-effective to build distribution and demand by working closely with resellers. When the demand outlook for a product is favorable because it has unique benefits, is superior to competing brands, or is very popular among consumers, a pull strategy may be appropriate. Companies often use a combination of push and pull strategies, with the emphasis changing as the product moves through its life cycle.

THE ROLE OF ADVERTISING AND PROMOTION

As shown in the marketing model in Figure 2–1, the marketing program includes promotion both to the trade (channel members) and to the company's ultimate customers. Marketers use the various promotional-mix elements—advertising, sales promotion, direct marketing, publicity/public relations, digital/Internet marketing, and personal selling—to inform consumers about their products, their prices, and places where the products are available. Each promotional-mix variable helps marketers achieve their promotional objectives, and all variables must work together to achieve an integrated marketing communications program.

To this point, we have discussed the various elements of the marketing plan that serves as the basis for the IMC program. The development and implementation of an IMC program is based on a strong foundation that includes market analysis, target marketing and positioning, and coordination of the various marketing-mix elements. Throughout the following chapters of this text, we will explore the role of various IMC elements in helping achieve marketing objectives.

Summary

Promotion plays an important role in an organization's efforts to market its product, service, or ideas to its customers. Figure 2–1 shows a model for analyzing how promotions fit into a company's marketing program. The model includes a marketing strategy and analysis, target marketing, program development, and the target market. The marketing process begins with a marketing strategy that is based on a detailed situation analysis and guides for target market selection and development of the firm's marketing program.

In the planning process, the situation analysis requires that the marketing strategy be assumed. The promotional program is developed with this strategy as a guide. One of the key decisions to be made pertains to the target marketing process, which includes identifying, segmenting,

targeting, and positioning to target markets. There are several bases for segmenting the market and various ways to position a product.

Once the target marketing process has been completed, marketing program decisions regarding product, price, distribution, and promotions must be made. All of these must be coordinated to provide an integrated marketing communications perspective, in which the positioning strategy is supported by one voice. Thus all product strategies, pricing strategies, and distribution choices must be made with the objective of contributing to the overall image of the product or brand. Advertising and promotion decisions, in turn, must be integrated with the other marketing-mix decisions to accomplish this goal.

Key Terms

Discussion Questions

1. The lead-in to this chapter discusses Buick's attempt to reposition its cars to a younger audience. Explain why this may or may not work. (LO 2-4)

2. Many companies compete in a number of market segments. Discuss an example of one such company and describe how it communicates with its customers in different market segments. (LO 2-4)

3. Discuss the role that IMC assumes in the marketing mix. That is, how is this element of the mix coordinated with pricing, distribution, and product functions? (LO 2-5)

4. As the media environment changes, explain how this impacts the role of advertising and promotion. Why is the IMC process different than it was, say, 20 years ago? (LO 2-1)

5. Discuss the difference between benefit and demographic segmentation. Give examples of companies employing each. Is it possible for a company to employ both forms of segmentation simultaneously? (LO 2-4)

6. IMC Perspective 2–1 discussed the millennial generation. Discuss some of the ways that this market segment is different from previous age cohorts. (LO 2-3)

7. IMC Perspective 2–2 discusses the importance of the Hispanic market. What makes this subculture different, and what must marketers do to successfully target it? (LO 2-2)

8. What is meant by *repositioning*? Discuss some companies that have successfully employed this strategy. (LO 2-4)

9. Many companies have maintained their same brand identity for years by keeping the same logos, packaging, and so on while others have made changes. Give examples of companies employing both of these strategies and discuss their results. (LO 2-5)

10. Some marketers feel that grouping consumers into age cohorts like millennials, baby boomers, and so forth results in unreliable generalizations and that such strategies might not be successful. Give the pros and cons of this argument. (LO 2-2)

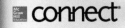

Digital users can access their personalized and adaptive SmartBook, Ad Forum Video Cases, and interactive exercises to review chapter concepts.

3

Organizing for Advertising and Promotion: The Role of Ad Agencies and Other Marketing Communication Organizations

© Maksim Kabakou/Shutterstock RF

LEARNING OBJECTIVES

LO1 Describe how companies organize for advertising and integrated marketing communications functions.

LO2 Compare the advantages and disadvantages of different ways to organize for advertising and promotion.

LO3 Identify the types of advertising agencies and the roles they play.

LO4 Explain how to select, compensate, and evaluate advertising agencies.

LO5 Identify the role and functions of specialized marketing communication organizations.

LO6 Compare the pros and cons of using an integrated marketing services agency.

CAN ADVERTISING AGENCIES SURVIVE THE DIGITAL REVOLUTION?

In July 2007, the cable network AMC aired the first episode of a new drama series called "Mad Men" that was set in the 1960s and focused on the lives of men and women working in the fictional Sterling Cooper advertising agency on Madison Avenue in New York City. The lead character in the show was Don Draper, who was the talented creative director at the agency and then became one of the founding partners at a new agency after he and his superiors left the previous agency in advance of an unwanted acquisition. The Don Draper character was inspired by Draper Daniels, the creative director at the Leo Burnett agency in Chicago who helped create the legendary Marlboro Man campaign that made the iconic brand the leading brand of cigarettes in the world. "Mad Men" ran for seven seasons and received 16 Emmys and five Golden Globe Awards as well as critical acclaim for its writing, acting, and depiction of the inner workings of Madison Avenue during a time period that many called the glory years of the advertising industry.

Much has changed since the "Mad Men" era of advertising when the primary focus of agencies was on developing big ideas for creative ad campaigns that would be executed through television commercial or print ads in magazines and newspapers. During the 1980s and 1990s many of the changes that impacted the agency business occurred on the business and management side. One of the most significant developments was the merger of three major agencies (BBDO, Doyle Dane Bernbach, and Needham Harper) into a new holding company called the Omnicom Group. *Advertising Age* termed the merger the "Big Bang" as it served as the catalyst for a flurry of mergers and acquisitions that led to consolidation of the agency business and the formation of the four major agency holding companies that dominate the industry today. The holding companies recognized that the advertising business was changing and many of the services that were traditionally provided by large full-service agencies were becoming unbundled such as media, research, and public relations. They responded by forming large media specialist companies as part of their agency networks that could use their size and clout to extract better media prices and cost savings for their clients. They also began acquiring many of the leading public relations, direct-marketing, sales promotion, and event marketing firms so they could tout their ability to serve all other clients' integrated marketing communications needs under one roof.

During the first decade of the new millennium, agencies recognized that the Internet and digital media were becoming an increasingly important part of the IMC program for their clients. Many agencies responded by expanding their in-house capabilities as well as by acquiring companies with expertise in digital and social media. However, many agencies are finding that the marketing communications industry is changing too fast to keep pace just by expanding their digital capabilities or making acquisitions. The advertising and marketing services landscape has changed dramatically over the past five years and continues to become more complex. Much of this is due to the complexities and challenges associated with digital media and other emerging technologies that are impacting the way marketers communicate with consumers. Marketers are looking for new and better ways to connect with their customers and many are utilizing the detailed analytics that come from digital media and other tools to evaluate the effectiveness of their efforts to do so.

The disruptions being created by the digital revolution are squeezing agencies from all sides. Media buying is becoming automated and done by software, particularly for digital and social messages, and big data are driving the planning and evaluation of the advertising strategies and tactics used by marketers. Companies that provide digital advertising platforms such as Google and Facebook are becoming very powerful players in the marketing communication ecosystem as are data/customer relationship marketing companies such as Epsilon, Axiom, and Experian Marketing. Information technology service companies such as IBM, Accenture, McKinsey, and Deloitte are also providing advertising and media-related services for marketers. In addition to their advertising agencies, marketers are using a multitude of vendors and technology providers. One report found that marketers are using as many as 30 different tools to help them plan, manage, and evaluate their IMC campaign and the data associated with them.

The challenge facing many agencies is how to respond to all of the factors that are disrupting the advertising industry and their business models. Many are doing so at a time when they are facing growing creative challenges and workloads as well as clients who are looking for ways to cut their marketing spending and battling with agencies over compensation fees. Moreover, more marketers are bringing their advertising in-house rather than using an outside agency or are limiting the services they provide. Many companies are no longer looking for a traditional agency of record (AOR) relationship whereby the agency plays a lead role in their IMC programs, but rather are looking to work with best-in-class marketing partners with specialized expertise in various areas.

Some experts are very pessimistic about the future of the advertising agency business. In his new book *Madison Avenue Manslaughter,* industry consultant Michael Farmer suggests that agencies are on a path to self-destruction. He argues that the problems they face are the result of the balkinization of the agency business, which he describes as the process of dividing a state or region into smaller parts that are hostile or noncooperative with each other. Farmer argues that agencies have clung to shortsighted beliefs in specialization rather than integrating various disciplines such as digital, direct, and traditional advertising. He also is critical of agencies for their lack of knowledge in managing, analyzing, and drawing insights from big data. Farmer notes that the only way out of this mess is for agencies to rethink their primary mission from creativity and big ideas to results for their clients.

The changes occurring in the world of marketing and advertising present tremendous challenges for advertising agencies and require that they transform themselves if they want to survive and prosper. It is likely that some agencies will resist changing and hope for a return to the glory days of advertising depicted in "Mad Men." As one agency marketing executive notes: "Mad Men made people nostalgic for a time when a beautiful piece of advertising in a single channel could grab the attention of the country and cause a hug number of people to change their behavior." However, most recognize that those days are long gone and agencies that fail to adapt may find themselves watching reruns of "Mad Men" and yearning for the good-old days of advertising—after their clients have moved on to a new agency.

Sources: Alexandra Bruell, "Agency of the Future," *Advertising Age,* May 2, 2016, pp. 232–35; Patrick Coffee, "Why Today's Ad Agencies Are Reluctant to Call Themselves 'Ad Agencies,'" *Adweek,* November 10, 2015, www.adweek.com/news/advertising-branding/why-todays-ad-agencies-are-reluctant-call-themselves-ad-agencies-167971; Rance Crain, "Did Agencies Specialize Themselves to Death?" *Advertising Age,* September 14, 2015, p. 58; Terence Kawaja, "Back to 'Mad Men'—What the Future Holds for Ad Agencies," *Advertising Age,* September 3, 2015, http://adage.com/article/guest-columnists/back-mad-men-future-holds-ad-agencies/300195/; Jami Oetting, "What Does the Ad Agency of the 2020 Look Like?" January 11, 2016, http://blog.hubspot.com/agency/agency-2020.

Developing and implementing an integrated marketing communications program is usually a complex and detailed process involving the efforts of many persons. As consumers, we generally give little thought to the individuals or organizations that create the clever advertisements that capture our attention, the websites we visit, the videos we watch online, or the contests and sweepstakes we hope to win. But for those involved in the marketing process, it is important to understand the nature of the industry and the structure and functions of the organizations involved. As discussed in the first two chapters, the advertising and promotions business is changing as marketers search for better ways to communicate with their customers. These changes are impacting the way marketers organize for integrated marketing communications, as well as their relationships with advertising agencies and other communication specialists.

This chapter examines the various organizations that participate in the IMC process, their roles and responsibilities, and their relationship to one another. We discuss how companies organize internally for advertising and promotion. For most companies, advertising is planned and executed by an outside ad agency. Many large agencies offer a variety of other IMC capabilities, including public relations, digital/Internet, sales promotion, and direct marketing. Thus, we will devote particular attention to the ad agency's role and the overall relationship between company and agency.

Other participants in the promotional process (such as direct-marketing, sales promotion, and digital/interactive agencies and public relations firms) are becoming increasingly important as more companies take an integrated marketing communications approach to promotion. We examine the role of these specialized marketing communication organizations in the promotional process as well. The chapter concludes with a discussion of whether marketers are best served by using the integrated services of one large agency or the separate services of a variety of communications specialists.

PARTICIPANTS IN THE INTEGRATED MARKETING COMMUNICATIONS PROCESS: AN OVERVIEW

Before discussing the specifics of the industry, we'll provide an overview of the entire system and identify some of the players. As shown in Figure 3–1, participants in the integrated marketing communications process can be divided into five major groups: the advertiser (or client), advertising agencies, media organizations, specialized communication services, and collateral services. Each group has specific roles in the promotional process.

The advertisers, or **clients**, are the key participants in the process. They have the products, services, or causes to be marketed, and they provide the funds that pay for the IMC program. The advertisers also assume major responsibility for developing the marketing plan and making the final decisions regarding the advertising and promotional program that will support it. The organization may perform most of these efforts itself either through its own advertising or marketing communications department or by setting up an in-house agency.

However, many organizations use an **advertising agency**, an outside firm that specializes in the creation, production, and/or placement of the communications message and that may provide other services to facilitate the marketing and promotions process. Many large advertisers retain the services of a number of agencies, particularly when they market a number of products. For example, Kraft Foods uses as many as eight advertising agencies for its various brands, while General Motors uses seven primary agencies for its various automotive divisions, which include Buick, Cadillac, Chevrolet, and GMC, along with a major media buying service. GM also uses a public relations agency as well as several digital, promotional, and experiential marketing agencies; an entertainment marketing agency; a retail marketing agency; and an agency that specializes in sports marketing. Many large companies often use additional agencies that specialize in developing ads for multicultural markets. For example, in addition to its primary agency of record, Saatchi & Saatchi, L.A., Toyota Motor Corporation uses additional agencies in the United

FIGURE 3–1

Participants in the Integrated Marketing Communications Process

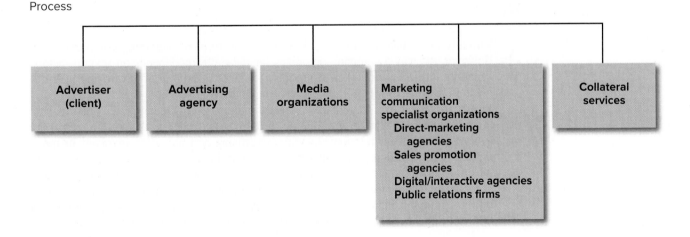

NATIONAL GEOGRAPHIC TRAVEL

How We Connect to 28 Million Consumers

15 LOCAL LANGUAGE EDITIONS

TABLET

TRAVEL EVENTS & PHOTO WORKSHOPS

SOCIAL
10+ MILLION FANS

Travel Opportunities Across a Variety of Touch Points

BOOKS & MAPS

DIGITAL
2.5 MILLION MONTHLY VISITORS

MOBILE

NAT GEO EXPEDITIONS

EXHIBIT 3–1

National Geographic promotes the various ways marketers can use its media platforms to connect with consumers

Source: National Geographic Society

States to create ads for the African American, Hispanic, and Asian American markets. More and more, ad agencies are acting as partners with advertisers and assuming more responsibility for developing the marketing and promotional programs.

Media organizations are another major participant in the advertising and promotions process. The primary function of most media is to provide information or entertainment to their subscribers, viewers, or readers. But from the perspective of the promotional planner, the purpose of media is to provide an environment for the firm's marketing communications messages. The media must have editorial or program content that attracts consumers so that advertisers and their agencies will want to buy time or space with them. Exhibit 3–1 shows an ad run in advertising trade publications promoting the value of *National Geographic* magazine and its family of media products as a way to reach consumers around the world. While the media perform many other functions that help advertisers understand their markets and their customers, a medium's primary objective is to sell itself as a way for companies to reach their target markets with their messages effectively.

The next group of participants are organizations that provide **specialized marketing communication services**. They include direct-marketing agencies, sales promotion agencies, digital/interactive agencies, and public relations firms. These organizations provide services in their areas of expertise. A direct-response agency develops and implements direct-marketing programs, while sales promotion agencies develop promotional programs such as contests and sweepstakes, premium offers, or sampling programs. Digital/interactive agencies are being retained to develop websites for the Internet and help marketers as they move deeper into the realm of interactive media. Public relations firms are used to generate and manage publicity for a company and its products and services as well as to focus on its relationships and communications with its relevant publics.

The final participants shown in the promotions process of Figure 3–1 are those that provide **collateral services**, the wide range of support functions used by advertisers, agencies, media organizations, and specialized marketing communication firms. These individuals and companies perform specialized functions the other participants use in planning and executing advertising and other promotional functions. We will now examine the role of each participant in more detail. (Media organizations will be examined in Chapters 10 through 14.)

ORGANIZING FOR ADVERTISING AND PROMOTION IN THE FIRM: THE CLIENT'S ROLE

LO3-1

Virtually every business organization uses some form of marketing communication. However, the way a company organizes for these efforts depends on several factors, including its size, the number of products it markets, the role of advertising and promotion in its marketing mix, the advertising and promotion budget, and its marketing organization structure. Many individuals throughout the organization may be involved in the advertising and promotion decision-making process. Marketing personnel have the most direct relationship with advertising and are often involved in many aspects of the decision process, such as providing input to the campaign plan, agency selection, media strategy, and evaluation of the effectiveness of the IMC program. Top management is usually interested in how the advertising and other forms of marketing communication represent the firm, and this may also mean being involved in IMC decisions even when the decisions are not part of its day-to-day responsibilities.

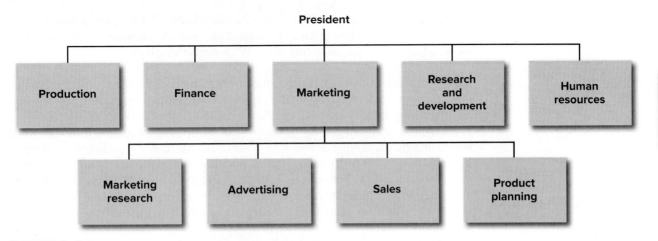

President

| Production | Finance | Marketing | Research and development | Human resources |

| Marketing research | Advertising | Sales | Product planning |

FIGURE 3–2

The Advertising Department under a Centralized System

While many people both inside and outside the organization have some input into the advertising and promotion process, direct responsibility for administering the program must be assumed by someone within the firm. Many companies have an advertising department headed by an advertising manager operating under a marketing director. In some companies this department may be called marketing communications (marcom). An alternative used by many large multiproduct firms is a decentralized marketing (brand management) system. A third option is to form a separate agency within the firm, an in-house agency. Each of these alternatives is examined in more detail in the following sections.

The Centralized System

In many organizations, marketing activities are divided along functional lines, with advertising placed alongside other marketing functions such as sales, marketing research, and product planning, as shown in Figure 3–2. The **advertising manager** is responsible for all promotions activities except sales (in some companies this individual has the title of marketing communications manager). In the most common example of a **centralized system**, the advertising or marcom manager controls the entire promotions operation, including budgeting, coordinating creation and production of ads, planning media schedules, and monitoring and administering the sales promotions programs for all the company's products or services.

The specific duties of the advertising or marketing communications manager depend on the size of the firm and the importance it places on promotional programs. Basic functions the manager and staff perform include the following.

Administration and Execution The manager must organize the advertising department and supervise and control its activities. The manager also supervises the execution of the plan by subordinates and/or the advertising agency. This requires working with such departments as production, media, art, copy, digital/interactive, and sales promotion. If an outside agency is used, the advertising department is relieved of much of the executional responsibility; however, it must review and approve the agency's plans.

Coordination with Other Departments The manager must coordinate the advertising department's activities with those of other departments, particularly those involving other marketing functions. For example, the advertising department must communicate with marketing research and/or sales to determine which product features are important to customers and should be emphasized in the company's communications. Research may also provide profiles of product users and nonusers for the media department before it selects broadcast or print media.

The advertising department may also be responsible for preparing material the sales force can use when calling on customers, such as brochures, sales promotion tools, advertising materials, and point-of-purchase displays.

Coordination with Outside Agencies and Services Many companies have an advertising or marketing communications department but still use an advertising agency as well as other outside services such as digital agencies. For example, companies may develop their advertising programs in-house while employing media buying services to place their ads and/or use collateral services agencies to develop brochures, point-of-purchase materials, and so on. The department serves a liaison between the company and any outside service providers and also determines which ones to use. Once outside services are retained, the manager will work with other marketing managers to coordinate their efforts and evaluate their performances.

A centralized organizational system is often used when companies do not have many different divisions, product or service lines, or brands to advertise. For example, airlines such as Southwest, American, and JetBlue have centralized advertising or marcom departments, as do major retailers such as Target, Walmart, and Best Buy. Many companies prefer a centralized department because developing and coordinating advertising and marketing programs from one central location facilitates communication regarding the promotions program, making it easier for top management to participate in decision making. A centralized system may also result in a more efficient operation because fewer people are involved in the program decisions, and as their experience in making such decisions increases, the process becomes easier.

At the same time, problems are inherent in a centralized operation. First, it may be difficult for advertising department staff members to understand the overall marketing strategy for the brand, particularly if they are not brought into the planning process. The department may also be slow in responding to specific needs and problems of a product/service or brand. As companies become larger and develop or acquire new products, services, brands, or even divisions, the centralized system may become impractical.

The Decentralized System

In large corporations with multiple divisions and many different products, it is very difficult to manage all the advertising, promotional, and other functions through a centralized department. These types of companies generally have a **decentralized system**, with separate manufacturing, research and development, sales, and marketing departments for various divisions, product lines, or businesses. Many companies that use a decentralized system, such as Procter & Gamble, Unilever, PepsiCo, Google, and Nestlé, assign each product/service or brand to a **brand manager** who is responsible for the total management of the brand, including planning, budgeting, sales, and profit performance. (The term *product manager* is also used to describe this position.) The brand manager, who may have one or more assistant brand managers, is also responsible for the planning, implementation, and control of the marketing program.[1]

Under this system, the responsibilities and functions associated with advertising and promotions are transferred to the brand manager, who works closely with the outside advertising agency and other marketing communications specialists as they develop the promotional program.[2] In a multiproduct or service firm, each brand may have its own ad agency and may compete against other brands within the company, not just against outside competitors. For example, Exhibit 3–2 shows ads for Tide and Gain, which are both Procter & Gamble products that compete for a share of the laundry detergent market.

As shown in Figure 3–3, the advertising department is part of marketing services and provides support for the brand managers. The role of marketing services is to assist the brand managers in planning and coordinating the integrated marketing

EXHIBIT 3–2

Many of Procter & Gamble's brands compete against each other

(Left): Source: Tide by Procter & Gamble; (Right): Source: Gain by Procter & Gamble

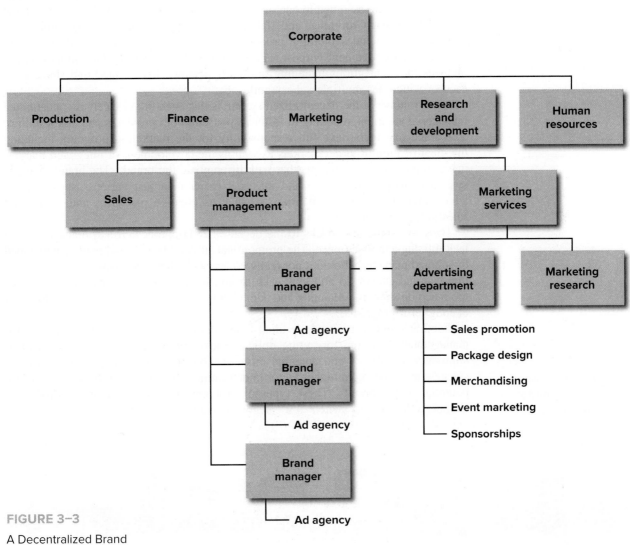

FIGURE 3–3

A Decentralized Brand
Management System

communications program. In some companies, the marketing services group may include sales promotion. The brand managers may work with sales promotion people to develop budgets, define strategies, and implement tactical executions for both trade and consumer promotions. Marketing services may also provide other types of support services, such as package design and merchandising.

Some companies may have an additional layer(s) of management above the brand managers to coordinate the efforts of all the brand managers handling a related group of products. This system—generally referred to as a **category management system**—includes category managers as well as brand and advertising managers. The category manager oversees management of the entire product category and focuses on the strategic role of the various brands in order to build profits and market share.[3] Each category manager will have one or more brand managers reporting to him or her for each specific brand as well as an advertising manager.

The advertising or marcom manager may review and evaluate the various parts of the IMC program and advise and consult with the brand managers. This person may have the authority to override the brand manager's decisions on advertising and other forms of promotion. In some multiproduct firms that spend a lot on advertising and promotion, the advertising manager may coordinate the work of the various agencies to obtain media discounts for the firm's large volume of media purchases. Category management is often used in large multiproduct or divisional companies. For example, Procter & Gamble's broad portfolio includes 10 product categories with about 65 brands (21 of which generate more than a billion dollars in revenue each year) that are assigned to one of four major divisions: Beauty; Fabric and Home Care; Health and Grooming; and Baby, Feminine and Family Care (Exhibit 3–3). Each division includes multiple product categories to which individual brands are assigned for management purposes. For example, the Health and Grooming division includes three categories including oral care, personal health care, and shave care, each of which has multiple subcategories.

An advantage of the decentralized system is that each brand receives concentrated managerial attention, resulting in faster response to both problems and opportunities. The brand managers have full responsibility for the marketing program, including the identification of target markets as well as the development of integrated marketing communications programs that will differentiate the brand.[4] The brand manager system is also more flexible and makes it easier to adjust various aspects of the advertising and promotional program, such as creative platforms and media and sales promotion schedules.[5]

There are some drawbacks to the decentralized approach. Brand managers often lack training and experience. The promotional strategy for a brand may be developed by a brand manager who does not really understand what advertising or sales promotion can and cannot do and how each should be used. Brand managers may focus too much on short-run planning and administrative tasks, neglecting the development of long-term programs.

Another problem is that individual brand managers often end up competing for management attention, marketing dollars, and other resources, which can lead to unproductive rivalries and potential misallocation of funds. The manager's persuasiveness may become a bigger factor in determining budgets than the long-run profit potential of the brands. These types of problems were key factors in Procter & Gamble's decision to switch to a category management system.

EXHIBIT 3–3

P&G's broad portfolio of brands are assigned to various categories for management

Source: Procter & Gamble

Finally, the brand management system has been criticized for failing to provide brand managers with authority over the functions needed to implement and control the plans they develop.[6] Some companies have dealt with this problem by expanding the roles and responsibilities of the advertising and sales promotion managers and their staff of specialists. The staff specialists counsel the individual brand managers, and advertising or sales promotion decision making involves the advertising and/or sales promotion manager, the brand manager, and the marketing director. For example, General Motors, which is one of the largest advertisers in the United States, decided to drop its brand management system and give division marketing directors more control of the advertising and promotion for its various models.[7] The traditional brand management system has come under attack recently as critics argue that brand managers spend too much time on internal issues such as planning and budgeting and do not devote enough effort to external matters or to creativity and problem solving.[8]

A new challenge facing the brand management system is training managers to keep abreast of the rapidly changing world of digital marketing and managing the identity of a brand across various social media platforms. Brand managers may be involved in deciding which platforms to utilize and how to use them, what to consider when creating internal social media guidelines, whether to handle social media in-house or outsource it, and metrics that should be used to evaluate the effectiveness of and return on investment for various social media tools. Brand managers are often involved in developing social media strategies that include playbooks for various social media sites such as Facebook, Google+, Pinterest, Instagram, YouTube, and Foursquare (Exhibit 3–4).[9]

EXHIBIT 3–4

Brand managers must understand how to use social media to manage brand identity

© Crain Communications Inc., Courtesy of Ad Age

In-House Agencies

Some companies, in an effort to reduce costs and maintain greater control over agency activities, have set up their own advertising agencies internally. An **in-house agency** is an advertising agency that is set up, owned, and operated by the advertiser. Some in-house agencies are little more than advertising departments, but in other companies they are given a separate identity and are responsible for the expenditure of large sums of advertising dollars. Large advertisers that use in-house agencies include Hyundai/Kia, Avon, Revlon, Land Rover, and Benetton. Many companies use in-house agencies exclusively; others combine in-house efforts with those of outside agencies. For example, retail giant Target has an internal creative department that handles the design of its weekly circulars, direct-mail pieces, in-store displays, promotions, and other marketing materials. However, the retailer uses outside agencies to develop most of its branding and image-oriented ads and for specific TV and print assignments. Other retailers such as Benetton and Banana Republic also have in-house advertising departments that work with outside agencies.

A major reason for using an in-house agency is to reduce advertising and promotion costs. Companies with very large advertising budgets pay a substantial amount to outside agencies in the form of media commissions or negotiated fees. With an internal structure, these commissions or fees go to the in-house agency. An in-house agency can also provide related work such as production of collateral materials, digital media, package design, and public relations at a lower cost than outside agencies. In-house agencies are also preferred by some companies because they keep the marketing communications function more closely tied to top management. A study by Forrester Research found that nearly 60 percent of in-house agencies report directly to the company's chief executive officer (CEO) or chief marketing officer (CMO).[10] Another reason is the stability an in-house agency provides because external agencies have much higher turnover levels which can take a toll on the client–agency relationship. In contrast, in-house agencies are known for retaining their personnel and have a turnover rate of less than 5 percent.[11]

Saving money is not the only reason companies use in-house agencies. Time savings, bad experiences with outside agencies, and the increased knowledge and understanding of the market that come from working on advertising and promotion for the product or service day by day are also reasons. Companies can also maintain tighter control over the process and more easily coordinate promotions with the firm's overall marketing program.

Some companies use an in-house agency simply because they believe it can do a better job than an outside agency could.[12] They may feel they have more knowledge about the market and competitors as well as a better understanding of the intricacies and complexities of their business. For example, Google launched an in-house agency in 2007 to handle its advertising. The company did very little advertising during its first 10 years in business because it relied primarily on the extensive publicity the company received and promotions done by other companies that would mention its search engine. However, as Google introduced more products and services, the company recognized the need to promote them to a broader audience and felt this could be done effectively using its own internal capabilities.[13] Thus, the company created a type of in-house agency known as the Google Creative Lab which develops much of its advertising, and hired several former agency executives to run it. However, in recent years as Google has grown and expanded beyond online search and introduced new products and services such as its Chrome web browser, Nexus tablets, and Android operating system, it has begun to use outside agencies. Google has used large agencies—such as Bartle Bogle Hagarty, which has developed advertising for the Chrome browser and Google Play app store—as well as a number of small independent agencies that fit well with the company's culture.[14]

Opponents of in-house agencies say they can give the advertiser neither the experience and objectivity of an outside agency nor the range of services. They argue that outside agencies have more highly skilled specialists and attract the best creative talent and that using an external firm gives a company a more varied perspective on its advertising problems and greater flexibility. Outside agencies also can provide greater strategic planning capabilities, outside perspectives on customers, and more creative experience with certain media such as television.[15] In-house personnel may become narrow or grow stale while working on the same product line, but outside agencies may have different people with a variety of backgrounds and ideas working on the account. Flexibility is greater because an outside agency can be dismissed if the company is not satisfied, whereas changes in an in-house agency could be slower and more disruptive.

The cost savings of an in-house agency must be evaluated against these considerations. For many companies, high-quality advertising is critical to their marketing success and should be the major criterion in determining whether to use in-house services. Companies like Rockport and Redken Laboratories have moved their in-house work to outside agencies in recent years. Redken cited the need for a "fresh look" and objectivity as the reason, noting that management gets too close to the product to come up with different creative ideas. Companies often hire outside agencies as they grow and their advertising budgets and IMC needs increase. For example, Under Armour has been growing rapidly in the athletic shoe and apparel market and expects to reach $10 billion in revenue by 2020. As the company grew and expanded into new product categories, Under Armour management recognized that it would be difficult to handle all of its advertising

EXHIBIT 3–5

Under Armour uses Droga5 to handle much of its advertising

Source: Under Armour, Inc.

in-house, and in late 2015 named Droga5 its first-ever agency of record.[16] The company first used Droga5 to handle work for its women's business and the agency responded by developing several award-winning ads including the "I Will What I Want" viral campaign featuring Gisele Bundchen and ballerina Misty Copeland (Exhibit 3–5).[17] Droga5 now handles nearly all of Under Armour's advertising for training, running, basketball, soccer, and connected fitness. However, the company still handles advertising for football in-house.

The ultimate decision as to which type of advertising organization to use depends on which arrangement works best for the company. As discussed in Digital and Social Media Perspective 3–1, the number of companies using in-house agencies to handle their advertising and other IMC functions is increasing, due in part to the explosion of digital advertising tools that require marketers to produce more content and do so more quickly. The advantages and disadvantages of the three systems are summarized in Figure 3–4. We now turn our attention to the functions of outside agencies and their roles in the promotional process.

ADVERTISING AGENCIES

Many major companies use an advertising agency to assist them in developing, preparing, and executing their promotional programs. An ad agency is a service organization that specializes in planning and executing advertising programs for its clients. More than 10,000 U.S. and international agencies are listed in the *Advertising Red Books*; however, most are individually owned small businesses employing fewer than five people. The U.S. ad agency business is highly concentrated. Nearly two-thirds of the domestic **billings** (the amount of client money agencies spend on media purchases and other equivalent activities) are handled by the top

FIGURE 3–4

Comparison of Advertising Organizational Systems

Organizational System	Advantages	Disadvantages
Centralized	■ Facilitated communications ■ Fewer personnel required ■ Continuity in staff ■ Allows for more top-management involvement	■ Less involvement with and understanding of overall marketing goals ■ Longer response time ■ Inability to handle multiple product lines
Decentralized	■ Concentrated managerial attention ■ Rapid response to problems and opportunities ■ Increased flexibility	■ Ineffective decision making ■ Internal conflicts ■ Misallocation of funds ■ Lack of authority ■ Internal rather than external focus
In-house agencies	■ Cost savings ■ More control ■ Increased coordination ■ Stability ■ Access to top management	■ Less experience ■ Less objectivity ■ Less flexibility ■ Less access to top creative talent

MORE COMPANIES ARE BRINGING ADVERTISING IN-HOUSE

Traditionally, most major companies have used outside agencies to plan, develop, and implement their advertising campaigns rather than doing so internally, or *in-house*. Many marketers argue that outside agencies bring a valuable external perspective as they have the benefit of working for a variety of companies across diverse industries. This often gives them a better understanding of market trends and developments, changes in customer behavior and ways they consume media, and other important factors. Ad agencies are also perceived as having the best creative talent and thus a good source for the big creative ideas that lead to break-through advertising campaigns and messages.

The perception in the marketing and advertising industries has usually been that in-house agencies are used primarily by companies looking to save money and avoid paying for the services of an outside agency or wanting to maintain control of their advertising and promotional programs. For example, smaller companies with limited marketing budgets have often used in-house agencies in their early stages and then moved to an external agency as their revenue and marketing budgets increased. The use of an in-house agency is also viewed as a preferable model in some industries such as financial services or retailing where a large amount of marketing content must be created

and distributed including collateral pieces, direct mail, promotions, videos, and materials to support events and promotions.

Several recent studies show that the use of an in-house agency is expanding beyond small companies and/or specific industries and is becoming prevalent in many large corporations as well. A report released by the Association of National Advertisers titled "The Rise of the In-House Agency" found that the use of in-house agencies increased from 42 percent in 2008 to nearly 60 percent five years later. The report defined an in-house agency as a department group or person that has responsibilities typically performed by an external advertising or other marketing communications agency, not including an internal PR function. The results from the ANA study do not suggest that marketers using in-house agencies have stopped using outside agencies as many continue to use both. However, a more recent report by the Society of Digital Agencies found that the percentage of companies that do not rely on any outside agencies reached 27 percent in 2015, up from 13 percent a few years earlier.

There are a number of reasons why marketers are taking more of their advertising and other IMC functions in-house. While cost savings was cited as one of the reasons for the

500 agencies. In fact, just 10 U.S. agencies handle nearly 30 percent of the total volume of business done by the top 900 agencies in the United States. The top agencies also have foreign operations that generate substantial billings and income. The top 10 agencies, ranked by their U.S. gross revenue, are listed in Figure 3–5.

FIGURE 3–5

Top 10 U.S. Advertising Agencies, 2015

Source: *Advertising Age*, 2016 Agency Report, May 2, 2016, p. 20.

Rank	Agency	Headquarters	U.S. Revenue (millions)
1	BBDO Worldwide (Omnicom)	New York	$603
2	McCann (Interpublic)	New York	562
3	J. Walter Thompson Co. (WPP)	New York	504
4	Y&R (WPP)	New York	455
5	TBWA Worldwide (Omnicom)	New York	362
6	Grey (WPP)	New York	336
7	DDB Worldwide (Omnicom)	New York	320
8	Leo Burnett Worldwide/ARC (Publicis)	Chicago	289
9	Publicis Worldwide (Publicis)	Paris	288
10	Saatchi & Saatchi (Publicis)	New York	282

increase in the use of in-house agencies, another major factor was the explosion of new digital advertising tools such as social media that require companies to produce more creative content and do so faster and more nimbly. Many companies feel that they can best handle the volume of content and the quick turnarounds required to keep pace with consumers who are online 24/7 in-house. Marketers also want more insights from analytics and the management of various data sources and view outside agencies' capabilities in these areas as limited.

Another reason companies are moving their advertising in-house is that agencies move too slowly and cannot keep pace with the fast-changing needs of their clients. Employees in many agencies are stretched thin and responsible for too many accounts, which makes it difficult for them to respond to their clients' needs. Some experts also argue that many agencies are too focused on traditional advertising while their clients prefer to connect with customers in new ways such as through social media and content marketing, and by using integrated models.

The trend toward taking advertising in-house is likely to continue. The In-House Agency Forum, which serves the needs of this growing community, has seen its membership increase dramatically and include major companies such as American Express, Coca-Cola, McDonald's, and Nestlé. The IHAF's former chair, Marta Stiglin, argues that in-house agencies can attract and retain the same level of strategic and creative talent as external agencies. She also notes that a major advantage of an in-house agency is that it has unlimited opportunity to learn from within, as those working inside a company can live and breathe the culture and the brand, which is difficult for external agencies to do.

It is important that agencies pay close attention to the increasing use of in-house agencies and consider how they can address the factors leading their clients to handle more of their advertising and other IMC functions in-house. The use of and need for external agencies is not likely to go away, but agencies must find ways to better serve the needs of their clients or risk having them take even more of their business in-house.

Sources: David Gianatasio, "What the In-House Agency Boom Means for CMOs and Outside Shops," *Adweek,* December 16, 2015, www.adweek.com/news/advertising-branding/what-house-agency-boom-means-cmos-and-outside-shops-168593; Mark W. Schaefer, "6 Reasons Marketing Is Moving In-House," *Harvard Business Review,* July 30, 2015, https://hbr.org/2015/07/6-reasons-marketing-is-moving-in-house; Jennifer Rooney, "The Rise of the In-House Agency: CMOs, Industry Respond to ANA Report," October 21, 2013, *Forbes,* www.forbes.com/sites/jenniferrooney/2013/10/21/the-rise-of-the-in-house-agency-cmos-industry-respond-to-ana-report/#2d296c15c671.

The figure shows that the advertising business is also geographically concentrated, with 8 of the top 10 agencies headquartered in New York City. Nearly 40 percent of U.S. agency business is handled by New York–based agencies. Other leading advertising centers in the United States include Boston, Chicago, Los Angeles, the Detroit area, Dallas, and Minneapolis. New York City is clearly the center of the advertising industry in the United States as nearly half of the top 100 agencies are headquartered in the city or the surrounding area (Exhibit 3–6). In addition to advertising agencies, 7 of the top 10 media specialist companies are based in the Big Apple as are many of the direct-marketing, digital, promotion, and marketing services agencies.[18] There are several reasons why New York City is the hub of the IMC business in the United States. Many of the major companies with large advertising and promotion budgets are based in the city or the surrounding area. In 2015, 48 of the companies ranked in the *Fortune* 500 were headquartered in New York City while another 40 or so of the top firms were located nearby in suburbs or in cities in Connecticut or New Jersey. New York is also the world's leading media center; nearly all of the major television and radio networks are based in the city as well as many magazine and news organizations.[19]

EXHIBIT 3–6

New York City is the center of the advertising industry in the United States

© Roberto Machado Noa/LighRocket/Getty Images

Agency Consolidation

During the late 1980s and into the 90s, the advertising industry underwent major changes as large agencies merged with or acquired other agencies and support organizations to form large advertising organizations, or superagencies. These **superagencies** were formed so that agencies could provide clients with integrated marketing communications services worldwide. Some advertisers became disenchanted with the superagencies and moved to smaller agencies that were flexible and more responsive.[20] However, during the mid-90s the agency business went through another wave of consolidation as a number of medium-size agencies were acquired and became part of large advertising organization holding companies such as Omnicom Group, WPP Group, and the Interpublic Group of Cos. Many of the midsize agencies were acquired by or forged alliances with larger agencies because their clients wanted an agency with international communications capabilities and their alignment with larger organizations gave them access to a network of agencies around the world. The consolidation of the agency business continued into the new millennium as large agencies such as Fallon Worldwide, Leo Burnett, Saatchi & Saatchi, and Kaplan Thaler were acquired by the giant French holding company Publicis Groupe. In 2015, the top four holding companies—WPP, Omnicom Group, Interpublic Group, and Publicis Groupe—accounted for a little more than half of U.S. agency revenue. The fifth major holding company is Tokyo-based Dentsu which controls nearly 30 percent of the media advertising in Japan and is also strong in several other Asian markets. Exhibit 3–7 shows the primary holdings of the top five agency holding companies.

With the move toward IMC, agencies are now getting much of their revenue from more than just traditional advertising services which now account for less than 30 percent of the revenue for U.S. agencies. In 2015, agencies' revenue came from other areas such as digital and media buying (41%), public relations (9%), CRM/direct marketing (15%), healthcare (10%), and promotion (10%).[21] Many of the advertising organizations and major agencies have been acquiring companies specializing in areas such as digital/interactive communications, public relations, customer relationship management (CRM), direct marketing, health care, and sales promotion so that they can offer their clients an ever-broader range of integrated marketing communications services. Particularly noteworthy in these numbers is the percentage of agency revenue that is being generated by digital media. Overall, U.S. agencies now generate over 40 percent of their revenue from digital media versus only 25 percent in 2009. About 60 percent of this revenue comes from digital-specialty agencies that focus on digital "pure-plays" such as search marketing, social media, and mobile marketing. The tremendous increase in digital is not limited to the United States. Major agency holding companies such as Publicis Groupe (52%) and WPP (37%) generate much of their worldwide revenue from various forms of digital activities.[22]

EXHIBIT 3–7

Primary holdings of the world's top five agency holding companies

© Crain Communications Inc., Courtesy of Ad Age

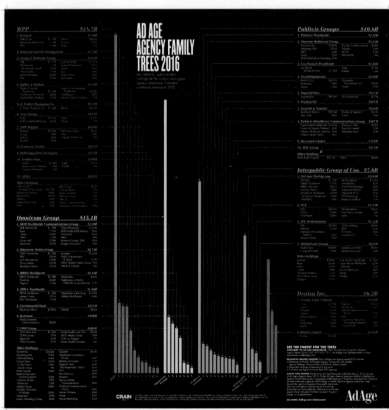

The Ad Agency's Role

The functions performed by advertising agencies might be conducted by the clients themselves through one of the designs discussed earlier in this chapter, but most large companies use outside firms. This section discusses some reasons advertisers use external agencies.

Reasons for Using an Agency Probably the main reason outside agencies are used is that they provide the client with the services of highly skilled individuals who are specialists in their chosen fields. An advertising agency staff may include artists, writers, media analysts, researchers, and others with specific skills, knowledge, and experience who can help market the client's products or services. Many agencies specialize in a particular type of business and use their knowledge of the industry to assist their clients with strategic marketing as well as branding. For example, The Lambesis Agency specializes in using integrated marketing communications to help its clients develop strong brands (Exhibit 3–8).

An outside agency can also provide an objective viewpoint of the market and its business that is not subject to internal company policies, biases, or other limitations. The agency can draw on the broad range of experience it has gained while working on a diverse set of marketing problems for various clients. For example, an ad agency that is handling a travel-related account may have individuals who have worked with airlines, cruise ship companies, travel agencies, hotels, and other travel-related industries. The agency may have experience in this area or may even have previously worked on the advertising account of one of the client's competitors. Thus, the agency can provide the client with insight into the industry (and, in some cases, the competition).

Types of Ad Agencies

Since ad agencies can range in size from a one- or two-person operation to large organizations with over 1,000 employees, the services offered and functions performed will vary. This section examines the different types of agencies, the services they perform for their clients, and how they are organized.

Full-Service Agencies Many companies employ what is known as a **full-service agency**, which offers its clients a full range of marketing, communications, and promotions services, including planning, creating, and producing the advertising; performing research; and selecting media. A full-service agency may also offer nonadvertising services such as strategic market planning; sales promotions, direct marketing, and digital/interactive capabilities; package design; and public relations and publicity.

The full-service agency is made up of departments that provide the activities needed to perform the various advertising functions and serve the client, as shown in Figure 3–6.

Account Services Account services, or account management, is the link between the ad agency and its clients. Depending on the size of the client and its advertising budget, one or more account executives serve as liaison. The **account executive** is responsible for understanding the advertiser's marketing and promotions needs and interpreting them to agency personnel. He or she coordinates agency efforts in planning, creating, and producing ads. The account executive also presents agency recommendations and obtains client approval.

As the focal point of agency–client relationships, the account executive must know a great deal about the client's business and be able to communicate this to

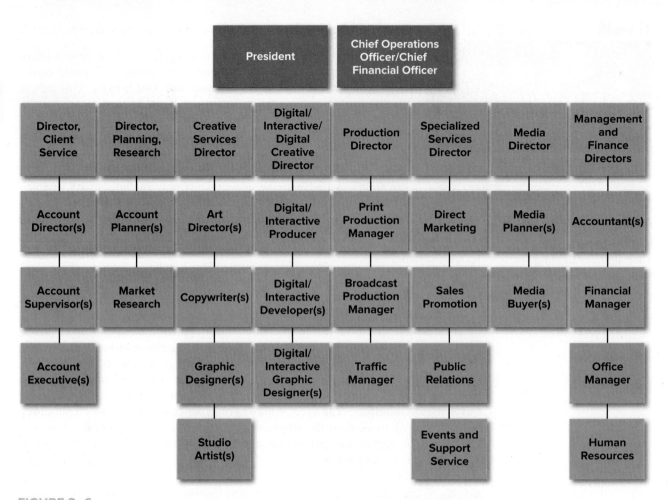

FIGURE 3–6

Full-Service Agency
Organizational Chart

specialists in the agency working on the account.[23] The ideal account executive has a strong marketing background as well as a thorough understanding of all phases of the advertising process. College graduates with undergraduate and graduate degrees in marketing, advertising, and other disciplines are often hired for account executive positions and go on to have careers in account management. However, with the revolutionary changes sweeping the advertising business, the role of account reps is changing dramatically and they are struggling to remain relevant.[24] Cost-cutting by marketers has thinned the once-bloated ranks of account management personnel in agencies by as much as 30 percent in recent years. Moreover, for those who remain, the expectations and demands of the position are changing. Agencies want account executives who are good strategic thinkers and have broad-based business acumen, not just expertise in advertising. And as other integrated marketing communications tools such as direct, digital, and social media become more central, they want them to have an understanding of and be able to coordinate activities and relationships in these areas. They also want individuals whose skill set includes solving complex communication problems, communicating in a mature fashion, selling the agency and its capabilities, and knowing when to push back on a client.

Some agencies are developing client-services training programs for their account executives that are designed to educate them in a variety of areas, including basic agency business issues, strategic marketing, the procurement process, and relationship building. Agencies and clients often work together to address this problem by developing communication and indoctrination programs that provide agency personnel with an overview of their clients' business objectives and marketing strategy as well as their financial/budget situation. This allows them to understand the limits within which creative solutions have to be developed.[25] Account representatives will continue to serve an important role in managing the relationships between agencies and their clients. However, the days of the old-school account executive in the gray wool suit are long gone as agencies look for more from those who work most closely with their clients (Exhibit 3–9).

Marketing Services   Over the past two decades, use of marketing services has increased dramatically. One service gaining increased attention is research, as agencies realize that to communicate effectively with their clients' customers, they must have a good understanding of the target audience. As was discussed in Chapter 1, the advertising planning process begins with a thorough situation analysis, which is based on research and information about the target audience.

Most full-service agencies maintain a *research department* whose function is to gather, analyze, and interpret information that will be useful in developing advertising for their clients. This can be done through primary research—where a study is designed, executed, and interpreted by the research department—or through the use of secondary (previously published) sources of information. Sometimes the research department acquires studies conducted by independent syndicated research firms or consultants. The research staff then interprets these reports and passes on the information to other agency personnel working on that account. The research department may also design and conduct research to pretest the effectiveness of advertising the agency is considering. For example, focus groups as well and other copy testing methods are often used to determine how messages developed by the creative specialists are likely to be interpreted by the target audience.

In many large agencies, the marketing services department may include **account planners** who are individuals that gather information that is relevant to the client's product or service and can be used in the development of the creative strategy as well as other aspects of the IMC campaign. Account planners work with the client as well as other agency personnel including the account executives, creative team members, media specialists, and research department personnel to collect information that can be helpful in gaining a better understanding of the client's target audience and the best ways to communicate with them. They gather and organize information about consumers as well as developments in the marketplace that can be used to prepare the *creative brief,* which is a document that the agency's creative department uses to guide the development of advertising ideas and concepts. Account planners may also be involved in assessing consumers' reactions to the advertising and other elements of the IMC program and providing the creative staff as well as other agency personnel with feedback regarding performance.

Account planning has become a very important function in many agencies because it provides the creative team, as well as other agency personnel, with more insight into consumers and how to use advertising and other IMC tools to communicate with them.[26] However, the account planning function has also become more demanding as the number of marketing communication channels and ways of contacting consumers increases. Account planners increasingly find themselves interacting with individuals from a variety of marketing communication disciplines and have to keep up with developments that are occurring in all of these areas. John Thorpe, the global brand strategy director for Goodby Silverstein & Partners, an agency that is known for its account planning, notes: "No longer can planners just be good at strategy. It's a cross-silo activity. They have to be good at a lot of things that run across advertising. Ambidexterity is required across the house."[27]

The advertising industry recognizes the importance of account planning and the important role it plays in the development of successful IMC campaigns. For example, the 4As, which is the leading trade association representing the advertising agency business in the United States, gives the Jay Chiat Awards for Strategic Excellence each year to agencies in various categories. These awards honor strategic thinking and account planning by planners and other agency professionals who have

EXHIBIT 3–9

The role of account executives has changed

© John Kuczala/Stone/Getty Images

JAY CHIAT AWARDS

NOW IN ITS 20TH YEAR, THE JAY CHIAT AWARDS RECOGNIZE THE BEST STRATEGIC THINKING IN MARKETING, MEDIA AND ADVERTISING AROUND THE WORLD.

The world of marketing is changing faster than ever before. But no matter how quickly marketing communications evolve and multiply, excellent strategy remains a cornerstone of impactful consumer engagements.

The global 4A's Jay Chiat Awards recognize the best strategic thinking in our industry. This year's winners showed that great strategies lead to ideas that engaged us, moved us to action, and even changed the way we see the world.

The Jay Chiat Awards celebrate the contribution of strategy and planning to great ideas.

Creative and effectiveness awards reward the output; the Jay Chiat Awards recognize the input.

A great Jay Chiat entry should capture breakthrough thinking that led to breakthrough execution. If you can point to the extraordinary

EXHIBIT 3–10

The Jay Chiat Awards recognize excellence in account planning

© American Association of Advertising Agencies

developed innovative insights and ideas that are implemented through creative advertising campaigns (Exhibit 3–10). Previously called the 4As Awards for Account Planning, the awards were renamed in 2004 in honor of advertising legend Jay Chiat, who is credited with introducing the discipline of planning to agencies in the United States.[28]

The *media department* of an agency analyzes, selects, and contracts for space or time in the media that will be used to deliver the client's advertising message. The media department is expected to develop a media plan that will reach the target market and effectively communicate the message. Since most of the client's ad budget is spent on media time and/or space, this department must develop a plan that both communicates with the right audience and is cost-effective.

Media specialists must know what audiences the media reach, their rates, and how well they match the client's target market. The media planning department reviews information on demographics, magazine and newspaper readership, radio listenership, and consumers' Internet/social media usage and TV viewing patterns to develop an effective media plan. The media buyer implements the media plan by purchasing the actual time and space.

Media planning and buying has become a very important part of the agency business. An agency's ability to negotiate prices and effectively use the vast array of media vehicles, as well as other sources of customer contact, is becoming as important as its ability to create ads. Some of the major agencies and/or their holding companies have formed independent media services companies to better serve their clients. These media specialist firms, which are discussed later in the chapter, serve the media needs of the agencies that are part of their parent holding companies but may also offer media services to other clients.

The research and media departments perform most of the functions that full-service agencies need to plan and execute their clients' advertising programs. Some agencies offer additional marketing services to their clients to assist in other promotional areas. An agency may have a sales promotion department, or merchandising department, that specializes in developing contests, premiums, promotions, point-of-sale materials, and other sales materials. It may have direct-marketing specialists and package designers, as well as a PR/publicity department. Many agencies have developed digital/interactive media departments to create websites for their clients. The growing popularity of integrated marketing communications has prompted many full-function agencies to develop capabilities and offer services in these other promotional areas. Traditional advertising agencies are recognizing that they must develop integrated marketing capabilities that extend beyond media advertising.

Creative Services   The creative services department is responsible for the creation and execution of advertisements. The individuals who conceive the ideas for the ads and write the headlines, subheads, and body copy (the words constituting the message) are known as **copywriters**. They may also be involved in determining the basic appeal or theme of the ad campaign and often prepare a rough initial visual layout of the print ad or television commercial.

While copywriters are responsible for what the message says, the *art department* is responsible for how the ad looks. For print ads, the art director and graphic designers prepare *layouts,* which are drawings that show what the ad will look like and from which the final artwork will be produced. For TV commercials, the layout is known as a *storyboard,* a sequence of frames or panels that depict the commercial in still form.

Members of the creative department work together to develop ads that will communicate the key points determined to be the basis of the creative strategy for the client's product or service. Writers and artists generally work under the direction of the agency's creative director, who oversees all the advertising produced by the organization. The director sets the creative philosophy of the department and may even become directly involved in creating ads for the agency's largest clients.

Once the copy, layout, illustrations, and mechanical specifications have been completed and approved, the ad is turned over to the *production department*. Most agencies do not actually produce finished ads; they hire printers, engravers, photographers, typographers, and other suppliers to complete the finished product. For broadcast production, the approved storyboard must be turned into a finished commercial. The production department may supervise the casting of people to appear in the ad and the setting for the scenes as well as choose an independent production studio. The department may hire an outside director to turn the creative concept into a commercial. For example, Nike has used film directors such as David Fincher and Spike Lee to direct some of its commercials; BMW has used well-known film directors such as Guy Ritchie and Ang Lee to direct some of its commercials and webisodes. Academy Award winner Martin Scorsese has directed commercials for Dolce & Gabbana including a spot for The One fragrance line that featured actors Matthew McConaughey and Scarlett Johansson as the spokesmodels. Copywriters, art directors, account managers, people from research and planning, and representatives from the client side may all participate in production decisions, particularly when large sums of money are involved.

Creating an advertisement often involves many people and takes several months. In large agencies with many clients, coordinating the creative and production processes can be a major problem. A *traffic department* coordinates all phases of production to see that the ads are completed on time and that all deadlines for submitting the ads to the media are met. The traffic department may be located in the creative services area of the agency, or be part of media or account management, or be separate.

Management and Finance Like any other business, an advertising agency must be managed and perform basic operating and administrative functions such as accounting, finance, and human resources. It must also attempt to generate new business. Large agencies employ administrative, managerial, and clerical people to perform these functions. The bulk of an agency's income (approximately 64 percent) goes to salary and benefits for its employees. Thus, an agency must manage its personnel carefully and get maximum productivity from them.

Agency Organization and Structure Full-function advertising agencies must develop an organizational structure that will meet their clients' needs and serve their own internal requirements. Most medium-size and large agencies are structured under either a departmental or a group system. Under the **departmental system**, each of the agency functions shown in Figure 3–6 is set up as a separate department and is called on as needed to perform its specialty and serve all of the agency's clients. Ad layout, writing, and production are done by the creative department; marketing services is responsible for any research or media selection and purchases; and the account services department handles client contact. Some agencies prefer the departmental system because it gives employees the opportunity to develop expertise in servicing a variety of accounts.

Many large agencies use the **group system**, in which individuals from each department work together in groups to service particular accounts. Each group is headed by an account executive or supervisor and has one or more media people, including media planners and buyers; a creative team, which includes copywriters, art directors, artists, and production personnel; and one or more account executives. The group may also include individuals from other departments such as marketing research, direct marketing, or sales promotion. The size and composition of the

IMC Perspective 3–1 > > >

Droga5—Creatively Led, Strategically Driven

If you were to ask people working in advertising their opinion regarding the hottest agency in the ad business and/or the one they admire most, it is very likely they would say Droga5 and for good reason. The agency, which began as a small creative boutique in New York City in 2006, has received agency of the year awards nine times over the past decade from various industry organizations such as the Cannes Lions, The One Show, and the Effies, as well as by *Adweek* and *Advertising Age,* which are the two major publications that cover advertising. Droga5 is the only agency to be named to *Advertising Age*'s A-List six consecutive years and in 2016 was selected as *Ad Age*'s Agency of the Year while receiving the same award from its Creativity division, making it only the fourth agency to receive both honors in the same year. Recognition of Droga5 has extended beyond the advertising industry as *Fast Company* magazine named it one of the World's Most Innovative Companies in 2013.

The agency was founded by David Droga, who grew up in an Australian ski resort and envisioned himself traveling the world as a ski instructor. However, it was his creative talent that took him abroad as he embarked on an advertising career at the OMON agency in Sydney, and by age 22 he was a partner and executive creative director. He moved to Singapore in 1996 to become the creative director of Saatchi & Saatchi Singapore; three years later he was promoted to executive creative director of the agency's London office. In 2003 he moved to New York City as the first-ever worldwide chief creative officer of the Publicis Network. However, after nearly a decade of helping grow agencies owned by major holding companies he decided to start his own agency and launched Droga5 (which is named for how his mother would label her fifth son's school shirts).

When asked to describe why his agency has been so successful and its biggest strength, David Droga describes it as caring and an obsession about doing work that stands out creatively, drives business, and has an impact in the real world. He notes that the agency aspires to do things differently and push the boundaries of creativity while helping its clients ascend to new places. And while creativity permeates the agency's thinking, it is also known for its strategic thinking. Clients such as JPMorgan Chase and Georgia Pacific have praised Droga5 for its research and analytical capabilities and how the agency synthesizes and uses information to develop creative insights and determine directions.

Droga5 describes itself as creatively led, strategically driven, digitally native, and humanity obsessed, all of which are reasons for its tremendous success and the accolades it has received. The agency has definitely lived up to its reputation as a creative powerhouse, as evidenced by the work it has done for clients and brands such as New Castle Brown Ale, Google, and Under Armour. The agency won a Facebook Blue Award for its "If We Made It" initiative for Newcastle that used social media and content to drive people online to view a would-be Super Bowl commercial featuring actor Ana Kendrick that never aired. The campaign

group vary depending on the client's billings and the importance of the account to the agency. For very important accounts, the group members may be assigned exclusively to one client. In some agencies, they may serve a number of smaller clients. Many agencies prefer the group system because employees become very knowledgeable about the client's business and there is continuity in servicing the account.

Other Types of Agencies and Services

Not every agency is a large full-service agency. Many smaller agencies expect their employees to handle a variety of jobs. For example, account executives may do their own research, work out their own media schedule, and coordinate the production of ads written and designed by the creative department. Many advertisers, including some large companies, are not interested in paying for the services of a full-service agency but are interested in some of the specific services agencies have to offer. Over the past few decades, several alternatives to full-service agencies have evolved, including creative boutiques and media buying services.

Creative Boutiques **Creative boutiques** are small ad agencies that provide only creative services and have long been an important part of the advertising industry. These specialized agencies have creative personnel such as writers and artists on staff but do not have media, research, or account planning capabilities. Creative boutiques have developed in response to some companies' desires to use only the

Source: Droga5

in real-time social media insults about her to emphasize that she used her strength and will to block out noise from even her nastiest critics. The agency has also developed the "Rule Yourself" campaign that features NBA star Stephen Curry, golfer Jordan Spieth, and ballerina Misty Copeland striving to be their best. The critically acclaimed work Droga5 has done for Under Armour has helped the company expand beyond football and into other sports and connect with women.

Droga5 has experienced tremendous growth over the past 10 years and is widely recognized as one of the leading independent agencies. In addition to all of the awards, its track record includes at least 31 percent year-over-year growth since its founding. Of course with this growth comes many challenges such as the hiring of new personnel as well as maintaining the unique culture that has made it so unique and successful. However, most people in the advertising industry fully expect Droga5 to continue to come up with great creative ideas for its clients as the agency seems only to get better each year under the leadership of David Droga. The ski industry's loss has clearly been a gain for the world of advertising.

Sources: Ann-Christine Diaz, "Agency of the Year," *Advertising Age,* January 25, 2016, pp. 6–7; Tim Nudd, "Droga5's Gisele Campaign for Under Armour Scores the Cyber Grand Prix at Cannes," *Adweek,* June 24, 2015, www.adweek.com/news/advertising-branding/droga5s-gisele-campaign-under-armour-scores-cyber-grand-prix-cannes-165541; Christopher Heine, "Droga5 Nabs Top Facebook Studio Award for Newcastle Brown Ale Work," *Adweek,* April 29, 2014, www.adweek.com/news/technology/droga5-nabs-top-facebook-studio-award-newcastle-brown-ale-work-157337.urce.

was really a parody on the marketing circus that surrounds the Super Bowl and included a salty "Suck It" response from Kendrick to Newcastle for hiring her for a would-be ad on the big game only to pull the plug that generated over 5 million views on social media. Droga5 also created the "Friends Furever" campaign for Google Android which paired images of unlikely animals playing together and was set to the "Oo-De-Lally" song from the Disney movie *Robin Hood.* The ads were immensely popular and among the most socially shared of all time.

Droga5 also has done outstanding creative work for Under Armour including the "I Will What I Want" campaign that won the Grand Prix Award at the 2015 Cannes International advertising festival. Part of the campaign included supermodel Gisele Bundchen and featured a website that pulled

creative services of an outside agency while maintaining control of other marketing communication functions internally. While most creative boutiques work directly for companies, full-service agencies often subcontract work to them when they are very busy or want to avoid adding full-time employees to their payrolls. They are usually compensated on a project or hourly fee basis.

Many creative boutiques have been formed by members of the creative departments of full-service agencies who leave the firm and take with them clients who want to retain their creative talents. An advantage of these smaller agencies is their ability to turn out inventive creative work quickly and without the cumbersome bureaucracy and politics of larger agencies. Many companies also prefer working directly with a smaller creative boutique because they can get more attention and better access to creative talent than they would at a larger agency.

Creative boutiques will continue to be an important part of the advertising industry. However, they face challenges as many find themselves competing against larger agencies for business, particularly when there are cutbacks in advertising spending. Moreover, many clients want the range of services that large agencies provide as they are often looking for strategic and business-building ideas rather than just creative work. Many creative boutiques offer additional services as they grow and acquire more clients and become very large and successful independent agencies. IMC Perspective 3–1 discusses Droga5, an independent agency that has become widely recognized for its outstanding creative work as well as strategic planning and received numerous industry awards.[29]

Media Specialist Companies   **Media specialist companies** are organizations that specialize in the buying of media, particularly for television and digital advertising. The task of purchasing advertising media has grown more complex, especially with the fragmentation of media audiences and the growth of digital media. Media buying services have found a niche by specializing in the analysis and purchase of advertising time and space. Agencies and clients often develop their own media strategies and hire a media buying service to execute them. However, some media buying services do help advertisers plan their media strategies. Because media buying services purchase such large amounts of time and space, they receive large discounts and can save the small agency or client money on media purchases. A major development in the purchasing of advertising media in recent years has been the rapid growth of **programmatic buying** which refers to wide range of technologies that are automating the buying, placement, and optimization of advertising media.[30] Programmatic buying originated in the purchase of digital advertising space where there are a myriad of options available to marketers and the purchase process is automated and often based on real-time bidding. However, programmatic buying is expanding beyond digital media as it is being used to purchase television advertising time as well.[31] Media buying services are generally paid a fee or commission for their work.

Media buying services have been experiencing strong growth in recent years as clients seek alternatives to full-service agency relationships. Many companies have been unbundling agency services and consolidating media buying to get more clout from their advertising budgets. Nike, Revlon, and Hyundai/Kia are among those that have switched some or all of their media buying from full-service agencies to independent media buyers. As noted earlier, many of the major agencies have formed independent media services companies that handle the media planning and buying for their clients and also offer their services separately to companies interested in a more specialized or consolidated approach to media planning, research, and/or buying. A number of large advertisers have consolidated their media buying with these large media specialist companies to save money and improve media efficiency. Major marketers such as PepsiCo, Unilever, Coca-Cola and L'Oréal also use media specialist companies to handle all of their global media buying, which helps them achieve economies of scale and more uniform media strategies and implementation across various countries.

The rise of the independent media buying services, operating outside the structure of the traditional ad agency media department, and the divestment of these departments from the agency system are two of the most significant developments that have occurred in the advertising industry in recent years. A study conducted for the Association of National Advertisers found a small percentage of companies still use a "general" ad agency to handle their media planning and buying as the vast majority use a media agency specialist to handle these functions. These media specialists are often part of the same agency holding company as the primary agency that handles their creative work, particularly for large advertisers. However, about a third of the time the media specialist agency is not related to the primary agency.[32] As the media landscape becomes more complex, technological developments such as the use of programmatic buying, big data and analytics will become even more important in the media planning and buying process. This will lead marketers to carefully review their media planning and buying processes and may result in even more use of media specialist companies.[33] Exhibit 3–11 shows how Initiative, which is one of the largest media specialist companies and is part of the Interpublic Group, promotes its services.

AGENCY COMPENSATION

As you have seen, the type and amount of services an agency performs vary from one client to another. As a result, agencies use a variety of methods to get paid for their services. Agencies are typically compensated in three ways: commissions, some type of fee arrangement, or percentage charges.

EXHIBIT 3–11

Initiative is one of the leading media specialist companies

Source: Initiative

initiative

who we are | what we think | what we do | news | contact

| RETHINKING MEDIA BY DESIGN | THE NEW POWER OF TELEVISION | THE AGE OF SOCIAL INFLUENCE | DON'T STOP AT THE DOOR OF THE STORE |

Read the report

Commissions from Media

The traditional method of compensating agencies is through a **commission system**, where the agency receives a specified commission (usually 15 percent) from the media on any advertising time or space it purchases for its client. (For outdoor advertising, the commission is 16⅔ percent.) This system provides a simple method of determining payments, as shown in the following example.

Assume an agency prepares a full-page magazine ad and arranges to place the ad on the back cover of a magazine at a cost of $100,000. The agency places the order for the space and delivers the ad to the magazine. Once the ad is run, the magazine will bill the agency for $100,000, less the 15 percent ($15,000) commission. The media will also offer a 2 percent cash discount for early payment, which the agency may pass along to the client. The agency will bill the client $100,000 less the 2 percent cash discount on the net amount, or a total of $98,300, as shown in Figure 3–7. The $15,000 commission represents the agency's compensation for its services.

Appraisal of the Commission System
While the commission system was the primary agency compensation method for many years, it has always been controversial. Critics of the commission system have long argued that it encourages agencies to recommend high-priced media to their clients to increase their commission level. The system has also been criticized on the grounds that it ties agency compensation to media costs, which have been skyrocketing over the past decade. Still others charge that the system encourages agencies to recommend mass-media advertising

FIGURE 3–7

Example of Commission System Payment

Media Bills Agency		Agency Bills Advertiser	
Costs for magazine space	$100,000	Costs for magazine space	$100,000
Less 15% commission	−15,000	Less 2% cash discount	−1,700
Cost of media space	85,000	Advertiser pays agency	$ 98,300
Less 2% cash discount	−1,700		
Agency pays media	$ 83,300	Agency income	$ 15,000

and avoid noncommissionable IMC tools such as direct mail, sales promotion, public relations, and event sponsorships unless they are requested by the clients.

Defenders of the commission system argue that it is easy to administer and keeps the emphasis in agency compensation on nonprice factors such as the quality of the advertising developed for clients. Proponents of the system argue that agency services are proportional to the size of the commission, since more time and effort are devoted to the large accounts that generate high revenue for the agency. They also note that the system is more flexible than it appears as agencies often perform other services for large clients at no extra charge as a way of justifying the large commission they receive.

Companies began moving away from the commission system during the 1990s, and most companies no longer use it as the basis for compensating their agencies. The most recent study of agency compensation conducted by the Association of National Advertisers (ANA) found that only 6 percent of major advertisers in the United States still paid commissions to their agencies, down from 16 percent in 2007.[34] Among those companies that do pay commissions, most do not pay the traditional 15 percent. Many advertisers have gone to a **negotiated commission** system whereby the commissions average from 8 to 10 percent or are based on a sliding scale that becomes lower as the clients' media expenditures increase. Agencies are also relying less on media commissions for their income as their clients expand their IMC programs to include other forms of promotion and cut back on mass-media advertising. The amount of agency income coming from media commissions is declining as many companies are now using other methods of agency compensation such as fees and performance-based incentives. The ANA survey was the first study of global ad agency compensation, and found that reliance on commissions is a more common practice outside the United States as more than a third of global marketers still use traditional media commissions to compensate their agencies. One reason for the higher use of commissions is that in some countries, such as Brazil and Japan, the use of commissions to compensate agencies is mandated by law or is a common practice.[35]

Fee, Cost, and Incentive-Based Systems

Since many believe the commission system is not equitable to all parties, many agencies and their clients have developed some type of fee arrangement or cost-plus agreement for agency compensation. Some are using incentive-based compensation, which is a combination of a commission and a fee system.

Fee Arrangement   There are two basic types of fee arrangement systems. In the straight or **fixed-fee method**, the agency charges a basic monthly fee for all of its services and credits to the client any media commissions earned. Agency and client agree on the specific work to be done and the amount the agency will be paid for it. Sometimes agencies are compensated through a **fee–commission combination**, in which the media commissions received by the agency are credited against the fee. If the commissions are less than the agreed-on fee, the client must make up the difference. If the agency does much work for the client in noncommissionable media, the fee may be charged over and above the commissions received.

Both types of fee arrangements require that the agency carefully assess its costs of serving the client for the specified period, or for the project, plus its desired profit margin. To avoid any later disagreement, a fee arrangement should specify exactly what services the agency is expected to perform for the client. The ANA study found that a fee-based structure, whereby agencies are paid fixed or labor-based fees for services provided, is the dominant form of compensation, with 57 percent of global marketers using this type of plan. Blended compensation plans that use a combination of fees and commissions to compensate agencies were used by 37 percent of the companies surveyed.

Cost-Plus Agreement Under a **cost-plus system**, the client agrees to pay the agency a fee based on the costs of its work plus some agreed-on profit margin (often a percentage of total costs). This system requires that the agency keep detailed records of the costs it incurs in working on the client's account. Direct costs (personnel time and out-of-pocket expenses) plus an allocation for overhead and a markup for profits determine the amount the agency bills the client.

Fee agreements and cost-plus systems are commonly used in conjunction with a commission system. The fee-based system can be advantageous to both the client and the agency, depending on the size of the client, advertising budget, media used, and services required. Many clients prefer fee or cost-plus systems because they receive a detailed breakdown of where and how their advertising and promotion dollars are being spent. However, these arrangements can be difficult for the agency, as they require careful cost accounting and may be difficult to estimate when bidding for an advertiser's business. Agencies are also reluctant to let clients see their internal cost figures.

Incentive-Based Compensation Many clients are demanding more accountability from their agencies and tying agency compensation to performance through some type of **incentive-based system**. Recently a new variation of this system has emerged in the form of *value-based compensation* whereby agencies are compensated above their basic costs, if they achieve or exceed results as measured by agreed-upon metrics.[36] The costs are determined by the tasks that the agency is expected to perform, staffing required, and hourly rates. While there are many variations, the basic idea is that the agency's ultimate compensation level will depend on how well it meets predetermined performance goals. These goals often include objective measures such as sales or market share as well as more subjective measures such as evaluations of the quality of the agency's creative work. Companies using incentive-based systems determine agency compensation through media commissions, fees, bonuses, or some combination of these methods. The use of performance incentives varies by the size of the advertiser, with large advertisers the most likely to use them. Figure 3–8 shows the various performance criteria used along with the basis for the incentive.

Recognizing the movement toward incentive-based systems, some agencies have agreed to tie their compensation to performance. Agency executives note that pay for performance works best when the agency has complete control over a campaign. Thus, if a campaign fails to help sell a product or service, the agency is willing to assume complete responsibility and take a reduction in compensation. On the other hand, if sales increase, the agency can receive greater compensation for its work.

Percentage Charges

Another way to compensate an agency is by adding a markup of **percentage charges** to various services the agency purchases from outside providers. These may include market research, artwork, printing, photography, and other services or materials. Markups usually range from 17.65 to 20 percent and are added to the client's overall bill. Since suppliers of these services do not allow the agency a commission, percentage charges cover administrative costs while allowing a reasonable profit for the agency's efforts. (A markup of 17.65 percent of costs added to the initial cost would yield a 15 percent commission. For example, research costs of $100,000 × 17.65% = $100,000 + $17,650 = $117,650. The $17,650 markup is about 15 percent of $117,650.)

FIGURE 3–8

Performance Criteria Used for Incentive Plans

Performance reviews	82%
Sales goals	53
Brand/ad awareness	51
Achieve project objectives	44
Brand perceptions	33
Copy test results	24
Market share goals	24
Profit goals	24
Other criteria	13
Basis for Incentives	
Agency performance	27%
Company performances	13
Both agency and company	53

Source: Association of National Advertisers, *Trends in Agency Compensation,* 14th ed., 2007.

Agencies Face Off with Procurement Specialists and Debate Rebates with Clients

For many years Madison Avenue was a world unto itself. Advertising agencies were compensated based on a 15 percent commission on the media purchases they made for their clients: Every time an ad appeared on television, played on radio, or was placed in a magazine, the cash registers rang on Madison Avenue. Agencies were dominated by "creatives" who came up with big ideas that could be translated into TV, print, radio, or billboard ads that would be run through these mass media to be seen or heard by the millions of consumers comprising the mass markets.

During the late 90s, the ad industry prospered and many agencies were still able to get many of their clients to agree to pay them based on a percentage of their media billings. However, during the first decade of the new millennium, many major advertisers did away with commissions entirely. The vast majority of clients now compensate their agencies by paying fees based on the agency's labor costs. To make matters more complicated, some companies now have their procurement officers negotiate contracts with their advertising agencies rather than their marketing or advertising managers. Many agencies are finding the procurement people to be much more difficult to negotiate with on issues such as their allocation of labor costs, employee salaries, overhead, and reasonable profit. The agencies argue that procurement departments really do not understand the advertising business and the role they play in brand building. Some agencies have tried to take a stand against clients who view them as vendors rather than marketing partners. However, other agencies are often willing to accept lower margins to gain new business, which has resulted in a loss of pricing power for many agencies.

The intervention of procurement departments into the advertising process is also receiving a cold reception from many marketing executives who argue that the advertising process is different from sourcing raw materials for manufacturing. They note that creating ideas is different from creating widgets and also express concern over procurement executives and chief financial officers (CFOs) trying to take over the agency selection process. They argue that too much emphasis is put on policing the financial aspects of the client–agency relationship and advertising, and agency fees are viewed as an expense rather than an investment. Many marketing executives and the majority of those on the agency side feel that it is difficult to judge the value of an agency's work on the basis of the number of hours they log on a client's account but recognize that this is becoming the new model under which they must operate.

A new issue has emerged from the increased emphasis on procurement-driven cost cutting: the practice of media rebates, which are loosely defined as an agency's receipt of a volume discount or compensation from media buys that is not passed on to the client. Many of the holding companies have spun off their media divisions into freestanding firms that handle only media buying. These large media buying firms can use their size and clout to extract better media prices and cost savings for their clients. However, the issue is whether these savings make their way to the clients or stay with the media buyers. Media rebates are a reviled but tolerated practice outside the United States and a survey conducted by the Association of National Advertisers (ANA) revealed that they may be becoming more commonplace here as well. The

The Future of Agency Compensation

As you can see, there is no one method of agency compensation to which everyone subscribes. Companies have continued to make significant changes in their agency compensation plans over the past decade, including the use of incentive-based compensation systems. The ANA study found that 49 percent of the advertisers surveyed said they have a performance incentive component in their agency compensation agreements and a significant number are considering doing so.[37]

As more companies adopt IMC approaches, they are reducing their reliance on traditional media advertising, and this is leading to changes in the way they compensate their agencies. The changes in agency compensation are also being driven by economic factors as most companies cut their advertising and promotion budgets during the recession as part of their efforts to save money across all areas of their marketing programs. Most marketers have not increased their marketing budgets and continue to be conservative with their spending for advertising and other forms of marketing communications. While clients recognize that their agencies must be able to make a profit, many are likely to continue to challenge them to reduce internal expenses, identify areas for cost reductions, and tightly manage their controllable spending.[38]

ANA, which represents nearly 700 companies that collectively spend over $250 billion on marketing and advertising each year, released a report showing that nearly a third of U.S. marketers are aware of rebates and incentives offered by media companies that may not be reimbursed to the advertiser. The report also noted that the vast majority of marketers surveyed believed agencies should turn over any rebates they receive to their clients as keeping the payments could impair their objectivity in media choices. Marketers are concerned that media rebates might affect their agencies' media-purchasing decisions and result in less than optimal allocations of their marketing budgets.

Marketers and agencies agree that rebates are not a problem if they are disclosed and passed on to clients. However, a problem arises in defining exactly what constitutes a media rebate and what should be passed on to clients because rebates seldom take the form of a simple cash payment from the media seller to the agency for reaching a volume target. Industry experts note that they often take more creative forms such as discounts for early payment of invoices, payment from the media company to the agency for research or other services, or bonus inventory, which the media agency may then be able to sell to clients that do not require an invoice. Rebates can also flow into specialized agency holding-company entities, where they become very difficult to track.

The ANA report recommends that language used in agency contracts calling for rebates be fully disclosed and documented and require that any discounts be passed on to clients. However, even those in the industry who are critical of rebates argue that they are a natural result of marketers' efforts to squeeze agency costs and procurement procedures that have narrowed margins to the point where they are seeking these incentives. Many marketers respond by arguing that their concerns involve more than just cost savings as they are also looking for more effectiveness from their media spending, particularly as digital spending increases and more media purchasing is done programmatically.

While agency executives may not like the changes that are occurring in the world of advertising, most recognize that they have little choice but to adapt to the changes. The involvement of clients' procurement departments is here to stay and one former agency executive's response to those who complain about it is "Welcome to the real world." He notes that most of those on the client side have had to deal with a purchasing department or hard-nosed buyer almost from the day they started work. The concerns over media rebates are having an impact on the industry as a number of marketers have been reviewing their media business and many industry experts note that these reviews are a result of the rebate debate. The ANA is also continuing to focus on the issue and in late 2015 hired two consulting firms to examine whether undisclosed rebates are influencing media agencies' work on behalf of their clients.

Many persons working in the advertising industry argue that the two sides must find a way to work together. Marketers must recognize that a relationship in which the agency is barely making any money is not sustainable and respect the right of agencies to make a reasonable profit, while agencies will have to continue to find ways to reduce their costs and accept smaller profit margins. However, they note that clients who continue to tighten the vise on their agencies may be cutting off their nose to spite their face as the quality of service they receive may suffer when the agency caves in to their demands.

Sources: Alexandra Bruell, "In Unilateral Decision, ANA Hires Two Firms to Probe Agency Rebates," *Advertising Age,* October 26, 2015, pp. 2, 4; Alexandra Bruell, "Unprecedented Wave of Media Reviews Partly Driven by Rebate Debate," *Advertising Age,* June 1, 2015, p. 8; Jack Neff, "The Great Rebate Debate: Are Media Buyers Getting Cash Back?" *Advertising Age,* September 10, 2012, pp. 52–54; Bob Liodice, "Transparency Is the Only Way to Avoid Abuse of Media Rebates and Incentives," *Advertising Age,* October 1, 2012, p. 49; Chris Ingram, "Time for Ad World to Meet the Real World," *Advertising Age,* July 2, 2006, p. 14; Rupal Parekh, "Fed-Up Shops Pitch a Fit at Procurement," *Advertising Age,* October 26, 2009, pp. 1, 17.

Companies are also making their agencies more accountable for the fees they charge them for services and are asking for more transparency in how agencies structure, determine, and present fee compensation.[39] One of the most significant findings from the ANA global agency compensation survey was the increased involvement of corporate procurement departments in the management and negotiation of agency compensation. Seventy-five percent of the global respondents indicated that their procurement departments are involved in the agency compensation negotiations, with nearly half reporting that the process is procurement led with marketing support and only 28 percent saying the process is marketing led. IMC Perspective 3–2 discusses how the involvement of procurement specialists is impacting agency compensation as well as concerns that this may be leading to a practice known as media rebates, whereby discounts from media buys are not passed on from the agency to the client.

EVALUATING AGENCIES

Given the substantial amounts of money being spent on advertising and promotion, demand for accountability of the expenditures has increased. Regular reviews of the agency's performance are necessary. The agency evaluation process usually involves two types of assessments, one financial and operational and the other more qualitative. The **financial audit** focuses on how the agency conducts its business. It is designed to verify costs and expenses, the number of personnel hours charged to an account, and payments to media and outside suppliers. The **qualitative audit** focuses on the agency's efforts in planning, developing, and implementing the client's advertising programs and considers the results achieved.

The agency evaluation is often done on a subjective, informal basis, particularly in smaller companies where ad budgets are low or advertising is not seen as the most critical factor in the firm's marketing performance. However, some companies have developed formal, systematic evaluation systems, particularly when budgets are large and the advertising function receives much emphasis. The top management of these companies wants to be sure money is being spent efficiently and effectively. As the costs of advertising and other forms of promotion rise, more companies are adopting formal procedures for evaluating the performance of their agencies. For example, a survey conducted by the Association of National Advertisers found that 76 percent of marketers have a formal evaluation process for traditional creative agencies while 68 percent have one for traditional media agencies. The survey also found that qualitative performance is weighted more heavily than quantitative factors. Among the leading qualitative performance criteria identified in the survey were innovation, ideas, teamwork, meeting deadlines, strategy, and implementation. An interesting finding of the study was that formal reviews were much less likely to be conducted for digital, public relations, direct, and multicultural agencies.[40]

An important consideration in evaluating agencies is the *value* they provide to their client's business. The American Association of Advertising Agencies and Association of National Advertisers conducted a major study to understand how both agencies and clients define value and the agency activities that provide the most value to the client's business.[41] The top seven dimensions of agency activity that advertisers indicated add the most value to their business are shown in Figure 3–9. The study also considered how clients add value to the client–agency relationship and found that the key value drivers include understanding the brand's problems/opportunities, giving the agency the necessary time and resources to do its best work, articulating expected outcomes, giving clear direction, and providing constructive feedback.[42]

Gaining and Losing Clients

The evaluation process described previously provides valuable feedback to both the agency and the client, such as indicating changes that need to be made by the agency and/or the client to improve performance and make the relationship more productive.

FIGURE 3–9

How Agencies Add Value to a Client's Business

Source: "Report on the Agency–Advertiser Value Survey," American Association of Advertising Agencies and Association of National Advertisers, August 2007.

1. Developing and producing creative ideas that are fresh and appropriate.

2. Ensuring that agency disciplines and functions are integrated and that agency teams and divisions collaborate well on behalf of the client.

3. Working in a collaborative way with the client by creating an environment of low egos and high mutual respect.

4. Developing ideas and programs that can be integrated into multiple communication channels.

5. Assigning its best people to the client's business and making its top executives available when needed.

6. Evaluating brand drivers like awareness, consideration, and purchase intent.

7. Providing guidance and solutions in new media and technologies.

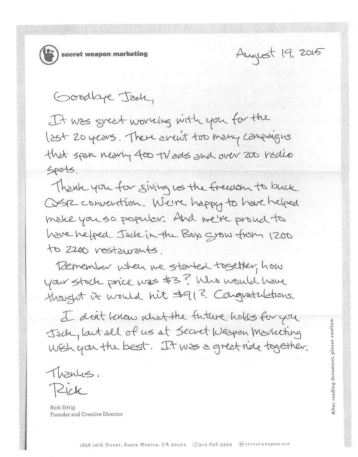

Many agencies have had very long-lasting relationships with their clients. For example, General Electric has been with the BBDO Worldwide agency for nearly a century.[43] Other well-known companies or brands that have had long-lasting relationships include Marlboro/Leo Burnett (60 years), McDonald's/DDB Worldwide (47 years), and Chevrolet/Campbell Ewald (94 years).

While many successful agency–client relationships go on for years, loyalty to a single agency is becoming less common as marketers seek new ways of connecting with consumers.[44] In recent years, a number of long-standing client relationships have been terminated. For example, ExxonMobil ended one of the longest-running relationships ever when the energy giant moved its account from McCann Erickson to BBDO. McCann had been Exxon's agency for nearly 100 years as it first began working with the company after the breakup of the Standard Oil empire in 1911.[45] In 2016 the Olive Garden restaurant chain parted ways with the Grey agency and moved to mcgarrybowen, citing the new agency's proven track record of creativity across multiple channels, while Jack in the Box ended its 20-year relationship with its longtime agency Secret Weapon Marketing. Exhibit 3–12 shows an ad the agency ran in several industry publications citing its role in helping the fast-food chain achieve tremendous growth during its tenure.

Some companies switch agencies quite often in search of better creative work or for a variety of other reasons such as reorganizations that lead to changes in top management, changes in marketing or advertising strategy, or conflicts that might arise from mergers and acquisitions among both clients and agencies. A company may also switch agencies in order to consolidate all of its advertising and marketing efforts in one shop. A number of global marketers such as Samsung, IBM, Colgate, Microsoft, and others have reduced the number of agencies they work with in recent years as a way to gain more control over their marketing communications and create a consistent brand image worldwide.[46]

In 2009, Hyundai Motor America moved all of the creative work for its Hyundai automotive brand to Innocean Worldwide America. Innocean is the U.S. arm of its Seoul-based agency of the same name, which is a subsidiary of the Korean parent company Hyundai Motor Group. The move was partly due to Hyundai wanting a more cohesive and consistent brand image worldwide. Innocean has done excellent creative work that has helped make Hyundai one of the fastest-growing automotive brands in the U.S. market over the past five years.[47] The agency has developed advertising and digital campaigns for models such as the Elantra and Sonata and has also helped Hyundai move into the upscale luxury sedan market with ads for the Genesis and Equus (Exhibit 3–13).

There are a number of reasons clients switch agencies. Understanding these potential problems can help the agency avoid them.[48] In addition, it is important to understand the process agencies go through in trying to win new clients.

EXHIBIT 3–12

The Secret Weapon Marketing agency says goodbye to its long-time client Jack in the Box in this ad. Gaining and losing clients is a challenging part of the agency business.

Source: Secret Weapon Marketing

EXHIBIT 3–13

Ads created by Innocean have helped make Hyundai one of the fastest-growing automotive brands in the United States

Source: Hyundai Motor America

Why Agencies Lose Clients   Some of the more common reasons agencies lose clients follow:

- *Poor performance or service.* The client becomes dissatisfied with the quality of the advertising and/or the service provided by the agency.
- *Poor communication.* The client and agency personnel fail to develop or maintain the level of communication necessary to sustain a favorable working relationship.
- *Unrealistic demands by the client.* The client places demands on the agency that exceed the amount of compensation received and reduce the account's profitability.
- *Personality conflicts.* People working on the account on the client and agency sides do not have enough rapport to work well together.
- *Personnel changes.* A change in personnel at either the agency or the advertiser can create problems. New managers may wish to use an agency with which they have established ties. Agency personnel often take accounts with them when they switch agencies or start their own.
- *Changes in size of the client or agency.* The client may outgrow the agency or decide it needs a larger agency to handle its business. If the agency gets too large, the client may represent too small a percentage of its business to command attention.
- *Conflicts of interest.* A conflict may develop when an agency merges with another agency or when a client is part of an acquisition or merger. In the United States, an agency cannot handle two accounts that are in direct competition with each other. In some cases, even indirect competition will not be tolerated.
- *Changes in the client's corporate and/or marketing strategy.* A client may change its marketing strategy and decide that a new agency is needed to carry out the new program. As more companies adapt an integrated marketing communications approach, they are looking for agencies that have integrated capabilities and can handle more than just their media advertising. A number of companies have changed agencies recently and moved their business to shops that have strong digital marketing capabilities.
- *Declining sales.* When sales of the client's product or service are stagnant or declining, advertising may be seen as contributing to the problem. A new agency may be sought for a new creative approach. For example, Anheuser Busch has changed agencies several times in recent years for Budweiser and Bud Light to try and reverse declining sales and market share for the two brands.[49]
- *Conflicting compensation philosophies.* Disagreement may develop over the level or method of compensation. As more companies move toward incentive-based compensation systems, disagreement over compensation is becoming more commonplace.

Copyright © 1982 Tom K. Ryan

- *Changes in policies.* Policy changes may result when either party reevaluates the importance of the relationship, the agency acquires a new (and larger) client, or either side undergoes a merger or acquisition.

- *Disagreements over marketing and/or creative strategy.* Agencies sometimes disagree with clients over the marketing strategy they want to pursue or the creative approach that might be best for the brand. For example, the Crispin Porter + Bogusky agency terminated relationships with several clients including Gateway and the Miller Brewing Co. over disagreements regarding marketing and creative strategy.

- *Lack of integrated marketing capabilities.* Many clients are changing agencies in search of a shop with a broader range of capabilities across various integrated marketing communication areas or greater expertise in a particular area such as digital marketing. In some cases clients are looking for an agency that can provide more integrated marketing services under one roof. However, many marketers are moving toward an open source model whereby they hire agencies and other marketing communication partners on a project basis, based on their special talents and expertise.[50]

If the agency recognizes various warning signs in its client relationship, it can try to adapt its programs and policies to make sure the client is satisfied. Some of the situations discussed here are unavoidable, and others are beyond the agency's control. But to maintain the account, problems within the agency's control must be addressed.

The time may come when the agency decides it is no longer in its best interest to continue to work with the client. Personnel conflicts, changes in management philosophy, and/or insufficient financial incentives are just a few of the reasons for such a decision. An agency may also decide to leave for a better business opportunity that allows it to grow and make more money. When agencies become known for doing excellent work and developing effective IMC campaigns, they often have the opportunity to pursue larger clients, which may include a company in the same industry. Conflict of interest policies preclude an agency from working for more than one company in a product or service category.[51]

How Agencies Gain Clients Competition for accounts in the agency business is intense, since most companies have already organized for the advertising function and only a limited number of new businesses require such services each year. While small agencies may be willing to work with a new company and grow along with it, larger agencies often do not become interested in these firms until they are able to spend at least $1 million per year on advertising. Many of the top agencies won't accept an account that spends less than $5 million per year. Once that expenditure level is reached, competition for the account intensifies.

In large agencies, most new business results from clients that already have an agency but decide to change their relationships. Thus, agencies must constantly search and compete for new clients. Some of the ways they do this follow.

Referrals Many good agencies obtain new clients as a result of referrals from existing clients, media representatives, and even other agencies. These agencies maintain good working relationships with their clients, the media, and outside parties that might provide business to them.

Solicitations One of the more common ways to gain new business is through direct solicitation. In smaller agencies, the president may solicit new accounts. In most large agencies, a new business development group seeks out and establishes contact with new clients. The group is responsible for writing solicitation letters, making cold calls, and following up on leads. The cutbacks in ad spending by many companies during the recent recession have resulted in many agencies pitching their services on an unsolicited basis to marketers who are satisfied with their agencies. Senior executives recognize that new business is the lifeblood of their agencies and some may encourage their business development teams to pursue advertisers who have not even put their accounts up for review.[52]

Presentations A basic goal of the new business development group is to receive an invitation from a company to make a presentation. This gives the agency the opportunity to sell itself—to describe its experience, personnel, capabilities, and operating procedures, as well as to demonstrate its previous work.

The agency may be asked to make a speculative presentation, in which it examines the client's marketing situation and proposes a tentative communications campaign that includes creative ideas. Because spec presentations require a great deal of time and preparation and may cost the agency a considerable amount of money without a guarantee of gaining the business, many firms refuse to participate in "creative shootouts." They argue that agencies should be selected on the basis of their experience and the services and programs they have provided for previous clients. Critics also note that in addition to the costs, which can be hundreds of thousands of dollars to pitch a major account, the creative work developed for speculative presentations is often not used and they do not always give a true indication of how the agency and client will work together.[53] However, many marketers still feel that spec presentations are an important part of the process of selecting a new agency and continue to use them. Thus, most agencies do participate in this form of solicitation, either by choice or because they must do so to gain accounts.

Due in part to the emphasis on speculative presentations, a very important role has developed for *ad agency review consultants,* who specialize in helping clients choose ad agencies. These consultants are often used to bring an objective perspective to the agency review process and to assist advertisers who may lack the resources, experience, or organizational consensus needed to successfully conduct a review. The use of search consultants is increasing as studies have shown that they are used in 30 to 40 percent of the agency reviews where the ad budget for the account is worth $10 million or more.[54] Because their opinions are respected by clients, the entire agency review process may be structured according to their guidelines. However, one study found that while many companies use search consultants to help them with their reviews, they do not always have a direct influence on the final decision regarding which agency they hire.[55]

Public Relations Agencies also seek business through publicity/public relations efforts. They often participate in civic and social groups and work with charitable organizations pro bono (at cost, without pay) to earn respect in the community. Participation in professional associations such as the American Association of Advertising Agencies and the Advertising Research Foundation can also lead to new contacts. Successful agencies often receive free publicity throughout the industry as well as in the mass media.

Image and Reputation Perhaps the most effective way an agency can gain new business is through its reputation for doing excellent work for the clients it serves. Word travels fast through the advertising and marketing industry regarding the agencies that are doing outstanding creative work in advertising as well as in other areas of IMC. There are many award competitions in which advertisers may enter their work and have it recognized, such as the Effie Awards, which are given each year to IMC campaigns based on the results they achieve as well as the strategy that goes into creating them. There are many other awards that recognize outstanding advertising creativity as well as work done in specific areas such as media planning and strategy, digital media, public relations, and sales promotion. For example, the Cannes Lions Awards are presented each year as

Extremely honored to be named @adage's 2016 B2B Agency of the Year! adage.com/article /specia ...

EXHIBIT 3–14

gyro was recognized by *Advertising Age* as the 2016 B-to-B Agency of the Year

© gyro

LO3-5

EXHIBIT 3–15

Direct marketing agencies such as Anderson provide clients a variety of direct and digital marketing services

Source: Anderson Direct & Digital

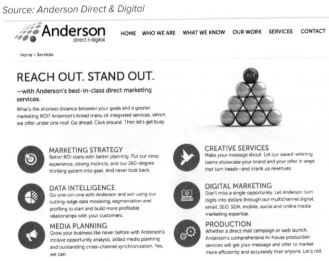

part of the Cannes International Advertising Festival and have become one of the most prestigious awards in the marketing communications industry. The CLIO Awards are also one of the world's most recognized international advertising, design, and communications competitions and reward creative excellence across a variety of categories and media types.

The major industry publications such as *Advertising Age* and *Adweek* also recognize the top agencies each year based on the quality of their creative work.[56] Being recognized by these publications, as well as other industry groups and associations, enhances the reputation and image of an agency. Exhibit 3–14 shows how gyro used Twitter to promote its being named B-to-B Agency of the Year by *Advertising Age*.

SPECIALIZED SERVICES

Many companies assign the development and implementation of their promotional programs to an advertising agency. But several other types of organizations provide specialized services that complement the efforts of ad agencies. Direct-response agencies, sales promotion agencies, and public relations firms are important to marketers in developing and executing IMC programs in the United States as well as international markets. Let us examine the functions these organizations perform.

Direct-Marketing Agencies

One of the fastest-growing areas of IMC is direct marketing, where companies communicate with consumers through telemarketing, direct mail, television, the Internet, and other forms of direct-response advertising. As this industry has grown, numerous direct-response agencies have evolved that offer companies their specialized skills in both consumer and business markets. Many of the top direct-marketing agencies such as Rapp, Wunderman, and OgilvyOne are subsidiaries of large agency holding companies. However, there are also a number of independent direct-marketing agencies including those that serve large companies as well as smaller firms that handle the needs of local companies. Many of these agencies have added digital capabilities as direct marketing and are utilizing the Internet and other digital channels to reach their target audiences (Exhibit 3–15).

Direct-marketing agencies provide a variety of services, including database analytics and management, direct mail, research, media services, and creative and production capabilities. While direct mail was traditionally their primary weapon, many direct-response agencies are expanding their services to include such areas as infomercial production, digital marketing, analytics, and database management. Database development and management is becoming one of the most important services provided by direct-response agencies. Many companies are using database marketing to pinpoint new customers and build relationships and loyalty among existing customers.

A typical direct-response agency is divided into three main departments: account management, creative, and media. Some agencies also have a department whose function is to develop and manage databases for their clients. The account managers work with their clients to plan direct-marketing programs and determine their role in the overall integrated marketing communications process. The creative department consists of copywriters, artists, and producers. Creative is responsible for developing the direct-response message, while the media department is concerned with its placement.

Like advertising agencies, direct-response agencies must solicit new business and have their performance reviewed by their existing clients, often through formal assessment programs. Most direct-response agencies are compensated on a fee basis.

Sales Promotion Agencies

Developing and managing sales promotion programs such as contests, sweepstakes, refunds and rebates, premium and incentive offers, and sampling programs are very complex tasks. Most companies use a **sales promotion agency** to develop and administer these programs. Some large ad agencies have created their own sales promotion department or acquired a sales promotion firm. However, most sales promotion agencies are independent companies that specialize in providing the services needed to plan, develop, and execute a variety of sales promotion programs.

Sales promotion agencies often work in conjunction with the client's advertising and/or direct-response agencies to coordinate their efforts with the advertising and direct-marketing programs. Services provided by large sales promotion agencies include promotional planning, creative research, tie-in coordination, fulfillment, premium design and manufacturing, catalog production, and contest/sweepstakes management. Many sales promotion agencies are also developing direct/database marketing and telemarketing to expand their integrated marketing services capabilities. Sales promotion agencies are generally compensated on a fee basis. Exhibit 3–16 shows a page from the website of Don Jagoda Associates, one of the leading sales promotion agencies.

Public Relations Firms

Many large companies use both an advertising agency and a PR firm. The **public relations firm** develops and implements programs to manage the organization's

publicity, image, and affairs with consumers and other relevant publics, including employees, suppliers, stockholders, government, labor groups, citizen action groups, and the general public. The PR firm analyzes the relationships between the client and these various publics, determines how the client's policies and actions relate to and affect these publics, develops PR strategies and programs, implements these programs using various public relations tools, and evaluates their effectiveness.

The activities of a public relations firm include planning the PR strategy and program, generating publicity, conducting lobbying and public affairs efforts, becoming involved in community activities and events, preparing news releases and other communications, conducting research, promoting and managing special events, and managing crises. As companies adopt an IMC approach to promotional planning, they are increasingly coordinating their PR activities with advertising and other promotional areas. Many companies are integrating public relations and publicity into the marketing communications mix to increase message credibility and save media costs.[57] Public relations firms are generally compensated on a fee basis or by retainer. We will examine their role in more detail in Chapter 17.

Digital/Interactive Agencies

With the rapid growth of the Internet and other forms of interactive media, a new type of specialized marketing communications organization has evolved—the interactive agency. Many marketers are using **digital/interactive agencies** that specialize in the development and strategic use of various digital marketing tools such as websites for the Internet, banner ads, search engine optimization, mobile marketing, and social media campaigns. They recognize that the development of successful interactive marketing programs requires expertise in digital technology as well as areas such as creative website design, database marketing, digital media, and customer relationship management. In addition to their advertising agencies, many marketers now choose to work with agencies that specialize in digital media. This has led many large agencies to develop their own digital shops that operate as separate entities within the agency such as Digital@Ogilvy and Arc, which is part of the Leo Burnett Group. Also, a number of other large digital agencies such as AKQA, Razorfish, Digitas, and R/GA are owned by major agency holding companies, which provides other agencies in their network with a digital resource. Many traditional advertising agencies have developed digital/interactive capabilities ranging from a few specialists within the agency to entire digital departments that work closely with other parts of the agency in developing integrated campaigns for their clients. For example, the digital arm of the Deutsch agency develops and manages the websites, social media, and online campaigns for clients such as Volkswagen, Taco Bell, and Target. Exhibit 3–17 shows how Deutsch promotes the creative work the agency did in redesigning the website for Volkswagen by incorporating ideas from dating sites. The site uses matchmaking functionality to help shoppers find their VW based on whatever criteria they're interested in—a specific model, certain features, favorite color, or price. Then it pairs them with new or used Volkswagen cars in their area. Each car has its own profile page with images, features, specs, and a payment estimator.[58]

While many agencies have or are developing interactive capabilities, a number of marketers are turning to more specialized interactive agencies to develop websites and interactive media. They feel these companies have more expertise in

EXHIBIT 3–17

Deutsch LA handles the digital/interactive part of Volkswagen's IMC program

Source: Volkswagen® Group of America, Inc.

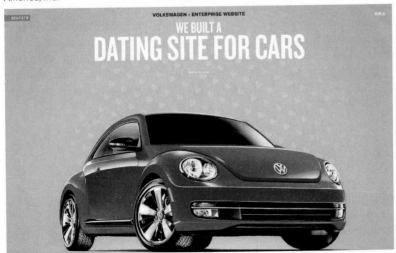

EXHIBIT 3-18

LYFE provides social media services for its clients

Source: LYFE Marketing

designing and developing websites as well as managing and supporting them. Interactive agencies range from smaller companies that specialize in website design and creation to full-service interactive agencies that provide all the elements needed for a successful digital/interactive marketing program. These services include strategic consulting regarding the use of the Internet and online branding, technical knowledge, systems integration, and the development of electronic commerce capabilities.

Full-service digital agencies, such as AKQA, have created successful digital marketing programs for a number of companies and brands, including Nike, Audi, Budweiser, and Gap. As the Internet and social media become increasingly important marketing tools, more companies will be turning to digital agencies to help them develop successful interactive marketing programs. The growth of social media and mobile marketing is also giving rise to companies that specialize in developing applications and campaigns for Facebook, Twitter, Instagram, Snapchat, and other social platforms. For example, there are a number of companies that help marketers build, monitor, manage, and measure their social media efforts across a variety of social and mobile platforms. These companies work with marketers to develop various ways to engage consumers, including various types of promotions as well as through user-generated photo, essay, and video contests. Exhibit 3–18 shows how LYFE Marketing, an Atlanta-based agency that works with companies in developing and implementing their social media programs, promotes its services. The number of digital agencies, as well as companies that specialize in the development of campaigns for social and mobile media, will continue to grow, as will their importance as marketers move more of their IMC efforts away from traditional media into the digital space.

COLLATERAL SERVICES

The final participants in the promotional process are those that provide various collateral services. They include marketing research companies, package design firms, consultants, photographers, graphic design companies, talent agencies, video production houses, and event marketing services companies. One of the more widely used collateral service organizations is the marketing research firm. Companies are increasingly turning to marketing research to help them understand their target audiences and to gather information that will be of value in designing and evaluating their advertising and promotions programs. Even companies with their own marketing research departments often hire outside research agencies to perform some services. Marketing research companies offer specialized services and can gather objective information that is valuable to the advertiser's promotional programs. They conduct *qualitative* research such as in-depth interviews and focus groups, as well as *quantitative* studies such as market surveys.

INTEGRATED MARKETING COMMUNICATIONS SERVICES

You have seen that marketers can choose from a variety of specialized organizations to assist them in planning, developing, and implementing an integrated marketing communications program. But companies must decide whether to use a different organization for each marketing communications function or consolidate them with a large advertising agency that offers all of these services under one roof. Many large agencies have broadened their IMC capabilities by developing internal expertise or by acquiring specialists in various fields. We have also seen how many companies are handling more of their IMC programs in house, not only to save money but also because of the need to have more control over their digital marketing.

Pros and Cons of Integrated Services

There has been an ongoing debate for years as to whether control of the IMC program should be maintained by the client or should be in the hands of the agency. It has been argued that the concept of integrated marketing is nothing new, particularly in smaller companies and communication agencies that have been coordinating a variety of promotional tools for years. And larger advertising agencies have been trying to gain more of their clients' promotional business for over 20 years. However, in the past, the various services were run as separate profit centers. Each was motivated to push its own expertise and pursue its own goals rather than develop truly integrated marketing programs.

Proponents of integrated marketing services contend that past problems are being solved and the various individuals in the agencies and their subsidiaries are learning to work together to deliver a consistent message to the client's customers. They argue that maintaining control of the entire IMC process achieves greater synergy among each of the communications program elements. They also note that it is more convenient for the client to coordinate all of its marketing efforts—media advertising, direct marketing, digital/social, events, sales promotions, and public relations—through one agency. An agency with integrated marketing capabilities can create a single image for the company or brand and address everyone with one voice.

But not every company wants to turn the entire IMC program over to one agency. Opponents say the providers become involved in political wrangling over budgets, do not communicate with each other as well and as often as they should, and do not achieve synergy. They also claim that agencies' efforts to control all aspects of the promotional program are nothing more than an attempt to hold on to business that might otherwise be lost to independent providers. They note that synergy and economies of scale, while nice in theory, have been difficult to achieve and competition and conflict among agency subsidiaries have been a major problem.[59]

Many companies use a variety of vendors for communication functions, choosing the specialist they believe is best suited for each promotional task, be it advertising, sales promotion, or public relations. While many ad agencies are working to master integration and compete against one another, they still must compete against firms that offer specialized services. As marketing consultant Jack Trout notes, "As long as there are a lot of specialized players, integrating an agency will be tricky. Specialists walk in the door and say 'this is all we do and we're good at it,' which is a hell of an argument. An agency that has all marketing operations in-house will never be perceived as the best in breed."[60]

The already complex client–agency relationship is becoming even more challenging as a result of several other factors, such reductions in marketing budgets and the accompanying desire of companies to reduce the cost of their IMC programs and the tremendous increase in the use of social media, mobile marketing, and other nontraditional forms of communication. A study by Forrester Research called "The Future of Agency Relationship" suggests that one of the biggest challenges facing marketers today is knowing who to turn to when they want to change their advertising and/or IMC strategies. The study notes that many of the major agencies are trying to bundle all of the traditional and nontraditional services together and position themselves as being able to offer all of them.[61] However, the more likely scenario is that marketers will have a number of agencies from different areas working on their business and it is important that they get them to work together. They also must decide who is going to be in charge of managing and coordinating the IMC program. Some companies, particularly those involved heavily in e-commerce or having major technology components to their business, are now opting to have digital agencies lead their IMC programs. For example, a number of companies including Travelocity, Intel, and Sheraton designated the Publicis Groupe's Razorfish as the lead agency on their accounts.[62]

Responsibility for IMC: Agency versus Client

Surveys of advertisers and agency executives have shown that both groups believe integrated marketing is important to their organizations' success and that it will be even more important in the future.[63] However, marketers and agency executives have very different opinions regarding who should be in charge of the integrated marketing communications process. Many advertisers prefer to set strategy for and coordinate their own IMC campaigns, but some agency executives see this as their domain.

While agency executives believe their shops are capable of handling the various elements an integrated campaign requires, many marketers, particularly larger firms, disagree. Marketing executives say the biggest obstacle to implementing IMC is the lack of people with the broad perspective and skills to make it work. Internal turf battles, agency egos, and fear of budget reductions are also cited as major barriers to successful integrated marketing campaigns.[64] A study by the Corporate Executive Board's Advertising and Marketing Roundtable surveyed the heads of advertising and marketing communication departments at global companies as well as agency executives regarding the use of multiple agency partners. The study found that "the traditional, static model of a single ad agency or a fixed roster of agencies working on a brand is being supplanted by an open-source model for some marketers. Under this model, marketers hire numerous disparate marketing partners—sometimes on a project basis—to leverage their special talents and expertise as needed.[65] The CEB report notes that clients will increasingly be relegating their lead agencies to be brand stewards and coordinators of a network of specialists in various IMC areas.

Many advertising agencies do not accept the premise that they must accept a new role as stewards and coordinators of specialists. These agencies still view themselves as strategic and executional partners and are adding more resources to offer their clients a full line of services. They are expanding their agencies' capabilities in digital/interactive, multimedia advertising, database management, direct marketing, public relations, and sales promotion. However, many marketers still want to set the strategy for their IMC campaigns and seek specialized expertise, more quality and creativity, and greater control and cost-efficiency by using multiple providers. Steven Center, the former chief marketing officer for Honda of America, takes a position that is probably shared by most top marketing executives. He notes that "Agencies are exposed to much more than us, and they have to bring in raw ideas, market reconnaissance, and intelligence. But they will not tell us how to organize our company to accomplish our marketing mission. That responsibility should always fall entirely with the owner of the brand."[66]

Preparing for the Future

As noted throughout the chapter, much has changed in regard to client–agency relationships, particularly over the past two decades. Traditional advertising agencies are facing competition from a variety of specialist companies, particularly in the areas of digital marketing and information technology, as well as the clients themselves who are bringing more of their IMC functions in-house. Agencies must be able to prove their value to clients and show how they are providing solutions to their marketing communications problems, not just services. Tim Williams, founder of Ignition Consulting Group, a leading advertising agency consulting company, has created a framework that outlines fundamental elements that agencies must work on in order to transform themselves and be prepared for the future. Williams refers to these elements as the Foundations of the 2020 agency and groups them into eight different

FIGURE 3–10

Foundations of the 2020 Agency

CHAPTER 3

Areas	Foundational Elements
Accountability	■ Responsibility for outcomes, not just outputs ■ Attention to success metrics vs. just cost of service ■ Measuring what matters: results for clients instead of agency time
Agility	■ Agile philosophy applied to work flow ■ Prototyping and minimum viable products ■ Interdisciplinary teams vs. departments
Collaboration	■ Culture that values collaboration over managing hours ■ Teams of givers, not just takers ■ Agency partners as peaceful competitors
Digital Fitness	■ Individuals with high digital IQ ■ Digital as competency across agency, not just a department ■ Deep understanding of data and personalization
Effectiveness	■ Provider of solutions, not just services ■ True project management vs. tracking of hours ■ Focus on effectiveness for clients, not just efficiency for agency
Expertise	■ Knowledge of specific markets or audiences ■ Best-in-class business model vs. full service ■ Centers of excellence and best practices
Innovation	■ Revenue streams from intellectual property, not just work for hire ■ Labs as independent business units ■ Marketing invention business, not just service business
Pricing	■ Pricing as a core competency versus costing ■ Aligning the economic incentives of both client and agency ■ Professional sellers negotiating with professional buyers

areas as shown in Figure 3–10. These elements do not involve simple modifications, such as adding additional services and capabilities, but rather call for fundamental changes in the way advertising agencies view their business model and serve their clients. Williams argues that agencies need to consider how to refocus and redefine their offerings to clients to make themselves indispensable, which will require them to carefully examine their service models and the how they operate their business.[67]

Summary

The development, execution, and administration of an advertising and promotions program involve the efforts of many individuals, both within the company and outside it. Participants in the integrated marketing communications process include the advertiser or client, ad agencies, media organizations, specialized marketing communications firms, and providers of collateral services.

Companies use three basic systems to organize internally for advertising and promotion. Centralized systems offer the advantages of facilitated communications, lower personnel requirements, continuity in staff, and more top-management involvement. Disadvantages include a lower involvement with overall marketing goals, longer response times, and difficulties in handling multiple product lines.

Decentralized systems offer the advantages of concentrated managerial attention, more rapid responses to problems, and increased flexibility, though they may be limited by ineffective decision making, internal conflicts, misallocation of funds, and a lack of authority. In-house agencies, while offering the advantages of cost savings, control, and increased coordination, have the disadvantage of less experience, objectivity, and flexibility. However, there has been an increase in the number of companies that are using in-house agencies to handle all, or at least part, of their IMC programs. The move toward greater use of in-house agencies is being driven by the increased use of digital marketing which requires companies to produce more IMC content and to do so in a timely manner.

Many firms use advertising agencies to help develop and execute their programs. These agencies may take on a variety of forms, including full-service agencies, creative boutiques, and media buying services. The first offers the client a full range of services (including creative, account, marketing, and financial and management services); the other two specialize in creative services and media buying, respectively. Agencies are compensated through commission systems, percentage charges, and fee- and cost-based systems. Recently, the emphasis on agency accountability has increased. Agencies are being evaluated on both financial and qualitative aspects, and some clients are using incentive-based compensation systems that tie agency compensation to performance measures such as sales and market share.

In addition to using ad agencies, marketers use the services of other marketing communication specialists, including direct-marketing agencies, sales promotion agencies, public relations firms, and digital/interactive agencies. A marketer must decide whether to use a different specialist for each promotional function or have all of its integrated marketing communications done by an advertising agency that offers all of these services under one roof.

Recent studies have found that most marketers believe it is their responsibility, not the ad agency's, to set strategy for and coordinate IMC campaigns. The lack of a broad perspective and specialized skills in nonadvertising areas are seen as major barriers to agencies' increased involvement in integrated marketing communications. Agencies must be able to prove their value to clients and show how they are providing solutions to their marketing communications problems. A framework was presented that outlines fundamental elements that agencies must work on in order to transform themselves and be prepared for the future.

Key Terms

clients 71
advertising agency 71
media organizations 72
specialized marketing communication services 72
collateral services 72
advertising manager 73
centralized system 73
decentralized system 74
brand manager 74
category management system 76
in-house agency 77

billings 79
superagencies 82
full-service agency 83
account executive 83
account planner 85
copywriter 86
departmental system 87
group system 87
creative boutique 88
media specialist companies 90
programmatic buying 90
commission system 91

negotiated commission 92
fixed-fee method 92
fee–commission combination 92
cost-plus system 93
incentive-based system 93
percentage charges 93
financial audit 96
qualitative audit 96
direct-marketing agency 101
sales promotion agency 102
public relations firm 102
digital/interactive agency 103

Discussion Questions

1. Discuss how disruptions being created by the digital revolution are impacting advertising agencies. What changes do advertising agencies need to make to respond to the impact of digital technology? (LO 3-3, 3-5)

2. What are the challenges facing traditional, full-service advertising agencies given the changes occurring in the area of integrated marketing communications? It has been argued that the traditional model of a full-service, lead agency is becoming obsolete. Do you agree or disagree with this position? (LO 3-3, 3-5, 3-6)

3. Who are the various participants in the integrated marketing communications process? Briefly discuss the roles and responsibilities of each and how they are changing given the changes occurring in the marketing landscape. (LO 3-1)

4. Discuss the various challenges faced by companies that use the brand management system when organizing for advertising and promotion. What are some of the things that marketers can do to address these problems and ensure that their brand managers are keeping abreast of external changes occurring in the market? (LO 3-2)

5. Discuss the pros and cons of using an in-house advertising agency. What are some of the reasons why companies might change from using an in-house agency and hire an outside agency? (LO 3-2)

6. Discuss how technology and the emerging role of digital and social media are impacting the role of brand managers. What types of skills are needed to be a successful brand manager today? What can companies do to train brand managers so they can keep up with the changes occurring in digital and social media? (LO 3-2)

7. IMC Perspective 3-1 discusses the outstanding creative work done by the Droga5 agency. Find an example of an award-winning campaign Droga5 has created for companies/brands such as Google, Under Armour, or Newcastle beer. Discuss why this campaign has been recognized for its creative excellence. (LO 3-3)

8. Discuss the challenges advertising agencies face in negotiating compensation structures with their clients when the procurement department becomes involved in the process. How might an agency respond to clients who demand to see their labor costs, overhead, and profit margins as part of the negotiation process? (LO 3-4)

9. Discuss the various criteria that might be used by an automotive marketer such as Ford or Honda in evaluating its advertising agencies versus a consumer packaged-goods marketer such as Procter & Gamble. Which of these criteria do you think would receive the most weight and why? (LO 3-4)

10. Discuss the role of specialized marketing communication organizations such as sales promotion, public relations, and digital agencies in the IMC process. Why are marketers likely to use these specialists rather than a full-service agency? (LO 3-3, 3-5)

11. Discuss the reasons why advertising agencies lose accounts. Find an example of a company that changed advertising agencies and identify the factors that led the company to switch to another agency. (LO 3-4)

12. Discuss the pros and cons for a marketer having one company handle all of its integrated marketing communications needs versus using specialized marketing communications firms to handle the various components of the program. (LO 3-5, 3-6)

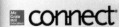

Digital users can access their personalized and adaptive SmartBook, Ad Forum Video Cases, and interactive exercises to review chapter concepts.

4

Perspectives on Consumer Behavior

Source: Mike Mozart, Flickr

LEARNING OBJECTIVES

LO1 Discuss why an understanding of consumer behavior is valuable in developing advertising and promotional programs.

LO2 Describe the steps in the consumer decision-making process.

LO3 Explain the influence on consumer behavior of psychological processes like perception and motivation.

LO4 Discuss behavioral learning theory and cognitive learning theory.

LO5 Explain the influence of external factors like culture and subculture influences.

LO6 Identify new ways to study consumer behavior.

IS SUCCESSFUL BRANDING JUST ABOUT EMOTIONS, COLOR, AND EMOJIS?

For years, marketers have been conducting research studies in an attempt to determine what makes a brand successful. Numerous articles and books have been written on the topic, and while they have provided very valuable insights, no one has come up with the "holy grail" of branding. Physiological research, attitude studies, along with sociology and cultural anthropology are just a few of the myriad approaches that have been explored in an attempt to gain insights. The one thing these studies have concluded is that there is no one thing that guarantees a brand will be successful.

But maybe it's not that hard after all! Is it possible that it's just about emotions, color, and emojis? Probably not, but it does appear that these factors certainly contribute to successful branding. Consider just a few of the following insights:

Emotions: A study conducted on befriending brands online by Dr. Tobias Langner, a marketing professor at the University of Wuppertal in Germany, and published in the journal *Psychology and Marketing,* concluded that "Some people feel more warmly to their favorite brands than they do toward their close friends." Langner and his research associates asked study participants to examine a series of photos including those of a close friend, a romantic partner, and a brand they claimed to love (including BMW and adidas) while they responded to a visual rating scale as well as a physiological measure. Respondents demonstrated a greater amount of love for their significant other than the brands. However, when it came to their friends, they reported more positive feelings and a greater physiological response toward the brands, leading the researchers to conclude that "the emotions we experience when we interact with our loved brands are as intensive as the emotions elicited by close friends."

In his exploration of the branding industry, Lucas Conley discusses *Obsessive Branding Disorder (OBD)* in relation to the high-end fashion industry. Conley claims that high-end fashions like Louis Vuitton have become so popular among Japanese women that some have admitted to eschewing motherhood in order to make the purchase of their beloved brand more attainable. He concludes that brands are replacing real-life networks of close friends, while sharing their values and never disagreeing with them. Emotional bonding with brands?

Color: Research on the impact of color in marketing has been like the weather—"everyone has to deal with it, but no one can do anything about it." In other words, while we all believe that color has an impact on the perceptions of brands, personal experiences hinder our ability to translated this impact into specific feelings. Recently, however, a number of studies have provided some important insights into how color impacts both branding and purchasing. These studies have concluded that (1) for some products, 90 percent of snap judgments made about products can be based on color alone; (2) color and brand "fit" (e.g., appropriateness) is important; (3) colors influence the perceived "personality" of the brand; and (4) consumers prefer recognizable brands, which makes color very important in creating a brand identity, among other viable conclusions.

Stanford professor Jennifer Aaker has spent years conducting studies on the relationship between color appropriateness and the product. Her studies on the dimensions of brand personality have led to the conclusion that there are five key dimensions to a brand's personality including sincerity, excitement, competence, sophistication, and ruggedness, and that colors *do* align with these specific traits (for example, brown with ruggedness, and red with excitement). While this research does not prescribe how to choose a color for a brand, it does clearly indicate that the feelings, mood, and image created by the color–brand interaction will have an impact on its persuasive capabilities.

Some additional studies on color have concluded that (1) gender impacts color preferences, (2) there is no single best color for impacting conversion rates on websites, and (3) the name of the color matters—fancy names are more liked (*mocha* was preferred to *brown*) and unusual and unique names can increase the intent to purchase. All of these studies come to the same conclusion—color will impact the perceptions of the brand.

Emojis: These studies, along with numerous others in consumer behavior add to our knowledge that a brand will be more successful if it has emotional value. Thus, as you might expect, companies are constantly trying to connect with consumers on an emotional level through advertising. The problem is that they only have a few seconds to do so. Could emojis be the answer? Companies are beginning to think so.

One such company is Emogi, the first to combine the use of pictograms with data science to create emotional ads. According to Travis Montague, founder and CEO of Emogi, including emojis in brand communications can deliver up to 10 times the average response rate and engagement up to six times while doubling the dwell rate. The belief is that advertising drives emotions, and emotions drive purchasing behavior. Emojis allow the advertiser to connect in the precious few seconds it has.

In 2016, Facebook added to its "like" button with five new "reaction" emojis. According to Mark Zuckerberg, the new emojis were added to provide Facebook users a better way to express their emotions quickly when responding to posts. To determine which emojis to use, Facebook hired University of California–Berkeley social psychology professor Dacher Keitner, who conducted research internationally to analyze the most frequently used stickers, emojis, and one-word comments. The result was Facebook's addition of the "love," "haha," "wow," "sad," and "angry" emoticons.

Some companies, like Coca-Cola, are already doing well at creating emotions. Coke has been "spreading smiles" for years in its quest to associate happiness with the brand. Coke has offered consumers a 10-step happiness guide, a happiness meter that analyzes mood-related words on Twitter, and more recently a "Choose Happiness" campaign that includes video, outdoor ads, bus wraps, and a #happiestselfie contest on social media.

Coke believes that linking the happy emotion to the brand can only help.

Competitor Pepsi has also jumped on the emotion bandwagon. The company's new "Say It with Pepsi" campaign has employed over 70 uniquely designed emojis to place on its cans and bottles in over 100 global markets. The "Pepsi-Mojis" are designed to deliver marketing messages "graphically, quickly and in a relatable way," according to a Pepsi spokesperson, and will constitute the centerpiece of the new campaign. The campaign will be supported by digital and traditional advertising and the emojis will be extended to PepsiMoji-inspired sunglasses. A soccer-themed campaign in Europe featuring soccer-inspired emojis includes soccer stars James Rodriguez of Real Madrid and Spanish goalkeeper great David de Gea of Manchester United. Additional strategies are already being developed.

It seems that Pepsi has been reading the research on emotions, brand personalities, and emojis and put them all together in one campaign.

Sources: E. J. Schultz and Jessica Wohl, "Pepsi Preps Global Emoji Can and Bottle Campaign," February 19, 2016, www.adage.com; Nathan Bomey, "Emojis to Grace Pepsi Products in Summer Campaign," February 19, 2016, www.usatoday; Chris Perez, "People Have Mixed Emojis over Facebook's New 'Likes,'" February 25, 2016, nypost.com; Tessa Wegert, "Emotion in Ads: Does Sentiment Sell?" July 30, 2015, www.clickz.com; "Does Your Wife Win Out over Your Favorite Brand?" July 30, 2015, www.ozy.com; "The Psychology of Color in Marketing and Branding," www.entrepreneur.com.

The introduction to this chapter demonstrates just some of the research that attempts to shed light on how consumers make purchase decisions and just how complicated this process can be. Consumer research is a major component in helping managers design marketing strategies. Marketers know that many factors may directly or indirectly influence consumers' decision making. What is important for them to know is how and why consumers' needs develop, what they are, and who is likely to use the product or service. Specifically, marketers will study consumer behaviors in an attempt to understand the many factors that lead to and impact purchase decisions. Often, in an attempt to gain insights, marketers will employ techniques borrowed from other disciplines. Research methods used in psychology, anthropology, sociology, and neuroscience are becoming more popular in businesses as managers attempt to explore consumers' purchasing motives. These motives along with consumers' attitudes, lifestyles, and decision-making processes need to be understood before effective marketing strategies can be formulated.

These are just a few of the aspects of consumer behavior that promotional planners must consider in developing integrated marketing communications programs. As you will see, consumer choice is influenced by a variety of factors.

It is beyond the scope of this text to examine consumer behavior in depth. However, promotional planners need a basic understanding of consumer decision making, factors that influence it, and how this knowledge can be used in developing promotional strategies and programs. We begin with an overview of consumer behavior.

AN OVERVIEW OF CONSUMER BEHAVIOR

A challenge faced by all marketers is how to influence the purchase behavior of consumers in favor of the product or service they offer. For companies like Visa, this means getting consumers to charge more purchases on their credit cards. For BMW, it means getting them to purchase or lease a car; for business-to-business marketers like UPS or FedEx, it means getting organizational buyers to purchase more of their products or use their services. While their ultimate goal is to influence consumers' purchase behavior, most marketers understand that the actual purchase is only part of an overall process.

Consumer behavior can be defined as the process and activities people engage in when searching for, selecting, purchasing, using, evaluating, and disposing of products and services to satisfy their needs and desires. For many products and services, purchase decisions are the result of a long, detailed process that may include an extensive information search, brand comparisons and evaluations, and other activities. Other purchase decisions are more incidental and may result from little more than seeing a product prominently displayed at a discount price in a store. Think of how many times you have made impulse purchases while in a store.

Marketers' success in influencing purchase behavior depends in large part on how well they understand consumer behavior. Marketers need to know the specific needs customers are attempting to satisfy and how they translate into purchase criteria. They need to understand how consumers gather information regarding various alternatives and use this information to select among competing brands, and how they make purchase decisions. Where do they prefer to buy a product? How are they influenced by marketing stimuli at the point of purchase? Marketers also need to

EXHIBIT 4–1

Telluride Ski Resort appeals to those who enjoy the skier lifestyle

Source: Telluride Ski & Golf Resort

understand how the consumer decision process and reasons for purchase vary among different types of customers. For example, purchase decisions may be influenced by the personality or lifestyle of the consumer. Notice how the ad shown in Exhibit 4–1 portrays excitement for those who enjoy the skier lifestyle.

The conceptual model in Figure 4–1 will be used as a framework for analyzing the consumer decision process. We will discuss what occurs at the various stages of this model and how advertising and promotion can be used to influence decision making. We will also examine the influence of various psychological concepts, such as motivation, perception, attitudes, and integration processes. Variations in the consumer decision-making process will be explored, as will perspectives regarding consumer learning and external influences on the consumer decision process. The chapter concludes with a consideration of alternative means of studying consumer behavior.

FIGURE 4–1

Basic Model of Consumer Decision Making

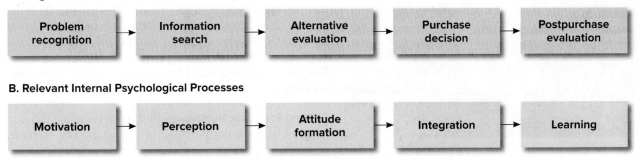

A. Stages in the Consumer Decision-Making Process

Problem recognition → Information search → Alternative evaluation → Purchase decision → Postpurchase evaluation

B. Relevant Internal Psychological Processes

Motivation → Perception → Attitude formation → Integration → Learning

THE CONSUMER DECISION-MAKING PROCESS

As shown in Figure 4–1, the consumer's purchase decision process is generally viewed as consisting of stages through which the buyer passes in purchasing a product or service. This model shows that decision making involves a number of internal psychological processes. Motivation, perception, attitude formation, integration, and learning are important to promotional planners, since they influence the general decision-making process of the consumer. We will examine each stage of the purchase decision model and discuss how the various subprocesses influence what occurs at this phase of the consumer behavior process. We will also discuss how promotional planners can influence this process.

Problem Recognition

Figure 4–1 shows that the first stage in the consumer decision-making process is **problem recognition**, which occurs when the consumer perceives a need and becomes motivated to solve the problem. The problem recognition stage initiates the subsequent decision processes.

Problem recognition is caused by a difference between the consumer's *ideal state* and *actual state*. A discrepancy exists between what the consumer wants the situation to be like and what the situation is really like. (Note that *problem* does not always imply a negative state. A goal exists for the consumer, and this goal may be the attainment of a more positive situation.)

Sources of Problem Recognition   The causes of problem recognition may be very simple or very complex and may result from changes in the consumer's current and/or desired state. These causes may be influenced by both internal and external factors.

Out of Stock   Problem recognition occurs when consumers use their existing supply of a product and must replenish their stock. The purchase decision is usually simple and routine and is often resolved by choosing a familiar brand or one to which the consumer feels loyal.

Dissatisfaction   Problem recognition is created by the consumer's dissatisfaction with the current state of affairs and/or the product or service being used. For example, a consumer may think her snow boots are no longer comfortable or stylish enough. Advertising may be used to help consumers recognize when they have a problem and/or need to make a purchase. The NicoDerm ad shown in Exhibit 4–2 offers assistance for those who may be dissatisfied with smoking and want to quit.

EXHIBIT 4–2

In this ad, NicoDerm offers to help those at the problem recognition stage

Source: GlaxoSmithKline

New Needs/Wants   Changes in consumers' lives often result in new needs and wants. For example, changes in one's financial situation, employment status, or lifestyle may create new needs and trigger problem recognition. As you will see, when you graduate from college and begin your professional career, your new job may necessitate a change in your wardrobe. (Good-bye blue jeans and T-shirts; hello suits and ties.) Having a baby may necessitate the purchase of a family-style car.

Not all product purchases are based on needs. Some products or services sought by consumers are not essential but are nonetheless desired. A **want** is a desire for something one does not have. Many products sold to consumers satisfy their wants rather than their basic needs.

Related Products/Purchases   Problem recognition can also be stimulated by the purchase of a product. For example,

EXHIBIT 4–3

Splat encourages consumers to be different by changing their hair color

© Developus

the purchase of a new iPhone may lead to the recognition of a need for accessories, such as a charger, ear phones, or a protective cover and apps. The purchase of an iPad may lead to buying a cover and screen cleaner. The purchase of a laptop may prompt the need for software programs, upgrades, a printer, and so on.

Marketer-Induced Problem Recognition Another source of problem recognition is marketers' actions that encourage consumers not to be content with their current state or situation. Ads for personal hygiene products such as mouthwash, deodorant, and foot sprays may be designed to create insecurities that consumers can resolve through the use of these products. Marketers change fashions and clothing designs and create perceptions among consumers that their wardrobes are out of style. Exhibit 4–3 shows how Splat encourages people to change their hair color.

Marketers also take advantage of consumers' tendency toward *novelty-seeking behavior*, which leads them to try different brands. Consumers often try new products or brands even when they are basically satisfied with their regular brand. Marketers encourage brand switching by introducing new brands into markets that are already saturated and by using advertising and sales promotion techniques such as free samples, introductory price offers, and coupons.

New Products Problem recognition can also occur when innovative products are introduced and brought to the attention of consumers. Marketers are constantly introducing new products and services and telling consumers about the types of problems they solve. For example, the smartphone has become much more than a telephone, as more and more apps are now available to do just about anything you can think of. Apple's applications (apps) store has over 1 million free and for-purchase apps for their smartphones and iPads (Exhibit 4–4). As more apps are added, these products will become appealing to more consumers.

Marketers' attempts to create problem recognition among consumers are not always successful. Consumers may not see a problem or need for the product the marketer is selling. Using the smartphone example just provided, for some, all of the potential provided by apps may be considered unnecessary—they just want to be able to send and receive phone calls, texts, and/or e-mails.

Examining Consumer Motivations

LO4-3

EXHIBIT 4–4

Apps for smartphones and iPads now number in the millions

© Maksym Yemelyanov/Alamy

Marketers recognize that while problem recognition is often a basic, simple process, the way a consumer perceives a problem and becomes motivated to solve it will influence the remainder of the decision process. For example, one consumer may perceive the need to purchase a new watch from a functional perspective and focus on reliable, low-priced alternatives. Another consumer may see the purchase of a watch as more of a fashion statement and focus on the design and image of various brands. To better understand the reasons underlying consumer purchases, marketers devote considerable attention to examining **motives**—that is, those factors that compel a consumer to take a particular action.

Hierarchy of Needs One of the most popular approaches to understanding consumer motivations is based on the classic theory of human motivation popularized many years ago by psychologist Abraham Maslow. His **hierarchy of needs** theory postulates five basic levels of human needs, arranged in a hierarchy based on their importance. As shown in Figure 4–2, the five needs are (1) *physiological*—the basic level of primary needs for things required to sustain life, such as food, shelter, clothing, and sex; (2) *safety*—the

FIGURE 4–2

Maslow's Hierarchy of
Needs

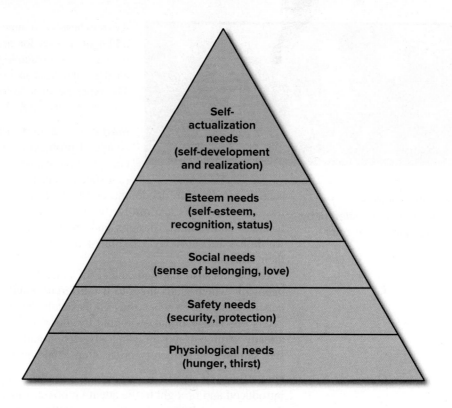

need for security and safety from physical harm; (3) *social/love and belonging*—
the desire to have satisfying relationships with others and feel a sense of love,
affection, belonging, and acceptance; (4) *esteem*—the need to feel a sense of
accomplishment and gain recognition, status, and respect from others; and
(5) *self-actualization*—the need for self-fulfillment and a desire to realize one's
own potential.

According to Maslow's theory, the lower-level physiological and safety
needs must be satisfied before the higher-order needs become meaningful. Once
these basic needs are satisfied, the individual moves on to attempting to satisfy higher-order needs such as self-esteem. In reality, it is unlikely that people
move through the needs hierarchy in a stairstep manner. Lower-level needs are
an ongoing source of motivation for consumer purchase behavior. However,
since basic physiological needs are met in most developed countries, marketers
often sell products that fill basic physiological needs by appealing to consumers'
higher-level needs.

While Maslow's needs hierarchy has flaws, it offers a framework for marketers to use in determining what needs they want their products and services to
be shown satisfying. Advertising campaigns can then be designed to show how
a brand can fulfill these needs. Marketers also recognize that different market
segments emphasize different need levels. For example, a young single person
may be attempting to satisfy social or self-esteem needs in purchasing a car,
while a family with children will focus more on safety needs. The Volvo ad in
Exhibit 4–5 focuses on security needs of consumers, while the Jaguar ad addresses
self-actualization.

Psychoanalytic Theory   A somewhat more controversial approach to the
study of consumer motives is the **psychoanalytic theory** pioneered by Sigmund
Freud. Although his work dealt with the structure and development of personality,
Freud also studied the underlying motivations for human behavior. Psychoanalytic
theory had a strong influence on the development of modern psychology and on

EXHIBIT 4–5

While Volvo uses an appeal to security needs by focusing on safety, why is the Jaguar ad an appeal to self-actualization?

© Volvo Cars of North America, LLC

Source: Jaguar Land Rover North America, LLC. All Rights Reserved

explanations of motivation and personality. It has also been applied to the study of consumer behavior by marketers interested in probing deeply rooted motives that may underlie purchase decisions.

Those who attempt to relate psychoanalytic theory to consumer behavior believe consumers' motivations for purchasing are often very complex and unclear to the casual observer—and to the consumers themselves. Many motives for purchase and/or consumption may be driven by deep motives one can determine only by probing the subconscious.

Among the first to conduct this type of research in marketing, Ernest Dichter and James Vicary were employed by a number of major corporations to use psychoanalytic techniques to determine consumers' purchase motivations. The work of these researchers and others who continue to use this approach assumed the title of **motivation research**.

Motivation Research in Marketing   Motivation researchers use a variety of methodologies to gain insight into the underlying causes of consumer behavior. Methods employed include in-depth interviews, projective techniques, association tests, and focus groups in which consumers are encouraged to bring out associations

FIGURE 4–3

Some of the Marketing Research Methods Used to Probe the Mind of the Consumer

In-depth interviews
Face-to-face situations in which an interviewer asks a consumer to talk freely in an unstructured interview using specific questions designed to obtain insights into his or her motives, ideas, or opinions.

Projective techniques
Efforts designed to gain insights into consumers' values, motives, attitudes, or needs that are difficult to express or identify by having them project these internal states upon some external object.

Association tests
A technique in which an individual is asked to respond with the first thing that comes to mind when he or she is presented with a stimulus; the stimulus may be a word, picture, ad, and so on.

Focus groups
A small number of people with similar backgrounds and/or interests who are brought together to discuss a particular product, idea, or issue.

related to products and brands (see Figure 4–3). As one might expect, such associations often lead to interesting insights as to why people purchase. For example:

- A man's purchase of a high-priced fur for his wife proves his potency.[1]
- Consumers prefer large cars because they believe such cars protect them from the "jungle" of everyday driving.[2]
- A man buys a convertible as a substitute mistress.
- Women like to bake cakes because they feel like they are giving birth to a baby.
- Women wear perfume to "attract a man" and "glorify their existence."
- Men like frankfurters better than women do because cooking them (frankfurters, not men!) makes women feel guilty. It's an admission of laziness.
- When people shower, their sins go down the drain with the soap as they rinse.[3]

As you can see from these examples, motivation research has led to some very interesting, albeit controversial, findings and to much skepticism from marketing managers. However, major corporations and advertising agencies continue to use motivation research to help them market their products.

Problems and Contributions of Psychoanalytic Theory and Motivation Research Psychoanalytic theory has been criticized as being too vague, unresponsive to the external environment, and too reliant on the early development of the individual. It also uses a small sample for drawing conclusions. Because of the emphasis on the unconscious, results are difficult if not impossible to verify, leading motivation research to be criticized for both the conclusions drawn and its lack of experimental validation. Since motivation research studies typically use so few participants, there is also concern that it really discovers the idiosyncrasies of a few individuals and its findings are not generalizable to the whole population.

Still, it is difficult to ignore the psychoanalytic approach in furthering our understanding of consumer behavior. Its insights can often be used as a basis for advertising messages aimed at buyers' deeply rooted feelings, hopes, aspirations, and fears. Such strategies are often more effective than rationally based appeals.

Some corporations and advertising agencies have used motivation research to gain further insights into how consumers think. Examples include the following:

- Chrysler had consumers sit on the floor, like children, and use scissors to cut words out of magazines to describe a car.[4]
- McCann Erickson asked women to draw and describe how they felt about roaches. The agency concluded that many women associated roaches with men who had abandoned them and that this was why women preferred roach killers that let them see the roaches die.
- Saatchi & Saatchi used psychological probes to conclude that Ronald McDonald created a more nurturing mood than did the Burger King (who was perceived as more aggressive and distant).
- Foote Cone & Belding gave consumers stacks of photographs of faces and asked them to associate the faces with the kinds of people who might use particular products.
- The advertising agency Marcus Thomas, LLC conducted in-depth one-on-one interviews and used projective techniques to determine underlying motivations for choosing one cardiovascular care facility over another.

While often criticized, motivation research has also contributed to the marketing discipline. The qualitative nature of the research is considered important in assessing how and why consumers buy. Focus groups and in-depth interviews are valuable methods for gaining insights into consumers' feelings, and projective techniques are often the only way to get around stereotypical or socially desirable responses. In addition, motivation research is the forerunner of psychographics (discussed in Chapter 2).

Finally, we know that buyers are sometimes motivated by symbolic as well as functional drives in their purchase decisions. Some believe that as competition for advertisers' dollars has increased, the amount and explicitness of sexual content on TV has increased as well as many programs and commercials now push the limits as to what is acceptable.[5] At the same time, some companies are using sex in advertising in less explicit ways. The Lexus ad in Exhibit 4–6 employed interactive technology and QR codes to send a sexy message. When the viewer scanned the QR codes placed in the ad, *Sports Illustrated* swimsuit models appeared in various scenes. While simply viewing the ad reveals no sexual content on the surface, when scanned, there is no doubt about the use of sex.

Information Search

The second stage in the consumer decision-making process is *information search*. Once consumers perceive a problem or need that can be satisfied by the purchase of a product or service, they begin to search for information needed to make a purchase decision. The initial search effort often consists of an attempt to scan information stored in memory to recall past experiences and/or knowledge regarding various purchase alternatives. This information retrieval is referred to as **internal search**. For many routine, repetitive purchases, previously acquired information that is stored in memory (such as past performance or outcomes from using a brand) is sufficient for comparing alternatives and making a choice.

If the internal search does not yield enough information, the consumer will seek additional information by engaging in **external search**. External sources of information include:

- *Internet sources*, such as organic and sponsored information available through companies' websites, consumer postings, and organizations like Angie's List, Yelp, and so on (Exhibit 4–7).
- *Personal sources*, such as friends, relatives, or co-workers.

- *Marketer-controlled (commercial) sources*, such as information from advertising, salespeople, or point-of-purchase displays and packaging.
- *Public sources*, including articles in magazines or newspapers and reports on TV and so on.
- *Personal experience*, such as actually handling, examining, or testing the product.

Determining how much and which sources of external information to use involves several factors, including the importance of the purchase decision, the effort needed to acquire information, the amount of past experience relevant, the degree of perceived risk associated with the purchase, and the time available. For example, the selection of a movie to see on a Friday night might entail simply talking to a friend or checking the movie guide with an app. A more complex purchase such as a new car might use a number of information sources—perhaps a review in *Kelley Blue Book* or *Consumer Reports* or on Carfax; discussion with family members and friends; an online search; or a test-drive of cars. At this point in the purchase decision, the information-providing aspects of advertising are extremely important.

Perception

Knowledge of how consumers acquire and use information from external sources is important to marketers in formulating communication strategies. Marketers are particularly interested in (1) how consumers sense external information, (2) how they select and attend to various sources of information, and (3) how this information is interpreted and given meaning. These processes are all part of **perception**, the process by which an individual receives, selects, organizes, and interprets information to create a meaningful picture of the world. Perception is an individual process; it depends on internal factors such as a person's beliefs, experiences, needs, moods, and expectations. The perceptual process is also influenced by the characteristics of a stimulus (such as its size, color, and intensity) and the context in which it is seen or heard (Exhibit 4–8).

Sensation Perception involves three distinct processes. **Sensation** is the immediate, direct response of the senses (taste, smell, sight, touch, and hearing) to a stimulus such as an ad, package, brand name, or point-of-purchase display. Perception uses these senses to create a representation of the stimulus. Marketers recognize that it is important to understand consumers' reactions to marketing stimuli. For example, the visual elements of an ad or package design must attract consumers' favorable attention, and stand out from competitors.

Marketers sometimes try to increase the level of sensory input so that their advertising messages will get noticed. For example, Bloomingdales's New York store sprayed Donna Karan's new perfume DKNY onto the sidewalks outside the store to introduce the perfume to consumers. Kraft Foods promoted the new DiGiorno Garlic Bread Pizza with scent strip cards in stores, while Avon uses scent strips for many products from perfumes to bubble baths in its catalogs. Scent strips have long been used in magazines, and a study of *Allure* magazine readers showed that 86 percent of readers said they had tried the scent strips, with 72 percent saying they purchased the product as a result.[6]

Selecting Information Sensory inputs are important but are only one part of the perceptual process. Other determinants of whether marketing stimuli will be attended to and how they will be interpreted include

Premium Carafe

ISN'T IT FUNNY HOW STEREO ADS ARE BORING UNTIL YOU WANT A STEREO?

We admit it. There are times when advertising isn't especially interesting.

For instance, stereo ads when you're not looking for a new stereo. Or insurance ads when you're not looking for a new insurance company. Or detergent ads when you're not looking for a new detergent.

But suppose your stereo breaks down. Or your insurance rates go up. Or your laundry comes out gray.

All of a sudden, stereo ads, insurance ads and detergent ads start looking a lot more interesting.

It's one of the basic truths of advertising. We try to be entertaining, but that's not really our job. Our job is to help you make the right choices

when you're in the market for any kind of product or service.

Of course, when you're not in the market, we recognize that advertising may seem beside the point. In that case, you're free to pretend it isn't there.

In fact, you're free to ignore advertising for as long as you choose.

Right up until your stereo breaks down.

ADVERTISING.
ANOTHER WORD FOR FREEDOM OF CHOICE.
American Association of Advertising Agencies

EXHIBIT 4–9

This ad reminds consumers of how advertising responds to their needs

© The American Association of Advertising Agencies

internal psychological factors such as the consumer's personality, needs, motives, expectations, and experiences. These psychological inputs explain why people focus attention on some things and ignore others. Two people may perceive the same stimuli in very different ways because they select, attend, and comprehend differently. An individual's perceptual processes usually focus on elements of the environment that are relevant to his or her needs and tune out irrelevant stimuli. Think about how much more attentive you are to advertising for smartphones, automobiles, or electronics when you are in the market for one of these products (a point that is made by the message from the American Association of Advertising Agencies in Exhibit 4–9).

Interpreting the Information Once a consumer selects and attends to a stimulus, the perceptual process focuses on organizing, categorizing, and interpreting the incoming information. This stage of the perceptual process is very individualized and is influenced by internal psychological factors. The interpretation and meaning an individual assigns to an incoming stimulus also depend in part on the nature of the stimulus. For example, many ads are objective, and their message is clear and straightforward. Other ads are more ambiguous, and their meaning is strongly influenced by the consumer's individual interpretation.

Selectivity occurs throughout the various stages of the consumer's perceptual process. Perception may be viewed as a filtering process in which internal and external factors influence what is received and how it is processed and interpreted. The sheer number and complexity of the marketing stimuli a person is exposed to in any given day require that this filtering occur. **Selective perception** may occur at the exposure, attention, comprehension, or retention stage of perception, as shown in Figure 4–4.

Selective Perception **Selective exposure** occurs as consumers choose whether or not to make themselves available to information. For example, a viewer of a television show may change channels or leave the room during commercial breaks.

Selective attention occurs when the consumer chooses to focus attention on certain stimuli while excluding others. One study of selective attention estimated that the typical consumer is exposed to nearly 1,500 ads per day yet perceives only 76 of these messages.[7] Other estimates range as high as 4,000 exposures per day, or as low as 362f.[8] While the numbers may vary, there is agreement that consumers screen out the majority of the ads. This means advertisers must make considerable effort to get their messages noticed. Advertisers often use the creative aspects of their ads to gain consumers' attention. For example, some advertisers set off their ads from others by showing their products in color against a black-and-white background. This creative tactic has been used in advertising for many products, among them Cherry 7UP, Nuprin, Pepto-Bismol, and Coca-Cola. Notice how the color red is used in the Coke ad to attract attention while also focusing on the brand identity in Exhibit 4–10. Coke almost seems to own this color, as the ad doesn't even mention the brand name.

FIGURE 4–4

The Selective Perception Process

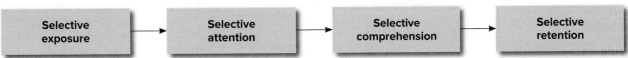

| Selective exposure | → | Selective attention | → | Selective comprehension | → | Selective retention |

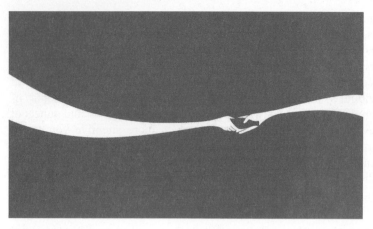

EXHIBIT 4–10

Color is used to attract attention to Coke products

Source: The Coca-Cola Company

Even if the consumer does notice the advertiser's message, there is no guarantee it will be interpreted in the intended manner. Consumers may engage in **selective comprehension**, interpreting information on the basis of their own attitudes, beliefs, motives, and experiences. They often interpret information in a manner that supports their own position. For example, an ad that disparages a consumer's favorite brand may be seen as biased or untruthful, and its claims may not be accepted.

The final screening process shown in Figure 4–4 is **selective retention**, which means consumers do not remember all the information they see, hear, or read even after attending to and comprehending it. Advertisers attempt to make sure information will be retained in the consumer's memory so that it will be available when it is time to make a purchase. **Mnemonics** such as symbols, rhymes, associations, and images that assist in the learning and memory process are helpful. Many advertisers use telephone numbers that spell out the company name and are easy to remember (for example, 1-800-GOFEDEX).

Subliminal Perception   Advertisers know consumers use selective perception to filter out irrelevant or unwanted advertising messages, so they employ various creative tactics to get their messages noticed. One controversial tactic advertisers have been accused of using is appealing to consumers' subconscious. **Subliminal perception** refers to the ability to perceive a stimulus that is below the level of conscious awareness. Psychologists generally agree it is possible to perceive things without being consciously aware of them.

As you might imagine, the possibility of using hidden persuaders such as subliminal audio messages or visual cues to influence consumers might be intriguing to advertisers but would not be welcomed by consumers. The idea of marketers influencing consumers at a subconscious level has strong ethical implications. IMC Perspective 4–1 discusses researchers' mixed opinions as to whether motivation research and subliminal advertising are likely to be effective in influencing consumer behavior.

Alternative Evaluation

After acquiring information during the information search stage of the decision process, the consumer moves to alternative evaluation. In this stage, the consumer compares the various brands or products and services he or she has identified as being capable of solving the consumption problem and satisfying the needs or motives that initiated the decision process. The various brands identified as purchase options to be considered during the alternative evaluation process are referred to as the consumer's *evoked set*.

The Evoked Set   The evoked set is generally only a subset of all the brands of which the consumer is aware. The consumer reduces the number of brands to be reviewed during the alternative evaluation stage to a manageable level. The exact size of the evoked set (sometimes referred to as the consideration set) varies from one consumer to another and depends on such factors as the importance of the purchase and the amount of time and energy the consumer wants to spend comparing alternatives.

IMC Perspective 4–1 > > >

Subliminal Advertising— Maybe It Does Work After All!

It has been more than half a century since Vance Packard's famous book *The Hidden Persuaders* shocked the world. In his book, Packard accused advertisers of using research techniques like "depth interviews" and "motivation research" to develop messages that appealed to consumers' subconscious. These appeals led consumers to be persuaded to make purchases without consciously being aware why they made their choices. At about the same time, James Vicary, a motivational researcher, introduced the concept of subliminal advertising, reporting that he had increased the sales of popcorn and Coke by subliminally flashing the messages "eat popcorn" and "drink Coca-Cola" across the screen. (2012 marked the 50th anniversary of Vicary's confession that his research study was a hoax.) Wilson Bryant Key further fueled the fires with his books claiming that subliminal advertising was, indeed, manipulating consumer behaviors.

© Deposit Photos/Glow Images RF

A rash of research studies, articles, and books designed to explore motivation research and subliminal advertising soon followed in an attempt to determine the veracity of these techniques. In a series of extensive reviews on the topic (1982, 1988), Timothy Moore concluded that there was no evidence to support the fact that subliminal messages can affect consumers' motivations, perceptions, or attitudes. For a long period of time subliminal advertising, motivation research, and the application of psychoanalytic theory to consumer behaviors seemed to go away, with members of society and academia apparently losing interest. But while the studies went away, they never really disappeared.

In the 1990s a number of studies surfaced arguing that subliminal advertising could work. Then in the 2000 Bush–Gore presidential campaign, the Republicans were accused of subliminally implanting the word *rats* into ads to attach the meaning to Al Gore. They ran the ad about 4,000 times before it was discovered and pulled due to protests. Eight years later political scientist Joel Weinberger, inspired by the controversy surrounding the ad, ran an experiment in which he found that flashing the word *RAT* in a TV commercial could increase the negative evaluations of a politician. Once again, motivation research was back in the spotlight.

More recently, scientists at the University College of London in the UK claimed that they proved conclusively that people can perceive the emotional value of subliminal messages. Another researcher also claimed that his series of research studies proved that music, country of origin, and even product weight have subliminal influences on consumers. Still another showed that in an experiment when viewers had the words *Lipton Iced Tea* flashed subliminally before them, when offered a drink after the experiment, 85 percent of them selected that drink out of a choice of three drinks, while only 20 percent did so without the exposure. Studies reported in the *Journal of Experimental Social Psychology* and the *Journal of Consumer Psychology* have provided evidence that under certain conditions—if the ad is goal relevant (for example, priming a soft-drink brand when the receiver is thirsty) and the consumer has not been warned of the subliminal message—subliminal ads may have an impact.

This time, however, no one seems to be getting alarmed, though Leonard Mlodinow—a best-selling author who teaches at California Institute of Technology—thinks they ought to be. Mlodinow believes that one of the more effective ways of using subliminal messages may be through product placements. He cites examples of product placements by Dr Pepper in the movie *Spider Man* and Pepsi in the movie *Home Alone* to support his position that subliminal placements work and are being used. After 50 years, consumers and researchers don't seem to be concerned that they need to worry about subliminal advertising. But they certainly haven't lost interest.

Sources: Thjs Verwijmeren, Stefan F. Bernitter, Wolfgang Stroebe, and Daniel H. J. Wgboldus, "Warning: You Are Being Primed! The Effect of a Warning on the Impact of Subliminal Ads," *Journal of Experimental Social Psychology* 40, no. 6 (November 2013), pp. 1124–29; Thjs Verwijmeren, Stefan F. Bernitter, Wolfgang Stroebe, and Daniel H. J. Wgboldus, "The Workings and Limits of Subliminal Advertising: The Role of Habits," *Journal of Consumer Psychology* 21, no. 2 (April 2011), pp 206–13; Johan C. Karremans and Martin Lindstrom, "How Subliminal Advertising Works," January 4, 2009, www.parade.com; "Hypnosis Reveals Ad Effects," *Adweek Asia*, January 29, 1999, p. 4; "Breaking French Connection," *Advertising Age*, March 22, 1999, p. 52; Kathryn Theus, "Subliminal Advertising and the Psychology of Processing Unconscious Stimuli: A Review of Research," *Psychology & Marketing* 11, no. 3 (1994), pp. 271–90; Timothy Moore, "Subliminal Advertising: What You See Is What You Get," *Journal of Marketing* 46, no. 2 (Spring 1982), pp. 38–47; Timothy Moore, "The Case against Subliminal Manipulation," *Psychology and Marketing* 5, no. 4 (Winter 1988), pp. 297–316; Kalpana Srinivasan, "FCC Ends Probe on Republican Ad," March 12, 2001, www.individual.com; George E. Condon Jr. and Toby Eckert, "Flap over 'RATS' Latest to Plague Bush's Drive," *San Diego Tribune*, September 13, 2000, p. A1; Richard Alleyne, "Subliminal Advertising Really Does Work, Claim Scientists," September 2009, www.telegraph.co.uk.

Chapter 4 PERSPECTIVES ON CONSUMER BEHAVIOR   123

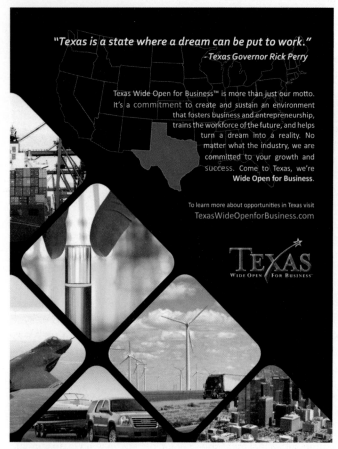

EXHIBIT 4–11

Texas wants to be in the evoked set of business locations

Source: Texas Economic Development and Tourism Division

The goal of most advertising and promotional strategies is to increase the likelihood that a brand will be included in the consumer's evoked set and considered during alternative evaluation. Marketers use advertising to create *top-of-mind awareness* among consumers so that their brands are part of the evoked set of their target audiences. Popular brands with large advertising budgets use *reminder advertising* to maintain high awareness levels and increase the likelihood they will be considered by consumers in the market for the product. Marketers of new brands or those with a low market share need to gain awareness among consumers and break into their evoked sets. The ad promoting Texas as a better place to live and do business (Exhibit 4–11) shows this strategy being used in a different context from products and brands. The ad presents the many benefits of Texas and encourages prospective businesses to consider it in their evoked set of places to locate or relocate.

Advertising is a valuable promotional tool for creating and maintaining brand awareness and making sure a brand is included in the evoked set. However, marketers also work to promote their brands in the actual environment where purchase decisions are made. Point-of-purchase materials and promotional techniques such as in-store sampling, end-aisle displays, and shelf tags touting special prices encourage consumers to consider brands that may not have initially been in their evoked set.

Evaluative Criteria and Consequences   Once consumers have identified an evoked set and have a list of alternatives, they must evaluate the various brands. This involves comparing the choice alternatives on specific criteria important to the consumer. **Evaluative criteria** are the dimensions or attributes of a product or service that are used to compare different alternatives. Evaluative criteria can be objective or subjective. For example, in buying an automobile, consumers use objective attributes such as price, warranty, and fuel economy as well as subjective factors such as image, styling, and performance.

Evaluative criteria are usually viewed as product or service attributes. Many marketers view their products or services as *bundles of attributes*, but consumers tend to think about products or services in terms of their *consequences* or *outcomes* instead. They distinguish between two broad types of consequences. **Functional consequences** are concrete outcomes of product or service usage that are tangible and directly experienced by consumers. The taste of a soft drink or a potato chip, the acceleration of a car, and the speed of the Internet service provider are examples of functional consequences. **Psychosocial consequences** are abstract outcomes that are more intangible, subjective, and personal, such as how a product makes you feel or how you think others will view you for purchasing or using it.

Product/service attributes and the consequences or outcomes consumers think they will experience from a particular brand are very important, for they are often the basis on which consumers form attitudes and purchase intentions and decide among various choice alternatives. Two subprocesses are very important during the alternative evaluation stage: (1) the process by which consumer attitudes are created, reinforced, and changed; and (2) the decision rules or integration strategies consumers use to compare brands and make purchase decisions. We will examine each of these processes in more detail.

Attitudes

Attitudes are learned predispositions to respond to an object and are some of the most heavily studied concepts in consumer behavior.[9] More recent perspectives view an attitude as a summary construct that represents an individual's overall feelings toward or evaluation of an object.[10] Consumers hold attitudes toward a variety of objects that are important to marketers, including individuals (celebrity endorsers such as Novak Djokovic or Danica Patrick), brands (Cheerios, Special K), companies (AT&T and Bank of America), product categories (beef, pork, tuna), retail stores (Walmart, Target), or even advertisements (Nike).

Attitudes are important to marketers because they theoretically summarize a consumer's evaluation of an object (or brand or company) and represent positive or negative feelings and behavioral tendencies. Marketers' keen interest in attitudes is based on the assumption that they are related to consumers' purchase behavior. But attitudes are very important to marketers. Advertising and promotion are used to create favorable attitudes toward new products/services or brands, reinforce existing favorable attitudes, and/or change negative attitudes. An approach to studying and measuring attitudes that is particularly relevant to advertising is multiattribute attitude models.

Multiattribute Attitude Models Consumer researchers and marketing practitioners have been using multiattribute attitude models to study consumer attitudes for two decades. A **multiattribute attitude model** views an attitude object, such as a product or brand, as possessing a number of attributes that provide the basis on which consumers form their attitudes. According to this model, consumers have beliefs about specific brand attributes and attach different levels of importance to these attributes. Using this approach, an attitude toward a particular brand can be represented as

$$A_B = \sum_{i=1}^{n} B_i \times E_i$$

where A_B = attitude toward a brand
B_i = beliefs about the brand's performance on attribute i
E_i = importance attached to attribute i
n = number of attributes considered

For example, a consumer may have beliefs (B_i) about various brands of toothpaste on certain attributes. One brand may be perceived as having fluoride and thus preventing cavities, tasting good, and helping control tartar buildup. Another brand may not be perceived as having these attributes, but consumers may believe it performs well on other attributes such as freshening breath and whitening teeth.

To predict attitudes, one must know how much importance consumers attach to each of these attributes (E_i). For example, parents purchasing toothpaste for their children may prefer a brand that performs well on cavity prevention, a preference that leads to a more favorable attitude toward the first brand. Teenagers and young adults may prefer a brand that freshens their breath and makes their teeth white and thus prefer the second brand.

Consumers may hold a number of different beliefs about brands in any product or service category. However, not all of these beliefs are activated in forming an attitude. Beliefs concerning specific attributes or consequences that are activated and form the basis of an attitude are referred to as **salient beliefs**. Marketers should identify and understand these salient beliefs and recognize that the saliency of beliefs varies among different market segments, over time, and across different consumption situations.

Attitude Change Strategies   Multiattribute models help marketers understand and diagnose the underlying basis of consumers' attitudes. By understanding the beliefs that underlie consumers' evaluations of a brand and the importance of various attributes or consequences, the marketer is better able to develop communication strategies for creating, changing, or reinforcing brand attitudes. The multiattribute model provides insight into several ways marketers can influence consumer attitudes, including:

- Increasing or changing the strength or belief rating of a brand on an important attribute (Colgate Optic White toothpaste has the best whitening power).
- Changing consumers' perceptions of the importance or value of an attribute (Michelin tires provide higher gas mileage and safety).
- Adding a new attribute to the attitude formation process (the product is environmentally friendly [Clorox Green]).
- Changing perceptions of belief ratings for a competing brand (GM shows its cars can compete with anyone's).

The first strategy is commonly used by advertisers. They identify an attribute or consequence that is important and remind consumers how well their brand performs on this attribute. In situations where consumers do not perceive the marketer's brand as possessing an important attribute or the belief strength is low, advertising strategies may be targeted at changing the belief rating. Even when belief strength is high, advertising may be used to increase the rating of a brand on an important attribute. BMW's "The Ultimate Driving Machine" campaign is a good example of a strategy designed to create a belief and reinforce it through advertising.

Marketers often attempt to influence consumer attitudes by changing the relative importance of a particular attribute. This second strategy involves getting consumers to attach more importance to the attribute in forming their attitude toward the brand. Marketers using this strategy want to increase the importance an attribute has to solve a problem (Exhibit 4–12).

The third strategy for influencing consumer attitudes is to add or emphasize a new attribute that consumers can use in evaluating a brand. Marketers often do this by improving their products or focusing on additional benefits or consequences associated with using the brand. For example, Tom's Shoes donates one pair of shoes for each pair sold to an impoverished person. The company does the same for each pair of eyeglasses sold.

A final strategy marketers use is to change consumer beliefs about the attributes of competing brands or product categories. This strategy has become much more common with the increase in comparative advertising, where marketers compare their brands to competitors' on specific product attributes.

Integration Processes and Decision Rules

Another important aspect of the alternative evaluation stage is the way consumers combine information about the characteristics of brands to arrive at a purchase decision. **Integration processes** are the way product knowledge, meanings, and beliefs are combined to evaluate two or more alternatives.[11] Analysis of the integration process focuses on the different types of *decision rules* or strategies consumers use to decide among purchase alternatives.

Consumers often make purchase selections by using formal integration strategies or decision rules that require examination

EXHIBIT 4–12

This Michelin ad stresses advantages over competitors' ads. What positioning strategy is being employed?

Source: Michelin North America, Inc.

EXHIBIT 4–13

This ad shows that market leader Levi's can use its strong brand image to appeal to consumer affect

Source: Levi Strauss & Co.

and comparison of alternatives on specific attributes. This process involves a very deliberate evaluation of the alternatives, attribute by attribute. When consumers apply such formal decision rules, marketers need to know which attributes are being considered to provide the information the consumers require.

Sometimes consumers make their purchase decisions using more simplified decision rules known as **heuristics**. For familiar products that are purchased frequently, consumers may use price-based heuristics (buy the least expensive brand) or promotion-based heuristics (choose the brand for which I can get a price reduction through a coupon, rebate, or special deal).

One type of heuristic is the **affect referral decision rule**, in which consumers make a selection on the basis of an overall impression or summary evaluation of the various alternatives under consideration. This decision rule suggests that consumers have affective impressions of brands stored in memory that can be accessed at the time of purchase.

Marketers selling familiar and popular brands may appeal to an affect referral rule by stressing overall affective feelings or impressions about their products. Market leaders, whose products enjoy strong overall brand images, often use ads that promote the brand by appealing to affect. Allstate's "You're in Good Hands," Gillette's "The Best a Man Can Get," and Nationwide's "Nationwide is on your side" are all examples of this strategy (Exhibit 4–13).

Purchase Decision

At some point in the buying process, the consumer must stop searching for and evaluating information about alternative brands in the evoked set and make a *purchase decision.* As an outcome of the alternative evaluation stage, the consumer may develop a **purchase intention** or predisposition to buy a certain brand. Purchase intentions are generally based on a matching of purchase motives with attributes or characteristics of brands under consideration. Their formation involves many of the personal subprocesses discussed in this chapter, including motivation, perception, attitude formation, and integration.

A purchase decision is not the same as an actual purchase. Once a consumer chooses which brand to buy, he or she must still implement the decision and make the actual purchase. Additional decisions may be needed, such as when to buy, where to buy, and how much money to spend. Often, there is a time delay between the formation of a purchase intention or decision and the actual purchase, particularly for highly involved and complex purchases such as automobiles, personal computers, and consumer durables.

For nondurable products, which include many low-involvement items such as consumer packaged goods, the time between the decision and the actual purchase may be short. Before leaving home, the consumer may make a shopping list that includes specific brand names because they have developed **brand loyalty**—a preference for a particular brand that results in its repeated purchase; of course, brand loyalty is not limited to nondurables. Consumers develop loyalties to many types of products and services. Marketers strive to develop and maintain brand loyalty among consumers. They use reminder advertising to keep their brand names in front of consumers, maintain prominent shelf positions and displays in stores, and run periodic promotions to deter consumers from switching brands.

Gaining and maintaining consumers' brand loyalty is not easy. Bank of America saw its loyalty go from number 1 to the bottom of the bank list in just one year. Competitors use many techniques to encourage consumers to try their brands, among them new product introductions and free samples. Figure 4–5 shows some of the brands that have achieved this goal. Marketers must continually battle to maintain their loyal consumers while replacing those who switch brands.

FIGURE 4–5
Brands That Have the Most Brand Loyalty

Category	Winner[a]
Airlines	JetBlue
Athletic footwear	Nike/New Balance
Automobiles	Ford/Hyundai
Bank	Wells Fargo
Car rental	Avis
Coffee	Dunkin' Donuts/Starbucks
Computers (laptop)	Apple
Credit cards	Discover
E-reader	Kindle
Evening news show	CBS
Flat-screen TV	Samsung
Hotels (luxury)	Ritz-Carlton
Insurance	Progressive
Online travel site	TripAdvisor
Soft drinks (reg/diet)	Pepsi/Diet Pepsi; Coke/Diet Coke
Toothpaste	Colgate
Vodka	Svedka
Wireless phone service	AT&T

[a]Brands listed have highest loyalty ranking in Brand Keys 2016 Customer Loyalty Engagement Index.
Source: www.brandkeys.com/awards, *2016.*

As seen, purchase decisions for nondurable, convenience items sometimes take place in the store, almost simultaneous with the purchase. Marketers must ensure that consumers have top-of-mind awareness of their brands so that they are quickly recognized and considered. Packaging, shelf displays, point-of-purchase materials, and promotional tools such as on-package coupons or premium offers can influence decisions made through constructive processes at the time of purchase.

Postpurchase Evaluation

The consumer decision process does not end with the purchase. After using the product or service, the consumer compares the level of performance with expectations and is either satisfied or dissatisfied. *Satisfaction* occurs when the consumer's expectations are either met or exceeded; *dissatisfaction* results when performance is below expectations. The postpurchase evaluation process is important because the feedback acquired from actual use of a product will influence the likelihood of future purchases. Positive performance means the brand is likely to be retained in the evoked set and increases the likelihood it will be purchased again. Unfavorable outcomes may lead the consumer to form negative attitudes toward the brand, lessening the likelihood it will be purchased again or even eliminating it from the evoked set.

EXHIBIT 4–14

Ally Bank attempts to capitalize on consumers' dissatisfaction with banks

© Ally Bank

Another possible outcome of a purchase is **cognitive dissonance**, a feeling of psychological tension or postpurchase doubt that a consumer experiences after making a difficult purchase choice. Dissonance is more likely to occur in important decisions where the consumer must choose among close alternatives (especially if the unchosen alternative has unique or desirable features that the selected alternative does not have).

Consumers experiencing cognitive dissonance may use a number of strategies to attempt to reduce it. They may seek out reassurance and opinions from others to confirm the wisdom of their purchase decision, lower their attitudes or opinions of the unchosen alternative, deny or distort any information that does not support the choice they made, or look for information that does support their choice. An important source of supportive information is advertising as consumers tend to be more attentive to advertising for the brand they have chosen.[12] Thus, it may be important for companies to advertise to reinforce consumer decisions to purchase their brands.

Marketers have come to realize that postpurchase communication is also important. Some companies send follow-up letters and brochures to reassure buyers and reinforce the wisdom of their decision. Many companies have set up toll-free numbers or e-mail addresses for consumers to call if they need information or have a question or complaint regarding a product. Some marketers also offer liberalized return and refund policies and extended warranties and guarantees to ensure customer satisfaction. Some have used customers' postpurchase dissatisfaction as an opportunity for gaining new business, as is reflected in Exhibit 4–14.

Variations in Consumer Decision Making

The preceding pages describe a general model of consumer decision making. But consumers do not always engage in all five steps of the purchase decision process or proceed in the sequence presented. They may minimize or even skip one or more stages if they have previous experience in purchasing the product or service or if the decision is of low personal, social, or economic significance. To develop effective promotional strategies and programs, marketers need some understanding of the problem-solving processes their target consumers use to make purchase decisions.

Many of the purchase decisions we make as consumers are based on a habitual or routine choice process. For many low-priced, frequently purchased products, the decision process consists of little more than recognizing the problem, engaging in a quick internal search, and making the purchase. The consumer spends little or no effort engaging in external search or alternative evaluation.

Marketers of products characterized by a routine response purchase process need to get and/or keep their brands in the consumer's evoked set and avoid anything that may result in their removal from consideration. Established brands that have strong market share position are likely to be in the evoked set of most consumers. Marketers of these brands want consumers to follow a routine choice process and continue to purchase their products. This means maintaining high levels of brand awareness through reminder advertising, periodic promotions, and prominent shelf positions in retail stores.

Marketers of new brands or those with a low market share face a different challenge. They must find ways to disrupt consumers' routine choice process and get them to consider different alternatives. High levels of advertising may be used to encourage trial or brand switching, along with sales promotion efforts in the form of free samples, special price offers, high-value coupons, and the like.

A more complicated decision-making process may occur when consumers have limited experience in purchasing a particular product or service and little or no knowledge of the brands available and/or the criteria to use in making a purchase decision. They may have to learn what attributes or criteria should be used in making a purchase decision and how the various alternatives perform on these dimensions. For products or services characterized by problem solving, whether limited or extensive, marketers should make information available that will help consumers decide. Advertising that provides consumers with detailed information about a brand and how it can satisfy their purchase motives and goals is important. Distribution channels should have knowledgeable salespeople available to explain the features and benefits of the company's product or service and why it is superior to competing products.

The Ameritrade ad in Exhibit 4–15 is a good example of how advertising can appeal to consumers who may be engaging in extended problem solving when considering financial planning. Notice how the ad communicates with consumers who may be concerned about achieving their dreams. The ad helps the consumer by offering expert advice and planning a variety of options.

THE CONSUMER LEARNING PROCESS

The discussion of the decision process shows that the way consumers make a purchase varies depending on a number of factors, including the nature of the product or service, the amount of experience they have with the product, and the importance of the purchase. One factor in the level of problem solving to be employed is the consumer's *involvement* with the product or brand. Chapter 5 examines the meaning of involvement, the difference between low- and high-involvement decision making, and the implications of involvement for developing advertising and promotional strategies.

Our examination of consumer behavior thus far has looked at the decision-making process from a *cognitive orientation*. The five-stage decision process model views the consumer as a problem solver and information processor who engages in a variety of mental processes to evaluate various alternatives and determine the degree to which they might satisfy needs or purchase motives. There are, however, other perspectives regarding how consumers acquire the knowledge and experience they use in making purchase decisions. To understand these perspectives, we examine various approaches to learning and their implications for advertising and promotion.

Consumer learning has been defined as "the process by which individuals acquire the purchase and consumption knowledge and experience they apply to future related behavior."[13] Two basic approaches to learning are the behavioral approach and cognitive learning theory.

Behavioral Learning Theory

Behavioral learning theories emphasize the role of external, environmental stimuli in causing behavior; they minimize the significance of internal psychological processes. Behavioral learning theories are based on the *stimulus–response orientation (S–R)*, the premise that learning occurs as the result of responses to external stimuli in the environment. Behavioral learning theorists believe learning occurs through the connection between a stimulus and a response. We will examine the basic principles of two behavioral learning theory approaches: classical conditioning and operant conditioning.

Classical Conditioning   **Classical conditioning** assumes that learning is an *associative process* with an already existing relationship between a stimulus and a response. Probably the best-known example of this type of learning comes from the studies done with animals by the Russian

FIGURE 4–6

The Classical Conditioning Process

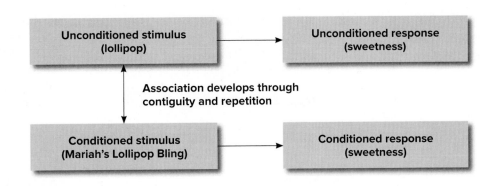

```
┌─────────────────────────┐                    ┌─────────────────────────┐
│ Unconditioned stimulus  │ ─────────────────▶ │ Unconditioned response  │
│ (lollipop)              │                    │ (sweetness)             │
└─────────────────────────┘                    └─────────────────────────┘
           ▲
           │        Association develops through
           │           contiguity and repetition
           ▼
┌─────────────────────────┐                    ┌─────────────────────────┐
│ Conditioned stimulus    │ ─────────────────▶ │ Conditioned response    │
│ (Mariah's Lollipop Bling)│                   │ (sweetness)             │
└─────────────────────────┘                    └─────────────────────────┘
```

EXHIBIT 4–16

Mariah Carey's new perfume associates its product with the looks and sweetness of lollipops

Source: Mariah Carey Beauty and EA Fragrances Co

psychologist Pavlov. Pavlov noticed that at feeding times, his dogs would salivate at the sight of food. The connection between food and salivation is not taught; it is an innate reflex reaction. Because this relationship exists before the conditioning process, the food is referred to as an *unconditioned stimulus* and salivation is an *unconditioned response*. To see if salivation could be conditioned to occur in response to another neutral stimulus, Pavlov paired the ringing of a bell with the presentation of the food. After a number of trials, the dogs learned to salivate at the sound of the bell alone. Thus, the bell became a **conditioned stimulus** that elicited a **conditioned response** resembling the original unconditioned reaction.

Two factors are important for learning to occur through the associative process. The first is contiguity, which means the unconditioned stimulus and conditioned stimulus must be close in time and space. In Pavlov's experiment, the dog learns to associate the ringing of the bell with food because of the contiguous presentation of the two stimuli. The other important principle is *repetition*, or the frequency of the association. The more often the unconditioned and conditioned stimuli occur together, the stronger the association between them will be.

Applying Classical Conditioning Learning through classical conditioning plays an important role in marketing. Buyers can be conditioned to form favorable impressions and images of various brands through the associative process. Advertisers strive to associate their products and services with perceptions, images, and emotions known to evoke positive reactions from consumers. Many products are promoted through image advertising, in which the brand is shown with an unconditioned stimulus that elicits pleasant feelings. When the brand is presented simultaneously with this unconditioned stimulus, the brand itself becomes a conditioned stimulus that elicits the same favorable response.

Figure 4–6 provides a diagram of this process, and the ad for Lollipop Splash in Exhibit 4–16 shows an application of this strategy. Notice how this ad associates the product with the look and sweetness of a lollipop. The brand's positioning plays off this association.

Classical conditioning can also associate a product or service with a favorable emotional state. A study by Gerald Gorn used this approach to examine how background music in ads influences product choice.[14] He found that subjects were more likely

FIGURE 4–7

Instrumental Conditioning in Marketing

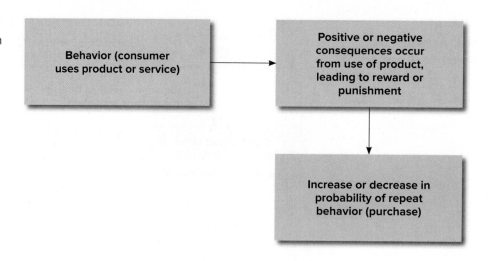

to choose a product when it was presented against a background of music they liked rather than music they disliked. These results suggest the emotions generated by a commercial are important because they may become associated with the advertised product through classical conditioning. Other studies have shown that music that was congruent with the message enhanced both ad recall and recognition[15] and that music can be used effectively as a mnemonic device to enhance the recall of advertising slogans. Advertisers often attempt to pair a neutral product or service stimulus with an event or situation that arouses positive feelings, such as humor, an exciting sports event, or popular music.

Operant Conditioning   Classical conditioning views the individual as a passive participant in the learning process who simply receives stimuli. Conditioning occurs as a result of exposure to a stimulus that occurs before the response. In the **operant conditioning** approach, the individual must actively *operate* or act on some aspect of the environment for learning to occur. Operant conditioning is sometimes referred to as *instrumental conditioning* because the individual's response is instrumental in getting a positive reinforcement (reward) or negative reinforcement (a form of reward that occurs when a negative outcome is removed when the desired behavior is performed).

Reinforcement, the reward or favorable consequence associated with a particular response, is an important element of instrumental conditioning. Behavior that is reinforced strengthens the bond between a stimulus and a response. Thus, if a consumer buys a product in response to an ad and experiences a positive outcome, the likelihood that the consumer will use this product again increases. If the outcome is not favorable, the likelihood of buying the product again decreases.

The principles of operant conditioning can be applied to marketing, as shown in Figure 4–7. Companies attempt to provide their customers with products and services that satisfy their needs and reward them to reinforce the probability of repeat purchase. Reinforcement can also be implied in advertising; many ads emphasize the benefits or rewards a consumer will receive from using a product or service. Reinforcement also occurs when an ad encourages consumers to use a particular product or brand to avoid unpleasant consequences. For example, the ad for Carfax in Exhibit 4–17 shows how using this service will help avoid negative consequences—that is, purchasing a used car with problems.

Two concepts that are particularly relevant to marketers in their use of reinforcement through promotional strategies are schedules of reinforcement and shaping. Different **schedules of reinforcement**

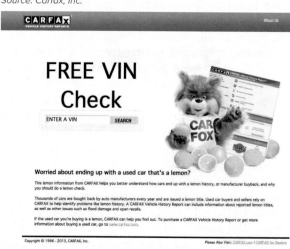

FIGURE 4–8

Application of Shaping
Procedures in Marketing

Terminal Goal: Repeat Purchase Behavior

Approximation Sequence	Shaping Procedure	Reinforcement Applied
Induce product trial	Free samples distributed; large discount coupon	Product performance; coupon
Induce purchase with little financial obligation	Discount coupon prompts purchase with little cost; coupon good for small discount on next purchase enclosed	Product performance; coupon
Induce purchase with moderate financial obligation	Small discount coupon prompts purchase with moderate cost	Product performance
Induce purchase with full financial obligation	Purchase occurs without coupon assistance	Product performance

result in varying patterns of learning and behavior. Learning occurs most rapidly under a *continuous reinforcement schedule*, in which every response is rewarded—but the behavior is likely to cease when the reinforcement stops. Marketers must provide continuous reinforcement to consumers or risk their switching to brands that do.

Learning occurs more slowly but lasts longer when a *partial* or *intermittent reinforcement schedule* is used and only some of the individual's responses are rewarded. Promotional programs have partial reinforcement schedules. A firm may offer consumers an incentive to use the company's product. The firm does not want to offer the incentive every time (continuous reinforcement), because consumers might become dependent on it and stop buying the brand when the incentive is withdrawn. A study that examined the effect of reinforcement on bus ridership found that discount coupons given as rewards for riding the bus were as effective when given on a partial schedule as when given on a continuous schedule.[16] The cost of giving the discount coupons under the partial schedule, however, was considerably less.

Reinforcement schedules can also be used to influence consumer learning and behavior through a process known as **shaping**, the reinforcement of successive acts that lead to a desired behavior pattern or response.

In a promotional context, shaping procedures are used as part of the introductory program for new products. Figure 4–8 provides an example of how samples and discount coupons can be used to introduce a new product and take a consumer from trial to repeat purchase. Marketers must be careful in their use of shaping procedures: If they drop the incentives too soon, the consumer may not establish the desired behavior; but if they overuse them, the consumer's purchase may become contingent on the incentive rather than the product or service.

Cognitive Learning Theory

Behavioral learning theories have been criticized for assuming a mechanistic view of the consumer that puts too much emphasis on external stimulus factors. They ignore internal psychological processes such as motivation, thinking, and perception;

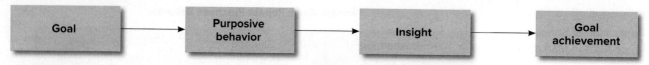

FIGURE 4–9

The Cognitive Learning
Process

they assume that the external stimulus environment will elicit fairly predictable responses. Many consumer researchers and marketers disagree with the simplified explanations of behavioral learning theories and are more interested in the complex mental processes that underlie consumer decision making. The cognitive approach to studying learning and decision making has dominated the field of consumer behavior in recent years. Figure 4–9 shows how cognitive theorists view the learning process.

Since consumer behavior typically involves choices and decision making, the cognitive perspective has particular appeal to marketers, especially those whose product/ service calls for important and involved purchase decisions. Cognitive processes such as perception, formation of beliefs about brands, attitude development and change, and integration are important to understanding the decision-making process for many types of purchases. The subprocesses examined during our discussion of the five-stage decision process model are all relevant to a cognitive learning approach to consumer behavior.

ENVIRONMENTAL INFLUENCES ON CONSUMER BEHAVIOR

The consumer does not make purchase decisions in isolation. A number of external factors have been identified that may influence consumer decision making. They are shown in Figure 4–10 and examined in more detail in the next sections.

 ## Culture

The broadest and most abstract of the external factors that influence consumer behavior is **culture**, or the complexity of learned meanings, values, norms, and customs shared by members of a society. Cultural norms and values offer direction and guidance to members of a society in all aspects of their lives, including their consumption behavior. It is becoming increasingly important to study the impact of culture on consumer behavior as marketers expand their international marketing efforts. Each country has certain cultural traditions, customs, and values that marketers must understand as they develop marketing programs.

FIGURE 4–10

External Influences on
Consumer Behavior

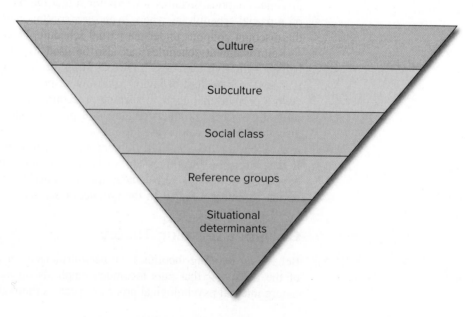

Marketers must also be aware of changes that may be occurring in a particular culture and the implications of these changes for their advertising and promotional strategies and programs. American culture continually goes through many changes that have direct implications for advertising. Marketing researchers monitor these changes and their impact on the ways companies market their products and services.

While marketers recognize that culture exerts a demonstrable influence on consumers, they often find it difficult to respond to cultural differences in different markets. The subtleties of various cultures are often difficult to understand and appreciate, but marketers must understand the cultural context in which consumer purchase decisions are made and adapt their advertising and promotional programs accordingly.

Subcultures

Within a given culture are generally found smaller groups or segments whose beliefs, values, norms, and patterns of behavior set them apart from the larger cultural mainstream. These **subcultures** may be based on age, geographic, religious, racial, and/or ethnic differences. A number of subcultures exist within the United States. The three largest racial/ethnic subcultures are African Americans, Hispanics, and various Asian groups. These racial/ethnic subcultures are important to marketers because of their size, growth, purchasing power, and distinct purchasing patterns. Marketers develop specific marketing programs for various products and services for these target markets. The ads in Exhibit 4–18 are just two of the many specifically designed to appeal to U.S. subcultures—in these cases, Ethiopians and Hispanics. Many others can easily be found that target teens, generations X and Y, older adults, and so on.

Social Class   Virtually all societies exhibit some form of stratification whereby individuals can be assigned to a specific social category on the basis of criteria important to members of that society. **Social class** refers to relatively homogeneous divisions in a society into which people sharing similar lifestyles, values, norms, interests, and behaviors can be grouped. While a number of methods for determining social class exist, class structures in the United States are usually based on occupational status, educational attainment, and income. Sociologists generally agree there are three broad levels of social classes in the United States: the upper (14 percent), middle (70 percent), and lower (16 percent) classes.

Social class is an important concept to marketers, since consumers within each social stratum often have similar values, lifestyles, and buying behavior. Thus, the various social class groups provide a natural basis for market segmentation. Consumers in the different social classes differ in the degree to which they use various

EXHIBIT 4–18

Ads targeted to subcultures

(Left): © Liya Kebede @ Viva Paris for L'Oréal Paris; (Right): Source: Estée Lauder Inc

EXHIBIT 4-19

This American Eurocopter ad attempts to appeal to the upper classes

© American Eurocopter Corp

products and services and in their leisure activities, shopping patterns, and media habits. Marketers respond to these differences through the positioning of their products and services, the media strategies they use to reach different social classes, and the types of advertising appeals they develop. The ad in Exhibit 4–19 shows how a product attempts to appeal to the upper classes in both copy and illustration.

Reference Groups

Think about the last time you attended a party. As you dressed for the party, you probably asked yourself (or someone else) what others would be wearing. Your selection of attire may have been influenced by those likely to be present. This simple example reflects one form of impact that groups may exert on your behavior.

A group has been defined as "two or more individuals who share a set of norms, values, or beliefs and have certain implicitly or explicitly defined relationships to one another such that their behavior is interdependent."[17] Groups are one of the primary factors influencing learning and socialization, and group situations constitute many of our purchase decisions.

A **reference group** is "a group whose presumed perspectives or values are being used by an individual as the basis for his or her judgments, opinions, and actions." Consumers use three types of reference groups (associative, aspirational, and disassociative) as a guide to specific behaviors, even when the groups are not present. In the party example, your peers—although not present—provided a standard of dress that you referred to in your clothing selection. Likewise, your college classmates, family, and co-workers, or even a group to which you aspire, may serve as referents, and your consumption patterns will typically conform to the expectations of the groups that are most important to you.

Marketers use reference group influences in developing advertisements and promotional strategies. The ads in Exhibit 4–20 are examples of *aspirational* reference groups (to which we might like to belong) and *disassociative* groups (to which we do not wish to belong), respectively.

Family Decision Making: An Example of Group Influences   In some instances, the group may be involved more directly than just as a referent. Family members may serve as referents to each other, or they may actually be involved in the purchase decision process—acting as an individual buying unit. As shown in Figure 4–11, family members may assume a variety of roles in the decision-making process. Each role has implications for marketers.

First, the advertiser must determine who is responsible for the various roles in the decision-making process so messages can be targeted at that person (or those people). These roles will also dictate media strategies, since the appropriate magazines, newspapers, or TV or radio stations must be used. Second, understanding the decision-making process and the use of information by individual family members is critical to the design of messages and choice of promotional program elements. In sum, to create an effective promotional program, a marketer must have an overall understanding of how the decision process works and the role that each family member plays.

Situational Determinants

The final external factor is the purchase and usage situation. The specific situation in which consumers plan to use the product or brand directly affects their perceptions,

EXHIBIT 4–20

The ad on the left shows an aspirational reference group; the one on the right stresses a disassociative reference group

(Left): Source: The United States Army; (Right): Source: Saskatchewan Ministry of Health

FIGURE 4–11

Roles in the Family Decision-Making Process

The initiator. The person responsible for initiating the purchase decision process—for example, the mother who determines she needs a new car.

The information provider. The individual responsible for gathering information to be used in making the decision—for example, the teenage car buff who knows where to find product information in specific magazines or collects it from dealers.

The influencer. The person who exerts influence as to what criteria will be used in the selection process. All members of the family may be involved. The mother may have her criteria, whereas others may each have their own input.

The decision maker(s). The person (or persons) who actually makes (make) the decision. In our example, it may be the mother alone or in combination with another family member.

The purchasing agent. The individual who performs the physical act of making the purchase. In the case of a car, a husband and wife may decide to choose it together and sign the purchase agreement.

The consumer. The actual user of the product. In the case of a family car, all family members are consumers. For a private car, only the mother might be the consumer.

preferences, and purchasing behaviors. Three types of **situational determinants** may have an effect: the specific usage situation, the purchase situation, and the communications situation.

Usage refers to the circumstance in which the product will be used. For example, purchases made for private consumption may be thought of differently from those that will be obvious to the public. The *purchase* situation more directly involves the environment operating at the time of the purchase. Time constraints, store environments, and other factors may all have an impact. The *communications* situation is the condition in which an advertising exposure occurs (in a car listening to the radio, with friends, etc.). This may be most relevant to the development of promotional strategies, because the impact on the consumer will vary according to the particular

IMC Perspective 4–2 > > >

Neuromarketing: Gaining Valuable Insights into the Consumer's Brain, or Overstepping the Bounds?

Decades ago when marketers first began to attempt to understand consumer behaviors, one of the first areas turned to in an attempt to gain insights was social psychology. Psychologists like Ernest Dichter and James Vicary researched the underlying motivations behind consumers' purchases, focusing on Freud's psychoanalytic theory and subconscious needs as the drivers of decisions. Numerous *Fortune* 500 companies employed their services, and the results were interesting to say the least.

For a variety of reasons, marketers moved away from trying to discover subconscious purchasing motives and moved on to other theories that examined consumers from a more conscious, information-processing, and problem-solving orientation. This approach has dominated marketing research ever since, with focus group and survey methodologies becoming the primary tools used to determine why consumers buy. (It is estimated that over $4.5 billion is spent yearly worldwide on qualitative research alone.)

But wait a minute. All of a sudden, the new "it" trend in marketing research has changed! Consumer research has once again (you guessed it!) begun to place more and more emphasis on the subconscious motives underlying consumer behaviors—albeit with a different research methodology. This new methodology, *neuroscience*, really isn't new at all. It has been adapted from the field of medicine, and already has archrival companies whose employees include neuroscientists, radiologists, and marketers who argue that their approach to understanding the relationships between brain functions and consumer behaviors is superior. The prestigious *Journal of Advertising Research (JAR)* devoted a four-part section titled "How Does Neuroscience Work in Advertising?" to explore the topic. The two most prevalent methodologies use functional magnetic resonance imaging (fMRI—scan of blood flow) and electroencephalography (EEG—electrical activity on the scalp) to, as one author said, "Hack into your brain." While the proponents of each method disagree as to which is better, both contend that neuroscience is superior to the traditional research methods used, such as focus groups and surveys. One of the articles published in the *JAR* issue agrees, providing research that shows that psychophysiology was more effective in determining consumers' emotional responses to messages. Another article, appearing in *Advertising Age*, argues that the more traditional methods are "sometimes just dead wrong." It appears that some major corporations agree.

Procter & Gamble, McDonald's, Viacom, L'Oréal, and Starcom are just a few of the companies that have used fMRI. Marketing guru Martin Lindstrom praised the methodology in his *New York Times* best-seller *Buyology*, and filmmaker Morgan Spurlock appeared inside an fMRI in his documentary *POM Wonderful: The Greatest Movie Ever Sold*. On the EEG side are Frito-Lay, CBS, ESPN, Intel, eBay, and PayPal, among others. Apple used EEG to determine why people like the iPad. The research organization NeuroFocus earned a Grand Ogilvy Award from the Advertising Research Foundation (its highest award for advertising research) for its work with Cheetos for "demonstrating the most successful use of research in the

situation. For example, a consumer may pay more attention to a commercial that is heard alone at home than to one heard in the presence of friends, at work, or anywhere distractions may be present. If advertisers can isolate a particular time when the listener is likely to be attentive, they will probably earn his or her undivided attention.

In sum, situational determinants may either enhance or detract from the potential success of a message. To the degree that advertisers can assess situational influences that may be operating, they will increase the likelihood of successfully communicating with their target audiences.

ALTERNATIVE APPROACHES TO CONSUMER BEHAVIOR

In addition to the perspectives discussed, consumer researchers complement these psychological approaches with perspectives driven from other scientific disciplines, such as economics, sociology, anthropology, philosophy, semiotics, neuroscience, and history. These cross-disciplinary perspectives have broadened the realm of methodologies used to study consumers and have provided additional insights into consumer decision processes. In addition new technologies have provided new means for exploring consumers' behaviors.

Deep inside the head

"Brain regions do a multitude of things, not just one," says neuroscientist Marco Iacoboni of Illuminare Labs. "This is not phrenology. We do know that brain regions are associated with a variety of tasks and mental states, but that some of these associations tend to be stronger than others." These results come from a test of car brands Iacoboni recently prepared for Illuminare.

The striatum is an important area for coding rewards—basic ones such as food and sex, but also more complex rewards such as cars. This area was especially active in the subject when watching the **Nissan Maxima.**

The posterior inferior frontal gyrus is an area known for, among other things, empathy and identification. Activity in this area when people look at marketing messages is a good sign because it indicates that people either empathize with the actor or identify with people using that product. In Illuminare's study, this region was particularly active for the **Chevy Malibu car.**

The medial prefrontal cortex is an important area for decision making, social cognition (thinking about other people and how to behave with other people), and sense of self. Activity in this region when thinking about or looking at products to buy is typically considered positive—and was especially activated by the **Honda logo.**

This Is Your Brain on Marketing

Up close and personal with fMRI. *By Chip Bayers*

ADWEEK / OCTOBER 3, 2011   31

© *Bryan Christie Design*

robust, stable and projectable sample sizes, these tools, as currently structured, often fail to reach the deeper emotional unconscious" (p. 23). His book discusses the overall superiority of neuroscience research to traditional methods.

But not everyone is on the bandwagon. Researchers are quick to criticize neuroscience research due to the fact that it is a relatively new science, and that most of the research has been funded by private corporations. Ray Poynter, a social media consultant, believes that it is far more hype than science and that neuromarketers "massively overclaim" their success stories. Poynter, among others, wants to wait to see more results before he buys in. So too do co-authors Duane Varan, Steven Bellman, Annie Lang, Patrick Barwise, and Rene Weber. Their article—appearing in the same issue of *JAR*—noted that "New neuromarketing methods that potentially can predict advertising effectiveness face a daunting process" and "there is no common truth, no single scientific reality exposed as a result of these new methods." Clearly, they are not buying into the physiological methods.

So, has the discipline of consumer behavior, which started with seeking subconscious motives for purchasing, returned to its roots? Does this new methodology suffer from the same weaknesses as motivation research did? Dr. Marco Iacoboni, founder of one of the neuromarketing research firms and professor of psychiatry and behavioral sciences at UCLA, seems to think so. Commenting on neuroscience research, Iacoboni said, "Well, this sounds like the same thing Freud said 100 years ago!"

Sources: "Cautious Eye Cast on Neuromarketing," June 26, 2015, www.warc.com; "Neuroscience Links Messages to Purchase," July 7, 2015, www.warc.com; "Marketers: Stop Asking Consumers 'Why' Market Research Needs to Catch Up to Neuroscience." April 15, 2015, www.adage.com; Douglas Van Praet, *Unconscious Branding: How Neuroscience Can Empower (and Inspire) Marketing* (New York: Palgrave Macmillan, 2012); Adam Penenberg, "They Have Hacked Your Brain," *Fast Company*, September 2011, pp. 85–89, 123–124; Chip Bayers, "This Is Your Brain on Marketing," *Adweek*, October 3, 2011, pp. 31–33.

creation of superior advertising that achieves a critical business objective." Douglas Van Praet, in his book *Unconscious Branding: How Neuroscience Can Empower (and Inspire) Marketing*, notes that "While quantitative surveys have more

New Methodologies

Whereas psychologists often study consumer responses to advertising and other forms of communication in controlled settings, where environmental variables can be kept constant, sociologists and anthropologists study behavior in context. For this reason, they often employ qualitative methodologies such as individual interviews, participant observation studies, and/or ethnographies. These methods help capture the social, cultural, and environmental influences that may affect consumer behavior, and may be even more effective in helping us understand than are traditional and/ or online survey methods. The humanities have also been a source of new methodologies for consumer research. Historians and semioticians focus their analyses on the advertising messages and other forms of communications themselves. These researchers examine the significance of communications from a linguistic or historical perspective. Research methods such as semiotic and structural analyses examine the symbolic meanings of advertising and different facets of consumption.

New Insights

These alternative perspectives and methodologies provide additional insights and expand our knowledge of consumers. For example, the cultural significance of advertising messages in shaping cultures and triggering communities is now better understood. Likewise, marketers now have a better understanding of how advertising campaigns become popular and help shape our culture. Thanks to the many interpretive analyses of advertisements over recent years, we are also more aware of the influence of advertising images on society.

Some consumer researchers believe that cross-disciplinary research is better suited for the study of consumers because it takes into account their complexity and multidimensionality. When considered along with psychological research, these alternative approaches help us better understand the impact of communications.

Summary

This chapter introduced you to the field of consumer behavior and examined its relevance to promotional strategy. Consumer behavior is best viewed as the process and activities that people engage in when searching for, selecting, purchasing, using, evaluating, and disposing of products and services to satisfy their needs and desires. A five-stage model of the consumer decision-making process consists of problem recognition, information search, alternative evaluation, purchase, and postpurchase evaluation. Internal psychological processes that influence the consumer decision-making process include motivation, perception, attitude formation and change, and integration processes.

The decision process model views consumer behavior primarily from a cognitive orientation. The chapter considered other perspectives by examining various approaches

to consumer learning and their implications for advertising and promotion. Behavioral learning theories such as classical conditioning and operant (instrumental) conditioning were discussed. Problems with behavioral learning theories were noted, and the alternative perspective of cognitive learning was discussed. New techniques, such as the use of neuroscience to determine what you buy and why you buy it, were covered as well.

The chapter also examined relevant external factors that influence consumer decision making. Culture, subculture, social class, reference groups, and situational determinants were discussed, along with their implications for the development of promotional strategies and programs. The chapter concluded with an introduction to alternative perspectives on the study of consumer behavior.

Key Terms

consumer behavior 113
problem recognition 114
want 114
motive 115
hierarchy of needs 115
psychoanalytic theory 116
motivation research 117
internal search 119
external search 119
perception 120
sensation 120
selective perception 121
selective exposure 121
selective attention 121

selective comprehension 122
selective retention 122
mnemonics 122
subliminal perception 122
evaluative criteria 124
functional consequences 124
psychosocial consequences 124
multiattribute attitude model 125
salient beliefs 125
integration processes 126
heuristics 127
affect referral decision rule 127
purchase intention 127
brand loyalty 127

cognitive dissonance 129
classical conditioning 130
conditioned stimulus 131
conditioned response 131
operant conditioning 132
reinforcement 132
schedules of reinforcement 132
shaping 133
culture 134
subcultures 135
social class 135
reference group 136
situational determinants 137

Discussion Questions

1. Neuroscience has been attacked by many as an invasion of privacy. Describe how marketers are using neuroscience research and discuss the pros and cons of this ethical argument. (LO 4-4)
2. The chapter discusses marketers' use of multiattribute attitude models. Explain what a multiattribute model

is and how a marketer might use it in an attempt to reach the consumer. (LO 4-3)
3. Explain what is meant by *cognitive dissonance*. Why is this concept important to marketers? (LO 4-3)
4. In attempting to segment the market, marketers often will segment on the basis of subcultures.

Citing the chapter, explain the advantages and potential pitfalls of this strategy. (LO 4-5)

5. Figure 4–1 presents a basic model of consumer decision making. Describe the model, and explain what happens at each step of the process. (LO 4-3)

6. Consumers experience different forms of problem recognition. Explain each type of problem recognition and give an example of a purchase of this type. (LO 4-2)

7. The chapter discusses a variety of research methodologies to examine consumers' behaviors. Discuss some of these, focusing on the advantages and disadvantages of each. (LO 4-1)

8. How might one's social class influence his or her consumer behaviors? Give examples of products and/or services that might be influenced by social class standing. (LO 4-5)

9. Explain the differences between functional and psychosocial consequences. Give examples of advertisements that focus on both types. (LO 4-3)

10. Marketers recognize that subcultures have an influence on consumer behaviors. Give examples of how various subcultures may impact one's buying decision. (LO 4-5)

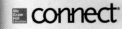

Digital users can access their personalized and adaptive SmartBook, Ad Forum Video Cases, and interactive exercises to review chapter concepts.

5 The Communication Process

Source: Tampax by © Procter & Gamble

LEARNING OBJECTIVES

LO1 Describe the communication process and its role in IMC.

LO2 Describe the basic model of the communication process.

LO3 Discuss the role of word-of-mouth influence and viral marketing.

LO4 Analyze receivers' responses to marketing communications and their implications for promotional planning and strategy.

LO5 Describe the influence of social media on the consumer decision process.

LO6 Discuss consumers' cognitive processing of marketing communications.

HOW A VIRAL CAMPAIGN FOR ALWAYS CHANGED THE MEANING OF "LIKE A GIRL"

Procter & Gamble's (P&G) Always has been one of the world's leading brands of feminine hygiene and protection products for nearly three decades. While the brand has been behind many product innovations that have helped improve women's lives, the marketing communications for Always focused on performance attributes whereas many of its competitors had moved on and were communicating with women and young girls in particular, in more emotional ways. Thus the marketing challenge for Always was to find a fresh and meaningful way to connect with the next generation of girls who are the future of the brand. The Always brand team asked its agency, Leo Burnett, to create a campaign that leveraged the brand's legacy of supporting girls as they make the transition from puberty to young women. Research conducted for the campaign showed that more than half of women surveyed indicated that they experienced a decline in confidence at puberty, which is the time when young girls first come into contact with Always, as well as competing brands. So empowering girls during this critical time of their lives when confidence was low was seen as an opportunity to reinforce the relevance of Always and help position it as a brand that understands the social issues and challenges girls face at puberty.

When the creative team at Leo Burnett began discussing ideas for the campaign, they explored various factors that influence girls' self-confidence during this vulnerable phase of their lives. Judy John, chief creative officer at Leo Burnett, noted that during the meeting someone taped a piece of paper to a board that read only "like a girl" to which they all were instantly drawn. The team discussed how the phrase has been around forever and is generally used in derogatory ways such as playground taunts about people running, throwing or fighting "like a girl." The phrase was the impetus for the big idea behind the campaign which was built around a social experiment designed to redefine the confidence of young girls and change the meaning of the "like a girl" phrase from an insult, which many women internalize to mean weakness and vanity, into a term of empowerment. The cornerstone of the campaign was a three-minute video showing how people of all ages interpret the phrase "like a girl" and the negative impact it has on society and young girls in particular. The video was directed by award-winning

documentary filmmaker Lauren Greenfield and featured a cast of men and women of all ages being asked to describe what they think the phrase "like a girl" means. It clearly showed how the phrase evokes negative and weak stereotypes. When adolescent girls, older women, and boys were asked to demonstrate how to run or fight like a girl, their arms flailed as they ran and awkwardly slapped instead of throwing powerful punches. However, when prepubescent girls were asked to do the same thing they ran as fast and hit as hard as they could, acting out athletic and deliberate motions. The video then asked: "When did doing something 'like a girl' become an insult?" The others soon realized their mistake and how they might be contributing to the self-esteem crisis among young women.

Once the video was produced, Leo Burnett developed a viral campaign around it to spread the message and spark a conversation that would change perceptions of what "like a girl" means. The goal was to empower women by showing that "like a girl" should be a meaningful and powerful statement all women should embrace. John notes that the social media hashtag #LikeAGirl was introduced to encourage people to change the meaning of the phrase by showing that it can mean amazing things. The video was released in the summer of 2014 by posting it on YouTube and Facebook and asking female celebrities and other influential women to share it across their social media accounts. In its first four days the video amassed 8.5 million views and nearly 250,000 Facebook interactions while the hashtag #LikeAGirl was mentioned in nearly 15,000 tweets. The viral activity was just getting started; by the end of 2014 the video was viewed more than 85 million times online worldwide, including 54 million views for the English-language version, making it among the top viral videos of the year. It has also been shared 1.5 million times on social media and generated more than 4.4 billion impressions worldwide. Moreover, the video was doing more than attracting viewers and being shared. A study conducted in late 2014 by the group Research Now found that among girls aged 16 to 24, 76 percent no longer said they saw the phrase "like a girl" as an insult after watching the video. The study also found that two out of three men who saw it said they would stop or think twice before using the phrase in a negative way.

While P&G was thrilled with the viral response to "Like a Girl," a decision was made to build on the momentum and take the message even further by creating a 60-second version of the video that would be shown during the 2015 Super Bowl. The global vice president for Always, noting that the Super Bowl is the most watched television event of the year with over 110 million viewers in the United States alone, explained the decision as follows: "We've only reached one half of our girls in the United States and . . . even fewer boys and men with the message, so I think with such a powerful message like this and the fact that we know it's already making an impact and changing perceptions, there's no better platform than the Super Bowl." The airing of the Always commercial was the first time a feminine care product was advertised during the Super Bowl, and proved to be another astute decision. The spot was the second most popular commercial that aired during the big game according to the USA Today Ad Meter survey, and P&G was praised for running the touching, stereotype-busting commercial and continuing the conversation about what it means to run, throw, or do pretty much any activity "like a girl."

The "Like a Girl" commercial received numerous accolades from the advertising community. It won an Emmy for outstanding commercial at the 2015 Creative Arts Emmy Awards as well as the Grand Clio Award, top honors at the Webby Awards, and several Gold Lion Awards at the Cannes Lions International Festival of Creativity. In addition to being a viral sensation, the "Like a Girl" video and campaign has produced very favorable results for the Always brand on key metrics such as brand awareness and purchase intentions. Brand equity ratings for Always showed double-digit increases during the course of the campaign while most of its competitors had slight declines. The Always brand team and Leo Burnett are continuing their efforts to empower young girls to build their self-confidence. The "Like a Girl" video was followed by another commercial/video called "Unstoppable" which features a group of girls and young women talking about the limitations they've experienced as a result of social norms and stereotyping. Always is also partnering with TED, the nonprofit organization devoted to disseminating ideas, to develop and spread confidence-inspiring content through its educational platform. P&G views "Like a Girl" as more than just a successful viral marketing campaign, but rather as the beginning of a grand social experiment to change the way young girls view themselves and to change the meaning of the phrase from an insult to the ultimate compliment.

Sources: Gabriel Beltrone, "Ad of the Day: Girls Are Unstoppable in Next Phase of Always 'Like a Girl' Campaign," *Adweek*, July 8, 2015, www.adweek.com/news/advertising-branding/ad-day-girls-are-unstoppable-next-phase-always-girl-campaign-165784; Jack Neff, "P&G Always Takes #LikeAGirl Viral Video to the Super Bowl," *Advertising Age*, January 29, 2015, http://adage.com/article/special-report-super-bowl/p-g-s-takes-likeagirl-super-bowl/296879/; Kelly Wallace, "How to Super Bowl #LikeAGirl," CNN, January 31, 2015, www.cnn.com/2015/01/29/living/feat-likeagirl-super-bowl-ad/; Case Study: Always #LikeAGirl, D&AD Awards 2015, www.dandad.org/en/case-study-always-likeagirl/.

The function of all elements of the integrated marketing communications program is to communicate. An organization's IMC strategy is implemented through the various communications it sends to current or prospective customers as well as other relevant publics. Organizations send communications and messages in a variety of ways, such as through advertisements, brand names, logos and graphic systems, websites, press releases, package designs, promotions, and visual images. As was discussed in the chapter opener, companies such as Procter & Gamble are developing more innovative ways to communicate with consumers and deliver their marketing messages as it is becoming increasingly difficult to do so through traditional media.

The way marketers communicate with their target audiences depends on many factors, including how much current and/or potential customers know and what they think about a company or brand and the image it hopes to create. Those involved in the planning and implementation of an IMC program need to understand the communication process and what it means in terms of how they create, deliver, manage, and evaluate messages about a company or brand. Developing an effective marketing communications program is far more complicated than just choosing a product feature or attribute to emphasize. Marketers must understand how consumers will perceive and interpret their messages and how these reactions will shape consumers' responses to the company and/or its product or service. And as the use of social media becomes more prevalent, it is important that marketers understand how consumers communicate with one another and how they can participate in and even influence these conversations.

This chapter reviews the fundamentals of communication and examines various perspectives and models regarding how consumers respond to advertising and promotional messages. Our goal is to demonstrate how valuable an understanding of the communication process can be in planning, implementing, and evaluating the marketing communications program.

THE NATURE OF COMMUNICATION

Communication has been variously defined as the passing of information, the exchange of ideas, or the process of establishing a commonness or oneness of thought between a sender and a receiver.[1] These definitions suggest that for communication to occur, there must be some common thinking between two parties and information must be passed from one person to another (or from one group to another). As you will see in this chapter, establishing this commonality in thinking is not always as easy as it might seem; many attempts to communicate are unsuccessful.

The communication process is often very complex. Success depends on such factors as the nature of the message, the audience's interpretation of it, and the environment in which it is received. The receiver's perception of the source and the medium used to transmit the message may also affect the ability to communicate, as do many other factors. Words, pictures, sounds, and colors may have different meanings to different audiences, and people's perceptions and interpretations of them vary. For example, if you ask for a soda on the East Coast or West Coast, you'll receive a soft drink such as Coke or Pepsi. However, in parts of the Midwest and South, a soft drink is referred to as pop. If you ask for a soda, you may get a glass of pop with ice cream in it. Marketers must understand the meanings that words and symbols take on and how they influence consumers' interpretation of products and messages.

EXHIBIT 5–1

This outdoor ad for milk targets Hispanic consumers by appealing to love for family

Source: The California Milk Advisory Board

Language is one of the major barriers to effective communication; there are different languages in different countries, different languages or dialects within a single country, and subtler problems of linguistic nuance and vernacular. This can be particularly challenging to companies marketing their products abroad, as discussed in Global Perspective 5–1. The growth of bilingual, multicultural ethnic markets in the United States is also creating challenges for domestic marketers. For example, while many marketers are recognizing the importance of appealing to the Hispanic market, they find that communicating with this fast-growing segment can be very challenging. They have to decide whether to use ads with a Hispanic-focused creative, dub or remake general market campaigns into Spanish, or run English-language ads and hope that they will be picked up by bilingual Hispanics. Many companies are creating ads specifically for the Hispanic market. Exhibit 5–1 shows an ad the California Milk Processor Board developed to target Hispanic consumers. Notice how the message in the ad focuses on how milk goes well with family traditions.

Communication Problems in International Marketing

Communication is a major problem facing companies that market their products and services in foreign countries. Language is one of the main barriers to effective communication; there can be different languages or dialects within a single country, and subtler problems of linguistic nuance and vernacular. For example, China has many languages and dialects, with differences great enough that people from different regions of the country often cannot understand each other. As another example, about 40 percent of the Canadian population does not use English as its preferred language. Of the non-English speakers, about 60 percent speak French, with the balance spread among a dozen or so other languages.

Mistranslations and faulty word choices have often created problems for companies in foreign markets, as well as for companies that are marketing their products and services to increasingly diverse and multicultural audiences in their domestic markets. International marketers must also be aware of the connotation of the words, signs, symbols, and expressions they use as brand names or logos or in various forms of promotion. Also, advertising copy, slogans, images, and symbols do not always transfer well into other languages. This not only impedes communication but also sometimes results in embarrassing blunders that can damage a company's or a brand's credibility or image and thereby cost it customers.

There are several widely cited examples of translation problems. For example, when Coca-Cola introduced its brand into China, the Chinese characters sounded like *Coca-Cola* but meant "bite the wax tadpole." With the help of a language specialist, the company substituted four Mandarin characters that retained the Coca-Cola sound but mean "can happy, mouth happy." KFC also encountered translation problems when the company first entered China in 1986 as its classic "Finger-lickin good" tagline was wrongly translated in Chinese to "Eat your fingers off." Then there is the classic story of when General Motors (GM) and Chevrolet introduced its

Nova to Latin America: The car did not do well because "no va" means "won't go" in Spanish. However, GM denied that the name was a problem, noting that the brand did pretty well in these markets and that in grammatical terms, "no va" is *not* how a Spanish speaker would describe a dead car. However, the company did change the name of the car to the Caribe in Spanish-speaking markets.

Global marketers sometimes try to internationalize various components of their marketing programs such as packaging, logos, and advertising messages to eliminate the time, effort, and costs required to adapt, or localize, a product or brand for international markets. One way of doing so is to rely on images rather than text or copy, which can be more susceptible to mistranslation. However, the use of images can present problems as well and can be subject to misinterpretation. For example, when Procter & Gamble started selling its Pampers diapers in Japan, it used an image of a stork delivering a baby on the packaging. While the advertising worked well in the United States, it never caught on with Japanese parents. After some research, the company learned that customers were concerned and confused by the image of a stork on the packaging, since the stories of storks bringing babies to parents isn't part of Japanese folklore. In Japan, the story goes that babies, particularly those who are special and whose lives and fates will play out differently than others, come from a giant peach that was floating down a river to their parents.

Marketers also have to be aware of how people read and process information in different languages when creating their ads. Swedish company Cederroth reportedly ran an ad for its Samarin brand of antacid in an Arabic newspaper using only a series of three images and the product name. The images were designed to tell the story: The first image showed a man looking as if he were ill, the second showed him drinking a glass of Samarin, and in the third image he appears happy and well. However, the ad did not account for the fact that Arabic speakers read from right to left and

BASIC MODEL OF COMMUNICATION

Over the years, a basic model of the various elements of the communication process has evolved, as shown in Figure 5–1.[2] Two elements represent the major participants in the communication process, the sender and the receiver. Another two are the major communication tools, message and channel. Four others are the major communication functions and processes: encoding, decoding, response, and feedback. The last element, noise, refers to any extraneous factors in the system that can interfere with the process and work against effective communication.

© inWhatLanguage.com – The Translation Management Cloud

often process advertising images the same way, and thus left consumers with the impression that the man became ill after consuming the product.

Another company that ran into problems in international markets over an advertising message is Burger King. A campaign created for BK's Texican Whopper that ran in the United Kingdom and Spain featured ads showing a short Mexican wrestler draped in a cape resembling his country's flag standing next to a lanky American cowboy and the tagline "the taste of Texas with a little spicy Mexican." Mexico's ambassador to Spain said the ad inappropriately displayed the Mexican flag, whose image is protected under national law, and requested that the ads be discontinued. Many Mexicans as well as Hispanic consumers in the United States were also critical of the ads, arguing that they were offensive. Burger King said that the ads were meant to show how influences from the southwestern United States and Mexico can mix, and were not meant to poke fun at Mexican culture. However, the company issued an apology and changed the advertising.

Many multinational companies are trying to develop global brands that can be marketed internationally using the same brand name and advertising campaigns. However, they must be careful that brand names, advertising slogans, signs, symbols, and other forms of marketing communication don't lose something in the translation. There are several things international marketers can do to avoid joining the top 10 list of language blunders. The first line of defense is to hire a translation service to review the material and make sure there are no problems. However, experts note that relying on translators alone may not be foolproof as they may not be steeped in current slang or the subtleties of a language. The experts recommend that translated materials be read by a linguistically mixed staff as well as by contacts in the local market who know dialects and slang. For example, the Internet-based, global translation company inWhatlanguage has more than 5,000 translators scattered across the globe, living in their respective countries, in constant contact with their fellow citizens and their national and regional media.

While the use of translators and native-speaker checks can help identify language problems, they do not solve the problem of how well an ad campaign translates into another culture. The vice president of marketing for the direct marketing agency Infocore notes that ad campaign concepts will never translate perfectly into another culture, which is a problem that many marketers do not want to acknowledge. He cites two basic problems, including multinational ad agencies being constrained by managers who do not want to surrender power to strangers in foreign markets and the "don't mess with the creative" mantra of marketers who assume that the magic of a campaign that works in one culture can be grafted onto another.

Time and again, problems with brand names, ad slogans, and visual signs and symbols have come back to haunt even the best of marketers. As Simon Anholt, a British marketing and branding expert, notes: "Language is in many respects such a silly little thing, but it has the power to bring marketing directors to their knees. That's where the terror lies."

Sources: Chad Brooks, "Lost in Translation: 8 International Marketing Fails," *Business News Daily*, October 7, 2013, www.businessnewsdaily.com/5241-international-marketing-fails.html; Adam Wooten, "International Business: The Wrong Marketing Picture Can Be a Thousand Words Lost in Translation," *Desert News*, March 26, 2011, www.desertnews.com/article/705369323; Rupal Parekh and Emily Bryson, "BK to Revise Ad after Complaint," *Advertising Age*, April 14, 2009, http://adage.com/article/global-news/burger-king-revise-ad-complaints-Mexican-official/135989/; Mark Laswell, "Lost in Translation," *Business 2.0*, August 2004, pp. 68–70; Deborah L. Venice, "Proper Message, Design in Global Markets Requires Tests," *Marketing News*, September 1, 2006, pp. 18, 24–25; Emily Maltby, "Expanding Abroad? Avoid Cultural Gaffes," *The Wall Street Journal*, January 19, 2010, p. B5.

Source Encoding

The sender, or **source**, of a communication is the person or organization that has information to share with another person or group of people. The source may be an individual (say, a salesperson or hired spokesperson, such as a celebrity, who appears in a company's advertisements) or a nonpersonal entity (such as the corporation or organization itself). For example, the source of many ads is the company, since no specific spokesperson or source is shown. However, many companies use a spokesperson to appear in their ads and to deliver their advertising messages. In some cases, a popular spokesperson can play a very important role in attracting attention

FIGURE 5–1

A Model of the
Communication Process

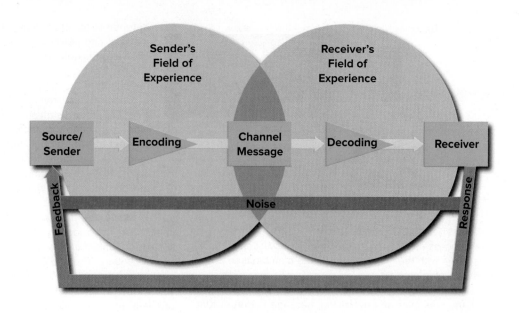

to a company's advertising and delivering the message, as well as influencing how well it is received by the target audience. For example, the Citizen Watch Company has featured a variety of athletes and celebrities as brand ambassadors/spokespersons in the "Better Starts Now" global campaign for its Eco-Drive watches. Exhibit 5–2 shows one of the ads from the campaign featuring singer Kelly Clarkson.

Because the receiver's perceptions of the source influence how the communication is received, marketers must be careful to select a communicator the receiver believes is knowledgeable and trustworthy or with whom the receiver can identify or relate in some manner. (How these characteristics influence the receiver's responses is discussed further in Chapter 6.)

The communication process begins when the source selects words, symbols, pictures, and the like to represent the message that will be delivered to the receiver(s). This process, known as **encoding**, involves putting thoughts, ideas, or information into a symbolic form. The sender's goal is to encode the message in such a way that it will be understood by the receiver. This means using words, signs, or symbols that are familiar to the target audience. Many symbols have universal meaning, such as the familiar circle with a line through it to denote no parking, no smoking, and so forth. Many companies also have highly recognizable symbols—such as McDonald's golden arches, Nike's swoosh, or the Coca-Cola trademark—that are known to consumers around the world. Marketers must pay very close attention to the symbols associated with their company or brand such as logos as they often become a shorthand way for consumers to identify them. In some cases marketers may change their logos as way of sending a different message to consumers. For example, in 2011 Starbucks changed its logo and dropped the green ring with the text "Starbucks Coffee" to more prominently display its iconic siren. The change was made to help consumers "think beyond coffee" when they see the Starbucks logo because the company is broadening

EXHIBIT 5–3

The image projected by an ad often communicates more than words

Source: Coach, Inc.

its strategic focus to include other product categories.[3] In some cases consumers may become very attached to a company's logo and react negatively when they change it. The Gap experienced this a few years ago when the retail chain introduced a redesigned logo that it felt was more contemporary. Responses to the new logo on social media were very negative and Gap returned to its old design after just four days.[4]

Message

The encoding process leads to development of a **message** that contains the information or meaning the source hopes to convey. The message may be verbal or nonverbal, oral or written, or symbolic. Messages must be put into a transmittable form that is appropriate for the channel of communication being used. In advertising, this may range from simply writing some words or copy that will be read as a radio message to producing an expensive television commercial. For many products, it is not the actual words of the message that determine its communication effectiveness but rather the impression or image the ad creates. Notice how the Coach ad shown in Exhibit 5–3 uses only a picture to deliver its message. However, the use of the brand name and picture is an effective way to communicate Coach's intended message of aspirational heritage mixed with an urban attitude. The ad is part of a campaign for the new Coach 1941 luxury line of handbags, apparel, and footwear which it describes as reinventing luxury and authenticity for a new generation.[5]

Marketers must make decisions regarding the *content* of the messages they send to consumers as well as the *structure* and *design* of these messages. Content refers to the information and/or meaning contained in the message while structure and design refer to the way the message is put together in order to deliver the information or intended meaning. More attention will be given to issues regarding message appeal and structure in the next chapter while message design is discussed in the chapters on creative strategy (Chapters 8 and 9).

Channel

The **channel** is the method by which the communication travels from the source or sender to the receiver. At the broadest level, channels of communication are of two types, nonpersonal and personal. *Nonpersonal channels* of communication are those that carry a message without direct, interpersonal contact between the sender and receiver. Nonpersonal channels are generally referred to as the **mass media** or mass communications, since the message they contain is directed to more than one person and is often sent to many individuals at one time. For example, a TV commercial broadcast on a prime-time show may be seen by 10 million people in a given evening while a print ad appearing in a popular magazine may be seen by millions of readers over the course of a week or month.

Nonpersonal channels of communication consist of two major types, print and broadcast. Print media include newspapers, magazines, direct mail, and billboards; broadcast media include radio and television. The Internet has characteristics of both nonpersonal as well as personal forms of communication. It has become a mass-media vehicle as it is now an important source of information for most consumers and many advertising messages are delivered through various forms of online advertising including banner ads, paid search, and ads on social media sites. In many

LO5-3

ways the Internet is nonpersonal in nature because consumers are often just consuming the information or content provided online and there is no personal contact between them and the companies that disseminate this information on their website or through online advertising. However, the Internet is increasingly becoming a form of personal communication since consumers can interact with marketers online as well as communicate and share information with one another through the use of various forms of social media.

Personal channels involve direct communication between two or more persons and can occur through interpersonal contact (face-to-face) or via other methods such as e-mail or through social media. Salespeople serve as personal channels of communication when they deliver a selling message or presentation to a buyer or potential customer. A major advantage of personal channels of communication is that the message or presentation can be tailored to the individual or audience and the sender receives direct feedback from them. Members of one's social networks such as friends, neighbors, associates, co-workers, or family members are also personal channels of communication. They often represent **word-of-mouth (WOM)** influence that involves informal communication among consumers about products and services and is a very powerful source of information.[6]

Many companies work hard to generate positive word-of-mouth discussion for their companies or brands using various buzz marketing techniques. **Buzz marketing** is just one of the new names for what used to be known simply as word-of-mouth communication while terms such as *consumer-generated marketing* and *viral marketing* are also used to describe the process.[7] The use of word-of-mouth marketing is really nothing new as marketers have long been handing out product samples and providing products to influential people and encouraging them to recommend the brand to others. For example, alcoholic beverage marketers have long understood the value of getting bartenders and servers to hype their brands while pharmaceutical companies have always worked to encourage influential physicians to talk up their products to their peers.

What makes buzz marketing different from traditional word-of-mouth communication is that it includes systematic and organized efforts to encourage people to speak favorably about a company, brand, organization, or issue and often to recommend it to others in their social network. What is also new is the number of companies that are now using buzz marketing, and the sophisticated ways they are going about it. Marketers often use techniques such as contests that encourage consumers to create user-generated content—such as photographs, videos, recipes, and product usage ideas—and then use social media as a way to disseminate it, which helps spread the word about their brands. In some cases consumers may be asked to vote on the user-generated content and also to share it with their friends and associates and encourage them to vote as well. For example, Frito-Lay sponsored the "Crash the Super Bowl" online commercial production competition for 11 years whereby consumers were invited to create 30-second commercials for its Doritos brand.[8] The company's advertising agency and marketing team would select the five finalists that were then posted to a website for a monthlong public vote, with the two spots receiving the most votes airing during the big game (Exhibit 5–4). Frito-Lay moved the contest to Facebook in 2013 and over the last four years of the contest the five finalist videos received nearly 100 million views each year as the social media site helped the contest go viral. During the 11 years that Frito-Lay ran the contest, three of the commercials that won the online vote and were aired during the big game were selected as the most popular ads in the USA Today Ad Meter competition which gauges consumer reactions to Super Bowl spots.[9]

Viral Marketing   The "Crash the Super Bowl" contest as well as the "Like a Girl" campaign discussed at the beginning of the chapter are excellent examples of the use

of **viral marketing**, which refers to the act of propagating marketing-relevant messages through the help and cooperation of individual consumers.[10] Many marketers along with their advertising and/or digital agencies now use a variety of tools and techniques to generate viral buzz about their brands, many of which take advantage of the emergence and growth of online communities and social media such as Facebook, Twitter, Pinterest, Instagram, Snapchat, and YouTube. However, successful viral marketing can be very difficult to achieve as the outcomes are affected by many factors that are often beyond a marketer's control.

Researchers have identified three major factors that affect the success of a viral marketing program, including message characteristics, individual sender or receiver characteristics, and social network characteristics.[11] Message characteristics relate to the content and creative design of a viral message and include factors such as whether the information is entertaining, engaging, novel, humorous, and/or informative. For example, many videos and commercials have a strong viral component that make them popular and encourage consumers to watch as well share them. The most shared ad in 2015 was the "Friends Furever" commercial for Google's Android which became not only the most shared ad for the year, but also of all time. The ad, which shows unlikely animals playing together and was part of Android's "Be together. Not the same." ad campaign, was shared more than 6.4 million times. Commercial featuring animals are often among the most shared on social media and in 2015 three other animal spots, all of them starring dogs, were in the top 10. They included the "Puppyhood" video for Purina Puppy Chow produced with BuzzFeed in which a man spontaneously adopts a puppy and they bond in typical roommate fashion; Budweiser's "Lost Dog" Super Bowl ad; and a video for Kleenex called "Unlikely Best Friends" which tells the story of a lovable dog who lost the use of his rear legs after being hit by a car and now gets around with

FIGURE 5–2

Motivations for Social
Sharing of Videos

Source: Adapted from "Why Some
Videos Go Viral" from *Harvard
Business Review,* September
2015. https://hbr.org/2015/09/
why-some-videos-go-viral.

Opinion Seeking	I want to see what my friends think
Shared Passion	It lets me connect with my friends about a shared interest
Conversation Starting	I want to start an online conversation
Social Utility	This could be useful to my friends
Self-Expression	It says something about me
Social in Real Life	It will help me socialize with my friends offline
Social Good	It's for a good cause and I want to help
Zeitgeist	It's about a current trend or event
Kudos: Authority	I want to demonstrate my knowledge
Kudos: Cool Hunting	I want to be the first to tell my friends

the help of wheels for legs. The dog is adopted by a man who is also disabled and bound to a wheelchair.[12]

In addition to the message, characteristics of the individual consumer also play an important role in the viral marketing process. Factors such as demographics, personality traits, and motivation for sharing content and messages as well as receiving them impact the effectiveness of viral campaigns.[13] For example, female and younger consumers tend to exert more influence on their target recipients and be more susceptible to viral influences than male and older consumers, while traits such as extroversion, innovativeness, and altruism are related to tendencies to share messages.[14] Insight into motivations for social sharing comes from a study done by Unruly, an ad marketing technology company that focuses on what is watched and shared online. Its analysis of over 430 billion video views and 100,00 consumer data points revealed that the two most powerful drivers of viral success are psychological response (how the content makes you feel) and social motivation (why you want to share it).[15] Unruly has identified 10 motivations for social sharing which are shown in Figure 5–2.

With regard to social network characteristics, the structure of networks through which a message spreads as well as the consumers' position in the social network, as defined by relationships with others, can influence the diffusion of a viral message. Many marketers try to identify individuals who are very influential in various social media domains, such as bloggers and persons with a large number of Facebook fans or Twitter followers; then they work hard to get their messages to them in hopes that they pass them on to others in their social network.

Another important aspect of viral marketing is what is often referred to as **seeding**, which involves identifying and choosing the initial group of consumers who will be used to start the diffusion or spreading of a message.[16] Companies that utilize viral marketing must develop a *seeding strategy* which involves determining how many initial consumers or "seeds" are needed and selecting the right consumers to start the viral process. For example, the Ford Motor Company introduced its new Fiesta subcompact car in the U.S. market in 2010 by using a social media campaign called the "Fiesta Movement" which involved enlisting a team of 100 "agents" to drive the new vehicle for six months and participate in monthly challenges that would allow them to share interesting content with their friends through social media. The Fiesta brand team and its advertising agency, Team Detroit, selected the agents based on their entrepreneurial spirit, number of social network followers

EXHIBIT 5–5

The Fiesta Movement used agents to generate buzz on social media for the car

Source: Ford Motor Company/Team Detroit, Inc.

or friends, social vibrancy, and creative vision.[17] The social media campaign was very successful in helping Ford launch the Fiesta in the United States and the company returned to social media to generate buzz around the redesigned 2014 model with its "Fiesta Movement: A Social Remix" campaign. Once again, Ford recruited 100 socially vibrant agents and gave them cars to drive and buzz about on social media (Exhibit 5–5).

There are advertising agencies and other companies that specialize in working with clients to develop viral marketing programs. Some companies are also building web communities so consumers can chat about their product experiences online. For example, in 2005 Procter & Gamble, which ironically is the world's largest advertiser, initiated a new word-of-mouth program brand community called Vocalpoint to reach the most influential group of shoppers in America: moms. Recently P&G has broadened the focus of Vocalpoint to include women aged 28 to 45 and now has more than 670,000 members. These women are very involved with their social networks through social media such as Facebook, Twitter, and various blogs and speak or interact with a number of other women during a typical day. P&G has also used the success of Vocalpoint to develop a new brand community called Orgullosa that targets Spanish-speaking women in the United States. Vocalpoint and Orgullosa are the flagship brand communities for P&G and are likely to be used as models for reaching other target audiences in the future (Exhibit 5–6).

Integrating Word of Mouth with IMC While viral techniques have become a popular way to generate buzz about a brand, research conducted by the Keller Fay Group—a market research company that focuses on word-of-mouth marketing—has shown that some 90 percent of conversations about products, services, and brands take place offline.[18] Face-to-face interaction accounts for the vast majority of word-of-mouth communications (75 percent) about a brand while phone conversations rank second (15 percent). Only 10 percent of word of mouth takes place through online channels such as e-mail/instant messages, blogs, and chat rooms. Their research also shows that nearly half the word-of-mouth conversations included references to the various IMC tools used for a brand, including print and television ads, websites, and other marketing tools such as point-of-sale displays and promotions.

EXHIBIT 5-6

Vocalpoint and Orgullosa are online communities where women can share information about products and various issues

Source: Procter & Gamble

Another important finding was that word-of-mouth conversations influenced by advertising are significantly more likely to involve recommendations to buy or try a brand when compared to other WOM-induced discussions about brands. Moreover, these WOM discussions are very powerful as consumers ascribe a high credibility to the information they hear from others; 50 percent say they are very likely to buy as a result of these conversations.[19]

Subsequent research by Keller Fay has found that the role of advertising in WOM is even stronger, as a quarter of all consumer conversations about brands involve discussions about advertising. And of the brand conversations in which consumers talk about advertising, television advertising is the most prevalent form, which is not surprising given that more money is spent on TV ads than any other medium. However, collectively, other forms of advertising including magazines, newspapers, the Internet, radio, and outdoor are about equal with respect to generating conversations about advertising, which suggests that a variety of IMC tools can be used to drive word of mouth.[20]

These findings are very important from an integrated marketing communications perspective in several respects. First, they show that that there can be powerful "pass-along" benefits from consumers talking favorably about a brand and referencing various elements of its IMC program. However, with consumers being bombarded by so many irrelevant marketing messages each day, it is very difficult to get them to talk about them. Thus, marketers must develop creative advertisements and other forms of communication that can trigger conversations and are worthy of sharing. They also reinforce the importance of marketers recognizing that all of the IMC elements work in unison to impact how consumers perceive a brand and the word-of-mouth discussion that is generated by it. The fact that consumers appear to be influenced the most by their conversations with other people shows that marketers need to finds ways to favorably influence these interactions. However, as Keller and Fay note, since most WOM discussions take place offline, marketers cannot rely only on social media to drive these conversations; they need to deploy a more robust set of IMC tools to drive brand advocacy.[21]

Marketers must be careful about the assumptions they make when using buzz marketing techniques. For example, a study conducted by David Godes and Diane Mayzlin on the effects of a word-of-mouth campaign for a chain store examined the characteristics of the most successful "agents" so that firms could better understand at whom they should target their buzz marketing efforts.[22] They found that agents who were not loyal customers of the store were more effective at generating sales through word of mouth than were loyal customers. The explanation offered for these somewhat counterintuitive findings is that loyal customers have already told their friends and acquaintances about a product and are already generating positive word of mouth. On the other hand, nonloyal customers may be more responsive to buzz marketing campaigns designed to encourage them to spread the word about a product. However, marketers still have to identify the best generators of buzz among both loyal and nonloyal customers such as those who are considered opinion leaders by their peers and "social butterflies" who have a high propensity to meet new people and connect with friends.

While the use of buzz and viral marketing campaigns is becoming more prevalent, concern has been expressed over its use and whether the person spreading the product message should disclose his or her affiliation. The Word of Mouth Marketing Association was formed in 2004 to promote and improve the use of word-of-mouth marketing and protect consumers and the industry by providing ethical guidelines for its use. WOMMA has developed a set of rules and guidelines that mandate that marketers must make sure that people recommending products or services disclose whom they are working for. Gary Ruskin, the former executive director of Commercial Alert, a nonprofit organization dedicated to protecting consumers from commercial exploitation, notes that without such disclosures there is "a danger of the basic commercialization of human relations, where friends treat one another as advertising pawns, undercutting social trust."[23]

Experts note that buzz marketing techniques are very resistant to manipulation and marketers must be careful about how they use them. Several companies have had buzz marketing campaigns backfire when consumers recognized that the companies were artificially trying to promote buzz for their brands. Some argue that the growing popularity of buzz marketing could well spell its downfall, because when consumers recognize that everyone is trying to create a buzz for their brand, they are likely to be turned off to the technique.[24] However, with the growth of social media and consumers becoming less attentive to and interested in traditional media advertising, it is likely that marketers will continue to seek ways to develop and deliver branded content and messages that consumers will share with one another. This will extend the reach and impact of their marketing messages and may add an implicit consumer endorsement as well.

The effective use of buzz marketing requires that marketers take a strategic approach in the development and implementation of campaigns that are designed to have strong WOM and viral components. For example, Keller and Fay note that marketers should think in terms of social consumers rather than just social media and focus on the stories that consumers share with one another about a brand or a product or service category to ensure that there is a good fit between the consumer story and the brand story. They also suggest that it is the job of brand strategists to identify the people who are most likely to talk about their brand or category and seek to understand when, where, and why people talk.[25]

Receiver/Decoding

The **receiver** is the person(s) with whom the sender shares thoughts or information. Generally, receivers are the consumers in the target market or audience who read, hear, and/or see the marketer's message and decode it. **Decoding** is the process of transforming the sender's message back into thought. This process is heavily influenced by the receiver's frame of reference or **field of experience**, which refers to the experiences, perceptions, attitudes, and values he or she brings to the communication situation.

For effective communication to occur, the message decoding process of the receiver must match the encoding of the sender. Simply put, this means the receiver understands and correctly interprets what the source is trying to communicate. As Figure 5–1 showed, the source and the receiver each have a frame of reference (the circle around each) that they bring to the communication situation. Effective communication is more likely when there is some *common ground* between the two parties. (This is represented by the overlapping of the two circles.) The more knowledge the sender has about the receivers, the better the sender can understand their needs, empathize with them, and communicate effectively. Exhibit 5–7 shows an ad for the Pew Environmental Group's Campaign for America's Wilderness that uses the concept of common ground by noting how both Republicans and Democrats agree on the importance of protecting the American wilderness by passing legislation to give permanent protection to wilderness land in 13 states.

While this notion of common ground between sender and receiver may sound basic, it often causes great difficulty in the advertising communications process. Marketing and advertising people often have very different fields of

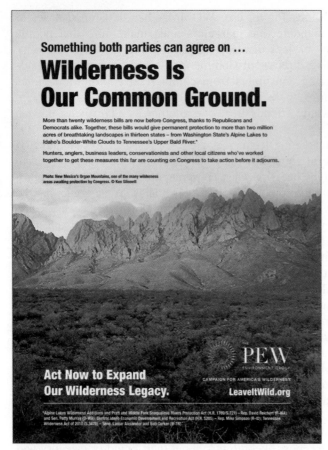

EXHIBIT 5–7

This ad uses the concept of common ground

© Ken Stinnett Photography

experience from the consumers who constitute the mass markets with whom they must communicate. Most are college-educated and work and/or reside in large urban areas such as New York, Chicago, or Los Angeles. Many of them are young, fashionable, upwardly mobile people with busy professional and social lives, avid interest in music and movies and the latest clubs and restaurants, and few distractions like children or elderly parents who need looking after. Yet they are often creating ads that must communicate with millions of consumers who have never attended college, work in blue-collar occupations, and/or live in rural areas or small towns. The executive creative director of a large advertising agency described how advertising executives become isolated from the cultural mainstream: "We pull them in and work them to death. And then they begin moving in sushi circles and lose touch with Velveeta and the people who eat it."[26]

Another factor that can lead to problems in establishing common ground between senders and receivers is age. As the population of the United States and many other countries grows older, concern has been expressed over the potential problems that might arise because of age differences between advertising agency personnel and older consumers. A study conducted for the Association of Advertising Agencies International found that professionals who work in advertising agencies are much younger than the general population. Nearly 60 percent of agency personnel staff is between the ages of 25 to 44 while only 30 percent of the U.S. adult population is in this age group.[27] The ads they create are often designed to appeal to younger consumers between 18 and 34 (or 49 at a stretch) and feature people who look and act just like them, despite the concentration of buying power among those over the age of 50. The youth bias is particularly evident in the creative departments as many of those who work in this area are under the age of 40. The age gap has become very prevalent in the digital/interactive area as well because these departments are dominated by younger people. Digital and Social Media Perspective 5–1 discusses how digital media are creating a new type of ageism in the marketing communications industry as many companies, as well as agencies, prefer to hire younger workers whom they view as more digital savvy than older people.

Critics argue that most advertising is really about the people who create it, not about the consumers who actually buy the products and services being advertised. It is important that marketers and their agencies understand the frame of reference and perspectives of the consumers in the target markets that are receiving their messages. Many companies spend a considerable amount of time and money pretesting advertising messages to make sure consumers understand them and decode them in the manner intended. Pretesting advertising messages is discussed in more detail in Chapter 18.

Noise

Throughout the communication process, the message is subject to extraneous factors that can distort or interfere with its reception. This unplanned distortion or interference is known as **noise**. Errors or problems that occur in the encoding of the message, distortion in a radio or television signal, and distractions at the point of reception are examples of noise. When you are watching an ad on TV or listening to a radio commercial and a problem occurs in the signal transmission, it will obviously interfere with your reception, lessening the impact of the commercial. Over the past decade a new type of noise has become prevalent in the television viewing environment which is the distraction of technology such as laptops, tablets, and mobile phones/smartphones. Many people now multitask while watching television: They may be online surfing the Internet, using apps, participating in social media, or texting. Figure 5–3 shows the results of a survey conducted by TiVo which looked at the frequency with which TV viewers in the United States multitask during commercials. The survey found that only 5 percent of the respondents indicated that they never, or almost never multitask during commercial breaks, while over 80 percent said they multitask almost every time or sometimes during a commercial break. Another survey conducted by TiVo found that live television is the format during which they are most likely to multitask (53 percent); multitasking while playing back a recorded show was lower (28 percent).[28]

Noise may also occur because the fields of experience of the sender and receiver don't overlap. Lack of common ground may result in improper encoding of the message—using a sign, symbol, or words that are unfamiliar or have different meaning to the receiver. The more common ground there is between the sender and the receiver, the less likely it is this type of noise will occur.

Response/Feedback

The receiver's set of reactions after seeing, hearing, or reading the message is known as a **response**. Receivers' responses can range from nonobservable actions such as storing information in memory to immediate action such as clicking through an online ad to go to a marketer's landing page or website or dialing a toll-free number to order a product advertised on television. Marketers are very interested in **feedback**, that part of the receiver's response that is communicated back to the sender. Feedback, which may take a variety of forms, closes the loop in the communications flow and lets the sender monitor how the intended message is being decoded and received.

For example, in a personal-selling situation, customers may pose questions, comments, or objections or indicate their reactions through nonverbal responses such as gestures and frowns.[29] The salesperson has the advantage of receiving instant feedback through the customer's reactions. But this is generally not the case when mass media are used. Because advertisers are not in direct contact with the customers, they must use other means to determine how their messages have been received.

While the ultimate form of feedback occurs through sales, it is often hard to show a direct relationship between advertising and purchase behavior. So marketers use other methods to obtain feedback, among them customer inquiries, store visits, coupon redemptions, and reply cards. Research-based feedback analyzes readership and recall of ads, message comprehension, attitude change, and other forms of response. With this information, the advertiser can determine reasons for success or failure in the communication process and make adjustments.

Successful communication is accomplished when the marketer selects an appropriate source, develops an effective message

FIGURE 5–3

Frequency of Multitasking by Television Viewers

Note: n = 856 ages 18+; numbers may not add up to 100% due to rounding.

Source: TiVO, "Second Annual Social Media & Multitasking," October 16, 2014.

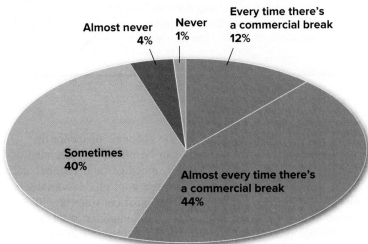

Almost never 4%

Never 1%

Every time there's a commercial break 12%

Sometimes 40%

Almost every time there's a commercial break 44%

Digital and Social Media Perspective 5–1 > > >

DIGITAL MEDIA CREATE A NEW TYPE OF AGEISM IN IMC

It has long been argued that there is a youth bias in the advertising industry. The claim is that marketers are fixated with reaching younger consumers while paying less attention to those over the age of 50, despite the fact that older consumers control half of the wealth, spend trillions of dollars on products and services each year, and comprise a large percentage of the population in most countries. Madison Avenue has been focused on the younger adult market (generally aged 18 to 49) for decades, and the media are obsessed with the under 50 demographic as well; most of the broadcast and cable networks have been filling their schedules with shows and programming aimed at people in their 20s, 30s, and 40s. Another area where advertising and marketing communications are often seen as having a youth bias is among agency personnel. Studies have shown that professionals who work in advertising agencies in the United States as well as other countries are much younger than the adult population. The youth bias is particularly evident in creative departments, where agency employment drops like a rock after age 40, particularly among those involved in creating the ads. It should be noted that the youth movement for those working in advertising is not limited to the United States. For example, in the United Kingdom the average age of advertising employees is 34, with more than 40 percent under age 30 and only 5 percent over age 50.

There are a number of reasons why agencies seem to be focusing their hiring toward young people. One reason is basic economics: Younger means cheaper, and in an industry notorious for taking every opportunity to cut costs, a 20-year veteran copywriter is much more expensive than a college graduate. (That younger, less experienced employees are paid less is, of course, true in most industries, not just advertising.) A second reason is creativity as agencies tend to think that younger employees are better suited to creative thinking, especially under tight deadlines and high pressure to perform. A third reason is the shift toward the use of digital media. Many agencies, as well as their clients, view the tried-and-true advertising methods used for decades—print, direct mail, and telemarketing—as suddenly being a thing

of the past. They are focusing their attention on new methods of reaching and engaging consumers such as through mobile marketing, and the use of social media platforms has become more prevalent and assumed to be better understood by the younger generation.

With the growth of digital and social media, a new type of ageism is taking place in the world of advertising, both in agencies and among companies that market their products and services to younger consumers. As technology continues to change and grow at an ever-expanding pace, ad agencies and marketing departments assume that young people are those best equipped to navigate the digital world. Whereas gray hair and work experience were once viewed as assets for marketing and advertising executives, Madison Avenue agencies are increasingly turning to freshly minted college grads who are (presumably) more in touch with the digital platforms that have become so vital for customer engagement.

Of course, industry veterans in the 50-and-over club—both employed and unemployed—will contend the industry has it all wrong, arguing that they too know the intricacies of the digital world and recognize that social media are more than a passing fad and have taken the time to learn about them. In fact, many creatives and account managers saw the writing on the wall years ago and have subsequently taken it upon themselves to learn how to use the various social media platforms such as Facebook, Snapchat, Instagram, and Twitter, along with search engine optimization and web analytics. Thus, this "ageism" is frustrating for "gray-haired" members of the work force who feel that they should be looked at as even *more* valuable to their companies and agencies because they can combine their new digital knowledge with significant work experience. Unfortunately, Madison Avenue firms, as well as most companies, do not seem to be budging as they delegate social media strategy and tasks to junior employees whom they assume know the platforms much better and will enjoy spending time in the space.

So what can older advertising and marketing professionals do to distinguish themselves as capable employees in

or appeal that is encoded properly, and then selects the channels or media that will best reach the target audience so that the message can be effectively decoded and delivered. In Chapter 6, we will examine the source, message, and channel decisions and see how promotional planners work with these controllable variables to develop communication strategies. Since these decisions must consider how the target audience will respond to the promotional message, the remainder of this chapter examines the receiver and the process by which consumers respond to advertising and other forms of marketing communications.

the digital age? First of all, they have to live in the present rather than the past and recognize that potential employers may not care about work they did or awards they won in the pre-digital era. For example, *Advertising Age* ran an article in 2016 that was a follow-up piece about David Shea, a 57-year-old advertising executive featured in a cover story the publication ran in 2012 on ageism in advertising. Shea had risen to the level of creative director at a major Madison Avenue agency and worked on accounts such as MTV, Mercedes, and numerous General Mills cereal brands. However, after losing his job due to agency cutbacks during the recession he struggled to find a new position as he had to fight the misconception that a creative past the age of 55 cannot be digitally savvy. When interviewed for the follow-up article in *Ad Age* and asked what he would have done differently, Shea noted: "After the article ran, there was one comment I took to heart. Somebody had written, 'Nice article, Dave, but the picture of you standing in your home office holding "Ogilvy on Advertising" with a bunch of relics from your career wasn't the best thing. You need to surround yourself with 2012, not the 1980s.' And I thought, 'You're right. Here I am a positioning expert, and in that shot it looked as if I was positioning myself for the past and not the future.'"

Most experts also recommend that older people take a long look in the mirror to determine exactly where the deficiencies in their digital skills may exist. Advertising professionals who grew up with a different generation of traditional media advertising must get up to speed on the most current trends in the digital world and be able to demonstrate their new knowledge. A "digital presence" is also essential through either a personal website or an extensive public profile on LinkedIn, Facebook, and Twitter. They also should consider many of the online tutorials that are available to educate themselves and stay current in various aspects of digital and social media. For example, Google offers online courses and training modules where one can learn how to use Google advertising and web marketing tools. It also offers certification tests for Google Analytics, AdWords, and other online tools. Facebook, which now owns Instagram, has websites that provide in-depth explanations for how to use each platform for advertising. Twitter also offers a best-practices guide for those interested in using the popular social media tool; Snapchat has similar information available.

With every passing year, older people who work in advertising and marketing are likely to find it harder to gain employment in an industry that is getting younger by the day. Thus, it is important that middle-aged managers and executives immerse themselves in digital media to stay relevant and, perhaps more importantly, gainfully employed. However, it is also important for advertising agencies, as well as their clients, to recognize that someone needs to train the young people they are hiring, many of whom have untapped potential and a hunger for knowledge but lack some of the skills needed to succeed in the industry. As *Advertising Age* writer Ken Wheaton notes: "Who better to teach them than the boomers and Gen Xers who were once hotshots, the ones who've stuck around out of love for the craft and loyalty to the company and know the business inside out, up and down, forward and backward."

Sources: Judann Pollack, "How One Man Beat the Odds," *Advertising Age*, March 21, 2016, p. 24; Ken Wheaton, "Think Twice Before You Kick All Those Middle Managers to the Curb," *Advertising Age*, March 21, 2016, p. 34; Rupel Parekh, "Aging in Adland: The Gray-Hair Phobia That's Hindering Older Execs," *Advertising Age*, January 30, 2012, pp. 1, 8–9.

ANALYZING THE RECEIVER

To communicate effectively with their customers, marketers must understand who the target audience is, what (if anything) it knows or feels about the company's product or service, and how to communicate with the audience to influence its decision-making process. Marketers must also know how the market is likely to respond to various sources of communication or different types of messages. Before

FIGURE 5–4

Levels of Audience
Aggregation

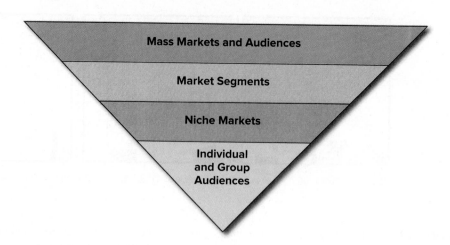

they make decisions regarding source, message, and channel variables, promotional planners must understand the potential effects associated with each of these factors. This section focuses on the receiver of the marketing communication. It examines how the audience is identified and the process it may go through in responding to a promotional message. This information serves as a foundation for evaluating the controllable communication variable decisions in the next chapter.

Identifying the Target Audience

The marketing communication process really begins with identifying the audience that will be the focus of the firm's advertising and promotional efforts. The target audience may consist of individuals, groups, niche markets, market segments, or a general public or mass audience (Figure 5–4). Marketers approach each of these audiences differently.

The target market may consist of *individuals* who have specific needs and for whom the communication must be specifically tailored. This often requires person-to-person communication and is generally accomplished through personal selling. Other forms of communication, such as advertising, may be used to attract the audience's attention to the firm, but the detailed message is carried by a salesperson who can respond to the specific needs of the individual customer. Life insurance, financial services, and real estate are examples of products and services promoted this way.

A second level of audience aggregation is represented by the *group.* Marketers often must communicate with a group of people who make or influence the purchase decision. For example, organizational purchasing often involves buying centers or committees that vary in size and composition. Companies marketing their products and services to other businesses or organizations must understand who is on the purchase committee, what aspect of the decision each individual influences, and the criteria each member uses to evaluate a product. Advertising and other forms of marketing communication may be directed at each member of the buying center, and multilevel personal selling may be necessary to reach those individuals who influence or actually make decisions.

Marketers look for customers who have similar needs and wants and thus represent some type of market segment that can be reached with the same basic communication strategy. Very small, well-defined groups of customers are often referred to as *market niches.* They can usually be reached through personal-selling efforts or highly targeted media such as direct mail. The next level of audience aggregation is *market segments,* broader classes of buyers who have similar needs and can be reached with similar messages. As we saw in Chapter 2, there are various ways of segmenting markets and reaching the customers in these segments. As market segments get larger, marketers usually turn to broader-based media such as newspapers, magazines, and TV to reach them.

Marketers of most consumer products attempt to attract the attention of large numbers of present or potential customers (*mass markets*) through mass communication such as advertising or publicity. Mass communication is a one-way flow of information from the marketer to the consumer. Feedback on the audience's reactions to the message is generally indirect and difficult to measure.

TV advertising, for example, lets the marketer send a message to millions of consumers at the same time. But this does not mean effective communication has occurred. This may be only one of several hundred messages the consumer is exposed to that day. There is no guarantee the information will be attended to, processed, comprehended, or stored in memory for later retrieval. Even if the advertising message is processed, it may not interest consumers or may be misinterpreted by them. Studies by Jacob Jacoby and Wayne D. Hoyer have shown that nearly 20 percent of all print ads and even more TV commercials are miscomprehended by readers.[30]

Unlike personal or face-to-face communications, mass communications do not offer the marketer an opportunity to explain or clarify the message to make it more effective. The marketer must enter the communication situation with knowledge of the target audience and how it is likely to react to the message. This means the receiver's response process must be understood, along with its implications for promotional planning and strategy.

THE RESPONSE PROCESS

Perhaps the most important aspect of developing effective integrated marketing communications programs involves understanding the *response process* the receiver may go through in moving toward a specific behavior (like purchasing a product) and how the promotional efforts of the marketer influence consumer responses. In many instances, the marketer's only objective may be to create awareness of the company or brand name, which may trigger interest in the product. In other situations, the marketer may want to convey detailed information to change consumers' knowledge of and attitudes toward the company/brand and ultimately change their behavior.

Traditional Response Hierarchy Models

A number of models have been developed to depict the stages a consumer may pass through in moving from a state of not being aware of a company, product, or brand to actual purchase behavior. Figure 5–5 shows four of the best-known response hierarchy models. While these response models may appear similar, they were developed for different reasons.

The **AIDA model** was developed to represent the stages a salesperson must take a customer through in the personal-selling process.[31] This model depicts the buyer as passing successively through attention, interest, desire, and action. The salesperson must first get the customer's attention and then arouse some interest in the company's product or service. Strong levels of interest should create desire to own or use the product. The action stage in the AIDA model involves getting the customer to make a purchase commitment and closing the sale. To the marketer, this is the most important stage in the selling process, but it can also be the most difficult. Companies train their sales reps in closing techniques to help them complete the selling process. More detailed models of the personal-selling process have been developed over the years that go beyond the basic steps of the AIDA model and focus on approaches such as "solution selling" and "insight selling."[32]

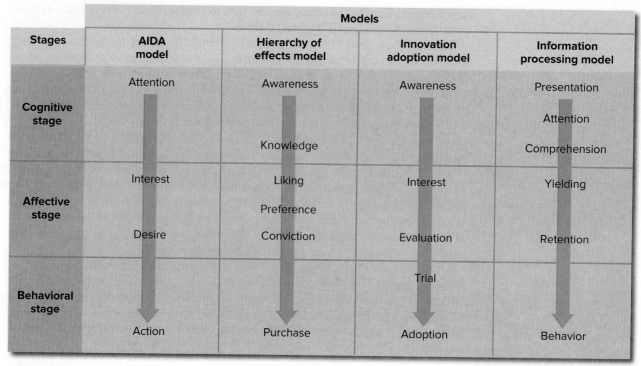

Stages	Models			
	AIDA model	**Hierarchy of effects model**	**Innovation adoption model**	**Information processing model**
Cognitive stage	Attention	Awareness	Awareness	Presentation
				Attention
		Knowledge		Comprehension
Affective stage	Interest	Liking	Interest	Yielding
		Preference		
	Desire	Conviction	Evaluation	Retention
Behavioral stage			Trial	
	Action	Purchase	Adoption	Behavior

FIGURE 5–5

Models of the Response Process

EXHIBIT 5–8

Sampling or demonstration programs encourage trial of new products such as disposable contact lenses, as shown in this offer from Acuvue

Source: VISTAKON®, Division of Johnson & Johnson Vision Care, Inc.

Perhaps the best known of these response hierarchies is the model developed by Robert Lavidge and Gary Steiner as a paradigm for setting and measuring advertising objectives.[33] Their **hierarchy of effects model** shows the process by which advertising works; it assumes a consumer passes through a series of steps in sequential order from initial awareness of a product or service to actual purchase. A basic premise of this model is that advertising effects occur over a period of time. Advertising communication may not lead to immediate behavioral response or purchase; rather, a series of effects must occur, with each step fulfilled before the consumer can move to the next stage in the hierarchy. This model is also the basis for the classic *purchase funnel* metaphor that is often used to depict the decision process consumers go through. The consumer starts at the top of funnel with a number of brands in mind, methodically reduces that number as he or she becomes familiar with and evaluates these alternatives, and then emerges with the brand he or she chooses to purchase.[34] As we will see in Chapter 7, the hierarchy of effects model as well as the purchase funnel have become the foundation for setting objectives and measuring the effectiveness of advertising and other IMC tools in many companies.

The **innovation adoption model** evolved from work on the diffusion of innovations.[35] This model represents the stages a consumer passes through in adopting a new product or service. Like the other models, it says potential adopters must be moved through a series of steps before taking some action (in this case, deciding to adopt a new product). The steps preceding adoption are awareness, interest, evaluation, and trial. The challenge facing companies introducing new products is to create awareness and interest among consumers and then get them to evaluate the product favorably. The best way to evaluate a new product is through actual use so that performance can be judged. Marketers often encourage trial by using demonstration or sampling programs or allowing consumers to use a product with minimal commitment (Exhibit 5–8). After trial, consumers either adopt the product or reject it.

The innovation adoption model is especially important to companies who are using IMC tools to introduce new products to the market. These marketers recognize that there are certain types of consumers who are of particular interest to them because of their interest in new products and their ability to influence others.[36] This influential group is commonly referred to as "early adopters," and they play a critical role in determining the success or failure of a new product because many consumers pay close attention to what they say and do. The high-tech industry is particularly interested in what are often referred to as "digital adopters," which is the group of consumers who are the first to use various new digital products and services such as smartphones, mobile apps, tablets, video gaming consoles, software, and apps (Exhibit 5–9). Companies marketing these new high-tech products recognize that one of the most effective ways they can launch them is to focus on the early digital adopters. This group of consumers is not only much more likely to buy new products, they also are respected for their opinions and thus can influence the purchase decision of others who look to them for advice. Studies have also shown that they are two to five times more likely to spread the word about new products and services than the average consumer.[37] Marketers are constantly looking for ways to identify and communicate with these early adopters.

The final hierarchy model shown in Figure 5–3 is the **information processing model** of advertising effects, developed by social psychologist William McGuire.[38] This model assumes the receiver in a persuasive communication situation like advertising is an information processor or problem solver. McGuire suggests that the series of steps a receiver goes through in being persuaded constitutes a response hierarchy. The stages of this model are similar to the hierarchy of effects sequence; attention and comprehension are similar to awareness and knowledge, and yielding is synonymous with liking. McGuire's model includes a stage not found in the other models: retention, or the receiver's ability to retain that portion of the comprehended information that he or she accepts as valid or relevant. This stage is important since most promotional campaigns are designed not to motivate consumers to take immediate action but rather to provide information they will use later when making a purchase decision.

Each stage of the response hierarchy is a dependent variable or outcome that must be attained and may serve as an objective of the communication process. As shown in Figure 5–6, each stage can be measured, providing the advertiser with feedback regarding the effectiveness of various strategies designed to move the consumer to purchase. The information processing model may be an effective framework for planning and evaluating the effects of a promotional campaign.

Implications of the Traditional Hierarchy Models The hierarchy models of communication response are useful to promotional planners from several perspectives. First, they delineate the series of steps potential purchasers must be taken through to move them from unawareness of a product or service to readiness to purchase it. Second, potential buyers may be at different stages in the hierarchy, so the advertiser will face different sets of communication problems. For example, a company introducing an innovative product like the Microsoft Surface tablet may use media advertising to make people aware of the product along with its features and benefits (Exhibit 5–10). Microsoft provides product information in its ads but also encourages consumers to visit retail stores as well as its website to learn more about the Surface. Consumers who visit the website or go to a retail store for a product demonstration will progress through the response hierarchy and move closer to purchase than those who only see an ad. Marketers of a mature brand that enjoys customer loyalty may need only supportive or reminder advertising to reinforce positive perceptions and maintain the awareness level for the brand.

The hierarchy models can also be useful as intermediate measures of communication effectiveness. The marketer needs to know where audience

EXHIBIT 5–9

Marketers often try to identify and target digital adopters

Source: Advertising Age Magazine, Crain Communications Inc.

FIGURE 5–6

Methods of Obtaining
Feedback in the Response
Hierarchy

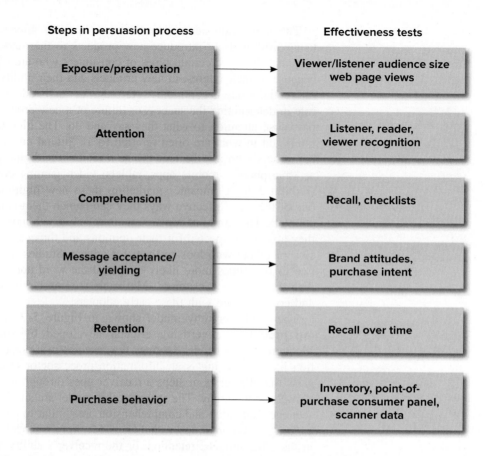

Steps in persuasion process

| Exposure/presentation |
| Attention |
| Comprehension |
| Message acceptance/ yielding |
| Retention |
| Purchase behavior |

Effectiveness tests

| Viewer/listener audience size web page views |
| Listener, reader, viewer recognition |
| Recall, checklists |
| Brand attitudes, purchase intent |
| Recall over time |
| Inventory, point-of-purchase consumer panel, scanner data |

EXHIBIT 5–10

Microsoft's Surface tablet is an innovative new product

Source: Microsoft

members are in the response hierarchy. For example, research may reveal that one target segment has low awareness of the advertiser's brand, whereas another is aware of the brand and its various attributes but has a low level of liking or brand preference. For the first segment of the market, the communication task involves increasing the awareness level for the brand. The number of ads may be increased, or a product sampling program may be used. For the second segment, where awareness is already high but liking and preference are low, the advertiser must determine the reason for the ambivalent or negative feelings and then attempt to address this problem in future advertising.

When research or other evidence such as social media monitoring reveals a company/brand is perceived favorably on a particular attribute or performance criterion, the company may want to take advantage of this in its advertising. This can be done by increasing the ad budget and/or creating ads that note the company or brand's popularity or favorable ratings.

Evaluating Traditional Response Hierarchy Models As shown in Figure 5–5, the four models presented all view the response process as consisting of movement through a sequence of three basic stages. The *cognitive stage* represents what the receiver knows or perceives about the particular product or brand. This stage includes awareness that the brand exists and knowledge, information, or comprehension about its attributes, characteristics, or benefits. The *affective stage* refers to the receiver's feelings or affect level (like or dislike) for the particular brand. This stage also includes stronger levels of affect such as desire, preference, or conviction. The *conative* or *behavioral stage* refers to the consumer's action toward the brand: trial, purchase, adoption, or rejection.

All four models assume a similar ordering of these three stages. Cognitive development precedes affective reactions, which precede behavior. One might assume that consumers become aware of and knowledgeable about a brand, develop feelings toward it, form a desire or preference, and then make a purchase. While this logical progression is often accurate, the response sequence does not always operate this way.

Over the past two decades, considerable research in marketing, social psychology, and communications has led to questioning of the traditional cognitive → affective → behavioral sequence of response. Several other configurations of the response hierarchy have been theorized.

Alternative Response Hierarchies

Michael Ray has developed a model of information processing that identifies three alternative orderings of the three stages based on perceived product differentiation and product involvement.[39] These alternative response hierarchies are the standard learning, dissonance/attribution, and low-involvement models (Figure 5–7).

The Standard Learning Hierarchy   In many purchase situations, the consumer will go through the response process in the sequence depicted by the traditional communication models. Ray terms this a **standard learning model**, which consists of a learn→feel→do sequence. Information and knowledge acquired or *learned* about the various brands are the basis for developing affect, or *feelings*, that guide what the consumer will *do* (e.g., actual trial or purchase). In this hierarchy, the consumer is viewed as an active participant in the communication process who gathers information through active learning.

Ray suggests the standard learning hierarchy is likely when the consumer is highly involved in the purchase process and there is much differentiation among competing brands. High-involvement purchase decisions such as those for industrial products and services and consumer durables like personal computers, printers, cameras,

FIGURE 5–7

Alternative Response Hierarchies—The Three-Orders Model of Information Processing

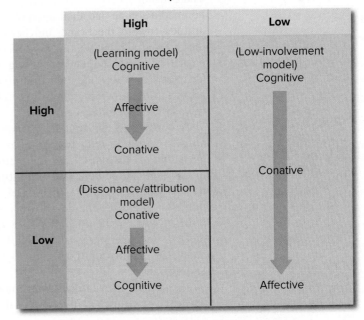

EXHIBIT 5–11

This Honda Pilot ad addresses the various stages in the standard learning hierarchy by focusing on an important product feature

Source: American Honda Motor Co., Inc. and Rubin Postaer and Associates

appliances, and automobiles are areas where a standard learning hierarchy response process is likely. Ads for products and services in these areas are often detailed and provide customers with information that can be used to evaluate brands and help them make a purchase decision. They also may focus on a specific product attribute or feature that is important to consumers in market segment they are targeting. For example, the ad for the new Honda Pilot SUV shown in Exhibit 5–11 appeals to the cognitive and affective steps in the standard learning hierarchy by showing how its Intelligent Traction Management system makes it adaptable to a variety of diverse conditions and uses.

The Dissonance/Attribution Hierarchy   A second response hierarchy proposed by Ray involves situations where consumers first behave, then develop attitudes or feelings as a result of that behavior, and then learn or process information that supports the behavior. This **dissonance/attribution model**, or do → feel → learn, occurs in situations where consumers must choose between two alternatives that are similar in quality but are complex and may have hidden or unknown attributes. The consumer may purchase the product on the basis of a recommendation by some nonmedia source and then attempt to support the decision by developing a positive attitude toward the brand and perhaps even developing negative feelings toward the rejected alternative(s). This reduces any *postpurchase dissonance* or anxiety the consumer may experience resulting from doubt over the purchase (as discussed in Chapter 4). Dissonance reduction involves *selective learning,* whereby the consumer seeks information that supports the choice made and avoids information that would raise doubts about the decision.

According to this model, marketers need to recognize that in some situations, attitudes develop *after* purchase, as does learning from the mass media. Ray suggests that in these situations the main effect of the mass media is not the promotion of original choice behavior and attitude change but rather the reduction of dissonance by reinforcing the wisdom of the purchase or providing supportive information. For example, the ad shown in Exhibit 5–12 notes that consumers who can afford to do so should purchase a Haiku fan. This ad reinforces the decision of those who have purchased a Haiku fan while also communicating a message about the quality of the brand to those who may be considering purchasing a ceiling fan.

As with the standard learning model, this response hierarchy is likely to occur when the consumer is involved in the purchase situation; it is particularly relevant

EXHIBIT 5-12

This ad reinforces the wisdom of the decision to purchase a Haiku fan

© *Big Ass Solutions*

for postpurchase situations. For example, a consumer may purchase a brand recommended by a friend and then develop a favorable attitude toward the company and pay close attention to its ads to reduce dissonance.

Some marketers resist this view of the response hierarchy because they can't accept the notion that the mass media have no effect on the consumer's initial purchase decision. But the model doesn't claim the mass media have no effect—just that their major impact occurs after the purchase has been made. Marketing communications planners must be aware of the need for advertising and promotion efforts not just to encourage brand selection but to reinforce choices and ensure that a purchase pattern will continue.

The Low-Involvement Hierarchy Perhaps the most intriguing of the three response hierarchies proposed by Ray is the **low-involvement hierarchy**, in which the receiver is viewed as passing from cognition to behavior to attitude change. This learn → do → feel sequence is thought to characterize situations of low consumer involvement in the purchase process. Ray suggests this hierarchy tends to occur when involvement in the purchase decision is low, there are minimal differences among brand alternatives, and mass-media (especially broadcast) advertising is important.

The notion of a low-involvement hierarchy is based in large part on Herbert Krugman's theory explaining the effects of television advertising.[40] Krugman wanted to find out why TV advertising produced a strong effect on brand awareness and recall but little change in consumers' attitudes toward the product. He hypothesized that TV is basically a low-involvement medium and the viewer's perceptual defenses are reduced or even absent during commercials. In a low-involvement situation, the consumer does not compare the message with previously acquired beliefs, needs, or past experiences. The commercial results in subtle changes in the consumer's knowledge structure, particularly with repeated exposure. This change in the consumer's knowledge does not result in attitude change but is related to learning something about the advertised brand, such as a brand name, ad theme, or slogan. According to Krugman, when the consumer enters a purchase situation, this information may be sufficient to trigger a purchase. The consumer will then form an attitude toward the purchased brand as a result of experience with it. Thus, in the low-involvement situation the response sequence is as follows:

Message exposure under low involvement →

Shift in cognitive structure → Purchase →

Positive or negative experience → Attitude formation

In the low-involvement hierarchy, the consumer engages in *passive learning* and *random information catching* rather than active information seeking. The advertiser must recognize that a passive, uninterested consumer may focus more on nonmessage elements such as music, characters, symbols, and slogans or jingles than actual message content. The advertiser might capitalize on this situation by developing a catchy jingle that is stored in the consumer's mind without any active cognitive processing and becomes salient when he or she enters the actual purchase situation.

Advertisers of low-involvement products also repeat simple product claims such as a key copy point or distinctive product benefit. A study by Scott Hawkins and

EXHIBIT 5–13

Heinz has been the leader in the ketchup market

© H.J. Heinz Company, used with permission

Stephen Hoch found that under low-involvement conditions, repetition of simple product claims increased consumers' memory of and belief in those claims.[41] They concluded that advertisers of low-involvement products might find it more profitable to pursue a heavy repetition strategy than to reach larger audiences with lengthy, more detailed messages. For example, Heinz has dominated the ketchup market for over 30 years by repeatedly telling consumers that its brand is the thickest and richest. Heinz has used a variety of advertising campaigns over the years. However, they all have communicated the same basic message that Heinz is the best and most preferred brand of ketchup (Exhibit 5–13).

Low-involvement advertising appeals prevail in much of the advertising we see for frequently purchased products such as consumer packaged goods: Wrigley's Doublemint gum invites consumers to "Double your pleasure." Bounty paper towels claim to be the "quicker picker-upper." Oscar Mayer uses the catchy jingle "I wish I were an Oscar Mayer wiener." Each of these slogans is designed to help consumers maintain top-of-mind awareness that can influence their purchase decisions when they are in the store and trying to complete a shopping trip.

Another popular creative strategy used by advertisers of low-involvement products is what advertising analyst Harry McMahan calls *VIP*, or *visual image personality*.[42] Advertisers often use symbols like the Pillsbury Doughboy, Morris the Cat, Tony the Tiger, and Mr. Clean to develop visual images that will lead consumers to identify and retain ads. Eveready began using the pink bunny in ads for its Energizer batteries in 1989, and he has helped sales of the brand keep going and going for nearly 30 years. As can be seen in Exhibit 5–14, the Energizer Bunny even has his own Facebook page with more than 400,000 fans.

Implications of the Alternative Response Models

Advertising and consumer researchers recognize that not all response sequences and behaviors are explained adequately by either the traditional or the alternative response hierarchies. Advertising is just one source of information consumers use in learning about products, forming attitudes, and/or making purchase decisions. Consumers are likely to integrate information from advertising and other forms of marketing communication as well as direct experience in forming judgments about a brand. For example, a study by Robert Smith found that advertising can lessen the negative effects of an unfavorable trial experience on brand evaluations when the ad is processed before the trial. However, when a negative trial experience precedes exposure to an ad, cognitive evaluations of the ad are more negative.[43] More recent research has also shown that advertising can affect consumers' objective sensory interpretation of their experiences with a brand and what they remember about it.[44]

EXHIBIT 5–14

The Energizer Bunny is still a popular personality symbol for the brand

Source: Eveready Battery Company, Inc.

The various response models offer an interesting perspective on the ways consumers respond to advertising and other forms of marketing communication. They also provide insight into promotional strategies marketers might pursue in different situations. A review of these alternative models of the response process shows that the traditional standard learning model does not always apply. The notion of a highly involved consumer who engages in active information processing and learning and acts on the basis of higher-order beliefs and a well-formed attitude may be inappropriate for some types of purchases. Sometimes consumers make a purchase decision on the basis of general awareness resulting from repetitive exposure to advertising, and attitude development occurs after the purchase, if at all. The role of advertising and other forms of promotion may be to induce trial, so consumers can develop brand preferences primarily on the basis of their direct experience with the product.

From a promotional planning perspective, it is important that marketers examine the communication situation for their product or service and determine which type of response process is most likely to occur. They should analyze involvement levels and product/service differentiation as well as consumers' use of various information sources and their levels of experience with the product or service. Once the manager has determined which response sequence is most likely to operate, the integrated marketing communications program can be designed to influence the response process in favor of the company's product or service. Several planning models have been developed that consider involvement levels as well as other factors including response processes and motives that underlie the attitude formation and subsequent brand choice.[45] These models can be of value to marketers as they develop IMC strategies because they recognize that advertising and other promotional tools work differently depending on the type of product involved and the decision process sequence that consumers are likely to follow.

The Social Consumer Decision Journey

The alternative response models discussed in the previous section have dominated much of the theorizing, research, and planning regarding how consumers respond to advertising and other IMC tools. However, over the past decade the environment in which consumers evaluate brands and make purchase decisions has changed dramatically as digital content—including social media—has become pervasive in our daily lives and is influencing consumer behavior. With the advent of social networking tools and the availability of digital devices such as smartphones and tablets, consumers are more empowered than ever before as they can access and retrieve information, connect with one another to share it, discuss products/services and brands, and interact with marketers quickly and easily.

A major study commissioned by the Advertising Research Foundation (ARF) examined how digital and social media are used in the purchase-decision process along with how and when consumers turn to them to help manage this process. One of the major findings of this study is that "consumers, in effect, are always on as they are constantly considering potential purchases and evaluating the various providers of products and service" and that they can be in both an active and passive shopping mode.[46] When they are in a "passive" shopping mode, the information and advice consumers need to make a purchase comes to them unsolicited, such as a comment on a social media site; an ad seen on a TV show, in a magazine, or on a website; or by observing someone using a product or service. At other times, consumers are in an "active" shopping mode whereby they are purposefully seeking information and/or assistance so they can make informed purchase decisions with confidence. Consumers in an active shopping mode may visit the website or Facebook page of a company or brand, go to a search engine such as Google, Yahoo!, or Bing, go to a retail store, or have a conversation with a friend or associate (either online or in person).

Another important conclusion from this study, as well as research conducted by the McKinsey & Company's Global Digital Marketing Strategy practice group, is that consumers do not make purchase decisions in the linear manner depicted by the traditional hierarchy of effects and purchase funnel models whereby they start at the wide part of the funnel with many brands in mind and narrow them down to a final choice.[47] The research conducted by McKinsey as well as the ARF study show that consumers go through a much more iterative and less reductive process and that they can enter a purchase path at various points, depending on whether they first engage with a brand, research a product or service, or hear about a product through their social networks. Based on these findings, David Edelman and his associates at McKinsey proposed a "consumer decision journey" framework for understanding how consumers interact with companies and brands during the purchase decision process. The decision journey has four basic stages: *consider, evaluate, buy,* and *enjoy-advocate-bond.*[48] This framework views the consumer decision-making process as a winding journey with multiple feedback loops rather than a linear, single uniform path to purchase based on active shopping and influenced by marketer dominated and controlled touch points such as media advertising.

Recognizing the increasing importance and influence of social media on consumer behavior, Edelman and his colleagues expanded the consumer decision journey framework to include social media, as shown in Figure 5–8. The social consumer decision journey framework recognizes that consumers connect with large numbers of brands through digital and social media channels that are often beyond the marketers' or retailers' control, evaluate a shifting array of them, and often expand the pool before narrowing it. After a purchase, consumers may remain very engaged and publicly promote or disparage the products or services they have purchased, often through digital and social media.[49] The McKinsey group note that "social media is a unique component of the consumer decision journey: it's the only form of marketing that can touch consumers at each and every stage, from when they're pondering brands and products right through the period after a purchase, as their experience influences the brands they prefer and their potential advocacy influences others."[50] As can be seen in Figure 5–8, there are a number of ways various digital and social media tools such as YouTube, Twitter, Facebook, and Foursquare can influence consumers at various stages of the decision journey.

FIGURE 5–8

The Social Consumer Decision Journey

1 Consumer considers purchase
Views your brand on retailer site and is impressed by enthusiastic user reviews

2 Consumer evaluates brand
Watches YouTube video posted by enthusiastic owner showing the product's innovative uses

3 Consumer buys product
Photographs the product in store, posts it for others to comment on, and receives personal message with coupon from the brand

6 Consumer bonds
"Tips" friends on Foursquare after revisiting your store to purchase again

5 Consumer advocates for brand
Comments on your representative's helpful advice in a user forum, then "likes" your Facebook page

4 Consumer interacts with brand after purchase
"Follows" your expert on Twitter to receive product updates; retweets to friends

Evaluate · Bond · Consider · Buy · Advocate · Experience

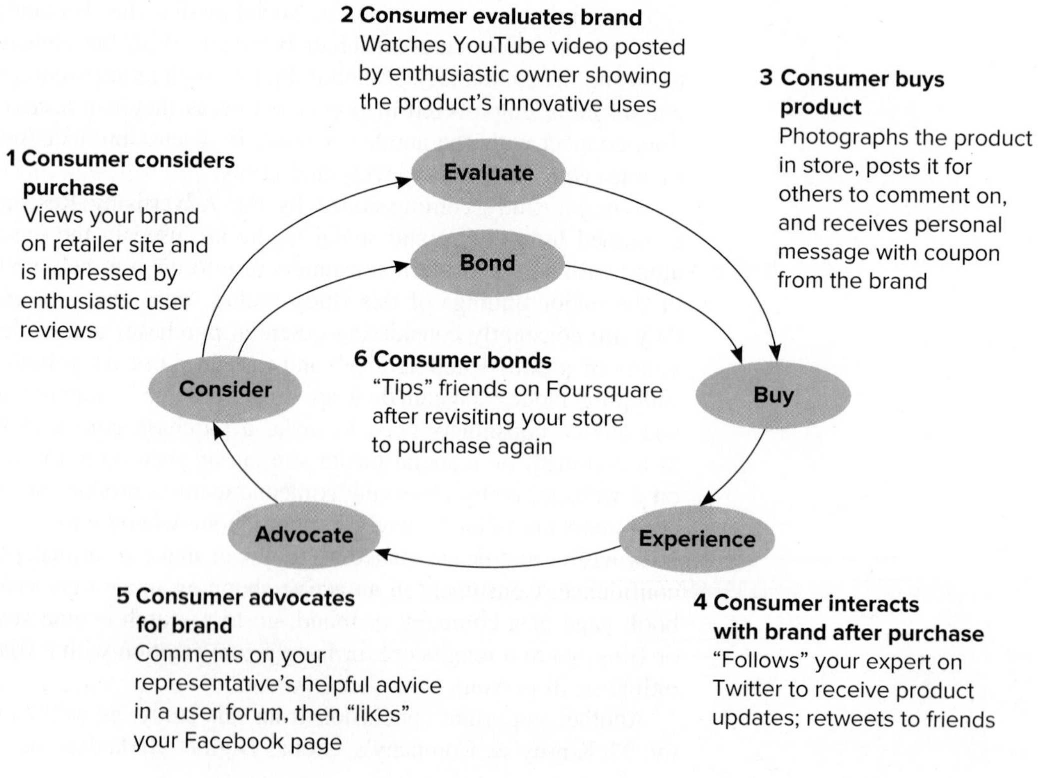

The consumer decision journey framework has a number of implications for marketers as they develop their IMC programs. Edelman notes that instead of determining how to allocate spending across the various IMC tools such as various forms of media advertising, marketers should target stages in the decision journey. Marketers often spend a large percentage of their IMC budgets on advertising and sales promotion which are designed to influence consumers at the consider and buy stages. However, consumers may often be influenced more during the evaluate and enjoy-advocate-bond stages. For many consumers the most important incentive to buy may be another person's advocacy or recommendation. He notes that it is also important for marketers to focus not only on the portion of their budget allocated to paid media—or what is sometimes referred to as "working media spend"—but also consider the role of *owned* media that a brand controls (such as websites and Facebook fan pages) as well as *earned media* (customer-created content on blogs, forums, and social media platforms).

Some of the findings from the ARF-commissioned study also are relevant to the role of social and digital media on the consumer decision journey. This study found that consumers like to tout their effectiveness and prowess as shoppers to others, which means that marketers can leverage this desire by providing forums for consumers to share their stories and experiences with others. The study also found that much online activity occurs after products are purchased, which points to an opportunity for marketers to develop a dialogue with consumers, engage them in discussions, and deepen their loyalty and affinity for their brands. The ARF study noted that the purchase journey of consumers varies by product or service category as high-risk/involvement products having longer cycles than lower-risk/involvement products. It is also important to note that the ARF research indicates that brand perceptions and offline advertising are still important in driving consideration throughout the cycle. Thus it is important for marketers to build and maintain strong brands and be visible and pervasive throughout the decision journey. Digital and Social Media Perspective 5–2 discusses how many marketers of low-involvement products such as consumer packaged are shifting more of their marketing budgets from traditional to digital media.

COGNITIVE PROCESSING OF COMMUNICATIONS

The hierarchical response models were for many years the primary focus of approaches for studying the receivers' responses to marketing communications. Attention centered on identifying relationships between specific controllable variables (such as source and message factors) and outcome or response variables (such as attention, comprehension, attitudes, and purchase intentions). This approach has been criticized on a number of fronts, including its black-box nature, since it can't explain what is causing these reactions.[51] In response to these concerns, researchers began trying to understand the nature of cognitive reactions to persuasive messages. Several approaches have been developed to examine the nature of consumers' cognitive processing of advertising messages.

The Cognitive Response Approach

One of the most widely used methods for examining consumers' cognitive processing of advertising messages is assessment of their **cognitive responses**, the thoughts that occur to them while reading, viewing, and/or hearing a communication.[52] These thoughts are generally measured by having consumers write down or verbally report their reactions to a message. The assumption is that these thoughts reflect the recipient's cognitive processes or reactions and help shape ultimate acceptance or rejection of the message.

Digital and Social Media Perspective 5–2 >>>

CONSUMER PACKAGED-GOODS MARKETERS TURN TO DIGITAL MEDIA

Consumer packaged-goods (CPG) companies such as Unilever, Nestlé, General Mills, Kraft Foods, Mondelēz International, and many others have traditionally relied on mass-media advertising such as television, magazines, and newspapers to market their products. CPG marketers account for about 13 percent of measured advertising spending in the United States and represent nearly half of the top 100 global advertisers and a third of the top 100 U.S. advertisers. The reliance on media advertising is not surprising, as many packaged goods are low-risk/reward types of products that are characterized by shorter purchase cycles and lower levels of involvement in the consumer decision-making process. CPG marketers have traditionally spent a large percentage of their IMC budgets on TV and print to build and maintain brand awareness, as well as on consumer and trade promotions that provide consumers with coupons, rebates, or some other type of extra incentive to buy. However, the age of digital marketing has definitely arrived for CPG marketers as many of them are shifting their media allocation from television and print in favor of digital ads.

The Interactive Advertising Bureau estimates that CPG companies spent only about 5 percent of their marketing budgets on digital advertising in 2012. By 2015 this number had increased to 8.5 percent, much lower than other industries such as automotive, telecom, and financial services that spend around 12 percent. However, while the percentage is low for the CPG industry, a number of major marketers are making major increases in their digital spending. Companies such as Unilever, Procter & Gamble, Kraft Foods, Hershey, and Campbell Soup Co. were spending or planning to spend as much as 25 to 40 percent of their media budgets on digital in 2016. Campbell, whose brands include Campbell's Soup, Prego, V8, and Pepperidge Farm, increased its digital

spending to 40 percent of its media while TV spending declined to 50 percent. Mondelēz International, which owns brands such as Oreos and Trident gum, planned to spend as much as half of its North American media budget on digital by 2016.

A number of industry experts predict that digital spending by CPG firms will continue to increase for a number of reasons. Many companies believe that the return on investment for monies spent on digital advertising media may be just as good as television or print. One reason for this is the conventional wisdom that digital is cheaper than traditional media since there is a vast supply of inventory and digital display space is relatively inexpensive, particularly ads purchased programmatically through real-time biding on ad exchanges. P&G is now purchasing 70 percent of its digital advertising through programmatic buying. Many CPG marketers are either cutting, or trying to control, the size and growth in their ad spending and feel that digital ads are a more efficient way to reach specific market segments. And of course marketers recognize that consumers are spending more time online, particularly on mobile devices, and thus digital is the best medium to reach them.

There are several other reasons why CPG firms are beginning to embrace digital media and make them a significant part of their IMC programs. First, companies such as Nielsen and ComScore are developing measurement systems for digital display and video viewing audiences using some of the same metrics that are available for television and which CPG marketers and their agencies are accustomed to using. A second reason is the advanced analytics that are now available from digital media that allow CPG marketers, many of whom are highly data-driven, to identify target audiences based on their purchase or other behavior. For example, in 2012 Facebook introduced a "Customer Audiences" program

The cognitive response approach has been widely used in research by both academicians and advertising practitioners. Its focus has been to determine the types of responses evoked by an advertising message and how these responses relate to attitudes toward the ad, brand attitudes, and purchase intentions. Figure 5–9 depicts the three basic categories of cognitive responses researchers have identified—product/message, source-oriented, and ad execution thoughts—and how they may relate to attitudes and intentions.

Product/Message Thoughts   The first category of thoughts comprises those directed at the product or service and/or the claims being made in the communication. Much attention has focused on two particular types of responses, counterarguments and support arguments.

Source: Campbell Soup Company

complementary, not just in terms of reaching additional consumers but as a way to engage consumers in different ways. Social media in particular are a way for CPG marketers to get consumers to endorse their brands to their friends and associates.

Another reason why CPG marketers are paying more attention to digital media is that they are conduits for price promotions. The average CPG company spends around two-thirds of its marketing budget on sales promotion, with much of this money going to trade promotions. Traditionally print has been the medium of choice for communicating price and promotional messages through freestanding inserts (FSIs) in newspapers as well as circulars. However, with the decline in newspaper readership, CPG marketers are looking for other ways to deliver promotional offers to bargain-minded consumers. Many are using social media sites such as Facebook, Instagram, and Twitter as a platform to offer promotional incentives to consumers and also as a way to engage consumers through contests and other types of promotions.

Traditional media advertising remains the key component of the IMC program for most packaged-goods marketers. However, CPG marketing and brand managers are learning from their counterparts in automotive, retail, telecom, travel, and other industries, with whom they often share best practices, about the value and return on investment (ROI) potential of digital and social media. Thus, it is very likely that the role of digital will become an increasingly important part of the IMC program for companies selling brands across the various CPG categories.

aimed at CPG marketers that allows them to upload their customer relationship management (CRM) databases and better target messages to their consumers on the social media site. In early 2013, Facebook entered into a partnership with several data mining firms to target ads to users based on their offline shopping habits and recent in-store purchases.

CPG markets are also recognizing the value of using digital and social media to build brand advocacy and as valuable tools for reaching consumers when they are at the consideration stage of the purchase process rather than just as a way of building brand awareness. For example, Campbell's CEO Denise Morrison notes that "We are moving away from brand marketing to brand experience where we earn consumers' trust." rather than buying it." She added that even when traditional advertising is used it will be complemented by dynamic real-time personalized communications driven by data. Campbell' s is not the only CPG marketer that recognizes the value of integrating digital media with traditional media. While many marketers view the use of digital media as a way to extend the reach and frequency of their offline advertising, others recognize that the two can be

Sources: E. J. Schultz, "Campbell Dives Deeper into Digital with Major Spending Hike," *Advertising Age*, July 23, 2015, http://adage.com/article/cmo-strategy/campbell-dives-deeper-digital-major-spending-hike/299631/; Jack Neff and E. J. Schultz, "Overdose?" *Advertising Age*, February 9, 2015, pp. 14–15; Jack Neff, "Why Digital Is Grabbing a Bigger of Consumer Product Budgets," *Advertising Age*, February 14, 2014, http://adage.com/article/news/cpg-execs-cagny-efficiency-digital-dollars/291814/; Jack Neff, "Does Digital Sell Soap?" *Advertising Age*, June 18, 2012, pp. 120–21.

Counterarguments are thoughts the recipient has that are opposed to the position taken in the message. For example, consider the ad for Ultra Tide shown in Exhibit 5–15. A consumer may express disbelief or disapproval of a claim made in an ad. ("I don't believe that any detergent could get that stain out!") Other consumers who see this ad may generate **support arguments**, or thoughts that affirm the claims made in the message. ("Ultra Tide looks like a really good product—I think I'll try it.")

The likelihood of counterarguing is greater when the message makes claims that oppose the receiver's beliefs. For example, a consumer viewing a commercial that attacks a favorite brand is likely to engage in counterarguing. Counterarguments relate negatively to message acceptance; the more the receiver counterargues, the less likely he or she is to accept the position advocated in the message.[53] Support

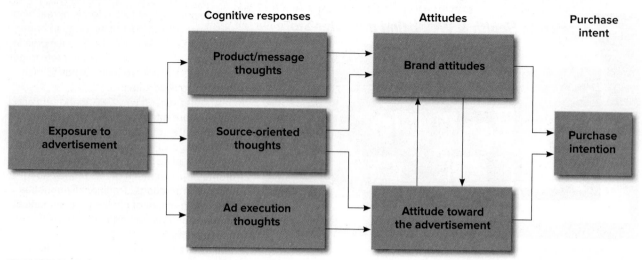

FIGURE 5–9

A Model of Cognitive Response

arguments, on the other hand, relate positively to message acceptance. Thus, the marketer should develop ads or other promotional messages that minimize counter-arguing and encourage support arguments.

Source-Oriented Thoughts   A second category of cognitive responses is directed at the source of the communication. One of the most important types of responses in this category is **source derogations**, or negative thoughts about the spokesperson or organization making the claims. Such thoughts generally lead to a reduction in message acceptance. If consumers find a particular spokesperson annoying or untrustworthy, they are less likely to accept what this source has to say.

Of course, source-related thoughts are not always negative. Receivers who react favorably to the source generate favorable thoughts, or **source bolsters**. As you would expect, most advertisers attempt to hire spokespeople their target audience likes to carry this effect over to the message. Considerations involved in choosing an appropriate source or spokesperson will be discussed in Chapter 6.

EXHIBIT 5–15

Consumers often generate support arguments in response to ads for quality products

Source: Tide by Procter & Gamble

Ad Execution Thoughts   The third category of cognitive responses shown in Figure 5–7 consists of the individual's thoughts about the ad itself. Many of the thoughts receivers have when reading or viewing an ad do not concern the product and/or message claims directly. Rather, they are affective reactions representing the consumer's feelings toward the ad. These thoughts may include reactions to ad execution factors such as the creativity of the ad, the quality of the visual effects, colors, and voice tones. **Ad execution–related thoughts** can be either favorable or unfavorable. They are important because of their effect on attitudes toward the advertisement as well as the brand.

Much attention has focused on consumers' affective reactions to ads, especially TV commercials.[54] **Attitude toward the ad** (A→ad) represents the receivers' feelings of favorability or unfavorability toward the ad. Advertisers are interested in consumers' reactions to the ad because they know that affective reactions are an important determinant of advertising effectiveness, since these reactions may be transferred to the brand itself or directly influence purchase intentions. One study found that people who enjoy a commercial are twice as likely as those who are neutral toward it to be convinced that the brand is the best.[55]

Consumers' feelings about the ad may be just as important as their attitudes toward the brand (if not more so) in determining an ad's effectiveness.[56] The importance of affective reactions and feelings generated by the ad depends on several factors, among them the nature of the ad and the type of processing engaged in by the receiver.[57] Many advertisers use emotional appeals designed to evoke positive feelings and affective reactions as the basis of their creative strategy. The success of this strategy depends in part on the consumers' involvement with the brand and their likelihood of attending to and processing the message. Another way marketers try to create favorable attitudes toward their ads in by using humor which can put consumers in a positive mood and increase their liking of not only the ad itself, but also the brand. For example, many of the ads shown during the Super Bowl each year use humorous appeals since marketers know consumers will be watching them closely and discuss them with others both during and after the game.

We end our analysis of the receiver by examining a popular model that considers how involvement and other factors that may influence the route to persuasion consumers follow and their cognitive processing of a message.

The Elaboration Likelihood Model

Differences in the ways consumers process and respond to persuasive messages are addressed in the **elaboration likelihood model (ELM)** of persuasion, shown in Figure 5–10.[58] The ELM was devised by Richard Petty and John Cacioppo to explain the process by which persuasive communications (such as ads) lead to persuasion by influencing attitudes. According to the ELM, the attitude formation or change process depends on the amount and nature of *elaboration,* or processing, of relevant information that occurs in response to a persuasive message. High elaboration means the receiver engages in careful consideration, thinking, and evaluation of the information or arguments contained in the message. Low elaboration occurs when the receiver does not engage in active information processing or thinking but rather makes inferences about the position being advocated in the message on the basis of simple positive or negative cues.

The ELM shows that elaboration likelihood is a function of two elements, motivation and ability to process the message. *Motivation* to process the message depends on such factors as involvement, personal relevance, and individuals' needs and arousal levels. *Ability* depends on the individual's knowledge, intellectual capacity, and opportunity to process the message. For example, an individual viewing a humorous commercial or one containing an attractive model may be distracted from processing the information about the product.

According to the ELM, there are two basic routes to persuasion or attitude change. Under the **central route to persuasion**, the receiver is viewed as a very active, involved participant in the communication process whose ability and motivation to attend, comprehend, and evaluate messages are high. When central processing of an advertising message occurs, the consumer pays close attention to message content and scrutinizes the message arguments. A high level of cognitive response activity or processing occurs, and the ad's ability to persuade the receiver depends primarily on the receiver's evaluation of the quality of the arguments presented. Predominantly favorable cognitive responses (support arguments and source bolsters) lead to favorable changes in cognitive structure, which lead to positive attitude change, or persuasion.

Conversely, if the cognitive processing is predominantly unfavorable and results in counterarguments and/or source derogations, the changes in cognitive structure are unfavorable and *boomerang,* or result in negative attitude change. Attitude change that occurs through central processing is relatively enduring and should resist subsequent efforts to change it.

Under the **peripheral route to persuasion**, shown on the right side of Figure 5–10, the receiver is viewed as lacking the motivation or ability to process information and is not likely to engage in detailed cognitive processing. Rather than evaluating the information presented in the message, the receiver relies on peripheral

FIGURE 5–10

The Elaboration Likelihood
Model of Persuasion

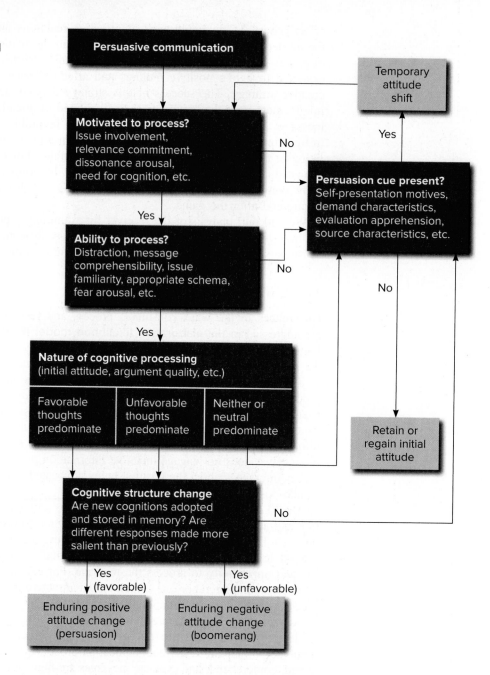

cues that may be incidental to the main arguments. The receiver's reaction to the message depends on how he or she evaluates these peripheral cues.

The consumer may use several types of peripheral cues or cognitive shortcuts rather than carefully evaluating the message arguments presented in an advertisement.[59] Favorable attitudes may be formed if the endorser in the ad is viewed as an expert or is attractive and/or likable or if the consumer likes certain executional aspects of the ad such as the way it is made, the music, or the imagery. Notice how the ad in Exhibit 5–16 for Peak Long Life antifreeze contains several positive peripheral cues, including an attractive and highly relevant celebrity endorser (race car driver Danica Patrick) and appealing visual imagery that is consistent with the brand positioning. These cues might help consumers form a positive attitude toward the brand even if they do not process the message portion of the ad.

Peripheral cues can also lead to rejection of a message. For example, ads that advocate extreme positions, use endorsers who are not well liked or have credibility problems, or are not executed well (such as low-budget ads for local retailers) may

EXHIBIT 5–16

This ad contains peripheral cues, most notably a celebrity endorser

Source: PEAK by Old World Industries

be rejected without any consideration of their information or message arguments. As shown in Figure 5–8, the ELM views attitudes resulting from peripheral processing as temporary. So favorable attitudes must be maintained by continual exposure to the peripheral cues, such as through repetitive advertising.

Implications of the ELM   The elaboration likelihood model has important implications for marketing communications, particularly with respect to involvement. For example, if the involvement level of consumers in the target audience is high, an ad or sales presentation should contain strong arguments that are difficult for the message recipient to refute or counterargue. If the involvement level of the target audience is low, peripheral cues may be more important than detailed message arguments.

An interesting test of the ELM showed that the effectiveness of a celebrity endorser in an ad depends on the receiver's involvement level.[60] When involvement was low, a celebrity endorser had a significant effect on attitudes. When the receiver's involvement was high, however, the use of a celebrity had no effect on brand attitudes; the quality of the arguments used in the ad was more important.

The explanation given for these findings was that a celebrity may serve as a peripheral cue in the low-involvement situation, allowing the receiver to develop favorable attitudes based on feelings toward the source rather than engaging in extensive processing of the message. A highly involved consumer, however, engages in more detailed central processing of the message content. The quality of the message becomes more important than the identity of the endorser. The ELM suggests that the most effective type of message depends on the route to persuasion the consumer follows. Many marketers recognize that involvement levels are low for their product categories and consumers are not motivated to process advertising messages in any detail. That's why marketers of low-involvement products often rely on creative tactics that emphasize peripheral cues and use repetitive advertising to create and maintain favorable attitudes toward their brand.

The ELM is one of the most frequently cited theories of how advertising impacts consumers and is considered one of the most influential theoretical contributions to the academic literature in advertising and other forms of persuasion.[61] However, the model has been the subject of debate and criticism by a number of academic researchers as attempts to replicate the findings from the study discussed previously have not been successful.[62] A recent effort to replicate this study with subjects from three countries (United States, United Kingdom, and Australia) was only partially successful and did not support the key finding that attitudes formed via the central route to persuasion are more predictive of behavior than those formed via the peripheral route. The authors suggest that changes in the media environment, particularly the shift to the dominance of digital and social media, call to question the relevancy of advertising theories developed during the era when traditional mass media was dominant.[63]

SUMMARIZING THE RESPONSE PROCESS AND THE EFFECTS OF ADVERTISING

As you have seen from our analysis of the receiver, the process consumers go through in responding to marketing communications can be viewed from a number of perspectives. Vakratsas and Ambler recently reviewed more than 250 journal articles and books in an effort to better understand how advertising works and affects the consumer.[64] On the basis of their review of these studies, they concluded that

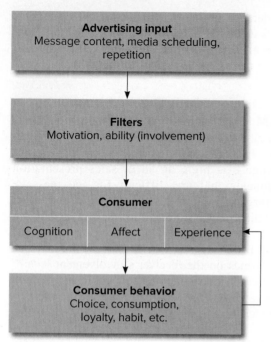

FIGURE 5–11

A Framework for Studying How Advertising Works

although effects hierarchies have been actively employed for nearly 100 years, there is little support for the concept of a hierarchy of effects in the sense of temporal sequence. They note that in trying to understand the response process and the manner in which advertising works, there are three critical intermediate effects between advertising and purchase (Figure 5–11). These include *cognition,* the "thinking" dimension of a person's response; *affect,* the "feeling" dimension; and *experience,* which is a feedback dimension based on the outcomes of product purchasing and usage. They conclude that individual responses to advertising are mediated or filtered by factors such as motivation and ability to process information, which can radically alter or change the individual's response to advertising. They suggest that the effects of advertising should be evaluated using these three dimensions, with some intermediate variables being more important than others, depending on factors such as the product category, stage of the product life cycle, target audience, competition, and impact of other marketing-mix components.

Other researchers have been critical of the hierarchy models as well. For example, Hall argues that advertisers need to move away from explicit and implicit reliance on hierarchical models of advertising effects and develop models that place affect and experience at the center of the advertising process.[65] The implication of these criticisms is that marketers should focus on cognition, affect, and experience as critical variables that advertising may affect. However, they should not assume a particular sequence of responses but, rather, engage in research and analysis to better understand how advertising and other forms of promotion may affect these intermediate variables in various product/market situations.

While a number of issues and concerns regarding hierarchy of effects models have been noted, many believe that they are of value to advertising practice and research. For example, Thomas Barry contends that despite their limitations, hierarchical models do help predict behavior. He notes that these models also provide insight into whether advertising strategies need to focus on impacting cognition, affect, and/or behavior based on audience or segmentation experiences and they provide valuable planning, training, and conceptual frameworks.[66]

Those responsible for planning the IMC program need to learn as much as possible about their target audience and how it may respond to advertising, along with other forms of marketing communication. For example, William Weilbacher has noted that marketing communications programs include more than just advertising.[67] Consumers are continually immersed in brand-sponsored communications that also include public relations, a broad range of sales promotion activities, social media, direct marketing, event sponsorships, movie and TV show product placements, and other forms of marketing communication. He argues that hierarchy models must move beyond just explaining the effects of advertising and consider how, and with what effects, consumers synthesize information from all the various integrated marketing communications activities for a brand. As we have seen from the discussion of the social consumer decision journey, information from the numerous forms of social media and other digital sources is adding to the number of factors that influence the consumer response process and decision making.

The various models discussed in this chapter are important as they present the basic elements of communication and provide insight into how consumers process and respond to advertising and other IMC tools. It is vital to understand the communication process as it provides a foundation for studying and evaluating integrated marketing communications. Those involved in various aspects of IMC find that understanding the communication process helps them make better decisions in planning, implementing, and evaluating their marketing communication programs.

Summary

The function of all elements of the IMC program is to communicate, so promotional planners must understand the communication process. This process can be very complex; successful marketing communications depend on a number of factors, including the nature of the message, the audience's interpretation of it, and the environment in which it is received. For effective communication to occur, the sender must encode a message in such a way that it will be decoded by the receiver in the intended manner. Feedback from the receiver helps the sender determine whether proper decoding has occurred or whether noise has interfered with the communication process.

Nonpersonal channels of communication are those that carry a message without direct, interpersonal contact between the sender and receiver and are generally referred to as the mass media. Personal channels involve direct communication between two or more persons and can occur through interpersonal contact (face-to-face) or via other methods such as e-mail or through social media. Members of one's social networks such as friends, neighbors, associates, co-workers, or family members are also personal channels of communication and represent word-of-mouth (WOM) influence, which can be a very powerful source of information. Marketers often try to generate WOM through viral marketing, which refers to the act of propagating marketing-relevant messages through the help and cooperation of individual consumers.

Promotional planning begins with the receiver or target audience, as marketers must understand how the audience is likely to respond to various sources of communication or types of messages. For promotional planning, the receiver can be analyzed with respect to both its composition (i.e., individual, group, or mass audiences) and the response process it goes through. A number of models of the response process have been developed, including the AIDA, hierarchy of effects, innovation adoption, and information processing model. Different orderings of the traditional response hierarchy include the standard learning, dissonance/attribution, and low-involvement models.

The environment in which consumers evaluate brands and make purchase decisions has changed dramatically as digital content—including social media—has become pervasive in our daily lives and is influencing consumer behavior. The social consumer decision journey framework recognized that consumers can enter the purchase path at various points, depending on whether they first engage with a brand, research a product or service, or hear about it through their social networks.

The cognitive response approach examines the thoughts evoked by a message and how they shape the receiver's ultimate acceptance or rejection of the communication. The elaboration likelihood model of attitude formation and change recognizes two forms of message processing, the central and peripheral routes to persuasion, which are a function of the receiver's motivation and ability to process a message. There are three critical intermediate effects between advertising and purchase, including cognition, affect, and experience. Those responsible for planning the IMC program should learn as much as possible about their target audience and how it may respond to advertising and other forms of marketing communications.

Key Terms

communication 145
source 147
encoding 148
message 149
channel 149
mass media 149
word-of-mouth (WOM) communications 150
buzz marketing 150
viral marketing 151
seeding 152
receiver 155

decoding 155
field of experience 155
noise 156
response 157
feedback 157
AIDA model 161
hierarchy of effects model 162
innovation adoption model 162
information processing model 163
standard learning model 165
dissonance/attribution model 166
low-involvement hierarchy 167

cognitive responses 171
counterargument 173
support argument 173
source derogations 174
source bolsters 174
ad execution–related thoughts 174
attitude toward the ad 174
elaboration likelihood model (ELM) 175
central route to persuasion 175
peripheral route to persuasion 175

Discussion Questions

1. The chapter opener discusses the award-winning "Like a Girl" campaign developed by the Leo Burnett agency for Procter & Gamble's Always brand. Why do you think this campaign was so successful and resulted in such a strong viral response among consumers? (LO 5-1, 5-2)

2. Global Perspective 5–1 discusses the problems marketers can encounter when developing advertising messages in different languages and for different cultures. Discuss some of the ways marketers can deal with this problem and avoid mistranslations and other communication problems. (LO 5-1)

3. What is meant by encoding? Discuss how encoding differs for various types of advertising messages such as radio and television commercials, print ads, and digital/online ads. (LO 5-2)

4. Explain the concept of viral marketing and how it relates to word-of-mouth communication. Find an example of a company that used viral marketing successfully and one that encountered problems when using this technique. (LO 5-3)

5. The chapter discusses the Fiesta Movement social media campaign used by Ford to launch its new Fiesta subcompact car in the U.S. market. Discuss the pros and cons of this program and assess the amount of risk Ford took in allowing the agents to use social media to communicate with their followers about the Fiesta? Do you agree with Ford's decision to use the Fiesta Movement: A Social Remix as part of its IMC program for the redesigned 2014 Fiesta? Why or why not? (LO 5-3)

6. Digital and Social Media Perspective 5–1 discusses the age bias that exists in advertising and digital agencies against older people, who may not be as digitally savvy as the younger generation. Do you think it is acceptable for agencies to favor younger people in the hiring process? How might an older person address the age bias problem? (LO 5-1, 5-3)

7. What is meant by the element of noise in marketing communications process? Discuss how mobile devices such as laptops, tablets, and smartphones are contributing to the noise problem for television advertising? What are some ways advertisers can deal with the noise distractions created by these devices? (LO 5-1, 5-2)

8. Discuss how the implications of the social consumer decision journey framework might differ for a marketer of a high-involvement product such as a tablet computer or smartphone versus a company marketing a low-involvement product such as soft drinks or paper towels. (LO 5-5)

9. Discuss some of the reasons consumer packaged-goods (CPG) marketers are allocating more of their IMC budgets to digital and social media versus traditional media such as television and print. Do you think marketers run any risks in allocating more of their budgets to digital and social versus traditional media? (LO 5-3)

10. Discuss the value to marketers of using a cognitive response approach to analyze consumers' reactions to and processing of their advertising messages. Choose a print ad or television commercial and discuss the types of cognitive responses that it might generate using the model shown in Figure 5–7. (LO 5-6)

11. Explain what is meant by a central versus peripheral route to persuasion and the factors that might determine when each might be used by consumers in response to an advertisement or other form of marketing communication. (LO 5-6)

6

Source, Message, and Channel Factors

AGGRESSIVE, YOUNG & FEARLESS

Source: Under Armour, Inc.

LEARNING OBJECTIVES

LO1 Discuss the variables in the communication system and how they influence consumers' processing of promotional messages.

LO2 Identify decision factors involved in selecting a source for a promotional message.

LO3 Compare the different types of message structures and appeals.

LO4 Explain how different types of channels influence the marketing communications process.

UNDER ARMOUR PROTECTS ITS HOUSE BY SPENDING WISELY ON ENDORSERS

Under Armour (UA) was founded in 1996 by Kevin Plank, a former University of Maryland football player, who began by selling compression shirts that could "wick" sweat away from the body to college sports teams out of the trunk of his car. Plank hated how the cotton T-shirts he wore under his shoulder pads and jersey became soaked with sweat as it was not only uncomfortable, but the extra weight hurt an athlete's performance. From the very beginning Under Armour's value proposition was based on selling athletic apparel that is functional and comfortable and enhances performance. However, the challenge facing Plank as an entrepreneur was how to build awareness of his innovative product and get athletes to wear it. As a former high school and college player, Plank had friends who were playing for more than a dozen National Football League (NFL) teams whom he would send shirts to wear as well as encourage them to get their teammates to do the same. As part of his grassroots approach he emphasized that if an Under Armour shirt helped them improve their performance even a little they would earn more money, thus positioning his pitch as a way to help the athletes rather than asking them to do him a favor. Thus, even in the nascent stages of the company, Kevin Plank was learning how to negotiate with athletes to get them to endorse Under Armour products.

Plank's first big break came in 1997 when the Miami Dolphins NFL team wore his product under their uniforms in a nationally televised game with the Under Armour logo visible on the neck of every shirt. The following year the football-oriented movie *Any Given Sunday* was being filmed in Baltimore where Under Armour is based. The producers of the movie were looking for a product that would represent the athletic nature of the movie and be comfortable to wear during filming. Under Armour agreed to provide products and its shirts were used throughout the filming and appeared in the movie itself, resulting in national exposure for the brand. A similar situation arose in 2003. This time it was sports cable giant ESPN that came calling, asking UA to be part of its new HBO series about football players called *Playmakers*. ESPN thought that since everyone in locker rooms seemed to be wearing Under Armour, it would be more realistic if the players in the movie were shown in UA clothing.

Under Armour achieved great success and grew very quickly in its early years by forming a brand identity that was associated with the raw emotion and muscle-filled world of football and other predominantly male team sports. The company developed a unique brand identity through its television advertising campaign that began in 2003 and used the slogan "Protect This House." The commercials featured well-conditioned football players working out while wearing Under Armour, and ended with the players gathering in a huddle and shouting "We must protect this house!" as if their lives depended on it. The iconic tagline became a symbol of what Under Armour stands for as a brand; and a few years ago the phrase "I will" was added to it as a call to action for athletes.

Under Armour went public in 2005 and the stock price nearly doubled the first day it was traded. Since going public the company has averaged more than 25 percent annual growth and reached $4 billion in revenue in 2016, and expects to hit $7 billion by 2018. The keys to Under Armour's success have included quality products, strong branding and positioning, and an incredible roster of athletes as endorsers, a number of whom it signed for much less money than its major competitors such as Nike and adidas. Even with its incredible growth, Under Armour is still only about an eighth the size of Nike, which had sales over of over $30 billion in 2016 and less than a quarter the size of adidas whose global revenue was nearly $20 billion. Nike spends nearly $1 billion a year on endorsement deals while adidas recently announced that it planned to sign 500 athletes in North America alone to deals. Nike's endorsers include basketball legend Michael Jordan and NBA superstars LeBron James and Kevin Durant, golfers Tiger Woods and Rory McIlroy, and soccer star Cristiano Rinaldo. Adidas top endorsers include soccer star Lionel Messi and Derrick Rose who plays for the New York Knicks in the NBA.

While Under Armour may not be able to spend as lavishly as its larger competitors on endorsement deals, most industry experts argue the company is spending its money more wisely. Under Armour's endorsers now include three of the best players and biggest stars in professional football, basketball, and baseball: Carolina Panthers quarterback Cam Newton, Golden State Warriors point guard

Stephen Curry, and Washington Nationals outfielder Bryce Harper. Newton is a former Heisman trophy winner who won the NFL's Most Valuable Player award in 2015 while leading his team to the Super Bowl. Harper was the National League Rookie of the Year in 2012 and won the league's MVP award in 2015.

Stephen Curry has been the key to Under Armour's newfound success in the basketball shoe market which is dominated by Nike. Under Armour approached Curry in 2013 when his contract with Nike was about to expire. Nike considered whether it was worth outbidding Under Armour for Curry and decided not to resign or offer him a coveted signature shoe line. Since signing with Under Armour, Curry has become one of the NBA's most prominent stars, winning the league's MVP award in both 2015 and 2016 while leading the Warriors to an NBA championship in 2015. Under Armour leveraged Curry's success by creating its first signature shoe, the UA Curry One, which is its best-selling shoe and has played a key role in helping the company reach nearly $800 million in footwear revenue.

Under Armour's eye for talent goes beyond team sports. The company signed swimmer Michael Phelps, a Baltimore native, to an endorsement deal in 2010. Phelps is the most decorated Olympian of all time with 22 medals, including 18 gold. In 2013 Under Armour signed golfer Jordan Spieth, who was a relative unknown right after he turned professional, but by 2015 was the number 1 ranked golfer in the world after winning two major championships including the Masters and U.S. Open.

Under Armour's roster of endorsers is not limited to male athletes. An important part of its growth strategy is to move beyond male-dominated sports such as football, baseball, and basketball and bring more women to the brand. Its roster of female athletes include skier Lindsey Vonn, a four-time Olympic gold medalist who has been with the company since 2006; up-and-coming tennis star Sloane Stephens; and Kelly O'Hara, who plays on the U.S. Women's National Soccer team that has won the FIFA World Cup and an Olympic gold medal. However, two of its most influential female endorsers are not athletes playing a professional sport, but rather a ballerina and a superstar model. The women are helping Under Armour in its efforts to position itself as a brand that can empower female athletes and compete against Lululemon and Nike in the fast-growing athleisure segment of the apparel market.

In 2014 Under Armour signed ballerina Misty Copeland to an endorsement deal. She went on to become only the third African American female soloist in the history of the American Ballet Theater. The company also signed Gisele Bundchen, one of the world's highest-paid models and wife of New England Patriots star quarterback Tom Brady, who is also an Under Armour endorser. Both women were featured in the award-winning "I Will, I Want" women's campaign that was a viral sensation racking up over 4 million views in just one week and helped make women's apparel 30 percent of Under Armour's revenue.

Under Armour recognizes that having the right athletes and other celebrities endorsing its products is a key success factor in the athletic shoe and apparel market. They not only help build the brand, but also are catalysts for sales. Kevin Plank notes that the success the company has had with Curry, Spieth, and Copeland has taught the company a valuable lesson regarding the need to think bigger, as all three have transcended their sports and become known by just their first names. In 2015 Under Armour overtook adidas, which also owns Reebok, to become the second most popular sportswear manufacturer in the United States and it has set its sights on the rest of the world. Watch out, Nike!

Sources: James Ellis and Dimitra Kessenides, "Under Armour's Most Valuable Players," *Bloomberg Businessweek,* February 14, 2016, pp. 20–21; Richard Feloni, "The Athlete Endorsements That Are Turning Under Armour into Nike's Strongest Competitor," *Business Insider,* June 16, 2015, www.businessinsider.com/the-athlete-endorsements-helping-under-armour-compete-with-nike-2015-6; Kevin Plank, "Under Armour's Founder on Learning to Leverage Celebrity Endorsements," *Harvard Business Review* 90, no. 5 (May 2012), pp. 45–48.

In this chapter, we analyze the major variables in the communication system: the source, the message, and the channel. We examine the characteristics of sources, how they influence reactions to promotional messages, and why one type of communicator is more effective than another. We then focus on the message itself and how structure and type of appeal influence its effectiveness. Finally, we consider how factors related to the channel or medium affect the communication process.

PROMOTIONAL PLANNING THROUGH THE PERSUASION MATRIX

To develop an effective advertising and promotional campaign, a firm must select the right spokesperson to deliver a compelling message through appropriate channels or media. Source, message, and channel factors are controllable elements in the communication model. The **persuasion matrix** (Figure 6–1) helps marketers see how each controllable element interacts with the consumer's response process.[1] The matrix has two sets of variables. *Independent variables* are the controllable components of the communication process, outlined in Chapter 5; *dependent variables* are the steps a receiver goes through in being persuaded. Marketers can choose the person or source who delivers the message, the type of message appeal used, and the channel or medium. And although they can't control the receiver, they can select their target audience. The destination variable is included because the initial message recipient may pass on information to others, such as friends or associates, through word of mouth.

Promotional planners need to know how decisions about each independent variable influence the stages of the response hierarchy so that they don't enhance one stage at the expense of another. A humorous message may gain attention but result in decreased comprehension if consumers fail to process its content. Many ads that use humor, sexual appeals, or celebrities capture consumers' attention but result in poor recall of the brand name or message. The following examples, which correspond to the numbers in various cells of Figure 6–1, illustrate decisions that can be evaluated with the persuasion matrix.

1. *Receiver/comprehension: Can the receiver comprehend the ad?* Marketers must know their target market to make their messages clear and understandable. A less educated person may have more difficulty interpreting a complicated message. Jargon may be unfamiliar to some receivers. The more marketers know about the target market, the more they see which words, symbols, and expressions their customers understand.
2. *Channel/presentation: Which media will increase presentation?* A popular prime-time-TV show such as *The Big Bang Theory* is seen by as many as

FIGURE 6–1

The Persuasion Matrix

Dependent variables: Steps in being persuaded	Independent variables: The communication components				
	Source	Message	Channel	Receiver	Destination
Message presentation			(2)		
Attention	(4)				
Comprehension				(1)	
Yielding		(3)			
Retention					
Behavior					

18 million people each week, while magazines such as *Time* and *People* reach over 3 million readers with each weekly publication and millions more through their digital editions. But the important point is how well a media vehicle reaches the marketer's target audience. A show such as *Keeping Up with the Kardashians,* which appears on the E! cable network, reaches around 2 million viewers each week and its audience primarily consists of young men and women between the ages of 18 and 24 who are very fashion conscious and tech savvy. Although the ratings of the show have declined recently, many companies still view it as a way to reach this audience which is highly coveted by many advertisers since they are prime prospects for clothing fashion, consumer electronics, and many other products.[2]

3. *Message/yielding: What type of message will create favorable attitudes or feelings?* Marketers generally try to create agreeable messages that lead to positive feelings toward the product or service. Humorous messages often put consumers in a good mood and evoke positive feelings that may become associated with the brand being advertised. Music adds emotion that makes consumers more receptive to the message. Many advertisers use explicit sexual appeals designed to arouse consumers or suggest they can enhance their attractiveness to the opposite sex. Some marketers compare their brands to the competition.

4. *Source/attention: Who will be effective in getting consumers' attention?* The large number of ads we are bombarded with every day makes it difficult for advertisers to break through the clutter. Marketers deal with this problem by using sources who will attract the target audience's attention—actors, athletes, rock stars, or attractive models.

SOURCE FACTORS

LO6-2

The source component is a multifaceted concept. When Tina Fey appears in a commercial for American Express, is the source Fey herself, the company, or some combination of the two? And, of course, consumers get information from friends, relatives, and neighbors; in fact, personal sources may be the most influential factor in a purchase decision. Word-of-mouth information transmitted from one individual to another is often perceived as more reliable and trustworthy than that received through more formal marketing channels such as advertising. As was discussed in Chapter 5, marketers are using buzz and stealth marketing methods to generate favorable word-of-mouth discussion and recommendations for their products and services.[3]

We use the term **source** to mean the person involved in communicating a marketing message, either directly or indirectly. A *direct source* is a spokesperson who delivers a message and/or endorses a product or service, like country music star Miranda Lambert who appears in an ad that is part of "The Breakfast Project" campaign sponsored by the Milk Processor Education Program. The campaign encourages people to eat a nutritious breakfast that includes milk (Exhibit 6–1). An *indirect source,* say, a model, doesn't actually deliver a message but draws attention to and/or enhances the appearance of the ad. Some ads use neither a direct nor an indirect source; the source is the organization with the message to communicate. Since most research focuses on individuals as a message source, our examination of source factors follows this approach.

Companies are very careful when selecting individuals to deliver their selling messages. Many firms spend huge sums of money for a specific person to endorse their product or company. They also spend millions recruiting, selecting, and training salespeople to represent the company and deliver sales presentations. They recognize that the characteristics of the source affect the sales and advertising message.

FIGURE 6–2

Source Attributes and
Receiver Processing Modes

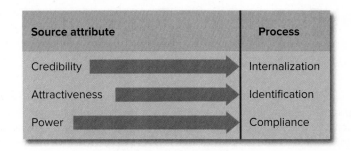

Source attribute	Process
Credibility	Internalization
Attractiveness	Identification
Power	Compliance

Marketers try to select individuals whose traits will maximize message influence. The source may be knowledgeable, popular, and/or physically attractive; typify the target audience; or have the power to reward or punish the receiver in some manner. Herbert Kelman developed three basic categories of source attributes: credibility, attractiveness, and power.[4] Each influences the recipient's attitude or behavior through a different process (see Figure 6–2).

Source Credibility

Credibility is the extent to which the recipient sees the source as having relevant knowledge, skill, or experience and trusts the source to give unbiased, objective information. There are two important dimensions to credibility, expertise and trustworthiness.

A communicator seen as knowledgeable—someone with expertise—is more persuasive than one with less expertise. But the source also has to be trustworthy—honest, ethical, and believable. The influence of a knowledgeable source will be lessened if audience members think he or she is biased or has underlying personal motives for advocating a position (such as being paid to endorse a product).

One of the most reliable effects found in communications research is that expert and/or trustworthy sources are more persuasive than sources who are less expert or trustworthy.[5] Information from a credible source influences beliefs, opinions, attitudes, and/or behavior through a process known as **internalization**, which occurs when the receiver adopts the opinion of the credible communicator since he or she believes information from this source is accurate. Once the receiver internalizes an opinion or attitude, it becomes integrated into his or her belief system and may be maintained even after the source of the message is forgotten.

A highly credible communicator is particularly important when message recipients have a negative position toward the product, service, company, or issue being promoted, because the credible source is likely to inhibit counterarguments. As discussed in Chapter 5, reduced counterarguing should result in greater message acceptance and persuasion.

Applying Expertise Because attitudes and opinions developed through an internalization process become part of the individual's belief system, marketers want to use communicators with high credibility. Companies use a variety of techniques to convey source expertise. Sales personnel are trained in the product line, which increases customers' perceptions of their expertise. Marketers of highly technical products recruit sales reps with specialized technical backgrounds in engineering, computer science, and other areas to ensure their expertise.

Spokespeople are often chosen because of their knowledge, experience, and expertise in a particular product or service area. Endorsements from individuals or groups recognized as experts, such as doctors or dentists, are also common in advertising. For example, Dove has promoted the fact that its skin cleansing products are the most recommended by dermatologists in ads for more than 60 years (Exhibit 6–2). The importance of using expert sources was shown in a study by Roobina Ohanian, who found that the

EXHIBIT 6–2

Dove promotes the fact that it is recommended by experts in skin care

Source: Dove by Unilever

Global Perspective 6–1 > > >

Celebrities Sell Out—but Only Abroad

While many celebrities make huge sums of money endorsing products and serving as advertising spokespeople, some big stars won't appear in ads in the United States because they don't want fans to think they've sold out. There has also long been a feeling among actors that appearing in commercials might devalue their image among the powerful Hollywood producers and directors. However, this has been changing in recent years and even some of the biggest names in entertainment have decided to cash in on their celebrity and appear in commercials. For example, Hollywood heavyweights Scarlett Johansson and Matthew McConaughey have been the faces of Dolce & Gabbanna's "The One" fragrance for a number of years. McConaughey also signed a lucrative endorsement deal with the Lincoln Motor Company division of Ford to help the luxury brand attract younger, more culturally progressive consumers. Nicole Kidman was paid $8 million to appear in commercials for the Chanel No. 5 fragrance line, and in 2012 Chanel hired Brad Pitt as its first male spokesperson for its signature fragrance. Using Pitt in Chanel ads may not have been a wise decision since the TV spot, which featured him

rambling on about journeys and fate, was widely criticized and parodied on YouTube and shows such as *Saturday Night Live*.

Some of the A-list celebrities still resist the temptation to cash in on their fame in the United States, but they are only too happy to appear in ads in foreign countries. Nowhere are ads starring American celebrities more prevalent than in Japan. Even the rich and famous have trouble saying no to Japanese advertisers who will pay them between $1 million and $3 million for a few hours' work to make 10-second spots that their Western fans across the Pacific will never see. In Japan, celebrities make more money for less work and because the commercials will never air in the United States, they think they can make the money without looking like they are selling their artistic souls.

Academy Award winner Leonardo DiCaprio, who is arguably one of the most famous actors in the world, appeared in a 15-second spot for the Jim Beam bourbon brand in which the only words he says are "cool bourbon, Jim Beam." The company said the ad would be used only in Japan, but it made its way to the United States and other countries via YouTube as soon as it was aired there.

Megastars such as Charlize Theron, Brad Pitt, Sean Connery, Kiefer Sutherland, Kevin Costner, and Harrison Ford have been paid millions for appearing in Japanese commercials. Theron has appeared in an ad for Honda and for Lux bath products, while Ford received several million dollars for appearing sweaty and bare-chested in Kirin beer commercials and print ads. Pitt has appeared in ads for canned coffee and blue jeans. Sometimes celebrities are forced to change their images or personalities to suit the advertising style of Japanese companies and the tastes of audiences in Japan. Japanese commercials have a totally different feel

© NC1 Wenn Photos/Newscom

perceived expertise of celebrity endorsers was more important in explaining purchase intentions than their attractiveness or trustworthiness. She suggests that celebrity spokespeople are most effective when they are knowledgeable, experienced, and qualified to talk about the product they are endorsing.[6] A number of other studies have shown that celebrities perceived as having expertise with a product or service can lend persuasive power to an advertising message.[7]

Applying Trustworthiness   While expertise is important, the target audience must also find the source believable. Finding celebrities or other figures with a trustworthy image is often difficult. Many trustworthy public figures hesitate to endorse products because of the potential impact on their reputation and image. E-Poll Market Research conducts ongoing consumer surveys to gauge the popularity and marketability of celebrities by surveying consumers and having them rate celebrities on 46 different personality attributes including items such as trustworthy, sincere, trendsetter, and influential. The company publishes its E-Score Celebrity Report each year which includes a spokesperson index score that reflects a celebrity's perceived credibility and authority and suggests his or her potential as a spokesperson.[8] The highest-scoring celebrities on its most recent lists have included than those in the United States and Europe and have often been described as "tacky" or "cheesy" by Western standards. For example, a commercial for Takara sake featured a kimono-clad Madonna wielding a sword and declaring "I'm pure," while another actor, Sean Connery, was shown carrying a ham into a room accompanied by the theme music from the James Bond movies.

There are several reasons why Japanese companies are willing to shell out huge sums of money for these stars. Many Japanese are fascinated by American culture and its celebrities, and endorsement of a brand by a star gives it a certain international cachet. Also, Japanese advertising emphasizes style and mood rather than substance; consumers expect to be entertained rather than bored by product information or testimonials. More than 80 percent of Japanese commercials are 10- or 15-second spots and around 85 percent use celebrities to capture viewers' attention.

Japan is not the only country where the Hollywood celebrities are hawking products. Actors Uma Thurman and Jeff Bridges appear in ads for the German fashion chain Marc O'Polo in Europe and Asia. Richard Gere has appeared in ads for Fiat in Europe, including a spot showing him driving a Lancia Delta from Hollywood to Tibet. Even though the ad aired in Italy, it created an uproar in China, where Gere is disliked for being an outspoken supporter of the Dalai Lama.

Some celebrities cashing in on endorsement deals abroad still try to protect their image at home and not be seen as selling out for money. Many stars have nondisclosure clauses in their contracts, specifying that the ads cannot be shown, or sometimes even discussed (oops!), outside Japan. They still see their appearance in TV ads as being potentially harmful to their reputations back home. However, with the growth of the Internet it is difficult to limit the viewing of the ads to one country; many of the commercials can now be found online on popular websites such as YouTube. Linda Thaler, chief executive officer of the Kaplan Thaler Group advertising agency, notes that "the days of Brad Pitt doing a commercial in Japan that he thought no one was going to see are gone." However, she also notes that the stigma that celebrities are selling out by doing a commercial has also gone by the wayside as Hollywood snobbery toward appearing in commercials declines.

While many celebrities are still unwilling to appear in ads in their home countries, some are softening their stance on the issue. For example, actor George Clooney appeared in ads for the Nestlé Nespresso coffee system only outside the United States for many years. However, in 2015 he agreed to use his star power to help Nespresso compete in the U.S. market which has proven to be resistant to smaller servings of coffee as consumers prefer to grab their java on the go from Starbucks, Dunkin Donuts, and other places. Clooney stars in humorous commercials alongside actor Danny DeVito where he trains him in the art of good taste. His Nespresso deal also includes an online film where he discussed how Nestlé supports farmers in war-torn South Sudan.

Syracuse professor Robert Thompson, an expert on television and popular culture, argues that appearing in commercials no longer carries a stigma for Hollywood celebrities. According to Thompson: "TV ads are much hipper and much cooler than a decade ago. I don't think people feel an obligation to hide it." However, celebrities are used to getting their way, and most would probably still prefer that the knowledge of their overseas endorsements stay there. Sorry about that.

Sources: Corine Gretler, "Nespresso to Bring George Clooney Coffee Ads to U.S. Market," *Bloomberg News,* October 20, 2015, www.bloomberg.com/news/articles/2015-10-29/nespresso-to-bring-george-clooney-coffee-ads-to-u-s-market; Bradford Wernie, "Lincoln Signs Matthew McConaughey to Help Win Younger Car Buyers," *Advertising Age,* August 21, 2014, http://adage.com/article/news/matthew-mcconaughey-signs-lincoln-boost-mkc/294661/; Jeff Labrecque, "Leonardo DiCaprio and the Easy Money of Foreign Commercials," *EW.com,* February 19, 2013, http://popwatch.ew.com/2013/02/19/leonardo-dicaprio-celebrity-foreign-commercials/; Rupal Parekh, "Brad Pitt Endorsing Chanel No. 5? Just Another Pretty Face," *Advertising Age,* May 9, 2012, http://adage.com/article/adages/brad-pitt-endorsing-chanel-5-pretty-face/234653/; James Parsons, "Japan's Ads Are Far from Being Lost in Translation," *Campaign,* September 14, 2007, p. 21; Louise Story, "Seeing Stars," *The New York Times,* October 12, 2006, p. C1.

actor Morgan Freeman, director Ron Howard, HGTV show host Mike Holmes, Tony Dungy (former NFL coach and analyst on NBC's Football Night in America), Michael J. Fox, Sandra Bullock, Betty White, and Tom Hanks. Talk-show host and entertainment producer Oprah Winfrey has also been a very trusted source through the years, and her "Favorite Things" list has served as a trusted source for product recommendations for many consumers. While many top celebrities could command large sums of money as endorsers and spokespersons, very few of them do often out of concern for how their image might be impacted. Global Perspective 6–1 discusses how some American celebrities protect their image by endorsing products in Japan and other countries rather than in the United States.

Advertisers use various techniques to increase the perception that their sources are trustworthy. Hidden cameras are used to show that the consumer is not a paid spokesperson and is making an objective evaluation of the product. Disguised brands are compared. (Of course, the sponsor's brand always performs better than the consumer's regular brand, and he or she is always surprised.) Advertisers also use the overheard-conversation technique to enhance trustworthiness. This involves creating a situation in a commercial where a person is shown overhearing a conversation in which favorable claims are made about a product or service. Most consumers are skeptical of these techniques, so they may have limited value in enhancing perceptions of an advertiser's credibility

Marketers can also deal with the source-trustworthiness issue by using other IMC tools such as publicity. Information received from sources such as newscasters is often very influential because these individuals are perceived as unbiased and thus more credible, even though they are often presenting stories that stem from press releases. In some situations celebrities may appear on news programs or talk shows and promote an upcoming cause or event such as the release of a new movie or music CD. With the increase in stealth marketing techniques, many consumers are becoming wary of endorsements made by celebrities on news programs and talk shows. For example, a *New York Times* article revealed that drug companies were making payments to celebrities or their favorite charities in return for the celebrities' touting the companies' pharmaceutical products on news and talk shows. As a result of the controversy from the article, CNN and the major broadcast networks announced that they would disclose any such financial deals during an interview.[9]

Concerns over potential bias in touting a product or service can involve more than celebrities. Several so-called consumer advocates and product experts have been criticized for giving favorable reviews and/or promoting specific products on local and national TV news programs and other shows without disclosing that they were being paid by the companies to mention their brands. Concern has been expressed over the practice as most television shows present the information presented by trend and fashion gurus or individuals with expertise in areas such as consumer electronics as unbiased and based solely on their expertise. However, the presentation is misleading to consumers if the experts have been paid to mention the products.[10]

With the growth of social media another area of concern has arisen regarding the trustworthiness of sources that endorse companies and brands and make recommendations on sites such as Facebook and Twitter as well as through online reviews or on blogs. In 2009 the Federal Trade Commission passed a set of guidelines requiring online endorsers and bloggers to disclose any material connection they might have to a company. The FTC developed the guidelines in response to studies that showed as many as 30 percent of online reviews were fake and were coming from someone who had been paid to write them or failed to reveal their association with a company or brand.[11]

Using Corporate Leaders as Spokespeople   Another way of enhancing source credibility is to use the company president or chief executive officer as a spokesperson in the firm's advertising. Many companies believe the use of their president or CEO is the ultimate expression of the company's commitment to quality and customer service. For some firms, the use of a president or CEO in their ads can help create an identity and personality for the company and/or brand. For example, Richard Branson's irreverence and zeal for life have helped personify the image of Virgin's empire of megastores, airlines, mobile phones, and soft drinks. Branson has been used occasionally in ads for various Virgin brands. A study by the research firm Ace Metrix found that the most effective CEO spokespersons currently are John Schnatter of the Papa John's pizza chain and Jim Koch, who is the head of the Boston Beer Company, which markets the popular Samuel Adams brands.[12] Schnatter has appeared in more than 50 ads for Papa John's and is perceived to be authentic and genuine, which are two important traits for the effective use of CEOs in ads for their companies (Exhibit 6–3). The practice of using company founders, owners, and presidents as advertising spokespersons is particularly prevalent among small and midsize companies such as retailers and auto dealers serving local markets.

Many marketing and advertising experts question the strategy of using company presidents or owners in ads and note that it is often ego rather than logic that is the reason for their use.[13] The experts suggest that businesspeople should get in front of the camera only if they exude credibility and possess the intangible quality of provoking a warm, fuzzy feeling in viewers. For example, Microsoft chair Bill Gates appeared in several TV commercials that were designed to help build a stronger image for the company. Gates was paired with comedian Jerry Seinfeld in the spots, which attempted to use quirky humor to get consumers to think about Microsoft in a different way. However, the ads aired for only a short time and many ad critics noted that Gates did not come across well in them.[14]

Another concern is that creating an image or culture around the CEO can make the corporate brand image more vulnerable if the individual becomes involved in any type of controversy such as a labor dispute, political issue, or personal problem. Critics of the practice also note that CEO spokespeople who become very popular may get more attention than their company's product/service or advertising message. And if a firm's image becomes too closely tied to a popular leader, there can be problems if that person leaves the company. For example, one of the most popular corporate spokespersons ever was Dave Thomas, the founder of Wendy's fast-food restaurants. Thomas appeared in more than 800 ads for Wendy's between 1989 and early 2002, when he passed away.[15] Wendy's had a difficult time replacing Thomas, who had become an advertising icon and was seen as the voice and personality of the company.[16] It has also been argued that the recent financial crisis and scandals involving top executives in some companies has eroded confidence in executives, which affects their ability to come across as trustworthy as they would have a few years ago. Moreover, in the new era of social media it is very easy to criticize corporate leaders who do not come across as trustworthy and believable.[17]

Major corporations are likely to continue to use their top executives in their advertising, particularly when they have celebrity value that helps enhance the firm's image. Some research suggests the use of a company president or CEO can improve attitudes and increase the likelihood that consumers will inquire about a company's product or service.[18] Defenders of the practice argue that the use of top executives or business owners in ads is an effective way of projecting an image of trust and honesty and, more important, the idea that the company isn't run by some faceless corporate monolith. As one expert notes: "These guys come into people's living rooms every night and, over the course of weeks and years, become like members of the family. It gets to the point that when you think of a certain product category, you think of the guy you see all the time on TV."[19]

Limitations of Credible Sources   Several studies have shown that a high-credibility source is not always an asset, nor is a low-credibility source always a liability. High- and low-credibility sources are equally effective when they are arguing for a position opposing their own best interest.[20] A very credible source is more effective when message recipients are not in favor of the position advocated in the message.[21] However, a very credible source is less important when the audience has a neutral position, and such a source may even be less effective than a moderately credible source when the receiver's initial attitude is favorable.[22]

Another reason a low-credibility source may be as effective as a high-credibility source is the **sleeper effect**, whereby the persuasiveness of a message increases with the passage of time. The immediate impact of a persuasive message may be inhibited because of its association with a low-credibility source. But with time, the association of the message with the source diminishes and the receiver's attention focuses more on favorable information in the message, resulting in more support. However, many studies have failed to demonstrate the presence of a sleeper effect.[23] Many advertisers hesitate to count on the sleeper effect, since exposure to a credible source is a more reliable strategy.[24]

Source Attractiveness

A source characteristic frequently used by advertisers is **attractiveness**, which encompasses similarity, familiarity, and likability.[25] *Similarity* is a supposed resemblance between the source and the receiver of the message, while *familiarity* refers to knowledge of the source through exposure. *Likability* is an affection for the source as a result of physical appearance, behavior, or other personal traits. Even when the sources are not athletes or movie stars, consumers often admire their physical appearance, talent, and/or personality.

Source attractiveness leads to persuasion through a process of **identification**, whereby the receiver is motivated to seek some type of relationship with the source and thus adopts similar beliefs, attitudes, preferences, or behavior. Maintaining this position depends on the source's continued support for the position as well as the receiver's continued identification with the source. If the source changes position, the receiver may also change. Unlike internalization, identification does not usually integrate information from an attractive source into the receiver's belief system. The receiver may maintain the attitudinal position or behavior only as long as it is supported by the source or the source remains attractive.

Marketers recognize that receivers of persuasive communications are more likely to attend to and identify with people they find likable or similar to themselves. Similarity and likability are the two source characteristics marketers seek when choosing a communicator.

Applying Similarity Marketers recognize that people are more likely to be influenced by a message coming from someone with whom they feel a sense of similarity.[26] If the communicator and receiver have similar needs, goals, interests, and lifestyles, the position advocated by the source is better understood and received. Similarity is used in various ways in marketing communications. Companies select salespeople whose characteristics match well with their customers'. A sales position for a particular region may be staffed by someone local who has background and interests in common with the customers. Global marketers often hire foreign nationals as salespeople so customers can relate more easily to them. Companies may also try to recruit former athletes to sell sporting goods or beer, since their customers usually have a strong interest in sports. Several studies have shown that customers who perceive a salesperson as similar to themselves are more likely to be influenced by his or her message.[27]

Similarity is also used by creating a situation where the consumer feels empathy for the person shown in the commercial. In a slice-of-life commercial, the advertiser usually starts by showing an event or predicament that consumers often with the hope of getting the consumer to think, "I can see myself in that situation." This can help establish a bond of similarity between the communicator and the receiver, increasing the source's level of persuasiveness. Marketers like to cast actors in their commercials that consumers will notice, recognize, identify with, and remember, as well as help differentiate their products and services. In some cases they try to create a personality figure for the company or brand that consumers will find likable. For example, one of the most popular advertising characters in recent years has been Lily, the retail store employee who appears in ads for AT&T's mobile service (Exhibit 6–4). Her perky enthusiasm and somewhat quirky wit and charm along with the way she presents the mobile plans to customers has made ad campaign very popular

EXHIBIT 6–4

The store employee in the AT&T commercials is very popular with consumers

Source: AT&T Inc.

with consumers.[28] Casting directors consider factors such as similarity and how the audience will identify with people when looking for talent to use in commercials.

Many companies feel that the best way to connect with consumers is by using regular-looking, everyday people with whom the average person can easily identify. For example, some of the most popular commercials for many years were those from the "Whassup?" campaign for Budweiser beer. In these ads the DDB agency cast a group of real-life friends from Philadelphia, rather than actors, who greet each other with the slang word "Whassup?" when they speak on the phone or get together to watch a game and enjoy a Bud. *Advertising Age* named "Whassup?" one of the top ad campaigns of the 21st century, noting how it was very effective at tapping into popular culture and what young people are actually like and how they speak to each other.[29]

Applying Likability: Using Celebrities Advertisers recognize the value of using spokespeople who are admired: TV and movie stars, athletes, musicians, and other popular public figures. Estimates of the percentage of all television commercials in the United States that feature a celebrity range from 14 to 20 percent, although an analysis of prime-time shows found only 9 percent.[30] The prevalence of celebrities in magazine ads is similar to television; a content analysis study of advertising appearing in 38 different magazines found that celebrities were used in only 10 percent of the ads. The use of celebrities was the highest for fashion, sports, and teen magazines and lowest for general news and business publications. With regard to product category, the use of celebrities was highest for athletic products, fashion/apparel, and cosmetics.[31] Globally, the market research company Millward Brown estimates that 18 percent of ads contain a celebrity spokesperson.[32] The use of celebrities in TV commercials is even higher in other countries such as South Korea and Japan.[33]

The top celebrity endorser in 2015 was Swiss tennis star Roger Federer, who made $58 million in endorsements, followed by pro golfers Tiger Woods at $50 million and Phil Michelson at $44 million. Other top American athlete endorsers include NBA stars LeBron James, Kevin Durant, and Kobe Bryant. The top international endorsers include soccer stars Cristiano Ronaldo and Lionel Messi, along with tennis stars Novak Djekovic and Rafael Nadal.[34]

For women, the top athlete endorser in 2015 was tennis star Maria Sharapova, who made nearly $30 million per year from her deals with Nike, Tiffany, Evian, Samsung, Head, Tag Heuer, and Cole Haan. Other top female endorsers include tennis stars Serena Williams and Caroline Wozniacki, along with actor-singer Jennifer Lopez and singers Beyoncé, Taylor Swift, and Katy Perry. Later in the chapter we discuss how Sharapova lost millions in endorsement deals when she failed a drug test at the 2016 Australian Open tennis tournament.

Why do companies spend huge sums to have celebrities appear in their ads and endorse their products? Many marketers think celebrities have *stopping power.* That is, they draw attention to advertising messages in a very cluttered media environment. They think a popular celebrity will favorably influence consumers' feelings, attitudes, and purchase behavior. And they believe celebrities can enhance the target audience's perceptions of the product in terms of image and/or performance. For example, a well-known athlete may convince potential buyers that the product will enhance their own performance.

A number of factors must be considered when a company decides to use a celebrity spokesperson, including the dangers of overshadowing the product and being overexposed, the target audience's receptivity, and risks to the advertiser.

Overshadowing the Product How will the celebrity affect the target audience's processing of the advertising message? Consumers may focus their attention on the celebrity and fail to notice or recall the brand or advertising message. Carsten Erfgen and his colleagues refer to this as the "vampire effect" and note that it occurs when the personality of the celebrity endorser overshadows the brand he

EXHIBIT 6–5

Soccer star David Beckham has a number of endorsement deals

© *Breitling, photo by Anthony Mandler*

or she is advertising and thus has a negative impact rather than helping to sell it.[35] Advertisers should select a celebrity spokesperson who will attract attention and enhance the sales message, yet not overshadow the brand. For example, high-end clothing brand St. John decided that it was best to drop actor Angelina Jolie from its advertising after a few years. The company felt that she was overshadowing the brand. Jolie was viewed as a very good fit for St. John, including her role as the voice of its children's charity—a cause she is well known for supporting. However, the company felt that she was simply too famous and decided to use a top British fashion model in its ads.[36] A recent study found that celebrity overshadowing can be particularly problematic when the consumers have low attachment to or interest in the celebrity.[37]

Overexposure Consumers are often skeptical of endorsements because they know the celebrities are being paid.[38] This problem is particularly pronounced when a celebrity endorses too many products or companies and becomes overexposed. For example, at one time cyclist Lance Armstrong had endorsement contracts with nearly 20 different companies, including Nike, PowerBar, General Mills, Oakley, and many others, and had to limit his endorsements so he did not become overexposed.[39] Soccer star David Beckham has endorsement contracts with a number of companies/brands including Gillette, Pepsi, Samsung, adidas, Armani, H&M, and Breitling watches (Exhibit 6–5). Advertisers can protect themselves against overexposure with an exclusivity clause limiting the number of products a celebrity can endorse. However, such clauses are usually expensive, and most celebrities agree not to endorse similar products anyway. Many celebrities, knowing their fame is fleeting, try to earn as much endorsement money as possible, yet they must be careful not to damage their credibility by endorsing too many products. For example, singer-actor Cher damaged her credibility as an advertising spokesperson by appearing in too many infomercials. When she realized that appearing in so many infomercials was hurting her acting career as well, she ceased doing them.[40]

Target Audiences' Receptivity One of the most important considerations in choosing a celebrity endorser is how well the individual matches with and is received by the advertiser's target audience. Former athletes such as Peyton Manning, Brett Favre, and Michael Jordan are still effective endorsers because they have very favorable images among baby boomers as well as Gen X consumers. NBA star LeBron James has been an effective spokesperson for several companies including Nike, Samsung, and Coca-Cola because he has tremendous name recognition and is very popular among younger consumers who are the primary target market for athletic shoes and soft drinks. McDonald's signed James to a multiyear endorsement deal, noting that his personal qualities make him a good fit for the company and that he is popular among young males who are heavy users of fast food. However, the the endorsement deal ended in 2015 as James began focusing more of his attention on Blaze Fast-Fire'd Pizza, a company in which he is was a founding investor.[41]

Consumers who are particularly knowledgeable about a product or service or have strongly established attitudes may be less influenced by a celebrity than those with little knowledge or neutral attitudes. One study found that college-age students were more likely to have a positive attitude toward a product endorsed by a celebrity than were older consumers.[42] The teenage market has generally been very receptive to celebrity endorsers, as evidenced by the frequent use of entertainers and athletes in ads targeted to this group for products such as apparel, cosmetics, and beverages. However, many marketers are finding that teenage consumers are more skeptical and cynical toward the use of celebrity endorsers and respond better to ads using humor, irony, and unvarnished truth. Some marketers targeting teenagers have responded to this by no longer using celebrities in their campaigns or by poking fun at their use.

EXHIBIT 6–6

New Balance has endorsement deals with more than 300 Major League Baseball players

Source: New Balance

Some companies avoid the use of celebrities entirely as they have determined that the market they are targeting is really not influenced by their endorsements. For example, New Balance became one of the leading brands of athletic footwear without the aid of celebrity endorsers. For many years, the company had a policy against hiring athletes to endorse its products and even ran ad campaigns that poked fun at its competitors for paying exorbitant amounts of money to athletes to wear their shoes. However, in 2013 the company began using athlete endorsers as it expanded beyond running shoes into other market segments such as baseball and soccer. The company now has endorsement deals with more than 300 Major League Baseball players and also signed a number of international soccer stars when it entered the soccer market in 2015 (Exhibit 6–6).[43]

Risk to the Advertiser A celebrity's behavior may pose a risk to a company.[44] A number of entertainers and athletes have been involved in activities that could embarrass the companies whose products they endorsed. Several companies including McDonald's, Coca-Cola, Spalding, and Nutella terminated endorsement deals with NBA superstar Kobe Bryant when he was charged with sexual assault in 2003. Other companies such as Nike and Upper Deck had long-term contracts with Bryant but limited their use of him as an endorser for a number of years. Even though the charges against Bryant were dropped, it took him years to repair his image and become a marketable endorser once again.[45] At one time Tiger Woods was making more than $100 million per year from various endorsement deals. However, a number of companies terminated their deals with him after issues regarding his infidelity became public in late 2009. IMC Perspective 6–1 discusses the risks marketers face when using high-profile athletes as endorsers and how companies such as Nike and others respond when a controversy arises involving one of their spokespersons.

Crisis situations regarding endorsers are not limited to athletes; problems can occur with other types of celebrities as well. For example, celebrity chef Paula Deen, who hosts popular cooking shows on the Food Network, became involved in a controversy after court documents released as part of a race and sex discrimination lawsuit against her showed she admitted to using racial epithets. Deen lost more than $12 million in endorsements and merchandising and licensing deals as companies such as JCPenney, Sears, Target, and Walmart removed her kitchen and cookware products from their stores; the Food Network terminated her as well.[46] Problems can also arise with individuals who have become celebrities based on their role as an advertising spokesperson. In 2015 Subway terminated its relationship with Jared Fogle, who had been a popular spokesperson for the company for more than 15 years, after he was arrested and later pleaded guilty to child pornography and sex charges.[47]

Marketers recognize that the use of celebrity endorsers can be a very expensive and high-risk strategy because what the celebrities do in their personal lives can impact their image and the way they are viewed by the public. Some companies may face a dilemma in selecting celebrity endorsers: While they prefer them to be upright, they still want them to have an edge or be somewhat irreverent to be able to connect with consumers. This may be particularly true for companies marketing their products to teens and young adults. To avoid problems, companies often research a celebrity's personal life and background. Many endorsement contracts include a morals clause allowing the company to terminate the contract if a controversy arises. Several companies, including luxury brands Burberry and Chanel as well as fashion retailer H&M, canceled their contracts with supermodel Kate Moss in the wake of a British tabloid photo that showed her using cocaine.[48] However, marketers should

IMC Perspectives 6–1 > > >

Marketers Run into Problems with Athlete Endorsers

Companies have been using popular athletes to endorse and pitch their products and services for years. Marketers realize the value of using athletes who are recognized and often admired by their target audience as a way to draw attention to their advertising messages. While sports stars are also frequently used to promote athletic products such as shoes, apparel, and sports equipment, the popularity of high-profile athletes often transcends sports and they are used to endorse a variety of other products and services including cars, fast food, soft drinks, clothing, airlines, watches, and consumer electronics. For example, watch companies such as Rolex, Omega, and TAG Heuer have used high-profile athletes such as Tiger Woods, Maria Sharapova, Lindsey Vonn, Roger Federer, and other sports icons as brand ambassadors while Samsung has used NBA star LeBron James in ads for its Galaxy smartphones.

There are a number of reasons why marketers use athletes to pitch their products. Consumers are likely to see athletes as experts who can reassure them about the quality of an athletic product or brand, particularly when it is perceived as being related to the athlete's performance level. Another reason is that many athletes achieve celebrity status because of their popularity and sports fans admire, and often idolize, them and view the use of a brand they endorse as a way of identifying with them. Avid sports fans often engage in a psychological process known as BIRGing or "basking in reflective glory" whereby they associate themselves with successful others such that another's success becomes their own.

But what happens when a controversy arises regarding an athlete and how might it affect the companies or brands he or she is endorsing and is closely aligned with? Recently several high-profile athletes have engaged in behaviors that have cost them very lucrative endorsement deals. One of the most costly, and perhaps most surprising, involved tennis star Maria Sharapova who for the past several years has been the world's highest-paid female athlete, earning nearly $30 million in prize money and endorsements in 2014 as well as 2015. The very attractive and popular tennis star has won five Grand Slam championships and is 1 of only 10 women to accomplish a career Grand Slam by winning all four major tournaments. However, Sharapova failed a drug test in January 2016 at the Australian Open when she tested positively for meldonium, a drug that is used to treat cardiac problems and can increase endurance. The World Anti-Doping Agency added the drug to its list of banned substances at the start of 2016 and Sharapova claimed that she had failed to read the update. The International Tennis Federation (ITF) took several months to investigate the case but in June 2016 she received a two-year suspension from the governing body.

While the ITF was taking some time to investigate the situation and make a decision, Sharapova's sponsors moved very quickly to distance themselves from her. German automotive company Porsche announced it was suspending its deal with Sharapova, while the Swiss watch maker TAG Heuer also announced it would not renew its deal with the 28-year-old star. Sharapova has endorsement deals with a number of other marketers, including Avon and Evian, who were reviewing their relationships with her, while her racquet sponsor Head did announce it would renew her endorsement contract. One of Sharapova's largest endorsement contracts is with Nike which initially announced that it was suspending its $12.5 million annual endorsement deal with her which is estimated to be worth $100 million over eight years and the company's biggest deal for a female athlete. However, a few months later the sportswear giant announced that it was standing by her, noting that an investigation by the International Tennis Federation found that she "did not intentionally break its rules" and had apologized for her mistake.

The swift action by TAG Heuer and Porsche to suspend their endorsement deals with Sharapova is an example of how marketers are reacting much more quickly to scandals involving athletes that they have under contract. In the past, companies would say or do nothing for months or even years, waiting for the dust to settle and story to die down before making a decision. By suspending its endorsement deal with an athlete but not terminating it, marketers leave the door open to renew the relationship if the athlete continues to perform well and remains popular with sports fans. For example, in late 2009 Nike had to make a decision regarding its endorsement deal with professional golfer Tiger Woods, who was involved

remember that adding morals clauses to their endorsement contracts only gets them out of a problem; it does not prevent it from happening. Thus, it is important that they carefully consider the character of a celebrity as well as the potential risk associated with using him or her as a spokesperson or endorser for the company or one of its brands.[49]

Return on Investment Perhaps the most important factor a company must consider regarding the use of celebrity endorsers is the return on investment from using them. Marketers use celebrities to increase awareness of and attention to their company and/or brands, as well as their advertisements, and to develop strong associations between

Never underestimate the competition.

NikeWomen.com

Source: NIKE Inc.

in a car accident outside his home following an argument with his wife. The intense media scrutiny of his personal life that followed led to revelations that the superstar, who was married with two young children, had been involved in numerous extramarital affairs. Nike had built the company's golf division around Woods and he singlehandedly helped make Nike one of the fastest-growing brands in the industry. Nike stood by Woods as surveys showed that attitudes toward him remained favorable among its target demographic of male golfers. However, Woods lost nearly $50 million in endorsement deals as a number of companies terminated their relationships with him, including Accenture, AT&T, Gatorade, and Gillette.

Three years later, Nike faced another major problem when seven-time Tour de France winner Lance Armstrong finally admitted to using performance-enhancing drugs. The company stood by Armstrong for a decade of allegations that the cyclist used PEDs throughout his career, but the evidence eventually became too overwhelming and Nike finally recognized that it could no longer afford to be associated with him. Armstrong also lost an estimated $70 million in endorsement deals with other companies including Oakley, UPS, Anheuser-Busch, Trek, 24 Hour Fitness, RadioShack, and Giro.

Some marketing experts noted that the problems Nike has encountered with endorsers is not surprising given that it has so many athletes under contract around the globe, including the superstars in most sports. They also note that Nike has a policy of standing by its athlete endorsers—except in the most extreme cases—and the brand is strong enough to withstand these setbacks. One such extreme case occurred in early 2016 when Nike terminated its relationship with Filipino boxing champion Manny Pacquiao one day after he made extremely derogatory statements about people in gay relationships during a media interview while he was running for political office in the Philippines. Pacquiao had won world championships in eight weight classes and was revered in the Philippines, as well as many other countries, for both his athletic success and his personal story, having risen from poverty to international stardom and political office. Nike announced that it found his comments abhorrent since the company opposes discrimination of any kind and has a history of supporting and standing up for the rights of the LGBT community.

While problems with endorsers may not do too much damage to larger companies that have a stable of celebrities endorsing their products, the effects can be very damaging to smaller companies whose brand is closely tied to, and often defined by, an athlete endorser. In an age where athletes and other celebrities have a myriad of platforms on which to speak such as Facebook and Twitter and the media are dedicating more resources than ever toward uncovering their transgressions, what can companies do to protect themselves? Aside from language in the contract barring such behavior, the simplest answer is—very little. No matter how much money a company pays endorsers, it cannot monitor them around the clock. Instead, companies must be very selective in selecting endorsers and in how much they pay them. Or as one agency executive suggests, marketers can go back to basics and hire real, credible experts and let the product be the star rather than the athletes. It is an interesting suggestion, but it is very unlikely that Nike or other companies will just do it.

Sources: Lara O'Reilly, "Maria Sharapova Is Losing Sponsorship Deal Worth Tens of Millions of Dollars after Her Failed Drug Test," *Business Insider,* March 8, 2016, www.businessinsider.com/nike-ends-100-million-maria-sharapova-deal-over-failed-drug-test-2016-3; Liam Stack, "Manny Pacquiao Loses Nike Sponsorship over Anti-Gay Remarks," *The New York Times,* February 18, 2016, http://nyti.ms/21OP731; Gabriel Beltrone, "Nike's Scandal Woes Just a Numbers Game," *Adweek,* February 17, 2013, www.adweek.com/news/advertising-branding/nikes-scandal-woes-just-numbers-game-147359; Jeremy Mullman, "For Nike, the Tiger Woods Brand Was Too Big to Fail," *Advertising Age,* April 12, 2010, pp. 1, 21.

the celebrity and the brand that will result in higher purchase intentions. Many companies do not reveal the increases in sales and/or market share that result from the use of celebrity endorsers. However, an interesting study was conducted by Anita Elberse and Jeroen Verleun that examined the economic impact of a sample of 347 endorsement deals for 180 athletes across six packaged-goods product categories. The results of their study found that sales did increase significantly over the first six months that the athlete endorsers were used—about 4 percent. However, subsequent major achievements by the athletes did not improve the sales of the brands studied relative to their competitors which calls into question the long-term value of endorsement deals.[50]

EXHIBIT 6–7

Marketers are using celebrities for more than just appearing in ads

© McGraw-Hill Companies/Mark Dierker, photographer

It should be noted that there are many examples of companies that have seen sales increase, and there can be other factors that marketers consider in determining the value gained from using a celebrity endorser. Thus it is likely that many marketers will continue to use them, despite some of the drawbacks associated with their use that have been discussed. Some companies are changing their relationships with celebrity endorsers and having them become more involved with their companies and brands rather than just appearing in advertisements (Exhibit 6–7). A number of high-profile celebrities have become involved in areas such as product design and development as well as the advertising creative process. For example, Anheuser-Busch InBev hired Justin Timberlake as the creative and musical curator for its Bud Light Platinum brand. However, the arrangement lasted only a year as the pop star changed allegiances and joined forces with Beam Inc. to market a new tequila called Sauza 901. His deal with Beam came after competitor Diageo announced a joint venture with Sean "Diddy" Combs for the acquisition of a luxury tequila brand called DeLeón.[51] BlackBerry retained singer Alicia Keys as a global creative director in 2013, but the relationship was short-lived and caused some embarrassment for the company after she tweeted out a message using an iPhone.[52] PepsiCo hired Beyoncé as a "brand ambassador" as part of a long-term $50 million endorsement deal that includes having her help create content and develop new ways to engage consumers and fans.[53] Some marketing experts argue that these celebrity deals are little more than window dressing while others argue that they can be valuable.

Marketers are also becoming more creative in the way they pay celebrities and even giving them a stake in the company. For example, rapper 50 Cent (Curtis Jackson) received a minority stake in Glacéau Vitaminwater which increased his involvement with the company. He developed a flavor, appeared in ads, and even mentioned the brand in some of this songs. When the company was acquired by Coca-Cola, Jackson made an estimated $400 million.[54] When Rihanna released the hit single "Umbrella" in 2007, Totes Isotoner, which had been manufacturing umbrellas for over 30 years, approached the pop singer about branding the company's umbrellas side-by-side with her and the song. What followed was an entirely new offering from Totes that allowed customers to design their own (sparkly, glittery) umbrellas that were consistent with Rihanna's image. Rihanna, in exchange for her commitment to the company and the use of her image and song, received a percentage of umbrella sales and other perks.[55] And when Under Armour signed New England Patriots quarterback Tom Brady to an endorsement deal, he received an equity stake in the company. According to Under Armour CEO Kevin Plank, it was an ideal arrangement for the firm as it makes Brady fully invested in the company's success.[56]

Understanding the Meaning of Celebrity Endorsers Advertisers must try to match the product or company's image, the characteristics of the target market, and the personality of the celebrity.[57] The image celebrities project to consumers can be just as important as their ability to attract attention. An interesting perspective on celebrity endorsement was developed by Grant McCracken.[58] He argues that credibility and attractiveness don't sufficiently explain how and why celebrity endorsements work and offers a model based on meaning transfer (Figure 6–3).

According to this model, a celebrity's effectiveness as an endorser depends on the culturally acquired meanings he or she brings to the endorsement process. Each celebrity contains many meanings, including status, class, gender, and age as well as personality and lifestyle. In explaining stage 1 of the meaning transfer process, McCracken notes:

> Celebrities draw these powerful meanings from the roles they assume in their television, movie, military, athletic, and other careers. Each new dramatic role brings the celebrity into contact with a range of objects, persons, and contexts. Out of these objects, persons, and contexts are transferred meanings that then reside in the celebrity.[59]

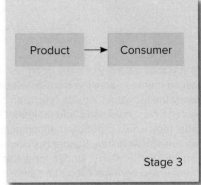

Culture

Objects
Persons
Context
Role 1
2
3

Celebrity

Stage 1

Endorsement

Celebrity → Product

Stage 2

Consumption

Product → Consumer

Stage 3

Key: → = Path of meaning movement

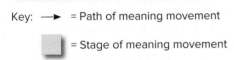 = Stage of meaning movement

FIGURE 6–3

Meaning Movement and the Endorsement Process

Examples of celebrities who have acquired cultural meaning that they bring to endorsements include actor Zooey Deschanel (from her role as the cute, quirky, and offbeat but lovable roommate on the sitcom *New Girl*) and Charlie Sheen (from his role as the free-spirited, bachelor/playboy on the hit show *Two and a Half Men* and then in his role as an anger management therapist on the show *Anger Management*). Deschanel's character image has been used in commercials for the Apple iPhone, while she also appears in ads for Rimmel cosmetics and Pantene Prov-V shampoo which capitalize on her attractiveness. Sheen's bad-boy image was utilized in a commercial for the Fiat Abarth which featured him driving the car around the inside of an opulent mansion as a group of attractive women cheer him on. The spot also poked fun at his personal problems as it showed him stepping out of the car and saying, "I love being under house arrest."[60] Actress-comedienne Tina Fey has developed cultural meaning through the various roles and characters she has played on *Saturday Night Live,* the sitcom *30 Rock,* and in movies such as *Mean Girls, Whiskey Tango Fox Trot,* and *Date Night* in which she played the role of a relatable woman trying to balance her life as a wife and mother. She is also an acclaimed writer and producer, which contributes to her cultural meaning as a successful, multitasking businesswoman.

McCracken suggests celebrity endorsers bring their meanings and image into the ad and transfer them to the product they are endorsing (stage 2 of the model in Figure 6–3). For example, American Express has been using Tina Fey in the advertising campaign for its Amex EveryDay Credit Card, which allows users to earn rewards on everyday purchases.[61] The company introduced the card to attract a new set of consumers and position the brand as more approachable and inclusive. American Express is also targeting working mothers who are living a very busy and somewhat hectic life. The TV commercials for the campaign show Fey in her trademark witty fashion as a busy, on-the-go working woman and mom, juggling her personal life with work other demands. She is an effective endorser for the brand since she represents the quintessential do-it-all woman with an endless things-to-do list but who gets it all done with the help of the Amex EveryDay Credit Card (Exhibit 6–8).

In the final stage of McCracken's model, the meanings the celebrity has given to the product are transferred to the consumer. By using Tina Fey in its ads, American Express can deliver on its branding and positioning platform by showing how its EveryDay Credit Card matches well with the lifestyle of busy people who are trying to balance demanding careers with their personal lives. McCracken notes that this final stage is complicated and difficult to achieve. The way consumers take possession of the meaning the celebrity has transferred to a product is probably the least understood part of the process.

Digital and Social Media Perspective 6–1 > > >

YOUTUBE STARS ARE THE NEW CELEBRITIES TO TEENS

If you took a survey of baby boomers or millennials and asked them to name the most influential celebrities, it is likely the list would include television and movie stars, entertainers, musicians, and athletes. Depending on their age, they would probably mention popular celebrities such as Jennifer Anniston, Sandra Bullock, George Clooney, Jimmy Kimmel, Carrie Underwood, Ellen DeGeneres, LeBron James, and perhaps even Kim Kardashian. However, if you were to ask American teenagers the same question, the list would be quite different and include names that most people have never heard of—such as Smosh, Shane Dawson, Jenna Marbles, and KSI—unless they spend a lot of time on YouTube and other popular social media sites.

A survey commissioned for *Variety* magazine and conducted by celebrity brand strategist Jeetendr Sehdev asked 1,500 respondents a list of questions assessing how 20 well-known personalities stacked up in terms of approachability, authenticity, and other criteria considered key aspects of overall influence. Half of the 20 were personalities with the most subscribers and views on YouTube while the other half were the celebrities with the highest Q-scores among U.S. teens aged 13 to 17. The results of the survey found that the five most influential personalities among the American teens 13 to 18 were all YouTube favorites, eclipsing the popular mainstream celebrities.

Heading the list was Smosh, the online comedy team of Ian Andrew Hecox and Anthony Padilla. Finishing second was another comedy duo, the Fine Brothers (Benny and Rafi), followed by the Swedish video gamer Felix Ulf Kjelberg, otherwise known as PewDiePie who has the most subscribers of all on YouTube. Rounding out the top five was a video gamer from the UK, Olajide Olatunji—better known by his alias KSIOlajidebt or KSI for short—followed by Ryan Higa who is known for his YouTube comedy videos. Higa, whose YouTube user name is Nigahiga, has over 16 million subscribers to his YouTube channel and his comedy videos have been viewed over 2.6 billion times. The only mainstream celebrities to score in the top 10 were Jennifer Lawrence, who ranked seventh, and Katy Perry, who was ninth.

Sehdev took a deeper dive into the survey data to better understand why the YouTube stars have more influence on teens. He found that they scored significantly higher than traditional celebrities across a range of characteristics that are seen as influencing the purchase behavior of teens. The YouTubers were judged to be more engaging, extraordinary, and relatable than mainstream stars, who were rated as being smarter and more reliable. The two types of celebrities were rated evenly in sex appeal. He also found that teens enjoy an intimate and authentic experience with YouTube personalities because they do not feel their images are

EXHIBIT 6–8

Tina Fey's image works well in ads for the Amex EveryDay Credit Card

Source: American Express Company

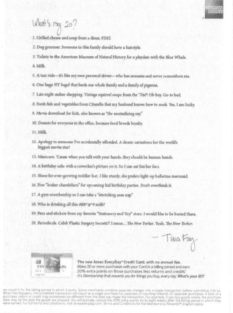

The meaning transfer model has some important implications for companies using celebrity endorsers. Marketers must first decide on the image or symbolic meanings important to the target audience for the particular product, service, or company. They must then determine which celebrity best represents the meaning or image to be

© Vivien Killilea/Getty Images

connected to their idols and have a sense of how they spend their lives.

There is no doubt that a new generation of talent who create their own content and deliver it on social sites such as YouTube, Vine, Instagram, Facebook, and other platforms are becoming household names among young consumers online and are legitimate influencers. Thus, marketers may have to rethink how they select and use celebrities since relying on mainstream celebs to endow their brands with star power may no longer be effective. Foster argues that a democratization of celebrity is taking place that includes three key factors—expertise, access, and identification—and popular social media personalities often stack up as well, if not better, on all three than Hollywood endorsers who are paid to hawk companies and brands. He notes that the use of endorsements in advertising will never go away but it is changing dramatically in ways that give it more meaning. Technology is making it easier for ordinary consumers to do the marketing for brands and do it in ways that are more authentic and may remove the need for celebrity endorsers. As Foster notes: "We've seen the future of celebrity endorsement. And it's us."

orchestrated by PR professionals. Teens also say they appreciate YouTube stars' more candid sense of humor, lack of filter, and risk-taking spirit, which are behaviors that are often managed carefully for mainstream celebrities.

Chris Foster, the chief operating officer of the Saatchi & Saatchi advertising agency, notes that the Internet and social media are clearly changing the nature of celebrity in ways that have major implications for advertising and other forms of marketing. He argues that the traditional image of a celebrity as remote and unknowable and highly controlled by publicists is no longer persuasive or effective since members of today's plugged-in generation want to feel

Sources: Chris Foster, "Why J-Law & George Clooney Don't Matter: Saatchi & Saatchi COO," *USA Today,* June 15, 2015, www.usatoday.com/story/opinion/2015/06/12/internet-celebrity-endorsement-advertising-column/71084290/; Susanne Alt, "Survey: YouTube Stars More Popular Than Mainstream Celebs among U.S. Teens," *Variety,* August 5, 2014, http://variety.com/2014/digital/news/survey-youtube-stars-more-popular-than-mainstream-celebs-among-u-s-teens-1201275245/; Todd Spangler, "New Breed of Online Stars Rewrite the Rules of Fame," *Variety,* August 5, 2014, http://variety.com/2014/digital/news/shane-dawson-jenna-marbles-internet-fame-1201271428/.

projected. An advertising campaign must be designed that captures that meaning in the product and moves it to the consumer. Marketing and advertising personnel often rely on intuition in choosing celebrity endorsers for their companies or products, but some companies conduct research studies to determine consumers' perceptions of celebrities' meaning.

Marketers may also pretest ads to determine whether they transfer the proper meaning to the product. When celebrity endorsers are used, the marketer should track the campaign's effectiveness. Does the celebrity continue to be effective in communicating the proper meaning to the target audience? Celebrities who are no longer in the limelight may lose their ability to transfer any significant meanings to the product.

CHOOSING A CELEBRITY ENDORSER

As we have seen, marketers must consider many factors when choosing a celebrity to serve as an advertising spokesperson for the company or a particular brand. Studies have shown that advertising and marketing managers take these various factors into account when choosing a celebrity endorser.[62] Among the most important factors are the celebrity's match with the target audience and the product/service or brand, the overall image of the celebrity, the cost of acquiring the celebrity, trustworthiness, the risk of controversy, and the celebrity's familiarity and likability among the target audience. Digital and Social Media Perspective 6–1 discusses how YouTube personalities have become more influential than mainstream celebrities who are less popular among young people.

While some advertising and marketing executives rely on their own intuition and gut feeling, many turn to research that measures a celebrity's familiarity and appeal among their target audience as well as other factors. Many companies and their advertising agencies rely on Q-scores that are commercially available from the New York–based firm Marketing Evaluations, Inc. To determine its Q-scores for sport personalities, actors, and entertainers, the company surveys a representative national panel of consumers several times a year. Respondents are asked to indicate whether they have ever seen or heard of the performer or sports personality and, if they have, to rate him or her on a scale that includes one of my favorites, very good, good, fair, and poor. The *familiarity score* indicates what percentage of people has heard of the person while the *one of my favorites score* is an absolute measure of the appeal or popularity of the celebrity. The well-known *Q-score* is calculated by taking the percentage of respondents who indicate that a person is "one of my favorites" and then dividing that number by the percentage of respondents who indicate they have heard of that person. Q-scores are important because they answer the question: How appealing is the person among those who do know him or her? The average Q-score for performers is generally around 18 and about 17 for sports personalities. Marketing Evaluation's Q-scores are also broken down on the basis of various demographic criteria such as a respondent's age, income, occupation, education, and race so that marketers have some idea of how a celebrity's popularity varies among different groups of consumers. Marketing Evaluations also now reports a negative Q-score which is the percentage of respondents who rate the personality as fair or poor divided by only those who are familiar with the person. Exhibit 6–9 shows a sample page from the Performer Q study. In addition to Q-scores, marketers use information provided by a number of other research firms that provide them with data on the popularity of various celebrities and insight into how well their image might fit with their company or brand.

Applying Likability Decorative Models

Advertisers often draw attention to their ads by featuring a physically attractive person who serves as a passive or decorative model rather than as an active communicator. Research suggests that physically attractive communicators generally have a positive impact and generate more favorable evaluations of both ads and products than less attractive models.[63] The gender appropriateness of the model for the product being advertised and his or her relevance to the product are also important considerations.[64] Products such as cosmetics or fashionable clothing are likely to benefit from the use of an attractive model, since physical appearance is very relevant in marketing these items.

Some models draw attention to the ad but not to the product or message. Studies show that an attractive model facilitates recognition of the ad but does not enhance copy readership or message recall. Thus, advertisers must ensure that the consumer's attention will go beyond the model to the product and advertising message.[65] Marketers must also consider whether the use of highly attractive models might negatively impact advertising effectiveness. Several studies have shown that some women experience negative feelings when comparing themselves with beautiful models used in ads and the images of physical perfection they represent.[66]

Some companies have developed marketing campaigns that undermine the traditional approach to beauty care advertising by telling women, as well as young girls, that they're beautiful just the way they are. For example, Unilever's Dove brand has long eschewed the use of supermodels in its ads and uses everyday women and girls who resemble its typical consumers. Since 2004 the company has been running an interesting global integrated marketing campaign designed to appeal to everyday women.[67] The "Campaign for Real Beauty" includes magazine ads, extensive public relations, and a website (www.campaignforrealbeauty.com) where women

	ONE OF MY FAVORITES	VERY GOOD	GOOD	FAIR/ POOR	TOTAL FAMILIAR	POSITIVE Q SCORE	NEGATIVE Q SCORE
PERSONALITY NAME							
TOTAL SAMPLE	9	18	30	25	83	11	31
6 - 11 YEARS	16	12	18	9	56	29	17
12 - 17 YEARS	11	21	30	23	86	13	27
18 - 34 YEARS	11	22	33	29	95	11	31
35 - 49 YEARS	11	20	34	26	90	12	29
50 AND OVER	4	13	28	27	72	6	37
18 - 49 YEARS	11	21	34	28	93	11	30
18 YEARS AND OVER	8	18	32	27	85	10	32
25 - 54 YEARS	11	20	32	28	91	12	31
TOTAL MALES							
6 AND OVER	9	16	31	25	81	11	31
18 - 34 YEARS	10	21	33	29	94	10	31
35 - 49 YEARS	13	18	33	25	89	15	28
50 AND OVER	4	11	28	25	67	5	36
18 - 49 YEARS	11	20	33	27	91	13	30
18 YEARS AND OVER	9	17	31	26	83	11	32
25 - 54 YEARS	12	21	30	27	90	13	30
TOTAL FEMALES							
6 AND OVER	10	19	30	26	84	12	31
18 - 34 YEARS	12	22	33	30	97	12	31
35 - 49 YEARS	8	21	35	27	91	9	30
50 AND OVER	5	15	28	29	76	7	38
18 - 49 YEARS	10	22	34	28	94	10	30
18 YEARS AND OVER	8	19	32	29	87	9	33
25 - 54 YEARS	10	20	34	29	92	11	31
HOUSEHOLD INCOME							
UNDER $20,000	8	13	30	20	71	11	28
$20,000 - $39,999	9	18	31	26	85	11	31
$40,000 - $59,999	11	14	34	27	86	13	31
$60,000 AND OVER	9	21	28	27	85	11	31
$75,000 AND OVER	9	19	29	28	85	11	32
EDUCATION (ADULT)							
HIGH SCHOOL GRADUATE/LESS	10	19	30	23	80	12	28
SOME COLLEGE/DEGREE	7	17	34	32	90	8	36
OCCUPATION (ADULT)							
WHITE COLLAR	7	21	35	29	91	7	32
BLUE COLLAR	10	16	32	28	85	12	32
RACE							
NON BLACK	7	17	31	27	81	9	33
BLACK	26	25	23	16	90	29	17
ETHNICITY							
HISPANIC	12	17	37	23	89	13	26
NIELSEN COUNTY SIZE							
A	11	18	32	26	87	12	30
B	9	19	30	25	83	11	30
C & D	8	16	28	24	75	10	32
REGION							
NORTHEAST	10	21	25	30	85	12	35
NORTH CENTRAL	9	19	32	24	83	11	28
SOUTH	11	18	32	21	82	13	26
WEST	7	13	30	30	80	9	38

EXHIBIT 6–9

Sample page from Marketing Evaluations, Inc. Performer Q Study

can discuss beauty-related issues (Exhibit 6–10). Dove has taken a social advocacy approach in the campaign, which it proclaims "aims to change the status quo and offer in its place a broader, healthier, more democratic view of beauty."[68]

Source Power

The final characteristic in Kelman's classification scheme is **source power**. A source has power when he or she can actually administer rewards and punishments to the receiver. As a result of this power, the source may be able to induce another person(s) to respond to the request or position he or she is advocating. The power of the source depends on several factors. The source must be perceived as being able to administer positive or negative sanctions to the receiver *(perceived control)* and the receiver must think the source cares about whether or not the receiver conforms

campaignforrealbeauty.com → | *Dove*

Let's face it, firming the thighs of a size 2 supermodel is no challenge. Real women have real curves. And according to women who tried new Dove Firming, it left their skin feeling firmer in just one week. What better way to celebrate the curves you were born with? New Dove Firming. Lotion, Cream and Body Wash. For beautifully firm skin.

EXHIBIT 6–10

Dove's "Campaign for Real Beauty" uses everyday women rather than supermodels in its ads

Source: Dove by Unilever Home and Personal Care-USA

(perceived concern). The receiver's estimate of the source's ability to observe conformity is also important *(perceived scrutiny).*

When a receiver perceives a source as having power, the influence process occurs through a process known as **compliance**. The receiver accepts the persuasive influence of the source and acquiesces to his or her position in hopes of obtaining a favorable reaction or avoiding punishment. The receiver may show public agreement with the source's position but not have an internal or private commitment to this position. Persuasion induced through compliance may be superficial and last only as long as the receiver perceives that the source can administer some reward or punishment.

Power as a source characteristic is very difficult to apply in a nonpersonal influence situation such as advertising. A communicator in an ad generally cannot apply any sanctions to the receiver or determine whether compliance actually occurs. An indirect way of using power is by using an individual with an authoritative personality as a spokesperson. For example, Take Pride in America uses actor-director Clint Eastwood, whose movie roles earned him an image as a rugged tough guy, in public service campaigns commanding people not to pollute or damage public lands (Exhibit 6–11). Eastwood has used his imposing image in TV commercials calling for people who abuse public lands "to clean up their act or get out of town."

The use of source power applies more in situations involving personal communication and influence. For example, in a personal-selling situation, the sales rep may have some power over a buyer if the latter anticipates receiving special rewards or favors for complying with the salesperson. Some companies provide their sales reps with large expense accounts to spend on customers for this very purpose. Representatives of companies whose product demand exceeds supply are often in a position of power; buyers may comply with their requests to ensure an adequate supply of the product. Sales reps must be very careful in their use of a power position, since abusing a power base to maximize short-term gains can damage long-term relationships with customers.

MESSAGE FACTORS

LO6-3

The way marketing communications are presented is very important in determining their effectiveness. Marketers must consider not only the content of their persuasive messages but also how this information will be structured for presentation and what type of message appeal will be used. Advertising, in all media except radio, relies heavily on visual as well as verbal information. Many options are available with respect to the design and presentation of a message. This section examines the structure of messages and considers the effects of different types of appeals used in advertising.

Message Structure

Marketing communications usually consist of a number of message points that the communicator wants to get across. An important aspect of message strategy is knowing the best way to communicate these points and overcome any opposing viewpoints audience members may hold. Extensive research has been conducted on how the structure of a persuasive message can influence its effectiveness, including order

EXHIBIT 6–11

Actor Clint Eastwood's authoritative image makes him an effective source

Source: Take Pride in America

of presentation, conclusion drawing, message sidedness, refutation, and verbal versus visual message characteristics.

Order of Presentation A basic consideration in the design of a persuasive message is the arguments' order of presentation. Should the most important message points be placed at the beginning of the message, in the middle, or at the end? Research on learning and memory generally indicates that items presented first and last are remembered better than those presented in the middle (see Figure 6–4).[69] This suggests that a communicator's strongest arguments should be presented early or late in the message but never in the middle.

Presenting the strongest arguments at the beginning of the message assumes a **primacy effect** is operating, whereby information presented first is most effective. Putting the strong points at the end assumes a **recency effect**, whereby the last arguments presented are most persuasive.

Whether to place the strongest selling points at the beginning or the end of the message depends on several factors. If the target audience is opposed to the communicator's position, presenting strong points first can reduce the level of counterarguing. Putting weak arguments first might lead to such a high level of counterarguing that strong arguments that followed would not be believed. Strong arguments work best at the beginning of the message if the audience is not interested in the topic, so they can arouse interest in the message. When the target audience is predisposed toward the communicator's position or is highly interested in the issue or product, strong arguments can be saved for the end of the message. This may result in a more favorable opinion as well as better retention of the information.

The order of presentation can be critical when a long, detailed message with many arguments is being presented. Most effective sales presentations open and close with strong selling points and bury weaker arguments in the middle. For short communications, such as a 15- or 30-second TV or radio commercial, the order may be less critical. However, many product and service messages are received by consumers with low involvement and minimal interest. Thus, an advertiser may want to present the brand name and key selling points early in the message and repeat them at the end to enhance recall and retention. Order of presentation is also an important consideration in other forms of marketing communication. For example, many press releases use the "pyramid style" of writing, whereby most of the important information is presented up front to ensure that it is read since editors often cut from the end of articles.

FIGURE 6–4

Ad Message Recall as a Function of Order of Presentation

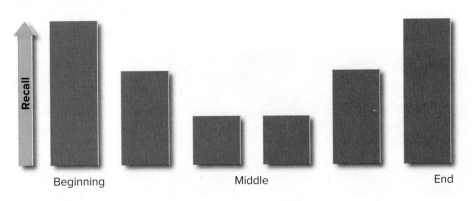

Conclusion Drawing Marketing communicators must decide whether their messages should explicitly draw a firm conclusion or allow receivers to draw their own conclusions. Research suggests that, in general, messages with explicit conclusions are more easily understood and effective in influencing attitudes. However, other studies have shown that the effectiveness of conclusion drawing may depend on the target audience, the type of issue or topic, and the nature of the situation.[70]

More highly educated people prefer to draw their own conclusions and may be annoyed at an attempt to explain the obvious or to draw an inference for them. But stating the conclusion may be necessary for a less educated audience, who may not draw any conclusion or may make an incorrect inference from the message. Marketers must also consider the audience's level of involvement in the topic. For highly personal or ego-involving issues, message recipients may want to make up their own minds and resent any attempts by the communicator to draw a conclusion. One study found that open-ended ads (without explicit conclusions) were more effective than closed-ended arguments that did include a specific conclusion—but only for involved audiences.[71]

Whether to draw a conclusion for the audience also depends on the complexity of the topic. Even a highly educated audience may need assistance if its knowledge level in a particular area is low. Does the marketer want the message to trigger immediate action or a more long-term effect? If immediate action is an objective, the message should draw a definite conclusion. This is a common strategy in political advertising, particularly for ads run close to election day. When immediate impact is not the objective and repeated exposure will give the audience members opportunities to draw their own conclusions, an open-ended message may be used.

Drawing a conclusion in a message may make sure the target audience gets the point the marketer intended. But many advertisers believe that letting customers draw their own conclusions reinforces the points being made in the message. For example, a health services agency in Kentucky found that open-ended ads were more memorable and more effective in getting consumers to use health services than were ads stating a conclusion. Ads that posed questions about alcohol and drug abuse and left them unanswered resulted in more calls by teenagers to a help line for information than did a message offering a resolution to the problem.[72] The ad shown in Exhibit 6–12, which is from the Montana Meth Project (MMP) drug prevention messaging campaign, is a good example of this strategy. The ad challenges teens to consider what they know about methamphetamine and prompts them to learn more by visiting the MMP website.

Message Sidedness Another message structure decision facing the marketer involves message sidedness. A **one-sided message** mentions only positive attributes or benefits. A **two-sided message** presents both good and bad points. The logic of a two-sided message is that acknowledging a limitation or short-coming can be a way to enhance credibility and make the message more effective. One-sided messages are most effective when the target audience already holds a favorable opinion about the topic. They also work better with a less educated audience.[73]

Two-sided messages are more effective when the target audience holds an opposing opinion or is highly educated. Two-sided messages may enhance the credibility of the source.[74] A better-educated audience usually knows there are opposing arguments, so a communicator who presents both sides of an issue is likely to be seen as less biased and more objective. Martin Eisend conducted a meta-analysis of the research conducted on the effects of one- versus two-sided advertising messages. The results of his analysis showed that the persuasive

impact of message sidedness depends on a number of factors including the amount and importance of negative information in the ad, attribute quality, placement of the negative information, the correlation between negative and positive attributes, and whether the advertiser discloses negative information voluntarily or because it is required to do so.[75]

Most advertisers use one-sided messages. They are concerned about the negative effects of acknowledging a weakness in their brand or don't want to say anything positive about their competitors. There are exceptions, however. Sometimes advertisers compare brands on several attributes and do not show their product as being the best on every one. There also may be situations in which a company feels that is best to acknowledge its shortcomings and let its customers know that it has addressed them.

An example of a company that used a two-sided message very effectively is the Domino's Pizza chain, which took the strategy to a whole new level in an integrated marketing campaign used to introduce its new, reformulated pizza. Domino's recognized that changes were needed after conducting research that revealed many consumers had issues with the taste of its pizza; As part of its "Pizza Turnaround" campaign Domino's used commercials showing the chain's new CEO in front of the camera admitting that he had heard what the focus groups had to say and that it took it to heart. The spots then pointed viewers to a special website (www.pizzaturnaround.com) that featured a four-minute documentary chronicling Domino's employees' reactions to the negative comments coming from the focus groups and telling about the company's quest to make a better pizza (Exhibit 6–13). The website also showed both positive and negative viewer comments that were linked in from Twitter. While Domino's and its agency knew the campaign might be risky, they moved forward with it and the results were very favorable. They received a great deal of publicity regarding the ads, much of which praised the company for conceding the shortcomings of its product and explaining what it was doing about it. The two-sided message strategy also had a very positive impact on sales as the chain generated a record increase in same-store sales during the campaign.[76]

Refutation   In a special type of two-sided message known as a **refutational appeal**, the communicator presents both sides of an issue and then refutes the opposing viewpoint. Since refutational appeals tend to "inoculate" the target audience against a competitor's counterclaims, they can be more effective than one-sided messages in making consumers resistant to an opposing message.[77]

Refutational messages may be useful when marketers wish to build attitudes that resist change and/or must defend against attacks or criticism of their products or the

FACT: WHALES LIVE
as long at SeaWorld.

My name is Chris, and I'm a veterinarian at SeaWorld. My entire professional life has been focused on the care and welfare of animals, including killer whales.

You might have heard attacks from PETA saying our killer whales live only a fraction as long as whales in the wild. They say, "In captivity, orcas' average life span plummets to just nine years."

But the author of an independent study, Dr. Douglas DeMaster, of the Alaska Fisheries Science Center, was quoted in *The Wall Street Journal* as saying, "Survival in the wild is comparable to survival in captivity."

There's no other way to say it ... PETA is not giving you the facts.

SeaWorld has several killer whales in their 30s and one that is close to 50 — right in line with what is seen in the wild. In fact, a July 2014 Associated Press (AP) report

analyzing 50 years of data from the federal Marine Mammal Inventory Report found that killer whales born at our parks "had an average life expectancy of 46 years."

It's frustrating that PETA gets a lot of attention by twisting statistics and falsely attacking us. As someone who cares for these incredible animals, their health and well-being is my priority every day. Just like doctors, we veterinarians take an oath. If PETA's accusations were true, I wouldn't work here.

When SeaWorld opened its doors 50 years ago, global understanding of killer whales was just beginning. The world has changed a lot since then, and SeaWorld has continued to change with it. Today, our whales live as long as those in the wild, and our study of them is helping conservationists better understand and protect killer whales and other marine animals everywhere.

Dr. Chris Dold
Veterinarian

Learn more at SeaWorldCares.com

EXHIBIT 6–14

A refutational appeal was used by SeaWorld to defend itself against criticism by PETA and other animal activist groups

Source: SeaWorld Parks & Entertainment, Inc.

company. For example, Exhibit 6–14 shows a refutational ad used by SeaWorld Entertainment that was part of an integrated campaign the company ran to defend itself against criticism by the animal activist group PETA. In addition to the refutational ads, SeaWorld created a website (seaworldcares.com) that provides information refuting many of the attacks made against the company regarding its treatment of killer whales as well as educate the public about the many programs and initiatives it has to protect and help marine life. Market leaders, who are often the target of comparative messages, may find that acknowledging competitors' claims and then refuting them can help build resistant attitudes and customer loyalty.

Verbal versus Visual Messages Thus far our discussion has focused on the information, or verbal, portion of the message. However, the nonverbal, visual elements of an ad are also very important. Many ads provide minimal amounts of information and rely on visual elements to communicate. Pictures are commonly used in advertising to convey information or reinforce copy or message claims.

Both the verbal and visual portions of an ad influence the way the advertising message is processed.[78] Consumers may develop images or impressions based on visual elements such as an illustration in an ad or the scenes in a TV commercial. In some cases, the visual portion of an ad may reduce its persuasiveness, since the processing stimulated by the picture may be less controlled and consequently less favorable than that stimulated by words.[79]

Pictures affect the way consumers process accompanying copy. A study showed that when verbal information was low in imagery value, the use of pictures providing examples increased both immediate and delayed recall of product attributes.[80] However, when the verbal information was already high in imagery value, the addition of pictures did not increase recall. Advertisers often design ads where the visual image supports the verbal appeal to create a compelling impression in the consumer's mind. Notice how the ad for Arrowhead Mountain Spring Water shown in Exhibit 6–15 uses a beautiful visual image of the mountains to communicate the key product attribute of purity.

Sometimes advertisers use a different strategy; they design ads in which the visual portion is incongruent with or contradicts the verbal information presented. The logic behind this strategy is that the use of an unexpected picture or visual image will grab consumers' attention and get them to engage in more effortful or elaborative processing.[81] A number of studies have shown that the use of a visual that is inconsistent with the verbal content leads to more recall and greater processing of the information presented.[82] The ad for Gain dishwashing liquid shown in Exhibit 6–16 is a good example of this technique. The visual image showing people happily washing dishes is not consistent with the ad copy stating that "dishwashing may never feel this great."

Message Appeals

One of the advertiser's most important creative strategy decisions involves the choice of an appropriate appeal. Some ads are designed to appeal to the rational, logical aspect of the consumer's decision-making process; others appeal to feelings in an attempt to evoke some emotional reaction. Many believe that effective advertising combines the practical reasons for purchasing a product with emotional values. In this section we will examine several common types of message appeals, including comparative advertising, fear, and humor.

EXHIBIT 6–15

Visual images are an effective way to communicate an important product attribute

Source: Arrowhead by Nestlé Waters North America

EXHIBIT 6–16

This ad uses a visual image that may encourage more elaborative processing

Source: Gain by Procter & Gamble

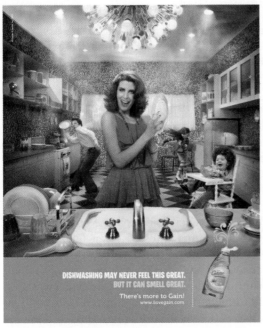

Comparative Advertising **Comparative advertising** is the practice of either directly or indirectly naming competitors in an ad and comparing one or more specific attributes.[83] This form of advertising became popular after the Federal Trade Commission (FTC) began advocating its use in 1972. The FTC reasoned that direct comparison of brands would provide better product information, giving consumers a more rational basis for making purchase decisions. Television networks cooperated with the FTC by lifting their ban on comparative ads, and the result was a flurry of comparative commercials.

Initially, the novelty of comparative ads resulted in greater attention. But since they have become so common, their attention-getting value has probably declined. Some studies show that recall is higher for comparative than noncomparative messages, but comparative ads are generally not more effective for other response variables, such as brand attitudes or purchase intentions.[84] Advertisers must also consider how comparative messages affect credibility. Users of the brand being attacked in a comparative message may be especially skeptical about the advertiser's claims.

Comparative advertising may be particularly useful for new brands, since it allows a new market entrant to position itself directly against the more established brands and to promote its distinctive advantages. Direct comparisons can help position a new brand in the evoked, or choice, set of brands the customer may be considering. Comparative advertising is often used for brands with a small market share. They compare themselves to an established market leader in hopes of creating an association and tapping into the leader's market.

The use of comparative advertising is not limited to new brands or those with a small market share; a number of high-profile marketers have been using comparative appeals to differentiate their brands in a competitive marketplace.[85] For example, comparative advertising has become common in the mobile phone industry as the four major providers (Verizon, AT&T, T-Mobile, and Sprint) often run ads comparing themselves against one another on key attributes such as network coverage, signal quality and price.[86] Apple made very effective use of comparative advertising for over three years with its comparative "Get a Mac" campaign, which poked fun at Microsoft's Windows operating system while promoting the user friendliness of Mac computers. The campaign included nearly 70 different TV spots that portrayed actor Justin Long as the hip, unflappable Mac and *New York Times Magazine* writer John Hodgman as the uptight and somewhat nerdy PC who is frustrated by the Mac's capabilities (Exhibit 6–17). It was credited with helping increase Apple's share of the PC market in the United States from 2 to 8 percent and was named the best advertising campaign of the first decade of the new century by industry trade publication *Adweek*.[87]

Ironically, several companies have been using comparative advertising effectively against Apple in recent years including Samsung and Microsoft. Samsung has used comparative ads to gain market share in the smartphone market by comparing its Samsung Galaxy smartphone to Apple's iPhone. For example, shortly after Apple launched the iPhone 5, Samsung ran a commercial for its Galaxy S III that mocked iPhone loyalists for waiting in line to get the new smartphone. The ad was one of several spots in Samsung's "The Next Best Thing Is Already Here" campaign that were very

EXHIBIT 6–17

Apple used comparative advertising in its "Get a Mac" campaign

© A. Miller/WENN Photos/Newscom

popular with consumers (Exhibit 6–18). Microsoft has also used comparative ads against Apple for its Surface Pro 3 tablet that show various features such as touchscreen display, detachable keyboard, stylus support, and connectivity ports—all of which are not available on Apple's popular MacBook Air. The comparative ads are part of Microsoft's strategy to position the Surface Pro as "the tablet that can replace your laptop."

Market leaders often hesitate to use comparison ads, as most believe they have little to gain by featuring competitors' products in their ads. There are exceptions, of course; Coca-Cola resorted to comparative advertising in response to challenges made by Pepsi that were reducing Coke's market share. Anheuser-Busch also responded to the comparative ads used by the Miller Brewing Company when its rival started gaining market share at the expense of Bud Light and other brands. A recent study by Fred Beard suggests that marketers must be careful when using comparative advertising because the potential for negative reactions by consumers is high when prominent brands compare themselves against one another. He also found that comparative ads work better with a younger audience than for older consumers.[88]

Another area where comparative messages are quite commonly used is political advertising. Political advertising is viewed as an important component of political speech and thus enjoys more First Amendment protection than commercial speech and less regulation by either government or self-policing agencies. Thus, it has become quite common for political ads to contain negative, one-sided attacks on an opposing candidate's weaknesses such as character flaws, voting record, public misstatements, broken promises, and the like.[89] The goal of these ads is to discredit the character, record, or position of an opponent and create doubt in voters' minds about his or her ability to govern effectively. A major reason why negative political ads are used successfully is that voters often tend to weight negative information more heavily than positive information when forming impressions of political candidates.[90] However, studies have shown that the use of "attack advertising" by politicians can result in negative perceptions of both candidates.[91] IMC Perspective 6–2 discusses how the use of attack ads has become very common in presidential elections in the United States and why they are often very effective.

EXHIBIT 6–18

Samsung's comparative ads positioned the Galaxy S III against the iPhone 5

Source: Samsung

Fear Appeals   Fear is an emotional response to a threat that expresses, or at least implies, some sort of danger. Ads sometimes use **fear appeals** to evoke this emotional response and arouse individuals to take steps to remove the threat. Some, like the antidrug ads used by the Partnership for a Drug-Free America, stress physical danger that can occur if behaviors are not altered. Others—like those for deodorant, mouthwash, or dandruff shampoos—threaten disapproval or social rejection. Fear appeals are often used to discourage unsafe behaviors such as drinking and driving

and more recently texting and driving. For example, the Ad Council, which is the leading producer of public service advertising in the United States, has created a number of campaigns that use fear appeal messages to deal with these behaviors. Exhibit 6–19 shows an ad created by the Ad Council to discourage buzzed driving by showing how getting arrested for a DUI can cost nearly $10,000 in legal fees. The ad was part of a campaign created by the council after its research found that too many drivers thought drunk driving messages didn't apply to them: that driving "buzzed" after only a few drinks was different than driving drunk.

EXHIBIT 6–19

The Ad Council uses a fear appeal to discourage buzzed driving

Source: National Highway Traffic Safety Administration and Ad Council

How Fear Operates Before deciding to use a fear appeal–based message strategy, the advertiser should consider how fear operates, what level to use, and how different target audiences may respond. One theory suggests that the relationship between the level of fear in a message and acceptance or persuasion is curvilinear, as shown in Figure 6–5.[92] This means that message acceptance increases as the amount of fear used rises—to a point. Beyond that point, acceptance decreases as the level of fear rises.

This relationship between fear and persuasion can be explained by the fact that fear appeals have both facilitating and inhibiting effects.[93] A low level of fear can have facilitating effects; it attracts attention and interest in the message and may motivate the receiver to act to resolve the threat. Thus, increasing the level of fear in a message from low to moderate can result in increased persuasion. High levels of fear, however, can produce inhibiting effects; the receiver may emotionally block the message by tuning it out, perceiving it selectively, or denying its arguments outright. Figure 6–5 illustrates how these two countereffects operate to produce the curvilinear relationship between fear and persuasion.

A study by Anand-Keller and Block provides support for this perspective on how fear operates.[94] They examined the conditions under which low- and high-fear appeals urging people to stop smoking are likely to be effective. Their study indicated that a communication using a low level of fear may be ineffective because it results in insufficient motivation to elaborate on the harmful consequences of engaging in the destructive behavior (smoking). However, an appeal arousing high levels of fear was ineffective because it resulted in too much elaboration on the harmful consequences. This led to defensive tendencies such as message avoidance and interfered with processing of recommended solutions to the problem.

Another approach to the curvilinear explanation of fear is the protection motivation model.[95] According to this theory, four cognitive appraisal processes mediate the individual's response to the threat: appraising (1) the information available regarding the severity of the perceived threat, (2) the perceived probability that the threat will occur, (3) the perceived ability of a coping behavior to remove the threat, and (4) the individual's perceived ability to carry out the coping behavior.

This model suggests that both the cognitive appraisal of the information in a fear appeal message and the emotional response mediate persuasion. An audience is more likely to continue processing threat-related information, thereby increasing the likelihood that a coping behavior will occur.

FIGURE 6–5

Relationship between Fear Levels and Message Acceptance

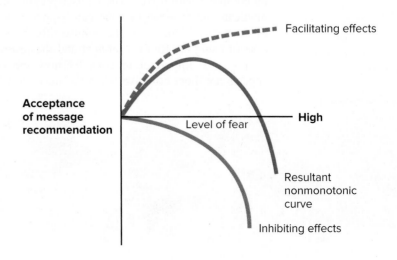

IMC Perspective 6–2 > > >

Political Attack Ads Become Pervasive

If you watch TV on any sort of regular basis, you've probably noticed that every two years the airwaves experience a huge influx of political advertising. Depending on the campaign cycle, the number of ads airing to promote candidates running for either local, state, or national political office will increase. Political ads generally fall into one of two categories. The first type is self-promoting, positive ads that highlight all of the great things the candidate has done throughout his or her career; the second type is negative or "attack ads" that target an opponent's platform, record, background, or character. These negative ads have become commonplace in political campaigns over the past decade and far outweigh the number of positive messages. And if you are like most voters, you are very annoyed by these ads and tired of seeing and/or hearing them.

While negative advertising in politics is indeed pervasive, the commonly held perception that negative ads are shown more often than their positive counterparts was not always the case. The 2004 presidential election between George W. Bush and John Kerry, for example, was viewed as the "most negative" presidential race since the 1950s, but only a little over 50 percent of all ads that aired were negative. Bush and Kerry were relatively kind to one another compared to the 2012 presidential election between Barack Obama and Mitt Romney, which set a record for most negative campaign ads in history. According to the Wesleyan Media Project, which tracks political advertising, 86 percent of Obama's TV ads and 79 percent of Romney's were negative. Political analysts noted that the campaign was so negative because

both candidates recognized that anything that moved even a small percentage of the voters could make a difference in the seven or eight key battleground states. While attack ads were used extensively by both Obama and Romney, the 2012 election was tame compared to the 2016 campaign between Hillary Clinton and Donald Trump, which was marked by disparaging messages from both sides, including accusations of racism and bigotry.

Of course the question most people ask when they become annoyed by all of the negative advertising that takes place during political campaigns is, does it work? Unfortunately for the voters who have to watch them, the answer appears to be yes. Studies have shown that negative ads are more powerful, memorable, and much more likely to discuss real issues in an election than positive ads. Positive ads can get away with flowery language and hyperbole to try to "prop up" a candidate, while negative ads must work hard to achieve credibility and provide evidence to support his or her claims. If a negative ad makes an assertion that is untrue, the candidate who created it may experience a backlash far worse than anything an opposing ad could provide. When negative ads do attack an opponent on a personal level, they usually highlight inexperience or dishonesty, two attributes that are very important when electing someone to public office. And attack ads may seem to be everywhere because they are having the intended effect whereby you may recall them long after seeing them.

Experts argue that another reason for the increase in attack ads is that they attract more attention from and coverage by the news media. Political science professor John Green has studied presidential campaigns over the past 25 years and

---

The protection motivation model suggests that ads using fear appeals should give the target audience information about the severity of the threat, the probability of its occurrence, the effectiveness of a coping response, and the ease with which the response can be implemented.[96] For example, the ad shown in Exhibit 6–20 uses a mild fear appeal for Seagate Technology's Replica product, which is used to back up computer hard drives. The ad uses playful illustrations in a graphic style to communicate the message of what can happen if your computer crashes and all of the files are lost. Notice how the ad also offers a solution to the threat by showing the ease of using the Replica product and the resulting peace of mind.

It is also important to consider how the target audience may respond. Fear appeals are more effective when the message recipient is self-confident and prefers

EXHIBIT 6–20

Seagate uses a mild fear appeal that alerts consumers to a problem and offers a solution

Source: Seagate Technology LLC

State 1

State 2

State 3

State 4

State 5

State 6

Source: Club for Growth

notes that the news media play a major role in the rise of negativity in presidential campaigns. Green argues that political consultants know that attack ads draw attention by the media which gives them an incentive to encourage candidates to use them. The news media's focus on negative advertising thus encourages its use and leads to a cycle of attack ads that is driven by political consultants and journalists.

Critics of negative political ads argue that they distract voters from the real issues by getting them to focus on meaningless personal attacks, encourage deception and incivility, and end up disillusioning voters. However, many political analysts are still very much in favor of them, arguing that if negativity were to disappear from our electoral battles so would the

democratic system in which we take so much pride. While a significant number of studies show that people are skeptical of and irritated by negative ads, political consultants point to studies showing that despite the public's feelings toward the moral or ethical nature of them, attack ads are often successful in shifting voters' perceptions of a candidate.

Politicians and their campaign managers realize that it is very difficult to win an election today without attacking their opponent. Candidates for public office often start a campaign by taking the high ground, but then waste little time turning to attack ads when they fall behind in the polls or feel they have to respond to an accusation made in one of their opponents' ads. It clearly looks like attack ads will remain the norm, and the question now is whether we will ever see a positive political ad again.

Sources: John Wihbey and Denise-Marie Ordway, "Negative Political Ad and Voter Effects: Research Roundup," *Journalist Resource,* February 6, 2016, http://journalistsresource.org/studies/politics/ads-public-opinion/negative-political-ads-effects-voters-research-roundup; Donovan Slack, "RIP Positive Ads in 2012," *Politicio,* November 4, 2012, www.politico.com/news/stories/1112/83262.html; Rance Crain, "Marketers Could Learn from Negative Political Ads: Keep It Simple," *Advertising Age,* February 20, 2012, http://adage.com/article/rance-crain/marketers-learn-political-ads-simple/232797/; Tom Denari, "Why Attack Ads and Disney Movies Are So Darned Effective," *Advertising Age,* October 19 2010, http://adage.com/article/146579/.

to cope with dangers rather than avoid them.[97] They are also more effective among non-users of a product than among users. Thus, a fear appeal may be better at keeping nonsmokers from starting than persuading smokers to stop.

In reviewing research on fear appeals, Herbert Rotfeld has argued that some of the studies may be confusing different types of threats and the level of potential harm portrayed in the message with fear, which is an emotional response.[98] He concludes that the relationship between the emotional responses of fear or arousal and persuasion is not curvilinear but rather is monotonic and positive, meaning that higher levels of fear do result in greater persuasion. However, Rotfeld notes that not all fear messages are equally effective, because different people fear different things. Thus they will respond differently to the same threat, so the strongest threats are not always the most persuasive. This suggests that marketers using fear appeals must consider the emotional responses generated by the message and how they will affect reactions to the message.

While research suggests that message recipients might tune out a message that uses too much fear, there are examples of advertising campaigns where high levels of fear have been effective at changing behavior. For example, the Montana Meth Project (MMP) is a large-scale prevention program aimed at reducing methamphetamine use, particularly among teenagers, through public service messaging, policy, and community outreach. The integrated campaign uses hard-hitting TV, radio, print, digital, and social media messaging to communicate the risks of meth use.[99]

NO ONE THINKS THEY'LL TRY TO TEAR OFF THEIR OWN SKIN. METH WILL CHANGE THAT.

THE METH PROJECT

METH
NOT EVEN ONCE.

MethProject.org

Many of the ads used in the campaign use a high level of fear to communicate the risks of meth use and addiction such as the one shown in Exhibit 6–21. The MMP has been very successful: meth use in Montana has declined significantly and the campaign has been expanded to a number of other states. A recent study of fear appeals by Andrea Morales, Eugenia Wu, and Gavan Fitzsimons suggests that ads such as those used in the MMP campaign may be effective because they activate disgust as well as fear through some of the disturbing images they contain.[100]

Humor Appeals Humorous ads are often the best known and best remembered of all advertising messages. Many advertisers, including FedEx, GEICO, Old Spice, Snickers, Budweiser, and Bud Light, use humor appeals effectively. Humor is usually presented primarily through TV commercials and online video and to a lesser extent through radio as these media lend themselves to the execution of humorous messages. However, humor is occasionally used in print ads as well as agency creatives can use images in combination with clever headlines and ad copy to develop humorous messages. The sermon ad for Listermint mouthwash shown in Exhibit 6–22 is a very good example of how humor can be used effectively in print media.

Advertisers use humor for many reasons.[101] Humorous messages attract and hold consumers' attention. They enhance effectiveness by putting consumers in a positive mood, increasing their liking of the ad itself and their feeling toward the product or service. And humor can distract the receiver from counterarguing against the message. A meta-analytic test of various models of how humor works in advertising showed that its effects are primarily based on affective processes and that it can distract from the processing of cognitive information such as brand beliefs and benefits. This suggests that the peripheral processing of humorous messages is dominant and that effort devoted to processing of ad-related affective elements comes at the expense of attention to brand-related cognitions.[102]

Critics argue that funny ads draw people to the humorous situation but distract them from the brand and its attributes. Also, effective humor can be difficult to produce and some attempts are too subtle for mass audiences. And, there is concern that humorous ads may wear out faster than serious appeals. **Wearout** refers to the tendency of a television or radio commercial to lose its effectiveness when it is seen and/or heard repeatedly.[103] Wearout may occur if consumers no longer pay attention to a commercial after several exposures or become annoyed at seeing or hearing an ad multiple times. Some experts argue that humorous

ads wear out faster than other formats because once the consumer gets the joke, the ad becomes boring. However, advocates of humor argue that funny ads are effective longer as consumers will respond more favorably to a well-executed humorous ad than a serious message.[104] One way marketers deal with the wearout problem is by creating "pool-outs" or multiple executions around a campaign theme that can be rotated so no one ad airs repeatedly during a short time period. For example, large advertisers such as GEICO, FedEx, and Anheuser-Busch InBev generally have a number of commercials available to rotate. However, this can be a problem for smaller companies that do not have a large enough budget to produce multiple commercials.

Clearly, there are valid reasons both for and against the use of humor in advertising. Not every product or service lends itself to a humorous approach. A number of studies have found that the effectiveness of humor depends on several factors, including the type of product or service and audience characteristics.[105] For example, humor has been more prevalent and more effective with low-involvement, feeling products than high-involvement, thinking products.[106] A recent study examined how audience involvement moderates the effects of humorous ads. The researchers found that for products that are not intrinsically humorous, the use of humor in an advertising message is more effective when involvement is relatively low rather than high. These findings support the idea that high-involvement products may not be as well suited for advertising humor as low-involvement products.[107]

CHANNEL FACTORS

The final controllable variable of the communication process is the channel, or medium, used to deliver the message to the target audience. While a variety of methods are available to transmit marketing communications, as noted in Chapter 5, they can be classified into two broad categories, personal and nonpersonal media.

Personal versus Nonpersonal Channels

There are a number of basic differences between personal and nonpersonal communications channels. Information received from personal influence channels is generally more persuasive than information received via the mass media. Reasons for the differences are summarized in the following comparison of advertising and personal selling:

> From the standpoint of persuasion, a sales message is far more flexible, personal, and powerful than an advertisement. An advertisement is normally prepared by persons having minimal personal contact with customers. The message is designed to appeal to a large number of persons. By contrast, the message in a good sales presentation is not determined in advance. The salesman has a tremendous store of knowledge about his product or service and selects appropriate items as the interview progresses. Thus, the salesman can adapt this to the thinking and needs of the customer or prospect at the time of the sales call. Furthermore, as objections arise and are voiced by the buyer, the salesman can treat the objections in an appropriate manner. This is not possible in advertising.[108]

Personal channels are used in several ways in an IMC program. As was discussed in Chapter 5, many marketers are recognizing the importance of word-of-mouth communications which is becoming more prevalent with the growth of social media. The more traditional use of personal communications is through sales programs which are implemented through a company's sales force as well as at the point of purchase through retail sales personnel. However, the advertising and promotion programs for most marketers rely heavily on traditional media advertising as well digital and social media. Thus, we will discuss some of the important factors that marketers must consider with respect to these media.

Effects of Alternative Mass Media

The various mass media that advertisers use to transmit their messages differ in many ways, including the number and type of people they reach, costs, information processing requirements, and qualitative factors. The mass media's costs and efficiency in exposing a target audience to a communication will be evaluated in Chapters 10 through 12. However, we should recognize differences in how information is processed and how communications are influenced by context or environment.

Differences in Information Processing   There are basic differences in the manner and rate at which information from various forms of media is transmitted and can be processed. Information from ads in print media, such as newspapers, magazines, or direct mail, as well as online through websites and other forms of owned media is *self-paced;* readers process the ad or information at their own rate and can study it as long as they desire. In contrast, information from the broadcast media of radio and television is *externally paced;* the transmission rate is controlled by the medium.

The difference in the processing rate for print and broadcast media has some obvious implications for advertisers. Self-paced print media make it easier for the message recipient to process a long, complex message. Advertisers often use print ads when they want to present a detailed message with a lot of information. Broadcast media are more effective for transmitting shorter messages or, in the case of TV, presenting images along with words.

While there are limits to the length and complexity of broadcast messages, advertisers can deal with this problem. One strategy is to use a radio or TV ad to get consumers' attention and direct them to a website for a more detailed message. Some advertisers develop broadcast and digital/print versions of the same message. The copy portion is similar in both media, but the print ad can be processed at a rate comfortable to the receiver.

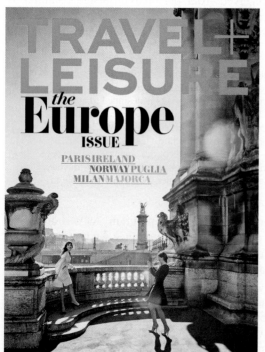

Effects of Context and Environment

Interpretation of an advertising message can be influenced by the context or environment in which the ad appears. Communication theorist Marshall McLuhan's thesis, "The medium is the message," implies that the medium communicates an image that is independent of any message it contains.[109] A **qualitative media effect** is the influence the medium has on a message. The image of the media vehicle can affect reactions to the message. For example, an ad for a high-quality men's clothing line might have more of an impact in a fashion magazine like *GQ* than in *Sports Afield.* Airlines, destination resorts, and travel-related services advertise in publications such as *Travel + Leisure* partly because the articles, pictures, and other ads help excite readers about travel (Exhibit 6–23).

A media environment can also be created by the nature of the program in which a commercial appears. One study found that consumers reacted more positively to commercials seen during a happy TV program than a sad one.[110] Advertisers pay premium dollars to advertise on popular programs that create positive moods, like sitcoms, sporting events, award shows such as the Oscars and Grammys, and holiday specials. Conversely, advertisers tend to avoid programs that create a negative mood among viewers or may be detrimental to the company or its products. Many companies won't advertise on programs with excessive violence or sexual content. Coca-Cola never advertises on TV news programs because it thinks bad news is inconsistent with Coke's image as an upbeat, fun product. A study by Andrew Aylesworth and Scott

MacKenzie found that commercials placed in programs that induce negative moods are processed less systematically than ads placed in programs that put viewers in positive moods.[111] They suggest that media buyers might be well advised to follow the conventional wisdom of placing their ads during "feel-good" programming, especially if the message is intended to work through a central route to persuasion. However, messages intended to operate through a peripheral route to persuasion might be more effective if they are shown during more negative programs, where presumably viewers will not analyze the ad in detail because of their negative mood state.

Clutter

Another aspect of the media environment which is important to advertisers is the problem of **clutter**, which has been defined as the amount of advertising in a medium.[112] However, for television, clutter is often viewed as including all the nonprogram material that appears in the broadcast environment—commercials, promotional messages for shows, public service announcements (PSAs), and the like. Clutter is of increasing concern to advertisers since there are so many messages in various media competing for the consumer's attention. Half of the average magazine's pages contain ads, and in some publications the ratio of ads to editorial content is even higher. On average, around a quarter of a broadcast hour on TV is devoted to commercials, while most radio stations carry an average of 10 to 12 minutes of commercial time per hour. The average length of a commercial break during prime time on the major networks is just over three minutes which means viewers are exposed to a large number of ads in a short time period, making it difficult for commercials to attract and hold the attention of viewers as well as communicate effectively.

Clutter has become a major concern among television advertisers as a result of increases in nonprogram time and the trend toward shorter commercials. While the 30-second commercial replaced 60-second spots as the industry standard in the 1970s, many advertisers are now using 15-second spots. The advertising industry continues to express concern over the highly cluttered viewing environment on TV; the amount of clutter increased as much as 30 percent during the 1990s and has continued to increase over the past two decades.[113] Several factors are causing the increased clutter including lower rating for TV shows as consumers spend more time online and the fact that many marketers are reducing their spending on television advertising and shifting these monies into digital ads. Thus, TV networks are inserting more commercials into programs to offset these factors and avoid revenue declines.

Clutter levels have been increasing as the four major broadcast networks and cable networks have also increased the amount of time allocated to commercials. Broadcast networks average just over 14 minutes of commercial time per hour while cable averages 15 and a half minutes, with some networks averaging more than 18 minutes.[114] Thus, a viewer watching three hours of prime-time programs on the major networks would be exposed to more than 100 commercials in addition to programming promotions, and PSAs.[115] The problem is even greater during popular shows, to which the networks add more commercials because they can charge more. And, of course, advertisers and their agencies perpetuate the problem by pressuring the networks to squeeze their ads into top-rated shows with the largest audiences.

The clutter problem is even higher on many cable networks and during daytime programs. Recently some cable networks such as TBS and TNT have been using compression technology to speed up the transmission of programs and allow more time for commercials, which is adding to the clutter problem.[116] Advertisers and agencies want the networks to commit to a minimum amount of program time and then manage the nonprogram portion however they see fit. If the networks wanted to add more commercials, it would come out of their promos, PSAs, or program credit time. The problem is not likely to go away, however, and advertisers will continue to search for ways to break through the clutter, such as using humor, celebrity spokespeople, or novel creative approaches.[117]

Summary

This chapter focuses on the controllable variables that are part of the communication process—source, message, and channel factors. Decisions regarding each of these variables should consider their impact on the various steps of the response hierarchy the message receiver passes through. The persuasion matrix helps assess the effect of controllable communication decisions on the consumer's response process.

Selection of the appropriate source or communicator to deliver a message is an important aspect of communications strategy. Three important attributes are source credibility, attractiveness, and power. Marketers enhance message effectiveness by hiring communicators who are experts in a particular area and/or have a trustworthy image. The use of celebrities to deliver advertising messages has become very popular; advertisers hope they will catch the receivers' attention and influence their attitudes or behavior through an identification process. The chapter discusses the meaning a celebrity brings to the endorsement process and the importance of matching the image of the celebrity with that of the company or brand.

The design of the advertising message is a critical part of the communication process. There are various options regarding message structure, including order of presentation of message arguments, conclusion drawing, message sidedness, refutation, and verbal versus visual traits. The advantages and disadvantages of different message appeal strategies were considered, including comparative messages and emotional appeals such as fear and humor.

Finally, the channel or medium used to deliver the message was considered. Differences between personal and nonpersonal channels of communication were discussed. Alternative mass media can have an effect on the communication process as a result of information processing and qualitative factors. The context in which an ad appears and the reception environment are important factors to consider in the selection of mass media. Clutter has become a serious problem for advertisers, particularly on TV, where commercials have become shorter and more numerous.

Key Terms

persuasion matrix 185
source 186
credibility 187
internalization 187
sleeper effect 191
attractiveness 192
identification 192

source power 203
compliance 204
primacy effect 205
recency effect 205
one-sided message 206
two-sided message 206
refutational appeal 207

comparative advertising 209
fear appeals 210
wearout 214
qualitative media effect 216
clutter 217

Discussion Questions

1. The chapter opener discusses how Under Armour has been very successful in its use of athletes as endorsers for the company/brand. Evaluate the strategy used by Under Armour in selecting and signing athletes to endorsement deals. Why do you think the company has been able to compete so effectively against larger companies such as Nike and adidas in signing athletes as endorsers? (LO 6-2)

2. Discuss how marketers can use the persuasion matrix shown in Figure 6–1 to plan their integrated marketing communications programs. Choose a TV commercial or print ad and use the persuasion matrix to evaluate how it might influence consumers' response processes. (LO 6-1)

3. Discuss the three primary source attributes noted by Herbert Kelman and the different processes by which they can influence attitude and/or behavior change. Find an example of an advertisement or other type of promotional message that utilizes each attribute. (LO 6-2)

4. Find examples of an advertising message or campaign that uses the company CEO, president, or founder as the spokesperson. Do you think this individual is an effective spokesperson for the company? Why or why not? (LO 6-2)

5. IMC Perspective 6–1 discusses the series of problems Nike has had with some of its endorsers because of controversies that have arisen in their personal lives. Discuss how the problems surrounding these endorsers might impact the image and reputation of Nike. How long do you think Nike should stand by endorsers when they run into personal problems? (LO 6-2)

6. Find a celebrity who is currently appearing in an advertising campaign for a particular company or brand

and use McCracken's meaning transfer model (shown in Figure 6–4) to analyze the use of this individual as a spokesperson. (LO 6-2)

7. Discuss the rise in popularity of YouTube stars such as Smosh, the Fine Brothers and PewDiePie among young people. Do you think these YouTube personalities can replace more traditional celebrities such as athletes, actors/actresses, and entertainers as advertising spokespersons? (LO 6-2)

8. Evaluate Domino's decision to run an advertising campaign acknowledging the problems with the taste of its pizza as a way to promote its new recipe. Do you think this strategy was an effective way to promote its reformulated product? (LO 6-3)

9. Visit the website for the Montana Meth Project (www.methproject.org) and choose three ads that use various levels of fear in the message. Discuss why each ad may or may not be effective. (LO 6-3)

10. Discuss the pros and cons of using humor as the basis for an advertising appeal. Find an example of an advertising message that uses humor and evaluate its effectiveness. (LO 6-3)

11. Discuss the problem of advertising clutter and how it is a problem in various media such as magazines, television, and radio. What are some of the ways the media can address the clutter problem? (LO 6-4)

12. What is meant by a qualitative media effect? Select a television program or a magazine and discuss the nature of the media reception environment created by the show or the publication. What type of companies or brands might be attracted to advertising on this program or in this publication? (LO 6-4)

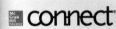

Digital users can access their personalized and adaptive SmartBook, Ad Forum Video Cases, and interactive exercises to review chapter concepts.

7 Establishing Objectives and Budgeting for the Promotional Program

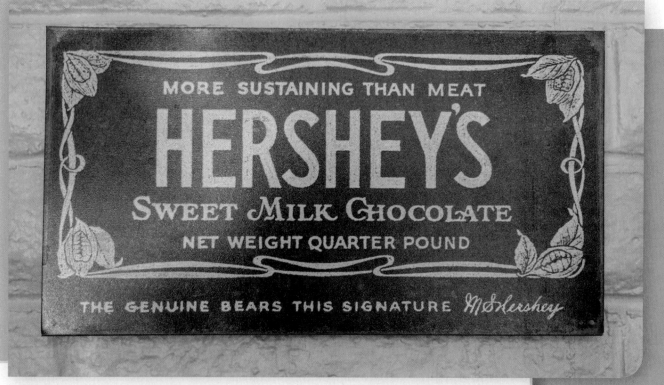

Source: Ed Rhee/Flickr/CC BY 2.0

LEARNING OBJECTIVES

LO1 Discuss the value of setting objectives for advertising and promotion.

LO2 Describe the relationship between promotional objectives and marketing objectives.

LO3 Discuss sales versus communications objectives.

LO4 Compare the value of sales objectives and communications objectives as goals for promotional programs.

LO5 Describe the process of budgeting for IMC.

LO6 Compare the economic and sales response perspectives on budgeting.

LO7 Compare different methods of setting budgets.

CHANGING MEDIA HABITS MEANS CHANGING BUDGET ALLOCATIONS. IS DIGITAL THE NEW KING?

Marketers have for some time been aware that the media environment has changed and that the younger generations are much less engaged with traditional media like television, newspapers, and magazines. These younger segments—particularly millennials—live in a digital world. What marketers may not have been aware of is how quickly and how significantly this change has been. The change has led to a whole new world of strategy development.

For the first time ever, predictions are that by 2017 digital ad spending will surpass that of TV—a "major milestone" in both the media and budgeting environments. *eMarketer* predicts that in 2017 digital's share of total advertising expenditures will account for 38.4 percent of total advertising expenditures, reaching $77.37 billion and surpassing that of television which will account for 35.8 percent or $72.01 billion. By 2020 it is predicted that TV will account for less than one-third of the total expenditures.

Does this mean the end for television? Not quite. While expenditures in television may be losing share relative to the growth of digital, it is still expected to grow over the long term at a rate of 2 percent a year. What it does mean is that advertisers expect to achieve greater returns from digital and are moving their monies to these media.

This movement is partly a result of the fascination with mobile. Expenditures in mobile were expected to grow by 38 percent to $43.6 billion in 2016. That number means that mobile spending will account for 63.4 percent of the total *digital* spend! So digital is king of media spending, but mobile is clearly the king of the digital world. Marketers have also indicated they will continue to increase investments in other areas as well, with an increased emphasis on data-driven marketing spending, e-mail, website enhancements, and social media. A survey of marketing executives indicates that the majority of them planned to increase their expenditures on Facebook, YouTube, and Twitter.

One of the companies making the switch is the traditional chocolate company Hershey.

Established in 1894, Hershey never advertised but continued to grow successfully. Sales took a big leap forward after Hershey bars became "Ration D" as part of the food kits provided to U.S. soldiers in World War II. When the soldiers returned, their brand loyalty to Hershey came with them. It wasn't until 1970 that the company deemed it necessary to start advertising with the initial ad in a Sunday newspaper supplement. The brand, which includes Hershey, Reese's, and Jolly Rancher, now spends about $700 million per year and plans on tripling the amount going to digital, which would constitute 20 percent of the overall ad budget. Forty percent of this would go to mobile. The balance would continue to go to traditional media, as the company still believes in the "exceptional reach of traditional TV" according to Hershey president for North America Michelle Buck. Digital expenditures are expected to give the brands an incremental reach, according to Buck, while increasing behavioral targeting opportunities.

So as more and more advertisers move their monies to digital, are they doing the right thing? According to Nathalie Tadena, writing in the *Wall Street Journal,* they may not be. Tadena cites a Forrester Research study that indicated that almost half of marketers plan to boost their investments in digital channels, despite the fact that a full 43 percent are still experimenting with digital and are not sure if it works. Less than half said that their marketing teams were "extremely successful" in developing and executing digital ad programs, and that they were more tactical than strategic.

So why the mad rush to digital? That's a very good question.

Sources: "Digital Ad Spending to Surpass TV Next Year," www.emarketer.com, March 8, 2016; "Hershey Plans to Triple Digital Ad Spending: The Spending Increase Will Target Mobile," www.adage.com, February 18, 2015; "Digital Marketers Continue Love Affair with Data," www.emarketer.com, March 18, 2015; Nathalie Tadena, "Marketers' Digital Push Continues, Despite Questions about What Works," www.blogs.wsj.com, April 7, 2015.

EXHIBIT 7–1

The objective of this ad is to demonstrate Allianz's support for the future.

Source: Allianz Life Insurance Company of North America

The lead-in to this chapter discusses how the changing media environment is forcing marketers to reallocate their advertising expenditures. As indicated, the monies previously allocated to traditional media are increasingly being moved to digital media. At the same time, not everyone is on board with what they consider to be more of a knee-jerk reaction than a sound strategy, as many managers admit they don't yet know if their digital expenditures are paying off. Those managers who have been hesitant to move strongly into digital argue that it is necessary to establish concrete communications objectives to guide their media strategies. These objectives should be based on purchase decision models that guide the budget allocation to various media, and not just the fact that a particular media category is trending. As you will see, many large companies have been using these purchase decision models for a number of years, and continue to do so. At the same time not everyone agrees with their use or their validity, arguing that the models are either outdated or should never have been used in the first place. As the media environment continues to change, marketers continue to examine these models and their value in guiding the IMC program. As this chapter will demonstrate, the success of a program can and should be measured by both marketing and communications objectives. The chapter will examine how the goals for the integrated marketing communications program follow the company's overall marketing strategy and how these goals determine and are determined by the promotional budget.

Unfortunately, many companies have difficulty with the most critical step in the promotional planning process—setting realistic objectives that will guide the development of the IMC program. Complex marketing situations, conflicting perspectives regarding what advertising and other promotional-mix elements are expected to accomplish, and uncertainty over resources make the setting of marketing communications objectives "a job of creating order out of chaos." While the task of setting objectives can be complex and difficult, it must be done properly because specific goals and objectives are the foundation on which all other promotional decisions are made. Budgeting for advertising and other promotional areas, as well as creative and media strategies and tactics, evolves from these objectives. They also provide a standard against which performance can be measured.

Setting specific objectives should be an integral part of the planning process. However, many companies either fail to use specific marketing communications objectives or set ones that are inadequate for guiding the development of the promotional plan or measuring its effectiveness. Many marketers are uncertain as to what integrated marketing communications should be expected to contribute to the marketing program. The goal of their company's advertising and promotional program is simple: to generate sales. They fail to recognize the specific tasks that advertising and other promotional-mix variables must perform in preparing customers to buy a particular product or service.

As we know, advertising and promotion are not the only marketing activities involved in generating sales. Moreover, it is not always possible or necessary to measure the effects of advertising in terms of sales. For example, the Allianz ad shown in Exhibit 7–1 has a goal beyond just supporting its company and attracting new customers.

Consider Procter and Gamble's "Like a Girl" campaign ad shown in Exhibit 7–2. What objectives might the company have for this ad? How might its effectiveness be measured?

EXHIBIT 7–2

Procter and Gamble's objectives for this campaign are other than generating sales

Source: Procter & Gamble

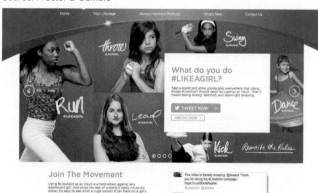

This chapter examines the nature and purpose of objectives and the role they play in guiding the development, implementation, and evaluation of an IMC program. Attention is given to the various types of objectives appropriate for different situations. We will also examine the budget-setting process and the interdependence of objective setting and budgeting.

THE VALUE OF OBJECTIVES

Perhaps one reason many companies fail to set specific objectives for their integrated marketing communications programs is that they don't recognize the value of doing so. Another may be disagreement as to what the specific objectives should be. Advertising and promotional objectives are needed for several reasons, including the functions they serve in communications, planning and decision making, and measurement and evaluation.

Communications

Specific objectives for the IMC program facilitate coordination of the various groups working on the campaign. Many people are involved in the planning and development of an integrated marketing communications program on the client side as well as in the various promotional agencies. The advertising and promotional program must be coordinated within the company, inside the ad agency, and between the two. Any other parties involved in the promotional campaign, such as public relations and/or sales promotion firms, research specialists, and media buying services, must also know what the company hopes to accomplish through its marketing communications program. Many problems can be avoided if all parties have written, approved objectives to guide their actions and serve as a common base for discussing issues related to the promotional program.

Planning and Decision Making

Specific promotional objectives also guide development of the integrated marketing communications plan. All phases of a firm's promotional strategy should be based on the established objectives, including budgeting, creative, and media decisions as well as direct-marketing, public relations/publicity, sales promotion, and/or reseller support programs.

Meaningful objectives can also be a useful guide for decision making. Promotional planners are often faced with a number of strategic and tactical options in terms of choosing creative options, selecting media, and allocating the budget among various elements of the promotional mix. Choices should be made based on how well a particular strategy matches the firm's promotional objectives.

Measurement and Evaluation of Results

An important reason for setting specific objectives is that they provide a benchmark against which the success or failure of the promotional campaign can be measured. Without specific objectives, it is extremely difficult to determine what the firm's advertising and promotion efforts accomplished. One characteristic of good objectives is that they are *measurable;* they specify a method and criteria for determining how well the promotional program is working. By setting specific and meaningful objectives, the promotional planner provides a measure(s) that can be used to evaluate the effectiveness of the marketing communications program. Most organizations are concerned about the return on their promotional investment, and comparing actual performance against measurable objectives is the best way to determine if the return justifies the expense.

DETERMINING INTEGRATED MARKETING COMMUNICATIONS OBJECTIVES

Integrated marketing communications objectives should be based on a thorough situation analysis that identifies the marketing and promotional issues facing the company or a brand. The situation analysis is the foundation on which marketing objectives are determined and the marketing plan is developed. IMC objectives evolve from the company's overall marketing plan and are rooted in its marketing objectives. Advertising and promotional objectives are not the same as marketing objectives (although many firms tend to treat them as synonymous).

Marketing versus Communications Objectives

Marketing objectives are generally stated in the firm's marketing plan and are statements of what is to be accomplished by the overall marketing program within a given time period. Marketing objectives are usually defined in terms of specific, measurable outcomes such as sales volume, market share, profits, or return on investment. Good marketing objectives are *quantifiable;* they delineate the target market and note the time frame for accomplishing the goal (often one year). For example, a copy machine company may have as its marketing objective "to increase sales by 10 percent in the small-business segment of the market during the next 12 months." To be effective, objectives must also be *realistic* and *attainable.*

A company with a very high market share may seek to increase its sales volume by stimulating growth in the product category. It might accomplish this by increasing consumption by current users or encouraging nonusers to use the product. Some firms have as their marketing objectives expanding distribution and sales of their product in certain market areas. Companies often have secondary marketing objectives that are related to actions they must take to solve specific problems and thus achieve their primary objectives.

Once the marketing communications manager has reviewed the marketing plan, he or she should understand where the company hopes to go with its marketing program, how it intends to get there, and the role advertising and promotion will play. Marketing goals defined in terms of sales, profit, or market share increases are usually not appropriate promotional objectives. They are objectives for the entire marketing program, and achieving them depends on the proper coordination and execution of all the marketing-mix elements, including not just promotion but product planning and production, pricing, and distribution. For example, a company may be very successful in its promotional program, creating interest and/or trial for a product. But what if the product is unavailable when the consumer goes to buy it, or what if, once in the store, the consumer feels the product is overpriced and decides not to buy? Should the promotional program be blamed when the product's poor performance is due to other marketing strategies or tactics?

Integrated marketing communications objectives are statements of what various aspects of the IMC program will accomplish. They should be based on the particular communications tasks required to deliver the appropriate messages to the target audience. Managers must be able to translate general marketing goals into communications goals and specific promotional objectives.

Sometimes companies do not have a formal marketing plan, and the information needed may not be readily available. In this case, the promotional planner must attempt to gather as much information as possible about the product and its markets from sources both inside and outside the company.

After reviewing all the information, the promotional planner should see how integrated marketing communications fits into the marketing program and what the firm hopes to achieve through advertising and other promotional elements. The next step is to set objectives in terms of specific communications goals or tasks.

Many planners approach promotion from a communications perspective and believe the objective of advertising and other promotional-mix elements is usually to communicate information or a selling message about a product or service. Other managers argue that sales or some related measure, such as market share, is the only meaningful goal for advertising and promotion and should be the basis for setting objectives. These two perspectives have been the topic of considerable debate and are worth examining further.

SALES VERSUS COMMUNICATIONS OBJECTIVES

Sales-Oriented Objectives

To many managers, the only meaningful objective for their promotional program is sales. They take the position that the basic reason a firm spends money on advertising and promotion is to sell its product or service. Promotional spending represents an investment of a firm's resources that requires an economic justification. Managers generally compare investment options on a common financial basis, such as return on investment (ROI). However, determining the specific return on advertising and promotional dollars is often quite a difficult task. A recent study by Webmarketing123 of both business-to-business (B2B) and business-to-consumer (B2C) marketers indicated that a majority admit they don't know which channels make the biggest impact on revenues. For example, while 87 percent of B2B marketers used social media, only 17 percent claimed they were able to measure ROI. Likewise, with B2C marketers, 87 percent said they used social media with only 27 percent able to measure ROI.[1] At the same time, many managers believe that monies spent on advertising and other forms of promotion should produce measurable results, such as increasing sales volume by a certain percentage or dollar amount or increasing the brand's market share. They believe objectives (as well as the success or failure of the campaign) should be based on the achievement of sales results.

As a result, many managers have increased their efforts to make agencies more accountable for their performances. In turn, some agencies have developed their own tools to attempt to provide more ROI information in regard to how their integrated communications programs are performing. These agencies often attempt to differentiate themselves from others on this premise.

Some managers prefer sales-oriented objectives to make the individuals involved in advertising and promotion think in terms of how the promotional program will influence sales. For example, GEICO, once ranked fourth behind State Farm, Allstate, and Progressive insurance companies, increased its advertising budget by 75 percent—nearly double that of its competitors—and broadened its media placements. As a result, GEICO took over as the number 1 insurance company in new customer acquisitions.[2] Likewise, Coca-Cola increased its ad spending by double digits to promote its mini-cans and bottles and the global "Share a Coke" campaign.[3] While the company would not disclose specific numbers, it did indicate that it saw a pay-off from the increased spend. The success of these advertising and promotional campaigns was judged by attainment of these goals (Exhibit 7–3).

EXHIBIT 7–3

Coca-Cola's "Share a Coke" campaign benefited from increased promotional spending

Source: The Coca-Cola Company

Problems with Sales Objectives It appears that increases in advertising expenditures seemed to work for GEICO and Coke as both experienced sales increases. Does this mean that these results can be attributed directly to the increased advertising budgets? Not necessarily. It might help to compare this situation to a football game and think of advertising as a quarterback. The quarterback is one of the most important players on

FIGURE 7–1

Factors Influencing Sales

the team but can be effective only with support from the other players. If the team loses, is it fair to blame the loss entirely on the quarterback? Of course not. Just as the quarterback is but one of the players on the football team, promotion is but one element of the marketing program, and there are many other reasons why the targeted sales level was not reached. The quarterback can lead his team to victory only if the linemen block, the receivers catch his passes, and the running backs help the offense establish a balanced attack of running and passing. Even if the quarterback plays an outstanding game, the team can still lose if the defense gives up too many points.

In the business world, sales results can be due to any of the other marketing-mix variables, including product design or quality, packaging, distribution, or pricing. Advertising can make consumers aware of and interested in the brand, but it can't make them buy it, particularly if it is not readily available or is priced higher than a competing brand. As shown in Figure 7–1, sales are a function of many factors, not just advertising and promotion. There is an adage in marketing that states, "Nothing will kill a poor product faster than good advertising." Taken with the other factors shown in Figure 7–1, this adage demonstrates that all the marketing elements must work together if a successful plan is to be implemented.

Another problem with sales objectives is that the effects of advertising often occur over an extended period. Many experts recognize that advertising has a lagged or **carryover effect**; monies spent on advertising do not necessarily have an immediate impact on sales.[4] Advertising may create awareness, interest, and/or favorable attitudes toward a brand, but these feelings will not result in an actual purchase until the consumer enters the market for the product, which may occur later. A review of econometric studies that examined the duration of cumulative advertising effects found that for mature, frequently purchased, low-priced products, advertising's effect on sales lasts up to nine months.[5] Models have been developed to account for the carryover effect of advertising and to help determine the long-term effect of advertising on sales.[6] The carryover effect adds to the difficulty of determining the precise relationship between advertising and sales.

Another problem with sales objectives is that they offer little guidance to those responsible for planning and developing the promotional program. The creative and

media people working on the account need some direction as to the nature of the advertising message the company hopes to communicate, the intended audience, and the particular effect or response sought. As you will see shortly, communications objectives are recommended because they provide operational guidelines for those involved in planning, developing, and executing the advertising and promotional program.

Where Sales Objectives Are Appropriate While there can be many problems in attempting to use sales as objectives for a promotional campaign, there are situations where sales objectives are appropriate. Certain types of promotion efforts seek direct action in nature; they attempt to induce an immediate behavioral response from the prospective customer. A major objective of most sales promotional programs is to generate short-term increases in sales. At the same time, short-term strategies hopefully will lead to longer-term gains as well. A good example is that of Kayem Foods of Chelsea, Massachusetts. To celebrate its 100th anniversary, Kayem changed the design of its frankfurter package. After consumer research suggested changing the copy and label on the package, the product was reintroduced. In the first 12 weeks Kayem saw sales rise by 15.7 percent[7] (Exhibit 7–4). Ten years later the company maintains the same label and has become the official hot dog of the Boston Red Sox, Florida Marlins, Jacksonville Jaguars, and Washington Nationals, among other sports teams.

Direct-response advertising is one type of advertising that evaluates its effectiveness on the basis of sales. Merchandise is advertised in material mailed to customers, in newspapers and magazines, through the Internet, or on television. The consumer purchases the merchandise by mail, on the Internet, or by calling a toll-free number. The direct-response advertiser generally sets objectives and measures success in terms of the sales response generated by the ad. For example, objectives for and the evaluation of a direct-response ad on TV are based on the number of orders received each time a station broadcasts the commercial. Because advertising is really the only form of communication and promotion used in this situation and response is generally immediate, setting objectives in terms of sales is appropriate. The American Airlines credit card ad shown in Exhibit 7–5 is an example of a product sold through direct-response advertising.

Retail advertising, which accounts for a significant percentage of all advertising expenditures, is another area where the advertiser often seeks an immediate response, particularly when sales or special events are being promoted. The ad for JCPenney's 60 percent off sale shown in Exhibit 7–6 is designed to attract consumers to stores during the sales period (and to generate sales volume). JCPenney's management can determine the effectiveness of its promotional effort by analyzing store traffic and sales volume during the sale and comparing them to figures for nonsale days. But retailers may also allocate advertising and promotional dollars to image-building campaigns designed to create and enhance favorable perceptions of their stores. For example, after Subway spokesperson Jarod Fogle pleaded guilty of having sex with minors and possessing child pornography, Subway immediately disassociated

Turn business expenses into travel experiences

Earn 30,000 bonus miles

EXHIBIT 7–6

JCPenney seeks sales from this ad

Source: jcp Media Inc.

EXHIBIT 7–7

This ad satisfies its communication objective by creating a favorable image of Consolidated Edison

Source: Consolidated Edison Co. of New York, Inc.

itself with Fogle, who had been in its ads for 15 years. Fogle had lost 245 pounds and had become the center of the Subway campaign stressing a healthy diet and weight-loss benefits of eating at the sandwich chain rather than at hamburger outlets. Subway's new campaign focused on the 50-year history of the brand and reminded people that it had been selling "fresh" long before Chipotle and Panera—who the company felt got all the credit for "fresh." The campaign was successful and Subway experienced little or no negative impact from the Fogle association, and enhanced the "fresh" image for the brand.

Sales-oriented objectives are also used when advertising plays a dominant role in a firm's marketing program and other factors are relatively stable. For example, many packaged-goods companies compete in mature markets with established channels of distribution, stable competitive prices and promotional budgets, and products of similar quality. They view advertising and sales promotion as the key determinants of a brand's sales or market share, so it may be possible to isolate the effects of these promotional-mix variables. Many companies have accumulated enough market knowledge with their advertising, sales promotion, and direct-marketing programs to have considerable insight into the sales levels that should result from their promotional efforts. Mark Baynes, vice president of Kellogg's Morning Foods Division, attributed a turnabout in sales to effective advertising, brand repositioning, and more emotional appeals that generate interest.[8] Thus, many companies believe it is reasonable to set objectives and evaluate the success of their promotional efforts in terms of sales results.

Advertising and promotional programs tend to be evaluated in terms of sales, particularly when expectations are not being met. Marketing and brand managers under pressure to show sales results often take a short-term perspective in evaluating advertising and sales promotion programs. They are often looking for a quick fix for declining sales or loss of market share. They ignore the pitfalls of making direct links between advertising and sales, and campaigns, as well as ad agencies, may be changed if sales expectations are not being met. As discussed in Chapter 3, many companies want their agencies to accept incentive-based compensation systems tied to sales performance. Thus, while sales may not be an appropriate objective in many advertising and promotional situations, managers are inclined to keep a close eye on sales and market share figures and make changes in the promotional program when these numbers become stagnant or decline.

Communications Objectives

Some marketers do recognize the problems associated with sales-oriented objectives. They recognize that the primary role of an IMC program is to communicate and that planning should be based on communications objectives. Advertising and other promotional efforts are designed to achieve such communications as brand knowledge and interest, favorable attitudes and image, and purchase intentions. Consumers are not expected to respond immediately; rather, advertisers realize they must provide relevant information and create favorable predispositions toward the brand before purchase behavior will occur.

For example, the ad in Exhibit 7–7 is designed to inform consumers of the company's focus on building for the future. While there is no call for immediate action, the ad creates

FIGURE 7–2

Communications Effects
Pyramid

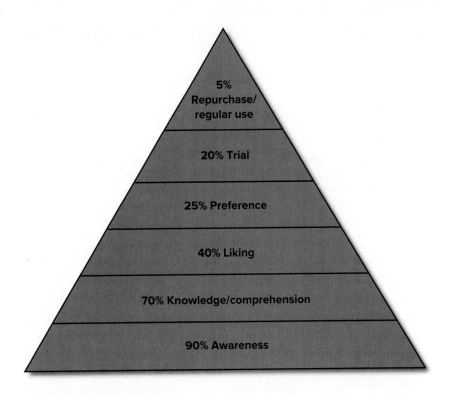

5%
Repurchase/
regular use

20% Trial

25% Preference

40% Liking

70% Knowledge/comprehension

90% Awareness

favorable impressions about the company by using pictures of children in action on computers to create a distinct image of the company. It is hoped that viewers will consider this image when they think about Consolidated Edison.

Advocates of communications-based objectives generally use some form of the hierarchical models discussed in Chapter 5 when setting advertising and promotional objectives. In all these models, consumers pass through three successive stages: cognitive (thinking), affective (feeling), and conative (behavioral). As consumers proceed through the three stages, they move closer to making a purchase.

EXHIBIT 7–8

Vans set different
communications objectives as
it grew

Source: Vans, A VF Company

Communications Effects Pyramid   Advertising and promotion perform communications tasks in the same way that a pyramid is built, by first accomplishing lower-level objectives such as awareness and knowledge or comprehension. Subsequent tasks involve moving consumers who are aware of or knowledgeable about the product or service to higher levels in the pyramid (Figure 7–2). The initial stages, at the base of the pyramid, are easier to accomplish than those toward the top, such as trial and repurchase or regular use. Thus, the percentage of prospective customers will decline as they move up the pyramid (or down the funnel).

The communications pyramid can also be used to determine promotional objectives for an established brand. The promotional planner must determine where the target audience lies with respect to the various blocks in the pyramid. If awareness levels for a brand and knowledge of its features and benefits are low, the communications objective should be to increase them. If these blocks of the pyramid are already in place, but liking or preference is low, the advertising goal may be to change the target markets' image of the brand and move consumers through to purchase. Think about the iconic shoe brand Vans for example (Exhibit 7–8). Vans started in 1966 in a small storefront in Anaheim, California, with shoe boxes on the shelves that didn't even have shoes in them. Once an order was placed, the shoes would be manufactured on the spot ready to be picked up the next day. Targeted to surfers and skateboarders, you could buy a pair for $8 or just one shoe for $4 (skateboarders tend to wear out one shoe

ARE SOCIAL, DIGITAL, AND MOBILE MEDIA CHANGING THE WAYS MARKETERS USE CONSUMER FUNNELS—OR ARE THESE FUNNELS EVEN RELEVANT?

Discussions of consumer response hierarchies have appeared in the marketing literature for over a half century and have had probably as many opponents as proponents regarding their usefulness in developing marketing and communications strategies. Nevertheless, a number of large companies including Sprint, Honda, and General Motors have employed their own hierarchies, typically referring to them as purchase funnels. These purchase funnels have been used as a planning guide to move consumers from awareness to final purchase. The number of consumers who continue through the stages of the funnel decreases, with fewer making a purchase than are actually aware of the product or brand. While consumer purchase funnels have their advocates, there are still some nonbelievers out there who contend that the funnels are too linear and the impact of digital, social, and mobile have changed the way consumers make decisions.

For example, Joe Ayyoub calls the funnel paradigm aged and says it's time for a reboot, arguing that we can no longer capture customers by taking them through the linear awareness to purchase sequence. Ayyoub describes the new decision sequence as more akin to a kid browsing at a fair than plunging down a slope. He attributes this change to the increase in digital information including product reviews, pricing information, and social media recommendations as well as the use of mobile by the customer while in the store. Because mobile is now replacing the desktop, says Ayyoub, the additional time spent online offers marketers more opportunity to reach potential consumers providing them with information as well as discounts or coupons. According to Ayyoub, it is time to split the funnel, with the top focusing on awareness, but once customers become aware, they are

moved to the bottom half where monies should be allocated to conversion strategies. At that point marketers can focus on delivering the right offers at the right time on the right platform and to the right audience. Essentially, one-to-one marketing replaces mass marketing.

Cynthia Clark agrees with Ayyoub, noting that the funnel has "morphed considerably from a decade ago." Clark contends that the buying journey has changed, with control shifting from the organization to the consumers who are taking it upon themselves to learn as much as they can about a brand before making a purchase. Forrester Research agrees, saying that in the past consumers would have gone through about 90 percent of the funnel before making first contact with a vendor to get a price quote. Control gives them the power right at the beginning of the process in the new paradigm. The best way to succeed now is to know your consumers. And the best way to know the consumers is through effective data gathering which allows the salesperson to speak directly to the needs of individual consumers through targeted conversations.

According to Jonathan Gray, VP of marketing at Revana Inc., because consumers use the Web, smartphones, and social media to do their research they leave a trail of information behind that companies can easily access and specifically address. Social media should be "mined" because these channels provide information about consumers and their interests, such as personality factors. In addition, marketers can continue to follow consumers after a sales interaction or purchase to determine the optimal time to reach out to them.

Mark Osborn, SAP's global lead for consumer products—who also believes the linear funnel no longer works—loves

---

that they use to drag or as a brake). With successful advertising, a spot in the movie *Fast Times at Ridgemont High,* and the attractiveness of the Southern California image, sales took off. Vans is now a $2.2 billion international brand that continues to grow.[9] Think about the company's movement through the communications pyramid and how the objectives and strategies had to change to achieve such success.

Problems with Communications Objectives   Not all marketing and advertising managers accept communications objectives; some say it is too difficult to translate a sales goal into a specific communications objective. But at some point a sales goal must be transformed into a communications objective. If the marketing plan for an established brand has an objective of increasing sales by 10 percent, the promotional planner will eventually have to think in terms of the message that will be communicated to the target audience to achieve this. Possible objectives include the following:

- Increasing the percentage of consumers in the target market who associate specific features, benefits, or advantages with our brand.
- Increasing the number of consumers in the target audience who prefer our product over the competition's.

the power of the smartphone. Osborn notes that the smartphone allows marketers to reach out to potential consumers anytime and anywhere and that its biggest impact for sales and marketing is "the ability to determine where a customer is at a given moment in time." If they opt in, companies can even tell where they are in the store and deliver more information to them.

There are many other marketers out there who contend that the funnel is dead and no longer of value to marketers. Most contend that with the advent of new media, consumers have changed and can't be treated like they were in the past. And, given the new technologies that provide a seemingly endless amount of data to marketers, they shouldn't be. Mass marketing is being replaced by one-to-one marketing.

However, not everyone is convinced that we need to bury the funnel.

One of the more in-depth examinations of how the consumer decision process works comes from an extensive three-phase study commissioned by the Advertising Research Foundation (ARF), which examined many of the issues addressed in the previously mentioned studies while adding valuable new insights. This study (which was noted in Chapter 5 under the social consumer decision journey framework) provides valuable insight into the important questions many marketers are asking such as, Have social and digital media altered the way in which consumers make purchase decisions? The study both supports and refutes some of the previous articles.

The ARF study does not consider the traditional decision-making models to be dead or even of limited value. Rather, the study was based on the assumption that the models have value, but need to be examined in a new light given

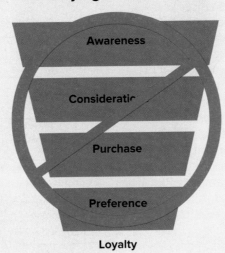

The Buying Funnel Is Dead

Awareness

Consideratic

Purchase

Preference

Loyalty

the impact of social and digital media. As was noted in Chapter 5, the ARF study contends that consumers are constantly considering potential purchases and evaluating brands, but at some times are in a more active shopping mode and purposefully seeking assistance so they can make a purchase decision with confidence. While various media may have an impact in the more passive state, it is the active state where consumers rely more heavily on social media to gain information from websites, friends, product experts, and so on. Interestingly, the goal may be more of a confirmation process; in most cases the brand or product has already been decided on by this stage. Thus, no single source is driving the purchase decision, but all can make a contribution in different ways. Another key finding was that trust is important, as social media expand the range of people that consumers feel they can trust, including family, friends, colleagues, and others. Feeling comfortable that they are making the right decision is critical. The ability to rely on these sources increases the confidence that consumers are making the right decision.

If all this is true, then one has to wonder if all these new technologies actually increase the consumers' trust and confidence. Are they likely to purchase just because they are being reached at the right time and place? The ARF study also showed that purchase decisions are often emotional and well thought out. Maybe consumers don't respond only to the last best offer?

Sources: Joe Ayyoub, "How to Break Out of the Funnel," www.clickzcom, July 2, 2015; Cynthia Clark, "Winning in the New and Improved Sales and Marketing Funnel," www.1to1media.com, May 12, 2014; Todd Powers, Dorothy Advincula, Manila Austin, Stacy Graiko, and Jasper Snyder, "Digital and Social Media in the Purchase Decision Process," *Journal of Advertising Research,* December 2012, pp. 479–89.

- Encouraging current users of the product to use it more frequently or in more situations.
- Encouraging consumers who have never used our brand to try it.

In some situations, promotional planners may gain insight into communications objectives' relationship to sales from industry research. Figure 7–3 provides an example of the GfK International purchase funnel used by many in the automobile industry as a diagnostic model of consumer decision making. Digital and Social Media Perspective 7–1 discusses how the changing media environment may be impacting the consumer decision-making process.

In attempting to translate sales goals into specific communications objectives, promotional planners often are not sure what constitutes adequate levels of awareness, knowledge, liking, preference, or conviction. There are no formulas to provide this information. The promotional manager will have to use his or her personal experience and that of the brand or product managers, as well as the marketing history of this and similar brands. Average scores on various communications measures for this and similar products should be considered, along with the levels achieved by competitors' products. This information can be related to the amount of money and

FIGURE 7–3

GfK Purchase Funnel

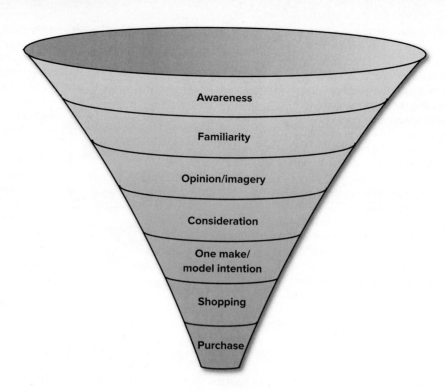

time spent building these levels as well as the resulting sales or market share figures. However, at some point, sales-oriented objectives must be translated into what the company hopes to communicate and to whom it hopes to communicate it.

Many marketing and promotional managers recognize the value of setting specific communications objectives and their important role as operational guidelines to the planning, execution, and evaluation of the promotional program. Communications objectives are the criteria used in the DAGMAR approach to setting advertising goals and objectives, which has become one of the most influential approaches to the advertising planning process.

DAGMAR: AN APPROACH TO SETTING OBJECTIVES

In 1961, Russell Colley prepared a report for the Association of National Advertisers titled *Defining Advertising Goals for Measured Advertising Results* (DAGMAR).[10] In it, Colley developed a model for setting advertising objectives and measuring the results of an ad campaign. The major thesis of the **DAGMAR** model is that communications effects are the logical basis for advertising goals and objectives against which success or failure should be measured.

Under the DAGMAR approach, an advertising goal involves a **communications task** that is specific and measurable. A communications task, as opposed to a marketing task, can be performed by, and attributed to, advertising rather than to by a combination of several marketing factors. Colley proposed that the communications task be based on a hierarchical model of the communication process with four stages:

- *Awareness*—making the consumer aware of the existence of the brand or company.
- *Comprehension*—developing an understanding of what the product is and what it will do for the consumer.
- *Conviction*—developing a mental disposition in the consumer to buy the product.
- *Action*—getting the consumer to purchase the product.

As discussed earlier, other hierarchical models of advertising effects can be used as a basis for analyzing the communications response process. Some advertising theorists prefer the Lavidge and Steiner hierarchy of effects model, since it is more specific and provides a better way to establish and measure results.[11]

While the hierarchical model of advertising effects was the basic model of the communications response process used in DAGMAR, Colley also studied other specific tasks that advertising might be expected to perform in leading to the ultimate objective of a sale. He developed a checklist of 52 advertising tasks to characterize the contribution of advertising and serve as a starting point for establishing objectives.

Characteristics of Objectives

A second major contribution of DAGMAR to the advertising planning process was its definition of what constitutes a good objective. Colley argued that advertising objectives should be stated in terms of concrete and measurable communications tasks, specify a target audience, indicate a benchmark starting point and the degree of change sought, and specify a time period for accomplishing the objective(s).

Concrete, Measurable Tasks   The communications task specified in the objective should be a precise statement of what appeal or message the advertiser wants to communicate to the target audience. Advertisers generally use a copy platform to describe their basic message. The objective or copy platform statement should be specific and clear enough to guide the creative specialists who develop the advertising message. For example, Hyundai, after years of being at or near the bottom of the list of automobiles in customer satisfaction ratings, focused its attention on increasing the quality, as well as improving consumers' perceptions, of its cars. The result is that the Hyundai Sonata is now at the very top of the list in customer satisfaction for midsize cars (Exhibit 7–9). According to DAGMAR, the objective must also be measurable. As can be seen in Exhibit 7–9, the various awards won along the way provided a measure of Hyundai's success.

Target Audience   Another important characteristic of good objectives is a well-defined target audience. The primary target audience for a company's product or service is described in the situation analysis. It may be based on descriptive variables such as geography, demographics, and psychographics (on which advertising media selection decisions are based) as well as on behavioral variables such as usage rate or benefits sought.

Benchmark and Degree of Change Sought   To set objectives, one must know the target audience's present status concerning response hierarchy variables

EXHIBIT 7–9

Hyundai has moved to the top of the list in customer satisfaction

Source: Hyundai Motor America

such as awareness, knowledge, image, attitudes, and intentions and then determine the degree to which consumers must be changed by the campaign. Determining the target market's present position regarding the various response stages requires **benchmark measures**. Often a marketing research study must be conducted to determine prevailing levels of the response hierarchy. In the case of a new product or service, the starting conditions are generally at or near zero for all the variables, so no initial research is needed.

Establishing benchmark measures gives the promotional planner a basis for determining what communications tasks need to be accomplished and for specifying particular objectives. For example, a preliminary study for a brand may reveal that awareness is high but consumer perceptions and attitudes are negative. The objective for the campaign must then be to change the target audience's perceptions of and attitudes toward the brand.

Quantitative benchmarks are not only valuable in establishing communications goals and objectives but also essential for determining whether the campaign was successful. Objectives provide the standard against which the success or failure of a campaign is measured. An ad campaign that results in a 90 percent awareness level for a brand among its target audience cannot really be judged effective unless one knows what percentage of the consumers were aware of the brand before the campaign began. A 70 percent precampaign awareness level would lead to a different interpretation of the campaign's success than would a 30 percent level.

Specified Time Period   A final consideration in setting advertising objectives is specifying the time period in which they must be accomplished. Appropriate time periods can range from a few days to a year or more. Most ad campaigns specify time periods from a few months to a year, depending on the situation facing the advertiser and the type of response being sought. For example, awareness levels for a brand can be created or increased fairly quickly through an intensive media schedule of widespread, repetitive advertising to the target audience. Repositioning of a product requires a change in consumers' perceptions and takes much more time.

Assessment of DAGMAR

The DAGMAR approach to setting objectives has had considerable influence on the advertising planning process. Many promotional planners use this model as a basis for setting objectives and assessing the effectiveness of their promotional campaigns. DAGMAR also focused advertisers' attention on the value of using communications-based rather than sales-based objectives to measure advertising effectiveness and encouraged the measurement of stages in the response hierarchy to assess a campaign's impact. Colley's work has led to improvements in the advertising and promotional planning process by providing a better understanding of the goals and objectives toward which planners' efforts should be directed. This usually results in less subjectivity and leads to better communication and relationships between client and agency.

Criticism of DAGMAR   While DAGMAR has contributed to the advertising planning process, it has not been totally accepted by everyone in the advertising field. A number of problems have led to questions regarding its value as a planning tool:[12]

- *Problems with the response hierarchy.* A major criticism of the DAGMAR approach is its reliance on the hierarchy of effects model. The fact that consumers do not always go through this sequence of communications effects before making a purchase has been recognized, and alternative response models have been developed. As indicated in the lead-in to this chapter, much of the criticism stems from the argument that digital and social media have significantly changed the consumer's decision-making process from a linear one-to-one in which consumers can enter or leave at any stage, resulting in a more circular process (Exhibit 7–10). DAGMAR MOD II recognizes that the appropriate response model depends on the situation and emphasizes identifying the sequence of decision-making steps that apply in a buying situation.[13]

- *Sales objectives.* Another objection to DAGMAR comes from those who argue that the only relevant measure of advertising objectives is sales. They have little tolerance for ad campaigns that achieve communications objectives but fail to increase sales. Advertising is seen as effective only if it induces consumers to make a purchase. The problems with this logic were addressed in our discussion of communications objectives.

- *Practicality and costs.* Another criticism of DAGMAR concerns the difficulties involved in implementing it. Money must be spent on research to establish quantitative benchmarks and measure changes in the response hierarchy. This is costly and time-consuming and can lead to considerable disagreement over method, criteria, measures, and so forth. Many critics argue that DAGMAR is practical only for large companies with big advertising and research budgets. Many firms do not want to spend the money needed to use DAGMAR effectively.

- *Inhibition of creativity.* A final criticism of DAGMAR is that it inhibits advertising creativity by imposing too much structure on the people responsible for developing the advertising. Many creative personnel think the DAGMAR approach is too concerned with quantitative assessment of a campaign's impact on awareness, brand-name recall, or specific persuasion measures. The emphasis is on passing the numbers test rather than developing a message that is truly creative and contributes to brand equity.

PROBLEMS IN SETTING OBJECTIVES

Although the DAGMAR model suggests a logical process for advertising and promotion planning, most advertisers and their agencies fail to follow these basic principles. They fail to set specific objectives for their campaigns and/or do not have the proper evidence to determine the success of their promotional programs. Many advertising agencies do not state appropriate objectives for determining success and thus can't demonstrate whether a supposedly successful campaign was really a success. Even though these campaigns may be doing something right, they generally did not know what it is.

One study examined the advertising practices of business-to-business marketers to determine whether their ads used advertising objectives that met Colley's four DAGMAR criteria.[14] Entries from the annual Business/Professional Advertising Association Gold Key Awards competition, which solicits the best marketing communications efforts from business-to-business advertisers, were evaluated with respect to their campaigns' objectives and summaries of results. Most of these advertisers did not set concrete advertising objectives, specify objective tasks, measure results in terms of stages of a hierarchy of effects, or match objectives to evaluation measures.

Improving Promotional Planners' Use of Objectives

As we have seen, it is important that advertisers and their agencies pay close attention to the objectives they set for their campaigns. They should strive to set specific and measurable objectives that not only guide promotional planning and decision making but also can be used as a standard for evaluating performance. Unfortunately, many companies do not set appropriate objectives for their integrated marketing communications programs.

Many companies fail to set appropriate objectives because top management has only an abstract idea of what the firm's IMC program is supposed to be doing. In an extensive review of thousands of case studies, Jerry Thomas concluded that most advertisers don't know if their advertising works and some ads may have a negative impact on sales. Thomas notes that the advertising industry has a very poor quality assurance system, and turns out a very inconsistent product (the ads). He cites a number of reason why this happens, one of which is the fact that clients don't define the role of advertising in the marketing program and do not precisely specify communications objectives.[15]

Few firms will set objectives that meet all the criteria set forth in DAGMAR. However, promotional planners should set objectives that are specific and measurable and go beyond basic sales goals. Even if specific communications response elements are not always measured, meeting the other criteria will sharpen the focus and improve the quality of the IMC planning process.

Setting Objectives for the IMC Program

One reason so much attention is given to advertising objectives is that for many companies advertising has traditionally been the major way of communicating with target audiences. Other promotional-mix elements such as sales promotion, direct marketing, and publicity are used intermittently to support and complement the advertising program.

Another reason is that traditional advertising-based views of marketing communications planning, such as DAGMAR, have dominated the field for so long. These approaches are based on a hierarchical response model and consider how marketers can develop and disseminate advertising messages to move consumers along an effects path. This approach, shown in Figure 7–4, is what professor Don Schultz calls *inside-out planning*. He says, "It focuses on what the marketer wants to say, when the marketer wants to say it, about things the marketer believes are important about his or her brand, and in the media forms the marketer wants to use."[16]

Schultz advocates an *outside-in planning* process for IMC that starts with the customer and builds backward to the brand. This means that promotional planners study the various media customers and prospects use, when the marketer's messages might be most relevant to customers, and when they are likely to be most receptive to the message.

A similar approach is suggested by Professor Tom Duncan, who argues that IMC should use **zero-based communications planning**, which involves determining

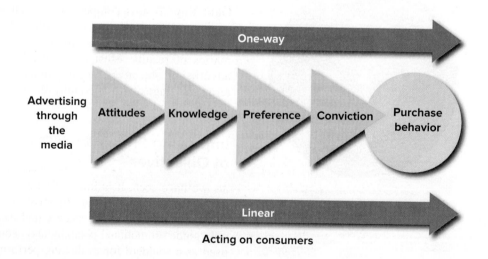

FIGURE 7–4

Traditional Advertising-Based View of Marketing Communications

One-way

Advertising through the media

Attitudes   Knowledge   Preference   Conviction   Purchase behavior

Linear

Acting on consumers

FIGURE 7–5

Objectives and Strategies
in the Social Consumer
Decision Journey

*Sources: Expert interviews;
McKinsey analysis.*

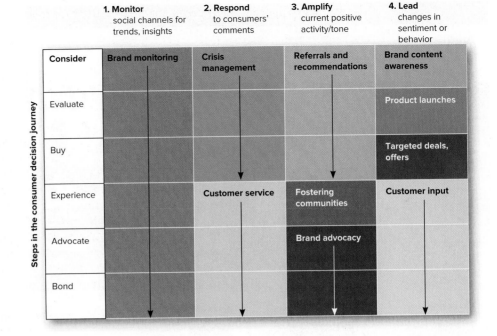

what tasks need to be done and which marketing communications functions should be used and to what extent.[17] This approach focuses on the task to be done and searches for the best ideas and media to accomplish it. Duncan suggests that an effective IMC program should lead with the marketing communications function that most effectively addresses the company's main problem or opportunity and should use a promotional mix that draws on the strengths of whichever communications functions relate best to the particular situation.

While Schultz and Duncan discuss strategies for setting objectives based on traditional response hierarchies, attention should also be given to competing models. As seen in Chapter 5, considering decision making as a "social consumer decision journey" necessitates the establishment of communications objectives as viewed from a different perspective. The rows in Figure 7–5 show the steps in the consumer decision journey ranging from consideration to bonding. The columns depict the objectives that marketers need to accomplish at each stage, while the 10 marketing responses necessary to achieve these objectives are listed within the matrix. In this perspective, the marketer must *monitor*—that is, know what is being said online about the product or brand to gain insights as to how it is being perceived in the marketplace and then respond accordingly. This process—according to the model—must take place continuously. Second, marketers must *respond* to specific issues at a personal level. Responses may be positive in nature (customer service or sales leads) or (more likely) be part of crisis management, dealing with negative issues regarding the product or brand. *Amplification* deals with designing the communications program—particularly as it relates to social media—to foster engagement and sharing, as well as loyalty. The objective of amplifying is to get consumers more involved in the brand, extending the experience the brand has to offer, and have them communicate their positive experiences to others in the social network. The final objective, *lead,* is designed to take the consumer to long-term behavioral changes. At the early stages of the process it may simply include creating more brand awareness. Later in the process, lead may be designed to create buzz or promote time-sensitive issues like sales or promotions. The model also advocates the solicitation of consumer input upon completion of the purchase for the purpose of creating continuous inputs.

While the social consumer decision journey may differ from traditional response hierarchies, it is also similar in that it envisions going through stages in the purchase decision. Like the traditional model, marketers need to take specific marketing actions to help consumers along through the process.

EXHIBIT 7–11

The Auckland Zoo attempts to attract visitors through a variety of media

Source: The Auckland Zoo

Many of the considerations for determining advertising objectives are relevant to setting goals for other elements of the integrated marketing communications program. The promotional planner should determine what role various sales promotion techniques, publicity and public relations, direct marketing, digital media, and personal selling will play in the overall marketing program and how they will interact with advertising as well as with one another.

For example, the marketing communications program for the Auckland Zoo has a number of objectives. First, it must provide funding for the zoo's programs and maintain a large and powerful base of supporters for financial strength. The communications must educate the public about the zoo's various programs and maintain a favorable image on a local, regional, and even international level. A major objective of the IMC program is drawing visitors to the zoo and its many experiences (Exhibit 7–11).

Like the Auckland Zoo, other zoos may establish similar objectives. As can be seen in Figure 7–6 these programs may employ a variety of integrated marketing communications tools. When setting objectives for these promotional elements, planners must consider what the firm hopes to communicate through the use of this element, among what target audience, and during what time period. As with advertising, results should be measured and evaluated against the original objectives, and attempts should be made to isolate the effects of each promotional element. Objectives for marketing communications elements other than advertising are discussed more thoroughly in Part Five of the text.

ESTABLISHING AND ALLOCATING THE PROMOTIONAL BUDGET

If you take a minute to look back at the IMC planning model in Chapter 1, you will see that while the arrows from the review of the marketing plan and the promotional situation analysis to analysis of the communication process are *unidirectional,* the flow between the communications analysis and budget determination is a *two-way interaction.* What this means is that whereas establishing objectives is an important part of the planning process, recognizing the limitations of the budget is important too. No organization has an unlimited budget, so objectives must be set with the budget in mind.

Advertising

Objectives: Drive attendance to Zoo. Uphold image and educate target audience and inform them of new attractions and special events and promotions.

Audience: Members and nonmembers of Zoological Society. Households in primary and secondary geographic markets consisting of Allegheny Country and 5 other countries in the tri-state regional area. Tertiary markets of 7 states. Tourist and group sales markets.

Timing: As allowed and determined by budget. Mostly timed to coincide with promotional efforts.

Tools/media: Television, radio, newspaper, magazines, direct mail, outdoor, tourist media (television and magazine).

Sales Promotions

Objectives: Use price, product, and other variables to drive attendance when it might not otherwise come.

Audience: Targeted, depending on co-op partner, mostly to Western Pennsylvania market.

Timing: To fit needs of Zoo and co-sponsoring partner.

Tools/media: Coupons, sweepstakes, tours, broadcast tradeouts, direct mail: statement stuffers, fliers, postcards, online ticket discounts.

Public Relations

Objectives: Inform, educate, create, and maintain image for Zoological Society and major attractions; reinforce advertising message.

Audience: From local to international, depending on subject, scope, and timing.

Timing: Ongoing, although often timed to coincide with promotions and other special events. Spur-of-the-moment animal news and information such as acquisitions, births, etc.

Tools/media: Coverage by major news media, articles in local, regional, national and international newspapers, magazines and other publications such as visitors' guides, tour books and guides, appearances by Zoo spokepersons on talk shows (such as *The David Letterman Show*), zoo newsletter, adopt an animal program, support conservation program.

Cause Marketing/Corporate Sponsorships/Events Underwriting

Objectives: To provide funding for Zoological Society programs and promote special programs and events done in cooperation with corporate sponsor. Must be win-win business partnership for Society and partner.

Audience: Supporters of both the Zoological Society and the corporate or product/service partner.

Timing: Coincides with needs of both partners, and seasonal attendance generation needs of Zoo.

Tools: May involve advertising, publicity, discount co-op promotions, ticket trades, hospitality centers. Exposure is directly proportional to amount of underwriting by corporate sponsor, both in scope and duration, education programs.

Direct Marketing

Objectives: Maintain large powerful base of supporters for financial and political strength.

Audience: Local, regional, national and international. Includes children's program, seniors (60+), couples, single memberships, and incremental donor levels.

Timing: Ongoing, year-round promotion of memberships.

Tools: Direct mail and on-grounds visibility.

Group Sales

Objectives: Maximize group traffic and revenue by selling group tours to Zoo.

Audience: Conventions, incentive groups, bus tours, associations, youth, scouts, schools, camps, seniors, clubs, military, organizations, domestic and foreign travel groups.

Timing: Targeted to drive attendance in peak seasons or at most probable times such as convention season.

Tools: Travel and tourism trade shows, telemarketing, direct mail, trade publication advertising.

Internet

Objectives: Provide information regarding the Zoo, programs, memberships and public relations activities.

Audience: All audiences interested in acquiring more information about the Zoo.

Timing: Ongoing, updated frequently over time.

Tools: Website, blog, including videos, Facebook, Twitter, and other social media.

FIGURE 7–6 An Example of a Zoo's Objectives for Various Promotional Elements

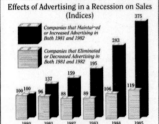

IN A RECESSION, THE BEST DEFENSE IS A GOOD OFFENSE.

It's a recession. Your instincts demand that you cut the ad budget. But, as the McGraw-Hill Research analysis of business-to-business advertising expenditures during the 1981-82 recession shows, it's those with the courage to maintain or increase advertising in a recession who reap a major sales advantage over their competitors who panic and fall back into a defensive posture. And this advantage continues to expand long after the recession is over.

Effects of Advertising in a Recession on Sales (Indices)

Recessions last an average of 11 months, but any advertising decision made during one can have permanent repercussions. The McGraw-Hill study demonstrates that nervous advertisers lose ground to the brave and can't gain it back. In 1980, according to the chart seen here, sales indices were identical, but by 1985 the brave had racked up a 3.2 to 1 sales advantage. A similar study done by McGraw-Hill during the 1974-75 recession corroborates the 1980's research.

A recession is the single greatest period in which to make short- and long-term gains. And, surprisingly, increasing advertising modestly during one has much the same effect on your profits as cutting advertising does. According to The Center for Research & Development's October 1990 study of consumer advertising during a recession, advertisers who yield "to the natural inclination to cut spending in an effort to increase profits in a recession find that it doesn't work." This study, relying on the PIMS database, also uncovered that aggressive recessionary advertisers picked up 4.5 times as much market share gain as their overcautious competitors, leaving them in a far better position to exploit the inevitable recovery and expansion.

Chevrolet countered its competitors during the 1974-75 recession by aggressively beefing up its ad spending and attained a two percent market share increase. Today, two share points in the automotive industry are worth over $4 billion. Delta Airlines and Revlon also boosted ad spending in the 1974-75 recession and achieved similar results.

Continuous advertising sustains market leadership. And it's far easier to sustain momentum than it is to start it up again. Consider this list of market category leaders: Campbell's, Coca-Cola, Ivory, Kellogg, Kodak, Lipton and Wrigley. This is the leadership list for 1925. And 1990. These marketers have maintained a relentless commitment to their brands in both good times and bad. Kellogg had the guts to pump up its ad spending during the Great Depression and cemented a market leadership it has yet to relinquish.

These are the success stories. Space and diplomacy don't allow the mention of the names of those who lacked gusto and chose to cut their ad spending in recessionary times.

But if you would like to learn more about how advertising can help make the worst of times the best of times, please write to Department C, American Association of Advertising Agencies, 666 Third Avenue, New York, New York 10017, enclosing a check for five dollars. You will receive a booklet covering the pertinent research done on all the U.S. recessions since 1923. Please allow 4 to 6 weeks for delivery.

AAAA

EXHIBIT 7–12

The American Association of Advertising Agencies (4As) promotes the continued use of advertising in a recession

© American Association of Advertising Agencies

Often when we think of promotional expenditures of firms, we think only about the huge amounts being spent. We don't usually take the time to think about how these monies are being allocated and about the recipients of these dollars. The budgeting decisions have a significant impact not only on the firm itself but also on numerous others involved either directly or indirectly. The remainder of this chapter provides insight into some underlying theory with respect to budget setting, discusses how companies budget for promotional efforts, and demonstrates the inherent strengths and weaknesses associated with these approaches. Essentially, we focus on two primary budgeting decisions: establishing a budget amount and allocating the budget.

Establishing the Budget

The size of a firm's advertising and promotions budget can vary from a few thousand dollars to more than a billion. When companies like AT&T and Verizon spend more than $2 billion per year to promote their products, they expect such expenditures to accomplish their stated objectives. The budget decision is no less critical to a firm spending only a few thousand dollars; its ultimate success or failure may depend on the monies spent. One of the most critical decisions facing the marketing manager is how much to spend on the promotional effort.

Unfortunately, many managers fail to realize the value of advertising and promotion. They treat the communications budget as an expense rather than an investment. Instead of viewing the dollars spent as contributing to additional sales and market share, they see budget expenses as cutting into profits. As a result, when times get tough, the advertising and promotional budget is the first to be cut—even though there is strong evidence that exactly the opposite should occur, as Exhibit 7–12 argues. Figure 7–7 shows the results of an extensive review of research involving advertising during a recession. The review covers 40 studies in the United States over an 83-year period. As can be seen, the argument for continuing to advertise during an economic downturn outweighs that of decreasing ad expenditures.[18] As shown in IMC Perspective 7–1, a number of successful companies agree, as indicated by their ad expenditures. Moreover, the decision is not a one-time responsibility. A new budget is formulated every year, each time a new product is introduced, or when either internal or external factors necessitate a change to maintain competitiveness.

While it is one of the most critical decisions, budgeting has perhaps been the most resistant to change. A comparison of advertising and promotional texts over the past 10 years would reveal the same methods for establishing budgets. The theoretical basis for this process remains rooted in economic theory and marginal analysis. (Advertisers also use an approach based on **contribution margin**—the difference between the total revenue generated by a brand and its total variable costs. But, as Robert Steiner says, *marginal analysis* and *contribution margin* are essentially synonymous terms.)[19] We begin our discussion of budgeting with an examination of these theoretical approaches.

Theoretical Issues in Budget Setting Most of the models used to establish advertising budgets can be categorized as taking an economic or a sales response perspective.

FIGURE 7–7

Conclusions on Research of Advertising in a Recession

Source: G. Tellis and K. Tellis, "Research on Advertising in a Recession," *Journal of Advertising Research* 49, no. 3 (2009), pp. 304–27.

- Advertising is strongly related to economic cycles across major world economies.

- The single most compelling reason for cutting back advertising during a recession is that sales during a recession are likely to be lower than they would be during an expansion.

- There is strong, consistent evidence that cutting back on advertising can hurt sales during and after a recession.

- Not cutting back on advertising during a recession could increase sales during and after the recession.

- Firms that increased advertising during a recession experienced higher sales, market share, or earnings during or after the recession.

- Most firms tend to cut back on advertising during a recession, reducing noise and increasing the effectiveness of advertising of the firm that advertises.

Marginal Analysis Figure 7–8 graphically represents the concept of **marginal analysis**. As advertising/promotional expenditures increase, sales and gross margins also increase to a point, but then they level off. Profits are shown to be a result of the gross margin minus advertising expenditures. Using this theory to establish its budget, a firm would continue to spend advertising/promotional dollars as long as the marginal revenues created by these expenditures exceeded the incremental advertising/promotional costs. As shown on the graph, the optimal expenditure level is the point where marginal costs equal the marginal revenues they generate (point *A*). If the sum of the advertising/promotional expenditures exceeded the revenues they generated, one would conclude the appropriations were too high and scale down the budget. If revenues were higher, a higher budget might be in order. (We will see later in this chapter that this approach can also be applied to the allocation decision.)

Whereas marginal analysis seems logical intuitively, certain weaknesses limit its usefulness. These weaknesses include the assumptions that (1) sales are a direct result of advertising and promotional expenditures and this effect can be measured and (2) advertising and promotion are solely responsible for sales. Let us examine each of these assumptions in more detail.

1. *Assumption that sales are a direct measure of advertising and promotion efforts.* Earlier in this chapter we discussed the fact that the advertiser needs to set communications objectives that contribute to accomplishing overall marketing objectives but at the same time are separate. One reason for this

FIGURE 7–8

Marginal Analysis

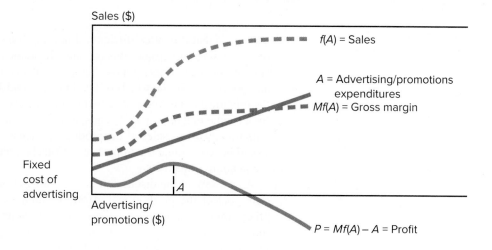

IMC Perspective 7–1 > > >

Companies Like Coca-Cola, Kraft, P&G, and 7UP Believe That Advertising Works

That's a pretty impressive list of companies. It's probably not that surprising that successful companies like these believe in advertising—maybe that's why they are so successful. Take Coca-Cola, for example. In just one quarter in 2015 Coke's revenues were almost $6 billion—just in North America! Part of the reason can be attributed to a double-digit percentage in increased advertising spending according to CEO Muhtar Kent. And the gains came in a period of increased competition in the overall beverage industry as well as in the amount of negative publicity the industry was experiencing as a whole. To pay for the increased spending, Coca-Cola cut expenses in other areas in the company. Clearly, the company feels the investment is worth it.

For most companies, when things aren't going well, belts get tightened. For example, a downturn in the economy leads to spending cutbacks. Unfortunately, one of the first areas to feel the pain of these cutbacks is marketing—particularly advertising. Take the last recessionary period experienced in the United States as an example. In a survey conducted at that time by the Association of National Advertisers, a staggering 77 percent of marketers indicated that they had plans to reduce their advertising media budgets. Seventy-two percent planned to reduce their production budgets, 48 percent were considering reducing agency compensation, and 68 percent said they would challenge their agencies to find ways to cut costs. Clearly, these companies were looking at ways to save money. But were they doing the right thing? It appears that some of the leading advertisers don't agree with this strategy.

Two of the most successful consumer packaged-goods companies in the United States do not subscribe to this strategy. During what might be considered the height of the recession in 2010, Procter and Gamble (P&G) increased its advertising spending by $1 billion in an attempt to grow sales and market share. Most of the increase went to campaigns

© Apic/Hulton Archive/Getty Images

for Gillette Fusion ProGlide razors, Pantene shampoo, and the launch of Pampers Dry Max diapers. The result was an increase of 4 share points in men's shaving and 0.5 point in shampoo. Pampers also rose by 1.5 share points in all marketing channels. When questioned about the wisdom of increasing ad spending in the midst of a recession, CFO Jon Moeller said, "Put simply, we would have been crazy to do anything else."

Like P&G, Kraft Foods agrees with the strategy of increasing expenditures when others are cutting. Kraft also increased its advertising spending in the latter half of 2010, noting that

strategy is that it is often difficult, if not impossible, to demonstrate the effects of advertising and promotions on sales. In studies using sales as a direct measure, it has been almost impossible to establish the contribution of advertising and promotion. In the words of David Aaker and James Carman, "Looking for the relationship between advertising and sales is somewhat worse than looking for a needle in a haystack."[20] Thus, to try to show that the size of the budget will directly affect sales of the product is misleading. A more logical approach would be to examine the impact of various budgets on the attainment of communications objectives.

As we saw in the discussion of communications objectives, sales are not the only goal of the promotional effort. Awareness, interest, attitude change, and other communications objectives are often sought, and while the bottom line may be to sell the product, these objectives may serve as the basis on which the promotional program is developed.

the company "would not tolerate the widespread use of promotions to enhance its position." Irene Rosenfeld, Kraft's CEO, stated that along with the increase in ad spending, the emphasis on aggressive promotional pricing and discounts would be reduced significantly. Rosenfeld believes that aggressive brand building would pay significant benefits going forward. The numbers seem to support her strategy as Tang and Oreo both saw 30 to 40 percent growth due to effective advertising and communications initiatives. Other Kraft brands also benefited from increased expenditures, including Capri-Sun, Kool-Aid, and Maxwell House Coffee.

Yet another successful brand, 7UP, also agreed with the P&G and Kraft strategy. The soft-drink brand had never fully recovered from its elimination from the soft-drink line of PepsiCo and being replaced by Sierra Mist and then sold to Dr Pepper's Snapple Group. Sales in the recession year 2008 were off by 8.1 percent, and in the first six months of 2009, they declined by another 7.7 percent. To make things worse, the overall soft-drink category was in a decline, with lemon-lime flavors among the hardest hit. Rather than cut back, 7UP's plans for 2010 were ambitious, including the first new advertising campaign in three years, new positioning, product line extensions, and an in-store facelift. The new budget was significantly increased over the $21 million (not including online) spent the year before. When asked "Why spend now?" David Falk, director of 7UP and flavors at the Dr Pepper Snapple Group, had a simple response: "Brands that advertise during economic lulls come out of those times a lot stronger."

Similar thinking is apparent at Burger King. The fast-food company announced a double-digit (20–25 percent) increase in ad spending over its $294 million in 2008, beginning in late 2009, with a big boost in the summer of 2010, the biggest season for fast-food sales. Interestingly, not only was Burger King going against the grain in spending, but the largest increases were targeted for television ads as opposed to those in digital media, at a time when many advertisers were going the other way. As noted by Russ Klein, Burger King's chief marketing officer at the time, "There is no way to replace television," underscoring the medium's broad reach. Klein also noted, "With the economic downturn, it's important for us to be front and center with value messaging, innovation and strategy. . . . There is strong historical evidence about companies that step up with their innovation and advertising and their ability to move through economic downturns and then emerge with stronger brands on the other end."

Another proponent of increased ad spending comes from General Mills. As the recession lingered on, General Mills's research indicated that more Americans were eating at home due to uncertainty about their fortunes in the years ahead. After a 25 percent increase in ad spending in the first quarter, the cereal company announced another high single-digit increase later in the year, believing that "the reinvestment is fueling net sales growth." (General Mills's retail sales increased 12 percent and operating profits were up 30 percent even with the increased ad spending.)

A number of other retailers also bucked the cutback trend in an attempt to fuel Christmas holiday sales. Kmart, Walmart, and JCPenney all doubled their advertising spending from the previous year, while Home Depot and Lowe's were up by 50 percent. Gap increased its spending by $25 million in the third quarter and by $45 million in the fourth. Gap also went back to television advertising for the first time in two years. According to a Walmart spokesperson, the world's number 1 retailer has always believed in maintaining spending even during a recession, noting that it benefits from media cost deflation.

Looking at the names on this list of companies that are not cutting—and actually increasing—advertising expenditures during a downturn, one wonders if maybe they know something the other 77 percent don't know. One thing is clear, they must believe that advertising works.

Sources: Mark J. Miller, "Coca-Cola Sees Pay-Off from Increased Marketing Spend," www.brandchannel.com, July 30, 2015; Kenneth Hein, "To Counter Downward Sales Trend, 7UP Ups Ad Spend," *Brandweek,* October 12, 2009, p. 5; Suzanne Vranica, "Retailers Boost Spending on Holiday Advertising," www.wsj.com, November 9, 2009; Emily Bryson York, "Burger King to Boost Ad Spending," www.adage.com, April 17, 2009; David Goetzl, "General Mills to Increase Ad Spending," www.mediapost.com, July 6, 2009; David Goetzl, "Coca-Cola, P&G to Keep Spending," www.warc.com, April 23, 2009; Jack Neff, "P&G Hikes Ad Spending by $1 Billion to Grow Share Sales," www.adage.com, August 3, 2010; Seeking Alpha, "Kraft Boosts AdSpend, CHTS Back on Promotions," www.warc.com, August 9, 2010.

2. *Assumption that sales are determined solely by advertising and promotion.* This assumption ignores the remaining elements of the marketing mix—price, product, and distribution—which do contribute to a company's success. Environmental factors may also affect the promotional program, leading the marketing manager to assume the advertising was or was not effective when some other factor may have helped or hindered the accomplishment of the desired objectives.

Overall, you can see that while the economic approach to the budgeting process is a logical one, the difficulties associated with determining the effects of the promotional effort on sales and revenues limit its applicability. Marginal analysis is seldom used as a basis for budgeting (except for direct-response advertising).

Sales Response Models You may have wondered why the sales curve in Figure 7–8 shows sales leveling off even though advertising and promotions efforts continue to increase. The relationship between advertising and sales has been the topic of much research and discussion designed to determine the shape of the response curve.

Almost all advertisers subscribe to one of two models of the advertising/sales response function: the concave-downward function or the S-shaped response curve.

- *The concave-downward function.* After reviewing more than 100 studies of the effects of advertising on sales, Julian Simon and Johan Arndt concluded that the effects of advertising budgets follow the microeconomic law of diminishing returns.[21] That is, as the amount of advertising increases, its incremental value decreases. The logic is that those with the greatest potential to buy will likely act on the first (or earliest) exposures, while those less likely to buy are not likely to change as a result of the advertising. For those who may be potential buyers, each additional ad will supply little or no new information that will affect their decision. Thus, according to the **concave-downward function model**, the effects of advertising quickly begin to diminish, as shown in Figure 7–9A. Budgeting under this model suggests that fewer advertising dollars may be needed to create the optimal influence on sales.

- *The S-shaped response function.* Many advertising managers assume the **S-shaped response curve** (Figure 7–9B), which projects an S-shaped response function to the budget outlay (again measured in sales). Initial outlays of the advertising budget have little impact (as indicated by the essentially flat sales curve in range *A*). After a certain budget level has been reached (the beginning of range *B*), advertising and promotional efforts begin to have an effect, as additional increments of expenditures result in increased sales. This incremental gain continues only to a point, however, because at the beginning of range *C* additional expenditures begin to return little or nothing in the way of sales. This model suggests a small advertising budget is likely to have no impact beyond the sales that may have been generated through other means (for example, word of mouth). At the other extreme, more does not necessarily mean better: Additional dollars spent beyond range *B* have no additional impact on sales and for the most part can be considered wasted. As with marginal analysis, one would attempt to operate at that point on the curve in area *B* where the maximum return for the money is attained.

Weaknesses in these sales response models render them of limited use to practitioners for direct applications. Many of the problems seen earlier—the use of sales as a dependent variable, measurement problems, and so on—limit the usefulness of these models. At the same time, keep in mind the purpose of discussing such models. Even though marginal analysis and the sales response curves may not apply directly, they give managers some insight into a theoretical basis of how

FIGURE 7–9

Advertising Sales/Response Functions

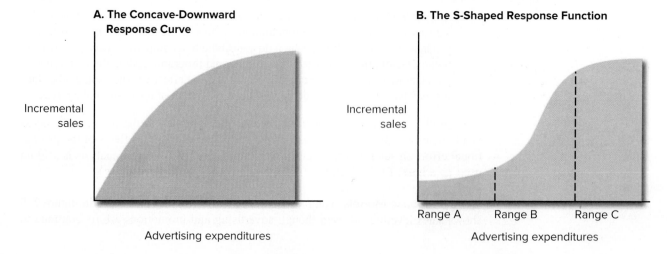

A. The Concave-Downward Response Curve

Incremental sales

Advertising expenditures

B. The S-Shaped Response Function

Incremental sales

Range A   Range B   Range C

Advertising expenditures

the budgeting process should work. There's some empirical evidence indicating the models may have validity.

The studies discussed in earlier chapters on learning and the hierarchy of effects also demonstrate the importance of repetition for gaining awareness and for subsequent higher-order objectives such as adoption. Thus, while these models may not provide a tool for setting the advertising and promotional budget directly, we can use them to guide our appropriations strategy from a theoretical basis. As you will see later in this chapter, such a theoretical basis has advantages over many of the methods currently being used for budget setting and allocation.

Additional Factors in Budget Setting   While the theoretical bases just discussed should be considered in establishing the budget appropriation, a number of other issues must also be considered. A weakness in attempting to use sales as a *direct* measure of response to advertising is that various situational factors may have an effect. Some of the factors that have been shown to affect the advertising/sales ratio are shown in Figure 7–10. For a product characterized by emotional buying motives, hidden product qualities, and/or a strong basis for differentiation, advertising would have a noticeable impact on sales. Products characterized as large-dollar purchases and those in the maturity or decline stages of the product would be less likely to benefit.

As we will see later in this chapter, the percentage-of-sales method of budgeting has inherent weaknesses in that the advertising and sales effects may be reversed. So we cannot be sure whether the situation actually led to the advertising/sales relationship or vice versa. Thus, while these factors should be considered in the budget appropriation decision, they should not be the sole determinants of where and when to increase or decrease expenditures.

FIGURE 7–10

Factors Influencing Advertising Budgets

Factor	Relationship of Advertising/Sales	Factor	Relationship of Advertising/Sales
Product Factors		Competition:	
Basis for differentiation	+	Active	+
Hidden product qualities	+	Concentrated	+
Emotional buying motives	+	***Customer Factors***	
	–	Concentration of users	+
	–	***Strategy Factors***	
Purchase frequency	Curvilinear	Early stage of brand life cycle	+
Market Factors		Long channels of distribution	+
Stage of product life cycle:		High prices	+
Introductory	+	High quality	+
Growth	+	Media strategy	+
Maturity	–	Creative strategy	+
Decline	–	Promotional strategy	+
Inelastic demand	+	***Cost Factors***	
Market share	–	High profit margins	+

Note: + relationship means the factor leads to a positive effect of advertising on sales; – relationship indicates little or no effect of advertising on sales.

FIGURE 7–11

Factors Considered in
Budget Setting

Changes in advertising strategy and/or creative approach	51%
Competitive activity and/or spending levels	47
Profit contribution goal or other financial target	43
Level of previous year's spending, with adjustment	17
Senior management dollar allocation or set limit	11
Volume share projections	8
Projections/assumptions on media cost increases	25
Modifications in media strategy and/or buying techniques	17

The *Advertising Age* Editorial Sounding Board consists of 92 executives of the top 200 advertising companies in the United States (representing the client side) and 130 executives of the 200 largest advertising agencies and 11 advertising consultants (representing the agency side). A survey of the board yielded the factors shown in Figure 7–11 that are important in budget setting.

Overall, the responses of these two groups reflect in part their perceptions as to factors of importance in how budgets are set. To understand the differences in the relative importance of these factors, it is important to understand the approaches currently employed in budget setting. The next section examines these approaches.

Budgeting Approaches

The theoretical approaches to establishing the promotional budget are seldom employed. In smaller firms, they may never be used. Instead, a number of methods developed through practice and experience are implemented. This section reviews some of the more traditional methods of setting budgets and the relative advantages and disadvantages of each. First, you must understand two things: (1) Many firms employ more than one method, and (2) budgeting approaches vary according to the size and sophistication of the firm.

Top-Down Approaches   The approaches discussed in this section may be referred to as **top-down approaches** because a budgetary amount is established (usually at an executive level) and then the monies are passed down to the various departments (as shown in Figure 7–12). These budgets are essentially predetermined and have no true theoretical basis. Top-down methods include the affordable method, arbitrary allocation, percentage of sales, competitive parity, and return on investment (ROI).

The Affordable Method In the **affordable method** (often referred to as the "all-you-can-afford method"), the firm determines the amount to be spent in various areas such as production and operations. Then it allocates what's left to advertising and promotion, considering this to be the amount it can afford. The task to be performed by the advertising/promotions function is not considered, and the likelihood of under- or overspending is high, as no guidelines for measuring the effects of various budgets are established.

Strange as it may seem, this approach is common among small firms. Unfortunately, it is also used in large firms, particularly those that are not marketing-driven and do not understand the role of advertising and promotion. For example, many high-tech firms focus on new product development and engineering and assume that

FIGURE 7–12

Top-Down versus Bottom-Up Approaches to Budget Setting

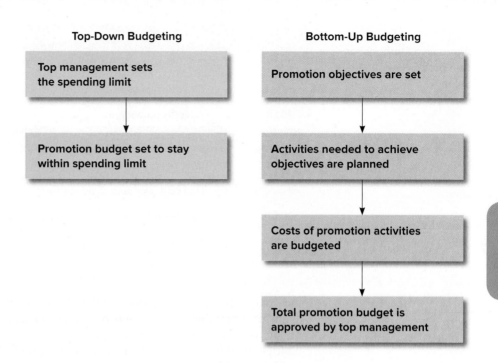

Top-Down Budgeting

Top management sets the spending limit

↓

Promotion budget set to stay within spending limit

Bottom-Up Budgeting

Promotion objectives are set

↓

Activities needed to achieve objectives are planned

↓

Costs of promotion activities are budgeted

↓

Total promotion budget is approved by top management

the product, if good enough, will sell itself. In these companies, little money may be left for performing the advertising and promotions tasks.

The logic for this approach stems from "We can't be hurt with this method" thinking. That is, if we know what we can afford and we do not exceed it, we will not get into financial problems. While this may be true in a strictly accounting sense, it does not reflect sound managerial decision making from a marketing perspective. Often this method does not allocate enough money to get the product off the ground and into the market. In terms of the S-shaped sales response model, the firm is operating in range A. Or the firm may be spending more than necessary, operating in range C. When the market gets tough and sales and/or profits begin to fall, this method is likely to lead to budget cuts at a time when the budget should be increased.

Arbitrary Allocation Perhaps an even weaker method than the affordable method for establishing a budget is **arbitrary allocation**, in which virtually no theoretical basis is considered and the budgetary amount is often set by fiat. That is, the budget is determined by management solely on the basis of what is felt to be necessary. In a discussion of how managers set advertising budgets, Melvin Salveson reported that these decisions may reflect "as much upon the managers' psychological profile as they do economic criteria."[22] While Salveson was referring to larger corporations, the approach is no less common in small firms and nonprofit organizations.

The arbitrary allocation approach has no obvious advantages. No systematic thinking has occurred, no objectives have been budgeted for, and the concept and purpose of advertising and promotion have been largely ignored. Other than the fact that the manager believes some monies must be spent on advertising and promotion and then picks a number, there is no good explanation why this approach continues to be used. Yet budgets continue to be set this way, and our purpose in discussing this method is to point out only that it is used—not recommended.

Percentage of Sales Perhaps the most commonly used method for budget setting (particularly in large firms) is the **percentage-of-sales method**, in which

FIGURE 7–13

Alternative Methods for
Computing Percentage of
Sales

METHOD 1: STRAIGHT PERCENTAGE OF SALES		
2017	Total dollar sales	$1,000,000
	Straight % of sales at 10%	$100,000
2018	Advertising budget	$100,000

METHOD 2: PERCENTAGE OF UNIT COST		
2017	Cost per product to manufacturer	$4.00
	Unit cost allocated to advertising	$1.00
2017	Forecasted sales, 100,000 units	
2018	Advertising budget (100,000 × $1)	$100,000

the advertising and promotions budget is based on sales of the product. Management determines the amount by either (1) taking a percentage of the sales dollars or (2) assigning a fixed amount of the unit product cost to promotion and multiplying this amount by the number of units sold. These two methods are shown in Figure 7–13.

A variation on the percentage-of-sales method uses a percentage of projected future sales as a base. This method also uses either a straight percentage of projected sales or a unit cost projection. In the straight-percentage method, sales are projected for the coming year based on the marketing manager's estimates. The budget is a percentage of these sales, often an industry standard percentage like those presented in Figure 7–14.

One advantage of using future sales as a base is that the budget is not based on last year's sales. As the market changes, management must factor the effect of these changes on sales into next year's forecast rather than relying on past data. The resulting budget is more likely to reflect current conditions and be more appropriate.

Figure 7–14 reveals that the percentage allocated varies from one industry to the next. Some firms budget a very small percentage (for example, 0.4 percent in bakery products), and others spend a much higher proportional amount (13.0 percent in distilled and blended liquors; 11.2 percent in dolls and stuffed toys). Actual dollar amounts spent vary markedly according to the company's total sales figure. Thus, a smaller percentage of sales in the construction machinery industry may actually result in significantly more advertising dollars being spent.

Proponents of the percentage-of-sales method cite a number of advantages. It is financially safe and keeps ad spending within reasonable limits, as it bases spending on the past year's sales or what the firm expects to sell in the upcoming year. Thus, there will be sufficient monies to cover this budget, with increases in sales leading to budget increases and sales decreases resulting in advertising decreases. The percentage-of-sales method is simple, straightforward, and easy to implement. Regardless of which basis—past or future sales—is employed, the calculations used to arrive at a budget are not difficult. Finally, this budgeting approach is generally stable. While the budget may vary with increases and decreases in sales, as long as these changes are not drastic the manager will have a reasonable idea of the parameters of the budget.

At the same time, the percentage-of-sales method has some serious disadvantages, including the basic premise on which the budget is established: sales. Letting the level of sales determine the amount of advertising and promotions dollars to be spent reverses the cause-and-effect relationship between advertising and sales. It treats advertising as an expense associated with making a sale

FIGURE 7–14   Advertising-to-Sales Ratios by Industry Sector

Industry Name	SIC Code No.	2014 Ad Spending ($ millions)	2015 Ad Spending ($ millions)	Annual Ad Growth Rate (%)	Annual Sales Growth Rate (%)	2015 Ad $ as % of Sales	2015 Ad $ as % of Margin
ABRASIVE, ASBESTOS, MISC MINRL	3290	507.787	528.905	3.3	1.3	8.2	31.4
ACCIDENT & HEALTH INSURANCE	6321	229	219.83	−4.3	−3.4	1	4.4
ACCOUNT, AUDIT, BOOKKEEP SVCS	8721	20.7	19.97	−3.4	3.1	1.1	3
ADHESIVES AND SEALANTS	2891	0.02	0.016	−21.6	7.3	1.5	5.6
ADVERTISING	7310	132.165	133.913	2.6	4.2	2	4
ADVERTISING AGENCIES	7311	10.033	8.666	−11.1	3.5	0	0
AGRIC PROD-LVSTK, ANIMAL SPEC	200	12.26	13.823	12.4	13.3	0.6	2.2
AGRICULTURAL CHEMICALS	2870	3564.254	3312.839	−7.1	−2.2	5	14.4
AGRICULTURE PRODUCTION–CROPS	100	173.612	171.539	0.5	6.4	0.7	1.5
AIR COURIER SERVICES	4513	517.178	529.505	2.4	2.1	0.7	2.7
AIR TRANSPORT, SCHEDULED	4512	2707.697	2634.352	−1.7	5.2	0.7	3
AIR-COND, HEATING, REFRIG EQ	3585	175.501	179.851	2.2	2.2	1.1	3.1
AIRCRAFT	3721	7.938	8.009	0.9	3	0.1	0.5
AIRPORTS & TERMINAL SERVICES	4581	0.117	0.15	25.9	6.7	0.8	1.6
AMUSEMENT & RECREATION SVCS	7900	335.555	366.011	8.8	9.2	3.7	12.8
AMUSEMENT PARKS	7996	232.1	236.695	1.6	2.3	6.2	13
APPAREL & OTHER FINISHED PDS	2300	1847.697	2014.898	8.8	9.6	4.4	8.7
APPAREL AND ACCESSORY STORES	5600	581.487	616.822	5.9	3.8	3.5	9.3
APPAREL, PIECE GDS, NOTNS-WHSL	5130	11.633	12.678	6.9	3.9	2.8	7.7
ARRANGE TRANS-FREIGHT, CARGO	4731	3.988	4.104	2.9	8.8	0.1	0.3
AUTO AND HOME SUPPLY STORES	5531	359.426	387.553	7.7	9	1.2	2.5
AUTO DEALERS, GAS STATIONS	5500	839.213	912.892	8.2	5.6	0.6	4.5
AUTO RENT & LEASE, NO DRIVERS	7510	423.479	456.462	7.8	7	1.4	3.1
AUTO REPAIR, SERVICES, PARKING	7500	2.585	3.177	21.2	14.7	0.1	0.9
BAKERY PRODUCTS	2050	3.67	4.187	13.2	9.3	0.4	1.2
BALL AND ROLLER BEARINGS	3562	0.2	0.1	−100	−9.4	0.1	0.3
BEVERAGES	2080	2300	2482.292	6	1	3.7	6.4
BIOLOGICAL PDS, EX DIAGNSTICS	2836	1296.288	1488.055	14.9	17	1.4	1.9
BITUMINOUS COAL, LIGNITE MNG	1220	1	0	−100	−10.3	0	0
BLANKBOOKS, BINDERS, BOOKBIND	2780	222.737	230.423	2.4	1.5	6.7	13.3
BLDG MATL, HARDWR, GARDEN-RETL	5200	118.122	126.044	6.5	8.3	1.2	3.5
BOOKS: PUBG, PUBG & PRINTING	2731	2155.239	2044.664	−6.2	−1.8	18.1	33
BRDWOVEN FABRIC MILL, COTTON	2211	1.903	1.926	1.3	0.5	0.2	1.1
BTLD & CAN SOFT DRINKS, WATER	2086	5168.45	5155.193	−0.5	−1.5	4.9	9.1
BUSINESS SERVICES, NEC	7389	132.936	126.346	−2.4	3.8	0.4	2.2
CABLE AND OTHER PAY TV SVCS	4841	5688.916	6230.451	9.8	5.5	2.8	6.5
CALCULATE, ACCT MACH, EX COMP	3578	328.418	378.028	14.1	3.3	2.4	7.3
CAN FRUIT, VEG, PRESRV, JAM, JEL	2033	138.093	140.996	2.2	2.3	1.7	4.9
CAN, FROZN, PRESRV FRUIT & VEG	2030	928.558	903.301	−3	1.8	3.3	9
CARPETS AND RUGS	2273	45.487	50.792	10.7	12.3	0.6	1.7
CATALOG, MAIL-ORDER HOUSES	5961	6094.508	7040.926	14.6	14.4	3.8	13.4
CEMENT, HYDRAULIC	3241	3.316	3.201	−3.8	−6.5	0.8	1.6
CHEMICALS & ALLIED PRODUCTS	2800	0.093	0.12	27.1	−3	0.9	2.1
CIGARETTES	2111	720.445	763.118	5.6	−1.9	0.7	1.4

Source: 2015 Ad-to-Sales Ratios, www.outburstadvertising.com.

rather than an investment. As shown in Figure 7–15, companies that consider promotional expenditures an investment reap the rewards (as was shown in IMC Perspective 7–1).

A second problem with this approach was actually cited as an advantage earlier: stability. Proponents say that if all firms use a similar percentage, that will bring stability to the marketplace. But what happens if someone varies from this standard percentage? The problem is that this method does not allow for changes in strategy either internally or from competitors. An aggressive firm may wish to allocate more monies to the advertising and promotions budget, a strategy that is not possible with a percentage-of-sales method unless the manager is willing to deviate from industry standards.

The percentage-of-sales method of budgeting may result in severe misappropriation of funds. If advertising and promotion have a role to perform in marketing a product, then allocating more monies to advertising will, as shown in the S-shaped curve, generate incremental sales (to a point). If products with low sales have smaller promotion budgets, this will hinder sales progress. At the other extreme, very successful products may have excess budgets, some of which may be better appropriated elsewhere.

The percentage-of-sales method is also difficult to employ for new product introductions. If no sales histories are available, there is no basis for establishing the budget. Projections of future sales may be difficult, particularly if the product is highly innovative and/or has fluctuating sales patterns.

Finally, if the budget is contingent on sales, decreases in sales will lead to decreases in budgets when they most need to be increased. Continuing to cut the advertising and promotion budgets may just add impetus to the downward sales trend. On the other hand, some of the more successful companies have allocated additional funds during hard times or downturns in the cycle of sales as shown earlier. Companies that maintain or increase their ad expenditures during recessions achieve increased visibility and higher growth in both sales and market share (compared to those that reduce advertising outlays).

FIGURE 7–15

Investments Pay Off in Later Years

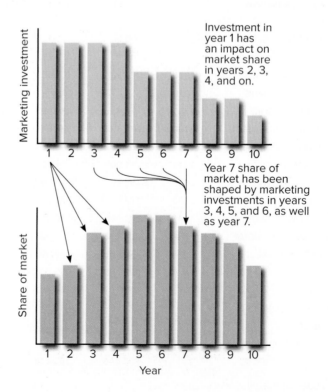

While the percentage-of-future-sales method has been proposed as a remedy for some of the problems discussed here, the reality is that problems with forecasting, cyclical growth, and uncontrollable factors limit its effectiveness.

Competitive Parity If you asked marketing managers if they ever set their advertising and promotions budgets on the basis of what their competitors allocate, they would probably deny it. Yet if you examined the advertising expenditures of these companies, both as a percentage of sales and in respect to the media where they are allocated, you would see little variation in the percentage-of-sales figures for firms within a given industry. Such results do not happen by chance alone. Companies that provide competitive advertising information, trade associations, and other advertising industry periodicals are sources for competitors' expenditures. Larger corporations often subscribe to services such as Competitive Media Reporting, which estimates the top 1,000 companies' advertising in 10 media and in total. Smaller companies often use a **clipping service**, which clips competitors' ads from local print media, allowing the company to work backward to determine the cumulative costs of the ads placed.

In the **competitive parity method**, managers establish budget amounts by matching the competition's percentage-of-sales expenditures. The argument is that setting budgets in this fashion takes advantage of the collective wisdom of the industry. It also takes the competition into consideration, which leads to stability in the marketplace by minimizing marketing warfare. If companies know that competitors are unlikely to match their increases in promotional spending, they are less likely to take an aggressive posture to attempt to gain market share. This minimizes unusual or unrealistic ad expenditures.

The competitive parity method has a number of disadvantages, however. For one, it ignores the fact that advertising and promotions are designed to accomplish specific objectives by addressing certain problems and opportunities. Second, it assumes that because firms have similar expenditures, their programs will be equally effective. This assumption ignores the contributions of creative executions and/or media allocations, as well as the success or failure of various promotions. Further, it ignores possible advantages of the firm itself; some companies simply make better products than others. A study by Yoo and Mandhachitara indicates that a competitive parity strategy must consider the fact that a competitor's advertising can actually benefit one's own firm, and that one competitor's gain is not always the other's loss. As shown in Figure 7–16 there are four different situations to determine how the competitive budgets may impact sales—only one of which involved the zero-sum scenario.[23]

Also, there is no guarantee that competitors will continue to pursue their existing strategies. Since competitive parity figures are determined by examination of competitors' previous years' promotional expenditures (short of corporate espionage), changes in market emphasis and/or spending may not be recognized until the competition has already established an advantage. Further, there is no guarantee that a competitor will not increase or decrease its own expenditures, regardless of what other companies do. Finally, competitive parity may not avoid promotional wars. Coke versus Pepsi and AT&T versus Verizon have been notorious for their spending wars, each responding to the other's increased outlays.

In summary, few firms employ the competitive parity method as a sole means of establishing the promotional budget. This method is typically used in conjunction with the percentage-of-sales or other methods. It is never wise to ignore the competition; managers must always be aware of what competitors are doing. But they should not just emulate them in setting goals and developing strategies.

Return on Investment (ROI) In the percentage-of-sales method, sales dictate the level of advertising appropriations. But advertising causes sales. In the marginal

FIGURE 7–16

Competitors' Advertising
Outlays Do Not Always Hurt

analysis and S-shaped curve approaches, incremental investments in advertising and promotions lead to increases in sales. The keyword here is *investment*. In the **ROI budgeting method**, advertising and promotions are considered investments, like plant and equipment. Thus, the budgetary appropriation (investment) leads to certain returns. Like other aspects of the firm's efforts, advertising and promotion are expected to earn a certain return. ROI has received a great deal of attention by practitioners over the past few years, with many still disagreeing as to how it should be measured. Figure 7–17 shows the results of *Advertising Age*'s report of the Aegis Group rating of how various media perform under this criterion (5 equals best).

While the ROI method looks good on paper, the reality is that it is rarely possible to assess the returns provided by the promotional effort—at least as long as sales continue to be the basis for evaluation. Thus, while managers are certain to ask how much return they are getting for such expenditures, the question remains unanswered and, as shown in the chapter introduction, depends on the criteria used to determine effectiveness. ROI remains a difficult method to employ.

Summary of Top-Down Budgeting Methods You are probably asking yourself why we even discussed these budgeting methods if they are not recommended for use or have severe disadvantages that limit their effectiveness. But you must understand the various methods used in order to recognize their limitations, especially since these flawed methods are commonly employed by marketers. Research conducted over a number of years by various researchers indicates that the affordable, competitive parity, percentage of sales, and objective and task methods are the most commonly employed budgeting methods. As noted, the emphasis on ROI has dramatically increased over the past few years.[24–28] Tradition and top management's desire for control are probably the major reasons why top-down methods continue to be popular.

Build-Up Approaches The major flaw associated with the top-down methods is that these judgmental approaches lead to predetermined budget appropriations often not linked to objectives and the strategies designed to accomplish them. A more effective budgeting strategy would be to consider the firm's communications objectives and budget what is deemed necessary to attain these goals. As noted

FIGURE 7–17 Aegis-Rated ROI of Various Media

Medium	The Measurement Challenge	ROI Measurability
Direct Response	Direct mail, telemarketing, and other forms are the most measurable of media listed here. Direct can have a synergistic effect, especially for pharma, telecom, and financial services.	5
Sales Promotion	Offers such as coupons and discounts generate a lot of consumer response and therefore a bounty of data. The data lend themselves to measurement, especially for package goods via syndicated scanner data. Freestanding inserts generate much valuable data.	5
Internet	The Internet can be influential for big-ticket purchases like cars. Very measurable, with the cautionary note that "Internet is a very broad net," ranging from search engines to ads in content to websites such as in the auto market, where such marques as Saab get lots of hits, and all should be looked at separately. The goal is to understand how the consumer is interacting online with the brand.	5
TV	While promotions have very pronounced, short-term effects that allow precise measurement, TV has a subtler and more gradual effect that may show greater variability. But ROI can be measured with a high degree of accuracy, and there's no excuse for TV not to show a measurable effect. MMA clients have been using a lot more analysis to create a better mix between :15s and :30s, and better allocation across dayparts.	4.5
Print	The experts can slice and dice print by weekly vs. monthly publications, by targeted vs. general market, by promotional ads vs. equity-building. Print promotional materials, like freestanding inserts, are a separate—and much more measurable—matter. As with all other media, accuracy and timing of the data are crucial in determining how measurable the medium is. Print can play a strong role in expanding the reach of the media mix.	4.5
Public Relations	There are companies that specialize in the measurement of PR campaigns' quality; they can measure the number of impressions delivered—via positive or negative PR—for a brand name or category. PR can have a measurable impact on sales (think trans fats in food). The problem: Many marketers aren't buying these PR data.	4
Video Games	Whether the game is played online or offline is crucial. An ad embedded in a game cartridge is very hard to measure because there's no way to know how often it's played, though there's no denying "True Crime's" Nick Kang is a big hit. With online games, there are great data available through the Internet.	Online Offline
	Scale: 5 = Best	
Radio	The available data typically aren't as strong as those for its traditional-media colleagues of TV and print, and this hampers radio.	3
Cinema	Movie advertising can be measured by the number of impressions delivered, much like outdoor or kiosk advertising would be measured.	3
Sponsored Events	Measurability depends on whether sponsorship is likely to spark short-term effect. A major recurring event like the Olympics is very measurable. Others can be difficult to measure short term. Measurement can be complex because events have so many pieces, including how the event is advertised, the PR buzz, signage, and the recollection of the event itself.	3
Product Placement	There are companies that measure quality of placement as well as the quantity of exposures. Treated much like TV advertising, with the caveat that not every product placement is the same. Fox's *American Idol* is a great example: AT&T Wireless's tie-in, which involves voting by text message, is interactive—even part of the entertainment—while the judges drinking from a Coke cup is not. (P.S. AT&T Wireless, now owned by Cingular, isn't an MMA client.) So the question becomes: How do you score the quality of placement?	3
Outdoor	Available data are limited due to the nature of outdoor advertising; there's no syndicated vendor that sells the needed data on outdoor. And outdoor lacks "variance"—the billboard is up X number of months and seen by an unchanging X number of people each day.	2
Guerrilla Marketing	Hard to measure if the variable you're using is sales. If 10,000 people at an event get free T-shirts, it's difficult to measure the effect on the 400,000 people living in that market. Because guerrilla can encompass so many different kinds of tactics, getting useful data can be a problem—it depends on how measurable the response is. Marketers' ROI expectations for guerrilla are lower than for other media, so the urgency to measure is less. Not to mention they spend a lot less on guerrilla than on traditional media like TV.	1

CHAPTER 7

earlier, the promotional planning model shows the budget decision as an interactive process, with the communications objectives on one hand and the promotional-mix alternatives on the other. The idea is to budget so these promotional-mix strategies can be implemented to achieve the stated objectives.

Objective and Task Method It is important that objective setting and budgeting go hand in hand rather than sequentially. It is difficult to establish a budget without specific objectives in mind, and setting objectives without regard to how much money is available makes no sense. For example, a company may wish to create awareness among *X* percent of its target market. A minimal budget amount will be required to accomplish this goal, and the firm must be willing to spend this amount.

The **objective and task method** of budget setting uses a **buildup approach** consisting of three steps: (1) defining the communications objectives to be accomplished, (2) determining the specific strategies and tasks needed to attain them, and (3) estimating the costs associated with performance of these strategies and tasks. The total budget is based on the accumulation of these costs.

Implementing the objective and task approach is somewhat more involved. The manager must monitor this process throughout and change strategies depending on how well objectives are attained. As shown in Figure 7–18, this process involves several steps:

1. *Isolate objectives.* When the promotional planning model is presented, a company will have two sets of objectives to accomplish—the marketing objectives for the product and the communications objectives. After the former are established, the task involves determining what specific communications objectives will be designed to accomplish these goals. Communications objectives must be specific, attainable, and measurable, as well as time limited.

2. *Determine tasks required.* A number of elements are involved in the strategic plan designed to attain the objectives established. (These strategies constitute the remaining chapters in this text.) These tasks may include advertising in various media, sales promotions, and/or other elements of the promotional mix, each with its own role to perform.

3. *Estimate required expenditures.* Buildup analysis requires determining the estimated costs associated with the tasks developed in the previous step. For example, it involves costs for developing awareness through advertising, trial through sampling, and so forth.

FIGURE 7–18

The Objective and Task Method

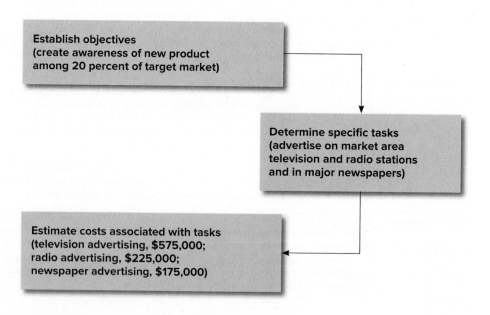

4. *Monitor.* As you will see in Chapter 18 on measuring effectiveness, there are ways to determine how well one is attaining established objectives. Performance should be monitored and evaluated in light of the budget appropriated.

5. *Reevaluate objectives.* Once specific objectives have been attained, monies may be better spent on new goals. Thus, if one has achieved the level of consumer awareness sought, the budget should be altered to stress a higher-order objective such as evaluation or trial.

The major advantage of the objective and task method is that the budget is driven by the objectives to be attained. The managers closest to the marketing effort will have specific strategies and input into the budget-setting process.

The major disadvantage of this method is the difficulty of determining which tasks will be required and the costs associated with each. For example, specifically what tasks are needed to attain awareness among 50 percent of the target market? How much will it cost to perform these tasks? While these decisions are easier to determine for certain objectives—for instance, estimating the costs of sampling required to stimulate trial in a defined market area—it is not always possible to know exactly what is required and/or how much it will cost to complete the job. This process is easier if there is past experience to use as a guide, with either the existing product or a similar one in the same product category. But it is especially difficult for new product introductions. As a result, budget setting using this method is not as easy to perform or as stable as some of the methods discussed earlier. Given this disadvantage, many marketing managers have stayed with those top-down approaches for setting the total expenditure amount.

The objective and task method offers advantages over methods discussed earlier but is more difficult to implement when there is no track record for the product. The following section addresses the problem of budgeting for new product introductions.

Payout Planning The first months of a new product's introduction typically require heavier-than-normal advertising and promotion appropriations to stimulate higher levels of awareness and subsequent trial. After studying more than 40 years of Nielsen figures, James O. Peckham estimated that the average share of advertising to sales ratio necessary to launch a new product successfully is approximately 1.5:2.0.[29] This means that a new entry should be spending at approximately twice the desired market share, as shown in the two examples in Figure 7–19. For example, in the food industry, brand 101 gained a 12.6 percent market share by spending 34 percent of the total advertising dollars in this category. Likewise, brand 401 in the toiletry industry had a 30 percent share of advertising dollars to gain 19.5 percent of sales.

To determine how much to spend, marketers often develop a **payout plan** that determines the investment value of the advertising and promotion appropriation. The basic idea is to project the revenues the product will generate, as well as the costs it will incur, over two to three years. Based on an expected rate of return, the payout plan will assist in determining how much advertising and promotions expenditure will be necessary and when the return might be expected. A three-year payout plan is shown in Figure 7–20. The product would lose money in year 1, almost break even in year 2, and finally begin to show substantial profits by the end of year 3.

The advertising and promotion figures are highest in year 1 and decline in years 2 and 3. This appropriation is consistent with Peckham's findings and reflects the additional outlays needed to make as rapid an impact as possible. (Keep in mind that shelf space is limited, and store owners are not likely to wait around for a product to become successful.) The budget also reflects the firm's guidelines for new product expenditures, since companies generally have established deadlines by which the product must begin to show a profit. Finally, keep in mind that building market share may be more difficult than maintaining it—thus the substantial dropoff in expenditures in later years.

FIGURE 7–19

Share of Advertising
Sales Relationship
(Two-Year Summary)

A. New Brands of Food Products

Brand	Average share of advertising	Attained share of sales	Ratio of share of advertising to share of sales
101	34%	12.6%	2.7
102	16	10.0	1.6
103	8	7.6	1.1
104	4	2.6	1.5
105	3	2.1	1.4

B. New Brands of Toiletry Products

Brand	Average share of advertising	Attained share of sales	Ratio of share of advertising to share of sales
401	30%	19.5%	1.5
402	25	16.5	1.5
403	20	16.2	1.2
404	12	9.4	1.3
405	16	8.7	1.8
406	19	7.3	2.6
407	14	7.2	1.9
408	10	6.0	1.7
409	7	6.0	1.2
410	6	5.9	1.0
411	10	5.9	1.7
412	6	5.2	1.2

While the payout plan is not always perfect, it does guide the manager in establishing the budget. When used in conjunction with the objective and task method, it provides a much more logical approach to budget setting than the top-down approaches previously discussed. Yet on the basis of the studies reported on earlier, payout planning does not seem to be a widely employed method.

Quantitative Models Attempts to apply *quantitative models* to budgeting have met with limited success. For the most part, these methods employ **computer simulation models** involving statistical techniques such as multiple regression

FIGURE 7–20

Example of Three-Year
Payout Plan ($ millions)

	Year 1	Year 2	Year 3
Product sales	15.0	35.50	60.75
Profit contribution (@ $0.50/case)	7.5	17.75	30.38
Advertising/promotions	15.0	10.50	8.50
Profit (loss)	(7.5)	7.25	21.88
Cumulative profit (loss)	(7.5)	(0.25)	21.63

analysis to determine the relative contribution of the advertising budget to sales. Because of problems associated with these methods, their acceptance has been limited, and quantitative models have yet to reach their potential. As requirements for accountability continue to increase, more sophisticated models may be forthcoming. Specific discussion of these models is beyond the scope of this text, however. Such methods do have merit but may need more refinement before achieving widespread success.

Summary of Budgeting Methods   There is no universally accepted method of setting a budget figure. Weaknesses in each method may make it unfeasible or inappropriate. As earlier studies have shown, the use of the objective and task method continues to stay high, whereas less sophisticated methods vary in their rates of adoption. More advertisers are also employing the payout planning approach.

In a study of how managers make decisions regarding advertising and promotion budgeting decisions, George Low and Jakki Mohr interviewed 21 managers in eight consumer-product firms. Their research focused on the decision processes and procedures used to set spending levels on the factors that influence the allocation of advertising and promotion dollars.

On the basis of their results (shown in Figure 7–21), the authors concluded that the budget-setting process is still a perplexing issue to many managers and that institutional pressures led to a greater proportion of dollars being spent on sales

FIGURE 7–21

How Advertising and Promotions Budgets Are Set

The Nature of the Decision Process

- Managers develop overall marketing objectives for the brand.
- Financial projections are made on the basis of the objectives and forecasts.
- Advertising and promotions budgets are set on the basis of quantitative models and managerial judgment.
- The budget is presented to senior management, which approves and adjusts the budgets.
- The plan is implemented (changes are often made during implementation).
- The plan is evaluated by comparing the achieved results with objectives.

Factors Affecting Budget Allocations

- The extent to which risk taking is encouraged and/or tolerated.
- Sophistication regarding the use of marketing information.
- Managerial judgment.
- Use of quantitative tools.
- Brand differentiation strategies.
- Brand equity.
- The strength of the creative message.
- Retailer power.
- Short- versus long-term focus.
- Top-down influences.
- Political sales force influences.
- Historical inertia.
- Ad hoc changes.

promotions than managers would have preferred. In addition, the authors concluded that to successfully develop and implement the budget, managers must (1) employ a comprehensive strategy to guide the process, avoiding the piecemeal approach often employed, (2) develop a strategic planning framework that employs an integrated marketing communications philosophy, (3) build in contingency plans, (4) focus on long-term objectives, and (5) consistently evaluate the effectiveness of programs.[30]

By using these approaches in combination with the percentage-of-sales methods, these advertisers are likely to arrive at a more useful, accurate budget. For example, many firms now start the budgeting process by establishing the objectives they need to accomplish and then limit the budget by applying a percentage-of-sales or another method to decide whether or not it is affordable. Competitors' budgets may also influence this decision.

Allocating the Budget

Once the budget has been appropriated, the next step is to allocate it. The allocation decision involves determining which markets, products, and/or promotional elements will receive which amounts of the funds appropriated.

Allocating to IMC Elements   As noted earlier, many advertisers are shifting some of their budget dollars away from traditional advertising media and into digital and social media. Figure 7–22 shows that most traditional media advertisers expect to decrease their expenditures in these media into the future as well.

Some marketers have also used the allocation decision to stretch their advertising dollar and get more impact from the same amount of money. Companies have taken a number of steps, including consolidating and cutting division expenditures, reducing agency fees, producing fewer campaigns, and relying more on targeted media.

Client–Agency Policies   Another factor that may influence budget allocation is the individual policy of the company or the advertising agency. The agency may discourage the allocation of monies to sales promotion, preferring to spend them on the advertising area. The agency may take the position that these monies are harder to track in terms of effectiveness and may be used improperly if not under its control. (In many cases commissions are not made on this area, and this fact may contribute to the agency's reluctance.)

The orientation of the agency or the firm may also directly influence where monies are spent. Many ad agencies are managed by officers who have ascended through the

FIGURE 7–22

Marketing Spending Plans, 2016

Source: Adapted from 2016 Marketing Budget Trends, by Channel. Retrieved February 2016, www.marketingcharts .com/online/2016-marketing-budget- trends-by-channel-64987.

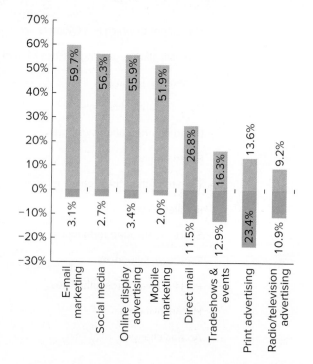

creative ranks and are inclined to emphasize the creative budget. Others may have preferences for specific media. For example, some agencies position themselves as experts in nontraditional media and often spend more client money in this medium. Both the agency and the client may favor certain aspects of the promotional program, perhaps on the basis of past successes, that will substantially influence where dollars are spent.

Market Size While the budget should be allocated according to the specific promotional tools needed to accomplish the stated objectives, the *size* of the market will affect the decision. In smaller markets, it is often easier and less expensive to reach the target market. Too much of an expenditure in these markets will lead to saturation and a lack of effective spending. In larger markets, the target group may be more dispersed and thus more expensive to reach. Think about the cost of purchasing media in Chicago or New York City versus a smaller market like Columbus, Ohio, or Birmingham, Alabama. The former would be much more costly and would require a higher budget appropriation.

Market Potential For a variety of reasons, some markets hold more potential than others. Marketers of snow skis would find greater returns on their expenditures in Denver, Colorado, than in Fort Lauderdale, Florida. Imported Mexican beers sell better in the border states (Texas, Arizona, California) than in the Midwest. A disproportionate number of imported cars are sold in California and New England. When particular markets hold higher potential, the marketing manager may decide to allocate additional monies to them. (Keep in mind that just because a market does not have high sales does not mean it should be ignored. The key is *potential*—and a market with low sales but high potential may be a candidate for additional appropriations.)

Market Share Goals Two studies in the *Harvard Business Review* discussed advertising spending with the goal of maintaining and increasing market share.[31] John Jones compared the brand's share of market with its share of advertising voice (the total value of the main media exposure in the product category). Jones classified the brands as "profit taking brands, or underspenders" and "investment brands, those whose share of voice is clearly above their share of market." His study indicated that for those brands with small market shares, profit takers are in the minority; however, as the brands increase their market share, nearly three out of five have a proportionately smaller share of voice.

Jones noted that three factors can be cited to explain this change. First, new brands generally receive higher-than-average advertising support. Second, older, more mature brands are often "milked"—that is, when they reach the maturity stage, advertising support is reduced. Third, there's an advertising economy of scale whereby advertising works harder for well-established brands, so a lower expenditure is required. Jones concluded that for larger brands, it may be possible to reduce advertising expenditures and still maintain market share. Smaller brands, on the other hand, have to continue to maintain a large share of voice.

James Schroer addressed the advertising budget in a situation where the marketer wishes to increase market share. His analysis suggests that marketers should:

- Segment markets, focusing on those markets where competition is weak and/or underspending instead on a national advertising effort.
- Determine their competitors' cost positions (how long the competition can continue to spend at the current or increased rate).
- Resist the lure of short-term profits that result from ad budget cuts.
- Consider niching strategies as opposed to long-term wars.

Figure 7–23 shows Schroer's suggestions for spending priorities in various markets.

Economies of Scale in Advertising Some studies have presented evidence that firms and/or brands maintaining a large share of the market have an advantage over smaller competitors and thus can spend less money on advertising and realize

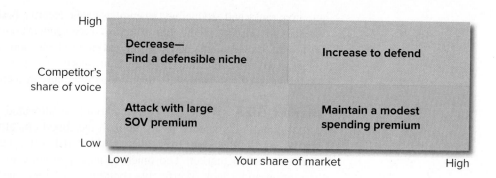

a better return.[32] Larger advertisers can maintain advertising shares that are smaller than their market shares because they get better advertising rates, have declining average costs of production, and accrue the advantages of advertising several products jointly. In addition, they are likely to enjoy more favorable time and space positions, cooperation of middle people, and favorable publicity. These advantages are known as **economies of scale**.

Reviewing the studies in support of this position and then conducting research over a variety of small package products, Kent Lancaster found that this situation did not hold true and that in fact larger brand share products might actually be at a disadvantage.[33] His results indicated that leading brands spend an average of 2.5 percentage points more than their brand share on advertising. More specifically, his study concluded:

1. There is no evidence that larger firms can support their brands with lower relative advertising costs than smaller firms.
2. There is no evidence that the leading brand in a product group enjoys lower advertising costs per sales dollar than do other brands.
3. There is no evidence of a static relationship between advertising costs per dollar of sales and the size of the advertiser.

The results of this and other studies suggest there really are no economies of scale to be accrued from the size of the firm or the market share of the brand.[34]

Organizational Characteristics   In a review of the literature on how allocation decisions are made between advertising and sales promotion, George Low and Jakki Mohr concluded that organizational factors play an important role in determining how communications dollars are spent.[35] The authors note that the following factors influence the allocation decision. These factors vary from one organization to another, and each influences the relative amounts assigned to advertising and promotion:

- The organization's structure—centralized versus decentralized, formalization, and complexity.
- Power and politics in the organizational hierarchy.
- The use of expert opinions (for example, consultants).
- Characteristics of the decision maker (preferences and experience).
- Approval and negotiation channels.
- Pressure on senior managers to arrive at the optimal budget.

One example of how these factors might influence allocations relates to the level of interaction between marketing and other functional departments, such as accounting and operations. The authors note that the relative importance of advertising versus sales promotion might vary from department to department. Accountants, being dollars-and-cents minded, would argue for the sales impact of promotions, while operations would argue against sales promotions because the sudden surges in demand that might result would throw off production schedules. The marketing department might be influenced by the thinking of either of these groups in making its decision.

The use of outside consultants to provide expert opinions might also affect the allocation decision. Trade journals, academic journals, and even books might also be valuable inputs into the decision maker's thinking. In sum, it seems obvious that many factors must be taken into account in the budget allocation decision. Market size and potential, specific objectives sought, and previous company and/or agency policies and preferences all influence this decision.

Summary

This chapter has examined the role of objectives in the planning and evaluation of the IMC program and how firms budget in an attempt to achieve these objectives. Specific objectives are needed to guide the development of the promotional program, as well as to provide a benchmark against which performance can be measured and evaluated. Objectives serve important functions as communications devices, as a guide to planning the IMC program and deciding on various alternatives, and for measurement and evaluation.

Objectives for IMC evolve from the organization's overall marketing plan and are based on the roles various promotional-mix elements play in the marketing program. Many managers use sales or a related measure such as market share as the basis for setting objectives. However, many promotional planners believe the role of advertising and other promotional-mix elements is to communicate because of the various problems associated with sales-based objectives. They use communications-based objectives like those in the response hierarchy as the basis for setting goals.

Much of the emphasis in setting objectives has been on traditional advertising-based views of marketing communications. However, many companies are moving toward zero-based communications planning, which focuses on what tasks need to be done, which marketing communications functions should be used, and to what extent. Many of the principles used in setting advertising objectives can be applied to other elements in the promotional mix.

As you have probably concluded, the budget decision is not typically based on supporting experiences or strong theoretical foundations. Nor is it one of the more soundly established elements of the promotional program. The budgeting methods used now have some major problems. Economic models are limited, often try to demonstrate the effects on sales directly, and ignore other elements of the marketing mix. Some of the methods discussed have no theoretical basis and ignore the roles advertising and promotion are meant to perform.

One possible way to improve the budget appropriation is to tie the measures of effectiveness to communications objectives rather than to the broader-based marketing objectives. Using the objective and task approach with communications objectives may not be the ultimate solution to the budgeting problem, but it is an improvement over the top-down methods. Marketers often find it advantageous to employ a combination of methods.

As with determining the budget, managers must consider a number of factors when allocating advertising and promotions dollars. Market size and potential, agency policies, and the preferences of management itself may influence the allocation decision.

Key Terms

marketing objectives 224
integrated marketing communications objectives 224
carryover effect 226
DAGMAR 232
communications task 232
benchmark measures 234
zero-based communications planning 236

contribution margin 240
marginal analysis 241
concave-downward function model 244
S-shaped response curve 244
top-down approaches 246
affordable method 246
arbitrary allocation 247
percentage-of-sales method 247

clipping service 251
competitive parity method 251
ROI budgeting method 252
objective and task method 254
buildup approach 254
payout plan 255
computer simulation models 256
economies of scale 260

Discussion Questions

1. Explain some of the factors that might lead to success in increasing sales and achieving communications when competitors decrease their budgets. (LO 7-7)

2. Discuss why some marketers consider the allocation of media dollars to digital and social media at the expense of traditional media to be a "knee-jerk reaction." (LO 7-5)

3. Why are the affordable and arbitrary allocation budgeting methods considered to be very poor budgeting methods? (LO 7-5)

4. Explain why communications measures may be better to use than sales or market share objectives when developing the IMC plan. (LO 7-1)

5. Explain the S-shaped response curve and the concave-downward curve as they relate to budget setting. What are the differences in these two curves? Give examples of how each might be more appropriate for different products. (LO 7-6)

6. Companies like P&G and Kraft Foods have found success by increasing their IMC budgets while other companies reduce theirs during a recession. Explain why they have likely achieved this success. (LO 7-7)

7. Some marketers feel that the hierarchy of effects models may no longer reflect the characteristics of the consumer decision-making process. Discuss the pros and cons of these arguments. (LO 7-4)

8. Explain why it is so difficult to directly measure the impact of advertising on sales. What factors may inhibit this determination? (LO 7-3)

9. Explain some of the reasons marketers are shifting their budget allocations from traditional to digital and social media. What are some of the advantages and disadvantages with this reallocation? (LO 7-5)

10. Why is it important for marketers to set specific objectives for advertising and promotion? What criteria must these objectives meet to be valid? (LO 7-1)

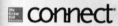

Digital users can access their personalized and adaptive SmartBook, Ad Forum Video Cases, and interactive exercises to review chapter concepts.

8 Creative Strategy: Planning and Development

Zero hidden costs

1040EZ/A

AbsoluteZero

$0 Fed $0 NEW State $0 To File

intuit TurboTax ✓ Federal Free Edition

Source: TurboTax by Intuit, Inc.

LEARNING OBJECTIVES

LO1 Describe the role of creative strategy in advertising.

LO2 Identify inputs to the creative process.

LO3 Describe the development of creative strategy.

LO4 Examine approaches to developing the major selling ideas that are used as the basis for an advertising campaign.

TURBOTAX SHOWS CONSUMERS A BETTER WAY TO DO THEIR TAXES

If you were to ask most people what things creates the most anxiety in their lives, many would put filing tax returns at or near the top of their list. Even though more than 75 percent of all taxpayers get a refund each year that averages around $3,000, filing their own taxes is scarier than speaking in public for most people. Even for digitally savvy millennials, fear rules during tax season. A survey of people who planned to file taxes in 2016, commissioned by the financial information site NerdWallet, found that 80 percent report concerns such as making a mistake, not getting a full refund, or paying too much. And of course there is always the fear of getting audited by the IRS if your taxes are not done properly and/or you did not pay your fair share of taxes.

Today there are companies and services to aid in tax preparation and help reduce people's anxiety. The tax preparation business has historically been divided into two major segments: the assisted or do-it-for-me (DIFM) segment and the do-it-yourself (DIY) segment. Consumers in the DIFM segment use a tax preparation service or tax professional while those in the DIY segment use manual forms, software, or online services. For the past 25 years, TurboTax has been the leader in the DIY segment of the market; its products have been continuously ranked as the best-selling tax software. TurboTax is a division of Intuit, a company that creates business and financial management solutions for small businesses, consumers, and accounting professionals and whose other flagship products include Quick-Books and Mint.com.

While online tax preparation service has made tax filing much easier, fear, uncertainty, and doubt persist. Intuit has been on a journey the past few years to reinvent the TurboTax brand and transform the way taxes are done through product innovation that makes it superior to all other tax preparation methods. Its Brand Purpose is to put hardworking, self-determined Americans in charge of their own money, starting with taxes, and continue to deliver unmatched value to them. TurboTax has identified a core target segment called "On My Way" that it is focusing on to grow the DIY category. This is a large segment consisting of 17 million early life stage filers who are the most open to doing their taxes online but still use DIFM services. Most of these people are millennials who are younger, optimistic, and confident as well as generally early adopters of, and very comfortable with, technology that gives them a sense of control over their financial lives.

TurboTax has set course on a business model transformation that is directly addressing the needs of the On My Way consumer by building familiarity among prospects and disrupting the tax preparation category. One key strategy for doing this is through the introduction of TurboTax Absolute Zero which disrupts the category by offering federal and state tax preparation free of charge for the 60 million value-conscious 1040EZ/A Simple Filers in the United States who can least afford to pay to have their taxes prepared for them. TurboTax monetizes these customers by offering a value-added bundle of services that they can voluntarily choose to add. By offering these filers a completely free solution, TurboTax is betting that it can build trust and familiarity with them and as their tax situation becomes more complex, they will come back to the company and pay for one of its higher-end solutions. The way TurboTax will deliver superior value on these higher-end solutions is through its incredible product innovations.

During the 2016 tax season, Intuit decided it was time to take the next step in its journey to disrupt people's notion and communicate how it was delivering superior value through its product innovation. Intuit developed an insight-driven, integrated marketing campaign designed to reinforce the positioning of TurboTax as the smarter way to do taxes. The campaign dramatized and celebrated "ownable moments" in the TurboTax experience that demonstrate key customer benefits in ways that change people's current beliefs about and expectations of TurboTax.

To execute on its strategy and show how TurboTax has transformed the tax filing process into something anyone can do, Intuit's advertising agency, Wieden+Kennedy, created a big idea–led campaign titled "It Doesn't Take a Genius to Do Your Taxes." The campaign included seven 30-second TV spots featuring some of the world's greatest minds appearing in amusing commercials showing that TurboTax is so simple and intuitive that even real-life geniuses can't make it any easier to use or understand. Among the brainiacs appearing in the spots are a physicist, a mathematician, and a computer scientist. TurboTax's integrated marketing campaign not only leveraged the product innovation in its TV campaign, but also promoted the "ownable moments" on the TurboTax.com website and the payoff people experience from using the product.

Another important goal of the campaign was to prove that Intuit has transformed the tax filing process into something anyone can do by promoting how TurboTax was giving 60 million Americans with simple tax returns the ability to file their federal and state states for free by using its Absolute Zero service. For example, one commercial features theoretical physicist Michio Kaku explaining the concept of "absolute zero" as it applies to TurboTax—which charges nothing for its basic, easy-filing service—by noting that "Nothing is the absence of something. Zero is absolute nothing."

At the peak of the tax season, Intuit ran a clever commercial on the 2016 Super Bowl featuring Sir Anthony Hopkins being interviewed as an award-winning actor who has resisted the temptation to sell out in his illustrious career. However, as Hopkins explains that he would never impugn his integrity or tarnish his name by selling a product, he lifts a teacup to his mouth with the TurboTax logo. He's also wearing blue slippers promoting the tax service and his dog is wearing a TurboTax sweater. Hopkins notes that he has "way more integrity" than to sell out and rationalizes that he really is not doing so since it's free to file taxes with TurboTax Absolute Zero, noting that "It's free, there's nothing to sell."

To leverage its Super Bowl ad message, Intuit also utilized digital and social media to extend the Absolute Zero message across online channels and keep it in the forefront of consideration during the offer period. TurboTax took home the 2016 Merkle Digital Bowl crown which is given each year to the brands that best leverage digital marketing tools such as social media, SEO, paid search, and e-mail marketing to support their Super Bowl advertising.

Intuit is well on its way to repositioning the TurboTax brand and building meaningful connections with the core target of On My Way consumers. The company plans to continue to disrupt people's notions of with it's like to do their own taxes with TurboTax, supporting its brand purpose of putting hardworking Americans in charge of their money, starting with taxes

Sources: Internal Communications with Intuit, Inc.; "Millennials Fear Filing Taxes More Than Most Americans," *Nerdwallet,* February 17, 2016, www.nerdwallet.com/blog/taxes/millennials-fear-filing-taxes/; Davide Gianatasio, "Physics Geniuses Illustrate the Mind-Bending Simplicity of TurboTax in W+K's New Ads Campaign," *Adweek,* January 4, 2016, www.adweek.com/adfreak/physics-geniuses-illustrate-mind-bending-simplicity-turbotax-wks-new-ads-168817.

One of the most important components of an integrated marketing communications program is the advertising message. While the fundamental role of an advertising message is to communicate information, it does much more. The commercials we watch on TV or hear on radio, the print ads we see in magazines and newspapers, and the videos, banner ads, and other forms of advertising on the Internet and social media sites are a source of entertainment, motivation, fascination, fantasy, and sometimes irritation as well as information. Ads and commercials appeal to, and often create or shape, consumers' problems, desires, and goals. From the marketer's perspective, the advertising message is a way to tell consumers how the product or service can solve a problem or help satisfy desires or achieve goals. Advertising can also be used to create images or associations and position a brand in the consumer's mind as well as transform the experience of buying and/or using a product or service. Many consumers who have never driven or even ridden in a BMW perceive it as "the ultimate driving machine" (Exhibit 8–1). Many people feel good about sending Hallmark greeting cards because they have internalized the company's advertising theme, "when you care enough to send the very best."

One need only watch an evening of commercials or peruse a few magazines to realize there are a myriad of ways to convey an advertising message. Underlying all of these messages, however, are a **creative strategy** that determines what the advertising message will say or communicate and **creative tactics** for how the message strategy will be executed. In this chapter, we focus on advertising creative strategy. We consider what is meant by creativity, particularly as it relates to advertising, and examine a well-known approach to creativity in advertising.

Because one cannot drive a Van Gogh.

The new 7 series.

The ultimate driving machine.

We also examine the creative strategy development process and various approaches to determining the *big idea* that will be used as the central theme of the advertising campaign and translated into attention-getting, distinctive, and memorable messages. Creative specialists are finding it more and more difficult to come up with big ideas that will break through the clutter and still satisfy the concerns of their risk-averse clients. Yet their clients are continually challenging them to find the creative message that will strike a responsive chord with their target audience.

Some of you may not be directly involved in the design and creation of ads; you may choose to work in another agency department or on the client side of the business. However, because creative strategy is often so crucial to the success of the firm's IMC effort, everyone involved in the promotional process should understand the creative strategy and tactics that underlie the development of advertising campaigns and messages, as well as the creative options available to the advertiser. Also, individuals on the client side as well as agency people outside the creative department must work with the creative specialists in developing the advertising campaign, implementing it, and evaluating its effectiveness. Thus, marketing and product managers, account representatives, researchers, and media personnel must appreciate the creative process and develop a productive relationship with creative personnel.

THE IMPORTANCE OF CREATIVITY IN ADVERTISING

For many students, as well as many advertising and marketing practitioners, the most interesting aspect of advertising is the creative side. We have all at one time or another been intrigued by an ad and admired the creative insight that went into it. A great ad is a joy to behold and often an epic to create, as the cost of producing a TV commercial can exceed $1 million. Many companies see this as money well spent. They realize that the manner in which the advertising message is developed and executed is often critical to the success of the promotional program, which in turn can influence the effectiveness of the entire marketing program. Major advertisers such as Procter & Gamble, Verizon, AT&T, Unilever, GEICO, FedEx, Apple, McDonald's, Coca-Cola, and many other companies spend millions of dollars each

Digital and Social Media Perspective 8–1 > > >

THE TOP AD CAMPAIGNS OF THE 21ST CENTURY MOVE BEYOND TRADITIONAL MEDIA

For nearly a century advertising has played a very important role in powering our economic system by not only providing consumers with information about products and services, but also by encouraging them to improve their standard of living and purchase brands that help them do so. In the process advertising has had a profound impact on society and culture, which critics are quick to point out has been both good and bad. However, many also agree that examining society though the lens of marketing, advertising, and media can provide great insight into the people who consume it and how it influences them.

Even the critics would agree that those who create the impactful advertising messages often have tremendous insight into consumers and what entertains, moves, and motivates them. Thus, it is always interesting to look back and see how the advertising industry, including those who work in it and write about it, evaluates the work of advertising creatives and what they consider the best advertising campaigns. *Advertising Age* is the leading trade publication of the ad world and has provided in-depth coverage of the industry in weekly editions since 1930. In 1999 *Ad Age* selected the Top 100 Campaigns of the Century and number 1 was the famous "Think Small" campaign for the Volkswagen Beetle, which was created by the Doyle Dane Bernbach agency. The top five also included campaigns for Coca-Cola ("The pause that refreshes"), Marlboro cigarettes ("The Marlboro Man"), Nike ("Just Do It"), and McDonald's ("You deserve a break today").

Of the top 100 campaigns only a few are, like the iconic Nike campaign, still in use today: "Got Milk?," the "Energizer Bunny," Wheaties' "Breakfast of Champions," "The Ultimate Driving Machine" for BMW, and "A Diamond Is Forever," which has appeared in every ad for a DeBeers engagement ring since 1948. While it is interesting to take a walk down advertising's memory lane and talk about the great campaigns of the past century, you are more likely interested in campaigns that are relevant to your generation and may have impacted your purchase decisions. The good news is that *Advertising Age* extended its list of the best ad campaigns in 2015 by selecting the 15 best campaigns of the 21st century thus far by having some of the most influential and acclaimed industry creatives and executives judge the nominees.

The campaign selected as the best of the 21st century thus far is Dove's "Campaign for Real Beauty" (discussed in Chapter 6) that originated in the UK and Canada and was turned into a global IMC campaign by Unilever, which owns the brand. Rather than using traditional models like most ads for beauty products, the Dove campaign featured real women whose physical appearance was outside the stereotypical norms of beauty and triggered conversations and debates about society's notions of female standards of beauty. It also arrived at a time when the Internet, and then social media, allowed consumers to interact and share messages such as the popular "Evolution" and "Real Beauty Sketches" videos which are two of the most viral videos of all time. The *Ad Age* Panel used terms such as *groundbreaking, bold, transparent,* and *authentic* to describe the "Campaign for Real Beauty," which has led other companies to run purpose-driven campaigns such as the "Like a Girl" movement for P&G's Always brand.

Other campaigns on the 21st century list include Apple's "Get a Mac" series of comparative ads that aired 66 TV commercials over a three-year period poking fun at Microsoft's Windows operating system. The ads featured actor Justin Long as the cool, hip, and unflappable Mac and writer John Hodgman as the uptight and somewhat nerdy PC. Other top campaigns include Procter & Gamble's "Thank You, Mom" campaign that featured U.S. Olympic athletes' moms cheering them on in the Olympic Games; the "Whassup?" campaign for Budweiser that made the catchphrase a part of popular youth culture; Burger King's "Subservient Chicken" which included a website where users could submit more than 300

year to develop advertising messages that will win the hearts and minds of consumers. They also spend hundreds of millions of dollars more to purchase media time and space to run these messages. While these companies sell excellent products and services, they realize creative advertising is also an important part of their marketing success. The importance of creativity is summarized very well by Stephan Vogel, the chief creative officer of Ogilvy & Mather Germany: "Nothing is more efficient than creative advertising. Creative advertising is more memorable, longer lasting, works with less media spending, and builds a fan community . . . faster."[1]

Good creative strategy and execution can often be central to determining the success of a product or service or reversing the fortunes of a struggling brand. For example, creative advertising was able to revive Procter & Gamble's Old Spice brand and make it the market leader in the body wash category as well as one of different commands and a chicken character would respond; and the "Truth" antismoking campaign for the American Legacy Foundation which is the largest, and arguably most effective, effort to discourage young people from smoking. The campaign uncovered and undermines the marketing tactics used by Big Tobacco and relies on unconventional methods such as public stunts and bold billboards, as well as social media, to expose the negative health effects and social consequences of smoking.

Source: Old Spice by Procter & Gamble

Several of the top campaigns capitalized on the popularity of social media and viral marketing. Chipotle's "Back to the Start" campaign started with an animated short film posted on YouTube about a farmer abandoning his traditional operations in favor of more sustainable farming practices. Chipotle waited for the buzz to build through social media and public relations before taking a shorter version of the video to television. Red Bull also used viral marketing for its "Stratos" video which captured the record-breaking, 24-mile free-fall of Felix Baumgartner from the stratosphere in 2012. The video racked up 171 million views online in addition to a tremendous number of earned media mentions and helped increase Red Bull sales by 7 percent in the first six months following the jump.

Another campaign that used the power of social media and viral marketing to leverage great creative work was "The Man Your Man Could Smell Like" effort for Old Spice body wash which helped revive a mostly forgotten brand. The tongue-in-cheek ads developed for the campaign featured a bare-chested, Casanova-like character (played by Isaiah Mustafa, a former NFL wide receiver and obscure actor with a magnetic presence to go along with his six-pack abs) who tells female viewers that Old Spice body wash will make their male partners smell like him. The most popular spot in the series opens with Mustafa stepping out of the shower with a towel around his waist brandishing a bottle of Old Spice body wash and saying: "Hello ladies, look at your man. Now back to me. Now back at your man. Now back to me. Sadly it isn't me. But if he stopped using lady-scented body wash and switched to Old Spice, he could smell like me."

The agency for Old Spice, Wieden+Kennedy, built on the popularity of the ads with the "Responses" campaign which involved having questions solicited for the "Old Spice Guy" via Twitter and Facebook and having him answer them in short video clips online. Thousands of questions and comments poured in from fans and W+K shot nearly 200 video clips with Mustafa's responses, including one in which he proposed to a man's girlfriend for him. Within a week, online views of the new videos soon eclipsed the original TV spots and Google searches for "Old Spice" increased by 2,000 percent. Old Spice became the most-viewed brand in online videos in 2010 and the campaign helped make it the market leader in the body-wash category.

While the most popular campaigns of the 20th century relied on traditional media, particularly television, most of the 15 added to the list are integrated marketing efforts that are combining paid, owned, and earned media. The top campaigns of the 21st century also reflect changes that have occurred in society because they are tapping into important social issues such as health and sustainability as well as asking consumers to rethink the way they view women. The famous communication theorist Marshall McLuhan, who is best known for coining the phrase "the medium is the message," once stated, "Historians and archaeologists will one day discover that the ads of our time are the richest and most faithful daily reflections any society ever made of its whole range of activities." It is interesting to think about what these campaigns are saying about modern-day society.

Sources: *Ad Age* Staff, "Top Ad Campaigns of the 21st Century," *Advertising Age,* January 12, 2015, pp. 14–22; Nina Bahadur, "Dove 'Real Beauty' Campaign Turns 10: How a Brand Tried to Change the Conversation about Female Beauty," *The Huffington Post,*" January 21, 2014, www.huffingtonpost.com/2014/01/21/dove-real-beauty-campaign-turns-10_n_4575940.html; Jack Neff, "Meet the Man Your Man Could Smell Like," Advertising Age, March 29, 2010, pp. 2, 3; Cotton Delo, "Online Video: Old Spice the Most Viral Brand of the Year—Again," Advertising Age, December 28, 2011, http://adage.com/article/the-viral-video-chart/spice-viral-brand-year-video/231780/; Bob Garfield, "Ad Age Advertising Century: The Top 100 Campaigns," *Advertising Age,* March 29, 1999, http://adage.com/article/special-report-the-advertising-century/ad-age-advertising-century-top-100-campaigns/140918/.

the leading brands of other personal care products for men. Digital and Social Media Perspective 8–1 discusses the top advertising campaigns of the 21st century and how many of them are not only using outstanding creative work, but are also combining paid, owned, and earned media to communicate with consumers. Conversely, an advertising campaign that is poorly conceived or executed can be a liability. Many companies have solid marketing and promotional plans and spend substantial amounts of money on advertising, yet have difficulty coming up with a creative campaign that will differentiate them from their competitors.

It is important to understand that just because an ad or commercial is creative or popular does not mean it will increase sales or revive a declining brand. Many ads have won awards for creativity but failed to increase sales.[2] For example, Anheuser-Busch InBev terminated its 30-year relationship with the DDB agency, which had created

EXHIBIT 8–2

The "Climb On" campaign for Coors Light is designed to make an emotional connection with beer drinkers

Source: 72 and Sunny and MillerCoors

a number of award-winning campaigns for Budweiser such as the "Whassup?" ads as well as many critically acclaimed commercials featuring the iconic Clydesdales.[3] Sales of both Budweiser and Bud Light had declined over the past several years and AB InBev felt that a change was needed in creative strategy for the brands. The two major competitors in the U.S. beer industry, Anheuser-Busch InBev and MillerCoors, have both experienced major sales declines in the light beer category recently as craft beers become more popular. Both companies switched agencies several times as they struggled to find ad campaigns that will help move the sales needle for brands such as Bud Light, Miller Lite, and Coors Light.[4] In 2015 Coors Light dropped its popular cold activation campaign which helped position it as the "World's Most Refreshing Beer." Its new agency, 72 and Sunny, launched the new "Climb On" dual-gender campaign in 2016 that encourages men and women to celebrate the mountains they climb with a refreshing Coors Light. The ads still focus on the cold refreshment aspect of the brand but also are designed to make a stronger emotional connection with beer drinkers (Exhibit 8–2).[5]

Many advertising and marketing people have become ambivalent toward, and in some cases even critical of, advertising awards.[6] They argue that agency creative people are often more concerned with creating ads that win awards than ones that sell their clients' products. Other advertising people believe awards are a good way to recognize creativity that often does result in effective advertising. As we saw in Chapter 7, the success of an ad campaign cannot always be judged in terms of sales. However, many advertising and marketing personnel, particularly those on the client side, believe advertising must ultimately lead the consumer to purchase the product or service. Finding a balance between creative advertising and effective advertising is difficult. To better understand this dilemma, we turn to the issue of creativity and its role in advertising.

ADVERTISING CREATIVITY

What Is Creativity?

Creativity is probably one of the most commonly used terms in advertising. Ads are often called creative. The people who develop ads and commercials are known as creative types. And advertising agencies develop reputations for their creativity. Perhaps so much attention is focused on the concept of creativity because many people view the specific challenge given to those who develop an advertising message as being creative. It is their job to turn all of the information regarding product features and benefits, marketing plans, consumer research, and communication objectives into a creative concept that will bring the advertising message to life. This begs the question: What is meant by *creativity* in advertising?

Different Perspectives on Advertising Creativity

Perspectives on what constitutes creativity in advertising differ. At one extreme are people who argue that advertising is creative only if it sells the product. An advertising message's or campaign's impact on sales counts more than whether it is innovative or wins awards. At the other end of the continuum are those who judge the creativity of an ad in terms of its artistic or aesthetic value and originality. They contend creative ads can break through the competitive clutter, grab the consumer's attention, and have some impact.

As you might expect, perspectives on advertising creativity often depend on one's role. A study by Elizabeth Hirschman examined the perceptions of various individuals involved in the creation and production of TV commercials, including management types (brand managers and account executives) and creatives (art director, copywriter, commercial director, and producer).[7] She found that product managers and account executives view ads as promotional tools whose primary purpose is to communicate favorable impressions to the marketplace. They believe a commercial should be evaluated in terms of whether it fulfills the client's marketing and communicative objectives. The perspective of those on the creative side was much more self-serving, as Hirschman noted:

> In direct contrast to this client orientation, the art director, copywriter, and commercial director viewed the advertisement as a communication vehicle for promoting their own aesthetic viewpoints and personal career objectives. Both the copywriter and art director made this point explicitly, noting that a desirable commercial from their standpoint was one which communicated their unique creative talents and thereby permitted them to obtain "better" jobs at an increased salary.[8]

In her interviews, Hirschman also found that brand managers were much more risk-averse and wanted a more conservative commercial than the creative people, who wanted to maximize the impact of the message.

What constitutes creativity in advertising is probably somewhere between the two extremes. To break through the clutter and make an impression on the target audience, an ad often must be unique and entertaining. As noted in Chapter 5, research has shown that a major determinant of whether a commercial will be successful in changing brand preferences is its "likability," or the viewer's overall reaction.[9] TV commercials, videos, and print ads that are well designed and executed and generate emotional responses can create positive feelings that are transferred to the product or service being advertised. Many creative people believe this type of advertising can come about only if they are given considerable latitude in developing advertising messages. But ads that are creative only for the sake of being creative often fail to communicate a relevant or meaningful message that will lead consumers to purchase the product or service.

Everyone involved in planning and developing an advertising campaign must understand the importance of balancing the "it's not creative unless it sells" perspective with the novelty/uniqueness and impact position. Marketing and brand managers or account executives must recognize that imposing too many sales- and marketing-oriented communications objectives on the creative team can result in mediocre advertising, which is often ineffective in today's competitive, cluttered media environment. At the same time, the creative specialists must recognize that the goal of advertising is to assist in selling the product or service and good advertising must communicate in a manner that helps the client achieve this goal. Despite having different perspectives on creativity, both sides are likely to agree that creative advertising is important because it often garners more attention and can lead to deeper processing by consumers.[10] Marketing professor Scott Koslow also notes that "creativity gives permission to consumers to be open to what appears to be new information about a brand and brings a fresh perspective—the ultimate "new-news.""[11]

Determinants of Creativity

Advertising creativity is the ability to generate fresh, unique, and appropriate or relevant ideas that can be used as solutions to communication problems. Those who study as well as work in advertising generally agree on these two central determinants of creativity, which are often viewed in terms of divergence and relevance.[12] **Divergence** refers to the extent to which an ad contains elements that are novel, different, or unusual. Robert Smith and his colleagues have identified five major factors that could account for the ways divergence can be achieved in advertising, which they describe as follows:[13]

1. *Originality.* Ads that contain elements that are rare, surprising, or move away from the obvious and commonplace.

2. *Flexibility.* Ads that contain different ideas or switch from one perspective to another.
3. *Elaboration.* Ads that contain unexpected details or finish and extend basic ideas so they become more intricate, complicated, or sophisticated.
4. *Synthesis.* Ads that combine, connect, or blend normally unrelated objects or ideas.
5. *Artistic value.* Ads that contain artistic verbal impressions or attractive shapes and colors.

There are other ways divergence can be achieved in developing creative advertising such as through the use of humor, fantasy, emotion, and imagery, which are discussed in Chapter 9 as the basis for advertising execution techniques. In some cases the focus of the creative strategy may be to achieve *fluency* which refers to the ability to generate a variety of messages around a creative idea. For example, the popular "Got Milk?" campaign developed by the California Milk Processor Board has been running for nearly two decades. A myriad of humorous TV commercials, print ads, and even interactive games have been developed around the basic creative idea of showing people in uncomfortable situations because they have run out of milk, encouraging them to keep an ample supply on hand (Exhibit 8–3).

The second major determinant of creativity is **relevance**, which reflects the degree to which the various elements of the ad are meaningful, useful, or valuable to the consumer.[14] Smith et al. suggest that relevance can be achieved in two ways. *Ad-to-consumer relevance* refers to situations where the ad contains execution elements that are meaningful to consumers. For example, advertisers may use celebrities with whom consumers identify, music that they like, or visual images and other execution techniques that capture their interest and attention. *Brand-to-consumer relevance* refers to situations where the advertised brand of a product or service is of personal interest to consumers. Relevance or appropriateness can also be viewed in terms of the degree to which an advertisement provides information or an image that is pertinent to the brand. Ads for many products such as fashionable clothing, jewelry, cosmetics, and liquor often rely on visual images to deliver their message rather than providing specific product information. However, these images are important to consumers in forming impressions and attitudes toward these brands and deciding whether to select one brand over another.

The ad for the Volkswagen Beetle convertible shown in Exhibit 8–4 is a good example of creative advertising that relies on the originality aspect of divergence. The humorous spot shows a man entering a convenience store wearing a ski mask and stocking up on chips and candy, totally unaware that he is terrifying everyone else in the store as they think he is committing a robbery. As the 60-second spot unfolds, the other shoppers cringe while the man at the counter becomes increasingly tense. And when the masked man goes to pay for his items, the cashier says, "I don't want any trouble," to which he innocently responds: "I don't want any trouble either." The masked man then goes outside to join his friends in the VW convertible with its top down and the driver says to him: "You know you forgot to take your mask off, right?" As a police siren wails in the background, one of the other men notes that they should probably get out of there. The spot ends with the men driving through a

winter wonderland as the voiceover says: "Introducing the new Beetle convertible, now every day is a top-down day." The spot is a creative way to grab and hold the attention of the viewer and has an element of suspense and surprise to it with the unexpected ending. Douglas Van Praet, who was the director of the account planning team at Volkswagen's agency (Deutsch LA) at the time the ad was created, provides the following perspective on the commercial:[15]

> Launching a convertible in the middle of winter can be a challenge. But for Volkswagen, it was an opportunity to tell a simple, human story in a clever way. The Beetle is the soul of Volkswagen—the original and iconic car everyone knows. And in "Mask," Deutsch and Volkswagen married those elements into a clever and relatable story. "Mask" follows a young man perusing a mini-mart, grabbing a few items for a road trip with his friends. Only, they are road tripping in the middle of winter, in the Beetle Convertible wearing ski masks. Our shopper forgot to take his mask off, frightening everyone in the store. The unexpected misdirect, which leaves viewers wondering if they're watching a robbery until the end of the spot—when the car is revealed driving through a snowy mountain scene—is classic Volkswagen advertising. A clever surprise and a unique approach to play up the launch of the Beetle Convertible during winter.

A number of studies have been conducted showing that advertising creativity impacts consumers' responses to advertising messages across various stages of the response hierarchy, including cognitive, affective, and behavioral responses.[16] For example, advertising that is more novel has been shown to require consumer processing time, resulting in longer exposure and greater attention. Studies have also shown that creative ads draw more attention to the advertised brand, higher levels of recall, greater motivation to process the information, and deeper levels of processing.[17] In addition to these cognitive outcomes, studies have also shown that creative advertising positively impacts emotional reactions including attitudes and purchase intentions.[18]

While most of the research on advertising creativity has by focused on measures such as attention, attitudes and purchase intentions, German professors Reinartz and Saffert conducted an interesting study that related the five creativity factors to purchase behavior.[19] They analyzed more than 400 German television ad campaigns across nine different consumer packaged-goods categories, examining the impact of creativity on actual sales figures for the products. Their findings showed that highly creative campaigns had a greater impact on sales than campaigns that were low in creativity, although the impact of creativity differed by product category. They also found big variations in the impact that different creative elements had on advertising effectiveness. Although all of the creativity factors had a positive impact, elaboration was the most powerful followed by artistic value while synthesis was least important. However, an important finding from their study is that it was the combination of different creative elements that accounted for the most variation in sales. As can be seen in Exhibit 8–5, campaigns that combined originality with elaboration had the greatest impact followed by those combining originality with artistic value.

Several of these studies have shown that divergence achieved through novelty/originality and/or elaboration is a particularly important component of advertising creativity. However, clients often favor relevance over divergence as they want their agencies to create ads that communicate pertinent information such as specific product features and benefits. Smith and his colleagues suggest that clients should be less resistant to divergent approaches and note that there is a fundamental need for divergent thinkers in the ad development process.[20] Considering that most advertising messages are seen and/or heard in a very cluttered media environment where marketers must compete for the attention of consumers, it is important that attention be given to creating ads that are novel and divergent as well as relevant and meaningful. The findings from Reinartz and Saffert's research show that advertising creativity has a significant impact on sales and marketers need to pay close attention to creative elements of their ads.

Those who work in agencies, particularly in the creative departments, recognize the importance of developing advertising messages that are novel and unique but still

EXHIBIT 8-5

Impact of combinations of
creative elements on sales

What Creativity Combinations Work Best?		% Relative Effectiveness (Sales Uplift of Pairing Relative to Average Effectiveness)
Originality + Elaboration	**More effective**	+96
Originality + Artistic value		+89
Elaboration + Artistic value		+28
Originality + Synthesis		+ 1
Originality + Flexibility		− 1
Synthesis + Elaboration		− 5
Flexibility + Synthesis		−20
Synthesis + Artistic value		−29
Flexibility + Elaboration		−59
Flexibility + Artistic value	**Less effective**	−99

communicate relevant information to the target audience. For example, the former D'Arcy Masius Benton & Bowles agency developed a set of principles to guide its creative efforts and help achieve superior creative work. The agency views a creative advertising message as one that is built around a core or power idea (which will be discussed later in this chapter) and uses excellent design and execution to communicate information that is relevant to the target audience. The agency used these principles to develop outstanding creative work for clients such as Procter & Gamble's Charmin and Pampers brands, Norelco, Budweiser, and many other popular brands. The agency was integrated into the Publicis Groupe in 2002, but these Universal Advertising Standards are still used by the various agencies that are part of the Publicis's agency family.

PLANNING CREATIVE STRATEGY

The Creative Challenge

Those who work on the creative side of advertising often face a real challenge. They must take all the research, creative briefs, strategy statements, communications objectives, and other input and transform them into an advertising message. Their job is to write copy, design layouts and illustrations, or produce commercials that effectively communicate the central theme on which the campaign is based. Rather than simply stating the features or benefits of a product or service, they must put the advertising message into a form that will engage the audience's interest and make the ads memorable.[21]

The job of the creative team is challenging because every marketing situation is different and each campaign or advertisement may require a different creative approach. Numerous guidelines have been developed for creating effective advertising,[22] but there is no magic formula. As copywriter Hank Sneiden notes in his book *Advertising Pure and Simple:*

> Rules lead to dull stereotyped advertising, and they stifle creativity, inspiration, initiative, and progress. The only hard and fast rule that I know of in advertising is that there are no rules. No formulas. No right way. Given the same problem, a dozen creative talents would solve it a dozen different ways. If there were a sure-fire formula for successful advertising, everyone would use it. Then there'd be no need for creative people. We would simply program robots to create our ads and commercials and they'd sell loads of product—to other robots.[23]

EXHIBIT 8–6

Wieden+Kennedy's belief in taking risks has led to creative advertising for clients such as Nike

Source: NIKE Inc.

Taking Creative Risks

Many creative people follow proven formulas when creating ads because they are safe. Clients often feel uncomfortable with advertising that is too different. Bill Tragos, former chair of TBWA, the advertising agency noted for its excellent creative work for Absolut vodka, Evian, and many other clients, says, "Very few clients realize that the reason that their work is so bad is that they are the ones who commandeered it and directed it to be that way. I think that at least 50 percent of an agency's successful work resides in the client."[24] Koslow and his colleagues have examined the influence of clients on the creativity of their agencies and found that the main reason some marketers receive better creative work than other is that they are open to exploring new ideas. They also found that access to consumer research is important as it provides agencies with insights needed to produce highly creative works. They noted that highly creative campaigns do not just appear; planning and insightful research are important for agencies to develop new ideas.[25]

Many who work on the creative side in agencies argue that it is important for clients to take some risks if they want breakthrough advertising that gets noticed. One agency that has been successful in getting its clients to take risks is Wieden+Kennedy, best known for its excellent creative work for companies such as Nike and ESPN over the years and more recently for clients such as Intuit/TurboTax (Exhibit 8–6). The agency's founders believe a key element in its success has been a steadfast belief in taking risks when most agencies and their clients have been retrenching and becoming more conservative.[26] The agency can develop great advertising partly because clients like Nike are willing to take risks and go along with the agency's priority system, which places the creative work first and the client–agency relationship second. The agency has even terminated relationships with large clients like Gallo when they interfered too much with the creative process. Several major advertisers including Procter & Gamble and Coca-Cola have added Wieden+Kennedy to their agency roster in efforts to increase the creativity of their advertising.[27] The Old Spice campaign discussed earlier in the chapter is an example of the excellent creative work being done by W+K.

Not all companies or agencies agree that advertising has to be risky to be effective, however. Many marketing managers are more comfortable with advertising that simply communicates product or service features and benefits and gives the consumer a reason to buy. They see their ad campaigns as multimillion-dollar investments whose goal is to sell the product rather than finance the whims of their agency's creative staff. They argue that some creative people have lost sight of advertising's bottom line: Does it sell? There has been an ongoing debate over the artsy, image-oriented approach to advertising taken by many creative types versus the more hard-sell approach that many clients prefer.

The Perpetual Debate: Creative versus Hard-Sell Advertising

For decades there has been a perpetual battle over the role of advertising in the marketing process. The war for the soul of advertising has been endlessly fought between those who believe ads should move people and those who just want to move product. On one side are the "suits" or "rationalists" who argue that advertising must sell the product or service, and that the more selling points or information in an ad, the better its chance of moving the consumer to purchase. On the other side are the "poets" or proponents of creativity who argue that advertising has to build an emotional bond between consumers and brands or companies that goes beyond product advertising. The debate over the effectiveness of creative or artsy advertising is not new. The rationalists have taken great delight in pointing to long lists of creative and award-winning campaigns over the years that have failed in the marketplace. Some note that even legendary advertising executive David Ogilvy, whom many consider the greatest copywriter of all time, once said: "If it doesn't sell, it's not creative."[28]

The "poets" argue that the most important thing good advertising does is make an emotional connection with consumers. They note that consumers do not want to be bombarded by ads; they want to be entertained and inspired. Indeed numerous studies have found that consumers look for ways to avoid TV commercials as well as online video and banners ads rather than watch or click through on them.[29] Thus, advertising has to be creative and enjoyable enough that consumers will not avoid it, yet still be able to help sell a product or service. It is the second part of this mandate that causes concern among the "suits." They note that there are many examples of creative campaigns that moved consumers' emotions but were terminated because they did not increase sales and/or market share and put accounts and reputations on the line. As noted earlier, a number of major advertisers have dismissed agencies that earned critical acclaim and awards for their creative work but failed to move the sales needle.[30]

Most of the "poets" who support advertising that connects on an emotional level insist that selling product is as much a priority for them as it is for those on the rational side of the debate. One top agency executive notes that "we've proven that this kind of advertising works, otherwise we wouldn't be in business, us or the agencies that practice the craft at this level." However, Brent Bouchez, former executive creative director at the Bozzell agency, argues the poets are losing sight of the fact that advertising is about selling things and being really creative in advertising means solving problems and building interesting brands that people want to buy. He notes, "It's time we stopped teaching young creative people to consider it a victory if the logo in an ad is hard to find, or if the product doesn't appear in the commercial at all. It's time we stopped using 'break through the clutter' as an excuse to say nothing about what it is we're selling or why you should buy it."[31]

The issue of how much latitude creative people should be given and how much risk the client should be willing to take is open to considerable debate. However, clients and agency personnel generally agree that the ability to develop novel yet appropriate approaches to communicating with the customer makes the creative specialist valuable—and often hard to find.

Creative Personnel

The image of the creative advertising person perpetuated in novels, movies, and TV shows is often one of a freewheeling, freethinking, eccentric personality. The educational background of creative personnel is often in nonbusiness areas such as art, literature, music, humanities, or journalism, so their interests and perspectives tend to differ from those of managers with a business education or background. Creative people tend to be more abstract and less structured, organized, or conventional in their approach to a problem, relying on intuition more often than logic. For example, Arthur Kover conducted a study of advertising copywriters and found that they work without guidance from any formal theories of communication. However, those interviewed in his study did have similar informal, implicit theories that guide them in creating ads. These theories are based on finding ways to break through the ad clutter, open the consciousness of consumers, and connect with them to deliver the message.[32]

It is important to note that creativity is not the exclusive domain of those who work in the creative department of ad agencies. Integrated marketing communications requires creative thinking from everyone involved in the planning and execution of IMC programs. Personnel from other parts of the agency such as account services and planning, media planners, digital media specialists and researchers, as well as those on the client side, such as marketing and brand managers, must all seek creative solutions to challenges faced in planning developing, and executing an IMC campaign. For example, awards are given each year for creativity in areas such as media

EXHIBIT 8–7

Awards for creativity are given for media planning as well as other components of an IMC program

Source: UM (Universal McCann)

planning, sales promotion, and digital and interactive media. In 2016 UM, which is part of the Interpublic Group, was selected as Media Agency of the Year by both *Advertising Age* and *Adweek* (Exhibit 8–7). UM was honored for its creativity in media planning and strategy for its clients including Coca-Cola, Sony Pictures, CVS, and Johnson & Johnson brands such as Tylenol and Clean & Clear.

It is also important that those working on the client side do not create a relationship with their agencies that inhibits the creative processes required to produce good advertising. Shelia Sasser and Scott Koslow point out that the most highly skilled creatives aspire to work with open-minded clients who are receptive to new ideas. They also note some of the best creative work developed by agencies does not get used because clients are resistant to taking creative risks, unless they are under pressure to perform.[33] Advertising agencies as well as other IMC specialist organizations thrive on creativity because it is at the heart of what they do. Thus, agencies, as well as clients, must create an environment that fosters the development of creative thinking and creative advertising. Clients must also understand the differences between the perspectives of the creative personnel and marketing and product managers. Differences between creative and managerial personalities and perspectives must be recognized and tolerated so that creative people can do their best work and all those involved in the advertising process can cooperate. While the client has ultimate approval of the advertising, the opinions of creative specialists must be respected when advertising ideas and content are evaluated. (Evaluation of the creatives' ideas and work is discussed in more detail in Chapter 9.)

THE CREATIVE PROCESS

Some advertising people say creativity in advertising is best viewed as a process and creative success is most likely when some organized approach is followed. This does not mean there is an infallible blueprint to follow to create effective advertising; as we saw earlier, many advertising people reject attempts to standardize creativity or develop rules. However, most do follow a process when developing an ad.

One of the most popular approaches to creativity in advertising was developed by James Webb Young, a former creative vice president at the J. Walter Thompson agency. Young said, "The production of ideas is just as definite a process as the production of Fords; the production of ideas, too, runs an assembly line; in this production the mind follows an operative technique which can be learned and controlled; and that its effective use is just as much a matter of practice in the technique as in the effective use of any tool."[34] Young's model of the creative process contains five steps:

1. *Immersion.* Gathering raw material and information through background research and immersing yourself in the problem.
2. *Digestion.* Taking the information, working it over, and wrestling with it in the mind.
3. *Incubation.* Putting the problems out of your conscious mind and turning the information over to the subconscious to do the work.
4. *Illumination.* The birth of an idea—the "Eureka! I have it!" phenomenon.
5. *Reality or verification.* Studying the idea to see if it still looks good or solves the problem; then shaping the idea to practical usefulness.

Young's process of creativity is similar to a four-step approach outlined much earlier by English sociologist Graham Wallas in his classic book *The Art of Thought*.[35]

1. *Preparation.* Gathering background information needed to solve the problem through research and study.
2. *Incubation.* Getting away and letting ideas develop.

3. *Illumination.* Seeing the light or solution.

4. *Verification.* Refining and polishing the idea and seeing if it is an appropriate solution.

Models of the creative process are valuable to those working in the creative area of advertising, since they offer an organized way to approach an advertising problem. Preparation or gathering of background information is the first step in the creative process. As we saw in earlier chapters, the advertiser and agency start by developing a thorough understanding of the product or service, the target market, and the competition. They also focus on the role of advertising and other IMC tools in the marketing and promotional program.

These models do not say much about how this information will be synthesized and used by the creative specialist because this part of the process is unique to the individual. In many ways, it's what sets apart the great creative minds and strategists in advertising. However, many agencies are now using a process called *account planning* to gather information and help creative specialists as they go through the creative process of developing advertising.

Account Planning

To facilitate the creative process, many agencies now use **account planning**, which is a process that involves conducting research and gathering all relevant information about a client's product or service, brand, and consumers in the target audience. Account planning began in Great Britain during the 1960s and 70s and has spread to agencies in the United States as well as throughout Europe and Asia. The concept has become very popular in recent years as many agencies have seen the successful campaigns developed by agencies that are strong advocates of account planning.[36] One such agency is Goodby, Silverstein & Partners, which has used account planning to develop highly successful campaigns for clients such as Marmot, Adobe, Frito-Lay, Häagen-Dazs as well as the popular "Got Milk?" ads for the California Milk Processor Board.

Jon Steel, a former vice president and director of account planning at the agency's San Francisco office, has written an excellent book on the process titled *Truth, Lies & Advertising: The Art of Account Planning.*[37] He notes that the account planner's job is to provide the key decision makers with all the information they require to make an intelligent decision. According to Steel, "Planners may have to work very hard to influence the way that the advertising turns out, carefully laying out a strategic foundation with the client, handing over tidbits of information to creative people when, in their judgment, that information will have the greatest impact, giving feedback on ideas, and hopefully adding some ideas of their own."

Account planning plays an important role during creative strategy development by driving the process from the customers' point of view. Planners will work with the client as well as other agency personnel, such as the creative team and media specialists. They discuss how the knowledge and information they have gathered can be used in the development of the creative strategy as well as other aspects of the advertising campaign. Account planners are usually responsible for all the research (both qualitative and quantitative) conducted during the creative strategy development process. In the following section we examine how various types of research and information can provide input to the creative process of advertising. This information can be gathered by account planners or others whose job it is to provide input to the process.

Inputs to the Creative Process: Preparation, Incubation, Illumination

Background Research   Only the most foolish creative person or team would approach an assignment without first learning as much as possible about the client's product or service, the target market, the competition, and any other relevant background information. The creative specialist should also be knowledgeable about general trends, conditions, and developments in the marketplace, as well as research on specific advertising approaches or techniques that might be effective. The creative specialist can acquire background information in numerous ways. Some informal fact-finding techniques have been noted by Sandra Moriarty:

- Reading anything related to the product or market—books, trade publications, general interest articles, research reports, and the like.
- Asking everyone involved with the product for information—designers, engineers, salespeople, and consumers.
- Listening to what people are talking about. Visits to stores, malls, restaurants, and even the agency cafeteria can be informative. Listening to the client can be particularly valuable, since he or she often knows the product and market best.
- Using the product or service and becoming familiar with it. The more you use a product, the more you know and can say about it.
- Working in and learning about the client's business to understand better the people you're trying to reach.[38]

To assist in the preparation, incubation, and illumination stages, many agencies provide creative people with both general and product-specific preplanning input. **General preplanning input** can include books, periodicals, trade publications, websites, scholarly journals, pictures, and clipping services, which gather and organize magazine, newspaper, and online articles on the product or service, the market, and the competition, including the latter's ads. This input can also come from research studies conducted by the client, the agency, the media, or other sources.

Another useful general preplanning input concerns trends, developments, and happenings in the marketplace. Information is available from a variety of sources, including local, state, and federal governments, secondary research suppliers, and various industry trade associations, as well as advertising and media organizations. For example, advertising industry groups like the American Advertising Federation (AAF), the 4As (formerly called the American Association of Advertising Agencies), and media organizations like the Video Advertising Bureau, Radio Advertising Bureau, and the Association of Magazine Media publish research reports and newsletters that provide information on market trends and developments and how they might affect consumers. Those involved in developing creative strategy can also gather relevant and timely information by reading publications like *Adweek, Advertising Age,* and *Marketing News.* Many individuals who work in creative departments read *Communication Arts* magazine which covers topics such as design, advertising, illustration, photography, interactive media, and typography (see Exhibit 8–8).

Product- or Service-Specific Research

In addition to getting general background research and preplanning input, creative people receive **product- or service-specific preplanning input**. This information generally comes in the form of specific studies conducted on the product or service, the target audience, or a combination of the two. Quantitative and qualitative consumer research such as attitude studies, market structure, and positioning studies such as perceptual mapping and lifestyle research, focus group interviews, and demographic and psychographic profiles of users of a particular product, service, or brand are examples of product-specific preplanning input.

Many product- or service-specific studies helpful to the creative team are conducted by the client or the agency. More than 40 years ago, the BBDO ad agency developed an approach called **problem detection** for finding ideas around which creative strategies could be based.[39] This research technique involves asking consumers

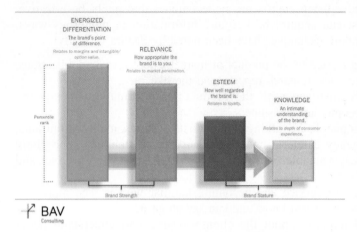

EXHIBIT 8–9

BrandAsset Valuator is used to manage brands

Source: Reprinted with permission of BrandAsset Consulting. © BAV Consulting.

familiar with a product (or service) to generate an exhaustive list of things that bother them or problems they encounter when using it and how often they arise. The consumers rate these problems in order of importance and evaluate various brands in terms of their association with each problem. A problem detection study can provide valuable input for product improvements, reformulations, or new products. It can also give the creative people ideas regarding attributes or features to emphasize and guidelines for positioning new or existing brands. Many marketers and/or their agencies still use variations of the problem detection technique today.

Some agencies conduct lifestyle studies annually and construct detailed psychographic or lifestyle profiles of product or service users. DDB Worldwide conducts a large-scale study each year that surveys 7,000 men and women to measure their activities, interests, opinions, and attitudes as well as their usage of a wide range of products and services. The information is used to construct a psychographic profile of the target audiences for whom they are developing ads as well as to gain insight into general consumer trends. The DDB Life Style Study® has been conducted annually since 1975 and is the nation's longest-running and largest longitudinal study of attitudes and behaviors. The sample is balanced to the U.S. Census on gender, age, and race.

A number of advertising agencies conduct branding research to help better identify clients' customers and how they connect to their brands. For example, the Y&R Group developed a proprietary tool called the BrandAsset Valuator (BAV™) for building and managing a brand. The model uses four pillars: energized differentiation, relevance, esteem, and knowledge. These pillars identify cores issues for the brand and evaluate current and future financial performance and potential (Exhibit 8–9). The agency formed a separate corporate research group to handle the BAV which is now the world's largest database of brand perceptions; it contains ratings from consumers in 51 countries on more than 43,000 brands on 72 dimensions.

Nearly all of the major agencies are conducting branding research and/or developing models or systems that they can use to gain better insight into consumers and develop more effective campaigns for their clients. The importance of building and maintaining strong brands is likely to become even greater in the future. This will put even more pressure on agencies to develop new and better tools and techniques that can be used to guide their clients' advertising campaigns.

Qualitative Research Input Many agencies, particularly larger ones with strong research departments, have their own research programs and specific techniques they use to assist in the development of creative strategy and provide input to the creative process. In addition to the various quantitative research studies, qualitative research techniques such as in-depth interviews or focus groups can provide the creative team with valuable insight at the early stages of the creative process. **Focus groups** are a research method whereby consumers (usually 10 to 12 people) from the target market are led through a discussion regarding a particular topic. Focus groups give insight as to why and how consumers use a product or service, what is important to them in choosing a particular brand, what they like and don't like about various products or services, and any special needs they might have that aren't being satisfied. A focus group session might also include a discussion of types of ad appeals to use or evaluation of the advertising of various companies.

Focus group interviews bring the creative people and others involved in creative strategy development into contact with the customers. Listening to a focus group gives copywriters, art directors, and other creative specialists a better sense of who the target audience is, what the audience is like, and whom the creatives need to write,

EXHIBIT 8-10

Marketers often use online focus group services to pretest ads

Source: Invoke

design, or direct to in creating an advertising message. Focus groups can also be used to evaluate the viability of different creative approaches under consideration and suggest the best direction to pursue.[40] Many marketers are now conducting focus groups online using groups of consumers who are part of an online community, as well as Internet research panels of 80 to 100 consumers organized by research firms such as Greenfield Online and Invoke Solutions. Concepts can be presented to these panels using instant-message and chat room styles, and detailed feedback can be gathered and processed in a few hours versus several weeks that are needed to get comparable results from traditional focus groups.[41] Exhibit 8-10 shows how Invoke promotes the value of its online focus groups by showing how they were used by Orbitz and its agency, BBDO, in developing the "Take Vacation Back" ad campaign which won a David Ogilvy Award from the Advertising Research Foundation.

EXHIBIT 8-11

The Aflac duck did not test well in focus groups but has been the basis for a very successful campaign

Source: Aflac Incorporated

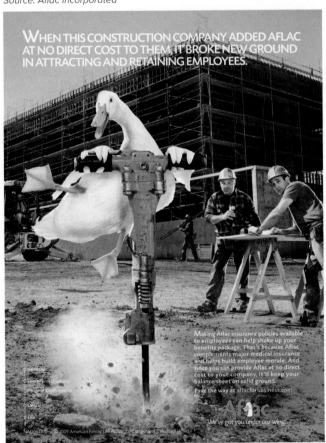

Agency creative personnel have long expressed concern over the idea of having their ideas and work critiqued by consumers. Many creatives insist that good ideas don't need to be tested and that testing can often weaken a creative execution. Moreover, they argue that it interferes with the creative process and limits their ability to develop innovative and breakthrough advertising messages.[42] Those critical of focus groups note that highly successful campaigns such as the one featuring the Aflac duck would never have made it on the air if the company had heeded the responses of focus group participants. While many participants found the duck funny, others found it insulting. The duck survived only after executives from the Kaplan Thaler Group convinced the company to allow the Ipsos-ASI research firm to test the ad along with four others it created and four spots from other agencies competing for the account.[43] The recall score of the spot featuring the duck was the highest score Ipsos-ASI had seen in the insurance category at the time. Kaplan Thaler won the account, and the award-winning campaign featuring the duck debuted in late 1999 and has been running ever since (Exhibit 8-11). It also has helped raise awareness of Aflac and led to significant increases in sales for the supplemental insurance provider.

While some creative personnel may be opposed to having their ideas scrutinized in a focus group, there

Digital and Social Media Perspective 8–2 > > >

DIGITAL'S NEED FOR SPEED CHALLENGES PRETESTING OF CREATIVE WORK

Major marketers often spend hundreds of thousands of dollars to develop and test creative ideas and concepts that will be turned into advertising campaigns for their brands and for good reason. Many of the commercials you see on television for big brands cost an average of $400,000 just to produce while some, such as those created for the Super Bowl, can cost more than $1 million when all of the preproduction, production, and postproduction costs are added up. And once a commercial is produced, marketers may spend several hundred million more on television media time to run the spot. In addition to the development, production, and media costs, marketers also have to consider opportunity costs which refer to the cost of an alternative that must be forgone in order to pursue a certain action. From an advertising perspective this simply means, Would another creative approach have worked better than the one chosen?

Given that marketers spend so much money on advertising one would think that they would also be willing to invest in research to test creative concepts as well as commercials to determine whether they are going to be effective. Traditionally, most major marketers have used some form of copy or A/B testing to compare the effectiveness of various creative concepts or advertising messages prior and make a decision on which one to use. Various forms of copy testing have been used for years and there are many examples of how marketers have relied on the tests to avoid costly mistakes and choose the best alternative. Today most copy testing methods involve showing ads online to a panel of consumers and measuring their reactions using measures such as recall, likability, persuasiveness, and purchase intentions. Ads can be tested in various stages of production ranging from early versions shown in rough animated form such as animatics, all the way through to a finished commercial. Survey results are often compared to norms with previous ads, category averages, or other popular ads currently running.

Copy or pretesting has long been a research stalwart for marketers and many companies such as Frito-Lay still pretest TV commercials or videos that will be used online, particularly those backed by large media budgets. However, copy testing, like so many other areas of advertising and marketing communication, is changing as a result of the digital revolution and marketers' desire to move more quickly and keep pace with the new media consumption patterns of consumers. Many marketers feel that today's digital and social media environment requires them to create multiple executions of TV commercials, videos, and other content to keep pace

---

are, of course, numerous examples of situations where input from focus groups has proved to be very valuable and insightful. Creative personnel must recognize that companies want to ensure that the ads that are being developed for their brands have the best possible chance of evoking favorable reactions from consumers and encouraging them to purchase their product and/or services. Joe Plummer, the former chief research officer of the Advertising Research Foundation, explains their position pretty well by noting that "Any creative director worth his salt who really thinks a client is going to lay down $100 million without a high level of confidence of success is naïve."[44] However, Digital and Social Media Perspective 8–2 discusses how pretesting of advertising messages is changing as a result of the digital revolution and marketers' desire to develop more message content and move more quickly.

Another form of qualitative input that has become popular among advertising agencies is **ethnographic research**, which involves observing consumers in their natural environment.[45] This form of research has its roots in the social science discipline of anthropology, where it has long been used to gather information on human societies and cultures. It has been adapted for use in marketing by sending anthropologists or trained researchers into the field to study and observe consumers in their homes, at work, or at play. For example, the Ogilvy & Mather agency has a research unit called the Discovery Group, which moves into consumers' homes, follows consumers in their leisure pursuits, or trails them as they move through their daily lives. For Ogilvy client MillerCoors, Discovery staffers traveled around the country filming Miller drinkers, as well as those drinking competitive brands. They used the tapes to study group dynamics and how the dynamics changed while people were drinking. The agency used the insights gained from the study to help develop a new advertising campaign for Miller Lite beer.

with consumers who are spending more time online and can easily avoid or skip their ads and other messages. Some are also critical of traditional copy testing methods arguing that it is based on outdated thinking regarding how advertising works and is no longer valid. They note that while pretesting methods may be effective for evaluating informational ads, it does not work well for emotional messages, as most only scratch the surface of which emotions an ad can evoke and how a consumer will respond after viewing it.

Resistance to pretesting of advertising messages is nothing new; many advertisers have respected their ad agencies' request not to subject their creative ideas and work to the metrics that copy testing services churn out. For example, Wieden+Kennedy has a reputation for resisting copy testing, and the former director of global marketing for Nike claimed that he had an agreement with W+K's founder Dan Kennedy not to pretest its ads noting that "It makes you dull. It makes you predictable. It makes you feel safe." The former brand manager for Old Spice also notes that the popular "The Man Your Man Could Smell Like" spot was not copy tested. Other popular campaigns that have gone live without pretesting include the "Mayhem" ads for All State Insurance which are very popular with young people. The campaign has used a number of different executions featuring a villainous character who wreaks havoc on cars and property as a way of showing that many accidents involve more than your average fender bender. Allstate's senior VP of marketing noted that while there was some internal pressure to kill the ads, the company did not do any market testing or focus groups; she just asked herself, "Would I want to watch those ads?"

Not all marketers are willing to go with their gut feelings when it comes to approving their agencies' creative work. For example, Anheuser-Busch InBev has a reputation for using strict copy testing standards and PepsiCo, which owns brands such as Frito-Lay and Gatorade, pretests most of its ads. However, PepsiCo did forego testing for a short film that was created as part of a viral marketing campaign for its Pepsi Max brand that featured NASCAR driver Jeff Gordon disguised a regular guy shopping for a car and taking the car salesperson on a scary ride. The video was part of the "Zero Calorie in Disguise" campaign for Pepsi Max and received more than 40 million views on YouTube and other social media sites.

The debate over the value of pretesting TV commercials as well as videos and other types of digital content is likely to continue. Leading market research companies such as Ace Metrix, Ipsos, and Millward Brown are adapting their testing methods and developing ways to pretest commercials and videos more quickly online as well as incorporating new types of measures such as biometrics and online behavioral data. However, as more marketers feel the need for speed in developing content, they are likely to forego copy testing and use tools such as social media monitoring to decide whether their messages are resonating with consumers and then respond accordingly.

Sources: E. J. Schultz, "Fired Up," *Advertising Age*," September 14, 2015, pp. 21–23; Molly Soat, "The Case for Earlier Insights," *Marketing News*, July 2015, pp. 16–17; Time Peterson, "How the Top Ad Agencies Win on YouTube: Great Creative, Lots of Ads," *Advertising Age*, February 14, 2014, http://adage.com/article/digital/meet-top-creative-media-agencies-youtube/291707/.

Many marketing and agency researchers prefer ethnographic research over the use of focus groups, as the latter technique has a number of limitations. Strong personalities can often wield undue influence in focus groups, and participants often will not admit, or may not even recognize, their behavior patterns and motivations. However, ethnographic studies can cost more to conduct and are more difficult to administer.

Generally, creative people are open to any research or information that will help them understand the client's target market better and assist in generating creative ideas. The advertising industry is recognizing the importance of using research to guide the creative process. The Advertising Research Foundation initiated the David Ogilvy Awards, named after the advertising legend who founded Ogilvy & Mather. These awards are presented to teams of advertising agencies, client companies, and research companies in recognition of research that has been used successfully to determine the strategy and effectiveness of ad campaigns.

The Grand Ogilvy Award winner in 2016 was a campaign developed by Grey Advertising and digital agency 360i for Nestlé's Lean Cuisine frozen meals. The brand was facing six years of sales declines and embarked on a major rebranding effort that included new packaging and entrée options as well as an integrated campaign developed to link it to healthy eating habits rather than calorie counting. Insights from 360i's Tribe Analysis and Brand Compass research were used to create an emotionally focused video featuring women weighing their life accomplishments in lieu of their bodies to start a conversation around weight and body perception. The campaign included a two-minute video posted on social media that opens with the question: "How much do you weigh?" However, instead of weighing their bodies the women weigh their personal accomplishments such as a long,

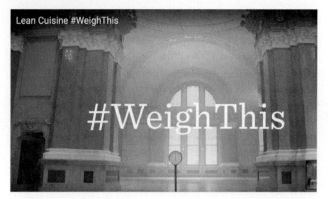
Lean Cuisine #WeighThis

#WeighThis

happy marriage; a backpack representing trips around the world; making the Dean's list in college; and donating bone marrow to a sister. The spot is accompanied by the message "If you're going to weigh something, weigh what matters" and ends by inviting viewers to share how they'd like to be weighed with the hashtag #WeighThis (Exhibit 8–12). The campaign also included television and print ads that show how eating Lean Cuisine can be part of a healthy lifestyle for busy women with hectic schedules. The campaign played an integral role in the turnaround strategy for Lean Cuisine and helped it achieve its first sales increase in six years.[46]

Inputs to the Creative Process: Verification, Revision

The verification and revision stage of the creative process evaluates ideas generated during the illumination stage, rejects inappropriate ones, refines and polishes those that remain, and gives them final expression. Techniques used at this stage include directed focus groups to evaluate creative concepts, ideas, or themes; message communication studies; portfolio tests; and evaluation measures such as viewer reaction profiles.

At this stage of the creative process, members of the target audience may be asked to evaluate rough creative layouts and to indicate what meaning they get from the ad, what they think of its execution, or how they react to a slogan or theme. The creative team can gain insight into how a TV commercial might communicate its message by having members of the target market evaluate the ad in storyboard form. A **storyboard** is a series of drawings used to present the visual plan or layout of a proposed commercial. It contains a series of sketches of key frames or scenes along with the copy or audio portion for each scene (see Exhibit 8–13).

EXHIBIT 8–13

Marketers can gain insight into consumers' reactions to a commercial by showing them a storyboard or an animatic

Source: Campari America, San Francisco, CA

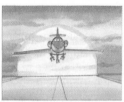

Testing a commercial in storyboard form can be difficult because storyboards are too abstract for many consumers to understand. To make the creative layout more realistic and easier to evaluate, the agency may produce an **animatic**, a videotape of the storyboard along with an audio soundtrack. Storyboards and animatics are useful for research purposes as well as for presenting the creative idea to other agency personnel or to the client for discussion and approval.

At this stage of the process, the creative team is attempting to find the best creative approach or execution style before moving ahead with the campaign themes and going into actual production of the ad. The verification/revision process may include more formal, extensive pretesting of the ad before a final decision is made. Pretesting and related procedures are examined in detail in Chapter 18.

CREATIVE STRATEGY DEVELOPMENT

Advertising Campaigns

Most ads are part of a series of messages that make up an IMC or **advertising campaign**, which is a set of interrelated and coordinated marketing communications activities that center on a single theme or idea that appears in different media across a specified time period. Determining the unifying theme around which the campaign will be built is a critical part of the creative process, as it sets the tone for the individual ads and other forms of marketing communications that will be used. A **campaign theme** should be a strong idea, as it is the central message that will be communicated in all the advertising and other promotional activities. The theme for the advertising campaign is usually expressed through a **slogan (tagline)** that reduces the key idea into a few words or a brief statement. The advertising slogan should serve as a summation line that succinctly expresses the company or brand's positioning, as well as the message it is trying to deliver to the target audience.[47] The slogan usually appears in every advertisement and is often used in other forms of marketing communications to serve as a reminder of, and to reinforce, the marketer's branding message. Kohli, Leuthesser, and Suri note that slogans are a key element of a brand's identity as they can enhance a brand's image, aid in its recognition and recall, and help differentiate it in the minds of consumers, thus contributing to brand equity.[48] They note that while a brand name and/or logo cannot say much in a literal sense, slogans can bridge this gap and say something about the image of the product or service. They can also serve as a "hook" or "handle" that helps capture the meaning of a brand and help relay what makes it special.[49]

Advertising campaign plans are short term in nature and, like marketing and IMC plans, are done on an annual basis. However, the campaign themes are usually developed with the intention of being used for a longer time period. Unfortunately, many campaign themes last only a short time, usually because they are ineffective or market conditions and/or competitive developments in the marketplace change. IMC Perspective 8–1 discusses some of the reasons why many advertising slogans do a poor job of communicating a distinctive identity for a company or brand, and offers some guidelines for developing more effective taglines.

While some marketers change their campaign themes often, a successful campaign

FIGURE 8–1

Examples of Effective Advertising Slogans

Company or Brand	Slogan
1. Nike	Just do it.
2. Home Depot	More saving. More doing.
3. Gillette	The Best a Man Can Get
4. McDonald's	I'm Lovin' It!
5. De Beers	A Diamond Is Forever
6. Walmart	Save Money. Live Better.
7. Bounty	The Quicker Picker-Upper
8. Gatorade	Win From Within
9. Under Armour	We Must Protect This House. I Will.
10. Macy's	The Magic of Macy's

IMC Perspective 8–1 > > >

Creating More Effective Ad Slogans

Consumers are exposed to hundreds of advertising messages as we go through our daily media consumption routines of reading newspapers and magazines, listening to radio, watching television, surfing the Internet, and staying in touch through social media. Most of the ads that we see and/or hear contain a slogan or tagline that is designed to serve as a summation line that succinctly expresses the company's or brand's positioning as well as the message it is trying to deliver to the target audience. Stop and think for a moment about Nike's "Just Do It" tagline, which has been used in its advertising for more than two decades and is recognized by nearly everyone. The tagline is designed to encourage personal athletic achievement, whether through playing a sport or engaging in some type of exercise or workout routine such as running, biking, aerobics, or even walking. Of course Nike wants us all to do it while wearing its shoes or exercise apparel, which millions of consumers around the world proudly do. Even when we see a Nike ad that does not contain the slogan, the famous "swoosh" trademark often prompts consumers to rehearse the "Just Do It" line in their minds.

Nike's tagline was chosen as one of the top five ad slogans of all time and has even been enshrined in the Smithsonian Institution. Some of the other top taglines that effectively communicate the benefits or unique features of a product/service or brand include "M&M's: Melts in your mouth, not in your hands"; Allstate Insurance's "You're in Good Hands with Allstate"; Kay Jewelers's "Every kiss begins with Kay"; and the

Source: Kumail Hemani

iconic "Got Milk?" tagline. Great slogans can also help make a brand part of popular culture such as Under Armour's "Protect This House" and "What Happens Here Stays Here" for the Las Vegas Convention and Visitors Authority.

While there are many other examples of good taglines, there are probably many more of poor slogans that are very

theme may last for decades. Philip Morris has been using the "Marlboro country" campaign for over 50 years, General Mills has positioned Wheaties cereal as the "Breakfast of Champions" since 1933, and BMW has used "the ultimate driving machine" theme since 1974. Even though BMW has changed agencies several times over the past four decades, the classic tagline has been retained. Figure 8–1 lists some of the advertising slogans currently being used by marketers that are recognized as being very effective because they are memorable and communicate a unique message for the company or brand.

Like any other area of the marketing and promotional process, the creative aspect of advertising and the development of the campaign theme is guided by specific goals and objectives. A creative strategy that focuses on what must be communicated will guide the selection of the campaign theme and the development of all messages used in the ad campaign. The creative strategy is based on several factors, including identification of the target audience; the basic problem, issue, or opportunity the advertising must address; the major selling idea or key benefit the message needs to communicate; and any supportive information that needs to be included in the ad. Once these factors are determined, a creative strategy statement should describe the message appeal and execution style that will be used. Many ad agencies outline these elements in a document known as the copy or creative platform.

Creative Brief

The written **creative brief** specifies the basic elements of the creative strategy. Different agencies may call this document a *creative platform* or *work plan, creative*

broad and vague and are meaningless phrases to most consumers. Branding expert Laura Ries cites recent taglines of three of the largest automotive advertisers as examples of slogans that lack motivation and do not provide a reason for buying the brand. As you read them, try to connect them with the brand they are advertising: "Go Further," "Find New Roads," and "Let's go places." The slogans are for Ford, Chevrolet, and Toyota, respectively. You can ask yourself if they really inspire you to consider one of these brands. Ries argues that many slogans do little to position a company or brand or differentiate them from competitors.

Marketing experts note that a good tagline must break through the advertising clutter, differentiate the company or brand, and be memorable. John Mathes, director of brand services at Bancography, a bank branding and positioning consulting company, notes that "The tagline is a hardworking collection of words that should give you that 'aha' moment every time you see or hear it." He reminds marketers that a tagline is your brand's sound bite and is often all you can expect consumers to remember. The importance of slogans in the branding process is also noted by digital marketing manager Kumail Hemani, who notes that they often play an important strategic role in influencing the minds of consumers. His guidelines for creating effective slogans, which are shown in the chart, include recognizing that a slogan is a shadow for a brand as it is used everywhere along with it and thus has a key role in communicating the essence of a brand. He also notes that slogans should be simple, catchy, and predictable as well as connect with the consumer on an emotional level.

Many marketers and their agencies spend a great deal of time and effort developing slogans for their companies and brands, but some experts argue that taglines are becoming less important as many brands do not use them. Brand-building consultant Denise Yohn notes that admired brands such as Starbucks, Whole Foods, and Lululemon do not use slogans whereas Apple has not used its famous "Think different" tagline for many years. Yohn maintains that advertisers relied on slogans more in the past as a way to summarize lengthy ad copy with a memorable catchphrase. However, she argues that many marketers are relying more on targeted social media campaigns and word of mouth and running fewer big campaigns that require taglines. Yohn also points out that taglines work best when a brand's differentiation is derived from a product or service attribute. However, today many brands try to distinguish themselves by connecting with consumers' values and personalities, which can be difficult to convey through a tagline.

The next time you see an ad, pay attention to the tagline and think about whether it communicates anything unique or relevant and/or contributes to the images of the company or brand. If the experts are correct, many will fail to do so. However, those that do can help make a company's or brand's marketing message more memorable and effective and give it a leg up on the competition.

Sources: Laura Ries, "Slogans vs. Taglines: What Is Your Brand's Battle Cry?" *Advertising Age,* November 9, 2015, p. 27; Denis Lee Yohn, "The Death of the Tagline," *Adweek,* September 9, 2013, www.adweek.com/news/advertising-branding/death-tagline-152255; Stephen Winzenburg, "Your Advertising Slogans Are Crummy. Can't You Do Better?" *Advertising Age,* January 14, 2008, p. 15; John Mathes, "Taglines That Stick: Here's How to Create an Effective Brand Summation Line," *ABA Bank Marketing,* December 1, 2008, pp. 22–25; Kumail Hemani, "Impact of Slogans on Branding," *Social Media Today,* March 26, 2012, http://socialmediatoday.com/node/475582.

blueprint, or *creative contract.* The account representative or manager assigned to the account usually prepares the creative brief. In larger agencies, an individual from research or the strategic account planning department may write it. People from the agency team or group assigned to the account, including creative personnel as well as representatives from media and research, have input. The advertising manager and/or the marketing and brand managers from the client side ultimately approve the creative brief. Figure 8–2 shows a sample copy platform outline that can be used to guide the creative process. Just as there are different names for the creative brief, there are variations in the outline and format used and in the level of detail included.

FIGURE 8–2

Creative Brief Outline

1. Basic problem or issue the advertising must address.

2. Advertising and communications objectives.

3. Target audience.

4. Major selling idea or key benefits to communicate.

5. Creative strategy statement (campaign theme, appeal, and execution technique to be used).

6. Supporting information and requirements.

7. Schedule (what is needed and when).

Lambesis

2800 Roosevelt Street, Carlsbad California, 92008 Main 760.547.2333 Fax 760.547.2331 lambesis.com

Creative Brief

Client: Tacori

Assignment
Develop new print concepts for the launch of the 18K925 line by Tacori

Objectives
• Support the long-term goal of growing 18K925 to become 50% of Tacori's business by clearly establishing the new Tacori collection as a more accessible, fashion jewelry line

Target
• Women, Age 25-49, HHI $75K+, Urban dwellers, Brand driven consumers, in market for fashion jewelry for self or as a gift for someone special.

• *What do they currently think?*
  I know and love Tacori as a high-end jewelry brand that's gifted for special occasions (=expressions of love)

• *What do we want them to think?*
  Tacori is also a brand with bold, statement-making, accessible designs that still have that distinctly artisanal Tacori touch (=expressions of style)

Product positioning
Tacori's 18K925 designer jewelry line is the ultimate expression of passion, with modern, accessible style and lasting quality.

Reasons to believe
• Accessible price points between $400 - $3000
• Bold, fun, wearable designs fuse colorful gemstones and gold+silver metals, with classic Tacori design cues
• Distinct Tacori brand name and image

Tonality
Modern meets heirloom, bold, aspirational, unique

Creative considerations
• Develop concepts within the Iconic Passion campaign
• Creative requirements:
  • Demonstrate aspirational, yet attainable luxury
  • Accommodate a variety of product imagery including necklaces, bracelets and/or rings to showcase the range of jewelry
  • Use the Tacori logo
• Other considerations that need be addressed:
  • Concepts must be able to work for print and horizontal OOH and B&W newspaper
  • Concepts need to ensure that retailer tags added to the bottom of the ad are legible

EXHIBIT 8–14A

Creative brief for Tacori jewelry

TACORI

EXHIBIT 8–14B

Print ad created based on creative brief to establish Tacori as an accessible fashion jewelry line

Source: Tacori

Several components of the creative brief were discussed in previous chapters. For example, Chapter 7 examined the DAGMAR model and showed how the setting of advertising objectives requires specifying a well-defined target audience and developing a communication task statement that spells out what message must be communicated to this audience. Determining what problem the product or service will solve or what issue must be addressed in the ad helps in establishing communication objectives for the campaign to accomplish. Two critical components of the brief are the development of the major selling idea and creative strategy development. These two steps are often the responsibility of the creative team or specialist and form the basis of the advertising campaign theme.

Many creative briefs also include supporting information and requirements (brand identifications, disclaimers, and the like) that should appear in any advertising message. This information may be important in ensuring uniformity across various executions of the ads used in a campaign or in meeting any legal requirements. Exhibits 8–14A and B show an example of a creative brief used by the Lambesis agency to create a print campaign for Tacori and an ad that was created based on the brief. As noted in the brief, the primary objective of the advertising for Tacori is to establish the Tacori collection as a more accessible fashion jewelry line.

Obtaining information regarding customers, the product or service, and the market that can be used in developing the creative brief is an important part of the creative planning process. While it is important that this basic information is provided to agency creatives, this may not always occur due to breakdowns in communication on the client as well as the agency side or between the two. John Sutherland, Lisa Duke, and Avery Abernethy developed a model of the flow of marketing information from clients to the agency creative staff, shown in Figure 8–3.[50] The model

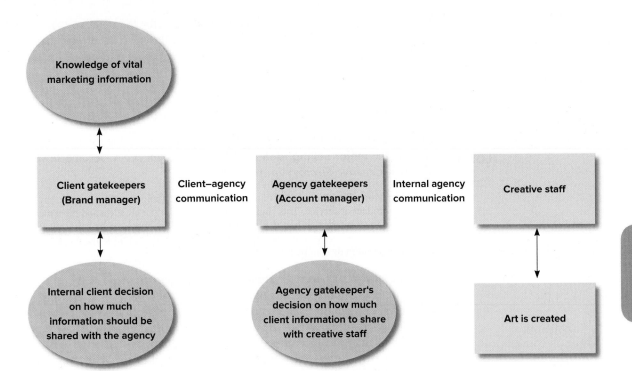

FIGURE 8–3

Model of Marketing Information Flow from the Marketing Manager to the Creative Staff

Source: John Sutherland, Lisa Duke, and Avery Abernethy, "A Model of Marketing Information Flow," *Journal of Advertising* 33, no. 4 (Winter 2004), p. 42. Copyright © 2004 by American Academy of Advertising.

shows that there are five major communication interfaces and decision points where gatekeepers can impede the flow of information to agency creatives.

A great deal of attention has been paid to the client–agency communication interface that occurs between the brand manager and/or advertising manager on the client side and the account manager on the agency side. Communication problems can occur between clients and their agencies, which can make the job of the creative staff much more difficult. However, this model shows that there are four other potential communication interface failure points, including (1) the client or client gatekeeper lacking knowledge of some or all of the information needed for effective advertising; (2) the client deciding not to share with the agency all of the available information that is relevant to creating effective advertising; (3) the agency gatekeeper(s) deciding not to share with creative staffers all of the client information received; and (4) internal agency communication failures that may result in the creative staff not receiving all of the relevant information received from the client.

Sutherland and colleagues conducted an extensive survey of agency creative directors, copywriters, and art directors on the specific types of marketing information that is made available to them for use in developing and executing a creative strategy. They identified six specific types of marketing information, including the demographic profile of the target audience, customer product usage information, client's product performance information, competitors' product performance information, marketing strategy information, and the main selling point supplied by the client. Their study showed that agency creative personnel often lack the information needed to effectively design and execute creative strategies. They found that information in these specific categories was provided to creatives only around one-half to two-thirds of the time. Even the most basic target demographic profile was not provided 30 percent of the time. This study indicates that there is a gap in the information that creative personnel need to develop effective advertising and what they are being provided and points to the need for better communication between clients and agencies.

The information contained in the copy platform provides the creative staff with important background information and the basic elements of the overall advertising strategy. The next step in the creative process is the development of the message strategy and begins with the search for the *big idea* that will build on the strategy and bring it to life. One of the major challenges for the creative team is determining the major selling idea that will be used as the basis of the campaign. We will examine some approaches often used for determining the major selling idea and campaign theme.

The Search for the Major Selling Idea

An important part of creative strategy is determining the central theme that will become the **major selling idea** of the ad campaign. As A. Jerome Jeweler states in his book *Creative Strategy in Advertising*:

> The major selling idea should emerge as the strongest singular thing you can say about your product or service. This should be the claim with the broadest and most meaningful appeal to your target audience. Once you determine this message, be certain you can live with it; be sure it stands strong enough to remain the central issue in every ad and commercial in the campaign.[51]

Some advertising experts argue that for an ad campaign to be effective it must contain a big idea that attracts the consumer's attention, gets a reaction, and sets the advertiser's product or service apart from the competition's. Well-known ad executive John O'Toole describes the *big idea* as "that flash of insight that synthesizes the purpose of the strategy, joins the product benefit with consumer desire in a fresh, involving way, brings the subject to life, and makes the reader or audience stop, look, and listen."[52]

Of course, the real challenge to the creative team is coming up with the big idea to use in the ad. Many products and services offer virtually nothing unique, and it can be difficult to find something interesting to say about them. The late David Ogilvy, generally considered one of the most creative advertising copywriters ever to work in the business, has stated:

> I doubt if more than one campaign in a hundred contains a big idea. I am supposed to be one of the more fertile inventors of big ideas, but in my long career as a copywriter I have not had more than 20, if that.[53]

While really great ideas in advertising are difficult to come by, there are many big ideas that became the basis of very creative, successful advertising campaigns. Classic examples include "We Try Harder," which positioned Avis as the underdog car-rental company that provided better service than Hertz; the "Pepsi Generation" theme and subsequent variations like "The Taste of a New Generation" and "GenerationNext"; the "Be All You Can Be" theme used in recruitment ads for the U.S. Army; the "Intel Inside" campaign for Intel microprocessors that go in personal computers; Nike's "Just Do It"; the "Got Milk?" and milk moustache themes used to promote milk consumption; and Apple's "Think Different" campaign. More recent big ideas that have resulted in great advertising campaigns include the "Priceless" campaign for MasterCard which has helped the company grow brand value and revenue every years since it was launched in 1997, the "I'm Lovin' It!" campaign for McDonald's, and the "Imported From Detroit" campaign for Chrysler which used its big idea to position the company against import automotive brands and tout the revival of U.S. automakers.[54]

Another example of a big idea that became the basis of a long-running and effective IMC program is "The Most Interesting Man in the World" campaign created by Havas Worldwide for Dos Equis beer. Research conducted by the agency with import beer drinkers revealed that they were annoyed by much of the beer advertising, which used images of sexy women, sophomoric humor, and tired clichés. The research also revealed that they felt misrepresented and misunderstood and, more than anything, wanted to be perceived as interesting and conversely, not boring. Based on these insights, the agency creative team came up with a big idea of creating a personality symbol for brand who they labeled "The Most Interesting Man in the World." The agency created a fictitious character played by veteran actor

EXHIBIT 8–15

Dos Equis's "The Most Interesting Man in the World" campaign is an example of an effective big idea

Source: Heineken USA

Jonathan Goldsmith, who is portrayed in the ads as a suave and debonair gentleman with an exotic accent, silver beard, and no-nonsense attitude (Exhibit 8–15). The commercials show him in highly exotic and intriguing situations and locales such as leading mysterious expeditions, running with the bulls in Pamplona, or arm wrestling with Fidel Castro. At the end of every ad he acknowledges that he does not always drink beer, but when he does, he prefers Dos Equis and then delivers the signature line "Stay thirsty my friends." The implied message from the ads is that all beer drinkers could and should be living a more interesting life and, of course, can vicariously do so by drinking Dos Equis.

The campaign launched in 2007 and helped make Dos Equis, which was once a low-profile brand sold mostly in Texas and California, the six largest imported beer in the United States. The final ad featuring Goldsmith aired in 2016 and showed him headed for a one-way trip to Mars, leaving the impression that the character will never come back. He delivers his classic line "Stay Thirsty My Friends" aboard a rocket ship, as the campaign's familiar voiceover states that "his only regret is not knowing what regret feels like." Dos Equis has continued the campaign with a new actor playing the role of the most interesting man.[55]

Big ideas are important in business-to-business advertising, and B2B marketers are recognizing the importance of building awareness as well as a clear brand identity for their companies. B2B marketers such as General Electric, IBM, Xerox, Siemens, and many others also face the challenge of communicating how their products and services can be used to solve complex business problems and help other companies run their businesses and achieve their goals.[56] For example, Siemens, the German-based electronics and engineering company, recently launched a new campaign called "Ingenuity for Life," which is designed to show how its technology impacts not only business, but society as well.[57] The campaign includes print ads as well as videos being shown online and through social media that discuss how Siemens's digital and manufacturing technologies are used in various industries and how they benefit people and communities (Exhibit 8–16).

Developing the Major Selling Idea

EXHIBIT 8–16

Siemens's "Ingenuity for Life" campaign is a big idea for a business-to-business marketer

Source: Siemens AG

It is difficult to pinpoint the inspiration for a big idea or teach advertising creatives an easy way to find one. As noted earlier, Arthur Kover conducted a study of advertising copywriters to understand how they approach the creative process and search for big ideas. He found that they view the purpose of a big idea as breaking through the advertising clutter and delivering a message.[58] Advertising professor John Rossiter argues that most copywriters focus on communicating the *key benefit claim,* which refers to the benefit thought by the copywriter to be the key to selling the advertised product. He notes that most creative ideas are based on finding ways to dramatically and effectively convey the key benefit claim.[59] As noted earlier, the key benefit claim is often explicit in the tagline that is used as the basis for the advertising campaign such as the "I'm Lovin It!" theme for McDonald's or "The Ultimate Driving Machine" for BMW. However, the creative team must still work to develop effective ways to communicate this message in the executions of the advertising and other components of the IMC program.

There are myriad ways that creative personnel can approach the search for big ideas

EXHIBIT 8–17

This ThermaCare ad uses a unique selling proposition

Source: ThermaCare

and how to execute them. However, over the years several classic approaches have emerged that can guide the creative team's search for a major selling idea and the development of effective advertising. Among the four best-known approaches are the following:

- Using a unique selling proposition.
- Creating a brand image.
- Finding the inherent drama.
- Positioning.

Unique Selling Proposition   The concept of the **unique selling proposition (USP)** was developed by Rosser Reeves, former chair of the Ted Bates agency, and is described in his influential book *Reality in Advertising*. Reeves noted three characteristics of unique selling propositions:

1. Each advertisement must make a proposition to the consumer. Not just words, not just product puffery, not just show-window advertising. Each advertisement must say to each reader: "Buy this product and you will get this benefit."
2. The proposition must be one that the competition either cannot or does not offer. It must be unique either in the brand or in the claim.
3. The proposition must be strong enough to move the mass millions, that is, pull over new customers to your brand.[60]

Reeves said the attribute claim or benefit that forms the basis of the USP should dominate the ad and be emphasized through repetitive advertising. An example of a brand that uses a USP approach for its advertising is ThermaCare heatwraps (Exhibit 8–17). The brand has patented heat cells that penetrate to increase circulation and accelerate healing as well as provide relief from back pain, which is a problem for many people.

For Reeves's approach to work, there must be a truly unique product or service attribute, benefit, or inherent advantage that can be used in the claim. The approach may require considerable research on the product and consumers, not only to determine the USP but also to document the claim. As we will see in Chapter 20, the Federal Trade Commission objects to advertisers' making claims of superiority or uniqueness without providing supporting data. Also, some companies have sued their competitors for making unsubstantiated uniqueness claims.[61]

Advertisers must also consider whether the unique selling proposition affords them a *sustainable competitive advantage* that competitors cannot easily copy. In the packaged-goods field in particular, companies quickly match a brand feature for feature, so advertising based on USPs becomes obsolete. For example, a few years ago MillerCoors introduced MGD 64, a 64-calorie version of its Miller Genuine Draft brand and the lowest-calorie domestic beer on the market. However, within a year its major rival Anheuser-Busch launched Bud Select 55, which contained only 55 calories, after noting the success Miller had with its ultra-low-calorie beer.[62]

Creating a Brand Image   In many product and service categories, competing brands are so similar that it is very difficult to find or create a unique attribute or benefit to use as the major selling idea. Many of the packaged-goods products that account for most of the advertising dollars spent in the United States are difficult to differentiate on a functional or performance basis. The creative strategy used to sell these products is based on the development of a strong, memorable identity for the brand through **image advertising**.

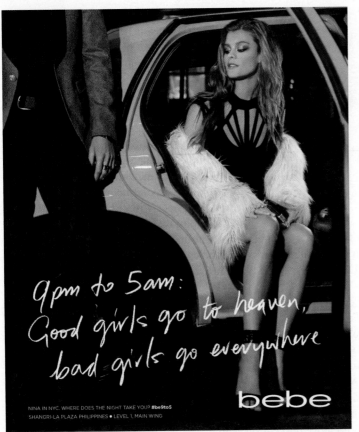

EXHIBIT 8–18

bebe uses advertising to build an image as a sexy and stylish brand

Source: bebe Stores, Inc.

David Ogilvy popularized the idea of brand image in his famous book *Confessions of an Advertising Man*. Ogilvy said that with image advertising, "every advertisement should be thought of as a contribution to the complex symbol which is the brand image." He argued that the image or personality of the brand is particularly important when brands are similar:

> The greater the similarity between brands, the less part reason plays in brand selection. There isn't any significant difference between the various brands of whiskey, or cigarettes, or beer. They are all about the same. And so are the cake mixes and the detergents and the margarines. The manufacturer who dedicates his advertising to building the most sharply defined personality for his brand will get the largest share of the market at the highest profit. By the same token, the manufacturers who will find themselves up the creek are those shortsighted opportunists who siphon off their advertising funds for promotions.[63]

Image advertising has become increasingly popular and is used as the main selling idea for a variety of products and services, including soft drinks, liquor, cigarettes, cars, airlines, financial services, perfume/colognes, and clothing. Many consumers wear various brands of designer jeans, such as True Religion or AG, and drink certain brands of beer or soft drinks because of the image of these brands. The key to successful image advertising is developing an image that will appeal to product users. This is often done by associating a brand with certain symbols or artifacts that have cultural meaning. For example, Marlboro became the leading brand of cigarettes by using advertising that associates the brand with the cowboy, who is perceived as rugged, individualistic, and a symbol of freedom and independence. Many fashion brands build an image by using ads that feature attractive models and visual appeals that convey psychosocial associations and feelings such as sexy, stylish, glamorous, and sophisticated. Advertising for bebe embodies many of these image characteristics as a way of building an emotional connection with young women who are interested in style and fashion (Exhibit 8–18).

Finding the Inherent Drama Another approach to determining the major selling idea is finding the **inherent drama** or characteristic of the product that makes the consumer purchase it. The inherent drama approach expresses the advertising philosophy of Leo Burnett, founder of the Leo Burnett agency in Chicago. Burnett believed that there is almost always something about a brand that separates it from all other brands and keeps it in the marketplace. He argued that this inherent drama "is often hard to find but it is always there, and once found it is the most interesting and believable of all advertising appeals."[64] Burnett believed that good creative minds know how to bring inherent drama to life through advertising based on a foundation of consumer benefits with an emphasis on the dramatic element in expressing those benefits.

Burnett advocated a down-home type of advertising that presents the message in a warm and realistic way. Some of the more famous ads developed by his agency using the inherent-drama approach are for McDonald's, Maytag appliances, Kellogg's cereals, and Hallmark cards. Leo Burnett has created a number of poignant and dramatic advertising campaigns for Hallmark cards over the past 25 years based on the approach. A recent example was the "Put Your Heart to Paper" online campaign for Mother's Day which encouraged people to express how they feel about their

EXHIBIT 8–19

Advertising for Hallmark such as the "Put Your Heart to Paper" campaign often uses inherent drama

Source: Hallmark Licensing, LLC

moms by going beyond the usual stereotypical expressions such as "I Love You" and "Thank You." To capture how much their words meant to them, the participants were interviewed on camera and were unaware their mothers were secretly listening to their loving words in another room. The moms were then invited to join them and the emotional reactions were recorded in a series of videos that became the basis for the ad campaign.[65] Digital ads were used to promote the message: "Don't say, 'I love you . . .' say something more," and put your heart to paper with a Hallmark card. Visitors to a Hallmark website, YouTube channel, and social media sites were encouraged to join in using the hashtag #PutYourHeart-ToPaper. Leo Burnett has created versions of the campaign for other holidays as well such as Valentine's Day, as shown in Exhibit 8–19.

Positioning   The concept of *positioning* as a basis for advertising strategy was introduced by Jack Trout and Al Ries in the early 1970s and has become a popular basis of creative development.[66] The basic idea is that advertising is used to establish or "position" the product or service in a particular place in the consumer's mind. Positioning is done for companies as well as for brands. Many of the top brands in various product and service categories have retained their market leadership because they have established and maintained a strong position or identity in the minds of consumers.[67] For example, Crest has built and maintained the success of its toothpaste based on the position of cavity prevention, while BMW's positioning of its car as "the ultimate driving machine" transcends and helps differentiate its entire product line.

Positioning is also done for entire companies as well as various divisions of large corporations. For example, General Electric positions itself as an innovative and imaginative digital industrial company that is making a difference in the world by building the energy, health, transportation, and technology infrastructure for the new millennium. General Electric recently launched a major campaign designed to reinforce its position as a digital company that brings hardware, software, and big data together and also help recruit young people to join GE. The "What's the Matter with Owen?" campaign includes TV commercials as well as social media ads featuring a college graduate named Owen who has just been hired and is thrilled with his new job as an industrial digital developer for GE. However, his classmates and family don't understand his excitement because they think GE is still only a manufacturing company. For example, in one humorous spot his father gives him a hammer that was his grandfather's, thinking he will be working on building industrial equipment. Each spot ends with "GE, The digital company. That's also an industrial company" (Exhibit 8–20).

EXHIBIT 8–20

General Electric positions itself as an innovative digital industrial company in its recruiting campaign

Source: General Electric

EXHIBIT 8–21

Advertising for Special K reflects the new positioning strategy for the brand

Source: Kellogg Co.

Trout and Ries originally described positioning as the image consumers had of the brand in relation to competing brands in the product or service category, but the concept has been expanded beyond direct competitive positioning. As discussed in Chapter 2, products can be positioned on the basis of product attributes, price/quality, usage or application, product users, cultural symbols, or product class. Any of these can spark a major selling idea that becomes the basis of the creative strategy and results in the brand's occupying a particular place in the minds of the target audience. Since positioning can be done on the basis of a distinctive attribute, the positioning and unique selling proposition approaches can overlap. Positioning approaches have been used as the foundation for a number of successful creative strategies. In some situations marketers recognize that they must adapt their positioning strategy for different market segments or modify it to respond to connect better with their target market. For example, the Kellogg Company has changed its positioning strategy for its Special K cereal brand by moving away from using diet-based appeals to touting its positive nutrition benefits and how it helps women stay strong.[68] For many years, ads for Special K were accompanied by images of scales and diet challenges. However, Kellogg recognized that women no longer want to strictly count calories but rather want to eat foods with broader nutritional benefits. The new tagline for Special K is "Fortify" and the advertising is designed to appeal to the inner strength women exude every day with ads such as the one for new Special K Nourish shown in Exhibit 8–21.

Positioning is often the basis of a firm's creative strategy when it has multiple brands competing in the same market. For example, the two top-selling brands of motor oil, Pennzoil and Quaker State, became part of the same company following a merger a few years ago and are now owned by the Shell Oil Company. The company creates separate identities for the two brands by positioning them differently and targeting a slightly different group of motor oil consumers for each.[69] Pennzoil is positioned as a brand that stands for protection and is targeted at the "Active Specifier" or person who will most likely pay to have their oil changed. Quaker State/Q uses a performance positioning and targets the "Enthusiast" segment that is involved in maintaining their car and will most likely purchase their own oil and install it themselves. Exhibit 8–22 shows ads for each brand reflecting these positioning themes.

EXHIBIT 8–22

Advertising for Pennzoil and Quaker State positions the brands differently

Source: Pennzoil and Quaker State by Shell International B.V.

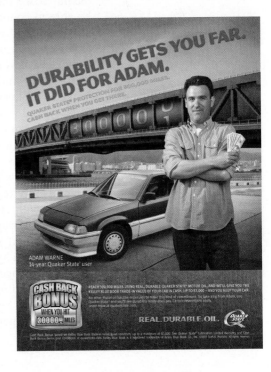

Contemporary Approaches to the Big Idea

The USP, brand image, inherent-drama, and positioning approaches are often used as the basis of the creative strategy for ad campaigns. These creative styles have become associated with some of the most successful creative minds in advertising and their agencies.[70] However, agencies are by no means limited to any one creative approach. For example, the famous "Marlboro Country" campaign, a classic example of image advertising, was developed by Leo Burnett Co. Many different agencies have followed the unique selling proposition approach advocated by Rosser Reeves at Ted Bates. The challenge to the creative specialist or team is to find a major selling idea—whether it is based on a unique selling proposition, brand image, inherent drama, position in the market, or some other approach—and use it as a guide in developing an effective creative strategy.

While these classic approaches are used by many creative specialists, many other styles are available and are indeed necessary given the changes that have occurred in media and technology over the past two decades. Some of the more contemporary advertising visionaries who have had a major influence on modern-day advertising include Hal Riney of Hal Riney & Partners, Lee Clow and Jay Chiat of TBWA/Chiat/Day, Dan Wieden of Wieden+Kennedy, and Jeff Goodby and Rich Silverstein of Goodby, Silverstein & Partners. In describing these creative leaders, Anthony Vagnoni of *Advertising Age* writes:

> The modern creative kings don't write books, rarely give interviews or lay out their theories on advertising. They've endorsed no set of rules, professed no simple maxims like Mr. Ogilvy's famous "When you don't have anything to say, sing it." If pronouncements and books are out the window, what's replaced them is a conscious desire to lift the intelligence level of advertising. Today's leaders see advertising as an uplifting social force, as a way to inspire and entertain.[71]

Goodby and Silverstein note: "Advertising works best when it sneaks into people's lives, when it doesn't look or feel like advertising. It's about treating people at their best, as opposed to dealing with them at their lowest common denominator." They describe their creative formula as doing intelligent work that the public likes to see and that, at the same time, has a sales pitch.[72] Lee Clow says, "No rule book will tell you how to target the masses anymore. The best of us understand the sociocultural realities of people and how they interact with the media. If we didn't, we couldn't make the kinds of messages that people would be able to connect with."[73]

Advertisers are facing major challenges in their search for the big idea in the today's world. They must develop creative ideas that can differentiate their brands and extend beyond traditional mass media. Most marketers and their agencies recognize that they must come up with big ideas that can be used across a variety of media, engage consumers, and enter into a dialogue with them. Many of the approaches that have worked well in the traditional media-centric world of print and television advertising may not be effective in the complex, multiscreen world in which consumers live today. Jean Lin, CEO of the digital network Isobar, argues that technology and accessibility to information has forever changed people's relationship with brands along with how they form perceptions and opinions. She argues that the role of a contemporary creative agency must change, and notes: "In this new world, how we come up with creative solutions has to change. We must embrace interactive and nonlinear messaging. Hand-held devices and mobility means everywhere; stories need to be told seamlessly across screens. And business ideas need to be nurtured through creativity, innovation, and imagination."[74]

The challenge of developing creative advertising that captures the attention of consumers and impacts them has clearly become even greater with the proliferation of new media. Lee Clow, now the chair of TBWA/Media Arts Lab, which is Apple's lead creative agency and the 2013 honoree of the prestigious Lion of St. Mark Award given to an individual for his or her contribution to creativity in advertising, was asked to comment on how advertising has changed over the past several decades and the creative challenge facing agencies. Clow responded as follows: "Brands have the ability to connect with people in all kinds of ways and have an ongoing dialogue and relationship with them as opposed to the monologue, how it used to be. We haven't come close to figuring out how to use all these new-media opportunities and most clients are very conflicted about what media they should use and why. They keep thinking there's some new silver bullet in the new media world that will allow them save money or find a new way to twist consumers' arms."[75] Clow summarizes the challenge facing those who work on the creative side in the new world of advertising quite well. However, marketers will continue to challenge their agencies, as well as themselves, to find innovative ideas and creative solutions for advertising and other forms of marketing communications.

Summary

The creative development and execution of the advertising message are crucial parts of a firm's integrated marketing communications program and are often the key to the success of a marketing campaign. Marketers generally turn to ad agencies to develop, prepare, and implement their creative strategy since these agencies are specialists in the creative function of advertising. The creative specialist or team is responsible for developing an effective way to communicate the marketer's message to the customer. Other individuals on both the client and the agency sides work with the creative specialists to develop the creative strategy, implement it, and evaluate its effectiveness.

The challenge facing the writers, artists, and others who develop ads is to be creative and come up with fresh, unique, and appropriate ideas that can be used as solutions to communications problems. Creativity in advertising is a process of several stages, including preparation, incubation, illumination, verification, and revision. Various sources of information are available to help the creative specialists determine the best campaign theme, appeal, or execution style. Many companies use research for input to the creative process including including qualitative techniques such as focus groups and ethnographic studies. Research is also used to pretest advertising messages to determine how consumers evaluate and will respond to them, although some companies are foregoing copy testing as the changing media consumption environment of consumers requires them to develop more content and move more quickly.

Most advertising is part of a series of messages that make up an IMC or advertising campaign that is based on a central theme or idea. The campaign theme is usually expressed through a slogan or tagline. Creative strategy development is guided by specific goals and objectives and is based on a number of factors, including the target audience, the basic problem the advertising must address, the objectives the message seeks to accomplish, and the major selling idea or key benefit the advertiser wants to communicate. These factors are generally stated in a copy platform, which is a work plan used to guide development of the ad campaign. An important part of creative strategy is determining the major selling idea that will become the central theme of the campaign. There are several approaches to doing this, including using a unique selling proposition, creating a brand image, looking for inherent drama in the brand, and positioning.

Advertisers are facing major challenges in their search big ideas that extend beyond traditional mass media. They must develop big ideas that can be used across a variety of media, engage consumers, and enter into a dialogue with them. Many of the approaches that have worked well in the traditional media-centric world of print and television advertising may not be effective in the complex, multiscreen world in which consumers live today.

Key Terms

creative strategy 266
creative tactics 266
advertising creativity 271
divergence 271
relevance 272
account planning 278
general preplanning input 279
product- or service-specific preplanning
    input 279

problem detection 279
focus groups 280
ethnographic research 282
storyboard 284
animatic 285
advertising campaign 285
campaign theme 285
slogan (tagline) 285
creative brief 286

major selling idea 290
unique selling proposition (USP) 292
image advertising 292
inherent drama 293

Discussion Questions

1. Discuss the creative challenges Intuit and the Wieden+Kennedy agency face in developing advertising campaigns for a tax preparation software product such as TurboTax. Evaluate the creative strategy W+K used for the "It Doesn't Take a Genius to Do Your Taxes" campaign that is discussed in the chapter opener. (LO 8-1, 8-3)

2. Discuss the role and importance of creativity in advertising. Do you think advertising agencies often emphasize creativity at the expense of developing ads that can help generate sales for a product or service? What can clients do to avoid this problem? (LO 8-1)

3. Digital and Social Media Perspective 8–1 discusses some of the advertising campaigns that were selected as the best of the 21st century. Choose one of these campaigns and analyze it from a creative perspective giving attention to the strategy used for the campaign and the reasons why it has been effective. (LO 8-1)

4. The chapter discusses how advertising agencies are sometimes fired even though they create award-winning ads and campaigns for their clients. Evaluate the decision by companies such as AB InBev to dismiss their ad agency and Hire a new one even though the agency has done award winning creative work for the company/brand. (LO 8-1)

5. Advertising creativity is viewed as the ability to generate unique and appropriate ideas that can be used as solutions to communication problems. This definition suggests that a creative ad is one that is novel but also relevant or appropriate. Find an example of an advertisement (either a print ad, TV commercial, or online ad/video) that is novel but not necessarily relevant to the product or service. Discuss why the client would have approved this ad. (LO 8-1)

6. Discuss the various factors that account for the way divergence can be achieved in advertising creativity. Find an example of an advertisement that reflects these various characteristics and explain how it does so. (LO 8-1)

7. Discuss the types of research that can be used by an advertising agency during the preparation, illumination, and incubation stages of the creative process. Find an example of an advertising campaign that has used research as input to the creative process and discuss how it was done. (LO 8-2, 8-3)

8. Many advertising creative personnel are opposed to focus group research as they argue that it may inhibit the creative process. Discuss the problems with, as well as the value of, using focus groups to evaluate advertising creative work. (LO 8-2)

9. Digital and Social Media Perspective 8–2 discusses the pros and cons of pretesting advertising creative work and how it is being impacted by the digital revolution. Discuss the pros and cons of the pretesting of creative work done by agencies and how the shift to digital media is impacting copy testing. (LO 8-2, 8-3)

10. Assume that you have been hired as an account planner by an advertising agency and assigned to work on the advertising campaign for a new brand of bottled water. Describe the various types of general and product-specific preplanning input you might provide to the creative team. (LO 8-2)

11. Discuss the role an advertising slogan plays in the development of an advertising campaign as well as some of the factors that should be considered in developing an effective tagline. Find an example of a good tagline as well as one that does not communicate effectively. Discuss the reasons why you view these as either good or bad examples of advertising slogans. (LO 8-3)

12. Find an example of an ad or campaign that you think reflects one of the approaches used to develop a major selling idea such as unique selling proposition, brand image, inherent drama, or positioning. Discuss how the major selling idea is reflected in this ad or campaign. (LO 8-4)

connect

Digital users can access their personalized and adaptive SmartBook, Ad Forum Video Cases, and interactive exercises to review chapter concepts.

9

Creative Strategy: Implementation and Evaluation

Source: Dasani by The Coca-Cola Company

LEARNING OBJECTIVES

LO1 Compare the different types of appeals used in advertising.

LO2 Identify creative execution styles and their most appropriate applications.

LO3 Compare tactics for the creation of print ads and TV commercials as well as online advertising.

LO4 Discuss guidelines for clients to evaluate creative work.

DASANI: DESIGNED TO MAKE A DIFFERENCE

For many years, the marketing battles in the beverage industry were fought over market share for carbonated soft drinks. During the latter decades of the 20th century Coke and Pepsi traded salvos in the "cola wars" as the two brands dominated the market for soft drinks that have long been America's most popular beverages. Up until the 1990s, bottled water was only a sliver of the U.S. beverage industry and the market was dominated by upscale brands such as Perrier and Evian. However, during the last decade of the millennium beverage consumption patterns were changing as soft drink sales began to stagnate while bottled water became the fastest-growing segment of the mass market beverage category. Beverage companies recognized that consumers were increasingly choosing healthy, convenient, zero-calorie bottled water over other beverages and were launching new products to grab a share of the market.

While the bottled water market was growing rapidly, The Coca-Cola Company was skeptical as to whether consumers would be willing to buy bottled water and remained focused on soft drinks and other beverages. But the success of Pepsi's Aquafina, Nestlé's Poland Spring, and other brands in the fast-growing market finally moved the soft-drink giant to change course and enter the bottled water market. The Coca-Cola Company launched DASANI bottled water in 1999. Strong growth in the bottled water category, along with The Coca-Cola Company's extensive distribution system, helped the brand achieve 20 percent compounded growth through 2006 and become a $1 billion brand in retail sales. However, by 2007 the marketing environment for bottled water was beginning to change. Mainstream brands such as DASANI, Aquafina, Arrowhead, and others had become more commoditized and began losing market share to private label brands and enhanced water beverage brands, such as **vitamin**water®. The Coca-Cola Company found its DASANI brand stuck in the middle and being squeezed between premium, prestige brands such as **smart**water®, Voss, ETHOS, FIJJI and EVIAn and low/value-priced private label brands. The bottled water category was also facing environmental concerns with many consumers and retailers questioning the sheer number of brands on the market and the disposal of plastic bottles. By 2009, Walmart and other major retailers began dropping DASANI and other mainstream brands of bottled water.

In 2009, The Coca-Cola Company retained Lambesis as the new advertising agency for the DASANI brand. Lambesis quickly recognized that its first challenge was to defend against the market squeeze from the high- and low-end brands, which required positioning DASANI bottled water as the most aspirational, yet accessible mainstream brand. The bottled water category was dominated by competitors making taste claims as well as functional or wellness claims which proved to be difficult to credibly or successfully sustain. Research conducted as part of the strategic account planning process found that heavy bottled water users didn't think about "water" in terms of a bottled beverage, but instead as something that invigorates the mind, body, and soul. They also view the functional benefits of water as something more fundamental, as water is viewed as a life-giving source. Based on these findings Lambesis developed an integrated marketing communications strategy to position DASANI bottled water as the feel-good, crisp-tasting companion that invigorates you—whenever, wherever—helping body and mind stay refreshed and feel good during all moments throughout the day.

The Coca-Cola Company and Lambesis also recognized that the environmental concerns regarding bottled water also had to be addressed and could be a point of differentiation. Coca-Cola had created PlantBottle® packaging, a 100 percent recyclable bottle made from up to 30 percent plant-based material that was being used for some of its other beverages. The Company was ready to reintroduce its DASANI brand in this new, more environmentally friendly bottle and knew that the launch had to make the brand likable and relevant to both consumers as well as retailers. Lambesis recognized that the relaunch campaign could serve the DASANI brand in two ways—by appealing to "light green" consumers who were seeking simple ways to be more environmentally conscious and by positioning the DASANI brand as a more premium brand in the highly competitive bottled water market. The agency created a fully integrated rebranding campaign that combined environmentally conscious messaging with premium high design to celebrate the DASANI brand, the PlantBottle packaging, and the brand's sustainability platform. A sleek and minimalist aesthetic was used throughout all of the creative work to reflect the pure, clean, refreshing feeling of water. Lambesis utilized these design elements for the website as well as for high-impact online display ads, both of which helped educate consumers about the PlantBottle packaging.

Print and outdoor advertising used for the campaign centered around an impactful image of natural plant life "growing" the PlantBottle packaging. Lambesis created an innovative print insert on 100 percent recycled paper with a peel-off plantable seeded paper leaf to showcase the environmentally conscious design of the packaging. Seeded leaf paper with eco-conscious messaging was also placed on products in retail stores to further communicate DASANI's commitment to sustainability. The integrated campaign also used television advertising, as the first TV spot used bright, clean, nature-inspired imagery to showcase the brand's commitment to being more sustainable and to portray DASANI bottled water as clean, crisp, and refreshing. A second spot was set to music from the classic Chubby Checker song "The Twist" and leveraged its enduring appeal to demonstrate to consumers how easy it is to twist and recycle the new PlantBottle packaging. The entertaining "Twist" spot ranked as the second most memorable commercial that aired during the 2012 Olympic Games in research conducted by Ace Metrix, rating higher than spots for companies and brands such as Nike, Samsung, and Old Spice that aired much more frequently.

The integrated campaign was very successful as it helped the DASANI line regain distribution in key retail accounts and positioned it as the mass prestige brand that stands out as the clear choice between higher-priced premium brands and lower-priced private label options. Building on the successful repositioning of DASANI bottled water, The Coca-Cola Company launched a new product named DASANI Drops® which is a zero-calorie flavor enhancer with various flavors that can be added to water. DASANI Drops flavor enhancers give consumers a new way to enjoy drinking water by enhancing the taste of water with a simple squeeze of an easy-to-carry bottle and targets mothers and health-conscious people who are very busy with their daily routine. An integrated campaign themed "Turn Your Flavor On" supported the introduction of the Dasani Drops enhancers, and included print, digital, and outdoor advertising along with in-store promotions and sampling at stores, on college campuses, and at concerts.

The successful repositioning of DASANI has made the brand the market leader in the bottled water category and The Coca-Cola Company decided to leverage the brand equity created through the excellent integrated marketing campaigns by introducing DASANI Sparkling, a carbonated water beverage. The new product is produced by adding carbonation to filtered water, has no sweeteners, and comes naturally flavored with lime, lemon, berry, and apple. The Coca-Cola Company was already selling Seagram's Sparkling Seltzer water in bottles and cans but decided to introduce the DASANI line extension to take advantage of the brand's strong identity as well as the strong growth in carbonated water, which is one of the fastest-growing segments of the beverage industry. For many years, sparkling water was associated with the higher-end Perrier brand, which is naturally carbonated spring water from France, as well as San Pellegrino from Italy. However, the market has become more crowded with brands such as LaCroix as well as some sparkling waters such as Cascade Ice and AquaFina FlavorSplash which are artificially sweetened. In 2016 The Coca-Cola Company debuted new flavors and introduced fresh packaging for the DASANI Sparkling line and supported these efforts with an integrated marketing campaign called "Break for Bubbles" which encourages people to take a break from everyday stresses with a refreshing beverage. The integrated marketing campaign includes television, digital, print, and out of home advertising that delivers a message of how the DASANI Sparkling brand enlivens any moment with a refreshing and rejuvenating escape so you can renew, recharge, and restart your day fresh.

Over the past seven years the excellent creative work done by the Lambesis agency has helped propel DASANI bottled water from a brand that was struggling to avoid commodity status to the highest-ranked branded water in dollar volume. Moreover, bottled water has become the fastest-growing mass market beverage category in the United States with annual sales of nearly $15 billion. The DASANI brands have also become an important part of the Coca-Cola Company's product portfolio as consumers continue to move toward healthy, convenient, and refreshing beverages. And as they do so, DASANI bottled water will be there to deliver pure, crisp taste with a clean, fresh style.

Sources: The Lambesis Agency; Nielsen Scanning, YTD AMC, July 30 2016; Elizabeth Whitman, "The Ad Campaign That Convinced Consumers to Pay for Water," *Priceonomics*, June 2016, http://priceonomics.com/the-ad-campaign-that-convinced-americans-to-pay/; Betsy McKay, "Pepsi, Coke Take Opposite Tacks in Bottled Water Marketing Battle," *The Wall Street Journal*, April 18, 2002, www.wsj.com/articles/SB1019079736646644200.

APPEALS AND EXECUTION STYLES

The **advertising appeal** refers to the approach used to attract the attention of consumers and/or to influence their feelings toward the product, service, or cause. An advertising appeal can also be viewed as "something that moves people, speaks to their wants or needs, and excites their interest."[1] The **creative execution style** is the way a particular appeal is turned into an advertising message presented to the consumer. According to William Weilbacher:

> The appeal can be said to form the underlying content of the advertisement, and the execution the way in which that content is presented. Advertising appeals and executions are usually independent of each other; that is, a particular appeal can be executed in a variety of ways and a particular means of execution can be applied to a variety of advertising appeals. Advertising appeals tend to adapt themselves to all media, whereas some kinds of executional devices are more adaptable to some media than others.[2]

Advertising Appeals

Many different appeals can be used as the basis for advertising messages. At the broadest level, these approaches are generally broken into two categories: informational/rational appeals and emotional appeals. In this section, we focus on ways to use rational and emotional appeals as part of a creative strategy. We also consider how rational and emotional appeals can be combined in developing the advertising message.

Informational/Rational Appeals **Informational/rational appeals** focus on the consumer's practical, functional, or utilitarian need for the product or service and emphasize features of a product or service and/or the benefits or reasons for owning or using a particular brand. The content of these messages emphasizes facts, learning, and the logic of persuasion.[3] Rational-based appeals tend to be informative, and advertisers using them generally attempt to convince consumers that their product or service has a particular attribute(s) or provides a specific benefit that satisfies their needs. Their objective is to persuade the target audience to buy the brand because it is the best available or does a better job of meeting consumers' needs. For example, Exhibit 9–1 shows an ad for the Honda Accord that uses a rational appeal by promoting the fact that it was named to the 10 Best list by *Car and Driver* magazine, a very influential automotive magazine, and has received this honor a record 30 times.

Many rational motives can be used as the basis for advertising appeals, including comfort, convenience, economy, health, and sensory benefits such as touch, taste, and smell. Other rational motives or purchase criteria commonly used in advertising include quality, dependability, durability, efficiency, efficacy, and performance. The particular features, benefits, or evaluative criteria that are important to consumers and can serve as the basis of an informational/rational appeal vary from one product or service category to another as well as among various market segments.

Weilbacher identified several types of advertising appeals that fall under the category of rational approaches, among them feature, competitive advantage, price, news, and product/service popularity appeals.

Ads that use a *feature appeal* focus on the dominant traits of the product or service. These ads tend to be highly informative and present the customer with a number of important product attributes or features that will lead to favorable attitudes and can be used as the basis for a rational purchase decision. Technical and high-involvement products such as automobiles often use this type of advertising appeal. However, a feature appeal can be used for a

EXHIBIT 9–1

A rational appeal is used to promote the awards received by the popular Honda Accord

Source: American Honda Motor Co., Inc. and Rubin Postaer and Associates

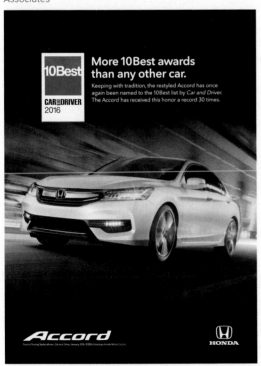

TURNS ZZZ'S INTO A'S.

Red Bull Energy Drink is a unique combination of Taurine, Glucuronolactone, B-vitamins and other important nutrients. It improves performance, increases endurance and concentration, improves reaction speed and stimulates the metabolism. In short, Red Bull vitalizes both body and mind.

RED BULL GIVES YOU WIIINGS.

EXHIBIT 9–2

Red Bull uses a feature appeal to promote its product benefits to students

Source: Red Bull GmbH

EXHIBIT 9–3

Southwest Airlines uses a variation of a price appeal in the "Transfarency" campaign

Source: Southwest Airlines Co.

variety of products and services. These types of appeals often show how product attributes can result in specific benefits for consumers. For example, Exhibit 9–2 shows an ad for Red Bull that focuses on the various ingredients contained in the energy drink and the benefits they provide such as enhanced performance, endurance, and concentration. This particular ad is targeted to students, who are an important target market for energy drinks, and suggests that Red Bull can help you stay awake and alert when studying for exams.

When a *competitive advantage appeal* is used, the advertiser makes either a direct or an indirect comparison to another brand (or brands) and usually claims superiority on one or more attributes. This type of appeal was discussed in Chapter 6 under Comparative Advertising.

A *favorable price appeal* makes the price offer the dominant point of the message. Price appeal advertising is used most often by retailers to announce sales, special offers, or low everyday prices. Price appeal ads are often used by national advertisers, particularly during during economic down times or to reach price sensitive market segments. Most fast-food chains have made price an important part of their marketing strategy through promotional deals and "value menus" or lower overall prices, and their advertising strategy is designed to communicate this. Price-based appeals are also often used by business-to-business marketers to advertise products and/or services and promote their value or affordability. Many other types of advertisers use price appeals as well, such as airlines and car-rental companies. For example, Southwest Airlines recently used a variation of a price appeal with its "Transfarency" campaign with ads such as the one shown in Exhibit 9–3. The goal of the campaign, which coins a word for transparency in airfares, is that Southwest tells customers up front what to expect in terms of fees and doesn't surprise them with hidden charges.

News appeals are those in which some type of news or announcement about the product, service, or company dominates the ad. This type of appeal can be used for a new product or service or to inform consumers of significant modifications or improvements. This appeal works best when a company has important news it wants to communicate to its target market. For example, airlines sometimes use news appeals when they begin offering service to new cities or opening new routes as a way of informing consumers as well as generating media interest that can result in publicity for them.

Product/service popularity appeals stress the popularity of a product or service by pointing out the number of consumers who use the brand, the number who have switched to it, the number of experts who recommend it, or its leadership position in the market. The main point of this type of advertising appeal is that the wide use of the brand proves its quality or value and other customers should consider using it. The ad shown in Exhibit 9–4 uses a popularity appeal by noting how the TaylorMade M1 and M2 drivers are played by more professional golfers on tour than any other brand. Ads such as this are used to implement TaylorMade's marketing strategy, which focuses on innovation, the technological superiority of its golf equipment, and the popularity and use of its clubs by tour professionals who exert a strong influence on the purchase decisions of amateur golfers. This particular ad features professional tour player Jason Day who is one of the top golfers in the world.

Emotional Appeals **Emotional appeals** relate to the customers' social and/or psychological needs for purchasing a product or service. Many consumers' motives for their purchase decisions are emotional, and their feelings about a brand can be more important than knowledge

of its features or attributes. Advertisers for many products and services view rational, information-based appeals as dull. Many advertisers believe appeals to consumers' emotions work better at selling brands that do not differ markedly from competing brands, since rational differentiation of them is difficult.[4]

Many feelings or needs can serve as the basis for advertising appeals designed to influence consumers on an emotional level, as shown in Figure 9–1. These appeals are based on the psychological states or feelings directed to the self (such as pleasure or excitement), as well as those with a more social orientation (such as status or recognition). The ad shown in Exhibit 9–5, featuring actor/singer Victoria Justice, appeals to emotional motives such as self-esteem and pride and is part of the "Body by Milk" integrated marketing campaign created by America's Milk Processors. The ads are targeted at teens and designed to educate them about the nutritional benefits of milk and how it can help them look their best.

Advertisers can use emotional appeals in many ways in their creative strategy. Kamp and Macinnis note that commercials often rely on the concept of *emotional integration*, whereby they portray the characters in the ad as experiencing an emotional

FIGURE 9–1

Bases for Emotional Appeals

Personal States or Feelings		Social-Based Feelings
Safety	Arousal/stimulation	Recognition
Security	Sorrow/grief	Status
Fear	Pride	Respect
Love	Achievement/accomplishment	Involvement
Affection	Self-esteem	Embarrassment
Happiness	Actualization	Affiliation/belonging
Joy	Pleasure	Rejection
Nostalgia	Ambition	Acceptance
Sentiment	Comfort	Approval
Excitement		

Look good. Feel victorious. got milk?

EXHIBIT 9–5

This milk ad appeals to emotional motives such as self-esteem and pride

Source: The California Milk Advisory Board

benefit or outcome from using a product or service.[5] Ads using humor, sex, and other appeals that are very entertaining, arousing, upbeat, and/or exciting can affect the emotions of consumers and put them in a favorable frame of mind. Many TV advertisers use poignant ads that bring a lump to viewers' throats. Hallmark, Campbell's Soup, Nike, and McDonald's often create commercials that evoke feelings of warmth, nostalgia, and/or sentiment. Marketers use emotional appeals in hopes that the positive feeling they evoke will transfer to the brand and/or company. Research shows that positive mood states and feelings created by advertising can have a favorable effect on consumers' evaluations of a brand.[6] Studies also show that emotional advertising is better remembered than nonemotional messages.[7]

The effectiveness of emotion-based appeals has also been documented in research conducted by Hamish Pringle and Peter Field and is discussed in their book *Brand Immortality*.[8] Pringle and Field analyzed 880 case studies of successful advertising campaigns submitted for the United Kingdom–based Institute of Practitioners in Advertising Effectiveness Award competition over the past three decades and included campaigns from the UK as well as international competitions. Their analysis compared advertising campaigns that relied primarily on emotional appeals versus those that used rational persuasion and information. A key finding from their study is that advertising campaigns with purely emotional content are nearly twice as likely to generate large profit gains than campaigns using only rational content. The emotional-only campaigns were also more effective than those that used a combination of emotional and rational content. Their research also showed that one of the reasons why emotional campaigns work so well is that they reduce price sensitivity and strengthen the ability of brands to charge a price premium which contributes to profitability. They also found that emotional campaigns continue to work well during economic downturns such as the recent global recession.[9]

While emotional appeals are often executed through television commercials, many marketers are now implementing them online through videos that provide an opportunity for popular messages to go viral. An example of this is the "Love Has No Labels" public service advertising campaign that was sponsored by the Ad Council, to get people to examine and challenge their own prejudices and biases. The digital agency R/GA created a three-minute video for the campaign by filming at a live event in which a large x-ray screen depicts different sets of people as only two skeletons embracing. As the skeleton images separate and walk out from behind the screen, the audience discovers who they really are (Exhibit 9–6). This process occurs a number of times in the video, each highlighting different pairings of gender, race, sexual orientation, religion, ability, and age to encourage viewers' to take a closer look at their own expectations and implicit bias. The heartwarming video uses the song "She Keeps Me Warm" by Mary Lambert to help set the sentimental tone for the message. The video amassed more than 110 million views online and is the second most viewed community and activism campaign of all time.[10]

Another reason for using emotional appeals is to influence consumers' interpretations of their product usage experience. One way of doing this is through what is known as transformational advertising. A **transformational ad** is defined as "one which associates the experience of using (consuming) the advertised brand with a unique set of psychological characteristics which would not typically be associated with the brand experience to the same degree without exposure to the advertisement."[11]

Transformational ads create feelings, images, meanings, and beliefs about the product or service that may be activated when consumers use it, transforming their interpretation of the usage experience. Christopher Puto and William Wells note that a transformational ad has two characteristics:

1. It must make the experience of using the product richer, warmer, more exciting, and/or more enjoyable than that obtained solely from an objective description of the advertised brand.
2. It must connect the experience of the advertisement so tightly with the experience of using the brand that consumers cannot remember the brand without recalling the experience generated by the advertisement.[12]

Transformational advertising can help differentiate a product or service by making the consumption experience more enjoyable by suggesting the type of experiences consumers might have when they consume the product or service. This type of advertising is often used by companies in the travel industry to help consumers envision the experience or feeling they might have when they take a trip such as a cruise or visit a particular destination.

Image advertising, which is designed to give a company or brand a unique association or personality, is often transformational in nature. It is designed to create a certain feeling or mood that is activated when a consumer uses a particular product or service. An excellent example of this type of advertising is the "Find Your Beach" campaign for the import beer brand Corona Extra. Advertising for Corona over the years has helped establish the brand as the beer to drink when relaxing on a white-sand tropical beach. The "Find Your Beach" campaign extends this theme to other consumption situations by showing people enjoying Corona on a city rooftop, during a break from skiing, on an airplane, or in a bar in the city with a group of friends. However, the final scene in all of the spots takes the viewer back to the familiar tropical-beach scene and concludes with an onscreen super that instructs viewers to "Find your beach." The ads are designed to preserve Corona's iconic beach image while extending the Corona state of mind beyond the sun, sand, and surf. The campaign also includes print ads that help position the brand as a little more urban, and are designed to appeal to consumers in major markets[13] (Exhibit 9–7).

MARKETERS USE VIRTUAL REALITY TO CREATE IMMERSIVE EXPERIENCES FOR CONSUMERS

Distracted driving has become a tremendous problem in countries around the world; sending or reading a text message or talking on a cell phone while behind the wheel of a car can be deadly. Studies show that those who text while driving are much more likely to be involved in a crash, yet people of all ages continue to ignore the warning and pleas not to do so. In 2010 telecommunications giant AT&T launched the "It Can Wait" campaign, which has a simple message: "Keep your eyes on the road, not your phone." The campaign has included a variety of IMC tools such as TV commercials, a website (itcanwait.com), online videos that tell the intimate story of people whose lives were changed forever by people who were texting while driving, and even mobile apps that can provide a shortcut message to respond when in the car ("#X I'm about to drive. Will text you when I'm done.").

The "It Can Wait" campaign has had to evolve as smartphone driving distractions have grown beyond texting to include social media posting, web surfing, video chatting, e-mailing, and more. So in 2015 AT&T turned to a more powerful tool to get people to realize the consequences of distracted driving—*virtual reality (VR)*, which is a fully immersive digital simulated environment that gives the user feeling and sensation of being in it. AT&T launched a nationwide virtual reality tour to help people understand that it's not possible to drive safely while using a smartphone and to immerse them in the horrific sensation of being in a car accident.

As part of the tour, people had the chance to immerse themselves in the world of distracted driving by strapping on a VR headset and getting behind the wheel of a car that drives along suburban streets as the driver narrowly misses everyday obstacles—such as kids in crosswalks, cyclists, joggers, and other vehicles—as he reads and sends text messages. The distracted driving ends with a devastating sensation when the car is involved in a wreck and its airbag explodes as the driver is shown being thrown around the inside of the vehicle. The company that created the VR experience for AT&T also has developed an app that can be downloaded to a mobile device and watched using a Google Cardboard VR viewer.

AT&T is not the only company using the immersive power of virtual reality. The United States Soccer Federation redesigned its most conspicuous symbol, the red, white, and blue crest that adorns the jerseys of the men's and women's national teams. When the time came to unveil the new crest, the federation elected to bypass the traditional news media channels and deliver a more immersive VR experience directly to soccer fans. USSF worked with STRIVR Labs, a company that specializes in developing applications of VR for sports training and fan experiences, to create a promotional video that allows the viewer to experience what it is like to be a player on the U.S. national team by participating in a training session and going inside the locker room with the U.S. National team. The video, along with a Google Cardboard VR viewer and USSF scarf, was sent to 8,000 registered club supporters as well as an additional 2,000 development academy players and other soccer fans across the country.

STRIVR has also created fan experience videos for a number of professional sports teams including the Boston Red

Combining Rational and Emotional Appeals In many advertising situations, the decision facing the creative specialist is not whether to choose an emotional or a rational appeal but, rather, determining how to combine the two approaches. As noted copywriters David Ogilvy and Joel Raphaelson have stated:

> Few purchases of any kind are made for entirely rational reasons. Even a purely functional product such as laundry detergent may offer what is now called an emotional benefit—say, the satisfaction of seeing one's children in bright, clean clothes. In some product categories the rational element is small. These include soft drinks, beer, cosmetics, certain personal care products, and most old-fashioned products. And who hasn't experienced the surge of joy that accompanies the purchase of a new car?[14]

Consumer purchase decisions are often made on the basis of both emotional and rational motives, and attention must be given to both elements in developing effective advertising. Purchase decisions regarding services can also be based on both rational and emotional motives. For example, many consumers choose an airline based on factors such as price, availability, arrival and/or departure time, and the ability to earn miles or points for their travel. However, airlines recognize that it is also important to appeal to emotional factors in competing for passengers. Frequent flyers in particular often become loyal to one airline based on emotional as well as

© STRIVR Labs, Inc.

Sox baseball team, New England Patriots of the NFL, and New York Rangers of the National Hockey League. The VR experience developed for the Rangers made it possible for a fan to experience what it is like to be an NHL goalie in Madison Square Garden. STRIVR partnered with MSG to develop the world's first virtual reality goaltender simulator, which was set up on a concourse inside the arena, and allowed viewers to put on the goaltender equipment in the team's locker room before going onto the ice and then attempting to stop a series of shots from actual Rangers players. Afterward they were sent an e-mail with their stats and a photo showing them in goal.

A number of retailers are also using virtual reality by adding an experiential dimension to in-store shopping. For example, North Face has set up VR viewing stations in some of its stores and shoppers can watch videos that show what it is like to rock climb in Yosemite National Park and the Moab Desert in Utah or climb mountains in Nepal. The VR experience is designed to let people see the beauty of these places as well as get them excited and motivated to purchase outdoor gear such as hiking boots and apparel.

Toms Shoes is using virtual reality as part of its one-for-one campaign through which it donates a pair of shoes to needy children for every pair it sells. The company has put VR headsets into more than 100 stores around the world so shoppers can watch panoramic views of a schoolyard in Peru as children are given a pair of Toms shoes. VR allows the viewers to experience their excitement while creating a sense of altruism.

Many experts feel that virtual reality is going to revolutionize the way we live, play, learn, and shop as marketers continue to find ways to connect with consumers through the new technology. Facebook is betting big on virtual reality; the company paid $2 billion in 2014 to purchase Oculus Rift which makes high-end VR headsets and is developing handheld controllers that let users see and incorporate their hands in VR games and other experiences. Samsung, Sony, HTC, and Google are also investing heavily in VR. Several companies are developing online ads that utilize VR and in the future it is likely that we will be immersed in TV commercials rather than just watching them. There is a scene in the hit movie *The Matrix* that may be applicable to the current state of VR as Morpheus says to Meo: "Unfortunately, no one can be told what the Matrix is. You have to see it for yourself." The same holds true for virtual reality, but it is very likely that marketers will make sure we not only see it, but experience their companies and brands through it as well.

Sources: Shan Li, "Introducing Shoppers to a New Reality," *Los Angeles Times*, April 10, 2016, www.latimes.com/business/la-fi-retail-vr-20160410-story.html; Zach Shonburn, "U.S. Soccer's Rebranding Gets an Assist from Virtual Reality," *The New York Times*, February 29, 2016, http://mobile.nytimes.com/2016/02/29/business/media/us-soccers-rebranding-gets-an-assist-from-virtual-reality.html?referer=https://www.google.com/; Steve Hall, "AT&T Adds Virtual Reality Component to 'It Can Wait' Campaign," *Marketing Land*, July 20, 2015, http://marketingland.com/att-adds-virtual-reality-component-can-wait-campaign-135749.

rational motives, and some airlines use ads that are designed to connect to these travelers on an emotional level. For example, Delta has been running its "Keep Climbing" campaign since 2010 and is a declaration of the company's commitment to making flying better where the airline is headed. The TV commercials, videos, and print and online ads used in the campaign show how Delta is keeping up with the needs of travelers and helping them navigate through their entire travel experience. For example, the ad shown in Exhibit 9–8 promotes how Delta is adding Wi-Fi on all long-haul international flights.

Marketers continue to search for ways to connect with consumers on an emotional level. One way of doing so is by using the emerging technology of virtual reality (VR) to interact with consumers and immerse them into different environments. Digital and Social Media Perspective 9–1 discusses how a number of companies are using VR to transform consumer experiences that are relevant to their products and services.

Additional Types of Appeals   Not every ad fits neatly into the categories of rational or emotional appeals. For example, ads for some brands can be classified as **reminder advertising**, which has the objective of building brand awareness and/or keeping the brand name in front of consumers. Well-known brands and market

EXHIBIT 9-8

Advertising for Delta Air Lines often appeals to emotional as well as rational motives

Source: Delta Air Lines, Inc.

EXHIBIT 9-9

This clever ad reminds active people of the nutritional value of California almonds

Source: Almond Board of California

leaders often use reminder advertising to maintain top-of-mind awareness among consumers in their target markets. For example, the Almond Board of California runs ads such as the one shown in Exhibit 9–9 in men's and women's health- and fitness-oriented magazines to remind active people about the nutritional value of almonds and how they are an excellent source of protein. Products and services that have a seasonal pattern to their consumption also use reminder advertising, particularly around the appropriate period. For example, marketers of candy products often increase their media budgets and run reminder advertising around Halloween, Valentine's Day, Christmas, and Easter.

Online ads often serve as a form of reminder advertising. Many of the banner ads that are pervasive on Internet websites have very low click-through rates but still can be effective and serve a valuable function by fostering familiarity, even though most consumers may never click through to the source of the ads. Research into the psychology of online advertising has shown that repeated exposure to banner advertising can enhance familiarity with and generate positive feelings toward a brand.[15] These favorable feelings often occur through what psychologists have identified as the *mere exposure effect*, whereby repeated exposure to a stimulus (such as a brand name) can result in favorable feelings toward it.[16] While digital advertising may have positive effects through the incidental exposure that takes place when consumers visit a website, many advertising experts argue that consumers tune out most of the banner ads, as well as other forms of Internet advertising. They note that it is becoming increasingly difficult to get people visiting a website to attend to, let alone engage with, digital ads.[17]

Advertisers introducing a new product often use **teaser advertising**, which is designed to build curiosity, interest, and/or excitement about a product or brand by talking about it but not actually showing it. Teasers, or *mystery ads* as they are sometimes called, are also used by marketers to draw attention to upcoming product launches and/or advertising campaigns and generate interest and publicity for them.

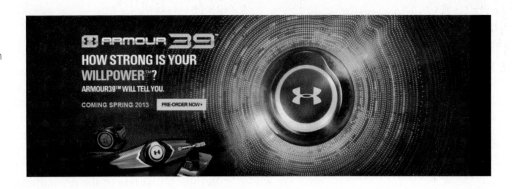

CHAPTER 9

For example, Under Armour has used teaser ads to create interest and excitement around new product introductions such as running and basketball shoes. The company recently used teaser ads as part of its prelaunch campaign for its Armour39™ performance monitoring system, as shown in Exhibit 9–10.

Teaser ads also are often used for new movies or TV shows and for major product launches. They are especially popular among automotive advertisers for introducing a new model or announcing significant changes in a vehicle. A recent study by Thorbjorsen and his colleagues found that online teaser advertising pre-announcing a new product is more effective in generating product interest and positive word of mouth than merely advertising a new product at the time of launch.[18] While teaser campaigns can generate interest in a new product, advertisers must be careful not to extend them too long or they will lose their effectiveness. As one advertising executive says, "Contrary to what we think, consumers don't hold seminars about advertising. You have to give consumers enough information about the product in teaser ads to make them feel they're in on the joke."[19]

Another form of advertising that is becoming increasingly popular is **user-generated content (UGC)**, whereby ads are created by consumers rather than by the company and/or its agency.[20] A number of marketers have developed contests that involve having consumers create ads and submit them for consideration. As discussed in Chapter 5, Frito-Lay was one of the first marketers to use UGC on a major level when it sponsored a "Crash the Super Bowl" creative competition and ran a user-generated ad that was entirely conceived and produced by amateurs rather than advertising professionals. A number of other marketers have made UGC part of their advertising campaigns by using TV commercial or print ads that have been crowdsourced. However, Ford took the use of UGC to an entirely new level by making all of the TV, print, and digital advertising used to launch its 2014 Fiesta model crowdsourced.[21] The reason for having the campaign entirely based on UGC was to extend the rekindling of the "Fiesta Movement" beyond social media platforms and make it a totally integrated campaign. Exhibit 9–11 shows one of the UGC ads created as part of the campaign. The increasing use of digital and social media such as YouTube, Facebook, and Snapchat is likely to result in greater use of UGC by marketers as a way of getting consumers involved with their brands.[22]

Many ads are not designed to sell a product or service but rather to enhance the image of the company or meet other corporate goals such as soliciting investment or recruiting employees. These are generally referred to as corporate image advertising and are discussed in detail in Chapter 17.

Advertising Execution

Once the specific advertising appeal that will be used as the basis for the advertising message has been determined, the creative specialist or team begins its execution. *Creative execution* is the way an advertising appeal is presented.

While it is obviously important for an ad to have a meaningful appeal or message to communicate to the consumer, the manner in which the ad is executed is also important.

One of the best-known advocates of the importance of creative execution in advertising was William Bernbach, founder of the Doyle Dane Bernbach agency. In his famous book on the advertising industry, *Madison Avenue*, Martin Mayer notes Bernbach's reply to David Ogilvy's rule for copywriters that "what you say in advertising is more important than how you say it." Bernbach replied, "Execution can become content, it can be just as important as what you say. A sick guy can utter some words and nothing happens; a healthy vital guy says them and they rock the world."[23] Bernbach was one of the revolutionaries of his time who changed advertising creativity on a fundamental level by redefining how headlines and visuals were used, how art directors and copywriters worked together, and how advertising could be used to arouse feelings and emotions.

An advertising message can be presented or executed in numerous ways. We will examine some of the most frequently used execution approaches including the following:

- Straight-sell or factual message
- Scientific/technical evidence
- Demonstration
- Comparison
- Testimonial
- Slice of life
- Animation
- Personality symbol
- Imagery
- Dramatization
- Humor
- Combinations

EXHIBIT 9–12

This ad for the Mach3 Sensitive razor uses a creative straight-sell execution

Source: Gillette by Procter & Gamble

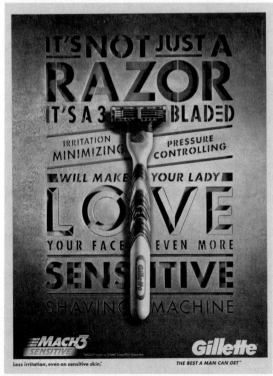

Straight-Sell or Factual Message One of the most basic types of creative executions is the straight-sell or factual message. This type of ad relies on a straightforward presentation of information concerning the product or service. The execution is often used with informational/rational appeals, where the focus of the message is the product or service and its specific attributes and/or benefits.

Straight-sell executions are commonly used in print ads. A picture of the product or service occupies part of the ad, and the factual copy takes up the rest of the space. They are also used in TV advertising, with an announcer generally delivering the sales message while the product/service is shown on the screen. Ads for high-involvement consumer products as well as industrial and other business-to-business products generally use this format. Straight-sell advertising executions are often used for various types of consumer products and services as well and can be very effective when done creatively. For example, the ad for the Gillette Mach3 Sensitive razor shown in Exhibit 9–12 uses a very clever and creative execution to communicate the product's features and benefits. The Mach3 Sensitive was launched by Gillette in response to a market research study that found a high percentage of men don't shave every day because they have sensitive skin that can be aggravated by shaving and leave their faces raw and irritated.[24] Notice how the ad copy addresses these issues while using a little hyperbole by suggesting that using the Mach3 will make your lady love your face even more.

Scientific/Technical Evidence   In a variation of the straight sell, scientific or technical evidence is presented in the ad to support performance or efficacy claims. Advertisers often cite technical information, results of scientific or laboratory studies, or endorsements by scientific bodies, doctors or agencies to support their advertising claims. For example, an endorsement from the American Council on Dental Therapeutics on how fluoride helps prevent cavities was the basis of the campaign that made Crest the leading brand of toothpaste. The ad for Alcon's Opti-Free multipurpose disinfecting solution for contact lens care treatment shown in Exhibit 9–13 uses this execution style by noting how the product is the number 1 doctor-recommended brand and how its performance is driven by science.

Demonstration   Demonstration advertising is designed to illustrate the key advantages of the product/service by showing it in actual use or in some staged situation. Demonstration executions can be very effective in convincing consumers of a product's utility or quality and of the benefits of owning or using the brand. TV and online videos are particularly well suited for demonstration executions, since the benefits or advantages of the product can be shown on the screen using sight, sound and motion. Although perhaps a little less dramatic than TV, demonstration ads can also work in print. The ad for Varilux Progressive Lenses shown in Exhibit 9–14 is an excellent example of the use of this technique. The ad shows the superiority of its progressive lens with W.A.V.E. technology over ordinary progressive lens by contrasting the clarity of the two images. The company also uses demonstrations in TV and online ads.

Comparison   Brand comparisons can also be the basis for the advertising execution. The comparison execution approach is increasingly popular among advertisers, since it offers a direct way of communicating a brand's particular advantage over its competitors or positioning a new or lesser-known brand with industry leaders. Comparison executions are often used to execute competitive advantage appeals, as discussed earlier.

Testimonial   Many advertisers prefer to have their messages presented by way of a testimonial, where a person praises the product or service on the basis of his or her personal experience with it. Testimonial executions can have ordinary satisfied customers discuss their own experiences with the brand and the benefits of using it. This approach can be very effective when the person delivering the testimonial is someone with whom the target audience can identify or who has an interesting story to tell. The testimonial must be based on actual use of the product or service to avoid legal problems, and the spokesperson must be credible.

A number of marketers, such as weight-loss companies, use testimonials to advertise their products, services, and programs. For example, Jenny Craig uses television commercials and print ads featuring ordinary consumers as well as celebrities discussing how they have been able to lose weight by following the company's programs. Exhibit 9–15 shows an ad with a testimonial from a person who lost weight using the Jenny Craig program.

A related execution technique is the *endorsement*, where a well-known or respected individual such as a celebrity or expert in the product or service area speaks on behalf of the company

CHAPTER 9

We guarantee
you'll lose weight or
your money back!*

WEIGHT
LOSS

Leah F.
LOST 126 LBS**

CALL NOW! **1-800-Jenny20**
jennycraig.com

*Clients following our program,
on average, lose 1-2 lbs per week.

EXHIBIT 9-15

Jenny Craig uses
testimonials to advertise its
weight-loss program

Source: Jenny Craig

or the brand. When endorsers promote a company or its products or services, the message is not necessarily based on their personal experiences.

Slice of Life   A widely used advertising format, particularly for packaged-goods products, is the slice-of-life execution, which is generally based on a problem–solution approach. This type of ad portrays a problem or conflict that consumers might face in their daily lives. The ad then shows how the advertiser's product or service can resolve the problem.

Slice-of-life executions are often criticized for being unrealistic and irritating to watch because they are often used to remind consumers of problems of a personal nature, such as dandruff, bad breath, body odor, and laundry problems. Often these ads come across as contrived, silly, phony, or even offensive to consumers. However, many advertisers still prefer this style because they believe it is effective at presenting a situation to which most consumers can relate and at registering the product feature or benefit that helps sell the brand. For many years, Procter & Gamble was known for its reliance on slice-of-life advertising executions as many of the company's commercials used either the slice-of-life or testimonial format. However, P&G has begun using humor, animation, and other less traditional execution styles and now relies less on slice of life or testimonials.[25]

Slice-of-life or problem–solution execution approaches are not limited to consumer-product advertising. Many business-to-business marketers use this type of advertising to demonstrate how their products and services can be used to solve business problems.[26] Some business-to-business marketers use a variation of the problem–solution execution that is sometimes referred to as *slice-of-death advertising.*[27] This execution style is used in conjunction with a fear appeal, as the focus is on the negative consequences that result when businesspeople make the wrong decision in choosing a supplier or service provider. For example, FedEx has used this type of advertising for nearly three decades through humorous but to-the-point commercials that show what might happen when important packages and documents aren't received on time.

Execution is critical in using the technique effectively as these ads are designed to be dramatizations of a supposedly real-life situation that consumers might encounter. Getting viewers to identify with the situation and/or characters depicted in the ad can be very challenging. Since the success of slice-of-life ads often depends on how well the actors come across and execute their roles, professional actors are often used to achieve credibility and to ensure that the commercial is of high quality. Smaller companies and local advertisers often do not have ad budgets large enough to hire the talent or to pay for the production quality needed to effectively create slice-of-life spots. Thus, this execution technique is more likely to be used by companies with ad budgets that are large enough to fund the use of professional talent and production of quality commercials.

Many marketers like to use the slice-of-life genre as they believe it can be an effective way of addressing a problem or issue and offering a solution. Slice-of-life commercials can also be used as an effective way to execute humor appeals. For example, the most popular commercial on the 2016 Super Bowl was a humorous ad for the Hyundai Genesis automobile featuring actor/comedian Kevin Hart. In the "First Date" spot Hart plays an overprotective father who lends his new Genesis—equipped with Hyundai's Blue Link Finder feature—to his daughter's date so he can track the couple's whereabouts throughout the night. The ad includes various scenes showing Hart spying on the couple such as when he puts his arm around her in a movie theater and wins her a prize at a carnival. The funniest scene shows the Genesis parked at a scenic spot overlooking the city and Hart stopping the boy from kissing his daughter while suspended from a helicopter and yelling: "You're

messing with the wrong daddy!" The boy decides to take the girl home early and the spot ends with him nervously returning the keys to the father while the daughter angrily walks into the house, and Hart smiles and asks, "Honey, what did you guys do tonight?" (see Exhibit 9–16).

Animation   An advertising execution approach that has become popular in recent years is animation. With this technique, animated scenes are drawn by artists or created on the computer, and cartoons, puppets, or other types of fictional characters may be used. Cartoon animation is especially popular for commercials targeted at children. Animated cartoon characters have also been used in many campaigns, including Green Giant vegetables (the Jolly Green Giant) and Keebler cookies (the Keebler elves). Kraft Foods revitalized its Mr. Peanut character a few years ago to make him more appealing to younger consumers and has run animated commercials with actor Robert Downey Jr. doing the voice and more recently comedian Bill Hader from *Saturday Night Live*.[28]

An excellent example of a commercial created using computer-generated animation is a spot called "Back to the Start" which was commissioned by Chipotle Mexican Grill for its Cultivate Foundation. The two-minute short film depicts the life of a farmer as he slowly turns his family farm into an industrial animal factory before seeing the errors of his ways and realizes the benefits of sustainable farming and turns it back (Exhibit 9–17). The film has a specially commissioned track of Coldplay's "The Scientist" sung by Willie Nelson; Chipotle encouraged viewers to

EXHIBIT 9–17

This "Back to the Start" Cannes Lions Film Grand Prix Winner 2012 for the Chipotle Cultivate Foundation uses computer-generated animation

Source: Chipotle/Cannes Lions International Advertising Festival Winner

EXHIBIT 9–18

KFC has brought back Colonel Sanders as a personality symbol for the brand

Source: KFC Corporation

download the song on iTunes, with proceeds going to the Cultivate Foundation. The spot ran online, in movie theaters, and as Chipotle's first national TV ad and won the Grand Prix and Gold Lion awards at the Cannes International Advertising Festival and was named one of the top 15 commercials of the 21st century by *Advertising Age*. The use of animation as an execution style may increase as creative specialists find more ways to use computer-generated graphics and other technological innovations.[29]

Personality Symbol Another type of advertising execution involves developing a central character or personality symbol that can deliver the advertising message and with which the company or brand can be identified. This character can be a person, like the iconic Mr. Whipple, who asked shoppers, "Please don't squeeze the Charmin," or the Maytag repairman, who sits anxiously by the phone but is never needed because the company's appliances are so reliable. Recall in Chapter 8 we discussed "The Most Interesting Man in the World" character for Dos Equis beer who has been a popular personality symbol in advertising for the brand for more than 10 years. Another popular personality symbol is Flo, the white-clad, perky salesclerk character who has appeared in ads for Progressive insurance.

A very interesting twist on the use of a personality symbol is a recent campaign created by the Wieden+Kennedy agency for KFC that resurrected Colonel Harland Sanders, who founded the company (originally known as Kentucky Fried Chicken) in 1940 and appeared in ads for decades for the popular chicken restaurant chain. Although Sanders died over 35 years ago, KFC decided to harken back to its past by having comedians Darrell Hammond and Norm Macdonald play the bespectacled founder (Exhibit 9–18). A major goal of the campaign is to appeal to millennials, many of whom have never tried KFC, by adding a modern, comedic twist to his character. The integrated campaign includes new packaging, menu items, websites, and social media and has helped increase KFC sales since its launch.[30]

Personality figures can also be built around animated characters and animals. As discussed in Chapter 5, personality symbols such as Morris the Cat, Tony the Tiger, and Charlie the Tuna have been used for decades to promote 9-Lives cat food, Kellogg's Frosted Flakes, and Star-Kist tuna, respectively. Other popular personality symbols that have been used more recently include the Energizer Bunny, GEICO insurance's gecko, and the Burger King character. One of the most popular and effective advertising personality symbols has been the Aflac duck which has been very successful in raising awareness, as well as sales, for the supplemental insurance company over the past five years.[31] Aflac has even integrated the duck into the company's redesigned corporate logo to take advantage of the tremendous equity that has resulted from the ads featuring the character.

Imagery You have probably noticed that some ads contain little or no information about the brand or company and are almost totally visual. These advertisements use imagery executions whereby the ad consists primarily of visual elements such as pictures, illustrations, and/or symbols rather than information. An imagery execution is used when the goal is to encourage consumers to associate the brand with the symbols, characters, and/or situation shown in the ad. Imagery ads are often the basis for emotional appeals that are used to advertise products or services where differentiation based on physical characteristics is difficult, such as soft drinks, liquor, designer clothing, and cosmetics. However, image is important for all types of products and services as marketers want the target audience to hold a favorable set of psychosocial associations for their company or brand.

An imagery execution may be based on *usage imagery* by showing how a brand is used or performs and the situation in which it is used. For example, advertising for trucks and SUVs often shows the vehicles navigating tough terrain or in challenging situations such as towing a heavy load. Usage imagery executions are also often used in the marketing of services as well as experiences such as hotels and destination resorts to show favorable images related to the use of a company's service offering. An excellent example of this is the ad shown in Exhibit 9–19 for The Peaks Resort & Spa in Telluride, Colorado. The visual images used in the ad are a very effective way to promote the resort by showing its beautiful location, rooms, and amenities. This type of execution can also be based on *user imagery* where the focus is on the type of person who uses the brand. Ads for cosmetics, jewelry, and designer clothing brands often use very attractive models in the hope of getting consumers to associate his or her physical attractiveness with the brand (see Exhibit 9–20). Image executions rely heavily on visual elements such as photography, color, tonality, and design to communicate the desired image to the consumer. Marketers who rely on image executions have to be sure that the usage or user imagery with which they associate their brand evokes the right feelings and reactions from the target audience.

Dramatization Another execution technique particularly well suited to television is dramatization, where the focus is on telling a short story with the product or service as the star. Dramatization is somewhat akin to slice-of-life execution in that it often relies on the problem–solution approach, but it uses more excitement and suspense in telling the story. The purpose of using drama is to draw the viewer into the action it portrays. Advocates of drama note that when it is successful, the audience becomes lost

EXHIBIT 9–19

This ad for the Peaks Resort & Spa utilizes usage imagery to promote the property

Source: The Peaks Resort and Spa

EXHIBIT 9–20

This bebe ad uses an attractive model to create a favorable image for the brand

Source: Bebe Stores, Inc.

in the story and experiences the concerns and feelings of the characters.[32] According to Sandra Moriarty, there are five basic steps in a dramatic commercial:

> First is exposition, where the stage is set for the upcoming action. Next comes conflict, which is a technique for identifying the problem. The middle of the dramatic form is a period of rising action where the story builds, the conflict intensifies, the suspense thickens. The fourth step is the climax, where the problem is solved. The last part of a drama is the resolution, where the wrap-up is presented. In advertising that includes product identification and call to action.[33]

In his excellent book *Creative Advertising*, Mario Pricken lists several relevant questions that should be considered when telling a story through a dramatic execution: What everyday situations could you develop around the product to show its advantages in the best light? What sort of story could involve the product as best friend or partner? In what everyday situation could it attract attention in a provocative way? In what situation could it become a star, a lifesaver, or a helper? In what everyday story could it make people laugh? He also notes that there are a number of dramatic styles that might be best suited for telling the story. These include, but are not limited to, genres such as thriller, adventure, comedy, slapstick, love story, and documentary.[34]

The challenge facing the creative team when using a dramatic execution is how to encompass the various elements and tell the story effectively in 30 seconds, which is the length of the typical commercial.

An example of the effective use of a dramatization execution in a commercial is a recent spot for the Buick Enclave sport-utility vehicle created by Leo Burnett Detroit (Exhibit 9–21). The commercial opens with an aura of tension as it shows a family on an airplane landing in a snowstorm; the pilot announces that the windchill outside is 10 below and the flight attendant tells the passengers "there are record lows out there so bundle up." As the plane touches down on the snowy runway, the man takes out his smartphone and uses the MyBuick remote start feature to start the Enclave, which is sitting in the airport parking lot, and sets the temperature to 82 degrees and activates the heated seats. The tone of the commercial then turns upbeat as the song "Not a Care" begins to play and the voiceover says: "With MyBuick remote start the new Buick Enclave makes sure you're ready for anything." The commercial ends with the family getting off the parking bus and into their warm and comfortable car.

EXHIBIT 9–21

This Buick Enclave commercial uses a dramatization execution

Source: General Motors and Leo Burnett Detroit

Humor Like comparisons, humor was discussed in Chapter 6 as a type of advertising appeal, but this technique can also be used as a way of presenting other advertising appeals. Humorous executions are particularly well suited to television or radio, although some print ads attempt to use this style. The pros and cons of using humor as an executional technique are similar to those associated with its use as an advertising appeal.

Combinations Many of the execution techniques can be combined to present the advertising message. For example, animation is often used to create personality symbols or present a fantasy. Slice-of-life ads are often used to demonstrate a product or service or as the basis for various types of emotional appeals. Comparisons are sometimes made using a humorous approach. FedEx uses humorous executions of the slice-of-death genre depicting business people experiencing dire consequences when they use another delivery service and an important document doesn't arrive on time. It is the responsibility of the creative specialist(s) to determine whether more than one execution style should be used in creating the ad. IMC Perspective 9–1 discusses how Taco Bell used a variety of execution styles as part of its "Live Más" campaign which has helped make the fast-food chain more attractive and relevant to young, hip, and cross-cultural consumers.

CREATIVE TACTICS

Our discussion thus far has focused on the development of creative strategy and various appeals and execution styles that can be used for the advertising message. Once the creative approach, type of appeal, and execution style have been determined, attention turns to creating the actual advertisement. The design and production of advertising messages involve a number of activities, among them writing copy, developing illustrations and other visual elements of the ad, and bringing all of the pieces together to create an effective message. In this section, we examine the verbal and visual elements of an ad and discuss tactical considerations in creating print ads and TV commercials.

Creative Tactics for Print Advertising

The basic components of a print ad are the headline, the body copy, the visual or illustrations, and the layout (the way they all fit together). The headline and body copy portions of the ad are the responsibility of the copywriters; artists, often working under the direction of an art director, are responsible for the visual presentation. Art directors also work with the copywriters to develop a layout, or arrangement of the various components of the ad: headlines, subheads, body copy, illustrations, captions, logos, and the like. We briefly examine the three components of a print ad and how they are coordinated.

Headlines The **headline** is the words in the leading position of the ad—the words that will be read first or are positioned to draw the most attention. Headlines are usually set in larger type and are often set apart from the body copy or text portion of the ad to give them prominence. Most advertising people consider the headline the most important part of a print ad.

The most important function of a headline is attracting readers' attention and interesting them in the rest of the message. While the visual portion of an ad is obviously important, the headline often shoulders most of the responsibility of attracting readers' attention. Research has shown the headline is generally the first thing people look at in a print ad, followed by the illustration. Only 20 percent of readers go beyond the headline and read the body copy.[35] So in addition to attracting attention, the headline must give the reader good reason to read the copy

IMC Perspective 9-1 > > >

Taco Bell Gets Consumers to Live Más

Taco Bell Corp. is a subsidiary of Yum! Brands, Inc., the world's largest restaurant company with nearly 40,000 restaurants in more than 125 countries. The Yum! brands, which also include KFC and Pizza Hut, are the global leaders in the chicken, pizza, and Mexican-style food categories. Taco Bell is the leading Mexican-inspired quick-service restaurant in the United States with nearly 6,000 locations across the country that serve more than 36 million customers every week. The company has had a number of creative advertising campaigns over the years, including the popular "Yo Quiero Taco Bell" campaign that featured a Chihuahua with an attitude who became a pop-culture and advertising icon. The ads featuring the dog helped generate the highest advertising awareness ever for the chain as well as burnish Taco Bell's image as a hip place to eat. Over the past decade Taco Bell ran a number of other successful advertising campaigns, including those using the "Run for the Border" and "Think Outside the Bun" themes.

Taco Bell is the largest and most profitable Yum! Brands chain in the United States, but during the Great Recession sales stagnated. The company was following a food as fuel philosophy and a "fill them up, move them out" marketing strategy that relied on humorous ads and promotions to pitch its products to young males. At the end of 2011, Taco Bell was coming off its third year of flat or declining sales and was looking for ideas to grow its store traffic and tweak its positioning to broaden its appeal beyond young males. As part of its turnaround strategy, the marketing and agency teams decided it was time to move beyond the "Think Outside the Bun" campaign that had been running for a number of years and make the brand more vital and exciting to its core target market of cross-cultural millennials.

In early 2012 Taco Bell introduced a new campaign slogan, "Live Más" (*más* is Spanish for "more"), which it views as a bilingual phrase that sums up why the brand is attractive and relevant to young, hip, and cross-cultural consumers. The tagline also represents a movement of the brand from the idea of "food as fuel" to food as an experience and lifestyle. DraftFCB, the agency that created the new campaign theme, explained the thinking behind it: "The brand has moved past the point of the idea of 'food

Source: Taco Bell Corp.

as fuel.' Young people in our new multicultural landscape don't see it that way. They look at food as an experience. That's what the new Taco Bell will provide. And that's the story we're telling."

As part of its new strategy, Taco Bell rolled out a slate of new products and a new upscale menu called Cantina Bell, featuring higher-quality ingredients, that was aimed at more health-conscious consumers. However, Taco Bell sales really took off in the spring of 2012 when a new product line was introduced called Doritos Locos Tacos (DLTs), which was the product of a co-branding effort with snack food giant Frito-Lay. A variety of flavors were tested before deciding on Nacho Cheese for the initial launch. The taco has a shell made from Nacho Cheese Doritos Chips and is served in custom packaging to prevent cheese dust from getting on consumers' fingers.

There was tremendous buzz prior to the launch of the new tacos, and Taco Bell took advantage of the excitement surrounding the introduction. A clock on Taco Bell's website ticked down the Doritos Locos Tacos launch and the winner of a Twitter contest was sent a truck loaded with the tacos. Consumers went "loco" for the new tacos; more than 100 million were sold in the first 10 weeks and within a year DLTs

portion of the ad, which contains more detailed and persuasive information about the product or service. To do this, the headline must put forth the main theme, appeal, or proposition of the ad in a few words. Some print ads contain little if any body copy, so the headline must work with the illustration to communicate the entire advertising message.

Headlines also perform a segmentation function by engaging the attention and interest of consumers who are most likely to buy a particular product or service. Advertisers begin the segmentation process by choosing to advertise in certain types of publications (e.g., a business, travel, or fashion magazine). An effective were accounting for nearly a quarter of all the taco sales at Taco Bell. In 2012 Taco Bell posted an 8 percent increase in same-store sales, more than double the 3.3 percent of industry leader McDonald's. And in early 2013, Taco Bell launched the second flavor of the new tacos, Cool Ranch, with its largest integrated marketing and consumer engagement effort ever as Doritos Locos Tacos became the most successful product launch in the company's 50-year history.

To reach the target market of cross-cultural millennials, Taco Bell has utilized social media in ways never done before in the fast-food category. A number of the TV spots for DLT used consumer-generated ideas that were tied to buzz about the new product as the marketing team searched social media for user experiences and reactions to the new product. For example, one of the commercials was based on a YouTube video showing a consumer who drove 900 miles to find a DLT, while another featured a series of Instagram posts strung together showing consumers taking their first bite of the Cool Ranch DLT. To build awareness and buzz prior to the launch of the Cool Ranch DLT, social media sites such as YouTube, Twitter, and Facebook were used to provide sneak peeks of the new flavor. Fans identified as social media influencers were invited to sample the product early by giving them a secret passcode and prompted to spread the word so others could try the new DLT.

The launch was also supported by a robust television campaign inspired by consumer responses to the original Nacho Cheese DLT and subsequent demand for the Cool Ranch version. The launch spot, "World's Most Obvious Idea," capitalized on the group swell of consumers wondering when Taco Bell would make a Cool Ranch version. Fifteen-second spots were also created that featured the reaction of consumers and celebrities as they try the new taco for the first time. The campaign also invited fans to post to Instagram or tweet their best #wow or #duh face—using those specific hashtags, followed by #CoolRanchDLT—for a chance to see their photo reactions on a giant billboard in Times Square. The invitations also appeared on DLT packages as well as beverage cups as part of the integrated campaign.

A commercial created for the Super Bowl based on the "Live Más" theme was also a big hit. The 60-second spot called "Viva Young" features a group of senior citizens sneaking out of their retirement home late at night and embarking on an epic night of partying that includes dancing, getting tattoos, sneaking into neighbors' swimming pools, and going on other escapades. They eventually end up, of course, at a Taco Bell for a "Fourthmeal" before returning to the home as the sun comes up. A Spanish version of Fun's hit song "We Are Young" was used in the commercial to help convey authenticity. The ad was one of the most popular spots in the Super Bowl and received the most buzz on social media.

Taco Bell was named *Advertising Age*'s Marketer of the Year in 2013, but the company is not resting on its laurels as it continues to find ways to leverage the "Live Más" theme and keep growing. In 2014 it rolled out a breakfast menu to capitalize on the rapid growth in the daypart category, and also launched the Taco Bell Mobile Ordering and Payment App. A year later it began offering delivery by partnering with the on-demand delivery service Doordash.

The marketing team is also testing the waters with the generation of consumers following the millennials who have been dubbed generation Z. Taco Bell's insights team has been researching this cohort to understand how they differ from the millennials and has found that they are even more empowered, entrepreneurial, and creative. To connect with them, Taco Bell is experimenting with emerging social media platforms such as Twitter's Periscope to test its ability to drive awareness and store traffic as well as building promotions around cultural moments such as "promposals." For example, Periscope was used for a live-streaming newscast to unveil its Breakfast Biscuit Taco, alerting consumers of a giveaway on Cinco de Mayo.

Taco Bell is also introducing new products in hope of replicating the tremendous success of the Doritos Locos Tacos. The Quesalupa, which is a hybrid of a quesadilla and a chalupa, was unveiled during Super Bowl 50 in 2016 with its playful "Bigger Than Everything" campaign that was designed to create mystery around and overblow the hype surrounding its release. The TV spot used hyperbole to promote its debut as bigger than cultural phenomena such as Tinder, drones, aliens, man buns, and even football. Taco Bell continues to engage consumers and get them to experience more and "Live Más."

Sources: Jeanne Poggi, "Inside Taco Bell's Not-So-Secret Product Launch," *Advertising Age*, February 7, 2016, http://adage.com/article/special-report-super-bowl/inside-taco-bell-s-secret-super-bowl-product-launch/302553/; Ashley Rodriguez, "Informed by Millennial Misses, Brands Retool for Gen Z," *Advertising Age*, May 18, 2015, p. 32; Maureen Morrison, "Marketer of the Year: Taco Bell," *Advertising Age*, September 2, 2013, p. 15; Emma Bazilian, "Taco Bell, Doritos Dominated Super Bowl Social Media," *Adweek*, February 4, 2013, www.adweek.com/news/advertising-branding/taco-bell-doritos-dominated-super-bowl-social-media-147029; Mike Hammer, "Taco Bell Gets a More Relevant Attitude," *Adweek*, March 11, 2012, www.adweek.com/sa-article/taco-bell-gets-more-relevant-attitude-138823.

headline goes even further in selecting good prospects by addressing their specific needs, wants, or interests. For example, the headline in the UPS ad shown in Exhibit 9–22 is designed to appeal to small business owners who rely on daily deliveries to operate and serve their customers. The headline attracts attention by using an unlikely premise and draws people into the ad copy which explains how UPS Accent Point locations serve more than 8,000 neighborhood businesses. The ad is part of the "United Problem Solvers" campaign that focuses on how UPS can solve problems for all types of customers ranging from small businesses to large enterprises.[36]

EXHIBIT 9–22

The headline of this UPS ad is designed to attract the attention of small business owners

Source: United Parcel Service of America, Inc.

EXHIBIT 9–23

This ad for the American Indian College Fund uses an indirect headline that encourages people to read the body copy

Source: American Indian College Fund

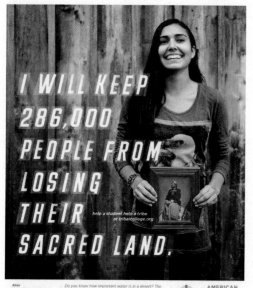

Types of Headlines There are numerous headline possibilities. The type used depends on several factors, including the creative strategy, the particular advertising situation (e.g., product type, media vehicle[s] being used, timeliness), and its relationship to other components of the ad, such as the illustration or body copy. Headlines can be categorized as direct and indirect. **Direct headlines** are straightforward and informative in terms of the message they are presenting and the target audience they are directed toward. Common types of direct headlines include those offering a specific benefit, making a promise, or announcing a reason the reader should be interested in the product or service.

Indirect headlines are not straightforward about identifying the product or service or getting to the point. But they are often more effective at attracting readers' attention and interest because they provoke curiosity and lure readers into the body copy to learn an answer or get an explanation. Techniques for writing indirect headlines include using questions, provocations, how-to statements, and challenges.

Indirect headlines rely on their ability to generate curiosity or intrigue so as to motivate readers to become involved with the ad and read the body copy to find out the point of the message. This can be risky if the headline is not provocative enough to get the readers' interest. Advertisers deal with this problem by using indirect headlines that are interesting enough to generate interest or curiosity as well as employing a strong visual appeal that will attract attention and offer a reason for reading more of the message. For example, the ad for the American Indian College Fund shown in Exhibit 9–23 uses an indirect headline (I Will Keep 286,000 People from Losing Their Sacred Land) that might create curiosity among magazine readers and encourage them to read the copy below for an explanation of what is meant by it. The body copy at the bottom of the ad explains how Northwest Indian College has one of the best environmental science study programs in the country and gives students such as Alssa knowledge they can use to help their tribes, thus encouraging people to support the American Indian College Fund.

Subheads While many ads have only one headline, it is also common to see print ads containing the main head and one or more secondary heads, or **subheads**. Subheads are usually smaller than the main headline but larger than the body copy. Subheads are often used to enhance the readability of the message by breaking up large amounts of body copy and highlighting key sales points. Their content reinforces the headline and advertising slogan or theme. The ad for GEICO auto insurance shown in Exhibit 9–24 is a good example of the effective use of subheads to present a large amount of advertising copy and highlight the major points of the message.

Body Copy The main text portion of a print ad is referred to as the **body copy** (or sometimes just *copy*). While the body copy is usually the heart of the advertising message, getting the target audience to read it is often difficult. The copywriter faces a dilemma: The body copy must be long enough to communicate the advertiser's message yet short enough to hold readers' interest.

Body copy content often flows from the points made in the headline or various subheads, but the specific content depends on the type of advertising appeal and/or execution style being used. For example, straight-sell copy that presents relevant information, product features and benefits, or competitive advantages is often used with the various types of rational appeals discussed earlier in the chapter. Emotional

EXHIBIT 9–24

This GEICO ad uses subheads to make the copy easier to read as well as to highlight features and benefits

Source: GEICO

EXHIBIT 9–25

This ad uses a clever visual image to provide insight into the process of designing the new Honda Civic

Source: American Honda Motor Co., Inc. and Rubin Postaer and Associates

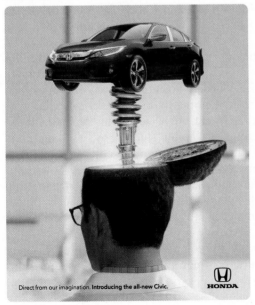

Direct from our imagination. Introducing the all-new Civic.

HONDA

appeals often use narrative copy that tells a story or provides an interesting account of a problem or situation involving the product.

Advertising body copy can be written to go along with various types of creative appeals and executions—comparisons, price appeals, demonstrations, humor, dramatizations, and the like. Copywriters choose a copy style that is appropriate for the type of appeal being used and effective for executing the creative strategy and communicating the advertiser's message to the target audience.

Visual Elements   The third major component of a print ad is the visual element. The illustration is often a dominant part of a print ad and plays an important role in determining its effectiveness. The visual portion of an ad must attract attention, communicate an idea or image, and work in a synergistic fashion with the headline and body copy to produce an effective message. In some print ads, the visual portion of the ad is essentially the message and thus must convey a strong and meaningful image. For example, the ad shown in Exhibit 9–25 uses a whimsical visual image to promote the new, redesigned Honda Civic. The print ad was part of a new campaign designed to go inside the head of a Honda engineer and provide insight into the thinking process of designing a car. The simple line of copy at the bottom reinforces the message presented by the visual image.

Many decisions have to be made regarding the visual portion of the ad: what identification marks should be included (brand name, company or trade name, trademarks, logos); whether to use photos or hand-drawn or painted illustrations; what colors to use (or even perhaps black and white or just a splash of color); and what the focus of the visual should be.

Layout   While each individual component of a print ad is important, the key factor is how these elements are blended into a finished advertisement. A **layout** is the physical arrangement of the various parts of the ad, including the headline, subheads, body copy, illustrations, and any identifying marks. The layout shows where each part of the ad will be placed and gives guidelines to the people working on the ad. The layout helps the copywriter determine how much space he or she has to work with and how much copy should be written. It can also guide the art director in determining the size and type of photos.

While the layout of a print ad is often straightforward, some creative executions can be challenging but also provide marketers with a very effective way to deliver a branding message. For example, The Lambesis Agency created a unique print ad for DASANI purified water that was part of an integrated campaign designed to communicate the Earth-inspired design for the brand's new bottle. The advertising used to launch the new PlantBottle™ packaging included a print ad with a peel-off plantable seeded paper leaf insert (Exhibit 9–26). As discussed in the chapter opener, the campaign helped enhance consumer perceptions of DASANI as being innovative and environmentally conscious. Layouts are often done in rough form and presented to the client so that the advertiser can visualize what the ad will look like before giving preliminary approval. The agency should get client approval of the layout before moving on to the more costly stages of print production.

Creative Tactics for Television

As consumers, we see so many TV commercials that it's easy to take for granted the time, effort, and money that go into making them. Creating and producing commercials that break through the clutter

EXHIBIT 9-26

This creative print ad was used to launch DASANI's new PlantBottle™ packaging

Source: Dasani by The Coca-Cola Company

on TV and communicate effectively is a detailed, expensive process. On a cost-per-minute basis, commercials are the most expensive productions seen on television.

TV is a unique and powerful advertising medium because it contains the elements of sight, sound, and motion, which can be combined to create a variety of advertising appeals and executions. Unlike print, the viewer does not control the rate at which the message is presented, so there is no opportunity to review points of interest or reread things that are not communicated clearly. As with any form of advertising, one of the first goals in creating TV commercials is to get the viewers' attention and then maintain it. This can be particularly challenging because of the clutter and because people often view TV commercials while doing other things (reading a book or magazine, talking).

Like print ads, TV commercials have several components. The video and audio must work together to create the right impact and communicate the advertiser's message.

Video The video elements of a commercial are what is seen on the TV screen. The visual portion generally dominates the commercial, so it must attract viewers' attention and communicate an idea, message, and/or image. A number of visual elements may have to be coordinated to produce a successful ad. Decisions have to be made regarding the product, the presenter, action sequences, demonstrations, and the like, as well as the setting(s), the talent or characters who will appear in the commercial, and such other factors as lighting, graphics, color, and identifying symbols.

Audio The audio portion of a commercial includes voices, music, and sound effects. Voices are used in different ways in commercials. They may be heard through the direct presentation of a spokesperson or as a conversation among various people appearing in the commercial. A common method for presenting the audio portion of a commercial is through a **voiceover**, where the message is delivered or action on the screen is narrated or described by an announcer who is not visible. A number of major advertisers have celebrities with distinctive voices do the voiceovers for their commercials.[37] Actor Morgan Freeman does the voiceover commercials for Visa, Patrick Dempsey does State Farm Insurance, and Hyundai has used actors Paul Rudd and Judd Apatown in some of its TV spots. Other celebrities who have been paid large sums of money to do voiceovers for commercials include *Madmen* star Jon Hamm for Mercedes-Benz, George Clooney for Budweiser, Julia Roberts for Nationwide Insurance, and Lisa Kudrow for Yoplait.

While some companies use celebrities or professionals to do the voiceover for their commercials, digital disruption is rapidly changing the voiceover industry as an online marketplace has emerged that connects voice actors to companies who need them. For decades voiceovers were done primarily by professionals who were members of the Screen Actors Guild (SAG) and often had agents represent them. However, today voice actors are setting up home studios by hooking up a microphone and mixer and marketing their services through companies such as Voices.com, Voice123.com, and others that connect companies with voiceover talent (Exhibit 9–27). Voice actors often still need agents and SAG membership for most of the high-paying jobs such as advertising campaigns done by major marketers. However, many smaller companies are using online voice services for their commercials and videos.[38]

Music is also an important part of many TV commercials and can play a variety of roles.[39] In many commercials, the music provides a pleasant background or helps

EXHIBIT 9–27

Companies such as Voices.com connect companies with voiceover talent

Source: Interactive Voices Inc

create the appropriate mood. Advertisers often use **needledrop**, which Linda Scott describes as follows:

> Needledrop is an occupational term common to advertising agencies and the music industry. It refers to music that is prefabricated, multipurpose, and highly conventional. It is, in that sense, the musical equivalent of stock photos, clip art, or canned copy. Needledrop is an inexpensive substitute for original music; paid for on a one-time basis, it is dropped into a commercial or film when a particular normative effect is desired.[40]

In some commercials, music is much more central to the advertising message. It can be used to get attention, break through the advertising clutter, communicate a key selling point, help establish an image or position, or add feeling.[41] For example, the David & Goliath agency has used music very effectively in commercials it has created for the Kia Soul subcompact car which feature the animated hamster characters shown driving the car and wearing hip-hop gear (Exhibit 9–28). Advertising for the Kia Soul is targeted at millennials and four pillars of their lifestyle: music, sports, pop culture, and "connected life" which includes a connection to technology and close ties to friends and family.[42] A number of hit songs have been used in the commercials, including "Animals" by Maroon 5, Lady Gaga's "Applause," hip-hop duo Black Sheep's song "This or That," and LMFAO's hit song "Party Rock Anthem."

Another example of the effective use of music is advertising for various Nico-Derm nicotine replacement products that are used by many smokers who are trying to quit the habit. Classic songs such as Rare Earth's "I Just Want to Celebrate" and Marvin Gaye and Tammi Terrell's hit "Ain't No Mountain High Enough" are used in its commercials to reinforce the message that every time someone trying to stop smoking says no to a cigarette, it is cause for celebration as he or she is moving closer to achieving the goal. Honda's agency, RPA, also integrated music very well into the TV commercial that was part of "The Dreamer" campaign for the newly designed Honda Civic which included the print ad shown earlier in Exhibit 9–25. In the TV spot as the engineer designs the new Civic, the car escapes from his imagination and goes on a magical journey around his workspace as the techno song "Walking on a Dream" by Empire of the Sun plays. The car drives across winding roads and past sun-splashed waterfalls before landing at the bottom of a rainbow slide.

EXHIBIT 9–28

Music is an integral part of the TV commercials for the Kia Soul that feature the hip-hop hamsters

Source: Kia Motors America

Steve Oakes conducted a review and analysis of research on consumers' cognitive and affective responses to music in advertising.[43] He found that increased congruity between the music and advertising with respect to variables such as mood, genre, score, image, and tempo contributes to the communication effectiveness of an advertisement by enhancing recall, brand attitude, affective response, and purchase intention. Research has also shown that music can work through a classical conditioning process to create a positive mood that makes consumers more receptive to an advertising message.[44] These studies underscore the importance of considering the mood induced by music and how it might influence responses to ads.

Because music can play such an important role in the creative strategy, many companies have paid large sums for the rights to use popular songs in their commercials. There are two kinds of works to which companies negotiate rights when licensing music for use in commercials. The *musical composition* includes the music notes and the words, while the *master recording* includes the voice(s) of the original artist.[45] The latter is usually much more expensive to buy, so advertisers will often negotiate for the rights to use the music and have it performed by someone with a similar voice. Rights to music can be held by various parties, such as the original artist, the artist's estate, or a music publishing company. For example, the rights to songs done by the late reggae star Bob Marley are held by his estate, while the rights to songs by the Beatles as well as Michael Jackson are controlled by music publishing company Sony/ATV.

Some advertising experts argue that music can account for as much as 50 percent of the effectiveness of a commercial and are encouraging their clients to invest in popular songs and soundtracks that can help them connect with their customers on an emotional level. They note that marketers who align themselves with popular songs and artists are often perceived as more cutting-edge and trendy, particularly if they are seen as exposing consumers to new artists and/or songs. There was a time when artists felt having their music used in commercials or creating songs for ads was "selling out." However, most artists now recognize that it is more beneficial and lucrative to "sell in" and become open to having their music used in commercials.

Some advertisers are willing to pay millions of dollars to use the voices of the original artists in their commercials. A recent study by Nielsen, "I Second That Emotion: The Emotive Power of Music in Advertising," found that commercials with some form of music performed better across four important metrics—creativity, empathy, emotive power, and information power—than those that did not have music. The study notes that music can not only create a positive emotional response but can also help motivate consumers buy a brand. For example, advertising for the HP x360 tablet that featured Meghan Trainor's hit song "Lips Are Movin" resulted in a 26 percent increase in sales among her fan base of teens and young adults. Ford Motor Co. also had great success with music when it licensed Rachel Platten's hit "Fight Song" for use in commercials for its Edge SUV in 2015, as sales increased significantly after it began airing ads with the popular song.[46]

Another important musical element in both TV and radio commercials is **jingles**, catchy songs about a product or service that usually carry the advertising theme and a simple message. For example, Subway Restaurants's "Five-dollar foot-long" jingle has been an integral part of one of the most effective promotional campaigns ever developed in the fast-food industry. The catchy jingle ("Five. Five. Five dollar. Five dollar foot-long") repeats the word *five* several times to help register the price of the product and help promote the value of the large sandwiches.[47] In 2016 Armour updated the jingle it had been using in its advertising since 1967 as part of a new campaign to update the image of its hot dogs and other meat products. The jingle originally ended with the line "Armour hot dogs, the dogs kids love to bite" and now ends "Armour great moms, the moms we love so much."[48] Other popular jingles include those for retailer Toys "Я" Us ("I don't wanna grow up, I'm a Toys "Я" Us kid"), Folgers coffee ("The best part of waking up is Folgers in your cup"), and Kay Jewelers ("Every kiss begins with Kay").

In some commercials, jingles are used more as a form of product identification and appear at the end of the message. Jingles are often composed by companies that specialize in writing commercial music for advertising. These jingle houses work with the creative team to determine the role music will play in the commercial and the message that needs to be communicated.

While the use of jingles dates back to the 1950s, they are used less frequently today than in the past as many advertisers are using current and classic pop songs in their ads. The director of music at the Leo Burnett agency notes that companies using jingles must be careful, noting that "we are living in a world of iPods, MTV, and video and jingles sound corny."[49] However, despite these concerns, many marketers still use jingles. In fact, jingles have made somewhat of a comeback in recent years as many marketers want to include original music as part of their advertising messages.[50] A number of companies have been reinventing their own jingles for a new generation of consumers such as State Farm, which did a hip-hop version of its classic "Like a good neighbor, State Farm is there" jingle and Meow Mix cat food, which recently had artist Cee Lo Green do a remix of the iconic Meow Mix jingle.[51]

Jingles are also still commonplace in the television and radio commercials used by local advertisers; these companies view them as an effective way to keep their company name and/or slogan in the minds of their customers and prospects. The position of many advertisers regarding the use of jingles is perhaps best summed up by a Procter & Gamble brand manager who stated that the company believes jingles still work, noting that "if they are humming it, they are buying it."[52]

Planning and Production of TV Commercials   One of the first decisions that has to be made in planning a TV commercial is the type of appeal and execution style that will be used. Television is well suited to both rational and emotional advertising appeals or combinations of the two. Various execution styles used with rational appeals, such as a straight sell or announcement, demonstration, testimonial, or comparison, work well on TV. Television is particularly well suited to emotional appeals such as humor, fear, romance, and fantasies, which are often executed using dramatizations and slice-of-life commercials.

Advertisers recognize that they need to do more than talk about, demonstrate, or compare their products or services. Their commercials have to break through the clutter and grab viewers' attention, which is becoming increasingly difficult in today's multitasking viewing environment. Television is essentially an entertainment medium, and many advertisers recognize that their commercials are most successful when they entertain as well as inform. Many of the most popular advertising campaigns are characterized by commercials with strong entertainment value, like the engaging ads for Apple and AT&T as well as humorous spots for companies/brands such as GEICO, Hyundai, FedEx, and Budweiser/Bud Light.

Television commercials are an integral part of the IMC program for most marketers, particularly larger companies that are advertising their products and services to mass markets. However, the costs of planning and producing a TV commercial can be very high and must be considered as part of the budget for an advertising campaign. While it is possible to produce a commercial for a few thousand dollars (such as many spots that air for local retailers and businesses), marketers recognize that a poorly produced TV ad will not be effective and may have a negative impact on the company and/or brand's image. Thus, large amounts of money are often required to produce high-quality TV commercials. For 25 years a Television Production Cost Survey was done by the American Association of Advertising Agencies (4As) that provided an estimate of revealed that the average cost for producing a 30-second commercial for a national brand. However, the last survey done was five years ago and cost data supplied by 10 agencies for 506 national commercials of varying length estimated the average cost to be $354,000.[53] It is likely that the production costs for quality commercials have increased since the last 4As survey, particularly for major marketers who rely heavily on TV ads. Figure 9–2 shows an example of the production costs for a commercial that was produced for a major fast-food chain.

There are many factors that contribute to the costs of producing a TV commercial, including production personnel, equipment, location fees, video editing, sound recording and mixing, music fees, and talent. Increases in television commercial

FIGURE 9–2

Production Costs for a
30-Second Television
Commercial

Big Time Productions
1234 Production Place
Santa Monica, CA 90404

Bid Date 3/25/10			Firm Bid (x) Cost Plus Fixed Fee ( )		
Production Co:	Big Time Productions		Agency:	Awesome Ads	
Address:	1234 Production Place		Address:	1234 Advertising Way	
	Santa Monica, CA 90404			Santa Monica, CA 90404	
Telephone:	(310)555-5555		Telephone:	(310)555-5555	
Fax:	(310)444-4444		Fax:	(310)444-4444	
Job #:	M10-340		Agency Prod:	Ashley Producer	
Director:			Agency Art Dir:	Brian Artist	
Executive Producer:			Agency Writer:	Deborah Writer	
Production Contact:			Agency Bus Mgr:	Alan Business	
DP:			Client:	FAST FOOD CHAIN	
Art Director:			Product:	Sandwich, Burger,	
Editor:	Fine Edits		Bid Name:		
Pre-Production					
Days:					
Build & Strike Days:			Commercial Title:		Length:
Pre-Light Days:	One		1) "Delicious Sandwich"		:30
Studio Shoot Days:			2) "Yummy Burger"		:30
Location Days:	Two	Hours: 10 & 14			
Locations(s)	Los Angeles				

SUMMARY OF PRODUCTION COSTS	TOTAL
PRE-PRODUCTION & WRAP	$76,676
SHOOTING LABOR	$93,901
LOCATIONS & TRAVEL	$65,690
PROPS, WARDROBE & ANIMALS	$18,670
STUDIO & SET CONSTRUCTION	$88,056
EQUIPMENT	$42,750
FILMSTOCK DEVELOP & PRINT	$22,920
DIRECTOR/CREATIVE FEES	$32,400
INSURANCE	$12,288
PRODUCTION MARK UP	$92,153
NEEDLEDROP MUSIC	$2,000
EDITING	$66,504
TALENT	$33,905
GRAND TOTAL	$647,913

production costs are a major concern among marketers, and many companies are looking for ways to reduce them. For example, a large expense item is talent costs as actors who appear in commercials receive *residuals* that are based primarily on how many times a commercial airs. The Joint Policy Committee on Broadcast Relations, an advertising industry group that represents advertisers and agencies in bargaining with talent unions, proposed a new compensation system that will base pay for commercial actors on the size of the audience the spot reaches as well as the number of times it is run. In 2016 the talent unions and the Joint Policy Committee reached a tentative agreement on terms for successor television and radio commercials contracts and also includes provisions for digital and social media. However, this new compensation system is still in the approval stage.[54]

Planning the Commercial The various elements of a TV commercial are brought together in a **script**, a written version of a commercial that provides a detailed description of its video and audio content. The script shows the various audio components of the commercial—the copy to be spoken by voices, the music, and sound effects. The video portion of the script provides the visual plan of the commercial—camera actions and angles, scenes, transitions, and other important descriptions. The script also shows how the video corresponds to the audio portion of the commercial.

Once the basic script has been conceived, the writer and art director get together to produce a storyboard, a series of drawings used to present the visual plan or layout of a proposed commercial. The storyboard contains still drawings of the video scenes and descriptions of the audio that accompanies each scene. Like layouts for print ads, storyboards provide those involved in the production and approval of the commercial with a good approximation of what the final commercial will look like. In some cases an animatic (a videotape of the storyboard along with the soundtrack) may be produced if a more finished form of the commercial is needed for client presentations or pretesting.

Production Once the storyboard or animatic of the commercial is approved, it is ready to move to the production phase, which involves three stages:

1. *Preproduction*—all the work and activities that occur before the actual shooting/recording of the commercial.
2. *Production*—the period during which the commercial is filmed or videotaped and recorded.
3. *Postproduction*—activities and work that occur after the commercial has been filmed and recorded.

The various activities of each phase are shown in Figure 9–3. Before the final production process begins, the client must usually review and approve the creative strategy and the various tactics that will be used in creating the advertising message.

Creative Tactics for Online Advertising

While a great deal of attention has been given to advertising creativity over the years, much of the focus has been on its application to traditional forms of advertising such as print, television, radio or outdoor. However, marketers are allocating more of their media budgets to digital ads that appear on websites, social media and mobile devices which are creating a new set of challenges from a creative perspective. Compared to traditional media such as television or magazines, the Internet is a more goal-oriented medium. Getting consumers to pay attention to, let alone engage or interact with, a digital ad is very difficult since doing so takes them away from the content on the web page or social media site they are visiting on their computers, tablets, or phones. Online ads often interrupt our viewing sessions, and unless they are providing relevant information and/or are very creative or entertaining, it is likely they will be ignored. Doubleclick, which is the display advertising division of Google, reports that the click-through rates (CTRs) for online display advertising across all format and placements is just 0.17 percent.[55] Video ads have the highest average click-through rate (1.84 percent) of all digital ad formats but the CTR is still very low. Moreover, many of the pre-roll ads shown prior to a video being viewed do not give the viewer the option to skip the advertisement and thus are often perceived as intrusive and annoying.

Role of Digital Ads A variety of digital advertising formats are available to marketers including banner ads, search ads, interstitials, native ads, and videos.

FIGURE 9–3

The Three Phases of Production for Commercials

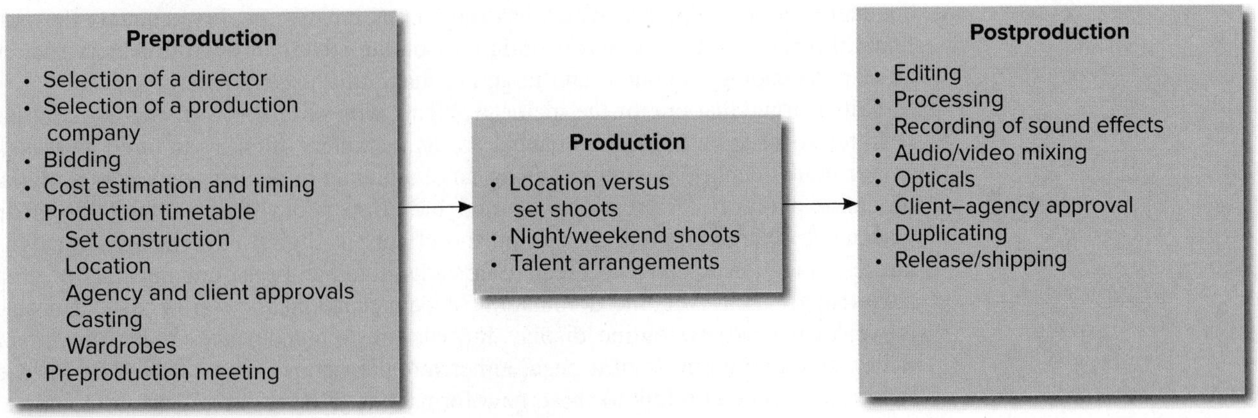

Preproduction
- Selection of a director
- Selection of a production company
- Bidding
- Cost estimation and timing
- Production timetable
    Set construction
    Location
    Agency and client approvals
    Casting
    Wardrobes
- Preproduction meeting

Production
- Location versus set shoots
- Night/weekend shoots
- Talent arrangements

Postproduction
- Editing
- Processing
- Recording of sound effects
- Audio/video mixing
- Opticals
- Client–agency approval
- Duplicating
- Release/shipping

The type of online ad used by marketers will vary depending on the goal(s) they are trying to achieve. Peter Minnium of the Internet Advertising Bureau notes that digital advertising is trifurcating into three types of advertising—concept, content, and commerce ads—and their use varies based on the goals and/or objectives the marketer is trying to achieve all along the purchase funnel.

The goal of digital concept ads is to drive top-of-the-funnel goals such as awareness and interest which can be achieved through banner ads or videos such as commercials. Content ads typically have a mid-funnel goal of enhancing consumers' knowledge or understanding of a product or service which can be done by providing high-quality content with which the viewer can engage. Different types of online ads can be used to provide content such as videos, webisodes, in-feed ads to Facebook or Twitter with sponsored content, and native ads. **Native advertising** is a type of paid placement designed to fit seamlessly into the content that surrounds it. The design, content, and writing style of a native ad mirrors the nonpaid content around it, giving the user the impression that it really belongs. Native advertising is becoming a dominant form of content advertising, particularly in digital editions of magazines and newspapers.

The third form of digital advertising is commerce ads which primarily have a bottom-of-the-funnel goal of getting consumers to take action and make a purchase. Commerce ads are the dominant form of display advertising, particularly retargeting types that follow consumers across the Web, and typically are not visually rich as their success is based on serving the right offer to consumers and can be easily measured in terms of clicks and conversions. While digital advertising is discussed in more detail in Chapter 15, we will consider the creative issues associated with display ads and online videos which are the dominant forms used by marketers.

Display Ads There are many different formats available for online display advertising. Many online display ads use large-size ad formats such as rectangular ads, horizontally oriented leaderboards, or skyscrapers that are vertically oriented and give advertisers the ability to place an ad adjacent to the website content. A study conducted by Dynamic Logic study analyzed results from 4,800 online campaigns and found that the best-performing ad unit in terms of metrics such as brand awareness, recall, and purchase intent was the traditional 180×150 pixel rectangular banner ad, noting that ads surrounding content, such as well-worn skyscraper and leaderboard units, are the least effective, as people have developed "banner blindness."[56] Rectangular banner ads can be more effective because they are often closer to and interrupt the content, which means that as you read the information on the site, your eye naturally has to roll over the ad. However, ads that cover content are also among the most annoying online advertising formats.

In another study the company analyzed the highest and lowest performers from its database of more than 170,000 digital ads and found that creative factors such as persistent branding, strong calls to action, and the use of human faces result in better ad recall, brand awareness, and purchase intentions rather than highly targeted or high-profile online ad placements. The results of the study support past research conducted by the company, which has shown that creative quality accounts for more than 50 percent of the success or failure of online advertising while factors such as ad size, technology, context, and targeting make up the remainder.

Critics argue that one of the major problems with online advertising is that it has been too focused on ubiquitous banner ads as marketers often try to build awareness and/or brand identity by simply buying large amounts of banner ads across a myriad on online platforms. A great deal of time and effort is devoted to optimizing media placement, retargeting, and measuring the effects of digital advertising campaigns, but less attention is given to creative considerations and the fundamentals of great advertising.[57] However, the domination of banner ads at the top or side of a page is weakening as new online display formats are being developed that are larger, richer, and take up more of a page, either initially or upon expansion. The Internet Advertising Bureau refers to these new formats as "Rising Stars" which include ad unit formats such as billboard sidekicks and sliders as well as various video formats. One format that has become very popular is expanding pushdown ad units that push page content down rather than expanding over it, which helps address the annoyance issue. Exhibit 9–29 shows examples of these various formats offered on the website of Cox Media. These formats are also available for online videos; we now turn our attention to this form of digital advertising.

Online Video The use of online video advertising is growing rapidly and is part of the tremendous growth in the viewing of videos across all online platforms including websites, YouTube, Facebook, Twitter, Snapchat, and other popular social media sites. The use of video for online advertising can include multiple formats ranging from the airing of a digital video or commercial in a program streaming online to more customized formats for viewing on mobile devices. Online advertisers using video can choose from a number of options regarding the placement of the ad such as pre-roll, which runs before the piece of video content that is being viewed; mid-roll, which runs somewhere in the middle of the content; or post-roll, where the video plays at the completion of the content. They can also choose to use interactive ads that take over the full screen and preempt or pause the video content and allow a variety of interactions, like clicking for more information, signing up for a newsletter, or locating a store. These types of ads allow for further viewer engagement with the brand as well as interactivity that either expands in player or clicks out to an advertiser website. Different online advertising formats have also been developed as part of the IAB's "Rising Stars" program such as control bars that allow viewers to do things such as sharing ads, watching extended versions, or overlaying videos with ad content.

Creative decisions regarding online videos and ads are often similar to those for television as far as the type of appeal, execution style, and use of video and audio elements. However, online video advertising must consider other factors such as intrusiveness, length, and content. For example, most online video ads are inserted pre-roll and shown prior to the video being viewed and provide little or no options to skip the advertisement which means they can interfere with intended viewer activity. A recent study by Goodrich, Schiller, and Galletta found that online ads that are perceived as intrusive had a negative impact on attitudes and intentions toward both the advertised brand and the host website and also resulted in higher abandonment of ad viewing.[58] Length of the online video or ad is also an important factor because consumers are likely to be annoyed by longer ad formats or abandon them if they have the option to do so, unless they find them as useful or entertaining. However, short-form commercials such as five-second spots may have trouble delivering a meaningful message.

Content is also an important consideration when creating online videos and advertisements. However, many creative directors note that the content of video ads that work well online is not that different from their TV counterparts. Videos and ads that provide relevant and/or valuable information are less likely to be perceived as intrusive and thus avoided. Emotional appeals often work better for longer videos, while humor can be very effective for online ads and perhaps have a greater likelihood of being shared. Marketers are recognizing that more attention has to be given to developing commercials and videos specifically for online use rather than simply uploading the same ads they use for television. Digital and Social Media Perspective 9–2 discusses the award-winning "Unskippable" campaign the Martin Agency developed for GEICO which consisted of a series of ads created specifically for use as pre-roll to YouTube videos.

EXHIBIT 9-29

Online Display Ad Formats

Source: Cox Media, LLC

THE BENEFITS OF COX.COM

- A quality, uncluttered environment to display your advertisements online
- The ability to reach Cox Subscribers on highly-trafficked pages within My Connection and WebMail
- Monthly reporting to help you measure success and maximize your return on investment
- Quality creative production to drive engagement and achieve campaign goals
- A great complement to your TV campaign

AD PLACEMENTS ON COX.COM

Digital and Social Media Perspective 9–2 > > >

GEICO'S "UNSKIPPABLE" CAMPAIGN BRINGS CREATIVITY To ONLINE PRE-ROLL ADVERTISING

Before reading this page, take a moment to think about the last time you went to YouTube to watch a video and a pre-roll commercial appeared before the video started. Did you watch the commercial or did you quickly hit the skip button so you could get on with watching the video? Advertisers are given less than five seconds on YouTube to convince the audience their ad is worth watching to the end before giving them the option to skip it; 94 percent of people skip pre-roll ads after that five-second mark. Even though they are paying YouTube to run the pre-roll ad, most marketers do little to get consumers to watch them since often they are uploading the same commercial they ran on television and hoping that viewers will not hit the skip button. Very few companies are creating advertising messages that are designed specifically for use as pre-roll ads on YouTube, Facebook, or various websites where consumers might encounter them.

However, one company that found a way to get people to watch its pre-roll ads is GEICO, which spends nearly $1 billion per year on various forms of advertising including television, print, outdoor, and digital to promote its auto, home, and property insurance. Like most marketers, GEICO is spending more of its advertising dollars online to run ads encouraging consumers to compare rates with its "15 Minutes Could Save You 15%" message. However, the Martin Agency, which handles all of GEICO's advertising, was well aware of the research showing that more than 90 percent of people skip pre-roll ads because they fail to hook people before they

get a chance to press the skip button. To address this problem the agency decided to develop ads specifically for use as pre-roll that put the emphasis on the first five seconds in a humorous way. Martin Agency account director Brad Higdon explained the challenge as follows: "We had the research. We knew the skip rate after five seconds was 96 percent, so we collectively challenged ourselves to find a workaround. If we're going to interrupt someone on their way to watch something they actually sought out, and want to watch, we better make it worth their while."

The first ad in the "Unskippable" campaign was called "Family," and opens with a family eating dinner and the mother smiling and saying, "don't thank me, thank the savings." After a few seconds the video freezes and an off-screen voiceover tells viewers: "You can't skip this Geico ad because it's already over." Then, the GEICO logo appears and the mother, father, son, and daughter remain as frozen mimes. However, the giant logo that typically signals the end of the commercial actually signals the beginning of the spot and the humor begins as the family's large Saint Bernard dog leaps up on the table and scarfs down everybody's spaghetti for the remaining 45 seconds of the ad. Right after it was launched the family dinner table pre-roll ad received 725,000 unaided views on YouTube and ended up receiving millions more over the next several months.

The Martin Agency created three additional pre-roll commercials for the "Unskippable" campaign using the

Marketers will continue to spend more of their advertising budgets online since this is where their target audiences are spending their time. Moreover, many feel that the targeting and measurement capabilities of digital more than make up for the creative limitations of online advertising. However, it is also important for marketers to challenge their agencies to adopt and experiment with new types of formats and develop digital ads that are informative, entertaining, and/or engaging rather than continuing to bombard consumers with banner and/or video ads that they can easily avoid by clicking a mouse or button.

CLIENT EVALUATION AND APPROVAL OF CREATIVE WORK

While the creative specialists have much responsibility for determining the advertising appeal and execution style to be used in a campaign, the client must evaluate and approve the creative approach before any ads are produced. A number of people on the client side may be involved in evaluating the creative work of the agency, including the advertising or communications manager, product or brand managers, marketing director or vice president, representatives from the legal department, and sometimes even the president or chief executive officer (CEO) of the company or the board of directors.

Source: GEICO

there is a gigantic logo of the brand in middle of screen the entire time. To us it's a deceptively simple piece of communication and really showed us how film can reinvent the way we look at media, even the least-sexy media in the world, which is pre-roll."

The Martin Agency and GEICO followed up on the award-winning "Unskippable" campaign in 2016 with a series of entertaining 15-second pre-roll ads that viewers find hard to skip. In the "Fast Forward" campaign the ads start with routine situations but after a few seconds a large GEICO logo appears and the voiceover announces, "We now fast forward to the end of this GEICO ad so you can get to your video faster." The ads then jump to some bizarre endings. For example, one spot opens with a pair of hikers treading the side of a cliff and after the interruption cuts to them hanging from the claws of a giant bird with one of them playing a saxophone. Another shows two lumberjacks engaged in chit-chat when they encounter an angry grizzly bear, then skips to show one of the men and the bear in a warm embrace.

Consumers are very likely to continue watching online videos and marketers will keep trying to get them to watch their pre-roll ads before doing so. Perhaps more will follow the lead of GEICO and create pre-roll ads that are worth watching.

freeze-frame format including one called "High Five" that showed two friends who celebrate saving money by performing a jumping high-five. During the freeze frame, the stunt wires become visible and one of the actor's feet catches fire. The campaign did more than generate a lot of buzz on social media; many advertising critics argue that it was a landmark moment in advertising when online video advertising took a turn for the better. The family dinner pre-roll ad earned the Film Grand Prix Award at the 2015 Cannes Lions International Festival of Creativity while the campaign was selected as Best Ad Campaign of 2015 by *Adweek* and also received *Advertising Age's* first ever Campaign of the Year Award in 2016. Critics loved the campaign because it brought innovation to the creatively barren world of pre-roll advertising and broke many of the rules for advertising. As the Cannes Jury president noted in discussing its selection of the family dinner spot for its top honor: "Instead of begging you to watch this ad, it challenges you not to watch it. Instead of a long story with a tenuous link to the brand at the end,

Sources: Anne-Christine Diaz, "Geico's New Campaign Is Really Unskippable," *Advertising Age*, February 29, 2016, http://adage.com/article/advertising/geico-s-campaign-unskippable/302851/; Anne-Christine Diaz, "Geico's 'Unskippable' from the Martin Agency Is Ad Age's 2016 Campaign of the Year," *Advertising Age*, January 25, 2016, http://adage.com/article/special-report-agency-alist-2016/geico-s-unskippable-ad-age-s-2016-campaign-year/302300/; Tim Nudd, "How the Best Ad Campaign of 2015 Hilariously Hacked the Lowly Preroll Ad," *Adweek*, December 13, 2015, www.adweek.com/news/advertising-branding/how-best-ad-campaign-2015-hilariously-hacked-lowly-preroll-ad-168614.

EXHIBIT 9–30

Apple's famous "1984" commercial almost never made it to the Super Bowl

Source: Apple Inc.

The amount of input each of these individuals has in the creative evaluation and approval process varies depending on the company's policies, the importance of the product to the company, the role of advertising in the marketing program, and the advertising approach being recommended. For example, the Chiat/Day agency had to convince Apple's board of directors to air the famous "1984" commercial used to introduce the Macintosh personal computer (Exhibit 9-30). Apple's board thought the commercial, which was based on the concept of Big Brother from George Orwell's classic novel *1984*, was too controversial and might have a negative impact on its image, particularly in the business market. The spot used stark images of Orwell's dystopia, and a dramatic scene of a young woman dressed in athletic gear and being chased by helmeted militia, running into a theater and hurling a sledgehammer into the screen, causing an explosion that shatters Big Brother. While the agency creative director who worked on the ad notes that Big Brother was supposed to symbolize a collective fear of technology, many still argue that it was really Apple's major competitor IBM that he represented. The agency convinced Apple's board to run the commercial during the

EXHIBIT 9–31

Advertising for SKYY Infusions builds off the core brand equity base and is consistent with marketing objectives

Source: Campari America, San Francisco, CA

1984 Super Bowl, which is the only time it appeared as a commercial on TV (other than in a local market prior to the game), and the impact was tremendous as it was the focus of attention in the media as well as the advertising world.

Many articles and stories have been written about the "1984" spot, and it has accumulated numerous accolades over the years. In 1999, *TV Guide* named the spot the greatest TV commercial of all time and *Advertising Age* recognized it as the best commercial of the 20th century. The spot is also credited with helping make the Super Bowl the advertising showcase it has become, and was the beginning of the new era of integrated marketing communications.[59]

In many cases, top management is involved in selecting an ad agency and must approve the theme and creative strategy for the campaign. Evaluation and approval of the individual ads proposed by the agency often rest with the advertising and product managers who are primarily responsible for the brand. The account executive and a member of the creative team present the creative concept to the client's advertising and product and/or marketing managers for their approval before beginning production. A careful evaluation should be made before the ad actually enters production, since this stage requires considerable time and money as suppliers are hired to perform the various functions required to produce the actual ad.

The client's evaluation of the print layout or commercial storyboard can be difficult, since the advertising or brand manager is generally not a creative expert and must be careful not to reject viable creative approaches or accept ideas that will result in inferior advertising. However, personnel on the client side can use the guidelines discussed next to judge the efficacy of creative approaches suggested by the agency.

Guidelines for Evaluating Creative Output

Advertisers use numerous criteria to evaluate the creative approach suggested by the ad agency. In some instances, the client may want to have the rough layout storyboard or animatic pretested to get quantitative information to assist in the evaluation. (Various methods for pretesting print ads and TV commercials will be discussed in Chapter 18.) However, the evaluation process is usually more subjective; the advertising or brand manager relies on qualitative considerations. Basic criteria for evaluating creative approaches are discussed next:

- *Is the creative approach consistent with the brand's marketing and advertising objectives?* One of the most important factors the client must consider is whether the creative appeal and execution style recommended by the agency are consistent with the marketing strategy for the brand and the role advertising and promotion have been assigned in the overall marketing program. This means the creative approach must be compatible with the image of the brand and the way it is positioned in the marketplace and should contribute to the marketing and advertising objectives. For example, SKYY Spirits extended its product line by introducing an all-natural, infused super-premium vodka to capitalize on the growth in the flavored segment of the vodka market. Advertising for the new SKYY Infusions line uses bold creative featuring strong visual images that communicate the natural flavor ingredients, as well as the brand's distinctive cobalt blue bottle (Exhibit 9–31). These ads are consistent with the core brand equity base of SKYY, from which several new product lines have been launched. The SKYY Infusions line extension also contributes to the equity of the core SKYY brand, which helps build the strength and value of the overall brand franchise.

- *Is the creative approach consistent with the creative strategy and objectives? Does it communicate what it is supposed to?* The advertising appeal and execution must meet the communications objectives laid out in the copy platform, and the ad must say what the advertising strategy calls for it to say. Creative specialists can lose sight of what the advertising message is supposed to be and come up with an approach that fails to execute the advertising strategy. Individuals responsible for approving the ad should ask the creative specialists to explain how the appeal or execution style adheres to the creative strategy and helps meet communications objectives.

- *Is the creative approach appropriate for the target audience?* Generally, much time has been spent defining, locating, and attempting to understand the target audience for the advertiser's product or service. Careful consideration should be given to whether the ad appeal or execution recommended will appeal to, be understood by, and communicate effectively with the target audience. This involves studying all elements of the ad and how the audience will respond to them. Advertisers do not want to approve advertising that they believe will receive a negative reaction from the target audience. For example, it has been suggested that advertising targeted to older consumers should use models who are 10 years younger than the average age of the target audience, since most people feel younger than their chronological age.[60] Advertisers also face a considerable challenge developing ads for the teen market because teenagers' styles, fashions, language, and values change so rapidly. They may find they are using an advertising approach, a spokesperson, or even an expression that is no longer popular among teens.

- *Does the creative approach communicate a clear and convincing message to the customer?* Most ads are supposed to communicate a message that will help sell the brand. Many ads fail to communicate a clear and convincing message that motivates consumers to use a brand. While creativity is important in advertising, it is also important that the advertising communicate information attributes, features and benefits, and/or images that give consumers a reason to buy the brand.

- *Does the creative execution keep from overwhelming the message?* A common criticism of advertising, and TV commercials in particular, is that so much emphasis is placed on creative execution that the advertiser's message gets overshadowed. Many creative, entertaining commercials have failed to register the brand name and/or selling points effectively. For example, Aflac had to modify the commercials using its iconic duck character after several research studies showed that many consumers were not exactly sure what Aflac insurance was. Consumers indicated that the advertising didn't explain what supplemental insurance is and what Aflac does, so recent ads focus more attention on explaining the product and the company.[61]

  With the increasing amount of clutter in most advertising media, it may be necessary to use a novel creative approach to gain the viewer's or reader's attention. However, the creative execution cannot overwhelm the message. Clients must walk a fine line: Make sure the sales message is not lost, but be careful not to stifle the efforts of the creative specialists and force them into producing dull, boring advertising.

- *Is the creative approach appropriate for the media environment in which it is likely to be seen?* Each media vehicle has its own specific climate that results from the nature of its editorial content, the type of reader or viewer it attracts, and the nature of the ads it contains. Consideration should be given to how well the ad fits into the media environment in which it will be shown. For example, the Super Bowl has become a showcase for commercials. People who care very little about advertising know how much a 30-second commercial costs and pay as much attention to the ads as to the game itself, so many advertisers feel compelled to develop new ads for the Super Bowl or to save new commercials

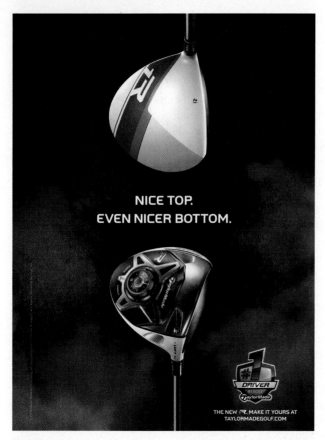

EXHIBIT 9–32

This clever ad was created specifically for the special swimsuit edition of *Sports Illustrated*

Source: TaylorMade Golf Company, Inc.

for the game. In some cases marketers may develop ads specifically for certain media vehicles such as magazines. For example, many of the ads run in the popular *Sports Illustrated Swimsuit Issue* that is published each February are adapted to fit with the theme of the magazine. Exhibit 9–32 shows an example of a clever ad done by TaylorMade Golf for the annual *SI* swimsuit edition.

- *Is the ad truthful and tasteful?* Marketers also have to consider whether an ad is truthful, as well as whether it might offend consumers. For example, Bloomingdale's created a controversy during the 2015 holiday season with an ad that appeared in the department store's holiday catalog. The ad featured a woman laughing and looking away as a man is shown looking at her suggestively. Next to the photo is a caption that reads "Spike your best friend's eggnog when they're not looking." Critics say the ad encourages men to "date rape" their female companions. Bloomingdale's apologized for the ad and acknowledged that it was inappropriate and in poor taste. However, despite the apology, the ad could not be pulled as it was part of a mailed catalog and resulted in a considerable amount of negative publicity for the retailer.[62]

The ultimate responsibility for determining whether an ad deceives or offends the target audience lies with the client. It is the job of the advertising or brand manager to evaluate the approach suggested by the creative specialists against company standards. The firm's legal department may be asked to review the ad to determine whether the creative appeal, message content, or execution could cause any problems for the company. It is much better to catch any potential legal problems before the ad is shown to the public.

The chief marketing officer, brand manager, advertising manager, and/or other personnel on the client side can use these basic guidelines in reviewing, evaluating, and approving the ideas offered by the creative specialists. There may be other factors specific to the firm's advertising and marketing situation. Also, there may be situations where it is acceptable to deviate from the standards the firm usually uses in judging creative output. As we will see in Chapter 18, the client may want to move beyond these subjective criteria and use more sophisticated pretesting methods to determine the effectiveness of a particular approach suggested by the creative specialist or team.

Summary

In this chapter, we examined how the advertising message is implemented and executed. Once the creative strategy that will guide the ad campaign has been determined, attention turns to the specific type of advertising appeal and execution format to carry out the creative plan. The appeal is the central message used in the ad to elicit some response from consumers or influence their feelings. Appeals can be broken into two broad categories, rational and emotional. Rational appeals focus on consumers' practical, functional, or utilitarian need for the product or service; emotional appeals relate to social and/or psychological reasons for purchasing a product or service. Numerous types of appeals are available to advertisers within each category.

The creative execution style is the way the advertising appeal is presented in the message. A number of common execution techniques were examined in the chapter, along with considerations for their use. Attention was also given to tactical issues involved in creating print, television, and digital advertising. The components of a print ad include headlines, body copy, illustrations, and layout. We also examined the video and audio components of TV commercials and various considerations involved in the planning and production of commercials. The role of creativity in digital advertising was discussed along with tactical considerations for display and online video ads.

Creative specialists are responsible for determining the advertising appeal and execution style as well as the tactical aspects of creating ads. However, the client must review, evaluate, and approve the creative approach before any ads are produced or run. A number of criteria can be used by advertising, product, or brand managers and others involved in the promotional process to evaluate the advertising messages before approving final production.

Key Terms

advertising appeal 303
creative execution style 303
informational/rational appeals 303
emotional appeals 304
transformational ad 306
reminder advertising 309
teaser advertising 310

user-generated content (UGC) 311
headline 319
direct headline 322
indirect headline 322
subhead 322
body copy 322
layout 323

voiceover 324
needledrop 325
jingle 326
script 328
native advertising 330

Discussion Questions

1. The chapter opener discusses how DASANI was able to use creative advertising to reposition the brand and make it the leading brand of bottled water. Evaluate the creative strategy used by the Lambesis Agency for DASANI bottled water as well as the two line extensions, DASANI Drops and DASANI Sparkling. Why have they been effective? (LO 9-1, 9-2)

2. Discuss some of the reasons why emotion-based advertising appeals are effective. Find an example of a company or brand that is using an advertising campaign based on emotional appeals and analyze its effectiveness. (LO 9-1)

3. Explain the concept of transformational advertising. Find an example of a company that is using transformational ads and discuss how the ads might enhance the experience of using the product or service. (LO 9-1)

4. Discuss the value of virtual reality (VR) as a way for marketers to communicate with consumers. What are some of the applications of VR to integrated marketing communications? What challenges will marketers face in using virtual reality as a way to connect with consumers? (LO 9-1, 9-2)

5. IMC Perspective 9–1 discusses the "Live Más" campaign for Taco Bell. Analyze the creative strategy used for this campaign, giving attention to the type of creative appeals used as well as the advertising execution. (LO 9-1, 9-2)

6. Choose three of the advertising execution techniques discussed in the chapter and find examples of advertisements that are using them. Discuss why the marketers might be using these particular ad execution techniques. (LO 9-2)

7. Discuss some of the reasons a marketer might choose to create a personality symbol or character to represent the company or brand. Analyze KFC's decision to bring back Colonel Sanders as a personality symbol for the brand. Do you agree with this decision? (LO 9-2)

8. Discuss the role of headlines in a print advertisement. What is the difference between a direct headline and an indirect headline and when might each type be used? (LO 9-3)

9. Discuss the role of music in advertising. Find an example of a television commercial that is using a specific song and discuss the role the music plays in delivering the message. (LO 9-3)

10. Discuss the challenges marketers face in developing online advertising messages. How will the creative strategy for online advertising differ depending on whether the goal is for concept, content, or commerce types of online advertising? (LO 9-3)

11. Digital and Social Media Perspective 9–2 discusses the "Unskippable" online advertising campaign created by the Martin Agency for GEICO. Why do you think this campaign was so popular among consumers? Do you think the technique used for the GEICO campaign could be used by other marketers as a way to draw attention to their online video ads?

12. Choose a current advertising campaign and analyze it with respect to the creative guidelines discussed in the last section of the chapter. Identify any areas where you feel the campaign does not meet the guidelines and discuss why this is so. (LO 9-4)

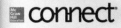

Digital users can access their personalized and adaptive SmartBook, Ad Forum Video Cases, and interactive exercises to review chapter concepts.

10 Media Planning and Strategy

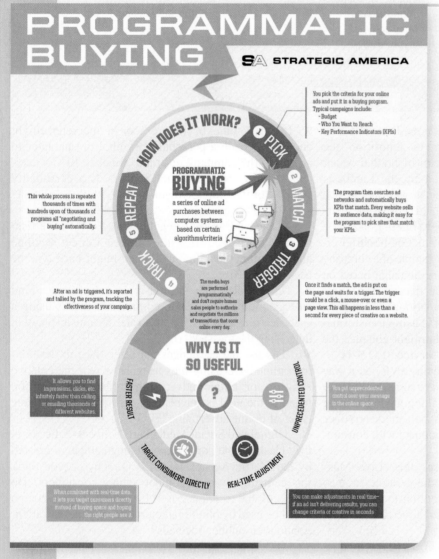

© Strategic America

PROGRAMMATIC: ADVERTISING'S NEWER, BETTER MOUSETRAP—IS BUYING BETTER WITH ROBOTS?

Not long ago, if marketers wanted to purchase an online display ad they had to contact the website, negotiate the terms for each ad placement, and sign an insertion order. If they wanted to do the same in traditional media, the process would be essentially the same—that is, determine which medium they wanted the ad in, negotiate the deal, and place an order. Now, thanks to big data, algorithms, and something called real-time bidding (RTB) all this can be done through technology almost instantly and, depending on who you believe, more effectively. The latest trend in media buying, known as programmatic buying, is upon us and online and social ad buyers seemingly can't adopt it fast enough.

Consider these numbers: In 2012, advertisers spent just shy of $2 billion on real-time bidding. By 2013 that number had risen to $36 billion—with only 7 percent of advertisers saying they spent more than 50 percent on automated buying. By 2016, 66 percent of buyers surveyed said they would spend the majority of their monies in this area, with 87 percent saying they experienced greater returns through programmatic.

But what is programmatic? It's hard to pin down exactly what the term means. While it started off as an acceptable synonym to *real-time bidding*, as it has grown in usage it has also become more confusing. According to *Adweek*, real-time bidding essentially means the use of big data to figure out the right ad, targeted to the right person, at the right time. A more formal definition is offered by Peter Naylor, former executive vice president at NBC Universal: "Programmatic is a catchall term that many people are using to categorize everything from behavioral and intent-based targeting to real-time bidding and exchange-based buying of inventory." So basically programmatic is computer-based advertising buying using a real-time bidding process. When an opening is available the software advises advertisers which page it is, and supplies demographic and behavioral data about the user. Each advertiser's software puts in its bid and in real time the transaction is completed along with the ad of the winning bidder. While originally used to buy and sell online display advertising, and used primarily by direct marketers, programmatic is now commonly used to buy mobile and video display advertising, and many expect that it will become the way to purchase ads on television as well. It is considered highly targeted resulting in improved results and efficiencies, and because it is automated it makes the buyer's life easier. Proponents believe that it will replace all other types of ad buying in the not-too-distant future.

A variety of companies are committed to programmatic already. As Kellogg moves more monies into digital advertising, the company continues to use TV and print. However, for its digital ad placements, programmatic is the method most commonly used. The company believes that it has increased return on investment (ROI) primarily through the improved frequency, control, and targeting using programmatic. Movies Unlimited, an online store for movie collectors specializing in hard-to-find titles while also carrying nearly every title currently available, had a tremendous amount of site traffic but also a 75 percent cart abandonment problem. By using programmatic to assist in e-mail retargeting efforts, the online company experienced a 500 percent increase in ROI. Melia Hotels International, McDonald's, and Telstra also claim success using programmatic, and P&G continues to increase its use to the point where the majority of the company's online buying will employ the automated method.

But, as to be expected, not everyone is so enthralled with the concept. There are those who believe they have found the Holy Grail of media buying, but there are others who are not convinced. Fraud, brand safety, and viewability are of major concern to many programmatic buyers. So too is transparency—or concrete evidence the ad is even being placed. These concerns are reflected in the brand managers' not knowing where the ads are being placed: What if the ad appears somewhere that is surrounded by offensive content? How would this impact their brand image? Another issue is what many consider to be "remnant inventory'"—that is, leftover availabilities that no one else wanted, and not providing information that allows buyers to know why this inventory was not sold. Reports have also indicated that more than 50 percent of the placements can't even be viewed. In addition, many ads may be placed on illegal, inappropriate, and low-quality sites. Many, if not all, of these concerns are eliminated in direct buying, providing the manager with a greater sense of comfort.

Despite these concerns, however, it appears that programmatic is here to stay (at least in the near future) and is likely to find its way into television and maybe even radio ad buying. When companies like P&G, Time, Inc., News Corp., and ESPN continue to embrace it, it will seemingly take a lot to stop the train!

Sources: "Programmatic TV Ushers in 'Golden Era,'" www.warc.com, March 14, 2016; "US Advertisers Are Investing Heavily in Programmatic, but Obstacles Remain," www.eMarketer.com, March 29, 2016; Tim Nichols, "Why Programmatic Ad Buying Is More Important Than You Think," www.clickz.com, November 13, 2015; "Programmatic Buyers Demand Placement Transparency," www.eMarketer.com, April 8, 2015; "Fraud, Brand Safety Take Center Stage among Ad Buyers," www.eMarketer, January 12, 2015; Jamie Turner, "What Every Advertising Agency Executive and CMO Should Know about Digital Media," www.60secondcommunications.com, January 12, 2015; Mike Shields, "Programmatic for Dummies," www.adweek.com, November 3, 2013.

The discussion in this chapter's opening vignette involves a major change taking place in the media buying arena. Prior to the arrival of the Internet and digital media, media buying was pretty much a standardized process. Buyers identified the target market, established objectives for the advertising, and conducted research to determine the best medium in which to place the ad. Then they would contact the medium directly (or through a media buying service) to negotiate the rates and placements and buy the time and/or space. Buyers knew when and where the ad would appear, and barring any mishaps, the deal was done. Once the Internet and digital came along all of this changed. The ability to gain even more data on the target audience, and to place the ad in pretty much real time, as well as the use of different metrics resulted in a whole new media buying landscape. As a result, media planning has become more complex than ever before—despite the contention that programmatic simplifies it. As you will see in the following chapters, these changes offer marketers opportunities not previously available, but they also require in-depth knowledge of all the media alternatives. Integrated marketing communications programs are no longer a luxury; they are a necessity. Media planners must now consider multiple new options as well as recognize the changes that are occurring in traditional sources. New and evolving media contribute to the already difficult task of media planning. Planning when, where, and how the message will be delivered is a complex and involved process that is constantly evolving. The primary objective of the media plan is to develop a framework that will deliver the message communicating what the product, brand, and/or service can do to the target audience in the most efficient, cost-effective manner possible.

This chapter presents the various methods of message delivery available to marketers, examines some key considerations in making media decisions, and discusses the development of media strategies and plans. Later chapters will explore the relative advantages and disadvantages of the various media and examine each in more detail.

It should be noted that while new media often use their own terms and concepts, many also use the more traditional metrics as well. Much of the focus in this chapter will be on traditional concepts, with subsequent chapters dealing with media-specific terminology. For example, in social media a medium would be user-generated video, YouTube is a platform, and a channel would be 60secondmarketer.com.[1] Nevertheless, the value and necessity of a planning framework still exists across media.

AN OVERVIEW OF MEDIA PLANNING

The media planning process is not an easy one. Options include mass media such as television, newspapers, radio, and magazines (and the choices available within each of these categories) as well as out of home media such as outdoor advertising,

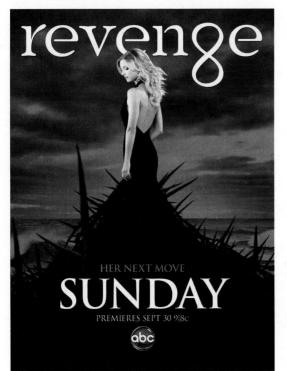

EXHIBIT 10–1

Revenge cast members appeared in commercials during the show

Source: American Broadcasting Companies, Inc.

transit advertising, and electronic billboards. A variety of other media such as direct marketing, promotional products, sales promotions, and in-store point-of-purchase options must also be considered. A proliferation of new media, including branded entertainment, social media, the Internet, and mobile, have also provided marketers with many options to consider.

While at first glance the choices among these alternatives might seem relatively straightforward, this is rarely the case. Part of the reason media selection becomes so involved is the nature of the media themselves. TV combines both sight and sound, an advantage not offered by most other media. Magazines can convey more information and may keep the message available to the potential buyer for a much longer time. Newspapers also offer their own advantages, as do outdoor, direct media, and each of the others. The new digital media offer many of the advantages of other media but also have limitations in their capabilities. The characteristics of each alternative must be considered, along with many other factors. This process becomes even more complicated when the manager has to choose between alternatives within the same medium—for example, between *Time* and *The Week* in print or between *The Big Bang Theory* and *NCIS* on TV, or Facebook and Instagram on the Internet.

Many companies, large and small, have come to realize the importance of a sound media strategy. They are focusing additional attention on the integration of creative work and media as well as the use of multiple media vehicles to achieve the optimal impact. For example, ads that have been shown on TV now appear for viewing on the company's Internet site. In the past the commercials to be shown on the Super Bowl were surrounded by secrecy in an attempt to heighten expectations. Now, many of the commercials that appear on the Super Bowl were first released on YouTube or other media outlets to gain more exposure. Advertisers still disagree as to which strategy is more effective. Some commercials now feature the television program's actors in commercials shown during the program. For example, Target and Neiman Marcus partnered to purchase all of the commercials in the former TV hit *Revenge* for an evening. The long-form commercials were approximately two minutes in length and featured different actors from the show receiving Christmas presents. Target and Neiman Marcus hoped that by integrating the show's characters, viewers would be more likely to pay attention to the commercials (Exhibit 10–1). Michael J. Fox and Julianna Margulies appeared in a commercial spot in *The Good Wife* to promote the TV show *CBS Cares*.

The product and/or service being advertised affects the media planning process. As demonstrated in Figure 10–1, firms have found some media more useful than others in conveying their messages to specific target audiences. For example, Procter & Gamble spends more of its budget in measured media (traditional media like TV, magazines) while American Express spends more in unmeasured media (digital, mobile, etc.). Note that many of these companies have decreased their spending in traditional media while at the same time increasing unmeasured expenditures. The result is placement of advertising dollars in these preferred media—and significantly different media strategies.

Some Basic Terms and Concepts

Before beginning our discussion of media planning, we review some basic terms and concepts used in the media planning and strategy process.

Media planning is the series of decisions involved in delivering the promotional message to the prospective purchasers and/or users of the product or brand. Media planning is a process, which means a number of decisions are made, each of which may be altered or abandoned as the plan develops.

FIGURE 10–1 Leading National Advertisers, Ranked by Total U.S. Advertising Spending, 2014–2015—$ Millions

RANK 2015	RANK 2014	MARKETER	HEADQUARTERS	TOTAL U.S. ADVERTISING SPENDING 2015	2014	% CHG	TOTAL U.S. MEASURED-MEDIA SPENDING 2015	2014	% CHG	TOTAL U.S. UNMEASURED-MEDIA SPENDING 2015	2014	% CHG
1	1	Procter & Gamble Co.	Cincinnati	$4,264.8	$4,434.6	−3.8	$2,221.4	$2,699.6	−17.7	$2,043.5	$1,735.0	17.8
2	2	AT&T	Dallas	3,865.5	3,857.9	0.2	1,700.0	1,794.6	−5.3	2,165.4	2,063.3	5.0
3	3	General Motors Co.	Detroit	3,495.3	3,219.9	8.6	1,418.2	1,560.5	−9.1	2,077.1	1,659.5	25.2
4	4	Comcast Corp.	Philadelphia	3,435.6	3,028.6	13.4	1,494.8	1,338.2	11.7	1,940.8	1,690.3	14.8
5	5	Verizon Communications	New York	2,749.0	2,526.0	8.8	1,040.6	1,138.3	−8.6	1,708.4	1,387.7	23.1
6	6	Ford Motor Co.	Dearborn, Mich.	2,678.0	2,467.1	8.5	1,026.6	797.9	29.2	1,651.4	1,672.3	−1.2
7	7	American Express Co.	New York	2,348.6	2,328.3	0.9	235.4	216.2	8.9	2,113.1	2,112.0	0.1
8	8	Fiat Chrysler Automobiles	London	2,250.0	2,249.8	0.0	932.7	1,001.6	−6.9	1,317.3	1,248.2	5.5
9	16	Amazon	Seattle	2,197.5	1,789.6	22.8	417.3	381.3	9.4	1,780.2	1,408.3	26.4
10	9	Samsung Electronics Co.	Seoul, South Korea	2,122.5	2,102.9	0.9	612.1	618.2	−1.0	1,510.4	1,484.7	1.7
11	13	Walmart Stores	Bentoville, Ark	2,090.3	1,940.1	7.7	689.3	884.6	−22.1	1,401.0	1,055.5	32.7
12	14	JPMorgan Chase & Co.	New York	2,063.0	1,902.7	8.4	259.7	304.8	−14.8	1,803.4	1,597.9	12.9
13	11	Johnson & Johnson	New Brunswick, N.J.	2,008.6	1,967.8	2.1	1,115.9	1,033.3	8.0	892.7	934.5	−4.5
14	12	L'Oréal	Clichy, France	1,994.4	1,941.9	2.7	1,267.3	1,457.7	−13.1	727.1	484.1	50.2
15	17	Pfizer	New York	1,926.4	1,673.2	15.1	1,588.7	1,385.0	14.7	337.6	288.2	17.2
16	10	Toyota Motor Corp.	Toyota City, Japan	1,801.9	2,090.3	−13.8	964.1	1,118.3	−13.8	837.9	971.9	−13.8
17	15	Walt Disney Co.	Burbank, Calif.	1,797.9	1,897.8	−5.3	660.7	755.8	−12.6	1,137.2	1,142.0	−0.4
18	24	Time Warner	New York	1,690.3	1,526.6	10.7	1,048.0	962.8	8.9	642.2	563.8	13.9
19	19	Berkshire Hathaway	Omaha, Neb.	1,683.0	1,625.2	3.6	1,455.8	1,400.7	3.9	227.2	224.5	1.2
20	23	Anheuser-Busch InBev	Leuven, Belgium/St. Louis	1,682.8	1,568.3	7.3	532.8	519.1	2.6	1,150.0	1,049.2	9.6
21	26	Capital One Financial Corp.	McLean, Va.	1,650.7	1,464.4	12.7	292.2	313.6	−6.8	1,358.6	1,150.8	18.1
22	22	21st Century Fox	New York	1,632.5	1,583.5	3.1	670.5	736.6	−9.0	962.0	846.8	13.6
23	29	Deutsche Telekom (T-Mobile)	Bonn, Germany/Bellevue, Wash.	1,600.0	1,400.0	14.3	957.0	800.1	19.6	643.0	599.9	7.2

Source: "The 200 Leading National Advertisers," *Advertising Age, July 13, 2015.*

The media plan is the guide for media selection. It requires development of specific **media objectives** and specific **media strategies** (plans of action) designed to attain these objectives. Once the decisions have been made and the objectives and strategies formulated, this information is organized into the media plan.

The **medium** is the general category of available delivery systems, which includes broadcast media (like TV and radio), print media (like newspapers and magazines), direct marketing, outdoor advertising, and other support media. The **media vehicle** is the specific carrier within a medium category. For example, *Vanity Fair* and *In Style* are print vehicles; *The Voice* and *60 Minutes* are broadcast vehicles; Facebook and Instagram are social media vehicles. As you will see in later chapters, each vehicle has its own characteristics as well as its own relative advantages and disadvantages. Specific decisions must be made as to the value of each in delivering the message.

Reach is a measure of the number of different audience members exposed at least once to a media vehicle in a given period of time. **Coverage** refers to the potential audience that might receive the message through a vehicle. Coverage relates to potential audience; reach refers to the actual audience delivered. (The importance of this distinction will become clearer later in this chapter.) Finally, **frequency** refers to the number of times the receiver is exposed to the media vehicle in a specified period. While there are numerous more media planning terms that are important and commonly used (for a useful reference see *Media Planning & Buying in the 21st Century*),[2] we will begin our discussion with these as they are critical to your understanding of the planning process.

The Media Plan

The media plan determines the best way to get the advertiser's message to the market. In a basic sense, the goal of the media plan is to find that combination of media that enables the marketer to communicate the message in the most effective manner to the largest number of potential customers at the lowest cost.

The activities involved in developing the media plan and the purposes of each are presented in Figure 10–2. As you can see, a number of decisions must be made throughout this process. As the plan evolves, events may occur that necessitate changes. Many advertisers find it necessary to alter and update their objectives and strategies frequently.

Problems in Media Planning

Unfortunately, the media strategy decision has not become a simple task. A number of problems contribute to the difficulty of establishing the plan and reduce its effectiveness. These problems include insufficient information, inconsistent terminologies, time pressures, and difficulty measuring effectiveness.

Insufficient Information While a great deal of information about markets and the media exists, media planners often require more than is available. Some data are just not measured, either because they cannot be or because measuring them would be too expensive. For example, continuous measures of radio listenership exist, but only periodic listenership studies are reported due to sample size and cost constraints. There are problems with some measures of audience size in other media as well. As seen in the lead-in to this chapter, there is often a lack of information and transparency in using programmatic buying.

The timing of measurements is also a problem; some audience measures are taken only at specific times of the year. (For example, **sweeps periods** in February, May, July, and November are used for measuring TV audiences and setting advertising rates.) This information is then generalized to succeeding months, so future planning decisions must be made on past data that may not reflect current behaviors.

FIGURE 10-2 Activities Involved in Developing the Media Plan

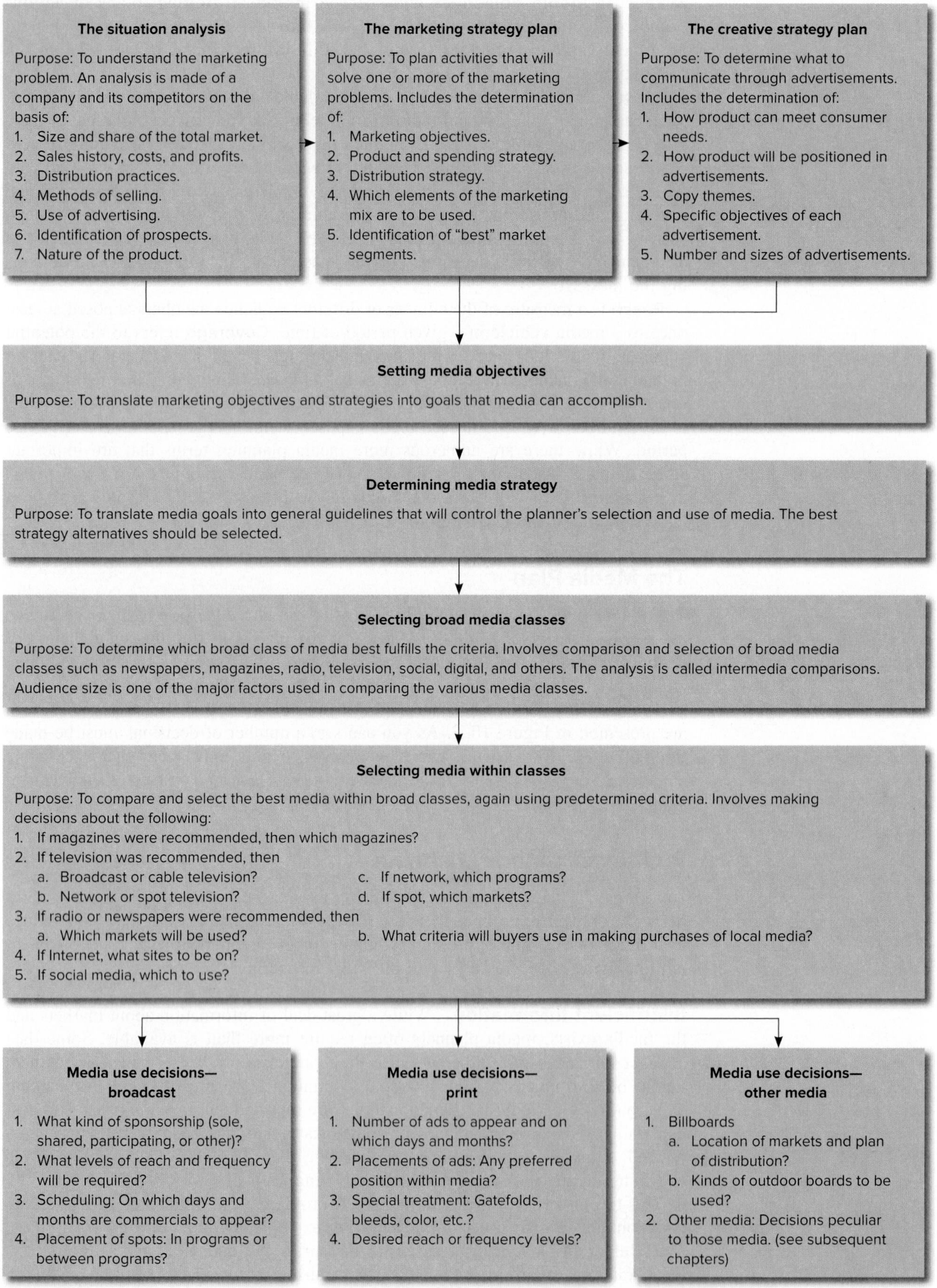

The situation analysis

Purpose: To understand the marketing problem. An analysis is made of a company and its competitors on the basis of:
1. Size and share of the total market.
2. Sales history, costs, and profits.
3. Distribution practices.
4. Methods of selling.
5. Use of advertising.
6. Identification of prospects.
7. Nature of the product.

The marketing strategy plan

Purpose: To plan activities that will solve one or more of the marketing problems. Includes the determination of:
1. Marketing objectives.
2. Product and spending strategy.
3. Distribution strategy.
4. Which elements of the marketing mix are to be used.
5. Identification of "best" market segments.

The creative strategy plan

Purpose: To determine what to communicate through advertisements. Includes the determination of:
1. How product can meet consumer needs.
2. How product will be positioned in advertisements.
3. Copy themes.
4. Specific objectives of each advertisement.
5. Number and sizes of advertisements.

Setting media objectives

Purpose: To translate marketing objectives and strategies into goals that media can accomplish.

Determining media strategy

Purpose: To translate media goals into general guidelines that will control the planner's selection and use of media. The best strategy alternatives should be selected.

Selecting broad media classes

Purpose: To determine which broad class of media best fulfills the criteria. Involves comparison and selection of broad media classes such as newspapers, magazines, radio, television, social, digital, and others. The analysis is called intermedia comparisons. Audience size is one of the major factors used in comparing the various media classes.

Selecting media within classes

Purpose: To compare and select the best media within broad classes, again using predetermined criteria. Involves making decisions about the following:
1. If magazines were recommended, then which magazines?
2. If television was recommended, then
    a. Broadcast or cable television?
    b. Network or spot television?
    c. If network, which programs?
    d. If spot, which markets?
3. If radio or newspapers were recommended, then
    a. Which markets will be used?
    b. What criteria will buyers use in making purchases of local media?
4. If Internet, what sites to be on?
5. If social media, which to use?

Media use decisions—broadcast

1. What kind of sponsorship (sole, shared, participating, or other)?
2. What levels of reach and frequency will be required?
3. Scheduling: On which days and months are commercials to appear?
4. Placement of spots: In programs or between programs?

Media use decisions—print

1. Number of ads to appear and on which days and months?
2. Placements of ads: Any preferred position within media?
3. Special treatment: Gatefolds, bleeds, color, etc.?
4. Desired reach or frequency levels?

Media use decisions—other media

1. Billboards
    a. Location of markets and plan of distribution?
    b. Kinds of outdoor boards to be used?
2. Other media: Decisions peculiar to those media. (see subsequent chapters)

(In the largest 56 TV markets meters are used to provide information.) Think about planning for TV advertising for the fall season. There are no data on the audiences of new shows, and audience information taken on existing programs during the summer may not indicate how these programs will do in the fall because summer viewership is generally much lower. While the advertisers can review these programs before they air, all markets do not have actual audience figures.

The lack of information is even more of a problem for small advertisers, or smaller markets, who may not be able to afford to purchase the information they require. As a result, their decisions are based on limited or out-of-date data that were provided by the media themselves, or no data at all.

Inconsistent Terminologies   Problems arise because the cost bases used by different media often vary and the standards of measurement used to establish these costs are not always consistent. For example, print media may present cost data in terms of the cost to reach a thousand people (cost per thousand, or CPM), broadcast media use the cost per ratings point (CPRP), and outdoor media use the number of showings. The advent of the Internet brought about a whole new lexicon of terminologies. Audience information that is used as a basis for these costs has also been collected by different methods. Finally, terms that actually mean something different (such as *reach* and *coverage*) may be used synonomously by some, adding to the confusion.

In 2006, a joint task force composed of members of the Association of National Advertisers (ANA), American Association of Advertising Agencies (4As), Direct Marketing Association (DMA), Advertising Research Foundation (ARF), Interactive Advertising Bureau (IAB), and Advertising Research Foundation (ARF) launched an initiative to determine a better way to measure consumer exposure to an advertisement. The group unveiled an initiative that would significantly change the way exposure was measured, essentially replacing the use of frequency (the number of exposures to an ad) with engagement, a measure they said would better reflect the growing number of media choices available to consumers. Although the committee agreed on backing the new term, others were not so willing, asking for a more precise definition of *engagement*. The committee agreed to further examine and validate the concept.[3] However, even today there is no consensus as to the meaning of the term.[4]

At the same time, the importance of engagement has been recognized by marketers. The Nielsen Company, which provides TV ratings data, is just one of many firms now providing engagement data. Figure 10–3 shows the results of a study that demonstrates that there is a strong correlation between program involvement and ad recall.

FIGURE 10–3

The Relationship between Engagement and Ad Recall

Source: The Nielsen Company.

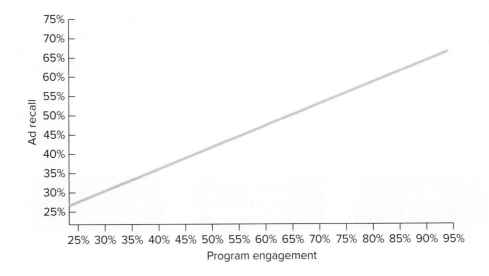

Time Pressures It seems that advertisers are always in a hurry—sometimes because they need to be, other times because they think they need to be. Actions by a competitor—for example, the cutting of airfares by one carrier—require immediate response. But sometimes a false sense of urgency dictates time pressures. In either situation, media selection decisions may be made without proper planning and analysis of the markets and/or media.

Difficulty Measuring Effectiveness Because it is so hard to measure the effectiveness of advertising and promotions in general, it is also difficult to determine the relative effectiveness of various media or media vehicles. (Recall the discussion of ROI from Chapter 7.) While progress is being made in this regard, the media planner may have little more than an estimate of or a good guess at the impact of these alternatives. In fact, in a study reported in *eMarketer* only 25 percent of brand marketers reported that they were confident that their media mix was optimal, due to the inability to make this determination.[5]

Because of these problems, not all media decisions are quantitatively determined. Sometimes managers have to assume the image of a medium in a market with which they are not familiar, anticipate the impact of recent events, or make judgments without full knowledge of all the available alternatives.

While these problems complicate the media decision process, they do not render it an entirely subjective exercise. The remainder of this chapter explores in more detail how media strategies are developed and ways to increase their effectiveness.

DEVELOPING THE MEDIA PLAN

The promotional planning model in Chapter 1 discussed the process of identifying target markets, establishing objectives, and formulating strategies for attaining them. The development of the media plan and strategies follows a similar path, except that the focus is more specifically keyed to determining the best way to deliver the message. The process, shown in Figure 10–4, involves a series of stages: (1) market analysis, (2) establishment of media objectives, (3) media strategy development and implementation, and (4) evaluation and follow-up. Each of these is discussed in turn, with specific examples.

MARKET ANALYSIS AND TARGET MARKET IDENTIFICATION

The situation analysis stage of the overall promotional planning process involves a complete review of internal and external factors, competitive strategies, and the like. In the development of a media strategy, a market analysis is again performed, although this time the focus is on the media and delivering the message. The key questions at this stage are these: To whom will we advertise (who is the target market)? What internal and external factors may influence the media plan? Where (geographically) and when should we focus our efforts?

FIGURE 10–4

Developing the Media Plan

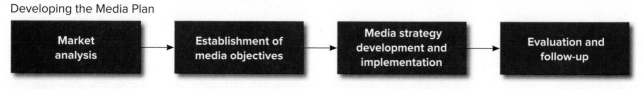

To Whom Will We Advertise?

While a number of target markets might be derived from the situation analysis, to decide which specific groups to go after, the media planner may work with the client, account representative, marketing department, and creative directors. A variety of factors can assist media planners in this decision. Some will require primary research, whereas others will be available from published (secondary) sources.

Experian Simmons, formerly the Simmons Market Research Bureau (SMRB), provides information through its annual *Experian National Consumer Study*. The study provides information regarding traditional media usage (English and Spanish languages), product, brands and services used, and demographic and psychographic characteristics. Experian also provides a *New Media Study* providing insights into Americans' use of mobile phones, social networking, and dozens of other new emerging technologies. The company's competitor GfK-Mediamark Research, Inc. (GfK MRI) also provides consumer information and media usage characteristics of the population.

Media planners are often more concerned with the percentage figures and index numbers than with the raw numbers. This is largely due to the fact that they may have their own data from other sources, both primary and secondary; the numbers provided may not be specific enough for their needs; or they question the numbers provided because of the methods by which they were collected. The total (raw) numbers provided by Experian and GfK MRI are used in combination with the media planner's own figures.

On the other hand, the **index number** is considered a good indicator of the potential of the market. This number is derived from the formula

$$\text{Index} = \frac{\text{Percentage of users in a demographic segment}}{\text{Percentage of population in the same segment}} \times 100$$

An index number over 100 means use of the product is proportionately greater in that segment than in one that is average (100) or less than 100. For example, the GfK MRI data in Figure 10–5 show that people in the age groups 18–24 and 25–34, respectively, are more likely to engage in snowboarding, while those who did not graduate high school, lower-income groups, and older adults are the least likely to snowboard. Men are more likely than women to participate. Depending on their overall strategy, marketers may wish to use this information to determine which groups are now using the product and target them or to identify a group that is currently using the product less and attempt to develop that segment. Figure 10–6 provides more instruction on how to read a GfK MRI report. (There is also an instructional video on YouTube—Google "GfK MRI-PLUS.")

While the index is helpful, it should not be used alone. Percentages and product usage figures are also needed to get an accurate picture of the market. Just because the index for a particular segment of the population is very high, that doesn't always mean it is an attractive segment to target. The high index may be a result of a low denominator (a very small proportion of the population in this segment). In Figure 10–7, the 18- to 24-year-old age segment has the highest index, but it also has both the lowest product usage and the lowest population percentage. A marketer who relied solely on the index would be ignoring a full 82 percent of product users.

Keep in mind that while Experian and GfK MRI provide demographic, geographic, and some psychographic information, other factors may also be useful in defining specific markets and media usage. IMC Perspective 10–1 shows how other factors may have an impact.

FIGURE 10-5 GfK MRI Report on Snowboarders
Spring 2014 Product: Leisure/Sports Snowboarding: Participated in Last 12 Months

		Total '000	UNW	'000	% Detail	% Target	Index
Total		237,011	329	3,566	100	1.5	100
Men		114,141	233	2,524	70.8	2.21	147
Women		122,870	96	11,041	29.2	.85	56
Educ: graduated college plus		67,714	94	842	23.61	1.24	83
Educ: attended college		68,224	141	1,410	39.54	2.07	137
Educ: graduated high school		70,520	76	1,075	30.16	1.52	101
Educ: did not graduate HS	*	30,552	18	239	6.69	0.78	52
Educ: post graduate	*	24,233	31	241	6.75	0.99	66
Educ: no college		101,072	94	1,314	36.85	1.3	86
Age 18–24		30,221	102	1,421	39.85	4.7	313
Age 25–34		41,706	127	1,182	33.15	2.83	188
Age 35–44		40,126	56	586	16.44	1.46	97
Age 45–54	*	43,941	28	244	6.85	0.56	37
Age 55–64	*	38,390	9	96	2.68	0.25	17
Age 65+	*	42,626	7	37	1.03	.09	6
Occupation: Professional and Related Occupations		32,190	52	568	15.93	1.76	117
Occupation: Management, Business and Financial Opera	*	22,675	45	387	10.84	1.7	113
Occupation: Sales and Office Occupations	*	32,545	47	574	16.09	1.76	117
Occupation: Natural Resources, Construction and Maintenance	*	13,108	26	301	8.45	2.3	153
Occupation: Other employed		41,958	89	916	25.69	2.18	145
HHI: $150,000+		26,233	51	561	15.73	2.14	142
HHI: $75,000–$149,999		68,105	107	1,297	36.38	1.9	127
HHI: $60,000–$74,999	*	25,109	41	370	10.37	1.47	98
HHI: $50,000–$59,999	*	18,815	27	304	8.52	1.61	107
HHI: $40,000–$49,999	*	20,600	26	1200	5.61	0.97	65
HHI: $30,000–$39,999	*	22,631	23	313	8.78	1.38	92
HHI: $20,000–$29,999	*	23,014	24	208	5.84	0.90	60
HHI: <$20,000	*	32,503	30	313	8.78	0.96	64
Race: White		178,734	253	2,761	77.44	1.54	103
Race: Black/African American	*	29,411	32	385	10.79	1.31	87
Race: American Indian/Alaskan	*	2,858	5	25	0.69	0.86	57
Race: Asian	*	6,958	24	203	5.69	2.91	194
Race: Other	*	23,339	24	262	7.35	1.12	75
Race: White Only		175,782	244	2,691	75.48	1.53	102
Race: Black/African American Only	*	28,166	30	381	10.69	1.35	90
Race: Other Race/Multiple Classifications		33,063	55	493	13.82	1.49	99
Spanish or Hispanic Origin	*	35,316	32	349	9.78	0.99	66
HH Subscribe to Cable		116,969	142	1,443	40.47	1.23	82
HH Subscribe to Digital Cable		95,351	129	1,266	35.5	1.33	88
HH Have a Satellite Dish		62,823	87	1,117	31.33	1.78	118
Watched any Pay-Per-View/Last 12 Months		31,468	52	571	16.02	1.81	121
Watched any Video on Demand/Last 12 Months		58,744	118	1,096	30.73	1.87	124
Any Cable Viewing/Last Week		191,554	253	2,701	75.76	1.41	94

* Indicates unstable sample of less than 50 responses.

Source: Mediamark Research, GfK MRI.

How to read a GfK MRI University Internet Reporter Worksheet

The numbers shown below are the number of people who used *Bottled Water & Seltzer* in the last 6 months.

Base Total '000: in the GfK MRI Spring 2014 study the Base Total (projected population) is **237,011**, when calculated in thousands represents **237,011,000** Adults 18+ (Base: All).

'000: projected to population is **84,983,000** Women (18+) drank Bottled Water & Seltzer in the Last 6 Months.

% Detail: 54.69% of Adults 18+ who drank Bottled Water & Seltzer in the Last 6 Months are Women.

% Target: 69.17% of Women 18+ drank Bottled Water & Seltzer in the Last 6 Months.

Index: Women 18+ are 6% more likely than the general population 18+ to drink Bottled Water & Seltzer in the Last 6 Months.

Target	Base Total '000	'000	% Detail	% Target	Index
Total	237,011	155,382	100	65.5	100
Men	114,141	70,399	45.31	61.8	94
Women	122,870	84,983	54.69	69.17	106
Educ: graduated college plus	67,714	45,929	29.56	67.83	103
Educ: attended college	68,224	46,503	29.93	68.16	104
Educ: graduated high school	70,520	44,265	28.49	62.77	96
Educ: did not graduate HS	30,552	18,685	12.03	61.16	93
Educ: post graduate	24,233	15,881	10.22	65.53	100
Educ: no college	101,072	62,950	40.51	62.28	95
Age 18-24	30,221	21,586	13.89	71.43	109
Age 25-34	41,706	29,020	18.68	69.58	106
Age 35-44	40,126	28,060	18.06	69.93	107
Age 45-54	43,941	30,044	19.34	68.37	104
Age 55-64	38,390	24,759	15.93	64.49	98
Age 65+	42,626	21,914	14.1	51.41	78
Occupation: Professional and Related Occupations	32,190	22,567	14.52	70.11	107
Occupation: Management, Business and Financial Operations	22,675	16,227	10.44	71.56	109
Occupation: Sales and Office Occupations	32,545	23,686	15.24	72.78	111

FIGURE 10–6

How to Read a GfK MRI Reporter Worksheet

Source: Mediamark Research & Intelligence, LLC (GfK MRI). Reprinted with permission.

What Internal and External Factors Are Operating?

Media strategies are influenced by both internal and external factors operating at any given time. *Internal factors* may involve the size of the media budget, managerial and administrative capabilities, or the organization of the agency. *External factors* may include the economy (the rising costs of media), changes in technology (the availability of new media and new buying methods), competitive factors, and the like. While some of this information may require primary research, much information is available through secondary sources, including magazines, syndicated services, news sources, and online.

One service's competitive information was shown in Figure 10–1. Another is Competitrack which provides media spending figures for various industries down to the campaign or product level. Competitive information is also available from many other sources.

Where to Promote?

The question of where to promote relates to geographic considerations. As noted in Chapter 7, companies often find that sales are stronger in one area of the country

FIGURE 10–7

How High Indexes Can Be Misleading

Age Segment	Population in Segment (%)	Product Use in Segment (%)	Index
18–24	15.1	18.0	119
25–34	25.1	25.0	100
35–44	20.6	21.0	102
45 +	39.3	36.0	91

IMC Perspective 10–1 > > >

BEING SOCIAL, COSMOPOLITAN, AND OTHER FACTORS MAY DETERMINE WHICH MEDIA YOU USE

By now we all know that the media habits of the younger generation have changed dramatically. Television viewing is down, newspaper readership is down, radio listenership is down, and on and on. But it is not just an age thing that has an impact on our media use. Other factors enter into the equation as well. And while advertisers continue to focus on demographics, they may be missing opportunities.

For example, while social media usage takes away time that one might be watching TV, it can also can drive others to watch. A study from *ShareThis* shows a strong correlation between social engagement and higher tune-in rates. The study shows that social media users who click on shared content about a particular TV series are nearly 2.5 times more likely to become viewers. The study also indicated that the genre of the show will impact social engagement rates, with reality and variety shows generating the most social sharing and comedy shows the least. The timing of the sharing also differs, with reality and variety show sharing most often taking place during the show (70 percent), while drama fans share about 24 hours later.

Being cosmopolitan can also make a difference. Recent studies have shown that cosmopolitan consumers are especially receptive to ads that signal the advertiser is addressing them. They are more likely to engage with communications that are consistent with their cosmopolitan values and lifestyles. Not only are they more likely to be reached through upscale magazines like *Luxury* and *Cosmopolitan,* but they are also more likely to use media that report on social causes, environmental issues, and so on.

A study conducted by the Entertainment Technology Center at the University of Southern California, the Hallmark Channel, and E-Poll Market Research concludes that a better predictor of media usage than demographics is the user's lifestyle. Identifying nine lifestyle groups (teens, college students, recent

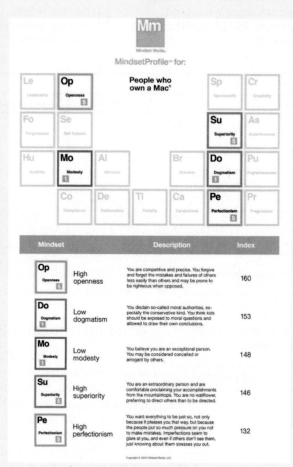

Source: Mindset Media LLC

or the world than another and may allocate advertising expenditures according to the market potential of an area. For example, the Mexican beer Pacifico has a much greater brand share of the beer market in the Pacific census region than in the Midwest census region. The question is, where will the ad dollars be more wisely spent? Should Pacifico allocate additional promotional monies to those markets where the brand is already among the leaders to maintain and expand market share, or does more potential exist in those markets where the firm is not doing as well and there is more room to grow? Perhaps the best answer is that the firm should spend advertising and promotion dollars where they will be the most effective—that is, in those markets where they will achieve the desired objectives. Unfortunately, as we have seen so often, it is not always possible to measure directly the impact of promotional efforts. At the same time, certain tactics can assist the planner in making this determination.

graduates, single, no kids, new nesters, established families, married couples with no children, and empty nesters), the researchers concluded that whereas cohorts of these groups may have similar demographic profiles, they may have different attitudes and media usage habits. For example, new nesters rate family relationships as more important than do childless couples (70 versus 56 percent). New nesters also watch more TV than other groups, and place high value on devices that filter content, like DVRs, video on demand services, and DVD players, to display family-appropriate programming. Childless couples, on the other hand, tend to be engaged more outside the home, relying less on TV; when they do watch TV, they prefer drama to family programming. Differences also exist in regard to other media, for example, social networking. New nesters use social networks to stay in touch with friends and family, and are the most satisfied with the technology. Childless couples are less satisfied, primarily using the networking sites for professional purposes. The conclusion of the study is that there are clear and distinct differences between these groups that offer media buyers an advantage over demographics.

Another study, conducted by the psychographic research company Mindset Media, provided similar findings. Examining both demographic data and personalities, this study concluded that younger people use new media more than their elders; older generations prefer print; and women read magazines more than men. Not much new there. But the study also concluded that the more exciting findings are related to the influence of one's personality on media usage. For example, while almost everyone uses the Internet for a variety of reasons, the heaviest users tend to be high in openness and bravado, while low-level users are high in dogmatism, socially conservative, and religious. Liberals are most likely to have the Internet as their most consumed medium. Newspaper readers are more likely to be optimists, recycle, purchase a luxury car, and are dynamic and leaders. Magazine readers are also dynamic, but are more open than newspaper readers. They are comfortable with their emotions, like the movies, and have music collections. Introverts and those low in self-motivation are less likely to read magazines. On the other hand, dynamic people don't watch TV, nor do those who exhibit high openness and leadership. Those high in bravado and risk takers are TV watchers, as are those who score low on openness

and leadership, and are less likely to plan. Finally, there are the radio listeners. The most dynamic of media users, they watch very little TV and always have the radio on in the car or at home. Introverts use almost no radio, are most likely to watch TV for five or more hours a day, and rarely plan. They also discourage their children from using the Internet. Overall, the study concludes, personality may be a better predictor of media usage than are age, gender, and income, and researchers may be better off using a personality test rather than focus groups and demographic data to determine media usage.

Looking at it from the other side, a study of Facebook users also yielded some interesting findings. Researchers from the University of Cambridge examined data from Facebook members who agreed to take online personality and intelligence tests, and were able to determine that what they "liked" on the popular media website told a lot about them and their personalities. Besides easily predicting one's gender and ethnicity, political and religious affiliations could be determined as well. In addition, the researchers were able to find personality traits that correlated with the endorsements. For example, those who "liked" NASCAR and *The Bachelor* tended to be more conservative and less open to new ideas. If you "like" the *Colbert Report* you are more likely to have a high IQ and like curly fries. Curly fries? Another study conducted by Pew Internet and American Life Project researchers concluded that social network users are more trusting and more willing to share information than those not on a social network, and are less concerned with privacy issues. The same holds true for Internet users who check into Facebook more than once a day than for those who don't. As noted by Fred Wolens, a public policy manager for Pew, "No matter the vehicle for information—a bumper sticker, yard sign, logos on clothing or other data found online—it has already been proven that it is possible for social scientists to draw conclusions about personal attributes based on these characteristics." Yikes!

Sources: Mel Prince, "Strategies for Marketing to Cosmopolitan Consumers," www.Quirks.com, February 2016; Gavin O'Malley, "Study: Social Media Drives TV Viewership," www.mediapostg.com, May 6, 2015; Geoffrey Mohan, "On Facebook, You Are What You 'Like,' Researchers Say," *Los Angeles Times*, March 12, 2013, p. A8; Steve McClellan, "Are Demographics Dead?" www.adweek.com, February 23, 2010, pp. 1–2; Beth Snyder Bulik, "How Personality Can Predict Media Usage," www.adage.com, May 4, 2009, pp. 1–4.

Using Indexes to Determine Where to Promote   In addition to the indexes from Experian Simmons and GfK MRI, three other indexes may also be useful:

1. The **survey of buying power index** is conducted for every major metropolitan market in the United States and is based on a number of factors, including population, effective buying income, and total retail sales in the area. Each of these factors is individually weighted to drive a buying power index that charts the potential of a particular metro area, county, or city relative to the United States as a whole. The resulting index gives media planners insight into the relative value of that market, as shown in Figure 10–8. When used in combination with other market information, the survey of buying power index helps the marketer determine which geographic areas to target.

2. The **brand development index (BDI)** helps marketers factor the rate of product usage by geographic area into the decision process.

FIGURE 10–8 Survey of Buying Power Index

DMA	Total Population	Households	Asian/ Pacific Islander	African-American Pop.	Hispanic Pop.	Population by Age Group					
						2–11	12–17	18–24	25–34	35–49	50+
Ft. Myers-Naples, FL	1,217,708	508,145	15,343	84,084	247,548	141,863	80,224	85,712	149,848	222,580	508,015
Gainesville, FL	322,150	129,627	12,118	55,007	22,018	34,805	22,127	59,388	47,021	57,414	93,993
Jacksonville, FL	1,758,602	680,711	44,550	384,062	99,011	240,379	142,160	158,680	235,808	379,557	552,285
Miami-Ft. Lauderdale, FL	4,300,579	1,561,568	90,165	886,325	1,979,958	542,344	334,111	384,710	502,057	984,256	1,443,731
Orlando-Daytona Beach-Melbourne, FL	3,723,526	1,464,418	105,286	488,912	640,945	457,847	276,477	323,235	493,413	775,064	1,304,938
Panama City, FL	368,863	148,310	4,522	50,011	12,953	43,900	26,555	31,351	51,089	76,883	129,719
Tallahassee-Thomasville, FL-GA	725,699	281,591	10,361	230,056	36,005	92,149	54,215	95,867	106,825	142,844	213,904
Tampa-St. Petersburg (Sarasota), FL	4,368,468	1,821,660	98,189	464,796	620,598	519,526	310,946	343,185	531,163	867,935	1,691,454
West Palm Beach-Ft. Pierce, FL	1,905,978	786,561	37,615	272,071	318,530	223,654	134,638	144,177	218,045	372,294	768,673

DMA	Total EBI	Retail Sales	Buying Power Index
Ft. Myers-Naples, FL	31,562,042,500	21,286,463,216	0.4633
Gainesville, FL	5,844,027,500	4,651,926,011	0.0968
Jacksonville, FL	37,164,647,500	28,725,730,663	0.5906
Miami-Ft. Lauderdale, FL	89,188,970,000	75,015,224,126	1.4625
Orlando-Daytona Beach-Melbourne, FL	77,523,552,500	59,556,677,892	1.2333
Panama City, FL	7,087,285,000	5,238,076,874	0.1133
Tallahassee-Thomasville, FL-GA	12,952,682,500	10,535,214,913	0.2166
Tampa-St. Petersburg (Sarasota), FL	96,233,265,000	65,492,720,766	1.4595
West Palm Beach-Ft. Pierce, FL	51,014,940,000	35,632,927,152	0.7529

Source: Copyright © 2009 by Nielsen Claritas Inc., a part of the Nielsen Company, and/or infoUSA, Inc. (as applicable): This product contains proprietary and confidential property of Nielsen Claritas Inc. and/or infoUSA, Inc. (as applicable). Unauthorized use, including copying of the product, is expressly prohibited.

FIGURE 10–9

Calculating BDI

$$BDI = \frac{\text{Percentage of brand sales in South Atlantic region}}{\text{Percentage of U.S. population in South Atlantic region}} \times 100$$

$$= \frac{50\%}{16\%} \times 100$$

$$= 312$$

$$BDI = \frac{\text{Percentage of brand to total U.S. sales in the market}}{\text{Percentage of total U.S. population in the market}} \times 100$$

The BDI compares the percentage of the brand's total U.S. sales in a given market area with the percentage of the total population in the market to determine the sales potential for that brand in that market area. An example of this calculation is shown in Figure 10–9. The higher the index number, the more market potential exists. In this case, the index number indicates this market has high potential for brand development.

3. The **category development index (CDI)** is computed in the same manner as the BDI, except it uses information regarding the product category (as opposed to the brand) in the numerator:

$$CDI = \frac{\text{Percentage of product category total sales in market}}{\text{Percentage of total U.S. population in market}} \times 100$$

The CDI provides information on the potential for development of the total product category rather than specific brands. When this information is combined with the BDI, a much more insightful promotional strategy may be developed. For example, consider the market potential for coffee in the United States. One might first look at how well the product category does in a specific market area. In Utah and Idaho, for example, the category potential is low (see Figure 10–10). The marketer analyzes the BDI to find how the brand is doing relative to other brands in this area. This information can then be used in determining how well a particular product category and a particular brand are performing and figuring what media weight (or quantity of advertising) would be required to gain additional market share, as shown in Figure 10–11.

While these indexes provide important insights into the market potential for the firm's products and/or brands, this information is supplemental to the

FIGURE 10–10

Using CDI and BDI to Determine Market Potential

$$CDI = \frac{\text{Percentage of product category sales in Utah/Idaho}}{\text{Percentage of total U.S. population in Utah/Idaho}} \times 100$$

$$= \frac{1\%}{1\%} \times 100$$

$$= 100$$

$$BDI = \frac{\text{Percentage of total brand sales in Utah/Idaho}}{\text{Percentage of total U.S. population in Utah/Idaho}} \times 100$$

$$= \frac{2\%}{1\%} \times 100$$

$$= 200$$

FIGURE 10–11

Using BDI and CDI Indexes

	High BDI	Low BDI
High CDI	High market share Good market potential	Low market share Good market potential
Low CDI	High market share Monitor for sales decline	Low market share Poor market potential

High BDI and high CDI	This market usually represents good sales potential for both the product category and the brand.
High BDI and low CDI	The category is not selling well, but the brand is; probably a good market to advertise in but should be monitored for declining sales.
Low BDI and high CDI	The product category shows high potential but the brand is not doing well; the reasons should be determined.
Low BDI and low CDI	Both the product category and the brand are doing poorly; not likely to be a good place for advertising.

overall strategy determined earlier in the promotional decision-making process. In fact, much of this information may have already been provided to the media planner. Since it may be used more specifically to determine the media weights to assign to each area, this decision ultimately affects the budget allocated to each area as well as other factors such as reach, frequency, and scheduling.

ESTABLISHING MEDIA OBJECTIVES

Just as the situation analysis leads to establishment of marketing and communications objectives, the media situation analysis should lead to determination of specific media objectives. The media objectives are not ends in themselves. Rather, they are designed to lead to the attainment of communications and marketing objectives. Media objectives are the goals for the media program and should be limited to those that can be accomplished through media strategies. An example of media objectives is this: Create awareness in the target market through the following:

- Use broadcast media to provide coverage of 80 percent of the target market over a six-month period.
- Reach 60 percent of the target audience at least three times over the same six-month period.
- Create a positive brand image through mood and creativity.

DEVELOPING AND IMPLEMENTING MEDIA STRATEGIES

Having determined what is to be accomplished, media planners consider how to achieve these objectives. That is, they develop and implement media strategies, which evolve directly from the actions required to meet objectives and involve the criteria in Figure 10–12.

The Media Mix

A wide variety of media and media vehicles are available to advertisers. While it is possible that only one medium and/or vehicle might be employed, it is much more

FIGURE 10–12

Criteria Considered in the Development of Media Plans

- The media mix
- Target market coverage
- Geographic coverage
- Scheduling
- Reach and frequency
- Recency
- Creative aspects and mood
- Flexibility
- Budget considerations

likely that a number of alternatives will be used. The objectives sought, the characteristics of the product or service, the size of the budget, and individual preferences are just some of the factors that determine what combination of media will be taken into consideration.

As an example, consider a promotional situation in which a product requires a visual demonstration to be communicated effectively. In this case, TV or the Internet may be the most effective medium. If the promotional strategy calls for coupons to stimulate trial, print media may be necessary. (Many companies also provide the capability to print coupons from their websites.) For in-depth information the Internet may be best, while for spreading the word among friends it may be social media.

By employing a media mix, advertisers can add more versatility to their media strategies, since each medium contributes its own distinct advantages (as demonstrated in later chapters). By combining media, marketers can increase coverage, reach, and frequency levels while improving the likelihood of achieving overall communications and marketing goals.

Target Market Coverage

The media planner determines which target markets should receive the most media emphasis. Developing media strategies involves matching the most appropriate media to this market by asking, "Through which media and media vehicles can I best get my message to prospective buyers?" The issue here is to get coverage of the market, as shown in Figure 10–13. The optimal goal is full market coverage, shown in the second pie chart. But this is a very optimistic scenario. More realistically, conditions shown in the third and fourth charts are most likely to occur. In the third chart, the coverage of the media does not allow for coverage of the entire market, leaving some potential customers without exposure to the message. In the fourth chart, the marketer is faced with a problem of overexposure (also called **waste coverage**), in which the media coverage exceeds the targeted audience. If media coverage reaches people who are not sought as buyers and are not potential users, then it is wasted. (This term is used for coverage that reaches people who are not potential buyers and/or users. Consumers may not be part of the intended target market but may still be considered as potential—for example, those who buy the product as a gift for someone else.)

The goal of the media planner is to extend media coverage to as many of the members of the target audience as possible while minimizing the amount of waste coverage. The situation usually involves trade-offs. Sometimes one has to live with less coverage than desired; other times, the most effective media expose people not sought. In this instance, waste coverage is justified because the media employed are likely to be the most effective means of delivery available and the cost of the waste coverage is exceeded by the value gained.

FIGURE 10–13

Marketing Coverage Possibilities

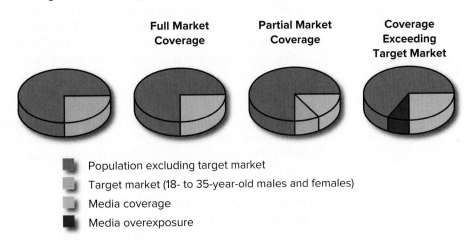

Full Market Coverage   Partial Market Coverage   Coverage Exceeding Target Market

■ Population excluding target market
■ Target market (18- to 35-year-old males and females)
■ Media coverage
■ Media overexposure

When watching football games on TV, you may have noticed commercials for stock brokerage firms such as Charles Schwab, Ameritrade, and E*Trade. Not all viewers are candidates for stock market services, but a very high percentage of potential customers can be reached with this strategy. So football programs are considered a good media buy because the ability to generate market coverage outweighs the disadvantages of high waste coverage.

Figure 10–14 shows how information provided by GfK MRI can be used to match media to target markets. This excerpt is from the report that profiles magazines read, cable TV show types watched, websites visited, and so forth by the snowboarders identified in Figure 10–5. (You can practice using index numbers here.) From Figure 10–14, you can see that Fuse and FX would likely be wise selections, whereas Bloomberg TV and Galavision would be less likely to lead to the desired exposures.

Geographic Coverage

Snow skiing is much more popular in some areas of the country than in others. It would not be the wisest of strategies to promote skis in those areas where interest is not high, unless you could generate an increase in interest. It may be possible to promote an interest in skiing in the Southeast, but a notable increase in sales of ski equipment is not very likely, given the market's distance from snow. The objective of weighting certain geographic areas more than others makes sense, and the strategy of exerting more promotional efforts and dollars in those areas follows naturally.

Scheduling

Obviously, companies would like to keep their advertising in front of consumers at all times as a constant reminder of the product and/or brand name. In reality, this is not possible for a variety of reasons (not the least of which is the budget). Nor is it necessary. The primary objective of *scheduling* is to time promotional efforts so that they will coincide with the highest potential buying times. For some products these times are not easy to identify; for others they are very obvious. Three scheduling methods available to the media planner—continuity, flighting, and pulsing—are shown in Figure 10–15. Appendix A shows how running shoe brand ASICS uses scheduling in its media plan.

Continuity refers to a continuous pattern of advertising, which may mean every day, every week, or every month. The key is that a regular (continuous) pattern is developed without gaps or nonadvertising periods. Such strategies might be used for advertising for food products, laundry detergents, toiletries, or other products consumed on an ongoing basis without regard for seasonality.

A second method, **flighting**, employs a less regular schedule, with intermittent periods of advertising and nonadvertising. At some time periods there are heavier promotional expenditures, and at others there may be no advertising. Many banks, for example, spend no money on advertising in the summer but maintain advertising throughout the rest of the year. Snow skis are advertised heavily between October and April; less in May, August, and September; and not at all in June and July.

Pulsing is actually a combination of the first two methods. In a pulsing strategy, continuity is maintained, but at certain times promotional efforts are stepped up. In the beer industry, advertising continues throughout the year but may increase at holiday periods such as Memorial Day, Labor Day, or the Fourth of July. The scheduling strategy depends on the objectives, buying cycles, and budget, among other factors. There are certain advantages and disadvantages to each scheduling method, as shown in Figure 10–16. One recent and comprehensive study (acclaimed by many in the TV research community as "the most comprehensive study ever to shed light on scheduling") indicates that continuity is more effective than flighting.

FIGURE 10–14   GfK MRI Provides Media Usage of Snowboarders
Fall 2014 Product: Leisure/Sports—Snowboarding: Participated in Last 12 Months—Total Adults

Cable Services: #Disney Junior	*	10,568	12	93	2.61	0.88	59
Cable Services: #Esquire Network	*	1,513	2	7	0.19	0.46	30
Cable Services: ABC Family		51,374	67	740	20.75	1.44	96
Cable Services: #FXM (FX Movies)	*	8,304	15	160	4.48	1.92	128
Cable Services: Adult Swim		16,603	51	582	16.32	3.51	233
Cable Services: #FXX	*	6,753	20	215	6.02	3.18	211
Cable Services: A&E		61,895	79	843	23.63	1.36	90
Cable Services: AMC		50,921	88	866	24.3	1.7	113
Cable Services: Animal Planet		51,891	84	926	25.98	1.79	119
Cable Services: BBC America	*	17,325	26	262	7.33	1.51	100
Cable Services: Al Jazeera America	*	2,773	3	20	0.56	0.73	48
Cable Services: BET (Black Entertainment)	*	23,291	31	420	11.79	1.8	120
Cable Services: American Heroes	*	15,657	29	231	6.49	1.48	98
Cable Services: Bloomberg Television	*	4,255	4	20	0.55	0.46	30
Cable Services: Bravo	*	32.814	40	367	10.28	1.12	74
Cable Services: Cartoon Network		27,997	58	644	18.06	2.3	153
Cable Services: CBS Sports Network	*	25,150	37	394	11.04	1.56	104
Cable Services: Centric	*	5,411	5	68	1.9	1.25	83
Cable Services: Chiller	*	7,237	8	103	2.88	1.42	94
Cable Services: CMT (Country Music)	*	21,162	25	251	7.05	1.19	79
Cable Services: CNBC	*	25,096	34	387	10.84	1.54	102
Cable Services: CNN		64,556	86	1,007	28.24	1.56	104
Cable Services: Comedy Central		33,921	103	1,074	30.11	3.16	210
Cable Services: CLOO	*	3,434	2	23	0.66	0.68	45
Cable Services: Cooking Channel	*	31,334	30	309	8.66	0.98	65
Cable Services: The Discovery Channel		68,273	130	1,389	38.71	2.02	134
Cable Services: Disney Channel	*	36,445	38	388	10.88	1.06	71
Cable Services: Disney XD	*	13,853	20	253	7.11	1.83	122
Cable Services: DIY (Do It Yourself)	*	17,705	20	152	4.26	0.86	577
Cable Services: Destination America	*	4,543	12	98	2.74	2.15	143
Cable Services: E! (Entertainment)	*	27,625	45	540	15.15	1.96	130
Cable Services: Discovery Fit & Health	*	6,666	9	96	2.69	1.44	96
Cable Services: ESPN		69,569	119	1,303	36.55	1.87	125
Cable Services: ESPN2		41,979	80	885	24.83	2.11	140
Cable Services: ESPN Classic	*	9,160	13	88	2.45	0.96	63
Cable Services: ESPNews	*	23,676	49	518	14.54	2.19	146
Cable Services: FamilyNet	*	2,754	6	62	1.74	2.25	150
Cable Services: Flix	*	3,749	3	45	1.27	1.21	80
Cable Services: Food Network		56,594	83	876	24.56	1.55	103
Cable Services: Fox News Channel		68,365	81	919	25.78	1.34	89
Cable Services: ESPNU	*	13,409	30	282	7.9	2.1	140
Cable Services: Fuse	*	6,118	21	267	7.48	4.36	290
Cable Services: FX		40,966	95	1,162	32.6	2.84	189
Cable Services: Fox News Network	*	11,835	12	154	4.3	1.3	86
Cable Services: Galavision	*	8,469	2	46	1.3	0.55	36
Cable Services: Fox Sports 1	*	128,507	45	406	11.39	1.43	95
Cable Services: GSN (Game Show Network)	*	10.022	11	166	4.66	1.66	100
Cable Services: Fox Sports 2	*	9.236	25	233	6.55	2.53	168
Cable Services: Golf Channel	*	11,109	19	188	5.28	1.69	113
Cable Services: GAC (Great American Country)*	*	8,126	10	95	2.66	1.17	78

* Indicates unstable sample of less than 50 responses.

Source: Mediamark Research, GfK MRI.

FIGURE 10–15

Three Methods of
Promotional Scheduling

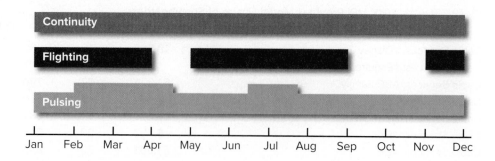

On the basis of the idea that it is important to get exposure to the message as close as possible to when the consumer is going to make the purchase, the study concludes that advertisers should continue weekly schedules as long as possible.[6] The key here may be the "as long as possible" qualification. Given a significant budget, continuity may be more of an option than it is for those with more limited budgets.

Reach versus Frequency

Since advertisers have a variety of objectives and face budget constraints, they usually must trade off reach and frequency. They must decide whether to have the message be seen or heard by more people (reach) or by fewer people more often (frequency).

How Much Reach Is Necessary?   Thinking back to the hierarchies discussed in Chapter 5, you will recall that the first stage of each model requires awareness of the product and/or brand. The more people are aware, the more they are likely to move to each subsequent stage. Achieving awareness requires reach—that is, exposing potential buyers to the message. New brands or products need a very

FIGURE 10–16

Characteristics of
Scheduling Methods

	Continuity
Advantages	Serves as a constant reminder to the consumer
	Covers the entire buying cycle
	Allows for media priorities (quantity discounts, preferred locations, etc.)
Disadvantages	Higher costs
	Potential for overexposure
	Limited media allocation possible

	Flighting
Advantages	Cost efficiency of advertising only during purchase cycles
	May allow for inclusion of more than one medium or vehicle with limited budgets
Disadvantages	Weighting may offer more exposure and advantage over competitors
	Increased likelihood of wearout
	Lack of awareness, interest, retention of promotional message during nonscheduled times
	Vulnerability to competitive efforts during nonscheduled periods

	Pulsing
Advantages	All of the same as the previous two methods
Disadvantages	Not required for seasonal products (or other cyclical products)

high level of reach, since the objective is to make all potential buyers aware of the new entry. High reach is also desired at later stages of the hierarchy. For example, at the trial stage of the adoption hierarchy, a promotional strategy might use cents-off coupons or free samples. An objective of the marketer is to reach a larger number of people with these samples in an attempt to make them learn of the product, try it, and develop favorable attitudes toward it. (In turn, these attitudes may lead to purchase.)

The problem arises because there is no known way of determining how much reach is required to achieve levels of awareness, attitude change, or buying intentions, nor can we be sure an ad placed in a vehicle will actually reach the intended audience. (There has been some research on the first problem, which will be discussed in the following section on effective reach.)

If you buy advertising time on *60 Minutes,* will everyone who is tuned to the program see the ad? No. Many viewers will leave the room, be distracted during the commercial, and so on, as shown in Figure 10–17 (which also provides a good example of the difference between reach and coverage). If I expose everyone in my target group to the message once, will this be sufficient to create a 100 percent level of awareness? The answer again is no. This leads to the next question: What frequency of exposure is necessary for the ad to be seen and to have an impact?

What Frequency Level Is Needed?   With respect to media planning, *frequency* carries a slightly different meaning. (Remember when we said one of the problems in media planning is that terms often take on different meanings?) Here frequency is the number of times one is exposed to the media vehicle in a specified time period (usually 13 weeks), not necessarily to the ad itself. Figure 10–17 demonstrates that depending on the program, this number may range from 12 to 40 percent. Marketers have always known that everyone who is watching a program is not going to stay in the room to watch the commercials. Given the rise in the number of people able to skip ads, one can be sure the number of those not exposed to the ad is on the increase. As noted, marketers continue to seek ways to increase engagement, hoping to reduce the number leaving the room during commercial breaks.

Most advertisers do agree that a 1:1 exposure ratio does not exist. So while your ad may be placed in a certain vehicle, the fact that a consumer has been exposed to that vehicle does not ensure that your ad has been seen. As a result, the frequency level expressed in the media plan overstates the actual level of exposure to the ad.

FIGURE 10–17

Who's Still There to Watch the Ads?

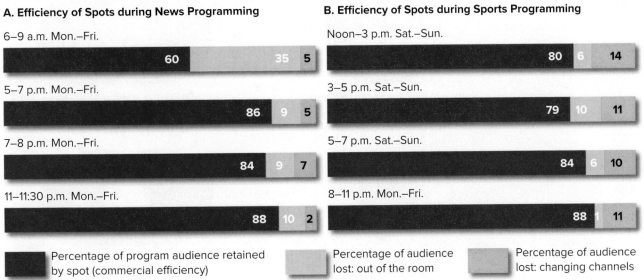

A. Efficiency of Spots during News Programming

6–9 a.m. Mon.–Fri.

60 35 5

5–7 p.m. Mon.–Fri.

86 9 5

7–8 p.m. Mon.–Fri.

84 9 7

11–11:30 p.m. Mon.–Fri.

88 10 2

B. Efficiency of Spots during Sports Programming

Noon–3 p.m. Sat.–Sun.

80 6 14

3–5 p.m. Sat.–Sun.

79 10 11

5–7 p.m. Sat.–Sun.

84 6 10

8–11 p.m. Mon.–Fri.

88 1 11

Percentage of program audience retained by spot (commercial efficiency)

Percentage of audience lost: out of the room

Percentage of audience lost: changing channels

This overstatement has led some media buyers to refer to the reach of the media vehicle as "opportunities to see" an ad rather than actual exposure to it.

Because the advertiser has no sure way of knowing whether exposure to a vehicle results in exposure to the ad, the media and advertisers have adopted a compromise: One exposure to the vehicle constitutes reach, given that this exposure must occur for the viewer even to have an opportunity to see the ad. Thus, the exposure figure is used to calculate reach and frequency levels. But this compromise does not help determine the frequency required to make an impact. The creativity of the ad, the involvement of the receiver, noise, and many other intervening factors confound any attempts to make a precise determination.

At this point, you may be thinking, "If nobody knows this stuff, how do they make these decisions?" That's a good question, and the truth is that the decisions are not always made on hard data. Says Joseph Ostrow, executive vice president/director of communications services with Young and Rubicam, "Establishing frequency goals for an advertising campaign is a mix of art and science but with a definite bias toward art."[7] Let us first examine the process involved in setting reach and frequency objectives and then discuss the logic of each.

Establishing Reach and Frequency Objectives   It is possible to be exposed to more than one media vehicle with an ad, resulting in repetition (frequency). If one ad is placed on one TV show one time, the number of people exposed is the reach. If the ad is placed on two shows, the total number exposed once is **unduplicated reach**. Some people will see the ad twice. The reach of the two shows, as depicted in Figure 10–18, includes a number of people who were reached by both shows (C). This overlap is referred to as **duplicated reach**.

Both unduplicated and duplicated reach figures are important. Unduplicated reach indicates potential new exposures, while duplicated reach provides an estimate of frequency. Most media buys include both forms of reach. Let us consider an example.

A measure of potential reach in the broadcast industry is the TV (or radio) **program rating**. This number is expressed as a percentage. For an estimate of the total number of homes reached, multiply this percentage times the number of homes with TV sets. For example, if there are 116.4 million homes with TV sets in the United States and the program has a rating of 30, then the calculation is 0.30 times 116.4, or 34.92 million homes. (We go into much more detail on ratings and other broadcast terms in Chapter 11.)

FIGURE 10–18

Representation of Reach and Frequency

A. Reach of One TV Program

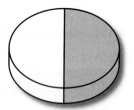

Total market audience reached

B. Reach of Two Programs

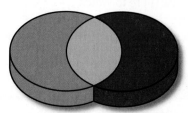

Total market audience reached

C. Duplicated Reach

Total market reached
with both shows

D. Unduplicated Reach

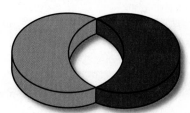

Total reach less
duplicated reach

Using Gross Ratings Points   To determine how much advertising volume or weight is necessary to accomplish advertiser's objectives, marketers rely on ratings (the number of people reached) and frequency (the average number of times exposed) figures. A summary measure that combines the program rating and the average number of times the home is reached during this period (frequency of exposure) is a commonly used reference point known as **gross ratings points (GRPs)**:

$$\text{GRP} = \text{Reach} \times \text{Frequency}$$

GRPs are based on the total audience the media schedule may reach using a duplicated reach estimate. **Target ratings points (TRPs)** refer to the number of people in the primary target audience the media buy will reach—and the number of times. Unlike GRP, TRP does not include waste coverage.

Given that GRPs do not measure actual reach, the advertiser must ask: How many GRPs are needed to attain a certain reach? How do these GRPs translate into effective reach? For example, how many GRPs must one purchase to attain an unduplicated reach of 50 percent, and what frequency of exposure will this schedule deliver? The following example may help you to understand how this process works.

First you must know what these ratings points represent. A purchase of 100 GRPs could mean 100 percent of the market is exposed once or 50 percent of the market is exposed twice or 25 percent of the market is exposed four times, and so on. As you can see, this information must be more specific for the marketer to use it effectively. To know how many GRPs are necessary, the manager needs to know how many members of the intended audience the schedule actually reaches. The graph in Figure 10–19 helps make this determination.

In Figure 10–19, a purchase of 100 TRPs on one network would yield an estimated reach of 32 percent of the total households in the target market. This figure would climb to 37.2 percent if two networks were used and 44.5 percent with three. Working backward through the formula for GRPs, the estimate of frequency of exposure—3.125, 2.688, and 2.247, respectively—demonstrates the trade-off between reach and frequency.

An interesting example of the use of GRPs is provided by a race to be the Republican candidate for California governor. With the election to be held in June, the advertising schedule for March for the leading candidate consisted of 1,000 GRPs per week in 11 California media markets. This buy was expected to yield a frequency of approximately 10 exposures per week to the average TV watcher in the largest markets, and approximately 6 per week in the smaller ones. The opposing candidate spent an estimated 15 to 50 percent of this amount, depending on the specific market.[8] The candidate that spent the most won the race.

The overriding question is, how many GRPs are necessary to achieve our objectives? According to Scott Walker, most advertisers prefer to get 500 to 700 GRPs

FIGURE 10–19

Estimates of Reach for Network TRPs

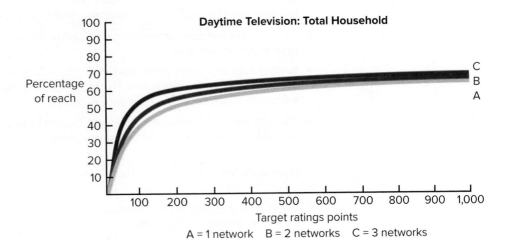

to be sure their message is seen and seen often.[9] A number of researchers have explored this issue. David Berger, vice president and director of research at Foote Cone & Belding, has determined that 2,500 GRPs are likely to lead to roughly a 70 percent probability of high awareness, 1,000 to 2,500 would yield about a 33 percent probability, and less than 1,000 would probably result in almost no awareness.[10] David Olson obtained similar results and further showed that as awareness increased, trial of the product would also increase, although at a significantly slower rate.[11] In both cases, it was evident that high numbers of GRPs were required to make an impact.

Figure 10–20 summarizes the effects that can be expected at different levels of exposure, on the basis of research in this area. A number of factors may be operating, and direct relationships may be difficult to establish. In addition to the results shown in Figure 10–20, Joseph Ostrow has shown that while the number of repetitions increases awareness rapidly, it has much less impact on attitudinal and behavioral responses.[12]

You can imagine how expensive it was for the candidate mentioned earlier to purchase 1,000 GRPs per week in 11 markets well before the election. To spend at that level for an extended period of time could result in overexposure (not to mention a major hit on the pocketbook), as viewers might get tired of the ads.

Determining Effective Reach   Since marketers have budget constraints, they must decide whether to increase reach at the expense of frequency or increase the frequency of exposure but to a smaller audience. A number of factors influence this decision. For example, a new product or brand introduction will attempt to maximize reach, particularly unduplicated reach, to create awareness in as many people as possible as quickly as possible. At the same time, for a high-involvement product or one whose benefits are not obvious, a certain level of frequency is needed to achieve effective reach.

Effective reach represents the percentage of a vehicle's audience reached at each effective frequency increment. This concept is based on the assumption that one exposure to an ad may not be enough to convey the desired message. As we saw earlier, no one knows the exact number of exposures necessary for an ad to make an impact, although advertisers have settled on three as the minimum. Effective reach (exposure) is shown in the shaded area in Figure 10–21 in the range of 3 to 10 exposures. Fewer than 3 exposures is considered insufficient reach, while more than 10 is considered overexposure and thus ineffective reach. This exposure level

FIGURE 10–20

The Effects of Reach and Frequency

1. One exposure of an ad to a target group within a purchase cycle has little or no effect in most circumstances.

2. Since one exposure is usually ineffective, the central goal of productive media planning should be to enhance frequency rather than reach.

3. The evidence suggests strongly that an exposure frequency of two within a purchase cycle is an effective level.

4. Beyond three exposures within a brand purchase cycle or over a period of four or even eight weeks, increasing frequency continues to build advertising effectiveness at a decreasing rate but with no evidence of decline.

5. Although there are general principles with respect to frequency of exposure and its relationship to advertising effectiveness, differential effects by brand are equally important.

6. Nothing we have seen suggests that frequency response principles or generalizations vary by medium.

7. The data strongly suggest that wearout is not a function of too much frequency; it is more of a creative or copy problem.

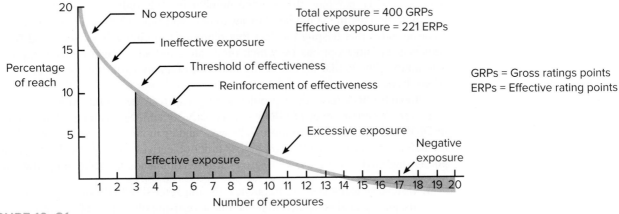

FIGURE 10–21

Graph of Effective Reach

is no guarantee of effective communication; different messages may require more or fewer exposures. For example, Jack Myers, president of Myers Reports, argues that the three-exposure theory was valid in the 1970s when consumers were exposed to approximately 1,000 ads per day. Now that they are exposed to 3,000 to 5,000 per day, three exposures may not be enough.[13] Adding in the fragmentation of television, the proliferation of magazines, and the advent of a variety of alternative media leads Myers to believe that 12 exposures may be the *minimum* level of frequency required. Also, Jim Surmanek, president/CEO of Media Analysis Plus, contends that the complexity of the message, message length, and recency of exposure also impact this figure.[14]

Since they do not know how many times the viewer will actually be exposed, advertisers typically purchase GRPs that lead to more than three exposures to increase the likelihood of effective reach and frequency. Surmanek also argues that effective reach can be as low as one exposure, if the exposure is very recent or close to the purchase occasion (thus, recency is more important than frequency). He contends that more exposures are necessary when the message is complex and requires several exposures to be understood.

Erwin Ephron, an expert in media planning, disagrees. Ephron notes that while increasing reach at minimum frequency was popular in the 1990s, it is no longer a viable strategy as changes in the marketplace (commercial avoidance, multitasking, and technological innovations like the DVR) have made it more difficult to get exposure to an ad. As a result, it is important to create plans that value both reach and frequency to ensure that the ad gets seen and has an impact. In other words, higher frequency results in higher reach.[15] Determining effective reach is further complicated by the fact that when calculating GRPs, advertisers use a figure that they call **average frequency**, or the average number of times the target audience reached by a media schedule is exposed to the vehicle over a specified period. The problem with this figure is revealed in the following scenario:

> Consider a media buy in which:
> 50 percent of audience is reached 1 time.
> 30 percent of audience is reached 5 times.
> 20 percent of audience is reached 10 times.
> Average frequency = 4

In this media buy, the average frequency is 4, which is slightly more than the number established as effective. Yet a full 50 percent of the audience receives only one exposure. Thus, the average frequency number can be misleading, and using it to calculate GRPs might result in underexposing the audience.

Complicating this even further, Sheree Johnson reports on research conducted by Media Dynamics, Inc. in 2014 examining how many daily ads consumers are exposed to in a day. Johnson distinguishes between ad and/or brand exposures and "ad only" exposures. While she agrees that the number of brand and ad exposures may be 5,000+ per day, the average number of "ads only" exposures is closer to 362, with 86 creating some level of awareness and only 12 making an impression.[16] Johnson notes that despite the fact that commercials clutter has risen steadily, consumers have more options by which they can avoid ads, which impacts exposures. The bottom line is that no one really knows how many exposures occur in one day, so we have to use our best estimates.

Although GRPs have their problems, they can provide useful information to the marketer. A certain level of GRPs is necessary to achieve awareness, and increases in GRPs are likely to lead to more exposures and/or more repetitions—both of which are necessary to have an effect on higher-order objectives. Perhaps the best advice for purchasing GRPs is offered by Ostrow, who recommends the following strategies:[17]

1. Instead of using average frequency, the marketer should decide what minimum frequency goal is needed to reach the advertising objectives effectively and then maximize reach at that frequency level.
2. To determine effective frequency, one must consider marketing factors, message factors, and media factors. (See Figure 10–22.)

Effective Frequency   While the previous discussion focused on the number of exposures that are necessary to achieve effective reach, it is also necessary to know how much frequency is necessary to impact other communications objectives. In research presented in the *Journal of Advertising*, Susanne Schmidt and Martin Eisend report on a meta-analysis that examined 37 studies that impact consumers' response to an ad. Specifically, the focus was on the number of exposures necessary to impact recall and attitude toward the brand. The results indicated that 10 exposures are necessary to maximize attitudes while recall increases linearly. The authors also note that other factors including consumer's involvement and time between exposures will also have an effect.[18]

In summary, the reach-versus-frequency decision, while critical, is very difficult to make. A number of factors must be considered, and concrete rules do not always apply. The decision is often more of an art than a science.

Recency   As noted by Ephron, the idea that one exposure to an ad had a greater impact than additional exposures did if it was shown in the week preceding a purchase led many advertisers to focus more attention on reach, less on frequency, and an emphasis on **recency**. Campaigns employed **recency planning**—focusing on short interval reach at minimum frequency levels as close to the purchase decision as possible. Rather than focusing on a four-week planning period for reach, recency planning calls for a continuous schedule over a one week period, and less targeting to gain exposure to reach as many potential consumers as possible.[19] While one might argue that many of the exposures are then wasted, Ephron would disagree, noting that people are in the market at different times and that awareness and image building also can benefit by the exposures. Both Ephron and Herbert Krugman suggest that advertising needs to act like a brand and that "Advertising needs to be like a product sitting on the shelf, because you never know when the consumer is going to be looking for you, so advertising has to rent the shelf-space all the time."[20]

Creative Aspects and Mood

The context of the medium in which the ad is placed may also affect viewers' perceptions. A specific creative strategy may require certain media. Because TV provides both sight and sound, it may be more effective in generating emotions than other media; magazines may create different perceptions from newspapers. In developing a media strategy, marketers must consider both creativity and mood factors. Let us examine each in more detail.

FIGURE 10–22

Factors Important in
Determining Frequency
Levels

Marketing Factors

- *Brand history.* Is the brand new or established? New brands generally require higher frequency levels.
- *Brand share.* An inverse relationship exists between brand share and frequency. The higher the brand share, the lower the frequency level required.
- *Brand loyalty.* An inverse relationship exists between loyalty and frequency. The higher the loyalty, the lower the frequency level required.
- *Purchase cycles.* Shorter purchasing cycles require higher frequency levels to maintain top-of-mind awareness.
- *Usage cycle.* Products used daily or more often need to be replaced quickly, so a higher level of frequency is desired.
- *Competitive share of voice.* Higher frequency levels are required when a lot of competitive noise exists and when the goal is to meet or beat competitors.
- *Target group.* The ability of the target group to learn and to retain messages has a direct effect on frequency.

Message or Creative Factors

- *Message complexity.* The simpler the message, the less frequency required.
- *Message uniqueness.* The more unique the message, the lower the frequency level required.
- *New versus continuing campaigns.* New campaigns require higher levels of frequency to register the message.
- *Image versus product sell.* Creating an image requires higher levels of frequency than does a specific product sell.
- *Message variation.* A single message requires less frequency; a variety of messages requires more.
- *Wearout.* Higher frequency may lead to wearout. This effect must be tracked and used to evaluate frequency levels.
- *Advertising units.* Larger units of advertising require less frequency than smaller ones to get the message across.

Media Factors

- *Clutter.* The more advertising that appears in the media used, the more frequency is needed to break through the clutter.
- *Editorial environment.* The more consistent the ad is with the editorial environment, the less frequency is needed.
- *Attentiveness.* The higher the level of attention achieved by the media vehicle, the less frequency is required. Low-attention-getting media require more repetitions.
- *Scheduling.* Continuous scheduling requires less frequency than does flighting or pulsing.
- *Number of media used.* The fewer media used, the lower the level of frequency required.
- *Repeat exposures.* Media that allow for more repeat exposures (for example, monthly magazines) require less frequency.

Creative Aspects   It is possible to increase the success of a product significantly through a strong creative campaign. But to implement this creativity, you must employ a medium that will support such a strategy. For example, the campaign for Lollipop Splash shown in Chapter 4 used print media to communicate the message effectively. Hallmark, among many others, has effectively used TV to create emotional appeals. In some situations, the media strategy to be pursued may be the driving force behind the creative strategy, as the media and creative departments work closely together to achieve the greatest impact with the audience of the specific media.

CHAPTER 10

Mood   Certain media enhance the creativity of a message because they create a mood that carries over to the communication. For example, think about the moods created by the following magazines: *Gourmet, Skiing, Travel and Leisure,* and *House Beautiful.* Each of these special-interest vehicles puts the reader in a particular mood. The promotion of fine wines, ski boots, luggage, and home products is enhanced by this mood. What different images might be created for your product if you advertised it in the following media?

> *The New York Times* versus the *National Enquirer*
> *Architectural Digest* versus *Reader's Digest*
> A highly rated prime-time TV show versus an old rerun
> Television versus the Internet

The message may require a specific medium and a certain media vehicle to achieve its objectives. Likewise, certain media and vehicles have images that may carry over to the perceptions of messages placed within them.

A study reported in the *Journal of Marketing* showed that TV viewers skip commercials based on the feeling created by a television program and a "mood mismatch," and the mismatch also makes it more difficult to recall when it is watched. For example, a show that creates a sad, quiet mood when interrupted by a loud and active commercial annoys viewers, resulting in a lower likelihood of remembering the brand message and an increased likelihood of ignoring or skipping through it.[21] While advertisers typically create exciting ads to get attention and interest, the study suggests that the advertiser may want to tone down the ad to fit the mood of the context within which it is shown.

Flexibility

An effective media strategy requires a degree of flexibility. Because of the rapidly changing marketing environment, strategies may need to be modified. If the plan has not built in some flexibility, opportunities may be lost and/or the company may not be able to address new threats. Flexibility may be needed to address the following:

1. *Market opportunities.* Sometimes a market opportunity arises that the advertiser wishes to take advantage of. For example, wine companies have attempted to capitalize on the increasing interest in this drink created by changing trends in the U.S. marketplace. The development of a new advertising medium may offer an opportunity that was not previously available.
2. *Market threats.* Internal or external factors may pose a threat to the firm, and a change in media strategy is dictated. For example, a competitor may alter its media strategy to gain an edge. Failure to respond to this challenge could create problems for the firm.
3. *Availability of media.* Sometimes a desired medium (or vehicle) is not available to the marketer. Perhaps the medium does not reach a particular target segment or has no time or space available. There are still some geographic areas that certain media do not reach. Even when the media are available, limited advertising time or space may have already been sold or cutoff dates for entry may have passed. Alternative vehicles or media must then be considered.
4. *Changes in media or media vehicles.* A change in the medium or in a particular vehicle may require a change in the media strategy. For example, the advent of cable TV opened up new opportunities for message delivery, as will the introduction of interactive media. The Internet has led many consumer companies to adopt this medium while a number of new technologies have provided additional options. New special-interest magazines, mobile phones, social networks, and video game ads are just a few. Likewise, a drop in ratings or a change in editorial format may lead the advertiser to use different alternatives.

Fluctuations in these factors mean the media strategy must be developed with enough flexibility to allow the manager to adapt to specific market situations.

Budget Considerations

One of the more important decisions in the development of media strategy is cost estimating. The value of any strategy can be determined by how well it delivers the message to the audience with the lowest cost and the least waste. We have already explored a number of factors, such as reach, frequency, and availability, that affect this decision. The marketer tries to arrive at the optimal delivery by balancing cost with each of these. As the following discussion shows, understanding cost figures may not be as easy as it seems.

Advertising and promotional costs can be categorized in two ways. The **absolute cost** of the medium or vehicle is the actual total cost required to place the message. For example, a full-page ad in *The Week* magazine costs about $72,800. **Relative cost** refers to the relationship between the price paid for advertising time or space and the size of the audience delivered; it is used to compare media vehicles. Relative costs are important because the manager must try to optimize audience delivery within budget constraints. Since a number of alternatives are available for delivering the message, the advertiser must evaluate the relative costs associated with these choices. The way media costs are provided and problems in comparing these costs across media often make such evaluations difficult.

Determining Relative Costs of Media To evaluate alternatives, advertisers must compare the relative costs of media as well as vehicles within these media. Unfortunately, the broadcast, print, and out of home media do not always provide the same cost breakdowns, nor necessarily do vehicles within the print media. Following are the cost bases used:

1. **Cost per thousand (CPM).** For years the magazine industry has provided cost breakdowns on the basis of cost per thousand people reached. The formula for this computation is

$$CPM = \frac{\text{Cost of ad space (absolute cost)}}{\text{Circulation}} \quad \text{Cost of ad space} \times 100$$

   Figure 10–23 provides an example of this computation for two vehicles in the same medium—*Time* and *The Week*—and shows that (all other things being equal) *Time* is a more cost-effective buy, even though its absolute cost is higher. (We will come back to "all other things being equal" in a moment.)

2. **Cost per ratings point (CPRP).** The broadcast media provide a different comparative cost figure, referred to as cost per ratings point or *cost per point (CPP)*, based on the following formula:

$$CPRP = \frac{\text{Cost of commercial time}}{\text{Program rating}}$$

   An example of this calculation for a spot ad in a local TV market is shown in Figure 10–24. It indicates that *The Middle* would be more cost-effective than *The Big Bang Theory.*

FIGURE 10–23

Cost per Thousand Computations: *Time* versus *The Week*

	Time	The Week
Cost per page	$229,200	$72,800
Circulation	3 million	500,000
Calculation of CPM	$229,200 × 1,000	$72,800 × 1,000
	3,000,000	500,000
CPM	$76.40	$145.60

FIGURE 10–24

Comparison of Cost per
Ratings Point

	The Middle	The Big Bang Theory
Cost per ad	$147,826	$327,000
Rating	2.0	3.7
Reach (millions HH)	8.18	14.9
Calculation	$147,826/2.0	$327,000/3.7
CPRP (CPP)	$73,913.00	$88,378.00

3. **Daily inch rate.** For newspapers, cost-effectiveness is based on the daily inch rate, which is the cost per column inch of the paper. Like magazines, newspapers now use the cost-per-thousand formula discussed earlier to determine relative costs. As shown in Figure 10–25, the *Pittsburgh Post Gazette* costs significantly less to advertise in than does the *Cleveland Plain Dealer* (again, all other things being equal).

FIGURE 10–25

Comparative Costs in
Newspaper Advertising

	Pittsburgh Post Gazette	Cleveland Plain Dealer
Cost per page	$20,969	$59,598
Cost per inch	303.90	473
Circulation	184,234	271,180
Calculation	$\text{CPRP} = \dfrac{\text{Page cost} \times 1{,}000}{\text{Circulation}}$	
	$\dfrac{\$20{,}969 \times 1{,}000}{184{,}234}$	$\dfrac{\$59{,}598 \times 1{,}000}{271{,}180}$
	$113.81	$219.77

As you can see, it is difficult to make comparisons across various media. What is the broadcast equivalent of cost per thousand or the column inch rate? In an attempt to standardize relative costing procedures, the broadcast and newspaper media have begun to provide costs per thousand, using the following formulas:

$$\text{Television:} = \frac{\text{Cost of 1 unit of time} \times 1{,}000}{\text{Program rating}} \qquad \text{Newspapers:} \frac{\text{Cost of ad space} \times 1{,}000}{\text{Circulation}}$$

While the comparison of media on a cost-per-thousand basis is important, intermedia comparisons can be misleading. The ability of TV to provide both sight and sound, the longevity of magazines, and other characteristics of each medium make direct comparisons difficult. The media planner should use the cost-per-thousand numbers but must also consider the specific characteristics of each medium and each media vehicle in the decision.

The cost per thousand may overestimate or underestimate the actual cost-effectiveness. Consider a situation where some waste coverage is inevitable. The circulation (using the *Time* magazine figures to demonstrate our point) exceeds the target market. If the people reached by this message are not potential buyers of the product, then having to pay to reach them results in too low a cost per thousand, as shown in scenario A of Figure 10–26. We must use the potential reach to the target market—the destination sought—rather than the overall circulation figure. A medium with a much higher cost per thousand may be a wiser buy if it is reaching more potential receivers. (Most media buyers rely on **target CPM [TCPM]** which calculates CPMs based on the target audience, not the overall audience.)

FIGURE 10–26

Cost-per-Thousand
Estimates

Scenario A: Overestimation of Efficiency	
Target market	18–49
Magazine circulation	3,250,000
Circulation to target market	65% (2,112,500)
Cost per page	$287,440

$$\text{CPM} = \frac{\$287,480}{3,250.00} = \frac{\$88.40}{\$287,480}$$

$$\text{CPM (actual target audience)} = \frac{\$287,440 \times 1,000}{2,112,500} = \$136.07$$

Scenario B: Underestimation of Efficiency	
Target market	All age groups, male and female
Magazine circulation	3,250,000
Cost per page	$287,440
Pass-along rate	3* (33% of households)

$$\text{CPM (based on readers per copy)} = \frac{\text{Page cost} \times 1,000}{\text{Circulation} + 3(1,072,500)} = \frac{(287,440 \times 1,000)}{4,322,500} = \$66.50$$

*Assuming pass-along was valid.

CPM may also underestimate cost-efficiency. Magazine advertising space sellers have argued for years that because more than one person may read an issue, the actual reach is underestimated. They want to use the number of **readers per copy** as the true circulation. This would include a **pass-along rate**, estimating the number of people who read the magazine without buying it. Scenario B in Figure 10–26 shows how this underestimates cost-efficiency. Consider a family in which a father, mother, and two teenagers read each issue of *Time.* Assume such families constitute 33 percent of *Time*'s circulation base, based on 3,250,000. While the circulation figure includes only one magazine, in reality there are four potential exposures in these households, increasing the total reach to 4.32 million.

While the number of readers per copy makes intuitive sense, it has the potential to be extremely inaccurate. The actual number of times the magazine changes hands is difficult to determine. How many people in a fraternity read each issue of *Sports Illustrated* or *GQ* that is delivered? How many people in a sorority or on a dorm floor read each issue of *Cosmopolitan* or *Vanity Fair*? How many of either group read each issue of *Bloomberg Businessweek*? While research is conducted to make these determinations, pass-along estimates are very subjective and using them to estimate reach is speculative. These figures are regularly provided by the media, but managers are selective about using them. At the same time, the art of media buying enters, for many magazines' managers have a good idea how much greater the reach is than their circulation figures provided.

In addition to the potential for over- or underestimation of cost-efficiencies, CPMs are limited in that they make only *quantitative* estimates of the value of media. Although they may be good for comparing very similar vehicles (such as *Time* and *The Week*), they are less valuable in making intermedia comparisons, for example, CPM for magazines versus Internet banner ads. We have already noted some differences among media that preclude direct comparisons.

You can see that the development of a media strategy involves many factors. Ostrow may be right when he calls this process an art rather than a science, as so much of it requires going beyond the numbers.

AD AGE BEST MEDIA PLANS: NO LONGER JUST TV

Years ago, the creative department pretty much dictated what the commercial or ad would be and then conveyed that information to the media department to place it. Then the realization hit that without good media placement even the best creative would be of much less value. Now, with the advent of so many more options for media placement, companies and their agencies recognize the importance of a good media plan. To many it is now the media plan that is arguably the most important part of the marketing process.

One of the advertising industry's most respected media is *Adweek*. For more than 20 years, *Adweek* has run the Media Plan of the Year competition. Over the last two decades these plans have evolved from a traditional media focus to much more of an IMC focus, as evidenced by the following 2015 award winners.

P&G "Like a Girl"—The first-place winner of the Media Plan of the Year for 2015 was targeted to young women experiencing puberty and their first period. P&G won the competition in the $5–10 million Overall Campaign category as well as for the Best Use of Social Media ($4 million). The "Like a Girl" objective was designed to instill confidence in young millennials, who often lose confidence as a result of their experience. The "Like a Girl" campaign's objective was to take the phrase and turn it into a sense of power for young women. The primary media focus was on mobile—the constantly used medium of choice among the target audience—and was designed to be shared on other media channels. And it worked! Over 90 million views of the campaign have already occurred, with 65 percent the first week through social media

sharing. But P&G didn't stop there. A "Like a Girl" commercial was shown on the Super Bowl right after Katie Perry performed. The results were amazing as the movement went worldwide: 59 percent of men and 76 percent of women ages 16–24 say they changed perceptions as a result of the campaign, and the Always brand purchase intent number rose by 92 percent. The campaign also won two gold, three silver, and a bronz Clio.

NIKE "Risk Everything"—The most-watched event in the world is the World Cup. The most popular shoe brand in the world is Nike. Nike wanted to make a major presence at the World Cup 2014, and it did. The idea was to reach out to the football-crazy teen market and immerse them in the 2014 games by getting them to "experience the World Cup as a mobile-first combination of digital games and social content." One day before the World Cup started, Nike launched the five-minute *Last Game* film, which led to more than 210 million views across social, digital, TV, and Xbox. The campaign theme "Risk Everything" was designed to encourage athletes from around the world to not just play the game but also to think differently and take risks. During the 26-day World Cup event, Nike aired custom animated films every day as well as original content delivered along with the TV commercials in real time. Nike believed that its communications efforts should also "risk everything" rather than just employ standard game coverage and advertising. The risk payed off, earning 410 million online views for its "Risk Everything" films, 23 million engagements, 6.2 million new social media followers, and a 21 percent increase in

EVALUATION AND FOLLOW-UP

All plans require some evaluation to assess their performance. The media plan is no exception.

In outlining the planning process, we stated that objectives are established and strategies developed for them. Having implemented these strategies, marketers need to know whether or not they were successful. Measures of effectiveness must consider two factors: (1) How well did these strategies achieve the media objectives? (2) How well did this media plan contribute to attaining the overall marketing and communications objectives? If the strategies were successful, they should be used in future plans. If not, their flaws should be analyzed.

The problem with measuring the effectiveness of media strategies is probably obvious to you at this point. At the outset of this chapter, we suggested the planning process was limited by problems with measurements and lack of consistent terminology (among others). While these problems limit the degree to which we can assess the relative effectiveness of various strategies, it is not impossible to make

Source: Media Markt

brand revenue. The campaign also earned Nike first place in the $15+ million campaign category as well as in the International category of $5+ million.

Media Markt "Rabbit Race"—The winning campaign in the $10–15 million category is a company you may never have heard of. The German entertainment electronics company Media Markt has long been known for its loud and sometimes ridiculous commercials. Its agency developed branded content sporting events featuring three rabbit races that became almost as popular as the World Cup itself. The races were hosted by one of Germany's best-known sports pundits and filmed at an "arena" built specifically for the event. They were broadcasted simultaneously on YouTube, Germany's nine largest TV stations, and the homepage of the nation's largest newspaper. In addition, bloggers and traditional print media covered the event. "Behind the scene" press coverage and "exclusive background stories" of each of the competing bunnies were part of the mix, as was a promotional element that offered a 50 percent cash back to shoppers who made a purchase in a Media Markt store the next day if their receipt contained a picture of the winning rabbit. As the event took off on social media, the project generated 250 million impressions, with 21 million live viewers and social media followers. The event created 250 percent more interactions than usual,

a 40 percent Facebook follower boost, and an 18.2 percent increase in overall customers. More people watched these running rabbits than the World Cup semifinal between the Netherlands and Argentina—the game that determined which team would play Germany for the title.

In addition to these winning campaigns, a number of other brands also had winning plans. A brief synopsis of some of these follows:

Oreo, "The Oreo Eclipse" ($450,000–$1 million)—Capitalizing on the first solar eclipse to be seen in the UK in 16 years, the company used digital outdoor screens to re-create the eclipse as it happened in different parts of the kingdom with a floating Oreo. Ten-second videos of the event were shown on the company's digital channels within one-half hour after the event. Britain's largest newspaper *The Sun* participated by having a special edition the morning of the event.

Taco Bell "Blackout" (less than $500,000)—Seeking rapid adoption of its mobile app that took two years to develop, Taco Bell hired ad agency Digitas Lbi to find a way to reach a goal of 2 million fans and get them to download the new app. When the app was deemed ready to go, all of Taco Bell's other apps went dark for 72 hours. The only thing shown was the message *"The new way to Taco Bell isn't on Twitter, it's #OnlyInTheApp."* Facebook, Instagram, and various online sites carried a similar message. Taco Bell reached its goal with over 2.5 million new downloads.

As these award-winning media plans clearly show, you don't have to spend millions of dollars to put together an award-winning campaign. A lot of creativity and a successful media strategy go a long way. And it is also quite clear that integration is the key!

Source: Katie Richards, Patrick Coffee, and Marty Swant, "The Year's 32 Best Media Plans, from Always and Nike to Oreos and Taco Bell," www.adweek.com, September 6, 2015.

such determinations. Sometimes it is possible to show that a plan has worked, as shown in IMC Perspective 10–2.

Even if the evaluation procedure is not foolproof, it is better than no attempt. We will discuss more about measuring effectiveness in Chapter 18.

CHARACTERISTICS OF MEDIA

To this point, we have discussed the elements involved in the development of media strategy. One of the most basic elements in this process is the matching of media to markets. In the following chapters, you will see that each medium has its own characteristics that make it better or worse for attaining specific objectives. First, Figure 10–27 provides an overall comparison of media and some of the characteristics by which they are evaluated. This is a very general comparison, and the various media options must be analyzed for each situation. Nevertheless, it is a good starting point and serves as a lead-in to subsequent chapters.

FIGURE 10–27

Media Characteristics

Media	Advantages	Disadvantages
Television	Mass coverage High reach Impact of sight, sound, and motion High prestige Low cost per exposure Attention getting Favorable image	Low selectivity Short message life High absolute cost High production costs Clutter
Radio	Local coverage Low cost High frequency Flexible Low production costs Well-segmented audiences	Audio only Clutter Low attention getting Fleeting message
Magazines	Segmentation potential Quality reproduction High information content Longevity Multiple readers	Long lead time for ad placement Visual only Lack of flexibility
Newspapers	High coverage Low cost Short lead time for placing ads Ads can be placed in interest sections Timely (current ads) Reader controls exposure Can be used for coupons	Short life Clutter Low attention-getting capabilities Poor reproduction quality Selective reader exposure
Outdoor	Location specific High repetition Easily noticed	Short exposure time requires short ad Poor image Local restrictions
Direct mail	High selectivity Reader controls exposure High information content Opportunities for repeat exposures	High cost/contact Poor image (junk mail) Clutter
Digital/ interactive	User selects product information User attention and involvement Interactive relationship Direct selling potential Flexible message platform	Privacy concerns Potential for deception Clutter Few valid measurement techniques

Summary

This chapter has presented an overview of the determination of media objectives, development of the media strategy, and formalization of objectives and strategy in the form of a media plan. Sources of media information, characteristics of media, and key media decisions were also discussed.

The media strategy must be designed to supplement and support the overall marketing and communications objectives. The objectives of this plan are designed to deliver the message the program has developed.

The basic task involved in the development of media strategy is to determine the best matching of media to the target market, given the constraints of the budget. The media planner attempts to balance reach and frequency and to deliver the message to the intended audience with a minimum of waste coverage. At the same time, a number of additional factors affect the media decision. Media strategy development has been called more of an art than a science because while many quantitative data are available, the planner also relies on creativity and nonquantifiable factors.

This chapter discussed many factors, including developing a proper media mix, determining target market and geographic coverage, scheduling, and balancing reach and frequency.

Creative aspects, budget considerations, the need for flexibility in the schedule, and the use of programmatic buying programs in the media planning process were also considered.

The chapter also introduced a number of resources available to the media planner. A summary chart of advantages and disadvantages of various media was provided.

Key Terms

media planning 341
media objectives 343
media strategies 343
medium 343
media vehicle 343
reach 343
coverage 343
frequency 343
sweeps periods 343
index number 347
survey of buying power index 351
brand development index (BDI) 351

category development index (CDI) 353
waste coverage 355
continuity 356
flighting 356
pulsing 356
unduplicated reach 360
duplicated reach 360
program rating 360
gross ratings points (GRPs) 361
target ratings points (TRPs) 361
effective reach 362
average frequency 363

recency 364
recency planning 364
absolute cost 367
relative cost 367
cost per thousand (CPM) 367
cost per ratings point (CPRP) 367
daily inch rate 368
target CPM (TCPM) 368
readers per copy 369
pass-along rate 369

Discussion Questions

1. Discuss some of the advantages of using programmatic media buying. Given that the majority of digital display ads are purchased this way, do you think this will be the only method media buyers use in the future? (LO 10-1)

2. There is new research that indicates that the number of ads one is exposed to in a day may be much lower than the thousands previously reported. Which numbers do you consider correct and why? (LO 10-4)

3. Marketers rely heavily on demographics when purchasing media. IMC Perspective 10–1 talks about additional factors that may be important. Discuss some of these factors and why they might impact media usage. (LO 10-4)

4. What are GRPs and target GRPs? Explain what these terms mean and discuss some of the strengths and weaknesses of using them. (LO 10-1)

5. The media landscape is rapidly changing. Explain what is meant by this statement. Then discuss some of the reasons why this is occurring. What can traditional media do to continue to exist? A number of studies have examined the role that personality and/or other personal characteristics may have on consumers' media usage. Discuss some of these studies. Do you

think that these characteristics may have an impact, or should marketers rely primarily on demographic characteristics? (LO 10-5)

6. Explain the differences between CPM and readers per dollar. Which is the most valuable relative cost comparison for advertisers to use? Why? (LO 10-1)

7. Figure 10–27 discusses the advantages and disadvantages of media. Describe any factors that may be taking place that might change the disadvantages or advantages of various media. (LO 10-5)

8. One of the more popular metrics now being used in nontraditional media (Internet, social media, etc.) is *engagement*. This term has also been used in evaluating traditional media. Explain what is meant by engagement. Is this term being used the same way in referring to both traditional and nontraditional media? (LO 10-1)

9. Discuss the differences between CDI and BDI. When would an advertiser use these indexes? (LO 10-2)

10. A number of studies have examined the role that personality and/or other personal characteristics may have on consumers' media usage. Discuss some of these studies. Do you think that these characteristics may have an impact, or should marketers rely primarily on demographic characteristics? (LO 10-2)

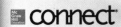

Digital users can access their personalized and adaptive SmartBook, Ad Forum Video Cases, and interactive exercises to review chapter concepts.

ASICS America Summary Flowchart

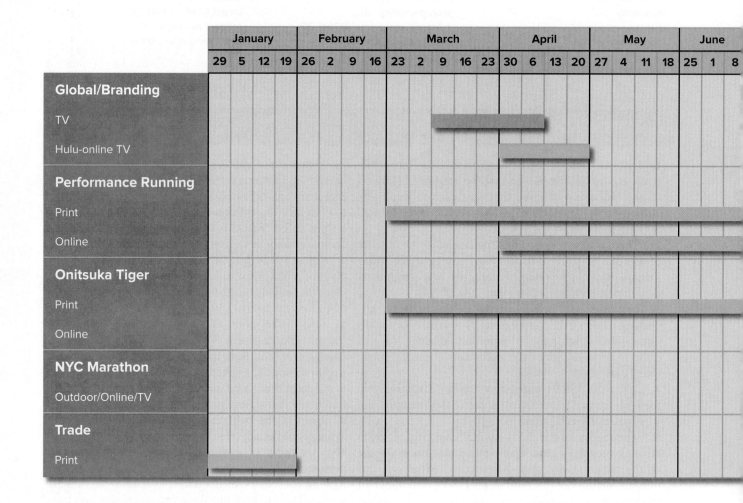

	January				February				March					April				May				June	
	29	5	12	19	26	2	9	16	23	2	9	16	23	30	6	13	20	27	4	11	18	25	1	8
Global/Branding																								
TV																								
Hulu-online TV																								
Performance Running																								
Print																								
Online																								
Onitsuka Tiger																								
Print																								
Online																								
NYC Marathon																								
Outdoor/Online/TV																								
Trade																								
Print																								

June			July				August					September				October				November				December			
8	15	22	29	6	13	20	27	3	10	17	24	31	7	14	21	28	5	12	19	26	2	9	16	23	30	7	14	21

11 Evaluation of Media: Television and Radio

LEARNING OBJECTIVES

LO1 Describe the role of television as an advertising medium and its advantages and limitations.

LO2 Discuss how television advertising time is purchased for network and local television as well as cable television.

LO3 Discuss how television viewing audiences are measured and developments in audience measurement.

LO4 Discuss the role of radio as an advertising medium and its advantages and limitations.

LO5 Discuss how radio advertising time is purchased.

LO6 Discuss how radio audiences are measured and developments in audience measurement.

THE FUTURE OF TELEVISION AND HOW IT WILL IMPACT ADVERTISING

Television has long been the medium of choice for marketers who want to reach large audiences and deliver an impactful message; the TV commercial has been considered the quintessential form of advertising by many marketers. The number of U.S. households with television has more than doubled over the past half century, going from 55 million in 1965 to 116.4 million in 2016. For much of this time period television was dominated by the three major broadcast networks and by the mid-90s, Fox had joined them as the fourth major network. The most significant development in the television industry prior to the turn of the century was the increasing penetration of cable TV and alternative delivery systems (ADS) such as direct broadcast by satellite, which dramatically increased the number of channels available to viewers. The number of homes with cable or ADS went from 13 percent in 1975 to nearly 90 percent today. As penetration increased, so did the number of channels available. At the end of the 1980s only a third of cable households could receive 30+ channels, but by the beginning of the new millennium the average household with cable had more than 100 channels available and today that number has nearly doubled.

One of the most significant factors impacting the television industry, as well as its use as an advertising medium, is the fragmentation of the viewing audience that has occurred with the increase in channels available through cable and ADS. Total viewership of the four major networks has declined dramatically over the past two decades and collectively accounts for less than 25 percent of the prime-time viewing audience. The top-rated shows used to be watched by nearly 20 percent of all TV households. However, it is rare for the top-rated TV shows to reach this many people and most top 10 shows struggle to get double-digit ratings. Many of these viewers are being lost to cable channels that offer programs appealing to more specific audiences interested in news, sports, fashion, music, cooking, travel, entertainment, and other areas.

While audience fragmentation is clearly impacting television, of even more concern to the industry is the effect technology is having on television viewing patterns. TiVo introduced the first digital video recorder (DVR) in 1999 and cable companies and ADS now make low-cost DVRs available to consumers who subscribe to their services. Just over half of TV households now have a DVR, which means they can record a show and watch it whenever they want and also fast-forward through the commercials. However, the impact of technology extends beyond DVRs because many people, particularly those in the 18–49 demographic target that advertisers covet, are not watching TV in the traditional linear fashion whereby they view a scheduled TV program at the specific time it's offered, and on the particular channel it's presented on. In addition to time-shifted viewing on DVRs, TV shows are being streamed online over personal computers, tablets, and smartphones as well as through connected streaming video devices and gaming consoles such as Apple TV, Amazon Fire TV, Google Chromecast, Xbox, and PlayStation—as well as smart TVs. Just 10 years ago most television shows were being watched live, but it is likely that by 2020 only 50 percent of viewership will be live while the other half will be nonlinear.

Compounding the problem facing the television and cable networks is concern over cord-cutting, which refers to households that are dropping their traditional pay-TV services such as cable or satellite TV. It is estimated that the number of pay-TV households will decline by a little over 1 percent per year and that by 2020 the total number of households that don't subscribe to pay-TV—a combination of cord-cutters and "cord-nevers" who had never signed up in the first place—will reach 23 percent of U.S. households. Moreover, many of the pay-TV providers plan to offer subscribers "skinny bundles" which will include fewer channels so they save money on their monthly bills. ESPN, the cable network with the most subscribers but also the highest monthly subscriber fee at just over $7, has lost an estimated 10 million subscribers since 2013 and now has its lowest subscriber total in nearly a decade at just under 90 million.

Whereas all of these factors have led to predictions of television's imminent demise as a major advertising medium, many experts are much more positive about it future. They note that while the viewing audience is clearly fragmented and viewing patterns are changing, TV advertising will remain valuable and important to marketers. Nielsen, the company that measures television viewing audiences, launched a new measurement system in 2016 that will account for linear as well as nonlinear TV viewing, which means advertisers will no longer have to pay for eyeballs that are not watching their commercials. It is also likely that TV commercials will become much more targeted and even personalized, which should make them more relevant and engaging to viewers.

It is also likely that television will remain important for marketers trying to reach large numbers of consumers in an impactful way. Even with the increase in cord-cutting, more than 90 million households will still subscribe to a pay-TV service; popular shows on the broadcast and cable networks will still reach millions of people. Sporting events on the major networks as well as cable channels such as ESPN and Fox Sports1 will be watched live and thus be DVR-proof, while major events such as the Super Bowl, Grammys, and Oscars will deliver large viewing audiences to marketers.

David Poltrack, chief research officer for the CBS television network, notes that the audience for its programming has actually grown in the past decade and expects it to continue to do so. He points to data showing that as previous generations grew older, their viewing of prime-time TV increased and that millennials appear to be following the same pattern as differences in viewing level have always been related to life stage. He notes that as millennials leave their parents' homes, settle down, and start families of their own, "many of them will, like the generations before them, purchase the biggest-screen television they can afford and start watching broadcast television."

The television networks cannot just assume they can sell commercial time based on TV's mass appeal. They will have to find ways to give viewers a better experience and provide more value to advertisers by reducing the number of commercials during a program as well as creating more engaging advertising formats. Just as technology is threatening television's viability as an advertising medium, it will also lead to more creative and efficient uses of TV for marketers. Television advertising will be used not just to create awareness or aspiration, but also to impact consumers further down the purchase funnel and at different points in their paths to purchase. Irwin Gotlieb, chair of GroupM which is one of the world's largest media companies, suggests that TV has a bright road ahead and perhaps summarizes the changes quite well: "It won't be your father's TV, nor would you want it to be."

Sources: Irwin Gotleib, "What We're Seeing Is the Evolution of TV, Not Its Decline," *Advertising Age,* April 18, 2016, p. 28; Jeanine Poggi, "The Future of TV Advertising," *Advertising Age,* April 18, 2016, pp. 10–14; Keach Hagey, "Cord-Cutting Is Accelerating," *The Wall Street Journal,* December 10, 2015, www.wsj.com/articles/cord-cutting-is-accelerating-1449745201; Jason Lynch, "Don't Panic, Says CBS: More People Are Watching TV Now Than a Decade Ago," *Adweek,* August 10, 2015, www.adweek.com/news/television/dont-panic-says-cbs-more-people-are-watching-tv-now-decade-ago-166313.

Television has been the dominant form of entertainment in most households for more than three quarters of a century. Advertising has been the lifeblood of the industry for nearly as long. Ever since Bulova ran the first TV ad in 1941 at a cost of ten dollars, the commercial has been considered the quintessential form of advertising for many marketers. Television advertising has gone through many changes over the past 75 years. For decades it was dominated by three major broadcast networks (ABC, CBS, and NBC), which could deliver more than 90 percent of the prime-time viewing audience on any given evening. However, with the growth of cable and direct broadcast satellite services, most television households can receive more than 100 channels that offer various types of shows, news, sports, music, information, and other entertainment genres. The device that delivers all of this into our homes has evolved, as well as the squat cubes that are rapidly being replaced by larger, flat-panel, high-definition televisions (HDTVs) that offer sharper and brighter digital images along with high-quality sound. Moreover, these HDTVs in our homes are often connected to other devices including digital video recorders (DVRs), gaming consoles, and computers, while the cable and satellite companies that deliver the signals also offer access to movies, sports, and other forms of entertainment through their on-demand services. Many experts argue that it is only a matter of time before all of this content is delivered to TV sets online via the Internet.

The changes that are occurring in the television industry are important because they are having a profound impact on the largest advertising medium. TV has virtually saturated households throughout the United States and most other countries and is still a very important part of the lives of most people. The average American household watches nearly five hours of TV a day, and "the tube" has become the predominant source of news and entertainment for many people. Over 90 percent of TV households in the United States have a DVD player, nearly 50 percent have digital video recorders (DVRs), and over 80 percent have HDTVs on which they can watch their favorite television programs and movies. On any given evening during the prime-time hours of 8 to 11 P.M., more than 100 million people are watching TV. Popular shows like *Empire, The Voice,* and *The Big Bang Theory* can draw between 10 to 15 million viewers each week. The large numbers of people who watch television are important to the TV networks and stations because they can sell time on these programs to marketers who want to reach that audience with their advertising messages. Moreover, the qualities that make TV a great medium for news and entertainment also make it an excellent medium for creative ads that can have a strong impact on consumers.

Radio is also an integral part of our lives. Many of us wake up to clock radios and rely on radio programs to inform and/or entertain us while we drive to work or school. For many people, radio is a constant companion in their cars, at home, even at work. The average American listens to the radio nearly three hours each day.[1] Like TV viewers, radio listeners are an important audience for marketers.

In this chapter, we examine the media of TV and radio, including the general characteristics of each as well as their specific advantages and disadvantages. We examine how advertisers use TV and radio as part of their advertising and media strategies, how they buy TV and radio time, and how audiences are measured and evaluated for each medium. We also examine the factors that are changing the role of TV and radio as advertising media.

TELEVISION

It has often been said that television is the ideal advertising medium. Its ability to combine visual images, sound, motion, and color presents the advertiser with the opportunity to develop the most creative and imaginative appeals of any medium. However, TV does have certain problems that limit or even prevent its use by many advertisers.

Advantages of Television

TV has numerous advantages over other media, including creativity and impact, coverage and cost-effectiveness, captivity and attention, and selectivity and flexibility.

Creativity and Impact   Perhaps the greatest advantage of TV is the opportunity it provides for presenting the advertising message. The interaction of sight and sound offers tremendous creative flexibility and makes possible dramatic, lifelike representations of products and services. TV commercials can be used to convey a mood or image for a brand as well as to develop emotional or entertaining appeals that help make a dull product appear interesting.

Television is also an excellent medium for demonstrating a product or service as well as telling a story about a brand to highlight its features and benefits or create an emotional attachment. For example, the Carmichael Lynch agency created a poignant commercial for Subaru called "Cut the Cord," which shows a father putting his daughter on the school bus for the first time and then driving alongside it to make sure she's okay (Exhibit 11–1). As he drives the dad says, "I'm

EXHIBIT 11–1

Subaru uses television commercials to create an emotional attachment to its cars

Source: Subaru of America, Inc.

overprotective. That's why I got a Subaru," while the voiceover at the end of the spot says, "Love. It's what makes a Subaru, a Subaru." Television commercials such as this that rely on slice-of-life stories revolving around themes such as longevity, safety, versatility, and adventure have helped Subaru of America record significant sales increases for seven consecutive years.[2]

Coverage and Cost-Effectiveness Television advertising makes it possible to reach large audiences. Nearly everyone, regardless of age, sex, income, or educational level, watches at least some TV. Most people do so on a regular basis. According to Nielsen Media Research estimates, nearly 297 million people aged 2 or older live in the nation's 116.4 million TV households, close to 77 percent of whom are 18 or older.

Marketers selling products and services that appeal to broad target audiences find that TV lets them reach mass markets, often very cost-efficiently. The average prime-time TV show reaches 4.6 million homes; a top-rated show like *The Big Bang Theory* may reach nearly 10 million homes and almost twice that many viewers. In 2015, the average cost per thousand (CPM) homes reached was nearly $24 for network evening shows and $5.85 for daytime weekly shows.[3]

Because of its ability to reach large audiences in a cost-efficient manner, TV is a popular medium among companies selling mass-consumption products. Companies with widespread distribution and availability of their products and services use TV to reach the mass market and deliver their advertising messages at a very low cost per thousand. Television has become indispensable to large consumer packaged-goods marketers, telecommunication companies, automotive manufacturers, and major retailers. Telecommunication companies like Verizon, AT&T, and Sprint spend around two-thirds of their measured media budgets on various forms of television advertising—network, spot, cable, and syndicated programs—while major retailers such as JCPenney, Sears, and Walmart allocate nearly 60 percent. Figure 11–1 shows the top 10 network and cable TV advertisers and their expenditures.

Captivity and Attention Television is basically intrusive in that commercials impose themselves on viewers as they watch their favorite programs. Unless we make a special effort to avoid commercials, most of us are exposed to thousands of them each year. The increase in viewing options and the penetration of DVDs, DVRs, remote controls, and other automatic devices have made it easier for TV viewers to avoid commercial messages.[4] However, the remaining viewers are likely to devote some attention to many advertising messages. As discussed in Chapter 5, the low-involvement nature of consumer learning and response processes may mean TV ads have an effect on consumers simply through heavy repetition and exposure to catchy slogans and jingles.

Selectivity and Flexibility Television has often been criticized for being a nonselective medium, since it is difficult to reach a precisely defined market segment through the use of TV advertising. But some selectivity is possible due to variations in the composition of audiences as a result of program content, broadcast time, and geographic coverage. For example, Saturday morning TV caters to children;

FIGURE 11–1

Top 10 Network and Cable
Network Advertisers, 2015

Network TV		
Rank	Company	Measured Broadcast (millions)
1	Procter & Gamble Co.	$743.0
2	AT&T	731.2
3	General Motors Co.	551.5
4	Ford Motor Co.	551.2
5	Pfizer	495.6
6	Verizon Communications	480.7
7	Time Warner	465.6
8	Deutsche Telekom (T-Mobile)	446.1
9	Apple	427.6
10	Johnson & Johnson	424.3
Cable TV Networks		
1	Procter & Gamble Co.	$606.3
2	AT&T	522.2
3	Berkshire Hathaway	499.0
4	PepsiCo	404.5
5	General Motors Co.	395.2
6	Time Warner	388.9
7	Yum Brands	380.8
8	Comcast Corp.	358.1
9	Hershey Co.	313.4
10	General Mills	307.8

Source: "200 Leading National Advertisers," *Advertising Age*, June 27, 2016, p. 18. Copyright © 2016 Crain Communications.

Saturday and Sunday afternoon programs are geared to the sports-oriented male; and weekday daytime shows appeal heavily to homemakers.

With the growth of cable TV, advertisers refine their coverage further by appealing to groups with specific interests such as sports, news, history, the arts, or music, as well as specific demographic groups. Exhibit 11–2 shows an ad promoting the Oxygen cable network and how it reaches young, upscale women who like to try new products, as well as recommend them to others.

Advertisers can also adjust their media strategies to take advantage of different geographic markets through local or spot ads in specific market areas. Television ads can be scheduled to run repeatedly to achieve continuity in media scheduling or flighting or pulsing can be used to take advantage of special events or occasions as well as time periods. For example, marketers targeting males often advertise during sporting events such as golf and tennis tournaments as well as MLB, NBA, or NFL games. Sports programming has become particularly popular among advertisers since sporting events are usually watched live. This increases the likelihood of viewers seeing an advertiser's commercial rather than fast-forwarding through them

IMC Perspective 11–1 > > >

Television Broadcast Rights Pay the Way for College Sports

Collegiate sports have long been an important part of the college experience; many students love football weekends at their schools or going to a basketball game and often stay connected to their alma maters by cheering for their sports teams. Despite their popularity, these are challenging times for intercollegiate sports as only a fraction of college athletic department's support themselves. Most rely on student fees and support from the school's general fund. Only about 20 percent of the 128 athletic departments in college football's top division, the Division 1 NCAA Football Bowl Subdivision (FBS), make a profit each year. However, the schools that do make a profit all have one thing in common: a big-time, high-profile football program. As colleges scramble to cover the budget shortfalls in their athletic departments, they have recognized that the best opportunity to do so is by leveraging college football, which is their most marketable asset. The good news for athletic directors is that the television networks are welcoming them with open arms because they know that college football is one of the best ways for them to reach the most important segment of their target audience—the millions of viewers who want to watch live sports.

College football, like most sporting events, is nearly always watched live on TV, which reduces the number of people who record the games and fast-forward through commercials. Advertisers are willing to pay more for broadcast rights for sporting events such as college football games because they are a good way to reach young men who are a valuable and elusive target audience for marketers. The television networks have agreed to pay about $30 billion in rights fees to college conferences and their member schools over the next 15 years, including a deal whereby ESPN paid

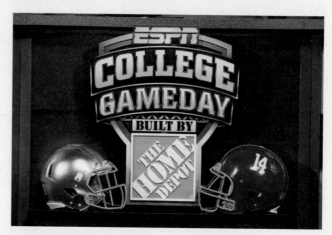

© Cal Sport Media/AP Images

an estimated $7 billion for the rights to televise major college football's FBS playoff for 12 years, a four-team tournament that began in 2014. To accommodate the networks' golden goose, college football teams are doing whatever they can to maximize television revenue including adding conference championship games, jumping to new conferences, abandoning long-standing rivalries, and dismantling the old system of postseason bowl games. Over the past few years a number of conferences including the Big Ten and Pac-12 have expanded and added new teams from major media markets. For example, Maryland and Rutgers were invited to join the Big Ten Conference while the universities of Colorado and Utah joined the Pac-12, largely for the TV markets they brought with them.

as is often the case when playing back a program on a DVR. IMC Perspective 11–1 discusses how college football and basketball have become very popular among marketers, which has led to tremendous increases in revenue for many universities from rights fees.

Limitations of Television

Although television is unsurpassed from a creative perspective, the medium has several disadvantages that limit or preclude its use by many advertisers. These problems include high costs, the lack of selectivity, the fleeting nature of a television message, commercial clutter, limited viewer attention, and distrust of TV ads.

Costs Despite the efficiency of TV in reaching large audiences, it is an expensive medium in which to advertise. The high cost of TV stems not only from the expense of buying airtime but also from the costs of producing a quality commercial. Production costs for a national brand 30-second spot average more than $350,000 and can reach over $1 million for more elaborate commercials.[5] Many advertisers also develop

The major television networks are willing to pay the NCAA, as well as the conferences, large sums of money for rights fees to televise games because college football is more popular than ever, which means millions of eyeballs are watching the games. Marketers spend more than a billion dollars per season to air national ads on college football games and several hundred million more for local ad time. There are a number of reasons why marketers are advertising on college football games and making them a major part of their IMC programs. While college football games are a way to reach young males (and often females), they also provide marketers with a way of connecting with affluent males through live sports programming, but at a lower price than National Football League games. About 16 percent of homes that watch college football regularly make more than $75,000 per year, while 28 percent earn over $100,000.

Another reason why college football is popular among marketers is the integrated marketing opportunities it offers them. For example, automotive marketer Nissan has been the official sponsor of the Heisman Memorial Trophy Award, which is given to the top college football player each year, for the past five seasons and has built an integrated marketing campaign around its sponsorship. The Nissan Heisman House campaign stars past Heisman Trophy winners in a series of TV spots that air during broadcasts of college football games on ESPN throughout the season. In addition, there are print ads, radio ads, and an interactive website that houses over 20 shareable online videos, as well as the annual Heisman House Tour that travels to college campuses throughout the season. A number of other companies and brands are using football games as a way to connect with students on college campuses, including Allstate, Home Depot, Aflac, and Chevrolet. Home Depot sponsors ESPN's popular "College Game Day" which airs from the campus where one of the biggest games of the week is being played and televised. Chevrolet sets up kiosks at the event where students can learn more about its cars, offers tailgaters rides to the stadium, and sponsors college football–themed sweepstakes.

Football is not the only collegiate sport that is generating revenue for colleges. In 2010 the NCAA signed a 14-year deal with CBS and Turner Broadcasting, which is a division of Time Warner Inc., to pay $740 million annually to televise the men's basketball tournament that has become known as "March Madness." In 2016, CBS and Turner agreed to pay another $8.8 billion to extend the deal for an additional eight years and lock in the rights to the popular tournament until 2032. The deal will funnel $1.1 billion annually to NCAA member colleges, which is much needed revenue for athletic programs that have been experiencing major budget cuts. Revenue from TV broadcast rights helps fund collegiate athletic programs, including women's sports programs as well as many minor sports that generate little revenue.

College sports programs have become very dependent on the monies the networks are willing to pay to broadcast their football and basketball games. However, the future success of the relationship between college sports, advertisers, and the TV networks will depend on several factors, including viewers' willingness to pay higher monthly bills as cable operators pass on the rights fees to subscribers, many of whom do not watch sports. It will also depend on whether the networks raise their advertising rates and make it prohibitive for companies to advertise during the games. There is also concern that the airways will become oversaturated with football and basketball games and the colleges themselves will slay the goose that is laying the golden egg. However, given the popularity of college football and basketball, this seems very unlikely.

Sources: Joe Flint, "CBS, Turner Strike $8.8 Billion Deal to Televise NCAA's March Madness through 2032,"*The Wall Street Journal,* April 12, 2016, pp. B1, B4; "Nissan's Popular 'Heisman House' Returns for 2015 College Football Season on ESPN," September 2, 2015, www.reuters.com/article/tn-nissan-idUSnBw026121a+100+BSW2015090; Michael McCarthy, "How Much Longer Can Sports Prices Defy Gravity—While Still Delivering ROI?" *Advertising Age,* April 8, 2013, p. 10; Rachel Bachman and Matthew Futterman, "College Football's Big-Money, Big-Risk Business Model," *The Wall Street Journal,* December 10, 2012, pp. B1, B4.

commercials specifically for certain ethnic markets such as African Americans and Hispanics.[6] More advertisers are using media-driven creative strategies that require production of a variety of commercials, which drive up their costs. Even local ads can be expensive to produce and often are not of high quality. The high costs of producing and airing commercials often price small and medium-size advertisers out of the market.

Lack of Selectivity   Some selectivity is available in television through variations in programs and cable TV. But advertisers who are seeking a very specific, often small, target audience find the coverage of TV often extends beyond their market, reducing its cost effectiveness (as discussed in Chapter 10). Geographic selectivity can be a problem for local advertisers such as retailers, since a station bases its rates on the total market area it reaches. For example, stations in Pittsburgh, Pennsylvania, reach viewers in western and central Pennsylvania, eastern Ohio, northern West Virginia, and even parts of Maryland. The small company whose market is limited to the immediate Pittsburgh area may find TV an inefficient media buy, since the stations cover a larger geographic area than the merchant's trade area. Geographic selectivity can be particularly problematic in large media markets.

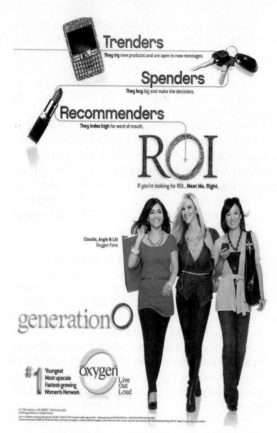

EXHIBIT 11–2

Oxygen promotes its ability to reach young, upscale women

Source: Oxygen Media LLC

Audience selectivity is improving as advertisers target certain groups of consumers through the type of program or day and/or time when they choose to advertise. However, TV still does not offer as much audience selectivity as radio, magazines, direct mail, or online ads for reaching precise segments of the market.

Fleeting Message Most TV commercials last only 30 seconds or less and leave nothing tangible for the viewer to examine or consider. Commercials have become shorter and shorter as the demand for a limited amount of broadcast time has intensified and advertisers try to get more impressions from their media budgets. Thirty-second commercials became the norm in the mid-1970s, and in 1986, the three major networks began accepting 15-second spots across their full schedules (except during children's viewing time). For the next two decades these shorter spots accounted for a little more than a third of all network commercials and around 15 percent of nonnetwork commercials. However, 15-second spots have become more prevalent over the past five years and now account for a similar amount of commercial activity on network TV; (46 percent each); 15-second spots are used even more than :30s on cable networks (47 vs. 42 percent). The 30-second format remains the dominant commercial length for nonnetwork advertising, accounting for 62 percent of spot TV ads versus 28 percent for 15-second spots.[7]

An important factor in the decline in commercial length has been the increase in media costs over the past decade, particularly for prime-time programs. With the average cost of a prime-time spot now exceeding $100,000, and the most popular shows commanding nearly $300,000 or more, advertisers see shorter commercials as the only way to keep their media costs in line. A 15-second spot typically sells for half the price of a 30-second spot. By using 15- or even 10-second commercials, advertisers can run additional spots to reinforce the message or reach a larger audience. Many advertisers also believe shorter commercials can deliver a message just as effectively as longer spots for much less money.

Clutter The problems of fleeting messages and shorter commercials are compounded by the fact that the advertiser's message is only one of many spots and other nonprogramming material seen during a commercial break, so it may have trouble being noticed. As noted in Chapter 5, one of advertisers' greatest concerns with TV advertising is the potential decline in effectiveness because of such *clutter*.

While the use of shorter commercials by advertisers has contributed to the problem, clutter also increases when the networks and individual stations run promotional announcements for their shows, make more time available for commercials, and redistribute time to popular programs. The next time you watch TV, count the number of commercials, promotions for the news or upcoming programs, or public service announcements that appear during a station break and you will appreciate why clutter is a major concern.

With all of these messages competing for our attention, it is easy to understand why the viewer comes away confused or even annoyed and unable to remember or properly identify the product or service advertised. Advertisers and agencies have been pressuring the networks to cut back on the commercials and other sources of clutter. However, the networks argue that they must maintain the number of commercials they show or increase advertising rates. Clutter has become even more of a problem on cable television as many networks have been packing in more ads to offset declines in viewership and a stagnant market for advertising sales.[8] Marketers worry that an oversaturation of commercials will reduce the effectiveness of their spots and drive more viewers away from watching traditional TV to commercial-free streaming services such Netflix and Amazon.[9]

Limited Viewer Attention   When advertisers buy time on a TV program, they are not purchasing guaranteed exposure but rather the opportunity to communicate a message to large numbers of consumers. But there is increasing evidence that the size of the viewing audience shrinks during a commercial break. People leave the room to go to the bathroom or to get something to eat or drink, or they are distracted in some other way during commercials.

Getting consumers to pay attention to commercials has become an even greater challenge in recent years; nearly half of television homes have a DVR while nearly 80 percent of households with income over $75,000 have one.[10] Most households have either cable or satellite service and receive an average of more than 100 channels, which means there are more viewing options available. These factors have contributed to the problems of zipping and zapping. **Zipping** occurs when viewers fast-forward through commercials as they play back a previously recorded program. With the increased penetration of DVRs, more people are watching recorded shows and fast-forwarding through the commercials. The problem is being compounded by the fact that many of the networks schedule their most popular shows against one another on the same nights and in the same time slots. Thus, the most popular shows also end up being the most recorded. Moreover, the audience for these shows is composed of upscale viewers in the 18-to-49 age group that are highly coveted by many advertisers. TiVo, the company that is the leading provider of digital video recorders, and Nielsen Media Research have conducted studies of TV viewers who fast-forward through ads and have found that men and women between the ages of 18 and 34 skip more commercials; older women tend to skip fewer ads than younger women.[11] TiVo Research & Analytics sells advertisers information with second-by-second program and spot-specific metrics for more than 110 national networks as well as live and time-shifted ratings under its Stop//Watch program. Television programmers and advertisers can use this information to analyze zipping behavior and determine the impact of DVRs on commercial viewership (Exhibit 11–3).

Zapping refers to changing channels to avoid commercials. Nearly all televisions come with remote controls, which enable viewers to switch channels easily. Studies have shown that as much as a third of program audiences may be lost to zapping when commercials appear.[12] Research by Nielsen has also found that most commercial zapping occurs at the beginning and, to a lesser extent, the end of a program. Zapping at these points is likely to occur because commercial breaks are so long and predictable. Research also shows that young adults zap more than older adults and that men are more likely to zap than women.[13]

Studies conducted on zapping behavior among television viewers have found that people stop viewing TV during a commercial break because they have a reason to stop watching television altogether or they want to find out what is being shown on other channels. The number of people zapping in and out was not related to the type of product being advertised or specific characteristics of the commercials.[14] Research has also shown that zappers recalled fewer of the brands advertised than nonzappers and that most of the brands that were recalled by zappers were placed near the end

EXHIBIT 11–3

TiVo tracks the viewing patterns of its subscribers

Source: TiVo

CONGRATULATIONS, YOU JUST SPENT $2 MILLION ON A TV CAMPAIGN TO REACH THIS GUY.

Just because your spot aired doesn't mean it was seen. With regular TV, you'll never know. Because 45% of network prime time advertising is fast-forwarded. At TiVo, we've found a way to catch them looking. Our ad solutions deliver your brand message at a time when we know viewers are engaged: on pause, while fast-forwarding, or when clicking through interactive tags to make a purchase right from that screen. And only TiVo provides data on a second-by-second basis to prove they're watching, remote in hand. It's the only way to know you're actually reaching someone who is, well, conscious.

Call now—the first 50 responses receive a free commercial fast forward analysis. For more information on TiVo Ad Solutions reach us at 212.520.1890, or tivoresearch@tivo.com.

GET WITH THE PROGRAM.

"My boyfriend preferred sports to *Blue Bloods*. I'll miss him."

ioneffects

Feeling the effects?
Tell us why you're hooked on *Blue Bloods*.
#IONeffects

EXHIBIT 11–4

ION Television promotes the engagement level of its viewers

Source: Ion Media Networks

of the commercial break, which is when viewers would be likely to return to a program.[15]

As more consumers become turned off by advertising and the number of channels available to them increases, the level of zapping is likely to increase. Thus, the challenge facing the networks, as well as advertisers, is how to discourage viewers from changing channels during commercial breaks and be more receptive to the advertising. Exhibit 11–4 shows an ad for the ION Television Network promoting how it has higher engagement with its programming, as more ION viewers watch live, stay tuned longer, and have higher brand recall than DVR viewers. Some advertisers believe that producing different executions of a campaign theme is one way to maintain viewers' attention. Others think the ultimate way to zap-proof commercials is to produce creative advertising messages that will attract and hold viewers' attention. However, this is easier said than done; many consumers just do not want to watch commercials.

Advances in technology are likely to continue to lead to changes in television viewing habits, which will impact the number of consumers who watch TV commercials. DVRs are expected to continue to present a problem for advertisers, particularly if devices such as the Dish Network's Hopper, which allows viewers to automatically skip ads on all TV programs they record, become more prevalent.[16] Also of concern to the television industry is how TV viewing patterns are being impacted by another time-shifting technology—video on demand (VOD)—that is offered by cable operators as well as satellite services. VOD services allow users to select and watch programs interactively, and pause, fast-forward, or rewind the program just as they might do with a DVR player.

For a number of years, TV shows available through VOD did not contain any ads and the networks made a limited number of shows available as they were reluctant to allow viewers access to shows without commercials since they were concerned they would become accustomed to that type of viewing experience. However, the networks have begun to make their programs available with commercials and the cable operators and other distributors have, in some cases, agreed to disable a viewer's ability to fast-forward through them. Some of the networks have also begun to include VOD viewership in the advertising packages they make available to advertisers, along with viewership on their websites as well as other devices such as tablets and smartphones.[17]

Viewers' interest in watching TV shows in alternative ways and on their own time schedule will increase as more homes acquire DVRs and VOD services. More people, particularly millennials, are also watching TV shows online through video-streaming subscription services including Netflix, Amazon, and Hulu Plus which are easily accessible through digital media services such as Roku, Apple TV, and apps integrated into smart TV sets. Television and cable networks and local TV stations are making more shows available on their websites. The challenge facing the TV industry is how to accommodate the demand for these alternative viewing methods and capture revenue from them while protecting their traditional advertising business model. They also must consider that the way many people watch television is changing as viewers are using their laptops, tablets, and smartphones to multitask when watching TV. Digital and Social Media Perspective 11–1 discusses how multitasking and social media are changing the way we watch television and the implications for advertisers.

Distrust and Negative Evaluation To many critics of advertising, TV commercials personify everything that is wrong with the industry. Critics often single out TV commercials because of their pervasiveness and the intrusive nature of the medium. Consumers are seen as defenseless against the barrage of TV ads, since they cannot control the transmission of the message and what appears on their screens.

Viewers dislike TV advertising when they believe it is offensive, uninformative, or shown too frequently or when they do not like its content.[18] Studies have shown that of the various forms of advertising, distrust is generally the highest for TV commercials.[19] Also, concern has been raised about the effects of TV advertising on specific groups, such as children or older adults.[20]

The results from the 2015 Nielsen Global Trust in Advertising Report, which are based on a survey of more than 30,000 people in 60 countries, showed that 63 percent of consumers say they completely or somewhat trust television advertising which was slightly higher trust in newspaper and magazine ads. Trust was much higher for TV ads than for online video (48 percent), search (47 percent), and banner ads (42 percent) as well as mobile ads (43 percent).[21]

BUYING TELEVISION TIME

A number of options are available to advertisers that choose to use TV as part of their media mix. They can purchase time in a variety of program formats that appeal to various types and sizes of audiences. They can purchase time on a national, regional, or local basis. Or they can sponsor an entire program, participate in the sponsorship, or use spot announcements during or between programs.

The purchase of TV advertising time is a highly specialized phase of the advertising business, particularly for large companies spending huge sums of money. Large advertisers that do a lot of TV advertising generally use agency media specialists or specialized media buying services to arrange the media schedule and purchase TV time. Decisions have to be made regarding national or network versus local or spot purchases, selection of specific stations, sponsorship versus participation, different classes of time, and appropriate programs. Local advertisers may not have to deal with the first decision, but they do face all the others.

Network versus Spot

A basic decision for all advertisers is allocating their TV media budgets to network versus local or spot announcements. Most national advertisers use network schedules to provide national coverage and supplement this with regional or local spot purchases to reach markets where additional coverage is desired.

Network Advertising   A common way advertisers disseminate their messages is by purchasing airtime from a **television network**. A network assembles a series of affiliated local TV stations, or **affiliates**, to which it supplies programming and services. These affiliates, most of which are independently owned, contractually agree to preempt time during specified hours for programming provided by the networks and to carry the national advertising within the program. The networks share the advertising revenue they receive during these time periods with the affiliates. The affiliates are also free to sell commercial time in nonnetwork periods and during station breaks in the preempted periods to both national and local advertisers.

The three traditional major networks are NBC, ABC, and CBS. The Fox Broadcasting Co. broadcasts its programs over a group of affiliated independent stations and has become the fourth major network. A number of Fox's prime-time programs, such as *Empire, Family Guy,* and *The Simpsons,* are very popular, particularly among the 18-to-49 age group that is often targeted by advertisers. Fox has also become a major player in sports programming with its contracts to broadcast sporting events such as NFL football and Major League Baseball.[22]

The other television network in the United States is CW, which was formed in 2006 when two 11-year-old networks, WB and UPN, decided to merge.[23] The

Digital and Social Media Perspective 11–1 > > >

THE WAY WE WATCH TELEVISION IS CHANGING THANKS TO DIGITAL AND SOCIAL MEDIA

Television has long been the medium of choice for marketers who want to reach large audiences and deliver an impactful message. However, developments in digital technology over the past decade or so have had a profound impact on the way people watch TV and are challenging its role as the quintessential advertising medium. For nearly 60 years consumers watched TV on huge, boxlike tube sets with screen sizes that slowly evolved from 19 to 36 inches in size. However, today nearly 90 percent of homes have high-resolution, pixel-perfect HDTVs and as the prices decline, the size of the television in many homes gets larger; the average screen size today is 42 inches. Over 80 percent of homes also have broadband wireless Internet, and many have video gaming consoles or other connected devices such as Apple TV, Roku, Amazon Fire TV, or Google Chromecast that help them stream video content to their televisions.

While HDTVs get larger and various devices are making TV viewing like surfing the Internet, not everyone is opting for "bigger is better" when it comes to watching television. Many people are going the opposite direction and are turning to their laptops, tablets, and even smartphones to watch their favorite movies, shows, and sports programs. In some cases, tablet owners will stare at a 10-inch screen for hours when there is a 42-inch HDTV in the same room. He or she may be viewing the smaller screen because a spouse or roommate is watching another program or because the Internet connection is better through a computer or tablet than a video-streaming device. However, a growing number of people have become tired of paying $100-plus monthly bills for cable or satellite TV service and don't even use an antenna to get free signals over the air. The Nielsen Co. estimates that there are now more than 5 million of these "Zero-TV" households that watch TV shows and movies on the Internet via Netflix, Hulu, or Amazon's Prime service, often via their smartphone connections.

There are other ways in which TV viewing is being transformed by computers, tablets, and smartphones. In fact, it's a similar concept to what you're probably doing while reading this book: multitasking. When is the last time you watched TV without surfing the Internet, texting friends, tweeting, going on Facebook, or playing games such as Words with Friends or Clash Royale? You probably can't remember, meaning you're among the 86 percent of TV watchers whom a recent Nielsen and Yahoo! study found watch TV while multitasking on your computer or mobile device. Within that group, 40 percent use their mobile devices for social networking, 33 percent utilize various apps, and over half text family and friends.

CW Network is co-owned by CBS/Viacom and Warner Bros., which is part of the Time Warner media conglomerate. The CW Network targets the 18-to-49 demographic but does not offer a full prime-time schedule. It airs 20 hours of regularly scheduled programming each week over six days that includes 10 hours of prime-time programming from Monday through Friday, 8:00 to 10:00 P.M. The new network has a number of popular programs, including *Crazy Ex-Girlfriend, The Flash, Arrow,* and *America's Next Top Model* (Exhibit 11–5). In addition to CW and the four major networks, there are also several Spanish-language networks in the United States.[24]

Spanish-language television networks such as Univision and Telemundo are becoming increasingly popular and provide advertisers a way to reach the fast-growing Hispanic market (Exhibit 11–6). Univision has become the nation's leading Hispanic media company and now challenges the four major broadcast TV networks with respect to size of its viewing audience. Hispanics now account for more than 52 million, or nearly 17 percent, of the U.S. population and advertising spending on Hispanic television continues to grow. The Hispanic population is also younger and is having a greater influence on the direction of pop culture, which makes them an important market for advertisers.[25]

The networks have affiliates throughout the nation for almost complete national coverage. When an advertiser purchases airtime from one of these national networks, the commercial is transmitted across the nation through the affiliate station network. Network advertising truly represents a mass medium, as the advertiser can broadcast its message simultaneously throughout the country.

President Kanye @President_Kanye · 30 Aug 2015

What do I and America have in common? We're both the greatest of all time. Who better to lead? #Kanye2020 #VoteForKanye

↩   ♺ 17   ♥ 21   •••

President Kanye @President_Kanye · 30 Aug 2015

#Kanye2020

↩   ♺ 49   ♥ 52   •••

Source: Twitter

The widespread multitasking and social media consumption during TV viewing is having a major effect on the television industry. One way is by bringing eyeballs to shows that otherwise would not be there. A Nielsen study showed that 46 percent of TV watchers started watching a show as a result of hearing about it through Facebook while Twitter came in second at 14 percent, websites of TV shows at 9 percent, and online discussion boards at 8 percent. Additionally 70 percent indicated that they talked about a show through social media while it was on the air. Most television shows also have a Facebook page where fans can read up on the latest episodes, learn more about the actors, and enter to win prizes related to the show. This keeps fans more interested in the shows. Some television shows even provide sneak-peak videos through Facebook to get fans excited about upcoming episodes.

Twitter is impacting television as well; many TV networks are using the social media platform to engage with their fans. For instance, many TV shows display hashtags in the bottom corner of the screen during shows so fans can easily get on Twitter and see what others are saying about the show and often chime in themselves. Millions of TV fans come on Twitter each week to discuss TV's biggest moments as they happen live without leaving the comfort of their own couches. Nielsen has ranked the top series, specials, and sports events on Twitter for the past several years, along with the most-tweeted-about minute in each category. For the past three years an AMC cable network program topped the list of top series on Twitter. In 2015 an average of 4 million people saw at least one tweet about new episodes of *The Walking Dead,* and viewers sent an average of 424,000 tweets about each episode.

Award shows are also popular on Twitter since people love to tweet about celebrities. For example, 248,000 tweets were sent in the minute following Kayne West's announcement on the 2015 MTV Music Awards that he would be running for president of the United States in 2020, making it the most-tweeted TV minute of 2015. We will probably have to wait awhile to see if he makes good on his announcement and whether Kim Kardashian becomes the first lady. If so, it is very likely people will be tweeting about it.

Sources: Adrianne Pasquarellli, "The Next Generation Learns to Live without TV Sets," *Advertising Age,* April 18, 2016, p. 26; "Tops of 2015: TV and Social Media," *Nielsen Newswire,* December 8, 2015, www.nielsen.com/us/en/insights/news/2015/tops-of-2015-tv-and-social-media.html; Kevin Sintumuang, "Is a Tablet the Only TV You Need?" *The Wall Street Journal,* September 28, 2012, pp. D1, D2; John Jannarone, "When Twitter Fans Steer TV," *The Wall Street Journal,* September 5, 2012, p. B6.

CHAPTER 11

EXHIBIT 11–5

The CW Network has a number of popular shows such as *America's Next Top Model*

Source: The CW Television Network

Número Uno is the New #1.

Univision swept ABC, CBS, NBC and FOX. For the first time ever, the Network's no-repeat lineup of **primetime novelas, variety** and **sports** made Univision **America's New #1 Network** among both adults 18-34 and 18-49, including men and women, in any language.

Thank you, viewers, for making history with us.

UNIVISION
#UnivisionMakesHistory
univision.net

Source: Nielsen, NPM, 6/2913-3/13/13. Mon-Sat 8-11pm/Sun 7-11pm, AA (000), A/W/M 18-34, A/W/M 18-49, Live+SD.

EXHIBIT 11–6

Univision is the leading Spanish-language network

© *Univision Communications Inc.*

A major advantage of network advertising is the simplification of the purchase process. The advertiser has to deal with only one party or media representative to air a commercial nationwide. The networks also offer many of the most popular and widely watched programs, particularly during prime time. Advertisers interested in reaching large national audiences generally buy commercials on shows that air during the prime-time viewing hours of 8 to 11 P.M. (7 to 10 P.M. in the Central and Mountain time zones).

While network advertising is an effective way to reach large audiences, the cost of advertising on prime-time shows is much higher because of the number of viewers they reach. Many of the popular prime-time shows such as *Empire, The Voice,* and *Scandal* can charge well over $200,000 for a 30-second spot. TV shows that do well among viewers in the 18-to-49 age group can often charge a premium since this demographic segment is very important to many advertisers. The most expensive TV program for the past several television seasons has been *NBC's Sunday Night Football,* which airs during the fall and charged more than $700,000 for a 30-second commercial during the 2016–2017 TV season. Many of the most watched shows on television are comedies, which are very popular among the coveted 18-to-49 audience.[26]

Availability of time can also be a problem because more advertisers turn to network advertising to reach mass markets. Traditionally, most prime-time commercial spots, particularly on the popular shows, are sold during the **up-front market**, a buying period that occurs before the TV season begins. Advertisers hoping to use prime-time network advertising must plan their media schedules and often purchase TV time as much as a year in advance. Demands from large clients who are heavy TV advertisers requires agencies and media specialist companies to participate in the up-front market. However, TV time is also purchased during the **scatter market** that runs through the TV season. Some key incentives for buying up front, such as cancellation options and lower prices, are becoming more available in the quarterly scatter market. Network TV can also be purchased on a regional basis, so an advertiser's message can be aired in certain sections of the country with one media purchase.

The major networks as well as their cable counterparts often reserve at least 10 percent or more of their inventory of advertising time rather than offering all of it for sale during the up-front market. This is done when sales during the up-front buying period are weak in hopes of being able to sell the advertising time at higher prices on the scatter market.[27] Networks can also get higher prices for commercial time on the scatter market for new shows that end up attracting large audiences over the course of the television season. Fluctuations in supply and demand for network time can also work to the benefit of advertisers as often they can take advantage of weak demand for ad time on certain programs and purchase it at lower rates on the scatter market.

Spot and Local Advertising **Spot advertising** refers to commercials shown on local TV stations, with time negotiated and purchased directly from the individual stations. All nonnetwork advertising done by a national advertiser is known as **national spot advertising**; airtime sold to local firms such as retailers, restaurants, banks, and auto dealers is known as **local advertising**. Local advertisers want media whose coverage is limited to the geographic markets in which they do business. This may be difficult to accomplish with TV, but many local businesses are large enough to make efficient use of TV advertising.

Spot advertising offers the national advertiser flexibility in adjusting to local market conditions. The advertiser can concentrate commercials in areas where market potential is greatest or where additional support is needed. This appeals to advertisers with uneven distribution or limited advertising budgets, as well as those interested in test marketing or introducing a product in limited market areas. National advertisers often use spot television advertising through local retailers or dealers as part of their cooperative advertising programs and to provide local dealer support.

A major problem for national advertisers is that spot advertising can be more difficult to acquire, since the time must be purchased from a number of local stations. Moreover, there are more variations in the pricing policies and discount structure of individual stations than of the networks. However, this problem has been reduced somewhat by the use of **station reps**, individuals who act as sales representatives for a number of local stations in dealings with national advertisers.

Spot ads are subject to more commercial clutter, since local stations can sell time on network-originated shows only during station breaks between programs, except when network advertisers have not purchased all the available time. Viewership generally declines during station breaks, as people may leave the room, zap to another channel, attend to other tasks, or stop watching TV.

While spot advertising is mostly confined to station breaks between programs on network-originated shows, local stations sell time on their own programs, which consist of news, movies, syndicated shows, or locally originated programs. Most cities have independent stations that spot advertisers use. Local advertisers find the independent stations attractive because they generally have lower rates than the major network affiliates.

The decision facing most national advertisers is how to combine network and spot advertising to make effective use of their TV advertising budget. Another factor that makes spot advertising attractive to national advertisers is the growth in syndication.

Syndication   Advertisers may also reach TV viewers by advertising on **syndicated programs**, shows that are sold or distributed on a station-by-station, market-by-market basis. A syndicator seeks to sell its program to one station in every market. There are several types of syndicated programming. *Off-network syndication* refers to reruns of network shows that are bought by individual stations. Shows that are popular in off-network syndication include *The Big Bang Theory, Modern Family,* and *Family Guy.* Off-network syndication shows are very important to local stations because they provide quality programming with an established audience. The syndication market is also very important to the studios that produce programs and sell them to the networks. Most prime-time network shows initially lose money for the studios, since the licensing fee paid by the networks does not cover production costs. Over four years (the time it takes to produce the number of episodes needed to break into syndication), half-hour situation comedies often run up a deficit of millions, and losses on a one-hour drama show are even higher. However, the producers recoup their money when they sell the show to syndication.

First-run syndication refers to shows produced specifically for the syndication market. The first-run syndication market is made up of a variety of shows, including some that did not make it as network shows. Examples of popular first-run syndication shows include talk shows such as *The Ellen Degeneres Show* and *The Dr. Phil Show,* entertainment shows such as *TMZ, Inside Edition,* and *Entertainment Tonight,* and court shows such as *Judge Judy.*

Advertiser-supported or *barter syndication* is the practice of selling shows to stations in return for a portion of the commercial time in the show, rather than (or in addition to) cash. The commercial time from all stations carrying the show is packaged into national units and sold to national advertisers. The station sells the remaining time to local and spot advertisers. Both off-network and first-run syndicated programs are offered through barter syndication. Usually, more than half of the advertising time is presold, and the remainder is available for sale by the local advertiser. Barter syndication allows national advertisers to participate in the syndication market with the convenience of a network-type media buy, while local stations get free programming and can sell the remainder of the time to local or spot advertisers. Top-rated barter syndicated programs include *Wheel of Fortune* and *Jeopardy.*

Syndication now accounts for more than a third of the national broadcast audience and has become a very big business, generating ad revenue comparable to any of the big-four networks. Syndicated shows have become more popular than network shows in certain dayparts, such as daytime, early prime time, and late fringe. In some markets, syndicated shows like *Wheel of Fortune* draw a larger audience than the network news.

Many national advertisers use syndicated shows to broaden their reach, save money, and target certain audiences. For example, off-network syndication shows such as *The Big Bang Theory, Family Guy,* and *Modern Family* are popular with advertisers because they reach the highly sought after, and often difficult to reach, young-adult audience (ages 18 to 34) and are lower on a cost-per-thousand basis than network shows. Figure 11–2 shows the top 10 regularly scheduled syndicated programs in 2014–2015. Syndication continues to gain in popularity, and more advertisers are making syndicated shows part of their television media schedules.

Syndication has certain disadvantages. The audience for some syndicated shows is often older and more rural, and syndicators do not supply as much research information as the networks do. Syndication also creates more problems for media buyers, since a syndicated show may not be seen in a particular market or may be aired during an undesirable time period. Thus, media buyers have to look at each market and check airtimes and other factors to put together a syndication schedule.

Methods of Buying Time

In addition to deciding whether to use network versus spot advertising, advertisers must decide whether to sponsor an entire program, participate in a program, or use spot announcements between programs. Sponsorship of a program and participations are available on either a network or a local market basis, whereas spot announcements are available only from local stations.

Sponsorship   Under a **sponsorship** arrangement, an advertiser assumes responsibility for the production and usually the content of the program as well as the advertising that appears within it. In the early days of TV, most programs were produced and sponsored by corporations and were identified by their name, for example, *Texaco Star Theater* and *The Colgate Comedy Hour.* Today most shows are produced by either the networks or independent production companies that sell them to a network. Sole sponsorship of programs is usually limited to specials and has been declining. However, some companies, including Ford, Hallmark, AT&T, General Electric, and IBM, do sponsor programs occasionally.

FIGURE 11–2

Top 10 Regularly Scheduled Syndicated Programs for 2014–2015 Season

Rank	Program	Household Rating
1	*The Big Bang Theory* (AT)	3.5
2	*Law & Order*	2.8
3	*The Big Bang Theory* (weekend) B	2.6
4	*Family Feud*	2.5
5	*Modern Family*	2.4
6	*Judge Judy*	2.3
7	*Wheel of Fortune*	1.9
8	*Jeopardy*	1.8
9	*Two and a Half Men*	1.6
10	*Family Guy*	1.5

Source: The Nielsen Company.

A company might choose to sponsor a program for several reasons. Sponsorship allows the firm to capitalize on the prestige of a high-quality program, enhancing the image of the company and its products. Companies also sponsor programs to gain more control over the shows carrying their commercials including the number, placement, and content of commercials. Commercials can be of any length as long as the total amount of commercial time does not exceed network or station regulations. Advertisers introducing new products or brands sometimes sponsor a program and run commercials that are several minutes long to launch them. While these factors make sponsorship attractive to some companies, the high costs of sole sponsorship limit this option to large firms. Most commercial time is purchased through other methods, such as participations.

Participations   Most advertisers either cannot afford the costs of sponsorship or want greater flexibility than sole sponsorship permits. Nearly 90 percent of network advertising time is sold as **participations**, whereby network advertisers pay for commercial time during one or more programs. An advertiser can participate in a certain program once or several times on a regular or irregular basis. Participations provide advertisers with more flexibility in market coverage, scheduling and budgeting. The advertiser has no long-term commitment to a program, and expenditures can be adjusted to buy whatever number of participation spots fits within the budget. This is particularly important to small advertisers with a limited budget. The second advantage is that the TV budget can be spread over a number of programs, thereby providing for greater reach in the media schedule.

The disadvantage of participations is that the advertiser has little control over the placement of ads, and there may also be problems with availability. Preference is given to advertisers willing to commit to numerous spots, and the firm trying to buy single spots in more than one program may find that time is unavailable in certain shows, especially during prime time.

Spot Announcements   As discussed previously, spot announcements are bought from the local stations and generally appear during time periods adjacent to network programs (hence the term **adjacencies**), rather than within them. Spot announcements are most often used by purely local advertisers but are also bought by companies with no network schedule (because of spotty or limited distribution) and by large advertisers that use both network and spot advertising.

Selecting Time Periods and Programs

Another consideration in buying TV time is selecting the right period and program for the advertiser's commercial messages. The cost of TV advertising time varies depending on the time of day and the particular program, since audience size varies as a function of these two factors. TV time periods are divided into **dayparts**, which are specific segments of a broadcast day.

The time segments that make up the programming day vary from station to station. However, a typical classification of dayparts for a weekday is shown in Figure 11–3. The various daypart segments attract different audiences in both size and nature, so advertising rates vary accordingly. Prime time draws the largest audiences, with 8:30 to 9 P.M. being the most watched half-hour time period and Sunday the most popular night for television. Since firms that advertise during prime time must pay premium rates, this daypart is dominated by the large national advertisers.

The various dayparts are important to advertisers since they attract different demographic groups. For example, daytime TV generally attracts women; early morning attracts women and children. The late-fringe (late-night) daypart period has become popular among advertisers trying to reach young adults who tune in to *The Late Show with Stephen Colbert* on CBS, *Jimmy Kimmel Live!* on ABC, and NBC's *The*

FIGURE 11–3

Common Television
Dayparts

Early morning	5:00 A.M.–9:00 A.M.	Monday through Friday
Daytime	9:00 A.M.–3:00 P.M.	Monday through Friday
Early fringe	3:00 P.M.–5:00 P.M.	Monday through Friday
Early news	5:00 P.M.–7:00 P.M.	Monday through Saturday
Prime access	7:00 P.M.–8:00 P.M.	Monday through Saturday
Prime	8:00 P.M.–11:00 P.M. 7:00 P.M.–11:00 P.M.	Monday through Saturday and Sunday
Late news	11:00 P.M.–11:30 P.M.	Sunday through Saturday
Late fringe	11:30 P.M.–2:00 A.M.	Monday through Friday
Overnight	2:00 A.M.–5:00 A.M.	Monday through Friday

Note: Times shown are for Eastern and Pacific time zones. Times may vary by market and station.

Tonight Show with Jimmy Fallon. Audience size and demographic composition also vary depending on the type of program.

Cable Television

The Growth of Cable Perhaps the most significant development in the television industry has been the expansion of **cable television**. Cable, or CATV (community antenna television), which delivers TV signals through fiber or coaxial wire rather than the airways, was developed to provide reception to remote areas that couldn't receive broadcast signals. Cable then expanded to metropolitan areas and grew rapidly due to the improved reception and wider selection of stations it offered subscribers. Alternative delivery systems (ADS) such as direct broadcast satellite (DBS) also provide access to TV signals in areas where wired cable is not available. In 2016, 86 percent of the nation's 116.4 million households watched TV either through wired cable (56 percent) or alternative delivery systems (30 percent) such as DirecTV and Dish Network. Cable and ADS carry programming from the four major TV networks as well as cable networks. However, most of the ADS homes cannot receive advertising run on local cable stations.

Cable TV and ADS subscribers pay a monthly fee for which they receive an average of nearly 200 channels, including the local network affiliates and independent stations, various cable networks, superstations, and local cable system channels. Cable networks have a dual revenue stream; they are supported by both subscriber fees and ad revenue. Cable operators also offer programming that is not supported by commercial sponsorship and is available only to households willing to pay a fee beyond the monthly subscription charge. These premium channels include HBO, Showtime, and The Movie Channel.

Cable TV broadens the program options available to the viewer as well as the advertiser by offering specialty channels, including all-news, pop music, country music, sports, weather, educational, and cultural channels as well as children's programming. Figure 11–4 shows the most popular cable networks along with the types of programming they carry. Many cable and ADS also carry **superstations**, independent local stations that send their signals nationally via satellite to cable operators to make their programs available to subscribers. Programming on superstations such as TBS and WGN generally consists of sports, movies, and reruns of network shows. The superstations carry national advertising and are a relatively inexpensive option for reaching cable households across the country.

FIGURE 11–4 Major Cable Networks

ABC Family	Family/general/original	ABC Family	Family/general/original
A&E Network	Biographies/dramas/movies/documentaries	Golf Channel	Golf
		Hallmark Channel	Original movies/miniseries
Adult Swim	Young adult entertainment/programs	Headline News	News/information
		HGTV	Decorating/gardening
AMC	Movies/documentaries	History Channel	Historical documentaries/movies
American Heroes	Military-focused programming/drama	History En Espanol	Historical programming/documentaries (Spanish language)
Animal Planet	Wildlife and nature documentaries/adventure/children's entertainment	Lifetime Networks	News/information/women's interests
BBC America	Drama/comedy/news/arts		
BET	Entertainment/information for African Americans	Logo TV	Movies/documentaries/gay-themed programming
Big 10 Network	College Sports	MLB Network	Major League Baseball
Bloomberg Television	Business and financial news	MSNBC	News/information
Bravo	Drama/movies/reality shows	MTV	Music/reality shows/drama
Cartoon Network	Cartoons	MTV 2	Music/videos/popular culture
CBS Sports Network	College sports/events	mun2 Television	Bilingual programming for Hispanics/Latino youth culture
Centric	Entertainment/information for African Americans	NBCSN	Sports
CMT Country	Country music video/concert/specials	NGC (National Geographic Channel)	Adventure/exploration/science/culture
CNBC	Financial and business news/interviews and discussions	NFL Network	NFL football
		Nickelodeon/Nick at Nite	Youth interest/cartoons/comedy/game shows
CNN	News/information		
CNN Espanol	News/information (Spanish language)	OWN (Oprah Winfrey Netwok)	Entertainment/movies/talk/specials
Comcast Sports Net	Regional sports	Oxygen	Movies/news/comedy/women's interests
Comedy Central	Comedy programs/original		
Cooking Channel	Food/cooking	Pac-12 Network	Colleges sports/Pac-12 Conference
Discovery Channel	Family/health/technology/science		
Disney XD	Children's programming/entertainment	SOAPnet	Soap operas/drama
		Syfy Channel	Science fiction
DIY Network	Home improvement/projects/crafts	Spike TV	Original programming/sports/entertainment for men
E! Entertainment Television	Entertainment/celebrities/pop culture		
		Superstation WGN	Movies/dramas/sports/sitcoms/reality-based programs
ESPN	Sports/specials/events		
ESPN 2	Sports	TBS	Entertainment/movies/sports
ESPN Sports Classics	Sports history/biographies	Telemundo	Entertainment/news/sports (Spanish language)
ESPN Deportes	Sports (Spanish language)		
ESPNEWS	Sports news	Tennis Channel	Tennis/health and fitness/lifestyle
Food Network	Food/cooking/entertainment	TLC (Learning Channel)	Science/history/adventure/behavior
Fox Business Network	Business news		
Fox News Channel	News/information	TNT	Movies/general entertainment/sports
Fox Soccer Plus	Soccer/rugby/sports	tru TV	Real-life stories/drama
Fox Sports1	Sports	Travel Channel	Travel information
Freeform	Family/general/original	TV Guide Channel	Television entertainment information
Fuse	Music/concerts		
FX	Entertainment/original programs	USA Network	Entertainment/movies/sports/drama
GAC: Great American Country	Country music/concerts	VH1	Music videos/movies/concerts/documentaries
Galavision	Programming/entertainment for Hispanics	Weather Channel	Weather
		WGN	Entertainment/sports/movies
GSN: Game Show Network (GSN)	Game shows	WE tv	Women's entertainment/fashion/health

EXHIBIT 11–7

Chicago Interconnect reaches over 3 million households

Source: Comcast Spotlight

EXHIBIT 11–8

The Travel Channel promotes programming its ability to deliver a very influential audience. What types of advertisements would you expect to see on the Travel Channel?

Source: The Travel Channel

Cable has had a considerable influence on the nature of television as an advertising medium. First, the expanded viewing options have led to considerable audience fragmentation. Much of the growth in cable audiences has come at the expense of the four major networks. Cable channels now have more of the prime-time viewing audience than the major networks. Many cable stations have become very popular among consumers, leading advertisers to reevaluate their media plans and the prices they are willing to pay for network and spot commercials on network affiliate stations.

Advertising on Cable Like broadcast TV, cable time can be purchased on a national, regional, or local (spot) level. Many large marketers advertise on cable networks to reach large numbers of viewers across the country with a single media buy. Regional advertising on cable is available primarily through sports and news channels that cover a certain geographic area.

Many national advertisers are turning to spot advertising on local cable systems to reach specific geographic markets. Spot cable affords them more precision in reaching specific markets, and they can save money by using a number of small, targeted media purchases rather than making one network buy. The growth in spot cable advertising is also being facilitated by the use of **interconnects,** where a number of cable systems and networks in a geographic area are joined for advertising purposes. These interconnects increase the size of the audience an advertiser can reach with a spot cable buy. For example, the Comcast Spotlight interconnect in Chicago reaches more than 2.4 million cable TV households in the greater Chicago metropolitan area; the Adlink Digital Interconnect delivers 3 million cable subscribers in Los Angeles and four surrounding counties (Exhibit 11–7).

Advantages of Cable Cable TV has experienced tremendous growth as an advertising medium because it has some important advantages. A primary one is selectivity. Cable subscribers tend to be younger, more affluent, and better educated than nonsubscribers and have greater purchasing power. Moreover, the specialized programming on the various cable networks reaches very specific target markets.

Many advertisers have turned to cable because of the opportunities it offers for **narrowcasting,** or reaching very specialized markets. For example, ESPN has become synonymous with sports and is very popular among advertisers who want to target men of all ages. ESPN has become more than just a 24-hour sports network; it has changed the way sports are covered and played a major role in making sports programming very popular and lucrative. CNBC is now the worldwide leader in business news and reaches a highly educated and affluent audience. The Travel Channel reaches an upscale and very influential audience that likes to explore and try new things and recommend them to others, including various products and services, as shown in Exhibit 11–8.

Advertisers are also interested in cable because of its low cost and flexibility. Advertising rates on cable programs are much lower than those for the shows on the major networks. Advertising time on network shows can cost two to three times as much on a cost-per-thousand basis in some time periods. Spot advertising is also considerably cheaper on most cable stations, while local cable is the most affordable television advertising vehicle available. This makes TV a much more viable media option for smaller advertisers with limited budgets and those interested in targeting their commercials to a well-defined target audience. Also, cable advertisers generally do not have to make the large up-front commitments the networks require, which may be as much as a year in advance.

The low costs of cable make it a very popular advertising medium among local advertisers. Car dealers, furniture stores, restaurants, and many other merchants are switching advertising spending from traditional media such as radio, newspapers, and even magazines to take advantage of the low rates of local cable channels. Local cable advertising is one of the fastest-growing segments of the advertising market, and cable systems are increasing the percentage of revenue they earn from local advertising.

Limitations of Cable   While cable has become increasingly popular among national, regional, and local advertisers, it still has some drawbacks. One major problem is that cable is still somewhat overshadowed by the major networks, as households with basic cable service watch considerably more network and syndicated programming than cable shows. This stems from the fact that cable generally has less popular programming than broadcast TV.

Another drawback of cable is audience fragmentation. Although cable's share of the TV viewing audience has increased significantly, the viewers are spread out among the large number of channels available to cable subscribers. The number of viewers who watch any one cable channel is generally quite low. Even popular cable networks such as ESPN, CNN, and MTV have prime-time ratings of only about 1 or 2 for their regular programming. The large number of cable stations has fragmented audiences and made buying procedures more difficult, since numerous stations must be contacted to reach the majority of the cable audience in a market. There are also problems with the quality and availability of local ratings for cable stations as well as research on audience characteristics.

Cable also still lacks total penetration, especially in some major markets. In 2016, overall cable penetration from both wired and alternative delivery systems such as satellite was 86 percent in the Los Angeles–designated market area (DMA), 82 percent in Houston, and 81 percent in the Dallas–Fort Worth DMA. In some designated market areas, wired cable penetration is low as many households receive cable programming from alternative delivery systems that do not offer local advertising. For example, penetration of wired cable is under 60 percent in some major DMAs such as Los Angeles, Denver, and Dallas–Fort Worth. Thus, local advertisers in these markets would not be able to reach a significant number of households by advertising on local cable networks.

The Future of Cable   Cable TV should continue to grow as its audience share increases and advertisers spend more money to reach cable viewers. The future of cable as an advertising medium will ultimately depend on the size and quality of the audiences cable networks can reach with their programs. This in turn will depend on cable's ability to offer programs that attract viewers and subscribers. Cable's image as a stepchild in program development and acquisition has changed. Cable networks such as VH1, E!, TBS, FX, CNN, ESPN, and others have been creating original films, documentaries, and other programs that draw significant ratings. Networks like A&E, the Discovery Channel, the National Geographic Channel, and the History Channel provide outstanding cultural and educational programming.

Many advertising and media experts note that many people, particularly children and young adults, really do not differentiate between cable and traditional broadcast television.[28] Cable programs generally cannot deliver the broad reach and mass audiences of popular network shows. However, cable networks have been developing high-quality and critically acclaimed programs such as AMC's *The Walking Dead* which is a drama series about a postapocalyptic world overrun by zombies. The show has been one of the most popular programs on cable and attracts viewing audiences similar in size to those of network programs, particularly among the 18-to-49 age group. Other popular shows on cable networks include HGTV's *Fixer Upper,* USA's *WWE Monday Night Raw,* and Lifetime's *Project Runway.*

Cable TV will continue to be a popular source of sports programming and is very important to advertisers interested in reaching the male market. For example,

IMC Perspective 11–2 > > >

MTV Returns to Its Roots to Connect with Viewers

MTV was launched in 1981 as a joint venture between American Express and Warner Communications. Almost from the outset, the pioneering 24-hour music video cable channel put young viewers in a trance and its iconic ad slogan "I Want My MTV!" became part of popular culture. The company that all but invented music videos quickly became one of the most powerful forces in the music world. It also became a popular platform for marketers who recognized that young people liked and trusted MTV, and it had a strong influence on how they looked, talked, and shopped. In 1986 Viacom International purchased MTV and a year later the company launched its first international channel in Europe; a few years later MTV Asia was operating music channels in China, India, Japan, South Korea, and other countries. By the turn of the century MTV was being watched in 136 countries and more than 300 million households around the world, and every week nearly 190 million people would watch the cable network.

For nearly two decades music videos were all the rage, and MTV was the hippest cable TV channel on the planet. The network continued to dominate the music scene on television by broadcasting live from concerts and spring breaks, serving up videos to the biggest hits, and introducing a host of new talent. MTV's popularity extended into the new millennium as it began to diversify its programming with a variety of reality shows such as *The Real World, The Hills, Road Rules, Jersey Shore,* and *Teen Mom 2.* However, MTV is now just one of many cable and online channels trying to attract young viewers and is no longer seen as a cutting-edge source for music or entertainment. Viewership has been on a steep and steady decline, particularly among the millennials that marketers

Source: Viacom International Inc.

covet, as MTV's prime-time ratings declined by 22 percent from 2013 to 2015.

A number of factors have been cited as reasons why MTV has lost its mojo, such as the tendency for teens and millennials to spend less time watching television and more time watching videos on YouTube, Snapchat, and Facebook or streaming movies and TV shows on Netflix, Amazon Prime, or Hulu. MTV's problems have been complicated by questions as to whether Nielsen is accurately measuring its viewing audiences. Viacom CEO Philippe Dauman argues that MTV really has not lost viewers but rather Nielsen's ratings fail to account for people watching television via apps on their smartphones and tablets, streaming devices such as Roku and Apple TV, websites on desktops and laptops, or various video-on-demand services.

While Viacom may blame the loss in MTV viewers on Nielsen's measurement system, others argue that the real problem is that the cable network is struggling to find programming that appeals to young audiences since reality programs

ESPN has become synonymous with sports and is very popular among advertisers who want to target men of all ages. ESPN has become more than just a 24-hour sports network; it has changed the way sports are covered and played a major role in making sports programming very popular and lucrative. In addition to reaching nearly 90 million homes in the United States, ESPN has grown to include ESPN2, ESPN News, ESPNU, ESPN Deportes, and 47 international channels (Exhibit 11–9). ESPN receives more than $7 per household in subscriber fees, which is far and away the highest of any television network.

A number of collegiate sport networks as well as regional sports networks (RSNs) provide sports programming to local markets. The most important programming on these RSNs is live broadcasts of professional and college sports, events such as football, basketball, and baseball. Many of these regional networks are associated with Fox Sports, Time Warner Cable SportsNet, and Comcast SportsNet. Thus, advertisers purchase ads in multiple regions with one media buy.

As cable penetration increases, its programming improves, and more advertisers discover its efficiency and ability to reach targeted market segments, cable's popularity as an advertising medium should continue to grow. Many agencies and media specialist companies have developed specialists to examine the use of cable in their clients' media schedules. However, cable is facing many of the same challenges no longer draw well and some of MTVs recent shows such as *Catfish, Broke A$$ Game Show, Awkward,* and *Eye Candy* have been too juvenile, trashy, and/or vulgar. One former MTV executive has argued that several years of cost cutting have hurt Viacom's creative culture and its shows have been bad. It has been noted that MTV has not had a major hit show since *Jersey Shore,* which premiered in 2009. Even shows on network television such as *The Voice, Empire,* or *Scandal* are more appealing to young people than MTV's programming.

In 2016, Viacom initiated a new programming strategy to try and reconnect with younger viewers who are increasingly turning to nontraditional platforms such as YouTube, Snapchat, Facebook, and Netflix to consume video and content. As part of its new strategy, MTV will once again put music front and center as well as bring back its news division and develop new programs. MTV has introduced several music-oriented shows including *Wonderland,* which is its first weekly live music performance series in nearly two decades, and launched an updated version of its classic *MTV Unplugged* series which showcases popular musical artists. MTV has also partnered with reality show producer Mark Burnett—who has produced hit shows such as *Survivor, The Voice,* and *Shark Tank*—to create a music competition series and launched the music documentary series *Year One,* which uses archived footage to explore the breakthrough year of the career of a music superstar.

MTV is also reviving it news division, which was once a vital source of pop culture and political journalism but was essentially shut down for many years. The company has hired more than two dozen journalists to cover music, politics, film, celebrities, and other aspects of popular culture and write stories that will air during news and pop-culture segments as well as on MTV's website, in podcasts, and on social media channels such as Facebook, Instagram, Snapchat, and YouTube. *MTV News* will also air on mtvU, its cable channel that reaches students on 750 college campuses around the country.

MTV's new strategy will not be limited to music-focused programming. The network's new president, Sean Atkins, notes that "MTV's goal is to create content that is beyond 'surface level' TV, unexpected and diverse in both types of people represented and points of view." To that end, MTV's new programming includes *Sweet/Vicious,* which is a dark dramedy about avenging sexual assault victims on a college campus; a docuseries called the *Outsiders* that follows families living on the fringe of society; and *Mary + Jane,* a comedy about enterprising marijuana dealers learning to navigate the hipster culture in Los Angeles.

Viacom is also taking steps to make MTV—as well its other cable channels such as Comedy Central, VH1, Nickelodeon, and Spike—more attractive to marketers. It is working with companies that collect and sell data gathered by cable, satellite, and Internet distributors to gather richer information about its viewers that can be used to help more precisely match advertisers with viewers. MTV has also made an effort to adapt to the changing viewing patterns of young people by launching an initiative called MTV Always On, whereby a team of pop-culture savants whip up batches of short-form video, GIFS, and memes that are injected into MTV advertising blocks to retain viewers' attention during commercial breaks and keep them from checking their smartphones or changing channels.

Viacom's goal is to make MTV exciting and relevant again and reclaim the grip it held on youth culture for several decades. If the new programming strategy works as planned, the network will be able to reconnect with young audiences and once again have them saying: "I Want My MTV!"

Sources: Jeanine Poggi, "How MTV Plans to Put the 'M' Back in Its Name," *Advertising Age,* April 21, 2016, http://adage.com/article/special-report-tv-upfront/mtv-plans-put-m-back/303628/; "MTV News Is Back, with Veterans from Grantland to Take on Vice," *Advertising Age,* February 11, 2016, http://adage.com/article/media/mtv-news-back-vets-grantland-vice/302668/; Felix Gillette and Lucas Shaw, "Why No One Wants Their MTV," *Bloomberg Businessweek,* July 6–12, 2015, pp. 46–51.

EXHIBIT 11–9

ESPN is the television industry's most powerful network

Source: ESPN Internet Ventures

as the major broadcast networks such as cord-cutting and competition from other viewing options such as streaming content on Netflix, Amazon Prime, Hulu, and YouTube. IMC Perspective 11–2 discusses how MTV has been losing viewers and the new programming strategy the network is implementing to reconnect with younger audiences.

Measuring the TV Audience

LO11-3

One of the most important considerations in TV advertising is the size and composition of the viewing audience. Audience measurement is critical to advertisers as well as to the networks and stations. Advertisers want to know the size and characteristics of the audience they are reaching when they purchase time on a particular program. And since the rates they pay are a function of audience size, advertisers want to be sure audience measurements are accurate.

Audience size and composition are also important to the networks and television stations, since they determine the amount they can charge for commercial time. Shows are frequently canceled because they fail to attract enough viewers to make their commercial time attractive to potential advertisers. Determining audience size is not an exact science and has been the subject of considerable controversy through the years. In this section, we examine how audiences are measured and how advertisers use this information in planning their media schedules.

Audience Measures   The size and composition of television audiences are measured by ratings services. The sole source of network TV and local audience information is the Nielsen Company. Nielsen gathers viewership information from a sample of TV homes and then projects this information to the total viewing area. The techniques used to gather audience measurement information include electronic metering technology, diaries, and embedded software in devices. Nielsen provides various types of information that can be used to measure and evaluate a network and/or station's viewing audience. These measures are important to media planners because they weigh the value of buying commercial time on a program.

Television Households An important metric needed to measure the size of a viewing audience is an estimate of the number of households in a market that own a television or a computer that can be used to watch TV shows. Nielsen now defines a **television household** as a home with at least one operable TV or monitor with the ability to deliver video via traditional means of antenna, cable set-top-box, or satellite receiver and/or with a broadband connection. This updated definition accounts for households that do not have antenna, cable, or satellite access but can still watch video over the Internet. Since more than 98 percent of U.S. households own a TV and have access to TV shows, television households generally correspond to the number of households in a given market. According to Nielsen's National Television Household Universe Estimates there were 116.4 million television households in the United States for the 2015–2016 TV season.

Program Rating Probably the best known of all audience measurement figures is the **program rating**, the percentage of TV households in an area that are tuned to a specific program during a specific time period. The program rating is calculated by dividing the number of households tuned to a particular show by the total number of households in the area. For example, if 10 million households (HH) watched *The Big Bang Theory,* the national rating would be 8.7, calculated as follows:

$$\text{Rating} = \frac{\text{HH tuned to show}}{\text{Total U.S. HH}} = \frac{10,000,000}{116,400,000} = 8.6$$

A **ratings point** represents 1 percent of all the television households in a particular area tuned to a specific program. On a national level, 1 ratings point represents 1,164,000 households. Thus, if a top-rated program like *The Big Bang Theory* averages a rating of 9, it would reach 10.5 million households each week (9 × 1,164,000).

The program rating is the key number to the television networks and stations, since the amount of money they can charge for commercial time is based on it.

A 1 percent change in a program's ratings over the course of a viewing season can mean millions of dollars in advertising revenue to a broadcast or cable network. Advertisers also follow ratings closely, since they are the key measure for audience size and commercial rates.

Households Using Television The percentage of homes in a given area where TV is being watched during a specific time period is called **households using television (HUT)**. This figure, sometimes referred to as *sets in use,* is always expressed as a percentage. For example, if 70 million of the U.S. TV households have their sets turned on at 9 P.M. on a Thursday night, the HUT figure is 60 percent (70 million out of 116.4 million). Television usage varies widely depending on the time of day and season of the year.

Share of Audience Another important audience measurement figure is the **share of audience**, which is the percentage of households using TV in a specified time period that are tuned to a specific program. This figure considers variations in the number of sets in use and the total size of the potential audience, since it is based only on those households that have their sets turned on. Audience share is calculated by dividing the number of households (HH) tuned to a show by the number of households using television (HUT). Thus, if 70 million U.S. households had their sets turned on during the 8 P.M. time slot when *The Big Bang Theory* is shown, the share of audience would be 14.3, calculated as follows:

$$\text{Share} = \frac{\text{HH tuned to show}}{\text{U.S. households using TV}} = \frac{10{,}000{,}000}{70{,}000{,}000} = 14.3$$

Audience share is always higher than the program rating unless all the households have their sets turned on (in which case they would be equal). Share figures are important since they reveal how well a program does with the available viewing audience. For example, late at night the size of the viewing audience drops substantially, so the best way to assess the popularity of a late-night program is to examine the share of the available audience it attracts relative to competing programs.

Ratings services also provide an audience statistic known as **total audience**, the total number of homes viewing any five-minute part of a telecast. This number can be broken down to provide audience composition figures that are based on the distribution of the audience into demographic categories.

National Audience Information Nielsen has a national TV ratings service that provides daily and weekly estimates of the size and composition of the national viewing audiences for programs aired on the broadcast and major cable networks. To measure the viewing audience, Nielsen uses a national sample of approximately 25,000 homes carefully selected to be representative of the population of U.S. households. The widely cited Nielsen ratings are based on the viewing patterns of this cross section of homes, which are measured using electronic metering technology. The **people meter** is an electronic measuring device that incorporates the technology of the old-style audimeter in a system that records not only what is being watched but also by whom in the measured households. The actual device is a small box with eight buttons—six for the family and two for visitors—that can be placed on the top of the TV (Exhibit 11–10). A remote-control unit permits electronic entries from anywhere in the room. Each member of the sample household is assigned a button/number that indicates his or her presence as a viewer. The device is also equipped with a sonar sensor to remind viewers entering or leaving the room to log in or out on the meter.

The viewership information the people meter collects from the household is stored in the home system until it is retrieved by Nielsen's

computers. Data collected include when the TV is turned on, which channel is viewed, when the channel is changed, and when the TV is off, in addition to who is viewing. The demographic characteristics of the viewers are also in the system, and viewership can be matched to these traits. Nielsen's operation center processes all this information each week for release to the TV and advertising industries. Nielsen uses a sample of metered households in 56 markets across the country to provide overnight viewing results.

Local Audience Information   Information on local audiences is important to both local advertisers and firms making national spot buys. Nielsen's local market measurement service is called the Nielsen Station Index (NSI), which measures viewing audiences in 210 local markets known as **designated market areas (DMAs)**. DMAs are nonoverlapping areas used for planning, buying, and evaluating TV audiences and are generally a group of counties in which stations located in a metropolitan or central area achieve the largest audience share. NSI reports information on viewing by time periods and programs and includes audience size and estimates of viewing over a range of demographic categories for each DMA.

In addition to the national audience measurement, Nielsen also measures TV viewership in the 56 largest local markets using electronic or metered technology. Local people meters (LPMs) are used in 25 of these markets while electronic set meters are used in the 31 markets just below the LPM level and measure only the channel to which the TV set is tuned. This information is augmented at least four times a year with demographic data that are collected from separate samples of households that fill out seven-day paper viewing diaries (or eight-day diaries in homes with DVRs). Smaller markets (DMAs ranked over 60) are currently measured using paper diaries only, although Nielsen plans to extend electronic measurement to some of these markets as well.

Nielsen measures viewing audiences in every local television market at least four times a year during rating periods known as **sweeps periods** . The term dates back to the 1950s, when Nielsen began mailing diaries to households and reporting the results, beginning with the East Coast markets before *sweeping* across the country. Sweeps rating periods are held in November, February, May, and July. In some of the larger markets, diaries provide viewer information for up to three additional sweeps months. The viewing information gathered during the sweeps periods is used for program scheduling decisions by local television stations and cable systems and is a basis for pricing and selling advertising time. Exhibit 11–11 shows how WJZ, the CBS affiliate in Baltimore, promotes its dominance of the sweeps ratings in various categories.

EXHIBIT 11–11

WJZ promotes its dominance of the sweeps rating period for local news

Source: WJZ-TV

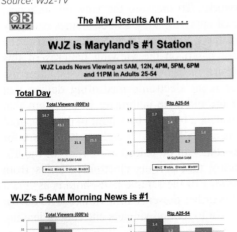

Many advertising executives and media buyers are skeptical of the local audience estimates gathered during the sweeps periods. They argue that special programming and promotion efforts are often used by the networks and their local affiliates to bolster their ratings during the sweeps and that the numbers gathered during these periods are not indicative of audience size for the remaining weeks of the year.[29]

Much of the concern over the measurement system used by Nielsen involves the use of the paper diaries to measure viewing in local markets. The system requires households in the sample to keep a tally of what is being watched and by whom. With so many channels now available, along with the increase in viewing through DVRs and on smartphones, tablets, and computers, it has become very challenging for the Nielsen panelists to accurately record all of their television viewing in the diaries. Many homes do not return completed diaries and many of those that are returned are often not filled out. Nielsen has acknowledged the problems with its measurement system for local markets and is working to correct them.[30]

Developments in Audience Measurement For years the television and advertising industries has been calling for changes in the way TV viewing audiences are measured at both the local and national levels. They have argued that new digital technologies are leading to major changes with regard to when, where, and how people watch television. Many of those working for the television networks as well as in advertising argue that the Nielsen measurement system is being overwhelmed by the explosion in the number of TVs, delivery systems, program options, and viewing platforms available. Advertisers and media planners have argued that these developments are having a major impact on audience size and composition and on the way advertisers use and should pay for TV as an advertising medium. A major issue in television audience measurement over the past decade has been the need to move beyond **linear TV** where the viewer has to watch a scheduled TV program at the particular time it's offered, and on the particular channel it's presented on.

One of the major concerns of advertisers for years has been the need to measure ratings for television commercials, not just for programs. In 2007 Nielsen began providing **commercial ratings** data, known as "C3," which includes measures of the average viewership of the commercials both live and up to three days after the ads are played back on a DVR.[31] The new ratings did not track individual ads or specific time slots, but rather offered an average viewership of all the national commercial minutes in a program. Thus advertisers began paying for advertising time on network shows based not just on linear TV usage, but based on measures of how many viewers watched commercials live and on DVR-recorded playback within three days of the airing of the show, rather than simply on the traditional program ratings.

While Nielsen's C3 ratings were an improvement over the old measurement system, many in the television and advertising industries were still dissatisfied with them, particularly as live viewing of television programs continued to decline and time-shifted viewing through DVRs and video on demand (VOD) became more prevalent. Many television network executives began pushing for "C7" ratings that include viewership of programs and commercials as many as seven days after live airing of a TV show, arguing that viewership of many programs continued to increase over a seven-day period.[32] By 2014 Nielsen was providing C3 as well as C7 viewership numbers; however, the industry continued to argue that better measurement was still needed to account for viewership across all platforms to determine total viewership of a program as well as viewing patterns.

In 2016 Nielsen began rolling out its Total Audience Measurement system, which is a single-sourced platform that accounts for all viewing across linear TV, DVRs, VOD, and connected TV devices including streaming video devices and game consoles, enabled smart TVs, tablets, smartphones, and personal computers.[33] The new measurement system accounts for viewers currently overlooked by current C3 and C7 metrics and also provides more insight into viewing patterns for television shows. The new system will be able to determine how much time people spend with devices overall and link program viewing to those specific devices. For example, in early tests of its measurement system, Nielsen broke viewership of a television show into the six categories shown in Figure 11–5. As can be seen in this chart, 45 percent of viewers watched the show during its live airing while an additional 32 percent watched the show by playing it back on a DVR within seven days after it aired. The remaining 23 percent of viewership came from people watching it digitally by streaming it on a PC or mobile device, watching it on VOD within 35 days, watching it on a DVR between 8 and 35 days, or watching it on a connected TV device. Nielsen is also developing a new metric called Total Use of Television (TUT), which adds connected TV usage to linear viewing to provide a complete view of TV usage.[34]

As part of its new Total Audience Measurement system, Nielsen is also increasing the sample size of its national TV panel to 40,000 households, which will represent a total of 100,000 viewers and include more than 100,00 TV sets and more than 50,000 connected devices.[35] While advertisers view Nielsen's new system as

FIGURE 11–5

Viewership Categories for Television Programs

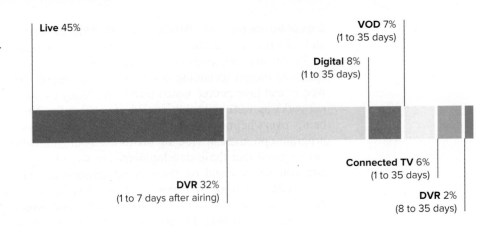

Live 45%

VOD 7%
(1 to 35 days)

Digital 8%
(1 to 35 days)

Connected TV 6%
(1 to 35 days)

DVR 32%
(1 to 7 days after airing)

DVR 2%
(8 to 35 days)

a significant improvement, there is still concern over how viewing audiences are measured. Expanded use of the people meter is seen as an improvement over the use of paper diaries, but critics note that these devices still require cooperation on an ongoing basis from people in the metered homes. Panelists in the Nielsen households, including children, must enter a preassigned number on the remote-control device every time they start or stop watching. Media researchers argue that children in particular often forget and adults tire of the task over the two years they are in the Nielsen sample. There has been a call for the use of more passive measurement systems that require less involvement by people in the metered homes and can produce more accurate measures of the program, as well as commercial, viewing audiences.[36]

Nielsen is continually working to address the ongoing challenges of audience measurement. The company now measures away-from-home viewing for a number of networks at places like health clubs, hotels, bars and restaurants, and transit locations.[37] Nielsen has begun measuring the television viewing patterns of college students by gathering information on the TV viewing patterns of students who live in households that are part of its national sample but live away at college. Nielsen's Extended Home study used people meters installed in dormitories and common areas, sorority and fraternity houses, and off-campus houses at colleges across the country to track the viewing patterns of students.

One of the more interesting findings from the Extended Home study was that college students watch as much television as other 18- to 24-year-olds. Students watch the tube up to 30 hours per week and they also watch a lot of late-night TV (after 11 P.M.). The ratings showed that Comedy Central's *South Park* was the number 1 cable program among male college students between the ages of 18 and 24 (Exhibit 11–12). The results also showed that animated TV programming is very popular among college students and that the number of women watching sports is higher than media experts expected.[38]

EXHIBIT 11–12

South Park is one of the most widely watched TV shows by male college students

© Comedy Central/PhotoFest

South Park (Comedy Central) season 5
Episode: The Super Best Friends, July 4, 2001
Shown: Kenny McCormick, Butters, Kyle Broflovski, Stan Marsh, Eric Cartman
Credit: Comedy Central/Photofest   © Comedy Central

Rentals grant one-time, EDITORIAL use only, unless otherwise negotiated. Please inform us about usage or new image as soon as possible. Research fees may apply if no images are used.

Please Credit:
PHOTOFEST
(212) 633-6330

RADIO

LO11-4

Television has often been referred to as the ideal advertising medium, and to many people it personifies the glamour and excitement of the industry. Radio, on the other hand, is often viewed as old-school and is not the first medium that comes to mind when developing a media strategy. Dominated by network programming and national advertisers before the growth of TV, radio has evolved into a primarily local advertising medium. Network advertising generally accounts for less than 5 percent of radio's revenue. However, radio boasts the broadest mass reach among all media while simultaneously affording advertisers narrow targeting capabilities through numerous formats and networks. Radio has also become a medium characterized by highly specialized programming appealing to very narrow segments of the population.

The importance of radio to advertisers is best demonstrated by the numbers, as it is a pervasive medium. There are more than 11,300 commercial radio stations in the United States, including 4,700 AM and 6,600 FM stations. There are over 576 million radios in use, which is an average of 5.6 per household. Radio reaches 77 percent of all Americans over the age of 12 each day and has grown into a ubiquitous background to many activities, among them reading, driving, running, working, and socializing. The average American listens to radio over 2 hours every weekday and 3 hours every weekend. Commercial radio dominates the time spent listening to some form of news or entertainment in a car, as nearly two-thirds of in-car listening time is on AM/FM radio. People are spending more time listening to the radio on computers and/or mobile devices; the online radio audience has doubled in the past six years and now exceeds more than 103 million monthly listeners. In 2015, the percentage of Americans 12 years of age or older who reported listening to radio online rose to 53 percent—nearly double the percentage who had done so only five years earlier with smartphones, becoming the device of choice for doing so. Online listening to radio is expected to continue to grow, and this audience complements rather than substitutes for broadcast radio.[39] The pervasiveness of this medium has not gone unnoticed by advertisers; radio has continued to hold its own in attracting advertising revenue in a highly competitive media environment, with total ad revenue holding steady at just over $17 billion from 2011 to 2016.

Radio plays an integral role in the lifestyle of consumers and has the power to reach and influence their purchase behavior. It has survived and flourished as an advertising medium because it has a number of advantages that make it an effective way for marketers to communicate with consumers. The radio industry promotes these advantages to advertisers to encourage use of the medium (Exhibit 11–13).

Advantages of Radio

Radio has many advantages over other media, including cost and efficiency, receptivity, selectivity, flexibility, mental imagery, and integrated marketing opportunities.

Cost and Efficiency   One of the main strengths of radio as an advertising medium is its low cost. Radio commercials are very inexpensive to produce. They require only a script of the commercial to be read by the radio announcer or a copy of a prerecorded message that can be broadcast by the station. The cost for radio time is also low. A minute on network radio may cost only $5,000, which translates into a cost per thousand of only $3 to $4. Local advertising on radio is lower on a cost-per-thousand basis, compared to local TV advertising. The low relative costs of radio make it one of the most efficient of all advertising media, and the low absolute cost means the budget needed for an effective radio campaign is often lower than that for other media.

The low cost of radio means advertisers can build more reach and frequency into their media schedule within a certain budget. They can use different stations to broaden the reach of their messages and multiple spots to ensure adequate

EXHIBIT 11–13

The Radio Advertising Bureau promotes the value of radio to advertisers

Source: Radio Advertising Bureau

frequency. Advertisers can use radio as a fast and relatively inexpensive way to get their names known. Radio commercials can be produced more quickly than TV spots, and the companies can run them more often. Many national advertisers also recognize the cost-efficiency of radio and use it as part of their media strategy.

Receptivity Radio often provides advertisers with a very receptive environment for their advertising messages. The Radio Advertising Bureau has conducted studies in conjunction with several research firms which show that consumers perceive radio advertising to be more personally relevant to them than ads on television or the Internet.[40] The studies have found that radio listeners have a unique relationship with radio as a medium because they often are more emotionally connected to the radio stations to which they listen. This emotional connection can make consumers more receptive to radio ads when the message is designed and placed properly. Figure 11–6 shows the main reasons consumers gave for listening to radio in a recent study that surveyed over 41,000 listeners of 220 radio stations in North America.[41] The survey found that while the primary reason cited was "to hear my favorite songs," many of the reasons for listening to radio are emotion-based as well as informational. Research has also shown that consumers perceive radio advertising as being more personally relevant to them. This may be due to the nature of radio ads usually being targeted to the demographic and psychographic characteristics of the listeners of particular stations, as discussed below.

Selectivity Another major advantage of radio is the high degree of audience selectivity available through the various program formats and geographic coverage of the numerous stations. Radio lets companies focus their advertising on specialized audiences such as certain demographic and lifestyle groups. Most areas have radio stations with formats such as adult contemporary, easy listening, classical music, country, news/talk shows, jazz, and all news, to name a few. Figure 11–7 shows the percentage of the radio listening audience captured by radio formats for various age groups. As can be seen in these numbers, the Rock, CHR/Top 40, Rhythmic, and Alternative formats get a high percentage of their listeners from the 18-to-24 and 24-to-34 age groups while News/Talk and Adult Standards formats get most of their

FIGURE 11–6

Main Reasons for Listening to Radio

Source: Radio Advertising Bureau and Jacobs Tech Survey.

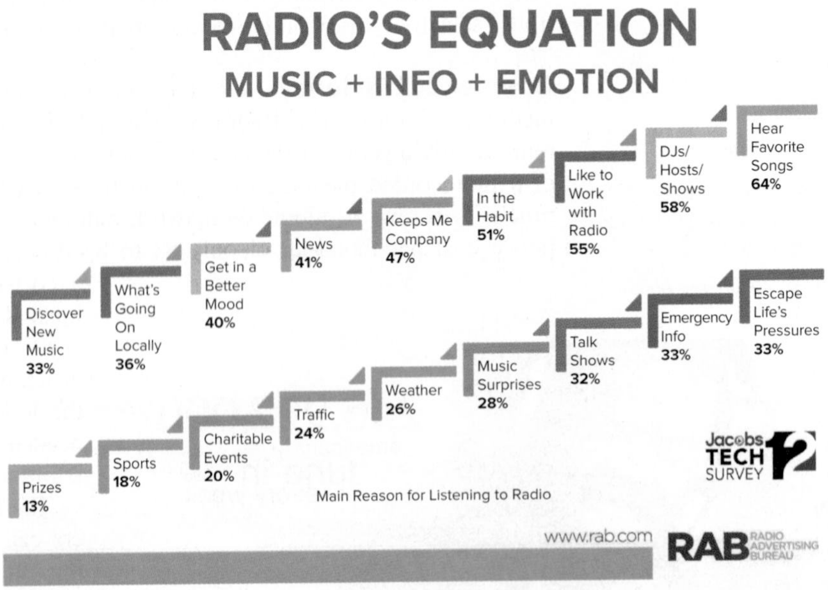

RADIO'S EQUATION
MUSIC + INFO + EMOTION

Discover New Music **33%**
What's Going On Locally **36%**
Get in a Better Mood **40%**
News **41%**
Keeps Me Company **47%**
In the Habit **51%**
Like to Work with Radio **55%**
DJs/Hosts/Shows **58%**
Hear Favorite Songs **64%**

Prizes **13%**
Sports **18%**
Charitable Events **20%**
Traffic **24%**
Weather **26%**
Music Surprises **28%**
Talk Shows **32%**
Emergency Info **33%**
Escape Life's Pressures **33%**

Main Reason for Listening to Radio

Jacobs TECH SURVEY 12

www.rab.com RAB RADIO ADVERTISING BUREAU

FIGURE 11–7

Radio Format Profiles by
Age Group

Format	18–24	25–34	35–44	45–54	55–64	65+
Adult Contemporary	14.1%	20.3%	22.4%	21.8%	14.0%	6.2%
Adult Hits	12.5%	17.0%	24.4%	28.7%	12.4%	2.8
Adult Standards	2.1%	1.5%	7.3%	14.8%	22.4%	45.9
All News	4.4%	7.8%	14.2%	23.1%	24.2%	22.8
All Sports	4.7%	19.8%	22.9%	21.8%	17.0%	10.9
All Talk	2.9%	12.9%	18.7%	22.4%	22.6%	21.3
Alternative	19.1%	26.9%	22.2%	17.0%	10.4%	2.0
CHR/Top 40	27.2%	28.4%	22.3%	14.5%	5.6%	1.7
Classic Hits	9.2%	13.2%	15.4%	26.7%	23.9%	7.3
Classic Rock	11.2%	16.5%	20.4%	30.1%	18.2%	2.5
Classical	6.0%	11.2%	14.6%	18.9%	15.1%	29.6
Country	15.9%	20.7%	16.6%	18.9%	15.1%	13.0
Easy Listening	0.8%	3.8%	6.7%	14.2%	23.0%	59.6
Ethnic	8.5%	8.2%	25.9%	29.7%	16.3%	15.3
Gospel	6.3%	11.6%	16.6%	21.0%	23.2%	22.6
Hispanic (all genres)	12.2%	21.6%	22.6%	22.0%	10.8%	7.7
Hot AC (subset of adult contemporary)	18.4%	22.6%	25.1%	18.6%	10.9%	
Jazz	4.0%	10.2%	13.8%	21.5%	24.8%	17.5
Mexican/Tejano/Ranchera (subset of Hispanic)	15.1%	25.5%	21.4%	22.4%	9.0%	4.4
News/Talk	3.6%	10.6%	15.1%	20.6%	23.3%	24.9
Oldies	9.6%	11.6%	10.6%	22.5%	26.6%	15.0
Public/Non-Commercial	5.5%	15.9%	19.3%	19.4%	20.0%	15.1
Religious/Christian	9.9%	15.9%	20.5%	22.2%	17.6%	10.8
Rhythmic	32.6%	29.6%	19.3%	11.8%	4.7%	0.8
Rock	19.5%	25.5%	23.1%	20.3%	9.3%	1.4
Soft AC/Lite Rock	7.8%	17.6%	17.7%	23.5%	17.6%	12.6
Spanish AC (subset of Hispanic)	12.8%	22.7%	23.3%	21.8%	11.4%	4.7
Tropical (subset of Hispanic)	13.5%	23.2%	23.4%	20.7%	8.6%	7.1
Urban	25.4%	24.6%	18.3%	16.2%	10.2%	4.4
Variety/Other	9.4%	18.1%	17.8%	20.2%	20.0%	10.6

Note: Numbers based on: *GfK MRI, 2015 Doublebase—Audience Composition Based on Total Week Cume, Adults 18+* (may not add to 100% due to rounding).

Source: Radio Format Profiles, Why Radio Fact Sheet, Radio Advertising Bureau, 2016.

listeners from adults over age 45. Elusive consumers like teenagers, college students, and working adults can be reached more easily through radio than most other media.

Radio can reach consumers other media can't. Light television viewers spend considerably more time with radio than with TV and are generally an upscale market in terms of income and education level. Light readers of magazines and newspapers also spend more time listening to radio. Radio has become a popular way to reach specific non-English-speaking ethnic markets. Los Angeles, New York City, Dallas, and Miami have several radio stations that broadcast in Spanish and reach these areas' large Hispanic markets. As mass marketing gives way to market segmentation and regional marketing, radio will continue to grow in importance.

Flexibility   Radio is probably the most flexible of all the advertising media because it has a very short closing period, which means advertisers can change their message almost up to the time it goes on the air. Radio commercials can usually be produced and scheduled on very short notice. Radio advertisers can easily adjust their messages to local market conditions and marketing situations.

Mental Imagery   A potential advantage of radio that is often overlooked is that it encourages listeners to use their imagination when processing a commercial message. While the creative options of radio are limited, many advertisers take advantage of the absence of a visual element to let consumers create their own picture of what is happening in a radio message.

Radio may also reinforce television messages through a technique called **image transfer**, where the images of a TV commercial are implanted into a radio spot.[42] First the marketer establishes the video image of a TV commercial. Then it uses a similar, or even the same, audio portion (spoken words and/or jingle) as the basis for the radio counterpart. The idea is that when consumers hear the radio message, they will make the connection to the TV commercial, reinforcing its video images. Image transfer offers advertisers a way to make radio and TV ads work together synergistically. This promotional piece put out by the Radio Advertising Bureau shows how the image transfer process works (Exhibit 11–14).

Integrated Marketing Opportunities   Radio provides marketers with a variety of integrated marketing opportunities. It can be used in combination with other media, including television, magazines, newspapers, the Internet, and social media, to provide advertisers with synergistic effects in generating awareness and communicating their message. The radio industry has sponsored research studies to determine how radio works in combination with other media. These studies have shown that the synergistic use of radio, television, newspapers, and the Internet has a positive impact on various measures such as brand awareness, brand consideration, emotional connections, purchase intentions, and website visitation.[43] Marketers can also use radio in conjunction with digital and social media applications such as Facebook and Twitter to allow listeners to publish audio content as well as receive song and station updates. Radio station websites as well as their Facebook, Instagram, and Twitter pages can be used to create listener databases and engage them by offering promotions and deals.

Radio can also be used in conjunction with a variety of other IMC tools such as sales promotion, event marketing, and cause-related marketing. Radio stations are an integral part of many communities and the deejays and program hosts are often popular and influential figures. Advertisers often use radio stations and personalities to enhance their involvement with a local market and to gain influence with local retailers. Radio also works very effectively in conjunction with place-based/point-of-purchase promotions. Retailers often use on-site radio broadcasts combined with special sales or promotions to attract consumers

EXHIBIT 11–14

The Radio Advertising Bureau promotes the concept of imagery transfer

Source: Radio Advertising Bureau

LOCAL MATTERS
CONNECTION TO LISTENERS

- Local content and promotions that strengthen local community connections
- Audience engagement with sites that offer local music talent and playlist interactivity between listeners and station
- Community events driven by stations prove local radio connection

EXHIBIT 11–15

Radio stations are often involved in local community events

Source: Radio Advertising Bureau

to their stores and get them to make a purchase. Live radio broadcasts are also used in conjunction with event marketing. Marketers often sponsor live broadcast promotions at beaches, sporting events, and festivals, setting up product booths for sampling and giveaways. Exhibit 11–15 shows how the Radio Advertising Bureau promotes the value of radio by showing how it can be used to strengthen local community connections.

Limitations of Radio

Several factors limit the effectiveness of radio as an advertising medium, among them creative limitations, fragmentation, difficult buying procedures, limited research data, limited listener attention, competition from digital media, and clutter. The media planner must consider them in determining the role the medium will play in the advertising program.

Creative Limitations   A major drawback of radio as an advertising medium is the absence of a visual image. The radio advertiser cannot show the product, demonstrate it, or use any type of visual appeal or information. A radio commercial is, like a TV ad, a short-lived and fleeting message that is externally paced and does not allow the receiver to control the rate at which it is processed. Because of these creative limitations many companies tend to ignore radio, and agencies often assign junior people to the development of radio commercials.

Fragmentation   Another problem with radio is the high level of audience fragmentation due to the large number of stations. The percentage of the market tuned to any particular station is usually very small. The top-rated radio station in many major metropolitan areas with a number of AM and FM stations may attract less than 10 percent of the total listening audience. Advertisers that want a broad reach in their radio advertising media schedule have to buy time on a number of stations to cover even a local market.

Difficult Buying Procedures   It should be readily apparent how difficult the media planning and purchasing process can become for the advertiser that wants to use radio on a nationwide spot basis. Acquiring information and evaluating and contracting for time with even a fraction of the 11,300 commercial stations that operate across the country can be very difficult and time-consuming. This problem has diminished somewhat in recent years as the number of radio networks and of syndicated programs offering a package of several hundred stations increases.

Limited Research Data   Audience research data on radio are often limited, particularly compared with TV, magazines, or newspapers. Most radio stations are small operations and lack the revenue to support detailed studies of their audiences. And most users of radio are local companies that cannot support research on radio listenership in their markets. Thus, media planners do not have as much audience information available to guide them in their purchase of radio time as they do with other media.

Limited Listener Attention   Another problem that plagues radio is that it is difficult to retain listener attention to commercials. Radio programming, particularly music, is often the background to some other activity and may not receive the listeners' full attention. Thus they may miss all or some of the commercials. One environment where radio has a more captive audience is in cars. But getting listeners to pay attention to commercials can still be difficult. Most people preprogram their

EXHIBIT 11–16

Radio promotes audience retention during commercial breaks

Source: Arbitron

car radio and change stations during commercial breaks. A study by Avery Abernethy found large differences between exposure to radio programs versus advertising for listeners in cars. They were exposed to only half of the advertising broadcast and changed stations frequently to avoid commercials.[44] However, a study by the companies Arbitron Inc. and Coleman Research analyzed the audience retained during commercial breaks by comparing the audience level for each minute of a commercial break to the audience for the minute before the commercials began.[45] The study found that on average 92 percent of the lead-in audience was retained during commercial breaks. Nearly the entire audience was retained during one-minute commercial pods (Exhibit 11–16). Another factor that is detracting from radio listening in automotive vehicles is the high penetration of mobile phones. Studies have found that commuters surveyed who own a mobile phone reported listening to less radio than they previously did.[46] Many consumers spend time on their phones while driving and also can listen to music stored on their phones or through streaming services.

Competition from Digital Media   Radio is also facing threats from several digital-based technologies that are impacting the listening audience for commercial radio. A major source of competition for conventional broadcast radio is the growth of satellite radio, which bounces signals off satellites stationed over the East and West Coasts and back down to receivers that encode the signals digitally. The major satellite radio company is SiriusXM which was formed by the merger of the major two satellite radio companies (Sirius and XM Radio) in 2008 and now has nearly 30 million subscribers.[47] The primary market for satellite radio is vehicle owners who choose it as an option when purchasing a new car or who purchase a receiver for about $100 and pay a monthly subscription fee of around $13 for the digital quality radio service that includes 140+ channels of music, news, talk, sports, and children's programming. However, SiriusXM also targets other markets for its service, including homes, businesses, Internet/mobile devices, portable radios, boats, and planes.

The music stations on SiriusXM are commercial free, while talk channels have approximately six minutes of commercials every hour. Programming on SirusXM features big-name entertainers and personalities such as shock jock Howard Stern, Jenny McCarthy, Dr. Laura, and other personalities. The satellite network has also spent large amounts of money to acquire the broadcast rights for professional and college sports as well as NASCAR. SiriusXM has also been adding more locally tailored programming such as traffic and weather reports, which make them more competitive against terrestrial stations in local markets.

In addition to satellite, terrestrial radio is also being impacted by the popularity of MP3 players such as Apple's iPod as well as music services that are being streamed over the Internet such as Pandora, Spotify, and Apple Music. However, the Radio Advertising Bureau has done studies that show that over 80 percent of drivers cite AM/FM radio as their primary in-car entertainment device (Exhibit 11–17).

EXHIBIT 11–17

Radio is the most popular in-car entertainment device

Source: Radio Advertising Bureau

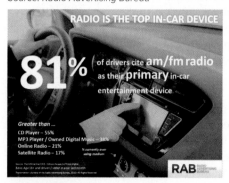

Clutter   Clutter is just as much a problem with radio as with other advertising media. Most radio stations carry an average of 10 minutes of commercials every hour. During the popular morning and evening rush hours, the amount of commercial time may exceed 12 minutes. Also contributing to the clutter problem is the practice of some stations offering "commercial-free" blocks of music to attract listeners. This practice results in more commercials being aired in a short time period and may also result in listeners switching to another station rather than listening through a long block of ads. Advertisers must create commercials that break through the clutter or use heavy repetition to make sure their messages reach consumers. In a study of radio listeners conducted by Edison Research, perceptions of increased ad clutter were cited by participants as a reason for spending less time listening to radio.[48]

The radio industry is looking for other ways to make radio advertising more valuable to marketers. In 2010 Clear Channel, which is now known as iHeartMedia, Inc., began offering advertisers a new service known as contextual radio ads that can automatically insert radio commercials immediately after specific programming or certain kinds of content, including other ads.[49] A number of companies have been using the service to better target their radio advertising messages. For example, Walmart ran ads for AC/DC's *Black Ice* album, which was sold exclusively at its stores, on various rock stations immediately after songs by the group were played. GEICO also used the service to air commercials with its "Save 15 percent on insurance" after ads for cars, motorcycles, or RVs aired.

Buying Radio Time

The purchase of radio time is similar to that of television, as advertisers can make either network, spot, or local buys. Since these options were reviewed in the section on buying TV time, they are discussed here only briefly.

Network Radio   Advertising time on radio can be purchased on a network basis using one of the national networks. There are currently seven major national radio networks such as CBS Radio, Cumulus, Westwood One, and Premiere. There are also more than 100 regional radio networks across the country. Using networks minimizes the amount of negotiation and administrative work needed to get national or regional coverage, and the costs are lower than those for individual stations. However, the number of affiliated stations on the network roster and the types of audiences they reach can vary considerably, so the use of network radio reduces advertisers' flexibility in selecting stations.

An important trend in radio is the increasing number of radio networks and syndicated programs that offer advertisers a package of several hundred stations. For example, *The Dan Patrick Show* is a syndicated radio and television sports talk show hosted by former ESPN personality Dan Patrick. It is syndicated nationally by Premiere Radio Networks and carried by more than 275 stations reaching 1.4 million people weekly (Exhibit 11–18). The show is particularly popular among the 18-to-49 male audience. Syndication reduces audience fragmentation and purchasing problems and increases radio's appeal to national advertisers.

EXHIBIT 11–18

The Dan Patrick Show is syndicated nationally

Source: The Dan Patrick Show

Spot Radio   National advertisers can also use spot radio to purchase airtime on individual stations in various markets. The purchase of spot radio provides greater flexibility in selecting markets, individual stations, and airtime and adjusting the message for local market conditions. Spot radio accounts for about 20 percent of radio time sold.

Local Radio   By far the heaviest users of radio are local advertisers; nearly 79 percent of radio advertising time is purchased from individual stations by local companies. Auto dealers, retailers, restaurants, and financial institutions are among the heaviest users of local radio advertising. But a number of radio advertisers are switching to local cable TV because the rates are comparable and there is the added advantage of TV's visual impact.

FIGURE 11-8

Dayparts for Radio

Morning drive time	6:00–10:00 A.M.
Midday	10:00 A.M.–3:00 P.M.
Afternoon/evening drive time	3:00–7:00 P.M.
Nighttime	7:00 P.M.–12:00 A.M.
All night	12:00–6:00 A.M.

Time Classifications

As with television, the broadcast day for radio is divided into various time periods or dayparts, as shown in Figure 11–8. The size of the radio listening audience varies widely across the dayparts, and advertising rates follow accordingly. The largest radio audiences (and thus the highest rates) occur during the early morning and late afternoon drive times. Radio rates also vary according to the number of spots or type of audience plan purchased, the supply and demand of time available in the local market, and the ratings of the individual station. Rate information is available directly from the stations and is summarized in SRDS's Radio Advertising Source, which provides format detail, demographics, spot radio rates, and other data for both local stations and radio networks. Some stations issue rate cards showing their ad rates across various dayparts. However, many stations do not adhere strictly to rate cards and the rates published in SRDS. Their rates are negotiable and depend on factors such as availability, time period, and number of spots purchased.

Audience Information

One problem with radio is the lack of audience information. Because there are so many radio stations and thus many small, fragmented audiences, the stations cannot support the expense of detailed audience measurement. Also, owing to the nature of radio as incidental or background entertainment, it is difficult to develop precise measures of who listens at various time periods and for how long. The major radio ratings service is Nielsen Audio which provides audience information for local stations and network audiences. For many years radio audience information was provided by Arbitron. However, Nielsen acquired Arbitron in 2012 and the deal was approved by the Federal Trade Commission in 2013. The acquisition of Arbitron gives Nielsen nearly total control of the television and radio measurement industry.[50]

Nielsen Audio   Nielsen Audio covers nearly 300 local radio markets with two to four ratings reports per year. Nielsen has a sample of representative listeners in each market who maintain a diary of their radio listening for seven days. Audience estimates for the market are based on these diary records and reported by time period and selected demographics in the *Radio Market Report*, to which clients subscribe. Figure 11–9 provides a sample page from the ratings report for people in the 18-to-49 age target audience across the various dayparts. The three basic estimates in the radio ratings report are

- Person estimates—the estimated number of people listening.
- Rating—the percentage of listeners in the survey area population.
- Share—the percentage of the total estimated listening audience.

These three estimates are further defined by using quarter-hour and cume figures. The **average quarter-hour (AQH) figure** expresses the average number of people estimated to have listened to a station for a minimum of five minutes during any quarter-hour in a time period. For example, station KCBQ has an average quarter-hour listenership of 2,500 during the weekday 6 to 10 A.M. daypart. This means that any weekday, for any 15-minute period during this time period, an

	Target Audience, Persons 18–49							
	Monday–Friday 6–10 A.M.				Monday–Friday 10 A.M.–3 P.M.			
	AQH (00)	CUME (00)	AQH Rtg	AQH Shr	AQH (00)	CUME (00)	AQH Rtg	AQH Shr
KCBQ								
METRO	25	263	.2	.8	40	365	.3	1.3
TSA	25	263			40	365		
KCBQ-FM								
METRO	101	684	.7	3.1	117	768	.9	3.7
TSA	101	684			117	768		
KCEO								
METRO	11	110	.1	.3	8	81	.1	.3
TSA	11	110			8	81		
KFMB								
METRO	171	790	1.3	5.3	106	678	.8	3.3
TSA	171	790			106	678		

EXHIBIT 11–19

Arbitron promotes its Portable People Meter

Source: Arbitron

average of 2,500 people between the ages of 18 and 49 are tuned to this station. This figure helps determine the audience and cost of a spot schedule within a particular time period.

Cume stands for "cumulative audience," the estimated total number of different people who listened to a station for at least five minutes in a quarter-hour period within a reported daypart. In Figure 11–9, the cumulative audience of people 18 to 49 for station KCBQ during the weekday morning daypart is 26,300. Cume estimates the reach potential of a radio station.

The **average quarter-hour rating (AQH RTG)** expresses the estimated number of listeners as a percentage of the survey area population. The **average quarter-hour share (AQH SHR)** is the percentage of the total listening audience tuned to each station. It shows the share of listeners each station captures out of the total listening audience in the survey area. The average quarter-hour rating of station KCBQ during the weekday 6 to 10 A.M. daypart is 0.2, while the average quarter-hour share is 0.8.

In 2008 Arbitron introduced the **Portable People Meter (PPM),** which is a wearable, page-size device that electronically tracks what consumers listen to on the radio by detecting inaudible identification codes that are embedded in the programming. The PPM was developed in response to calls from the radio and advertising industries for Arbitron to provide more detailed measures of radio audiences.[51] Advertisers have welcomed the use of PPMs as they provide more detailed demographic information on radio listeners. Nielsen Audio now uses the PPM to measure radio audiences in the top 50 markets and is expected to continue to expand its use to other markets over the next several years.[52] Exhibit 11–19 shows an ad promoting the value of the Portable People Meter when it was developed by Arbitron.

RADAR   Another rating service that is now owned by Nielsen is RADAR National Network Ratings, which is supported by radio networks, media services companies, and advertisers. RADAR measurements are based on information collected throughout the year by means of diary interviews from a probability sample of 200,000 respondents age 12 and older who live in telephone households. Respondents are instructed to record all radio listening as well as the day of the week, time of day, and location for a one-week period. Demographic information is also collected in the diaries.

RADAR reports are issued four times a year and provide network audience measures, along with estimates of audience and various segments. The audience estimates are time-period measurements for the various dayparts. RADAR also provides estimates of network audiences for all commercials and commercials within various programs.

As with TV, media planners must use the audience measurement information to evaluate the value of various radio stations in reaching the advertiser's target audience and their relative cost. The media buyer responsible for the purchase of radio time works with information on target audience coverage, rates, time schedules, and availability to optimize the advertiser's radio media budget.

Summary

Television and radio, are the most pervasive media in most consumers' daily lives and offer advertisers the opportunity to reach vast audiences. Both media are time- rather than space-oriented and organized similarly in that they use a system of affiliated stations belonging to a network, as well as individual stations, to broadcast their programs and commercial messages. Advertising on radio or TV can be done on national or regional network programs or purchased in spots from local stations.

TV has grown faster than any other advertising medium in history and has become the leading medium for national advertisers. No other medium offers its creative capabilities; the combination of sight, sound, and movement gives the advertiser a vast number of options for presenting a commercial message with high impact. Television also offers advertisers mass coverage at a low relative cost. Variations in programming and audience composition, along with the growth of cable, are helping TV offer more audience selectivity to advertisers. While television is often viewed as the ultimate advertising medium, it has several limitations, including the high cost of producing and airing commercials, a lack of selectivity relative to other media, the fleeting nature of the message and shorter commercials, the problem of commercial clutter, limited viewer attention, and distrust of TV ads. The latter two problems have been compounded in recent years by the trend toward shorter commercials. Television viewing is being impacted by the Internet as more television programs are now available online and consumers are watching television on personal computers, tablets, and smartphones. Social media are also changing the way people watch television and how they interact with TV programs.

Information regarding the size and composition of national and local TV audiences is provided by the Nielsen Company. The amount of money networks or stations can charge for commercial time on their programs is based on its audience measurement figures. This information is also important to media planners, as it is used to determine the combination of shows needed to attain specific levels of reach and frequency with the advertiser's target market.

Future trends in television include the continued growth of cable, competition to local cable operators from direct broadcast satellite systems, and a resulting increase in channels available to television households. The television industry is being impacted by cord-cutting as the number of households subscribing to cable TV continues to decline as more consumers watch television online. Changes have also occurred in the measurement of viewing audiences—such as the move to C3 and C7 ratings that includes measures of viewing audiences both live and up to three and seven days after a program airs live on television.

The role of radio as an entertainment and advertising medium has changed with the rapid growth of television. Radio has evolved into a primarily local advertising medium that offers highly specialized programming appealing to narrow segments of the market. Radio offers advertisers the opportunity to build high reach and frequency into their media schedules and to reach selective audiences at a very efficient cost. It also offers opportunities for integrated marketing programs such as place-based promotions and event sponsorships.

The major drawbacks of radio include its creative limitations owing to the absence of a visual image, the highly fragmented nature of the radio audience, difficult buying procedures, limited research data and listener attention, and clutter. Radio stations are also facing increased competition from online music services such as Pandora, Spotify, and Apple Music.

As with TV, the rate structure for radio advertising time varies with the size of the audience delivered. The primary sources of audience information are Nielsen Audio for local radio and its RADAR studies for network audiences.

Key Terms

Discussion Question

1. The chapter opener discusses the major developments impacting the television industry. Discuss these developments and how they are likely to impact TV's role as an advertising medium. How might these factors impact the way marketers use television as part of their IMC programs? (LO 11-1, 11-2, 11-3)

2. Discuss the advantages and limitations of television as an advertising medium and how these factors affect its use by major national advertisers as well as smaller local companies. (LO 11-2)

3. IMC Perspective 11–1 discusses how intercollegiate athletic programs have become very dependent on revenue from broadcast rights for football and basketball games. Discuss the reasons behind the growing popularity of sports programming on television and why television networks are willing to pay such large sums of money for the rights to televise college and professional sports. Discuss the impact this is having on colleges and their athletic programs in particular. (LO 11-1, 11-2)

4. Discuss how digital and social media are influencing the way people watch television. What are some of the ways television advertisers can leverage social media to work to their advantage? (LO 11-2)

5. What are the various options available to advertisers for purchasing advertising time on television? How does the use of these options differ for national versus local advertisers? (LO 11-2)

6. Choose one of the major cable networks listed in Figure 11–4 and analyze it as an advertising medium. Discuss the audience profile for viewers of programming on this cable network and the type of advertisers that might want to reach them. You might visit the website of the cable network for information on its viewing audience. (LO 11-2)

7. Evaluate the use of sweeps rating periods as a method for measuring local television viewing audiences. Do you think sweeps ratings provide reliable and valid estimates of local television viewing audiences? How might they be improved? (LO 11-3)

8. Discuss recent developments in the measurement of television viewing audiences and their implications for advertisers. Do you think advertisers should have to pay for viewers who watch TV shows on a time-shifted basis on their DVRs or video on demand? (LO 11-3)

9. What is a commercial rating, and how does this measure differ from a program rating? Discuss why advertisers and media planners prefer commercial ratings rather than program ratings. (LO 11-3)

10. What are the advantages and disadvantages of advertising on radio? Discuss how radio advertising can be used by national versus local advertisers. (LO 11-4)

11. Discuss the way Nielsen measures the listening audience for radio stations. Do you think the rating methods are providing reliable measures of radio audiences? (LO 11-6)

12. Discuss how radio stations, as well as advertisers, can deal with the clutter problem on radio and draw attention to their commercials. (LO 11-5)

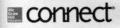 **connect**

Digital users can access their personalized and adaptive SmartBook, Ad Forum Video Cases, and interactive exercises to review chapter concepts.

12 Evaluation of Media: Magazines and Newspapers

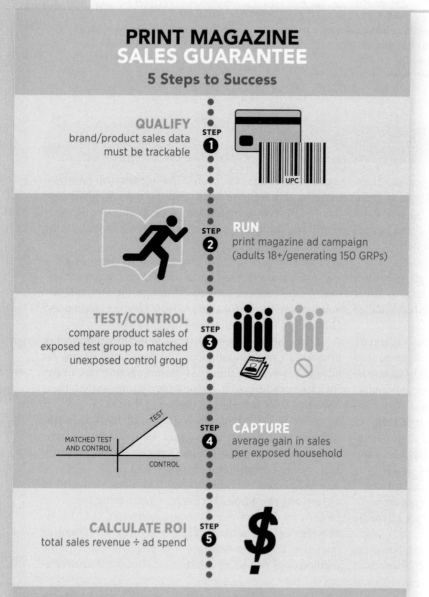

PRINT MAGAZINE
SALES GUARANTEE
5 Steps to Success

STEP 1 — **QUALIFY**
brand/product sales data must be trackable

STEP 2 — **RUN**
print magazine ad campaign (adults 18+/generating 150 GRPs)

STEP 3 — **TEST/CONTROL**
compare product sales of exposed test group to matched unexposed control group

STEP 4 — **CAPTURE**
average gain in sales per exposed household

MATCHED TEST AND CONTROL / TEST / CONTROL

STEP 5 — **CALCULATE ROI**
total sales revenue ÷ ad spend

Source: The Association of Magazine Media

LEARNING OBJECTIVES

LO1 Compare magazines and newspapers in terms of their value as advertising media.

LO2 Discuss magazine circulation and readership as well as audience information and research for magazines.

LO3 Describe how advertising space is purchased for magazines.

LO4 Discuss future trends and developments for magazines and how they will influence their use as an advertising media.

LO5 Describe the newspaper audience and audience information and research for newspapers.

LO6 Discuss how advertising space is purchased for newspapers and rates are determined.

LO7 Discuss future trends and developments for newspapers and how they will influence their use as an advertising media.

MAGAZINES GUARANTEE ADVERTISERS THAT PRINT ADS WORK

The past decade has not been kind to the traditional media of magazines and newspapers as they have been facing major challenges on a number of fronts. Both of these print media were impacted by a weak economy that led many companies to reduce their advertising budgets and, as spending returned, they have shifted more of their marketing dollars to digital media. One of the major problems facing magazines, just like newspapers, is that more people are now going online to get their news, information, and entertainment as well as to read the magazines and newspapers that they are no longer willing to purchase. Nearly all of the major magazines and newspapers now offer online versions of their publications, but the problem is that consumers are used to getting this content for free and are not willing to pay for it. And, as is the case with newspapers, most magazines are not generating enough money from digital advertising to make up for the loss in revenue from traditional print ads.

Digital disruption has had a major impact on the magazine industry; most magazines have experienced declines in circulation and lower advertising revenue for their print editions. Advertising revenue for print magazines declined from nearly $25 billion in 2007 to a little over $17 billion in 2015 while the number of ad pages in consumer magazines has not shown an industrywide increase since 2005. Magazine publishers recognize that consumers are becoming very comfortable reading magazines online and many have also begun offering digital "app" versions of their publications for the iPad as well as tablets that use the Android operating system. However, while the magazine industry recognizes that it must embrace its digital future, most publishers are not ready to abandon their traditional print publications. They still feel that there are inherent advantages of magazines to advertisers and have gone on the offensive to promote them.

The magazine industry has taken several steps recently to counter the perception that magazines are losing their clout with readers as well as their value as an advertising medium. The MPA—The Association of Magazine Media, the industry association that represents consumer magazines and works closely with them to represent their interests, is leading several initiatives. In late 2015 the magazine industry began making advertisers an offer that is difficult to refuse by launching the Print Magazine Sales Guarantee that is designed to counter years of declining ad page sales. Under this program magazine publishers are guaranteeing that advertising in print magazines will increase advertisers' brand sales and provide a positive return on investment or they will get their money back.

The primary goal of the sales guarantee program is to prove the value of print magazine advertising to marketers by showing them that it can move the sales needle for their brands. There are certain requirements an advertiser must meet to qualify for the guarantee. First, the products and brands being advertised in a print campaign must be sold by retailers whose sales results are measured by third-party research firms such as Nielsen Catalina Solutions, which tracks sales from grocery stores, supermarkets, drugstores, and mass merchants like Target and Walmart. A second requirement is that the advertiser must buy a minimum of 150 gross ratings points (GRPs) within one magazine media company over 12 months. This means that a print campaign must reach about 125 million adults 18 years and over an average of three times during the 12-month period. To determine the print campaign's impact on sales of the advertiser's product, Nielsen matches magazine subscriber data to shopper loyalty cards and then links them to anonymous households. Magazine publishers compare product sales among a panel of households exposed to their ads to results from a similar control panel not exposed to them to determine if sales were increased by exposure to the print ads.

According to the MPA, 16 major media companies representing 72 percent of the total magazine audience in the United States qualify to offer the Print Magazine Sales Guarantee program including Time Inc., Hearst Magazines, Conde Naste, and Meredith Corp. Many of these publishers have conducted similar programs over the past several years. For example, Time Inc. has offered a print ad sales guarantee across all of its magazines since January 2015, whereas Meredith Corp. launched its print magazine and ROI guarantee in 2011. Time says that its program has shown that on average every dollar invested in print advertising returns $17 in sales; Meredith claims that it has never had to provide a refund or free advertising space to a marketer. The publisher has results from 35 campaigns and all of them have shown that advertising in print magazines drives sales and ROI.

The MPA and magazine publishers are obviously confident in the ability of magazine advertising to drive sales, and feel that it is important to show advertisers that print is still a valuable medium and can play an important role in an integrated marketing campaign using multiple platforms. The MPA has undertaken several other initiatives to increase the credibility of magazine advertising with marketers. The trade group retained Millward Brown, one of the leading marketing and advertising research companies, to conduct a meta-analysis of nearly 100 advertising effectiveness studies commissioned by advertisers between 2007 and 2015 covering a variety of product/service categories and brands. The study examined how advertising in different media channels—including print, TV, and online—impacted consumers as they moved through the purchase funnel, with a specific focus on metrics measuring brand awareness, ad comprehension and recall, and persuasion.

The results of the meta-analysis showed that print advertising led to the greatest increases in metrics closest to purchasing behavior: brand favorability and purchase intent. The Millward Brown study also showed that when advertisers used print in combination with other media platforms such as television they had the most success in impacting metrics such as aided awareness, brand favorability, and purchase intentions. The meta-analysis also showed that print advertising does not wear out as quickly as other types of ads. While television and online showed diminishing returns after four exposures, print continued to improve ad awareness and persuasion at higher exposure levels (five or more).

The MPA and magazine publishers are hoping that the Print Magazine Sales Guarantee as well as the research studies and other initiatives they are pursuing will encourage marketers to spend more of their advertising budgets in print magazines. The trade group's former chief executive who led the development of the guarantee program notes that "print is the heritage format of this industry and advertisers have pulled their business back disproportionately." Magazine publishers will continue to expand their reach through digital versions of their publications. However, they are also hoping that they can get advertisers to realize that the digital versions of their magazines are rooted in print publications that still are valuable advertising platforms.

Sources: Jeffrey A. Trachtenberg, "Magazines Offer Money Back on Ads," *The Wall Street Journal*, October 13, 2015, p. B7; Nate Ives, "Magazines Create 'Industry-Wide Guarantee of Print Ads' Results," *Advertising Age*, October 12, 2015, http://adage.com/article/media/magazines-create-industry-wide-guarantee-print-ad-roi/300874/; "The Case for Print Magazines: Print in the Mix," *Adweek*, February 3, 2016, www.adweek.com/sa-section/case-print-magazines.

Magazines and newspapers have been advertising media for more than two centuries; for many years, they were the only major media available to advertisers. With the growth of the broadcast media, particularly television, reading habits declined. More consumers turned to TV viewing not only as their primary source of entertainment but also for news and information. But despite the competition from the broadcast media, newspapers and magazines remained important media vehicles to both consumers and advertisers.

Thousands of magazines are published in the United States and throughout the world. They appeal to nearly every specific consumer interest and lifestyle, as well as to thousands of businesses and occupations. By becoming a highly specialized medium that reaches specific target audiences, the magazine industry has prospered. Newspapers are still one of the primary advertising media in terms of both ad revenue and number of advertisers. They are particularly important as a local advertising medium for hundreds of thousands of retail businesses and are often used by large national advertisers as well.

Magazines and newspapers are an important part of our lives. For many consumers, newspapers are their primary source of product information. They would not think of going shopping without checking to see who is having a sale or clipping coupons from the weekly food section or Sunday inserts. Many people read a number of different magazines each week or month to become better informed or simply entertained. Individuals employed in various occupations rely on business magazines to keep them current about trends and developments in their markets and industries as well as in business in general.

While most of us are very involved with the print media, it is important to keep in mind that few newspapers or magazines could survive without the support of advertising revenue. Consumer magazines generate an average of 54 percent of their revenues from advertising; business publications receive nearly 73 percent. Newspapers generate nearly two-thirds or 70 percent of their total revenue from advertising. In many cities, the number of daily newspapers has declined because they could not attract enough advertising revenue to support their operations. The print media must be able to attract large numbers of readers or a very specialized audience to be of interest to advertisers.

As discussed in the chapter opener, both magazines and newspapers are facing significant challenges from digital media, which is impacting the number of people who read the traditional print version of each medium and is also attracting an increasingly larger amount of marketers' advertising budgets each year. Many magazines and newspapers are struggling to get consumers to pay for their online editions and continue to look for ways to monetize them. Although they can sell banners and other forms of online advertising to marketers, the ad rates they can charge on the Web cannot match those in print and generate enough revenue to make up for the losses they are incurring from the decline in the sale of print ads. Thus, in the short term magazines and newspapers have to continue to search for ways to attract and retain readers as well as the advertising pages and revenue that accompanies them. Despite the challenges they face, magazines and newspapers are still important media vehicles for most advertisers.[1]

THE ROLE AND VALUE OF MAGAZINES AND NEWSPAPERS

The role of magazines and newspapers in the advertiser's media plan differs from that of the broadcast media because they allow the presentation of detailed information that can be processed at the reader's own pace. The print media (including digital versions) are not intrusive like radio and TV, and they generally require some effort on the part of the reader for the advertising message to have an impact. For this reason, newspapers and magazines are often referred to as *high-involvement media*.[2] Magazine readership has remained strong despite the growth of new media options; over 90 percent of adults 18+ read print and digital editions of magazines, and they read an average of seven issues per month.[3]

The vast majority of U.S. adults read a newspaper each week across a variety of technology platforms. In a typical week nearly 70 percent of adults read newspapers in print or online, whereas 59 percent of young adults aged 18 to 24 read newspaper content. Major newspapers still reach a very broad target audience while specialized papers reach narrower or more specialized markets. Magazines are different from newspapers because the majority of them reach a selective audience and can be valuable in reaching specific types of consumers and market segments. Magazines and newspapers are the major forms of print media and online editions of most publications are now available, but the two are quite different as are the types of advertising each attracts. This chapter focuses on these two major forms of print media (including their online versions) and examines the specific advantages and limitations of each, along with factors that are important in determining their role in the media plan, as well as the overall IMC program.

MAGAZINES

Over the past several decades, magazines have grown rapidly to serve the educational, informational, and entertainment needs of a wide range of readers in both the consumer and business markets. Magazines are the most specialized of all advertising

EXHIBIT 12–1

Magazines targeted to a
specific industry or profession

© *Virgo Publishing, LLC*

media. While some magazines—such as *People* and *Reader's Digest*—are general mass-appeal publications, most are targeted to a very specific audience. There is a magazine designed to appeal to nearly every type of consumer in terms of demographics, lifestyle, activities, interests, or fascination. Numerous magazines are targeted toward specific businesses and industries as well as toward individuals engaged in various professions (Exhibit 12–1).

The wide variety makes magazines an appealing medium to a vast number of advertisers. Although TV accounts for the largest dollar amount of advertising expenditures among national advertisers, more companies advertise in magazines than in any other medium. Users of magazine ads range from large consumer-product companies such as Procter & Gamble and L'Oréal, which spend over $500 million a year on magazine advertising, to a small company advertising scuba equipment in the *Skin-Diver*, which is an online magazine.

Classifications of Magazines

To gain some perspective on the various types of magazines available and the advertisers that use them, consider the way magazines are generally classified. The media research company Kantar Media SRDS, the primary reference source on periodicals for media planners, divides magazines into three broad categories based on the audience to which they are directed: consumer (which includes farm), business, and health care publications. Each category is then further classified according to the magazine's editorial content and audience appeal.

Consumer Magazines Consumer magazines are bought by the general public for information and/or entertainment. The Kantar Media SRDS Consumer Media Advertising Source™ provides comprehensive planning data on U.S. print magazines and websites that reach consumer audiences. Kantar Media SRDS divides 2,700 domestic consumer magazines into 80 classifications, among them news, men's, sports, lifestyle, fitness, travel, and women's. Another way of classifying consumer magazines is by distribution: They can be sold through subscription or circulation, store distribution, or both. For example, whereas magazines such as *Time, People*, and *Sports Illustrated* are sold both through subscription and in stores, magazines such as *Woman's World* are sold primarily through stores. Magazines can also be classified by frequency; weekly, monthly, and bimonthly are the most common.

Consumer magazines represent the major portion of the magazine industry, accounting for nearly two-thirds of all advertising dollars spent in magazines. Consumer magazines are best suited to marketers interested in reaching general consumers of products and services as well as to companies trying to reach a specific target market. The most frequently advertised categories in consumer magazines are toiletries and cosmetics; drugs and remedies; food and food products; apparel and accessories; retail; and automotive.[4] Marketers of tobacco products spend most of their media budget in magazines, since they are prohibited from advertising in the broadcast media.

While large national advertisers tend to dominate consumer magazine advertising in terms of expenditures, the 2,700 consumer magazines are also important to smaller companies selling products that appeal to specialized markets. Special-interest magazines assemble consumers with similar lifestyles or interests and offer marketers an efficient way to reach these people with little wasted coverage or circulation. For example, companies marketing women's apparel, such as J.Crew, Anthropologie, H&M, and Forever 21, that target young adult females might find magazines such

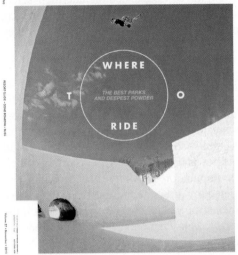

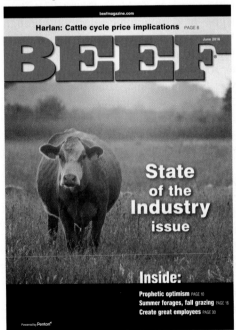

as *Seventeen, Elle, Allure,* or *Cosmopolitan* effective media vehicles for advertising to them.

Not only are these specialty magazines of value to firms interested in reaching a specific market segment, but their editorial content often creates a very favorable advertising environment for relevant products and services. For instance, avid skiers and snowboarders cannot wait for the first snowfall after reading the season's first issues of *Transworld Snowboarding* or *Skiing* magazine and may be quite receptive to the ads they carry for skiing and snowboarding equipment and destination ski resorts (Exhibit 12–2).

Farm Publications The consumer SRDS category also consists of all the magazines directed to farmers and their families. About 300 publications are tailored to nearly every possible type of farming or agricultural interest. SRDS breaks farm publications into nine classifications, ranging from general-interest magazines aimed at all types of farmers (e.g., *Farm Journal, Successful Farming, Progressive Farmer*) to those in specialized agricultural areas such as poultry (*Gobbles*), hog farming (*National Hog Farmer*), or cattle raising (*Beef*—see Exhibit 12–3). A number of farm publications are directed at farmers in specific states or regions, such as *Nebraska Farmer* or *Montana Farmer Stockman.* Farm publications are not classified with business publications because historically farms were not perceived as businesses.

Business and Health Care Publications Business publications are those magazines or trade journals published for specific businesses, industries, or occupations. Kantar Media SRDS breaks down nearly 5,000 print and 4,800 digital U.S. magazines and trade journals into nearly 200 market classifications. There are also approximately 2,700 publications in the health care category, of which 1,225 are digital. The major classifications include:

1. Magazines directed at specific professional groups, such as *National Law Review* for lawyers and *Architectural Forum* for architects.
2. Industrial magazines directed at businesspeople in various manufacturing and production industries—for example, *Automotive News, Chemical Week,* and *Industrial Engineer.*
3. Trade magazines targeted to wholesalers, dealers, distributors, and retailers, among them *Progressive Grocer, Drug Store News, Women's Wear Daily,* and *Restaurant Business.*
4. General business magazines aimed at executives in all areas of business, such as *Forbes, Fortune,* and *Bloomberg Businessweek.* (General business publications are also included in SRDS's consumer publications edition.)
5. Health care publications targeted to various areas including dental, medical and surgical, nursing, biotechnological sciences, hospital administration, veterinary medicine, and dentistry. Examples include *Modern Healthcare, Veterinary Practice News,* and *Dentistry Today.*

The numerous business publications reach specific types of professional people with particular interests and give them important information relevant to their industry, occupation, and/or careers. Business and health care publications are important to advertisers because they provide an efficient way of reaching the specific types of individuals who constitute their target market. Much marketing occurs at the trade and business-to-business level, where one company sells its products or services directly to another.

EXHIBIT 12–4

Magazine expert Samir Husni tracks the launch of new magazines each month

Source: Dr. Samir A. Husni

Advantages of Magazines

Magazines have a number of characteristics that make them attractive as an advertising medium. Strengths of magazines include their selectivity, excellent reproduction quality, creative flexibility, permanence, prestige, readers' high receptivity and involvement, and services they offer to advertisers.

Selectivity   One of the main advantages of using magazines as an advertising medium is their **selectivity**, or ability to reach a specific target audience. Magazines are the most selective of all media except direct mail. Most magazines are published for special-interest groups. The thousands of magazines published in the United States reach all types of consumers and businesses and allow advertisers to target their advertising to segments of the population who buy their products. For example, *PC Magazine* is targeted toward computer buffs, *Rolling Stone* reaches those with an avid interest in music, and *Ebony* focuses on the upscale African American market. Many new magazines are introduced each year targeting new interests and trends. According to Dr. Samir Husni, who has been tracking magazine launches since 1985, more than 800 new publications were launched in 2016 (Exhibit 12–4). New consumer magazines are continually being introduced to meet the changing needs, interests, and passions of the public in areas such as sports/recreation, gaming, entertainment/celebrity, travel, fashion/apparel, and beauty/grooming.[5] New business publications are also frequently launched to respond to developments in business and industry.

In addition to providing selectivity based on interests, magazines can provide advertisers with high demographic and geographic selectivity. *Demographic selectivity*, or the ability to reach specific demographic groups, is available in two ways. First, as a result of editorial content, most magazines are aimed at fairly well-defined demographic segments. *Ladies' Home Journal, Shape*, and *Cosmopolitan* are read predominantly by women; *Esquire, Maxim, ESPN The Magazine*, and *Sports Illustrated* are read mostly by men. Older consumers can be reached through publications like *AARP The Magazine*. Celebrity-focused magazines, which are read primarily by women, have become extremely popular in recent years.

A second way magazines offer demographic selectivity is through special editions. Even magazines that appeal to broader audiences, such as *Reader's Digest, Time*, and *Good Housekeeping*, can provide a high degree of demographic selectivity through their special demographic editions. Most of the top consumer magazines publish different editions targeted at different demographic markets.

Geographic selectivity lets an advertiser focus ads in certain cities or regions. One way to achieve geographic selectivity is by using a magazine that is targeted toward a particular area. Magazines devoted to regional interests include *Yankee* (New England), *Southern Living* (South), *Sunset* (West), and *Texas Monthly* (guess where), among many others. One of the more successful media developments of recent years has been the growth of city magazines in most major American cities. *Los Angeles Magazine, Philadelphia*, and *Boston*, to name a few, provide residents of these areas with articles concerning lifestyle, events, and the like, in these cities and their surrounding metropolitan areas. City and regional magazines make it possible for advertisers to focus on specific local markets that may be of interest to them. They also have a readership profile that appeals to marketers of upscale brands: high income, college educated, loyal, and influential in their communities. Most of these publications belong to the City and Regional Magazine Association, which represents magazines in 64 different markets (Exhibit 12–5). An advertiser can run an ad in all of the magazines that belong to the association with one media buy.

Another way to achieve geographic selectivity in magazines is through purchasing ad space in specific geographic editions of national or regional magazines. A number of publications divide their circulation into groupings based on regions

EXHIBIT 12—5

City magazines offer
advertisers high geographic
selectivity

*Source: City and Regional Magazine
Association*

or major metropolitan areas and offer advertisers the option of concentrating their ads in these editions. A magazine may break the United States into geographic areas and offer regional editions for each and/or offer advertisers their choice of editions directed to specific states or metropolitan areas. Many magazines allow advertisers to combine regional or metropolitan editions to best match the geographic market of interest to them.

Kantar Media SRDS lists more than 350 consumer magazines offering geographic and/or demographic editions. Regional advertisers can purchase space in editions that reach only areas where they have distribution, yet still enjoy the prestige of advertising in a major national magazine. National advertisers can use the geographic editions to focus their advertising on areas with the greatest potential or those needing more promotional support. They can also use regional editions to test-market products or alternative promotional campaigns in various regions of the country.

Ads in regional editions can also list the names of retailers or distributors in various markets, thus encouraging greater local support from the trade. The trend toward regional marketing is increasing the importance of having regional media available to marketers. The availability of regional and demographic editions can also reduce the cost per thousand for reaching desired audiences.

Reproduction Quality   One of the most valued attributes of magazine advertising is the reproduction quality of the ads. Magazines are generally printed on high-quality paper stock and use printing processes that provide excellent reproduction in black and white or color. Since magazines are a visual medium where illustrations are often a dominant part of an ad, this is a very important property. The reproduction quality of most magazines is far superior to that offered by the other major print

EXHIBIT 12–6

This creative Lexus ad becomes animated when placed over an iPad with a microsite loaded

© Photographer: John Higginson, Associate Creative Director: Fabio Simoes Pinto/Molly Grubbs, Art Producer: Lisa Matthews. Agency: Team One Advertising

medium of newspapers, particularly when color is needed. The use of color has become a virtual necessity in most product categories, and more than two-thirds of all magazine ads now use color. The excellent reproduction quality of magazines provides the opportunity for innovative creative work by agencies. Many marketers are now integrating digital technology with print advertising. For example, the Team One agency developed a very creative ad for Lexus that becomes animated—the engine revs, the headlights flash, the wheels spin, and the background pulses with color, all to a musical soundtrack—when placed over an iPad that has a Lexus microsite loaded (Exhibit 12–6). Lexus and Team One developed a special technology called "CinePrint" that was used to create the dynamic ad.[6]

Creative Flexibility   In addition to their excellent reproduction capabilities, magazines also offer advertisers a great deal of flexibility in terms of the type, size, and placement of the advertising material. Some magazines offer (often at extra charge) a variety of special options that can enhance the creative appeal of the ad and increase attention and readership. Examples include gatefolds, bleed pages, inserts, and creative space buys.

Gatefolds enable an advertiser to make a striking presentation by using a third page that folds out and gives the ad an extra-large spread. Gatefolds are often found at the inside cover of large consumer magazines or on some inside pages. Advertisers use gatefolds to make a very strong impression, especially on special occasions such as the introduction of a new product or brand. For example, automobile advertisers often use gatefolds to introduce new versions of their cars each model year. Not all magazines offer gatefolds, however, and they must be reserved well in advance and are sold at a premium.

Bleed pages are those where the advertisement extends all the way to the end of the page, with no margin of white space around the ad. Bleeds give the ad an impression of being larger and make a more dramatic impact. Many magazines charge an extra 10 to 20 percent for bleeds.

In addition to gatefolds and bleed pages, creative options available through magazines include unusual page sizes and shapes. Some advertisers have grabbed readers' attention by developing three-dimensional pop-up ads that jump off the page. Various other *inserts* are used in many magazines. These include return cards, recipe booklets, coupons, records, and even product samples. Cosmetic companies use scratch-and-sniff inserts to introduce new fragrances, and some companies use them to promote deodorants, laundry detergents, or other products whose scent is important. Inserts are also used in conjunction with direct-response ads and as part of sales promotion strategies.

Scented ads, pop-ups, singing ads, heavy card stock, stickers, and digital devices are among the types of inserts used by advertisers in magazines. Advertisers sometimes use special inserts to break through the clutter in magazines and to capture readers' attention. Marketers are becoming very strategic with regard to the type of inserts they are using in magazines and also continue to take advantage of technological advances in developing them. For example, the CW Television Network developed a unique magazine insert designed to use Twitter to promote its new television shows for the upcoming television season.[7] The first-of-its-kind print insert was put inside an October issue of *Entertainment Weekly* magazine and featured a

EXHIBIT 12–7

The CW network used a creative insert to promote its new television shows

Source: The CW Television Network

small LCD screen that displayed a video preview of new shows and a live Twitter feed of the last six tweets from the @CW Network account (Exhibit 12–7).

Many magazine publishers are willing to work with advertisers who want to use creative inserts because they are eager to show that magazines can compete with new media as a way to showcase products. While the inserts pose challenges to production staff and printers, these costs along with any extra postage fees are generally passed on to the advertisers. The total cost of manufacturing inserts varies depending on the complexity, weight, assembly requirements, and other factors. Some of the very elaborate inserts can cost advertisers as much as several million dollars.[8]

Creative space buys are another option of magazines. Some magazines let advertisers purchase space units in certain combinations to increase the impact of their media budget. For example, WD-40, an all-purpose lubrication product, has used half- or quarter-page ads on consecutive pages of several magazines, mentioning a different use for the product on each page, as shown in Exhibit 12–8. This strategy gives the company greater impact for its media dollars and is helpful in promoting the product's variety of uses.

Permanence   Another distinctive advantage offered by magazines is their long life span. TV and radio are characterized by fleeting messages that have a very short life span; newspapers are generally discarded soon after being read. Magazines, however, are generally read over several days and are often kept for reference. They are retained in the home longer than any other medium and are generally

EXHIBIT 12–8

WD-40 uses quarter-page ads to get greater impact from its media budget

Source: WD-40 Company

referred to on several occasions. A study of magazine audiences found that readers devote nearly an hour over a period of two or three days to reading an average magazine.[9] Studies have also found that nearly 75 percent of consumers retain magazines for future reference.[10] One benefit of the longer life of magazines is that reading occurs at a less hurried pace and there is more opportunity to examine ads in considerable detail. This means ads can use longer and more detailed copy, which can be very important for high-involvement and complex products or services. The permanence of magazines also means readers can be exposed to ads on multiple occasions and can pass magazines along to other readers.

Prestige   Another positive feature of magazine advertising is the prestige the product or service may gain from advertising in publications with a favorable image. Companies whose products rely heavily on perceived quality, reputation, and/or image often buy space in prestigious publications with high-quality editorial content whose consumers have a high level of interest in the advertising pages. For example, *Esquire* and *GQ* cover men's fashions in a very favorable environment, and a clothing manufacturer may advertise its products in these magazines to enhance the prestige of its lines. *Architectural Digest* provides an impressive editorial environment that includes high-quality photography and artwork. The magazine's upscale readers are likely to have a favorable image of the publication that may transfer to the products advertised on its pages. *Good Housekeeping* has a unique consumer policy that states that if a product bearing its famous seal proves to be defective within two years of purchase, the magazine will replace the product or refund the purchase price. The research division of the company, now known as the Good Housekeeping Research Institute, has been evaluating products for more than a century. The seal may be used only by products whose ads have been reviewed and accepted for publication in *Good Housekeeping*. The seal can increase consumer confidence in a particular brand and reduce the amount of perceived risk associated with a purchase since it really is a money-back guarantee (Exhibit 12–9).[11]

While brands may enhance their prestige by advertising in magazines with a favorable image and high-quality editorial content, the type of ads that appear in a magazine may also influence readers' perceptions of a publication. The results of a study by Sara Rosengren and Micael Dahlén found that advertising content influences the perceptions of a magazine. Advertising for high-reputation brands or ads that were high in execution quality was beneficial to the evaluations of a magazine, while ads for brands with a poor reputation or that were low in execution quality were detrimental to the image of the publication.[12] These findings suggest that it is important for publishers to manage the advertising content of their magazines in both print and online editions. Some publishers have design guidelines stating that advertising should be treated as content and note that relevant, attractive advertising is an important part of the magazine experience as editorial content for readers.

EXHIBIT 12–9

The Good Housekeeping seal gives consumers confidence in products advertised in the magazine. What are the benefits to including the Good Housekeeping Seal on advertisements?

Source: Hearst Communications, Inc.

While most media planners recognize that the environment created by a magazine is important, it can be difficult to identify it. Subjective estimates based on media planners' experience are often used to assess a magazine's prestige, as are objective measures such as reader opinion surveys.[13]

Consumer Receptivity and Engagement With the exception of newspapers, consumers are more receptive to advertising in magazines than in any other medium. Magazines are generally purchased because the information they contain interests the reader, and ads provide additional information that may be of value in making a purchase decision. Studies have shown that magazines are consumers' primary source of information for a variety of products and services, including automobiles, beauty and grooming, clothing and fashion, financial planning, and personal and business travel.[14]

Media planners recognize that one of the major advantages of advertising in magazines is the ability of the medium to engage readers and hold their attention. Numerous studies have shown that consumers become involved with magazines when they read them and are also more likely to find ads acceptable, enjoyable, and even a valuable part of a publication. Intrusive media such as television, radio, and the Internet struggle with problems such as inattention and consumers trying to avoid advertising messages. And as advertisers try harder to get their commercials seen and heard in these media, the more consumers search for ways to tune them out. However, magazine readers recognize that they control the rate and duration of their exposure to editorial content as well as advertisements and view ads as less disruptive to their media consumption experience.

Research has shown that engagement with an advertising medium is important because it is directly related to increased advertising recall and specific actions taken such as searching for additional information about an advertiser's brand, visiting its website, saving an ad for future reference, and purchasing a product or service, as well as recommending it to others. Exhibit 12–10 shows the various actions magazine readers take or plan as a result of exposure to specific magazine ads based on research by GfK MRI Starch, which is the leading producer of media and consumer research in the United States.

Services A final advantage of magazines is the special services some publications offer advertisers. Some magazines have merchandising staffs that call on trade intermediaries like retailers to let them know a product is being advertised in their publication and to encourage them to display or promote the item. Another service offered by magazines (usually the larger ones) is research studies that they conduct on consumers. These studies may deal with general consumer trends, changing purchase patterns, and media usage or may be relevant to a specific product or industry.

An important service offered by some magazines is **split runs**, where two or more versions of an ad are printed in alternate copies of a particular issue of a magazine. This service is used to conduct an A/B or split-run test, which allows the advertiser to determine which ad generates the most responses or inquiries, providing some evidence of their effectiveness. Technological developments have also made it possible for magazines to offer advertisers the opportunity to deliver personalized messages to tightly targeted audiences

Disadvantages of Magazines

Although the advantages offered by magazines are considerable, they have certain drawbacks too. These

EXHIBIT 12–10

Actions taken by consumers after exposure to magazine advertising

Source: The Association of Magazine Media

Print magazine advertising inspires action

Advertising effectiveness by position

	noted	action taken
first quarter of book	55%	61%
second quarter of book	50	61
third quarter of book	49	62
fourth quarter of book	50	62

Note: Includes all ads, size/color and cover positions.
Source: GfK MRI Starch, July 2013–June 2014.

Action taken includes:
• have a more favorable opinion about the advertiser
• consider purchasing the advertised product or service
• gather more information about the advertised product or service
• recommend the product or service
• visit the advertiser's website
• purchase the product or service
• clip or save the ad
• visit or plan to visit a dealership

Source: GfK MRI Starch.

MPA THE ASSOCIATION OF MAGAZINE MEDIA | magazine.org

include the costs of advertising, their limited reach and frequency, the long lead time required in placing an ad, and the problem of clutter and heavy advertising competition.

Costs The costs of advertising in magazines vary according to the size of the audience they reach and their selectivity. Advertising in large mass-circulation magazines like *Time, Reader's Digest*, and *Better Homes and Gardens* can be very expensive. For example, a full-page, four-color ad in *Time* magazine's national edition (circulation rate base of 3 million) cost $352,000 in 2016. Popular positions such as the back cover cost nearly $500,000.

Like any medium, magazines must be considered not only from an absolute cost perspective but also in terms of relative costs. Most magazines emphasize their effectiveness in reaching specific target audiences at a low cost per thousand. Also, an increasing number of magazines are offering demographic and geographic editions, which helps lower their costs. Media planners generally focus on the relative costs of a publication in reaching their target audience. However, they may recommend a magazine with a high cost per thousand because of its ability to reach a small, specialized market segment. Of course, advertisers with limited budgets will be interested in the absolute costs of space in a magazine and the costs of producing quality ads for these publications.

Limited Reach and Frequency Magazines are generally not as effective as other media in offering reach and frequency. While nearly 90 percent of adults in the United States read one or more consumer magazines each month, the percentage of adults reading any individual publication tends to be much smaller, so magazines have a thin penetration of households. For example, *Better Homes and Gardens* has the third-highest circulation of any magazine, at 7.6 million, but this represents only 6 percent of the 124.6 million households in the United States.

The top 25 consumer magazines based on total paid and verified circulation are shown in Figure 12–1. (It should be noted that publications such as *AARP The Magazine* and *AARP Bulletin* have a high circulation because they are included as part of the benefits package to members of the organization.) As can be seen in Figure 12–1, even the most popular consumer magazines have a circulation of under 5 million, which means that they reach only about 2 to 4 percent of the households in the United States. While total readership of these magazines may be higher since there will be multiple readers of the publication, marketers seeking broad reach must run ads in a number of different magazines, which adds to the complexity of the media buying process. Marketers whose media plan calls for broad reach will often use magazines in conjunction with other media such as television as well the Internet and social media. Since most magazines are monthly or at best weekly publications, the opportunity for building frequency through the use of the same publication is limited. Using multiple ads in the same issue of a publication is an inefficient way to build frequency. Most advertisers try to achieve frequency by adding other magazines with similar audiences to the media schedule.

Long Lead Time Another drawback of magazines is the long lead time needed to place an ad. Most major publications have a 30- to 60-day lead time, which means space must be purchased and the ad must be prepared well in advance of the actual publication date. No changes in the art or copy of the ad can be made after the closing date. This long lead time means magazine ads cannot be as timely as other media, such as radio or newspapers, in responding to current events or changing market conditions. However, as magazines face declines in ad pages and advertising revenue, many are shortening the lead times required to run ads in their publications. Advances in digital publishing and the use of computer-based production methods are also reducing the amount of lead time required to run an ad in a publication.

AARP The Magazine	23,428,878
AARP Bulletin	22,402,422
Better Homes and Gardens	7,624,910
Game Informer	6,901,964
AAA Living	4.987,965
Good Housekeeping	4,345,871
Family Circle	4,051,403
People	3,486,478
National Geographic	3,317,102
Woman's Day	3,289,258
Cosmopolitan	3,038,365
Time	3,036,602
Sports Illustrated	3,023,939
Southern Living	2,851,106
Reader's Digest	2,706,599
Shape	2,528,293
O, The Oprah Magazine	2,370,305
Glamour	2,313,279
Redbook	2,222,115
Taste of Home	2,207,689
ESPN The Magazine	2,153,657
FamilyFun Magazine	2,119,045
Martha Stewart Living	2,083,395
Parents	2,072,318
American Rifleman	2,055,137

Note: Figures are averages for total paid and verified circulation for December 31, 2015, based on
Alliance for Audited Media Snapshot reports, www.auditedmedia.com.

Clutter and Competition   While the problem of advertising clutter is generally discussed in reference to the broadcast media, magazines also have this drawback. The clutter problem for magazines is something of a paradox: The more successful a magazine becomes, the more advertising pages it attracts, and this leads to greater clutter. In fact, magazines generally gauge their success in terms of the number of advertising pages they sell.

Magazine publishers do attempt to control the clutter problem by maintaining a reasonable balance of editorial pages to advertising. The average consumer magazine is around 47 percent ad pages and 53 percent editorial.[15] However, many magazines contain ads on much more than half of their pages. This clutter makes it difficult for an advertiser to gain readers' attention and draw them into the ad. Thus, many print ads use strong visual images, catchy headlines, or some of the creative techniques discussed

EXHIBIT 12–11

P&G everyday is an online custom magazine published by Procter & Gamble

Source: Procter & Gamble

earlier to grab the interest of magazine readers. Some advertisers create their own custom magazines to sidestep the advertising clutter problem as well as to have control over editorial content. A number of companies have also been publishing their own magazines to build relationships with their customers. For example, Farmers Insurance sends its customers a magazine called *The Friendly Review* that contains useful articles on a variety of topics. Custom-published magazines have also become very popular among tobacco companies, such as Philip Morris, which direct-mail them to their customer base.[16] Some companies have begun offering online versions of their custom magazines. For example, Procter & Gamble began publishing *Home Made Simple* several years ago and the custom publication branched into a television program on the OWN Network and shopper marketing programs. The online publication is now called P&G *everyday* (Exhibit 12–11). Kraft Foods also publishes an online magazine called *Kraft Food & Family*, and the success of the online version led the company to begin offering a print version, which is sent to more than 3 million consumers.[17]

Clutter is not as serious an issue for the print media as for radio or TV, since consumers tend to be more receptive and tolerant of print advertising. They can also control their exposure to a magazine ad simply by turning the page.

Magazine Circulation and Readership

Two of the most important considerations in deciding whether to use a magazine in the advertising media plan are the size and characteristics of the audience it reaches. Media buyers evaluate magazines on the basis of their ability to deliver the advertiser's message to as many people as possible in the target audience. To do this, they must consider the circulation of the publication as well as its total readership and match these figures against the audience they are attempting to reach.

Circulation   Circulation figures represent the number of individuals who receive a publication through either subscription or store purchase. The number of copies distributed to these original subscribers or purchasers is known as *primary circulation* and is the basis for the magazine's rate structure. Circulation fluctuates from issue to issue, particularly for magazines that rely heavily on retail or newsstand sales. Many publications base their rates on *guaranteed circulation* and give advertisers a rebate if the number of delivered magazines falls below the guarantee. To minimize rebating, most guaranteed circulation figures are conservative; that is, they are set safely below the average actual delivered circulation. Advertisers are not charged for any excess circulation.

Many publishers became unhappy with the guaranteed circulation concept, since it requires them to provide refunds if guarantees are not met but results in a bonus for advertisers when circulation exceeds the guarantee. Thus, many publications have gone to a circulation rate base system. Rates are based on a set average circulation that is nearly always below the actual circulation delivered by a given issue but carries no guarantee. However, circulation is unlikely to fall below the rate base, since this would reflect negatively on the publication and make it difficult to attract advertisers at prevailing rates.

Circulation Verification   Given that circulation figures are the basis for a magazine's advertising rates and one of the primary considerations in selecting a publication, the credibility of circulation figures is important. Most major publications are audited by one of the circulation verification services. Consumer magazines and farm publications are audited by the Alliance for Audited Media (AAM, formerly known as Audit Bureau of Circulations, or ABC) which is a membership organization consisting of North America's leading advertisers, advertising agencies, and content providers. AAM provides independently verified data and information critical to evaluating and purchasing media including consumer magazines and has also begun auditing digital replica editions of magazines that are available for tablets such as the iPad. A digital replica edition must include the print edition's full editorial content, including photography. In addition, any advertiser appearing in the print edition must have the opportunity to appear in the digital replica edition.

AAM collects and evaluates information regarding the subscriptions and sales of magazines and newspapers to verify their circulation figures. Only publications with 70 percent or more paid circulation are eligible for verification audits by AAM. In 2002 the former ABC approved new guidelines for counting magazine circulation and sales. The changes did away with the long-standing "50 percent rule," in which copies that sold for less than half the basic price of a magazine could not be counted as paid circulation. Under the new rules copies sold at any price may be counted, but the magazine must disclose sales and prices in its circulation statements.[18] More than 2,000 business publications are audited by the Business Publications Audit (BPA) of Circulation. Many of these are published on a **controlled-circulation basis**, meaning copies are sent (usually free) to individuals the publisher believes can influence the company's purchases.

Circulation verification services provide media planners with reliable figures regarding the size and distribution of a magazine's circulation that help them evaluate its worth as a media vehicle. The AAM statement also provides other important information. It shows how a magazine is distributed by state and size, as well as percentage of the circulation sold at less than full value and percentage arrears (how many subscriptions are being given away). Many advertisers believe that subscribers who pay for a magazine are more likely to read it than are those who get it at a discount or for free.

EXHIBIT 12–12

Example of an Alliance for Audited Media publisher's statement

Source: Alliance for Audited Media

(2) Paid and Verified with Digital

Alliance for Audited Media
TRANSACT WITH TRUST

Publisher's Statement
6 months ended December 31, 2015, Subject to Audit

Prototype Magazine

Annual Frequency: 10

Field Served: Consumers interested in healthy living.

Published by Magazine Inc.

EXECUTIVE SUMMARY: TOTAL AVERAGE CIRCULATION

Total Paid & Verified Subscriptions	Single Copy Sales	Total Circulation	Rate Base	Variance to Rate Base
758,987	49,699	808,686	806,250	2,436

TOTAL CIRCULATION BY ISSUE

Issue	Paid Subscriptions Print	Digital Issue	Total Paid Subscriptions	Verified Subscriptions Print	Digital Issue	Total Verified Subscriptions	Total Paid & Verified Subscriptions	Single Copy Sales Print	Digital Issue	Total Single Copy Sales	Total Paid & Verified Circulation - Print	Total Paid & Verified Circulation - Digital Issue	Total Paid & Verified Circulation
July	630,818	70,000	700,818	59,000	1,000	60,000	760,818	52,365	2,000	54,365	742,183	73,000	815,183
Aug.	631,848	70,000	701,848	57,000	1,000	58,000	759,848	44,601	2,000	46,601	733,449	73,000	806,449
* Sept.	629,100		629,100	57,000		57,000	686,100	46,436		46,436	732,536		732,536
Oct.	626,899	70,000	696,899	57,000	1,000	58,000	754,899	49,802	2,000	51,802	733,501	73,000	806,501
Nov./Dec.	622,381	70,000	702,381	57,000	1,000	58,000	760,381	44,228	2,000	46,228	733,609	73,000	806,609
Average	630,487	70,000	700,487	57,500	1,000	58,500	758,987	47,699	2,000	49,699	735,686	73,000	808,686

SUPPLEMENTAL ANALYSIS OF AVERAGE CIRCULATION

	Print	Digital Issue	Total	% of Circulation
Paid Subscriptions				
Individual Subscriptions	545,973	59,000	604,973	74.8
Association: Deductible	2,001		2,001	0.3
Association: Nondeductible	1,003		1,003	0.1
Club/Membership: Deductible	10,114		10,114	1.3
Club/Membership: Nondeductible	1,001		1,001	0.1
Deferred	1,200		1,200	0.1
Partnership Deductible Subscriptions	48,210	1,000	49,210	6.1
School	1,000		1,000	0.1
Sponsored Subscriptions	19,985	10,000	29,985	3.7
Total Paid Subscriptions	630,487	70,000	700,487	86.6
Verified Subscriptions				
Public Place	50,500		50,500	6.2
Individual Use	7,000	1,000	8,000	1
Total Verified Subscriptions	57,500	1,000	58,500	7.2
Total Paid & Verified Subscriptions	687,987	71,000	758,987	93.8
Single Copy Sales				
Single Issue	46,091	2,000	48,091	6.0
Partnership Deductible Single Issue				
Sponsored Single Issue	1,608		1,608	0.2
Total Single Copy Sales	47,699	2,000	49,699	6.0
Total Paid & Verified Circulation	735,686	73,000	808,686	100.0

VARIANCE OF LAST THREE RELEASED AUDIT REPORTS

Audit Period Ended	Rate Base	Audit Report	Publisher's Statements	Difference	Percentage of Difference
12/31/2014	800,000	802,392	802,392		
12/31/2013	775,000	775,647	774,623	1,024	0.1
12/31/2012	700,000	705,825	706,250	-425	-0.0

Visit www.auditedmedia.com Media Intelligence Center for audit reports.

PRICES

	Suggested Retail Prices (1)	Average Price (2) Net	Average Price (2) Gross (Optional)
Average Single Copy	$3.95		
Subscription	$24.95		
Average Subscription Price Annualized (3)		$15.80	$21.00
Average Subscription Price per Copy		$1.58	$2.10

(1) For statement period
(2) Represents subscriptions for the 12 month period ended June 30, 2015
(3) Based on the following issue per year frequency: 10

04-0000-0

48 W. Seegers Road • Arlington Heights, IL 60005-3913 • T: 224-366-6939 • F: 224-366-6949 • www.auditedmedia.com

Media buyers are generally skeptical about publications whose circulation figures are not audited by one of the verification services, and some companies will not advertise in unaudited publications. Circulation data, along with the auditing source, are available from SRDS or from the publication itself. Exhibit 12–12 shows two pages of a sample publisher's statement from the Alliance for Audited Media for both print and digital editions. The publisher's statement includes information such as number of print and digital subscriptions as well as single-copy sales; circulation by issues, regions, and demographic editions; a trend analysis; and subscriptions and sales by state and county size.

Readership and Total Audience Advertisers are often interested in the number of people a publication reaches as a result of secondary, or pass-along, readership. **Pass-along readership** can occur when the primary subscriber or purchaser gives a magazine to another person or when the publication is read in doctors' waiting rooms or beauty salons, on airplanes, and so forth.

Advertisers generally attach greater value to the primary in-home reader than the pass-along reader or out of home reader, as the former generally spends more time with the publication, picks it up more often, and receives greater satisfaction from it. Thus, this reader is more likely to be attentive and responsive to ads. However, the value of pass-along readers should not be discounted. They can greatly expand a magazine's readership. *People* magazine commissioned a media research study to determine that its out of home audience spends as much time reading the publication as do its primary in-home readers.

You can calculate the **total audience/readership** of a magazine by multiplying the readers per copy (the total number of primary and pass-along readers) by the circulation of an average issue. For example, a magazine such as *Time* may have a circulation base of 3 million but an audience of over 19 million readers since it has a high pass-along rate that yields up to six readers per copy. However, rate structures are generally based on the more verifiable primary circulation figures, and many media planners devalue pass-along readers by as much as 50 percent. Total readership estimates are reported by major syndicated magazine research services (discussed next), but media buyers view these numbers with suspicion.

Audience Information and Research for Magazines

A very valuable source for information on magazines is Kantar Media SRDS, whose print and online service provides complete planning information on domestic and international consumer magazines as well as business and health care trade publications. The SRDS Consumer Media Advertising Source™ provides comprehensive planning data on U.S. print magazines and websites that reach consumer audiences including standardized ad rates, circulation figures, dates, general requirements, contact information, and links to online media kits, websites, and audit statements that provide additional information on readership and positioning. The SRDS Business Media Advertising Source™ database provides this information for trade media, including print journals and websites that reach business-to-business audiences.

While circulation and total audience size are important in selecting a media vehicle, the media planner is also interested in the match between the magazine's readers and the advertiser's target audience. Information on readers is available from several sources, including the publication's own research and syndicated studies. Most magazines now have online media kits that provide basic information such as reader demographics, circulation, editorial calendars, rates, specifications, contact information, and other valuable data for advertisers. Exhibit 12–13 shows a page from the online media kit for *Rolling Stone* magazine that provides a profile of readers for its digital edition. Magazines generally provide media planners with even more detail than is available in online media kits. SRDS compiles these detailed media kits from most magazines and makes them available to advertisers and their agencies. Most magazines provide media planners with reports detailing readers' demographics, financial profile, lifestyle, and

2016 ONLINE CONTENT

Audience

DEMOGRAPHICS
MALE 63%
FEMALE 37%
A18-34 5.9 MILLION USERS, INDEX 157
A25-54 7.7 MILLION USERS, INDEX 131
MEDIAN HHI $87,919
Source: comScore Media Metrix, 10 month average (Jan - Oct 2015)

TRAFFIC
• 22.2 MILLION UNIQUE VISITORS
• 183.3 MILLION PAGE VIEWS
• 2:41 MINUTES PER VISIT
Source: Google Analytics, 11 month average (Jan - Nov 2015)

SOCIAL EXTENSIONS
FACEBOOK: 4.3 MILLION FANS
TWITTER: 4.8 MILLION FOLLOWERS
Source: Facebook/Twitter fans/followers as of 11/30/15

MOBILE (SMARTPHONE + TABLET)
• 13.2 MILLION UNIQUE VISITORS
• 80.2 MILLION PAGE VIEWS
Source: Google Analytics, 11 month average (Jan - Nov 2015)

SMARTPHONE: 11.1 MILLION UNIQUE VISITORS
TABLET: 2.1 MILLION UNIQUE VISITORS
Source: Google Analytics, 11 month average (Jan - Nov 2015)

EXHIBIT 12–13

Rolling Stone's online media kit contains useful information for advertisers

Source: Rolling Stone

product usage characteristics. The larger the publication, the more detailed and comprehensive the information it usually can supply about its readers.

Syndicated research studies are also available. For consumer magazines, primary sources of information are Experian Simmons and the studies of GfK, which was discussed in Chapter 10. These studies provide a broad range of information on the audiences of major national and regional magazines, including demographics, lifestyle characteristics, and product purchase and usage data. Most large ad agencies and media buying services also conduct ongoing research on the media habits of consumers. All this information helps determine the value of various magazines in reaching particular types of product users.

Audience information is generally more limited for business publications than for consumer magazines. The widely dispersed readership and nature of business publication readers make audience research more difficult. Media planners generally rely on information provided by the publication or by sources such as Business Publication Audits, which provide the titles of individuals who receive the publication and the type of industry in which they work. This information can be of value in understanding the audiences reached by various business magazines.

Purchasing Magazine Advertising Space

Cost Elements   Magazine rates are primarily a function of circulation. Other variables include the size of the ad, its position in the publication, the particular editions (geographic, demographic) chosen, any special mechanical or production requirements, and the number and frequency of insertions.

An important consideration for advertisers when buying space in a magazine is whether they want some type of preferred placement or pay for a run-of-book ad that can appear anywhere in the magazine, at the discretion of the publisher. Most of the various preferred positions that magazines make available to advertisers are **first cover** (outside front), **second cover** (inside front), **third cover** (inside back), and **fourth cover** (outside back). These are considered to be very desirable positions in the magazine—particularly the fourth or back cover, for which there is often a waiting list. Because a cover ad position is a preferred position, it is almost always sold at a higher rate than any position inside the magazine. Very few publishers sell advertising space on the front cover of their magazines as the American Society of Magazine Editors guidelines discourage the practice. The front cover has always been considered editorial space and off limits to advertisers.[19]

Advertising space is generally sold on the basis of space units such as full page, half page, and quarter page, although some publications quote rates on the basis of column inches. The larger the ad, the greater the cost. However, many advertisers use full-page ads since they result in more attention and readership. Studies have found that full-page ads generated 30 percent more readership than half-page ads.[20]

Ads can be produced or run using black and white, black and white plus one color, or four colors. The more color used in the ad, the greater the expense because of the increased printing costs. On average, a four-color ad costs 30 percent more than a black-and-white ad. Advertisers generally prefer color ads because they have greater visual impact and are superior for attracting and holding attention.[21] Roper Starch Worldwide analyzed the effect of various factors on the readership of magazine ads. The "noted" scores (the percentage of readers who remember seeing the ad in a publication they read) are anywhere from 6 to 59 percent higher for a four-color full-page ad than for a black-and-white ad, depending on the product category. "Read-most" scores (the percentage who say they read more than half of the copy of an ad) are also higher for four-color versus black-and-white ads, by

IMC Perspective 12–1 > > >

Playboy Magazine Tries to Rebrand Itself

For several generations of American men, reading *Playboy* magazine was a cultural rite of passage that once held a forbidden fascination as well an illicit thrill. *Playboy* was launched in 1953 by Hugh Hefner and the first issue featured legendary actress Marilyn Monroe on the cover and inside as the magazine's "Sweetheart of the Month." In the days before *Playboy* landed on the magazine racks, nudity was taboo. However, *Playboy* showcased the female physique by featuring sexy centerfolds and other women and is widely considered a key driver of the sexual revolution. The centerfolds and other pictures of unclothed women included many celebrities through the years such as Madonna, Sharon Stone, Pamela Anderson, Kate Moss, and Naomi Campbell. However, *Playboy* was never completely about nudity. The photos were surrounded with high-end journalism that included articles from famous writers such as Jack Kerouac, Kurt Vonnegut, Marshal McLuhan, and Norman Mailer, as well as groundbreaking interviews of high-profile people and newsmakers such as Malcolm X, Martin Luther King Jr., former president Jimmy Carter, Apple cofounder Steve Jobs, and Donald Trump. One of the key selling points of the magazine was that it was created for literate, cultured men who also happened to enjoy photos of nude women. Indeed, the long-running joke made by many men seen reading *Playboy* was that they "read it for the articles."

Playboy was very successful for several decades as Hugh Hefner built a business empire around the magazine that included the once popular Playboy Clubs in various

Source: Theo Wenner, Playboy

cities as well as a television and film division. *Playboy*'s circulation peaked at 7.2 million in 1972, and for a number of years the magazine was able to cover all of its costs through money paid to buy the magazine, which meant that all of the advertising revenue was pure profit. However, *Playboy* faced increasing competition from other male-focused magazines such as *Penthouse* and *Hustler*, which bordered on hard-core pornography with their raunchy photos. *Playboy*'s circulation dropped to 3.4 million by 1986 and stabilized. However, in the late 90s a new set of competitors emerged—"lad mags" such as *Maxim, FHM*, and *Details*—which also competed for male

---

about 25 percent on average.[22] Other studies have examined the impact of size and color and found that a four-color spread (two facing pages) outperforms a one-page color ad by 30 percent and a black-and-white spread by 35 percent in terms of ad recall.[23] Ads requiring special mechanical production such as bleed pages or inserts may also cost extra.

Rates for magazine ad space can also vary according to the number of times an ad runs and the amount of money spent during a specific period. The more often an advertiser contracts to run an ad, the lower are the space charges. Volume discounts are based on the total space purchased within a contract year, measured in dollars. Advertisers can also save money by purchasing advertising in magazine combinations, or networks.

Magazine networks offer the advertiser the opportunity to buy space in a group of publications as a package deal. The publisher usually has a variety of magazines that reach audiences with similar characteristics. Networks can also be publishers of a group of magazines with diversified audiences or independent networks that sell space in groups of magazines published by different companies. For example, the Ivy League Magazine Network is a consortium of alumni magazines of Ivy League schools and two non-Ivies, Stanford University and the University of Chicago. Advertisers can purchase ad space and reach the well-educated, affluent alumni of all nine schools with one media purchase through the network (Exhibit 12–14).

EXHIBIT 12–14

Advertisers can reach alumni of Ivy League schools through the Ivy League Network

Source: Ivy League Magazine Network

Passion & Diversity. We're not talking about the Ivy League's commitment to diversity in academia or our audience's activities, but rather the incredibly diverse mix of editorial content our nine magazines feature with each issue.

eyeballs by featuring pictures of celebrities and supermodels baring not-quite-everything and editorial content that was more focused on lifestyle and fashion. And young men did not have to worry about being embarrassed if their mother found them reading a copy.

The lad mags along with the growth of the Internet had an impact on *Playboy* as its circulation dropped to 3 million by 2006. However, over the past 10 years its circulation has taken a nosedive, dropping to just over 800,000 by the end of 2015. The primary reason for the decline is that *Playboy*'s appeal was disrupted by the digital revolution when nudity and porn became virtually free and easily accessible online. Thus, sex is no longer a way to sell magazines; men who want to look at salacious pictures of women can get what they want on their computers, tablets, and smartphones. In addition, there has been a cultural shift with many experts arguing that younger generations of men are more respectful of women and there is a decreased tolerance for sexual aggression in modern society.

To respond to these developments Playboy Enterprises, which owns the magazine as well as related media and licensing activities, made a major strategic decision in late 2015 when it was announced that the magazine was moving away from full-frontal nudity as part of a larger redesign and rebranding effort aimed at appealing to more millennial men. Beginning with its March 2016 issue, *Playboy* no longer featured full nudity, although it does continue to show "sexy, seductive pictorials of the world's most beautiful women." The magazine is continuing to feature a "Playmate of the Month" and will go on publishing long-form journalism, interviews, and fiction. In a press release announcing the changes, Playboy Enterprises CEO Scott Flanders said: "The political and sexual climate of 1953, the year Hugh Hefner introduced *Playboy* to the world, bears almost no

resemblance to today. We are more free to express ourselves politically, sexually and culturally today, and that's in large part thanks to Hef's heroic mission to expand those freedoms. We will stay true to those core values with this new vision of *Playboy*'s future."

Playboy is hoping the changes being made to the magazine will make it more appealing to millennials as well as the advertisers trying to reach them. The decision to drop nudity from its pages means that the magazine will get more prominent placement in stores and no longer be relegated to the adult-only racks and wrapped in polybags. However, it remains to be seen if its new business model will work since the print magazine industry is in the middle of a sustained and seemingly irreversible decline as it competes against digital content. It is possible that we may never have the opportunity to see if the iconic magazine can successfully rebrand itself; the private equity company that owns the magazine announced that it was putting the entire Playboy Enterprises operation up for sale.

Many experts are skeptical that *Playboy* magazine can survive. Magazine analyst Samir "Mr. Magazine" Husni has argued that *Playboy* has no future because the reasons for its existence are no longer in place. Husni argues that "despite high brand recognition, *Playboy* does not appear to have a ready way to access a younger generation of consumers. Short of a foreign buyer with a ready overseas market looking to tap the *Playboy* lifestyle ideal, there's little to reflect it in contemporary cultural aspirations and ideals."

Sources: Edward Helmore, "Playboy Business on Sale for $500 m—But Is There Still Money in the Bunny?," *The Guardian*, April 2, 2016, www.theguardian.com/us-news/2016/apr/02/playboy-business-sale-future; Neil Powell, "The Real Reason Playboy Is Getting Rid of Nude Pics," *Fortune*, October 17, 2015, http://fortune.com/2015/10/17/playboy-stops-nude-photos/; Ravi Somaiya, "Nudes Are Old News at Playboy," *The New York Times*, October 13, 2015, pp. A1,3.

The Future for Magazines

The past few years have been very difficult for the magazine industry; many publications are experiencing reductions in revenue as advertisers shift more of their spending to digital media and other IMC tools and have been slow to increase their ad spending following the recession. Many publications have seen their number of advertising pages decline and have found it difficult to raise rates to offset the reduction in ad pages.[24] And while advertising revenue has been decreasing, publishers' other major revenue stream, circulation, has also been declining for most magazines. Many magazines have gone out of business in recent years including some that were published for decades such as *Gourmet, Metropolitan*, and *Vibe*, whereas a number of magazines have ceased publishing their print editions and are now available only online, including *Teen People* and *PC Magazine*. Other well-known magazines that have shuttered their print editions and gone online are *Newsweek, Sporting News, Jet*, and *Lucky*.[25] IMC Perspective 12–1 discusses how *Playboy* magazine has experienced a major decline in circulation over the past 10 years and as part of its rebranding efforts is doing away with full nudity in pictures of women appearing in the publication.

While the health of the economy has a major impact on the magazine industry, there are a number of other important issues facing the industry. The costs of paper and ink continue to rise, and the industry has had to weather several significant increases in postal rates which have had a major impact on their cost structure.[26] Magazines are also facing strong competition from other media such

EXHIBIT 12–15

Men's Journal and *Men's Health* magazines have been very successful in attracting the male audience

© McGraw-Hill Companies/Mark Dierker, photographer

as television, the Internet, social media, and direct mail. Publishers are looking at a number of ways to improve their position—including stronger editorial platforms, better circulation management, cross-magazine and media deals, database marketing, technological advances, and electronic delivery methods—to make advertising in magazines more appealing to marketers as well as to survive.

Stronger Editorial Platforms Magazines with strong editorial platforms that appeal to the interests, lifestyles, and changing demographics of consumers as well as business and market trends are in the best position to attract readers and advertisers. For example, broadly focused magazines such as *Time, People,* and *Reader's Digest* have experienced declines in circulation as well as advertising pages. However, fashion and lifestyle magazines targeted to women such as *Allure, Marie Claire, InStyle,* and *Vogue* have done well as have publications such as *Food Network Magazine* and *Bon Appetit.*[27] Several publications with strong editorial platforms that appeal to younger male readers have also done very well, including *ESPN The Magazine, Men's Journal,* and *Men's Health* (Exhibit 12–15).

Circulation Management One of the major challenges facing magazine publishers is trying to increase or even maintain their circulation bases. Circulation is the second major source of revenue for most publications, and publishers must carefully manage the costs of attracting and maintaining additional readers or subscribers. The cost of acquiring subscribers has increased dramatically over the past decade. However, publishers have not been able to pass on these increased costs because the prices consumers pay for subscriptions as well as single copies of magazines have increased only slightly. Thus, publishers have to pay more to maintain their rate bases (the circulation level guaranteed to advertisers), but they make less money on each subscription sold.

Publishers are also facing a drop in sweepstakes-generated circulation as a result of the controversy that developed over consumer confidence in the sweepstakes-related subscription offers. Agents such as Publishers Clearing House have been going through changes, both self-imposed and externally dictated, that have greatly reduced the number of subscriptions they generate for publishers. In 2014 a Senate committee investigation says Publishers Clearing House may be misleading consumers by sending out sweepstakes solicitations that "push the limits" of federal law and legal settlements between the company and dozens of states.[28] To compensate for losses from sweepstakes agents, publishers are looking to other methods of generating subscribers, such as making subscriptions available through websites, offering free trial copies online, conducting special promotions, and using other agents such as school-related subscription services.[29] Some publications such as *InStyle* have begun selling magazine subscriptions on Facebook by allowing users of the social media site to expand blurbs of magazine content that are common in news feeds into full articles that contain ads as well as options to subscribe.[30] Publishers have also been turning to daily-deal sites such as Groupon and Living Social as magazines such as *Esquire, Us Weekly, Reader's Digest, Allure, Men's Health,* and others have found them useful for attracting new subscribers. However, a major challenge publishers will face is getting subscribers to renew at higher rates once the discounted deals expire.[31]

Digital Magazines Many magazines are keeping pace with the digital revolution and the continuing consumer interest in technology by making their publications available online.[32] The number of consumer and business magazine websites has nearly doubled over the past five years. Online versions of magazines offer the many advantages of the Internet to publishers as well as advertisers. They provide advertisers with the opportunity for sponsorships as well as running video and banner ads and promotions on the online versions of the magazines. More and more people are becoming comfortable with reading magazines online rather than in traditional print form, which is leading many publications to expand beyond their basic

Forbes BrandVoice
A Content Marketing Platform

Brand content is just as relevant, engaging and informative as other kinds of content.

Publish it—with transparent labeling—to the same streams as Forbes editorial content.

70,593,266 All-Time Brand Voice Page Views

EXHIBIT 12–16

Forbes BrandVoice is a form of native advertising

Source: Forbes Media LLC

EXHIBIT 12–17

The Association for Magazine Media promotes the value of print advertising

© MPA-The Association of Magazine Media

This Is Your Brain on Print

print publications. A number of publishers are extending their magazine brands to include online, social networking, mobile, and user-generated content, which provides increasing readership as well as advertising reach opportunities.

Marketers are also recognizing that there are opportunities to integrate their advertising in online publications with the environment and editorial content by using **native advertising**, which takes on the look and feel of the surrounding content. There has been considerable debate over what the advertising industry means by native advertising; many argue that it is just a digital version of an editorial that might appear in a magazine or newspaper. However, some industry experts describe them as digital advertising formats that integrate more seamlessly into the aesthetics of a website or online publication as well as the editorial content to provide more value to both advertisers and readers.[33] What this means basically is that an online ad takes on the look and feel of the surrounding content and its visual design and user experience are native or specific to the online site. A number of magazine and newspaper brands have been working with marketers to create native ads for their online publications, including *Forbes*, the *Washington Post*, and *The Atlantic. Forbes* has been at the forefront in the use of native advertising an approach called BrandVoice that allows marketers to connect directly with its readers by enabling them to create content on the *Forbes* digital platforms. All content on the platforms is clearly labeled and transparent so readers know who is talking and the perspective from which they speak. Exhibit 12–16 shows how *Forbes* promotes its BrandVoice content marketing platform.

Another form of online delivery is digital editions of magazines developed specifically for tablets such as the iPad and devices using the Android operating system. There are more than 2,000 apps for magazines available in the United States. The number of digital app editions of magazines will continue to grow as more consumers become comfortable with reading them on their tablets and advances in technology make the reading experience similar to that of a print publication. Digital editions of many magazines are now able to offer ads that can deliver the impact of full-page magazine ads, include video and TV commercials, and link directly to an advertiser's website. However, while consumers who opt to read magazines on a mobile device enjoy the experience, magazine apps still account for a small share of total magazine readership. According to the Association of Magazine Media, research shows that 16 percent of adults read digital editions of magazines. Moreover, like print, digital editions of magazines must compete for the attention of readers who are searching the Web, visiting social media sites, and playing games.

The magazine industry recognizes that it must continue to respond to the changes in media consumption patterns and the challenges it faces as more marketers shift their advertising monies to digital. However, publishers still feel there are inherent advantages of traditional print magazines to advertisers and have gone on the offensive to promote them. For example, the MPA—Association for Magazine Media recently published a white paper titled "What Can Neuroscience Tell Us About Why Print Advertising Works?" that summarized the findings of numerous research papers, books, and reports regarding how consumers' brains process paper-based information.[34] The report concludes that print advertising is superior to online ads with regard to its ability to deliver a reading experience that supports comprehension of and connection with an advertisers message. Exhibit 12–17 shows how the MPA is promoting the key finding from the study regarding the value of print advertising.

NEWSPAPERS

Newspapers, the second major form of print media, like magazines are increasingly being read online through digital formats. In 2015, nearly $20 billion was spent on newspaper advertising, including print

CHAPTER 12

and digital, which was about 10 percent of the total advertising expenditures in the United States. Newspapers are an especially important advertising medium to local advertisers, particularly retailers. However, newspapers are also valuable to national advertisers. Many of the advertising dollars spent by local retailers are actually provided by national advertisers through cooperative advertising programs (discussed in Chapter 16). Newspapers vary in terms of their characteristics and their role as an advertising medium.

Types of Newspapers

The traditional role of newspapers has been to deliver prompt, detailed coverage of news as well as to supply other information and features that appeal to readers. The vast majority of newspapers are daily publications serving a local community. However, weekly, national, and special-audience newspapers have special characteristics that can be valuable to advertisers.

Daily Newspapers Daily newspapers, which are published each weekday, are found in cities and larger towns across the country. Many areas have more than one daily paper. Readership of daily newspapers varies by age as 40 percent or more of older adults (55+) read a newspaper every day but only around 20 percent of younger adults (18 to 34).[35] Newspapers provide detailed coverage of news, events, and issues concerning the local area as well as business, sports, and other relevant information and entertainment. Daily newspapers can further be classified as morning, evening, or Sunday publications. In 2016 there were just over 1,300 daily newspapers in the United States; of these, 30 percent were evening papers and 70 percent morning. There were also a little more than 900 Sunday newspapers, most of which were published by daily newspapers.

PEOPLE WHO DON'T HAVE TIME MAKE TIME TO READ THE WALL STREET JOURNAL.

See what Sir Martin Sorrell makes time to read at WSJ.com/SirMartin

THE WALL STREET JOURNAL.
Read ambitiously

Weekly Newspapers Most weekly newspapers originate in small towns or suburbs where the volume of news and advertising cannot support a daily newspaper. These papers focus primarily on news, sports, and events relevant to the local area and usually ignore national and world news, sports, and financial and business news. There are approximately 6,700 weekly newspapers published in the United States, and they have an average circulation of close to 7,500. Weeklies appeal primarily to local advertisers because of their geographic focus and lower absolute cost. Most national advertisers avoid weekly newspapers because of their duplicate circulation with daily or Sunday papers in the large metropolitan areas and problems in contracting for and placing ads in these publications. However, the contracting and scheduling problems associated with these papers have been reduced by the emergence of syndicates that publish them in a number of areas and sell ad space in all of their local newspapers through one office.

National Newspapers Newspapers in the United States with national circulation include *USA Today, The Wall Street Journal*, and *The New York Times*. All three are daily publications and have editorial content with a nationwide appeal. *The Wall Street Journal* has the largest circulation of any newspaper in the country with just over 2 million readers for its print and online editions. *The Wall Street Journal* is an excellent media vehicle for reaching businesspeople and also has a very affluent readership base, as shown in the ad in Exhibit 12–18. Another popular national newspaper is *USA Today*, which positions itself as "the nation's newspaper." *USA Today* has become a popular daily newspaper, particularly among business and leisure travelers, with its coverage of national news as well as its money, sports, lifestyle, and entertainment sections. National newspapers appeal primarily to large national advertisers

EXHIBIT 12–19

Most college newspapers now publish digital editions

Source: San Diego State University, The Daily Aztec

and to regional advertisers that use specific geographic editions of these publications. For example, *The Wall Street Journal* has three geographic editions covering 21 regions in which ads can be placed, while *USA Today* offers advertisers the opportunity to run ads in its national edition or any of 25 regional markets.

Special-Audience Newspapers A variety of papers offer specialized editorial content and are published for particular groups, including labor unions, professional organizations, industries, and hobbyists. Many people working in advertising read *Advertising Age*, while those in the marketing area read *Marketing News*. Specialized newspapers are also published in areas with large foreign-language-speaking ethnic groups, among them Polish, Chinese, Hispanics, Vietnamese, and Filipinos. In the United States, there are newspapers printed in more than 40 languages.

Newspapers targeted at various religious groups compose another large class of special-interest papers. For example, more than 140 Catholic newspapers are published across the United States. Another type of special-audience newspaper is one most of you probably read regularly during the school year, the college newspaper. More than 1,300 colleges and universities publish newspapers and offer advertisers an excellent medium for reaching college students, who are a difficult target audience for marketers to reach. Many college newspapers are now being published online and either eliminating or reducing the number of print editions they publish each week (Exhibit 12–19).

Newspaper Supplements Although not a category of newspapers per se, many papers include magazine-type supplements, primarily in their Sunday editions. Sunday supplements have been part of most newspapers for many years and come in various forms. One type is the nationally syndicated Sunday magazine, such as *Parade*, which is distributed through more than 500 newspapers and reaches over 50 million readers in markets across the country. These publications are similar to national magazines and carry both national and regional advertising. *Parade* is the only remaining nationally syndicated Sunday magazine since *USA Weekend* suspended publication in late 2014.

Some large newspapers publish local Sunday supplements distributed by the parent paper. These supplements contain stories of local interest, and both local and national advertisers buy ad space. *The New York Times Sunday Magazine* is the best-known local supplement. *The Washington Post, San Francisco Examiner*, and *Los Angeles Times* have their own Sunday magazines. In some areas, papers have begun carrying regional supplements as well as specialized weekday supplements that cover specific topics such as food, sports, or entertainment. Supplements are valuable to advertisers that want to use the newspaper yet get four-color reproduction quality in their ads.

Types of Newspaper Advertising

The ads appearing in print editions of newspapers can also be divided into different categories. The major types of newspaper advertising are display and classified. Other special types of ads and preprinted inserts also appear in newspapers.

Display Advertising **Display advertising** is found throughout the newspaper and generally uses illustrations, headlines, white space, and other visual devices in addition to the copy text. The two types of display advertising in newspapers are local and national (general).

Local advertising refers to ads placed by local organizations, businesses, and individuals who want to communicate with consumers in the market area served by the newspaper. Supermarkets and department stores are among the leading local display advertisers, along with numerous other retailers and service operations such as banks and travel agents. Local advertising is sometimes referred to as retail advertising because retailers account for 85 percent of local display ads.

National or *general advertising* refers to newspaper display advertising done by marketers of branded products or services that are sold on a national or regional level. These ads are designed to create and maintain demand for a company's product or service and to complement the efforts of local retailers that stock and promote the advertiser's products. Major retail chains, automakers, and airlines are heavy users of newspaper advertising.

Classified Advertising   **Classified advertising** also provides newspapers with a substantial amount of revenue. These ads are arranged under subheads according to the product, service, or offering being advertised. Employment, real estate, and automotive are the three major categories of classified advertising. While most classified ads are just text set in small type, some newspapers also accept classified display advertising. These ads are run in the classified section of the paper but use illustrations, larger type sizes, white space, borders, and even color to stand out.

Special Ads and Inserts   Special advertisements in newspapers include a variety of government and financial reports and notices and public notices of changes in business and personal relationships. **Preprinted inserts** are another type of advertising distributed through newspapers. These ads do not appear in the paper itself; they are printed by the advertiser and then taken to the newspaper to be inserted before delivery. Many retailers use inserts such as circulars, catalogs, or brochures in specific circulation zones to reach shoppers in their particular trade areas. Inserts are used most often in Sunday editions of major newspapers since consumers spend more time with the Sunday paper and often look for inserts from retailers on weekends. Exhibit 12–20 shows how the *San Diego Union-Tribune* promotes its insert distribution service to advertisers.

EXHIBIT 12–20

Newspaper inserts are used to reach target markets

Source: The San Diego Union-Tribune, LLC

INSERT DISTRIBUTION AND U-TMC SHARE MAIL

TARGET MARKETING ON YOUR TERMS
The Union-Tribune's flexible preprint insert options enable you to choose when and where you want your message delivered. You can target specific ZIP codes, within ZIP codes, or saturate the entire county — It's up to you.

SCHEDULING OPTIONS
Full-run preprinted supplements, or single-sheet flyers appearing in paid circulation, can be distributed any day, Tuesday through Sunday. Inserts running in U-TMC are delivered via USPS mail on Thursday/Friday.

ZIP CODE DISTRIBUTION
Choose the ZIP codes you want to reach based on geographic, demographic or psychographic marketing variables. Our Marketing department can help you identify your customers, show you where they live, what they like to do and more.

DIRECT-MAIL DISTRIBUTION (U-TMC)
For total market coverage, the Union-Tribune provides you with shared-mail delivery to the households of non-subscribers, via U-TMC. Capturing the attention of weekend shoppers, our shared-mail package of colorful inserts is mailed to approximately 670,000 non-subscribers every Thursday/Friday via the U.S. Postal Service (USPS), ensuring extremely reliable delivery.

• **HIGH PENETRATION**
U-TMC reaches over 89 percent of San Diego County households when combined with Union-Tribune daily circulation. And our database of subscribers and non-subscribers is updated monthly, to virtually eliminate overlap.

• **MICRO TARGET ZONES (MTZ'S)**
Now you can zoom-in on zones within ZIP codes with the Union-Tribune's Micro Target Zones (MTZs). Available in the U-TMC, this enables you to reach non-subscribers in a highly efficient manner.

MEXICO DISTRIBUTION
Our weekly distribution program to Mexico reaches 80,000 middle- and upper-class homes in Tijuana, and 50,000 in Mexicali. An estimated 90 percent of these targeted consumers shop in San Diego once a month or more. Make sure you include this valuable group of shoppers.

TOPPER PROGRAM – HIGH VISIBILITY
When delivered via the Union-Tribune, your insert can go on top of the newspaper so it's the first thing readers see. Ask your account manager about Topper pricing.

Sources: The San Diego Union-Tribune 1996 La Roka Acxi Distribution Study, 2006. Claritas, Inc., March 2007 Union-Tribune Circulation Department.

For advertising information, call (619) 293-1544 • www.utads.com

Advantages of Newspapers

Newspapers have a number of characteristics that make them popular among both local and national advertisers. These include their extensive penetration of local markets, flexibility, geographic selectivity, reader involvement, and special services.

Market Penetration   One of the advantages of newspapers is the high market coverage or penetration they offer an advertiser, particularly for older adult households. In most areas, 40 percent or more of these households read a daily newspaper, and the reach figure may reach 50 percent among households with higher incomes and education levels. The penetration of newspapers provides advertisers with an opportunity for reaching various segments of the population with their message. Also, since many newspapers are published and read daily, the advertiser can build a high level of frequency into the media schedule.

Flexibility   Another advantage of newspapers is the flexibility they offer advertisers. First, they are flexible in terms of requirements for producing and running the ads. Newspaper ads can be written, laid out, and prepared in a matter of hours. For most dailies, the closing time by which the ad must be received is usually only 24 hours before publication (although closing dates for special ads, such as those using

CONGRATULATIONS

San Diego's Own Callaway Golf Company
Congratulates San Diego's Own Phil Mickelson.

Champion Golfer of the Year.
#BRINGIT

EXHIBIT 12-21

Callaway Golf used a
newspaper ad for a timely
ad congratulating golfer
Phil Mickelson

Source: Callaway Golf

color, and Sunday supplements are longer). The short production time and closing dates make newspapers an excellent medium for responding to current events or presenting timely information to readers. For example, the Callaway Golf Company ran a newspaper ad congratulating professional golfer Phil Mickelson for winning the British Open golf tournament the day following the final round of the prestigious event. Mickelson is a member of the Callaway Golf team, and the ad was a very timely way to acknowledge his accomplishment and promote his use of Callaway golf equipment (Exhibit 12–21).

A second dimension of newspapers' flexibility stems from the creative options they make available to advertisers. Newspaper ads can be produced and run in various sizes, shapes, and formats; they can use color or special inserts to gain the interest of readers. Ads can be run in Sunday magazines or other supplements, and a variety of scheduling options are possible, depending on the advertiser's purpose.

Geographic Selectivity Newspapers generally offer advertisers more geographic or territorial selectivity than any other medium except direct mail. Advertisers can vary their coverage by choosing a paper—or combination of papers—that reaches the areas with the greatest sales potential. National advertisers take advantage of the geographic selectivity of newspapers to concentrate their advertising in specific areas they can't reach with other media or to take advantage of strong sales potential in a particular area. For example, BMW, Mercedes, and Land Rover use heavy newspaper media schedules in major metropolitan markets such as major cities in California and the New York/New Jersey area to capitalize on the high sales potential for luxury import cars in these markets. A number of companies use newspapers in their regional marketing strategies. Newspaper advertising lets them feature products on a market-by-market basis, respond and adapt campaigns to local market conditions, and tie into more retailer promotions, fostering more support from the trade.

Local advertisers like retailers are interested in geographic selectivity or flexibility within a specific market or trade area. Their media goal is to concentrate their advertising on the areas where most of their customers are. Many newspapers now offer advertisers various geographic areas or zones for this purpose. For example, the *Chicago Tribune* offers advertisers five different circulation area zones, as shown in Exhibit 12–22.

Reader involvement and Acceptance Another important feature of newspapers is consumers' level of acceptance and involvement with papers and the ads they contain. The typical daily newspaper reader spends time each day reading the weekday newspaper and even more time reading the Sunday paper. Recent studies have shown that around 56 percent of newspaper readers consume newspapers only in their printed form and are news enthusiasts. However, these print-only readers are older than those who read newspapers online and are less likely to have gone to college.[36] These consumers rely heavily on newspapers not only for news, information, and entertainment but also for assistance with consumption decisions.

Many consumers actually purchase a newspaper *because* of the advertising it contains. Consumers use retail ads to determine product prices and availability and to see who is having a sale. One aspect of newspapers that is helpful to advertisers is readers' knowledge about particular sections of the paper. Most of us know that ads for automotive products and sporting goods are generally found in the sports section, while ads for financial services are found in the business section. The weekly food section in many newspapers is popular for recipe and menu ideas as well as for the grocery store ads and coupons offered by many stores and companies.

The value of newspaper advertising as a source of information has been shown in several studies. One study found that consumers look forward to ads in newspapers more than in other media. In another study, 80 percent of consumers said newspaper ads were most helpful to them in doing their weekly shopping. Newspaper advertising has also been rated the most believable form of advertising in numerous studies.

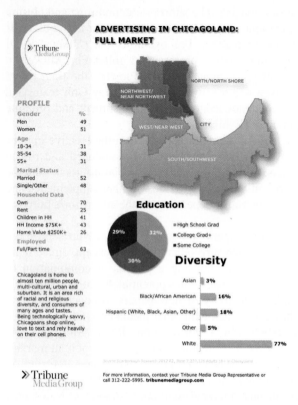

EXHIBIT 12–22

The *Chicago Tribune* offers advertisers combinations of different circulation area zones

© *Chicago Tribune Media Group*

EXHIBIT 12–23

Newspaper publishers are often an excellent source for information on local markets

Source: The San Diego Union-Tribune, LLC

Services Offered

The special services newspapers offer can be valuable to advertisers. For example, many newspapers offer merchandising services and programs to manufacturers that make the trade aware of ads being run for the company's product and help convince local retailers they should stock, display, and promote the item.

Many newspapers are also excellent sources of local market information through their knowledge of market conditions and research like readership studies and consumer surveys. For example, the publisher of the *San Diego Union-Tribune*, the major daily newspaper in San Diego, provides information on the local market through various reports and market studies (Exhibit 12–23).

Newspapers can also assist small companies through free copywriting and art services. Small advertisers without an agency or advertising department often rely on the newspaper to help them write and produce their ads.

Limitations of Newspapers

While newspapers have many advantages, like all media they also have disadvantages that media planners must consider. The limitations of newspapers include their reproduction problems, short life span, lack of selectivity, and clutter.

Poor Reproduction

One of the greatest limitations of newspapers as an advertising medium is their poor reproduction quality. The coarse paper stock used for newspapers, the absence of color, and the lack of time papers have available to achieve high-quality reproduction limit the quality of most newspaper ads. Newspapers have improved their reproduction quality in recent years, and color reproduction has become more available. Also, advertisers desiring high-quality color in newspaper ads can turn to such alternatives as freestanding inserts or Sunday supplements. However, these are more costly and may not be desirable to many advertisers. As a general rule, if the visual appearance of the product is important, the advertiser will not rely on newspaper ads. Ads for food products and fashions generally use magazines to capitalize on their superior reproduction quality and color.

Short Life Span

Unlike magazines, which may be retained around the house for several weeks, a daily newspaper is generally kept less than a day. So an ad is unlikely to have any impact beyond the day of publication, and repeat exposure is very unlikely. Compounding this problem are the short amount of time many consumers spend with the newspaper and the possibility they may not even open certain sections of the paper. Media planners can offset these problems somewhat by using high frequency in the newspaper schedule and advertising in a section where consumers who are in the market for a particular product or service are likely to look.

Lack of Selectivity

While newspapers can offer advertisers geographic selectivity, they are not a selective medium in terms of demographics or lifestyle characteristics. Most newspapers reach broad and very diverse groups of consumers, which makes it difficult for marketers to focus on

Innovative Advertising

Bookend   Stairstep

14

● Los Angeles Times | MEDIA GROUP

EXHIBIT 12–24

The *Los Angeles Times* promotes the innovative advertising shapes it now offers

Source: Los Angeles Times

narrowly defined market segments. For example, manufacturers of fishing rods and reels will find newspapers very inefficient because of the wasted coverage that results from reaching all the newspaper readers who don't fish. Thus, they are more likely to use special-interest magazines such as *Field & Stream* and *Fishing World.* Any newspaper ads for their products will be done through cooperative plans whereby retailers share the costs or spread them over a number of sporting goods featured in the ad.

Clutter   Newspapers, like most other advertising media, suffer from clutter as the advertiser's message must compete with numerous other ads for consumers' attention and interest. Moreover, the creative options in newspapers are limited by the fact that most ads are black and white. Thus, it can be difficult for a newspaper advertiser to break through the clutter without using costly measures such as large space buys or color.

Many newspapers are now offering advertisers the opportunity to use innovative shape-based ads that utilize unconventional sizes and formats such as stairsteps, bookends, U-shapes, island ads, spadea ads, and half-page spreads. Many newspapers are also now accepting ads on the front page of their publications as well as on the first page of various sections of the paper. The use of these innovative formats makes it possible for advertisers to more easily attract the attention of readers and increase recall of their advertising message. Exhibit 12–24 shows a page from the media kit for the *Los Angeles Times* promoting several of the innovative ad forms that the paper now offers advertisers.

The Newspaper Audience

As with any medium, the media planner must understand the nature and size of the audience reached by a newspaper in considering its value in the media plan. Since newspapers as a class of media do an excellent job of penetrating their market, the typical daily newspaper gives advertisers the opportunity to reach most of the households in a market. But, while local advertisers aim to cover a particular market or trade area, national advertisers want to reach broad regions or even the entire country. They must purchase space in a number of papers to achieve the desired level of coverage.

The basic sources of information concerning the audience size of newspapers come from the circulation figures available through rate cards, publishers' statements, or Kantar Media SRDS's *Newspaper Advertising Source.* Circulation figures for many newspapers are verified by the Alliance for Audited Media (AAM), which was discussed earlier. Advertisers that use a number of papers in their media plan generally find SRDS the most convenient source.

Newspaper circulation figures are generally broken down into three categories: the city zone, the retail trading zone, and all other areas. The **city zone** is a market area composed of the city where the paper is published and contiguous areas similar in character to the city. The **retail trading zone** is the market outside the city zone whose residents regularly trade with merchants within the city zone. The "all other" category covers all circulation not included in the city or retail trade zone.

Sometimes circulation figures are provided only for the primary market, which is the city and retail trade zones combined, and the other area. Both local and national advertisers consider the circulation patterns across the various categories in evaluating and selecting newspapers.

National advertisers often buy newspaper space on the basis of the size of the market area they cover. For example, General Motors might decide to purchase

CHAPTER 12

Find, consider and understand newspaper media.

The SRDS.com Newspaper Advertising Source® gives you comprehensive planning data on daily U.S. papers, newspaper groups, community papers, alternatives, shoppers, classifieds and their websites.

• 6,000+ national and local newspapers
• 3,400+ digital media listings
• 90+ media brands with iPad and tablet apps at the SRDS Tablet Media Library

Media research, your way

Search for media and advertising opportunities any way that makes sense to you. Get in, find your options and apply powerful filters and sorting capabilities to help you evaluate huge lists of media quickly.

• Media types (newspapers, digital media)
• Keywords and titles
• Geography (national papers or in 210 DMAs)
• Newspaper types
• Reps and press associations

Actionable data in one place

SRDS listings include all the data points you need to compile a plan.

• Rates and contact information
• Audience metrics and circulation
• Many media include audience profile links, publisher's positioning statements, featured marketing opportunities, logos, front-page and website images.

Make your media planning more efficient.
Learn more at srds.com or call 800.232.0772 x8002.

srds.com

EXHIBIT 12–25

SRDS *Newspaper Advertising Source* provides advertisers with valuable Information on newspapers

Source: Kantar Media

advertising in the top 10 markets, the top 50 markets, the top 100 markets, and so on. A national advertiser gets different levels of market coverage depending on the number of market areas purchased.

Audience Information Circulation figures provide the media planner with the basic data for assessing the value of newspapers and their ability to cover various market areas. However, the media planner also wants to match the characteristics of a newspaper's readers with those of the advertiser's target audience. Data on newspaper audience size and characteristics are available from studies conducted by the papers as well as from commercial research services. As with magazines, a valuable source for information on newspapers is Kantar Media SRDS, whose print and online service provides complete planning information on daily papers, newspaper groups, ethnic newspapers, college newspapers, comics, and newspaper-distributed magazines. The SRDS *Newspaper Advertising Source* data contain standardized ad rates, circulation figures, dates, general requirements, contact information, and other valuable information for media (Exhibit 12–25).

Companies such as Experian Simmons and GfK MRI provide syndicated research studies on lifestyles, media behavior, and product/brand preferences that include information on newspapers. These studies can be valuable for comparing newspapers with other media vehicles.

Many newspapers commission their own audience studies to provide current and potential advertisers with information on readership and characteristics of readers such as demographics, shopping habits, and lifestyles. These studies are often designed to promote the effectiveness of the newspaper in reaching various types of consumers. Since they are sponsored by the paper itself, many advertisers are skeptical of their results. Careful attention must be given to the research methods used and conclusions drawn by these studies.

Purchasing Newspaper Space

Advertisers are faced with a number of options and pricing structures when purchasing newspaper space. The cost of advertising space depends not only on the newspaper's circulation but also on factors such as premium charges for color or special sections as well as discounts available. The purchase process and the rates paid for newspaper space differ for general and local advertisers.

General versus Local Rates Newspapers have different rate structures for general or national advertisers and local or retail advertisers. **General advertising rates** apply to display advertisers outside the newspaper's designated market area (DMA) and to any classification deemed by the publisher to be "general" in nature. This includes ads run by national advertisers such as automotive, tobacco, packaged-goods, and pharmaceutical companies. **Retail or local advertising rates** apply to advertisers that conduct business or sell goods or services within the DMA. The rates paid by general advertisers are, on average, 75 percent higher than those paid by local advertisers. Newspaper publishers claim the rate differential is justified for several reasons. First, they argue it costs more to handle general advertising since ad agencies get a 15 percent commission and commissions must also be paid to the independent sales reps who solicit nonlocal advertising. Second, they note that general advertising is less dependable than local advertising; general advertisers usually don't use newspapers on a continual basis the way local advertisers do. Finally, newspaper publishers contend that demand for general advertising is inelastic—it will not increase if rates are lowered or decrease if rates are raised. This means there is no incentive to lower the national advertisers' rates.

National advertisers do not view these arguments as valid justification for the rate differential. They argue that the costs are not greater for handling national advertising than for local business and that many national advertisers use newspapers on a regular basis. Since they use an agency to prepare their ads, national advertisers are less likely to request special services. The large and costly staff maintained by many newspapers to assist in the design and preparation of advertising is used mostly by local advertisers. Many marketers sidestep the national advertiser label and the higher rates by channeling their newspaper ads through special category plans, cooperative advertising deals with retailers, and local dealers and distributors that pay local rates. However, the rate differential does keep many national advertisers from making newspapers a larger part of their media mix.

Rate Structures   While the column inch and **standard advertising unit (SAU)** are used to determine basic newspaper advertising rates, the media planner must consider other options and factors. Many newspapers charge **flat rates**, which means they offer no discount for quantity or repeated space buys. Others have an **open-rate structure**, which means various discounts are available. These discounts are generally based on frequency or bulk purchases of space and depend on the number of column inches purchased in a year.

Newspaper space rates also vary with an advertiser's special requests, such as preferred position or color. The basic rates quoted by a newspaper are **run of paper (ROP)**, which means the paper can place the ad on any page or in any position it desires. While most newspapers try to place an ad in a requested position, the advertiser can ensure a specific section and/or position on a page by paying a higher **preferred position rate**. Color advertising is also available in many newspapers on an ROP basis or through preprinted inserts or Sunday supplements.

Advertisers can also buy newspaper space based on **combination rates**, where they get a discount for using several newspapers as a group. Typically, a combination rate occurs when a publisher owns both a morning and an evening newspaper in a market and offers a reduced single rate for running the same ad in both newspapers, generally within a 24-hour period. Combination discounts are also available when the advertiser buys space in several newspapers owned by the publisher in a number of markets or in multiple newspapers affiliated in a syndicate or newspaper group.

The Future for Newspapers

Newspapers remain an important advertising medium; however, advertising revenue for traditional print papers has declined dramatically over the past several years. They generate most of their advertising revenue from local advertisers, particularly retailers who use display ads to advertise their products and services and inform consumers of sales and other types of promotions. Newspapers account for less than 5 percent of advertising expenditures for national advertisers, so they are very dependent on regional and local marketers for their advertising revenue.

Newspapers' major strength lies in their role as a medium that can be used effectively by local advertisers on a continual basis. However, there are a number of problems and issues newspapers must address to maintain their strong position as a dominant local advertising medium and to gain more national advertising. These include competition from other advertising media, maintenance and management of circulation, cross-media opportunities, and declining readership.

Competition from Other Media   The newspaper industry's battle to increase its share of advertising revenue has been difficult. In addition to the problems of reproduction quality and rate differentials, newspapers face competition from other media for both national and local advertisers' budgets.

Digital and Social Media Perspective 12–1 > > >

CAN NEWSPAPERS SURVIVE THE DIGITAL REVOLUTION?

The past decade has been very challenging for the newspaper industry. Total advertising spending in newspapers declined by more than 60 percent, from $42 billion in 2007 to $20 billion in 2015. Revenue from advertising is the primary source of income for newspapers in the United States, so the impact on publishers is obvious. However, advertising revenue is dependent on the number of eyeballs that newspapers can deliver to advertisers, and most papers have been struggling to retain readers. As you have likely noticed, newspapers are not what they used to be as the industry has undergone major changes in recent years. The rise of the Internet along with the increasing use of mobile devices, such as tablets and smartphones, to access content has had a dramatic impact on the newspaper industry. This digital disruption has changed the nature of the newspaper as a vehicle for information as well as its value as an advertising medium.

Traditionally newspapers bundled together an array of content that is offered in various sections such as national, international, and local news; business; sports; entertainment; local stories, editorials, and opinions; comics; and classified advertising for automobiles, real estate, rental, employment, and other products and services. Display advertising is interspersed throughout the paper and along with classified ads generates more than half of the revenue used to cover the costs of printing and distributing a physical paper. However, digital technology has led to the unbundling of the content provided by newspapers with the explosion of the news and information sources available on the Internet. Moreover, aggregation sites such as the Huffington Post, Google News, and Reddit consolidate news and information from a myriad of websites that are constantly updated, which means the news delivered by newspapers is "old news"

when it is delivered a day later. There are also aggregation sites for specific topics such as sports, business, entertainment, and most other areas of interest to readers.

Newspapers have also been impacted by the growth of online sites that have taken away much of their revenue from classified advertising. For example, employment sites such as Monster or CareerBuilder and many others are now used for recruiting employees; sites such as AutoTrader and Cars.com are used to buy and sell cars; while Craigslist has classified sections for virtually every product and service category. Newspapers have experienced an 80 percent decline in their revenue from classified advertising over the past decade; it has dropped from nearly $17 billion in 2003 to just over $3 billion in 2015. Revenue from display advertising has also been declining with many local retailers as well as national advertisers shifting their ad spending from newspapers to an array of digital alternatives.

The newspaper industry's initial response to the digital disruption was to put content online for free, which resulted in a tremendous growth in the number of online readers. Most newspapers began offering online versions of their publications and selling display advertising on their sites, primarily in the form of banner ads, to generate revenue. However, revenue from online advertising has not been able to compensate for the decline in monies received for print advertising because online ad rates are significantly lower than those for print ads. Digital advertising revenue for U.S. newspapers was just under $3.5 billion in 2014, only 11 percent more than in 2007. Marketers are not willing to pay as much for online newspaper ads because there is an enormous number of advertising options on the Internet, driving down prices, and the click-through rates on most of the banner ads that appear in online newspapers are minuscule.

The intermedia battle that newspapers find themselves involved in is no longer limited to other forms of traditional media. Many companies are using the Internet as a marketing tool and a place to invest advertising dollars that might otherwise go to newspapers. Local radio and TV stations (particularly cable stations), as well as the expanding number of Yellow Pages publishers, are aggressively pursuing local advertisers. Newspapers will have to fight harder to retain those advertisers. Digital and Social Media Perspective 12–1 discusses how the newspaper industry has been disrupted by the growth of digital media.

Newspapers are also facing strong competition from various online sites for classified and employment advertising, which have long been important major profit centers. Classified advertising revenue for U.S. newspapers has dropped steadily since 2000, declining from nearly $20 billion to just $3.2 billion in 2015. As shown in Figure 12–2, reductions in classified advertising have occurred across all three of the major categories, including automotive, real estate, and recruitment ads. Newspapers must now compete against online employment sites such as Monster.com and Job.com for job listings as well as social media sites such LinkedIn. Websites such as eBay and Craigslist have become popular ways for selling a variety of merchandise

© Ian Dagnall/Alamy

In essence, newspapers have been trading traditional print advertising dollars for digital pennies.

Newspapers trying to attract digital display and video advertising from marketers must also compete with other online media and websites as well as social media sites such as Facebook, LinkedIn, Instagram, and Snapchat that offer advertisers sophisticated ad-targeting techniques. The problem has become even greater recently with the growth in programmatic media buying whereby online ads are purchased in bulk through automated software programs that seek to maximize target audience coverage with little regard for the type of medium where the ad appears.

The challenges facing newspaper publishers have forced them to undergo significant cost-cutting measures while continuing to look for new sources of revenue. Many newspapers have tried to implement digital pay plans or "paywalls" that require readers to pay for a digital subscription or lose access. These digital pay plans may allow a certain number of free articles each month; however, users must pay for full access to the newspaper, which provides newspaper publishers with an additional source of revenue. They also help stabilize a newspaper's print circulation as digital access is typically offered free or at a reduced rate to print subscribers. However, most newspapers have not been successful in implementing paywalls and only a few major newspapers such as *The New York Times, The Wall Street Journal, Los Angeles Times*, and *Boston Globe* have a significant number of digital subscribers willing to pay for access to their content. Most of these paywalls are easy to get around and readers can generally find other ways to access articles such as through their social media feeds or through search engines.

Newspapers are responding in other ways to the digital disruption they have faced over the past decade and will continue to face in the future. Like magazines, many newspapers are turning to native advertising to make their online editions more appealing to advertisers. Many newspaper publishers are transforming their business model to generate revenue from a variety of new offerings, such as providing digital agency and marketing services, helping businesses connect directly with consumers through e-commerce transactions, and expanding their integrated marketing capabilities to include areas such as event marketing and promotional services. However, many experts are still questioning whether newspapers can respond to the disruption they are facing and survive in the new digital world.

Sources: "Up against the Paywall," *The Economist*, November 21, 2015, p. 62; Michael Sebastian, "Magazine Revenue to Climb Slightly as Newspaper Decline Continues," *Advertising Age*, June 2, 2015, http://adage.com/article/media/magazine-revenue-ticks-newspaper-decline-continues/298861/; Michael Barthel, "State of the News Media 2015: Newspapers," Pew Research Center, April 29, 2015, www.journalism.org/2015/04/29/newspapers-fact-sheet/.

FIGURE 12–2

Decline in Newspaper Classified Advertising Revenue

Source: Newspaper Association of America.

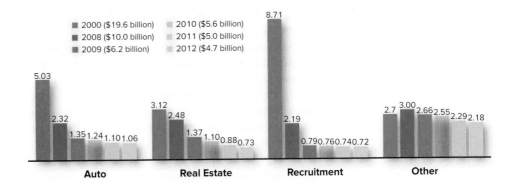

Legend: 2000 ($19.6 billion), 2008 ($10.0 billion), 2009 ($6.2 billion), 2010 ($5.6 billion), 2011 ($5.0 billion), 2012 ($4.7 billion)

Auto: 5.03, 2.32, 1.35, 1.24, 1.10, 1.06
Real Estate: 3.12, 2.48, 1.37, 1.10, 0.88, 0.73
Recruitment: 8.71, 2.19, 0.79, 0.76, 0.74, 0.72
Other: 2.7, 3.00, 2.66, 2.55, 2.29, 2.18

that traditionally was sold through classified ads in local newspapers. Craigslist, which began as a type of counterculture message board for young people in the San Francisco area, has now expanded to most major cities and has become popular among people of all ages. The online site includes sections for selling merchandise, apartment rentals, services, personals, and job listings. Some newspapers are recognizing that it is very difficult to compete against online sites for classified ads and are responding by offering free classified ads for merchandise under certain price points as a way to grow readership.

Newspapers are doing a number of other things to respond to the challenges from other media. Many papers have expanded their marketing capabilities and are making efforts to develop and sustain relationships with their advertisers. Some have created sophisticated databases and direct-mail capabilities, which they offer as value-added services. Others are increasing their marketing research departments, preparing comprehensive market studies for major customers, and, in some cases, serving as media advisors and marketing partners.

Circulation   The newspaper industry has been struggling for years to reverse declining circulation.[37] Most of the major newspapers in the United States have been experiencing a decline in circulation and are seeking ways to respond to the problem, such as by emphasizing readership measures and developing online versions of their papers. Like magazines, many newspapers are taking a closer look at their circulation and analyzing whether the cost of getting additional circulation is justified by the advertising revenue it generates. Many papers are raising newsstand and home delivery rates, and circulation revenue is accounting for more of their total revenue.

Several major metropolitan newspapers have found that advertisers use newspapers to reach consumers within specific geographic areas and do not want to pay for readers in outlying areas. Thus, some papers are eliminating what has been called "ego circulation" and focusing more on regional editions in their immediate trade area.

Newspapers have found that it is more cost-effective to focus on retaining subscribers rather than spending large sums of money to acquire new ones. The cancellation rate for newspaper subscribers has leveled off according to statistics from the Newspaper Association of America. These numbers reflect the fact that many newspapers are focusing more on retention of their core readers and offering programs such as discounts for automatic renewal payment plans.[38]

Attracting and Retaining Readers   The problems with newspapers as an advertising medium stem from the reduced popularity of the medium itself. Newspaper readership has been on a steady decline over the past decade.[39] The decline in newspaper readership can be attributed to several factors, including the fast-paced, time-poor lifestyle of the modern dual-income household and the increase in viewing options of TV, and of course, competition from the Internet as many of those who do read newspapers now read them digitally.[40] Of particular concern to publishers is the decline in newspaper readership among important market segments such as women and young adults. Surveys show that the percentage of women who read a newspaper on a typical day declined from 67 percent in 1981 to 39 percent recently.[41] Newspapers and advertisers are concerned because women are far more likely than men to make buying decisions. Many newspapers are introducing new women's sections and revising old ones to make them more appealing to modern women. This means including articles on such issues as health, parenting, and careers—for example, how women with children and jobs manage their time.

Newspapers are also concerned about where their future readers will come from, since many young people are heavy TV viewers and also are spending more and more time surfing the Internet and on social media. A number of newspapers have been redesigned to be more interesting and easier and faster to read. Changes include the increased use of color and graphics as well as expanded coverage of sports and entertainment. Some papers have begun providing short summaries of

EXHIBIT 12–26

The "Smart Is the New Sexy" campaign promotes the value of newspapers

© *Newspaper Association of America*

articles in each section of the paper so readers can skim them and decide what they want to read.

The newspaper industry is taking steps to address the problem of declining readership and to promote the value of newspapers. For example, the Newspaper Association of America (now known as the News Media Alliance) recently sponsored the "Smart Is the New Sexy" ad campaign to reinforce the value of newspapers to existing and prospective readers (Exhibit 12–26). The campaign uses a series of ads with engaging illustrations to point out the distinctive editorial, advertising, and community attributes delivered by newspapers. The integrated campaign also uses digital and social media to promote online dialogue around newspapers and to highlight the multiplatform experience provided by newspapers. QR codes and digital prompts link audiences to the website for the campaign (www.naa.org/smartsexy), where they can read more about the "Smart–Sexy" newspaper connection. They are also encouraged to share their own connection with newspapers by tweeting with the #smartsexy hashtag or by posting comments or video clips to the NAA's Facebook page.[42]

Online Delivery and Multiple Platforms

As discussed in Digital and Social Media Perspective 12–1, the digital transformation of media has hit the newspaper industry particularly hard and resulted in newspaper publishers broadening their portfolios well beyond the traditional print editions. Nearly every major newspaper now has a website, and most make their papers available online and through apps for mobile devices. The number of daily and weekly U.S. newspapers available online increased from less than 100 in 1995 to more than 3,200 in 2016. The digital newspaper audience increased from 70 million unique users per month in 2007 to nearly 179 million in 2015, with half of the newspaper digital audience composed of those using mobile devices (smartphones and tablets) to access newspaper content.[43] Publishers recognize that they must offer online versions of their newspapers as this has become the preferred mode of reading for many people, particularly younger consumers. Studies have shown that people who use online newspapers are highly engaged and are an upscale audience—they spend more time online, are better educated, and have higher incomes than online audiences in general. They are also more likely to make purchases online and to use the Internet to help them decide what to buy.[44]

Many newspapers are working to attract advertising dollars from both local and national advertisers. Networks are also forming to help local newspapers sell online ads on their websites to national advertisers. These networks provide national advertisers with access to newspaper websites across the country and facilitates the purchase of online ads in the same way it does with traditional print ads. While newspaper publishers are focusing more attention on the sale of online advertising, they are also facing strong competition from the major Internet search players such as Google, Yahoo!, Bing, and Local.com because these companies have made it inexpensive and easy for local companies to run ads with them. Many newspapers are forming alliances with these Internet search competitors whereby they can use their technology to sell more sophisticated ad offerings, such as behaviorally targeted ads.[45]

Most newspaper publishers are transforming themselves into *media* companies with products that include print and online newspapers, apps for those who read newspapers on mobile devices, and websites that include multiple products and services. By creating a variety of products and engaging consumers across multiple platforms, these companies can capitalize on new revenue opportunities that will undoubtedly present themselves in the future.

Summary

Magazines and newspapers, the two major forms of print media, play an important role in the media plans and strategy of many advertisers. Magazines are a very selective medium and are valuable for reaching specific types of customers and market segments. The three broad categories of magazines are consumer (which includes farm), business, and health care publications. Each of these categories can be further classified according to the publication's editorial content and audience appeal.

In addition to their selectivity, the advantages of magazines include their excellent reproduction quality, creative flexibility, long life, prestige, and readers' high receptivity to magazine advertising, as well as the services they offer to advertisers. Disadvantages of magazines include their high cost, limited reach and frequency, long lead time, and the advertising clutter in most publications.

Advertising space rates in magazines vary according to a number of factors, among them the size of the ad, position in the publication, particular editions purchased, use of color, and number and frequency of insertions. Rates for magazines are compared on the basis of the cost per thousand, although other factors such as the editorial content of the publication and its ability to reach specific target audiences must also be considered.

Newspapers are a very important medium to local advertisers, especially retailers. They are also used by national advertisers, although the differential rate structure for national versus local advertisers is a source of controversy. Newspapers are a broad-based medium that reaches a large percentage of households in a particular area. Newspapers' other advantages include flexibility, geographic selectivity, reader involvement, and special services. Drawbacks of newspapers include their lack of high-quality ad reproduction, short life span, lack of audience selectivity, and clutter.

Trends toward market segmentation and regional marketing are prompting many advertisers to make more use of newspapers and magazines. However, both magazines and newspapers face increasing competition from other media such as radio, cable TV, direct marketing, and the Internet. Both magazines and newspapers are working to improve the quality of their circulation bases, offer database marketing services, and initiate cross-media deals. Rising costs and declining readership are problems for many magazines and newspapers. The growth of the Internet along with the increasing use of mobile devices, such as tablets and smartphones, to access content has had a dramatic impact on traditional magazines and newspapers. This digital disruption has changed the nature of both forms of print media as a vehicle for information as well as their value as advertising media.

Key Terms

selectivity 422
gatefold 424
bleed page 424
split runs 427
controlled-circulation basis 431
pass-along readership 432
total audience/readership 432
first cover 433
second cover 433

third cover 433
fourth cover 433
magazine network 434
native advertising 437
display advertising 439
classified advertising 440
preprinted insert 440
city zone 443
retail trading zone 443

general advertising rates 444
retail or local advertising rates 444
standard advertising unit (SAU) 445
flat rate 445
open-rate structure 445
run of paper (ROP) 445
preferred position rate 445
combination rate 445

Discussion Questions

1. Discuss the digital disruption that is impacting the traditional print media of newspapers and magazines. Do you think magazine and newspaper publications can respond to these changes and attract and retain readers and in turn advertisers? (LO 12-1, 12-7)

2. The chapter opener discuss the Print Magazine Sales Guarantee that is being used by a number of major magazine media companies to encourage advertisers to run ads in print editions of their publications. Evaluate the decision by magazine publishers to offer this guarantee. Do you think it will help increase the number of ad pages they can sell to advertisers? (LO 12-1, 12-2)

3. Discuss the role of magazines as part of an advertiser's media strategy. What are the advantages and limitations of magazines? (LO 12-1, 12-2)

4. What is meant by native advertising? Do you think it is appropriate for advertisers to run native ads that appear to be editorial content rather than sponsored advertising? Why or why not? (LO 12-4)

5. If you were purchasing magazine advertising space for a marketer of running shoes such as Nike, ASICS, or New Balance what factors would you consider? Would your media plan be limited to running magazines or would you run ads in other types of publications? Explain. (LO 12-3, 12-5)

6. IMC Perspective 12–1 discusses how Playboy Enterprises is trying to rebrand *Playboy* magazine in order to attract male millennials and the advertisers trying to reach them. Do you think the company will be successful in rebranding *Playboy*? Why or why not? (LO 12-3)

7. The Association for Magazine Media promotes the value of advertising in traditional print magazines by citing research showing that print advertising is superior to online ads with regard to its ability to deliver a reading experience that supports comprehension of and connection with an advertisers message. Discuss some of the reasons why print ads may be superior to online ads. (LO 12-4)

8. Discuss some of the reasons why marketers advertise in college newspapers. Analyze the types of companies that advertise in the newspaper published by your university. (LO 12-1, 12-3)

9. What are the major challenges facing the newspaper industry and the use of newspapers as an advertising medium? How can newspapers respond to these challenges? (LO 12-7)

10. Find a copy of a national newspaper such as *USA Today* or your local newspaper and analyze the types of companies that are advertising in it and how they vary by section. Why do you think these companies are advertising in this newspaper? (LO 12-5)

11. What are some reasons for the dramatic decline in newspaper readership? What might newspaper publishers do to address this problem? (LO 12-5, 12-7)

12. What are some of the advantages online newspapers offer for advertisers? Find the online media kit of a newspaper and analyze how the publisher is promoting the digital edition to prospective advertisers. (LO 12-7)

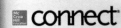

Digital users can access their personalized and adaptive SmartBook, Ad Forum Video Cases, and interactive exercises to review chapter concepts.

13 Support Media

Source: Jurassic World/Universal Pictures

LEARNING OBJECTIVES

LO1 Describe the role of support media in an IMC program.

LO2 Identify traditional and nontraditional support media in the development of an IMC program.

LO3 Compare the advantages and disadvantages of support media.

LO4 Describe how audiences for support media are measured.

THE BRANDCHANNEL PRODUCT PLACEMENT AWARDS: PRODUCT PLACEMENTS, INTEGRATIONS, AND BRANDED ENTERTAINMENT REMAIN POPULAR

As you no doubt know, the Academy Awards are given annually to the best movies of the year. But you probably didn't know that product placements have an annual awards show as well. For the last 10 years brandchannel has sponsored the Brandcameo Product Placement Awards—on the eve of the Oscars. Unlike the Oscars, the Brandcameo Awards honor the best, worst, and most product placements, or as noted by brandchannel, "here are the winners and losers for the past year in cinematic product placement, brand integration and scene-stealing branding" (2016 winners for movies in 2015):

Overall Product Placement Award Winner: Mercedes-Benz—The German automaker appeared in 9 of the top 31 movies of 2015 in roles ranging from cameo appearances to "scene stealers." In the movie *Fifty Shades of Grey* heroine Anastasia Steele drives a Mercedes CLK. In the James Bond thriller *Spectre*, Bond is collected in the desert by a caravan of villains driving black Mercedes AMGs—quite a coup for Mercedes given that both Aston Martin and Land Rover had official promos with the movie. Mercedes had placements in *Furious 7* and *Spy* as well, and got a double dip in the movie *Focus*. As the holder of naming rights to the New Orleans Superdome, when events take place at the Dome Mercedes benefits from name exposure. In *Focus*, much of the action appears in scenes taken while actor Will Smith is attending a Super Bowl game, with the Mercedes-Benz logo clearly visible in the background. But perhaps the clincher was the tie-in between the auto company and the movie *Jurassic World*. The two have had an ongoing relationship on and off the screen since the original *Jurassic* movie appeared in 1995!

Second-place-winner Apple appeared in a number of movies, including *Daddy's Home, Sisters, Our Brand Is Crisis, The Last Witch Hunter*, and *The Intern*, but none was a box office winner. While often a winner on a Brandcameo, Apple has been cutting back on placements. Tied with Apple was Sony, appearing in *San Andreas, Chappie, War Room*, and *Hotel Transylvania*.

Achievement for Product Placements in a Single Film: Fast and Furious—This award is given for the most product placements in a single movie. The award winner is a movie about automobiles, and is full of automobile placements. Interestingly, the most notable placement is for Corona Beer. In total, *Furious* has 48 identifiable brands. In second place is the film *Focus*, another auto movie (must be something about those movies that start with an F and are about cars!). *Focus* has 41 placements. The most product placements ever recorded in a movie was in the 2001 film *Driven* starring Sylvester Stallone—102. And, of course, it was a movie about F1 auto racing. The winners were followed by *Jurassic World* (35), *San Andreas* (27), *Straight Outta Compton* (26), *Spy* (24), *Taken 3* (23), *American Sniper* (23), and *Pitch Perfect 2* (21). That is a lot of product placements!

One of the other awards handed out by brandchannel may not be something you want to brag about:

Achievement in Shameless Product Placement: Mark Wahlberg—While the Brandcameos typically go to movies, this case is different. Mark Wahlberg plays himself in the movie *Entourage*. In one scene where Wahlberg and his entourage show up in a bus, it is completely covered by the brand names Marked and Ultra Hydrate. Marked is a brand of body building supplements launched by Wahlberg himself, while he is an investor in Ultra Hydrate—a bottled water brand. The beer brand Churchkey is co-owned by the star of the movie, Adrian Grenier, and also appears in the movie. Another of Wahlberg's movies, *Daddy's Home*, is more of a product integration as the Indian motorcycle brand has an extended subplot. Indian sells a Mark Wahlberg Collection of apparel, and Wahlberg (of course) is its spokesperson. He has also worn an Indian T-shirt in promos for the movie *Ted 2* and an Indian hat in the film *Transformers: The Age of Extinction*. By the way, *Ted 2* and *Entourage* each had a total of 66 product placements and/or integrations.

So what, you might say? If companies can do product placements, why can't individuals? Can't they also be brands? Those would be very legitimate questions to ask; to answer them, we need to know if and how product placements work.

Consumers seem to be avoiding commercials at an increasing rate due to oversaturation and the fact that new technologies make it easier to skip ads, so many marketers have turned to product placements and integrations—getting the product into the program (or movie or book)—as part of the context rather than as a separate communication. The growth in this industry has shown constant increases over the past decade both in the United States and internationally and, according to PQ Media's *Global Product Placement Spending Forecast*, will continue do so in the foreseeable future. This has led PQ Media to refer to product placement as a "strategic must-have" in a company's consumer marketing mix. Indeed, for many companies, product placements are very much an integral part of their IMC strategy. As noted by Simon Hudson, there exists a continuum of product placement branded entertainment types ranging from a verbal- or visual-only placement to product integration, where the brand is woven into the plot of the film.

While it is usually the case that companies are trying to get their brands placed in TV shows or movies, sometimes they don't want them placed and take steps to stop them or have them removed. Brands like Slip 'N Slide, Pepsi, and InSinkErator have brought suit against depictions of their products in movies, and more recently, so has Budweiser. In the movie *Flight,* Denzel Washington is portrayed as an airline pilot who is a functioning alcoholic—often drinking Bud, even while behind the wheel. As one might expect, Anheuser-Busch was not happy with the association and asked Paramount Pictures Corporation to obscure or remove the Budweiser logo from the film. So far, Paramount has refused, and there doesn't appear to be much Anheuser-Busch can do about it. Unfortunately for them, movie studios are not obligated to get permission before featuring a product in a movie. Stolichnaya vodka also was unhappy with the use of its brand in the movie without permission. Not exactly the kind of placement companies strive for.

Sources: Abe Sauer, "Announcing the 2016 Brand-cameo Product Placement Awards," February 24, 2016, www.brandchannel.com; Simon Hudson, "From Product Placement to Branded Entertainment," April 12, 2016, www.hotelexecutive.com; "Budweiser Seeks Removal from 'Flight,'" November 5, 2012, www.movies.msn.com.

The lead-in to this chapter demonstrates how pervasive product placements have become, appearing everywhere from movies to television to videos and video games. Given the increasing concern with consumers' abilities to avoid advertising, advertisers have turned to other ways to get their messages in front of prospective buyers. The result of this is increased attention to getting exposure, which, in turn, has led to significant changes in the media industry. Over the past few years there has been significant growth in the use of support media—both traditional and new media forms. In many ways, the consumers' efforts to avoid commercial exposure may have had an opposite effect, as it seems ads now appear in many places not previously home to such messages.

Ads have appeared on manhole covers, inside restroom stalls, on bus shelters, in grocery stores, on hubcaps, on cell phones, and even on people's bodies. In this chapter, we review a number of support media, some that are new to the marketplace and others that have been around awhile. We discuss their relative advantages and disadvantages, how they are used, and audience measurement of each. We refer to them as **support media** because the media described in the previous chapters dominate the media strategies of large advertisers, particularly national advertisers. Support media are used to reach those people in the target market the primary media may not have effectively reached and to reinforce, or support, their messages. It is important to remember that some of these media are not used only for support, but for some companies they may be the primary or sole medium used.

You may be surprised at how many different ways there are to deliver the messages and how often you are exposed to them. Let's begin by examining the scope of the support media industry and some of the many alternatives available to marketers.

THE SCOPE OF THE SUPPORT MEDIA INDUSTRY

LO13-1

Support media are referred to by several titles, among them **alternative media**, **below-the-line media**, **nonmeasured media**, and **nontraditional media**. These terms describe a vast variety of channels used to deliver communications and to promote products and services. In this chapter we will discuss many of these media (though, as you might imagine, it would be impossible for us to discuss them all).

Many advertisers, as well as the top 100 advertising agencies, have increased their use of support media, and as new alternatives are developed, this use will continue to grow. Given the rapid emergence of a variety of new media, we will further divide support media into *traditional* and *nontraditional* support media categories. There are actually hybrids as well because some traditional media have adapted to the new media environment by updating their offerings. There is no particular necessity for this further distinction other than to demonstrate that many of the various forms of support media have been around for quite some time, while others have surfaced only recently. Let us examine some of these in more detail.

TRADITIONAL SUPPORT MEDIA

LO13-2

Out of home (OOH) advertising media encompass many advertising formats found out of the home (see Figure 13–1). As can be seen, the Outdoor Advertising Association of America (OAAA) categorizes these media as out of home—including billboards, street furniture, place-based media, and transit. As shown in Figure 13–2, billboards and street furniture together constitute the majority of the outdoor billings. Given the similarity of these forms, we will discuss them together while addressing transit and place-based media subsequently.

CHAPTER 13

FIGURE 13–1

Out of Home Media: A Diverse Cross Section of Formats Comprise Outdoor Advertising Today

Source: Reprinted with permission of Outdoor Advertising Association of America.

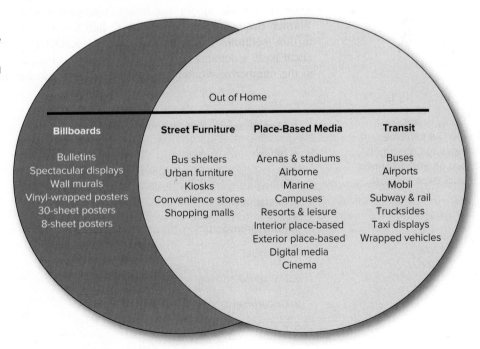

Out of Home

Billboards

Bulletins
Spectacular displays
Wall murals
Vinyl-wrapped posters
30-sheet posters
8-sheet posters

Street Furniture

Bus shelters
Urban furniture
Kiosks
Convenience stores
Shopping malls

Place-Based Media

Arenas & stadiums
Airborne
Marine
Campuses
Resorts & leisure
Interior place-based
Exterior place-based
Digital media
Cinema

Transit

Buses
Airports
Mobil
Subway & rail
Trucksides
Taxi displays
Wrapped vehicles

FIGURE 13–2

Four Major Product
Categories, 2015 Total OOH
Revenue: $7.3 Billion

Notes: Figures in millions.

Source: Outdoor Advertising
Association of America.

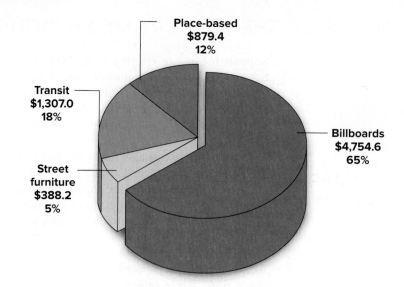

Place-based
$879.4
12%

Transit
$1,307.0
18%

Street
furniture
$388.2
5%

Billboards
$4,754.6
65%

Out of Home Advertising (OOH)

OOH advertising has probably existed since the days of cave dwellers. Both the Egyptians and the Greeks used it as early as 5,000 years ago. OOH is certainly one of the more pervasive communication forms, particularly if you live in an urban or suburban area.

While showing steady growth since 2000, OOH advertising—like most other media—saw a decline in billings during the recession but is now again on the increase with expenditures of approximately $7.3 billion in 2015—a total of approximately 5 percent of all advertising dollars.[1] The medium was once dominated by tobacco advertisers (25 percent of its $1.5 billion revenue came from cigarette advertising in 1991), so there were concerns in the industry when an agreement was reached with 46 states in November 1998 to ban all cigarette ads. Increased expenditures from local services and amusements, insurance, real estate, and telecom companies have more than made up for the losses. Companies like McDonald's, Apple, Verizon, Warner Brothers, Samsung, AT&T, and Coca-Cola are some of the top spenders in this medium. As shown in Figure 13–3, OOH continues to be used by a broad client base, a demonstration of its continued acceptance in the industry. The increase in the number of women in the work force has led to more advertising of products

1. Miscellaneous services and amusements

2. Retail

3. Media and advertising

4. Restaurants

5. Public transportation, hotels, and resorts

6. Financial

7. Insurance and real estate

8. Government, politics, and organizations

9. Communications

10. Automotive dealers and services

Source: Outdoor Advertising Association of America, 2016.

EXHIBIT 13-1

Billboards can be attention-getting

© Ray Allen/Alamy

targeted to this segment, and the increases in the number of vehicles on the road and the number of miles driven have led to increased expenditures by gas companies, food and lodging providers, and other media.

A major reason for the continued success of outdoor is its ability to remain innovative through technology. As Exhibit 13-1 shows, billboards are no longer limited to standard sizes and two dimensions; 3-D forms and extensions are now used to attract attention. Digital OOH media have also contributed to the success. Digital messages on billboards, transit signs, and in stores have allowed more advertisers to participate since messages can be changed quickly and often. In addition, it allows OOH advertising to appear in places previously unavailable, and in a timely fashion (Exhibit 13-2). You probably have been exposed to either signboards or electronic billboards at sports stadiums, in supermarkets, in the campus bookstores and dining halls, in shopping malls, on the freeways, or on the sides of buildings, from neon signs on skyscrapers in New York City to Mail Pouch Tobacco signs painted on the sides of barns in the Midwest. This is truly a pervasive medium.

Out of home advertising, particularly billboards, does have its critics. Ever since Lady Bird Johnson tried to rid the interstate highways of billboard advertising during her husband's presidency with the Highway Beautification Act of 1965, there has been controversy regarding its use. As previously noted, legislation has passed in 46 states banning the advertising of cigarettes on billboards. In addition, a number of cities and states in the United States and internationally have banned or restricted the use of billboards.

Digital Out of Home (DOOH)   One of the fastest-growing out of home industries is that of **digital out of home (DOOH) media**. DOOH media take three forms: (1) video advertising networks, which include digital video screens that appear in offices, stores, theaters, inside transit networks, and entertainment venues such as health clubs, sporting arenas, bars, and restaurants; and (2) digital billboards, or screens that transmit in LED (light-emitting diode) or LCD (liquid crystal display) technologies. Digital billboards include large boards found at sports and entertainment venues, retail locations (like malls), in transit locations (terminals, etc.), and at roadsides or large traffic locations. Place-based advertising, which is not a purely DOOH medium, often uses digital technology to send its messages. These typically include smaller signs that appear in restrooms, on stairs, on personal vehicles, and on specialty items. The global DOOH signage segment is expected to reach $20 billion by 2020 due to its ability to be creative, attract attention, and engage the consumer (see Digital and Social Media Perspective 13-1).[2]

EXHIBIT 13-2

Absolut promotes through a billboard in New York

© Jorge Vasconcelos/Flickr/Getty Images

Place-Based Out of Home Media

Several other forms of OOH advertising are also available, including aerial advertising, interior and exterior place-based, mobile boards, and more. OAAA classifies these as place-based media. Let's examine a few of these.

Aerial Advertising   Airplanes pulling banners, skywriting (in letters as high as 1,200 feet), and blimps all constitute another form of outdoor advertising available to the marketer: **aerial advertising**. Generally these media are not expensive in absolute terms and can be useful for reaching specific target markets. For example, Coppertone has often used skywriting over beach areas to promote its tanning lotions, beer companies (among others) commonly employ aerial advertising at sporting events, and

Digital and Social Media Perspective 13–1 > > >

BILLBOARDS COME INTO THE DIGITAL AGE

Imagine you are driving down the highway in your Toyota and as you glance over at a billboard a message tells you that you are driving the wrong car because the new Chevy Malibu gets better gas mileage than your car. Or imagine it is early morning and as you are driving at sunrise you see an Egg McMuffin rising on a billboard in sync with the sun (or setting with the sun if it is sunset). Now, what if you passed a different billboard and it had the ability to determine you were there and where you went afterward.

It has always been hard to ignore billboards, whether you want to or not, which is part of the reason the outdoor medium has continued to be attractive to advertisers. Now due to advances in digital technology, it may be even harder to ignore them. The growth of digital billboards (and other OOH advertising vehicles) may actually lead to consumers wanting to see—and even to interact with—a medium that many would like to see go away. (You have to admit it would be interesting to watch the McMuffin rise with the sun!) Some believe that the enhanced creativity that digital offers over traditional billboards may be putting the latter's future existence at risk.

There are a number of advantages to the digital versions. The creativity of the Egg McMuffin board is just one of many examples of the attention-getting capabilities being employed. Interestingly, McDonald's had a billboard about 10 years ago that employed the location of the sun to cast a shadow on which menu item to eat at that

time of day. The two boards were created by different agencies.

To launch the 2016 Malibu, Chevrolet and its agencies Posterscope USA—an OOH communications specialist agency—and Lamar Advertising Co. used vehicle-recognition technology that could identify certain types of vehicles and immediately generate dynamic, customized messages to the drivers. The vehicle-recognition campaign was the first of its kind, and was designed to create awareness of the Malibu's safety and fuel efficiency among other features of the car. As noted by Posterscopes's previous CEO, Helma Larkin, "By integrating vehicle-recognition technology into the campaign, we are able to deliver personalized content to drivers of competitive vehicles, increasing the likelihood that messages will be noticed and remembered." When a camera mounted on a pole next to the billboard recognizes a Ford Fusion, Toyota Camry, Nissan Altima, or Hyundai Sonata, the otherwise generic Malibu ad message shifts to a competitor-specific one, giving the driver 7 seconds to read it—and no doubt freak out!

Coke erected a "Drinkable" billboard to get potential customers attending the NCAA March Madness basketball finals to try a sample of Coke Zero. The billboard dispensed samples of the soda through 4,500 feet of straw tubing that spelled out "Taste It." By going to #OpenToTry, Coke Zero made it simple to get a taste test of the product. Coke has

---

local advertisers promote special events, sales, and the like. Exhibit 13–3 shows one of the many products, services, and/or events that have used this medium.

Mobile Billboards Another OOH medium is **mobile billboards**. Some companies paint their cars with ads; others paint trucks and vans. Still others put ads on small billboards, mount them on trailers, and drive around and/or park in the geographic areas being targeted (Exhibit 13–4). Costs depend on the area and the mobile board company's fees, though even small and large organizations have found the medium affordable. A number of studies have shown that mobile billboards can lead to a high number of impressions, while a study conducted by the Product Acceptance and Research Organization indicates that mobile ads lead to high levels of recall and readership, and were likely to have an impact on sales.[3]

A number of companies including Walmart, Home Depot, and State Farm are frequent users of mobile ads.

In-Store Media

Advertisers use **in-store media** such as in-store ads, aisle displays, store leaflets, shopping cart signage, and in-store TV to reach shoppers at the place where

© Tribune Content Agency LLC/Alamy

also developed drinkable stadium HD video boards, interactive mail kiosks, and flyers that turn into straws to further its efforts.

Perhaps one of the pioneering innovations is the billboard that can tell you have driven by and where you went afterward. Developed by Clear Channel Outdoor Americas, which has tens of thousands of billboards across the United States, and AT&T, the technology allows for tracking the movements of drivers who pass the billboards through their mobile phones. The data will assist in identifying the age and gender of persons driving by, and subsequently determine if they visit a store and where. Clear Channel and AT&T say the data will be anonymous and aggregated so individual customers can't be identified.

Digital signage companies have also become integrated with social media like Flickr, Facebook, and

Twitter. For example, a number of bars now have social media–enabled screens that they use to stage interactive games that allow customers to text answers to the displays, as well as send tweets or text messages to others in the bar (so long as they are appropriate content-wise). Tweets of specific menu or drink recommendations pop up on the indoor screens instantaneously. The Independent Coffee Network has also used Twitter and Flickr to catch the attention of customers in its stores, finding that it is effective in increasing engagement among the customers.

Both Intel and NEC have developed digital billboards with a camera inside that can identify shoppers' age and gender as they walk by or stand in front of the display. Kraft Foods and adidas have also experimented with facial recognition capabilities, and both Facebook and Google have facial recognition capabilities but claim they don't use them. The FBI used a digital billboard in Times Square (New York) to ask the public to help identify fugitives at large in the New York area; the digital capabilities of the billboard allowed for constant changing of faces.

But not everyone is happy with this new technology. Privacy advocates has always been concerned that companies will collect data from persons without their knowledge or permission—which seems to be the case. The Electronic Privacy Information Center claims that the technology has the potential to violate one's civil liberties and violates the First Amendment. But no one seems to stifle the progress!

Sources: Christopher Hall, "Digital Signage Tells You You're Driving the Wrong Car," April 19, 2016, www.digital signage today.com; Dale Buss, "Coke Zero Scores with "Drinkable Billboard at March Madness Finals," April 3, 2015, www.brandchannel.com; Tim Nudd, "An Egg McMuffin Rises with the Sun on This Tasty McDonald's Billboard," February 9, 2015, www.adweek.com.

they buy. A study by MEC Sensor and BMRB International revealed that one-third of shoppers say in-store ads influence them to make a purchase decision, 44 percent say they notice such ads, and 75 percent of those who noticed the ads said they are likely to purchase the advertised brand.[4]

EXHIBIT 13–4

An interesting and unusual example of a mobile billboard in an international setting

© Michael Belch

Trucks often serve as mobile billboards

© Outdoor Advertising Association of America

Much of the attraction of point-of-purchase media is based on figures from the Point of Purchase Advertising International (POPAI) that states that approximately two-thirds of consumers' purchase decisions are made in the store; some impulse categories demonstrate an 82 percent rate.[5] Many advertisers are spending more of their dollars where decisions are made now that they can reach consumers at the point of purchase, providing additional product information while reducing their overall marketing efforts.

Miscellaneous Out of Home Media

As shown in Figure 13–4, there are numerous OOH media available, adding to the pervasiveness of this medium. The next time you are out, take a few moments to observe how many different forms of outdoor advertising you are exposed to.

Transit Advertising

Another form of OOH advertising is **transit advertising**. Transit is targeted at the millions of people who are exposed to commercial transportation facilities, including buses, taxis, commuter trains, trolleys, airplanes, and subways.

Transit advertising has been around for a long time, but recent years have seen a renewed interest in this medium. Due in part to the increased number of women in the work force (they can be reached on their way to work more easily than at home), audience segmentation, and the fact that many people spend more time outside of the home than inside, transit continues to be a popular medium. McDonald's, Sprint, Frito-Lay, the United Way, numerous state lotteries, and others like transit's lower costs, frequency of exposures, flexibility, and point-of-sale presence. Kellogg's has found transit to be an effective medium for marketing

FIGURE 13–4

Out of Home Displays

Number of Out of Home Displays (2016)			
Billboards	**Street Furniture**	**Transit**	**Place-Based**
Bulletins	**Bus Shelters**	**Airports**	**Arena & Stadiums**
158,868	49,082	68,560	1,352
Digital Billboards	**Urban Furniture, i.e.,**	**Buses**	**Cinema**
6,700	Bus benches	205,426	34,350
Posters	Newsracks	**Subway & Rail**	**Digital Place-Based/Video**
165,606 faces	Newstands	184,078 faces	1.25 million screens
Junior Posters	Phone kiosks	**Mobile Billboards**	**Interior Place-Based, i.e.,**
33,336 faces	**Digital Urban Furniture**	1,200	Convenience stores
Walls/Spectaculars	699	**Truckside**	Health clubs
4,029		2,732 vehicles	Restaurants/bars
		Taxis/Wrapped Vehicles	**Exterior Place-Based, i.e.,**
		46,194	Airborne
		Digital Transit	Marine
		3,760	Resorts & leisures
			Shopping Malls
			30,532
			Digital Shopping Malls
			120

Source: Outdoor Advertising Association of America (OAAA), 2016.

Nutri-Grain, while the California Beef Council found that 42 percent of rail commuters in Northern California saw its beef ads inside terminals in just one month and as a result developed more positive attitudes toward beef.[6]

Types of Transit Advertising

There are actually three forms of transit advertising: (1) inside cards, (2) outside posters, and (3) station, platform, or terminal posters.

Inside Cards If you have ever ridden a commuter bus, you have probably noticed the **inside cards** placed above the seats and luggage area advertising restaurants, TV or radio stations, or a myriad of other products and services. As noted earlier, companies now advertise on digital screens in transit vehicles, which deliver news, video ads, restaurant information, and so forth. The ability to change the message and the visibility provide the advertiser with a more attention-getting medium.

Transit cards can be controversial. For example, in the New York subway system, many of the ads for chewing gum, soup, and Smokey the Bear have given way to public service announcements about AIDS, unwanted pregnancies, rape, and infant mortality. While subway riders may agree that such issues are important, many of them complain that the ads are depressing and intrusive.

Outside Posters Advertisers use various forms of outdoor transit posters to promote products and services. These **outside posters** may appear on the sides, backs, and/or roofs of buses, taxis, trains, and subway and trolley cars.

The increasing sophistication of this medium is demonstrated by a technology, developed by Vert, Inc. (a division of Clear Channel), that transforms ads on top of taxicabs into real-time animated electronic billboards. A web server that communicates with a global positioning satellite (GPS) is built into the taxi-top screen. The GPS determines the taxi's location and sends it to the local server, which then delivers the relevant ads for a particular area. A taxi traveling through a Hispanic community can have a message in Spanish, stock quotes could appear in the financial district, and so on. The message can also be changed by time of day—for example, to advertise coffee in the mornings and dinner specials later in the day. The ads appear in color in a format similar to banner ads, at 10 times the brightness of a TV screen (see Exhibit 13–5).

Station, Platform, and Terminal Posters Floor displays, island showcases, electronic signs, and other forms of advertising that appear in train or subway stations,

EXHIBIT 13–5

Electronic outside posters often appear on taxicabs

© Andrew Burton/Getty Images

airline terminals, and the like are all forms of transit advertising. As Exhibit 13–6 shows, **terminal posters** can be very attractive and attention-getting. Bus shelters often provide the advertiser with expanded coverage where other outdoor boards may be restricted. Digital signs on subway platforms have become a common sight.

Advantages and Disadvantages of OOH advertising
OOH advertising offers a number of advantages:

1. *Wide coverage of local markets.* With proper placement, a broad base of exposure is possible in local markets, with both day and night presence. Think about the millions of people exposed to billboards in Times Square!
2. *Frequency.* Because purchase cycles are typically for 30-day periods, consumers are usually exposed a number of times, resulting in high levels of frequency.
3. *Geographic flexibility.* OOH can be placed along highways, near stores, or on mobile billboards, almost anywhere that laws permit. For local advertisers, outdoor can reach people in specific geographic and/or demographic areas. Local, regional, or even national markets may be covered.
4. *Creativity.* As shown earlier, OOH ads can be very creative. Large print, colors, and other elements like digital signs attract attention.
5. *Ability to create awareness.* Because of its impact (and the need for a simple message), OOH can lead to a high level of awareness.
6. *Efficiency.* OOH usually has a very competitive CPM when compared to other media. The average CPM of OOH is often one-half of radio and far less than that of TV, magazines, and newspapers. Transit is one of the least expensive media in both relative and absolute costs.
7. *Effectiveness.* OOH advertising can be effective, as demonstrated by the California Beef example. In a study reported by BBDO advertising, 35 percent of consumers surveyed said they had called a phone number they saw on an OOH ad.[7] A study reported by Mukesh Bhargava and Naveen Donthu showed that OOH advertising can have a significant effect on sales, particularly when combined with a promotion.[8]
8. *Production capabilities.* Modern technologies have reduced production times for OOH advertising to allow for rapid turnaround time, and digital messages can be changed in minutes.
9. *Timeliness.* Many outdoor ads appear in or near shopping areas or on or in the vehicles taking customers there, thus resulting in timely exposures.

At the same time, however, there are limitations to outdoor, many of them related to its advantages:

1. *Waste coverage.* While it is possible to reach very specific audiences, in many cases the purchase of OOH results in a high degree of waste coverage. It is not likely that everyone driving past a billboard is part of the target market.
2. *Limited message capabilities.* Because of the speed with which most people pass by OOH ads, exposure time is short, so messages are limited to a few words and/or an illustration. Lengthy appeals are not likely to be effective. Some transit forms are not conducive to creative messages.
3. *Wearout.* Because of the high frequency of exposures, OOH may lead to a quick wearout. People are likely to get tired of seeing the same ad every day.
4. *Cost.* Because of the decreasing signage available and the higher cost associated with inflatables, outdoor advertising can be expensive in both an absolute and a relative sense.
5. *Measurement problems.* One of the more difficult problems of OOH advertising lies in the accuracy of measuring reach, frequency, and other effects. (As you will see in the measurement discussion, this problem is currently being addressed, though it has not been resolved.)
6. *Image problems.* OOH advertising has suffered some image problems as well as some disregard among consumers.

In sum, OOH advertising has both advantages and disadvantages for marketers. Some of these problems can be avoided with other forms of out of home advertising.

Advantages and Disadvantages of Transit Advertising In addition to sharing some of the advantages and disadvantages of other outdoor media, transit has a few more specific to this medium. Advantages of using transit advertising include the following:

1. *Exposure.* Long length of exposure to an ad is one major advantage of indoor transit forms. The average ride on mass transit is 45 minutes, allowing for plenty of exposure time. As with airline tickets, the audience is essentially a captive one, with nowhere else to go and nothing much to do. As a result, riders are likely to read the ads—more than once. A second form of exposure transit advertising provides is the absolute number of people exposed. About 9 million people ride mass transit every week, and over 10.6 billion rides are taken each year, providing a substantial number of potential viewers.[9]
2. *Frequency.* Because our daily routines are standard, those who ride buses, subways, and the like are exposed to the ads repeatedly. If you rode the same subway to work and back every day, in one month you would have the opportunity to see the ad 20 to 40 times. The locations of station and shelter signs also afford high frequency of exposure.
3. *Cost.* The CPM for transit advertising is low on a relative cost basis.

Some disadvantages are also associated with transit:

1. *Reach.* While an advantage of transit advertising is the ability to provide exposure to a large number of people, this audience may have certain lifestyles and/or behavioral characteristics that are not true of the target market as a whole. For example, in rural or suburban areas, mass transit is limited or nonexistent, so the medium is not very effective for reaching these people.
2. *Mood of the audience.* Sitting or standing on a crowded subway may not be conducive to reading advertising, let alone experiencing the mood the advertiser would like to create. Controversial ad messages may contribute to this less than positive feeling. Likewise, hurrying through an airport may create anxieties that limit the effectiveness of the ads placed there.

Measurement in Out of Home Media

LO13-4

In 2010 the OAAA announced a new audience measurement system that had been in development for the previous five years. OOH Ratings is considered to be an improvement over the traditional measure of opportunity to see, with a "likely to see" metric that can also provide demographic and ethnographic data. The new data included a combination of eye tracking, circulation, and travel survey data all combined into one rating by a coalition of research companies.[10]

A number of other sources of audience measurement and information are available:

- Competitive Media Reports provides information on expenditures on outdoor media by major advertisers.
- Experian Simmons Market Research Bureau conducts research annually for the Institute of Outdoor Advertising, providing demographic data, exposures, and the like. GfK-Mediamark Research & Intelligence (MRI) provides similar data.
- Point of Purchase Advertising International is a trade organization of point-of-purchase advertisers collecting statistical and other market information on POP advertising.
- The Outdoor Advertising Association of America (OAAA) is the primary trade association of the industry. It assists members with research, creative ideas, and more effective use of the medium and has a website at www.oaa.org. OAAA commissions outside research as well as its own—for example, the Nielsen Outdoor Advertising Studies.
- Geopath generates standard audience measurements for OOH media, providing members with demographic-specific impressions, rating points, and reach & frequency measures for over a million pieces of OOH inventory.
- The American Public Transportation Association (APTA) provides ridership statistics, studies, and other transit usage information.

PROMOTIONAL PRODUCTS MARKETING

According to the Promotional Products Association International (PPAI), **promotional products marketing** is "the advertising or promotional medium or method that uses promotional products, such as ad specialties, premiums, business gifts, awards, prizes, or commemoratives." Promotional products marketing is the more up-to-date name for what used to be called specialty advertising. **Specialty advertising** has now been provided with a new definition:

> A medium of advertising, sales promotion, and motivational communication employing imprinted, useful, or decorative products called advertising specialties, a subset of promotional products.
>
> Unlike premiums, with which they are sometimes confused (called advertising specialties), these articles are always distributed free—recipients don't have to earn the specialty by making a purchase or contribution.[11]

As you can see from these descriptions, specialty advertising is often considered both an advertising and a sales promotion medium. In our discussion, we treat it as a supportive advertising medium in the IMC program.

There are thousands of *advertising specialty* items, including ballpoint pens, coffee mugs, key rings, calendars, T-shirts, and matchbooks. Unconventional specialties such as plant holders, wall plaques, and gloves with the advertiser's name printed on them are also used to promote a company or its product; so are glassware, trophies, awards, and vinyl products. In fact, advertisers spend over $18.1 billion per year on specialty advertising items (Figure 13–5).[12]

If you stop reading for a moment and look around your desk (or bed or beach blanket), you'll probably find some specialty advertising item nearby. It may be the pen you are using, a scratch pad, or even a book cover with the campus bookstore name on it. Specialty items are used for many promotional purposes: to thank a

FIGURE 13–5

2014 Sales by Product
Category

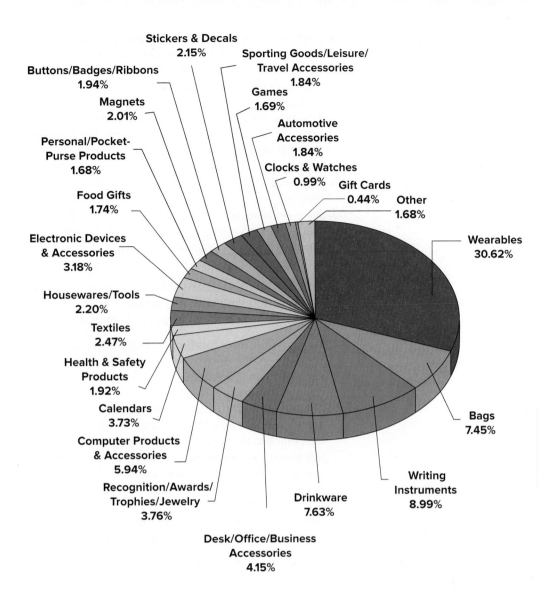

customer for patronage, keep the name of the company in front of consumers, introduce new products, or reinforce the name of an existing company, product, or service. Advertising specialties are often used to support other forms of product promotions.

Advantages and Disadvantages of Promotional Products Marketing

Like any other advertising medium, promotional products marketing offers the marketer both advantages and disadvantages. Advantages include the following:

1. *Selectivity.* Because specialty advertising items are generally distributed directly to target customers, the medium offers a high degree of selectivity. The communication is distributed to the desired recipient, reducing waste coverage.
2. *Flexibility.* As the variety of specialty items in Figure 13–5 demonstrates, this medium offers a high degree of flexibility. A message as simple as a logo or as long as is necessary can be distributed through a number of means. Both small and large companies can employ this medium for a variety of objectives limited only by their own creativity.
3. *Frequency.* Most forms of specialty advertising are designed for retention. Key chains, calendars, and pens remain with the potential customer for a long time, providing repeat exposures to the advertising message at no additional cost.

4. *Cost.* Some specialty items are rather expensive (for example, leather goods), but most are affordable to almost any size organization. While they are costly on a CPM basis when compared with other media, the high number of repeat exposures drives down the relative cost per exposure of this advertising medium.

5. *Goodwill.* Promotional products are perhaps the only medium that generates goodwill in the receiver. Because people like to receive gifts and many of the products are functional (key chains, calendars, etc.), consumers are grateful to receive them. The products also lead to a favorable impression of the advertiser.

6. *High recall.* Specialties lead to high recall of both the advertisers' name and message.

7. *Supplementing other media.* A major advantage of promotional products marketing is its ability to supplement other media. Because of its low cost and repeat exposures, the simplest message can reinforce the appeal or information provided through other forms.

Promotional products have also been used to support trade shows, motivate dealers, recognize employees, and promote consumer and sales force contests.

Disadvantages of promotional products marketing include the following:

1. *Image.* While most forms of specialty advertising are received as friendly reminders of the store or company name, the firm must be careful choosing the specialty item. The company image may be cheapened by a chintzy or poorly designed advertising form.

2. *Saturation.* With so many organizations now using this advertising medium, the marketplace may become saturated. While you can always use another ballpoint pen or scratch pad, the value to the receiver declines if replacement is too easy, and the likelihood that you will retain the item or even notice the message is reduced. The more unusual the specialty, the more value it is likely to have to the receiver.

3. *Lead time.* The lead time required to put together a promotional products message is significantly longer than that for most other media.

4. *Reach.* Use of other media—such as television—leads to greater reach.

Even with its disadvantages, promotional products marketing can be an effective medium.

Measurement in Promotional Products Marketing

Owing to the nature of the industry, specialty advertising has no established ongoing audience measurement system. Research has been conducted in an attempt to determine the impact of this medium, leading to the following results:

- 70 percent report having received a promotional product in the last 12 months.
- 88 percent recalled the advertiser's name.
- 83 percent say they like receiving promotional products.
- 38 percent say it is a constant reminder of the advertiser.
- 53 percent of those using the promotion used it once a week.
- 71 percent generally keep it.[13]

In a study conducted at Georgia Southern University, it was shown that promotional products had a positive impact on brand image, leading to a more positive perception of the business and a higher likelihood of recommending the business.[14] In addition, another study showed that by adding promotional products to an integrated media mix, brand impressions and purchase intent could be increased.[15]

The Promotional Products Association International (www.ppai.org) is the trade organization of the field. The PPAI helps marketers develop and use specialty advertising forms. It also provides promotional and public relations support for specialty advertising and disseminates statistical and educational information.

FIGURE 13–6

The Yellow Pages Page
Counts Continue to Decline

Source: Mike Blumenthal, "The
Annual Print Yellow Page Count and
Other Dead Horses," April 8, 2014,
www.blumenthalblog.com.

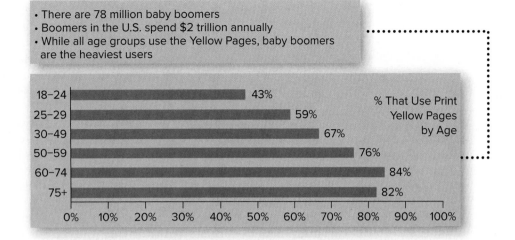

- There are 78 million baby boomers
- Boomers in the U.S. spend $2 trillion annually
- While all age groups use the Yellow Pages, baby boomers are the heaviest users

% That Use Print Yellow Pages by Age

Age	%
18–24	43%
25–29	59%
30–49	67%
50–59	76%
60–74	84%
75+	82%

Yellow Pages Advertising

How times have changed! While once a staple in almost everyone's home and a required medium for local advertisers, advertising expenditures in the **Yellow Pages** have been in serious decline. As younger consumers turn to search and online directories like Yelp to seek information, fewer and fewer are using the Yellow Pages print editions. At the same time the use of the online Yellow Pages (YP.com) has been increasing. YP.com notes that over 80 million people visited its website in 2014 where there are more than 20 million listings.[16] Leisure-related searches such as restaurant locations and movies, as well as many of those for retail and service businesses, have gone completely online, to the detriment of the hard-copy YP books.

The opportunity for the Yellow Pages does still exist, since local media advertising is still expected to reach $148 billion by 2017—an increase of 2.3 percent from 2012.[17] However, this opportunity seems to lie with the baby boomers segment, who have grown up with the Yellow Pages and remain heavy users even today. While the boomer market is an attractive and lucrative one, nevertheless, the long-range forecast for the Yellow Pages—particularly the print edition—is not promising (Figure 13–6).

The Yellow Pages are often referred to as a **directional medium** because the ads do not create awareness or demand for products or services; rather, once consumers have decided to buy, the Yellow Pages point them in the direction where their purchases can be made (Exhibit 13–7). For example, calls to businesses from Yellow Pages ads have a 50 percent conversion rate versus a 3 percent rate from online search.[18] The Yellow Pages are thus considered the final link in the buying cycle.

OTHER TRADITIONAL SUPPORT MEDIA

There are numerous other traditional ways to promote products. Some are reviewed here.

Advertising in Movie Theaters

Another method of delivering a message that is increasing quickly (to the dismay of many) is the use of movie theaters to promote

CHAPTER 13

products and/or services. Commercials shown before the film and previews, with both local and national sponsorships, are now regularly shown in movie theaters. In addition, ads in theater lobbies, at kiosks, and on popcorn tubs and drink cups are used. Automotive, food, and package-goods companies and regional and local companies are just some of the product categories that find this medium attractive. The growth rate of the number of theaters showing a commercial before the movie has increased steadily since the 1980s. Movie theater ad sales exceeded $716 million in 2015.[19]

Consumer reaction to ads in movie theaters is mixed. A number of earlier studies have shown that most people think these ads are annoying or very annoying, although now people may be becoming more used to them. The Cinema Advertising Council (CAC) reported that 63 percent of moviegoers say they do not mind ads before the movie starts.[20] Another CAC study indicated that 72 percent of moviegoers who recalled an ad in cinema had not seen the ad on TV. Of those who had seen both TV and cinema ads, 32 percent prefer the cinema ad.[21] On the other hand, many consumers complain that having paid for a ticket, they shouldn't have to sit through ads and/or commercials.

Nevertheless, a number of products and brands have used this advertising medium, including Allstate, BMW, Cadillac, Kmart, Old Navy, and Taco Bell, among others (Exhibit 13–8). Numerous brands have developed commercials specifically for the purpose of being shown before movies. In addition, a research study commissioned by one in-theater advertising broker showed that the ads were three times more likely to be remembered than TV ads.[22]

Advantages of Movie Theater Advertising   Movies provide a number of advantages to advertisers, including the following:

1. *Exposure.* While the number of people attending movies declined slightly in 2015 the audience continues to be substantial. Ticket sales were over $11 billion per year.[23]
2. *Emotional attachment.* One report found that 41.5 percent of moviegoers say they become emotionally attached to cinema ads and brands—more than the ads on the broadcasts of the *Super Bowl, Summer Olympics, World Series,* or the *Oscars.*[24] One neuromarketing research study showed movie-ad viewers to be much more engaged than those watching TV spots.[25]
3. *Cost.* The cost of advertising in a theater varies from one setting to the next. However, it is low in terms of both absolute and relative costs per exposure.

EXHIBIT 13–8

An M&M's bus driver asks moviegoers to silence their cell phones during this movie trailer ad that ends with the tagline: "movies are better with M."

Source: M&M's by Mars, Inc. and BBDO, New York

4. *Attention.* Movie watchers pay attention to the ads shown in theaters. Research indicates that cinema ads reach many consumers who say they are usually ad avoiders. These consumers are 157 percent more likely to see an ad in a movie than any other medium.[26]
5. *Clutter.* Lack of clutter is another advantage offered by advertising in movie theaters. Most theaters limit the number of ads.
6. *Proximity.* Since many theaters are located in or adjacent to shopping malls, potential customers are "right next door." (Of moviegoers, 74 percent combine the activity with dining out.[27])
7. *Segmentation.* A key advantage of movie advertising is the ability to target specific demographic segments. The profile of the moviegoer is above-average in education and affluence. The movie titles and ratings enable advertisements to reach specific groups.
8. *Quality.* The high-quality production including sight and sound allow more creative and attention getting ads.
9. *Integration.* Those who download movies online are actually more likely to attend a movie than is the typical adult.[28]

Disadvantages of Movie Theater Advertising   Some of the disadvantages associated with movie theaters as advertising media follow:

1. *Irritation.* Perhaps the major disadvantage is that many people do not wish to see advertising in these media. A number of studies suggest these ads may create a high degree of annoyance. If true, this dissatisfaction may carry over to the product itself, to the movies, or to the theaters.
2. *Cost.* While the cost of advertising in local theaters has been cited as an advantage because of the low rates charged, ads exposed nationally are often as much as 20 percent higher than an equal exposure on television. CPMs also tend to be higher than in other media.

While viewers seemingly either like or dislike cinema ads, it seems they are here to stay.

NONTRADITIONAL SUPPORT MEDIA

Branded Entertainment

As noted in the lead-in to this chapter, one of the major changes (along with the growth of social and mobile media) that has occurred in the area of integrated marketing communications over the past few years is the enormous growth associated with **branded entertainment**. Branded entertainment is a form of advertising that blends marketing and entertainment through television, film, music talent, and technology. Essentially, the goal is to use entertainment media to gain consumers' attention and exposure to products and/or brands. It is extremely difficult to place a dollar amount on branded entertainment, but there is no doubt that its use continues to increase yearly.

Let's take a look at the ways companies use branded entertainment. Simon Hudson, Endowed Chair in Tourism and Hospitality at the University of South Carolina, suggests that there is a subtle difference between product placements and branded entertainment that many overlook and the two should be considered at opposite ends of a continuum.[29] On one end of the continuum are product placements, which Hudson describes as only a visual or verbal passive placement of the brand, with no integration into the program, movie, and so on. At the other end is branded entertainment, in which the brand is woven into the story line at a much higher level of integration. At the same time the effectiveness of the strategy chosen (placement vs. branded entertainment) will be impacted by the media used, the brand characteristics, consumer attitudes toward brand placements, and other factors, including regulations.

Product Placements While **product placements** account for only a small portion of major advertisers' budgets, the use of this medium has increased tremendously in recent years and is likely to continue to do so. Estimates are that in 2015 paid product placement spending in the United States reached $6.0 billion—a growth of 13.2 percent.[30] It should be noted, however, that it is difficult to assess the accuracy of these figures, as many product placements are free or provided in exchange for trade. Product placement agencies contend that as much as 70 to 95 percent of their placements are for trade.[31] An in-depth study of the product placement industry by Russell and Belch supports this contention.[32] Industry analysts expect this trend to continue as placements move from traditional media to alternative media, as video recorder growth sales continue (allowing for increased avoidance of commercials), and as consumers' lifestyles change. Placements have caught on in Europe; the UK has now approved product placements on television, imposing more restrictions than in the United States.[33]

Interestingly, product placements are not a new phenomenon; placements are known to have existed as early as the 1930s and were commonly employed via soap operas in the 1950s. However, it was not until the turn of the century that the number of placements skyrocketed. Today, product placements are used to gain exposure by numerous companies large and small (Exhibit 13–9) and are a very important part of the IMC strategy for companies like Under Armour, adidas, Triumph Motorcycles, and Anheuser-Busch (just to name a few in addition to those mentioned in the chapter lead-in). Much of the logic behind product placement is that since the placement is embedded in the script or program setting, it cannot be avoided, thereby increasing exposure. Given the lack of intrusiveness of the placement, consumers may not have the same negative reactions to it as they may have to a commercial. Further, research has demonstrated that association with a program or movie—or particularly with a celebrity—may enhance the image of the product and, in some instances, lead to increased engagement and sales.[34]

Given the intense growth in the number of product placements, some marketers are concerned that placements may be becoming too common. It is rare to watch a movie or TV show without being exposed to one or more placements. Given the obvious attempt to gain exposure in many of these, placements may be becoming more obvious; consumers may perceive them more like ads and, as a result, they may have less impact on the viewer. Some industry watchdogs have called for more regulation of placements, contending that they blur the lines between advertising and programming and therefore may be deceptive. The FCC is currently considering this possibility.

At this time, however, product placements continue to increase both in number and in dollar amounts. As noted earlier, some films have included over 60 placements in less than a two-hour movie. In addition, placements are appearing in media and situations never before imagined, including music videos, video games, and books. Subway, Coca-Cola, and even President Obama (when running for president) have used product placements in video games, while Oreos, Hershey Kisses, and Netflix have received plugs in books. Some of these were paid placements; others were not.

Product Integration A more involved form of product placements actually leads to the placement being integrated throughout the program content and/or script. In **product integration** the product is woven throughout the program or becomes the program itself. Like product placements, product integrations are on the increase as the networks continue to search for new program content, and the proliferation of cable media channels affords

EXHIBIT 13–9

GM frequently uses product placement as seen in this ad featuring the Chevy Volt which was featured in the Disney movie *Tomorrowland*

Source: General Motors

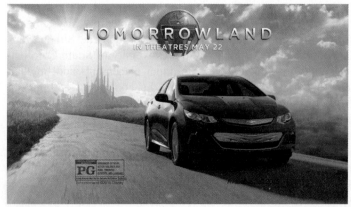

marketers with numerous integration opportunities. For example, on an episode of *Modern Family*, much of the show was devoted to the family's bumbling of the father's request for an Apple iPad for his birthday and their frantic efforts to find one (Exhibit 13–10).

When the family actually obtained one, the program ended with the father sitting on the couch with the iPad in his lap, enjoying the product.[35] In another instance, In the movie *Avengers*, 20 minutes of the action takes place in downtown Seoul, Korea, thanks to a contribution from the city of $3.6 million for production costs.[36] Under Armour collaborated with 20th Century Fox on production of the movie *The Martian* and created a microsite around star Matt Damon's training regimen.

EXHIBIT 13–10

An iPad Placement in *Modern Family*

© Eric McCandless/ABC via Getty Images

Advertainment   The creation of video and/or music content by an advertiser in an attempt to entertain viewers while advertising their products is known as **advertainment**. For example, Beyoncé's viral "I Was Here" music video designed to promote World Humanitarian Day was created by Droga5—an agency specializing in the creation of advertainment. The same agency created *Follow Phoenix* to promote Spotify's feature that allows users to follow musicians on their service with the click of a button. The 18-minute documentary, which lived on YouTube's homepage for a day, followed the band *Phoenix* for 24 hours in segments in an attempt to get more subscribers to Spotify. Perhaps the most classic piece of advertainment was Red Bull–sponsored Stratos space jump (Exhibit 13–11). The live stream of skydiver Felix Baumgartener jumping from 127,900 feet and landing on his feet while breaking the record for the world's highest free fall was viewed live by 7.1 million viewers. That was way back in 2012!

EXHIBIT 13–11

Red Bull sponsored the Stratos space jump

© Jay Nemeth/ZUMA Press/Newscom

Another form of advertainment is that of **advergames**. A number of companies including Chipotle and Burger King have developed online games designed to promote their products through electronic games. These games are designed to advertise products, brands, or organizations across social media, company websites, and mobile apps. For example, the Chipotle game called *Food With Integrity* guided players through 4 worlds and 20 levels. Those who made it through were rewarded with a "buy one, get one free" offer at Chipotle restaurants. The game led to 6.5 million users on YouTube in two weeks and a sales spike. On the flip side, the game (as well as those from other companies) has come under attack from some watchdog groups such as the Berkeley Studies Media Group and Bath University's Institute for Policy Research, among others, for being deceptive because those who played the games were not aware it was an advertisement.[37] Numerous other companies have created advergames with the purpose of getting potential consumers involved with their brand.

Content Sponsorship   Rather than developing their own content, some advertisers agree to sponsor specific programs, receiving product placements, integration, and promotions in return. HGTV offers sponsorships to companies built around remodeling, gardening, home decorating, and more. Heineken has collaborated with the FIFA, and Rolex with the ATP World Tennis Tour. North Face had a significant content sponsorship in the Masters of Snowboarding webcast, and The Food Network and Travel Channel offer a variety of sponsorship opportunities. Turner Broadcasting offers content sponsorship opportunities on the Cartoon Network and Boomerang as well as some of its other channels. Content sponsorships are also common on the Internet;

Calvin Klein and *Vanity Fair* and One a Day and *Eating Well* are just two examples of collaborations.

Ad-Supported Video on Demand (VOD)   VODs are specialized content programs offered online and by some cable TV networks that are developed by advertisers and provided to the cable operators for free. For example, General Motors produced a short feature on the history of the Corvette to be shown on CNN through Time Warner and Comcast's VOD channels. MTV launched a series called *How to Show* in which musicians, athletes, and celebrities offer the "tricks of their trades" (the U.S. Air Force was the first advertiser). Pinkbike offers hundreds of biking videos online. A number of TV shows have been made available as well; the San Diego Zoo provides a video tour to San Diego cable subscribers. A study conducted by *IPSOS* showed that running VOD ads in conjunction with regular TV advertising (versus just TV ads alone) could result in higher ad recall, purchase intent, and likelihood of talking about the brand with family and friends, as well as searching for the brand online and visiting the brand's website than TV ads alone.[38]

Others   While other forms of branded entertainment continue to develop through wireless, mobile, and "branded locations," space does not allow us to discuss each in detail. Suffice it to say that the use of branded entertainment continues to increase and will continue to do so as more and more technological innovations provide opportunities.

Advantages of Branded Entertainment   A number of advantages of branded entertainment have been suggested:

1. *Exposure.* In regard to product placements, a large number of people see movies each year (close to 2 billion admissions per year). The average film is estimated to have a life span of three and one-half years (with 75 million exposures), and most moviegoers are very attentive audience members. When this is combined with the home video market and network and cable TV (including HBO, Showtime, and the Movie Channel), the potential exposure for a product placed in a movie and on television is enormous. And this form of exposure is not subject to zapping, at least not in the theater. High exposure numbers are also offered for TV placements, based on the ratings and the possibility to direct the ad to a defined target market.
2. *Frequency.* Depending on how the product is used in the movie (or program), there may be ample opportunity for repeated exposures (many, for those who like to watch a program or movie more than once). For example, if you are a regular watcher of the programs containing placements and/or integrations, you will be exposed to the products placed therein a number of times. Syndication will result in additional exposures.
3. *Support for other media.* Branded entertainment supports other promotional tools. A trend is to have the client that is placing the product cross-promote the product and movie tie-in in multiple media venues. As noted, the tie-ins reinforce and are reinforced by ads and commercials. It is now very common for advertisers to tie in to movies (see the lead-in to this chapter.)
4. *Source association.* In Chapter 6 we discussed the advantages of source identification. When consumers see their favorite TV celebrities or movie stars using certain brands, the association may lead to a favorable product image or even to sales. In one study of 524 8- to 14-year-olds, 75 percent stated that they notice when brands are placed on their favorite shows, and 72 percent said that seeing a favorite character using a brand makes them want to purchase that brand.[39] Another study among adults showed that one-third of viewers said they try a product after seeing it on a TV show or movie.[40]
5. *Cost.* While the cost of branded entertainment may range from free samples to hundreds of thousands of dollars, the latter is an extreme. The CPM for this

form of advertising can be very low, owing to the high volume of exposures it generates. For many products, like the Apple iPad in the *Modern Family* episode, the placements may be free because they save the TV or movie producers the expense of having to pay for the cost of the products.

6. *Recall.* A number of firms have measured the impact of product placements on next-day recall. Results ranged, but most show recall is higher than for TV commercials.

7. *Bypassing regulations.* In the United States as well as many foreign countries, some products are not permitted to advertise on television or to specific market segments. Product placements and integrations have allowed the cigarette and liquor industries to have their products exposed, circumventing these restrictions. For example, in the popular cable TV show *Jersey Shore*, in one scene a sack of Marlboro cigarettes washed up onto the beach, raising the specter of a placement. Philip Morris disclaimed any involvement.[41] Recently there have been attempts to control the bypassing of regulations. The Marin Institute, an alcohol industry watchdog group, filed suit against Budweiser for its tie-ins to the movie *The Wedding Crasher*, arguing that the movie encouraged underage drinking. Spirits manufacturers Diageo, Bacardi USA, and Brown-Forman have also been named in lawsuits for similar reasons.[42]

8. Other companies have been accused of advertising junk foods to kids through placements, and—as noted—through video games.[43]

9. *Acceptance.* Studies have shown that viewers are accepting of product placements and in general evaluate them positively, though some products (alcohol, guns, cigarettes) are perceived as less acceptable. Other studies report similar results, with one showing that as many as 80 percent of consumers say they have a positive attitude toward placements.[44] In a study conducted with tweens, 43 percent said they found placements to be funny, 39 percent found them to be informative, and 35 percent found them entertaining and interesting.[45] A study by *eMarketer* reported similar results.[46]

10. *Targeting.* Content sponsorships and VOD may effectively reach potential customers with a strong interest in the subject matter (i.e., fashion, football, biking).

Disadvantages of Branded Entertainment   Some disadvantages are also associated with branded entertainment:

1. *High absolute cost.* While the CPM may be very low for various forms of branded entertainment, the absolute costs may be very high, pricing some advertisers out of the market. The increased demand branded entertainment, coupled with the rising emphasis by the studios on cross-promotions, drives costs up considerably. A study conducted by the National Association of Advertisers indicated that 79 percent of advertisers believe that the costs of branded entertainment deals are too high.[47] Some companies have ceased using this form of promotion citing the rising costs.

2. *Time of exposure.* The way some products are exposed to the audience has an impact, but there is no guarantee viewers will notice the product. Some product placements are more conspicuous than others. When the product is not featured prominently, the advertiser runs the risk of not being seen (although, of course, the same risk is present in all forms of media advertising).

3. *Limited appeal.* The appeal that can be made in some of these media forms is limited. There is no potential for discussing product benefits or providing detailed information. Rather, appeals are limited to source association, use, and enjoyment. The endorsement of the product is indirect, and the flexibility for product demonstration is subject to its use in the medium.

4. *Lack of control.* In many movies, the advertiser has no say over when and how often the product will be shown. Many companies have found that their placements in movies did not work as well as expected. Fabergé developed an entire

Christmas campaign around its Brut cologne and its movie placement, only to find the movie was delayed until February. Others have had their placements cut from the script.

5. *Public reaction.* Many TV viewers and moviegoers are incensed at the idea of placing ads in programs or movies. These viewers want to maintain the barrier between program content and commercials. If the placement is too intrusive, they may develop negative attitudes toward the brand. The increased use of placements and integrations has led many consumers to be annoyed by what they consider to be crass commercialization. The FTC has explored options for limiting placements without consumer notification, though they have not sought increased regulation to date. Still others are upset about programs such as *Undercover Boss* in which a CEO goes undercover in his or her own company to see how his employees work. Critics contend that these shows are nothing more than public relations disguised as programming.

6. *Competition.* The appeal of branded entertainment has led to increased competition to get one's product placed or integrated, increasing demand and costs. As noted, the number of product placements seems to be expanding exponentially.

7. *Negative placements.* Some products may appear in movie scenes that are disliked by the audience or create a less than favorable mood or reflect poorly on the brand. For example, in the movie *Missing*, a very good, loyal father takes comfort in a bottle of Coke, while a Pepsi machine appears in a stadium where torturing and murders take place—not a good placement for Pepsi. Emerson—the manufacturer of the garbage disposal brand In-Sink-Erator—sued NBC for showing a cheerleader getting her hand mangled in the program *Heroes*. NBC never received permission from Emerson to show the brand.

8. *Clutter.* The rapid growth of branded entertainment tie-ins has led to an overwhelming number of placements and integrations as noted previously. Like other forms of advertising, too many placements and integrations will eventually lead to clutter and loss of effectiveness.

Measurement in Branded Entertainment With the rapid growth in branded entertainment have come a number of research studies and companies attempting to monitor and measure the impact of this media form. At this time, there is no one accepted standard used by advertisers or industry members.[48] However, a number of high-profile companies now offer services in this area, including those listed below.

- *Nielsen Media Research.* The TV ratings company currently tracks product placements on network television. The company has plans to track cable programs in the near future.
- *Brandchannel Product Placement Watch.* While not specifically a measurement company, brandchannel provides up-to-date information as to what is currently going on in the branded entertainment industry including the annual Brandcameo Product Placement Awards.
- *Rentrak.* The branded entertainment measurement service and product integration valuation company iTVX have combined efforts to measure Results-Oriented-Integration. The method values the quality of each hundredth of a second of an integration, and then translates them into a Product Placement/ Commercial Cost Ratio to value the integration by comparing it to the value of a commercial.

Guerrilla Marketing

In addition to branded entertainment, another nontraditional way that advertisers are now attempting to reach consumers is referred to by a variety of names, including guerrilla marketing, stealth, street, buzz, ambush, or viral marketing. Whatever it is called, there seems to be no end in sight to where advertisers will attempt to reach you. While previously targeted primarily to college students and others of the same age group, these efforts have now been expanded to reach additional audiences as well. Guerrilla marketers have benefited by technology in that they can be even more creative, as well as the fact that cell phones now have cameras, and through social media viewers can send pictures to others instantly.

A variety of other well-known companies have used guerrilla tactics. Target rented an entire hotel during Fashion Week in New York, throwing open the curtains of exterior room windows to reveal 66 dancers clad in Day-Glo skeleton suits to catch the attention of eventgoers. Panasonic built a 9-foot-tall pigeon to promote the launch of a new camera, and Amnesty International painted hands on a manhole grate to make it appear someone was jailed underneath.

Some marketers wonder if the guerrilla tactics are being taken too far. To promote the movie *Dead Man Down*, a viral agency tagged a scene with two men fighting on the floor of an elevator to the shock and chagrin of unsuspecting onlookers. In another, the floor seemingly falls out of an elevator while riders are in it (of course, there was a glass bottom). To promote Carlsberg beer, an unsuspecting man is aroused from his sleep by a friend who says he is desperate for money and asks him to bring $400 to a seedy bar. When the friend delivers, everyone raises a glass to salute friendship while it is all being caught on tape.

The stunts often go viral, but they are often very expensive to produce, risky, and sometimes even dangerous. Robert Thompson, a professor of popular culture at Syracuse University, thinks that the pranks may have gone "over the top."[49] Many others agree.

Miscellaneous Other Media

The variety of options for placing ads appears endless. Obviously, we have reported on only a few of these. Chapter 15 will discuss a few more, specifically online vehicles. Before leaving this chapter, however, we would like to mention a few of the faster-growing and more widely used options.

- *Parking lot ads.* An out of home medium showing increased growth is that of parking lot signage. From signs on cart docks to painting the walls of indoor parking garages, more companies are finding this medium attractive—particularly for point-of-purchase items. The ads reach a variety of demographics, depending on where they are placed. PepsiCo is just one of a number of companies employing this medium.

- *Gas station pump ads.* Screens appearing on gas pumps now reach you while you are pumping gas. What else do you have to do?

- *Place-based media.* The idea of bringing the advertising medium to the consumers wherever they may be underlies the strategy behind place-based media. TV monitors and magazine racks have appeared in classrooms, doctors' offices, and health clubs, among a variety of other locations. PRN (the Premiere Retail Network) has TV channels in more than 10,000 locations, including Walmart, Costco, Best Buy, and Sam's Clubs in the United States, reaching an estimated 237 million consumers a month, and is now a $1.7 billion a year industry.[50] Place-based media have become a profitable venture and an attractive alternative for media buyers. Many advertisers, particularly pharmaceutical companies, have found place-based media an effective way to reach their markets. McDonald's now has a McDonald's TV Channel in its stores. Nielsen, Experian/Simmons, GfK MRI, and others all provide audience reports. A study conducted by Millward Brown regarding customers' reactions to video ads at checkout counters in grocery stores indicated that over 70 percent of customers said they would watch the screen while in the checkout lines, 78 percent said the screens caught their attention, and 85 percent said the screens were entertaining and pleasant to watch.[51]

- *Others.* Just a few other examples of the use of support media: Coca-Cola installed 1,000 feet of light boxes in the Atlanta subway to show motion picture ads for Dasani; Muzak, a provider of background music, teamed with Tyme

EXHIBIT 13–12

Advertising on people's bodies is becoming more common

© Marmaduke St. John/Alamy

ATMs to broadcast ads at bank ATM sites; ads now appear on luggage conveyors at some airports, on MetroCards, on hubcaps, in elevators, on bowling balls, bike wheels, in people's homes, and on fruit. People are even allowing ads to be placed on their bodies, including their heads, necks, and thighs. A store in Kentucky offers a 20 percent discount to shoppers with the store's name tattooed in a visible location on the body, while the New Zealand Tourism Bureau uses its head (Exhibit 13–12). There are many other examples, as is demonstrated in Exhibit 13–13 (at least he earned something from the fight!).

Advantages and Disadvantages of Miscellaneous Alternative Media   Advantages of alternative media include the following:

- *Awareness and attention.* Perhaps the major advantage of these tactics is their ability to attract attention. Given their novelty and the nontraditional locations in which they appear, they are likely to create awareness and gain attention.
- *Cost-efficiencies.* Because of the nontraditional nature of alternative media, many advertisers are using media not previously used for advertising, or that, in general, do not require high expenditures. As such, the absolute and relative costs are not yet that high.
- *Targeting.* Depending on the tactic used, the campaign can be very targeted. It can be exposed only to a specific event, location, age, or interest group.

Disadvantages of alternative media include the following:

- *Irritation.* Unless the advertiser is careful, advertising placed in the wrong medium may have a negative impact, resulting in irritation, negative attitudes toward the advertiser, or even opportunities for the competitor. When Microsoft logos were painted on sidewalks, the city and consumers were not impressed and Microsoft was fined. One of its competitors gained significant public relations benefits when the company announced it would be happy to remove the paintings. The City of New York was not very happy with Snapple when the company's giant Popsicle started to melt and created a flood in Union Square.
- *Wearout.* For now, many of these campaigns are novel and unique and are attracting consumer interest. As the number of efforts increases, however, there is the potential to lose the uniqueness associated with them.

EXHIBIT 13–13

Ads often appear in the strangest places

© AP Images

Summary

This chapter introduced you to the vast number of support media available to marketers. These media, also referred to as nontraditional or alternative media, are just a few of the many ways advertisers attempt to reach their target markets. We have barely scratched the surface here. Support media include out of home advertising (outdoor, in-store, and transit), promotional products, and movie theater advertising, among many others. The fastest-growing area is that of branded entertainment, including product placements, product integrations, and others.

Support media offer a variety of advantages. Cost, ability to reach the target market, and flexibility are just a few of those cited in this chapter. In addition, many of the media discussed here have effectively demonstrated the power of their specific medium to get results.

But each of these support media has disadvantages. Perhaps the major weakness with most is the lack of audience measurement and verification. Unlike many of the media discussed earlier in this text, most nontraditional media do not provide audience measurement figures. So the advertiser is forced to make decisions without hard data or based on information provided by the media.

As the number and variety of support media continue to grow, it is likely the major weaknesses will be overcome. When that occurs, these media may no longer be considered nontraditional or alternative.

Key Terms

support media 454
alternative media 455
below-the-line media 455
nonmeasured media 455
nontraditional media 455
out of home (OOH) advertising 455
digital out of home media 457
aerial advertising 457

mobile billboard 458
in-store media 458
transit advertising 460
inside cards 461
outside posters 461
terminal posters 462
promotional products marketing 464
specialty advertising 464

Yellow Pages 467
directional medium 467
branded entertainment 469
product placement 470
product integration 470
advertainment 471
advergame 471

Discussion Questions

1. Discuss some recent examples of product placements and/or integrations. Describe the context in which they were used, and how they intended to reach their target markets. Explain where these placements and/or integrations would fit on Hudson's branded entertainment continuum. (LO 13-4)

2. Place-based advertising has continued to expand to a variety of locations. Discuss some of the advantages and disadvantages of this medium. (LO 13-3)

3. What is in store for the Yellow Pages? Will this medium continue to survive in the future? Explain what the Yellow Pages must do to continue to exist. (LO 13-1)

4. Discuss some of the advantages and disadvantages of branded entertainment and give examples of both good and bad uses of this medium. (LO 13-3)

5. There are some who predict that traditional outdoor ads like billboards may soon cease to exist, in part due to the rapid growth of digital signage. Take a position in support of or opposition to this prediction, supporting your argument with examples. (LO 13-1)

6. Content sponsorship has been on the increase in a variety of media. Give examples of sponsorships in different media and explain why their use is increasing. (LO 13-3)

7. Explain why marketers have increased their use of product placements and integrations. Do you think that product placements and integrations are effective? Explain your answer. (LO 13-2)

8. Digital advertising media seem to be more and more effective, but at the same time, more and more controversial. Explain why both of these situations have arisen. (LO 13-2)

9. Why has the use of guerrilla marketing been on the increase? Take a position as to whether or not this form of marketing has become controversial, and explain whether or not this criticism is warranted. (LO 13-2)

10. What are some of the advantages and disadvantages of promotional products? What are some of the situations in which promotional products may be most valuable to marketers? (LO 13-2)

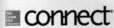 Digital users can access their personalized and adaptive SmartBook, Ad Forum Video Cases, and interactive exercises to review chapter concepts.

14 Direct Marketing

© SkyMall/Splash News/Newscom

LEARNING OBJECTIVES

LO1 Define direct marketing.

LO2 Discuss the role of direct marketing in an IMC program.

LO3 Identify strategies and tactics in the use of direct marketing.

LO4 Compare the advantages and disadvantages of direct marketing.

SKYMALL—WILL FLYING EVER BE THE SAME?

If you have taken a flight lately, you may have noticed that something is missing (besides the service!). If you look in the pocket in the seatback in front of you, there used to be a SkyMall catalog. For 25 years, when you got bored you could reach into the pocket, take out the catalog, and browse through hundreds of items you might not find anywhere else. For example, where would you find the Garden Yeti character shown in the photo in this lead-in? But, for now at least, the catalog is gone and boredom is back.

Where else could you find a shoulder saddle to carry a toddler, or a dry-erase board that can stick to any surface? Where would you to go to look for a super-slim neck pillow, a compression shirt that squeezes in your bulging belly—or a framed photo that spells out the names of colleges? If your name is Bob, you may have trouble finding a T-shirt specifically made for you and others named Bob. (The last four of these were the hottest sellers from the catalog in the last two years before it went away.)

At one time the SkyMall reached over 600 million air travelers, offering the captured audience something to do, and buy, while they had plenty of time to kill. Just a few years ago, SkyMall reported revenue of $27.6 million for the first three quarters, with the most profitable quarter—which usually accounts for approximately 40 percent of the yearly business—coming up. Then a year or so later the company was in debt and gone. What happened?

The Federal Aviation Administration (FAA) for one thing. When the FAA eased restrictions on the use of portable electronic devices such as smartphones and tablets, SkyMall felt the pinch. And now that airlines offer wireless Internet access on about 50 percent of their flights, passengers aren't searching for something to read or shop for. Sales fell by over 50 percent in one year. Others claim that SkyMall was a dinosaur and that time had passed it by just as it did the Montgomery Wards and Sears catalogs. Then there are those who contend that print catalogs are dying and will soon cease to exist.

But SkyMall was no ordinary catalog. It was a cultural icon of "Why didn't I think of that?" products. It was regularly referred to on television series such as *Breaking Bad, Weeds,* and *How I Met Your Mother,* among others. Is the catalog business that bad off?

For years, catalogs have come through the mail. Montgomery Ward published his first catalog (one page) in 1875, and eight years later his "Wish Book" that contained over 10,000 items and was over 240 pages long. The Sears & Roebuck Company (Sears) published its first catalog in 1894, and by the next year it contained over 300 pages. As noted by Charles Nicholls, the print catalog had "interruptive value" because it arrived in the mailbox. It also was convenient since it can be read in front of the TV, in bed, or wherever and whenever one pleases. Because it often lies on the table or is kept nearby on a shelf for an extended time, it is revisited and is an instant source of information. Research has demonstrated the success of the print catalog over the years, indicating that consumers who receive a catalog in the mail buy twice as often as those who don't.

But studies by research companies Adobe and Harris Interactive have shown that mobile shopping apps are beginning to take on the role of the catalog, with as many as 40 percent of tablet and smartphone users stating that they have retail apps. Not only do they have them, but they like them and use them in much the same way print catalogs are used. Many of those surveyed said the shopping apps created a stronger connection to the retailer, and that if the retailer did not offer this service they would consider the store to be "old-fashioned."

So, were the SkyMall catalog and, for that matter, all catalogs as we knew them relics of the past? Not quite yet. While digital catalogs offer some distinct advantages over print, the traditional versions still have their value. And even though retailers have found that digital catalog sales are on the increase, they have also found that it is more difficult to cross-sell products or get add-on sales than it is through print versions. After a decline in catalog printings from 2013 to 2014, print versions were on the increase and the Direct Marketing Association projects a 3.1 percent growth rate in the coming years.

But what about SkyMall? There is good news there as well! It appears that all of SkyMall's woes couldn't be attributed to what pundits said they were. Apparently, the company's losses accumulated due to other financial dealings that had little to do with the catalog, and SkyMall was purchased in a bankruptcy auction about a year later.

The new company said it would modernize the catalog, increasing its digital presence, and would soon be back on the market. After all, where else could you buy a Garden Yeti that comes in three sizes—21 or 28 inches tall, or 6 feet and 150 pounds (for only $2,250 + shipping)? A must have!!

Sources: Jessica Durando, "SkyMall Is Back!" May 29, 2015, www.usatoday.com; Jeff Goldman, "N.J. Company to Try to Revive SkyMall Catalog Found in Back of Airline Seat Pocket, Report Says," April 3, 2015, www.nj.com; Hugo Martin, "SkyMall Loses Its Captive Audience," *LA Times,* April 27, 2014, pp. B1, B7; "Are Shopping Apps Taking on the Role of Catalogs," January 23, 2013, www.eMarketer.

The discussion of the SkyMall catalog in the lead-in to this chapter in many ways reflects the nature of the direct-marketing industry today. For years consumers have relied on and used direct-marketing tools like catalogs and direct mail to do some of their shopping. Then a number of factors occurring in the environment forced direct marketers to adapt, or die. Like SkyMall, in most cases, the industry has responded quite effectively. Direct marketing has now become a very important component of the IMC program, often working with other media as opposed to attempting to be a stand-alone marketing tool. It is important to realize that there are numerous direct-marketing *tools* that can be used to reach one's target market. This chapter will discuss these direct media, their advantages and disadvantages, and their role in the IMC process.

DIRECT MARKETING

While many companies rely on a variety of promotional-mix elements to move their products and services through intermediaries, an increasing number are going directly to the consumer. These companies believe that whereas promotional-mix tools such as advertising, sales promotion, support media, and personal selling are effective in creating brand image, conveying information, and/or creating awareness, going direct can generate an immediate behavioral response. Direct marketing is a valuable tool in the integrated communications program, though it usually seeks somewhat different objectives.

In this chapter, we discuss direct marketing and its role as a communications tool. For many companies and organizations, direct marketing is a key element in their IMC program, and for some marketers it has become the medium of choice for reaching consumers. We begin by defining direct marketing and then examine direct-marketing media and their use in the overall communications strategy. The section concludes with a basis for evaluating the direct-marketing program and a discussion of the advantages and disadvantages of this marketing tool.

Defining Direct Marketing

As noted in Chapter 1, **direct marketing** is a system of marketing by which organizations communicate directly with target customers to generate a response or transaction. This response may take the form of an inquiry, a purchase, or even a vote. The Direct Marketing Association (DMA) defines direct marketing as

> an interactive system of marketing which uses one or more advertising media to effect a measurable response and/or transaction at any location.[1]

First we must distinguish between direct marketing and direct-marketing media. As you can see in Figure 14–1, direct marketing is an aspect of total marketing—that is, it involves marketing research, segmentation, evaluation, and the like, just as our planning model in Chapter 1 did. Direct marketing uses a set of **direct-response media**, including direct mail, telemarketing, interactive TV, print, the Internet, and

FIGURE 14–1 U.S. Direct-Marketing Expenditures by Medium and Market (in Billions of Dollars)

Channel	Market	2006	2010	2011	2012	2016	Compound Annual Growth Rate	
							2006–2011	2011–2016
Commercial E-Mail		**$0.8**	**$1.4**	**$1.6**	**$1.7**	**$2.3**	**13.8%**	**8.6%**
	Business	0.5	0.8	0.9	0.9	1.3	13.7	8.3
	Consumer	0.4	0.6	0.7	0.8	1.1	13.9	8.8
Direct Mail (catalog)		**20.1**	**16.4**	**17.3**	**17.7**	**20.5**	**–3.0**	**3.5**
	Business	7.7	6.4	6.8	7.0	8.2	–2.5	3.9
	Consumer	12.4	9.9	10.4	10.7	12.3	–3.3	3.3
Direct Mail (noncatalog)		**33.0**	**31.5**	**32.8**	**33.4**	**37.1**	**–0.1**	**2.5**
	Business	12.6	12.0	12.5	12.7	14.2	–0.1	2.5
	Consumer	20.5	19.5	20.3	20.7	22.9	–0.2	2.5
Insert Media		**1.9**	**2.1**	**2.1**	**2.2**	**2.3**	**2.4**	**1.7**
	Business	0.7	0.8	0.8	0.8	0.9	2.7	1.8
	Consumer	1.2	1.3	1.4	1.4	1.5	2.2	1.6
Internet Display		**5.0**	**7.2**	**8.5**	**9.5**	**14.1**	**11.3**	**10.6**
	Business	2.8	4.0	4.7	5.2	7.7	11.1	10.3
	Consumer	2.2	3.2	3.8	4.3	6.4	11.4	10.9
Internet Other		**1.9**	**3.2**	**3.9**	**4.4**	**5.9**	**15.7**	**8.8**
	Business	1.0	1.8	2.1	2.4	3.2	15.6	8.6
	Consumer	0.8	1.4	1.7	2.0	2.7	15.8	9.1
Internet Search		**8.4**	**11.8**	**13.9**	**15.6**	**22.4**	**10.6**	**9.9**
	Business	4.7	6.5	7.7	8.6	12.2	10.5	9.7
	Consumer	3.8	5.3	6.2	7.1	10.2	10.7	10.2
Internet Social Networking		**0.6**	**2.0**	**2.5**	**3.0**	**6.1**	**34.4**	**19.4**
	Business	0.3	0.9	1.1	1.4	2.8	34.5	19.7
	Consumer	0.3	1.1	1.4	1.6	3.3	34.2	19.1
DR Magazine		**8.4**	**6.9**	**7.0**	**6.9**	**7.2**	**–3.7**	**0.6**
	Business	4.3	3.6	3.7	3.7	3.9	–3.1	1.1
	Consumer	4.1	3.2	3.3	3.2	3.3	–4.4	0.0
Mobile		**0.1**	**0.6**	**0.9**	**1.2**	**3.1**	**75.2**	**28.7**
	Business	0.0	0.2	0.3	0.4	0.9	69.2	25.2
	Consumer	0.0	0.4	0.6	0.8	2.2	78.8	30.3
DR Newspaper		**16.1**	**8.4**	**7.8**	**7.0**	**4.9**	**–13.6**	**–9.0**
	Business	6.1	3.2	3.0	2.7	1.9	–13.1	–8.7
	Consumer	10.0	5.2	4.8	4.3	3.0	–13.9	–9.1

(continued)

CHAPTER 14

Channel	Market	2006	2010	2011	2012	2016	Compound Annual Growth Rate 2006–2011	2011–2016
DR Radio		**4.9**	**3.9**	**3.9**	**3.8**	**3.9**	**–4.4**	**–0.2**
	Business	2.4	2.0	2.0	2.0	2.0	–3.7	0.1
	Consumer	2.5	1.9	1.9	1.9	1.9	–5.2	–0.5
Telephone Marketing		**44.8**	**36.3**	**36.6**	**36.9**	**38.1**	**–3.9**	**0.8**
	Business	26.8	22.0	22.2	22.4	23.2	–3.7	0.9
	Consumer	17.9	14.4	14.4	14.5	14.9	–4.3	0.6
DR Television		**22.0**	**20.8**	**22.1**	**22.9**	**25.9**	**0.1**	**3.2**
	Business	9.7	9.5	10.2	10.6	12.2	0.9	3.7
	Consumer	12.3	11.3	11.9	12.3	13.7	–0.7	2.9
Other		**2.8**	**2.0**	**2.1**	**2.1**	**2.3**	**–5.2**	**1.4**
	Business	1.2	0.9	1.0	1.0	1.0	–4.5	1.9
	Consumer	1.6	1.1	1.2	1.2	1.2	–5.6	1.0
Total		**$170.8**	**$154.4**	**$163.0**	**$168.5**	**$196.0**	**–0.9%**	**3.8%**
	Business	80.8	74.6	79.1	81.8	95.6	–0.4	3.9
	Consumer	90.0	79.8	83.9	86.7	100.4	–1.4	3.6

Source: From the Direct Marketing Association, The Power of Direct Marketing, 2012.

other media. These media are the tools by which direct marketers implement the communication process.

The purchases of products and services through direct-response advertising currently exceed $2.05 trillion and are projected to reach $2.49 trillion by the year 2016.[2] Firms that use this marketing method range from major retailers such as the Gap, Restoration Hardware, and IKEA to airline companies to financial services and local companies. Business-to-business and industrial marketers have also significantly increased their direct-marketing efforts, with an estimated $1.09 trillion in sales forecast by 2016.[3]

The Growth of Direct Marketing

Direct marketing has been around since the invention of the printing press in the 15th century. Ben Franklin was a very successful direct marketer in the early 1700s, and Warren Sears and Montgomery Ward were using this medium in the 1880s.

The major impetus behind the growth of direct marketing may have been the development and expansion of the U.S. Postal Service, which made catalogs available to both urban and rural dwellers. Catalogs revolutionized America's buying habits; consumers could now shop without ever leaving their homes.

But catalogs alone do not account for the rapid growth of direct marketing. A number of factors in American society have led to the increased attractiveness of this medium for both buyer and seller:

- *Consumer credit cards.* There are now more than 1 billion credit cards—bank, oil company, retail, and so on—in circulation in the United States. This makes it feasible for consumers to purchase both low- and high-ticket items through direct-response channels and assures sellers that they will be paid. It is estimated that over $2.09 trillion is charged on credit cards each year.[4] Of course, not all of this was through direct marketing, but a high percentage of direct purchases do use this method of payment, and companies such as American Express, Diners Club, MasterCard, and Visa are among the heaviest direct advertisers.

- *The changing structure of American society and the market.* One of the major factors contributing to the success of direct marketing is that so many Americans are now "money-rich and time-poor." The rapid increase in dual-income families has meant more income. (It is estimated that in 2015 women made up about 57 percent of the labor force.)[5] At the same time, the increased popularity of physical fitness, do-it-yourself crafts and repairs, and home entertainment has reduced the time available for shopping and has increased the attractiveness of direct purchases.

- *Technological advances.* The rapid technological advancement of the electronic media and the Internet has made it easier for consumers to shop and for marketers to be successful in reaching the desired target markets. Well over 110 million television homes receive home shopping programs. The ease and speed of shopping on the Internet, for example on Amazon.com, while having the purchase delivered to one's door is an attractive option.

- *Miscellaneous factors.* A number of other factors have contributed to the increased effectiveness of direct marketing, including changing values and lifestyles, more sophisticated marketing techniques, more options, and the industry's improved image. These factors will also ensure the success of direct marketing in the future. The variety of companies employing direct marketing demonstrates its potential.

While some organizations rely on direct marketing solely to generate a behavioral response, for many others direct marketing is an integral part of the IMC program. They use direct marketing to achieve other than sales goals and integrate it with other program elements. We first examine the role of direct marketing in the IMC program and then consider its more *traditional* role.

The Role of Direct Marketing in the IMC Program

Long the stepchild of the promotional mix, direct marketing has now become an important component in the integrated marketing programs of many organizations. In fact, direct-marketing activities support and are supported by other elements of the promotional mix.

Combining Direct Marketing with Advertising   Obviously, direct marketing is in itself a form of advertising. Whether through mail, print, digital, or TV, the direct-response offer is an ad. It usually contains a toll-free number, always has a link, and sometimes has a form that requests mailing information. Sometimes the ad supports the direct-selling effort directly. For example, IKEA, Nordstrom, and Bloomingdale's among many others run image ads and commercials to support their store and catalog sales. Bose Audio also markets through stores and online, supporting its efforts through advertising (Exhibit 14–1). In the past, some advertisers were reluctant to sell directly to customers, worrying that to do so might result in lost sales to retail stores. A study conducted by Forrester Research, Inc. showed just the opposite. More than half of manufacturers who sell on their e-commerce sites reported that the sites actually benefited stores while only 9 percent said that it had a negative effect. In addition, 72 percent of responding companies said that selling online actually improved customer satisfaction.[6] Overall, the advertising was shown to support both direct and in-store sales positively.

EXHIBIT 14–1

Bose uses creative ads like this one to promote its products in stores and online

Source: Bose Corporation

Combining Direct Marketing with Public Relations   As you will see later in this text, public relations activities often employ direct-response techniques. Private companies may use telemarketing activities to solicit funds for charities or co-sponsor charities that use these and other direct-response techniques to raise funds. Likewise, corporations and organizations engaging in public relations activities may include toll-free numbers or website URLs in their ads or promotional materials. The DMA Nonprofit Federation has worked with numerous organizations and small and large companies in support of environmental issues and assisting them in the use of direct media in their PR efforts.

Combining Direct Marketing with Personal Selling   Telemarketing and direct selling are two methods of personal selling used to generate sales. Nonprofit organizations like charities often use telemarketing (along with direct mail) to solicit funds. As you will see, for-profit companies—particularly those in the business-to-business market—are also using telemarketing with much greater frequency to screen and qualify prospects (which reduces selling costs) and to generate leads. Direct-mail pieces are often used to invite prospective customers to visit auto showrooms to test-drive new cars; the salesperson then assumes responsibility for the selling effort. Automobile manufacturers and their dealers have both made effective use of this approach.

Combining Direct Marketing with Sales Promotions   How many times have you received a direct-mail piece notifying you of a sales promotion or event or inviting you to participate in a contest or sweepstakes? Ski shops regularly mail announcements of special end-of-season sales. Airlines send out mailers or e-mails announcing promotional airfares. Nordstrom and other retail outlets sometimes call their existing customers to notify them of special sales promotions. Each of these is an example of a company using direct-marketing tools to inform customers of sales promotions (Exhibit 14–2). In turn, the sales promotion event may support the direct-marketing effort. A study conducted by Vertis indicated that marketers could increase the effectiveness of their direct-mail campaigns by offering exclusive deals and/or coupons. Seventy two percent of adults surveyed said they had responded to a direct-mail offering of a buy-one-get-one free offer, and 63 percent said they had responded to an offer of a percentage discount on merchandise. Both of these numbers had increased since a previous study conducted in 2005. E-mails containing special offers, vouchers, or discounts have also been shown to be effective.[7] Databases are often built from the names and addresses acquired from a promotion, and direct mailers and/or telemarketing calls follow.

Combining Direct Marketing with Support Media   Adding a promotional product to a direct mailer has proven to increase response rates. One company included a promotional product in half of its 10,000 mailers and not in the other half. The former generated 65 percent more orders. 3M used a promotional product as an incentive for people responding to a direct-mail offer. The incentive generated a 23 percent response rate versus only 9 percent for the regular mailer. Promotional products like refrigerator magnets, bookmarkers, and other items that can be easily inserted into the mailer are commonly used. We will discuss the combination of direct marketing with the Internet in Chapter 15.

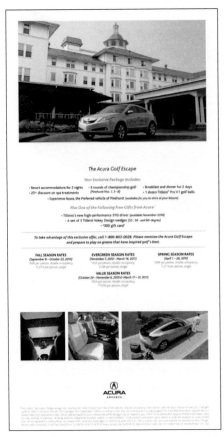

EXHIBIT 14-3

Acura and Pinehurst Golf Resort partner on a direct-mail program

Source: Acura and Pinehurst

To successfully implement direct-marketing programs, companies must make a number of decisions. As in other marketing programs, they must determine (1) what the program's objectives will be, (2) which markets to target (through the use of a list or marketing database), (3) what direct-marketing strategies will be employed, and (4) how to evaluate the effectiveness of the program.

Direct-Marketing Objectives

Though more marketers now understand the contribution that direct marketing offers to the IMC program, the direct marketer usually seeks a direct response. The objectives of the program are typically defined in terms of behaviors—for example, test drives, votes, contributions, and/or sales, and so on. A typical objective is defined through a sought response, perhaps a 2 to 3 percent response rate.

Not all direct marketing seeks a behavioral response, however. Many organizations use direct marketing to build an image, maintain customer satisfaction, and inform and/or educate customers in an attempt to lead to future actions. When President Obama kicked off his presidential reelection campaign in 2012, he did so with direct-response TV ads. The ads asked viewers to call an 888 phone number or visit JoinObama.com and enter their e-mail addresses and zip codes to get more involved in his reelection efforts. The success of the president's reelection campaign was attributed to these types of grassroots efforts. Exhibit 14–3 provides an example of how Acura and Pinehurst Golf Resort partnered to offer consumers a special three-hour use of an Acura—the "Preferred Vehicle of Pinehurst"—and a special package price for their vacation getaway. The two companies believe that they share a common target market profile and similar business philosophies of offering only the highest-quality product.

Direct-Marketing Strategies and Media

As with all other communications programs discussed in this text, marketers must decide the message to be conveyed, the size of the budget, and so on. Perhaps the major difference between direct-marketing programs and other promotional-mix programs regards the use of media.

As shown in Figure 14–1, direct marketing employs a number of media, including direct mail, telemarketing, direct-response broadcasting, the Internet, and print. Each medium is used to perform specific functions, although they all generally follow a one- or two-step approach.

In the **one-step approach**, the medium is used directly to obtain an order. You've probably seen TV commercials for products like wrench sets, workout equipment, or magazine subscriptions in which the viewer is urged to phone a toll-free number to place an order immediately. Their goal is to generate an immediate sale when the ad is shown.

The **two-step approach** may involve the use of more than one medium. The first effort is designed to screen, or qualify, potential buyers. The second effort generates the response (e.g., the order). For example, many companies use telemarketing to screen on the basis of interest and then follow up to interested parties with more information designed to achieve an order or use personal selling to close the sale. Some companies have evolved from a one-step to a two step-approach. For example, the magazine sales company Publishers Clearing House at one time employed a one-step approach by seeking subscriptions through direct mail. The company now has television commercials that tell potential consumers to watch for the mailers, or to go online to register to win (and buy magazine subscriptions!).

Direct Mail Direct mail is often called "junk mail"—the unsolicited mail you receive. More advertising dollars continue to be spent in direct mail than in almost any other advertising medium—an estimated $46 billion in 2014.[8] A typical U.S. household receives an average of 19 direct-mail pieces per week.[9] Direct mail is not restricted to small companies seeking our business. Respected large companies and organizations in the retail, financial services, and fund-raising sectors (among others) commonly employ this medium.

Many advertisers shied away from direct mail in the past, fearful of the image it might create or harboring the belief that direct mail was useful only for low-cost products. But this is no longer the case. For example, Porsche Cars North America, Inc. uses direct mail to target high-income, upscale consumers who are most likely to purchase its expensive sports cars. Jaguar and Maserati have also employed this strategy. In one example, Porsche developed a direct-mail piece that was sent to a precisely defined target market: physicians in specialties with the highest income levels. This list was screened to match the demographics of Porsche buyers and narrowed further to specific geographic areas. The direct-mail piece was an X-ray of a Porsche 911 Carrera 4 written in the language of the medical audience. This creative campaign generated one of the highest response rates of any mailing Porsche has done in recent years. The piece shown in Exhibit 14–4 is one sent by Jaguar to market its new F Pace automobile.

Keys to the success of direct mail are the **mailing lists**, which constitute the database from which names are generated, and the ability to segment markets and, of course the offer. It is now possible to buy mailing lists, e-mail lists, and sales leads. Lists have become more current and more selective, eliminating waste coverage. The data for these lists are derived from a variety of sources such as customer purchase history and third-party lists.

The importance of the list has led to a business of its own. It has been estimated that there are over 39 billion names on lists, and many companies have found it profitable to sell the names of purchasers of their products and/or services to list firms. (One of these companies claims to have over 245 million names on its e-mail list alone!) Companies like InfoUSA, Experian, and Nielsen Business Media (Exhibit 14–5) provide such lists on a national level, and in most metropolitan areas there are firms providing the same service locally.

While direct mail continues to be a favorite medium of many advertisers, and projections are that the market will grow, this medium has been seriously threatened by the Internet. The lower cost of e-mail and the convenience of the Internet have raised concerns among traditional direct-mail marketers. Interestingly, the Internet is both a threat and an opportunity, as Internet companies have increased their

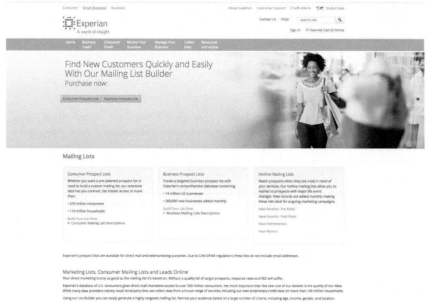

expenditures in direct mail to drive potential customers to their sites. Nevertheless, the traditional direct-mail business has experienced lower response rates from many consumers who see the offer first through direct mail and then go online to order. Many companies, have shifted from print to online catalogs, saving money and remaining more current. E-mail has also been shown to be an effective strategy for a variety of companies and organizations, as demonstrated in Digital and Social Media Perspective 14–1.

EXHIBIT 14–5

Experian (www.experian.com) offers a mailing list builder to help companies find new customers

Source: Experian Information Solutions, Inc.

Catalogs Major participants in the direct-marketing business include retailers and other catalog companies. The number of catalogs mailed and the number of traditional catalog shoppers has decreased each year since 2007, with an estimated 11.1 billion catalogs mailed in 2014 (down from 11.9 billion in 2013).[10] At the same time research by the Direct Marketing Association indicates that approximately one-third of marketers predict that they will increase their catalog mailings by 1 to 10 percent over the next few years.[11] Although some predicted that catalogs would cease to exist with more use of the Internet and the number of catalogs mailed continues to decrease, traditional catalogs are still an effective way to reach consumers. The emotional appeal of the traditional catalog exceeds that of online catalogs and ultimately is one of the best ways to drive consumers online.

Many companies use catalogs in conjunction with their more traditional sales and promotional strategies. For example, companies like Pottery Barn, Bloomingdale's, Nordstrom, and Illuminations sell directly through catalogs but also use them to inform consumers of product offerings available in the stores. Some companies (for example, Oriental Trading Company) rely solely on catalog sales. Others that started out exclusively as catalog companies have branched into retail outlets, among them Road Runner Sports, Eddie Bauer, Banana Republic, and Illuminations (Exhibit 14–6). The products being offered through this medium have reached new heights as well. The 2015 Neiman Marcus Christmas catalog featured:

- Keanu Reeves's designed and built motorcycles (only three were made) at $150,000 each
- A $400,000 dream trip to India
- A $95,000 Neiman Marcus Mustang
- A $90,000 balloon ride

Of course, these products were designed to attract publicity more than anything else—unless you have a lot of money!

In addition to the traditional hard copies, catalogs are now available on the Internet for both consumer and business-to-business customers. In some instances in the consumer market the catalog merchandise is available in retail stores as well. In others, the catalog and retail divisions are treated as separate entities. For example, if you purchase through the Eddie Bauer catalog, you can exchange or return the merchandise

EXHIBIT 14–6

Road Runner Sports is one of many successful catalog companies now in retail

Source: Road Runner Sports, Inc.

Digital and Social Media Perspective 14–1 > > >

SPORTS TEAMS FIND THAT DEALING "DIRECT" WITH FANS IS BEST STRATEGY

If you are a fan and follow professional sports you might think that owners don't need marketing to market their products. This is particularly true in MLB, the NFL, and NHL; coming by a ticket is not always so easy. As a result, secondary markets have developed—think StubHub—to help you find a seat for those hard-to-get games. These secondary markets allow ticketholders to sell their tickets at whatever price they wish, making money off commissions. There is no control over the pricing, so the secondary markets have become a competitor for the franchises themselves. StubHub by far is the largest ticket-selling marketplace in the world.

As you might expect, the franchises themselves have begun to discover ways to compete with secondary sellers to maintain direct relationships with their fan base. Ticket buyers now trust dealing with secondary marketers as much as they do with the teams' box offices, so the focus has moved away from competing on price to competing on the fan experience. In recent years there has been an extended effort to bring the fan back to the box office and the game by enhancing the overall experience by dealing with them directly and improving on the customer relationship management (CRM). The idea is to create "fans," not ticket buyers. Debbie Knowlan, of the Atlanta Falcons NFL football team, noted, "Being able to make the connection with fans on a one-to-one basis and delivering experience and game-day memories is the foundation to building solid relationships that go beyond a ticket purchase. In a world that is consumed with social and digital communications, people still look for that direct interaction with the team they support and are passionate for—this is what creates a fan."

To offer enhancements that create engagement, sports franchises have turned to direct marketing. Take the Detroit Pistons NBA basketball team as an example. The Pistons figured out a way to keep fans engaged at games, whether they are waiting in line at the restroom or in traffic on the way to get there: e-mail. Teaming with Movable Ink, a company that can update e-mails in real time after they have

been sent, the two have turned the static e-mail into a "real-time, dynamic second-screen experience." The e-mails are used before, during, and after the games to improve the fan experience. For example, before the game the e-mail goes out to ticket holders before tip-off and updates every time a recipient opens it. The e-mails show team matchups, records, stats, and so on as well as information about getting there (like traffic). During the game it shows live scores and stats for all 10 players on the floor at any given point, and at the end it displays the final box score. Both before and after the game the e-mails post a live traffic map to find the optimal route in and out of the arena. After a very short period of time the Pistons saw engagement increase by 45 percent and mobile engagement increase by 49 percent over the previous static e-mails.

Other teams have also turned to direct marketing, including the New York Jets, Phoenix Coyotes, and 59.2 percent of all colleges with sports teams.

A study conducted by Research and Markets collected detailed data from over 100 colleges regarding their spending patterns, practices, and plans for sports marketing, including baseball, basketball, football, lacrosse, and other sports. The research examined spending habits on a variety of media, including outdoor, print, and digital as well as other marketing vehicles. The study showed that for colleges with an enrollment of 20,000 or more, over 81 percent advertise in newspapers, while only 34 percent of those in schools of less than 20,000 students do. Regardless of size, more than 65 percent of Division I schools employed opt-in e-mail to promote their team. Most of these schools found their efforts to be successful; almost 37 percent report increases in basketball attendance, even though their teams may not have played better.

Borrowing an idea from the University of Minnesota, the Phoenix Coyotes professional hockey team ran a promotion designed to incentivize fans to attend their final 10 home games. The promotion used a GOALden ticket, in which fans purchased tickets based on the number of goals they expected the home team to allow in those games.

to the retail stores. Some companies' products must be returned to the catalog department. At the Gap, the catalog is used to supplement the inventory in stock, and phone orders for different sizes and so on can be made from the store and shipped for free.

E-mail Direct mail on the Internet (**e-mail**) is essentially an electronic version of regular mail. Like regular mail it is highly targeted, relies heavily on lists, and attempts to reach consumers with specific needs through targeted messages. The use of e-mail marketing by both business-to-business and business-to-consumer marketers continues to grow; both the low cost and the higher effectiveness than

Once the goals were reached (for example, 5 games for 5 goals) the tickets were void. Fans could purchase up to as many as 25 goals, at a greatly reduced price. At the game the fans swiped a Personal Identification Card letting them in and indicating how many goals they had left. The Coyotes would also send an e-mail after each game reminding the fans how many goals remained on their cards. To advertise the promotion, the Coyotes relied on only two media—an e-mail campaign geared to past package and season ticket holders and a direct-mail campaign to season ticket holders going back to five or six years prior.

It worked! The promotion led to the sales of 200 packages and an incremental $35,000 in revenue. In addition, there was a substantial increase in cross-selling sales for other packages and future games, and an unmeasurable amount of buzz!

The New York Jets football team has never had a home of its own. Even though the franchise has been around for 50 years, it has never had its own stadium. Starting as the New York Titans in the original American Football League in 1960, the team played its first game in the Polo Grounds. In 1964 it moved to Shea Stadium—a venue built for baseball and the home of the New York Mets. After 20 years, the Jets moved to the Meadowlands in New Jersey—as a tenant. To make matters worse, the team shared the stadium with its crosstown rival New York Giants in—of all things—Giants Stadium. In the 1970s, 80s, and 90s the Jets team was not very competitive and had troubles drawing fans. But by the turn of the century, the Jets once again began to compete for the division title and fill the stadium for almost every home game. Season tickets could not be bought for years, and it got so bad, fans gave up on trying to do so. So the Jets built a new facility: for the first time ever the team had its own stadium!

Good news, bad news! With the new Jets stadium set to open in fall 2010, marketing of season tickets started in 2008—right in the middle of the recession. While new

Source: Movable Ink and The Detroit Pistons

season tickets had not been available for decades, the new stadium would hold 82,500 people, many of whom were unaware of ticket availability. The Jets hired a Manhattan advertising agency to coordinate the IMC campaign, which included advertising, an interactive microwebsite, support media, public relations, and a heavy emphasis on direct marketing. The campaign was called "Opportunity Knocks," and the initial theme line was "Finally, we're the home team." A three-pronged approach was taken with phase 1 focusing on branding and awareness and accompanied with call-to-action direct-response media. Existing ticket holders were invited to tour the new stadium when completed and received glossy brochures to encourage them to buy seats in the new venue. Finally, follow-up phone calls, e-mails, and direct-mail pieces were used to close the deal. Existing ticket holders were offered the best seating options based on their seniority, but good seats were still available.

While the season ticket holders responded well, seats remained. After the existing ticket holders had their chance, the unsold seats (including club seats) were made available to the general public—with a "Ticket for everybody" program that included a wide variety of price options and a 15-year financing program for the more expensive seats. All of the media efforts including the TV spot, a print campaign, direct mail, web advertising, and e-mails again included a specific call to action. And, success was achieved.

It seems that going "directly" to the fans means using direct media to get there. Watch out StubHub!

Sources: Erik Wander, "The Detroit Pistons Are Sending Emails That Change Every Time Fans Check Them," www.adweek.com, April 6, 2016; Russell Scibetti, "How Teams Can Benefit from Direct Relationship with Fans," www.sportsbusinessdaily.com, September 22, 2014; Dylan Bohanan, "Coyotes Create a Goalden Promotion," www.sportsforum.com, April 3, 2013; Laura Wood, "The 2013 Survey of College Sports Marketing Practices: 59.62% of Schools Used Direct Mail in the Past Year to Market sporting Events," *Sports Techy*, April 17, 2013, p. 1; Thomas Haire, "Jets Audible into Direct Response," *Response*, January 2010.

traditional direct mail appeal to marketers. A study conducted by the Harvard Business School showed that e-mail campaigns were as much as 95 times more effective than traditional direct-marketing campaigns when return on investment (ROI) was used as the effectiveness measure.[12]

Sometimes users may also receive less-targeted and unwanted e-mails. The electronic equivalent of junk mail, these messages are referred to as **spam**. Because of the high volumes of spam and the fact that many consumers consider it a nuisance, the U.S. government has passed laws regulating its use. In addition, antispam software has become effective in blocking most of the unwanted messages. Nevertheless, all indications are that the end of this form of advertising is not in sight.

Infomercials: Shopping at 3 a.m.?

Way back in the "old days" many TV stations would go off the air after midnight until 6 a.m. If you happened to turn on your set during this time period you probably saw nothing more than a sign-off signal indicating there was no programming. There just weren't enough people out there watching to make it worthwhile to air anything. Often referred to as the "Graveyard Slot," the media during this period could be purchased at a very low rate, but there weren't many people awake. That has all changed. For some companies, the Graveyard Slot is their prime time. These are the direct-response companies that do their advertising—or even 30- to 60-minute direct-response programming called infomercials—at this time selling just about anything imaginable from Perfect Polly the plastic parakeet that chirps like an old car alarm to the UroClub, a nine-iron golf club that doubles as a portable urinal. Most people say they don't like this form of advertising, but research shows that as many as one-third of us have purchased products from an infomercial. The mere fact that you see them on TV is evidence that they work. Long-form ads, as they are often called, have successfully marketed a variety of product lines including weight-loss products, personal care items, exercise equipment, and even churches, doctors, and pet-bird stores. The infomercial market was expected to exceed $250 billion by 2015. You have probably heard of Proactiv (a skin care line that sells over $1.0 billion annually exclusively through infomercials), or PedEgg, a heel-scraping callus remover that has been on the market since 2007. Then there is the Pocket Hose, the Hurricane Spin Mop, the "Showtime rotisserie grill at home," the George Foreman Grill, and the ShamWow. Of course, we could go on but we will just talk about the top three grossing infomercials of all time to date. But before we do, take a guess! (*Hint:* It is not the Thighmaster, the Snuggie, or the George Foreman Grill. Nope, it is not the ShamWow either! Here are the top three:

Total Gym—Coming in at number three, this workout system sells for over $1,000 and is endorsed by Chuck Norris and Christie Brinkley. The machine allows you to work on toning many parts of your body through 80 different exercises and promises a full workout in 10–20 minutes. You can try it at home for 30 days for just $1.00, and if you don't like it you can send it back. (Good luck with that!) Total sales to date are over $1 billion!

P90X—Tony Horton's Beachbody Company, the second highest grossing infomercial, has been doing infomercials since at least 2005, and now grosses over $400 million a year. For just three payments of $39.95 you get Tony Horton's 90-day fitness workout system. Working out for just 30 minutes a day, you will be toned in only 90 days. You also get a nutrition plan and a video of success stories. You can try it free for 30 days.

Proactiv—And the winner, clocking in at $1.0 billion a year (and has been in the market since 1995), is the Proactiv acne system. The champion of all infomercials, the Proactiv anti-acne facial cleanser has used a

---

Broadcast Media The success of direct marketing in the broadcast industry has been truly remarkable; as far back as 1996 over 77 percent of the U.S. population reported that they had viewed a direct-response appeal on TV.[13] Direct-response TV is estimated to generate more than $13.73 billion in advertising billings in 2016.[14]

Two broadcast media are available to direct marketers: television and radio. While radio was used quite extensively in the 1950s, its use and effectiveness have dwindled substantially in recent years. Thus, the majority of direct-marketing broadcast advertising now occurs on TV, which receives the bulk of our attention here. It should be pointed out, however, that the two-step approach is still very common on the radio, particularly with local companies.

Direct marketing in the broadcast industry involves both direct-response advertising and support advertising. In **direct-response advertising**, the product or service is offered and a sales response is solicited, through either the one- or two-step approach previously discussed. Examples include ads for apparel, exercise equipment, collectables, and so on. Toll-free phone numbers are included so that the receiver can immediately call to order. **Support advertising** is designed to do exactly that— support other forms of advertising. Ads for Publishers Clearing House or *Reader's Digest* or other companies telling you to look in your mailbox for a sweepstakes entry are examples of support advertising.

Direct-response TV encompasses a number of media, including direct-response TV spots like those just mentioned, infomercials, and home shopping shows (teleshopping). And as noted in Chapter 10, Internet TV—for example, Amazon Prime Instant Video and Hulu Plus—has attracted a number of viewers.

variety of celebrities to promote the product, spending over $15 million a year in the process. Katy Perry, P. Diddy, Jessica Simpson, Kelly Clarkson, Lindsay Lohan, Britney Spears, and Vanessa Williams are just a few who have endorsed the product over the years. The ads have become so popular they have gone viral; Proactiv now has a You-Tube page that has had over 1.5 million hits!

These are just a few of the many successful infomercials. Whopper Choppers, George Foreman grills, Slap-Chops, and ShamWows can also be included in this list, as could Richard Simmons's "Sweatin to the Oldies."

"But why?" you might ask. How can some of these messages be so irritating but so successful? Numerous explanations have been offered over the years. One is that the high-volume, high-action scripts increase viewers' dopamine levels by creating (or at least making us recognize) problems we never knew we had, and then offer a solution. There is also the potential impact of the celebrities. Look at the Proactiv list mentioned earlier, then add in Chuck Norris, Susan Lucci, and George Foreman (among others)—all of whom have been successful infomercial product endorsers. Add in these factors and the ability to create and measure effective infomercials, and you have a remedy for success. So much success, in fact, that some retail stores—major competitors in the past—now carry some of these products. If you can't beat them, join them?

Sources: Ben Alberstadt, "The Ten Best Selling Infomercials of All Time," June 28, 2014, www.therichest.com; "Pitching to America at 3 a.m.," *The Week,* December 20, 2013, p. 36; Bob Fernandez, "Atlantic City TV Station Looking Beyond Infomercials," *McClatchy-Tribune Business News,* May 29, 2011, p. 1.

EXHIBIT 14–7

Bentley has successfully used an infomercial to attract buyers

Source: Bentley Motors

TV Spots Referred to in the direct-marketing industry as *short-form programs,* these spots include direct-response commercials commonly seen on television for products such as drugs and toiletries, audio and video supplies, household products, and more.

Infomercials The lower cost of commercials on cable and satellite channels has led advertisers to a new form of advertising. An **infomercial** is a long commercial that is designed to fit into a 30-minute or 1-hour time slot. Many infomercials are produced by the advertisers and are designed to be viewed as regular TV shows. Today's infomercials use both one- and two-step approaches. Programs such as *Liquid Luster, Amazing Discoveries,* and *Stainerator* (the so-called miracle-product shows) were the most common form of infomercial in the 1980s. While this form of show is still popular, the infomercial industry has been adopted by many large, mainstream marketers, including Coca-Cola, Braun, Disney, Nissan, Bentley, Apple, and Microsoft (see Exhibit 14–7).

As to their effectiveness, IMC Perspective 14–1 proves that infomercials are watched and sell products. The demographics of the infomercial shopper reflect a married female, mean age of 45, Caucasian, working full time with a household income of $55,000+ per year.[15] This advertising medium is indeed effective with a broad demographic base, not significantly different from the infomercial nonshopper in age, education, income, or gender. Retail stores are benefiting from infomercials as well, as brand awareness leads to increased in-store purchases. For example, a $500,000 print campaign combined with an infomercial for the George Foreman grill led to more sales at retail stores than through direct TV.[16]

The popularity of the infomercial has led companies to expand into the more frequently watched daytime TV market and the creation of infomercial networks. There is now an "As Seen on TV" website and catalog.

However, some people are not sold on the idea of ads disguised as programs. For example, infomercials disguised as "ultrahip" TV shows have been targeted at teenagers, raising fears that kids under the age of 13 will be susceptible to their lure. Consumer complaints are on the rise, and the FTC has already levied fines for deceptive endorsements against infomercial sponsors, and has taken legal action against those engaging in deceptive practices. Well-known infomercial promoter Kevin Trudeau was fined $37.6 million by the FTC for making false claims in his infomercials. Four consumer groups (the Consumer Federation of America, Center for the Study of Commercialism, Center for Media Education, and Telecommunications Research and Action Center) have asked the FCC to require all infomercials to display a symbol that indicates a "paid ad" or "sponsored by" so that viewers won't confuse them with regular programming.

Home Shopping   The development of toll-free telephone numbers, combined with the widespread use of credit cards, has led to a dramatic increase in the number of people who shop via their TV sets through home shopping channels. Jewelry, kitchenware, fitness products, insurance, household products, and a variety of items are now promoted (and sold) this way. The major shopping channel in the United States (QVC) broadcasts on TV 24 hours a day and online. While Internet e-commerce sales have hurt the TV home shopping channels, they have succeeded through adaptation: Both QVC and Home Shopping Network (HSN) have upgraded their product lines to include designer brand names and luxury goods at a lower price point. QVC has also purchased Zulily—a leading e-commerce site that targets millennial moms. Zulily, according to *The Wall Street Journal,* is "the web's version of QVC."[17] The success of home shopping networks has led to a proliferation of shopping channels, including the Gem Shopping Network, America's Auction Network, and the Liquidation Channel, to name just a few. As the demographics of shopping channel buyers continue to move younger and more upscale, the products offered on these channels continue to change as well. It is now possible to to shop on QVC on one's Apple Watch.

Print Media   Magazines and newspapers are difficult media to use for direct marketing. Because these ads have to compete with the clutter of other ads and because the space is relatively expensive, response rates and profits may be lower than in other media. Print direct-response ads can still be found in specific interest areas like financial newspapers or sports and hobby magazines, but they are being used less often.

Telemarketing   If you have a telephone, you probably do not have to be told about **telemarketing**, or sales by telephone. Both profit and charitable organizations have employed this medium effectively in one- and two-step approaches. Combined telemarketing sales (business-to-consumer and business-to-business) have continued to decrease since 2004. While business-to-business companies continue to employ this strategy with some success, in recent years the telemarketing industry has suffered from a decline due to a number of factors. Problems associated with telemarketing include its potential for fraud and deception and its potential for annoyance. These developments have led to the development of a Do Not Call list for both landline and cell phones and the resulting decline in sales in the consumer market.

EXHIBIT 14–8

Cutco is one of many companies using direct selling

© Cutco Cutlery Corp

Those in the telemarketing and telemedia industry have responded to public criticisms, while Dial-a-Porn and its ilk hold a diminishing share of 800, 900, and 976 offerings—the latter two being pay-per-call service typically used by adult chat lines, psychic services, and other content providers.

DIRECT SELLING

An additional element of the direct-marketing program is **direct selling**, the direct, personal presentation, demonstration, and sales of products and services to consumers in their homes. Amway, Avon, Cutco, Mary Kay, and Tupperware are some of the best-known direct-selling companies in the United States and have now extended these programs overseas (Exhibit 14–8). Amway, Avon, and Herbalife all have annual sales of over $5 billion; one of the relatively newcomers to the industry is the direct-selling jewelry company Stella & Dot, whose sales were expected to approach $1 billion by 2016. Approximately 18.2 million people engage in direct selling throughout the United States, and 99 percent of them are independent contractors (not employees of the firm they represent). Direct selling generates over $34 billion in sales, 94 percent of which is through person-to-person or party plan selling.[18]

The three forms of direct selling are:

1. *Repetitive person-to-person selling.* The salesperson visits the buyer's home, job site, or other location to sell frequently purchased products or services (for example, Amway). Mary Kay has given away over 100,000 Cadillacs—the company's symbol of sales success.
2. *Nonrepetitive person-to-person selling.* The salesperson visits the buyer's home, job site, or other location to sell infrequently purchased products or services (for example, Cutco).
3. *Party plans.* The salesperson offers products or services to groups of people through home or office parties and demonstrations (for example, Tupperware and PartyLite Gifts).

Whereas a number of products and services are sold through direct selling, home and family durables, weight-loss and wellness products, and personal services are the most popular. The "typical" direct-selling representative is female (over 74 percent), married (77 percent), and works part time (89 percent). For most of the representatives, direct selling is not a full-time job but an opportunity to earn additional income and a way to get the product at a discount for themselves. Over half of those in this industry spend fewer than 10 hours a week selling, and the vast majority spend less than 30 hours a week selling. Figure 14–2 reflects the means by which they sell.

FIGURE 14–2

Sales Strategy (methods used to generate sales)

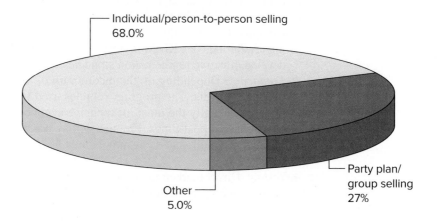

Individual/person-to-person selling
68.0%

Party plan/group selling
27%

Other
5.0%

EVALUATING THE EFFECTIVENESS OF DIRECT MARKETING

Because they generate a direct response, measuring the effectiveness of direct-marketing programs is not difficult. Using **cost per order (CPO)**, advertisers can evaluate the relative effectiveness of an ad in only a few minutes based on the number of calls generated. By running the same ad on different stations, a direct marketer can determine the relative effectiveness of the medium itself. For example, if the advertiser targets a $5 return per order and a broadcast commercial (production and print) costs $2,500, the ad is considered effective if it generates more than 500 orders. Similar measures have been developed for print and direct-mail ads.

Another commonly employed measure of effectiveness is **Customer Lifetime Value (CLTV)**. CLTV is a simple formula that is used to assist marketers in determining the dollar value associated with a long-term relationship with a customer, thus evaluating his or her worth. The value is used to determine whether or not a customer should be acquired, as well as to optimize service levels to existing customers. Companies use CLTV to assist them in assessing future revenues and profit streams from the customer, so that they can focus more on the satisfaction and retention of their more profitable customers. Thus, the company can focus more attention on profitable customers while spending less marketing effort on those with a low CLTV score.

Many companies use an **RFM analysis** (recency, frequency, monetary), a marketing technique used to determine quantitatively which customers are the most profitable by examining how recently a customer has purchased (recency), how often he or she purchases (frequency), and how much the customer spends (monetary).

For direct-marketing programs that do not have an objective of generating a behavioral response, traditional measures of effectiveness can be applied. (We discuss these measures in Chapter 18.)

Advantages and Disadvantages of Direct Marketing

Many of the advantages of direct marketing have already been presented. A review of these and some additions follow:

1. *Selective reach.* Direct marketing lets the advertiser reach a large number of people and reduces or eliminates waste coverage. Intensive coverage may be obtained through broadcast advertising or through the mail. While not everyone drives on highways where there are billboards or pays attention to TV commercials, virtually everyone receives mail. A good list allows for minimal waste, as only those consumers with the highest potential are targeted. For example, a political candidate can direct a message at a very select group of people (those living in a certain zip code or members of the Sierra Club, say); a book club can target recent purchasers or avid readers.

2. *Segmentation capabilities.* Marketers can rent or purchase lists of recent product purchasers, car buyers, bank-card holders, and so on. These lists may allow segmentation on the basis of geographic area, occupation, demographics, and job title, to mention a few. Combining this information with the geocoding capabilities of PRIZM or VALS (discussed in Chapter 2), marketers can develop effective segmentation strategies.

3. *Frequency.* Depending on the medium used, it may be possible to build frequency levels. The program vehicles used for direct-response TV advertising are usually the most inexpensive available, so the marketer can afford to purchase repeat times. Frequency may not be so easily accomplished through the mail, since consumers may be annoyed to receive the same mail repeatedly.

4. *Testing.* Direct marketing allows for a strong ability to test the effectiveness of the overall program as well as specific elements.

5. *Timing.* While many media require long-range planning and have long closing dates, direct-response advertising can be much more timely. Direct mail and e-mail, for example, can be put together very quickly and distributed to the target population. TV programs typically used for direct-response advertising are older, less viewed programs that are likely to appear on the station's list of available spots. Another common strategy is to purchase available time at the last possible moment to get the best price.

6. *Personalization.* No other advertising medium can personalize the message as well as direct media. Parents with children at different age levels can be approached, with their child's name included in the appeal. Car owners are mailed letters congratulating them on their new purchase and offering accessories. Computer purchasers are sent software solicitations. College students receive very personalized information that recognizes their specific needs and offers solutions, as well as college loan offers.

7. *Costs.* While the CPM for direct mail may be very high on an absolute and a relative basis, its ability to specifically target the audience and eliminate waste coverage reduces the actual CPM. Costs may be higher than in other media, but direct methods may be more profitable. The ads purchased on TV are often among the lowest-priced available. E-mail is extremely inexpensive. A second factor contributing to the cost-effectiveness of direct-response advertising is the cost per customer purchasing. Because of the low cost of media, each sale generated can be very inexpensive.

8. *Measures of effectiveness.* No other medium can measure the effectiveness of its efforts as well as direct response. Feedback is often immediate and almost always accurate.

Disadvantages of direct marketing include the following:

1. *Image factors.* As we noted earlier, the mail segment of this industry is often referred to as junk mail. Many people believe unsolicited mail promotes junk products, and others dislike being solicited. Even some senders of direct mail, including Motorola, GM, and Air Products & Chemicals, say they throw out most of the junk mail they receive. This problem is particularly relevant given the increased volume of mail being sent through e-mail. The Direct Marketing Association estimates that the typical household receive almost 19 pieces of direct mail a week.[19]

    Likewise, direct-response ads on TV are often low-budget ads for lower-priced products, which contributes to the image that something less than the best products are marketed in this way. (Some of this image is being overcome by the home shopping channels, which promote some very expensive products.) Telemarketing is found to be irritating to many consumers, as is "spam" or Internet junk mail. Other factors have also created image problems for the direct-marketing industry.

2. *Accuracy.* One of the advantages cited for direct mail and telemarketing was targeting potential customers specifically. But the effectiveness of these methods depends on the accuracy of the lists used. People move, change occupations, and so on, and if the lists are not kept current, selectivity will decrease. Computerization has greatly improved the currency of lists and reduced the incidence of bad names; however, the ability to generate lists is becoming a problem. The cost of generating a lead can range from a few dollars to as much as hundreds depending on its quality. Some states now have restrictions on how and where data on customers can be gathered.

3. *Content support.* In our discussion of media strategy objectives in Chapter 10, we said the ability of magazines to create mood contributes to the overall effectiveness of the ads they carry. In direct-response advertising, mood creation is limited to the surrounding program and/or editorial content. Direct-mail and online services are unlikely to create a desirable mood.

4. *Rising costs.* As postal rates increase, direct-mail profits are immediately and directly impacted. The same is true for print costs, which drives up the costs of mailers and catalogs. The low cost of e-mail has led many companies to switch to this medium.
5. *Do Not Call lists.* Do Not Call lists now exist for both landline and cell phones. A "Do Not Contact" list in which consumers can choose not to receive junk mail is under consideration by the FTC.

Summary

This chapter introduced you to the rapidly growing field of direct marketing, which involves a variety of methods and media beyond direct mail and telemarketing. The versatility of direct marketing offers many different types of companies and organizations a powerful promotional and selling tool.

Direct marketing continues to outpace other advertising and promotional areas in growth; many of the *Fortune* 500 companies now use sophisticated direct-marketing strategies. Database marketing has become a critical component of many marketing programs.

Advantages of direct marketing include its selective reach, segmentation, frequency, flexibility, and timing. Personalized and custom messages, low costs, and the ability to measure program effectiveness are also advantages of direct-marketing programs.

At the same time, a number of disadvantages are associated with the use of direct marketing. Image problems, deception, and the intrusive nature of the medium make some marketers hesitant to use direct-marketing tools. However, self-policing of the industry and involvement by large, sophisticated companies have led to significant improvements. As a result, the use of direct marketing will continue to increase.

Key Terms

direct marketing 480
direct-response media 480
one-step approach 485
two-step approach 485
mailing list 486

e-mail 488
spam 489
direct-response advertising 490
support advertising 490
infomercial 491

telemarketing 492
direct selling 493
cost per order (CPO) 494
Customer Lifetime Value (CLTV) 494
RFM analysis 494

Discussion Questions

1. What is an infomercial? What are some of the reasons that infomercials have been so successful? Which types of products and services do you think are likely to be candidates for successful infomercials? (LO 14-3)
2. Explain the role that direct marketing can play in the IMC program. Can direct marketing be used for anything other than a behavioral response? If so, give examples. (LO 14-4)
3. What is the future of the traditional home shopping channels like QVC and HSN? Given the decline in television viewership, what will these channels have to do to survive? (LO 14-3)
4. Some marketers believe that traditional catalogs are on the way out and that they will be replaced by digital catalogs. Explain why digital catalogs will or will not not drive the traditional catalog into extinction.

Cite some of the advantages of maintaining a traditional print catalog. (LO 14-3)
5. To many consumers, shopping through direct channels offers a number of distinct advantages over traditional shopping methods. At the same time, there are distinct disadvantages to this form of shopping. Give examples of the advantages and disadvantages of each form of shopping.
6. Explain what is meant by Customer Lifetime Value. How does this formula benefit the direct marketer? (LO 14-4)
7. A study by the Harvard Business School has shown that e-mail marketing is much more effective than traditional direct mail in that it provides a much greater return on investment (ROI). Explain some of the reasons why this would be. (LO 14-4).

8. Direct marketing has been an effective tool for marketers for a long time. Provide some reasons why direct marketing has been so effective. Do you think this trend will continue? (LO 14-1)

9. Direct marketers are very good at determining the effectiveness of their programs. Many direct marketers now measure the impact of the program on the consumer funnel. Explain how direct marketers measure effectiveness, and how they now use the consumer funnel for this purpose. (LO 14-4)

10. While a very effective medium, direct marketing also has a number of distinct disadvantages. Discuss some of these, and what marketers could do to decrease them. (LO 14-4)

Digital users can access their personalized and adaptive SmartBook, Ad Forum Video Cases, and interactive exercises to review chapter concepts.

15

The Internet: Digital and Social Media

Source: Solve Advertising & Branding

LEARNING OBJECTIVES

LO1 Describe the role of the Internet and digital and social media in an IMC program.

LO2 Discuss the use of Web 1.0 and Web 2.0 media platforms in the IMC process.

LO3 Explain how to evaluate the effectiveness of communications through the Internet and digital and social media.

LO4 Compare the advantages and disadvantages of the Internet and digital and social media.

LO5 Discuss the social and ethical issues associated with the Internet and digital and social media.

THE MAD RUSH TO DIGITAL: SMART MANAGEMENT OR LEMMINGS?

Throughout this text you have seen examples of marketers changing their media allocations from traditional media to digital, arguing that millennials don't watch television, read the newspapers, or listen to the radio anymore. In a one-year period from 2014 to 2015 digital spending rose 20 percent to a record $59.6 billion. Spending on mobile rose 66 percent, social 55 percent, and digital video 30 percent (nonmobile search was up 8 percent, and display revenues up 3 percent). In the same period television advertising was down 3.4 percent to $63 billion, with forecasts expecting digital to surpass TV in 2016. The Interpublic Group of Companies's (IPG) Magna Global ad buying agency announced in 2016 that it would be swinging $250 million in clients' ad spending from TV to YouTube over the next five quarters, while Procter & Gamble, among many others, has also followed suit. The fact that so many advertisers are allocating so much of their budgets to digital must reflect the collective wisdom of the industry, right? Well, not necessarily.

Advertisers cite a number of reasons for the shift. As already noted, many believe that the declining ratings and print readership among millennials is because of their fascination with digital, making it a much more effective medium in attaining reach while also more cost-effective. For example, an article by John McDermott at www.digiday.com described what advertisers could get if they took the cost of one 30-second ad in the 2015 Super Bowl and spent the $4.5 million online instead (the Super Bowl reached approximately 113 million viewers) including (1) a week's worth of Snapchat ads, (2) 3.5 billion display ads, (3) 50 million video views on Facebook, and (4) 6.4 million clicks on search ads. The CPM for the Super Bowl ad would also be higher than those of Facebook, Instagram, Twitter, LinkedIn, or Pinterest. Digital ads are also touted for their accountability and effectiveness and the ability to buy through programmatic targeting, which significantly reduces the time and effort of the media buying process (see lead-in to Chapter 10).

Not everyone is so enamored, however. Numerous articles have demonstrated the problems with the advertising on the Internet obsession, including problems with fraud, viewability, deception, and bots (web-surfing algorithms meant to mimic human traffic created by botnets and distributed by millions illegally hijacking web browsers), among other issues. Some managers consider programmatic a "lazy-man's excuse for media buying."

Malicious bots are now estimated to constitute as much as 61.5 percent of all website traffic, according to a report by Igal Zeifman, and the more desirable the audience the higher the likelihood the ad may be seen only by a bot, thus leading advertisers to think they are reaching (and paying for) more than is true. A number of studies have also indicated that as many as half of online display ads are nonviewable due to technical issues or never appear on the screen at all! The hottest topic of all—programmatic—attracts an estimated 14 percent more bots than display ads, while programmatic video attracts an estimated 73 percent more bot traffic, costing advertisers about $7.6 billion a year. Some advertisers still feel uncertain as to where their ads are placed on programmatic, and ad blocking is on the increase.

One very interesting study, *The Blank Video Project,* conducted by Minneapolis agency Solve, specifically looked at the validity of views on YouTube. The website estimates that 300 hours of content are uploaded to its platform every minute, and has become very attractive to many managers. In the study, Solve created a 4-minute blank video with no motion, sound, title, or description. "It consisted of nothing but a blank white slate," with a click-through URL that took the viewer to the solve-ideas.com website. The video was promoted through YouTube TrueView Advertising and the agency was charged only for viewers who watched at least 30 seconds. Viewers could opt out to skip the video after 5 seconds. Over 100,000 views were generated with the ad served 227,819 times, thus, 46 percent of the time the viewer threshold was reached. On average, viewers made it through 2 minutes and 26 seconds of the video before leaving and 22 percent made it to the end—of a blank video!

Solve explains that it had no intent to attack or denegrate YouTube.com, having used the platform itself many times, but rather the agency wanted to demonstrate to advertisers that they need to find a better way to evaluate the quality and performance of their content and recognize that what is being promised may not always hold true. The agency suggests that better metrics than "likes" or "thumbs up" are necessary to get a true picture of effectiveness.

The question is, are advertisers going to take the time and effort to make this commitment, or will they continue to follow the trend and continue to move monies to digital media in spite of its shortcomings?

Sources: "US Internet Adspend Surges 20%," April 22, 2016, www.warc.com; John McDermott, "What the Cost of a Super Bowl Ad Can Buy Online," January 30, 2015, www.digiday.com; Igal Zeifman, "Report: Bot Traffic Is Up to 61.5% of All Website Traffic," February 2016, www.incapsula.com; Christopher Heine, "Bots Will Cost Digital Advertisers $7.2 Billion in 2016, Says ANA Study," January 2016, www.adweek.com; "The Blank Video Project," 2015, www.solve-ideas.com.; "US Digital Ad Spending to Surpass TV This Year," www.eMarketer,.com, September 13, 2016.

As you can see from the lead-in to this chapter, as well as previous chapters, the Internet has changed media buying unlike any medium has in the past. The incredibly rapid growth has been spurred by a number of factors including the changing media habits of younger generations and the capabilities of digital media themselves. There appears to be no near end in sight to the move of dollars from traditional media to social media, mobile, platforms like YouTube, and other digital options. While the Internet itself required marketers to rethink their IMC programs, the advent of Web 2.0, which led to even more capabilities, has altered the environment forever for new and old brands and large and small companies.

This chapter will examine the role of the Internet and digital media in the IMC program. We will examine the growth of the Internet, how companies use the various platforms therein, and its role in an IMC program as well as some of the advantages and disadvantages associated with this medium. We will also discuss the various new media options that have resulted from the development of the Internet and their roles in an IMC program. The chapter will conclude with a discussion of the measurement of these media.

THE GROWTH OF THE INTERNET

Why the Rapid Adoption of the Internet?

The unprecedented growth of the Internet—the digital revolution—has led to changes in the marketing environment forcing marketers to rethink almost everything they do. As the World Wide Web evolves, so too do marketing communications programs. There are now close to 2 billion Internet users worldwide, and the growth since the year 2000 is staggering. A number of reasons can be cited as to why this growth has been so rapid. One is consumers' increased desire for information that they are now able to obtain easily. The speed and convenience of acquiring this information, as well as the ability to control what and how much is received, has had great appeal. The ability to conduct e-commerce through one's personal computer is also very attractive as it now seems there is almost nothing that one can't find or buy on the Web. It is as though the Internet has no bounds; every day one can find something new there.

Like the consumers', marketers' adoption of this medium has also soared. The ability to target customers effectively through the Net is attractive to marketers. The increased attention for accountability on the part of businesses has led to a view of the Internet as a medium that would provide more direct feedback on the value of marketing expenditures, customer satisfaction, trends, and the competition. As was true of direct marketing, companies liked the fact that, unlike traditional media, it was often easier to account for the ROI of their expenditures. In fact, in its earliest stages a number of marketing companies perceived the Internet as a direct-response medium. While a large component of the Web is still that of e-commerce, today's marketers now employ the medium for numerous other communications and marketing objectives (as we will discuss shortly).

EXHIBIT 15–1

Start-up company SweetBling.com has benefited from the use of the Internet

Source: SweetBling.com

Today's World Wide Web has evolved into a different medium than anyone could have expected 10 years ago. Unlike other media, which are essentially unidirectional and responsible for the content provided and products and services offered for sale, the Internet is interactive, allowing for a two-way flow. Consumers not only control when and which messages and content they are exposed to, but also now provide their own content, offer their own goods and services for sale, and provide feedback on the same as provided by others. As you will see, marketers are involving consumers in a way never seen before, through a variety of platforms that never existed just a few decades ago.

Web Objectives

When major corporations first began to conduct business on the Internet, they put up websites primarily for information purposes and a one-way flow of information resulted. Companies like Kmart and Maytag had sites that were really not much more than online catalogs, while those of other companies were designed for information purposes only. The role of the website quickly changed, however, as sites are now designed to accomplish a number of objectives and have become much more creative by promoting brand images, positioning, and offering promotions, product information, and products and services for sale, with many allowing interactivity. In addition, these sites allow for consumers' feedback and input that can be directly used by marketers to keep their customers engaged. This resulted in marketers utilizing the Internet in an entirely new way, moving beyond the purely informational role. As you will see, the objective of disseminating information and selling products remains, but additional communications and sales objectives are also being pursued.

Unlike other media discussed thus far in the text, the Internet is actually a hybrid of media. In part, it is a communications medium, allowing companies to create awareness, provide information, and influence attitudes, as well as pursue other communications objectives. Videos, display ads, and commercials—some of which may also appear on television—are commonly used for this purpose. For others, it is also a direct-response medium, allowing the user to both purchase and sell products through e-commerce, like Amazon and Craigslist. With the advent of social media, marketers have increasingly pursued a third objective of building brand image and developing a more direct and involved relationship with customers through engagement with the brand. Thus, we will discuss each of the objectives in this chapter. Let's first look at some of the communications objectives these companies want to achieve.

Create Awareness   Advertising on the Web can be useful in creating awareness of an organization as well as its specific product and service offerings. For small companies with limited budgets, the Web offers the opportunity to create awareness well beyond what might be achieved through traditional media. For example, a start-up company like the one shown in Exhibit 15–1 can almost immediately gain worldwide exposure at a reasonable cost—something that was not possible before the Internet. Although a valuable tool for creating awareness—particularly for smaller companies that may have limited advertising budgets—the Internet is not likely to be the most effective of the IMC elements for achieving this objective for larger companies. Mass-media advertising may be more useful for this purpose, given its larger reach and lower cost per exposure (as the TV people will be glad to remind you!). Studies have demonstrated the effectiveness of TV to drive visitors to websites. Nevertheless, even larger well-established companies have the creation of and increase in awareness as a primary objective.

Generate Interest   A visit to RedBull.com will quickly demonstrate how a site can be used to generate interest. The site provides news, live streams, videos, and more from the "World of Red Bull" (Exhibit 15–2). The objectives of this site and many others like it are simple: Create interest that will bring visitors back to learn more about the products—and, of course, to sell stuff.

Disseminate Information   One of the primary objectives for using the Web is to provide in-depth information about a company's products and services. Having a website has become a necessity, as more and more buyers expect that a company will have a site providing them with detailed information about its offerings, warranties, store locations, and so on. Think about the last time you tried to find information on a company on the Internet and it didn't have a website. It is extremely rare for this to happen, and if it did, you would likely be hesitant to pursue a relationship with the company. In the government sector, contracts are often put out to bid on the Internet. Information regarding requirements, specifications, submission dates, and so forth is disseminated more quickly, to more potential candidates, and at a much lower cost via the Net than it is through other media. Want information on filing federal income taxes? The first place you would look would likely be www.irs.gov. Websites serve as a means of communicating information about a company's products and services, philanthropic efforts, contact information, and the company itself.

Create an Image   Many websites are designed to reflect the image a company wants to portray. For example, check out the site www.nikawater.org (Exhibit 15–3). The site is an excellent example of a website used for image building. Visitors get a good feeling about the water company's concern for humanity. Interestingly, one of the difficulties traditional marketers have experienced is that of creating a brand image on the Internet. While some of these companies have been successful, others have not fared as well and have come to realize that branding and image-creating strategies must be specifically adapted to this medium.

Create a Strong Brand   The Internet—as part of an integrated marketing communications program—can be a useful tool for branding. While originally many companies had difficulty using the Internet to establish their brand, this is no longer the case. Red Bull has used its site (shown earlier) as an integral part of its IMC campaign focusing on the "Red Bull Gives You Wings" image, positioning itself as a brand dedicated to excitement and daring through its motorsports, biking, surfing, and snowboarding news and videos as well as music and event sponsorships. Red Bull is one of the many companies that have "figured it out" in regard to successful branding.

Stimulate Trial   Many marketers have found the Internet to be an effective medium for stimulating trial of their products or services. Often websites offer electronic coupons in an attempt to stimulate trial of their products. Others offer samples, promotions, and sweepstakes designed to encourage trial. Music sites, like iTunes.com, allow for a "sampling" of songs before you purchase, while some business-to-business sites allow you to test their software online before purchasing.

Create Buzz   One of the many advantages of the Web is the ability to create buzz. The viral nature of social networking and other sites makes them attractive to marketers intending to

EXHIBIT 15–4

eBay is one of the most popular e-commerce sites

Source: eBay.com

spread the word and use word of mouth. In a very successful effort to go viral, Dove recently created a video employing a sketch artist to draw women's self-perceptions and the way others saw them based on the descriptions they provided, without his ever seeing them. Titled "Dove Real Beauty Sketches," the amazing difference between these perceptions made the point that women often suffer self-esteem issues needlessly. In less than a month the viral video gained more than 114 million views, making it the most watched ad ever. The brand message was taken worldwide by Dove who uploaded the videos in 25 languages to 33 of its official YouTube channels, reaching customers in more than 110 countries. "Real Beauty Sketches" generated close to 3.8 million shares in its first month online, adding 15,000 new subscribers to Dove's YouTube channel over the following two months.[1]

Gain Consideration Many marketers believe that the Internet is an effective medium for achieving communications objectives such as consideration and/ or evaluation. Blogs and discussion boards are considered particularly useful for providing information useful in evaluating products and brands. The use of "mommy bloggers" and teen "haulers" as well as marketing influencers has become a powerful marketing strategy used by H&M, JCPenney, Dove, Ann Taylor, and Timex, among others.

E-Commerce

The Internet also offers the opportunity to sell directly to customers in both the consumer market and the business-to-business market. This direct selling of goods and services has been labeled **e-commerce**. Sales through e-commerce were expected to reach over $320 billion in the United States by 2016[2] (Exhibit 15–4). Many of the sites already mentioned in this chapter have a sales component—as either a primary or secondary goal.

Many companies maintain their existing "brick-and-mortar" stores while also selling through the Internet. Ann Taylor, Macy's, and Nordstrom are placing more emphasis on online sales; Samsung, and Apple have added kiosks inside their stores where consumers can order online.

We discussed e-commerce and strategies employed in this area in Chapter 14. Let's have a look at how the Internet can be used as part of an IMC program.

THE INTERNET AND INTEGRATED MARKETING COMMUNICATIONS

Up to this point, we have mentioned the need for using the Internet as part of an IMC program and the objectives sought. In this section, we discuss how the Web can be used with other program elements.

Wikipedia, among other sources, makes a distinction between Web 1.0 and Web 2.0. Web 1.0 is generally referred to as the first decade or so of the World Wide Web, ending with the "bursting of the dot-com bubble."[3] For the most part, Web 1.0 consists mainly of static sites resulting in a one-way flow of communication. Web 2.0 has led to dramatic changes in the World Wide Web, primarily as a result of decentralization of communications and interactivity, with information provided by users as contributors of content such as user-generated ads content and so on (Figure 15–1). In this chapter we are not concerned with the technical changes that have taken place, but rather the resulting impact on marketing communications. Everything we have discussed to this point still constitutes the way marketers use the Web; however, Web 2.0 has added some key components that have had a drastic impact on how the Internet is used in an IMC program; so we will discuss them separately, starting with Web 1.0.

FIGURE 15–1

Differences in the Way
Organizations Have
Interacted with Customers
on the Web

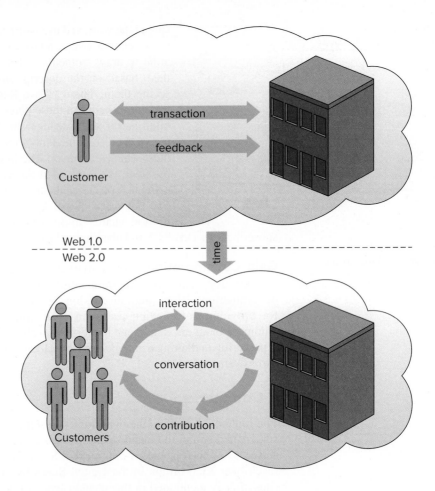

Advertising on the Internet—Web 1.0

Like broadcast or print, the Internet is an advertising medium. Companies and organizations working to promote their products and services must consider this medium as they would television, magazines, outdoor, and so on. Advertising on the Internet employs a variety of forms, display ads including banners, sponsorships, pop-ups and pop-unders, interstitials, paid searches, behavioral targeting, contextual ads, and rich media. Web 1.0 is the terminology used to refer to the early evolution of the World Wide Web in which users could view web pages and interface with them, but could not contribute to the content of the web page.

Banners   The most common form of advertising on the Web is **banner ads**. It has been estimated that the average Internet user sees over 1,700 banner ads per month, while those in the age group 25–34 see over 2,000.[4] Banner ads may be used for creating awareness or recognition, entering viewers into contests and sweepstakes, or direct-marketing objectives. Banner ads may take on a variety of forms, as shown in Exhibit 15–5, as well as a number of names such as *leader boards, rectangles, side panels, skyscrapers,* or *verticals.* They can also be static, animated, or in flash. Initially banner ads constituted the vast majority of advertising on the Net, but studies indicating their questionable effectiveness have led some companies to reduce their usage. Reports on click-through rates vary, but most studies indicate a less than 1 percent response rate.[5] At the same time, a number of studies have shown that although viewers may not click through the banners, they can still be effective in driving consumers to search or visit the ad's website. A study reported in the *Journal of Consumer Research* showed evidence that even with low click-through rates, banner ads may still create a favorable attitude toward the ads through repeated exposures.[6] However, many consumers find banner ads annoying, leading many companies to avoid this advertising format.

EXHIBIT 15–5

Banner ad formats

© *Darrell Coomes,* HeyBannerBanner. com

Sponsorships   Another common form of advertising is **sponsorships**. There are two types of sponsorships. *Regular sponsorships* occur when a company pays to sponsor a section of a site—for example, a *House Beautiful* magazine or *Cosmopolitan* magazine sponsorship on Design.com or a corporate sponsorship of a page on Forbes.com. A more involved agreement is the **content sponsorship**, in which the sponsor not only provides dollars in return for name association but also participates in providing the content itself. In some cases, the site is responsible for providing content and having it approved by the sponsor; in other instances, the sponsor may contribute all or part of the content. To position Bud Light as the leading purveyor of Canada's electronic dance music (EDM) culture, the brand partnered with Vice/Thump, a leading authority on EDM culture in Canada, to create the Bud Light Living Room. Thump produced all of the content in collaboration with the Bud Light Brand Team. The content consisted of year-round exclusive EDM coverage and special features on the state of electronic dance music.

Pop-Ups/Pop-Unders   When you access the Internet, you no doubt have seen a window or a creature of some sort appear on your screen in an attempt to get your attention. These advertisements are known as **pop-ups**, and they often appear when you access certain sites. Pop-ups are usually larger than banner ads but smaller than a full screen.

Pop-unders are ads that appear underneath the web page and become visible only when the user leaves the site. For example, if you have ever visited a travel website, you probably were hit with a pop-under ad for Orbitz, one of the heaviest users of this form of web advertising.

While some companies believe that pop-ups and pop-unders are effective forms of advertising, others disagree. Consumer complaints have led some sites to no longer accept these advertising forms. A study conducted by TNS revealed that 93 percent of respondents found pop-up ads annoying or very annoying.[7] The frequency and effectiveness of pop-ups and pop-unders have been greatly reduced given the advent of pop-up screeners, which will block the ads before they appear on your screen.

Interstitials   **Interstitials** are full-page ads that appear on your screen while you are waiting for a site's content to download. Unlike banner ads, interstitials require the viewer to click off the ad to continue to the site they want to go to. Yelp and LinkedIn are just two of the many companies to employ this advertising form. Because consumers have complained that mobile interstitials are irritating, in 2015 Google put into place a new policy to discourage their use by declaring the sites that use mobile interstitial apps as "mobile unfriendly."[8] Unfortunately for advertisers who may want to employ this medium, interstitials can also be blocked by pop-up blockers.

Paid Searches   Exhibit 15–6 shows the results of a **search** on Google. In general, the higher a site appears on a search page, the more visitors it will receive. (Often searchers will not go past the first page of results.) **Organic search results** are those that appear because of their relevance to the search terms, not advertisements. Advertisers will also attempt to reach consumers through **nonorganic (paid) search results** such as **pay-per-click** advertising by placing their ads on web pages that display results from search engine queries. Over $29 billion was spent on search advertising in 2016, with that number expected to increase to more than $40 billion by 2019.[9]

While there are a number of search engines offering their services, Google (Exhibit 15–6) is by far the dominant provider, accounting for 55 percent of all

EXHIBIT 15-6

Results of a Google search for flowers

Source: Google.com

search ad revenues.[10] In an effort to more specifically target customers who may be interested in their offerings, advertisers employ **search engine optimization (SEO)**. SEO is the process of improving the volume of traffic driven to one's site by a search engine through unpaid (organic) results as opposed to paid inclusions. The belief is that the higher a site appears on the search results list, the more visitors it will receive. SEO considers how search engines work and edits its HTML and coding to increase its relevance to keywords and to remove barriers to the indexing activities of search engines. SEO has now become an integral part of the Internet marketing strategy of companies and organizations of all sizes.

Behavioral Targeting Another Internet advertising strategy that has seen rapid growth is **behavioral targeting**. Behavioral targeting is based on advertisers' targeting consumers by tracking their website surfing behaviors, such as which websites they have visited and/or searches they have made. By compiling clickstream data and Internet protocol (IP) information, segments of potential buyers can be identified and ads directed specifically to them. For example, by tracking an individual's visits to a number of automobile websites, an ad for cars or a dealership could be served to that individual in real time. As will be seen later in this chapter, behavioral targeting has been shown to be an effective, albeit controversial, strategy.

Recently, advertisers have increased their use of **retargeting**. Once a user visits a website either on his or her desktop or mobile and leaves without purchasing the product, a specifically targeted ad will display on participating subsequent websites the user visits. Purchasing the space, however, is not a fixed transaction, but a bid process. Since each site has only so much space set aside for display ads, brands must bid against competitors for the space. The brand that puts in the highest bid is the one whose ads you will see. For example, let's say you were shopping for a pair of shoes at Nordstrom online, but didn't purchase. The next time you visited a website such as Yahoo! or Microsoft, an ad for Nordstrom shoes would appear. Because advertisers find retargeting more successful than banner or display ads, their use is increasing. The vast majority of over 1,000 marketers surveyed are already retargeting on mobile— and 87 percent plan to increase this investment in 2016.[11] Due to their rapid adoption, many advertisers are concerned that the ads may become as irritating as pop-up ads.

Contextual Ads Advertisers who target their ads based on the content of the web page are using **contextual advertising**. Whereas behavioral advertising tracks surfing behaviors, contextual ad placements are determined by the content on the web page. For example, an advertiser may place an airline ad on a travel site, or a golf club ad on a golf site, or even in or near a story about golf on another site. As another example, Google's AdSense targets ads to match the content of a publisher's site. The ads come in a variety of formats including images and video ads and can be targeted to geographic or local markets.

Recently, some marketers and policymakers have become concerned due to the increased popularity of native advertising. As defined by *Wikipedia*, **native advertising** is "a web advertising in which the advertiser attempts to gain attention by providing valuable content in the context of the user's experience; it is similar in concept to an advertorial which is a paid placement attempting to look like an article."[12]

The goal of native ads is to be less intrusive while catching the attention of the reader who is likely interested in the content matter he or she is reading. While these native ads have been shown to outperform the traditional banner ad, concern has been expressed over the fact that the ads sometimes appear as content, and not ads, leading the consumer to be misled (IMC Ethical Perspective 15–1).

Native Advertising: Are We Giving Customers What They Want or Deceiving Them?

One of the fastest-growing trends in digital advertising is the use of native advertising. Defined as "any paid advertising that takes the specific form and appearance of editorial content from the publisher," advertisers love native ads because they allow advertisers to cut through the clutter of display ads, and have been found to be much more effective than other ad forms. Users say the effectiveness of native ads is a result of the fact that readers find them less obtrusive and often interesting given the fact that they blend in with the content in which they appear. Some advertisers believe that native ads actually enhance the viewer's experience. *The Atlantic* website claims that the use of native ads has led to an increased audience that spent twice as much time as the industry average on the ads (viewing for as long as 4 to 5 minutes), that click-through rates have tripled, and that the format had contributed 60 percent of *The Atlantic*'s ad revenue and was expected to continue to grow. Jimmy Maymann, CEO of the *Huffington Post,* went so far as to suggest that native advertising "was the potential solution to many of the problems facing publishers." One-fifth of the content on the *Huffington Post* site is now native advertising, accounting for 35 percent of the brand's revenues.

Jason Hill, the global head of media strategy for General Electric, believes that native ads are more effective in generating engagement and interaction, and that "traditional digital advertising has become wallpaper." Hill says that most of the monies GE spent on display ads have now gone into native formats. The travel magazine *Afar* has found native ads to be effective in engaging readers in its Afar Collection which includes hotels and resorts such as the Ritz-Carlton, the Fairmont Olympic Hotel, the Loews Regency New York, and the Peninsula in Hong Kong—each of which has paid *Afar* $25,000 to become part of the collection of 19 lodges. Twitter's MoPub, which handles over 3 billion mobile ads a day, has opened to native ads targeted to mobile users, and expects the native ads to generate at least the same amount in the near future.

The fact that native ads may be effective because viewers are less likely to perceive them as ads is also a problem. In a study by the Reuters Institute for the Study of Journalism, 43 percent of readers said they felt disappointed or deceived after reading content they didn't realize was sponsored. In another study of 2,000 consumers conducted by Civic Science, 61 percent thought that the ads hurt a publication's credibility. Considering native ads as the digital equivalent version of the traditional advertorials (advertising material placed under the guise of editorial material) that appears in magazines and newspapers, the Federal Trade Commission (FTC) opened an investigation into their use and whether they might be deceptive. In 2015 the FTC issued a strong "policy statement" in which the conclusion was that "native ads may not be interpreted as such, and therefore, may be deceptive." The commission also concluded that

Source: AFAR Media

- "Misleading representations or omissions about an advertisement's true nature or source, including that a party other than the sponsoring advertiser is the source of the advertising, are likely to affect consumers' behavior with regard to the advertised product or the advertisement."
- "The Commission views as material any misrepresentations that advertising content is a news or feature article, independent product review, investigative report, or scientific research or other information from a scientific or other organization."

The policy statement also provided advertisers with examples of native ads and what advertisers should do to prevent deception, noting that the ads needed to make clear disclosures. The FTC provided guidelines for doing so.

Despite the FTC's guidelines and threats, a study conducted by Media Radar in which thousands of native ads were reviewed, found that four months after the policy statement was released, 70 percent of the ads still did not comply with the FTC regulations. Only 5 percent labeled the content as an "ad," while 12 percent used "promoted." A number of the ads still had no labeling at all, even though the FTC had already taken action against some advertisers for failing to do so. Many believe that the use of this form of advertising will continued unabated in the short run, or until the FTC starts to crack down harder. In the meantime, the appeal of not revealing that they are truly ads and not content seems to be just too hard to resist for many advertisers.

Sources: Bartosz W. Wojdynski and Nathaniel J. Evans, "Going Native: Effects of Disclosure Position and Language on the Recognition and Evaluation of Online Native Advertising," *Journal of Advertising,* May 3, 2016, pp. 157–168; David Rodnitzky, "Now That the FTC Has Spoken on Native Advertising, What's Next?" January 12, 2016, www.marketingland.com; Marty Swant, "Publishers Are Largely Not Following the FTC's Native Ad Guidelines," April 8, 2016, www.adweek.com; Mike O'Brien, "Native Advertising 101: The Good, the Bad and the Ugly," December 10, 2015, www.clickz.com; "Less Is More, *The Atlantic* Finds," October 16, 2015, www.warc.com; Yovee Koh, "Twitter MoPub Opens Up Native Advertising," December 12, 2013, www.wsj.com.

Rich Media The increased penetration of broadband into households has increased the attention given to streaming video. **Rich media**, defined as "a broad range of interactive digital media that exhibit dynamic motion, taking advantage of enhanced sensory features such as video, audio and animation."[13] Others state that rich media include all content that is created in flash.[14] The successful adoption of music videos, sports clips, news, and more has led advertisers to create a variety of forms of streaming video advertising content.

Types of rich media include the following:

Online Commercials The equivalent of traditional television commercials, **online commercials** are appearing more often on the Net. Some of these commercials appear before the content that the user is seeking. These ads, called **pre-rolls**, are becoming more commonly employed by online advertisers, with some requiring that you watch the ad prior to receiving the content. Some companies have created their own web commercials to be shown only on the Internet, while others run the same spots they show on TV. A number of commercials were released online prior to their being shown on the 2016 Super Bowl—a break from tradition in which the TV commercials always appeared first. Another trend has been to have consumers develop their own commercials to be shown online or on TV—or both. The Super Bowl has taken full advantage of this strategy. A number of companies have been successful in blending the two media, showing the commercial on TV and then directing interested viewers to the Web if they wish to see it again or to view longer versions. Online advertising spending continues to rise, and consumer acceptance of these ads is increasing.

Video on Demand As described in Chapter 13, **video on demand (VOD)** consists of video clips of various entertainment activities (which include ads or are sponsored) that are also available through the Internet. College basketball games, FIFA World Cup highlights, and demonstrations on how to use the Apple iPhone are just a few of the many options available.

Webisodes Short featured films created by the advertiser, such as those created by Jaguar and BMW, are examples of **webisodes**, in which companies create their own content to advertise their products. *The Walking Dead* and *Heroes* are examples of series that are now webisodes. IKEA, Target, Sara Lee, and Honda are just a few of the companies that have employed webisodes, but the range of these efforts also includes small jewelers, baking companies, cereal producers, and others.

Other Forms of Rich Media Advertising Advertising interactive banner ads, expandable ads, and rich media ads placed in video games, instant messaging, podcasts, and video ads within blogs are additional ways that rich media are currently employed.

IMC Using Social and Other Media—Web 2.0

As noted earlier in the chapter, after the dot-com bubble burst at the turn of the century, the World Wide Web underwent significant changes. These changes led to the adoption of and the referral to the new Web as "Web 2.0." The birth of Web 2.0 has led to the development of many **new media**. As shown in Figure 15–2, these new media are designed for a number of purposes and contain a wide variety of materials for consumer use. While it is beyond the scope of this text to cover all of these new media, we will discuss many of them and their relevance to an IMC program. We will start our discussion with social networking sites, as the growth in this area has been literally astounding, and marketers have adopted these sites as an integral and critical part of their IMC programs.

FIGURE 15–2   Types of New Media

Types of New Media	Primary Purpose	Material	Examples
Forums and Chat Rooms	Discussion on topics, interest group sharing of information	Forums, discussion boards	Hardwarezone.com Forums
E-mail	Sending of electronic mail with file attachments	Web-based and non-Web-based e-mail platforms	Hotmail, Gmail, Yahoo! Mail
Social Networking Sites	Peer networking	Fan sites, alumni networks, personal news updates	Facebook, Twitter, LinkedIn
Content Aggregators	Hosting of content for information and entertainment	Informative content, podcasts, videos, channels	YouTube, Hulu
Virtual Reality	3-D experience, alternate space	Simulated environments, experiences	Second Life
Online Gaming	Alternate fantasy, entertainment, gaming	MMORPG (massively multiplayer online role-playing games), multiplayer online games	World of Warcraft, StarCraft II
Blogs	Opinions, information, viewpoints	Helpdesk, viewpoints, opinions	MrBrown.com Xiaxue.com
Portals	Aggregating news, communication tools	News studies, sponsored pages, ads	Asiaone.com, Yahoo!
Social News Sites	Peer-ranked news stories	News stories, popular blog content	Digg.com

Social media have been defined in numerous ways. Using the simplest definition from the *Merriam-Webster* dictionary, social media is defined as: "Forms of electronic communication (such as Web sites) through which people create online communities to share information, ideas, personal messages, etc."[15] As can be seen in Figure 15–3 there are numerous ways for consumers to access these sites (desktops, laptops, tablets, smartphones, and connected devices), as well as a variety of reasons for using them, including sharing information, networking, and so forth. The most popular of these are **social networking sites**, which are platforms for networks or social relations among people who share interests, activities, backgrounds, or real-life connections. While there are hundreds of social networks in existence, a small number of these dominate in terms of membership. Prior to discussing each of them and how marketers have used them, let's first examine the characteristics of the platforms.

Who Uses Social Media and Why   The use of social media is truly a worldwide phenomenon; there is a presence on every continent, with an estimated 2.5 billion users in 2017.[16] Many of the top user sites are in China (where Facebook is not allowed). China is the most socially engaged social media market, with over 608 million mobile social network users.[17] As you will see when we discuss social networks, the demographics of the users of these sites vary, as do the reasons for using them. Let's start off by examining why users of these sites do so, and who they are.

Although a number of motivations for using social media have been identified (sharing ideas, activities, and events with others; community involvement, etc.), marketers are most interested in why individuals use these platforms from a consumer behavior perspective. In a series of studies, Muntinga examined the motivations for using social media in a brand-related context[18] (Consumers Online Brand-Related Activities—COBRAs). Specifically, the studies focused on why consumers

FIGURE 15-3

Social Media Landscape

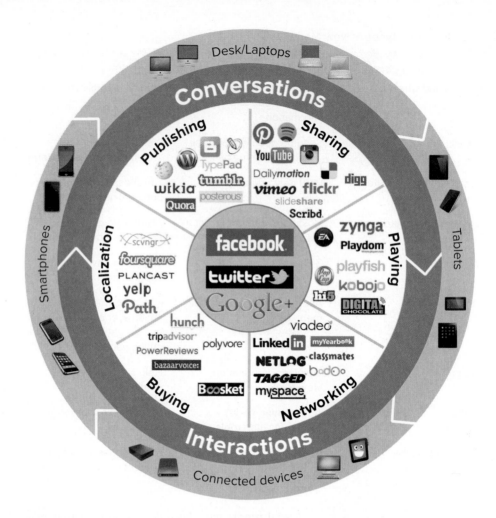

(1) consume, (2) contribute to, and/or (3) create brand-related content. His results indicated that these COBRAs are driven by three primary motivations: (1) to gain information, (2) entertainment, and (3) remuneration. Gaining information included gathering prepurchase information, knowledge about brands, and new ideas. Entertainment involved enjoyment, relaxation, and passing time. Remuneration involved the potential to get something in return—for example, money, job-related benefits, or other rewards (social attraction, etc.). As will be seen throughout our further discussions, the ability for marketers to satisfy these motivations directly reflects their potential for success.

A Pew Research study recently showed that as much as 65 percent of all Internet users say that they use social networks, which places the number in the billions of users (Facebook alone has over 1.4 billion users).[19] Although the networks are appealing to a range of demographics, they are particularly appealing to those between the ages of 18 and 29, and some are more appealing to women. As one might expect, the older age groups are less likely to engage in social media, particularly networks, though usage is on the increase in these segments as well. Overall growth and time spent on social media has slowed in the past few years, perhaps indicating maturity.

Prior to examining these social media, let's examine how and why marketers use them in an IMC program. Again, the examples provided are but a sampling of the many ways marketers have used these media.

How Marketers Use Social Media In a study of 3,000 marketers conducted by Social Media Examiner, an amazing 97 percent said they now include social media in their marketing plans, with 92 percent stating that social media are important to their marketing success.[20] As can be seen in Figure 15–4, the primary reasons

FIGURE 15–4 The Social Media Landscape

CMO.COM — Adobe
GOOD ☐ OK ☐ BAD ☐

	f (Facebook)	g+ (Google+)	Twitter	P (Pinterest)	in (LinkedIn)	YouTube
CUSTOMER COMMUNICATION	Facebook is an easy and efficient way to reach your entire demographic, but if you want to reach non-fans, you have to pay for sponsored posts. Facebook can be used to create and push content, or to help manage reputation.	Google+ still lacks the reach of Facebook and Twitter, but it does facilitate communication with customers—even if they are not in your circles.	Twitter is the best channel for direct communication with customers. Most under-24s prefer it as a forum for customer service.	Although businesses now have a presence on Pinterest, little opportunity exists for direct communication with customers.	LinkedIn provides the opportunity to connect with customers through groups with specific interests connected to your brand.	Video enables customer involvement in the most unique way possible. Customers can be entertained, informed, and engaged—all at the same time. They also can respond directly through comments.
BRAND EXPOSURE	Facebook is one of the easiest, quickest, and most cost-effective ways to gain brand exposure.	Because you can reach people who are outside your circles, Google+ offers excellent brand exposure. Google+ accounts also appear in branded search results, which adds credibility and increased exposure.	Twitter is an easy and cost-effective way to gain exposure for your brand.	Visual content is viewed 70% more than written content. This makes Pinterest a powerful tool for brand exposure. What's more, about 25% of users have purchased a product/service they discovered on Pinterest.	LinkedIn provides impressive exposure to the business world, allowing you to promote personal and business brands to professional contacts and communities.	YouTube is a community. As such, it allows sharing, channel creation, and advertising, which is becoming more accepted by users—provided the video is worth watching.
TRAFFIC TO YOUR SITE	It's as simple as this: Fan page + 1 like = 20 new site visitors.	Google+ provides more worthwhile traffic. Users tend to stay on the sites whose links they follow.	Twitter has an unmatched ability to drive traffic directly to a site.	Pinned images contain links back to a site, which is why Pinterest tends to be one of the top three traffic referral sites.	LinkedIn is not a huge referral source for sites yet, but numbers are climbing. Connections and search engines can generate traffic.	YouTube can drive traffic to a site through links in a video and ads before a video begins. Popular channels and videos are highly effective in driving traffic.
SEO	Although social sharing might hold more weight in the future, right now only shared links from fan pages matter, not personal links.	The Google +1 button allows users to search both public and privately shared information. This has a knock-on effect for SEO and search engine ranking.	Google gives authority ranks for Twitter profiles, so link juice is limited.	Pinterest does not pass much link juice, and pinning does not allow follow links.	LinkedIn doesn't have a huge effect on individual content yet, but its profiles remain some of the easiest and most frequently SEO-ranked social profiles on the Web.	Active YouTube channels bump up SEO rankings. Integrating keywords, site maps, titles, and robot text files help judge relevance.

for using social media are to (1) drive traffic to one's site, (2) communicate with customers, and (3) gain brand exposure. The most important benefit these marketers believe they derive from the use of social media is increased exposure (89 percent). A close examination of Figure 15–4 indicates that marketers find different media more effective for achieving specific objectives. For example, Twitter is considered the best channel for direct communication with consumers, while LinkedIn may be better for connecting with specific groups (like professionals). At the same time, LinkedIn may be the least effective for driving traffic. Each site contributes in more than one way.

Interestingly, although marketers strongly believe that social media are a necessary component in their marketing programs, they still feel uncertain as to how to use these media tactically and how to measure their effectiveness. Studies have shown that the ability to measure the effectiveness of these media is of major concern, and may hinder their increased adoption into marketing programs.

Let's examine some of the more popular social media, and how marketers use them in their IMC programs. We start our discussion with the most popular sites used by marketers.

The Most Popular Social Media

Facebook The largest of all social networks, Facebook has over 1.4 billion subscribers worldwide, covering six continents and 100 countries, who say they are on the site monthly. In 2016, sources estimated that the average time spent on the site per day was 50 minutes, constituting more than half of the 1.72 hours per day spent on all social media[21] (Figure 15–5). While the site has been somewhat controversial over the years as a result of frequently changing its privacy agreements, and other privacy-related issues, businesses have found Facebook to be a valuable communications medium. Based on advertising revenues, marketers consider Facebook to be the most important social platform for advertising; the site accounted for 31.2 percent ($10.29 billion) of all display ad spending in the United States in 2016.[22] Facebook leads all other social media in display advertising revenues.

Just as individuals can exchange information by posting on a "wall," companies can as well by posting information about the company and/or its products, photos, promotions, events, news, and so on. Facebook also allows advertising that can be targeted to subsets of Facebook users based on demographic and geographic data and interests and activities. In addition, because Facebook knows what pages its members like and visit, what their interests are, and even who is in their social network, targeting can become even more precise—and, as you might expect, create even more privacy concerns. Due to market place challenges, Facebook itself has evolved in an attempt to become an even more attractive medium for marketers by adding a number of new marketing tools, including sponsored stories, more targeted ads, and mobile video formats including Facebook Live. The increased time being spent on mobile and engagement with video have led Facebook to continue to develop new programs and attract new advertisers.

Facebook has become a "must have" medium for many marketers who have used the site in a variety of ways. Throughout this text we have shown numerous examples of how companies use Facebook. Some other companies that use the site are shown in Exhibit 15–7.

Now the site offers advertisers the opportunity to employ virtual reality–style ads that appear as sponsored posts in news feeds. Mountain Dew, Vice, and Mondelēz have already placed such ads,

EXHIBIT 15–7

An example of advertisements on Facebook

Source: SweetBling.com

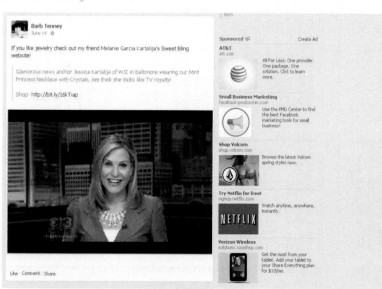

	2013	2014
All Internet Users	71%	71%
Men	66	66
Women	76	77
White, non-Hispanic	71	71
Black, non-Hispanic	76	67
Hispanic	73	73
18–29	84	87
30–49	79	73
50–64	60	63
65+	45	56*
High school grad or less	71	70
Some college	75	71
College+ (n = 685)	68	74*
Less than $30,000/yr	76	77
$30,000–$49,999	76	69
$50,000–$74,999	68	74
$75,000+	69	72
Urban	75	71
Suburban	69	72
Rural	71	69

Note: Percentages marked with an asterisk (*) represent a significant change from 2013. Results are significant at the 95% confidence level using an independent z-test.

Source: Pew Research Center's Internet Project. September Combined Omnibus Survey, September 11–14 and September 18–21, 2014. N = 1,597 Internet users ages 18+. The margin of error for all Internet users is +/− 2.9 percentage points. 2013 data from Pew Internet August Tracking Survey, August 7–September 16, 2013. N = 1,445 Internet users ages 18+.

EXHIBIT 15–8

In this AT&T Facebook virtual reality ad, viewers are able to get in the driver's seat, enjoy the 360° view, and hear how race car driver Ben Albano uses the AT&T network

Source: AT&T Inc.

and AT&T, Nestlé, and Samsung are soon to follow (Exhibit 15–8). As Facebook continues to move into the video arena, you can expect its ad revenues to continue to grow into the future.

Twitter Twitter is an online social network microblogging network that enables users to send and receive text-based messages (tweets) up to 140 characters in length (at the time of this writing Twitter was considering increasing the number of characters allowed to 10,000). Twitter has over 1.3 billion registered users, but only about 300 million who are active users (the others apparently just observe) and continues to grow.[23] Like Facebook, Twitter has international appeal, with the largest bases in the United States and Great Britain. Over half of all companies that use social media in their marketing plans use Twitter, given the finding that 50 percent of all users follow brands on Twitter and are likely to both buy and recommend brands they follow to others.[24]

Like Facebook, many marketers have found Twitter a useful tool for communicating with their customers and potential customers and, as noted in the CMO report shown earlier (Figure 15–4), may be the very best tool for establishing connections with customers. For example, a number of brands including AT&T, Capital One, Dove Men's Care, Nike, and Buick purchased promoted tweets in real time during the NCAA "March Madness" college basketball tourney. AT&T sent out courtside photos through Twitter, encouraging fans to be engaged in the games while connecting with other viewers.

When Mercedes-Benz introduced its new A-Class automobile, a commercial was run on the popular TV show *X Factor* integrating the cast into a chase scene. Viewers were in control of the action in the scene and by tweeting #evade or #hide they determined the action in the 30-second spot. The "commercial you drive" was viewed by hundreds of thousands of viewers, and was considered a contributor to the product's launch success.

The City of St. Louis also found Twitter to be an effective medium for reaching its market. In this case, the medium was used in a nonprofit effort to find ways to improve the city titled "Tweet Me in St. Louis." After establishing a community-based website (www.rallystl.org), the organization used Facebook and Twitter to crowdsource ideas on how to improve the city as well as crowdfunding to raise money to support the ideas generated. The public was asked to tweet ideas in regard to cultural arts, education, housing, or virtually anything else that they thought needed improvement. After the period for submitting ideas was closed, participants were asked to vote on the best ones—again by tweeting their vote. Those involved believed that the simplicity of the ability to tweet a response was a major factor contributing to the campaign's success. Virgin America, Sephora, and Starbucks, among others, have all used Twitter's enhanced promoted tweets program, which ensures that tweets from their brands will appear at the top of the timeline for those who follow the brand. Other companies have found that Twitter can be used to respond to customer complaints and/or inquiries, retweeting important information and monitoring the market to watch for opportunities or threats. Exhibit 15–9 shows a Twitter ad Hostess ran to celebrate the beginning of baseball season.

Like Facebook, Twitter has made substantial changes to the site in an effort to gain advertising revenues. Twitter now offers advertisers a "tailored audiences program" in which users who visit a website and also use Twitter could be found later for retargeting purposes. Brands can also share their e-mail lists with Twitter and deliver ads to their customers. The idea is that companies can create tailored audiences using lists of Twitter IDs to build a more potentially interested database.[25] Database marketing companies Acxiom, Merkle, and Mailchimp, among others are assisting brands in this endeavor.

Twitter actually scored a touchdown, so to speak, beating out competitors Facebook, Amazon, and Verizon to win the rights to Live-Stream NFL Thursday Night Football games along with pre- and postgame shows and behind-the-scenes coverage provided by Periscope. According to chief operating officer Adam Bain, Twitter "continues our strategy to build the world's best daily connected audience that watches together and can talk with one another in real-time."[26]

Instagram By far the fastest-growing social network is Instagram. The online photo-sharing and social networking site allows users to post and edit pictures and share them on a variety of social networks, such as Facebook or Twitter. In 2016 the site had almost 400 million users, a 15.1 percent gain over 2015 (compared to approximately 8 percent by Pinterest and Twitter).[27] Marketers in numerous industries worldwide have found Instagram useful for a variety of communications activities. Instragram's visual content allows companies to post pictures and video news, events, new product introductions,

nike   Follow

434k likes   70w

nike You don't have to stop to smell the flowers.

view all 2,264 comments

lcunneen1343 Lovely sene

nfrancenia Great

gyulia_ @aurynjosh97

kaylamarielindsay Let's go on a run @emmataylor_13

mukhlis_cr7 so prettyy

ridwan2300 so beutyful

paulas_life Awesome!!!

e_esta_foodie where? japan ?where"""nice area"

semra_k28

princes.af @nicoledevries1

s.a.b.18 Nice

Log in to like or comment.

EXHIBIT 15–10

Nike is considered one of the most successful users of Instagram

Source: NIKE Inc.

and other company- or brand-related activities to increase exposure, showcase products in a creative way, establish visual brand identity, and more. Many marketers consider Instagram to be the most engaging of all social networks. Companies have initiated very successful contests in which they engage consumers by having them post pictures related to their brands. In its #SonyLove contest, Sony asked people to first follow the company on Instagram and then post pictures of anything that represented "love" to them. One entry was chosen every day to win a $50 Sony Store gift card or other Sony merchandise based on their entry. Virgin America frequently surprises flyers with a gift and posts them in a picture on Instagram, or encourages its followers to do the same. Given the ability to post pictures to garner engagement, the variety of uses of this site for marketers seem almost endless (Figure 15–6).

Snapchat Originally developed as an app that had disappearing pictures, Snapchat has now evolved into a mix of private messaging and public content, including brand networks, publications, and live events such as sports and music. Nevertheless, studies have shown that the personal-oriented messaging was still being accessed by users more than the publicly offered content that was being presented. Seventy-one percent of users surveyed said that they preferred the app for its chat, messaging, and imaging services, versus 5 percent who almost exclusively chose the various events, brand features, and celebrity content on a daily basis. Twenty-four percent responded that they accessed all features equally. While at first wary of using the site, the fast growth, particularly among millennials, has become an attractive medium to advertisers. Amazon, Hollister, Macy's, Samsung, and Universal Pictures have all run Snapchat campaigns, and McDonald's, in particular, is placing a lot of emphasis on marketing through snaps. Luxury brand Michael Kors used Snapchat's "Stories" feature at New York's Fashion Week showing content from runway pictures, backstage shots, and front-row pictures[28] (Exhibit 15–11).

Snapchat attributes much of its newfound success to the fact that it is very mobile friendly—particularly with its vertical video feature—and well-liked and considered fun by millennials. The company is now experimenting with an e-commerce component.

FIGURE 15–6

How Brands Use Instagram

Here are just a few examples of how brands have successfully employed Instagram:

Nike—The most followed brand on Instagram, Nike keeps it simple. For example, one photo shows a woman jogging through a beautiful row of cherry blossom trees with the caption "You don't have to stop and smell the flowers." Simple, but eye-catching and interesting. Nike also uses influencers such as soccer star Cristiano Ronaldo and other athletes.

Reebok—Taking a different approach from Nike, ReebockWomen inspires women to be better, stronger, and more determined. Visual content focuses on effort, action, and sweat with an emphasis on action images and sports while striking a balance between athletes and everyday women.

Chanel—Keeping it plain and simple like Nike, the product is always front and center. One series included Gisele Bundchen talking about her makeup secrets.

Staples—Attention-getting vivid colors exaggerated by a white background that appear hypnotic. Over 8 percent of Staples customers say they view the posts.

Saks Fifth Avenue—With a Like2tobuy platform, the Saks posts are shoppable. The attractiveness and diversity of its photos including store windows, Gucci shoe displays, and Louis Vuitton shots lure consumers into the photos.

EXHIBIT 15–11

Luxury brand Michael Kors Snapchat ads

Source: Michael Kors

EXHIBIT 15–12

A number of companies have found Pinterest to be useful in their IMC programs

© *Southwest Airlines*

Pinterest Pinterest is a pinboard-style photo-sharing website that allows users to create and manage theme-based image collections such as events, interests, and hobbies. Users can browse other pinboards for images, "re-pin" images to their own pinboards, or "like" photos. Pinterest is most attractive to females, with approximately 71 percent of their users women.[29] As with Instagram, Sony has found this site to be quite useful in its marketing efforts as have numerous others such as Whole Foods, Southwest Airlines, and GE (Exhibit 15–12). Nordstrom has used Pinterest to post pictures of new product offerings, to make its blog more appealing, and to sponsor a bridal contest in which brides-to-be could win prizes including cash, a bridal consultant, and a hotel stay at a J.W. Marriott Resort. Many other marketers targeting women have found Pinterest to be an effective medium. As opposed to Facebook, Instagram, and Twitter, Pinterest offers the opportunity to see pinners' product preferences, plans, and aspirations. There were over 110 million active users of Pinterest in 2016.[30]

LinkedIn Another social networking site but with a different audience, LinkedIn now has over 400 million business professionals as members—128 million in the United States.[31] While the site is primarily used by professionals to network, businesses have used banner ads on the site in an attempt to reach this professional audience to promote their products and services. LinkedIn offers marketers the opportunity to connect to customers with specific interests that may be related to their brand.

YouTube Another powerful social medium, YouTube is a content aggregator, hosting content for information and entertainment. Users can upload and share their own videos, as well as those placed by others (including companies). The growth of YouTube has been, and continues to be, phenomenal; there are now more than 400 hours of video being uploaded to the site every minute (three times as much as just two years prior) and being sent to more than 1 billion unique users per month around the world. In the United States, YouTube now reaches a larger audience of adults 18 to 34 than any single television network. Projections are that by 2018 YouTube could become as large as CBS or Viacom.[32]

What makes YouTube so effective for marketers is the ability to use the site as an advertising medium or as a search platform (Exhibit 15–13). Marketers can post videos of their products or brands that can be informational (how to build an IKEA bookcase) or entertaining (as noted, companies posted TV commercials on the YouTube site prior to showing them on the Super Bowl). The site is particularly engaging to millennials, the much sought after segment by many marketers—so much so that YouTube has its own stars and vloggers and is now competing with advertising dollars that previously were targeted to broadcast television. Many companies have now established their own YouTube channel, which allows them to have a specifically branded URL and fully customized content. Among the top 10 advertisers on

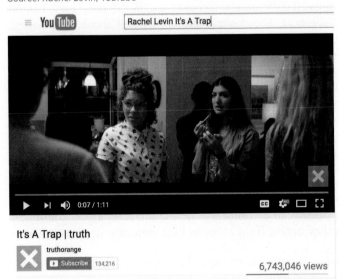

YouTube are Walmart, Target, Lowe's, Amazon, and Walgreens.[33]

The potential for exposure on YouTube is one of the major attractions for marketers large and small. For example, Rachel Levin, a beauty vlogger sometimes referred to as "YouTubes's Cover Girl," has had her antismoking commercial "It's A Trap" viewed 6.5 million times, while overall Levin's videos have been viewed over a billion times. Others, including makeup tutorialist Michelle Phan, has 7.9 million subscribers, Bethany Mota—a teen vlogger—has 9.3 million, and the spoof video Smosh has 21 million.[34] At the same time, a small brand, Orabrush, that had no sales online or offline was able to successfully pull its product into large retail stores like Walmart as a result of its successful YouTube video. In less than two years the Orabush channel garnered over 45 million views, and consumers' demands for the tongue cleaner led to retail distribution. A study conducted by Defy Media showed that for teens, YouTube stars were much more influential on their purchase decisions than were either TV or movie stars, and were fine with the fact that their stars were pushing products and trying to sell them things[35] (Exhibit 15–14).

Additional Social Media   While these are some of the most commonly used social media, there are others that are important to marketers as well:

Other Social Sites   As noted earlier, there are many more social media sites that are useful to marketers in their IMC programs. These sites have been used by marketers for marketing research, public relations, promotions, and a variety of other strategies.

Periscope   A new but quickly growing live streaming app, Periscope gives users 24 hours to watch a live stream and encourages engagement by having viewers use "likes." Brands are using Periscope in a variety of ways. For example, Nissan streamed the unveiling of its 2016 Maxima at the New York Auto Show to create buzz; Taco Bell hosted a mock press conference about a new breakfast menu item and encouraged fans to stop by Taco Bell on Cinco de Mayo to enjoy a free "Biscuit Taco"; JCPenney featured Eva Longoria, who introduced her new bedding collection while answering viewers' questions from a launch in Los Angeles. Coach and GE, among others, are quickly finding new ways to use the app.

What is interesting is that almost all of the social media we have discussed to this point employ many other IMC tools discussed earlier in the text (such as product placements, direct marketing, etc.) as well as blogging, marketing influencers, and native advertising, and their viewers recognize that they are being sold to. For some reason it does not seem to bother them as much as when traditional media try to do the same.

EXHIBIT 15–15

Podcasts have become popular with a number of advertisers

© Ian Dagnall/Alamy

Podcasting **Podcasting** is a medium that uses the Internet to distribute audio or video files for downloading into iPods, iPads, tablets, and other portable devices. As the market for these devices grows, the attractiveness of this medium does as well. Radio stations, including Clear Channel Communications and National Public Radio, and television programs, such as *60 Minutes,* now podcast entire programs or video clips. Traditional advertisers like Ford, Dunkin' Donuts, Wendy's, Allstate, and P&G are just a few of the many companies running ads or sponsorships in the medium, while others are finding it useful as well (Exhibit 15–15). For example, Durex, a condom manufacturer, has purchased product placements in podcasts—in part to reach young listeners with risque marketing messages while skirting FCC decency rules.

As noted by Steven Perlberg, advertising revenue growth in podcasting has been limited by a range of problems not unlike the issues that online media faced in its early days. It is difficult to measure how many people actually tune into a podcast, and ads in podcasts are relatively expensive, making it unclear whether the investment pays off. The process of buying and selling ads in podcasts is still complex and clunky.[36]

RSS **Really Simple Syndication (RSS)** is a specification that uses XML to organize and format Web-based content in a standard way. Content owners create an RSS feed, which usually consists of titles and brief descriptions of about 10 articles elsewhere on the site. The difference between Web content and an RSS feed is that the latter can send out notifications whenever new material is available. Because the alerts can be customized to the viewers' preferences, advertisers have found it useful for disseminating information to those who may be most interested. For example, the *Washington Post* allows for advertising in its RSS feeds, and companies like American Express, Continental Airlines, and Verizon have all run ads through RSS feeds.

Blogs A **blog** (or weblog) is a Web-based publication consisting primarily of periodic articles, normally presented in reverse chronological order. As noted, blogs may reflect the writings of an individual, a community, a political organization, or a corporation, and they offer advertisers a new way to reach their target audiences. For example, there are blogs about beer, current events, sports, raising children, and so on. In 2016 there were an estimated 295 million active blogs on the Internet.[37] Tumblr is the largest worldwide blog host. Some marketers are excited about the potential of blogs to reach large or targeted audiences at a small cost. Besides banner ads, companies can buy pay per click ads and/or become an affiliate. As a result, these marketers attempt to keep the bloggers happy by feeding them exclusives, releasing product news to them before it hits the mainstream, and so on. Others are a bit more skeptical, noting that there are a number of problems with the use of blogs, including the potential for deception and limited reach. These critics cite the use of mommy bloggers (there is a network of 23,000 in the United States) and teen bloggers who may support brands and promote them for compensation to unsuspecting audiences. These critics are also concerned about the ethics of companies employing other forms of "influencers" as shown in Ethical Perspective 15–2. Whether bloggers are full-time professionals or just hobbyists, many of them write about brands they love or hate (or love to hate!), and their influence on consumers is on the increase, as the consumers often use the information they obtain from blogs in their purchase decisions.

Other 2.0 Media Forms There are numerous other 2.0 media forms also available to marketers including the use of virtual and augmented reality and QR codes.

EXHIBIT 15–16

Yelp guides potential consumers using augmented reality

© Yelp.com

Virtual/Augmented Reality While it may seem like something out of the future, **virtual and augmented reality** are very much here. The virtual reality world Second Life has not lived up to expectations, but there are now thousands of augmented reality apps that are currently being used by marketers and consumers alike, and the future promises much more. For example, Wikitude World Browser is widely regarded as one of the best of all augmented reality browsers. As one travels around an area, Wikitude will provide just about any geographically relevant information needed, including *Wikipedia* articles for landmarks, ATM locations, YouTube videos, tweets, Foursquare locations, and so on. Yelp Monocle (Exhibit 15–16) uses cell phone GPS and compass data to display star rating and review counts for nearby businesses on top of the camera view in real time. Other AR apps can help one find subways, metros, and transit stops; calculate distances between locations; as well as provide many more forms of helpful information content. As noted in Chapter 14, companies are now incorporating augmented reality into their catalogs, brochures, and so on. IKEA is testing an interactive virtual reality kitchen on a gaming platform. The app creates a full-size virtual kitchen in which users can interact with objects as though they were there, and experiment with different kitchen designs, colors, and so forth. Lowe's, Toms, and North Face are also employing virtual reality in their stores to make shopping more fun and to enhance the shopping experience. Wheaties employed an augmented cereal box that allowed consumers to interact with and share their interactions via Facebook, Twitter, and e-mail.

QR Codes While **QR codes** may not have reached the potential expected, many marketers have used them effectively. A large percentage of print ads now carry the bar codes, but consumers have not used them as frequently as expected. An example of a successful application of this technology was a joint effort between Disney and Cargill (Honeysuckle White and Shady Brook Farms meats) that used mobile bar codes to entice consumers to buy through a "Wreck-It Ralph" Blu-ray combo pack promotion. Cargill placed QR bar codes on 7 million packages of turkey products that, when scanned, took consumers to a website where they could get a $5 mail-in rebate over their mobile device. The very popular app Shazam is another good example of the use of a form of QR code, in which radio listeners can immediately identify a song, artist, and album title through their cell phones. Just as it seems that QR codes may be beginning to grow in popularity, they are being threatened by a new technology, near field communication (NFC). NFC enables marketers to deliver content through an embedded chip that allows wireless communications just by touching the material or being in close proximity to the NFC tag. Essentially, the NFC tag performs the same function as a QR code but with much less effort required on the part of the consumer. Interestingly, and sadly, the famed 120-year-old Cracker Jack replaced its toy surprise that was in each and every box with a QR code that buyers could scan to see if they won anything. (Have we gone too far with digital?)

Sales Promotion on the Internet

Companies have found the Internet to be a very effective medium for disseminating sales promotions. Numerous companies tie in sales promotions to their

Influencer Marketing: Using Social Media Celebrities to Market Brands

What's the fastest-growing marketing tool on the Internet? The growth of the use of influencers. A poll of marketing professionals reported on in *Chief!Marketer* indicated that the use of social media celebrities in an attempt to stimulate word-of-mouth advertising was the fastest-growing channel being employed by business-to-consumer marketing execs. Companies now spend hours of time scanning the social media world or, alternatively, hiring agencies that already have the connections, to find "social standouts" whom they can hire to promote their products for them. But who are these standouts you ask? They can range from the girl next door to professional influencers, from mommy bloggers to fashionistas, and they are in the perfect position to succeed given the current state of the existing marketplace combining the dual worlds of millennials and the social media. Given the evidence that millennials trust their peers more than advertisements and use social media more than traditional media, the "perfect storm" has led to the use of peers who share common interests to become brand evangelists—for a fee, of course. Companies no longer need to find and vet influencers because there are now a number of talent agencies, networks, and matchmaking services that specialize in this business, many of whom are owned by large companies like the Walt Disney Company (Maker Studios) and Twitter (Niche). While it is hard to determine how much companies are spending in this market, it is obvious that the market is growing.

Take Robby Ayala, for example. Robby dropped out of law school to pursue a full-time video career making goofy six-second movies to post on the video service Vine and streamed to his 2.6 million followers each day. Getting paid thousands of dollars to create videos, Ayala turned his hobby into a business that works as a talent scouting service and ad agency rolled into one matching social media stars with marketers and advertisers who want to reach young users like his followers. His company, according to Niche, has nearly 3,000 social media accounts and has reached 500 million followers, working with 70 brands including the likes of Home Depot, General Electric, and Gap Kids. Niche itself is now valued at $11 million. And then there are fashion influencers Ann-Marie Hoang and Chriselle Lim, just two of hundreds of such individuals who make in excess of $100,000 a year by having their photos posted on Instagram and other social media while shopping and having them viewed by thousands of followers.

What is it about influencers—usually referred to as opinion leaders in the old days—that makes them so attractive to marketers? When asked, marketers usually cite a number of advantages: (1) Influencers are able to reach a very targeted audience (for example, cross-training fans); (2) they create trust; (3) they generate engagement; (4) they are social; (5) their followers are tired of paid ads; and (6) their title trends high and is classified as

© Gustavo Caballero/Getty Images

a "breakout," which means that the keyword *influencers experience* growth greater than 5,000 percent. The bottom line is they think the influencer strategy generates strong revenue at a low price. For example, when 50 influencers posted an Instagram picture of themselves wearing and touting the same Lord & Taylor dress on the same day, the dress sold out the following weekend!

Of course, not everyone is convinced. According to a study examining 48 influencer marketing programs across 15 U.S. industries and 662 influencers conducted by Burst Media, advertisers earned $6.85 for every $1.00 they spent on the programs. But the highest returns were limited to certain industries like consumer packaged goods, followed by retailers and apparel brands. Many other categories like supermarkets, shoes, toys and games, and garden products gained far less. Social engagement rates also varied, indicating that the use of the channel was not for everyone. In addition, most influencers now want cash for their sponsorship, with 70 percent preferring monetary compensation on a per-post-cost and only 11 percent opting for free products or affiliate partnerships (4 percent) or running ads on their blogs (4 percent). Whereas the endorsements are supposed to indicate that they are "sponsored" or "paid ads," many do not, leading to the potential for deception and a loss of self-image. Finally, companies like Pinterest actually lose advertising revenue when "Pinfluencers"—influencers who pin products—reduce the number of ads the products may have purchased on the Pinterest site.

Overall, one has to ask if influencers are really "deceivers."

Sources: "Influencer Marketing Is Rapidly Gaining Popularity among Brand Marketers," February 9, 2016, www.eMarketer.com; Mike Shields and Jack Marshall, "Paid 'Influencers' Undercut ads on Pinterest," *The Wall Street Journal,* January 16, 2015, pp. B1, B5; "Influencers Want Cash," November 6. 2015, www.warc.com; "Influencer Marketing: All It's Cracked Up to Be?" March 18, 2015, www.eMarketer; Paresh Dave, "Tapping Fashion 'Influencers,'" *Los Angeles Times,* January 2, 2015, pp. B1, B2.

EXHIBIT 15–17

Sales promotions are common on websites

Source: The Ghirardelli Chocolate Company

websites and/or through other forms of digital and social media. Approximately 57.5 percent of U.S. Internet users 18 and older redeemed digital coupons or codes in 2015.[38] Ghirardelli engages in the use of sales promotions with its website as do many others (Exhibit 15–17). Numerous companies now print online coupons. Other examples include the use of trivia games, contests, sweepstakes, instant win promotions, and so on.

Personal Selling on the Internet

The Internet has been both a benefit and a detriment to many of those involved in personal selling—particularly those in the business-to-business market. For some, the Internet has been a threat that might take away job opportunities. Companies have found that they can remain effective, or even increase effectiveness, by building a strong online presence. The high-cost and poor-reach disadvantages of personal selling are allowing these companies to reduce new hires and even cut back on their existing sales forces.

On the positive side, websites have been used quite effectively to enhance and support the selling effort. As noted earlier, digital and social media have become a primary source of information for millions of customers in the consumer and business-to-business markets. Visitors to websites can gain volumes of information about a company's products and services. In return, the visitors become a valuable resource for leads that both internal and external salespersons can follow up, and they become part of a prospect database. Not only can potential customers learn about the company's offerings, but the selling organization can serve and qualify prospects more cost-effectively.

The Web can also be used to stimulate trial. For many companies, personal salespersons can reach only a fraction of the potential customer base. Through trial demonstrations or samples offered online, customers can determine if the offering satisfies their needs and, if so, request a personal sales call. In such cases both parties benefit from time and cost savings.

Companies have used the Internet to improve their one-on-one relationships with customers. By providing more information in a more timely and efficient manner, a company enables customers to learn more about what it has to offer. This increases the opportunity for cross-selling and customer retention. Twitter has become a powerful tool for consumers to voice their opinions of companies or complaints, while also allowing the involved company to respond quickly.

In a well-designed IMC program, the Internet and personal selling are designed to be complementary tools, working together to increase sales. It appears that more and more companies are coming to this realization.

Public Relations on the Internet

The Internet is a useful medium for conducting public relations activities. Many sites devote a portion of their content to public relations activities, including the provision of information about the company, its philanthropic activities, annual reports, and more.

Companies, nonprofit organizations, and political parties have become quite adept at using the Internet for public relations purposes. An excellent example of the use of public relations on the Internet is provided by Chrysler (Exhibit 15–18). The site provides up-to-date news stories and other forms of content, photo images, and cross-references to other sites or media as well as press kits and a calendar of upcoming events. It also provides information about Chrysler automobiles and the corporation

itself and allows for customer feedback and registration for updates. In addition, Chrysler's homepage contains many of the articles written about the corporation, including awards won and philanthropic efforts achieved such as its concern for the environment and support for numerous causes.

Other examples of the effective use of public relations activities on the Internet are also available, as you will see in the chapter on public relations. The Web is a useful medium for conducting public relations activities, and its use for this function is on the increase.

At the same time, many philanthropic and nonprofit organizations have found the Internet to be a useful way to generate funds. As noted earlier, charitable organizations have also formed sites to handle public relations activities, provide information regarding the causes the charity supports, collect contributions, and so on. In an example of integrating the Internet with public relations and television, companies have found the Internet to be extremely useful for providing information in times of a crisis and for gathering feedback about their products and services and about themselves (particularly through blogs and RSS feeds).

Direct Marketing on the Internet

Our discussion of direct marketing and the Internet approached the topic from two perspectives: the use of direct-marketing tools for communications objectives and e-commerce (as discussed in Chapter 14). As we stated previously, many direct-marketing tools like direct mail, infomercials, and the like have been adapted to the Internet. At the same time, e-commerce—selling directly to the consumer via the Internet—has become an industry all its own.

MOBILE

As dramatic an impact that the Internet had on companies' IMC programs, it almost pales in comparison to the changes brought about by **mobile**. Spawned by the rapid adoption of smartphones and tablets, mobile is now receiving strong attention from marketers, and ad revenues continue to climb, primarily through applications (apps). A study reported by Comscore reported that by 2016 smartphone penetration in the United States had reached 79.3 percent or 198.9 million persons.[39] While all digital advertising revenues were expected to increase slightly through 2019, mobile was expected to grow by 59 percent in 2015 alone, surpassing desktop ads and print and accounting for 51.9 percent of total digital spending (Figure 15–7). As adoption of these phones and tablets increases, content consumption will grow right along with

FIGURE 15–7 U.S. Mobile Ad Spending, 2013–2019

	2013	2014	2015	2016	2017	2018	2019
Mobile ad spending (billions)	**$10.67**	**$19.15**	**$28.72**	**$40.50**	**$49.81**	**$57.78**	**$65.87**
—% change	120.0%	79.5%	50.0%	41.0%	23.0%	16.0%	14.0%
—% of digital ad spending	24.7%	37.7%	49.0%	60.4%	66.6%	69.7%	72.2%
—% of total media ad spending	6.3%	10.8%	15.3%	20.4%	23.9%	26.3%	28.6%

Note: Includes classified, display (banners and other, rich media, and video), e-mail, lead generation, messaging-based, and search advertising; ad spending on tablets is included.

Source: eMarketer, March 2015.

it, and so too will advertising spending to reach these users. Marketers see mobile as offering very strong potential and will continue to move monies from traditional media to mobile. Figure 15–8 shows where these dollars will be allocated within the digital platform.

While more dollars are being moved from traditional media to mobile, a number of studies have shown that tablets have led to increases in search behavior and online purchasing and have dramatically changed the way we view television. While one might think tablets may be responsible for decreasing TV watching, this is not the case; more than half of those tablet owners surveyed indicated it had no impact, while many respondents under the age of 50 said it actually *increased* their TV viewing.[40] The amount of TV watching may not be changing much, but the way that it is being watched has. Younger consumers are much more likely to report that they watch TV with their tablet with them, posting, e-mailing, and texting friends as well as seeking information about program content and commercials while viewing.

The appeal of mobile stems in part from the fact that younger generations media usage habits have changed. As we have seen throughout this text their use of print media is down, what was television viewing is now taking place on tablets, and sales of desktops and laptops are being replaced by smartphones and tablets. In fact, some studies show that many smartphone owners use their devices to make

CHAPTER 15

FIGURE 15–8

U.S. Digital Ad Spending, by Device, 2013–2019 (in Billions)

Note: Desktop includes spending primarily on desktop-based ads. Mobile includes classifieds, display (banners and other, rich media, and video), e-mail, lead generation, messaging-based advertising and search advertising; ad spending on tablets is included.

Source: eMarketer, March 2015.

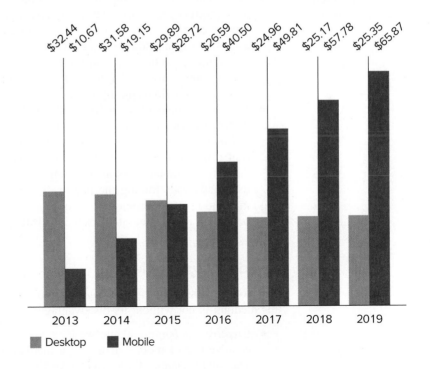

EXHIBIT 15–19

Scharffen Berger effectively uses mobile to advertise its brand

Source: Scharffen Berger Chocolate Maker

phone calls less than they do for other activities. Being in constant touch is critical for many millennials, which opens up the opportunity for marketers to reach potential consumers at almost any time and any place—even at the point of purchase. (Next time you are in a public place, take a minute to look around at how many people are on their cell phones!) As the technology continues to advance, marketers will continue to be more and more creative, and more effective with their sales messages—for example, vertical videos!

The Role of Mobile in the IMC Process

If you have been reading the previous sections of this chapter, you have already seen how mobile has already been integrated with other media. We have discussed mobile ads, provided examples of sales promotions and direct marketing and even product placements through the phones. We have also pointed out that marketing influencers can now reach consumers through their smartphones and when users access Facebook and/or other social networks on their phones, marketers are provided with even more opportunities to reach them. The use of native ads on smartphones and tablets has been deemed to be quite effective and on the increase.

Let's look at some specific examples of successful mobile marketing tactics:

- The automobile industry has found that marketing through mobile is effective throughout the purchase funnel. At the top of the funnel mobile, tablet, and video ads have all been shown to contribute to encouraging potential buyers to begin to look for a new car (exceeded only by direct mail). One study indicated that the automobile industry led all global industries in the number of video completions of mobile banner ads.[41]

- Advertising dollars being allocated to mobile search will continue to increase as marketers recognize that search on smartphone and tablet devices is on the increase. A study by FordDirect showed that 81 percent of auto shoppers used smartphones to research different autos. Twenty-five percent of these used smartphones exclusively, and once on the lot, 25 percent used their phones to access more sources of information.[42] Shoppers were also using their phones to arrange for financing options.

- In other examples, Burger King delivered mobile coupons to consumers within a geofence; Hershey's offered to sponsor data costs for consumers who watched a video for its Scharffen Berger chocolate brand (Exhibit 15–19); JetBlue sent different messages to tablet and smartphone users, and offered a video game to the tablet users as they might have more time to watch; McDonald's used native ads touting the nature of their coffee. As you can see, mobile is integrating other promotional components into their campaigns while itself becoming more integrated itself into IMC programs.

Disadvantages of Mobile

Lest you be mislead into believing that mobile is the be all and end all of media, this medium is not without its disadvantages:

- *Creative challenges*—While we have provided some excellent examples of the creative use of mobile, it is still a medium that challenges creative directors. The small screens limit what advertisers can do as compared to the larger screens of TV and even desktops. The JetBlue example provided earlier is one interesting approach to this challenge.

- *Time*—The very nature of being mobile means viewers may be on the move, thus providing less time to get attention, and limits message capabilities. Unlike the desktop and some traditional media, the viewer is not settled in to use the medium. Thus, it is more difficult to get, and hold, attention, and the message may have to be limited and short.
- *Sharing*—Maybe we should say *not sharing*. One study found that 99 percent of mobile devices users do not like to share what they see. Thus, one of the key objectives of digital advertisers is to get engagement, responding to the brand, providing feedback and extending the reach to make the message viral. Desktop users are 35 percent more likely to click on a sharing button than mobile users.[43]
- *Reach*—While mobile has certainly been adopted by the millennials, other segments are not as enamored with the medium. Gen Xers are less likely to be as favorably inclined toward mobile than are millennials; baby boomers don't seem to be enamored at all, with only 7.9 percent saying they are likely to purchase products advertised on mobile, and only 5.2 percent saying they would be interested in receiving an ad on their phone.[44]

Despite its potential weaknesses, mobile will continue to be adopted and is expected to constitute approximately 72 percent of all digital advertising by 2019.

INTERNET METRICS

LO15-3

Companies measuring the effectiveness of digital and social media employ a variety of methods, most of which are done electronically. As you will see, a number of companies provide Internet measures as part of a package; that is, they provide audience measurement information (demographics, psychographics, etc.) as "up-front" information as well as some of the effectiveness measures described below. First, we will discuss some of the measures used to determine the effectiveness of a website. Then we will discuss some of the companies providing these measures.

FIGURE 15–9

Example Internet Metrics

Source: IAB.net.

Clicks

Post-click conversions

Cost per conversion

Unique visitors

Average frequency

Frequency to conversion ratios

Advertising exposure time

Ad interaction rate

View-through rate

Visits

Webpage eye tracking

Offline sales lift

Cross-media models

Audience Measures and Measures of Effectiveness

When the Internet industry first developed its own measures of effectiveness, problems with these measures led to a slower rate of adoption by traditional media buyers. In an attempt to respond to criticism of the audience metrics employed, as well as to standardize some of the measures used to gauge effectiveness of the Internet, the Interactive Advertising Bureau (IAB)—the largest and most influential trade group—formed a task force in November 2004 consisting of major global corporations involved in advertising and research. The task force was created to examine and create standardized measures to measure advertising impact that could be used to assess the impact of ads and to eliminate confusion. The three key points of the new recommendations are detailed in a 20-page report available from IAB.net. Industry experts believe that the adoption of these guidelines, along with objective auditing, would make the Internet a more attractive medium for many of those who advertise in traditional media. The guidelines have the support of major online publishers, as well as the nearly 40 major proprietary online ad-server technologies and major associations worldwide.[45]

Internet-Specific Measures One of the perceived advantages of the Internet is a company's ability to measure commercial effectiveness, due in part to its ability to measure activity in real time. Figure 15–9 shows some of the measures that are currently used by companies. These measures include audience measures specific to the Internet and interactive industry. (For a detailed explanation of each of these terms, visit www.IAB.net.)

Traditional Measures In addition to the Internet-specific measures, companies employ a number of traditional marketing and communications measures. Some of these include the following:

- *Recall and retention.* A number of companies use traditional measures of recall and retention to test their Internet ads. These same measures have been used to pretest online commercials as well.
- *Surveys.* Survey research, conducted both online and through traditional methods, is employed to determine everything from site usage to attitudes toward a site.
- *Sales.* For the e-commerce marketers, a prime indicator of effectiveness is the volume of sales generated. Adding information regarding demographics, user behaviors, and so on can increase the effectiveness of this measure.
- *Tracking.* Some companies now offer more traditional tracking measures such as brand awareness, ad recall, message association, and purchase intent.
- *ROI.* A study conducted by comScore, MySpace, and dunnhumby measured the ROI of online sales generated by a $1 million campaign on MySpace.[46]

The previously mentioned measures reveal that digital media have their own set of criteria for measuring effectiveness and are also borrowing from traditional measures; for example, brand recall has become a major area of focus. The American Association of Advertising Agencies and the Association of National Advertisers use a system called Advertising Digital Identification (Ad-Id). Ad-Id assigns advertising across all media a specific media code to facilitate cross-media buys. In 2008 Ad-Id became the official media coding standard.[47] The goal of the coalition is to develop cross-media standards employing impression comparisons that include the Internet. Many of the companies that provide research information in traditional media (Nielsen, Ipsos-ASI) are now extending their reach into the Internet world. Others (Insights.com, Forrester) have developed measures specifically for online users. Two of the commonly used Internet advertising effectiveness measurement companies used are comScore and Media Metrix. These companies offer a combination of effectiveness measures for marketers to use. Academics are also beginning to publish articles related to measuring effectiveness of digital and social media. Studies on consumers' attitudes toward a site, response variations in e-mail surveys, and similarities between brick-and-mortar retailing and e-commerce are just a few of the many articles being published in academic journals to advance the measurement of Internet use.

In addition to the metrics provided here, there are numerous methods that have been suggested for measuring the effectiveness of social media. Note that the metrics shown in Figure 15–10 are not a complete list of effectiveness measures used, but they do provide an illustration of just some of the ways that marketers attempt to determine if they are accomplishing their goals when employing these media. Also keep in mind that many marketers are not enthralled with these measures, which has led to their reluctance to invest more monies in these new media, or to attempt to employ effectiveness measures at all.

Unfortunately, not all of the methods used to measure Internet activity and effectiveness are accurate. We discuss some of these problems next.

ADVANTAGES AND DISADVANTAGES OF THE INTERNET AND DIGITAL AND SOCIAL MEDIA

A number of advantages of the Internet and social media can be cited:

1. *Target marketing.* A major advantage of the Internet and digital and social media is the ability to target very specific groups of individuals with a minimum of waste coverage. For those in the business-to-business market, the

Social Media Application	Brand Awareness	Brand Engagement	Word of Mouth
Blogs	• Number of unique visits • Number of return visits • Number of times bookmarked • Search ranking	• Number of members • Number of RSS feed subscribers • Number of comments • Amount of user-generated content • Average length of time on site • Number of responses to polls, contests, surveys	• Number of references to blog in other media (online/offline) • Number of reblogs • Number of times badge displayed on other sites • Number of "likes"
Microblogging (e.g., Twitter)	• Number of tweets about the brand • Valence of tweets +/– • Number of followers	• Number of followers • Number of @replies	• Number of retweets
Cocreation (e.g., NIKEID)	• Number of visits	• Number of creation attempts	• Number of references to project in other media (online/offline)
Social bookmarking (e.g., StumbleUpon)	• Number of tags	• Number of followers	• Number of additional taggers
Forums and Discussion Boards (e.g., Google Groups)	• Number of page views • Number of visits • Valence of posted content +/–	• Number of relevant topics/threads • Number of individual replies • Number of sign-ups	• Incoming links • Citations in other sites • Tagging in social bookmarking • Offline references to the forum or its members • In private communities: number of pieces of content (photos, discussions, videos); chatter pointing to the community outside of its gates • Number of "likes"
Product Reviews (e.g., Amazon)	• Number of reviews posted • Valence of reviews • Number and valence of other users' responses to reviews (+/–) • Number of wish list adds • Number of times product included in users' lists (i.e., Listmanial on Amazon.com)	• Length of reviews • Relevance of reviews • Valence of other users' ratings of reviews (i.e., how many found particular review helpful) • Number of wish list adds • Overall number of reviewer rating scores entered • Average reviewer rating score	• Number of reviews posted • Valence of reviews • Number and valence of other users' responses to reviews (+/–) • Number of references to reviews in other sites • Number of visits to review site page • Number of times product included in users' lists (i.e., Listmanial on Amazon.com)
Social Networks (e.g., Bebo, Facebook, LinkedIn)	• Number of members/fans • Number of installs of applications • Number of impressions • Number of bookmarks • Number of reviews/ratings and valence +/–	• Number of comments • Number of active users • Number of "likes" on friends' feeds • Number of user-generated items (photos, threads, replies) • Usage metrics of applications/widgets • Impressions-to-interactions ratio • Rate of activity (how often members personalize profiles, bios, links, etc.)	• Frequency of appearances in timeline of friends • Number of posts on wall • Number of reposts/shares • Number of responses to friend referral invites
Video and Photosharing (e.g., Flickr, YouTube)	• Number of views of video/photo • Valence of video/photo ratings +/–	• Number of replies • Number of page views • Number of comments • Number of subscribers	• Number of embeddings • Number of incoming links • Number of references in mock-ups or derived work • Number of times republished in other social media and offline • Number of "likes"

Source: *MIT Sloan Management Review,* Fall 2010.

Internet resembles a combination trade magazine and trade show, as only those most interested in the products and/or services a site has to offer will visit the site (others have little or no reason to do so). In the consumer market, through personalization, retargeting, and other techniques, sites are becoming more tailored to meet one's needs and wants.

2. *Message tailoring.* As a result of precise targeting, messages can be designed to appeal to the specific needs and wants of the target audience, much of which comes from behavior tracking. The interactive capabilities of social media make it possible to carry on one-to-one marketing with increased success in both the business and the consumer markets.

3. *Interactive capabilities.* Because these media are interactive, they provide strong potential for increasing customer involvement, engagement, and satisfaction and almost immediate feedback for buyers and sellers.

4. *Information access.* Perhaps the greatest advantage of the Internet is its availability as an information source. Internet users can find a plethora of information about almost any topic of their choosing merely by conducting a search. Once they have visited a particular site, users can garner a wealth of information regarding product specifications, costs, purchase information, and so on. Links will direct them to even more information if it is desired. Google and YouTube also offer a search function.

5. *Sales potential.* The sales numbers generated by Amazon and eBay alone (not to mention many, many more) demonstrate the incredible sales numbers being generated in both the business-to-business and the consumer segments. Forecasts are for continued growth in the future. In addition, the number of persons who shop online and then purchase offline has continued to increase.

6. *Creativity.* Creatively designed sites can enhance a company's image, lead to repeat visits, and positively position the company or organization in the consumer's mind. Visit some of the sites mentioned earlier to see what we mean. Consumer-generated social media lead to even more creativity.

7. *Exposure.* For many smaller companies, with limited budgets, the World Wide Web enables them to gain exposure to potential customers that in the past would have been impossible (recall the example of the tongue cleaner). For a fraction of the investment that would be required using traditional media, companies can gain national and even international exposure in a timely manner.

8. *Speed.* For those requesting information on a company, its products, and/or its service offerings, the Internet is the quickest means of acquiring and providing this information. Well-designed sites keep this information current, and search allows for additional sources.

9. *Complement to IMC.* The Internet and digital and social media complement and are complemented by other IMC media. As such, they serve as vital links in the integrative process. Marketers understand that these media support and are supported by traditional media.

10. *Timeliness.* The ability to communicate quickly and currently offer an advantage that no other media can match. Using social media and mobile, companies can keep consumers up-to-date with pretty much anything and everything—for example, think about product recalls.

While potentially effective, the Internet and digital and social media also have disadvantages, including the following:

1. *Measurement problems.* One of the greatest disadvantages of the Internet and new media is the lack of reliability of the research numbers generated. A quick review of forecasts, and other statistics offered by research providers will demonstrate a great deal of variance—leading to a serious lack of validity and reliability. One company mentioned earlier, eMarketer, has attempted to reconcile such differences and explain the reasoning for the discrepancies (differences in methodologies employed), but the problem still exists. The actions taken by the IAB to standardize metrics will help in reducing some of this problem. But

due to difficulties involved in both measuring and forecasting in this medium, it remains necessary to proceed with caution when using these numbers. In a study of 410 marketing executives published by McKinsey, the primary reason cited for not investing more online was the lack of sufficient metrics.[48,49] As noted earlier, more recent studies indicate that this concern still exists as companies like AT&T still consider measurement a major problem.[50]

LO15-5

2. *Clutter.* As the number of ads proliferates, the likelihood of one's ad being noticed drops accordingly. The result is that some ads may not get noticed, and some consumers may become irritated by the clutter. Studies show that banner ads have lost effectiveness for this very reason, and that interstitials are irritating as well. Many ads others show consistently declining click-through rates.

3. *Potential for deception.* The Center for Media Education has referred to the Web as "a web of deceit" in regard to advertisers' attempts to target children with subtle advertising messages. The center, among others, has asked the government to regulate the Internet. In addition, data collection without consumers' knowledge and permission, hacking, and credit card theft are among the problems confronting Internet users. Bloggers, marketing influencers who endorse brands without revealing that they are being compensated to do so, and native ads can also be misleading. The problem with native ads may be particularly true on smartphones, where proper labeling of the ads as sponsored may be difficult to see.

4. *Privacy.* One of the many issues of concern for Internet users is that of privacy. Perhaps of most concern is the collection of personal data which are subsequently provided to marketers, sometimes without the users' knowledge. While many younger users seem to be less worried, actions taken by websites like Facebook, among others, have led to user boycotts as well as calls for more regulation. The IAB has issued a policy on privacy to which it asks companies to adhere (see www.iab.net).

5. *Irritation.* Numerous studies have reported on the irritating aspects of some Web tactics. These studies have shown consumers' discontent with clutter, e-mail spam, and pop-ups and pop-unders. There is also a growing sense of irritation with retargeting ads and pre-rolls. These irritating aspects can deter visitors from coming to or returning to the sites, or result in negative attributes toward the advertiser.

Overall, the Internet and digital and social media offer marketers some very definite advantages over traditional media. At the same time, disadvantages and limitations render this medium as less than a one-stop solution. However, as part of an IMC program, these media are very valuable tools.

Summary

This chapter introduced you to the Internet and a variety of digital and social media. It explained some of the objectives for these media and how they can be used in an IMC program.

The discussion of the Internet focused on understanding the growth of the Internet, the objectives sought when using the Internet, and Internet communications strategies. In addition, we discussed the role of the Internet in an IMC program, explaining how all the IMC program elements can be used with the Internet.

The chapter discussed a number of online tools including paid search, behavioral targeting, contextual ads, rich media, and a number of Web 2.0 platforms including social media, social networks, user-generated content, blogs, RSS, and podcasting. We noted advantages of the Web 2.0 including targeting markets, using interactive capabilities, and building

relationships. In addition, we reviewed disadvantages—including high costs, unreliable measurements and statistics, and relatively low reach (compared to that of some traditional media), and the potential for deception.

The Internet has been the most rapidly adopted medium of our time (until mobile). The growth of mobile, due to the adoption of smartphones and portable devices, and millions of applications has led to very rapid growth in advertising expenditures in this area. Mobile holds great potential for both business-to-business and consumer marketers. However, contrary to popular belief, digital media, like the Internet, social media, and mobile, are not stand-alone media. Their role in an integrated marketing communications program strengthens the overall promotional program as well as the effectiveness of these media themselves.

Key Terms

Discussion Questions

1. What is native advertising? Why do some believe that this form of advertising is deceptive? Explain what you think. (LO 15-5)

2. Marketers seem to be increasing their use of bloggers, vloggers, and influencers. Explain what these terms mean. Why do some consider the use of these as potentially deceptive? (LO 15-5)

3. Explain why some companies seem to be fascinated by digital and social media. What are some of the factors that might support this thinking? What are some that might lead to considering it misdirected? (LO 15-4)

4. In the chapter we said that social media and mobile are both part of an IMC program, and also use other media in their own programs. Explain what this means and give examples. (LO 15-1)

5. Explain the differences between Web 1.0 and Web 2.0. Give examples of how marketers use both. (LO 15-1)

6. Many marketers and policymakers believe the Internet and social media may constitute a "web of deceit."

Explain what they mean by this comment. Provide examples as to why they have this feeling. (LO 15-4)

7. The drive to go viral has resulted in some major marketing mistakes. Explain why marketers are seemingly obsessed with going viral. Then explain some of the consequences that might occur should these efforts fail. (LO 15-5)

8. The new media discussed in this chapter offer some distinct advantages over traditional media, but also have some disadvantages. Discuss some of the advantages and disadvantages of traditional and new media. (LO 15-4)

9. Discuss the role of social media in an IMC program. What can these media best contribute in regard to helping marketers achieve communications objectives? (LO 15-2, 15-4)

10. Policymakers are concerned that some bloggers may not be disclosing the fact that they are being compensated for product or brand endorsements. Explain why they may be concerned about this and why it may lead to negative impacts on the consumer. (LO 15-5)

---

connect

Digital users can access their personalized and adaptive SmartBook, Ad Forum Video Cases, and interactive exercises to review chapter concepts.

16 Sales Promotion

Source: Sports Authority

LEARNING OBJECTIVES

LO1 Describe the role of sales promotion in the IMC program.

LO2 Identify the objectives of sales promotion programs.

LO3 Explain how marketers use various types of consumer- and trade-oriented sales promotion tools.

LO4 Explain how to coordinate sales promotion with advertising.

LO5 Discuss potential problems in the use of sales promotion tools.

MARKETERS FALL INTO THE DISCOUNTING TRAP: AND THERE MAY BE NO WAY OUT

A key indicator of the strength of a nation's economy is the size and growth in its gross domestic product (GDP) which represents the total value of all goods and services produced. In countries such as the United States and many others, consumer spending accounts for nearly 70 percent of GDP which means that if consumers are not spending, the economy struggles to grow. For nearly a decade, the U.S. economy has been struggling to recover from the Great Recession that began in late 2007 and lasted for nearly two years and is considered the worst economic downturn since the Great Depression. During the recession, as well as the recovery period, consumers became more price-sensitive and value-conscious and companies in virtually every product and service category learned that it can be very difficult to get consumers to pay a premium for their brands. Many marketing and consumer behavior experts, as well as economists, have argued that the recession led to permanent changes in buyer behavior and that consumers have remained frugal and value-conscious ever since.

Based on the lackluster economic growth of the past few years, it appears that the experts may be right; fundamental changes in consumer behavior have occurred and we may never see a return to the free-spending days of yesteryear. It appears that the passion for consumption that helped drive the U.S. economy and make it world's largest for decades is waning. Consumers are no longer addicted to shopping and going to malls and supercenters to spend excessively. However, when they do shop they are often looking for a deal because they have become hooked on promotions and discounts, and for good reason. Nearly every retailer—as well as businesses such as hotels, rental cars, restaurants, and many others—now offers consumers the opportunity to save money through some type of promotion, which appeals to our primal desire for landing a bargain. The problem is that marketers have fallen so deeply into the bargain trap that discounting has become an expectation of consumers rather than a bonus or extra incentive.

It is not surprising that consumers are often looking for deals. Surveys have shown that more than 40 percent of the items American consumers buy today were bought on sales versus only 10 percent in the 1990s. Many consumers have become more disciplined in their spending and are carefully scrutinizing their purchases, rethinking their brand loyalties, and looking for ways to save money by doing comparison shopping, clipping coupons, or downloading offers from Groupon or other sites. Many consumers are always on the lookout for discounts and deals. And while many marketers are all too happy to give them one, they are creating a discount trap from which there is no easy escape. Some retailers who have become overly dependent on promotions and discounts have tried to reduce their dependence on them and move toward more of an "everyday low pricing approach."

Macy's tried to cut back on the number of "One-day sales" and the 15 to 25 percent discounts and coupons that accompanied them but the effort was short-lived as consumers across the country stayed away from the stores and sales dropped for four consecutive months. Later in the chapter we discuss how JCPenney hired a new CEO, Ron Johnson, a few years ago who was shocked to find that over 70 percent of the retailer's merchandise was being sold at discounts of 50 percent off or more when he took over. Johnson's efforts to wean JCPenney's customers off coupons and discounts resulted in a $4.3 billion drop in revenue in the first year of his experiment; many of its lost sales were scooped up by the likes of Macy's and Kohl's, who responded to Johnson's move with even more discounting. Johnson's tenure as CEO lasted only 16 months before being fired and JCPenney has returned to discounting.

JCPenney and Macy's, like many other companies, have learned the hard way that they had violated a basic law of human nature when it comes to marketing: consumers love a deal. Moreover, retailers, like many other marketers, often train consumers to wait for discounts through sales, special offers, coupons, and rebates which make it very difficult to sell their merchandise at full price. Compounding the problem today is the emergence of online retailers such as Amazon which had more than $120 billion in online sales in 2016 and has been growing at 20 percent annually. Not only are shoppers buying online, they now have the ability to "showroom" or compare prices on the Internet and use this information to negotiate with brick-and-mortar retailers or simply buy online.

In addition to online retailers, those benefiting most from the discounting are off-price retailers such as T.J.Maxx, Family Dollar, and Marshalls, while department stores as well as specialty retailers that they are squeezing look for ways to respond. Nordstrom and Saks Fifth Avenue are competing by opening outlet stores rather than traditional department stores; Nordstrom now has nearly twice as many Nordstrom Rack outlets as full-service stores, while Saks has nearly double the number of its OFF 5th outlet stores than traditional stores.

Some retailers are finding it very difficult to survive the intense discounting and competition and are either closing some of their underperforming stores or even going out of business. The Gap, which also owns Old Navy and Banana Republic, closed 40 of its North American stores in 2015 and plans to close nearly 175 over the next few years. The athletic shoe retailer Finish Line recently announced that it would close 150 stores by 2020 in an effort to boost its profitability. The good news for Finish Line is that it is still in business whereas other sporting goods retailers have not been so fortunate. In 2016 Sports Authority, which was once the largest sporting goods store chain in the United States, closed all of its 450 stores as it struggled to compete against online competitors and could not get shoppers to buy its merchandise without big discounts. Sports Chalet, a regional chain in California and Arizona, also closed all of its stores in 2016 and went out of business after 57 years of operation.

Retailers are not the only companies being impacted by the discounting trend; the vendors who supply them with merchandise are also being impacted. Many marketers have turned to coupons, rebates, and other forms of discounts to appeal to promotion-sensitive consumers. A number of the major hotel chains are turning to promotions to woo travelers away from third-party booking sites such as Expedia and Priceline that offer discounted rooms by either matching their prices or giving them perks such as room upgrades or extra reward points. For example, Hilton Worldwide launched one of the largest marketing campaigns ever to let its loyalty program members know they would receive discounts on rooms if they booked directly.

Many marketers and retailers have created a dilemma from which there is no easy escape. They know that discounts will increase sales in the short term, but the more marketers use these promotions, the more consumers become conditioned to purchase an item only when it is on sale or they have a coupon. Moreover, many consumers love to shop for deals and view it like playing a game; the money they save is how they keep score. The temptation for marketers to play the game and look for the quick fix and sales spike from a promotion will always be there as well. It is likely that many will continue to yield to the temptation and offer a discount rather than try to sell their brands at full price.

Sources: Stephanie Rosenbloom, "Book Directly, Hotels Advise," *San Diego Union Tribune*, May 22, 2016, p. C5; Chris Isidore, "Sports Authority to Close All Remaining Stores," *CNN Money*, May, 18, 2016, http://money.cnn.com/2016/05/18/news/companies/sports-authority-closing/; Adrianne Pasquarelli, "Retailers Combat Sliding Sales," *Advertising Age*, May 16, 2016; Jennifer Reingold and Phil Wahba, "Where Have All the Shoppers Gone?" *Fortune.com*, September 3, 2014, pp. 80–84.

As discussed in the chapter opener, marketers recognize that advertising alone is not always enough to move their products off store shelves and into the hands of consumers. They are using a variety of sales promotion methods targeted at both consumers and the wholesalers and retailers that distribute their products to stimulate demand. Most companies' IMC programs include consumer and trade promotions that are coordinated with their advertising, direct marketing, publicity/publications, and digital marketing as well as their personal-selling efforts.

This chapter focuses on the role of sales promotion in a firm's IMC program. We examine how marketers use both consumer- and trade-oriented promotions to influence the purchase behavior of consumers as well as wholesalers and retailers. We explore the objectives of sales promotion programs and the various types of sales promotion tools that can be used at both the consumer and trade level. We also consider how sales promotion can be integrated with other elements of the promotional mix and look at problems that can arise when marketers become overly dependent on consumer and trade promotions.

THE SCOPE AND ROLE OF SALES PROMOTION

Sales promotion has been defined as "a direct inducement that offers an extra value or incentive for the product to the sales force, distributors, or the ultimate consumer with the primary objective of creating an immediate sale."[1] Keep in mind several important aspects of sales promotion as you read this chapter.

First, sales promotion involves some type of inducement that provides an *extra incentive* to buy. This incentive is usually the key element in a promotional program; it may be a coupon or price reduction, the opportunity to enter a contest or sweepstakes, a money-back refund or rebate, or an extra amount of a product. The incentive may also be a free sample of the product, given in hopes of generating a future purchase or a premium such as the Mini Minion characters toy used by General Mills for Lucky Charms cereal (Exhibit 16–1). The Minion premium offer was part of a promotional tie-in to the movie *Despicable Me 2* that included packaging themed to the movie, eight collectible Minion premiums, and product integrations.[2] Most sales promotion offers attempt to add some value to the product or service. While advertising appeals to the mind and emotions to give the consumer a reason to buy, sales promotion appeals more to the pocketbook and provides an incentive for purchasing a brand.

Sales promotion can also provide an inducement to marketing intermediaries such as wholesalers and retailers. A trade allowance or discount gives retailers a financial incentive to stock and promote a manufacturer's products. A trade contest directed toward wholesalers or retail personnel gives them extra incentive to perform certain tasks or meet sales goals.

A second point is that sales promotion is essentially an *acceleration tool*, designed to speed up the selling process and maximize sales volume.[3] By providing an extra incentive, sales promotion techniques can motivate consumers to purchase a larger quantity of a brand or shorten the purchase cycle of the trade or consumers by encouraging them to take more immediate action.

Companies also use limited-time offers such as price-off deals to retailers or a coupon with an expiration date to accelerate the purchase process.[4] Sales promotion attempts to maximize sales volume by motivating customers who have not responded to advertising. The ideal sales promotion program generates sales that would not be achieved by other means. However, as we will see later, many sales promotion offers end up being used by current users of a brand rather than attracting new users.

A final point regarding sales promotion activities is that they can be *targeted to different parties* in the marketing channel. As shown in Figure 16–1, sales promotion can be broken into two major categories: consumer-oriented and trade-oriented promotions. Activities involved in **consumer-oriented sales promotion** include sampling, couponing, premiums, contests and sweepstakes, refunds and rebates, bonus packs, price-offs, loyalty programs, and event marketing. These promotions are directed at consumers, the end purchasers of goods and services, and are designed to induce them to purchase the marketer's brand.

As discussed in Chapter 2, consumer-oriented promotions are part of a promotional pull strategy; they work along with advertising to encourage consumers to purchase a particular brand and thus create demand for it. Consumer promotions are also used by retailers to encourage consumers to shop in their particular stores. Many grocery stores use their own coupons or sponsor contests and other promotions to increase store patronage.

Trade-oriented sales promotion includes dealer contests and incentives, trade allowances, point-of-purchase displays, sales training programs, trade shows, cooperative advertising, and other programs designed to motivate distributors and retailers to carry a product

EXHIBIT 16–1

A premium offer is used to provide extra incentive to purchase Lucky Charms

© McGraw-Hill Companies/Mark Dierker, photographer

FIGURE 16–1

Types of Sales Promotion
Activities

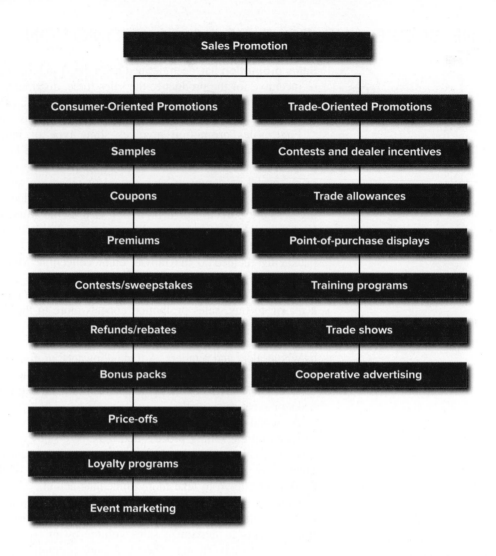

and make an extra effort to push it to their customers. Many marketing programs include both trade- and consumer-oriented promotions, since motivating both groups maximizes the effectiveness of the promotional program.

THE GROWTH OF SALES PROMOTION

While sales promotion has been part of the marketing process for a long time, its role and importance in a company's integrated marketing communications program have increased dramatically over the past decade. Consumer sales promotion–related spending increased from $56 billion in 1991 to over $300 billion in 2016.[5] Marketers also spend an estimated $150 billion each year on promotions targeted at retailers and wholesalers. Consumer packaged-goods (CPG) firms continue to be the core users of sales promotion programs and tools. However, sales promotion activity is also increasing in other categories, including health care, consumer electronics fast-food, retailing, and service industries.

Estimates are that marketers spend more than half of their promotional budgets on sales promotion, with the remainder being allocated to media advertising.[6] Allocation of marketing budgets among consumer promotions, trade promotions, and media advertising varies by industry and company. For example, trade promotion accounts for nearly 50 percent of the budget for consumer packaged-goods companies, with

EXHIBIT 16–2

Advertisements often use promotions such as sweepstakes to draw attention

Source: Channellock, Inc.

27 percent going to consumer promotion and 24 percent to media advertising.[7] Moreover, a significant amount of the monies that marketers allocate to media advertising is spent on ads that deliver promotional messages regarding contests, games, sweepstakes, and rebate offers.[8] Surveys have shown that marketers devote about 17 percent of their ad budgets to promotional messages.[9] Promotional messages are also used to help attract attention and to image-building ads. For example, Channellock used print and banners ads such the ad one in Exhibit 16–2 to promote its "Gridiron Garage Giveaway" sweepstakes which included a pair of season tickets to the winners favorite NFL team. The prize package also included a trip to the Channellock factory for a VIP tour so the winners could see how their new tools are made. The company has been running the sweepstakes for the past five years.

Reasons for the Increase in Sales Promotion

The increases in the percentage of the IMC budget allocated to sales promotion over the years concerned many marketers who still viewed media advertising as the primary tool for brand building and saw sales promotion programs as little more than gimmicks that contributed little to brand equity. However, most have recognized that consumers may love their brands but often want an extra incentive to buy them. Marketers also know they must partner effectively with trade accounts, and this often means providing them with an additional incentive to stock and promote their brands and participate in various promotional programs.

A major reason for the increase in spending on sales promotion is that the promotion industry has matured over the past several decades. Increased sophistication and a more strategic role and focus have elevated the discipline and its role in the IMC program of many companies. In the past, sales promotion specialists would be brought in after key strategic branding decisions were made. Promotional agencies were viewed primarily as tacticians whose role was to develop a promotional program such as a contest or sweepstakes or a coupon or sampling program that could create a short-term increase in sales. However, many companies are now making promotional specialists part of their strategic brand-building team, a move that puts sales promotion on par with media advertising. Many promotional agencies have expanded their capabilities and expertise and now offer clients a variety of integrated marketing services that extend beyond just sales promotion. For example, Exhibit 16–3 shows how Aspen Marketing Services, one of the largest providers of integrated marketing and promotional services, promotes its capabilities by including a variety of IMC tools such as experiential, direct, and digital marketing.

EXHIBIT 16–3

Aspen Marketing Services touts its IMC capabilities

Source: AspenMs.com

There are also a number of other factors that have led to the increase in the importance of sales promotion and the shift in marketing dollars from media advertising to consumer and trade promotions. Among them are the growing power of retailers, declining brand loyalty, increased promotional sensitivity, brand proliferation, and fragmentation of the consumer market, short-term focus of many marketers, increased accountability, competition, and growth of digital and social media.

The Growing Power of Retailers

One reason for the increase in sales promotion is the power shift in the marketplace from manufacturers to retailers. For many years, manufacturers of national brands had the power and influence; retailers were just passive distributors of their products. Consumer-product manufacturers created consumer demand for their brands by using heavy advertising and some consumer-oriented promotions, such as samples, coupons, and premiums, and exerted pressure on retailers to carry the products. Retailers did very little research and sales analysis; they relied on manufacturers for information regarding the sales performance of individual brands.

In recent years, however, several developments have helped transfer power from the manufacturers to the retailers. With the advent of optical checkout scanners and sophisticated in-store computer systems, retailers gained access to data concerning how quickly products turn over, which sales promotions are working, and which products make money.[10] Retailers use this information to analyze sales of manufacturers' products and then demand discounts and other promotional support from manufacturers of lagging brands. Companies that fail to comply with retailers' demands for more trade support often have their shelf space reduced or even have their product dropped.

Another factor that has increased the power of retailers is the consolidation of the retail industry, which has resulted in larger chains with greater buying power and clout. These large chains have become accustomed to trade promotions and can pressure manufacturers to provide deals, discounts, and allowances. Consolidation has also given large retailers more money for advancing already strong private-label initiatives, and sales promotion is the next step in the marketing evolution of private-label brands. Private-label brands in various packaged-goods categories such as foods, drugs, and health and beauty care products are giving national brands more competition for retail shelf space and increasing their own marketing, including the use of traditional sales promotion tools. Private-label products now account for nearly 17 percent of sales for packaged-goods products reaching $120 billion in 2014.[11] Well-marketed private-label products are forcing national brand leaders, as well as second-tier brands, to develop more innovative promotional programs and to be more price-competitive.[12]

One of the most significant developments among retailers is the tremendous growth of Walmart, which has become the largest company in the world as well as the most powerful retailer[13] (Exhibit 16–4). Walmart operates nearly 11,500 stores in 28 countries, including more than 5,200 in the United States, and had sales of $482 billion in fiscal 2016. It controls 20 percent of dry grocery, 29 percent of nonfood grocery, 30 percent of health and beauty aids, and 45 percent of general merchandise sales in the United States. Walmart accounts for a large share of the business done by every major U.S. consumer-products company and can use its power to influence the way marketers use sales promotions. Like many large retailers, Walmart often asks for account-specific promotions that are designed for and offered only through its stores. The company also has been known to mandate that marketers forgo promotional offers and use the monies to reduce prices.[14]

EXHIBIT 16–4

Walmart is the world's largest and most powerful retailer

© McGraw-Hill Education/John Flournoy, photographer

Declining Brand loyalty Another major reason for the increase in sales promotion is that consumers have become less brand loyal and are purchasing more on the basis of price, value, and convenience. Some consumers are always willing to buy their preferred brand at full price without any type of promotional offer. However, many consumers are loyal coupon users and/or are conditioned to look for deals when they shop. They may switch back and forth among a set of brands they view as essentially equal. These brands are all perceived as being satisfactory and interchangeable, and consumers purchase whatever brand is on a special sale or for which they have a coupon.

Increased Promotional Sensitivity Marketers are making greater use of sales promotion in their marketing programs because consumers respond favorably to the incentives it provides. A recent IRI Market Pulse Survey found that 25 percent of consumer are buying packaged-goods brands that are on sale over their preferred brands and 23 percent are making product selections based on loyalty card discounts.[15] An obvious reason for consumers' increased sensitivity to sales promotion offers is that they save money. Another reason is that many purchase decisions are made at the point of purchase by consumers who are increasingly time-sensitive and facing too many choices. Some studies have found that up to 70 percent of purchase decisions are made in the store, where people are very likely to respond to promotional deals.[16]

Many marketers, as well as retailers, often condition consumers to wait for discounts through sales, special offers, and coupons, which make it very difficult to sell their merchandise at full price. Surveys have shown that consumers are 50 percent more price-sensitive than they were 25 years ago and for good reason.[17] Marketers issue more than 300 billion coupons each year, or nearly 1,000 per person. They also use rebates, buy-one-get-one-free offers, special sales events, price-off deals, and other discounts to attract price-sensitive consumers. Consumers are not naive; they know that manufacturers or retailers will offer some type of promotion that encourages them to wait for the next deal rather than purchasing a product at full price.

Brand Proliferation A major aspect of many firms' marketing strategies over the past decade has been the development of new products. The market has become saturated with new brands, most of which lack any significant advantages. Research shows that about 75 percent of consumer packaged goods and retail products fail in their first year—in large part because of ingrained consumer shopping habits.[18] Thus, companies increasingly depend on sales promotion to encourage consumers to try these brands. In Chapter 4, we saw how sales promotion techniques can be used as part of the shaping process to lead the consumer from initial trial to repeat purchase at full price. Marketers are relying more on samples, coupons, rebates, premiums, and other innovative promotional tools to achieve trial usage of their new brands and encourage repeat purchase (Exhibit 16–5).

Promotions are also important in getting retailers to allocate some of their precious shelf space to new brands. The competition for shelf space for new products in stores is enormous. Supermarkets carry an average of 30,000 products (compared with 13,067 in 1982). Retailers favor new brands with strong sales promotion support that will bring in more customers and boost their sales and profits. Many retailers require special discounts or allowances from manufacturers just to handle a new product. These slotting fees or allowances, which are discussed later in the chapter, can make it expensive for a manufacturer to introduce a new product.

Marketers are also shifting more of their promotional efforts to direct and digital marketing, which often includes some form of sales promotion incentive. Many marketers use information they get from premium offers, trackable coupons, rebates, and sweepstakes to build databases for future direct-marketing efforts. As marketers continue to shift from media advertising to direct marketing, promotional offers will probably be used even more to help build databases. The technology is already in place to enable marketers to communicate individually with target consumers and transform mass promotional tools into ways of doing one-to-one marketing.

Short-Term Focus Many businesspeople believe the increase in sales promotion is motivated by marketing plans and reward systems geared to short-term performance and the immediate generation of sales volume as discussed in the

EXHIBIT 16–5

Sales promotion tools such as this coupon for Purina Dog Chow are often used to encourage trial of a new brand or a repeat purchase

Source: Nestlé Purina Petcare

opening vignette to the chapter. Some think the packaged-goods brand management system has contributed to marketers' increased dependence on sales promotion. Brand managers use sales promotions routinely, not only to introduce new products or defend against the competition but also to meet quarterly or yearly sales and market share goals. The sales force, too, may have short-term quotas or goals to meet and may also receive requests from retailers and wholesalers for promotions. Thus, reps may pressure marketing or brand managers to use promotions to help them move the products into the retailers' stores.

Many managers view consumer and trade promotions as the most dependable way to generate short-term sales, particularly when they are price-related. The reliance on sales promotion is particularly high in mature and slow-growth markets, where it is difficult to stimulate consumer demand through advertising. This has led to concern that managers have become too dependent on the quick sales fix that can result from a promotion and that the brand franchise may be eroded by too many deals.

Professors Leonard Lodish and Carl Mela have conducted research that suggests many companies are too focused on short-term results because the profusion of scanner data allows brand and marketing managers, as well as retailers, to see how sales often spike in response to promotional discounts.[19] They note that managers became enamored with these short-term increases in sales, which resulted in the allocation of the majority of their marketing budgets to consumer and trade promotions. Another problem they note is that many brand managers stay in their positions for a short time period, which motivates them to focus on the use of promotional tactics that can have more of an immediate impact. They often view investing in advertising or product development as benefiting the performance of subsequent managers rather than their own. When asked about why they take a short-term perspective, marketing and brand managers point out that they are judged on quarterly sales because investors focus on these numbers, and the link between promotion and sales is obvious.

Increased Accountability In addition to pressuring their marketing or brand managers and sales force to produce short-term results, many companies are demanding to know what they are getting for their promotional expenditures. Results from sales promotion programs are generally easier to measure than those from advertising. Many companies are demanding measurable, accountable ways to relate promotional expenditures to sales and profitability.

Managers who are being held accountable to produce results often use price discounts or coupons, since they produce a quick and easily measured jump in sales. It takes longer for an ad campaign to show some impact, and the effects are more difficult to measure. Marketers are also feeling pressure from the trade as powerful retailers demand sales performance from their brands. Real-time data available from computerized checkout scanners make it possible for retailers to monitor promotions and track the results they generate on a daily basis.

Competition Another factor that led to the increase in sales promotion is manufacturers' reliance on trade and consumer promotions to gain or maintain competitive advantage. The markets for many products are mature and stagnant, and it is increasingly difficult to boost sales through advertising. Exciting, breakthrough creative ideas are difficult to come by, and consumers' attention to mass-media advertising continues to decline. Rather than allocating large amounts of money to run dull ads, many marketers have turned to sales promotion.

Many companies are tailoring their trade promotions to key retail accounts and developing strategic alliances with retailers that include both trade and consumer promotional programs. A major development in recent years is **account-specific marketing** (also referred to as *comarketing*), whereby a manufacturer collaborates with an individual retailer to create a customized promotion that accomplishes mutual objectives. For example, Exhibit 16–6 shows an account-specific promotion the WD-40 Company ran in conjunction with the O'Reilly Auto Parts retail chain. The promotion included limited-edition, custom cans made to commemorate the

EXHIBIT 16–6

WD-40 developed an account-specific promotion for O'Reilly Auto Parts

Source: WD-40 Company

60th anniversary of WD-40's multiuse product, which has been made in the United States since 1953. The special cans were created as a salute to those who subscribe to the tradition of hard work and getting the job done.[20]

Retailers may use a promotional deal with one company as leverage to seek an equal or better deal with its competitors. Consumer and trade promotions are easily matched by competitors, and many marketers find themselves in a promotional trap where they must continue using promotions or be at a competitive disadvantage. (We discuss this problem in more detail later in the chapter.)

The Growth of Digital Marketing Another factor that has contributed to the increased use of sales promotion is the digital marketing revolution. Many marketers now use the various forms of online marketing to implement sales promotion programs as well as measure their effectiveness. Promotional offers have also become commonplace in various forms of online advertising including mobile marketing as a way of attracting the attention of consumers or encouraging them to take action. Various types of promotions such as coupons and discounts along with entry forms for contests and sweepstakes appear on marketers' websites as well as their social media pages on Facebook, Twitter, and Instagram.

Sales promotion offers are also used by marketers as a way to encourage consumers to "like" their brands on Facebook or follow them on Twitter. Figure 16–2 shows the results of a survey conducted by the research firm MarketingSherpa that examined why consumers follow brands on various social media platforms. The most popular reason cited by U.S. consumers who do connect with brands on social media

FIGURE 16–2

Reasons to connect on Social Media

Source: From MarketingSherpa; www.marketingsherpa.com/article/chart/why-customers-follow-brands-social-accounts.

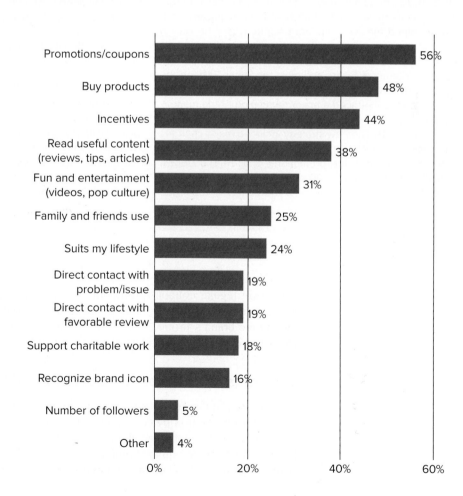

IMC Perspective 16–1 > > >

JCPenney Learns How Much Consumers Love Promotions

The JCPenney Company (JCP) has been a mainstay of the American retail scene for more than a century. The company was founded by James Cash Penney in 1902 on the principle of treating customers the way he wanted to be treated himself: fair and square. During the 20th century JCP became a powerhouse in the retail industry with more than 2,000 stores that would anchor large-scale shopping centers across the United States, offering a wide variety of products such as apparel, cosmetics, shoes, jewelry, household appliances, and furniture. JCP's primary target market has always been value-conscious consumers from middle-income families. Over the past several decades the retailing competitive landscape in the United States changed with the emergence of mass merchandisers such as Walmart and Target, which also target the mid-tier market. JCP also faces competition from retailers such as Marshalls and Kohl's as well as more upscale stores such as Macy's and Nordstrom. JCP has also been challenged in recent years by the emerging fast fashion retailers such as Zara, H&M, and Forever 21 as well as the growth in online sales of clothing. By 2010, the number of JCP stores had been cut nearly in half to just over 1,100 and the company was struggling to hold on to its position among the ranks of America's top retailers.

In 2011, JCP hired a new executive team that included Ron Johnson as its new CEO and Michael Francis as president. Johnson joined the company from Apple, where he was in charge of the company's highly successful retail stores, and had also been head of merchandising for Target. Francis was a 22-year veteran of Target and most recently had been the chain's chief marketing officer. In January 2012 the new management team announced a major revamping of the marketing strategy for JCP that would return the retailer to its "fair and square" roots. The new strategy included major changes in the company's pricing and promotion and a shift away from the pervasive use of sales, promotional deals, and coupons. JCP had been using nearly 600 sales and promotional events per year, and nearly 75 percent of the company's revenue came from merchandise that was discounted by at least 50 percent, more than double the industry average.

The new pricing and promotional model included three key elements: an everyday "fair" price that was close to the average price JCP customers typically paid based on historical sales data; a monthlong "value" price whereby some items would be discounted up to 30 percent off the everyday price; and a final "best" on select items that would be offered on the first and third Friday of every month to coincide with payday for many American consumers. The transformation also included a complete company rebranding, with a new logo and tagline: "Fair and Square." JCPenney's IMC program throughout 2012 focused on communicating the store's rebranding and new pricing strategy to consumers through the use of television and print advertisements, direct mail, online and social media, public relations, and event marketing.

The company kicked off the new strategy with a series of commercials featuring talk-show host Ellen DeGeneres, who was once a JCP employee, poking fun at their old way of pricing. The humorous spots showed DeGeneres going back in time to different periods such as trying to use a coupon in the old days of the Wild, Wild West or battling the crowd in an early morning door buster sale in the 1950s. The spots would end with taglines designed to communicate JCP's new pricing such as "no coupons, just great prices" or "no door busters, just great prices."

JCP's new pricing and promotional strategy took effect in all stores across the country on February 1, 2012, and it did not take long for consumers to let the retailer know how they felt about it. Just two months later, JCP announced that its first-quarter results were the worst year-over-year quarterly decline in more than seven years as the company recorded a quarterly loss of $163 million. JCP's overall sales declined by 20 percent while same-store sales, a key retail industry metric that measures the change in sales for stores open at least one year, declined by 19 percent and foot traffic in the stores was down 10 percent. Johnson and Francis defended the new

was to get regular coupons/promotions (56 percent). Forty-eight percent of consumers said they connected to brands' social accounts because they were interested in buying the brand's products, and 44 percent said they connected because there was an incentive (e.g., sweepstakes, discount, or gift card).[21]

Concerns about the Increased Role of Sales Promotion

As discussed in the previous section, many factors have contributed to the increased use of sales promotion by consumer-product manufacturers. Marketing and advertising executives are concerned about how this shift in the allocation of the promotional budget affects brand equity. Some critics argue that sales promotion increases come at the expense of brand equity and every dollar that goes into promotion rather than

Source: J.C. Penney Corporation, Inc.

strategy and responded to investors' concerns by telling them that it would take time for consumers to adjust to the new pricing and promotional strategy as they had been conditioned to primarily purchase items that were on sale, offered at a discount, or for which they had a coupon. Over the next several months JCP tried to stay the course with its "Fair and Square" model, but sales and store traffic continued to decline.

In June, JCP announced that Francis, who was responsible for the marketing and implementation of the new pricing plan, was leaving the company effective immediately. By July, JCP announced that it was moving away from its three-tier pricing and promotional strategy to a new two-tier model and also began promoting price-match guarantees, taking a page from discounters such as Target and Walmart. A JCP spokesperson noted that the retailer was committed to offering straightforward pricing that is fair and square but was making some enhancements to further clarify and simplify its pricing.

JCP's woes continued for the remainder of the year as the company's total revenue for 2012 fell by 23 percent, or nearly $4 billion, to $13.3 billion, while comparable store sales declined by 25 percent. In January 2013, JCP announced that it would begin bringing back many of the hundreds of sales that it had eliminated the prior year in hopes of luring shoppers who were turned off when the discounts and promotions disappeared. CEO Johnson noted that the return to old ways was not a deviation from his strategy but rather an "evolution." However, the JCP board of directors decided that they did not believe in evolution; four months later they announced that the company was parting ways with Johnson and replaced him with the company's previous CEO, Myron Ullman.

JCP lost more than $1 billion during Johnson's 16-month tenure as CEO and its stock price declined from $40 a share to a little over $8. Many industry analysts noted that Johnson greatly underestimated just how much shoppers like to hunt for deals and bargains and by cutting back on promotions they no longer had a reason to shop at JCP on a regular basis. Moreover, by taking away the regular sales and promotions customers loved, JCP abandoned its core shopping enthusiasts. For the past three years JCP has been struggling to win back these customers as its sales declined to $12.6 billion in fiscal 2016. Myron Ullman retired as CEO in 2015 and was replaced by Marvin Ellison, whose goal is to make JCP smarter and more efficient at keeping customers loyal and selling more products to each one. His strategy includes getting JCP's 87 million active customers to spend more time shopping in its stores, building on its in-house brands, and overhauling its website and shopping app to make it easier for in-store customers to find discounts and deals. It is likely that JCPenney will be sending them some coupons as well.

Sources: Phil Wahba, "The Man Who's Re-(Re-Re) Inventing J.C. Penney," *Fortune.com*, March 1, 2016, pp. 76–82; Jennifer Reingold, "How to Fail in Business While Really, Really Trying," *Fortune.com*, April 7, 2014, pp. 80–90; Joann S. Lublin and Dana Mattioli, "Penney CEO Out, Old Boss Back In," *The Wall Street Journal*, April 8, 2013, p. A1; Anne D'Innocenzio, "Penney Pitches Sales," *U-T San Diego*, January 29, 2013, pp. C1, C5; Natalie Zmuda, "JC Penney Reinvents Department-Store Retailing," *Advertising Age*, January 25, 2012, http://adage.com/article/news/jc-penney-reinvents-department-store-retailing/232339/.

advertising devalues the brand.[22] They say trade promotions in particular contribute to the destruction of brand franchises and equity as they encourage consumers to purchase primarily on the basis of price.

Marketers often struggle with the problem of determining the extent to which they should use promotions to help generate sales for their brands or drive traffic to their retail stores versus relying on advertising as a way to build their brand image and avoid discounting and price competition. Given a choice, many companies would prefer to minimize their reliance on promotions and discounts and compete on the basis of product quality and/or brand image. However, many companies find it very difficult to avoid using promotions, particularly when consumers have become accustomed to them. IMC Perspective 16–1 discusses how retailer JCPenney's efforts to reduce its reliance on promotions a few years ago resulted in

EXHIBIT 16–7

Macy's relies heavily on promotions to retain customers

© McGraw-Hill Education/Jill Braaten, photographer

a major decline in sales and led to the firing of the CEO who made the decision to do so.

JCPenney is not the only company that has failed in its efforts to lessen consumers' reliance on various types of promotions, including coupons and sales. For example, a few years ago Macy's, which is one of the nation's premier retailers, embarked on a new strategy designed to wean consumers off the 15 to 20 percent coupons as well as the "one-day sales" which it had become very reliant on to drive store traffic. The new strategy also called for more advertising to let consumers know about Macy's makeover and build a strong brand image for the chain. After implementing the new strategy, sales dropped for four consecutive months and Macy's had to backtrack on its plan and revert to the previous strategy, which relied heavily on various forms of discounts as well as one-day and other types of short-term sales (Exhibit 16–7).[23]

Proponents of advertising argue that marketers must maintain strong franchises if they want to differentiate their brands and charge a premium price for them. They say advertising is still the most effective way to build the long-term franchise of a brand: It informs consumers of a brand's features and benefits, creates an image, and helps build and maintain brand loyalty. However, many marketers are not investing in their brands as they take monies away from media advertising to fund short-term promotions. Professors Lodish and Mela suggest that managers need to develop and arm themselves with long-term measures of brand performance and use them to make smarter marketing decisions that will not undermine brand equity.[24] However, the temptation to look for the quick fix and sales spike from a promotion will always be there. And it is likely that many marketers will continue to yield to the temptation rather than try to sell their brands at full price, particularly when competitors are using promotional tactics to attract their customers. Many of these concerns are justified, but not all sales promotion activities detract from the value of a brand. It is important to distinguish between consumer franchise-building and nonfranchise-building promotions.

Consumer Franchise-Building versus Nonfranchise-Building Promotions

Sales promotion activities that communicate distinctive brand attributes and contribute to the development and reinforcement of brand identity are **consumer franchise-building (CFB) promotions**.[25] Consumer sales promotion efforts cannot make consumers loyal to a brand that is of little value or does not provide them with a specific benefit. But they can make consumers aware of a brand and, by communicating its specific features and benefits, contribute to the development of a favorable brand image. Consumer franchise-building promotions are designed to build long-term brand preference and help the company achieve the ultimate goal of full-price purchases that do not depend on a promotional offer.

For years, franchise or image building was viewed as the exclusive realm of advertising, and sales promotion was used only to generate short-term sales increases. But now marketers are recognizing the image-building potential of sales promotion and paying attention to its CFB value. Surveys have found that nearly 90 percent of senior marketing executives believe consumer promotions can help build brand equity while nearly 60 percent think trade promotions can contribute.[26] Most sales promotion agencies recognize the importance of developing consumer and trade promotions that can help build brand equity. For example, Exhibit 16–8 shows a classic ad for Ryan Partnership that stresses how the agency develops trade promotions that help build brand equity.

Companies can use sales promotion techniques in a number of ways to contribute to franchise building. Rather than using a one-time offer, many companies are developing frequency programs that encourage repeat purchases and long-term patronage. Many credit cards have loyalty programs where consumers earn bonus points every time they use their card to charge a purchase. These points can then be redeemed for various items. Most airlines and many hotel chains offer frequent-flyer or guest programs to encourage repeat patronage. Many retail stores have also begun using frequency programs to build loyalty and encourage repeat purchases.

Nonfranchise-building (non-FB) promotions are designed to accelerate the purchase decision process and generate an immediate increase in sales. These activities do not communicate information about a brand's unique features or the benefits of using it, so they do not contribute to the building of brand identity and image. Price-off deals, bonus packs, and rebates or refunds are examples of non-FB sales promotion techniques. Trade promotions receive the most criticism for being non-franchise building and for good reason. First, many of the promotional discounts and allowances given to the trade are never passed on to consumers. And most trade promotions that are forwarded through the channels reach consumers in the form of lower prices or special deals and lead them to buy on the basis of price rather than brand equity.

Many specialists in the promotional area stress the need for marketers to use sales promotion tools to build a franchise and create long-term continuity in their promotional programs. Whereas non-FB promotions merely borrow customers from other brands, well-planned CFB activities can convert consumers to loyal customers. Short-term non-FB promotions have their place in a firm's promotional mix, particularly when competitive developments call for them. But their limitations must be recognized when a long-term marketing strategy for a brand is developed.

CONSUMER-ORIENTED SALES PROMOTION

Marketers have been using various types of sales promotion for more than a hundred years and have found a variety of ways to give consumers an extra incentive to purchase their products and services. In this section, we examine the various sales promotion tools and techniques marketers can use to influence consumers. We study the consumer-oriented promotions shown in Figure 16–1 and discuss their advantages and limitations. First, we consider some objectives marketers have for sales promotion programs targeted to the consumer market.

Objectives of Consumer-Oriented Sales Promotion

As the use of sales promotion techniques continues to increase, companies must consider what they hope to accomplish through their consumer promotions and how they interact with other promotional activities such as advertising, direct marketing, and personal selling. Not all sales promotion activities are designed to achieve the same objectives. As with any promotional-mix element, marketers must plan consumer promotions by conducting a situation analysis and determining sales promotion's specific role in the integrated marketing communications program. They must decide what the promotion is designed to accomplish and to whom it should be targeted. Setting clearly defined objectives and measurable goals for their sales promotion programs forces managers to think beyond the short-term sales fix (although this can be one goal).

While the basic goal of most consumer-oriented sales promotion programs is to induce purchase of a brand, the marketer may have a number of different objectives for both new and established brands—for example, obtaining trial and repurchase, increasing consumption of an established brand, defending current customers, targeting a specific market segment, or enhancing advertising and marketing efforts.

Obtaining Trial and Repurchase One of the most important uses of sales promotion techniques is to encourage consumers to try a new product or service. While thousands of new products are introduced to the market every year, the vast majority of them fail within the first year. Many of these failures are due to the fact that the new product or brand lacks the promotional support needed either to encourage initial trial by enough consumers or to induce enough of those trying the brand to repurchase it. Sales promotion tools have become an important part of new brand introduction strategies; the level of initial trial can be increased through techniques such as sampling, couponing, and refund offers. The success of a new brand depends not only on getting initial trial but also on inducing a reasonable percentage of people who try the brand to repurchase it and establish ongoing purchase patterns. Promotional incentives such as coupons or refund offers are often included with a sample to encourage repeat purchase after trial. For example, Exhibit 16–9 shows an account-specific promotion Gillette used for its Fusion ProGlide razor. Razors were mailed to members of the Rite Aid drug chain wellness + rewards program to encourage trial, while a $5 off coupon for cartridges was included to encourage consumers to continue to use the product.

Increasing Consumption of an Established Brand Many marketing managers are responsible for established brands competing in mature markets, against established competitors, where consumer purchase patterns are often well set. Awareness of an established brand is generally high as a result of cumulative advertising effects, and many consumers have probably tried the brand. These factors can create a challenging situation for the brand manager. Sales promotion can generate some new interest in an established brand to help increase sales or defend market share against competitors.

Marketers attempt to increase sales for an established brand in several ways, and sales promotion can play an important role in each. One way to increase product

EXHIBIT 16–10

Arm & Hammer used this FSI to promote a specific use for the product

© Church & Dwight Co., Inc. Use of image is with the express written permission of Church & Dwight Co., Inc. Princeton, New Jersey

EXHIBIT 16–11

Miller Lite's Taste Challenge was a very successful promotion for attracting users of competing brands

Source: MillerCoors

consumption is by identifying new uses for the brand. Sales promotion tools like recipe books or calendars that show various ways of using the product often can accomplish this. One of the best examples of a brand that has found new uses is Arm & Hammer baking soda. Exhibit 16–10 shows a clever freestanding insert (FSI) that promotes the brand's fridge-freezer pack, which absorbs more odors in refrigerators and freezers.

Another strategy for increasing sales of an established brand is to use promotions that attract nonusers of the product category or users of a competing brand. Attracting nonusers of the product category can be very difficult, as consumers may not see a need for the product. Sales promotions can appeal to nonusers by providing them with an extra incentive to try the product, but a more common strategy for increasing sales of an established brand is to attract consumers who use a competing brand. This can be done by giving them an incentive to switch, such as a coupon, premium offer, bonus pack, or price deal. Marketers can also get users of a competitor to try their brand through sampling or other types of promotional programs. For example, MillerCoors used a Taste Challenge promotion to help regain market share for Miller Lite against Bud Light and other brands of light beer.[27] A key component of this integrated campaign was an interactive, on-premise promotion in bars, restaurants, and nightclubs where consumers were given the opportunity to compare the taste of Miller Lite against Bud Light (Exhibit 16–11).

Defending Current Customers With more new brands entering the market every day and competitors attempting to take away their customers through aggressive advertising and sales promotion efforts, many companies are turning to sales promotion programs to hold present customers and defend their market share. A company can use sales promotion techniques in several ways to retain its current customer base. One way is to load them with the product, taking them out of the market for a certain time. Special price promotions, coupons, or bonus packs can encourage consumers to stock up on the brand. This not only keeps them using the company's brand but also reduces the likelihood they will switch brands in response to a competitor's promotion.

Targeting a Specific Market Segment Most companies focus their marketing efforts on specific market segments and are always looking for ways to reach their target audiences. many marketers are finding that sales promotion tools such as contests and sweepstakes, events, coupons, and samplings are very effective ways to reach specific geographic, demographic, psychographic, and ethnic markets. Sales promotion programs can also be targeted to specific user-status groups such as nonusers or light versus heavy users. For example, MASS Hispanic, the promotional agency for Kimberly-Clark's Kleenex brand of facial tissues, created an award-winning promotion whose objective was to increase the relevance of the brand and build a better connection with the Hispanic market.

The agency created a promotion called "Con Kleenex Expresa tu Hispanidad" (Express Your Hispanic Pride with Kleenex) where Hispanic consumers were invited to express their traditions and cultural pride through an art contest (Exhibit 16–12). The contest called on aspiring amateur Hispanic artists and consumers around the country to submit an original design expressing their Latino pride for the opportunity to win $5,000 plus the privilege of having the artwork appear on a boutique-size Kleenex tissue carton during Hispanic Heritage month. The back end of the promotion included a chance for consumers to participate in selecting a "People's Choice" winner and to purchase special cartons of Kleenex that were displayed in retail stores during Hispanic Heritage month. Over 30,000 consumers voted online to pick the best design, and 18 of Kimberly-Clark's key retail accounts provided special

EXHIBIT 16–12

Kimberly-Clark used a contest targeted to Hispanic consumers to increase their involvement and connection to Kleenex

© *Kimberly-Clark Worldwide, Inc.*

retail displays of the winning cartons, which led to a 476 percent increase in Kleenex sales in the stores during the promotional period.[28]

Promotional programs also can be developed to coincide with peak sales periods for certain products and services. For example, candy companies such as Mars and Hershey often develop sales promotions that are run right before Halloween while clothing and school supply companies targeting children and teens run promotions in late summer, when most of the back-to-school shopping occurs.

Enhancing Integrated Marketing Communications and Building Brand Equity A final objective for consumer-oriented promotions is to enhance or support the integrated marketing communications effort for a brand or company. Building and/or maintaining brand equity was traditionally viewed as something that was done through media advertising, but it has also become an important goal for marketers as they develop their sales promotion programs. Companies are asking their advertising and promotion agencies to think strategically and develop promotional programs that can do more than simply generate short-term sales. They want promotions that require consumers to become more involved with their brands and offer a way of presenting the brand essence in an engaging way. Many marketers are recognizing that a well-designed and executed promotion can be a very effective way to engage consumers and to differentiate their brands. Sales promotion techniques such as contests or sweepstakes and premium offers are often used to draw attention to an advertising campaign, to increase involvement with the message and product or service, and to help build relationships with consumers.

CONSUMER-ORIENTED SALES PROMOTION TECHNIQUES

Sampling

Marketers use a variety of consumer-oriented sales promotion tools to accomplish the objectives just discussed. We will discuss how these various sales promotion tools are used and factors marketers must consider in using them, beginning with sampling.

Sampling involves a variety of procedures whereby consumers are given some quantity of a product for no charge to induce trial. Sampling is generally considered the most effective way to generate trial, although it is also the most expensive. As a sales promotion technique, sampling is often used to introduce a new product or brand to the market. However, sampling is used for established products as well. Some companies do not use sampling for established products, reasoning that samples may not induce satisfied users of a competing brand to switch and may just go to the firm's current customers, who would buy the product anyway. This may not be true when significant changes (new and improved) are made in a brand.

Manufacturers of packaged-goods products such as food, health care items, cosmetics, and toiletries are heavy users of sampling since their products meet the three criteria for an effective sampling program:

1. The products are of relatively low unit value, so samples do not cost too much.
2. The products are divisible, which means they can be broken into small sample sizes that are adequate for demonstrating the brand's features and benefits to the user.
3. The purchase cycle is relatively short, so the consumer will consider an immediate purchase or will not forget about the brand before the next purchase occasion.

EXHIBIT 16–13

Jack in the Box's "Free Fryday" promotion was an effective way to encourage consumers to try its new French fries

Source: Jack In The Box Inc.

Benefits and Limitations of Sampling   Samples are an excellent way to induce trial as they provide consumers with a risk-free way to try new products. A major study by the Promotion Marketing Association (now known as the Brand Activation Association) found that the vast majority of consumers receiving a sample either use it right away or save it to use sometime later.[29] Sampling generates much higher trial rates than advertising or other sales promotion techniques.

Getting people to try a product leads to a second benefit of sampling: Consumers experience the brand directly, gaining a greater appreciation for its benefits. This can be particularly important when a product's features and benefits are difficult to describe through advertising. Many foods, beverages, and cosmetics have subtle features that are most appreciated when experienced directly. Thus, marketers in these industries often use samples as a way to introduce consumers to their new products. For example, Jack in the Box, one of the major fast-food restaurant chains in the Western region of the United States, used a "Free Fryday" promotion to give consumers the opportunity to sample its new French fries (Exhibit 16–13). Nearly 70 percent of the respondents in the PMA survey indicated they have purchased a product they did not normally use after trying a free sample. The study also found that samples are even more likely to lead to purchase when they are accompanied by a coupon.

While samples are an effective way to induce trial, the brand must have some unique or superior benefits for a sampling program to be worthwhile. Otherwise, the sampled consumers revert back to other brands and do not become repeat purchasers. The costs of a sampling program can be recovered only if it gets a number of consumers to become regular users of the brand at full retail price.

Another possible limitation to sampling is that the benefits of some products are difficult to gauge immediately, and the learning period required to appreciate the brand may require supplying the consumer with larger amounts of the brand than are affordable. An example would be an expensive skin cream that is promoted as preventing or reducing wrinkles but has to be used for an extended period before any effects are seen.

Sampling Methods   One basic decision the sales promotion or brand manager must make is how the sample will be distributed. The sampling method chosen is important not only in terms of costs but also because it influences the type of consumer who receives the sample. The best sampling method gets the product to the best prospects for trial and subsequent repurchase. Some basic distribution methods include door-to-door, direct-mail, in-store, and on-package approaches. *Door-to-door sampling*, in which the product is delivered directly to a residence, is used when it is important to control where the samples are delivered. For many years newspapers were used to achieve mass distribution of samples such as by using poly bags, with a promotional message printed on them along with the sample. However, less than half of U.S. households now subscribe to a print newspaper, which reduces their value as a sampling method for marketers who want mass distribution of their samples

Sampling through the mail is common for small, lightweight, nonperishable products. A major advantage of this method is that the marketer has control over where and when the product will be distributed and can target the sample to specific market areas. Many marketers are using information from geodemographic target marketing programs such as Nielsen's PRIZM to better target their sample mailings. *In-store sampling* is increasingly popular, especially for food products since consumers get to taste the item and the demonstrator can give them more information about the product while it is being sampled. Although this sampling method can be very effective, it can also be expensive and requires a great deal of planning, as well as the cooperation of retailers.

EXHIBIT 16–14

Armor All uses on-package samples for related products

Source: The Armor All/STP Products Company

On-package sampling, where a sample of a product is attached to another item, is another common sampling method (see Exhibit 16–14). This procedure can be very cost-effective, particularly for multiproduct firms that attach a sample of a new product to an existing brand's package. A drawback is that since the sample is distributed only to consumers who purchase the item to which it is attached, the sample will not reach nonusers of the carrier brand. Marketers can expand this sampling method by attaching the sample to multiple carrier brands and including samples with products not made by their company.

Event sampling has become one of the fastest-growing and most popular ways of distributing samples. Many marketers are using sampling programs that are part of integrated marketing programs that feature events, media tie-ins, and other activities that provide consumers with a total sense of a brand rather than just a few tastes of a food or beverage or a trial size of a packaged-goods product. Event sampling can take place in stores as well as at a variety of other venues such as concerts, sporting events, and other places.

Other Methods of Sampling The four sampling methods just discussed are the most common, but several other methods are also used. Several companies also use specialized sample distribution service companies. These firms help the company identify consumers who are nonusers of a product or users of a competing brand and develop appropriate procedures for distributing a sample to them. Many college students receive sample packs at the beginning of the semester that contain trial sizes of such products as mouthwash, toothpaste, headache remedies, and deodorant.

The Internet is yet another way companies are making it possible for consumers to sample their products, and it is adding a whole new level of targeting to the mix by giving consumers the opportunity to choose the samples they want. Several companies offer websites where consumers can register to receive free samples for products that interest them. Exhibit 16–15 shows the homepage from the website of MyTownOffers.com promoting the samples and other promotional offers it makes available to consumers. The service asks consumers qualifying questions on product usage that can be used by marketers to target their samples and other promotional offers more effectively.

Marketers also use various forms of social media as a way to distribute samples. For example, Splenda used Facebook to distribute samples of a pocket-size spray form of its sweetener. The company used engagement ads to direct consumers to the Splenda Mist page, where they could sign up for a "first look" at the new product and provide the company with information about themselves. Splenda also used its Facebook page to solicit valuable feedback from consumers who received the samples.[30]

Couponing

The oldest, most widely used, and most effective sales promotion tool is the cents-off coupon. Coupons have been around since 1895, when the C. W. Post Co. started using the penny-off coupon to sell its new Grape-Nuts cereal. In recent years, coupons have become increasingly popular with consumers, which may explain their explosive growth among manufacturers and retailers that use them as sales promotion incentives. Coupons are the most popular sales promotion technique as they are used by nearly all the packaged-goods firms.

Coupon distribution and use for consumer packaged goods (CPG) in the United States increased significantly during the recent recession as the number of coupons distributed reached a record 332 billion in 2010, with 3.3 billion being redeemed. As the economy recovered, the number of coupons distributed declined to 307 billion in 2015, with 2.4 billion being redeemed. According to NCH Marketing Services, a company that tracks coupon distribution and redemption patterns, over 90 percent of consumers in the United States use coupons and 13 percent say they always use them when they shop. The average face value of the 307 billion CPG coupons distributed in 2015 was $1.79, while the average value for the 2.4 billion redeemed was $1.42. However the average face value of coupons redeemed for nonfood CPG was 20 percent higher than for food products.[31]

Adding more fuel to the coupon explosion of the past several decades has been the vast number of coupons distributed through retailers that are not even included in these figures. In some markets, a number of grocery stores make manufacturers' coupons even more attractive to consumers by doubling the face value.

Advantages and Limitations of Coupons   Coupons have a number of advantages that make them popular sales promotion tools for both new and established products. First, coupons make it possible to offer a price reduction only to those consumers who are price-sensitive. Such consumers generally purchase *because* of coupons, while those who are not as concerned about price buy the brand at full value. Coupons also make it possible to reduce the retail price of a product without relying on retailers for cooperation, which can often be a problem. Coupons are generally regarded as second only to sampling as a promotional technique for generating trial. Since a coupon lowers the price of a product, it reduces the consumer's perceived risk associated with trial of a new brand. Coupons can encourage repurchase after initial trial. Many new products include a cents-off coupon inside the package to encourage repeat purchase.

Coupons can also be useful promotional devices for established products. They can encourage nonusers to try a brand, encourage repeat purchase among current users, and get users to try a new, improved version of a brand. Coupons may also help coax users of a product to trade up to more expensive brands. The product category where coupons are used most is disposable diapers, followed by cereal, detergent, and deodorant. Some of the product categories where coupons are used the least are carbonated beverages, candy, and gum.

But there are a number of problems with coupons. First, it can be difficult to estimate how many consumers will use a coupon and when. Response to a coupon is rarely immediate; it typically takes several months to redeem one. A study of coupon redemption patterns by Inman and McAlister found that many coupons are redeemed just before the expiration date rather than in the period following the initial coupon drop.[32] Many marketers are attempting to expedite redemption by shortening the time period before expiration. The average length of time from issue date to expiration date for CPG coupons in 2015 was 6.3 weeks, with the time being longer for consumer food products than for nonfood products. However, coupons remain less effective than sampling for inducing initial product trial in a short period.

A problem associated with using coupons to attract new users to an established brand is that it is difficult to prevent the coupons from being used by consumers who already use the brand. Rather than attracting new users, coupons can end up reducing the company's profit margins among consumers who would probably purchase the product anyway. However, they can help retain users.

Other problems with coupons include low redemption rates and high costs. Couponing program expenses include the face value of the coupon redeemed plus costs for production, distribution, and handling of the coupons. Figure 16–3 shows the calculations used to determine the costs of a couponing program using an FSI (freestanding insert) in the Sunday newspaper and a coupon with a face value of $1.00. As can be seen from these figures, the cost of a couponing program can be very high. Marketers should track coupon costs very carefully to ensure their use is economically feasible.

Another problem with coupon promotions is misredemption, or the cashing of a coupon without purchase of the brand. Coupon misredemption or fraud occurs in a

FIGURE 16–3

Calculating Couponing
Costs

Cost per Coupon Redeemed: An Illustration	
1. Distribution cost: 55,000,000 circulation × $6.25/M	$343,750
2. Redemptions at 1.5%	825,000
3. Redemption cost: 825,000 redemptions × $1.00 face value	$825,000
4. Retailer handling cost and processor fees: 825,000 redemptions × $0.10	$82,500
5. Creative costs	$1,500
6. Total program cost: Items 1 + 3 + 4 + 5	$1,252,750
Cost per coupon redeemed Cost divided by redemption	$1.52
7. Actual product sold on redemption (misredemption estimated at 20%): 825,000 × 80%	660,000
8. Cost per product moved: Program cost divided by amount of product sold	$1.90

number of ways, including redemption of coupons by consumers for a product type or size not specified on the coupon; redemption by store managers and employees without the accompanying sales of the product; printing of coupons by criminals who sell them to unethical merchants, who in turn redeem them; and online fraud, whereby phony coupons are produced and distributed online. Coupon fraud and misredemption cost manufacturers an estimated $500 million a year in the United States alone.

Many manufacturers hold firm in their policy to not pay retailers for questionable amounts or suspicious types of coupon submissions. However, some companies are less aggressive, and this affects their profit margins. Marketers must allow a certain percentage for misredemption when estimating the costs of a couponing program. Ways to identify and control coupon misredemption, such as improved coding, are being developed, but it still remains a problem. Many retailers are tightening their policies regarding Internet coupons. For example, Walmart will not accept Internet coupons unless they have a valid expiration date, remit address, and bar code.

Coupon Distribution Coupons can be disseminated to consumers by a number of means, including freestanding inserts in Sunday newspapers, direct mail, newspapers (either in individual ads or as a group of coupons in a cooperative format), magazines, on packages, and online. Distribution through newspaper **freestanding inserts (FSIs)** is by far the most popular method for delivering coupons to consumers, accounting for more than 90 percent of all coupons distributed. An FSI is a four-color multipage printed advertising booklet that contains consumer packaged-goods coupon offers delivered with newspapers (usually in Sunday editions). FSIs can also be delivered in direct-mail packages along with local retailer ads or can be cooperative booklets such as *RedPlum* or *SmartSource* as well as solo books done by companies. For example, Procter & Gamble uses its own *P&G brandSAVER* FSI booklet each month in newspapers throughout the country (Exhibit 16–16).

There are a number of reasons why FSIs are the most popular way of delivering coupons, including their high-quality four-color

EXHIBIT 16–16

Procter & Gamble distributes its own FSI booklet

© McGraw-Hill Education/Mark Dierker, photographer

FIGURE 16–4

CPG Coupon Distribution by Media

*Remaining includes: Newspaper, all digital formats, military and miscellaneous, where no individual media format exceeds one sharp point of the total market, retailer in ads excluded.

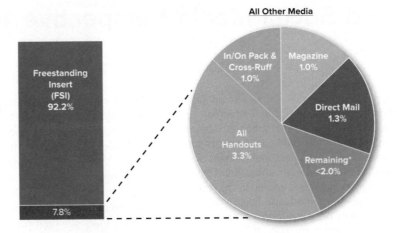

graphics, competitive distribution costs, national same-day circulation, market selectivity, and the fact that they can be competition-free due to category exclusivity (by the FSI company). Prices for a full-page FSI are currently about $6 to $7 per thousand, which makes FSI promotions very efficient and affordable. Because of their mass-market appeal among consumers and predictable distribution, coupons distributed in FSIs are also a strong selling point with the retail trade.

The increased distribution of coupons through FSIs has, however, led to a clutter problem. Consumers are being bombarded with too many coupons, and although each FSI publisher offers product exclusivity in its insert, this advantage may be negated when there are three inserts in a Sunday paper. Redemption rates of FSI coupons have declined from 4 percent to under 2 percent and even lower for some products. These problems are leading some marketers to look at other ways of delivering coupons that will result in less clutter and higher redemption rates, such as direct mail on by simply handing them out or dispensing the electronically in retail stores. Figure 16–4 shows the percentage of coupons delivered through methods other than FSIs.

Couponing Trends   Coupons continue to be the most effective sales promotion tool for influencing consumers' purchase decisions, as evidenced by the 3 billion that are redeemed each year by U.S. consumers. The popularity of coupons reflects the fact that they are a way for the average household to save a considerable amount of money each year. Coupon use has remained high even after the recent recession; nearly 80 percent of consumers use coupons on a regular basis and some use them very heavily. In fact, the term *extreme couponing* has been coined to describe the activity of combining shopping skills with coupon use in an effort to save as much money as possible while shopping. The TLC network still airs a reality show titled *Extreme Couponing*, which focuses on shoppers who save large amounts of money by using coupons (Exhibit 16–17).

The increased use of coupons also reflects the fact that more coupons are being distributed by marketers who are using them as a way to compete against lower-priced competitors as well as private-label store brands.[33] While consumers are using more coupons, there are still a number of problems facing marketers in using them. The average U.S. household is still barraged with nearly 3,000 coupons per year and consumers redeem less than 2 percent of the hundreds of billions of coupons distributed.

Concerns over the cost and effectiveness of coupons have led some marketers to cut back on their use and/or change the way they use them. For example, marketers

EXHIBIT 16–17

Extreme Couponing is a popular reality TV show

© McGraw-Hill Education/Mark Dierker, photographer

Digital and Social Media Perspective 16–1 > > >

MOBILE COUPONS ARE BECOMING POPULAR

Marketers have been bombarding consumers with coupons and other types of promotional discounts and offers for decades, with the vast majority of the more than 300 billion coupons being distributed through traditional methods such as FSIs in Sunday newspapers and direct-mail packets sent directly to consumers' homes. Marketers know that most of these coupons and promotional offers end up in the recycling bin of the more digitally oriented millennials who spend more time online, particularly on social media sites, than they do reading newspapers or sorting through direct-mail pieces. Thus, in recent years a number of companies have emerged that make coupons available to consumers online as well as through other methods, such as sending them directly to mobile devices.

Digital coupon use is still limited and represents less than 3 percent of all coupons redeemed. Scarborough research estimates that the number of consumers using digital coupons has grown 27 percent since 2012 to 68.4 million in 2016. However, consumers are becoming increasingly reliant on their digital devices to assist them in the shopping process and seek out coupons from a diverse set of sites. Though online shopping behavior is growing among all age groups, millennials lead the way in using digital devices to plan and carry out purchase decisions. The use of paperless coupons received via a smartphone or mobile device is higher for millennials (81 percent) versus Gen X (74 percent) and baby boomers (50 percent). It is also interesting to note that contrary to some expectations, affluent shoppers (households with income over $100,000) are just as likely to use coupons as other income groups and 70 percent of them use digital coupons. Studies show that affluent shoppers feel that by saving money with coupons they are doing something good for their budgets, and more than half feel that the money they save with coupons allows them to buy more products when shopping.

Consumers seek out coupons from a number of different digital channels including retailer, manufacturer, and coupon websites as well as search engines, coupon-specific apps, e-mails from retailers and coupon companies, push notifications, and QR codes on digital signage or catalogs and through search engines such as Google, Bing, and Yahoo!. Companies such as ScanLife, ShopSavvy, and Red-Laser provide shopping apps that allow consumers to just scan the UPC bar code with their phone to get a coupon for that product or a related one. Many consumers are downloading coupons linking mobile coupons and other promotional offers to their retailer loyalty cards. Some marketers work with companies such as Cellfire, which deliver coupons to mobile devices of consumers who sign up for its service. Cellfire is the leading provider of load-to-card (L2C) digital coupons in the consumer packaged-goods market and works with marketers as well as more than 22,000 stores nationwide to offer mobile couponing services.

have reduced the duration period, with expiration dates of three months or less becoming more common. Marketers are also moving to greater use of multiple-item purchase requirements for coupons, particularly for grocery products where nearly 40 percent of the coupons use this tactic. Despite the growing sentiment among major marketers that coupons are inefficient and costly, very few companies are likely to abandon them entirely. However, companies as well as the coupon industry are looking for ways to improve on their use.

Many marketers and retailers are looking to the Internet as a medium for distributing coupons. Several companies now offer online couponing services such as Cox. Target Media also offers consumers the opportunity to access coupons online, through Valpak.com. The website makes the same coupons and offers available to consumers that come in the Valpak direct-mail envelope. Another form of online couponing that has become very popular over the past 10 years is through deals and discounts offered by companies such as Groupon and Living Social.

The best-known company competing in this promotional space is Groupon, which was founded in 2008 in Chicago and is rapidly expanding throughout the world. Groupon's original foundation was the daily deal whereby it offered discounted deals for various products and services on its website, Groupon.com, that had to be purchased that day to take advantage of the discount. The offer would remain available only if a certain number of people agreed to purchase it. However, Groupon no longer uses a tipping point model and the deals it offers are now on from the start. Consumers can join the site for free and, once registered, receive e-mail notifications of discounted deals being offered in their market area each day. Exhibit 16–18 shows how Groupon's model works for both consumers and merchants.

Source: Cellfire Inc.

DIGITAL COUPONS FOR BIG BRANDS

Cellfire is the largest digital coupon provider in the world. Through the Cellfire Digital Offer Network, consumer packaged goods companies can deliver coupons and other offers to consumers electronically automatically loading to the customer's loyalty savings card. Consumers can find new deals with any smart phone or web browser while in one of more than 22,000 grocery and drug store locations. We work with more than 500 partners and deliver millions of coupons every day.

The Cellfire Digital Offer Network enables consumer packaged goods companies to drive and measure in-store purchases with an end-to-end solution:

- Offers implemented uniformly across all web-enabled devices
- Interactive, targeted and secure
- Easy and fast to implement
- Customized real-time reporting
- Efficient and controlled distribution
- Reliable/scalable
- Real time discounts

Another way consumers are accessing discounts and special offers through their mobile devices is through companies such as Groupon, Living Social, and others that connect local merchants as well as national brands with consumers looking for deals. Groupon has been moving from a demand-fulfillment model, such as where it helps fill empty seats in a restaurant on a slow night, to a demand-generation model, whereby customers will check its site or app for relevant deals. This means a shift from "pushing" deals to consumers through e-mails to "pulling" them to its website, Facebook page, or mobile app, where they can check out the deals that are available and then make

a purchase. Groupon also plans to utilize more mobile marketing since more than half of its transactions now take place over smartphones and other mobile devices. Nearly 120 million people worldwide have downloaded the Groupon Mobile app, which makes it possible for the company to use location-based marketing whereby deals are sent to consumers based on their proximity to a specific merchant such as a restaurant or retail store. The company also now offers a number of merchant services such as mobile payment offerings.

Mobile coupons are likely to become an even more important part of marketers' digital marketing programs because they recognize that mobile now represents nearly 65 percent of all digital media time for people online, with mobile apps dominating that usage. Another reason marketers are increasing their use of mobile coupons is that they are an effective way to measure the effectiveness of mobile advertising. *eMarketer* cites studies showing that almost two-thirds of U.S. marketers view mobile coupons as the most effective method for attributing in-store purchase to mobile ads.

The tremendous growth in mobile marketing is likely to continue as consumers spend more time on their smartphones and other digital devices and use them to plan and make purchases. And marketers will be there with coupons and other promotional offers.

Sources: *2k16 Valassis Coupon Intelligence Report,* NCH Resource Center, www2.nchmarketing.com/ResourceCenter/searchresults.aspx?q=coupon%20 Intelligence%20report; "Mobile Coupons Effective Way to Link Mobile Ad to In-Store Purchase," *eMarketer,* November 10, 2015; www.emarketer.com/ Article/Mobile-Coupons-Effective-Way-Link-Mobile-Ad-In-Store-Purchase/ 1013209; "Groupon's Goals for 2015 & Beyond," *Forbes,* March 3, 2015, www.forbes.com/sites/greatspeculations/2015/03/03/groupons-goals-for-2015-beyond/#fe843ff4d1c8.

EXHIBIT 16–18

Groupon has become a very popular way for merchants to offer discounts and deals to consumers

Source: Groupon, Inc.

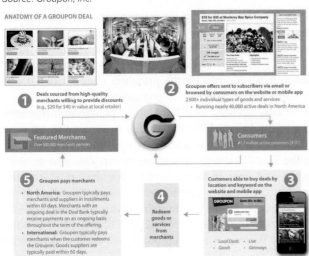

Another way to distribute coupons that is growing rapidly is through mobile marketing whereby coupons are sent directly to mobile phones. Marketers are using various social media platforms such as Facebook, Twitter, and Instagram and are also working with companies such as Cellfire that distribute coupons to mobile devices of consumers who sign up for its service. Mobile coupons have become particularly popular among millennials and younger generations of consumers, as discussed in Digital and Social Media Perspective 16–1.

Premiums

Premiums are a sales promotion device used by many marketers. A **premium** is an offer of an item of merchandise or service either free or at a low price that is an extra incentive for purchasers. Many marketers are eliminating toys and gimmicks in favor of value-added premiums that reflect the quality of the product and are consistent with its image and positioning in the market. Marketers spend over $4 billion a year on value-added premium incentives targeted at the consumer market. The two basic types of offers are the free premium and the self-liquidating premium.

Free Premiums Free premiums are usually small gifts or merchandise included in the product package or

EXHIBIT 16–19

McDonald's Happy Meals use toys as premium offers to help attract children

© urbanbuzz/Alamy

sent to consumers who mail in a request along with a proof of purchase. In/on-package free premiums include toys, balls, trading cards, or other items included in cereal packages, as well as samples of one product included with another. Package-carried premiums have high impulse value and can provide an extra incentive to buy the product. However, several problems are associated with their use. First, there is the cost factor, which results from the premium itself as well as from extra packaging that may be needed. Finding desirable premiums at reasonable costs can be difficult, particularly for adult markets, and using a poor premium may do more harm than good.

Free mail-in premium offers require the consumer to send in more than one proof of purchase and thus can encourage repeat purchase and reward brand loyalty. But a major drawback of mail-in premiums is that they do not offer immediate reinforcement or reward to the purchaser, so they may not provide enough incentive to purchase the brand. Few consumers take advantage of mail-in premium offers as the average redemption rate for them around 2 to 4 percent.

Free premiums have become very popular in the restaurant industry, particularly among fast-food chains such as McDonald's and Burger King, which use premium offers in their kids' meals to attract children. McDonald's has become the world's largest toymaker on a unit basis, commissioning about 750 million toys per year for its Happy Meals (Exhibit 16–19). Many of the premium offers used by the fast-food giants have cross-promotional tie-ins with popular movies and can be very effective at generating incremental sales. McDonald's negotiates movie tie-in deals with a number of studios, including DreamWorks Animation SKG and Pixar Animation Studios, as well as Disney. McDonald's uses movie tie-ins as the basis for many of its Happy Meal promotions.

One of the fastest-growing types of incentive offers being used by marketers is airline miles, which have literally become a promotional currency. U.S. airlines make more than an estimated $2 billion each year selling miles to other marketers. Consumers are now choosing credit-card services, phone services, hotels, and many other products and services on the basis of mileage premiums for major frequent-flyer programs such as American Airlines's AAdvantage program or United Airlines's Mileage Plus program. Exhibit 16–20 shows how American Airlines promotes the value of AAdvantage miles as a promotional incentive that companies can offer to help attract and retain customers.

EXHIBIT 16–20

American Airlines promotes the value of AAdvantage miles as a purchase incentive

© McGraw-Hill Education/Mark Dierker, photographer

Self-Liquidating Premiums
Self-liquidating premiums require the consumer to pay some or all of the cost of the premium plus handling and mailing costs. The marketer usually purchases items used as self-liquidating premiums in large quantities and offers them to consumers at lower-than-retail prices. The goal is not to make a profit on the premium item but rather just to cover costs and offer a value to the consumer.

In addition to cost savings, self-liquidating premiums offer several advantages to marketers. Offering values to consumers through the premium products can create interest in the brand and goodwill that enhances the brand's image. These premiums can also encourage trade support and gain in-store displays for the brand and the premium offer. Self-liquidating premiums are often tied directly to the advertising campaign, so they extend the advertising message and contribute to consumer franchise building for a brand. For example, Philip Morris offers Western wear, outdoor items, and other types of

Marlboro gear through its Marlboro Country catalog, which reinforces the cigarette brand's positioning theme.

Self-liquidating premium offers have the same basic limitation as mail-in premiums: very low redemption rates which can leave the marketer with a large supply of items with a logo or some other brand identification that makes them hard to dispose of. Thus, it is important to test consumers' reaction to a premium incentive and determine whether they perceive the offer as a value. Another option is to use premiums with no brand identification, but that detracts from their consumer franchise-building value.

Contests and Sweepstakes

Contests and sweepstakes are an increasingly popular consumer-oriented promotion as marketers spent over $2 billion on them each year. These promotions seem to have an appeal and glamour that such tools as cents-off coupons lack. Contests and sweepstakes are exciting because, as one expert has noted, many consumers have a "pot of gold at the end of the rainbow mentality" and think they can win the big prizes being offered.[34] The lure of sweepstakes and promotions has also been influenced by the "instant-millionaire syndrome" that has derived from huge cash prizes given by many state lotteries in recent years. Marketers are attracted to contests and sweepstakes as a way of generating attention and interest among a large number of consumers.

There are differences between contests and sweepstakes. A **contest** is a promotion where consumers compete for prizes or money on the basis of skills or ability. The company determines winners by judging the entries or ascertaining which entry comes closest to some predetermined criterion (e.g., picking the winning teams and total number of points in the Super Bowl or NCAA basketball tournament). Contests usually provide a purchase incentive by requiring a proof of purchase to enter or an entry form that is available from a dealer or advertisement. Some contests require consumers to read an ad or package or visit a store display to gather information needed to enter. Marketers must be careful not to make their contests too difficult to enter, as doing so might discourage participation among key prospects in the target audience.

A **sweepstakes** is a promotion where winners are determined purely by chance; it cannot require a proof of purchase as a condition for entry. Entrants need only submit their names for the prize drawing. While there is often an official entry form, handwritten entries must also be permitted. One form of sweepstakes is a **game**, which also has a chance element or odds of winning. Scratch-off cards with instant winners are a popular promotional tool. Some games occur over a longer period and require more involvement by consumers. Promotions where consumers must collect game pieces are popular among retailers and fast-food chains as a way to build store traffic and repeat purchases.

Because they are easier to enter, sweepstakes attract more entries than contests. They are also easier and less expensive to administer, since every entry does not have to be checked or judged. Choosing the winning entry in a sweepstakes requires only the random selection of a winner from the pool of entries or generation of a number to match those held by sweepstakes entrants. Experts note that the costs of mounting a sweepstakes are also very predictable. Companies can buy insurance to indemnify them and protect against the expense of awarding a big prize. In general, sweepstakes present marketers with a fixed cost, which is a major advantage when budgeting for a promotion.

Contests and sweepstakes can involve consumers with a brand by making the promotion product relevant or by connecting the prizes to the lifestyle, needs, or interests of the target audience. Marketers often look for creative themes for contests and sweepstakes that will capture the attention and interest of consumers and generate entries, as well as excitement, over a new product. For example, when

EXHIBIT 16-21

This contest for Axe Apollo fits well with the positioning of the new product line

Source: Axe by Unilever

Unilever introduced its new Axe Apollo line of men's grooming products, the branding strategy behind the product line was developed around the emerging reality of space tourism and perception of astronauts as heroes. Apollo is the name of the third human spaceflight program sponsored by NASA, the U.S. government agency that is responsible for the nation's civilian space program. The global IMC campaign used to introduce the Apollo product line included a contest offering consumers a chance to win a flight on the Lynx suborbital plane which will last about one hour, reach an altitude of 64 miles, and provide a weightlessness experience of about five minutes before descending back to Earth (Exhibit 16–21).

To build on the hero theme, the tagline for the contest was "Leave a man. Come back a hero" which fit well with the positioning of Axe as a brand that gives young men confidence they can use to make themselves more attractive to women. The actual contest to win one of the coveted Lynx flights, which was promoted in 60 countries and 45 languages, required contestants to go to a special website to complete an astronaut profile detailing why they should be chosen. Based on the number of votes received from the public, over 100 finalists were chosen from around the world to attend the Axe Apollo Space Academy and go through three days of training and testing that included in-space simulation exercises. Twenty-four men won tickets to space; 22 winners were chosen from the space academy competition, while the 22nd and final ticket was awarded to a U.S. resident in a sweepstakes that was a part of a tie-in with the Super Bowl, and one from a UK national promotion.

The nature of contests and sweepstakes, as well as the way they are deployed, is changing as many companies are delivering them online rather than through traditional entry forms that are submitted via the mail or dropped in an entry box. Marketers are using the Internet for their contests and sweepstakes because of its cost-efficiency, immediate data collection capabilities, and ability to keep consumers engaged. Promotions are being designed to ensure an engaging consumer experience by making them more entertaining and interactive and also developing prizes that are not only larger but more customized and experiential-based.[35] A number of companies are also integrating user-generated content into their contests, which are often promoted on their Facebook pages. Contests that rely on *crowdsourcing* whereby consumers enter ideas and they are voted on by others are becoming increasingly popular. For example, Frito-Lay has run create-a-chip contests for Doritos as well as Lay's potato chips, while Samuel Adams has run contests asking consumers to create a crowdsourced beer, and Arizona Beverages USA has prodded the public to create new iced tea flavors.[36]

Problems with Contests and Sweepstakes While the use of contests and sweepstakes continues to increase, there are some problems associated with these types of promotions. Many sweepstakes and/or contest promotions do little to contribute to consumer franchise building for a product or service and may even detract from it. The sweepstakes or contest often becomes the dominant focus rather than the brand, and little is accomplished other than giving away substantial amounts of money and/or prizes. Many promotional experts question the effectiveness of contests and sweepstakes. Some companies have cut back or even stopped using them because of concern over their effectiveness and fears that consumers might become dependent on them.

Another problem with contests and sweepstakes is the participation in them by hobbyists who submit entries but have no real interest in the product or service. Because most states make it illegal to require a purchase as a qualification for a sweepstakes entry, consumers can enter as many times as they wish. Entrants may enter a sweepstakes numerous times, depending on the nature of the prizes

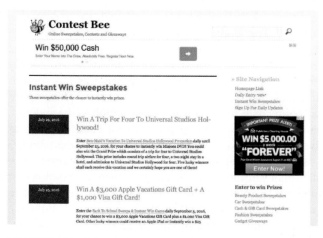

EXHIBIT 16–22

Contest Bee is a collection of online contests and sweepstakes. Do you think the problems associated with contests and sweepstakes outweigh their effectiveness?

Source: ContestBee.com

EXHIBIT 16–23

Pennzoil uses a refund offer that is tied to a future purchase

Source: Pennzoil by Shell International B.V.

and the number of entries allowed. There are numerous websites on the Internet such as sweepsadvantage.com that inform consumers of all the contests and sweepstakes being held, the entry dates, estimated probabilities of winning, how to enter, and solutions to any puzzles or other information that might be needed. The presence of the professional entrants not only defeats the purpose of the promotion but also may discourage entries from consumers who feel that their chances of winning are limited. Exhibit 16–22 shows a page from the website ContestBee.com, which provides consumers with information on contests and sweepstakes and how to enter them.

Numerous legal considerations affect the design and administration of contests and sweepstakes.[37] These promotions are regulated by several federal agencies, and each of the 50 states has its own rules. The regulation of contests and sweepstakes has helped clean up the abuses that plagued the industry for many years and has improved consumers' perceptions of these promotions. But companies must still be careful in designing a contest or sweepstakes and awarding prizes.[38] Most firms use consultants that specialize in the design and administration of contests and sweepstakes to avoid any legal problems, but they may still run into problems with them if they are not administered properly. Marketers are not the only ones who encounter problems with promotions; consumers who win contests and sweepstakes often learn that there may be unexpected tax consequences because the prizes are treated as income by the Internal Revenue Service. Many of the prizes offered in contests and sweepstakes go unclaimed because consumers do not want to pay taxes based on their face value.[39]

Refunds and Rebates

Refunds (also known as *rebates*) are offers by the manufacturer to return a portion of the product purchase price, usually after the consumer supplies some proof of purchase. Consumers are generally very responsive to rebate offers, particularly as the size of the savings increases. Rebates are used by makers of all types of products, ranging from packaged goods to major appliances, cars, and computer software.

Marketers often use refund offers to induce trial of a new product or encourage users of another brand to switch. Refund offers can also encourage repeat purchase. Many offers require consumers to send in multiple proofs of purchase. The size of the refund offer may even increase as the number of purchases gets larger. Some packaged-goods companies are switching away from cash refund offers to coupons or cash/coupon combinations. Using coupons in the refund offer enhances the likelihood of repeat purchase of the brand. For example, Exhibit 16–23 shows a coupon refund offer used by Pennzoil that can be redeemed on the next oil change.

Evaluating Refunds and Rebates   Rebates can help create new users and encourage brand switching or repeat purchase behavior, or they can be a way to offer a temporary price reduction. This offer can influence purchase even if the consumer fails to realize the savings, so the marketer can reduce price for much less than if a direct price-off deal is used.

Some problems are associated with refunds and rebates. Many consumers are not motivated by a refund or rebate offer because of the delay and the effort required to obtain the savings. They do not want to be bothered saving cash register receipts and proofs of purchase, filling out forms, and mailing in the offer.[40] A study of consumer perceptions found a negative relationship between the use of rebates and

the perceived difficulties associated with the redemption process.[41] The study also found that consumers perceive manufacturers as offering rebates to sell products that are not faring well. Nonusers of rebates were particularly likely to perceive the redemption process as too complicated and to suspect manufacturers' motives. This implies that companies using rebates must simplify the redemption process and use other promotional elements such as advertising to retain consumer confidence in the brand.

When small refunds are being offered, marketers may find other promotional incentives such as coupons or bonus packs more effective. They must be careful not to overuse rebate offers and confuse consumers about the real price and value of a product or service. Also, consumers can become dependent on rebates and delay their purchases or purchase only brands for which a rebate is available. Many retailers have become disenchanted with rebates and the burden and expense of administering them.[42]

However, despite the complaints consumers and retailers may have about them, marketers are unlikely to eliminate the use of rebates as they are a very effective promotion tool. A well-promoted, high-value rebate can increase sales significantly, and eliminating them can have a negative impact on sales, particularly in product categories where consumers have come to expect them. Marketers also recognize that they can accomplish a perceived price reduction among consumers who plan to redeem the rebates but never do so and factor the redemption rates into their pricing structure.[43]

Bonus Packs

Bonus packs offer the consumer an extra amount of a product at the regular price by providing larger containers or extra units (Exhibit 16–24). Bonus packs result in a lower cost per unit for the consumer and provide extra value as well as more product for the money. There are several advantages to bonus pack promotions. First, they give marketers a direct way to provide extra value without having to get involved with complicated coupons or refund offers. The additional value of a bonus pack is generally obvious to the consumer and can have a strong impact on the purchase decision at the time of purchase.

Bonus packs can also be an effective defensive maneuver against a competitor's promotion or introduction of a new brand. By loading current users with large amounts of its product, a marketer can often remove these consumers from the market and make them less susceptible to a competitor's promotional efforts. Bonus packs may result in larger purchase orders and favorable display space in the store if relationships with retailers are good. They do, however, usually require additional shelf space without providing any extra profit margins for the retailer, so the marketer can encounter problems with bonus packs if trade relationships are not good. Another problem is that bonus packs may appeal primarily to current users who probably would have purchased the brand anyway or to promotion-sensitive consumers who may not become loyal to the brand.

Price-Off Deals

Another consumer-oriented promotion technique is the direct **price-off deal**, which reduces the price of the brand. Price-off reductions are typically offered right on the package through specially marked price packs, as shown in Exhibit 16–25. Typically, price-offs range from 10 to 25 percent off the regular price, with the reduction coming out of the manufacturer's profit margin, not the retailer's. Keeping the retailer's margin during a price-off promotion maintains its support and cooperation.

EXHIBIT 16–26

Buy one/get one free deals are often used to encourage multiple purchases of a brand

Source: Nestlé Purina Petcare

Marketers use price-off promotions for several reasons. First, since price-offs are controlled by the manufacturer, it can make sure the promotional discount reaches the consumer rather than being kept by the trade. Like bonus packs, price-off deals usually present a readily apparent value to shoppers, especially when they have a reference price point for the brand and thus recognize the value of the discount.[44] So price-offs can be a strong influence at the point of purchase when price comparisons are being made. Price-off promotions can also encourage consumers to purchase larger quantities, preempting competitors' promotions and leading to greater trade support.

Price-off promotions may not be favorably received by retailers, since they can create pricing and inventory problems. Most retailers will not accept packages with a specific price shown, so the familiar *X* amount off the regular price must be used. Also, like bonus packs, price-off deals appeal primarily to regular users instead of attracting nonusers. Finally, the Federal Trade Commission has regulations regarding the conditions that price-off labels must meet and the frequency and timing of their use.

A popular variation of a price-off promotion is the buy one/get one free deal such as the offer for Purina Beneful dog food shown in Exhibit 16–26. These types of price promotions are an effective way to provide extra value for consumers and encourage them to make multiple purchases of a product.

Loyalty Programs

One of the fastest-growing areas of sales promotion is the use of **loyalty programs** (also referred to as *continuity* or *frequency programs*). American Airlines was one of the first major companies to use loyalty programs when it introduced its AAdvantage frequent-flyer program in 1981. Since then frequency programs have become commonplace in a number of product and service categories, particularly travel and hospitality, as well as among retailers. Virtually every airline, car rental company, casinos, and hotel chain has some type of frequency program. American Airlines has more than 70 million members in its AAdvantage program, while Marriott International has enlisted more than 20 million business travelers into its Rewards program. The loyalty marketing research firm COLLOQUY's biennial report on the scope of U.S. reward programs showed that in 2015 consumers held 3.3 billion memberships in customer loyalty programs, which was a 26 percent increase in just two years.[45]

Many packaged-goods companies are also developing loyalty programs. Pillsbury, Nestlé, Kraft, General Mills, and others have recently introduced continuity programs that offer consumers the opportunity to accumulate points for continuing to purchase their brands; the points can be redeemed for gifts and prizes. Supermarkets were among the first retailers to develop card-based shopper loyalty programs and more than 7,000 of them now have loyalty programs that offer members discounts, a chance to accumulate points that can be redeemed for rewards, newsletters, and other special services. Loyalty programs are also used by a variety of other retailers, including department stores, home centers, bookstores, and even local bagel shops. Many specialty retailers such as consumer electronics stores also have launched loyalty programs. For example, Best Buy launched its Rewards Zone program in 2003, and the program has grown to include more than 7 million members.

There are a number of reasons why loyalty programs have become so popular. Marketers view these programs as a way of encouraging consumers to use their products or services on a continual basis and as a way of developing strong customer loyalty. Many companies are also realizing the importance of customer retention and understand that the key to retaining and growing market share is building relationships with loyal customers.[46] Frequency programs also provide marketers with the opportunity to develop databases containing valuable information on their customers that can be used to better understand their needs, interests, and characteristics

EXHIBIT 16–27

The Plenti Rewards program allows consumers to earn points from a number of companies

Source: Plenti

as well as to identify and track a company's most valuable customers. These databases can also be used to target specific programs and offers to customers to increase the amount they purchase and/or to build stronger relationships with them. Many marketers find it more cost-efficient and effective to communicate with their customers through their loyalty programs than through mass-media advertising.

As frequency programs become more common, marketers will be challenged to find ways to use them as a means of differentiating their product, service, business, or retail store. According to the recent study by COLLOQUY, the average American household belongs to 29 loyalty programs but is active in only 12 of them.[47] It has been argued that many of the loyalty programs developed by marketers are really short-term promotions that over-reward regular users and do little to develop long-term loyalty.[48] A study by a loyalty marketing firm found that 66 percent of consumers say that discounts are the main reason they participate in loyalty programs. This study also found that many consumers drop out of loyalty programs because of the length of time it takes to accumulate reward points.[49] Marketers must find ways to make their loyalty programs more than just discount or frequent-buyer programs. This will require the careful management of databases to identify and track valuable customers and their purchase history and the strategic use of targeted loyalty promotions.

Some companies have already begun making changes in their loyalty programs to make them more appealing to members and encourage more purchases. For example, a number of companies including Macy's, AT&T, Rite Aid, Expedia, Nationwide, and ExxonMobile now participate in the Plenti loyalty program that is operated by American Express and allows shoppers to earn points with multiple retailers (Exhibit 16–27). A number of companies have also made changes in the way rewards are earned in their loyalty programs. Several airlines such as American, Delta, United, and Southwest now base rewards on the amount of money spent for airline tickets rather than miles flown. In early 2016, Starbucks made changes to its My Starbucks Rewards program and customers now earn reward stars based on the amount of money they spend at the coffee retailer. Previously customers earned one star per transaction no matter how much money they spent.[50]

Event Marketing

Another type of consumer-oriented promotion that has become very popular in recent years is the use of event marketing. It is important to make a distinction between *event marketing* and *event sponsorships*, as the two terms are often used interchangeably yet they refer to different activities. **Event marketing** is a type of promotion where a company or brand is linked to an event or where a themed activity is developed for the purpose of creating experiences for consumers and promoting a product or service. Marketers often do event marketing by associating their product with some popular activity such as a sporting event, concert, fair, or festival. However, marketers also create their own events to use for promotional purposes. For example, PepsiCo has created an irreverent brand image for its popular Mountain Dew brand by associating it with action sports. Extreme sports are about a nonconforming lifestyle from clothes to music, and young people respond to brands that make an authentic connection and become part of the action sports community. In 2005, the brand raised its involvement with action sports to a new level when it became a founding partner of the Dew Tour, a five-event series that features competition in snowboarding BMX, and freestyle motocross and skateboading (Exhibit 16–28). From an event marketing perspective, an important part of the Dew Tour is the promotional opportunities associated with the various events. These include custom

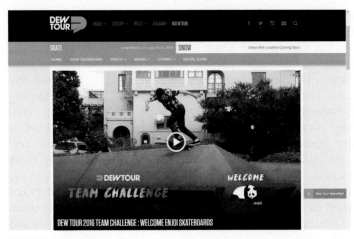

EXHIBIT 16–28

The Dew Tour provides Mountain Dew with event marketing opportunities

Source: The Enthusiast Network and Mountain Dew

art, interactive displays, athlete autograph sessions, lounges where fans can hang out and interact with their favorite extreme sport athletes, and the product sampling kitchen where they can try various Mountain Dew flavors, as well as other products.

An **event sponsorship** is an integrated marketing communications activity where a company develops actual sponsorship relations with a particular event and provides financial support in return for the right to display a brand name, logo, or advertising message and be identified as a supporter of the event. Event marketing often takes place as part of a company's sponsorship of activities such as concerts, the arts, social causes, and sporting events. Decisions and objectives for event sponsorships are often part of an organization's public relations activities and are discussed in Chapter 17.

Event marketing has become a very popular part of the integrated marketing communications programs of many companies as they view them as excellent promotional opportunities and a way to associate their brands with certain lifestyles, interests, and activities. Events can be an effective way to connect with consumers in an environment where they are comfortable with receiving a promotional message. Moreover, consumers often expect companies to be part of events and welcome their participation as they make the events more entertaining, interesting, and exciting. Marketers can use events to distribute samples as well as information about their products and services or to actually let consumers experience their brands.

Summary of Consumer-Oriented Promotions and Marketer Objectives

The discussion of the various sales promotion techniques shows that marketers use these tools to accomplish a variety of objectives. As noted at the beginning of the chapter, sales promotion techniques provide consumers with an *extra incentive* or *reward* for engaging in a certain form of behavior such as purchasing a brand. For some types of sales promotion tools the incentive the consumer receives is immediate, while for others the reward is delayed and is not realized immediately. Marketers often evaluate sales promotion tools in terms of their ability to accomplish specific objectives and consider whether the impact of the promotion will be immediate or delayed. Figure 16–5 outlines which sales promotion tools can be used to

FIGURE 16–5

Consumer-Oriented Sales Promotion Tools for Various Marketing Objectives

	Marketing Objective		
Consumer Reward Incentive	**Induce trial**	**Customer retention/loading**	**Support IMC program/ build brand equity**
Immediate	• Sampling • Instant coupons • In-store coupons • In-store rebates	• Price-off deals • Bonus packs • In- and on-package free premiums • Loyalty programs	• Events • In- and on-package free premiums
Delayed	• Media- and mail-delivered coupons • Mail-in refunds and rebates • Free mail-in premiums • Scanner- and Internet-delivered coupons	• In- and on-package coupons • Mail-in refunds and rebates • Loyalty programs	• Self-liquidating premiums • Free mail-in premiums • Contests and sweepstakes • Loyalty programs

accomplish various objectives of marketers and identifies whether the extra incentive or reward is immediate or delayed.[51]

It should be noted that in Figure 16–5 some of the sales promotion techniques are listed more than once because they can be used to accomplish more than one objective. For example, loyalty programs can be used to retain customers by providing both immediate and delayed rewards. Shoppers who belong to loyalty programs sponsored by supermarkets and receive discounts every time they make a purchase are receiving immediate rewards that are designed to retain them as customers. Some loyalty promotions such as frequency programs used by airlines, car rental companies, and hotels offer delayed rewards by requiring that users accumulate points to reach a certain level or status before the points can be redeemed. Loyalty programs can also be used by marketers to help build brand equity. For example, when an airline or car rental company sends its frequent users upgrade certificates, the practice helps build relationships with these customers and thus contributes to brand equity.

While marketers use consumer-oriented sales promotions to provide current and/ or potential customers with an extra incentive, they also use these promotions as part of their marketing program to leverage trade support. Retailers are more likely to stock a brand, purchase extra quantities, or provide additional support such as end-aisle displays when they know a manufacturer is running a promotion during a designated period. The development of promotional programs targeted toward the trade is a very important part of the marketing process and is discussed in the next section.

TRADE-ORIENTED SALES PROMOTION

Objectives of Trade-Oriented Sales Promotion

Like consumer-oriented promotions, sales promotion programs targeted to the trade should be based on well-defined objectives and measurable goals and a consideration of what the marketer wants to accomplish. Typical objectives for promotions targeted to marketing intermediaries such as wholesalers and retailers include obtaining distribution and support for new products, maintaining support for established brands, encouraging retailers to display established brands, and building retail inventories.

Obtain Distribution for New Products Trade promotions are often used to encourage retailers to give shelf space to new products. Manufacturers recognize that only a limited amount of shelf space is available in supermarkets, drugstores, and other major retail outlets. Thus, they provide retailers with financial incentives to stock and promote new products. While trade discounts or other special price deals are used to encourage retailers and wholesalers to stock a new brand, marketers may use other types of promotions to get them to push the brand. Merchandising allowances can get retailers to display a new product in high-traffic areas of stores, while incentive programs or contests can encourage wholesale or retail store personnel to push a new brand.

Maintain Trade Support for Established Brands Trade promotions are often designed to maintain distribution and trade support for established brands. Brands that are in the mature phase of their product life cycle are vulnerable to losing wholesale and/or retail distribution, particularly if they are not differentiated or face competition from new products. Trade deals induce wholesalers and retailers to continue to carry weaker products because the discounts increase their profit margins. Brands with a smaller market share often rely heavily on trade promotions, since they lack the funds required to differentiate themselves from competitors through media advertising. Even if a brand has a strong market position, trade promotions may be

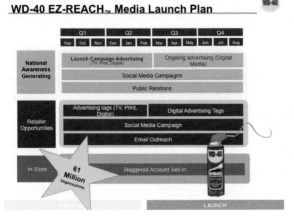

EXHIBIT 16–29

WD-40's program calendar shows the retailers the marketing support planned to support its new EZ-REACH product

Source: WD-40 Company

used as part of an overall marketing strategy. For example, Heinz has relied heavily on trade promotions to hold its market share position for many of its brands. Many consumer packaged-goods companies count on trade promotions to maintain retail distribution and support.

Encourage Retailers to Display Established Brands Another objective of trade-oriented promotions is to encourage retailers to display and promote an established brand. Marketers recognize that many purchase decisions are made in the store, and promotional displays are an excellent way of generating sales. An important goal is to obtain retail store displays of a product away from its regular shelf location. A typical supermarket has approximately 50 display areas at the ends of aisles, near checkout counters, and elsewhere. Marketers want to have their products displayed in these areas to increase the probability shoppers will come into contact with them. Even a single display can increase a brand's sales significantly during a promotion.

Manufacturers often use multifaceted promotional programs to encourage retailers to promote their products at the retail level. For example, Exhibit 16–29 shows a program calendar the WD-40 Company provides to retailers showing the various marketing support programs the company would be using to support the launch of its new EZ-REACH product. The program included a variety of IMC tools including targeted advertising on television and in magazines; online videos, and e-newsletters; social media banners and blogs; trade publication and blogger outreach; public relations; and various types of consumer and trade promotions.

Build Retail Inventories Manufacturers often use trade promotions to build the inventory levels of retailers or other channel members. There are several reasons manufacturers want to load retailers with their products. First, wholesalers and retailers are more likely to push a product when they have high inventory levels rather than storing it in their warehouses or back rooms. Building channel members' inventories also ensures they will not run out of stock and thus miss sales opportunities.

Some manufacturers of seasonal products offer large promotional discounts so that retailers will stock up on their products before the peak selling season begins. This enables the manufacturer to smooth out seasonal fluctuations in its production schedule and passes on some of the inventory carrying costs to retailers or wholesalers. When retailers stock up on a product before the peak selling season, they often run special promotions and offer discounts to consumers to reduce excess inventories.

Types of Trade-Oriented Promotions

Manufacturers use a variety of trade promotion tools as inducements for wholesalers and retailers. Next we examine some of the most often used types of trade promotions and some factors marketers must consider in using them. These promotions include contests and incentives, trade allowances, displays and point-of-purchase materials, sales training programs, trade shows, and co-op advertising.

Contests and Incentives Manufacturers may develop contests or special incentive programs to stimulate greater selling effort and support from reseller management or sales personnel. Contests or incentive programs can be directed toward managers who work for a wholesaler or distributor as well as toward store or department managers at the retail level. Manufacturers often sponsor contests for resellers and use prizes such as trips or valuable merchandise as rewards for meeting sales quotas or other goals.

Contests or special incentives are often targeted at the sales personnel of the wholesalers, distributors/dealers, or retailers. These salespeople are an important link in the distribution chain because they are likely to be very familiar with the market, more frequently in touch with the customer (whether it be another reseller or the ultimate consumer), and more numerous than the manufacturer's own sales organization. Manufacturers often devise incentives or contests for these sales personnel. These programs may involve cash payments made directly to the retailer's or wholesaler's sales staff to encourage them to promote and sell a manufacturer's product. These payments are known as **push money (pm)** or *spiffs*. For example, an appliance manufacturer may pay a $25 spiff to retail sales personnel for selling a certain model or size. In sales contests, salespeople can win trips or valuable merchandise for meeting certain goals established by the manufacturer. As shown in Figure 16–6, these incentives may be tied to product sales, new account placements, or merchandising efforts.

While contests and incentive programs can generate reseller support, they can also be a source of conflict between retail sales personnel and management. Some retailers want to maintain control over the selling activities of their sales staffs. They don't want their salespeople devoting an undue amount of effort to trying to win a contest or receive incentives offered by the manufacturer. Nor do they want their people becoming too aggressive in pushing products that serve their own interests instead of the product or model that is best for the customer.

Many retailers refuse to let their employees participate in manufacturer-sponsored contests or to accept incentive payments. Retailers that do allow them often have strict guidelines and require management approval of the program.

Trade Allowances Probably the most common trade promotion is some form of **trade allowance**, a discount or deal offered to retailers or wholesalers to encourage them to stock, promote, or display the manufacturer's products. Types of allowances offered to retailers include buying allowances, promotional or display allowances, and slotting allowances.

Buying Allowances A buying allowance is a deal or discount offered to resellers in the form of a price reduction on merchandise ordered during a fixed period. These discounts are often in the form of an **off-invoice allowance**, which means a certain per-case amount or percentage is deducted from the invoice. A buying allowance

FIGURE 16–6

Three Forms of Promotion Targeted to Reseller Salespeople

- Product or Program Sales

  Awards are tied to the selling of a product; for example:

    Selling a specified number of cases

    Selling a specified number of units

    Selling a specified number of promotional programs

- New Account Placements

  Awards are tied to:

    The number of new accounts opened

    The number of new accounts ordering a minimum number of cases or units

    Promotional programs placed in new accounts

- Merchandising Efforts

  Awards are tied to:

    Establishing promotional programs (such as theme programs)

    Placing display racks, counter displays, and the like

BUMBLE BEE®

WILD SARDINES

Pre-Packed Gourmet Brisling Wild Sardines Shippers Ready for Display!

★ Mixed Shippers Promote Trial and Impulse Sales. Perfect for secondary placements in perimeter areas to increase sales of related items

★ Generate higher category profit margin and larger basket rings

★ Customer friendly 48 count displays with eye catching graphics and clean designs

★ Available in two configurations

Extra Small Sardines: 48ct - 24/3.75oz Extra Virgin Olive Oil(EVOO) and 24/EVOO with Hot Jalapeño Peppers

Small Sardines: 48ct – 24/3.75oz Mediterranean-12/Water-12/Mango Habañero

EXHIBIT 16–30

Bumble Bee Seafoods uses a promotional allowance to encourage retailers to use in-store displays of its Wild Sardines products

Source: Bumble Bee Foods, LLC

can also take the form of *free goods;* the reseller gets extra cases with the purchase of specific amounts (for example, 1 free case with every 10 cases purchased).

Buying allowances are used for several reasons. They are easy to implement and are well accepted, and sometimes expected, by the trade. They are also an effective way to encourage resellers to buy the manufacturer's product, since they will want to take advantage of the discounts being offered during the allowance period. Manufacturers offer trade discounts expecting wholesalers and retailers to pass the price reduction through to consumers, resulting in greater sales. However, as discussed shortly, this is often not the case.

Promotional Allowances Manufacturers often give retailers allowances or discounts for performing certain promotional or merchandising activities in support of their brands. These merchandising allowances can be given for providing special displays away from the product's regular shelf position, running in-store promotional programs, or including the product in an ad. The manufacturer generally has guidelines or a contract specifying the activity to be performed to qualify for the promotional allowance. The allowance is usually a fixed amount per case or a percentage deduction from the list price for merchandise ordered during the promotional period.

Exhibit 16–30 shows a trade promotional piece used by Bumble Bee Seafoods to inform retailers of the merchandising opportunities available for its new Wild Sardines product and to encourage them to use in-store displays. An important goal of the company's trade marketing efforts is to get retailers to set up more displays of its products in various areas of their stores where related products are sold.

Slotting Allowances Some retailers demand a special allowance for agreeing to handle a new product. **Slotting allowances**, also called *stocking allowances, introductory allowances,* or *street money,* are fees retailers charge for providing a slot or position to accommodate the new product. Retailers justify these fees by pointing out the costs associated with taking on so many new products each year, such as redesigning store shelves, entering the product into their computers, finding warehouse space, and briefing store employees on the new product.[52] They also note they are assuming some risk, since so many new product introductions fail. Proponents of slotting fees argue argue that marketers often introduce new products with little consumer research and marketing support and do not consider the costs incurred by retailers when these products fail.[53]

Slotting fees can range from a few hundred dollars per store to $50,000 or more for an entire retail chain. Manufacturers that want to get their products on the shelves nationally can face several million dollars in slotting fees. Many marketers believe slotting allowances are a form of blackmail or bribery and say some 70 percent of these fees go directly to retailers' bottom lines.

Retailers can continue charging slotting fees because of their power and the limited availability of shelf space in supermarkets relative to the large numbers of products introduced each year. Some retailers have even been demanding **failure fees** if a new product does not hit a minimum sales level within a certain time. The fee is charged to cover the costs associated with stocking, maintaining inventories, and then pulling the product.[54] Large manufacturers with popular brands are less likely to pay slotting fees than smaller companies that lack leverage in negotiating with retailers.

In 1999, the Senate Committee on Small Business began taking action against the practice of using slotting fees in the grocery, drugstore, and computer software industries because of the fees' negative impact on small business.[55] The committee recommended that the Federal Trade Commission and Small Business Administration take steps to limit the use of slotting fees because they are anticompetitive. A study by Paul Bloom, Gregory Gundlach, and Joseph Cannon examined the views of manufacturers, wholesalers, and grocery retailers regarding the use of slotting fees. Their findings suggest that slotting fees shift the risk of new product introductions from retailers to manufacturers and help apportion the supply and demand of new products. They also found that slotting fees lead to higher retail prices, are applied in a discriminatory fashion, and place small marketers at a disadvantage.[56]

Despite the concerns over their use, many national and regional grocery store chains continue to charge slotting fees, arguing that there is a limit to the number of products they can carry on their shelves and these fees are warranted. However, some stores such as Costco, Whole Foods, and Walmart do not charge slotting fees. Walmart can us its size and buying power to negotiate low prices that it can pass on to its customers, while Costco and Whole Foods focus on selecting products that best fit their customers' needs.[57]

Displays and Point-of-Purchase Materials The next time you are in a store, take a moment to examine the various promotional materials used to display and sell products. Point-of-purchase (POP) displays are an important promotional tool because they can help a manufacturer obtain more effective in-store merchandising of products. Companies in the United States spend more than $20 billion a year on POP materials, including end-of-aisle displays, banners, posters, shelf cards, motion pieces, and stand-up racks, among others. Point-of-purchase displays are very important to marketers since many consumers make their purchase decisions in the store. In fact, some studies estimate that nearly two-thirds of a consumer's buying decisions are made in a retail store. Thus, it is very important for marketers to get the attention of consumers, as well as to communicate a sales or promotional message, through POP displays.

A measurement study from Point-of-Purchase Advertising International (an industry trade association) and the Advertising Research Foundation estimates that the cost-per-thousand-impressions figure for POPs is $6 to $8 for supermarket displays.[58] The CPM figure is based on findings that a grocery store display makes an average of 2,300 to 8,000 impressions per week, depending on store size and volume. Although this study has shown that POP displays are very effective at reaching consumers, difficulties in getting retail stores to comply with requests for displays often make it difficult for marketers to use them.[59] Moreover, many retailers are decreasing the amount of signage and displays they will accept as well as the messages they can communicate. Also, as account-specific promotions become more popular, some retailers are requiring customized POP materials. For example, 7-Eleven has taken over the responsibility for the production of all POP materials from vendors—who must still pay for them. The goal is to give 7-Eleven complete control over its in-store environment.

Despite these challenges, marketers recognize that point-of-purchase displays are an important part of their promotional programs. Many continue to develop innovative methods to display their products efficiently, make them stand out in the retail environment, and communicate a sales message to consumers. It should be noted that the importance of creative POP displays is not limited to grocery or convenience stores. Point-of-purchase displays are also important to companies that distribute their products through other types of retail outlets, such as home improvement, consumer electronic, and specialty retail stores. For example, Exhibit 16–31 shows an award-winning POP display created by E-B Display Co. to promote the SeaKlear family of pool and spa treatments. The display holds 16 different pool and spa products, and the unique octagonal shape allows for a 360-degree shoppable display in a relatively small footprint. The display also has large graphic areas to educate consumers regarding specific uses and applications and help them make their purchase decisions.

EXHIBIT 16–31

This award-winning point-of-purchase display plays an important role in the merchandising of SeaKlear pool and spa products

Source: SeaKlear

Many manufacturers help retailers use shelf space more efficiently through **plano-grams**, which are configurations of products that occupy a shelf section in a store. Some manufacturers are developing computer-based programs that allow retailers to input information from their scanner data and determine the best shelf layouts by experimenting with product movement, space utilization, profit yields, and other factors.[60]

Sales Training Programs   Another form of manufacturer-sponsored promotional assistance is sales training programs for reseller personnel. Many products sold at the retail level require knowledgeable salespeople who can provide consumers with information about the features, benefits, and advantages of various brands and models. Cosmetics, appliances, computers, consumer electronics, and sporting equipment are examples of products for which consumers often rely on well-informed retail sales personnel for assistance.

Manufacturers provide sales training assistance to retail salespeople in a number of ways. They may conduct classes or training sessions that retail personnel can attend to increase their knowledge of a product or a product line. These training sessions present information and ideas on how to sell the manufacturer's product and may also include motivational components. Sales training classes for retail personnel are often sponsored by companies selling high-ticket items or complex products such as smartphones, cars, or ski equipment.

Another way manufacturers provide sales training assistance to retail employees is through their own sales force. Sales reps educate retail personnel about their product line and provide selling tips and other relevant information. The reps can provide ongoing sales training as they come into contact with retail sales staff members on a regular basis and can update them on changes in the product line, market developments, competitive information, and the like.

Manufacturers also give resellers detailed sales manuals, product brochures, reference manuals, and other material. Many companies provide DVDs or digital files for retail sales personnel that include product information, product-use demonstrations, and ideas on how to sell their product. These selling aids can often be used to provide information to customers as well.

Trade Shows   Another important promotional activity targeted to resellers is the **trade show**, a forum where manufacturers can display their products to current as well as prospective buyers. According to the Center for Exhibition Industry Research, more than 100 million people attend the nearly 15,000 trade shows each year in the United States and Canada, and the number of exhibiting companies exceeds 1.3 million. In many industries, trade shows are a major opportunity to display one's product lines and interact with customers. They are often attended by important management personnel from large retail chains as well as by distributors and other reseller representatives.

A number of promotional functions can be performed at trade shows, including demonstrating products, identifying new prospects, gathering customer and competitive information, and even writing orders for a product. Trade shows are particularly valuable for introducing new products because resellers are often looking for new merchandise to stock. Shows can also be a source of valuable leads to follow up on through sales calls or direct marketing. The social aspect of trade shows is also important. Many companies use them to entertain key customers and to develop and maintain relationships with the trade. An academic study demonstrated that trade shows generate product awareness and interest and can have a measurable economic return.[61] An example of a very high-profile trade show is the International Consumer Electronics Show (CES) that is held in Las Vegas each January. The show is owned and produced by the Consumer Electronics Association (CEA) and is often used as a platform for the announcement and release of new products such as computers, smartphones, HDTVs, and various other types of consumer electronic items. CES also receives extensive coverage from the media, which makes it a valuable promotional opportunity for markets launching new products. Exhibit 16–32 shows a picture from a recent CES.

Cooperative Advertising The final form of trade-oriented promotion we examine is **cooperative advertising**, where the cost of advertising is shared by more than one party. There are three types of cooperative advertising. Although the first two are not trade-oriented promotion, we should recognize their objectives and purpose.

Horizontal cooperative advertising is advertising sponsored in common by a group of retailers or other organizations providing products or services to the market. For example, automobile dealers who are located near one another in an auto park or along the same street often allocate some of their ad budgets to a cooperative advertising fund. Ads are run promoting the location of the dealerships and encouraging car buyers to take advantage of their close proximity when shopping for a new automobile. Many cities and resort areas use horizontal cooperative advertising by having hotels, theme parks, tourist attractions and other businesses that benefit from tourism contribute monies to a fund to advertise and promote the area as a tourist destination and/or a place to hold meetings and conventions.

Ingredient-sponsored cooperative advertising is supported by raw materials manufacturers; its objective is to help establish end products that include the company's materials and/or ingredients. Companies that often use this type of advertising include DuPont, which promotes the use of its materials such as Teflon and Kevlar; 3M, which promotes Thinsulate; and NutraSweet, whose artificial sweetener is an ingredient in many food products and beverages.

Perhaps the best-known, and most successful, example of this type of cooperative advertising is the "Intel Inside" program, sponsored by Intel Corporation, which the company has been using since 1991.[62] Under this program, personal computer manufacturers get back 5 percent of what they pay Intel for microprocessors in return for showing the "Intel Inside" logo in their advertising as well as on their PCs. The monies received from Intel must be applied to ads paid for jointly by the PC maker and Intel. Many of the print and online ads for PCs run in the United States and other countries carry the "Intel Inside" logo, and the program has helped Intel grow its share of the microprocessor market from 56 percent in 1990 to nearly 80 percent.[63]

Another technology company that uses ingredient-sponsored advertising is Qualcomm, which has been running a brand-building campaign for its Snapdragon processor that powers many smartphones and other mobile devices. The company runs ads in the United States and several other countries to promote the features

EXHIBIT 16–33

Qualcomm uses ingredient-sponsored advertising for its Snapdragon processor

Source: Qualcomm

and benefits of the Snapdragon processor and how it contributes to the performance of mobile devices. Exhibit 16–33 shows an ad for the Snapdragon processor.

The most common form of cooperative advertising is the trade-oriented form, **vertical cooperative advertising**, in which a manufacturer pays for a portion of the advertising a retailer runs to promote the manufacturer's product and its availability in the retailer's place of business. Manufacturers generally share the cost of advertising run by the retailer on a percentage basis (usually 50–50) up to a certain limit.

The amount of cooperative advertising the manufacturer pays for is usually based on a percentage of dollar purchases. If a retailer purchases $100,000 of product from a manufacturer, it may receive 3 percent, or $3,000, in cooperative advertising money. Large retail chains often combine their co-op budgets across all of their stores, which gives them a larger sum to work with and more media options.

Cooperative advertising can take several forms. Retailers may advertise a manufacturer's product in, say, a newspaper ad featuring a number of different products, and the individual manufacturers reimburse the retailer for their portion of the ad. Or the ad may be prepared by the manufacturer and placed in the local media by the retailer. Exhibit 16–34 shows a cooperative ad format for Bumble Bee Seafoods that retailers in various market areas can use by simply inserting into a newspaper circular or use as a display ad by adding their store name and location.

Once a cooperative ad is run, the retailer requests reimbursement from the manufacturer for its percentage of the media costs. Manufacturers usually have specific requirements the ad must meet to qualify for co-op reimbursement, such as size, use of trademarks, content, and format. Verification that the ad was run is also required, in the form of a digital copy of the ad and an invoice.

EXHIBIT 16–34

This Bumble Bee Seafoods ad is provided to retailers for use as part of its vertical cooperative advertising program

Source: Bumble Bee Foods, LLC

As with other types of trade promotions, manufacturers have been increasing their cooperative advertising expenditures. Some companies have been moving money out of national advertising into cooperative advertising because they believe they can have greater impact with ad campaigns in local markets. Historically, retailers have spent most cooperative advertising monies in traditional media such as newspaper, direct mail and radio and until recently many marketers discouraged or did not allow the use of co-op funds in online channels. However, as audiences for newspapers and broadcast media decline, many companies have changed their policies and are allowing co-op funds to be spent in digital media.[64] Some retail chains now offer digital media buying platforms that are designed to help vendors better reach the retailers customers, not just through the retailer website but through other online channels. Mass merchants such as Walmart and Target as well as supermarket chains such as Safeway/Albertsons, Food Lion, and ShopRite have set up digital media exchanges and are encouraging vendors to allocate some of their trade promotion dollars to them.[65]

COORDINATING SALES PROMOTION WITH ADVERTISING AND OTHER IMC TOOLS

Those involved in the promotional process must recognize that sales promotion techniques usually work best in conjunction with advertising and other integrated marketing tools and that the effectiveness of an IMC campaign can be enhanced by

consumer-oriented sales promotion efforts. Rather than separate activities competing for a firm's promotional budget, advertising and sales promotion should be viewed as complementary tools. When properly planned and executed to work together, advertising and sales promotion can have a *synergistic effect* much greater than that of either promotional mix element alone.

Proper coordination of sales promotion with other IMC tools is essential for the firm to take advantage of the opportunities offered by each and get the most out of its promotional budget. Successful integration of advertising and sales promotion requires decisions concerning not only the allocation of the budget to each area but also the coordination of the ad and sales promotion themes, proper media support for, and timing of, the various promotional activities, and the target audience reached.

Budget Allocation

While many companies are spending more money on sales promotion than on media advertising, it is difficult to say just what percentage of a firm's overall promotional budget should be allocated to advertising versus consumer- and trade-oriented promotions. This allocation depends on a number of factors, including the specific promotional objectives of the campaign, the market and competitive situation, and the brand's stage in its life cycle.

Consider, for example, how allocation of the promotional budget may vary according to a brand's stage in the product life cycle. In the introductory stage, a large amount of the budget may be allocated to sales promotion techniques such as sampling and couponing to induce trial. In the growth stage, however, promotional dollars may be used primarily for advertising to stress brand differences and keep the brand name in consumers' minds.

When a brand moves to the maturity stage, advertising is primarily a reminder to keep consumers aware of the brand. Consumer-oriented sales promotions such as coupons, price-offs, premiums, and bonus packs may be needed periodically to maintain consumer loyalty, attract new users, and protect against competition. Trade-oriented promotions are needed to maintain shelf space and accommodate retailers' demands for better margins as well as encourage them to promote the brand. A study on the synergistic effects of advertising and promotion examined a brand in the mature phase of its life cycle and found that 80 percent of its sales at this stage were due to sales promotions. When a brand enters the decline stage of the product life cycle, most of the promotional support will probably be removed and expenditures on sales promotion are unlikely.

Coordination of Ad and Promotion Themes

To integrate the advertising and sales promotion programs successfully, the theme of consumer promotions should be tied in with the positioning platform for the company and/or their brand wherever possible. Sales promotion tools should attempt to communicate a brand's unique attributes or benefits and to reinforce the sales message or advertising campaign theme. In this way, the sales promotion effort contributes to the consumer franchise-building effort for the brand.

At the same time, media advertising and other IMC tools should be used to draw attention to a sales promotion program such as a contest, sweepstakes, or event or to a special promotion offer such as a price reduction or rebate program. An excellent example of this is the award-winning "Win 500 Flights" sweepstakes that was developed by MasterCard and its promotional agency, Armstrong Partnership. The sweepstakes was developed under the umbrella of MasterCard's "Priceless" campaign theme and thus was designed to deliver on the brand promise that MasterCard understands what matters most to consumers—in this case traveling for any reason at all. The primary objective of the integrated marketing campaign

flights to Ireland to find a four-leaf clover: $0

flights to Vegas to try it out: $0

flights to Ireland to return defective four-leaf clover: $0

(traveling for any reason at all: priceless)

EXHIBIT 16–35

MasterCard used media advertising to promote the "Win 500 Flights" sweepstakes

Source: MasterCard

EXHIBIT 16–36

Unilever coordinates the advertising and sales promotion for the Dove Men + Care line

Source: Dove by Unilever

was to drive MasterCard use during the key summer travel season. Consumers using their MasterCard from July 1 to August 31 were automatically entered in the sweepstakes for a chance to win 500 airline tickets to anywhere that could be shared with family and friends. Media advertising including television, print, out-of-home, and online banner ads were used to promote the sweepstakes, along with an extensive public relations campaign. Exhibit 16–35 shows one of the print ads used to promote the "Win 500 Flights" sweepstakes.

Media Support and Timing

Media support for a sales promotion program is critical and should be coordinated with the media program for the ad campaign. Media advertising is often needed to deliver such sales promotion materials as coupons, sweepstakes, contest entry forms, premium offers, and even samples. It is also needed to inform consumers of a promotional offer as well as to create awareness, interest, and favorable attitudes toward the brand.

By using advertising in conjunction with a sales promotion program, marketers can make consumers aware of the brand and its benefits and increase their responsiveness to the promotion. Consumers are more likely to redeem a coupon or respond to a price-off deal for a brand they are familiar with than one they know nothing about. Moreover, product trial created through sales promotion techniques such as sampling or high-value couponing is more likely to result in long-term use of the brand when accompanied by advertising.[66]

Using a promotion without prior or concurrent advertising can limit its effectiveness and risk damaging the brand's image. If consumers perceive the brand as being promotion dependent or of lesser quality, they are not likely to develop favorable attitudes and long-term loyalty. Conversely, the effectiveness of an ad can be enhanced by a coupon, a premium offer, or an opportunity to enter a sweepstakes or contest.

An example of the effective coordination of advertising and sales promotion is the introductory campaign Unilever developed for its Dove Men + Care line. Unilever sent samples of the body and face wash product to more than half the households in the United States along with high-value coupons and also used trade promotions targeted to retailers as part of its introductory marketing blitz. The sales promotion efforts were accompanied by heavy advertising in print and on television, including a commercial in the Super Bowl, and follow-up spots featuring New Orleans Saints quarterback Drew Brees. The launch campaign included the use of additional IMC tools, including public relations, mobile marketing, and digital and social media. Unilever continues to coordinate advertising and sales promotion for the Dove Men + Care line with ads such as the one shown in Exhibit 16–36.

To coordinate their advertising and sales promotion programs more effectively, many companies are getting their sales promotion agencies more involved in the advertising and promotional planning process. Rather than hiring agencies to develop individual, nonfranchise-building types of promotions with short-term goals and tactics, many firms are having their sales promotion and advertising agencies work together to develop integrated promotional strategies and programs. Figure 16–7 shows how the role of promotional agencies is changing.

FIGURE 16–7

The Shifting Role of the
Promotion Agency

Traditional	New and Improved
1. Primarily used to develop short-term tactics or concepts.	1. Used to develop long- and short-term promotional strategies as well as tactics.
2. Hired/compensated on a project-by-project basis.	2. Contracted on annual retainer, following formal agency reviews.
3. Many promotion agencies used a mix—each one hired for best task and/or specialty.	3. One or two exclusive promotion agencies for each division or brand group.
4. One or two contact people from agency.	4. Full team or core group on the account.
5. Promotion agency never equal to ad agency—doesn't work up front in annual planning process.	5. Promotion agency works on equal basis with ad agency—sits at planning table up front.
6. Not directly accountable for results.	6. Very much accountable—goes through a rigorous evaluation process.

SALES PROMOTION ABUSE

The increasing use of sales promotion in marketing programs is more than a passing fad. It is a fundamental change in strategic decisions about how companies market their products and services. The value of this increased emphasis on sales promotion has been questioned by several writers, particularly with regard to the lack of adequate planning and management of sales promotion programs.[67]

Are marketers becoming too dependent on this element of the marketing program? As was discussed earlier, consumer and trade promotions can be a very effective tool for generating short-term increases in sales, and many brand managers would rather use a promotion to produce immediate sales than invest in advertising and build the brand's image over an extended time. As the director of sales promotion services at one large ad agency noted: "There's a great temptation for quick sales fixes through promotions. It's a lot easier to offer the consumer an immediate price savings than to differentiate your product from a competitor's."[68]

Overuse of sales promotion can be detrimental to a brand in several ways. A brand that is constantly promoted may lose perceived value. Consumers often end up purchasing a brand because it is on sale, they get a premium, or they have a coupon, rather than basing their decision on a favorable attitude they have developed. When the extra promotional incentive is not available, they switch to another brand. A study by Priya Raghubir and Kim Corfman examined whether price promotions affect pretrial evaluations of a brand.[69] They found that offering a price promotion is more likely to lower a brand's evaluation when the brand has not been promoted previously compared to when it has been frequently promoted; that price promotions are used as a source of information about a brand to a greater extent when the evaluator is not an expert but does have some product or industry knowledge; and that promotions are more likely to result in negative evaluations when they are uncommon in the industry. The findings from this study suggest that marketers must be careful in the use of price promotions as they may inhibit trial of a brand in certain situations.

Alan Sawyer and Peter Dickson have used the concept of *attribution theory* to examine how sales promotion may affect consumer attitude formation.[70] According to this theory, people acquire attitudes by observing their own behavior and considering why they acted in a certain manner. Consumers who consistently purchase a brand because of a coupon or price-off deal may attribute their behavior to the

FIGURE 16–8

The Sales Promotion Trap

All Other Firms	Our Firm	
	Cut back promotions	Maintain promotions
Cut back promotions	Higher profits for all	Market share goes to our firm
Maintain promotions	Market share goes to all other firms	Market share stays constant; profits stay low

external promotional incentive rather than to a favorable attitude toward the brand. By contrast, when no external incentive is available, consumers are more likely to attribute their purchase behavior to favorable underlying feelings about the brand.

Another potential problem with consumer-oriented promotions is that a **sales promotion trap** or spiral can result when several competitors use promotions extensively.[71] Often a firm begins using sales promotions to differentiate its product or service from the competition. If the promotion is successful and leads to a differential advantage (or even appears to do so), competitors may quickly copy it. When all the competitors are using sales promotions, this not only lowers profit margins for each firm but also makes it difficult for any one firm to hop off the promotional bandwagon.[72] This dilemma is shown in Figure 16–8.

A number of industries have fallen into this promotional trap. In the cosmetics industry, gift-with-purchase and purchase-with-purchase promotional offers were developed as a tactic for getting buyers to sample new products. But they have become a common, and costly, way of doing business.[73] In many areas of the country, supermarkets fell into the trap of doubling coupons, which cut into their already small profit margins. Fast food chains have also fallen into the trap with promotions featuring popular menu items for 99 cents or one dollar. Fast food companies use their dollar menus to offer options to budget-conscious consumers and provide them with consistent everyday values. McDonald's introduced its value menu in 2003 and for many years it included popular items such as its double cheeseburger. However, competitors such as Burger King and Wendy's responded by putting popular items on their value meal menus in an effort to keep pace with the industry leader.[74] Other competitors also introduced dollar menu items such as Taco Bell, which introduced a "Cravings" value menu in 2013 (Exhibit 16–37).[75] That same year McDonald's revamped its Dollar Menu and renamed it Dollar Menu & More and added pricier items to its value offering. However, in 2016 McDonald's replaced this with the "McPick 2" menu, which allows customers to pay $2 for two items, including the McDouble, McChicken sandwiches, small fries, or mozzarella sticks.[76]

Marketers must consider both the short-term impact of a promotion and its long-term effect on the brand. The ease with which competitors can develop a retaliatory promotion and the likelihood of their doing so should also be considered. Marketers must be careful not to damage the brand franchise with sales promotions or to get the firm involved in a promotional war that erodes the brand's profit margins and threatens its long-term existence. Marketers are often tempted to resort to sales promotions to deal with declining sales and other problems when they should examine such other aspects of the marketing program as channel relations, price, packaging, product quality, or advertising.

EXHIBIT 16–37

In this ad, Taco Bell promotes its cravings menu and joins its fast food competitors in the sales promotion spiral of the value menu

Source: Taco Bell Corp.

CHAPTER 16

After reading this chapter you can see that there are a number of factors that marketers must consider in developing and implementing effective sales promotion programs as they involve much more than just offering consumers an extra economic incentive to purchase a product. Priya Raghubir, Jeffrey Inman, and Hans Grande suggest that there are three aspects to consumer promotions, including economic, informative, and affective effects.[77] They note that in addition to economic effects, marketers must consider the information and signals a promotional offer conveys to the consumer as well as the affective influences. These include the consumer feelings and emotions aroused by exposure to a promotion or associated with purchasing the brand or company that is offering a deal. By considering all of these effects, managers can design and communicate consumer promotions more efficiently as well as more effectively.

Summary

For many years, advertising was the major promotional-mix element for most consumer-product companies. Over the past two decades, however, marketers have been allocating more of their promotional dollars to sales promotion. There has been a steady increase in the use of sales promotion techniques to influence consumers' purchase behavior. The growing power of retailers, erosion of brand loyalty, increase in consumers' sensitivity to promotions, increase in new product introductions, fragmentation of the consumer market, short-term focus of marketing and brand managers, increase in advertising, and competition are some of the reasons for this increase.

Sales promotions can be characterized as either franchise building or nonfranchise building. The former contribute to the long-term development and reinforcement of brand identity and image; the latter are designed to accelerate the purchase process and generate immediate increases in sales.

Sales promotion techniques can be classified as either trade- or consumer-oriented. A number of consumer-oriented sales promotion techniques were examined in this chapter, including sampling, couponing, premiums, contests and sweepstakes, rebates and refunds, bonus packs, price-off deals, loyalty programs, and event marketing. The characteristics of these promotional tools were examined, along with their advantages and limitations. Various trade-oriented promotions were also examined, including trade contests and incentives, trade allowances, displays and point-of-purchase materials, sales training programs, trade shows, and cooperative advertising.

Advertising and sales promotion should be viewed not as separate activities but rather as complementary tools. When planned and executed properly, advertising and sales promotion can produce a synergistic effect that is greater than the response generated from either promotional-mix element alone. To accomplish this, marketers must coordinate budgets, advertising and promotional themes, media scheduling and timing, and target audiences.

Sales promotion abuse can result when marketers become too dependent on the use of sales promotion techniques and sacrifice long-term brand position and image for short-term sales increases. Many industries experience sales promotion traps when a number of competitors use promotions extensively and it becomes difficult for any single firm to cut back on promotion without risking a loss in sales. Overuse of sales promotion tools can lower profit margins and threaten the image and even the viability of a brand.

Key Terms

1. The chapter opener discusses how many retailers have become overly dependent on discounts and promotions and the problems this has created for them. Discuss some of the reasons retailers have increased their use of discounts and promotions. How might they reduce their dependency on them to drive store traffic and sales? (LO 16-1, 16-5)

2. Discuss the difference between consumer-oriented promotions and trade-oriented promotions and the role each plays in a marketer's IMC program. What are the various objectives for each category of sales promotion? (LO 16-1, 16-2, 16-3)

3. What are some of the reasons marketers are allocating more of their promotional budget to sales promotion rather than media advertising? Do you agree with critics who argue that the increased use of sales promotion is undermining brand equity for many once-powerful brands? (LO 16-1)

4. IMC Perspective 16–1 discusses the problems JCPenney encountered when it tried to cut back on the use of promotions and move to a "fair and square" pricing and promotion model. Why do you think JCP customers reacted so negatively to the retailer's reduction in promotional offers? Do you think JCP should have given the new strategy more time to take effect before abandoning it?

5. Discuss how mobile marketing is impacting marketers' use of sales promotion. (LO 16-1, 16-2)

6. What is the difference between a consumer franchise-building promotion and a nonfranchise-building promotion? Find an example of a promotion being used by a company that contributes to the equity of the brand and explain how it does so. (LO 16-2)

7. The chapter discusses the contest Unilever and its ad agency developed to launch the new Axe Apollo men's personal care product line. Evaluate this contest as a consumer franchise-building promotion for the Axe Apollo brand. (LO 16-2)

8. Evaluate the effectiveness of coupons as a sales promotion tool. How would you respond to critics who argue that they are inefficient since less than 2 percent of coupons are redeemed? (LO 16-3)

9. Discuss the type of company that would be likely to offer discounts to consumers using Groupon. What are the pros and cons of a company using Groupon to make promotional offers to consumers? (LO 16-3)

10. What are some of the problems marketers face in using contests and sweepstakes? Discuss steps they can take to avoid these problems. (LO 16-3)

11. A report by a rebate fulfillment service showed that the average redemption rate for a $50 rebate on a product that costs $200 is only 35 percent. Why do you think redemption rates for rebates are so low? How might these low redemption rates affect a marketer's decision regarding the use of rebates as a promotional tool? (LO 16-3)

12. Discuss the various type of trade promotions used by marketers, giving attention to the objectives as well as the pros and cons of each. (LO 16-3)

13. What is meant by a sales promotion trap or spiral? Find an example of an industry or market where a promotional battle is taking place. What are the options for companies in deciding whether to participate in the promotional war? (LO 16-5)

connect

Digital users can access their personalized and adaptive SmartBook, Ad Forum Video Cases, and interactive exercises to review chapter concepts.

17

Public Relations, Publicity, and Corporate Advertising

1.5 billion people

work in water-related sectors and nearly all jobs depend on water and those that ensure its safe delivery.

Better water, better jobs

www.worldwaterday.org

UN WATER
WORLD WATER DAY
22 MARCH 2016 - WATER AND JOBS

Source: UN-Water-World Water Day

LEARNING OBJECTIVES

LO1 Describe the roles of public relations, publicity, and corporate advertising in the promotional mix.

LO2 Compare the advantages, disadvantages, and effectiveness of public relations and publicity.

LO3 Discuss the advantages, disadvantages, and effectiveness of corporate advertising.

LO4 Compare the different forms of corporate advertising.

MARKETERS FIND THAT DOING GOOD HAS ITS REWARDS

Many small companies and corporations have been good citizens for years, but a lot of people didn't know it. In the past, advertising and promotion and public relations for the good of the corporation operated as separate managerial silos. While these companies and corporations often did many things that directly benefited the community—whether it be local or global—they usually did so without a lot of fanfare or "patting themselves on the back." Then someone must have turned on a light that said, "if you are doing these good things, why aren't you letting people know it?" Reluctantly, at first, the firms slowly started to let others know about their benevolence through corporate reports and maybe even a press release here and there. The first cracks started to appear in the silos. Then things started to change. Companies started to be less hesitant to let people know the good things they were doing—after all, the public always knew if they did something bad! Since there was no noticeable negative feedback, they expanded their PR efforts to be sure that people *did* know, and not long thereafter started to use PR more like a marketing tool. And why not? Many companies are doing very good things out there without recognition, and the positive publicity wouldn't hurt!

In 1992, the UN Conference on Environment and Development organized the first World Water Day. Based on the dire water conditions in many parts of the world today—663 million people, or 1 in 10, live without clean water; diseases from dirty water kill more people every year than all forms of violence, including war; access to clean water can save around 16,000 lives a week, and more—CleanWater.org called on brands and media support to bring attention to the problem. And respond they did! CNBC International broadcast some of the lesser known facts about water. The beer brand Stella Artois, through Twitter, asked consumers to purchase a limited-edition Chalice; the profits would help provide five years of clean water to a person in need. The children's TV show *Sesame Street* introduced Raya—a health superstar, whose birthday just happened to be on World Water Day. DAVIDsTEA created a whole new variety of tea, with each 50-gram purchase leading to a contribution of one month of clean water to a Kenyan child in need. Just a few of the other participants included Unilever,

Georgio Armani Fragrances, Arrowhead Brand Mountain Spring Water, and the Surfrider Foundation who asked people to pledge to skip a shower for one day, which would save one million gallons of water that day. Numerous companies directly or indirectly involved with the use of water including Speakman (maker of high-end shower heads and plumbing products), water resource management company WaterStart, and Delta Faucets, among many more have joined in the cause. All of the participants put their own unique twist on their contribution to the effort (including World of Warcraft!).

World Water Day is just one of thousands of causes being supported by numerous companies. Another is Earth Day. And just like World Water Day, companies have approached the cause in their own creative fashion. Earth Day—which is celebrated worldwide every April 22 since 1970—has now mobilized over 200 million people in 141 countries and over 20,000 companies, along with a billion people who participated in the event in 2016. Earth Day offers a variety of causes to engage in—all designed to protect the earth. For example, Hershey has focused on sustainability challenges, tracing back through its supply chain that covers 94 percent of the mills that supply its palm and palm kernel oil globally to be sure they are compliant with environmentally friendly procedures. Hershey announced major progress in its push for 100 percent certified and sustainable cocoa worldwide by 2020. McDonald's has earned high praise for its deforestation plan, and Chipotle received kudos for its stance in dropping a major supplier that didn't meet the company's strict standards set as part of its sustainability commitment despite the fact that the move cost it a 5 percent drop in stock value. Of course, there are thousands more companies also supporting the cause in various ways—and more than 1.5 million other causes. Americans themselves donate over $358 billion to various charities and causes alone.

You have probably never heard of any of these companies' endeavors. So why are they doing it?

Well, clearly, a staggering number of people become exposed to their positive actions, creating a lot of goodwill, while portraying the companies in a favorable light. Maybe some of that goodwill will directly benefit them through sales, financial investments, and so on. Being a good corporate brand certainly enhances their image as well—there are studies showing that many consumers prefer to purchase from "green" companies, all things being equal. Or, maybe they are just what they portend to be—good citizens that care about others!

As noted earlier, companies have only recently begun to recognize the power of public relations. In the past most PR activities were devoted to local activities, crisis management, or dealing with negative publicity. Once marketers realized the power and potential for integrating PR into the IMC mix, the nature and importance of this medium changed dramatically—not only for communicating positive information about the company's goodwill endeavors, but also for supporting their brands.

It is this last statement that has some PR people, and the general public as well, concerned that these small companies and large corporations are supporting causes in their own best interests. Or, maybe they just are altruistic and want to help others. If the world finds out about that, is that so bad?

Sources: Sheila Shayon, "World Water Day: Brands, Media Support Clean, Safe Water Efforts," March 22, 2016, www.brandchannel.com; Dale Buss, "Earth Day 2015: Hershey Puts Sustainability Where Its Mouth Is," April 22, 2015, www.brandchannel.com; Dale Buss, "Earth Day 2015: Chipotle Maintains Brand Integrity as Momentum Slows," April 22, 2015, www.brandchannel.com; "Giving USA: Americans Donated an Estimated $358.38 Billion to Charity in 2014: Highest Total in Report's 60-Year History," June 29, 2015, www.givingusa.org.

The lead-in to this chapter demonstrates the changing role that public relations now plays in the IMC programs of small companies to major corporations. In the examples provided you can see that from a more traditional and philanthropic perspective, marketers stand to gain through the use of this medium. At the same time, public relations has now assumed a much more important role in IMC programs. This role is less philanthropic and much more marketing-oriented. In this chapter we will examine the role of public relations in the IMC program and how this role has changed over recent years. Like every other aspect of IMC, the public relations function has been changed significantly by digital and social media. Simply put, news travels faster and wider now for most companies and organizations. As a result, the role of public relations and the importance of managing publicity has taken an increased importance.

The power of publicity can be positive or negative. The results often directly impact the companies involved financially as well as in respect to trust, image, and other nonfinancial aspects. Brands and/or companies have ceased to exist as a result of negative publicity, and others can attribute their success to positive messages. As you will see in this chapter, publicity is often out of the control of the marketer, but increasingly the management of publicity is being adopted as a marketing strategy. While attempts to generate positive publicity are nothing new, as these efforts increase, they signify changes in the public relations functions of companies and organizations. Although the importance and role of public relations in the IMC program may be argued, one thing is clear: The role of public relations in the communications program has changed.

Publicity, public relations, and corporate advertising all have promotional program elements that may be of great benefit to marketers. They are integral parts of the overall promotional effort that must be managed and coordinated with the other elements of the promotional mix. However, these three tools do not always have the specific objectives of product and service promotion, nor do they always involve the same methods you have become accustomed to as you have read this text. Typically, these activities are designed more to change attitudes toward an organization or issue than to promote specific products or affect behaviors directly (though you will see that this role is changing in some organizations). This chapter explores the roles of public relations, publicity, and corporate advertising; the advantages and disadvantages of each; and the processes by which they are employed.

What is public relations? How does it differ from other elements of marketing discussed thus far? Perhaps a good starting point is to define what the term *public relations* has traditionally meant and then to introduce its new role.

The Traditional Definition of PR

A variety of books define **public relations (PR)**, but perhaps the most comprehensive definition is that offered by *Public Relations News* (the weekly newsletter of the industry):

> The management function which evaluates public attitudes, identifies the policies and procedures of an organization with the public interest, and executes a program of action (and communication) to earn public understanding and acceptance.[1]

Public relations is indeed a management function. The term *management* should be used in its broadest sense; it is not limited to business management but extends to other types of organizations, including nonprofit institutions.

In this definition, public relations requires a series of stages, including:

1. The determination and evaluation of public attitudes.
2. The identification of policies and procedures of an organization with a public interest.
3. The development and execution of a communications program designed to bring about public understanding and acceptance.

This process does not occur all at once. An effective public relations program continues over months or even years.

Finally, this definition reveals that public relations involves much more than activities designed to sell a product or service. The PR program may involve some of the promotional program elements previously discussed but use them in a different way. For example, companies may send press releases to announce new products or changes in the organization, companies may organize special events to create goodwill in the community, and companies may use advertising to state the firm's position on a controversial issue.

The New Role of PR

An increasing number of marketing-oriented companies have established new responsibilities for public relations. In this new role PR takes on a much broader (and more marketing-oriented) perspective, designed to promote the organization as well as its products and/or services.

The way that companies and organizations use public relations might best be viewed as a continuum. On one end of the continuum is the use of PR from a traditional perspective. In this perspective, public relations is viewed as a non-marketing function whose primary responsibility is to maintain mutually beneficial relationships between the organization and its publics. In this case, customers or potential customers are only part of numerous publics—employees, investors, neighbors, special-interest groups, and so on. Marketing and public relations are separate departments; if external agencies are used, they are separate agencies. At the other end of the continuum, public relations is considered primarily a marketing communications function. All noncustomer relationships are perceived as necessary only in a marketing context.[2] In these organizations, public relations reports to marketing. At the same time, for many companies the PR function is moving more and more toward a new role, which is much closer to a marketing function than a traditional one.

In the new role of public relations, managers envision both strong marketing and strong PR departments. Rather than each department operating independently,

CHAPTER 17

the two work closely together, blending their talents to provide the best overall image of the firm and its product or service offerings. As noted by Jonah Bloom, there has always been a cultural gulf separating the two departments, but today's information age demands the two camps work together. Bloom comments, "You'll struggle to peddle your eco-friendly detergent if your company is being slammed for pouring chemicals into a river."[3] In a poll conducted among members of the Public Relations Society of America (PRSA) and subscribers to *PR News*, 76 percent of respondents stated that they regularly work with the marketing department; 78 percent thought that the marketing department had a positive perception of the PR department, and an equal number indicated the same perception about marketing. While the degree of coordination differed by activity, the study clearly reflects coordination and cooperation.[4]

Writing in *Advertising Age*, William N. Curry notes that organizations must use caution in establishing this relationship because PR and marketing are not the same thing, and when one department becomes dominant, the balance required to operate at maximum efficiency is lost.[5] He says losing sight of the objectives and functions of public relations in an attempt to achieve marketing goals may be detrimental in the long run. Others take an even stronger view that if public relations and marketing distinctions continue to blur, the independence of the PR function will be lost, and it will become much less effective.[6] In fact, as noted by Cutlip, Center, and Broom, marketing and public relations are complementary functions, "with each making unique but complementary contributions to building and maintaining the many relationships essential for organizational survival and growth. To ignore one is to risk failure in the other."[7] This position is consistent with our perception that public relations is an important part of the IMC process, contributing in its own way but also in a way consistent with marketing goals.

Integrating PR into the Promotional Mix

Given the broader responsibilities of public relations, the issue is how to integrate it into the promotional mix. Companies have a number of ways in which they organize the marketing and public relations functions. Others may outsource the public relations to outside agencies. In this text we regard public relations as an IMC program element. This means that its broad role must include traditional responsibilities, as well as new ones.

Whether public relations takes on a traditional role or a more marketing-oriented one, PR activities are still tied to specific communications objectives. Assessing public attitudes and creating a favorable corporate image are no less important than promoting products or services directly.

Marketing Public Relations Functions

Thomas L. Harris has referred to public relations activities designed to support marketing objectives as **marketing public relations (MPR)** functions.[8] Marketing objectives that may be aided by public relations activities include raising awareness, informing and educating, gaining understanding, building trust, giving consumers a reason to buy, and motivating consumer acceptance. MPR adds value to the integrated marketing program in a number of ways:

- *Building marketplace excitement before media advertising breaks.* The announcement of a new product, for example, is an opportunity for the marketer to obtain publicity and to dramatize the product, thereby increasing the effectiveness of ads. When Apple introduces any new product from its iPhones to Apple watches, a great deal of anticipation is created through public relations prior to the availability of the product. (Articles about the features in the iPhone 7 were being discussed at cnet.com well before the anticipated launch!)

EXHIBIT 17–1

Tesla receives a lot of press coverage prior to releasing models

EXHIBIT 17–2

Betty Crocker's website is designed to create goodwill and build loyalty for its consumers by offering ideas, recipes, coupons, and even an "ask Betty" section where consumers can submit questions

Source: Betty Crocker by General Mills Marketing Inc. (GMMI)

The result is that Apple receives a great deal of press coverage and word of mouth. It seems that upon release of any Apple product, consumers wait in lines—sometime for hours—to be the first to own the next innovation, with little or no advertising having been implemented.

- *Improving ROI.* By reducing overall marketing costs, while at the same time delivering meaningful marketing outcomes, MPR helps improve ROI.
- *Creating advertising news where there is no product news.* Ads themselves can be the focus of publicity. There seems to be as much hype about the ads on the Super Bowl as there is for the game itself. TV commercials frequently find their ways to social sites on the Internet, where they are viewed time and time again and forwarded to others.
- *Introducing a product with little or no advertising.* This strategy has been implemented successfully by a number of companies, including Tesla, Segway, Ty, Crayola, and, of course, Apple. Among others, Gillette uses PR as the lead medium in every new product launch. More and more companies seem to be taking this approach (Exhibit 17–1).
- *Providing a value-added customer service.* Butterball established a hotline where people can call in to receive personal advice on how to prepare their turkeys. The company handled 25,000 calls during the first holiday season. Many companies provide such services on their Internet sites. Chicken of the Sea provides recipes to visitors to its site (which, of course, suggest using Chicken of the Sea tuna).
- *Building brand-to-customer bonds.* The Pillsbury Bake-Off has led to strong brand loyalty among Pillsbury customers, who compete by submitting baked goods. The contest has taken place annually since 1949, and the winner now receives a $1 million prize! The winning recipes are posted on the Pillsbury website. Competitor Betty Crocker has used branded video to reach its MPR objectives and also has a helpful website (Exhibit 17–2).

- *Influencing the influentials.* That is, providing information to opinion leaders.
- *Defending products at risk and giving consumers a reason to buy.* By taking constructive actions to defend or promote a company's products, PR can actually give consumers a reason to buy the products. Energizer's national education campaign that urged consumers to change the batteries in their fire alarms when they reset their clocks in the fall resulted in a strong corporate citizen image and increased sales of batteries. Cessna's campaign to convince executives that there are legitimate reasons to buy corporate jets (Exhibit 17–3) is an excellent example of defending a product at risk. Figure 17–1 shows a few more examples.

As shown in Figure 17–2, Harris notes that there are a number of advantages of using MPRs.[9]

One of the major threats of using an MPR structure, as expressed by Harris, is that public relations functions may become subservient to marketing efforts—a concern expressed by many opponents of MPR. However, if employed properly and used in conjunction with other traditional public relations practices as well as IMC elements, MPR can continue to be used effectively. Weiner also notes that the key to the successful use of MPRs is integration with IMC, though such a task may prove to be difficult to accomplish.

FIGURE 17–1

Companies Use MPRs

Cessna

During the last big recession and auto industry sales slump, top executives of Detroit's Big Three car companies went to the nation's capital to ask for a bailout. When the execs traveled on a $50 million private plane rather than drive, the lawmakers and press bashed them for it. Unfortunately, the backlash had a profound negative effect on jet manufacturers, as numerous orders were canceled or deferred. Production was cut by as much as 56 percent, and as much as one-third of the industry's workers were laid off. One company, Cessna, decided to fight back and give corporate America a reason to buy.

In a hard-hitting print campaign starting in *The Wall Street Journal* called "Rise," Cessna challenged business leaders to not be timid, and recognize private planes are not about ego, but about having the right tools to be productive. Cessna said it was time for the other side of the story to be told. In addition to *The Wall Street Journal*, the ads were run in national business newspapers and magazines as well as aviation trade journals, together with an extensive PR campaign. Four years later Cessna was still receiving requests for reprints of the ads, and sales were on the increase.

Betty Crocker

Faced with the objective of getting more cake bakers to visit its website, Betty Crocker worked with digital video agency Touchstorm to create a series of informational videos targeted to mothers who bake their children's birthday cakes. Analyzing search terms, the two determined that when mothers want information or help in baking cakes, they don't search on brand names, but rather on specific solution terms like "birthday cake." Given this information, a series of high-quality HD videos approximately five minutes in length were created and posted on the Betty Crocker website. To convey the idea that the videos were instructional and not promotional, there was little reference to the Betty Crocker brand. The videos were very engaging, with an average of 75 percent of the content being watched. To date, the videos have driven over 70 million visitors to the website and, more important, are building brand loyalty due to their instructional nature.

Chipotle

Chipotle's slogan "food with integrity" took a hit when a handful of its restaurants across the United States were found to have an *E. coli* problem. The crisis grew to almost 200 stores, causing restaurant traffic and share prices to drop to the point where there were concerns that the company might not survive the crisis. Just when it appeared that things were under control, it happened again. But the company didn't just let the crisis take its course; instead PR and marketing teamed up to battle the bad news head on. CEO Steve Ells issued an open letter of apology in national print ads and on the website, gave interviews on television, and promised that the company would be the absolute leader in food safety from here on out. The company also embarked on a campaign to bolster the brand image and get customers to return to the stores. With the largest marketing budget in the company's history, Chipotle ran outdoor, print, digital, and direct mail to let customers know that safety will be the number 1 priority. A food safety website was created, and both mobile and social media were employed. Sales promotions ("buy one get one free") and online coupons were all enlisted to get customers back in the stores. While still not out of the woods, the company appears to be going to survive, as customers are coming back and the stock prices are rising.

FIGURE 17-2

Advantages and
Disadvantages of MPRs

Advantages

- It is a cost-effective way to reach the market.
- It is a highly targeted way to conduct public relations.
- It benefits from the endorsement of independent and objective third parties who have no association with the product.
- It achieves credibility.
- It supports advertising programs by making messages more credible.
- It breaks through the clutter.
- It circumvents consumer resistance to sales efforts.
- There can be improved media involvement among consumers.
- It can create influence among opinion leaders and trendsetters.
- It can improve ROI.

Disadvantages

- There is a lack of control over the media.
- It is difficult to tie in slogans and other advertising devices.
- Media time and space are not guaranteed.
- There are no standard effectiveness measures.

Sources: Thomas L. Harris, "Marketing PR—The Second Century," *Reputation Management*, January/February 1999, www.prcentral.com, pp. 1–6.

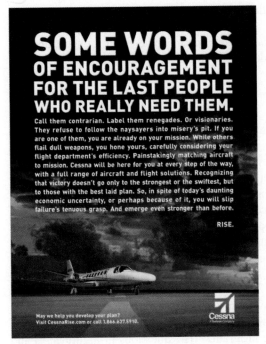

EXHIBIT 17-3

Cessna attempts to aid a
product at risk

© Cessna Aircraft Company, A
Textron Inc. Company

THE PROCESS OF PUBLIC RELATIONS

The actual process of conducting public relations and integrating it into the promotional mix involves a series of both traditional and marketing-oriented tasks.

Determining and Evaluating Public Attitudes

You have learned that public relations is concerned with people's attitudes toward the firm or specific issues beyond those directed at a product or service. The first question you may ask is why—why is the firm so concerned with the public's attitudes?

One reason is that these attitudes may affect sales of the firm's products. A number of companies have experienced sales declines as a result of consumer boycotts. BP, Nestlé, Nokia, and Walmart are just a few companies that have had to respond to organized pressures. PETA's six-year attack on SeaWorld for alleged mistreatment of the animals in captivity at the parks led SeaWorld to launch a $10 million ad campaign response addressing the allegations and presenting SeaWorld's position, while accusing PETA of disseminating false information. After a six-year fight, SeaWorld discontinued the killer whale program, noting that the "Shamu" image was no longer viable for the future.[10] Likewise, the media must be concerned with the attitudes of the public. *Fox News*, which is owned by News Corp., lost favor with many in the Republican base for its coverage of the 2016 Republican presidential primaries. Long known as a network favored by conservatives, the network saw a significant drop in perceptions of Fox as providing "fair and balanced coverage"; viewers were unhappy with the way *Fox News* treated candidate Donald Trump and ignored candidate Dr. Ben Carson. Fox's Buzz score, measured on a –100 to +100 with 0 being neutral, dropped from a high of 38 in 2013 to 17 by summer 2016

CHAPTER 17

according to a BrandIndex survey. If these perceptions were to continue, the result could be a significant drop in ad revenues during national election coverage as the conservative base tuned out.

On the other hand, companies can gain favorable impressions and positive attitudes from consumers by doing the right thing. For example, Intuit sent consumers an apology letter and a free upgrade for changing its TurboTax software and not including a number of forms that were in in previous versions but not taking adequate measures to inform it customer base that it was doing so and why. The apology was used as an example of great customer service by bloggers and helped improve attitudes toward the TurboTax product. You can view this letter at http://blog.turbotax.intuit.com/uncategorized/an-apology-to-our-turbotax-desktop-customers-18817/.

Second, no one wants to be perceived as a bad citizen. Corporations exist in communities, and their employees generally both work and live there. Negative attitudes carry over to employee morale and may result in a less-than-optimal working environment internally and in the community.

Due to their concerns about public perceptions, many privately held corporations, publicly held companies, utilities, and media survey public attitudes. The reasons for conducting this research are many, but include the following:

1. *It provides input into the planning process.* Once the firm has determined public attitudes, they become the starting point in the development of programs designed to maintain favorable positions or change unfavorable ones.
2. *It serves as an early warning system.* Once a problem exists, it may require substantial time and money to correct. By conducting research, the firm may be able to identify potential problems and handle them effectively before they become serious issues.
3. *It secures support internally.* If research shows a problem or potential problem exists, it will be much easier for the public relations arm to gain the support it needs to address this problem.
4. *It increases the effectiveness of the communication.* The better it understands a problem, the better the firm can design communications to deal with it.

Establishing a PR Plan

For some companies, their PR programs involve little more than press releases, press kits for the media, and/or trade shows and new product announcements.

Further, these tools are often not designed into a formal public relations effort but rather are used only as needed. In other words, no structured program for conducting PR is evident. As we noted earlier, the public relations process is an ongoing one, requiring formalized policies and procedures for dealing with problems and opportunities. Just as you would not develop an advertising and/or a promotions program without a plan, you should not institute public relations efforts haphazardly. Moreover, the PR plan needs to be integrated into the overall marketing communications program. Figure 17–3 provides some questions marketers should ask to determine whether their PR plan is workable.

Cutlip and colleagues suggest a four-step process for developing a public relations plan: (1) define public relations problems, (2) plan and program, (3) take action and communicate, and (4) evaluate the program.[11] The questions in Figure 17–3 and the four-step planning process tie in with the promotional planning process stressed throughout this text.

Developing and Executing the PR Program

Because of the broad role that public relations may be asked to play, the PR program may need to extend beyond promotion. A broader definition of the target market, additional communications objectives, and different messages and delivery systems may be employed. Let us examine this process.

FIGURE 17–3

Ten Questions for Evaluating
Public Relations Plans

1. Does the plan reflect a thorough understanding of the company's business situation?

2. Has the PR program made good use of research and background sources?

3. Does the plan include full analysis of recent editorial coverage?

4. Do the PR people fully understand the product's strengths and weaknesses?

5. Does the PR program describe several cogent, relevant conclusions from the research?

6. Are the program objectives specific and measurable?

7. Does the program clearly describe what the PR activity will be and how it will benefit the company?

8. Does the program describe how its results will be measured?

9. Do the research, objectives, activities, and evaluations tie together?

10. Has the PR department communicated with marketing throughout the development of the program?

EXHIBIT 17–4

An example of a newsletter used for internal communication by the College of Business Administration at San Diego State University

Newsletter: © San Diego State University, College of Business Administration; courtroom: © McGraw-Hill Education; flag: © Digital Archive Japan/Alamy RF; graduates: © McGraw-Hill Education

---

San Diego State University
College of Business Administration

Hallway Chat
August 2016

Hallway Chat was initiated to serve the College of Business faculty, staff and lecturers as a monthly means of communicating news and information relevant to the college and its stakeholders.

College of Business Administration

Notes from the Community: For those that don't know, SDSU management lecturer, Dr. Wendy Patrick, is a San Diego County deputy district attorney in her day job. During a recent case, a prospective juror said he couldn't be a fair and impartial juror because Wendy was his instructor at SDSU last semester and since she gave him an A, he already wanted to vote for her side. "Everyone cracked up, was a great way to start the day!" Wendy said.

A Little International Flair: Andy Baker taught a social media marketing course over the summer at SRH University Heidelberg. "In particular, we explored how current theory and practice of social media marketing can be applied to small and medium-sized businesses," he said. "I also ate too many plates of delicious schweinshaxe and drank plenty of tasty dunkelweizen."

CBA Renovation Update: The university is currently in the process of hiring an architect for the College of Business remodeling project. Stay tuned!

Obituary: Long-time CBA board member, Duane Roth, passed away on August 3 after a bicycle accident. Click here to read more.

College of Business Fun Fact

With over 5000 students, the College of Business at SDSU is the 55ʰ largest business school in the world and the 28ⁿᵈ largest business school in the U.S.

Determining Relevant Target Audiences The targets of public relations efforts may vary, with different objectives for each. Some may be directly involved in selling the product; others may affect the firm in a different way (e.g., they may be aimed at stockholders or legislators). These audiences may be internal or external to the firm.

Internal audiences may include the employees, stockholders, and investors of the firm as well as members of the local community, suppliers, and current customers. As noted in Figure 17–1, Cessna's public relations programs were designed, in part, to reach buyers as well as to improve morale among employees. Why are community members and customers of the firm considered internal rather than external? According to John Marston, it's because these groups are already connected with the organization in some way, and the firm normally communicates with them in the ordinary routine of work.[12] **External audiences** are those people who are not closely connected with the organization (e.g., the public at large).

It may be necessary to communicate with these groups on an ongoing basis for a variety of reasons, ranging from ensuring goodwill to introducing new policies, procedures, or even products. A few examples may help.

Employees of the Firm Maintaining morale and showcasing the results of employees' efforts are often prime objectives of the public relations program. Organizational newsletters, notices on bulletin boards, awards ceremonies and events, direct mail, and annual reports are some of the methods used to communicate with these groups. Exhibit 17–4 shows one such internal communication used by the College of Business Administration at San Diego State University.

Personal methods of communicating may be as formal as an established grievance committee or as informal as an office Christmas party. Other social events, such as corporate bowling teams or picnics, are also used to create goodwill.

Stockholders and Investors You may think an annual report like the one in Exhibit 17–5 provides stockholders and investors only with financial information regarding the firm. While this is one purpose, annual reports are also a communications channel for informing this

CHAPTER 17

EXHIBIT 17–5

In addition to providing information regarding its finances, GE's Annual Report serves a variety of purposes. To view the report in its entirety, visit www.ge.com/ar2015/

Source: General Electric

EXHIBIT 17–6

Citgo demonstrates concern for the community

Source: Citgo Petroleum Corporation

audience about why the firm is or is not doing well, outlining future plans, and providing other information that goes beyond numbers.

It has become very common for companies to use annual reports for public relations purposes—to generate additional investments, to bring more of their stocks "back home" (i.e., become more locally controlled and managed), and to produce funding to solve specific problems, as well as to promote goodwill.

Community Members People who live and work in the community where a firm is located or doing business are often the target of public relations efforts. Such efforts may involve ads informing the community of activities that the organization is engaged in, for example, reducing air pollution, cleaning up water supplies, or preserving wetlands. (The community can be defined very broadly.) As you can see in Exhibit 17–6, a number of oil companies are involved in this form of public relations by demonstrating to people that the organization is a good citizen with their welfare in mind.

Suppliers and Customers An organization wishes to maintain *goodwill* with its suppliers as well as its consuming public. If consumers think a company is not socially conscious, they may take their loyalties elsewhere. Suppliers may be inclined to do the same.

Sometimes sponsoring a public relations effort results in direct evidence of success. Certainly Betty Crocker achieved its goal of getting consumers to the website and getting engaged with the brand. Indirect indications of the success of PR efforts may include more customer loyalty, less antagonism, or greater cooperation between the firm and its suppliers or consumers.

MARKETING EDGE

EDUCATE | DEVELOP | GROW | EMPLOY

Public relations efforts are often targeted to more than one group and are a direct result of concerns initiated in the marketplace. As noted earlier, along with potential consumers, trade association members, human resource directors, buyers, and suppliers often constitute the target audience for PR efforts.

Relevant audiences may also include people not directly involved with the firm. The press, educators, civic and business groups, governments, and the financial community can be external audiences.

The Media Perhaps among the most critical external publics are the media, which determine what you will read in your newspapers or online, or see on TV and how this news will be presented. Because of the media's power, they should be informed of the firm's actions. Companies issue press releases and communicate through conferences, interviews, and special events. The media are generally receptive to such information as long as it is handled professionally; reporters are always interested in good stories. In turn, the media are also concerned about how the community perceives them. (Remember the *Fox News* example provided earlier.)

Educators A number of organizations provide educators with information regarding their activities. The Advertising Education Foundation (AEF), the Direct Marketing Association (DMA), the Promotional Products Association International (PPAI), and the Outdoor Advertising Association of America (OAAA), among others, keep educators informed in an attempt to generate goodwill as well as exposure for their causes on both a local and national level. These groups and major corporations provide information regarding innovations, state-of-the-art research, and other items of interest. Marketing EDGE, formerly the Direct Marketing Educational Foundation (DMEF), provides materials including case examples and lecture notes specifically designed for educators (Exhibit 17–7).

Educators are a target audience because, like the media, they control the flow of information to certain parties—in this case, people like you. *The Bloomberg News* and *Fortune* magazines attempt to have professors use their magazines in their classes, as does *The Wall Street Journal, The New York Times*, and *Advertising Age*, among others. In addition to selling more magazines and newspapers, such usage also lends credibility to the medium.

Civic and Business Organizations The local Jaycees, Kiwanis, and other nonprofit civic organizations also serve as gatekeepers of information. Companies' financial contributions to these groups, speeches at organization functions, and sponsorships are all designed to create goodwill. Corporate executives' service on the boards of nonprofit organizations also generates positive public relations.

Governments Public relations often attempts to influence government bodies directly at both local and national levels. Successful lobbying may mean immediate success for a product, while regulations detrimental to the firm may cost it millions. Imagine for a moment what FDA approval of a product can mean for sales, or what could happen to the beer and wine industries if TV advertising were banned. The pharmaceutical industry lobbied hard for permission to advertise prescription drugs directly to the consumer. Within the first five years of approval, an estimated 65 million consumers approached their doctors to inquire about the drugs as a result. The industry now spends over $5 billion a year on advertising, leading some organizations like the American Medical Association (AMA) to seek the ban to be reinstated[13] (Figure 17–4). In 2016, Rep. Rosa DeLauro (D-CT) proposed the Responsibility in Drug Advertising Act of 2016, seeking a three-year moratorium on direct-to-consumer (DTC) pharma advertising, though few expect it to pass. In turn, environmentalists, trade unions, and other groups with specific agendas will attempt to influence government legislation in their behalf.

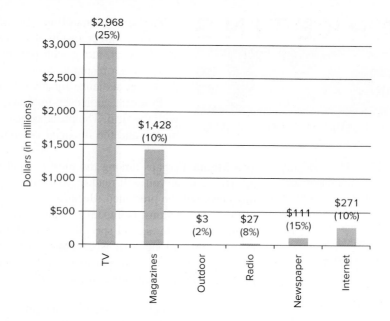

Financial Groups In addition to current shareholders, potential shareholders and investors may be relevant target markets for PR efforts. Financial advisors, lending institutions, and others must be kept abreast of new developments as well as of financial information, since they offer the potential for new sources of funding. Press releases and corporate reports play an important role in providing information to these publics.

Implementing the PR Program Once the research has been conducted and the target audiences identified, the public relations program must be developed and delivered to the receivers. A number of PR tools are available for this purpose, including press releases, press conferences, exclusives, interviews, and community involvement.

The Press Release One of the most important publics is the press. To be used by the press, information must be factual, true, and of interest to the medium as well as to its audience. The source of the **press release** can do certain things to improve the likelihood that the "news" will be disseminated, such as ensuring that it reaches the right target audience, making it interesting, and making it easy to pass along.

The information in a press release won't be used unless it is of interest to the users of the medium it is sent to. For example, financial institutions may issue press releases to business trade media and to the editor of the business section of a general-interest newspaper. Organizations like the PR Newswire and PRLog provide services to help disseminate information.

Press Conferences We are all familiar with **press conferences** held by political figures. Although used less often by organizations and corporations, this form of delivery can be very effective. The topic must be of major interest to a specific group before it is likely to gain coverage. Usually major accomplishments (such as the awarding of the next Super Bowl, FIFA, or Olympics location), and major breakthroughs (such as medical cures, emergencies, or catastrophes) warrant a national press conference. On a local level, community events, local developments, and the like may receive coverage. Companies often call press conferences when they have significant news to announce, such as the introduction of a new product

EXHIBIT 17-8

Lacrosse star Paul Rabil's foundation (www.paulrabilfoundation.org) gives back to the community in many various ways

Source: The Paul Rabil Foundation

or advertising campaign. Sports teams use this tool to attract fan attention and interest when a new star is signed.

Exclusives Although most public relations efforts seek a variety of channels for distribution, an alternative strategy is to offer one particular medium exclusive rights to the story if that medium reaches a substantial number of people in the target audience. Offering an **exclusive** may enhance the likelihood of acceptance. As you watch television over the next few weeks, watch for the various networks' and local stations' exclusives. Notice how the media actually use these exclusives to promote themselves.

Interviews When you watch TV or read magazines, pay close attention to the personal interviews. Usually someone will raise specific questions, and a spokesperson provided by the firm will answer them. For example, when the FBI announced that it was investigating Subway brand ambassador Jared Fogle in a pornography issue, Subway immediately issued press releases on Facebook and Twitter feeds saying Subway was immediately suspending the relationship and provided interviews with a company spokesperson to answer questions. Depending on how significant the issue is, sometimes even top management will get involved. When consumers protested Chick-fil-A's support of antigay Christian organizations, the president, Dan Cahy, stood by his decision in an interview with *The Baptist Press* newspaper.

Community Involvement Many companies and individuals enhance their public image through involvement in the local community. This involvement may take many forms, including membership in local organizations like the Kiwanis or Jaycees and contributions to or participation in community events (Exhibit 17–8).

The Internet As discussed in Chapter 15, the Internet has become a means by which companies and organizations can disseminate public relations information. Just as in the print media, companies have used the Web to establish media relations and government, investor, and community relationships; to deal with crises; and even to conduct cause marketing. Companies have used their websites to address issues, as well as to provide information about products and services, archive press releases, link to other articles and sites, and provide lists of activities and events. Many corporate websites have sections listing their press activities.

Social Networks and Blogs More and more companies and organizations are making use of social networks, blogs, and other Web 2.0 media (discussed in Chapter 15) for public relations purposes. It is now expected that companies will post information on their websites providing announcements and updates on product releases, recalls, or other issues. In addition, many of these companies are using 2.0 media to disseminate this information. Subway made valuable use of blogs, Facebook, Twitter, and other social media during and after the Jared Fogle incident. One of the many advantages cited for the use of social media is for PR purposes, keeping those on the networks current in events surrounding the company or or organization (see Digital and Social Media Perspective 17–1).

Digital and Social Media Perspective 17-1 > > >

USING SOCIAL MEDIA OFTEN LEADS TO GOOD RESULTS—FOR SOMEONE!

As noted earlier in this chapter, companies and organizations have turned to social and digital media to both create positive publicity and respond to negative news as well. One of the goals of nearly every company, large and small, is pretty simple: generate as much positive "buzz" as possible. If their "likes," "tweets," comments, and memes aren't increasing every day, these companies feel that they are probably falling behind the competition. Indeed, companies dedicate millions of dollars and thousands of hours of time to improve their social media presence, hoping that their efforts will help their messages spread throughout the digital world like wildfire. But what happens when a company or brand experiences negative publicity resulting in negative buzz? While social media can do wonders for a brand when news is positive, what happens when the news is likely to be detrimental? The business of "damage control" has been around for years, but how it is being done has fundamentally changed over the past decade. Newspapers, radios, and magazines are all but being replaced by computers, tablets, and mobile phones that power social platforms capable of spreading news at speeds previously unseen or unheard of. These social media provide a platform for both proponents and opponents of brands to "talk" directly to a company as well as numerous others. The old days of sending a company or a celebrity a letter in the mail hoping it gets read and responded to are long gone. Today's methods of providing feedback—posting on Facebook, Snapchat, or Twitter—have a better-than-average chance that someone will read it and pass it along.

One example of a brand responding to negative publicity and reversing course on a decision is whisky distiller Maker's Mark, which in 2013 abruptly changed its mind on a publicly announced plan to dilute its whisky from 45 percent alcohol by volume to 42 percent to meet unanticipated demand. The company announced the change in an e-mail to the brand's most loyal fans claiming that the change in alcohol content would not make for a dramatic difference in how the whisky tastes. Unfortunately (or fortunately), the e-mail quickly went viral among Maker's Mark drinkers through numerous social channels. The feedback was so negative that within just one week of the announcement, Marker's Mark reversed course and canceled plans to dilute the whisky. Or did it? There are many out there in the public relations industry who believe the entire announcement was designed to create publicity for the brand. The result was a public relations bonanza. Upon hearing the breaking news in February, fans of Maker's Mark began hording the product, rocketing sales up 44 percent. By the time the dust had settled Maker's Mark had very publicly reversed its decision and enjoyed the benefits of widespread, free publicity. While it is not certain whether the strategy was planned or whether Maker's Mark was lucky, it all turned out fine for the company.

Another example demonstrates that even the most popular and respected organizations are not immune to negative publicity. Just ask the Susan G. Komen Foundation, the nation's most prominent breast cancer advocacy organization, which decided to end its decades-long partnership with Planned Parenthood. Despite the fact that the funding Planned Parenthood would lose from the foundation

Advantages and Disadvantages of PR

Like the other program elements, public relations has both advantages and disadvantages.

Advantages include the following:

1. *Credibility.* Because public relations communications are not perceived in the same light as advertising—that is, the public does not realize the organization either directly or indirectly paid for them—they tend to have more credibility. The fact that the media are not being compensated for providing the information may lead receivers to consider the news more truthful and credible. For example, an article in newspapers or magazines discussing the virtues of aspirin may be perceived as much more credible than an ad for a particular brand of aspirin.

   Automotive awards presented in magazines such as *Motor Trend* have long been known to carry clout with potential car buyers. The influential J.D. Power Awards are now offered for a variety of reasons (quality, customer satisfaction, service, etc.) in a variety of industries (automobile, financial services, airports, etc.). It has become a common practice for car companies and others to promote their achievements (Exhibit 17–9). In one instance, the wife of a recently passed away spouse received a direct-mail piece from a funeral home touting

© Richard Drew/AP Images

organization attributing it to the negative publicity; it had not recovered by 2015. Another negative result was the black mark on Komen's image among its supporters. Meanwhile, 11 Komen for the Cure affiliates contributed hundreds of thousands of dollars to the Planned Parenthood cause.

Yet another well-respected foundation also felt the wrath of negative publicity when Nike announced that it would dissolve its partnership with the Livestrong Foundation. After nine years of standing by seven-time Tour de France winner and famed cancer survivor Lance Armstrong, a week after the U.S. Anti-Doping Agency released thousands of pages of documents showing the biker had used performance-enhancing drugs, Nike reversed course. While Nike said it would continue to support the foundation itself, as well as honor the contract through 2014, it terminated the sales of Livestrong gear, which helped bring in over $500 million to cancer research. RadioShack also terminated its relationship with Armstrong. His Twitter account was quiet after the announcement, and revenue fell to $38.1 million in 2012, from $46.8 million the previous year. It continued to fall throughout 2013. By 2014, 13 of Livestrong's 100 employees resigned. By 2016, under new leadership, and without Nike and RadioShack, the organization continues to survive and continues to help others, but with much less money to do so.

constituted only a tiny portion of its annual grants, Komen's decision ignited heavy opposition within its own ranks as well as from everyday citizens, politicians, and particularly breast cancer survivors. Komen's social media channels received thousands of threats by longtime supporters to put down their pink ribbons and no longer support their fund-raising efforts. At the same time, Planned Parenthood actually received thousands of donations directly from supporters who thought Komen's decision would forever cripple the organization. While the Komen foundation believed it had good reasons for curtailing its support for Planned Parenthood, one can argue that it did not voice the reasons adequately. Perhaps had the public been aware of these reasons, those opposed to Komen may have had a different opinion (or, again, maybe not!). The end results were the resignation of Komen's senior vice president of public policy and decreases in contributions: 2013 contributions were down $77 million from the previous year, with the

Sources: Steven Ertelt, "11 Komen for the Cure Affiliates Give Planned Parenthood Hundreds of Thousands in Donations," July 29, 2015, www.lifenews.com; Michael Hiltzik, "Susan G. Komen Foundation Discovers the Price of Playing Politics," January 8, 2014, www.latimes.com; James F. Thompson, "Maker's Mark Miracle: Best PR Disaster Ever Engineered," Adweek, May 2, 2013; "Nike and Livestrong Foundation Dissolve Lucrative Partnership," May 29, 2013, www.brandchannel.com; Chris Otts, "Maker's Mark Defends Watering Down Its Bourbon," February 12, 2013, www.courier-Journal.com; Mark Boxley, "Maker's Mark to Restore Alcohol Content of Whiskey," February 17, 2013, www.courier-Journal.com; Jennifer Preston and Gardiner Harris, "Outcry Grows Fiercer after Funding Cut by Cancer Group," February 2, 2012, www.nytimes.com; Shirley Brady, "Susan G. Komen for the Cure Policy Exec Resigns," February 7, 2012, www.brandchannel.

its services and the fact that it was the recipient of a J.D. Power Award for funeral service.

News about a product may in itself serve as the subject of an ad. Exhibit 17–10 demonstrates how General Mills used favorable publicity from a variety of sources to promote the importance of whole grain in a healthy diet and promote the use of whole grain in its cereals. Note that every cereal box prominently displays the whole-grain ingredients.

2. *Cost.* In both absolute and relative terms, the cost of public relations is very low, especially when the possible effects are considered. While a firm can employ public relations agencies and spend millions of dollars on PR, for smaller companies this form of communication may be the most affordable alternative available. As noted, many services exist to distribute this information at little or no cost. Many public relations programs require little more than the time and expenses associated with putting the program together and getting it distributed, yet they still accomplish their objectives.

3. *Avoidance of clutter.* Because they are typically perceived as news items, public relations messages are not subject to the clutter of ads. A story regarding a new product introduction or breakthrough is treated as a news item and is likely to receive attention.

4. *Lead generation.* Information about technological innovations, medical breakthroughs, and the like results almost immediately in a multitude of inquiries. These inquiries may give the firm some quality sales leads.
5. *Ability to reach specific groups.* Because some products appeal to only small market segments, it is not feasible to engage in advertising and/or promotions to reach them. If the firm does not have the financial capabilities to engage in promotional expenditures, the best way to communicate to these groups is through public relations. Social networks and blogs have become extremely valuable in this regard.
6. *Image building.* Effective public relations helps develop a positive image for the organization. A strong image is insurance against later misfortunes. The strength of the Toyota brand name made it possible for Toyota to get through a series of crises involving mechanical problems, while VW will likely survive the extensive negative press received when it was shown to have manipulated emissions tests on its diesel vehicles.

Perhaps the major disadvantage of public relations is the potential for not completing the communications process. While public relations messages can break through the clutter of commercials, the receiver may not make the connection to the source. Many firms' PR efforts are never associated with their sponsors in the public mind.

Public relations may also misfire through mismanagement and a lack of coordination with the marketing department. When marketing and PR departments operate independently, there is a danger of inconsistent communications, redundancies in efforts, and so on.

The key to effective public relations is to establish a good program, worthy of public interest, and to manage it properly. To determine if this program is working, the firm must measure the effectiveness of the PR effort.

Measuring the Effectiveness of PR

As with the other promotional program elements, it is important to evaluate the effectiveness of the public relations efforts. In addition to determining the contribution of this program element to attaining communications objectives, the evaluation offers other advantages:

1. It tells management what has been achieved through public relations activities.
2. It provides management with a way to measure public relations achievements quantitatively.
3. It gives management a way to judge the quality of public relations achievements and activities.

According to the **Public Relations Society of America**, organizations that understand and subscribe to the benefits of public relations evaluation can effectively:

- Validate the results of their efforts.

- Link the results to business outcomes that further the realization of organizational goals.
- Credibly merchandise the impact of the results to those who fund PR programs.
- Set smarter objectives, develop better strategies, and employ more compelling and engaging tactics.
- Make midcourse adjustments and corrections.
- Regularly adapt their measurement approaches based on changing objectives, new competitors, and emerging best practices.[14]

In an extensive review of criteria used to measure effectiveness, Professor Jim Macnamara of the University of Technology, Sydney, identified 30 metrics that are broadly used for measuring PR and corporate communication today.[15] In a review of emerging models for measuring public relations effectiveness, Amit Jain concluded that traditional methods no longer work. Jain notes that as digital becomes more and more of the public relations process, new criteria need to be added to previous measures, and new models must be developed.[16]

Mark Weiner, in discussing measures of effectiveness specific to MPRs, also suggests using the following methods:[17]

- *Media content analysis.* Systematically and objectively identifying the characteristics of messages that appear in the media, analyzing the content to determine trends and perceptions relevant to the product or brand.
- *Survey research.* Quantitatively assessing consumers' attitudes toward the product or brand.
- *Marketing-mix modeling.* Drawing data from multiple sources and integrating them to provide insight into the process.

The PESO model discussed in Chapter 1 has now been embraced by public relations practitioners. As noted, the model was developed and championed by Gini Dietrich, a leading voice for the PR industry.[18] An excellent example of how the model works when combined with marketing is reflected by Dell at the company's Dell World conference. To communicate information about their first annual Global Technology Adoption Index (GTAI) the PR and marketing teams involved press, native ads, and owned and social media.

In the Dell example, here's how it went:

- Michael Dell announced the Global Technology Adoption Index (GTAI) during the Dell World press conference.
- The GTAI results were shared across Dell's social media platforms (e.g., LinkedIn, Twitter, Facebook), including tweets from the @Dell handle, and the social community was encouraged to use the hashtag #delltechindex.
- Dell's owned media site, Tech Page One, released a story called "Tech Hype Meets Tech Reality" which outlined some of the key findings from the GTAI.
- The PR team pitched the story to journalists and secured media coverage including online tech and business sites like the *Irish Times*, ZDnet, and eWeek.
- The *New York Times* GTAI native advertising campaign was released a day after the news media covered the announcement.
- Online video and content syndication ran on business and technology sites.
- Paid social posts promoted the campaign on LinkedIn and Twitter.
- Infographics were used to accompany all of the above content.

In summary, the role of public relations in the promotional mix is changing. As PR has become more marketing-oriented, the criteria by which the programs are evaluated have also changed. At the same time, nonmarketing activities will continue to be part of the public relations department and part of the basis for evaluation.

PUBLICITY

Publicity refers to the generation of news about a person, product, or service that appears in broadcast or print media. To many marketers, publicity and public relations are synonymous. In fact, publicity is really a subset of the public relations effort.

But there are several major differences. First, publicity is typically a *short-term* strategy, while public relations is a concerted program extending over a period of time. Second, public relations is designed to provide positive information about the firm and is usually controlled by the firm or its agent. Publicity, on the other hand, is not always positive and is not always under the control of, or paid for by, the organization. Both positive and negative publicity often originates from sources other than the firm.

In most organizations, publicity is controlled and disseminated by the public relations department. In this section, we discuss the role publicity plays in the promotional program and some of the ways marketers use and react to these communications.

The Power of Publicity

One of the factors that most set off publicity from the other program elements is the sheer power this form of communication can generate. Unfortunately for marketers, this power is not always realized in the way they would like it to be. Publicity can make or break a product or even a company. At one point, BP's stock dropped to less than one-half of what it was prior to the Gulf spill. Samsung's value declined by billions of dollars when it suffered negative publicity as a result of it's exploding cell phone batteries.

Why is publicity so much more powerful than advertising or sales promotion—or even other forms of public relations? First, publicity is highly credible. Unlike advertising and sales promotions, publicity is not usually seen as being sponsored by the company (in negative instances, it never is). So consumers perceive this information as more objective and place more confidence in it. In fact, media often take great measures to ensure their objectivity and promote the fact that they are not influenced by advertisers or other outside sources.

Publicity information may be perceived as endorsed by the medium in which it appears. For example, publicity regarding a breakthrough in the durability of golf balls will go far to promote them if it is reported by *Golf* magazine. *Car & Driver*'s award for car of the year reflects the magazine's perception of the quality of the auto selected.

Still another reason for publicity's power is its news value and the frequency of exposure it generates. When the publicity is positive, companies stand to benefit. When it is not, companies may suffer negative consequences such as lost sales, impacts on image, and even litigation.

The bottom line is that publicity is news, and people like to pass on information that has news value. Publicity thus results in a significant amount of free, credible, word-of-mouth information regarding the firm and its products.

The Control and Dissemination of Publicity

In some of the examples cited previously, the control of publicity was not in the hands of the company. In some instances it is the firm's own blunder that allows information to leak out. Companies such as VW, Samsung, and BP could do nothing to stop the media from releasing negative information about them. When publicity becomes news, it is reported by the media, sometimes despite efforts by the firm. In these instances, the organization needs to react to the potential threat created by the news. Unfortunately, simply ignoring the problem will not make it go away.

EXHIBIT 17–11

Tree Top responds to the threat of negative publicity

© Tree Top, Inc.

A good example of one company's efforts to respond to adverse publicity is shown in Exhibit 17–11. Tree Top's problems began when all the major news media reported that the chemical Alar, used by some growers to regulate the growth of apples, might cause cancer in children. Despite published statements by reliable scientific and medical authorities (including the surgeon general) that Alar does not cause cancer, a few special-interest groups were able to generate an extraordinary amount of adverse publicity, causing concern among consumers and purchasing agents. A few school districts took apples off their menus, and even applesauce and juice were implicated. Tree Top ran the ad shown in Exhibit 17–11 to state its position and alleviate consumers' fears. It also sent a direct mailing to nutritionists and day care operators. The campaign was successful in assuring consumers of the product's safety and rebuilding their confidence.

Another example of effectively countering negative publicity is reflected in Budweiser's response to a class action lawsuit and negative publicity claiming that the brewer was watering down its beer, thereby reducing the alcoholic content and cheating consumers out of millions of dollars. Bud's response advertisement was particularly effective because it not only refuted the claim without giving it credence but at the same time turned the tables by indicating that not only does Bud maintain the brand's integrity, it also demonstrates the fact that they support causes by donating over 71 million cans of drinking water to those in need as shown in Exhibit 17–12.

Publicity can also work for marketers. Kids' toys frequently achieve significant sales due to high levels of positive publicity and word-of-mouth advertising. Sales of Cabernet Sauvignon increased an average of 45 percent in the month after a CBS *60 Minutes* report indicating that daily moderate consumption of red wine can reduce the risk of heart disease, and green tea sales skyrocketed when the word spread that consumption of the product was effective in preventing cancer. Products that contain antioxidents are now very popular due to their health benefits. There are many more examples of the positive impact publicity can have.

Marketers like to have as much control as possible over the time and place where information is released. One way to do this is with the **video news release (VNR)**, a publicity piece produced by publicists so that stations can air it as a news story. The videos almost never mention that they are produced by the subject organization, and most news stations don't mention it either. Many government agencies have used VNRs, as have the American Dental Association, GM, Motorola, and Nokia, among others. The use of VNRs without disclosing the source has led some consumer advocates to protest such actions. The Consumer Product Safety Commission has published guidelines for the appropriate use of VNRs at www.cpsp.gov.

In their efforts to manage publicity and public relations, marketers are continuously learning more about these activities. Courses are offered, websites are devoted to the topic, and books are written on how to manage publicity. These books cover how to make a presentation, whom to contact, how to issue a press release, and what to know about each medium addressed, including TV, radio, newspapers, magazines, the Internet, and direct-response advertising. They discuss such alternative media as news conferences, seminars, events, and personal letters, as well as insights on how to deal with government and other legislative bodies. Because this information is too extensive to include as a single chapter in this

THEY MUST HAVE TESTED ONE OF THESE.

DONATED BY ANHEUSER-BUSCH

WATER

drinking water

12 FL. OZ.

ANHEUSER-BUSCH
ST. LOUIS, MO

It would have been easy to get because we've done it 71 million times.
That's how many cans of pure drinking water we've donated to the
American Red Cross and disaster relief organizations worldwide.

But in every other circumstance, the Anheuser-Busch logo is our ironclad
guarantee that the beer in your hand is the best beer we know how to brew.
We take no shortcuts and make no exceptions. Ever.

Follow us @budweiser

ENJOY RESPONSIBLY ©2015 Anheuser-Busch, St. Louis, MO

EXHIBIT 17–12

Budweiser effectively responds to negative publicity

Source: Anheuser-Busch

text, we suggest you peruse one of the many books available on this subject for additional insights.

Advantages and Disadvantages of Publicity

Publicity offers the advantages of credibility, news value, significant word-of-mouth communications, and a perception of being endorsed by the media. Beyond the potential impact of negative publicity, other major problems arise from the use of publicity: lack of control, timing, and accuracy.

Lack of Control   In the viral world today, there is little control of what information is conveyed. Social networks, blogs, and so on have expanded the number of recipients of messages, while at the same time opening up the information stream to sources that are not confined by standards that may be imposed on traditional media. The result is that once public, the company or organization has lost control over the information. This can often become a costly experience.

Timing   Timing of the publicity is not always completely under the control of the marketer. Unless the press thinks the information has very high news value, the timing of the press release is entirely up to the media—if it gets released at all. Thus, the information may be released earlier than desired or too late to make an impact.

Accuracy   There are numerous ways to generate publicity. Quite often these means are not in the company's control. Unfortunately, the information sometimes gets lost in translation; that is, it is not always reported the way the provider wishes it to be. As a result, inaccurate information, omissions, or other errors may result. Sometimes when you see a publicity piece that was written from a press release, you wonder if the two are even about the same topic.

Measuring the Effectiveness of Publicity

The methods for measuring the effects of publicity are essentially the same as those discussed earlier under the broader topic of public relations. As noted at that point, traditional models of effectiveness are giving way to new measures as the digital world becomes a more important player in the communications programs of both large and small companies.

CORPORATE ADVERTISING

One of the more controversial forms of advertising is **corporate advertising**. Actually an extension of the public relations function, corporate advertising does not promote any one specific product or service. Rather, it is designed to promote the firm overall, by enhancing its image, assuming a position on a social issue or cause, or seeking direct involvement in something. Why is corporate advertising controversial? A number of reasons are offered:

1. *Consumers are not interested in this form of advertising.* Studies have shown that many consumers are not interested in corporate ads. At least part of this

may be because consumers do not understand the reasons behind such ads. Of course, much of this confusion results from ads that are not very good from a communications standpoint.

2. *It's a costly form of self-indulgence.* Firms have been accused of engaging in corporate image advertising only to satisfy the egos of top management. This argument stems from the fact that corporate ads are not easy to write. The message to be communicated is not as precise and specific as one designed to position a product, so the top managers often dictate the content of the ad, and the copy reflects their ideas and images of the corporation.

3. *The firm must be in trouble.* Some critics believe the only time firms engage in corporate advertising is when they are in trouble—either in a financial sense or in the public eye—and are advertising to attempt to remedy the problem. There are a number of forms of corporate advertising, each with its own objectives. These critics argue that these objectives have become important only because the firm has not been managed properly.

4. *Corporate advertising is a waste of money.* Given that the ads do not directly appeal to anyone, are not understood, and do not promote anything specific, critics say the monies could be better spent in other areas. Again, much of this argument has its foundation in the fact that corporate image ads are often intangible. They typically do not ask directly for a purchase; they do not ask for investors. Rather, they present a position or try to create an image. Because they are not specific, many critics believe their purpose is lost on the audience and these ads are not a wise investment of the firm's resources.

Despite these criticisms and others, corporate advertising still enjoys wide usage. A variety of business-to-business and consumer-product companies continue to run corporate image ads, and numerous others have also increased expenditures in this area.

Since the term *corporate advertising* tends to be used as a catchall for any type of advertising run for the direct benefit of the corporation rather than its products or services, much advertising falls into this category. For purposes of this text (and to attempt to bring some perspective to the term), we use it to describe any type of advertising designed to promote the organization itself rather than its products or services.

Objectives of Corporate Advertising

Corporate advertising may be designed with two goals in mind: (1) creating a positive image for the firm and (2) communicating the organization's views on social, business, and environmental issues. More specific applications include:

- Boosting employee morale and smoothing labor relations.
- Helping newly deregulated industries ease consumer uncertainty and answer investor questions.
- Helping diversified companies establish an identity for the parent firm rather than relying solely on brand names.[19]

As these objectives indicate, corporate advertising is targeted at both internal and external audiences and involves the promotion of the organization as well as its ideas.

Types of Corporate Advertising

Marketers seek attainment of corporate advertising's objectives by implementing image, advocacy, or cause-related advertising. Each form is designed to achieve specific goals.

Image Advertising   One form of corporate advertising is devoted to promoting the organization's overall image. **Image advertising** may accomplish a number of objectives, including creating goodwill both internally and externally, creating a position for the company, and generating resources, both human and financial. A number of methods are used:

1. *General image or positioning ads.* As shown in Exhibit 17–13, ads are often designed to create an image of the firm in mind. The exhibit shows how Toyota is attempting to create an image of itself as an innovator and leader in caring for the environment. The ad is designed to demonstrate Toyota's concern for conservation today and preservation for the future.

2. *Sponsorships.* Firms often run corporate image advertising on TV programs or specials. For example, on the National Geographic Channel, a number of companies including Nikon, American Airlines, and others provide sponsorships to associate themselves with the quality programming shown. These and others also sponsor programs on public TV and other educational programs designed to promote the corporation as a good citizen. By associating itself with high-quality or educational programming, companies like Siemens and Starbucks as well as local sponsors hope for a carryover effect that benefits their own images.

   Other examples of sponsorships include those run by American Express (Members Project), American Airlines (UNICEF), and Nike (The Girl Effect). Exhibit 17–14 shows Whirlpool's sponsorship of the Habitat for Humanity and its efforts to fight to eliminate poverty housing. Visa considers sponsorships an important part of its integrated marketing communications. It has sponsored the Olympics, the U.S. decathlon team, FIFA, NFL, NHL, the Toronto International Film Festival, and others. The sponsorships are designed to fulfill specific business objectives while providing support for the recipients. Figure 17–5 shows a few of the companies that decided an Olympic sponsorship would be good for them.

FIGURE 17–5

2016 U.S. Olympic Sponsors and Partners

| P&G |
| Coca-Cola |
| DOW |
| ATOS |
| McDonald's |
| Samsung |
| Visa |
| GE |
| Panasonic |
| Omega |
| Bridgestone |

EXHIBIT 17–13

Toyota uses corporate image advertising for positioning

© The Advertising Archives

EXHIBIT 17–14

Whirlpool supports the fight to eliminate poverty housing

Source: Whirlpool Corporation

We don't hire Turks, Greeks, Poles, Indians, Ethiopians, Vietnamese, Chinese or Peruvians.

Nor Swedes, South Koreans or Nicaraguans. We hire individuals. We don't care what your surname is. Because ambition and determination have nothing to do with your nationality. McDonald's is one of the most integrated companies in Sweden, with as many as ninety-five nationalities working for us. Join us at mcdonalds.se

i'm lovin' it

EXHIBIT 17–15

Corporate image advertising designed to attract employees

Source: McDonald's

3. *Recruiting.* The associated ad presented in Exhibit 17–15 is a good example of corporate image advertising designed to attract new employees. The ad—in McDonald's colors—would certainly catch one's attention. (The tagline underneath reads "We hire individuals.")

4. *Generating financial support.* Some corporate advertising is designed to generate investments in the corporation. By creating a more favorable image, the firm makes itself attractive to potential stock purchasers and investors. More investments mean more working capital, more monies for research and development, and so on. In this instance, corporate image advertising is almost attempting to make a sale; the product is the firm.

Although there is no concrete evidence that corporate image advertising leads directly to increased investment, many managers believe there is, and that there is a correlation between the price of stock and the amount of corporate advertising done. Firms that spend more on corporate advertising also tend to have higher-priced stocks (though a direct relationship is very difficult to substantiate).

This thing called *image* is not unidimensional. Many factors affect it. Figure 17–6 shows the results of three different rankings from three different sources. Note that none of the corporations appear on all three lists, which shows that companies can be respected and attain a strong corporate reputation in a number of ways. The most admired firms did not gain their positions merely by publicity and word of mouth (nor, we guess, did the least admired).

A positive corporate image cannot be created just from a few advertisements. Quality of products and services, innovation, sound financial practices, good corporate citizenship, and wise marketing are just a few of the factors that contribute to overall image. In addition, the type of product marketed and emotional appeal also contribute. The surveys cited above demonstrate that profits and stock performances have little to do with reputation and that once a reputation is acquired, it has lasting power. At the same time, IMC Perspective 17–1 demonstrates just how difficult it is to maintain a reputation.

Event Sponsorships   As we noted in the last section, corporate sponsorships of charities and causes have become a popular form of public relations. While some companies sponsor specific events or causes with primarily traditional public relations objectives in mind, a separate and more marketing-oriented use of sponsorships is also on the increase. Such **event sponsorships** take on a variety of forms, as shown

FIGURE 17–6

Corporate Reputations

World's Most Admired	Best Corporate Citizens	Global Rep Track
1. Apple	Microsoft	Rolex
2. Google (Alphabet)	Intel	Walt Disney
3. Amazon.com	Hasbro	Google (Alphabet)
4. Berkshire Hathaway	Johnson & Johnson	BMW
5. Walt Disney	Ecolab	Mercedes-Benz

Sources: "World's Most Admired Companies 2016—Fortune," www.money.cnn.com; "100 Best Forbes 2016," 2016, www.Forbes.com; "The World's Most Reputable Companies," 2016, www.forbes.com.

Holding on to a Good Reputation Is Not as Easy as It Seems

Procter & Gamble, Rolex, Google, Apple—for most consumers these names are considered marketing leaders. The companies are admired, considered good corporate citizens, and have excellent reputations. What you may not realize is how difficult it is for them to maintain these positions. You may have heard of the adage, What have you done for me lately? While we may typically think of this as applying to individuals, it holds just as true for corporations. Just one mistake can bring down a firm's image in a heartbeat. Sometimes the mistake may be of their own doing, but in other cases a slight error can create major damage. Consider these examples:

Bud Light—As part of its "Up for Whatever" campaign, the beer company stamped some bottles with the tagline "the perfect beer for removing 'no' from your vocabulary for the night." Unfortunately, photos of the bottles were immediately picked up and posted on Reddit and the *Consumerist.* The next day it was circulated on social media with users claiming that it promoted a rape culture. The buzz got so great that it resulted in a tweet from U.S. Representative Nita Lowey (D-NY), criticizing the company saying that Bud Light should "promote responsible—not reckless—drinking." Brand perception scores took a major hit. After issuing an apology, Alexander Lambrecht, VP of Anheuser-Busch's Bud Light division, stated that the company would never condone disrespectful or irresponsible behavior and that the slogan would not be printed on any more bottles. He also noted that now in its second year, the campaign developed more than 140 messages that have shown to lead to consumer engagement, but this one missed the mark, and it won't happen again.

Krispy Kreme—In a promotion of its *"Krispy Kreme Klub,"* the company posted the acronym *KKK* on its Facebook page. Of course, it immediately heard about it from social media followers, and issued an apology as well as the explanation for the mistake.

Tom's of Maine—As a company that built its reputation for using only natural ingredients in its toothpastes, it wasn't exactly telling the truth. Once discovered, the misrepresentation led to a class action lawsuit and an eventual agreement to shell out $4.5 million and change its labeling practices. As noted by Mark Miller at www.brandchannel.com, the agreement didn't bring any smiles to the faces at Tom's or its parent company Colgate.

Nationwide—In an ad shown on Super Bowl 2015, Nationwide Insurance attempted to bring attention to child safety. The commercial was based on a dead child's message to his parents about neglecting household safety—a good cause. The ad, titled "Make Safe Happen," focused on preventable accidents and showed an overflowing bathtub, a litter of dishwasher pods on the floor, and a scene of an overturned TV.

© George W. Bailey/Shutterstock

Unfortunately, viewer's didn't like the ad and the public outcry on social media overshadowed the message. The ad is considered by many to be the worst Super Bowl commercial ever, and damaged the company's image. The Nationwide CMO is no longer with the company.

Others—Urban Outfitters drew the ire of Kent State University for marketing a red-stained vintage sweatshirt with the college logo and what looked like blood stains. (In 1970 Ohio National Guardsmen shot and killed four Kent State students during Vietnam War protests.) Zara marketed a striped shirt with a six-pointed yellow badge that resembled uniforms worn at Holocaust concentration camps. Hermès, the maker of handbags that sell for $10,500 to $150,000, was asked by Jane Birkin (the actress and singer for whom the bags' line was named) to have her name taken off the bag line to protest the killing of crocodiles, ostriches, and lizards once it was brought to her attention by PETA.

How do these mistakes happen? Companies that are often cited for doing good things (Bud giving out cans of water; Tom's for supporting a number of environmental causes, etc.) can also be on the receiving end of negative publicity. Clearly someone in the organization had to have noticed the slogan "Up for Whatever," was aware of the meanings of the six-pointed badge, knew about Kent State, and realized the company would draw attention in this day and age—and not positive attention. Apologists claim that America is getting overly sensitive and that it was only a joke gone bad, or a mistake, and mistakes happen. Unfortunately, sometimes mistakes can be very detrimental to a company's health. Just ask ex-Nationwide CMO Matt Jachius.

Sources: Lindsey Rupp and Duane Stanford, "Bud Light Is Sorry for Slogan That Critics Say Endorsed Rape," April 28, 2015, www.bloomberg.com; Elizabeth Bell, "Hermès, Bagged by PETA, Sees Jane Birkin Protest Her Namesake Bag," July 29, 2015, www.brandchannel.com; Dale Buss, "For Former Nationwide CMO, Super Bowl Ad Was a Preventable Accident," May 6, 2015, www.brandchannel.com; Patricia Odell, "Krispy Kreme Gets Slammed for KKK Promo," February 9, 2015, www.chiefmarketer.com; Mark J. Miller, "Tom's of Maine Admits It's Not Totally Natural with $4.5M Settlement," July 29, 2015, www.brandchannel.com.

FIGURE 17–7   North American Sponsorship Spending by Property Type

	2014 Spending	2015 Spending	Increase from 2014	2016 Spending (Projected)	Increase from 2015 (Projected)
Sports	$14.35 billion	$14.99 billion	4.5%	$15.74 billion	5.0%
Entertainment	$2.05 billion	$2.13 billion	4.1%	$2.22 billion	4.2%
Causes	$1.85 billion	$1.92 billion	4.0%	$2 billion	3.7%
Arts	$923 million	$939 million	1.7%	$970 million	3.3%
Festivals, fairs, annual events	$847 million	$860 million	1.5%	$878 million	2.1%
Associations and membership organizations	$574 million	$591 million	3.0%	$612 million	3.6%

Sources: Adapted from *Cause Marketing Forum*, 2016; IEG.

in Figure 17–7. Anything from apparel and equipment (Under Armour's sponsors men's and womens' teams in a variety of sports, and at all levels) to concerts, stadiums, and college football bowl games are now commonly used for corporate sponsorship. Like any other relationship, however, risks must be assumed by both sides in such agreements. For example, many companies that have had their names placed on stadiums—TWA Dome (St. Louis), PSINet (Baltimore), Fruit of the Loom (Miami)—have gone bankrupt, while others have had their images tarnished—Enron (Enron Field), MCI (MCI Center)—which is not good for the cities or the companies themselves. A risk taken by a company in naming a stadium is the cost of hundreds of millions of dollars, which can cause stockholders and consumers concern over the value of such an investment. At the same time, naming a stadium can lead to increased name exposure—particularly for those companies that don't have strong brand recognition. For example, MetLife insurance, whose name is on the New York Jets and New York Giants stadium, believes it has been a very good investment, based on increased exposure alone. In addition, research has shown that 99 percent of fans can recall the name of the sponsors of their stadiums, and 35 percent say it causes them to have a more favorable impression of the brand.[20]

As can be seen, sponsorship expenditures across all categories have increased. Sponsorships of sports events still account for most of the spending.

For example, the NASCAR Sprint Cup Series remains an attractive event to numerous companies, despite the increasing costs of sponsorship (Exhibit 17–16). Many companies are attracted to event sponsorships because effective IMC programs can be built around them, and promotional tie-ins can be made to local, regional, national, and even international markets. Companies are finding event sponsorships an excellent platform from which to build equity and gain affinity with target audiences as well as a good public relations tool. For example, Hertz Rental Cars recently signed a three-year deal with Penske Racing and expects it to be extended. Hertz CEO Mark Frissora considers it one of the best ways to spend his advertising dollars given the ability to reach his specific target market, as well as the number of impressions received for the investment. He also notes that 20 percent of NASCAR's fan base rent cars and he wants them to think of Hertz when they do.[21]

Advocacy Advertising   A third major form of corporate advertising addresses social, business, or environmental issues. Such **advocacy advertising** is concerned with propagating ideas and elucidating controversial social issues of public importance in a manner that supports the interests of the sponsor.

While still portraying an image for the company or organization, advocacy advertising does so indirectly, by adopting a position on a particular issue rather than promoting the organization itself. An example of advocacy advertising sponsored by the American Heart Association and the American Stroke Association and targeting teens

EXHIBIT 17-16

Hertz believes a NASCAR
sponsorship is a good
investment

© Tom Pennington/Getty Images

to stop smoking is shown in Exhibit 17–17. Advocacy advertising has increased in use over the past few years and has also met with increased criticism. An advertising campaign sponsored by the Santa Fe Natural Tobacco company was designed to create a more positive image of tobacco. The two-page ad began with a statement, "There are some things in our past you should know about," and continues on side two with statements that include the fact that the company has been supporting American farmers since the early 1990s, their tobacco is 100 percent additive-free, and it is all grown in the United States. The image of the tobacco industry in the United States has been a negative one for decades despite many attempts to change it.

Advocacy ads may be sponsored by a firm or by a trade association and are designed to tell readers how the firm operates or explain management's position on a particular issue. Sometimes the advertising is a response to negative publicity or to the firm's inability to place an important message through its regular public relations channels. At other times, the firm just wants to get certain ideas accepted or to have society understand its concerns.

Another form of advocacy advertising, **issue ads** are increasingly appearing in the media (Exhibit 17–18). While considered a form of advocacy advertising, issue ads may have no affiliation with a corporate or trade sponsor but may be sponsored by an organization to bring attention to what they consider to be an important issue. For example, after failed negotiations between the Humane Society of the United States and grocery store chain Trader Joe's, the animal welfare organization placed an issue ad with the headline "Why Won't Trader Joe's Give an Inch?" The response from Trader Joe's customers was enormous, leading the company to publicly announce that it would convert all of its brand eggs to cage free within three months. In 2007, the U.S. Supreme Court ruled that corporate and union sponsorships of issue ads (previously banned) must be permitted to run. Many believed this decision would lead to a significant increase in issue advertising.[22]

Advocacy advertising has been criticized by a number of sources. But as you can see in Exhibit 17–19, this form of communication has been around for a long time. AT&T engaged in issues-oriented advertising way back in 1908 and has continued to employ this form of communication into the 21st century. Critics contend that companies

EXHIBIT 17-17

An example of an advocacy ad

Source: US Department of Health and Human Services

with large advertising budgets purchase too much ad space and time and that advocacy ads may be misleading, but the checks and balances of regular product advertising also operate in this area.

Cause-Related Advertising   An increasingly popular method of image building is **cause-related marketing**, in which companies link with charities or nonprofit organizations as contributing sponsors. Over 2.0 billion was spent on cause marketing in 2016.[23] The company benefits from favorable publicity, while the charity receives much-needed funds. Proponents of cause marketing say that association with a cause may differentiate one brand or store from another, increase consumer acceptance of price increases, generate favorable publicity, and even win over skeptical officials who may have an impact on the company. Indeed, one study showed that association with a cause will impact consumers' purchase decisions—making them more likely to buy from the sponsor, while another showed that consumers are more likely to trust a brand that supports causes.[24] Apple, Google, Microsoft, and Pepsi are just a few brands well known for their support of causes. Cause-marketing relationships can take a variety of forms. Making outright donations to a nonprofit cause, having companies volunteer for the cause, donating materials or supplies, running public service announcements, or even providing event refreshments are some of the ways companies get involved. Exhibit 17–20 shows an

EXHIBIT 17–18

Issue ads like this one from the NRDC.org against air pollution are on the increase

Source: National Resources Defense Council

EXHIBIT 17–19

AT&T has used advocacy ads for years

© *Jay Paul/Getty Images*

EXHIBIT 17–20

This ad was part of a campaign designed to stop domestic violence

Source: House of Ruth Maryland

event titled "High Heels for Hope." The proceeds from this event went directly to the House of Ruth in Baltimore, Maryland—a cause supporting women and youth who have suffered from domestic violence. The campaign was targeted to those attempting to overcome the impact of domestic violence.

At the same time, not all cause marketing is a guarantee of success. Cause marketing requires more than just associating with a social issue, and it takes time and effort. Companies have gotten into trouble by misleading consumers about their relationships, and others have wasted money by supporting a cause that offered little synergism. One survey showed that more than 300 companies associated themselves with breast cancer concerns, but most became lost in sponsorship clutter. Another has shown that consumers are becoming more skeptical and are demanding more accountability from companies' cause-marketing efforts.[25] Others have simply picked the wrong cause—finding that their customers and potential customers either have little interest in or don't support the cause. In some cases, cause marketing is considered nothing more than shock advertising. Finally, the results of cause-marketing efforts can sometimes be hard to quantify.

Advantages and Disadvantages of Corporate Advertising

A number of reasons for the increased popularity of corporate advertising become evident when you examine the advantages of this form of communication:

1. *It is an excellent vehicle for positioning the firm.* Firms, like products, need to establish an image or position in the marketplace. Corporate image ads are one way to accomplish this objective. A well-positioned product is much more likely to achieve success than is one with a vague or no image. The same holds true of the firm. Stop and think for a moment about the image that comes to mind when you hear the name Apple, Johnson & Johnson, or Procter & Gamble.

   Now what comes to mind when you hear Unisys, USX, or Navistar? How many consumer brands can you name that fall under ConAgra's corporate umbrella (Hunts, Chef Boyardee, Pam, Slim-Jims, and many others)? While we are not saying these latter companies are not successful—because they certainly are—we are suggesting their corporate identities (or positions) are not as well entrenched as the identities of those first cited. Companies with strong positive corporate images have an advantage over competitors that may be enhanced when they promote the company overall.

2. *It takes advantage of the benefits derived from public relations.* As the PR efforts of firms have increased, the attention paid to these events by the media has lessened (not because they are of any less value, but because there are more events to cover). The net result is that when a company engages in a public relations effort, there is no guarantee it will receive press coverage and publicity. Corporate image advertising gets the message out, and though consumers may not perceive it as positively as information from an objective source, the fact remains that it can communicate what has been done.

3. *It reaches a select target market.* Corporate image advertising should not be targeted to the general public. It is often targeted to investors and managers of other firms rather than to the general public. It doesn't matter if the general public does not appreciate this form of communication, as long as the target market does (remember the Hertz–Penske relationship?). In this respect, this form of advertising may be accomplishing its objectives.

Some of the disadvantages of corporate advertising were alluded to earlier in the chapter. To these criticisms, we can add the following:

1. *Questionable effectiveness.* There is no strong evidence to support the belief that corporate advertising works. Many doubt the data cited earlier that demonstrated a correlation between stock prices and corporate image advertising as some studies show little support for this effect.
2. *Constitutionality and/or ethics.* Some critics contend that since larger firms have more money, they can control public opinion unfairly. This point was resolved in the courts in favor of the advertisers. Nevertheless, many consumers still see such advertising as unfair given the great disparities that sometimes exist in financial resources available to some but not others, and immediately take a negative view of the sponsor.

A number of valid points have been offered for and against corporate advertising. Two things are certain: (1) No one knows who is right, and (2) the use of this communications form continues to increase.

Measuring the Effectiveness of Corporate Advertising

As you can tell from our discussion of the controversy surrounding corporate advertising, there needs to be methods for evaluating whether or not such advertising is effective:

- *Attitude surveys.* One way to determine the effectiveness of corporate advertising is to conduct attitude surveys to gain insights into both the public's and investors' reactions to ads. A study conducted by Janas Sinclair and Tracy Irani on advocacy advertising in the biotechnology industry employed a survey research methodology to demonstrate that public accountability was a good predictor of corporate trustworthiness, and this and the attitude toward the advertiser would predict consumers' attitude toward the ad, biotechnology, and purchase intentions.[26] Studies reported on earlier in this chapter show the many positive effects that companies that engage in corporate advertising might receive. The firm measured recall and attitude toward corporate advertisers and found that corporate advertising is more efficient in building recall for a company name than is product advertising alone. Frequent corporate advertisers rated better on virtually all attitude measures than those with low corporate ad budgets.
- *Studies relating corporate advertising and stock prices.* A number of studies have examined the effect of various elements of corporate advertising (position in the magazine, source effects, etc.) on stock prices. These studies have yielded conflicting conclusions, indicating that while the model for such measures seems logical, methodological problems may account for at least some of the discrepancies.
- *Focus group research.* Focus groups have been used to find out what investors want to see in ads and how they react after the ads are developed. As with product-oriented advertising, this method has limitations, although it does allow for some effective measurements.

While the effectiveness of corporate advertising has been measured by some of the methods used to measure product-specific advertising, reported research in this area has not kept pace with that of the consumer market. The most commonly offered reason for this lack of effort is that corporate ads are often the responsibility of those in the highest management positions in the firm, and these parties do not wish to be held accountable. It is interesting that those who should be most concerned with accountability are the most likely to shun this responsibility!

Summary

This chapter examined the role of the promotional elements of public relations, publicity, and corporate advertising. We noted that these areas are all significant to the marketing and communications effort and are usually considered differently from the other promotional elements. Nevertheless, companies are increasing their use of these touch points in their IMC programs.

Public relations was shown to be useful in its traditional responsibilities as well as in a more marketing-oriented role. In many firms, PR is a separate department operating independently of marketing; in others, it is considered a support system. Many companies now effectively use PR as an IMC tool, with established MPR objectives. Many large firms have an external public relations agency, just as they have an outside ad agency.

In the case of publicity, another factor enters the equation: lack of control over the communication the public will receive. In public relations and corporate advertising, the organization remains the source and retains much more control. Publicity often takes more of a reactive than a proactive approach, yet it may be more instrumental (or detrimental) to the success of a product or organization than all other forms of promotion combined.

Although not all publicity can be managed, the marketer must nevertheless recognize its potential impact. Press releases and the management of information are just two of the factors under the company's control. Proper reaction and a strategy to deal with uncontrollable events are also critical responsibilities.

Corporate advertising was described as controversial, largely because the source of the message is often top management, so the rules for other advertising and promoting forms are often not applied. This element of communication definitely has its place in the promotional mix. But to be effective, it must be used with each of the other elements, with specific communications objectives in mind. The growing importance of cause, issue, and advocacy marketing was also discussed.

Finally, we noted that measures of evaluation and control are required for each of these program elements, just as they are for all others in the promotional mix. We presented some methods for taking such measurements and some evidence showing why it is important to use them. As long as the elements of public relations, publicity, and corporate advertising are considered integral components of the overall communications strategy, they must respect the same rules as the other promotional-mix elements to ensure success.

Key Terms

public relations (PR) 581
marketing public relations (MPR) 582
internal audiences 587
external audiences 587
press release 590
press conference 590

exclusive 591
Public Relations Society of
America 594
publicity 596
video news release (VNR) 597
corporate advertising 598

image advertising 600
event sponsorship 601
advocacy advertising 603
issue advertising (issue ad) 604
cause-related marketing 605

Discussion Questions

1. The chapter discusses a number of public relations blunders, many of which might have been avoided with due diligence. Explain why these mistakes occur and who is ultimately responsible. (LO 17-2)

2. What impact do you think the millennial generation will have on cause marketing, issue advertising, and advocacy advertising? Explain your reasoning. (LO 17-1)

3. Explain the differences between traditional and the new public relations objectives (MPRs). What are the advantages and disadvantages of each? (LO 17-2)

4. Describe some of the measures used to measure public relations effectiveness. Critique these and provide an overall critique of their validity. (LO 17-4)

5. Describe the conflict between traditional PR agencies and those that see PR as more of a marketing function. Cite reasons why each of these groups holds the position it does. Who is right? (LO 17-1)

6. As noted in the chapter lead-in, many companies have suffered from the consequences of negative publicity. Discuss what companies might do to ward off the negative impact of bad press. How well did the companies in the chapter fare? (LO 17-2)

7. Research studies have indicated that cause marketing can actually lead to an increased intention to purchase a brand. Explain why this is the case and provide examples that you feel may pertain. (LO 17-5)

8. Putting one's name on a stadium can be an expensive proposition, and the prices continue to increase. Discuss whether this would be a good investment for a company, and why or why not. Give examples of companies for which this might be a good investment. (LO 17-3)

9. The chapter discusses cause marketing, advocacy advertising, and issue ads. Explain the differences between these forms of communication and give examples of each. (LO 17-5)

10. Social media have had a profound impact on the power of publicity. Explain what this means and whether you believe it to be true or not. Provide examples to support your position. (LO 17-2)

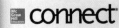 **connect**

Digital users can access their personalized and adaptive SmartBook, Ad Forum Video Cases, and interactive exercises to review chapter concepts.

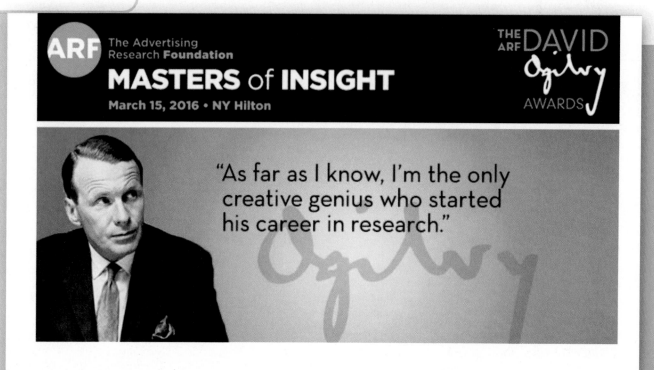

Source: ARF.org

LEARNING OBJECTIVES

LO1 Compare reasons for and against measuring the effectiveness of promotional programs.

LO2 Describe the tools and processes available for assessing promotional program effectiveness.

LO3 Discuss the limitations of current methods for measuring advertising effects.

LO4 Compare different methods of measuring effectiveness of other promotional programs.

One of the most prestigious awards an advertising agency and its client can receive is an Ogilvy Award. The award is named for longtime advertising executive David Ogilvy, who was always a strong advocate of the use of research in advertising. Sponsored by the Advertising Research Foundation (ARF), the awards are given for excellence in advertising research and/or the creative use of research in the advertising development process. While initially the awards were purely advertising related, awards are now given in a variety of communications areas. The 2016 Grand Ogilvy Award was won by Nestlé for the Lean Cuisine brand.

Campaign Title: *#WeighThis Brand: Nestlé Lean Cuisine*

Category: Social Media

Lean Cuisine—frozen meals targeted to the weight conscious and those on a diet—was in its fifth year of sales declines, and Nestlé knew it had to do something fast to save the brand. Since its peak in the 1980s, the brand had lost 70 percent of its customers and 12 percent of the shelf space being allocated to it by retailers. Through social segmentation and brand perception analysis, Nestlé and partner MetaVision discovered that when consumers had conversations about the brand, they were mostly functional and lacking emotional relevance. They also observed that while female consumers lead accomplished lives, they felt that they lived in a society that continues to judge women only by appearance. A social media campaign was developed, called #WeighThis, that focused on the accomplishments that fuel successful lifestyles for women. The centerpiece of the campaign was an emotionally powerful video featuring real women weighing their life accomplishments in lieu of their bodies. #WeighThis was an integral part of Lean Cuisine's turnaround strategy and largely contributed to the brand seeing its first sales increase in six years, despite a decline in media spending.

Research employed by MetaVision included social listening which entailed volume trend analysis, in-depth social sentiment analysis, 360i Tribe Analysis, and 360i Brand Compass to determine insights that would lead to the development of a campaign that would resonate with the existing Lean Cuisine audience and potential consumers. Through MetaVision's proprietary social segmentation research (Tribe Analysis) and brand perception analysis (Brand Compass), it was determined that the product was consistently the butt of jokes, and cultural references about who was perceived to be the Lean Cuisine consumer: "a lonely single female eating dinner at home alone." However, the research also showed that Lean Cuisine's core target was a woman who was actually quite successful (high-income earners, college graduates, hard workers that provided for others), but existing in a society that continued to judge her not by her accomplishments, but rather her appearance.

The creative strategy was designed to reposition the brand into more of an emotional space and promote conversation that would lead to an image that was about more than just dieting. The message focused less on functional attributes, and more on emotional drivers and accomplishments that lead to a successful lifestyle for women. The spots featured real women weighing their accomplishments—becoming a parent, making the dean's list as a single mother, and traveling the world—in lieu of weighing their bodies. The media strategy included placing the centerpiece video on Facebook, Twitter, and YouTube and utilized paid media, PR, and influencer marketing to communicate the message. Throughout the campaign, women were encouraged to share the ways in which they would like to be weighed using the hashtag #WeighThis on Lean Cuisine's social channels, promoting an open conversation about meaningful accomplishments.

As noted earlier, #WeighThis was an integral part of Lean Cuisine's turnaround strategy and largely contributed to the brand seeing its first sales increase in six years. Almost immediately, the brand experienced double-digit growth, and the #WeighThis video was an instant viral success, contributing to a 33 percent increase in positive brand perception. Within the first week of launch, the video reached the number 9 spot in the *Ad Age* Viral Video chart with a 6.5 million reach. Year-over-year conversations about Lean Cuisine increased by 178 percent across social media, and increased the brand's competitive share of voice by 19 percentage points. The campaign resonated emotionally with consumers describing how they wanted to be weighed, and reduced share of negative conversations around Lean Cuisine on social media to just 4 percent—a decrease from the previous year's share of 25 percent negativity. Lean Cuisine is no longer perceived as a lonely, single woman's quick-fix dinner, but rather an advocate for female empowerment—and is the *Grand Ogilvy Award Winner!*

Case studies of numerous other award winners can be found at the Ogilvy Awards website (www.thearf.org/2016-arf-david-ogilvy-awards). The awards are given in a variety of categories including (1) the use of big data, (2) creative effectiveness, (3) cross platform, (4) innovation, (5) media, (6) mobile, (7) new audiences, and (8) social media. Following is a sampling just to give you an idea, with the category winner in parentheses:

Use of Big Data (Warner Brothers)—Warner Brothers Home Entertainment team strategically aggregated big data from over 30 data sources to ensure its plan for promoting the movie *Pan* could be data driven to achieve maximum ROI. An integrative team was put together to include participants from creative, traditional media, digital media, social media, research/analytics, and others. The team was able to select the right TV networks/dayparts, identify the best programmatic segments to leverage, and uncover the right Facebook segments for targeting, which led to a successful media strategy and a successful launch of the movie.

Creative Effectiveness (Ontario Women's Directorate)—Because sexual violence and harassment are shockingly prevalent in Canadian society, the directorate worked on a program designed to help reduce the problem. After reviewing 20 years of behavioral studies on the issue of sexual violence and harassment, and interviewing two of the top Canadian behavioral experts on violence against women, the Ontario Women's Directorate reviewed sexual assault statistics in Canada. The directorate determined that to be successful, it was critical to understand the cultural norms and behavioral motivation surrounding the persistent issue of sexual violence and harassment. After reviewing surveys conducted by the Public Health Agency of Canada and Ipsos and Ipsos Reid, the directorate found that while 80 percent of people said they have an obligation to intervene in cases of harassment and 81 percent to intervene in cases of violence, the gap between intention and action was the most telling. Only 37 percent of respondents said they would actually take action and get involved when witnessing violence or harassment. This led to a launch of the provocative campaign #WhoWillYouHelp, which took a unique approach by targeting the bystander. In an Ipsos Reid Mid Campaign Tracking report, 71 percent of respondents strongly agreed that people should speak out more about sexual harassment and violence against women compared to 63 percent before the campaign. The campaign also encouraged intervention among bystanders in a variety of scenarios involving sexual harassment and assault. Half of Ontarians polled recalled the provocative advertisement, and research among those who recalled the ad resulted in their saying, "I have an obligation to intervene if I witness sexual harassment" (pre-campaign, 37 percent; post-campaign, 58 percent) and "If I witness sexual harassment and don't intervene, I'm making the decision to allow it to continue (pre-campaign, 37%; post-campaign, 53 percent).

These examples of using research to develop successful campaigns are just a few of the many out there. Each demonstrates how the research guides development and provides and indication of success or failure. Just as David Ogilvy drew it up!

Source: "2016 ARF David Ogilvy Awards," www.theARF.org.

As noted throughout this text, the increased emphasis on accountability is forcing many companies to evaluate, or reevaluate, their IMC plans. Both clients and agencies are continually striving to determine whether their communications are working and how well they are working relative to other options. A number of studies indicate that marketing managers are not confident in the metrics they are currently using and are searching for new methods designed to assist in this endeavor. Companies and organizations continue to work together in an attempt to provide answers to these questions and to develop new ways to measure communications effectiveness.

Measuring the effectiveness of the promotional program is a critical element in the IMC planning process. Research allows the marketing manager to evaluate the performance of specific program elements and provides input into the next period's situation analysis. It is a necessary ingredient to a continuing planning process, yet it is often not carried out.

In this chapter, we discuss some reasons firms should measure the effectiveness of their IMC programs, as well as why many decide not to. We also examine how, when, and where such measurements can be conducted. Most of our attention is devoted to measuring the effects of advertising because much more time and effort have been expended developing evaluation measures in advertising than in the other promotional areas. We will, however, discuss measurement in other areas of the IMC program as well. You'll recall that we addressed the methods used to evaluate many of the other promotional elements in previous chapters.

It is important to understand that in this chapter we are concerned with research that is conducted in an evaluative role—that is, to measure the effectiveness of advertising and promotion and/or to assess various strategies before implementing them. This is not to be confused with research discussed earlier in the text to help develop the promotional program, although the two can (and should) be used together, as you will see. While evaluative research may occur at various times throughout the promotional process (including the development stage), it is conducted specifically to assess the effects of various strategies. We begin our discussion with the reasons effectiveness should be measured as well as some of the reasons firms do not do so.

ARGUMENTS FOR AND AGAINST MEASURING EFFECTIVENESS

Almost anytime one engages in a project or activity, whether for work or for fun, some measure of performance occurs. In sports, you may compare your golf score against par or your time on a ski course to other skiers' performance. In business, employees are generally given objectives to accomplish, and their job evaluations are based on their ability to achieve these objectives. Advertising and promotion should not be an exception. It is important to determine how well the communications program is working and to measure this performance against some standards.

Reasons to Measure Effectiveness

Assessing the effectiveness of ads both before they are implemented and after the final versions have been completed and fielded offers a number of advantages:

1. *Avoiding costly mistakes.* The top three advertisers in the United States were expected to spend over $10 billion in advertising and promotion in 2015. The top 10 spent a total of over $25 billion.[1] This is a lot of money to be throwing around without some understanding of how well it is being spent. If the program is not achieving its objectives, the marketing manager needs to know so he or she can stop spending (wasting) money on it.

   Just as important as the out-of-pocket costs is the opportunity loss due to poor communications. If the advertising and promotional program is not accomplishing its objectives, not only is the money spent lost but so too is the potential gain that could result from an effective program. Thus, measuring the effects of advertising does not just save money. It also helps the firm maximize its investment.

2. *Evaluating alternative strategies.* Typically a firm has a number of strategies under consideration. For example, there may be some question as to the degree to which each medium should be used or whether one message is more effective than another. Or the decision may be between two promotional program elements. A key issue for the manager is to be able to determine how effective each one was. Numerous companies have also reallocated monies to nontraditional media. A number of studies have revealed that advertisers said they planned to spend more monies in digital and social media in the coming years. The question is, should research be spent on traditional, social, or digital advertising or other media and in what combination? Research may be designed to help the manager determine which strategy is most likely to be effective.

3. *Increasing the efficiency of advertising in general.* You may have heard the expression "can't see the forest for the trees." Sometimes advertisers get so

Digital and Social Media Perspective 18–1 > > >

THE ADVERTISING EFFECTIVENESS METRICS OF THE FUTURE—TESTING EMOTIONS?

It has always been a struggle for managers to get an idea of how well their advertising programs were working. To make matters worse, when they have taken efforts to determine the effectiveness of their programs, they often got pushback from their ad agencies, which argued (and still do!) that it is difficult to measure how ads are contributing to the overall marketing program, and that measuring could actually lead to *lower* effectiveness by stifling creativity. But then, shareholders and others arguing for some of the monies being spent on advertising began to have an impact and marketers started to pay more attention to metrics that might provide them with data to make better management decisions. With the rapid adoption of new digital media, it seems that marketers are (or at least some feel that they are) regressing to a time long ago because it is so difficult to measure the contribution that these new media are making to the overall marketing program. Add to this the fact that there are often more time pressures when placing ads in these media, and the problem increases.

Over the years advertisers came to an agreement as to what measures should be used to measure the effectiveness in traditional media. However, there is no such consensus with social and digital at this point, and there are still many companies that use new media metrics only to evaluate their IMC programs. At the same time, there are numerous studies that show that managers say they do not feel that they have a good understanding of marketing effectiveness in either

channel. Agencies are even more skeptical, believing that their clients' understanding of the effects range from nonexistent to "poor."

And the disagreement goes on. For example, one article appears contending that online metrics have replaced traditional measures of knowing the effect of ads on consumers in the purchase funnel. Another study also demonstrates that online metrics can be useful for this purpose. Score one for the digital folks! But then there are others, like Shane Snow, who argue that marketers are getting it all wrong, and that "the next big trend in media is going to require us to rethink publishing metrics entirely." Jack Marshall contends that attempts to measure native advertising are "all over the map." Some managers have even argued that since different companies have different objectives for their campaign, metrics are superfluous. In a survey conducted by the Association of National Advertisers, many managers said they were still trying to figure out exactly what they should measure. In reviewing the survey, the ANA's executive vice president, Bill Duggan, noted that the lack of standardized metrics may hamper future growth.

To make things even more complicated, there is a growing interest in measures that don't neatly fit into either the digital or traditional category. An article in *Advertising Age* says the future of measurement may not come from surveys but from smiles and/or smirks. The article notes that if

close to the project they lose sight of what they are seeking, and because they know what they are trying to say, they expect their audience will also understand. They may use technical jargon that not everyone is familiar with. Or the creative department may get too creative or too sophisticated and lose the meaning that needs to be communicated. How many times have you seen an ad and asked yourself what it was trying to say, or how often have you seen an ad that you really like, but you can't remember the brand name? Conducting research helps companies develop more efficient and effective communications. An increasing number of clients are demanding accountability for their promotional programs and putting more pressure on the agencies to produce. As the lead-in to this chapter discussing the Ogilvy Award winners demonstrates, effective research can be used for both of these purposes. The way to conduct this research is not so clear, as can be seen in Digital and Social Media Perspective 18–1).

4. *Determining if objectives are achieved.* In a well-designed IMC plan, specific communication objectives are established. If objectives are attained, new ones need to be established in the next planning period. An assessment of how program elements led to the attainment of the goals should take place, and/or reasons for less-than-desired achievements must be determined. Research should address whether the strategy delivers the stated objectives and how appropriate the measures used to make this assessment are.

© lipik/Shutterstock RF

has roots at the Machine Perception Lab at the University of California, San Diego. Emotient conducts facial recognition studies in controlled groups but is increasing its emphasis on testing ads "in the wild"—that is, analyzing the facial expressions of people viewing ads on digital signs in real life.

So what's the answer? As you will see in this chapter, marketers are trying a variety of methods to try to find out. Many of these measures are new, some have been around for a while, and some are a combination of old and new. New techniques like eye tracking, facial recognition, and neuroscience applications are being used alongside traditional recall and attitude measurement techniques. More and more retailers are using attribution modeling to attempt to determine how various media touch points are performing, and there has been an increase in measuring the effectiveness of emotional versus cognitive ads, the impact of creativity, storytelling versus hard sell, and so on.

Whereas marketers have disagreed on both the value of measuring effectiveness and how to measure for a long time, few these days argue against the need to determine the former. There also seems to be a movement to employ various methods at the same time. As noted by both Affectiva and Millward Brown, facial recognition should not be used in isolation, but as a complement to traditional copy testing methods. Maybe we can all agree to that?

you want to know how people react to an ad you need to measure how they feel, not ask them. A number of new companies now offer sophisticated "facial recognition" technologies. For example, Kellogg Company, Mars, Inc., and Unilever have used the services of Affectiva to measure and analyze moment-to-moment facial expressions of people watching videos on a smartphone or laptop. Affectiva's CEO Nicholas Langeveld says that "people have a really hard time articulating their feelings. And sometimes there is a subtle fleeting little emotion that people aren't even aware is happening." Facial recognition will capture these emotions, supporters say. Research company Millward Brown now offers facial recognition as part of its ad testing suites, and Nielsen and others do as well. A competitor of Affectiva is Emotient, which

Sources: "Facial-Recognition Lets Marketers Gauge Consumers' Real Responses to Ads," May 18, 2015, www.adage.com; Shane Snow, "Brands Are Measuring Their Content All Wrong," April 22, 2014, www.contently.com; Jack Marshall, "Native Advertising Measurement Is All over the Map," April 17, 2015, www.wsj.com; "Display Ad Effectiveness in the Purchase Funnel," October 22, 2015, www.msi.org; Laurie Sullivan, "Marketing Budgets Rise, Determining Multi-Channel ROI, Metrics Remains a Challenge," February 5, 2013, www.mediapost.com; Laurie Sullivan, "Retailers Use Attribution Modeling to Measure the Touchpoints Driving Sales," May 28, 2013, www.emarketer.com.

Reasons Not to Measure Effectiveness

While it seems obvious that it makes sense to measure effectiveness, the fact remains that in too many instances this is not done. Whereas advertisers know that it is important to measure effectiveness, with as many as 90 percent considering it a priority, many do not do so, or if they do, they are not confident of the results. On the positive side, 54 percent of these managers say they plan to increase their expenditures in this area.[2]

Companies give a number of reasons for not measuring the effectiveness of advertising and promotions strategies:

1. *Cost.* Perhaps the most commonly cited reason for not testing (particularly among smaller firms) is the expense. In one of the surveys cited, it was noted that while some companies spend as much as 25 percent of their revenue on marketing and advertising, 70 percent of them spend less than 2 percent on measuring effectiveness.[3] Good research can be expensive in terms of both time and money. Many managers decide that time is critical and they must implement the program while the opportunity is available. Many believe the monies spent on research could be better spent on improved production of the ad, additional media buys, and the like.

    While the first argument may have some merit, the second does not. Imagine what would happen if a poor campaign were developed or the incentive program did not motivate the target audience. Not only would you be spending money without the desired effects, but the effort could do more harm than good. Spending more money to buy media does not remedy a poor message or substitute for an improper promotional mix. For example, one of the nation's leading brewers watched its test-market sales for a new brand of beer fall short of expectations. The problem, it thought, was an insufficient media buy. The solution, it decided, was to buy all the TV time available that matched its target audience. After two months, sales had not improved and the product was abandoned in the test market. Analysis showed the problem was not in the media but rather in the message, which communicated no reason to buy. Research would have identified the problem, and millions of dollars and a brand might have been saved. The moral: Spending research monies to gain increased exposure to the wrong message is not a sound management decision. Also, keep in mind the Nationwide Insurance ad discussed in Chapter 17 about the little boy talking from his grave about avoidable accidents. It is very possible that this ad may never have been shown if properly tested prior to airing.

2. *Research problems.* A second reason cited for not measuring effectiveness is that it is difficult to isolate the effects of promotional elements. Each variable in the marketing mix affects the success of a product or service. Because it is often difficult to measure the contribution of each marketing element directly, some managers become frustrated and decide not to test at all. They say, "If I can't determine the specific effects, why spend the money?" In a study conducted by the Fournaise Marketing Group—a marketing performance and measurement business—reviewing over 500 marketing campaigns, briefs, and effectiveness reports, it concluded that the metrics being used were "shocking" in a very negative sense.[4] Simply put, the report concluded that marketers did not understand how to measure effectiveness.

   This argument that not being able to determine specific effects, so no measurement should take place, suffers from weak logic. While we agree that it is not always possible to determine the dollar amount of sales contributed by promotions, research can provide useful results and, as shown throughout this text, most have useful and specific metrics to evaluate their performance.

3. *Disagreement on what to test.* The objectives sought in the promotional program may differ by industry, by stage of the product life cycle, or even for different people within the firm. There are numerous ways to measure these and not always a consensus as to what measure should be used. The sales manager may want to see the impact of promotions on sales, top management may wish to know the impact on corporate image, and those involved in the creative process may wish to assess recall and/or recognition of the ad. The metrics used to measure effectiveness in traditional media are often quite different than those for digital media. Lack of agreement on what to test often results in no testing at all. A study conducted by the 4As and ANA revealed that many marketers were dissatisfied with their efforts to integrate traditional and digital media, and there is a need to develop appropriate metrics for doing so. At the same time there is much disagreement as to what to measure. As shown in Figure 18–1, a variety of metrics are used in measuring the effectiveness of social media alone, and these measures continue to change.

   Again, there is little rationale for this position. With the proper design, many or even all of the above might be measured. Since every promotional element is designed to accomplish specific objectives while contributing to the overall program, research can be used to measure its effectiveness in doing so.

4. *The objections of creative.* It has been argued by many (and denied by others) that the creative department does not want its work to be tested and many agencies are reluctant to submit their work for testing. This is sometimes true. Ad agencies' creative departments argue that tests are not true measures of the creativity and effectiveness of ads; applying measures stifles their creativity; and the more creative the ad, the more likely it is to be successful. They

FIGURE 18-1

Marketers Use a Variety of
Social Media Metrics

Metrics	Percentage of Respondents		
	August 2010	February 2013	August 2014
Page views/visits/hits	47.6%	40.9%	60.7%
How many friends or followers	24.0	30.5	45.0
Repeat visits	34.7	24.9	38.7
Convert from visitor to buyer	25.4	21.1	31.3
Web mentions	15.7	16.2	24.2
Levels of sales	17.9	8.7	16.8
Ratings for online products and services	8.2	6.0	14.0
Customer acquisition costs	11.8	10.2	13.7
Net promoter score	7.5	9.8	12.8
Revenue per customer	17.2	9.2	12.5
Ratings for other text analysis	6.6	8.5	11.7
Costs for customer retention	7.7	3.0	6.3
Shopping carts abandoned	3.8	2.8	6.0
Profits per customer	9.4	4.5	6.0

Source: eMarketer.com.

EXHIBIT 18-1

In this ad CHIAT/DAY
expresses its opinion of recall
tests by offering a case history
of the 1984 Apple Commercial

Source: TBWA/CHIAT/DAY

want permission to be creative without the limiting guidelines marketing may impose. The Chiat/Day ad shown in Exhibit 18–1 reflects how many people in the advertising business feel about this subject.

At the same time, the marketing manager is ultimately responsible for the success of the product or brand. Given the substantial sums being allocated to advertising and promotion, it is the manager's right, and responsibility, to know how well a specific program—or a specific ad—will perform in the market. As you have seen throughout this text, managers are placing much more emphasis on social and digital media at the expense of traditional strategies—not just media but creative strategies as well, much to the chagrin of creative directors. A very interesting study by comScore ARS measured the contribution that effective creative versus other marketing variables—ad quality, the media plan, and other elements (price, promotions, distribution, etc.)—made to campaign effectiveness (Figure 18–2).[5]

5. *Time.* A final reason given for not testing is a lack of time. Managers believe they already have too much to do and just can't get around to testing, and they don't want to wait to get the message out because they might miss the window of opportunity. Planning might be the solution to the first problem. An article in *Advertising Age* indicates that time pressures are actually on the increase, particularly when it comes to digital. The speed to get content out in the digital age puts a spotlight on previous processes used to validate ad concepts before they are put into the market. As a result, many marketers are eschewing traditional copy testing methods and taking the risk that their ads will succeed on a hunch or gut feel. Although many managers are overworked and time poor, research is just too important to skip.

Variables	Contribution to Sales Changes (Percent)*
Ad quality†	52%
Media plan‡	13
Other (price, promotion, distribution, etc.)	35

*Numbers represent the percent variance in market share shifts explained by the corresponding factors.

†Ad quality represents the quality of creative based on the ARS Persuasion Score, which measures changes in consumer preference through a simulated purchase.

‡Media plan includes variables such as GRPs, wearout, and continuity/flighting of airing.

Source: comScore ARS Global Validation Summary.

The second argument can also be overcome with proper planning. Responding to these needs, Millward Brown is in the process of developing new tools that will allow marketers to test different versions of creative ideas and get results back within hours. While timeliness is critical, getting the wrong message out is of little or no value and may even be harmful. There will be occasions where market opportunities require choosing between testing and immediate implementation. But even then some testing may help avoid mistakes or improve effectiveness.

CONDUCTING RESEARCH TO MEASURE ADVERTISING EFFECTIVENESS

What to Test

We now examine how to measure the effects of communications. This section considers what elements to evaluate, as well as where and how such evaluations should occur.

In Chapter 5 we discussed the components of the communication model (source, message, media, receiver) and the importance of each in the promotional program. Marketers need to determine how each is affecting the communication process. Other decisions made in the promotional planning process must also be evaluated.

Source Factors An important question is whether the spokesperson being used is effective and how the target market will respond to him or her. Or a product spokesperson may be an excellent source initially but, owing to a variety of reasons, may lose impact over time. As shown in Chapter 17, negative publicity can easily change the value of a source. The fact that so many of the companies using Lance Armstrong as a spokesperson terminated their contracts with him was based on the expectation that the target audiences would no longer have positive perceptions of him. The list of celebrities who have fallen out of favor is a long one.

Message Variables Both the message and the means by which it is communicated are bases for evaluation. For example, in the beer example discussed earlier, the message never provided a reason for consumers to try the new product. In other instances, the message may not be strong enough to pull readers into the ad by attracting their attention or clear enough to help them evaluate the product. Sometimes the message is memorable but doesn't achieve the other goals set by management. For example, one study examined what effect sexually themed print ads would have on viewers. Among the numerous results was that men favor sex appeals more than women do and that recall of the brands was lower for sexual ads than for nonsexual ones. Whereas men responded that sexual ads have "high stopping power" for them, their lower brand recall seems to indicate that they are paying more attention to other aspects of the ad than the marketers would prefer.[6] A number of companies are now attempting to determine the specific reactions that viewers have to product and brand messages, including excitement, engagement, stress, and anxiety responses.

Media Strategies   Research may be designed in an attempt to determine which media class (for example, broadcast versus print), subclass (newspapers versus magazines), or specific vehicles (which newspapers or magazines) generate the most effective results. Likewise, how does one digital medium compare relative to others, or to traditional media? Perhaps most importantly, how does each medium contribute to the achievement of overall IMC objectives?

An important factor is the **vehicle option source effect**, "the differential impact that the advertising exposure will have on the same audience member if the exposure occurs in one media option rather than another." People perceive ads differently depending on their context.[7]

Another factor to consider in media decisions involves scheduling. The evaluation of flighting versus pulsing or continuous schedules is important, particularly given the increasing costs of media time. As discussed in Chapter 10, there is evidence to support the fact that continuity may lead to a more effective media schedule than does flighting. Likewise, there may be opportunities associated with increasing advertising weights in periods of downward sales cycles or recessions. The manager experimenting with these alternative schedules and/or budget outlays should attempt to measure their differential impact.

As more and more companies and organizations move toward an integrated media mix, it becomes increasingly important to attempt to determine the individual contributions of various media as well as their synergistic effect. As you will see later in this chapter, progress is being made in this regard, but making such a determination is not a simple task.

Budgeting Decisions   A number of studies have examined the effects of budget size on advertising effectiveness and the effects of various ad expenditures on sales. Many companies have also attempted to determine whether increasing their ad budget directly increases sales. This relationship is often hard to determine, perhaps because using sales as an indicator of effectiveness ignores the impact of other marketing-mix elements. More definitive conclusions may be possible if other dependent variables, such as the communications objectives stated earlier, are used.

When to Test

Virtually all test measures can be classified according to when they are conducted. **Pretests** are measures taken before the campaign is implemented; **posttests** occur after the ad or commercial has been in the field. A variety of pretests and posttests are available to the marketer, each with its own methodology designed to measure some aspect of the advertising program. Figure 18–3 classifies these testing methods.

Pretesting   Pretests may occur at a number of points, from as early on as idea generation to rough execution to testing the final version before implementing it. More than one type of pretest may be used. For example, concept testing (which is discussed later in this chapter) may take place at the earliest development of the ad or commercial, when little more than an idea, basic concept, or positioning statement is under consideration. In other instances, layouts of the ad campaign that include headlines, some body copy, and rough illustrations are used. For TV commercials, storyboards and animatics may be tested. In these tests specific shortcomings may be identified, and changes made to enhance certain executional elements. As noted by Cramphorn, the best reason to pretest is to identify winners, to enhance good ads, and to eliminate bad ones. He notes that it is important to know the probable effect the ad will have before committing to its use.[8]

FIGURE 18–3

Classification of Testing Methods

Pretests		
Laboratory Methods		
Consumer juries	Theater tests	Readability tests
Portfolio tests	Rough tests	Comprehension and reaction tests
Physiological measures	Concept tests	
Field Methods		
Dummy advertising vehicles	On-air tests	Online theater testing
Posttests		
Field Methods		
Recall tests	Single-source systems	Recognition tests
Association measures	Inquiry tests	Tracking studies

The methodologies employed to conduct pretests vary. In focus groups, participants freely discuss the meanings they get from the ads, consider the relative advantages of alternatives, and even suggest improvements or additional themes. In addition to or instead of the focus groups, consumers are asked to evaluate the ad on a series of rating scales. (Different agencies use different measures.) In-home interviews, mall intercept, Internet surveys, or laboratory methods may be used to gather the data.

The advantage of pretesting at this stage is that feedback is relatively inexpensive. Any problems with the concept or the way it is to be delivered are identified before large amounts of money are spent in development. Sometimes more than one version of the ad is evaluated to determine which is most likely to be effective.

Because it costs so much less to find out that an ad may not work prior to making it public, rather than after doing so, it certainly makes sense to pretest.

The disadvantage is that mock-ups, storyboards, or animatics may not communicate nearly as effectively as the final product. The mood-enhancing and/or emotional aspects of the message are very difficult to communicate in this format. Another disadvantage is time delays. Many marketers believe being first in the market offers them a distinct advantage over competitors, so they forgo research to save time and ensure this position—even though this may be a risky strategy.

Posttesting   Posttesting is also common among both advertisers and ad agencies (with the exception of testing commercials for wearout). Posttesting is designed to (1) determine if the campaign is accomplishing the objectives sought and (2) serve as input into the next period's situation analysis.

Where to Test

In addition to when to test, decisions must be made as to *where*. These tests may take place in either laboratory or field settings.

Laboratory   In **laboratory tests**, people are brought to a particular location where they are shown ads and/or commercials. The testers either ask questions about them or measure participants' responses by other methods—for example, pupil dilation, eye tracking, or galvanic skin response.

The major advantage of the lab setting is the *control* it affords the researcher. Changes in copy, illustrations, formats, colors, and the like can be manipulated inexpensively, and the differential impact of each assessed. This makes it much easier for the researcher to isolate the contribution of each factor.

The major disadvantage is the lack of *realism.* Perhaps the greatest effect of this lack of realism is a **testing bias**. When people are brought into a lab (even if it has been designed to look like a living room), they may scrutinize the ads much more closely than they would at home. A second problem with this lack of realism is that it cannot duplicate the natural viewing situation, complete with the distractions or comforts of home. Looking at ads in a lab setting may not be the same as viewing at home on the couch, with the spouse, kids, dog, cat, and parakeet chirping in the background. (A bit later you will see that some testing techniques have made progress in correcting this deficiency. No, they did not bring in the dogs and the parakeets.) Overall, however, the control offered by this method probably outweighs the disadvantages, which accounts for the frequent use of lab methods.

Field Tests **Field tests** are tests of the ad or commercial under natural viewing situations, complete with the realism of noise, distractions, and the comforts of home. Field tests take into account the effects of repetition, program content, and even the presence of competitive messages.

The major disadvantage of field tests is the lack of control. It may be impossible to isolate causes of viewers' evaluations. If atypical events occur during the test, they may bias the results. Competitors may attempt to sabotage the research. And field tests usually take more time and money to conduct, so the results are not available to be acted on quickly. Thus, realism is gained at the expense of other important factors. It is up to the researcher to determine which trade-offs to make.

How to Test

Our discussion of what should be tested, when, and where was general and designed to establish a basic understanding of the overall process as well as some key terms. In this section, we discuss more specifically some of the methods commonly used at each stage. First, however, it is important to establish some criteria by which to judge ads and commercials.

Conducting evaluative research is not easy. Twenty-one of the largest U.S. ad agencies have endorsed a set of principles aimed at "improving the research used in preparing and testing ads, providing a better creative product for clients, and controlling the cost of TV commercials."[9] This set of nine principles, called **Positioning Advertising Copy Testing (PACT)**, defines *copy testing* as research "that is undertaken when a decision is to be made about whether advertising should run in the marketplace. Whether this stage utilizes a single test or a combination of tests, its purpose is to aid in the judgment of specific advertising executions."[10] The nine principles of good copy testing are shown in Figure 18–4.

FIGURE 18–4

Positioning Advertising Copy Testing (PACT)

1. Provide measurements that are relevant to the objectives of the advertising.

2. Require agreement about how the results will be used in advance of each specific test.

3. Provide multiple measurements (because single measurements are not adequate to assess ad performance).

4. Be based on a model of human response to communications—the reception of a stimulus, the comprehension of the stimulus, and the response to the stimulus.

5. Allow for consideration of whether the advertising stimulus should be exposed more than once.

6. Require that the more finished a piece of copy is, the more soundly it can be evaluated and require, as a minimum, that alternative executions be tested in the same degree of finish.

7. Provide controls to avoid the biasing effects of the exposure context.

8. Take into account basic considerations of sample definition.

9. Demonstrate reliability and validity.

FIGURE 18–5

The Five Guiding Principles
of Digital Measurement

Principle #1 Move to a "viewable impressions" standard and count real exposures online.

Principle #2 Online advertising must migrate to a currency based on audience impressions, not gross impressions.

Principle #3 Because all ad units are not created equal, we must create a transparent classification system.

Principle #4 Determine interactivity "metrics that matter" for brand marketers, so that marketers can better evaluate the online's contribution to brand building.

Principle #5 Digital media measurement must become increasingly comparable and integrated with other media.

Source: Author created from www.measurementnow.net.

On the digital side, a blue ribbon task force has been assembled in an industry-wide initiative dedicated to making digital media advertising friendlier to brands by evolving the way interactive advertising is measured. The project, titled "Making Measurement Make Sense," a joint effort of the 4As, the ANA, and the Interactive Advertising Bureau, has a goal of "making digital media measurements directly comparable to those of traditional media, while maintaining the ability to evaluate the unique value that interactivity brings to brand campaigns."[11] The committee has established five guiding principles for this purpose (Figure 18–5).

As you can see, advertisers and their clients are concerned about developing *appropriate* testing methods. Adherence to these principles may not make for perfect testing, but it goes a long way toward improving the state of the art and alleviates at least one of the testing problems cited earlier.

THE TESTING PROCESS

Testing may occur at various points throughout the development of an ad or a campaign: (1) concept generation research; (2) rough, prefinished art, copy, and/or commercial testing; (3) finished art or commercial pretesting; and (4) market testing of ads or commercials (posttesting).

Concept Generation and Testing

Figure 18–6 describes the process involved in advertising **concept testing**, which is conducted very early in the campaign development process in order to explore

FIGURE 18–6

Concept Testing

Objective
Explores consumers' responses to various ad concepts as expressed in words, pictures, or symbols.
Method
Alternative concepts are exposed to consumers who match the characteristics of the target audience. Reactions and evaluations of each are sought through a variety of methods, including focus groups, direct questioning, and survey completion. Sample sizes vary depending on the number of concepts to be presented and the consensus of responses.
Output
Qualitative and/or quantitative data evaluating and comparing alternative concepts.

FIGURE 18–7

Weaknesses Associated
with Focus Group Research

- The results are not quantifiable.

- Sample sizes are too small to generalize to larger populations.

- Group influences may bias participants' responses.

- One or two members of the group may steer the conversation or dominate the discussion.

- Consumers become instant "experts."

- Members may not represent the target market. (Are focus group participants a certain type of person?)

- Results may be taken to be more representative and/or definitive than they really are.

the targeted consumer's response to a potential ad or campaign or have the consumer evaluate advertising alternatives. Positioning statements, copy, headlines, and/or illustrations may all be under scrutiny. The material to be evaluated may be just a headline or a rough sketch of the ad. The colors used, typeface, package designs, and even point-of-purchase materials may be evaluated.

One of the more commonly used methods for concept testing is focus groups, which usually consist of 8 to 10 people in the target market for the product. Companies have tested everything from product concepts to advertising concepts using focus groups. For most companies, the focus group is the first step in the research process. The number of focus groups used varies depending on group consensus, strength of response, and/or the degree to which participants like or dislike the concepts. Some companies use 50 or more groups to develop a campaign, although fewer than 10 are usually needed to test a concept sufficiently.

While focus groups continue to be a favorite of marketers, they are often overused. The methodology is attractive in that results are easily obtained, directly observable, and immediate. A variety of issues can be examined, and consumers are free to go into depth in areas they consider important. Also, focus groups don't require quantitative analysis. Unfortunately, many managers are uncertain about research methods that require statistics; and focus groups, being qualitative in nature, don't demand much skill in interpretation. Weaknesses with focus groups are shown in Figure 18–7. Clearly, there are appropriate and inappropriate circumstances for employing this methodology.

Another way to gather consumers' opinions of concepts is mall intercepts, where consumers in shopping malls are approached and asked to evaluate rough ads and/or copy. Rather than participating in a group discussion, individuals assess the ads via questionnaires, rating scales, and/or rankings. New technologies allow for concept testing over the Internet, where advertisers can show concepts simultaneously to consumers throughout the United States, garnering feedback and analyzing the results almost instantaneously. In addition, online focus groups are being used more often to do concept testing (Exhibit 18–2). Internet methods are becoming increasingly popular given the cost savings and time efficiencies associated with these research methods, and some research firms now offer hybrid studies that involve a combination of online and traditional measures.

Rough Art, Copy, and Commercial Testing

Because of the high cost associated with the production of an ad or commercial (many network commercials cost hundreds of thousands of dollars to produce), advertisers are increasingly spending more monies testing a rendering of the final ad at early stages. Slides

EXHIBIT 18–2

Online focus groups are used
for concept testing

© InsideHeads.com, conducting
online focus groups since 1998

Virtual Focus Facility: Observer View

A rough commercial is an unfinished execution that may fall into three broad categories:

Animatic Rough	Photomatic Rough	Live-Action Rough
Succession of drawings/cartoons	Succession of photographs	Live motion
Rendered artwork	Real people/scenery	Stand-in/nonunion talent
Still frames	Still frames	Nonunion crew
Simulated movement:	Simulated movements:	Limited props/minimal opticals
Panning/zooming of frame/rapid sequence	Panning/zooming of frame/rapid sequence	Location settings

Finished Commercial Uses		
Live motion/animation		
Highly paid union talent		
Full union crew		
Exotic props/studio sets/special effects		

FIGURE 18–8

Rough Testing Terminology

of the artwork posted on a screen or animatic and photomatic roughs may be used to test at this stage. (See Figure 18–8 for an explanation of terminology.) Because such tests can be conducted inexpensively, research at this stage is becoming ever more popular.

But cost is only one factor. The test is of little value if it does not provide relevant, accurate information. Rough tests must indicate how the finished commercial would perform. Studies have demonstrated that these testing methods are reliable and the results typically correlate well with the finished ad.

Most of the tests conducted at the rough stage involve lab settings, although some on-air field tests are also available. Popular tests include comprehension and reaction tests and consumer juries. Again, the Internet allows field settings to be employed at this stage.

1. *Comprehension and reaction tests.* One key concern for the advertiser is whether the ad or commercial conveys the meaning intended. The second concern is the reaction the ad generates. Obviously, the advertiser does not want an ad that evokes a negative reaction or offends someone. **Comprehension and reaction tests** are designed to assess these responses (which makes you wonder why some ads are ever brought to the marketplace).

    Tests of comprehension and reaction employ no one standard procedure. Personal interviews, group interviews, and focus groups have all been used for this purpose, and sample sizes vary according to the needs of the client; they typically range from 50 to 200 respondents.

2. *Consumer juries.* This method uses consumers representative of the target market to evaluate the probable success of an ad. **Consumer juries** may be asked to rate a selection of layouts or copy versions presented in pasteups on separate sheets. The objectives sought and methods employed in consumer juries are shown in Figure 18–9.

    While the jury method offers the advantages of control and cost effectiveness, serious flaws in the methodology limit its usefulness:

    • *The consumer may become a self-appointed expert.* One of the benefits sought from the jury method is the objectivity and involvement in the product or service that the targeted consumer can bring to the evaluation process. Sometimes, however, knowing they are being asked to critique ads, participants try to become more *expert* in their evaluations, paying more attention and being more critical than usual. The result may be a less than objective evaluation or an evaluation on elements other than those intended.

FIGURE 18-9

Consumer Juries

Objective
Potential viewers (consumers) are asked to evaluate ads and give their reactions to and evaluation of them. When two or more ads are tested, viewers are usually asked to rate or rank order the ads according to their preferences.

Method
Respondents are asked to view ads and rate them according to either (1) the order of merit method or (2) the paired comparison method. In the former, the respondent is asked to view the ads and then rank them from one to *n* according to their perceived merit. In the latter, ads are compared only two at a time. Each ad is compared to every other ad in the group, and the winner is listed. The best ad is that which wins the most times. Consumer juries typically employ 50 to 100 participants.

Output
An overall reaction to each ad under construction as well as a rank ordering of the ads based on the viewers' perceptions.

- *The number of ads that can be evaluated is limited.* Whether *order of merit* or *paired comparison* methods are used, the ranking procedure becomes tedious as the number of alternatives increases. Consider the ranking of 10 ads. While the top 2 and the bottom 2 may very well reveal differences, those ranked in the middle may not yield much useful information.

  In the paired comparison method, the number of evaluations required is calculated by the formula

  $$\frac{n(n-1)}{2}$$

  If six alternatives are considered, 15 evaluations must be made. As the number of ads increases, the task becomes even more unmanageable.
- *A halo effect is possible.* Sometimes participants rate an ad good on all characteristics because they like a few and overlook specific weaknesses. This tendency, called the **halo effect**, distorts the ratings and defeats the ability to control for specific components. (Of course, the reverse may also occur—rating an ad bad overall due to only a few bad attributes.)
- *Preferences for specific types of advertising may overshadow objectivity.* Ads that involve emotions or pictures may receive higher ratings or rankings than those employing copy, facts, and/or rational criteria. Even though the latter are often more effective in the marketplace, they may be judged less favorably by jurists who prefer emotional appeals.

Some of the problems noted here can be remedied by the use of ratings scales instead of rankings. But ratings are not always valid either. Thus, while consumer juries have been used for years, questions of bias have led researchers to doubt their validity. As a result, a variety of other methods (discussed later in this chapter) are more commonly employed.

A/B Testing   The process of **A/B testing** has been employed by marketers for years. The process involves the testing of two versions of an advertisement or homepage to see which will be the more effective prior to launch. In the vast majority (if not all) of these cases the ads or web pages are finished products. In making a case for using A/B testing earlier in the development process, Molly Soat makes the argument that waiting so long to test could be costing companies money, and at the same time be less effective. She notes that a number of advertising experts call for the testing of display art, or scripts, for example to gain insights into consumers' thinking rather than waiting to just have them choose between two finished ads. Besides saving a lot of money by not developing and producing a potentially ineffective ad, the results would likely lead to ads that use consumers' insights. The experts argue for using A/B testing earlier in the developmental process and measuring consumer's emotional and neurological responses rather than just have them choose between two finish products. Of course, the finished ads could be A/B tested as well.[12]

Pretesting of Finished Ads

Pretesting finished ads is one of the more commonly employed studies among marketing researchers and their agencies. At this stage, a finished advertisement or commercial is used; since it has not been presented to the market, changes can still be made.

Many researchers believe testing the ad in final form provides better information. Several test procedures are available for print and broadcast ads, including both laboratory and field methodologies.

Print methods include portfolio tests, analyses of readability, and dummy advertising vehicles. Broadcast tests include theater tests and on-air tests. Both print and broadcast may use physiological measures.

Pretesting Finished Print Messages   A number of methods for pretesting finished print ads are available. One is *Gallup & Robinson's Impact System,* described in Figure 18–10. The most common of these methods are portfolio tests, readability tests, and dummy advertising vehicles.

Portfolio Tests Portfolio tests are a laboratory methodology designed to expose a group of respondents to a portfolio consisting of both control and test ads. Respondents are then asked what information they recall from the ads. The assumption is that the ads that yield the *highest recall* are the most effective.

While portfolio tests offer the opportunity to compare alternative ads directly, a number of weaknesses limit their applicability:

1. Factors other than advertising creativity and/or presentation may affect recall. Interest in the product or product category, the fact that respondents know they are participating in a test, or interviewer instructions (among others) may account for more differences than the ad itself.
2. Recall may not be the best test. Some researchers argue that for certain types of products (those of low involvement) ability to recognize the ad when shown may be a better measure than recall.

One way to determine the validity of the portfolio method is to correlate its results with readership scores once the ad is placed in the field. Whether such validity tests

FIGURE 18–10

G&R Research and Consulting

Objective
Understanding the performance of individual advertising executions or testing finished products. Research and testing gauge the potential of an idea behind potential advertising executions prior to fielding.
Methods
In-person interviewing; telephone; Internet; physiological; advertising response modeling; qualitative and quantitative research; facial EMG; others.
Output
Sales-validated methods for the development of messaging and the optimization of performance.

are being conducted or not is not readily known, although the portfolio method remains popular in the industry. A variety of the portfolio test is the **mock magazine test** in which an ad is placed in an actual magazine and a similar methodology is employed.

Readability Tests The communications efficiency of the copy in a print ad can be tested without reader interviews. This test uses the **Flesch formula**, named after its developer, Rudolph Flesch, to assess readability of the copy by determining the average number of syllables per 100 words. Human interest appeal of the material, length of sentences, and familiarity with certain words are also considered and correlated with the educational background of target audiences. Test results are compared to previously established norms for various target audiences. The test suggests that copy is best comprehended when sentences are short, words are concrete and familiar, and personal references are drawn.

The Flesch Kincaid Reading Ease Score method eliminates many of the interviewee biases associated with other tests and avoids gross errors in understanding. The norms offer an attractive standard for comparison. Other readibility measures also exist, including the SMOG Readability Formula and the Fry Graph Readability Formula.

Disadvantages are also inherent, however. The copy may become too mechanical, and direct input from the receiver is not available. Without this input, contributing elements like creativity cannot be addressed. To be effective, this test should be used only in conjunction with other pretesting methods.

New Print Pretesting Measures In an effort to improve upon the traditional print pretest measures, a number of companies have introduced new methodologies or improved-upon existing methods. Many of these involve hybrid measures that either measure effectiveness in different ways, or in different channels. For example, Ipsos-ASI Next*Connect has introduced an online copy testing tool (Figure 18–11) that can test ads on digital or traditional media. Consumers are recruited to complete an online survey where they are exposed to a variety of ad messages. The results are compared against a control group that was not exposed to the advertising. The methodology allows for testing ads in finished or rough formats, for individual executions or multiple campaign elements, and determine ads' impact in traditional and new media.

The PTG (PreTesting Group) methodology measures the time a respondent spends with a print ad or tablet or with a hidden camera in a store. The magazines contain a number of ads targeted toward the interests of the consumers. Unknown to the consumers, as they go through the magazines, hidden cameras using eye-tracking technology record where their eyes go on the page, how long they stay on the page,

FIGURE 18–11

Ipsos-ASI's Next*Connect

Objective
To assist advertisers in copy testing of rough or finished advertisements in traditional or digital form to determine the individual executions or multiple campaign elements across any platform.
Method
Consumers are recruited to complete an online survey where they are exposed to a variety of messages and results are compared against those from a control group not exposed to any ads.
Output
Standard scores, related recall, persuasion, and comprehensive diagnostics; potential ad-driven in-market sales.

and the stopping power of the ad. The studies can be conducted in person or online and can measure recall, main idea communication, and more.

Millward Brown offers its own trademarked methodology as well, called Link. According to the company, Link uses a comprehensive set of diagnostic questions to evoke viewer reactions to the ads. Nonverbal measures including eye tracking can also be used to determine consumers' enjoyment, comprehension, involvement, and other reactions to the ads. The three key metrics provided include awareness, persuasion, and short-term sales likelihood.

While other methods and measures are available, the most popular form of pretesting of print ads now involves a series of measures. The tests can typically be used for rough and/or finished ads and are most commonly conducted in a lab or online.

Pretesting Finished Broadcast Ads A variety of methods for pretesting broadcast ads are available. The tests can typically be used for rough and/or finished ads and are most commonly conducted in a lab or online. As noted, most of the companies that offer pretesting of print ads have expanded their services to include TV and other platforms. (The ASI method described in Figure 18–11 uses the same testing platform across media.) For example, MSW●ARS Research provides offerings that allow the advertiser to evaluate the impact of advertising messages and campaigns composed of any combination of touch points, including broadcast (television and radio), outdoor, and digital. The company provides research solutions in brand strategy, all stages of creative development from concept to fully finished ads, campaign evaluation across all channels, advertising and brand equity tracking, and additional consulting services.

Theater Tests In the past, one of the most popular laboratory methods for pretesting finished commercials was **theater testing**. In theater tests participants are invited to view pilots of proposed TV programs. In some instances, the show is actually being tested, but more commonly a standard program is used so audience responses can be compared with normative responses established by previous viewers. Sample sizes range from 250 to 600 participants, with 300 being most typical.

The methods of theater testing operations vary, though all measure brand preference changes. For example, many of the services now use programs with the commercials embedded for viewing in one's home or office rather than in a theater. Others establish viewing rooms in malls and/or hotel conference rooms. Some do not take all the measures listed here; others ask the consumers to turn dials or push buttons on a keypad to provide the continual responses. An example of one methodology is shown in Figure 18–12 (you may remember GfK from Chapter 10) and Exhibit 18–3.

FIGURE 18–12

GfK AD*VANTAGE Pulse Methodology

AD*VANTAGE Pulse surveys are based on tests carried out in a studio. The number of respondents is typically about $n = 125$, normally composed of category users defined by the client. Each participant is shown a TV program, with commercial breaks that include the test commercial, and then asked questions about the program. The closed- and open-ended questions are recorded via a touch-screen system. Key measures include (1) visibility (Will the commercial be remembered?); (2) branding (Will the brand be remembered?); (3) communications (What visuals and messages will be remembered?); (4) brand enhancement (Does the ad promote a positive feeling toward the brand?); and (5) persuasion (Will the commercial inspire nonusers to try the product, and will it enhance brand loyalty among existing customers?). The diagnostics include measures of viewers' awareness, comprehension, uniqueness, and involvement of the commercial. The AD*VANTAGE Pulse methodology also allows for scene-by-scene analysis, and can be used to test all traditional forms of advertising as well as digital.

EXHIBIT 18–3

This ad for GfK promotes its research and testing as a smart business decision. Do you agree or disagree?

Source: GfK

Those opposed to theater tests cite a number of disadvantages. First, they say the environment is too artificial. The recruiting and lab testing conditions are likely to lead to testing effects, and consumers are exposed to commercials they might not even notice in a more natural environment. Second, the contrived measure of brand preference change seems too phony to believe. Critics contend that participants will see through it and make changes just because they think they are supposed to. Finally, the group effect of having others present and overtly exhibiting their reactions may influence viewers who did not have any reactions themselves.

Proponents argue that theater tests offer distinct advantages. In addition to control, the established norms (averages of commercials' performances) indicate how one's commercial will fare against others in the same product class that were already tested. Further, advocates say the brand preference measure is supported by actual sales results.

Despite the limitations of theater testing, most major consumer-product companies have used it to evaluate their commercials. This method may have shortcomings, but it allows them to identify strong or weak commercials and to compare them to other ads. Companies like Ipsos-ASI and Consumer Quest now offer in-home and online theater testing (Exhibit 18–3).

On-Air Tests Some of the firms conducting theater tests also insert the commercials into actual TV programs in certain test markets. Typically, the commercials are in finished form, although the testing of ads earlier in the developmental process is becoming more common. This is referred to as an **on-air test** and often includes single-source ad research (discussed later in this chapter). Information Resources, Ipsos-ASI, MSW•ARS, and Nielsen are well-known providers of on-air tests.

On-air testing techniques offer all the advantages of field methodologies, as well as all the disadvantages. The most commonly employed metric used in an on-air test is **recall**—that is, the number of persons able to recall the ad and/or its message. In an examination of real-world advertising tests reported in the *Journal of Advertising Research,* Hu et al. conclude that recall and persuasion pretests, while often employed, do not fare well in respect to reliability and/or validity.[13] Nevertheless, most of the testing services have offered evidence of both validity and reliability for on-air pretesting of commercials. Both Ipsos-ASI and MSW•ARS claim their pretest and posttest results yield the same recall scores 9 out of 10 times—a strong indication of reliability and a good predictor of the effect the ad is likely to have when shown to the population as a whole.

In summary, on-air pretesting of finished or rough commercials offers some distinct advantages over lab methods and some indications of the ad's likely success. Whether the measures used are as strong an indication as the providers say remains in question.

Physiological Measures A less common but increasingly adopted method of pretesting finished commercials involves a laboratory setting in which physiological responses are measured. These measures indicate the receiver's *involuntary* response to the ad, theoretically eliminating biases associated with the voluntary measures reviewed to this point. (Involuntary responses are those over which the individual has no control, such as heartbeat and reflexes.) Physiological measures used to test both print and broadcast ads include pupil dilation, galvanic skin response, eye tracking, and brain waves:

1. *Pupil dilation.* Research in **pupillometrics** is designed to measure dilation and constriction of the pupils of the eyes in response to stimuli. Dilation is associated with action; constriction involves the body's conservation of energy.

Digital and Social Media Perspective 18–2 > > >

PHYSIOLOGICAL METHODS, EYE TRACKING, AND MOUSE HOVERING LEAD TO MORE EFFECTIVE TESTING

An increased emphasis on accountability and the pressure to determine an ad's effectiveness, along with the explosion of new media and changes and improvements to existing media, are just some of the reasons why marketers continue to seek new ways to examine how their messages are performing. As a result, new research methodologies are being developed, and existing technologies are being adapted to assist in making this determination. Many of these involve the application of neurosciences. Some of these are proving to be quite successful:

On the academic side, Innerscope and professors at Temple University joined together to measure physiological reactions to Super Bowl ads including heart rates and breathing patterns as well as fMRI data. Another team of marketing professors used visual-imagery theory to test whether consumers were making the connection between the sponsor and the event they were attending—their results indicated that "attendees who rated the event as 'higher quality' had a higher attitude toward the sponsors' products that were showcased at the tournament."

Practitioners have also joined in. For example, there is a methodology called "mouse hovering" in which a heat-mapping technology collects data as to where users have "moused" over an ad and for how long. The start-up company claims that the data will help advertisers better understand which parts of the ad users engage with and how intensely. Given that click-throughs are more important to direct marketers than those attempting to use the Internet for branding purposes, Moat—the developer of the technology—believes that its method of determining effectiveness is of more value than counting clicks. A competitor of Moat, RealVu, addresses this same problem from a different perspective, focusing on display advertising on the Internet. Rather than using heat-mapping technology, RealVu measures the seconds a user is actually exposed to an ad. While both companies agree that click-throughs are not effective measures of Internet advertising, they don't necessarily agree as to what is the best measure.

A methodology that seems to be gaining more and more acceptance in marketing circles has actually been around for quite some time. The usefulness of eye-tracking technology for measuring advertising effectiveness is not news for marketers. Back in the late 1970s and early 1980s, advertising researchers were employing this technology to determine where viewers were focusing when they looked at ads and/or TV commercials. One story is that one of the original Tab diet soft-drink commercials was changed when viewers focused on the female swimsuit model instead of the product. The commercial was supposedly changed to have her hold the can in front of her body to attract attention. For whatever reason, while proven to be useful, eye tracking never went away, but no one seemed to pay much attention it. Now all of that is changing.

One company heavily involved with using eye tracking to determine advertising effectiveness is Tobii. An international company with offices located in the United States, Norway, Germany, Japan, and China, Tobii was founded as a result of a research project at the Royal Institute of Technology in Stockholm, Sweden, and employs eye tracking for a variety of nonmarketing purposes, as well as for measuring ad effectiveness. The company offers its research services for studying online marketing, including determining the effectiveness of banner ads, e-mail campaigns, newsletters, and in-game advertising. More traditional testing includes copy testing print ads in the creative stage; assessing the impact of out-of-home ads in bars, airports, grocery stores, and so on; determining the effectiveness of product placements and TV commercials; and even testing promotional products.

There are a variety of reasons marketers have found a number of new applications for eye tracking. In addition to the effectiveness measures offered by Tobii and others, companies have used this methodology for:

- *Retail (interior displays/window design):* Eye-tracking studies enabling interior designers to choose color, lighting, architecture, and so on to subtly influence the

Advertisers have used pupillometrics to evaluate product and package design as well as to test ads. Pupil dilation suggests a stronger interest in (or preference for) an ad or implies arousal or attention-getting capabilities. Other attempts to determine the affective (liking or disliking) responses created by ads have met with less success.

Because of high costs and some methodological problems, the use of pupillometrics has waned over the past decade. But it can be useful in evaluating certain aspects of advertising.

2. *Galvanic skin response (GSR).* Also known as **electrodermal response (EDR)**, GSR measures the skin's resistance or conductance to a small amount of

customer's mood. This includes the use of eye catchers to attract passers-by and arouse their curiosity.

- *Package design:* Optimizing the look and feel of the packaging as well as the attention-getting capabilities.
- *Advertisements:* Allowing the advertiser to determine what customers see and to determine the effectiveness of copy and visuals.
- *Online marketing:* From web design to viewers' attention to display ads, marketers are finding eye tracking a valuable tool to enhance effectiveness.

Researchers use eye movements to tell specifically where viewers are looking, to see if they are reading or scanning, and what catches their first view. They can also tell how much time the viewers spend looking at a specific stimulus and the order in which they view others (if they do!). For example:

- An eye-tracking study conducted by Oneupweb asked participants to navigate Facebook, Twitter, and YouTube as they normally would. The study revealed that 65 percent of them engaged with a sponsor within 10 seconds of beginning their search, when asked to search for Pepsi on both Facebook and YouTube (Twitter was not included because it has no search tool). On Facebook, the results showed that their first attention was paid to the sponsored ads, and others were barely, if at all, viewed, while on YouTube, the top six organic results and the first sponsored ad got all the attention. The conclusion? Sponsored ads work better than expected.
- In another Internet study, Jakob Nielsen and Kara Pernice, authors of the book *Eyetracking Web Usability,* tracked how people navigate websites when looking for information. Searches included how to deal with heartburn, shopping for baby presents, and picking cell phone features, among others. Their results indicate that to be effective, an ad should be simple, with those that had only text or text and a separate image being most effective, while those that imposed text on top of images or included animation fared the worse. Although the study showed that people saw 36 percent of the ads on the pages they visited, the time spent viewing them was only one-third of a second. One of the most surprising results was the fact that text-only ads scored best. When asked for an explanation, the authors hypothesized that unlike television which is a passive medium, the Web is all about taking action, searching,

clicking, and so forth. On the Web, it is the value of content that makes it attractive.

- In a scarier application, a Canadian company now offers an eye-tracking device that can determine when someone looks at a billboard, where the person looks, and for how long, without one even knowing it—up to 33 feet. It then provides Google-like metrics that greatly improve on existing methods of data collection.
- In Germany, a pre- and posttest research study was designed to measure participants' perceptions and recall of ads through a virtual reality situation in which one drives a van down the street with advertisements on both sides. The eye-tracking and survey results are then combined to determine viewers' unaided/aided recall, recognition and design aspects of the ads. And yes, they can do it at different speeds!

Part of the reason for eye-tracking measures not hitting the mainstream is the high cost and obtrusiveness of the measurement equipment (usually the participants have to wear headgear, whether in a lab setting or in the field—for example, walking through a department store or supermarket looking weird). There was also the question about whether the fact that the participants knew they were in a study influenced their behaviors. However, P&G, working with an external eye-tracking firm, believes that eye tracking has saved the company substantial amounts of money by allowing P&G to cancel website display ads that are not being seen. The information is gathered from a panel of consumers using webcams to track their eye movements while on a site, and is then fed back to P&G's creative department indicating what works best.

Maybe eye tracking is here to stay!

Sources: Angeline G. Close, Russell Lacey, and T. Bettina Cornwell, "Visual Processing and Need for Cognition Can Enhance Event-Sponsorship Outcomes—How Sporting Event Sponsorships Benefit from the Way Attendees Process Them," *Journal of Advertising Research* 55, no. 2 (May 2015), pp. 206–15; Tom Avril, "Super Bowl Ads Get Look by Science," February 27, 2014, www.philly.com; Christopher Heine, "P&G Slashes Wasteful Display Ad Budgets Using Eye Tracking," May 30, 2013, www.adweek.com; "Advertising Research and Eye Tracking," June 10, 2013, www.tobii.com; Barbara Kiviat, "Why We Look at Some Web Ads and Not Others," November 8, 2009, www.time.com; Nathania Johnson, "Eye Tracking Study Shows Sponsored Ads Attract Social Media Searchers," July 19, 2009, blog.searchenginewatch.com; Dan Skeen, "Eye-Tracking Device Lets Billboards Know When You Look at Them," June 12, 2007, www.wired.com; G. Theuner, K. Pischke, and T. Bley, "Analysis of Advertising Effectiveness with Eye Tracking," *Proceedings of Measuring Behavior 2008*, Maastricht, The Netherlands, August 26–29, 2008, pp. 229–30.

current passed between two electrodes. Response to a stimulus activates sweat glands, which in turn increases the conductance of the electrical current. Thus, GSR/EDR activity might reflect a reaction to advertising. While there is evidence that GSR/EDR may be useful to determine the effectiveness of ads, difficulties associated with this testing method have resulted in its infrequent use at this time.

3. *Eye tracking.* As seen in Digital and Social Media Perspective 18–2 a methodology that is more commonly employed is **eye tracking** (Figure 18–13), in which viewers are asked to view an ad while a sensor aims a beam of infrared light at the eye. The beam follows the movement of the eye and shows the exact

FIGURE 18–13

Eye Movement Research

Objective
Track viewers' eye movements to determine what viewers read or view in print ads and where their attention is focused in TV commercials, at websites, or on billboards.

Method
Fiber optics, digital data processing, and advanced electronics are used to follow eye movements of viewers and/or readers as they process an ad.

Output
Relationship among what readers see, recall, and comprehend. Scan movement paths in print ads, on billboards, in commercials, in print materials, and on websites. (Can also be used to evaluate package designs.)

spot on which the viewer is focusing, and for how long (Exhibit 18–4). The continuous reading of responses demonstrates which elements of the ad are attracting attention, how long the viewer is focusing on them, and the sequence in which they are being viewed.

Eye tracking can identify strengths and weaknesses in an ad. For example, attractive models or background action may distract the viewer's attention away from the brand or product being advertised. The advertiser can remedy this distraction before fielding the ad. In other instances, colors or illustrations may attract attention and create viewer interest in the ad.

Eye tracking has increasingly been used to measure the effectiveness of websites and online ads and, as noted earlier, e-mails. Using eye tracking to examine how consumers view homepages, Steve Outing and Laura Roel were able to determine that (1) eyes first fixate on the upper left of the screen, (2) dominant headlines draw attention first, and (3) larger type promotes scanning, while small type encourages reading. The study drew other conclusions as well—too many to mention here.[14] Digital and Social Media Perspective 18–2 details some other applications of eye tracking and other physiological methods.

4. *Brain waves.* **Electroencephalographic (EEG) measures** can be taken from the skull to determine electrical frequencies in the brain. These electrical impulses are used in two areas of research, alpha waves and hemispheric lateralization:

   • **Alpha activity** refers to the degree of brain activation. People are in an alpha state when they are inactive, resting, or sleeping. The theory is that a person

in an alpha state is less likely to be processing information (recall correlates negatively with alpha levels) and that attention and processing require moving from this state. By measuring a subject's alpha level while viewing a commercial, researchers can assess the degree to which attention and processing are likely to occur.

- **Hemispheric lateralization** distinguishes between alpha activity in the left and right sides of the brain. It has been hypothesized that the right side of the brain processes visual stimuli and the left processes verbal stimuli. The right hemisphere is thought to respond more to emotional stimuli, while the left responds to logic. The right determines recognition, while the left is responsible for recall. If these hypotheses are correct, advertisers could design ads to increase learning and memory by creating stimuli to appeal to each hemisphere. However, some researchers believe the brain does not function laterally and an ad cannot be designed to appeal to one side or the other.

- Using technologies originally designed for the medical field such as positron emission tomography (PET), functional magnetic resonance imaging (fMRI), and electroencephalography (EEG), neuroscientists have teamed up with marketers to examine physiological reactions to ads and brands through brain scan imaging. By monitoring the brain activity directly, scientists are learning how consumers make up their minds by measuring chemical activity and/or changes in the magnetic fields of the brain as well as how they react to commercials.

EEG research has engaged the attention of academic researchers for some time, but recently the technology has gained in attractiveness to practioners as well. In addition to those examples cited earlier in the chapter and throughout this text, companies like the Nielsen Company—the world's largest audience measurement company—have invested in neuroscience measurement as *Fortune* 500 companies increasingly seek these services. Neuroscience measures have been used to determine viewers' responses to Super Bowl commercials, differences in responses to drinking Coke and Pepsi, political ads, and movie trailers, to name just a few of the many applications.

Market Testing of Ads

The fact that the ad and/or campaign has been implemented does not diminish the need for testing. The pretests were conducted on smaller samples and may in some instances have questionable merit, so the marketer must find out how the ad is doing in the field. In this section, we discuss methods for posttesting an ad. Many of the tests are similar to the pretests discussed in the previous section and are provided by the same companies.

Posttests of Print Ads A variety of print posttests are available, including inquiry tests, recognition tests, and recall tests.

Inquiry Tests Used in both consumer and business-to-business market testing, **inquiry tests** are designed to measure advertising effectiveness on the basis of inquiries generated from ads appearing in various print media, often referred to as "bingo cards" such as the one shown in Exhibit 18–5. While still used, the response card is employed less often today as viewers can seek information merely by searching on the URL provided in the ad. The inquiry may take the form of the number of coupons returned, phone calls generated, or direct inquiries through reader cards. If you called in a response to an ad in a local medium recently, perhaps you were asked how you found out about the company or product or where you saw the ad. This is a very simple measure of the ad's or medium's effectiveness.

More complex methods of measuring effectiveness through inquiries may involve (1) running the ad in successive issues of the same medium; (2) running

Receive the information you need to market smarter instantly!
Go to: **www.targetonline.com** and click on free information.

Or...Fill out this card and either FAX your request today: 215-238-5388 or mail.

Free Subscription

Do you wish to receive (continue to receive) a FREE subscription to
TARGET MARKETING? ☐ **YES** ☐ NO

Signature_____ Date_____

Name (please print) _____ Title _____

Company Name _____

Address _____

City/State/Zip _____

Telephone_____ FAX _____

Email Address:_____

1. **TYPE OF BUSINESS AT THIS LOCATION: (Check One)**
    04 ☐ Catalogers, Mail Order Companies
    05 ☐ Retailers, Wholesaler/Distributor
    06 ☐ On-line Merchant
    03 ☐ Financial Services: Banks, Insurance, Credit Cards, Investment
    21 ☐ Fund Raisers: Non-Profit Groups, Charities
    33 ☐ High Technology: Internet Services, Computers, Software,
         Telecommunications, Office Equipment
    12 ☐ Manufacturers, Package Goods and Other Business-to-Business Marketers
    31 ☐ Non Financial Services Marketers: Associations, Clubs, Educational,
         Government Agencies, Health Care, Membership Organizations, Personnel
         Services, Real Estate, Utilities, Communications, Tourism and Travel
    13 ☐ Publishers: Magazines, Books, Newsletters, Newspapers, Book & Record Clubs
         On-line publications
    01 ☐ Advertising/DM Agencies, Freelance Creative and Consultants
    09 ☐ Mailing List Professionals: Brokers, Compilers, Owners
    20 ☐ Other: (Please Specify) _____
2. **JOB FUNCTION: (Check One)**
    10 ☐ Corporate and General Management (Excluding Sales, Marketing and
         Advertising Management)
    02 ☐ Marketing, List and Sales Management
    01 ☐ Advertising Promotion and Public Relations Management
    08 ☐ Operational, Technical and Telemarketing Management
    06 ☐ Circulation Management
    11 ☐ Other: (Please Specify) _____
3. **MY FIRM'S MARKETING ACTIVITY: (Check All That Apply)**
    1 ☐ Catalog   5 ☐ Consumer
    2 ☐ Direct Mail   6 ☐ Business-to-Business
    09 ☐ Internet   7 ☐ International
    3 ☐ Telemarketing   8 ☐ None of the Above
    10 ☐ Alternate Media
4. **IN THE PERFORMANCE OF YOUR JOB, CHECK THE ONE THAT BEST DESCRIBES
    YOUR PURCHASING AUTHORITY: (Check One)**
    1 ☐ Authorize/Approve Purchase
    2 ☐ Recommend/ Specify Purchase
    3 ☐ No Purchasing Authority

Free Information

Circle the free info number for the products and services that interest you

001	002	003	004	005	006	007	008	009	010	011	012
013	014	015	016	017	018	019	020	021	022	023	024
025	026	027	028	029	030	031	032	033	034	035	036
037	038	039	040	041	042	043	044	045	046	047	048
049	050	051	052	053	054	055	056	057	058	059	060
061	062	063	064	065	066	067	068	069	070	071	072
073	074	075	076	077	078	079	080	081	082	083	084
085	086	087	088	089	090	091	092	093	094	095	096
097	098	099	100	101	102	103	104	105	106	107	108
109	110	111	112	113	114	115	116	117	118	119	120
121	122	123	124	125	126	127	128	129	130	131	132
133	134	135	136	137	138	139	140	141	142	143	144
145	146	147	148	149	150	151	152	153	154	155	156
157	158	159	160	161	162	163	164	165	166	167	168
169	170	171	172	173	174	175	176	177	178	179	180

For Information on Product/Service Categories

To request information on any of the following areas of interest, check the appropriate free
information number:

501 ☐ Agencies/Consultants/Creative Services	530 ☐ Internet Services
502 ☐ Alternate Media/Delivery	513 ☐ Lettershop Services
503 ☐ Broadcast Media/Services	514 ☐ Lists-Business-to-Business
504 ☐ Call Center Equipment	515 ☐ Lists-Consumer
505 ☐ Credit/Collection Services	528 ☐ Lists-E-mail
506 ☐ Database Management Systems/	516 ☐ Lists-International
Services/Software	517 ☐ List Services
507 ☐ Delivery Services	518 ☐ Mailing Equipment/Services
529 ☐ E-mail Marketing	520 ☐ Paper
508 ☐ Envelopes/Order Forms/Labels	521 ☐ Premiums/Promotional Products
509 ☐ Fulfillment Services/Operations	522 ☐ Prepress Equipment/Services
510 ☐ Int'l Call Centers	523 ☐ Printers
511 ☐ Int'l Delivery Services	527 ☐ Printing Systems/Equipment
512 ☐ Int'l DM Agencies	524 ☐ Telemarketing Services
525 ☐ International DM Services	RS0110

split-run tests, in which variations of the ad appear in different copies of the same newspaper or magazine; and/or (3) running the same ad in different media. Each of these methods yields information on different aspects of the strategy. The first measures the *cumulative* effects of the campaign; the second examines specific elements of the ad or variations on it. The final method measures the effectiveness of the medium rather than the ad itself.

While inquiry tests may yield useful information, weaknesses in this methodology limit its effectiveness. For example, inquiries may not be a true measure of the attention-getting or information-providing aspects of the ad. The reader may be attracted to an ad, read it, and even store the information but not be motivated to inquire at that particular time. Time constraints, lack of a need for the product or service at the time the ad is run, and other factors may limit the number of inquiries. But receiving a small number of inquiries doesn't mean the ad was not effective; attention, attitude change, awareness, and recall of copy points may all have been achieved. At the other extreme, a person with a particular need for the product may respond to any ad for it, regardless of specific qualities of the ad.

Major advantages of inquiry tests are that they are inexpensive to implement and they provide some feedback with respect to the general effectiveness of the ad or medium used. But they are usually not very effective for comparing different versions or specific creative aspects of an ad.

Recognition Tests Perhaps the most common posttest of print ads is the **recognition method**, most closely associated with GfK Starch. The *Starch Ad Readership Report,* which has existed for over 85 years, lets the advertiser assess the impact of an ad in a single issue of a magazine, over time, and/or across different magazines. Starch measures hundreds of thousands of print ads representing more than 180 consumer magazines per year and provides a number of measures of an ad's effectiveness. In addition to the traditional *Starch Ad Readership Report,* Starch

FIGURE 18–14

The GfK Starch Ad
Readership Report

Objective

Determining recognition of print ads and providing insight into the involvement readers have with specific ads. Starch now provides this service for ads appearing in magazines and/or digital.

Method

Personal interviewers screen readers for qualifications and determine exposure and readership to specific issues of newspapers, consumer magazines, and business and professional publications. Participants are asked to go through the magazines, looking at the ads, and provide specific responses.

Output

Starch Ad Readership Reports generate four recognition scores:

- Noting score—the percentage of readers who remember seeing the ad.
- Brand-associated score—the percentage of readers who recall seeing or reading any part of the ad identifying the product or brand.
- Read any score—the percentage of readers who read any of the ad's copy.
- Read-most score—the percentage of readers who report reading at least half of the copy portion of the ad. Ad norms provide a benchmark to provide a comparison to other ads in the issue.

These conventional scores have now been supplemented by additional measures, including brand disposition, purchase behavior or intention, actions taken, word-of-mouth opportunity, and publication and advertising engagement.

now offers syndicated and private studies, pretesting, out-of-home studies, and more. The measures used in the Starch test methodology are shown in Figure 18–14. An example of a Starch scored ad is shown in Exhibit 18–6.

Starch claims that (1) the pulling power of various aspects of the ad can be assessed through the control offered, (2) the effectiveness of competitors' ads can be compared through the norms provided, (3) alternative ad executions can be tested, and (4) readership scores are a useful indication of consumers' *involvement* in the ad or campaign. (The theory is that a reader must read and become involved in the ad before the ad can communicate. To the degree that this readership can be shown, it is a direct indication of effectiveness.)

Of these claims, perhaps the most valid is the ability to judge specific aspects of the ad. Some researchers have criticized other aspects of the Starch recognition method (as well as other recognition measures) on the basis of problems of false claiming, interviewer sensitivities, and unreliable scores:

1. *False claiming.* Research shows that in recognition tests, respondents may claim to have seen an ad when they did not. False claims may be a result of having seen similar ads elsewhere, expecting that such an ad would appear in the medium, or wanting to please the questioner. Interest in the product category also increases reporting of ad readership. Whether this false claiming is deliberate or not, it leads to an overreporting of effectiveness. On the flip side, factors such as interview fatigue may lead to an underreporting bias—that is, respondents not reporting an ad they did see.

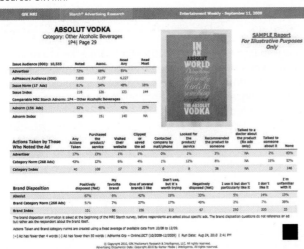

2. *Interviewer sensitivities.* Anytime research involves interviewers, there is a potential for bias. Respondents may want to impress the interviewer or fear looking unknowledgeable if they continually claim not to recognize an ad. There may also be variances associated with interviewer instructions, recordings, and so on, regardless of the amount of training and sophistication involved.

3. *Reliability of recognition scores.* Starch admits that the reliability and validity of its readership scores increase with the number of insertions tested, which essentially means that to test just one ad on a single exposure may not produce valid or reliable results.

In sum, despite critics, the Starch readership studies continue to dominate the posttesting of print ads. The value provided by norms and the fact that multiple exposures can improve reliability and validity may underlie the decisions to employ this methodology. In addition, the long-standing reliability and trustworthiness of the organization definitely comes into play, as the Starch methodology has been used for over 85 years, and has continued to evolve with the times.

Recall Tests There are several tests to measure recall of print ads. Perhaps the best known of these are the Ipsos-ASI Next*Correct test and the Gallup & Robinson Magazine Impact Research Service (MIRS) described in Figure 18–15. (A number of other companies, including Millward Brown and Decision Analyst, offer similar services.) These **recall tests** are similar to those discussed in the section on pretesting broadcast ads in that they attempt to measure recall of specific ads.

In addition to having the same interviewer problems as recognition tests, recall tests have other disadvantages. The reader's degree of involvement with the product and/or the distinctiveness of the appeals and visuals may lead to higher-than-accurate recall scores, although in general the method may lead to lower levels of recall than actually exist (an error the advertiser would be happy with). Critics contend the test is not strong enough to reflect recall accurately, so many ads may score as less effective than they really are, and advertisers may abandon or modify them needlessly.

On the plus side, it is thought that recall tests can assess the ad's impact on memory. Proponents of recall tests say the major concern is not the results themselves but how they are interpreted. Previous studies have shown that the correlation between ad recall and recognition is very high in both newspapers and magazines.

FIGURE 18–15

G&R Magazine Impact Research Service (MIRS)

Objective

Tracking recall of advertising (and client's ads) appearing in magazines to assess performance and effectiveness.

Method

Test magazines are placed in participants' homes and respondents are asked to read the magazine that day. Test ads are embedded with editorial content and other ads. A telephone interview is conducted the next day to assess recall of ads, idea communication, persuasion, brand rating, and ad liking. Both business-to-business and consumer magazine ads can be tested.

Output

Measures provided:

- Norms.
- Verbatim respondent playback.
- Performance summary.
- Diagnostics.

Posttests of Broadcast Commercials A variety of methods exist for posttesting broadcast commercials. The most common provide a combination of day-after recall tests, persuasion measures, and diagnostics. Test marketing and tracking studies, including single-source methods, are also employed.

Day-After Recall Tests The most popular method of posttesting employed in the broadcasting industry for decades was the *Burke Day-After Recall test*. While a number of companies offered day-after recall (DAR) methodologies, the "Burke test" for all intents and purposes became the generic name attached to these tests. While popular, day-after recall tests also had problems, including limited samples, high costs, and security issues (ads shown in test markets could be seen by competitors). Because of their common usage, numerous studies have been conducted to determine the efficacy of DAR tests. Although these studies have been conducted quite some time ago, the conclusions seem to be relevant today and merit consideration here. In addition, the following disadvantages with recall tests were also suggested:

1. DAR tests may favor unemotional appeals because respondents are asked to verbalize the message. Thinking messages may be easier to recall than emotional communications, so recall scores for emotional ads may be lower.[15] A number of other studies have also indicated that emotional ads may be processed differently from thinking ones; some ad agencies, for example, Leo Burnett and BBDO Worldwide among others, have gone so far as to develop their own methods of determining emotional response to ads.[16]
2. Program content may influence recall. The programs in which the ad appears may lead to different recall scores for the same brand. The net result is a potential inaccuracy in the recall score and in the norms used to establish comparisons.
3. A pre-recruited sample may pay increased attention to the program and the ads contained therein because the respondents know they will be tested the next day. This testing effect would lead to a higher level of recall than really exists.
4. In addition, studies have shown that recall is a measure that the ad has been received, but not necessarily accepted, and not predictive of sales.[17,18]

The major advantage of day-after recall tests is that they are field tests. The natural setting is supposed to provide a more realistic response profile. These tests are also popular because they provide norms that give advertisers a standard for comparing how well their ads are performing. In addition to recall, a number of different measures of the commercial's effectiveness are now offered, including persuasive measures and diagnostics. (The Burke test itself no longer exists under that name.)

Persuasive Measures As noted earlier in our discussion of pretesting broadcast commercials, a number of research firms now offer measures of a commercial's persuasive effectiveness. Some of the services offer additional persuasion measures, including purchase, intent, and frequency-of-purchase criteria.

Diagnostics In addition to measuring recall and persuasion, copy testing firms also provide diagnostic measures. These measures are designed to garner viewers' evaluations of the ads, as well as how clearly the creative idea is understood and how well the proposition is communicated. Rational and emotional reactions to the ads are also examined. A number of companies offer diagnostic measures, including G&R and Millward Brown, among many others.

Comprehensive Measures While each of the measures just described provides specific input into the effectiveness of a commercial, many advertisers are interested in more than just one specific input. Thus, some companies provide comprehensive

FIGURE 18–16

Ipsos-ASI's Next*TV test

Objectives

To assist advertisers in testing of their commercials through multiple measures to determine (1) the potential of the commercial for impacting sales, (2) how the ad contributes to brand equity, (3) how well it is in line with existing advertising strategies and objectives, and (4) how to optimize effectiveness.

Method

Consumers are recruited to evaluate a TV program, with ads embedded into the program as they would be on local prime-time television. Consumers view the commercial on a video-based system that self-erases in their homes to simulate actual field conditions. (The option to use local cable television programs with commercial inserts is also provided.)

Output

Related recall (day-after recall) scores; multiple persuasion scores, including brand preference shifts, purchase intent and frequency, in-market sales effectiveness, copy effect, comprehensive diagnostics to determine what viewers take away from the ad and how creative elements contribute to or distract from advertising effectiveness, and comparison to norms.

approaches in which each of the three measures just described can be obtained through one testing program. Figure 18–16 describes one such comprehensive program, Ipsos-ASI's Next*TV test (Exhibit 18–7).

Test Marketing Many companies conduct tests designed to measure their advertising effects in specific test markets before releasing them nationally. The markets chosen are representative of the target market. For example, a company may test its ads in Portland, Oregon; San Antonio, Texas; or Buffalo, New York, if the demographic and socioeconomic profiles of these cities match the product's market. A variety of factors may be tested, including reactions to the ads (for example, alternative copy points), the effects of various budget sizes, or special offers. The ads run in finished form in the media where they might normally appear, and effectiveness is measured after the ads run.

EXHIBIT 18–7

Ipsos-ASI offers a comprehensive testing measure

Source: Ipsos

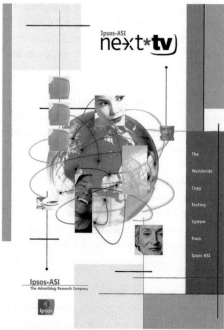

The advantage of test marketing of ads is realism. Regular viewing environments are used and the testing effects are minimized. A high degree of control can be attained if the test is designed successfully. For example, an extensive test market study was designed and conducted by Seagram and Time, Inc. over a period of three years to measure the effects of advertising frequency on consumers' buying habits. This study demonstrated just how much could be learned from research conducted in a field setting but with some experimental controls. It also showed that proper research can provide strong insights into the impact of ad campaigns. (Many advertising researchers consider this study one of the most conclusive ever conducted in the attempt to demonstrate the effects of advertising on sales.)

The Seagram study also reveals some of the disadvantages associated with test market measures, not the least of which are cost and time. Few firms have the luxury to spend three years and hundreds of thousands of dollars on such a test. In addition, there is always the fear that competitors may discover and intervene in the research process.

A number of companies, including Procter & Gamble and Toyota, have test-marketed interactive commercials. Reckitt—the world's largest manufacturer of household cleaning products—and Whirlpool have joined efforts to test iTV ads. Customers were offered three different enticements to interact with the campaign: (1) register to win a Whirlpool dishwasher, (2) register for free samples of Finish Dishwater Freshener, or (3) order money-off coupons for Finish Dishwater Tablets. After eight months of testing, Reckitt reported that the target goal of 35,000 responses was exceeded.[19]

Test marketing can provide substantial insight into the effectiveness of advertising if care is taken to minimize the negative aspects of such tests.

Single-Source Tracking Studies Since the 1980s the focus of many research efforts has been on single-source tracking methods. **Single-source tracking methods** track the behaviors of consumers from the television set to the supermarket checkout counter. Participants in a designated area who have cable TV and agree to participate in the studies use optical scanning equipment that identifies their household and gives the research company their demographics. The households are split into matched groups; one group receives an ad while the other does not, or alternate ads are sent to each. Their purchases are recorded from the bar codes of the products bought. Commercial exposures are then correlated with purchase behaviors.

Earlier we mentioned the use of single-source ad research in pretesting commercials. The single-source method can also be used effectively to posttest ads, allowing for a variety of dependent measures and tracking the effects of increased ad budgets and different versions of ad copy—and even ad effects on sales.

A 10-year study conducted by Information Resources's BehaviorScan service demonstrated long-term effects of advertising on sales. The study examined copy, media schedules, ad budgets, and the impact of trade promotions on sales in 10 markets throughout the United States and concluded that advertising can produce sales growth as long as two years after a campaign ends.[20] (The study also concluded that results of copy recall and persuasion tests were unlikely to predict sales reliably.) A number of single-source methods have been used, including the Nielsen Company's Catalina.

Many advertisers believe these single-source measures will change the way research is conducted due to the advantages of control and the ability to measure directly the ads' effects on sales. A number of major corporations and ad agencies are now employing this method, including companies and their agencies in the automotive, entertainment, financial services, packaged goods, and pharmaceutical industries among others. Nielsen has used Catalina to improve the marketing efforts of beer, frozen foods, and coffee companies.

Whereas single-source testing is a valuable tool, it still has some problems. One researcher says, "Scanner data focus on short-term sales effects, and as a result capture only 10 to 30 percent of what advertising does."[21] Others complain that the data are too complicated to deal with, as an overabundance of information is available. Still another disadvantage is the high cost of collecting single-source data. While the complexity of single-source data resulted in a slow adoption rate, this method of tracking advertising effectiveness became widely adopted in the 1990s by the research companies mentioned earlier (G&R, Millward Brown, and Ipsos-ASI).

Tracking Print/Broadcast Ads One of the more useful and adaptable forms of posttesting involves tracking the effects of the ad campaign by taking measurements at regular intervals. **Tracking studies** have been used to measure the effects of advertising on awareness, recall, interest, and attitudes toward the ad and/or brand as well as purchase intentions. (Ad tracking may be applied to both print and broadcast ads but is much more common with the latter.) Personal interviews, phone surveys, mall intercepts, and even mail surveys have been used. Sample sizes typically range from 250 to 500 cases per period (usually quarterly or semiannually). Tracking studies yield perhaps the most valuable information available to the marketing manager for assessing current programs and planning for the future. (See Exhibit 18–8.)

EXHIBIT 18–8

Firefly (www.fireflymb.com) was created by Millward Brown to drive brand success through tracking studies and other measurements

Source: Firefly Millward Brown

The major advantage of tracking studies is that they can be tailored to each specific campaign and/or situation. A standard set of questions can track effects of the campaign over time or through the consumer purchase funnel. In a study by the research organization Yankelovich and the Television Bureau of Advertising (TVB), it was shown that the effectiveness of advertising depends on the product category and where the consumer is in the purchase funnel. The advertising medium impact varied as the consumer moved through the stages.[22] The effects of various media can also be determined, although with much less effectiveness. Tracking studies have also been used to measure the differential impact of different budget sizes, the effects of flighting, brand or corporate image, and recall of specific copy points. As you will see later in the chapter, however, it is often difficult to quantify some of the measures suggested. Finally, when designed properly, as shown in Figure 18–17, tracking studies offer a high degree of reliability and validity.

Some of the problems of recall and recognition measures are inherent in tracking studies, since many other factors may affect both brand and advertising recall. Despite these limitations, however, tracking studies are a very effective way to assess the effects of advertising campaigns.

In summary, you can see that each of the testing methods considered in this chapter has its strengths and its limitations. You may wonder: Can we actually test advertising effectiveness? What can be done to ensure a valid, reliable test? The next section of this chapter suggests some answers.

ESTABLISHING A PROGRAM FOR MEASURING ADVERTISING EFFECTS

There is no surefire way to test advertising effectiveness. However, in response to pressures to determine the contribution of ads—traditional and online—to the overall marketing effort, steps are being taken to improve this measurement task. Let's begin by reviewing the major problems with some existing methods and then examine possible improvements.

FIGURE 18–17

Factors That Make or Break Tracking Studies

1. Properly defined objectives.
2. Alignment with sales objectives.
3. Properly designed measures (e.g., adequate sample size, maximum control over interviewing process, adequate time between tracking periods).
4. Consistency through replication of the sampling plan.
5. Random samples.
6. Continuous interviewing (that is, not seasonal).
7. Evaluation of measures related to behavior (attitudes meet this criterion; recall of ads does not).
8. Critical evaluative questions asked early to eliminate bias.
9. Measurement of competitors' performance.
10. Skepticism about questions that ask where the advertising was seen or heard (TV always wins).
11. Building of news value into the study.
12. "Moving averages" used to spot long-term trends and avoid seasonality.
13. Data reported in terms of relationships rather than as isolated facts.
14. Integration of key marketplace events with tracking results (e.g., advertising expenditures of self and competitors, promotional activities associated with price changes in ad campaigns, introductions of new brands, government announcements, changes in economic conditions).

Problems with Current Research Methods

When current testing methods are compared to the criteria established by PACT (see Figure 18–4) and Making Measurement Make Sense (Figure 18–5), it is clear that some of the principles important to good testing can be accomplished readily, whereas others require substantially more effort. For example, PACT principle 6 (providing equivalent test ads) should require a minimum of effort. The researcher can easily control the state of completion of the test communications. Also fairly easy are principles 1 and 2 (providing measurements relative to the objectives sought and determining *a priori* how the results will be used). In regard to Figure 18–5, and digital measurement, some of the principles (for example, principle 2, the currency issue, and 5, comparable measures) may not be difficult to achieve.

We have seen throughout this text that each promotional medium, the message, and the budget all consider the marketing and communications objectives sought. The integrated marketing communications planning model establishes the roles of these elements. So by the time one gets to the measurement phase, the criteria by which these programs will be evaluated should simply fall into place.

Slightly more difficult are PACT principles 3, 5, and 8, although again these factors are largely in the control of the researcher. Principle 3 (providing multiple measurements) may require little more than budgeting to make sure more than one test is conducted. At the most, it may require considering two similar measures to ensure reliability. Likewise, principle 5 (exposing the test ad more than once) can be accomplished with a proper research design. Finally, principle 8 (sample definition) requires little more than sound research methodology; any test should use the target audience to assess an ad's effectiveness. You would not use a sample of nondrinkers to evaluate new liquor commercials. Likewise principles 3 and 4 on the digital side might take some time and give and take, but can be accomplished.

The most difficult factors to control—and the principles that may best differentiate between good and bad testing procedures—are PACT requirements 4, 7, and 9. Fortunately, however, addressing each of these contributes to the attainment of the others. On the digital side, developing "viewable impressions" is proving to be a difficult task.

While it is important that marketers' attempts to measure effectiveness be guided by all of the principles stated, the research should be guided by a model of human response to communications that encompasses reception, comprehension, and behavioral response. It is the best starting point, in our opinion, because it is the principle least addressed by practicing researchers. If you recall, Chapter 5 proposed a number of models that could fulfill this requirement. Yet even though the models have existed for quite some time, few if any common research methods attempt to integrate them into their methodologies. Most current methods do little more than provide recall scores, despite the fact that many researchers have shown recall to be a poor measure of effectiveness. Models that do claim to measure such factors as attitude change or brand preference change are often fraught with problems that severely limit their reliability. Once again, a problem with digital metrics is that they often don't provide insights into the consumer response processes because the measures are behavioral and provide no insights into the emotional side. An effective measure must include some relationship to the communication process.

It might seem at first glance that PACT principle 7 (providing a nonbiasing exposure) would be easy to accomplish. But lab measures, while offering control, are artificial and vulnerable to testing effects. And field measures, although more realistic, often lose control. The Seagram and Time study may have the best of both worlds, but it is too large a task for most firms to undertake. Some of the improvements associated with the single-source systems help solve this problem. In addition, properly designed ad tracking studies provide truer measures of the impact of the communication. As technology develops and more attention is paid to this principle, we expect to see improvements in methodologies soon.

Last but not least is PACT principle 9, the concern for reliability and validity. This principle must carry over to online measures as well. Most of the measures discussed are lacking in at least one of these criteria, yet these are two of the most critical distinctions between good and bad research. If a study is properly designed, and by that we mean it addresses principles 1 through 8, it should be both reliable and valid. Studies designed to measure the impact of online advertising also need to adhere to the PACT principles as well as the Making Measurement Make Sense ones. As you have just read, many of the larger research firms mentioned here are now applying platforms to measure both traditional and digital ads. Given the history and credibility of these companies, they will no doubt make a valuable contribution to improving online measurements. However, for those companies not able or willing to employ large research companies, for there to be any validity in what they measure they must move beyond the exclusive use of digital measure like those shown in Figure 18–1.

Essentials of Effective Testing

Simply put, good tests of advertising effectiveness must address the nine principles established by PACT. One of the easiest ways to accomplish this is by following the decision sequence model in formulating promotional plans.

- *Establish communications objectives.* We have stated that except for a few instances (most specifically direct-response advertising), it is nearly impossible to show the direct impact of advertising on sales. So the marketing objectives established for the promotional program are not usually good measures of communication effectiveness. For example, it is very difficult (or too expensive) to demonstrate the effect of an ad on brand share or on sales. On the other hand, attainment of communications objectives can be measured and leads to the accomplishment of marketing objectives.
- *Use a consumer response model.* Early in this text we reviewed the hierarchy of effects models and cognitive response models, which provide an understanding of the effects of communications and lend themselves to achieving communications goals. Many companies including Honda, General Motors, Sprint, and others use hierarchy models to establish objectives and assess effectiveness in both the traditional and online environments.
- *Use both pretests and posttests.* From a cost standpoint—both actual cost outlays and opportunity costs—pretesting makes sense. It may mean the difference between success or failure of the campaign or the product. But it should work in conjunction with posttests, which avoid the limitations of pretests, use much larger samples, and take place in more natural settings. Posttesting may be required to determine the true effectiveness of the ad or campaign.
- *Use multiple measures.* Many attempts to measure the effectiveness of advertising focus on one major dependent variable—perhaps sales, recall, or recognition. As noted earlier in this chapter, advertising may have a variety of effects on the consumer, some of which can be measured through traditional methods and others that require updated thinking (recall the discussion on physiological responses). For a true assessment of advertising effectiveness, a number of measures may be required. The Ogilvy Award winners mentioned earlier all employed multiple measures to track the effects on communications objectives.
- *Understand and implement proper research.* It is critical to understand research methodology. What constitutes a good design? Is it valid and reliable? Does it measure what we need it to? There is no shortcut to this criterion, and there is no way to avoid it if you truly want to measure the effects of advertising.

A major study sponsored by the Advertising Research Foundation (ARF), involving interviews with 12,000 to 15,000 people, addressed some of these issues.[23] While we do not have the space to analyze this study here, note that the research was designed to evaluate measures of copy tests, compare copy testing procedures, and examine some of the PACT principles. ARF has published information on this study in a number of academic and trade journals.

MEASURING THE EFFECTIVENESS OF OTHER PROGRAM ELEMENTS

Throughout this text, we have discussed how and when promotional program elements should be used, the advantages and disadvantages of each, and so on. In many chapters we have discussed measures of effectiveness used to evaluate these programs. In the final section of this chapter, we add a few measures that were not discussed earlier.

Measuring the Effectiveness of Sales Promotions

Sales promotions are not limited to retailers and resellers of products. Sports marketers have found them a very effective way to attract crowds and have been able to measure their relative effectiveness by the number of fans attending games. Major League Baseball teams have seen their attendance increase for those games in which promotions are offered.

A number of organizations measure sales promotions. One firm, Market-Source, provides marketers with a basis for measuring the effectiveness of their sampling programs. While too involved to discuss in detail here, the program calculates a breakeven rate by dividing the sampling investment by the profit for the user. If the conversions exceed the breakeven rate, the sampling program is successful.[24] Promotion Decisions Inc. examines the impact of freestanding inserts (FSIs) in Figure 18–18.

Other measures of sales promotions are also available. For example, Prognos offers a Retail Promotion Effectiveness solution that gives retailers visibility into the factors that influence the effectiveness of all of their promotions, allowing the retailer to make the right decision about the right products to promote using promotional vehicles and understanding the required inventory levels. Other companies have

FIGURE 18–18

Measuring the Effects of FSIs

A study by Promotion Decisions Inc. examined the actual purchase data of users and nonusers of 27 coupon promotions in its National Shopper Lab (75,000 households) over a period of 18 months. The findings are as follows:

- FSI coupons generated significant trial by new and lapsed users of a product (53 percent).

- Repeat purchase rates were 11.8 percent higher among coupon redeemers than nonredeemers.

- 64.2 percent of repeat volume among coupon redeemers was without a coupon.

- There was no significant difference in share of volume between buyers who used coupons and those who did not.

- Coupons returned between 71 and 79 percent of their cost within 12 weeks.

- Full-page ads provided higher redemption rates, incremental volume, redemption by new users, and a higher number of repeat buyers than half-page ads.

- Consumers who used coupons were brand loyal.

used awareness tracking studies and count the number of inquiries, coupon redemptions, and sweepstakes entries. They also track sales during promotional and nonpromotional periods while holding other factors constant. The Nielsen Company's ScanTrack methodology helps marketers answer the questions regarding how many promotions to do and how this promotion compares to competitors', and what overall sales lifts are associated with individual promotions using scanner data. An article by SAS concludes that retailers that make promotion decisions without considering measurable customer behavior are at a great disadvantage in the marketplace.[25]

One interesting and useful technology designed to track the effectiveness of sales promotions at the point of sale is offered by Shopper Trak. Shopper Trak employs heat map technology in the store that views traffic; whether a person is coming or going; calculates the shopper's height (to differentiate between adults and children); and gauges traffic patterns and sales conversions, among other metrics. The system helps retailers evaluate the effectiveness of promotions or displays located throughout the store.[26]

Measuring the Effectiveness of Nontraditional Media

In Chapter 13, we noted that one of the disadvantages of employing nontraditional media is that it is usually difficult to measure the effectiveness of the programs. But some progress has been made, as shown in these examples:

- *The effects of shopping cart signage.* Earlier we discussed sales increases that occurred when shopping cart signage was used. We have also noted throughout this chapter that while increasing sales is a critical goal, many other factors may contribute to or detract from this measure. (It should be noted that these results are often provided by the companies that sell these promotional media.) At least one academic study examined the effectiveness of shopping cart signage on data besides sales.[27] This study used personal interviews in grocery stores to measure awareness of, attention to, and influence of this medium. Interestingly, it suggests shopping carts are much less effective than the sign companies claim.
- *The effectiveness of parking lot–based media.* In Chapter 13, we discussed advertising on parking lot signage and other areas to attempt to reach selective demographic groups. Now the Traffic Audit Bureau (TAB) is tracking the effectiveness of this form of advertising to give advertisers more reliable criteria on which to base purchase decisions. The TAB data verify ad placements, while the media vendors have employed Experian Simmons Market Research and Nielsen Media Research to collect ad impressions and advertising recall information. These measures are combined with sales tracking data to evaluate the medium's effectiveness.
- *The effects of in-store radio and television.* Interactive Market Systems (IMS) introduced software that enables clients to measure the effectiveness of in-store radio. The company planned to introduce similar software designed to measure in-store television advertising effectiveness.[28]
- *The effectiveness of other media.* A number of companies provide effectiveness measures to determine the impact of package designs, POP displays, trade show exhibits, and the like. Nielsen Entertainment and Massivemedia now offer a service to measure video game advertising effectiveness as well as that of other outdoor media. While it is not possible to list them all here, suffice it to say that if one wants to measure the impact of various IMC elements, the resources are available.

Measuring the Effectiveness of Sponsorships

In earlier chapters we discussed the growth in sponsorships and the reasons why organizations have increased their investments in this area. Along with the increased expenditures have come a number of methods for measuring the impact of sponsorships. Essentially, measures of sponsorship effectiveness can be categorized as exposure-based methods or tracking measures:[29]

- *Exposure methods.* Exposure methods can be classified as those that monitor the quantity and nature of the media coverage obtained for the sponsored event and those that estimate direct and indirect audiences. While commonly employed by corporations, scholars have heavily criticized these measures. For example, Michel Pham argues that media coverage is not the objective of sponsorships and should not be considered as a measure of effectiveness. He argues that the measures provide no indication of perceptions, attitude change, or behavioral change and should therefore not be considered as measures of effectiveness.[30]
- *Tracking measures.* These measures are designed to evaluate the awareness, familiarity, and preferences engendered by sponsorship based on surveys. A number of empirical studies have measured recall of sponsors' ads, awareness of and attitudes toward the sponsors and their products, and image effect, including brand and corporate images.

A number of companies now measure the effectiveness of sports and other sponsorships. For example, companies assign a value referred to as media equivalency and assign a monetary value to the amount of exposure the sponsor receives during the event. They review broadcasts and add up the number of seconds a sponsor's product name or logo can be seen clearly (for example, on signs or shirts). A total of 30 seconds is considered the equivalent of a 30-second commercial. (Such measures are of questionable validity.)

As with all other IMC touch points, marketers would like to measure the ROI of event sponsorships. But—like these other means of communication—this is usually not possible, so the focus will be on other more communication-oriented objectives. Figure 18–19 shows a Sponsorship Performance Matrix used by effectiveness measurement company SponsorMap. The vertical axis of this matrix measures the passion the target audience feels toward the sponsoring organization. The more emotionally attached to the property (sporting team, event, etc.), the higher the Passion Index. The horizontal axis measures sponsor appreciation—the Gratitude Index. According to SponsorMap, companies can achieve more appreciation by being more active, thus creating more goodwill. As can be seen in Figure 18–19,

FIGURE 18–19

Sponsorship Performance Matrix

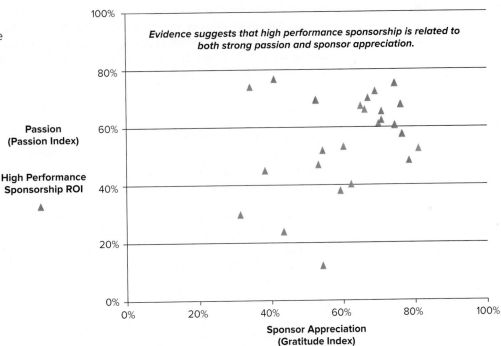

the sponsor would want to be in the upper right-hand corner to achieve maximum effectiveness.

Performance research measures impact on brand awareness and image shifts. Tracking the number of website visits and buzz generated are also criteria that have been used.

While each of these measures has its advantages and disadvantages, most do not go far enough. As noted by John Nardone and Ed See, most marketers limit their sponsorship evaluations to brand awareness and impressions. The key question that needs to be asked, they say, is "how do you do sponsorships that build brand equity and maintain financial responsibility?"[31] We suggest using several in assessing the impact of sponsorships. In addition to those mentioned here, the eight-step process suggested in Figure 18–20 could be used to guide these evaluations.

Measuring the Effectiveness of Other IMC Program Elements

Many of the organizations mentioned in this chapter offer research services to measure the effectiveness of specific promotional program elements. As we noted at the outset of this chapter, the increased use of integrated marketing communications programs has led to more interest in determining the synergistic effects of all program elements. A review of the Ogilvy Award winners from 1993 to date demonstrates the increased integration of additional media (as opposed to specifically the best advertising campaign) and the value of measuring their contribution to the program's success. Also departing from the specific focus on advertising are the awards given by the London-based *Institute of Practitioners,* which has opened the competition to nontraditional media as well as public relations, sales promotions, and other entries.

As noted, a number of studies have been implemented to determine the combined effects of two or more media as well as their synergistic impact. The number of studies being designed to specifically measure synergistic effects continues to increase—most of which demonstrate a higher effectiveness when multiple media are employed. For example, after receiving negative publicity from a number of sources, Walmart increased its public relations activities and its advertising designed to enhance its corporate image. In less than a year, Walmart was able to show significant improvement in its image, which the company directly attributes to the combined use of the two program elements.[32]

As previously stated, a number of research firms such as Millward Brown and Nielsen Media Research are applying traditional advertising effectiveness measures to their online advertising to assess their overall communications effects.[33]

Perhaps the major challenge facing the adoption of an IMC approach is determining the effectiveness and contribution of various elements of the IMC program. A number of academic studies have offered insights into this endeavor, as has at

FIGURE 18–20

Eight Steps to Measuring Event Sponsorship

1. Narrowly define objectives with specifics.

2. Establish solid strategies against which programming will be benchmarked and measure your programming and effectiveness against the benchmark.

3. Set measurable and realistic goals; make sure everything you do supports them.

4. Enhance, rather than just change, other marketing variables.

5. Don't pull Marketing Plan 101 off the shelf. Programming should be crafted to reflect the particulars of your company's constituencies and target audiences.

6. Define the scope of your involvement. Will it involve multiple areas within the company? Who internally and externally constitutes the team?

7. Think "long term." It takes time to build brand equity. Also, think of leveraging your sponsorship through programming for as long as possible, before and after the event.

8. Build evaluation and a related budget into your overall sponsoring program. Include items such as pre- and postevent attitude surveys, media analyses, and sales results.

FIGURE 18–21

Measuring Effectiveness, Not Only Efficiency

The most important issue for IMC planning is identifying the most appropriate contact mix, that is, which contacts to prioritize.

Questions: Are we . . .	
Being effective:	1. Doing the right things?
Being efficient:	2. Doing things right?

Current techniques measure only efficiency

Reach, frequency, GRPs (media surveys)

Weight of market activity (stochastic)

MCA by integration measures effectiveness and efficiency

Influence of contacts

Consumer brand experience

least one company. For example, Dinner et al. examined the "presence, magnitude, and carryover of cross-channel effects for online advertising (display and search) and traditional media."[34] Their conclusion was that cross-channel effects do exist and are important. A study conducted by John M. McGrath concluded that there is tentative evidence that an IMC approach might lead to positive effects on attitudinal and behavioral intentions measures. McGrath called for additional research into the area.[35]

One very effective approach to measuring the impact of the IMC program is that provided by the marketing communications research company Integration. The company's approach is based on the belief that integrated marketing communications improve both the efficiency and the effectiveness of a campaign. Integration contends that most traditional measurement techniques focus only on the former of these (see Figure 18–21). Noting the increased demand for marketing managers to prioritize the media vehicles used to promote their brands, Integration developed Market Contact Audit (MCA) to measure both the efficiency and the effectiveness of media used to establish contacts with consumers. By measuring consumers' understanding, evaluation, and perceptions of the contacts and their association with the brand, MCA allows marketers to assess the overall effectiveness as well as the relative contribution of individual IMC elements.[36]

Despite these efforts, it appears we still have a long way to go to determine the overall effectiveness of an IMC program. All the advertising effectiveness measures discussed here have their inherent strengths and weaknesses. They offer the advertiser some information that may be useful in evaluating the effectiveness of promotional efforts. While not all promotional efforts can be evaluated effectively, progress is being made.

Summary

This chapter introduced you to issues involved in measuring the effects of advertising and promotions. These issues include reasons for testing, reasons companies do not test, and the review and evaluation of various research methodologies. We arrived at a number of conclusions: (1) Advertising research to measure effectiveness is important to the promotional program, (2) not enough companies test their ads, and (3) problems exist with current research methodologies. In addition, we reviewed the criteria for sound research and suggested some ways to accomplish effective studies.

All marketing managers should want to know how well their promotional programs are working. This information is critical to planning for the next period, since program adjustments and/or maintenance are based on evaluation of current strategies. Problems often result when the measures taken to determine such effects are inaccurate or improperly used.

This chapter demonstrated that testing must meet a number of criteria (defined by PACT and Making Measurement Make Sense) to be successful. These evaluations should occur both before and after the campaigns are implemented.

A variety of research methods were discussed, many provided by syndicated research firms such as Ipsos-ASI, MSW•ARS, Millward Brown, and the Nielsen Co. All of these companies have expanded their service offerings

CHAPTER 18

to assist in the evaluation of online and other advertising platforms. Many companies have developed their own testing systems. There has been an increase in testing through the Internet.

Single-source research data were discussed. These single-source systems offer strong potential for improving the effectiveness of ad measures in the future, since commercial exposures and reactions may be correlated to actual purchase behaviors. However, to date their use has not met expectations.

It is important to recognize that different measures of effectiveness may lead to different results. Depending on the criteria used, one measure may show that an ad or promotion is effective while another states that it is not. This is why clearly defined objectives and the use of multiple measures are critical to determining the true effects of an IMC program.

Key Terms

vehicle option source effect 619
pretests 619
posttests 619
laboratory tests 620
testing bias 621
field tests 621
Positioning Advertising Copy Testing (PACT) 621
concept testing 622
comprehension and reaction tests 624
consumer juries 624

halo effect 625
A/B testing 625
portfolio test 626
mock magazine test 627
Flesch formula 627
theater test 628
on-air test 629
recall 629
pupillometrics 629
electrodermal response (EDR) 630
eye tracking 631

electroencephalographic (EEG) measures 632
alpha activity 632
hemispheric lateralization 633
inquiry tests 633
split-run test 634
recognition method 634
recall tests 636
single-source tracking method 639
tracking studies 639

Discussion Questions

1. A/B testing has been used by marketers for decades to evaluate two different versions of finished ads and/or web pages. Some experts now believe that A/B testing would be more effective if employed earlier in the campaign development process. Explain what they mean by this, and argue for or against this position. (LO 18-1)

2. Explain why it is so difficult to measure the overall IMC program effectiveness. (LO 18-3)

3. This chapter discussed the Ogilvy Awards. Describe what these awards are and how they have changed over time. Give examples of companies that have won these awards (you can find past winners online) and why they have won them. (LO 18-1)

4. Explain why it is important to pretest. When should this testing take place? Give examples of what might make ads or commercials that are pretested more successful. (LO 18-1).

5. Digital advertisers seem to want to have their own effectiveness measures, while eschewing those of traditional advertisers. What are the pros and cons of this position? Argue for one side or the other. (LO 18-4)

6. Most managers believe that they should be measuring the effectiveness of their advertising programs. However, studies have shown that they usually do not do so. Cite some of the reasons why managers should measure effectiveness and why they do not. (LO 18-1)

7. Marketers have turned to physiological measures in an attempt to determine the effectiveness of their advertising. Discuss some of the methods now being used and the advantages and disadvantages of each. (LO 18-3)

8. How have marketers employed the methodology of eye tracking? Give examples of companies that have employed this methodology. When does eye tracking seem to be most useful? (LO 18-3)

9. Describe the *Starch Ad Readership Report* and the measures provided in the report. Discuss how Starch has had to adapt this report due to changing market conditions, and the new metrics now provided. (LO 18-2)

10. Explain why different metrics may be more useful to marketers in determining the effectiveness of their advertising at different times. Give examples of which metrics may be useful as consumers go through the purchase decision process. (LO 18-4)

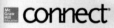

Digital users can access their personalized and adaptive SmartBook, Ad Forum Video Cases, and interactive exercises to review chapter concepts.

19 International Advertising and Promotion

Source: The Coca-Cola Company

LEARNING OBJECTIVES

LO1 Describe the role and importance of international marketing and promotion.

LO2 Discuss how economic, cultural, legal, and other factors in the international environment affect advertising and promotional decisions.

LO3 Compare global versus localized advertising and promotion.

LO4 Discuss the decision areas of international advertising.

LO5 Describe the role of other elements of the promotional mix in the international IMC program.

COCA-COLA WANTS PEOPLE AROUND THE WORLD TO "TASTE THE FEELING"

Coca-Cola is one of the most recognizable and valuable brands in the world, consistently ranking at or near the top of various brand value surveys. The flagship soft drink Coca-Cola, or Coke as it often referred to, is the world's number 1 beverage brand and is sold in more than 200 countries around the globe. The iconic brand has been around for more than 130 years and has never strayed from its timeless and basic ideals. While a number of different advertising campaigns have come and gone throughout the years, Coca-Cola has remained consistent in appealing to one basic emotion: pleasure. Many of the popular advertising campaigns used to sell Coca-Cola have been built around simple slogans using words such as *smile, enjoy*, and *happiness* that translate easily to consumers everywhere.

From 2009 until 2016, Coca-Cola's global IMC campaign used the slogan "Open Happiness" which was designed to appeal to consumers' desire for comfort and optimism and was an invitation to consumers around the world to refresh themselves with a Coke and enjoy life. The "Open Happiness" campaign won numerous awards: Coca-Cola was named *Advertising Age* Marketer of the Year in 2013 and was honored as Creative Marketer of the Year in 2013 at the Cannes Lions International Festival of Creativity. However, in 2016, Coca-Cola's new chief marketing officer, Marcos de Quinto, announced that the company would be making a major shift in its marketing strategy whereby all Coke trademark brands will be united in one global creative campaign called "Taste the Feeling." The new campaign puts the product at the center of every ad as Coca-Cola seeks to win over more drinkers in the struggling soda category.

In explaining the reasons for the change, de Quinto noted that "Open Happiness" had become a lofty, ideal-based campaign because it was being used to address various societal issues through initiatives such as its 2015 Super Bowl ad that focused on online bullying or messages that promoted peaceful co-existence among nations. He argued that the campaign had become a bit too preachy and was no longer focusing on simple pleasures, such as enjoying an ice-cold Coke on a hot day. Coca-Cola's global vice president for creative noted that Coke no longer wants to be about "fixing happiness" with high-level ideas; the new campaign is about living in the intimacy and simplicity of moments and is similar to the classic tagline "Have a Coke and a Smile." The "Taste the Feeling" campaign is designed to bring to life the idea that drinking a Coca-Cola product is a simple pleasure that makes everyday moments more special and celebrates the experience of doing so. The company also feels that the new campaign is more focused on the actual product and will build a strong connectivity with the feeling one has when drinking a Coke. CMO de Quinto notes: "We want to help remind people why they love the product as much as they love the brand."

The "Taste the Feeling" global campaign was launched in 2016 in 195 countries and includes print, TV, digital, out-of-home, and in-store marketing. The campaign kicked off with a lead commercial called "Anthem" which puts a Coke at the center of ordinary moments such ice skating with friends, a first date, and a first kiss and features rising pop star Conrad Swell doing the singing for the spot. Another commercial is set to the Queen and David Bowie song "Under Pressure" and showcases Coke as a way to release everyday pressures faced by teens. Music plays a key role in all of the communications for the campaign, with various spots including songs produced by Swedish artist Avicii.

Another major part of the new strategy is a "one-brand" approach that will unite various brands such as Coca-Cola Light/Diet Coke, Coke Zero, and Coca-Cola Life under one personality rather than running different campaigns for each. Diet Coke and Coke Zero are positioned as customized choices for drinkers who may want a sugar-free soft drink. The one-brand approach includes a global packaging shift as the new cans and bottles for the entire Coca-Cola trademark line will feature the brand's signature "Red Disc" which has become a signature element of the brand through the years. The new packaging was launched in Mexico and parts of Europe but is not expected to be used in North America until at least 2017. In some European countries such as Spain, a new can design features the color red on the top half of the cans, with different colors on the bottom representing varieties such as the flagship Coca-Cola brand, Coke Zero, and Coca-Cola Light (Diet Coke is marketed as Coca-Cola Light in all markets except North America, Australia, and the UK).

Implementation of the new global strategy is a major undertaking and 4 of the 10 agencies Coca-Cola works with worldwide are taking a lead role in the "Taste the Feeling" campaign, including Ogilvy New York, Sra. Rushmore of Madrid, Santo of Buenos Aires, and Mercado-McCann of Argentina. However, other agencies will contribute content to the integrated campaign as it evolves. Coca-Cola is phasing in the one-brand approach more slowly in North America where Diet Coke and Coke Zero have carved out unique identities and will continue to work with agencies for these brands in markets such as the United States. However, the company's long-term goal is to bring the two brands under the Coca-Cola branding umbrella to avoid consumers viewing them as having a separate identity.

Coca-Cola knows it has a lot riding on the new "Taste the Feeling" campaign, but feels that changes were needed to address the challenges it is facing in the global market such as declining soda consumption in many markets amid growing health concerns and a shift to healthier lifestyles. Marcos de Quinto believes that the new "Taste the Feeling" global IMC campaign, as well as the new packaging strategy, will help consumers around the world better connect with the brand and various Coke products. His goal is to keep things simple for consumers and return to the essence of what the Coca-Cola brand is about: a brand for everybody and one that makes them feel good.

Sources: Natalie Zmuda, "Coca-Cola Unveils New Global Packaging: All Coke Varieties Will Feature Brand's Global Trademark," *Advertising Age*, April 18, 2016, http://adage.com/article/cmo-strategy/coca-cola-unveils-global-packaging/303613/; E. J. Schultz, "Coke Replace 'Open Happiness' with 'Taste the Feeling' in Major Strategic Shift," *Advertising Age*, January 19, 2016, http://adage.com/article/cmo-strategy/coke-debuts-taste-feeling-campaign-strategic-shift/302184/; Jay Mole, "One Brand Strategy, New Global Campaign Unite Coca-Cola Trademark," *Coca-Cola Journey*, January 19, 2016, www.coca-colacompany.com/tastethefeeling.

The primary focus of this book so far has been on integrated marketing communications programs for products and services sold in the U.S. market. Many American companies have traditionally devoted most of their marketing efforts to the domestic market, since they often lack the resources, skills, or incentives to go abroad. This is changing rapidly, however, as U.S. corporations recognize the opportunities that foreign markets offer for new sources of sales and profits as well as the need to market their products internationally. Many companies are striving to develop global brands that can be advertised and promoted the world over.

In this chapter, we look at international advertising and promotion and the various issues marketers must consider in communicating with consumers around the globe. We examine the environment of international marketing and how companies often must adapt their promotional programs to conditions in each country. We review the debate over whether a company should use a global marketing and advertising approach or tailor it specifically for various countries.

We also examine how firms organize for international advertising, select agencies, and consider various decision areas such as creative strategy and media selection. While the focus of this chapter is on international advertising, we also consider other promotional-mix elements in international marketing, including sales promotion, publicity/public relations, and digital and social media. Let's begin by discussing some of the reasons international marketing has become so important to companies.

THE IMPORTANCE OF INTERNATIONAL MARKETS

One of the major developments in the business world over the past several decades has been the globalization of markets. The emergence of a largely borderless world has created a new reality for all types of companies. Today, world trade is driven by global competition among global companies for global consumers.[1] With the development of faster communication, transportation, and financial transactions, time and distance are no longer barriers to global marketing. Products and services

EXHIBIT 19–1

Tourism Australia promotes the country as a travel destination with the "There's Nothing Like Australia" campaign

Source: Tourism Australia

developed in one country quickly make their way to other countries, where they are finding enthusiastic acceptance. Consumers around the world wear Nike shoes and apparel and Levi's jeans, eat at McDonald's, shave with Gillette razors, use Dell and Lenovo computers as well as Apple and Samsung smartphones, drink Coca-Cola and Pepsi Cola soft drinks and Starbucks coffee, communicate on phones made by Samsung, Apple, and Xiaomi, and drive cars made by global automakers such as Ford, Honda, General Motors, Toyota, BMW, and Volkswagen.[2]

Companies are focusing on international markets for a number of reasons. Many companies in the United States and Western Europe recognize that their domestic markets offer them limited opportunities for expansion because of slow population growth, saturated markets, intense competition, and/or an unfavorable marketing environment. For example, soft-drink consumption in the United States has been declining over the past decade as consumers turn to healthier beverages such as juices, teas, and fortified waters. The industry has also been under pressure from public health groups and regulatory agencies in both the United States and the European Union because of concerns over the consumption of sugared soft drinks and childhood obesity.[3] Thus companies like PepsiCo and Coca-Cola are looking to international markets in Asia, Africa, and Latin America for growth opportunities.[4]

Many companies must focus on foreign markets to survive. Most European nations are relatively small in size and without foreign markets would not have the economies of scale to compete against larger U.S. and Japanese companies. For example, Swiss-based Nestlé and Netherlands-based Unilever are two of the world's largest consumer-product companies because they have learned how to market their brands to consumers in countries around the world. Australia's tourist industry is a major part of its economy and relies heavily on visitors from other countries. Tourism Australia, the federal government agency responsible for the country's international and domestic tourism marketing, has been running a global campaign called "There's Nothing Like Australia," which is designed to attract visitors by showcasing the diversity of places to visit and experiences available across the country.

In 2016, Tourism Australia launched a variation of its global IMC campaign that highlights the country's world-class aquatic and coastal experiences which are its key competitive advantages as a tourist destination. The campaign is based on research showing that 70 percent of Australia's international visitors enjoy these experiences as part of their trip to the country, but many tourists do not have a full appreciation of the breadth, depth, and quality of experiences such as visiting the Sydney Harbor and its famous opera house, snorkeling on the Great Barrier Reef, or taking a helicopter ride over the 12 Apostles (Exhibit 19–1). In addition to digital, print, and television advertising, Tourism Australia is using virtual reality (VR) at travel expos and events to give prospective travelers an immersive experience and capture what it feels like to visit many of its aquatic and coastal attractions.[5]

Companies are also pursuing international markets because of the opportunities they offer for growth and profits. The dramatic economic, social, and political changes around the world in recent years have opened markets in China and Eastern Europe. China's joining of the World Trade Organization in 2001 has provided foreign competitors with access to 1.3 billion potential Chinese consumers, and Western marketers are eager to sell them a variety of products and services.[6] The growing markets of the Far East, Latin America, Africa, and other parts of the world present tremendous opportunities to marketers of consumer products and services as well as business-to-business marketers.

Many companies in the United States, as well as in other countries, are also pursuing international markets out of economic necessity as they recognize that globalization is revolutionizing the world far more radically and rapidly than industrial development and technological changes of previous eras. In his influential book *The World Is Flat: A Brief History of the Twenty-First Century*, Thomas L. Friedman discusses how the economic flattening of the earth is being stimulated by technology

EXHIBIT 19–2

The WD-40 Co. gets much of its sales growth from foreign markets such as Latin America

Source: WD-40 Company

that is breaking down barriers that historically inhibited and restricted international trade. He notes that companies in the United States can prosper only if they are able to compete in the global marketplace that encompasses the 95 percent of the world's population that lives beyond our borders.[7]

Most major multinational companies have made the world their market and generate much of their sales and profits from abroad. However, international markets are important to small and midsize companies as well as the large multinational corporations. Many of these firms can compete more effectively in foreign markets, where they may face less competition or appeal to specific market segments or where products have not yet reached the maturity stage of their life cycle. For example, the WD-40 Co. has saturated the U.S. market with its lubricant product and now gets much of its sales growth from markets in Europe, Asia, Latin America, China, and Australia (Exhibit 19–2).

Another reason it is increasingly important for U.S. companies to adopt an international marketing orientation is that imports are taking a larger and larger share of the domestic market for many products. The United States has been running a continuing **balance-of-trade deficit**; the monetary value of our imports exceeds that of our exports. American companies are realizing that we are shifting from being an isolated, self-sufficient, national economy to being part of an interdependent *global economy*. This means U.S. corporations must defend against foreign inroads into the domestic market as well as learn how to market their products and services to other countries.

While many U.S. companies are becoming more aggressive in their pursuit of international markets, they face stiff competition from large multinational corporations from other countries. Some of the world's most formidable marketers are European companies such as Unilever, Nestlé, Siemens, Philips, and Reckitt Benckiser as well as the various Japanese and South Korean automotive and consumer electronic manufacturers such as Honda, Toyota, Sony, Samsung, Hyundai, and LG.

THE ROLE OF INTERNATIONAL ADVERTISING AND PROMOTION

Advertising and promotion are important parts of the marketing program of firms competing in the global marketplace. An estimated $183 billion was spent on advertising in the United States in 2015, with much of this money being spent by multinational companies headquartered outside this country. Advertising expenditures outside the United States have increased by nearly 70 percent since 1990, reaching almost $500 billion in 2015. Global marketers based in the United States, as well as European and Asian countries, increased their worldwide advertising, particularly on digital marketing.[8] Figure 19–1 shows the top 10 companies in terms of worldwide advertising spending.

In addition, estimates are that another $500 billion is spent on sales promotion efforts targeted at consumers, retailers, and wholesalers around the world. The United States is still the world's major advertising market, accounting for over one-third of the estimated $563 billion in worldwide ad expenditures. Nearly 90 percent of the money spent on advertising products and services around the world is concentrated in the United States and Canada along with the industrialized countries of Western Europe and the Pacific Rim, including Japan, South Korea, and Australia. However, advertising spending is increasing rapidly in markets outside North America, Europe, and Japan such as India, China, and Brazil.[9]

More and more companies recognize that an effective promotional program is important for companies competing in foreign markets. As one international marketing scholar notes:

> Promotion is the most visible as well as the most culture bound of the firm's marketing functions. Marketing includes the whole collection of activities the firm performs in

FIGURE 19–1 Top 10 Companies by Worldwide Advertising Spending

Rank	Advertiser	Headquarters	Measured Media Spending (millions U.S. dollars)		
			Worldwide	Outside the U.S.	U.S. Spending
1	Procter & Gamble Co.	Cincinnati, Ohio	$10,125	$7,206	$2,919
2	Unilever	Rotterdam/London	7,394	6,550	844
3	L'Oréal	Clichy, France	5,264	3,790	1,474
4	Coca-Cola Co.	Atlanta, Georgia	3,279	2,870	409
5	Toyota Motor Corp.	Toyota City, Japan	3,185	1,982	1,203
6	Volkswagen	Wolfsburg, Germany	3,171	2,566	605
7	Nestlé	Vevey, Switzerland	2,930	2,227	703
8	General Motors	Detroit, Michigan	2,849	1,189	1,660
9	Mars, Inc.	McClean, Virginia	2,569	1,762	807
10	McDonald's Corp.	Oak Brook, Illinois	2,494	1,558	936

Source: "Global Marketers," *Advertising Age*, December 7, 2015.

relating to its market, but in other functions the firm relates to the market in a quieter, more passive way. With the promotional function, however, the firm is standing up and speaking out, wanting to be seen and heard.[10]

Many companies have run into difficulties developing and implementing advertising and promotion programs for international markets. Companies that promote their products or services abroad face an unfamiliar marketing environment and customers with different sets of values, customs, consumption patterns, and habits, as well as differing purchase motives and abilities. Languages vary from country to country and even within a country, such as India or Switzerland. Media options are quite limited in many countries, owing to lack of availability or limited effectiveness. These factors demand different creative and media strategies as well as changes in other elements of the advertising and promotional program for foreign markets.

THE INTERNATIONAL ENVIRONMENT

Just as with domestic marketing, companies engaging in international marketing must carefully analyze the major environmental factors of each market in which they compete, including economic, demographic, cultural, and political/legal variables. Figure 19–2 shows some of the factors marketers must consider in each category when analyzing the environment of each country or market. These factors are important in evaluating the potential of each country as well as designing and implementing a marketing and promotional program.

The Economic Environment

A country's economic conditions indicate its present and future potential for consuming, since products and services can be sold only to countries where there is enough income to buy them. This is generally not a problem in developed countries such as the United States, Canada, Japan, and most of Western Europe, where consumers generally have higher incomes and standards of living. Thus, they can and want to purchase a variety of products and services. Developed countries have the

FIGURE 19–2

Forces in the International
Marketing Environment

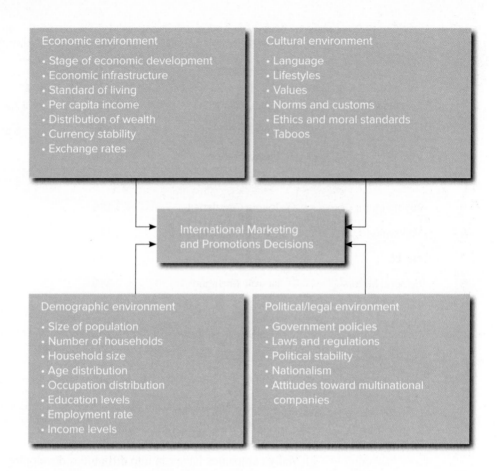

economic infrastructure in terms of the communications, transportation, financial, and distribution networks needed to conduct business in these markets effectively. By contrast, many developing countries lack purchasing power and have limited communications networks available to firms that want to promote their products or services to these markets.

For most companies, industrialized nations represent the greatest marketing and advertising opportunities. But most of these countries have stable population bases, and their markets for many products and services are already saturated. Many marketers are turning their attention to parts of the world whose economies and consumer markets are growing. For a number of years, the economies of the BRIC nations, which include Brazil, Russia, India, and China, grew faster than the world average and combined advertising spending in the four countries reached just over $100 billion in 2015. However, much of this growth recently has come from China and India as the economies of Russia and Brazil are experiencing high inflation and economic volatility.[11] Much of Brazil's growth prior to the recent economic downturn has come from an emerging lower middle class that now represents nearly half of the company's population.[12]

China and India in particular are two countries that are transforming the global economy. The two countries together account for a third of the world's population, and they both have had economic growth rates ranging from 6 to 10 percent over the past several years, which is much greater than other countries in the world. Each country has the fundamentals to sustain the high growth rates, including young populations, high savings, and a growing number of consumers who have the ability to purchase, as well as the need for, many products.[13]

Marketers of products such as mobile phones, TVs, personal computers, cars, as well as luxury items such as jewelry and designer clothing are focusing more

attention on consumers in India and China.[14] The growing middle class in these countries is also creating growth opportunities for marketers of consumer packaged-goods products, who are focusing a great deal of attention and spending more on advertising to reach these consumers. For example, China has become Nike's second-largest market, and the company is spending large amounts of money there on media advertising, promotions, events, and sponsorship of sports teams and athletes such as track star and Olympic gold medalist Liu Xiang (Exhibit 19–3). China has become the second-largest advertising market in the world, trailing only the United States, with Japan coming in third. Global Perspective 19–1 discusses the challenges and opportunities marketers face in China.

Many multinational companies are also turning their attention to other emerging markets such as Vietnam, the Philippines, and Bangladesh which are some of the fastest-growing economies because they have become manufacturing hubs with the migration of manufacturing away from China. Sub-Saharan African nations such as Nigeria and Kenya are also experiencing economic growth but are still underdeveloped, particularly in rural areas.[15]

Many multinational companies have also been focusing their attention on third-world countries and the 4 billion consumers who live in the remote, rural communities of developing countries where consumer markets are slowly emerging. Packaged-goods companies such as Procter & Gamble and Unilever sell soap, toothpaste, shampoo, and laundry detergents to consumers in remote villages. Often they adapt their products for these markets by making them available in single-use sachets that cost the equivalent of pennies rather than dollars and can be easily distributed and sold through the small kiosks found in rural villages. Many developing countries are becoming more stable and open to trade and direct foreign investment, while education levels are also improving. Although investment in these markets still requires a long-term perspective, many companies are recognizing that the billions of people in the third world are eager to become consumers and represent a major growth opportunity.

The Demographic Environment

Major demographic differences exist among countries as well as within them. Marketers must consider income levels and distribution, age and occupation distributions of the population, household size, education, and employment rates. In some countries, literacy rates are also a factor; people who cannot read will not respond well to print ads. Demographic data can provide insight into the living standards and lifestyles in a particular country to help companies plan ad campaigns.

Demographic information can reveal the market potential of various foreign markets. India's population was nearly 1.3 billion in 2016, half of whom are under the age of 25. Only China has a larger population with 1.36 billion. Latin America remains one of the world's largest potential markets, although the meager income of most consumers in the region is still a problem. Brazil, the largest consumer market in South America, now has a population of 205 million, although recent political and economic problems are impacting the country and consumer spending.[16] Many European countries as well as the United States, Canada, Japan, and China are experiencing low or even negative population growth and aging consumer base which is leading many companies to look to other parts of the world for growth. More than 50 percent of the Latin American market is younger than age 30; children are the fastest-growing demographic group in the region. These numbers have caught

Global Perspective 19–1 > > >

Marketers Look to China for Growth

For many years, marketers could only dream of selling their products to China's 1.36 billion consumers. However, with the end of the cultural revolution in 1979 and its massive modernization drive over the past four decades, China has become the fastest-growing consumer market in the world. Advertising, once banned as a capitalist scourge, is now encouraged by the Chinese government, which views it as a catalyst that can accelerate China's economic development. Underlying the growth of advertising in China is the tremendous economic growth of the country, particularly in the urban areas that are home to more than a half of the country's population versus 20 percent in 1985. There is also a new spirit of consumption, as reform in China has brought about dramatic increases in the purchasing power and size of the middle class. The average disposable income of Chinese consumers continues to rise and demand is increasing for many other products, including personal computers, mobile phones, automobiles, clothing, and luxury brands.

As China continues to develop, companies from the United States as well as other countries have been working to penetrate the Chinese market and for good reason. China's gross domestic product (GDP) in 2015 was nearly $11 trillion, making it the world's second-largest economy after the United States. While most countries have struggled to grow their economies, China has averaged nearly 8 percent GDP growth since 2010. The Middle Kingdom has become the world's largest automotive market with 24.9 million vehicles sold in the country in 2015 versus 17.4 million in the United States and 14 million in the European Union, and now accounts for 28 percent of global sales. In addition to automobiles, China has become the biggest market in the world for many other products including shoes, apparel, smartphones, and luxury goods such as watches, jewelry, and fashion accessories.

The newly emerging middle class in China is very brand conscious and demand for popular Western products from the United States and Europe, as well as goods from Japan and Korea, is increasing. Chinese consumers prefer foreign brands associated with technological innovation, status, and fashion while local brands prevail for more functional commoditized purchases such as washing machines, air conditioners, and refrigerators. However, Chinese consumers are no longer purchasing multinational brands based solely on country-of-origin; they have become much more savvy and discriminating. Many Western brands are struggling to stay relevant, particularly among millennials who have grown up under the one-child policy and during the boom years of double-digit economic growth. Millennials in China are very different from their parents and are focused on living an interesting and happy life and are very immersed in pop culture.

The size of the Chinese market and emerging middle class makes entering the market a no-brainer for most multinational companies. However, the realities of competing in the country are much more difficult since China's diverse customer base encompasses a broad range of economic disparity and cultural complexity. China lacks the marketing infrastructure that companies take for granted in the West. The country lacks quality consumer research data as well as distribution systems and it has very fragmented state-owned media. Advertisers are finding that television is the most effective way to reach China's masses—over 95 percent of Chinese consumers have a TV and they are more influenced by the attention of international advertisers such as Mattel, PepsiCo, Coca-Cola, Burger King, and others. Indonesia also has a very young population, with more people under the age of 16 than the United States, and they are very receptive to Western ways and products.

The Cultural Environment

Another important aspect of the international marketing environment is the culture of each country. Cultural variables that marketers must consider include language, customs, tastes, attitudes, lifestyles, values, and ethical/moral standards. Nearly every country exhibits cultural traits that influence not just the needs and wants of consumers but how they go about satisfying them.

Marketers must be sensitive not only in determining what products and services they can sell foreign cultures but also in communicating with them. Advertising is often the most effective way to communicate with potential buyers and create markets in other countries. But it can also be one of the most difficult aspects of the international marketing program because of problems in developing messages that will be understood in various countries.

© XiXinXing/Alamy RF

commercials than consumers in the West. However, China has only one national network, state-owned CCTV, which airs 16 channels 24 hours a day, seven days a week. Since there is only one national network, advertisers have little leverage when purchasing television time. They also find that it can be very challenging to develop TV ads that can communicate effectively with such a broad and diverse target audience that ranges from sophisticated urban dwellers to rural farmers.

The Internet and social media have also become very important IMC tools in China and are used by consumers to learn about brands. China has nearly 700 million Internet users, twice the entire U.S. population, and has also surpassed the United States to become the number 1 e-commerce market in world. E-commerce accounted for 22 percent of retail sales in China and is expected to increase to 38 percent by 2020. WeChat is an instant messaging app that has become particularly popular in China with nearly 700 million monthly active users. The app is used not only for communication purposes, but also includes services such as online payments, finance, taxi-hailing, and e-commerce. Social media are used extensively by consumers to research and share information about brands, and some experts suggest they have become substitutes for government enforcement of quality control.

Advertising agencies are also finding that doing business in China can be very challenging. Local clients are demanding and agency relationships last less than three years on average. Many multinational marketers are also breaking with global agency alignments in China and are working with local agencies as they expand deeper into the country. Nearly 75 percent of China's ad billings are in the hands of local agencies, which are becoming stronger and expanding their capabilities. One industry consultant noted that being a top executive for a multinational agency network in China is the toughest job in advertising because it is a market in transition with little or no account loyalty. Foreign agencies that want to be successful must also adapt to China's energy and culture. Local companies must be able to develop campaigns very quickly as well as work with country-specific digital platforms and understand the advanced mobile patterns of Chinese consumers.

Multinational companies recognize that the enormous size of the Chinese market, along with its strong economic development and growth, make it imperative for them to be there. By 2030, nearly two-thirds of the world's middle class will be in Asia while only 21 percent will reside in North America and Europe combined. The vice chair of the Omnicom Group summarized it best noting, "Asia is the future with the world's largest middle class, and China is at the center of it."

Sources: Angela Donald, "FF Shanghai Is *Ad Age*'s 2016 International Agency of the Year," *Advertising Age*, January 25, 2016, p. 46; "Why Foreign Brands Have to Figure Out China All over Again," *Advertising Age*, December 7, 2015, pp. 6–10; Angela Doland, "Five Insights on Marketing to China's Millennials," *Advertising Age*, August 13, 2015, http://adage.com/article/special-report-women-to-watch-china-2015/insights-marketing-china-s-millennials/299877; Hilary Masell Oswald, "A New Vantage Point," *Marketing News*, April 2013, pp. 38–42; Joan Voight, "The Great Brand of China," *Adweek*, October 29, 2012, p. 22.

International advertisers often have problems with language. The advertiser must know not only the native tongue of the country but also its nuances, idioms, and subtleties. International marketers must be aware of the connotations of words and symbols used in their messages and understand how advertising copy and slogans are translated. Marketers often encounter problems in translating their advertising messages and brand names into various languages. The ad for TaylorMade Burner Irons golf clubs shown in Exhibit 19–4 is one example. In the United States and other English-speaking countries, the tagline the advertising used is "The Set Is Dead." However, in Asian countries such as Japan and Korea, the word *dead* in the tagline did not translate well so it was changed to "The Set Is History," which made the meaning of the phrase easier to understand.

When the Colgate-Palmolive Co. launched its Colgate Max Fresh toothpaste brand in China, the company found that the brand name did not translate well, which led to it being changed to Icy Fresh. Colgate also had to change the description of the dissolvable mini breath strips that were part of the formulation of the product to cooling crystals since the concept of breath strips had no relevance to Chinese consumers.

Problems arising from language diversity and differences in signs and symbols that are used in marketing communications can usually be best solved with the help

EXHIBIT 19–4

The tagline used in this TaylorMade ad had to be changed for Asian countries because of translation problems

Source: TaylorMade Golf Company, Inc.

of local expertise. Marketers should consult local employees or use an ad agency knowledgeable in the local language that can help verify that the advertiser is saying what it wants to say. Many companies turn to agencies that specialize in translating advertising slogans and copy into foreign languages.[17]

Tastes, traditions, and customs are also an important part of cultural considerations. The customs of a society affect what products and services it will buy and how they must be marketed. In France, cosmetics are used heavily by men as well as women, and advertising to the male market is common. There are also cultural differences in the grooming and hygiene habits of consumers in various countries. For example, though many U.S. consumers use products like deodorant and shampoo daily, consumers in many other Western countries are not as fanatical about personal hygiene, so consumption of products such as deodorants and mouthwash is much lower than in the United States.

Another aspect of culture that is very important for international marketers to understand is values. **Cultural values** are beliefs and goals shared by members of a society regarding ideal end states of life and modes of conduct. Society shapes consumers' basic values, which affect their behavior and determine how they respond to various situations. For example, cultural values in the United States place a major emphasis on individual activity and initiative, while many Asian societies stress cooperation and conformity to the group. Values and beliefs of a society can also affect its members' attitudes and receptivity toward foreign products and services.[18] Values such as *ethnocentrism*, which refers to the tendency for individuals to view their own group or society as the center of the universe, or nationalism often affect the way consumers in various countries respond to foreign brands or even advertising messages.[19] For many years, consumers in many European countries were reluctant to buy American brands and there was even a backlash against American imagery. In fact, many U.S. companies doing business in Europe were careful not to flaunt their American roots.

In recent years, U.S. brands have become popular in many other European countries as well as in Asia. Marketers attribute the rising popularity of many U.S.-made products to the worldwide distribution of American music, films, and TV shows; the growth of the Internet; and the increase in travel to the United States. These factors have made consumers in foreign countries more familiar with American culture, values, and lifestyle.[20]

Japan is one of the more difficult markets for many American advertisers to understand because of its unique values and customs.[21] For example, the Japanese have a very strong commitment to the group; social interdependence and collectivism are as important to them as individualism is to most Americans. Ads stressing individuality and nonconformity have traditionally not done well in Japan, but Westernized values have become more prevalent in Japanese advertising in recent years.[22] However, the Japanese dislike ads that confront or disparage the competition and tend to prefer soft rather than hard sells.[23] A study found that Japanese and American magazine ads tend to portray teenage girls in different ways and that the differences correspond to each country's central concepts of self and society. In many American ads teens are associated with images of independence, rebelliousness, determination, and even defiance that are consistent with the American value of individuality. In contrast, Japanese ads tend to portray a happy, playful, childlike, girlish image that is consistent with the Japanese culture's sense of self, which is more dependent on others.[24] A study of the impact of the "Lost Decade," which refers to the period of economic stagnation and uncertainty that occurred during the 1990s and into the new millennium, on Japanese advertising resulted in a shift toward the use of more direct and persuasive selling approaches but being too blatantly direct could still be problematic.[25]

As advertisers turn their attention to China, more consideration is also being given to understanding the cultural system and values of the world's most populous country. Chinese values are centered on Confucianism, which stresses loyalty and interpersonal relationships. Chinese culture also emphasizes passive acceptance of fate by seeking harmony with nature; inner experiences of meaning and feeling; stability and harmony; close family ties; and tradition.[26]

Nike ran into a problem over a commercial that aired in China showing NBA basketball star LeBron James winning a battle with a Chinese dragon and a kung fu master. The commercial was banned by government regulators who stated that it created indignant feelings among Chinese television viewers because it showed an American sports icon defeating the dragon, a symbol of Chinese culture, and the martial arts master, a symbol of national pride. A statement posted on the website of China's State Administration for Radio, Film, and Television stated that the ad violated the regulation that "all advertisements must uphold national dignity and interest, and respect the motherland's culture." Nike's China marketing director said that it was not the company's intention to show disrespect to the Chinese culture, explaining that the ad was meant to inspire youth to overcome internal fear and obstacles in order to improve themselves. Toyota Motor Co. of Japan also had to retract an issue and apology for an ad that ran in magazines and newspapers in China depicting stone lions, a traditional sign of Chinese power, saluting and bowing to a Prado Land Cruiser sport-utility vehicle.[27] A recent study examined perceptions of offensive advertising among Chinese consumers living in Hong Kong and Shanghai. The study found that the central issue related to whether an ad was perceived as offensive by the type of execution and creative tactics used or by the offensiveness of the product or service being advertised. The researchers noted that despite the sophistication and modernization of these two major cities, consumers there remain conservative and, to some extent collectivist, as susceptibility to interpersonal influence affects this evaluation of offensive advertising. They recommended that marketers remain cautious when developing advertising for China and should not take too many risks with offensive advertising.[28]

Religion is another aspect of culture that affects norms, values, and behaviors and can have a strong influence on advertising in certain countries and regions. For example, in many Arab countries, religion has a major influence on cultural values and must be taken into consideration in developing advertising messages. Marketers must be aware of various taboos resulting from conservative applications of the Islamic religion. Alcohol and pork cannot be advertised. Human nudity is forbidden, as are pictures of anything sacred, such as images of a cross or photographs of Mecca. There are also strict guidelines regarding the use of women in advertising and the various roles to which they can be assigned. Women often do not appear in advertising and when they do only their eyes may be shown. In conservative Islamic countries, many religious authorities are opposed to advertising on the grounds that it promotes Western icons and culture and the associated non-Islamic consumerism. Restrictions on advertising still exist in some countries such as Iran, which has particularly averse feelings toward Western-style advertising. However, Western-style ads have become more prevalent in many Middle Eastern countries such as Qatar, the United Arab Emirates, and Lebanon.

Both Coca-Cola and PepsiCo have taken their cola wars to the Middle East and have been engaged in a battle to win the soft-drink allegiance of Arabs, especially the youth, in countries such as Lebanon, Saudi Arabia, Egypt, and Qatar. To reach the youth market, the two companies have used a variety of integrated marketing tools including media advertising, sponsorship of sports teams as well as sporting and musical events, and talent shows as well as branded entertainment. Global Perspective 19–2 discusses how the country of Qatar will be hosting the 2022 FIFA World Cup and the role IMC played in helping the Arab country secure the bid to host this popular sports event.

Expect Amazing from the 2022 FIFA World Cup in Qatar

The Fédération Internationale de Football Association (FIFA) World Cup is the largest single-event sporting competition in the world. The tournament, which is held once every four years, is FIFA's flagship event, involving the national soccer (or football, as it is referred to in most countries) teams from 32 qualifying nations. The FIFA World Cup is also the world's most widely viewed sporting event. Nearly 3 billion people worldwide tune in to the monthlong tournament on television, and over 3 million spectators usually attend the 64 matches played.

One of the goals of FIFA in awarding hosting rights is to promote the game of football around the globe, as well as in the host nation and region. The 2010 FIFA World Cup was played in South Africa, the 2014 tournament was held in Brazil, and Russia is hosting in 2018. In 2022, the small country of Qatar will become the first Middle Eastern and Arab nation to host the prestigious event.

Qatar is the smallest nation, both by population and by area, ever to have been awarded the right to host the FIFA World Cup; the country is approximately the size of the state of Connecticut and has a population of 2 million. Qatar recognized that its size could be perceived as a shortcoming in competing against Australia, Japan, South Korea, and the United States, the four other nations that bid for the right to host the 2022 FIFA World Cup. Rather than shying away from the issue, Qatar decided to turn its size into a positive by positioning itself as an environmentally and socially friendly host nation for the FIFA World Cup. As an example, the bid detailed how all of the stadiums, as well as nearly 90,000 hotel rooms and other amenities, would be within a 60-kilometer (37.3-mile) radius and easily accessible by public transportation from Doha, Qatar's capital. It also noted how the new, state-of-the-art stadiums would rely on solar power as part of a commitment to host the first ever carbon neutral FIFA World Cup, and use innovative cooling systems to provide maximum comfort for players and fans. The bid also outlined how most of the stadiums would be constructed using modular components, so they could be disassembled after the tournament and donated to developing countries, contributing to the tournament's legacy and leaving Qatar with stadiums suitable for its size.

Qatar's effort to win the right to host the 2022 FIFA World Cup entailed hard work and innovation, as well as an integrated marketing campaign designed to deliver the message of how this small country planned to transform various perceived challenges into unique assets. The process began with a positioning platform built around the tagline "Expect Amazing." The tagline was designed to communicate its intentions and dare people to believe in Qatar and its bid to host the FIFA World Cup. The "Expect Amazing" campaign was officially launched one year before FIFA would make its decision to award hosting rights, with a TV commercial called "Puzzles." The goal of the spot was to gain global support for the bid by showcasing Qatar as a beautiful and vibrant country that welcomed people of all nations and was capable of hosting the World Cup. In addition, Qatar launched its official bid website that included a blog that allowed football fans to learn what was happening behind the scenes and kept them informed of the latest news so they would feel like partners in the bidding process. Social media, including Facebook, Twitter, and a YouTube channel, were also used to engage fans and supporters and provide another digital platform for what became known as the Qatar 2022 marketing effort.

The next phase of the campaign included a social responsibility initiative called "Generation Amazing." Football tournaments were held for underprivileged children from various countries in the Middle East and Asia, including Nepal, Pakistan, Lebanon, Syria, and Qatar. A select group of participants, chosen based on their football and leadership skills, were taken to South Africa to attend the 2010 FIFA World Cup. A documentary was created to capture the experiences of the children and posted on the Qatar 2022 Bid's YouTube channel to help generate publicity for the cause. Leading up to the 2010 FIFA World Cup, another video, called "Stadiums," was created and posted on YouTube, showcasing several of the stadiums that had been designed to host the football matches. That video received more than 2 million views on the Qatar 2022 Bid's YouTube channel and helped generate

The Political/Legal Environment

The political and legal environment in a country is one of the most important factors influencing the advertising and promotional programs of international marketers. Regulations differ owing to economic and national sovereignty considerations, nationalistic and cultural factors, and the goal of protecting consumers not only from false or misleading advertising but, in some cases, from advertising in general. It is difficult to generalize about advertising regulation at the international level, since some countries are increasing government

Source: Qatar Foundation

buzz across various other social media channels. Throughout the campaign, Qatar repeatedly grabbed the spotlight by introducing various legendary soccer players as ambassadors for its bid. The finale of the marketing campaign occurred in November 2010, just a few weeks before the FIFA decision, when Qatar hosted a friendly soccer match between Brazil and Argentina, two of the world's top teams, showcasing the country and its ability to host the type of big international soccer matches for which the FIFA World Cup is rightfully known.

While Qatar utilized an excellent integrated marketing program to draw attention to its desire to host the FIFA World Cup, there were a number of other key strategic components to its bid. Qatar repeatedly emphasized the diversity of its population and the country's geographic location as a crossroads between the East and West. To demonstrate its diversity, Qatar's final presentation to the FIFA Executive Committee, the organization's voting body, was delivered in three different languages: French, Spanish, and English, punctuated by three videos that drove home the message that the Executive Committee had the chance to make history by bringing the FIFA World Cup to the Middle East for the first time. The last speaker at the final bid presentation was Her Highness Sheikha Moza, the wife of the country's then-emir, who challenged the Executive Committee, asking them, "When do you think is the right time for the World Cup to come to the Middle East?" She also noted the significant impact that

Qatar's hosting of the FIFA World Cup would have on the Middle East region and the world as a whole.

On December 2, 2010, FIFA's president pulled Qatar's name from an envelope, awarding hosting rights for the 2022 FIFA World Cup to Qatar, a small Middle Eastern nation that had defied the odds. Following the decision, the Qatar 2022 Supreme Committee (Q22) was created by Qatar's government to deliver the infrastructure required for this high-profile sporting event, while also achieving the social, economic, and environmental goals laid out during the bid. Qatar views hosting the FIFA World Cup as a catalyst for driving growth and economic development and an opportunity to leave a lasting legacy for Qatar, the Middle East, and beyond. Qatar recognizes that major sporting events such as the FIFA World Cup provide a unique opportunity to increase focus, awareness, and unity within society, and is actively promoting increased participation in sports, especially for women, and healthy lifestyles.

Since being selected to host the FIFA World Cup, Qatar has had to deal with a number of issues and concerns over its ability to host such a major supporting event. Concerns were also raised over holding the tournament during the summer given the intense heat in Qatar; FIFA decided to move the 2022 World Cup to November and December. However, this has created problems with television networks such as Fox and Telemundo, who paid large sums of money to televise the games and prefer to have them in the summer so they do not overlap with football season in the United States.

The Qatar Supreme Committee must continue to develop and implement effective IMC program that addresses the delivery of infrastructure, including the progress being made and the opportunities being created for firms in Qatar and around the world. The committee is also focused on raising awareness, addressing concerns, and building positive perceptions of Qatar as a culturally rich, dynamic, stable, and vibrant nation in the Gulf region. During the bidding process Qatar told the world to "Expect Amazing." Now it is time for the country to "Deliver Amazing" as it strives to host a successful FIFA World Cup in 2022.

Sources: Joshua Robinson, "FIFA to Move 2022 Qatar World Cup to Winter," *The Wall Street Journal*, March 19, 2015, www.wsj.com/articles/fifa-to-move-2022-qatar-world-cup-to-winter-1426786731; Vivienne Walt, "Qatar Takes over the World," *Fortune*, September 2, 2013, pp. 90–95; Qatar 2022 Strategic Plan, Qatar 2022 Supreme Committee; Building Towards 2022, Qatar 2022 Supreme Committee.

control of advertising while others are decreasing it. Government regulations and restrictions can affect various aspects of a company's advertising and IMC program, including:

- The types of products that may be advertised.
- The content or creative approach that may be used.
- The media that all advertisers (or different classes of advertisers) are permitted to employ.
- The use of social and digital media.

- The amount of advertising a single advertiser may use in total or in a specific medium.
- The use of foreign languages in ads.
- The use of advertising material prepared outside the country.
- The use of local versus international advertising agencies.
- The specific taxes that may be levied against advertising.

A number of countries ban or restrict the advertising of various products. Cigarette advertising is banned in some or all media in numerous countries besides the United States including Argentina, Canada, France, Italy, Norway, Sweden, and Switzerland. The Australian government limits tobacco advertising to point of purchase. The ban also excludes tobacco companies from sponsoring sporting events.

In 2012 Australia's high court upheld the country's Plain Packaging Act, making it the first country to ban brand logos on all tobacco packages. The new law requires tobacco and cigarettes to be sold in plain green packages that feature graphic pictures of the negative health effects of smoking such as blindness; mouth, throat, and lung cancer; and the dangers of secondhand smoke (Exhibit 19–5). The new law is being challenged by tobacco companies through the World Trade Organization; they have concerns that it could set a marketing precedent that is adopted by other countries.[29] In Malaysia, a government ban on cigarette-related advertising and sponsorship was initiated in 2003 in an effort to curb the rising number of smokers in the country.[30] In China, tobacco and liquor advertising are banned except in hotels for foreigners. In Europe there has been a long-standing ban on advertising for prescription-drug products, which is designed to keep government-subsidized health care costs under control. The European Union (EU) has argued that advertising increases the marketing budgets of drug companies and results in higher prices. The ban prevents prescription-drug companies from mentioning their products even on their websites or in brochures, although some relaxation of these restrictions is being considered by the European Commission for drugs used to treat AIDS, diabetes, and respiratory ailments.[31]

The advertising of tobacco and liquor is banned in India, although many companies have tried to get around the ban by using what are known as "surrogate advertisements." Instead of promoting tobacco and liquor products, these TV commercials and print ads market unrelated products that the company also happens to manufacture—such as CDs, playing cards, and bottled water—that carry the same brand name and allow them to build brand awareness. The Indian government has been clamping down on surrogate TV ads in response to complaints by health activists, which is leading marketers to look to other ways to promote their brands such as the branding of sports teams, concerts, and other entertainment events. They are also lobbying the Indian government for more flexibility in enforcing the crackdown such as allowing liquor ads on late-night television programs. Liquor marketers including beer and distilled spirits companies are also using social media to promote their brands since regulations as they are no clear rules covering the use of the medium in India.[32]

Many countries restrict the media that advertisers can use as well as the extent to which ads can appear in the media. In the EU, legislation limits the commercial time to 12 minutes per hour and some countries require less frequent but longer advertising breaks that can be as long as 6 minutes. In 1999, the European Commission threw out an appeal against Greece's national ban on toy advertising on daytime television. Thus, advertisers can advertise toys on TV only during the evening hours.[33] Some of the most stringent advertising regulations in the world are found in Scandinavian countries. Commercial TV advertising did not begin in Sweden until 1992, and both Sweden and Denmark limit the amount of time available for commercials. Both Sweden

EXHIBIT 19–6

Diet Coke must use a different name in some countries

© Francis Dean/Dean Pictures/Newscom

and Norway prohibit domestic advertising that targets children as their governments believe that young people are not able to differentiate between advertising and programming and are not capable of understanding the selling intent of commercials.[34] Saudi Arabia opened its national TV system to commercial advertising in 1986, but advertising is not permitted on the state-run radio system. Advertising in magazines and newspapers in the country is subject to government and religious restrictions.[35]

Many governments have rules and regulations that affect the advertising message. For example, comparative advertising is legal and widely used in the United States and Canada but is illegal in some countries, such as Korea and Belgium. In Europe, the European Commission has developed a directive to standardize the basic form and content of comparative advertising and develop a uniform policy. In 2012 the EU updated its Directive on Misleading and Comparative Advertising that specifies the conditions under which comparative advertising is permitted and requires marketers to make sure their advertisements are not misleading: compare "like with like"—goods and services meeting the same needs or intended for the same purpose; objectively compare important features of the products or services concerned; do not discredit other companies' trademarks; and do not create confusion among traders.[36] Comparative advertising is used on a limited basis in many EU countries, such as Germany.

Many Asian and South American countries have also begun to accept comparative ads. Brazil's self-regulatory advertising codes were so strict for many years that few advertisers were been able to create a comparative message that could be approved. However, comparative advertising has become more common in the country although the comparison must be objective and supported by verifiable data and evidence.[37] Many countries restrict the types of claims advertisers can make, the words they can use, and the way products can be represented in ads. In Greece, specific claims for a product, such as "20 percent fewer calories," are not permitted in an advertising message.[38] Copyright and other legal restrictions make it difficult to maintain the same name from market to market. For example, Diet Coke is known as Coca-Cola Light in Germany, France, and many other countries because of legal restrictions prohibiting the word *diet* (Exhibit 19–6).

China has also begun cracking down on advertising claims as consumer groups slowly become a more powerful force in the country. For years, government regulation of advertising was less stringent than in developed markets and many companies were very aggressive with their advertising claims. However, government officials have begun enforcing a 1995 law that stipulates that statistical claims and quotations "should be true and accurate with sources clearly indicated." In 2005, the Chinese government launched a crackdown on false and illegal ads with a focus on cosmetic, beauty, health, and pharmaceutical products.[39]

An area that is receiving a great deal of attention in Europe, as well as in the United States, is the marketing and advertising of food products that are considered to contribute to childhood obesity. The European Health Commission has called on advertisers of a variety of food products to set their own regulations to curb the advertising of so-called junk food to the 450 million consumers in the European Union. The commission has also recommended that these companies do not advertise directly to children and has even threatened to ban advertising icons such as Ronald McDonald and Tony the Tiger.[40]

GLOBAL VERSUS LOCALIZED ADVERTISING

The discussion of differences in the marketing environments of various countries suggests that each market is different and requires a distinct marketing and advertising program. However, through the years a great deal of attention has focused on the concept of **global marketing**, where a company uses a common marketing plan for all countries in which it operates, thus selling the product in essentially the same way everywhere in the world. **Global advertising** falls under the umbrella of global marketing as a way to implement this strategy by using the same basic advertising approach in all markets.

The debate over standardization versus localization of marketing and advertising programs began decades ago.[41] But the idea of global marketing was popularized by Professor Theodore Levitt, who says the worldwide marketplace has become homogenized and consumers' basic needs, wants, and expectations transcend geographic, national, and cultural boundaries.[42] More recently support for the idea of global marketing has come from advocates of global consumer culture theory (GCCT) who argue that the globalization of markets has led to the existence of a global consumer culture in which many consumers share consumption values regardless of the countries in which they reside.[43] An outgrowth of this theory is the concept of global consumer culture positioning which suggests that the shared consumption-related beliefs, symbols, and behaviors of many consumers across markets create an opportunity to use positioning strategies that transcend cultures. While this does not suggest complete homogenization or globalization of markets to the degree advocated by Levitt, it does suggest an opportunity for marketers of global brands to use global positioning and be advertised in similar ways across markets.[44]

Not everyone agrees with the practicality of global marketing, particularly with respect to advertising. Many argue that products and advertising messages must be designed or at least adapted to meet the differing needs of consumers in different countries.[45] We will consider the arguments for and against global marketing and advertising, as well as situations where it is most appropriate.

Advantages of Global Marketing and Advertising

A global marketing strategy and advertising program offers certain advantages to a company, including the following:

- Economies of scale in production and distribution.
- Lower marketing and advertising costs as a result of reductions in planning and control.
- Lower advertising production costs.
- Abilities to exploit good ideas on a worldwide basis and introduce products quickly into various world markets.
- A consistent international brand and/or company image.
- Simplification of coordination and control of marketing and promotional programs.

Advocates of global marketing and advertising contend that standardized products are possible in all countries if marketers emphasize quality, reliability, and low prices. They say people everywhere want to buy the same products and live the same way. Product standardization results in lower design and production costs as well as greater marketing efficiency, which translates into lower prices for consumers. Product standardization and global marketing also enable companies to roll out products faster into world markets, which is becoming increasingly important as product life cycles become shorter and competition increases.

A number of companies including IBM, De Beers, British Airways, and American Express have successfully used the global advertising approach. Gillette has used the "Best a Man Can Get" as its global advertising theme for over a decade and has launched a number of new razor products including the Sensor, Mach3, and Fusion using a global approach.[46] Gillette uses the same advertising theme in each country and maintains websites and social media pages with similar content and layout, with only language differences.

Frito-Lay launched its first global campaign for Doritos, which is the world's largest tortilla/corn-chip brand. Doritos had a different look and feel across the

EXHIBIT 19–7

Doritos uses global advertising to create a consistent image for the brand in various countries

Source: Doritos by Frito-Lay North America, Inc.

37 countries where the brand is sold; 25 packaging variations existed and different advertising approaches were used in various markets. Packaging for Doritos was standardized across all markets and the global campaign themed "For the Bold" was developed that included digital and television advertising, promotions on Facebook and Twitter, and sponsorship of concerts. The creative approach used in the campaign included humorous TV and print executions focusing on bold choices made to enjoy Doritos such as the ad shown in Exhibit 19–7. Frito-Lay's vice president of marketing explained the move to a global campaign: "With the rise of social media and technology, our world is smaller and more connected than ever before. We have found that our consumers across the world share very similar passions and interests, but until now may not have had a consistent way of speaking about the Doritos brand. The campaign is our way of connecting these fans worldwide, as we now provide a consistent storyline, and look and feel from the Doritos brand."[47]

Problems with Global Advertising

Opponents of the standardized global approach argue that very few products lend themselves to global advertising.[48] Differences in culture, market, and economic development; consumer needs and usage patterns; media availability; and legal restrictions make it extremely difficult to develop an effective universal approach to marketing and advertising. Advertising may be particularly difficult to standardize because of cultural differences in circumstances, language, traditions, values, beliefs, lifestyle, music, and so on. Moreover, some experts argue that cultures around the world are becoming more diverse, not less so. Thus, advertising's job of informing and persuading consumers and moving them toward using a particular brand can be done only within a given culture.

Consumer usage patterns and perceptions of a product may vary from one country to another, so advertisers must adjust their marketing and advertising approaches to different problems they may face in different markets. For example, while eating pizza is viewed as a casual affair in the United States and many other countries, in Japan it is perceived as an upscale meal that is consumed more on special occasions. Since entering the Japanese market in 1985, Domino's Pizza has been focusing on creating more usage occasions such as Valentine's Day and Mother's Day by delivering its pizza in heart-shaped, pink boxes. The company has also used clever promotions such as one where the chain offered 2.5 million yen (about $30,000) for one hour's work at a Domino's store. For another popular offbeat promotion Domino's announced that it was working with space agency JAXA (the Japanese equivalent of NASA), Honda, and other high-profile companies to build the first-ever pizza store on the moon.[49] The CEO of Domino's Japan participated in the promotion by appearing in a full spacesuit, customized with a Domino's patch, and displaying a big picture of the Moon Branch Project (Exhibit 19–8).

Many experts believe that marketing a standardized product the same way all over the world can turn off consumers, alienate employees, and blind a company to diversities in customer needs. Multinational companies can also encounter problems when they use global advertising as local managers in countries or regions often resent the home office standardizing the advertising function and mandating the type of advertising to be used in their markets. Sir Martin Sorrell, chair of the United Kingdom–based

EXHIBIT 19–8

Domino's Pizza used its humorous Moon Branch Project promotion in Japan

© *Domino's Pizza Japan*

WPP Group, argues that there are limits to global advertising and that the one-size-fits-all pendulum has gone too far. He urges his executives to focus on consumer needs in the countries they serve and advocates the use of country managers to build contacts and adapt campaigns to local markets.[50]

When Is Globalization Appropriate?

While globalization of advertising is viewed by many in the advertising industry as a difficult task, some progress has been made in learning what products and services are best suited to worldwide appeals:[51]

1. Brands or messages that can be adapted for a visual appeal, avoiding the problems of trying to translate words into dozens of languages.
2. Brands that are promoted with image campaigns that play to universal needs, values, and emotions.
3. High-tech products and new products coming to the world for the first time, not steeped in the cultural heritage of a country.
4. Products with nationalistic flavor if the country has a reputation in the field.
5. Products that appeal to a market segment with universally similar tastes, interests, needs, and values.

Many companies and brands rely on visual appeals that are easily adapted for use in global advertising campaigns. These companies are often marketing products in the secondary category, such as jewelry, cosmetics, liquor, and cigarettes, that appeal to universal needs, values, and emotions and lend themselves to global campaigns. Marketers recognize that emotions such as joy, sentiment, excitement, and pleasure are universal as are needs/values such as self-esteem, status, and achievement. Thus, it is common for global advertising campaigns to use emotional and image appeals.

High-tech products such as smartphones, personal computers, HDTV sets, video games, and fitness trackers are products in the third category. Many of the marketers of high-tech products use global campaigns to promote their brands. For example, Fitbit launched a global campaign in 2016 for its Blaze wearable device that focused on its modular design that allows consumers to remove and insert trackers into different frames and bands.[52] Taiwan-based HTC developed a global campaign for

its HTC One smartphone that focused on testimonials from real people rather than actors.[53] One of the spots featured a photographer using an HTC One phone to shoot a fashion model as they're both falling at 126 miles an hour in the Arizona desert. Pictures taken on the phone were run in print ads in U.S. publications such as *Wired, Sports Illustrated, People*, and *US Weekly* as well as publications in other countries (Exhibit 19–9).

Products in the fourth category are those that come from countries with national reputations for quality and/or a distinctive image that can be used as the basis for global advertising. These products capitalize on the **country-of-origin effect**, which refers to consumers' general perceptions of quality for products made in a given country.[54] Examples include Swiss watches, French wine, and German beer or automobiles. Many U.S. companies such as Apple, Google, and Nike are also taking advantage of the cachet American brands have acquired among consumers around the world in recent years.[55]

A number of studies have shown a pronounced effect of country of origin on the quality perceptions of products, with the reputation of specific countries impacting consumers' evaluative judgments of brands.[56] Thus, companies and brands that originate in countries associated with quality may want to take advantage of this in their advertising. However, some marketing experts argue that in today's world of globalization, consumers are only vaguely aware of the country of origin for many of the brands they buy.[57] Thus, marketers need to understand whether product origin is relevant to the consumers in their target market. A study conducted among a representative sample of 1,000 college students from over 375 universities across the United States found that the vast majority of them were unaware of the country of origin of most brands. However, while the students were not aware of where the brands came from, they did have definite opinions about which countries produce the best products. When students were asked whether they believe a country makes quality products, Japan was rated the highest at 82 percent, followed by the United States at 78 percent, Germany at 77 percent, and Italy at 74 percent. Countries rated the lowest for product quality were Russia, Mexico, and Vietnam.[58]

In the final category for which globalization is appropriate are products and services that can be sold to common market segments around the world, such as those identified by Salah Hassan and Lea Katsansis.[59] One such segment is the world's elite—people who, by reason of their economically privileged position, can pursue a lifestyle that includes fine jewelry, expensive clothing, quality automobiles, and the like. Marketers of high-quality, luxury brands such as Tiffany, Prada, Cartier, Gucci, Chanel, and Louis Vuitton can use global advertising to appeal to the elite market segment around the world. Well-known international brands competing in the luxury goods marketplace often present a singular image of prestige and style to the entire world.

An example of a marketer of luxury products that uses global advertising is Swiss watchmaker TAG Heuer, which targets upscale consumers, many of whom are world travelers. Thus, the company feels that it is important to have a consistent advertising message and image in each country and uses global advertising to do so. The only element of its advertising that changes from country to country is the celebrity ambassador who appears in the ad. For example, TAG Heuer recently launched its #Don't Crack Under Pressure global campaign that uses Brazilian soccer star Cristiano Ronaldo and British model/actress Cara Delevingne in Europe (Exhibit 19–10). In the United States, the ambassadors include actor Chris Hemsworth and NFL football star Tom Brady.

Another segment of global consumers who have similar needs and interests and seek similar features and benefits from products and services is teenagers. There are more than 500 million teens in Asia and Latin America, whose lifestyles are converging with those of the 80 million teens in Europe, and North America to

EXHIBIT 19–10

TAG Heuer uses a global campaign featuring different celebrity ambassadors for various countries

Source: TAG Heuer

create a vast, free-spending global market.[60] Teens now have intense exposure to the Internet, social media, television, movies, music, travel, and global advertising from companies such as Levi Strauss, Benetton, Nike, Coca-Cola, Pepsi, and many others.

Global Products, Local Messages

While the pros and cons of global marketing and advertising continue to be debated, many companies are taking an in-between approach by standardizing their products and basic marketing strategy but localizing their advertising messages. They recognize that it is difficult to create relevant and timely global advertising themes, positioning, and stories that appeal to consumers around the world and can be creatively executed across all touch points. The in-between approach recognizes similar desires, goals, needs, and uses for products and services but tailors advertising to the local cultures and conditions in each market. Some call this approach "think globally, act locally," others describe it as "global vision with a local touch," while more recently it has been referred to as *glocal* advertising strategy—locally adapting a universally embraced core idea that will resonate in any market anywhere in the world. Advocates of this approach argue that designers of global advertising strategy carry a creative concept most of the way to execution while regional marketers tailor the work to make it locally relevant and aligned to the different category and brand situations in different markets.[61]

Although some marketers use global ads with little or no modification, most companies adapt their messages to respond to differences in language, market conditions, and other factors. Many global marketers use a strategy called **pattern advertising**: their ads follow a basic approach, but themes, copy, and sometimes even visual elements are adapted to differences in local markets. For example, the TAG Heuer ads shown in Exhibit 19–10 are an example of pattern advertising. Creative elements of TAG Heuer ads such as the layout, logo, pictures of the product, slogan, and tagline remain clear, consistent, and visually recognizable all over the world.[62]

Another way global marketers adapt their campaigns to local markets is by producing a variety of ads with a similar theme and format and allowing managers in various countries or regions to select those messages they believe will work best in their markets. Some companies are also giving local managers more autonomy in adapting global campaign themes to local markets. They recognize that global advertising can rarely reflect the idiosyncratic characteristics of every market, but the alternative—locally designed advertising—often sacrifices a consistent global message and does not take advantage of economies of scale.

Most managers believe it is important to adapt components of their advertising messages—such as the language, models, scenic backgrounds, message content, and symbols—to reflect the culture and frame of reference of consumers in various countries. For example, global branding expert Nigel Hollis notes that research conducted by Millward Brown found that, all things being equal, brands that are identified with local culture will perform better than others.[63] He notes several reasons why it is important for brands to have a strong degree of identity to local culture and advises that the key to global brand success is to connect with consumers at the local level while capitalizing on the advantages offered by operating on a global scale.[64] Many companies are making these tactical adjustments to their advertising messages while still pursuing global strategies that will help them project a consistent global image and turn their products and services into global brands.

DECISION AREAS IN INTERNATIONAL ADVERTISING

Companies developing advertising and promotional programs for international markets must make certain organizational and functional decisions similar to those for domestic markets. These decisions include organization style, agency selection, creative strategy and execution, and media strategy and selection.

Organizing for International Advertising

One of the first decisions a company must make when it decides to market its products to other countries is how to organize the international advertising and promotion function. This decision is likely to depend on how the company is organized overall for international marketing and business. Three basic options are centralization at the home office or headquarters, decentralization of decision making to local foreign markets, or a combination of the two.

Centralization   Many companies prefer to *centralize* the international advertising and promotion function so that all decisions about agency selection, creative strategy and campaign development, media strategy, and budgeting are made at the firm's home office. Complete centralization is likely when market and media conditions are similar from one country to another, when the company has only one or a few international agencies handling all of its advertising, when the company can use standardized advertising, or when it desires a consistent image worldwide. Centralization may also be best when a company's international business is small and it operates through foreign distributors or licensees who do not become involved in the marketing and promotional process.

Many companies prefer the centralized organizational structure to protect their foreign investments and keep control of the marketing effort and corporate and/or brand image. Centralization can save money, since it reduces the need for staff and administration at the local subsidiary level. As the trend toward globalized marketing and advertising strategies continues, more companies are likely to move more toward centralization of the advertising function to maintain a unified world brand image rather than presenting a different image in each market. Some foreign managers may actually prefer centralized decision making, as it removes them from the burden of advertising and promotional decisions and saves them from defending local decisions to the home office. However, many marketing and advertising managers in foreign markets oppose centralized control. They say the structure is too rigid and makes it difficult to adapt the advertising and promotional program to local needs and market conditions.

Decentralization   Under a *decentralized* organizational structure, marketing and advertising managers in each market have the authority to make their own advertising and promotional decisions. Local managers can select ad agencies, develop budgets, conduct research, approve creative themes and executions, and select advertising media. Companies using a decentralized approach put a great deal of faith in the judgment and decision-making ability of personnel in local markets. This approach is often used when companies believe local managers know the marketing situation in their countries the best. They may also be more effective and motivated when given responsibility for the advertising and promotional program in their markets. Decentralization also works well in small or unique markets where headquarters' involvement is not worthwhile or advertising must be tailored to the local market.

International fragrance marketer Chanel, Inc. uses a decentralized strategy. Chanel found that many of its fragrance concepts do not work well globally and decided to localize advertising. For example, the U.S. office has the option of using ads created by the House of Chanel in Paris or developing its own campaigns for the U.S. market. Chanel executives in the United States think that the French concept of prestige is not the same as Americans' and the artsy ads created in France do not work well in this country.[65]

Combination   While there is an increasing trend toward centralizing the international advertising function, many companies combine the two approaches. The home office, or headquarters, has the most control over advertising policy, guidelines, and operations in all markets. The international advertising or marketing communication manager works closely with local or regional marketing managers and personnel from the international agency (or agencies) and sets advertising and promotional objectives, has budgetary authority, approves all creative themes and executions, and approves media selection decisions, especially when they are made on a regional basis or overlap with other markets.

Advertising managers in regional or local offices submit advertising plans and budgets for their markets, which are reviewed by the international advertising manager. Local managers play a major role in working with the agency to adapt appeals to their particular markets and select media.

The combination approach allows for consistency in a company's international advertising yet permits local input and adaptation of the promotion program. Most consumer-product companies find that local adaptation of advertising is necessary for foreign markets or regions, but they want to maintain control of the overall worldwide image they project. For example, Levi Strauss in 2010 hired its first global chief marketing officer to oversee the company's marketing operations in over 60 countries and try to make the Levi's brand more competitive against premium denim lines such as True Religion, Seven For All Mankind, and Joe's Jeans.[66] However, the company still provides a great deal of autonomy to regional marketing directors.

Agency Selection

One of the most important decisions for a firm engaged in international marketing is the choice of an advertising agency. The company has three basic alternatives in selecting an agency to handle its international advertising. First, it can choose a major agency with both domestic and overseas offices. Many large agencies have offices all over the world and have become truly international operations. For example, a number of agencies have moved their offices from Hong Kong to Shanghai to be closer to the world's largest consumer market on the mainland of China.[67]

Many American companies prefer to use a U.S.-based agency with foreign offices; this gives them greater control and convenience and also facilitates coordination of overseas advertising. Companies often use the same agency to handle international and domestic advertising. As discussed in Chapter 3, the flurry of mergers and acquisitions in the ad agency business in recent years, both in the United States and in other countries, has created large global agencies that can meet the international needs of global marketers. A number of multinational companies have consolidated their advertising with one large agency. The consolidation trend began in 1994 when IBM dismissed 40 agencies around the world and awarded its entire account to Ogilvy & Mather Worldwide.[68] Since then a number of multinational companies such as Johnson & Johnson and Samsung have consolidated their creative with one agency and/or holding company. Many large companies are also consolidating their media planning and buying as well.

There are a number of reasons why global marketers consolidate their advertising with one agency. Many companies recognize they must develop a consistent global image for the company and/or its brands and speak with one coordinated marketing voice around the world. For example, IBM officials felt the company had been projecting too many images when its advertising was divided among so many agencies. The consolidation enabled IBM to present a single brand identity throughout the world while taking advantage of one of the world's best-known brand names (Exhibit 19–11).

Companies are also consolidating their global advertising in an effort to increase cost-efficiencies and gain greater

HOW TO COMPETE IN THE ERA OF "SMART".

For five years, IBMers have been working with companies, cities and communities to build a Smarter Planet. We've seen enormous advances, as leaders have begun using the vast supply of Big Data to transform their enterprises and institutions through mobile technology, social business and the cloud.

Big Data has changed how these leaders work, how they make decisions and how they serve their customers. And the ability to harness Big Data is giving their enterprises a new competitive edge in today's era of "smart".

Police in Memphis used Big Data and analytics to verify patterns of criminal activity, which helped them change their strategy.

DECISIONS BASED ON ANALYTICS, NOT ON INSTINCT. Decision makers once viewed their intuition and experience as the keys to formulating strategy and assessing risk. But analytics increasingly helps them discern real patterns and anticipate events.

A decade ago, the Memphis Police Department developed an analytics platform that created multilayer maps to identify patterns of criminal

activity. The department then changed its patrolling strategy, reducing crime by 24 percent.

THE SOCIAL NETWORK IS THE NEW PRODUCTION LINE. In this knowledge economy, the exchange of ideas has become the new means of production. The advent of social and mobile technology is shifting the competitive edge from having workers who amass knowledge to having workers who impart it.

Cemex, a $15 billion cement maker, wanted to create its first global brand of concrete, which required a coordination of stakeholders from each country. Cemex didn't build

a new lab. It built a social business network. Employees in 50 countries formed one global active community whose collaboration helped launch its first global brand in a third of the anticipated time.

FROM YOU AS A SEGMENT TO YOU AS YOU. The age of Big Data and analytics is revealing customers not as demographic "segments"

Social networks shift value to the workplace from knowledge that people possess to knowledge that they can communicate.

but as individuals. And that's changing how companies serve customers. Call centers, once evaluated by how quickly they got callers off the phone, are training employees to engage *more* with customers by starting conversations and serving individuals.

FINDING SUCCESS ON A SMARTER PLANET. An organisation that adopts these principles is a Smarter Enterprise. But using emerging technology is only part of the story. The real challenge now is to use these new insights to change entrenched work practices. To learn more about the new principles of the Smarter Enterprise, visit us at ibm.com/smarterplanet/in

LET'S BUILD A SMARTER PLANET.

Effective marketing no longer aims publicity at broad demographic groups—it opens conversations with individuals.

IBM logo, ibm.com, Smarter Planet and the planet icon are trademarks of International Business Machines Corp, registered in many jurisdictions worldwide. A current list of IBM trademarks is available on the Web at www.ibm.com/legal/copytrade.shtml © International Business Machines Corporation 2013.

leverage over their agencies. When a major client puts all of its advertising with one agency, that company often becomes the agency's most important account. And, as one IBM executive notes, "You become a magnet for talent and attention."[69] Consolidation can also lead to cost-efficiencies not only for creative but for media planning and buying as well.

Advertising executives also noted that a major reason for all of the account consolidation is that agencies now have the ability to communicate and manage globally. The Internet, e-mail, and videoconferencing capabilities through platforms such as Skype, Google Hangouts, and FaceTime make it much easier to manage accounts around the globe. Of course, placing an entire global advertising account with one agency can be risky. If the agency fails to deliver an effective campaign, the client has no backup agency to make a fast rebound and the search for a new agency can be very time-consuming. Clients who consolidate also face the problem of selling the idea to regional offices, which often previously enjoyed their own local agency relationships. However, it appears that more and more companies are willing to take these risks and rely on one agency to handle their advertising around the world.

A second alternative for the international marketer is to choose an agency that rather than having its own foreign offices or branches is affiliated with agencies in other countries or belongs to a network of foreign agencies. A domestic agency may acquire an interest in several foreign agencies or become part of an organization of international agencies. The agency can then sell itself as an international agency offering multinational coverage and contacts. Many of the large agency holding companies such as the WPP Group, Publicis Groupe, Omnicom, and Interpublic Group own agencies throughout the world that can handle their clients' advertising in various countries.

The advantage of this arrangement is that the client can use a domestic-based agency yet still have access to foreign agencies with detailed knowledge of market conditions, media, and so on in each local market. There may be problems with this approach, however. The local agency may have trouble coordinating and controlling independent agencies, and the quality of work may vary among network members. Companies considering this option must ask the local agency about its ability to control the activities of its affiliates and the quality of their work in specific areas such as creative and media.

The third alternative for the international marketer is to select a local agency for each national market in which it sells its products or services. Since local agencies often have the best understanding of the marketing and advertising environment in their country or region, they may be able to develop the most effective advertising.

Some companies like local agencies because they may provide the best talent in each market. In many countries, smaller agencies may, because of their independence, be more willing to take risks and develop the most effective, creative ads. Choosing local agencies also increases the involvement and morale of foreign subsidiary managers by giving them responsibility for managing the promotion function in their markets. Some companies have the subsidiary choose a local agency, since it is often in the best position to evaluate the agency and will work closely with it.

Criteria for Agency Selection The selection of an agency to handle a company's international advertising depends on how the firm is organized for international marketing and the type of assistance it needs to meet its goals and objectives in foreign markets. Figure 19–3 lists some criteria a company might use in selecting an agency. In a study conducted among marketing directors of European companies, creative capability was ranked the most important factor in selecting an advertising agency network, followed by understanding the market, understanding marketing goals, and ability to produce integrated communications. Size of the agency and agency reputation were cited as important criteria by less than 2 percent of the respondents.[70] Another study found that most clients choose an agency based on its creative reputation and the creative presentation it had made. However, a

- Ability of agency to cover relevant markets.

- Quality of agency work.

- Market research, public relations, and other services offered by agency.

- Relative roles of company advertising department and agency.

- Level of communication and control desired by company.

- Ability of agency to coordinate international campaign.

- Size of company's international business.

- Company's desire for local versus international image.

- Company organizational structure for international business and marketing (centralized versus decentralized).

- Company's level of involvement with international operations.

large number of clients felt their agencies lacked international expertise and account coordination ability.[71]

Some companies choose a combination of the three alternatives just discussed because their involvement in each market differs, as do the advertising environment and situation in each country. Several experts in international marketing and advertising advocate the use of international agencies by international companies, particularly those firms moving toward global marketing and striving for a consistent corporate or brand image around the world. The trend toward mergers and acquisitions and the formation of mega-agencies with global marketing and advertising capabilities suggests the international agency approach will become the preferred arrangement among large companies.

Creative Decisions

Another decision facing the international advertiser is determining the appropriate advertising messages for each market. Creative strategy development for international advertising is basically similar in process and procedure to that for domestic advertising. Advertising and communications objectives should be based on the marketing strategy and market conditions in foreign markets. Major selling ideas must be developed and specific appeals and execution styles chosen.

An important factor in the development of creative strategy is the issue of global versus localized advertising. If the standardized approach is taken, the creative team must develop advertising that will transcend cultural differences and communicate effectively in every country. For example, Airbnb recently launched a global advertising campaign titled "Live There" that is designed to appeal to consumers around the world to use its online site to find lodging in a home or apartment rather than having a cookie cutter experience by staying in a hotel. The campaign was based on research conducted by the company showing that 86 percent of Airbnb users pick the platform because they want to live more like a local than a tourist when visiting a destination. The campaign includes television and digital ads as well as a series of print ads featuring Pinterest-style images of travelers who look at home in various locales such as a Tokyo artist's loft, a California poolside, or a cozy apartment in Paris (Exhibit 19–12). The various ads in the global campaign focus on the idea that people shouldn't simply go to a new place, they should live there, even if for only one night.[72]

When companies follow a **localized advertising strategy,** the creative team must determine what type of selling idea, ad appeal, and execution style will work

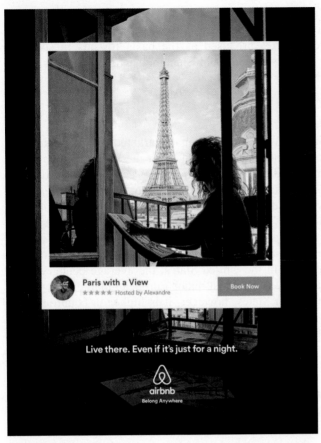

EXHIBIT 19–12

Airbnb's "Live There" global campaign appeals to consumers' desire to live like a local when they visit a destination

Source: Airbnb, Inc.

EXHIBIT 19–13

Television ads for Las Vegas were adapted for the Mexican market

Source: Las Vegas Convention and Visitors Authority

in each market. A product may have to be positioned differently in each market depending on consumers' usage patterns and habits. For example, the Las Vegas Convention and Visitors Authority took its popular "What Happens Here, Stays Here" campaign to several foreign markets, including the United Kingdom, Canada, and Mexico. Research conducted by the ad agency found that the creative ads were not provocative enough for the United Kingdom, needed to be toned down for Mexico, and could be left alone for western Canada.[73] However, French Canadians in the eastern part of the country are more European-like in their sensibilities and the agency plans to develop alternative taglines and stories for a French-language campaign there. Mexicans were more comfortable with storylines that fit with family customers and were not sexually provocative. For example, one spot featured a young man meeting a group of friends in a Mexican bar and trying to tell them about his first trip to Las Vegas, but being too excited to find the right words (Exhibit 19–13).

Marketers must also determine what type of advertising appeal or execution style will be most effective in each market. Emotional appeals such as humor may work well in one country but not in another because of differences in cultural backgrounds and consumer perceptions of what is or is not funny. While humorous appeals are popular in the United States and Britain, they are not used often in Germany, where consumers do not respond favorably to them. German advertising typically uses rational appeals that are text-heavy and contain arguments for a product's superiority.[74] France, Italy, and Brazil are more receptive to sexual appeals and nudity in advertising than are most other societies. The French government stepped up its efforts to convince advertisers and their ad agencies to tone down the use of sexual imagery and violence in their advertising.[75] France's Truth in Advertising Commission, which is the main self-regulatory body, has issued new standards regarding the presentation of human beings in advertising.

Countries such as Japan, Brazil, and Thailand appreciate creativity: Humorous and irreverent ads are often needed to catch the attention of consumers. In Thailand, which has become the creative nerve center of Asian advertising, the unusual blend of culture, religion, politics, and language influences the advertising. Thailand's *sabi-sabai* ("take it easy") attitude is partly a product of the country's Buddhist religion, which teaches disciples to forgive and look on the sunny side of life, as well as the country's heritage as a peaceful kingdom. Thailand has a very high literacy rate but few people read as a leisure activity, which results in most ads being visual in nature rather than based upon language.[76] Many marketers have found that ads that are more humorous, irreverent, or adventurous break through the clutter and attract the attention of Thai consumers.

Another country where there is a major emphasis on creativity is India, where consumers are not as cynical toward advertising as they are in many other countries such as the United States.[77] Multinational marketers are recognizing that they must create ads specifically for the Indian market rather than trying to adapt campaigns being used globally or in their domestic markets.

In China, marketers must deal with a very decentralized market with distinct differences in culture, language, food preferences, and lifestyles among the various regions and 2,000 cities. In general, the Chinese place a high emphasis on group and family values.

Advertisers must be careful when using humor and sexual appeal, particularly for national campaigns, since language and values vary greatly from province to province. Human interest stories are used as the basis for ads in southern China but less so in cities such as Beijing and Shanghai, where residents prefer more information-based ads.[78]

Media Selection

One of the most challenging areas for international marketers is media strategy and selection. Companies often find major differences in the media available outside their home markets, and media conditions may vary considerably from one country to another. Today advertising bombards consumers in countries around the world through a variety of media including print, television, out-of-home, and digital media. However, marketers still face a number of problems in attempting to communicate advertising and promotional messages to consumers in various countries. For example, the amount of time people spend watching television varies from one country to the next. In the United States, the average person spends nearly 5 hours a day watching television. Most major European markets spend less time watching TV than the United States; however, it is higher in countries such as Saudi Arabia as well as Croatia and Romania. A recent study of global media consumption showed that the United States and Western Europe watch a lot of TV, while Asia and other developing economies are disproportionately heavy in mobile and tablet use. But time spent online is increasing in the United States as well as other countries.[79]

In some countries, TV advertising is impacted by limits on the amount of commercial time available. For example, advertising time in countries that belong to the European Union have been limited to 12 minutes per hour. However, in 2016 the European Commission introduced proposals to lift this restriction and replace it with a daily limit of no more than 20 percent of time being devoted to advertising between 7:00 A.M. to 1:00 P.M., allowing broadcasters to choose more freely when air commercials. This is likely to result in broadcasters making more commercial time available during prime-time viewing hours and popular programs, while reducing the number of commercials aired during day-time broadcasting.[80]

The number of TV sets is increasing tremendously in India, but there is still controversy over TV advertising. Commercials are restricted to only 10 percent of programming time and must appear at the beginning or end of a program. Australia lifted a ban on cable TV advertising in 1997. However, some cable channels won't accept any advertising, and Australian consumers will not tolerate as much advertising on cable channels as on free TV networks.[81]

The characteristics of media differ from country to country in terms of coverage, cost, quality of reproduction, restrictions, and the like. In some countries, media rates are negotiable or may fluctuate owing to unstable currencies, economic conditions, or government regulations. For example, in China TV stations charge a local rate for Chinese advertisers, a foreign rate, and a joint venture rate. Although the more than a billion TV viewers make China the world's largest television market, the medium is strictly controlled by the Communist Party. State-owned China Central Television (CCTV) controls the national networks. Politics frequently intrude into program selection and scheduling: A show might be delayed for several months to coincide with a key political event, or programs from foreign countries may be pulled off the air.[82] CCTV has developed its own version of an up-front market, as an auction is held each November to sell advertising time on prime-time programming for the coming year. The annual auction is generally considered a barometer for China's media market as local and regional channels will often hold off setting their advertising rates to see the level of demand for advertising time. While CCTV is China's only national broadcaster, it accounts for just 12 percent of the total television advertising revenue in China, with the remainder going to local TV channels, provincial satellite channels, and provincial TV stations.[83]

Another problem international advertisers face is obtaining reliable media information such as circulation figures, audience profiles, and costs. Many countries that had only state-owned TV channels are now experiencing a rapid growth in commercial channels, which is providing more market segmentation opportunities. However, reliable audience measurement data are not available, and media buyers often rely on their instincts when purchasing TV time. A number of research companies are developing audience measurement systems for countries in Eastern Europe, Russia, and China. In China, AGB Nielsen Media Research monitors TV-viewing audiences in 11 of China's biggest cities including Beijing, Shanghai, and Guangzhou as well as in the rural parts of several provinces, using nearly 10,000 households with people meters.[84] Audience measurement information is also available from CSM Media Research, a company that is a joint venture between CTR Market Research (the leading market research company in China) and Kantar Media.

The goal of international advertisers is to select media vehicles that reach their target audience most effectively and efficiently. Media selection is often localized even for a centrally planned, globalized campaign. Local agencies or media buyers generally have more knowledge of local media and better opportunities to negotiate rates, and subsidiary operations can maintain control and adapt to media conditions and options in their market. Media planners have two options: using national or local media or using international media.

Local Media Many advertisers choose the local media of a country to reach its consumers. While the print media are struggling in the United States, they are still popular in many countries where magazines are circulated nationwide as well as national or regional newspapers that carry advertising directed to a national audience. Most countries also have magazines that appeal to special interests or activities, allowing for targeting in media selection. For example, Japan has numerous fashion magazines such as *Jelly*, which focuses on runway fashions, as well as street fashion and culture (Exhibit 19–14).

In addition to print and television, local media available to advertisers include radio, direct mail, billboards, cinema, and transit advertising. These media give international advertisers great flexibility and the opportunity to reach specific market segments and local markets within a country. Most international advertisers rely heavily on national and local media in their media plans for foreign markets.

International Media The other way for the international advertiser to reach audiences in various countries is through international media that have multimarket coverage. The primary focus of international media has traditionally been magazines and newspapers. A number of U.S.-based consumer-oriented publications have international editions, including *Time, Reader's Digest*, and *National Geographic* as well as the newspaper *USA Today*. Hearst Magazines International is the largest U.S. publisher of magazines worldwide and oversees the publication of nearly 300 print editions and more than 265 websites in 34 languages and 84 countries including *Esquire, Good Housekeeping, Cosmo Girl*, and *Elle*. Hearst also publishes *Cosmopolitan*, which with 64 international editions is the largest-selling young women's magazine and

EXHIBIT 19–14

Jelly is a popular fashion magazine in Japan

© McGraw-Hill Companies/Mark Dierker, photographer

EXHIBIT 19–15

International editions of *Cosmopolitan* magazine are distributed in more than 100 countries in 35 languages

© Hearst Magazines International

India and UK's No. 1 South Asian channel*

Diya Aur Baati Hum

Mon – Fri 9pm

www.startv.com/usa

India StarPlus

EXHIBIT 19–16

STAR India reaches more than 600 million people every month

© 21st Century Fox Star US LLC

has more editions than any other magazine in the world (Exhibit 19–15).[85] Other U.S.-based publications with foreign editions include *Bloomberg Businessweek, Fortune*, and *The Wall Street Journal*.

International publications offer advertisers a way to reach large audiences on a regional or worldwide basis. Readers of these publications are usually upscale, high-income individuals who are desirable target markets for many products and services. There are, however, several problems with these international media that can limit their attractiveness to many advertisers. Their reach in any one foreign country may be low, particularly for specific segments of a market. Also, while they deliver desirable audiences to companies selling business or upscale consumer products and services, they do not cover the mass consumer markets or specialized market segments very well. Other U.S.-based publications in foreign markets do offer advertisers ways to reach specific market segments.

Whereas print remains a popular medium for international advertising, many companies are turning their attention to television. Consumer product and service companies in particular view TV advertising as the best way to reach mass markets and effectively communicate their advertising messages. Satellite technology has helped spread the growth of TV in other countries through **direct broadcast by satellite (DBS)** to homes and communities equipped with small, low-cost receiving dishes. A number of satellite networks operate in Europe, Asia, and Latin America and beam entertainment programming across a number of countries. For example, Exhibit 19–16 shows an ad for StarPlus, one of the channels owned by STAR India, which has become the leading television company in India with 40 channels in 8 languages that reach more than 600 million people every month across India and other countries around the world.

THE ROLES OF OTHER PROMOTIONAL-MIX ELEMENTS IN INTERNATIONAL MARKETING

This chapter has focused on advertising, since it is usually the primary element in the promotional mix of the international marketer. However, as in domestic marketing, promotional programs for foreign markets generally include other elements such as sales promotion, public relations, and digital and social media. The roles of these other promotional-mix elements vary depending on the firm's marketing and promotional strategy in foreign markets.

Sales promotion and public relations can support and enhance advertising efforts; the latter may also be used to create or maintain favorable images for companies in foreign markets. For some firms, personal selling may be the most important promotional element and advertising may play a support role. This final section considers the roles of some of these other promotional-mix elements in the international marketing program.

Sales Promotion

Sales promotion activity in international markets is growing due in part to the transfer of promotion concepts and techniques from country to country and in part to the proliferation of media. The growth also stems from the liberalization of trade, the rise of global brands, the spread of cable and satellite TV, and the deregulation and/or privatization of media. Sales promotion and direct-response agencies have been becoming more common, particularly in Europe and more recently in South American, Asian, and Middle Eastern countries. In many less developed countries, spending on sales promotion often exceeds media spending on TV, radio, and print ads.

As we saw in Chapter 16, sales promotion is one of the fastest-growing areas of marketing in the United States. Companies increasingly rely on consumer- and trade-oriented sales promotion to help sell their products in foreign markets as well. Many of the promotional tools that are effective in the United States, such as free samples, premiums, event sponsorships, contests, coupons, and trade promotions, are also used in foreign markets. For example, Häagen-Dazs estimates it gave out more than 5 million free tastings of its ice cream as part of its successful strategy for entering the European market. Since taste is the major benefit of this premium product, sampling was an appropriate sales promotion tool for entering foreign markets. The WD-40 Co. uses samples in the United States as well as foreign markets to educate consumers about the versatility of the product and encourage trial. The sample shown in Exhibit 19–17, which uses the front headline "One Can. One Thousand Uses," was translated into 20 different languages. This makes it possible for the distributors in different countries to use a sampling tool in their local languages. Nestlé introduced its Nescafe brand to China by conducting the world's largest coffee-sampling program. Nescafe samples were passed out across 150 cities in China using 18 teams throughout the country. The sampling program helped increase sales by over 150 percent in the predominantly tea-drinking country.[86]

Unlike advertising, which can be done on a global basis, sales promotions must be adapted to local markets. Kamran Kashani and John Quelch noted several important differences among countries that marketers must consider in developing a sales promotion program.[87]

EXHIBIT 19–17

WD-40 uses product samples in various countries to encourage trial

Source: WD-40 Company

They include the stage of economic development, market maturity, consumer perceptions of promotional tools, trade structure, and legal restrictions and regulations:

- *Economic development.* In highly developed countries such as the United States, Canada, Japan, and Western European nations, marketers can choose from a wide range of promotional tools. But in developing countries they must be careful not to use promotional tools such as in- or on-package premiums that would increase the price of the product beyond the reach of most consumers. Free samples and demonstrations are widely used as effective promotional tools in developing countries. But coupons, which are so popular with consumers in the United States, are rarely used because of problems with distribution and resistance from retailers. In the United States and Britain, most coupons are distributed through newspapers (including FSIs) or magazines. Low literacy rates in some countries make print media an ineffective coupon distribution method, so coupons are delivered door to door, handed out in stores, or placed in or on packages. The use of coupons by both marketers as well as consumers is much greater in the United States than other countries as more than 300 billion coupons were distributed and nearly 3 billion redeemed in 2015. Coupon distribution and redemption in other countries drops dramatically from the levels seen in the United States; the United Kingdom is the second-largest user of coupons with just over 6 billion distributed and less than 100 million redeemed.

- *Market maturity.* Marketers must also consider the stage of market development for their product or service in various countries when they design sales promotions. To introduce a product to a country, consumer-oriented promotional tools such as sampling, high-value coupons, and cross-promotions with established products and brands are often effective. The competitive dynamics of a foreign market are also often a function of its stage of development. More competition is likely in well-developed mature markets, which will influence the types of sales promotion tools used. For example, there may be competitive pressure to use trade allowances to maintain distribution or consumer promotions that will maintain customer loyalty, such as bonus packs, price-off deals, or loyalty programs.

- *Consumer perceptions.* An important consideration in the design of sales promotion programs is how they are perceived by consumers as well as the trade. Consumer perceptions of various sales promotion tools vary from market to market. For example, Japanese women are less likely to take advantage of contests, coupons, or other promotions than are women in the United States. Premium offers in particular must be adapted to the tastes of consumers in various markets. A study by Huff and Alden examined consumers' opinions toward the use of coupons and sweepstakes in three Asian countries: Taiwan, Malaysia, and Thailand. The study found differences among the three countries, with consumers in Taiwan having more negative attitudes and lower levels of use of both sweepstakes and coupons than consumers in Malaysia and Thailand.[88]

- *Trade structure.* In areas with highly concentrated retailing systems, such as northern Europe, the trade situation is becoming much like the United States and Canada as pressure grows for more price-oriented trade and in-store promotions. In southern Europe, the retail industry is highly fragmented and there is less trade pressure for promotions. The willingness and ability of channel members to accommodate sales promotion programs must also be considered. Retailers in many countries do not want to take time to process coupons, post promotional displays, or deal with premiums or packaging that require special handling or storage. In countries like Japan or India, where retailing structures are highly fragmented, stores are too small for point-of-purchase displays or in-store sampling. In most Asian countries simple price-cut promotions that are supported by direct-mail leaflets and newspaper advertising are the primary promotional vehicles.[89]

- *Regulations.* An important factor affecting the use of sales promotions in foreign countries is the presence of legal restrictions and regulations. Laws affecting sales promotions are generally more restrictive in other countries than in the United States. Some countries ban contests, games, or lotteries, while others restrict the size or amount of a sample, premium, or prize. For example, fair-trade regulations in Japan limit the maximum value of premiums to 10 percent of the retail price; in France the limit is 5 percent. Canada prohibits games of pure chance unless a skill element is used to determine the winner. In Japan the amount of a prize offer is limited to a certain percentage of the product tied to the promotion.[90] In some countries, a free premium must be related to the nature of the product purchased. Many countries have strict rules when it comes to premium offers for children, and some ban them altogether.

  Variations in rules and regulations mean marketers must often develop separate consumer sales promotion programs for each country. Many companies have found it difficult to do any promotions throughout Europe because sales promotion rules differ so much from one country to another. While the European Commission has considered various proposals to standardize regulations for sales promotions in countries that are members of the European Union, it has not been successful in doing so. Thus, many companies use local agencies or international sales promotion companies to develop sales promotion programs in Europe as well as other foreign markets.

Public Relations

Many companies involved in international marketing are recognizing the importance of using public relations to support and enhance their marketing and advertising efforts.[91] Public relations activities are needed to deal with local governments, media, trade associations, and the general public, any of which may feel threatened by the presence of a foreign multinational. The job of PR agencies in foreign markets is not only to help the company sell its products or services but also to present the firm as a good corporate citizen concerned about the future of the country.

Companies generally need a favorable image to be successful in foreign markets. Those perceived negatively may face pressure from the media, local governments, or other relevant publics or even boycotts by consumers. Often, public relations is needed to deal with specific problems a company faces in international markets. For example, McDonald's and a number of other companies have had to deal with PR problems arising from concerns over the nutritional value of their food. The latest controversy erupted in response to a report showing child obesity in France had doubled to 16 percent in 10 years. Concerns over the problem of childhood obesity have spread to other European countries and other food companies such as Kraft and Kellogg are also being criticized. As noted earlier, the European Union called on the food industry to regulate so-called junk-food advertising aimed at consumers across the continent.[92]

Yum! Brand's KFC division ran into a public relations problem a few years ago in China, which is the restaurant chain's largest market, when Chinese media reported that several KFC suppliers used hormones and antibiotics to shorten the maturation cycle of chickens. The Chinese state television network (CCTV) ran an investigative piece on large-scale chicken farmers in the country, highlighting concerns over their practices; the food scare resulted in a 6 percent decline in sales for several months in KFC restaurants. In response to the PR crisis, KFC eliminated more than 1,000 farms from its supplier networks to ensure food safety and also pledged to step up self-inspections as well as enhance communication with the government and public.[93] As part of its response KFC used its various social media sites in the country such as Sina Weibo and Renren to respond to detail steps the company was taking to ensure the safety of its chicken, engage key media opinion leaders, and restore consumer confidence.[94]

Digital and Social Media

Worldwide Growth of the Internet

The Internet has clearly come of age as a global marketing medium and is now an important IMC tool as well for companies around the world, both large and small. Marketers are using digital and social media to promote their companies, build their brands, and engage in e-commerce transactions in their own countries as well as across borders. As of 2016, there were more than 3.4 billion Internet users around the world, with the largest number of users residing in Asia, followed by Europe and North America. China is now the country with the largest number of people online, with an estimated 721 million users, followed by India with 462 million, the United States with 281 million, and Japan with 115 million. There are also 614 million Internet users in Europe.[95]

As noted, China now has the world's largest Internet population. There are key differences in the demographic and usage behavior of China's "digital elite" as they are younger, better educated, and more likely to be employed full time versus Internet users in other countries. They also spend more time online and are more involved with Web 2.0 activities such as participating in blogs and chats, posting product ratings and reviews, and using social media. They are also more likely to access the Internet from mobile devices. The look, feel, and features of many Chinese websites are similar to those in the United States and Europe, and China has search and e-commerce sites that function like Google, Amazon, and eBay. Baidu dominates online search in China today since Google closed its China site in March 2010 because of censorship by the Chinese government and cyberattacks from within the country. It is expected that Google will work to resolve its disagreements with the Chinese government; the company will not want to turn its back on what has become the world's largest Internet and continues to grow. Google is working toward an agreement to offer an app store for Android devices that would include only government-approved apps.[96] Alibaba is China's largest online commerce company and its three main sites—Taobao, Tmall, and Alibaba.com—have hundreds of millions of users, and host millions of merchants and businesses. Alibaba handles more business than any other e-commerce company and is the most popular destination for online shopping in China, which is the world's fastest-growing e-commerce market.

Use of Digital and Social Media in International Marketing

Digital media are becoming an integral part of the IMC program of marketers at a global, regional, and local level as Internet penetration increases in countries around the world and marketers become more adept at using social media, mobile marketing, and other forms of digital communication. Most multinational marketers now have websites for specific countries and/or regions that allow them to tailor the information they provide to the needs, interests, lifestyles, and subtleties of consumers in these markets. For example, Exhibit 19–18 shows

EXHIBIT 19–18

TaylorMade Golf develops a website specifically for countries such as Japan

Source: TaylorMade Golf Company, Inc.

a page from the website used by the TaylorMade Golf Company in Japan. Marketers are also using mass-media advertising to drive consumers to their websites, where they provide them with detailed information about their products and services, encourage them to participate in promotions, or encourage them to make purchases.

International marketers are also allocating a large amount of their advertising budgets in various countries to digital media, with online advertising becoming the primary driver of global advertising spending growth. As is the case in the United States, much of this growth in digital advertising is being driven by ads on social media, online display and video, and paid search. The great majority of digital advertising is targeted at mobile devices, thanks to their widespread adoption and their ever-tighter integration into consumers' daily lives of consumers around the world.[97]

The use of social media is becoming very prevalent in countries around the world, and marketers are making social networking sites an integral part of their IMC programs. There are more than 2.3 billion active social media users worldwide, nearly half of whom live in Asian countries. Facebook has become the first truly global social networking brand and now has more than 1 billion users around the world. The company also owns Instagram which had over 400 million active users in 2016, 75 percent of whom live outside the United States. As discussed in Digital and Social Media Perspective 19–1, Facebook has become the leading social networking site in the United States as well as most other countries. Over the past few years it has become very popular in Brazil and replaced Orkut, which is owned by Google, as the most popular social media site in the country. However, Facebook has very little presence in China, where it is banned by the Chinese government along with several other social media sites, including Twitter. Its penetration is also very low in other countries such as Korea and Russia, since local social networking sites are thriving in these countries. One country where Facebook has overtaken a popular local social networking site is Japan; in 2012 it reached 15 million active users in the country, surpassing Japanese social network Mixi, and had 25 million users in 2016 (Exhibit 19–19). It is reported that several factors helped Facebook become very popular in Japan, including the popularity of the movie *The Social Network* and the huge number of social media interactions that occurred following the Tohoku earthquake and the Fukushima nuclear disaster.[98]

Twitter has also become a global social media platform as in 2016 the microblogging site had 313 million monthly active users. However, Twitter's growth has stagnated which is creating concern over its viability as a marketing platform.[99] The way people around the world are using Twitter is also changing. Research shows that usage is becoming much more commercial, with consumers posting comments about brands, using branded apps, and asking friends about products. It is likely that global marketers will continue to use Twitter, particularly for publicity and public relations, while looking for other ways to leverage it as an IMC tool such as through the use of Promoted Tweets as well as hashtag campaigns.

As the digital revolution continues, marketers will be making greater use of digital and social media in their global as well as regional and local IMC programs. The use of social networking sites will become more prevalent, and marketers are also expected to increase their use of mobile marketing techniques since more consumers are now using their smartphones and other mobile devices to access and surf the Internet. As consumers become more reliant on the Internet and various forms of digital media for information, entertainment, and socializing, marketers must develop ways to reach them through these contact points.

EXHIBIT 19–19

Mixi was the leading social networking site in Japan but has been overtaken by Facebook

© NetPhotos/Alamy

FACEBOOK WANTS TO DOMINATE THE SOCIAL MEDIA WORLD

Facebook was founded by Mark Zuckerberg in 2004 when he was a sophomore attending Harvard, and in a little more than a decade has grown from a social network meant only for Harvard students to a company whose goal is to connect everyone in the world. Nearly one-fourth of the world's population uses Facebook. And if the company has its druthers, the rest soon will too because its goal is to have 5 billion of the world's 7 billion people connected to its social network by 2030. In October 2012 Facebook reached a milestone when the popular social media site hit the 1 billion user mark; in less than five years it has added another 650 million users. It is important to note that the number of Facebook users does not represent the number of profiles—which could include repeats, fake users, or bots—but 1.65 billion *active* users who log on to their accounts at least once per month. Moreover, nearly two-thirds of Facebook monthly active users around the world spend an average of 20+ minutes per day on the social network site, liking, commenting, scrolling through news feeds and status updates, and looking at pictures and videos.

Facebook began in the United States and has grown rapidly here, but most of its users reside outside North America. As of 2016, nearly 85 percent of Facebook's worldwide users are from countries other than the United States and Canada. And, in much the same way that culture and traditions in everyday life vary from country to country, Facebook usage differs around the world as well. One country where Facebook, and overall social media usage, has exploded is Brazil, which is currently third behind the United States and India in number of Facebook users. Internet penetration is still a problem in Brazil as just over half of Brazilians have regular access, although the number continues to grow. The 110 million Internet users are very active online with average time spent on social media each day by Brazilian social media users at nearly 4 hours versus 2.7 in the United States.

Facebook is by far the most popular social platform with nearly 70 million users.

One explanation as to why social media usage in Brazil is increasing so rapidly is culture. Brazilians are known for their gregarious behavior in public spaces such as elevators and restaurants, their openness, and their passion for sharing information and pictures with friends and family. Brazilians, like an increasing number of mobile social media users in the United States, also show a propensity for being glued to social media platforms during sporting events and TV shows, since they are able to converse and share feelings in real time while watching.

Another reason for significant social media growth in Brazil is the very nature of its emerging economy, particularly the middle class's increasing access to the Internet at home and on mobile devices, and the expanding credit market among middle-class consumers. Brazilian consumers have shown an unusually strong willingness to make purchases online using credit cards, leading to increases in online advertising spending. Facebook, as well as Twitter and other social media platforms, have launched in-country operations in Brazil and plan to capitalize on online and mobile advertising opportunities on their respective platforms.

Another market of great interest to Facebook is India, where the number of Internet users has grown to nearly 400 million. While countries like Brazil represent significant opportunities for Facebook, India is the mother lode given its population of 1.3 billion. Growing Internet penetration and a large youth population has helped Facebook expand its user base in India to nearly 120 million, which is second only to the United States. Nearly 90 percent of those on Facebook in India are accessing the platform on their mobile phones at least one per month and nearly half are using their mobile phones every day to connect with friends on Facebook. The company has also added support for Hindi and seven other

Summary

Many companies are recognizing the opportunities as well as the necessity of marketing their products and services internationally because of saturated markets and intense competition from both domestic and foreign competitors. Advertising and promotion are important parts of the international marketing program of these companies. Global marketers based in the United States, as well as European and Asian countries, have increased their advertising spending, particularly in digital media.

International marketers must carefully analyze the major environmental forces in each market where they compete,

including economic, demographic, cultural, and political/legal factors. These factors are important not only in assessing the potential of each country as a market but also in designing and implementing advertising and promotional programs.

Much attention has focused on global marketing, where a standard marketing program is used in all markets. Part of global marketing is global advertising, where the same basic advertising approach is used in all markets. Opponents of the global (standardized) approach argue that differences in culture, market and economic conditions, and consumer

© NetPhotos/Alamy

Indian languages over the past year, and is working with software developers to get them to come up with more India-specific content that has high viral potential.

Over the next several years, however, Web access will become increasingly available to 900 million-plus mobile phone users. However, only about 10 percent of urban Indians have smartphones and ownership of the devices is miniscule in rural areas. One way Facebook is trying to reach Internet users in rural areas is with its "Free Basics" program which uses satellites, drones, and lasers to provide access to a host of basic services such as *Wikipedia*, health sites, weather reports, and, of course, Facebook. However, the company suffered a setback in 2016 when India's Telecom Regulatory Authority blocked Facebook's Free Basics service as part of a ruling that supports net neutrality arguing that the service violates neutrality by favoring some services over others.

And then there's China, which remains completely untapped by Facebook due to government censorship. Like India, China represents another tremendous growth opportunity based on its population of 1.36 billion people and the fact that the Chinese are avid users of social media. However, more than 3,000 Internet sites are banned in China, including Twitter as well as certain Google products such as YouTube, Gmail, and Google+. Facebook has been wooing the Chinese government for years in hope of getting a crack at China's nearly 700 million Internet users. However, even if China were to welcome Mark Zuckerberg and his social platform with open arms, there's no guarantee that Facebook could be successful in the Middle Kingdom. Chinese culture; the size, scope, and pace of China's Internet market; government protection and influence; and late entrance to a market already full of social media players are just a few of the challenges Facebook faces in China.

One of the most popular social media sites in China is a microblog called Sina Weibo that was launched by Chinese portal giant Sina.com in 2009. Sina Weibo, which is closer to Twitter than Facebook in terms of the user experience, has more than 300 million users. Another popular social media network in China has been Renren, which has nearly 200 million users, but has been losing ground to WeChat, which is an instant-messaging site developed by Tencent, China's largest Internet portal. WeChat has more than 700 million active users, most of whom reside in China. WhatsApp, the instant-messaging site that Facebook bought in 2014 for $19 billion, now has over a billion users globally but has been unable to gain significant market share in China. Many experts argue that if will be very difficult for Facebook to challenge WeChat's dominance in China, given that the homegrown platform is nearly a monopoly in the country.

While Facebook has been able to find its way into nearly every country in the world, penetrating the "great firewall of China" is likely to remain a challenge. In the meantime, Facebook will focus on other places in the world where it can connect people more easily without having to deal with the difficult issues it would face in China, such as government restrictions and censorship. Facebook still has plans to wire the world with Internet access through its Free Basics program since there are still billions of people in emerging markets in Southeast Asia, Latin America, and Africa that would welcome the opportunity to have access to the social media platform.

Sources: Yue Wang, "Facebook Still Wants to Crack China but It May Be Too Late," *Forbes*, March 21, 2016, www.forbes.com/sites/ywang/2016/03/21/facebook-still-wants-to-crack-china-but-it-maybe-too-late/#19e4411f50dc; Marco della Cava, "Facebook in 2030? 5 Billion Users Says Zuck," *USA Today*, February 4, 2016, www.usatoday.com/story/tech/news/2016/02/04/facebook-2030-5-billion-users-says-zuck/79786688/; Loretta Chao, "Brazil: The Social Media Capital of the Universe," *The Wall Street Journal*, February 5, 2013, pp. B1, B5; Amol Sharma, "India, a New Facebook Testing Ground," *The Wall Street Journal*, October 20, 2012, pp. B1, B5.

needs and wants make a universal approach to marketing and advertising impractical. Many companies use an in-between approach, standardizing their basic marketing strategy but localizing advertising messages to fit each market.

There are a number of important decision areas in the development of advertising and promotional programs for international markets. These include organization, agency selection, creative strategy and execution, and media strategy and selection. An important decision facing international advertisers is determining the appropriate advertising messages for each market. Creative strategy development for international advertising is basically similar in process and procedure to that for domestic advertising.

Sales promotion, personal selling, public relations, and the Internet are also part of the promotional mix of international marketers. Sales promotion programs usually must be adapted to local markets. Factors to consider include stage of market development, market maturity, consumer perceptions of promotional tools, trade structure, and legal restrictions and regulations. PR programs are also important to help international marketers develop and maintain favorable relationships with governments, media, and consumers in foreign countries. The use of digital and social media such as the Internet, social networking sites, and mobile marketing is becoming an important part of international marketers' IMC programs. Internet penetration is increasing rapidly in most countries, and as more consumers go online, marketers are developing websites for various countries and also using other forms of digital and social media to reach them.

Key Terms

Discussion Questions

1. The chapter opener discusses the "Taste the Feeling" global marketing launched by the Coca-Cola Company in 2016. Evaluate the creative strategy being used for this campaign as well as the "one-brand" approach that will unite various brands such as Coca-Cola Light/Diet Coke, Coke Zero, and Coca-Cola Life under one personality rather than running different campaigns for each. (LO 19-1, 19-2)

2. Why are international markets so important to U.S. companies as well as companies located in other countries? Discuss the various factors that companies must consider in developing IMC programs for various countries. (LO 19-1)

3. Discuss the factors that are leading to the economic growth of China and the market opportunities that are evolving. What challenges do marketers and their agencies face in developing IMC programs for the Chinese market? (LO 19-2)

4. Discuss how global marketers might use the 2022 FIFA World Cup soccer tournament that will be held in Qatar as an integrated marketing communications opportunity. What types of companies are best suited to use the World Cup for a global marketing platform? (LO 19-1, 19-2)

5. What are some of the cultural variables that marketers must consider in developing advertising and promotional programs in a foreign market? Choose one of these cultural variables and discuss how it has created a problem or challenge for a company in developing an advertising and promotional program in a specific country. (LO 19-2)

6. What is meant by a country-of-origin effect? Choose a product category for which there is a country-of-origin effect and find an example of a company or brand that is using it in its IMC campaign. (LO 19-3)

7. Discuss the advantages and disadvantages of using a global advertising campaign. For what type of products/services is a global advertising approach appropriate? (LO 19-3)

8. Discuss some of the differences in media that exist across various countries and how they might impact the media strategy used by marketers. (LO 19-4)

9. Discuss the evolving role of the Internet and other digital and social media in the IMC program of international marketers. How can marketers make effective use of digital and social media in marketing their products and services in various countries? (LO 19-5)

10. Why do you think Facebook has become so popular in countries around the world? Discuss the importance of social media in the IMC programs of international marketers. (LO 19-5)

connect

Digital users can access their personalized and adaptive SmartBook, Ad Forum Video Cases, and interactive exercises to review chapter concepts.

20 Regulation of Advertising and Promotion

Kobe Bryant @kobebryant · 4 Jun 2015
#UpgradeYourSportsDrink with @DrinkBODYARMOR #ThisIsNOW

> **Fortune** @FortuneMagazine
> Watch out Gatorade, this sports drink startup is coming for you for.tn/1M7VZzD

474   1K

Samir Mezrahi @samir · 4 Jun 2015
@kobebryant is this an advertisement?

10   28

Kobe Bryant ✓
@kobebryant

Follow

As in did I get $ to tweet it @samir? No, zero$ I ACTUALLY invested My own$ in @DrinkBODYARMOR because I believe in our product and our team

RETWEETS 612   LIKES 1,749

10:44 AM - 4 Jun 2015

Source: Twitter

LEARNING OBJECTIVES

LO1 Explain the role and function of various regulatory agencies.

LO2 Evaluate the effectiveness of self-regulation of advertising.

LO3 Describe how advertising is regulated by federal and state regulatory bodies.

LO4 Discuss the regulation of sales promotion, direct marketing, and Internet marketing.

MARKETERS FACE NEW RULES AND REGULATIONS FOR ONLINE ENDORSERS

Endorsements and testimonials have always been an important tool for advertisers who know they can be very persuasive. Consumers are often influenced by ads they see on TV or in a magazine showing how a product helped someone lose weight, get in shape, or make more money. Often these endorsements come from a celebrity such as an athlete, actor, or entertainer which can make them even more persuasive, particularly when consumers respect and admire these individuals. However, the Federal Trade Commission (FTC), which is the federal agency responsible for the regulation of advertising and other forms of marketing in the United States, has long recognized the power of endorsements and testimonials and thus requires them to be truthful and not misleading to the reasonable consumer. To help ensure that marketers meet this standard the FTC has provided them with guidelines titled *Guides Concerning the Use of Endorsements and Testimonials in Advertising.* The FTC guidelines in place for nearly three decades were designed to cover the use of endorsements and testimonials in traditional media such as TV, print, and radio. With the explosive growth of the Internet, the commission recognized that changes had to be made to cover endorsements that consumers might encounter online when watching a video on YouTube or reading a blog or social media post on Twitter or Facebook.

In 2009, the FTC revised its rules and regulations regarding the use of endorsements and testimonials in advertising for the first time since 1980. One of the goals of the revised guidelines is to clarify what an endorser such as a celebrity or blogger can say about a product or service in a testimonial. The new FTC rules state that celebrity endorsers can be held liable for false statements about a product or service and all endorsements must include results or outcomes that consumers can generally expect from using it. For example, advertisers are advised that using unrepresentative testimonials may be misleading if they are not accompanied by information describing what consumers can generally expect from use of the product or service. The old days of using a disclaimer such as "results not typical" or making claims that might be misleading without disclosing limitations or conditions are gone. In addition, the FTC guidelines

let endorsers know that they shouldn't talk about their experience with a product or service if they haven't tried it, or make claims about a product that would require proof they don't have.

The other major area covered in the revision to the FTC guidelines applies to the use of endorsements and testimonials made online, particularly through social media. The *Guides* point out that marketers using digital media are subject to the same truthful advertising laws that other forms of advertising always have been. That means, among other things, that anyone compensated to promote or review a product should disclose it. One of the goals of the FTC has been to clarify or establish when a blogger or even a consumer promoting a product on a social media platform or a review site such as Amazon or Yelp becomes an endorser. The FTC guidelines state that if there is a "material connection" between the endorser and the seller of the product or service, full disclosure is required. What this basically means is that anytime endorsers receive money or something of value, such as free products or services, it must be clearly and conspicuously disclosed when they are discussing or promoting the brand on social media. For example, an individual who maintains a fashion blog and receives a pair of jeans from a company and posts a review about how well they fit must disclose that she received them free of charge. Disclosures can also apply to celebrities who are promoting a brand in ad campaigns using both traditional and social media. While it may be clear that an athlete such as Kobe Bryant is endorsing a brand such as Body Armour sports drink when he promotes it in a TV commercial or print ad, the connection may not be obvious to consumers who read a tweet where he talks about the brand and a disclosure may be required.

The disclosure rule also applies to third-party networks that are paid by marketers and then turn around and pay bloggers or others to promote their brands online. For example, in 2015 the FTC settled a case against Machinima Inc., an online entertainment network, charging that it engaged in deceptive advertising by paying "influencers" to post YouTube videos endorsing Microsoft's Xbox One video system and several games as part of a marketing campaign being managed by Microsoft's ad agency. The influencers failed to adequately disclose their connection to Machinima and that they were being paid for their seemingly objective opinions. In another case, the FTC challenged the Deutsch LA advertising agency because its employees were encouraged to participate in an ad campaign by posting comments about one of its client's new products on Twitter without disclosing their connection to the ad agency or the client. The FTC argued that the tweets were misleading because they were not actual consumer views and they failed to disclose that they were posted by employees of the agency.

Another important part of the new FTC guidelines involves requirements for disclosures. In 2013 and 2015, the FTC issued updates to its endorsement guidelines that clarify how much disclosure is required and whether it applies to short-form platforms such as Twitter. In the updated guidelines the FTC discusses requirements related to factors such as proximity, prominence, and multimedia. With regard to proximity, even in a space-constrained ad or promotion, the disclosure must be physically close to the statement or endorsement. The FTC also requires that the disclosure be in understandable language, which means that using a hashtag such as #spon may not be acceptable. The FTC recommends using #Ad, "Ad:", or "Sponsored" in tweets. Prominence requirements mean that the disclosures must be prominent or viewable on any device and not buried within a web page or a page on a mobile platform. The multimedia guidelines require disclosure for audio or video claims and endorsements in the same clear and conspicuous ways as expected for written media. They also require that the form of the disclosure match the content, which means that if a video or sound file is used, the disclosure should be done in the native format rather than included in a post or annotation on a social media site.

The new FTC *Guides* and the recent updates require that marketers as well as their advertising agencies and third-party networks clearly understand how they can use endorsers and make sure that they are in compliance with the rules and regulations. It is important that they know what constitutes an endorsement because they do not always require explicit wording by the endorser stating that they approve of a product or service. Simply posting a video or photo on social media may convey that the poster likes and approves of the product and could be viewed as an endorsement. One legal expert notes that marketers must also track how they may be creating material connections such as by paying money to a celebrity or blogger to promote a brand; providing free products or discounts to bloggers offering entries into a contest or sweepstakes in exchange for posting pictures or statements about the brand; paying employees to post things about the brand on social media; or offering an incentive program to marketing affiliates.

As companies shift more of their marketing efforts online and make greater use of bloggers and other types of endorsers, it will be important for them to train their employees and monitor the way endorsers are being used. The FTC provides a helpful and simple mnemonic for marketers—MMM—which means *mandate* a disclosure policy that complies with the law; *make* sure people who work for you or with you know what the rules are; and *monitor* what they are doing on your behalf.

Sources: Linda Goldstein, "Advertisers Will Find It Harder to Balance Marketing Objectives with New Legal Guidelines in 2016," *Advertising Age*, January 11, 2016, p. 28; Heather Dunn, "Five Best Practices in Advertising Law," *Marketing News*, December 2015, pp. 20–22; Martin Beck, "FTC Puts Social Media Marketers on Notice with Updated Disclosure Guidelines," *Marketing Land*, June 12, 2015, http://marketingland.com/ftc-puts-social-media-marketers-on-notice-with-updated-disclosure-guidelines-132017; Abbey Klaasen and Michael Learmonth, "What You Need to Know about the New FTC Endorsement Rules—and Why," *Advertising Age*, October 12, 2009, http://adage.com/article/digital/ftc-endorsement-rules/139595/.

Suppose you are the advertising manager for a consumer-products company and have just reviewed a new commercial your agency created. You are very excited about the ad. It presents new claims about your brand's superiority that should help differentiate it from the competition. However, before you approve the commercial you need answers. Are the claims verifiable? Did researchers use proper procedures to collect and analyze the data and present the findings? Do research results support the claims? Were the right people used in the study? Could any conditions have biased the results?

Before approving the commercial, you have it reviewed by your company's legal department and by your ad agency's attorneys. If both reviews are acceptable, you send the ad to the major networks, which have their censors examine it. They may ask for more information or send the ad back for modification. (No commercial can run without approval from a network's Standards and Practices Department.)

Even after approval and airing, your commercial is still subject to scrutiny from such state and federal regulatory agencies as the state attorney general's office and the Federal Trade Commission. Individual consumers or competitors who find the ad misleading or have other concerns may file a complaint with the National Advertising Division of the Council of Better Business Bureaus. Finally, disparaged competitors may sue if they believe your ad distorts the facts and misleads consumers. If you lose the litigation, your company may have to retract the claims and pay the competitor damages, sometimes running into millions of dollars.

After considering all these regulatory issues, you must ask yourself if the new ad can meet all these challenges and is worth the risk. Maybe you ought to continue with the old approach that made no specific claims and simply said your brand was great.

Overview of Regulation

Regulatory concerns can play a major role in the advertising and promotion decision-making process. Advertisers operate in a complex environment of local, state, and federal rules and regulations. Additionally, a number of advertising and business-sponsored associations, consumer groups and organizations, and the media attempt to promote honest, truthful, and tasteful advertising through their own self-regulatory programs and guidelines. The legal and regulatory aspects of advertising are very complex. Many parties are concerned about the nature and content of advertising and its potential to offend, exploit, mislead, and/or deceive consumers.

Advertising has also become increasingly important in product liability litigation involving products that are associated with consumer injuries. In many of these cases the courts have been willing to consider the impact of advertising on behavior of consumers that leads to injury-causing situations. Thus advertisers must avoid certain practices and proactively engage in others to ensure that their ads are comprehended correctly and do not misrepresent their products or services.[1] The costs can be very high and consequences quite severe when companies become involved in legal proceedings regarding their advertising claims.

Numerous guidelines, rules, regulations, and laws constrain and restrict advertising. These regulations primarily influence individual advertisers, but they can also affect advertising for an entire industry. For example, cigarette advertising was banned from the broadcast media in 1970, and many groups continue to push for a total ban on the advertising of tobacco products, including e-cigarettes and other delivery forms.[2] As discussed later in the chapter, legislation is being considered that would either ban or impose major restrictions on direct-to-consumer advertising of drugs.[3] Advertising is controlled by internal self-regulation and by external state and federal regulatory agencies such as the Federal Trade Commission (FTC), the Federal Communications Commission (FCC), the Food and Drug Administration (FDA), and the U.S. Postal Service. State attorneys general also have become more active in advertising regulation. While only government agencies (federal, state, and local) have the force of law, most advertisers also abide by the guidelines and decisions of internal regulatory bodies. In fact, self-regulation from groups such as the media and the National Advertising Review Board probably has more influence on advertisers' day-to-day operations and decision making than government rules and regulations.

Decision makers on both the client and agency side must be knowledgeable about these regulatory groups, including the intent of their efforts, how they operate, and how they influence and affect advertising and other promotional-mix elements. In this chapter, we examine the major sources of advertising regulation, including

SELF-REGULATION

LO20-2

For many years, the advertising industry has practiced and promoted voluntary **self-regulation**. Most advertisers, their agencies, and the media recognize the importance of maintaining consumer trust and confidence. Advertisers also see self-regulation as a way to limit government interference, which, they believe, results in more stringent and troublesome regulations. Self-regulation and control of advertising emanate from all segments of the advertising industry, including individual advertisers and their agencies, business and advertising associations, and the media.

Self-Regulation by Advertisers and Agencies

Self-regulation begins with the interaction of client and agency when creative ideas are generated and submitted for consideration. Most companies have specific guidelines, standards, and policies to which their ads must adhere. Recognizing that their ads reflect on the company, advertisers carefully scrutinize all messages to ensure they are consistent with the image the firm wishes to project. Companies also review their ads to be sure any claims made are reasonable and verifiable and do not mislead or deceive consumers. Ads are usually examined by corporate attorneys to avoid potential legal problems and their accompanying time, expense, negative publicity, and embarrassment.

Internal control and regulation also come from advertising agencies. Most have standards regarding the type of advertising they either want or are willing to produce, and they try to avoid ads that might be offensive or misleading. Most agencies will ask their clients to provide verification or support for claims they might want to make in their advertising and will make sure that adequate documentation or substantiation is available. However, agencies will also take formal steps to protect themselves from legal and ethical perils through agency–client contracts. For example, many liability issues are handled in these contracts. Agencies generally use information provided by clients for advertising claims, and in standard contracts the agency is protected from suits involving the accuracy of those claims. Contracts will also absolve the agency of responsibility if something goes wrong with the advertised product and consumers suffer damages or injury or other product liability claims arise.[4] However, agencies have been held legally responsible for fraudulent or deceptive claims and in some cases have been fined when their clients were found guilty of engaging in deceptive advertising.[5] Many agencies have a creative review board or panel composed of experienced personnel who examine ads for content and execution as well as for their potential to be perceived as offensive, misleading, and/or deceptive. Most agencies also employ or retain lawyers who review the ads for potential legal problems. Exhibit 20–1 shows the homepage for the Olshan Frome Wolosky law firm in New York City, which specializes in advertising and integrated marketing communications law.

EXHIBIT 20–1

The Olshan firm specializes in advertising and integrated marketing communications law

© Olshan Frome Wolosky LLP

Self-Regulation by Trade Associations

Like advertisers and their agencies, many industries have also developed self-regulatory programs. This is particularly true in industries whose advertising is prone to controversy, such as liquor and alcoholic beverages, drugs, and various products marketed to children. Many trade and industry associations develop their own advertising guidelines or codes that member companies are expected to abide by including the Toy Industry Association, the Motion Picture Association of America, and the Pharmaceutical Research and Manufacturers of America. The Wine Institute, the U.S. Brewers Association, and the Distilled Spirits Council of the United States all have guidelines that member companies are supposed to follow in advertising alcoholic beverages.[6]

The advertising of hard liquor on television has been a very controversial issue as many consumer and public health groups argue that liquor is more dangerous than beer or wine because of its higher alcohol content. Critics also argue that airing liquor ads on TV glamorizes drinking and encourages children and teenagers to drink and were successful in keeping advertising for spirits off the major networks until recently. While no specific law prohibits the advertising of hard liquor on radio or television, it was effectively banned for over five decades as a result of a code provision by the National Association of Broadcasters and by agreement of liquor manufacturers and their self-governing body, the Distilled Spirits Council of the United States (DISCUS). However, in November 1996, DISCUS amended its code of good practice and overturned its self-imposed ban on broadcast advertising.[7]

After the DISCUS ban was lifted, the four major broadcast TV networks as well as major cable networks such as ESPN and MTV continued to refuse liquor ads, prompting consumer and public interest groups to applaud their actions.[8] However, the major networks cannot control the practices of affiliate stations they do not own and many of them began accepting liquor ads, as did local cable channels and independent broadcast stations. While the national broadcast networks continued their self-imposed ban for many years, the amount of liquor advertising on television continued to increase as more cable and local broadcast stations began accepting the commercials. Over the past several years the major networks have been accepting commercials for liquor, although most of the ads do not air before 10 P.M., unlike on cable, where many networks allow them anytime.[9]

The airing of hard liquor ads on a network TV show represents a major victory for the distilled spirits industry, which has argued there should be a level playing field for alcohol advertising and that liquor should be viewed the same way as beer and wine. They also note that the Federal Trade Commission (FTC) has said there is no basis for treating liquor ads differently than advertising for other types of alcohol. Thus, it appears that TV advertising for distilled spirits is here to stay and it's likely that you will see a lot more liquor ads on network TV shows as well as on cable. However, as might be expected, public advocacy groups such as the Center for Science in the Public Interest and the Center on Alcohol Marketing and Youth remain opposed to the networks' softening of their stance, arguing that youth exposure to liquor ads on TV has already increased significantly (Exhibit 20–2).

Many professions also maintain advertising guidelines through local, state, and national organizations. For years professional associations like the American Medical Association (AMA) and the American Bar Association (ABA) restricted advertising by their members on the basis that such promotional activities lowered members' professional status and led to unethical and fraudulent claims. However, such restrictive codes have been attacked by both government regulatory agencies and consumer groups. They argue that the public has a right to be informed about a professional's services, qualifications, and background and that advertising will improve professional services as consumers become better informed and are better able to shop around.[10]

In 1977, the Supreme Court held that state bar associations' restrictions on advertising are unconstitutional and that attorneys have First Amendment freedom of speech rights to advertise.[11] Many professional associations subsequently removed their restrictions, and advertising by lawyers and

EXHIBIT 20–2

In this advertisement for The Center on Alcohol Marketing and Youth, it is apparent that they are opposed to the advertising of hard liquor on television

Source: The Center on Alcohol Marketing and Youth

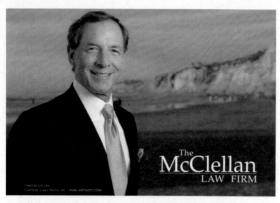

The McClellan Law Firm handles the
most complex cases in the most creative way

Catastrophic Personal Injury | Products Liability | Business Litigation | Intellectual Property

By limiting the number of cases and taking a team-based approach,
The McClellan Law Firm devotes all of our time, energy and resources to your case.

- Over 95 verdicts and settlements in excess of $1million—more than any other San Diego Lawyer
- Only San Diego lawyer inducted into the Inner Circle of Advocates
- 2012 San Diego Product Liability Litigation Lawyer of the Year by Best Lawyers
- 2012 Daniel T. Broderick III Award winner
- Fellow, American College of Trial Lawyers
- Top 50 San Diego Super Lawyers list 2007-2013
- Designated Tier 1 Personal Injury law firm by U.S. News & World Report

(619) 231-0505
www.mcclellanlaw.com

EXHIBIT 20–3

Advertising is often used by
attorneys to promote their
services

© McClellan Law Firm, photo by
J.Kat Photo, Inc., www.jkatphoto.
com

other professionals is now common (Exhibit 20–3).[12] Although industry associations are concerned with the impact and consequences of members' advertising, they have no legal way to enforce their guidelines. They can only rely on peer pressure from members or other nonbinding sanctions to get advertisers to comply. In 1982, the Supreme Court upheld an FTC order permitting advertising by dentists and physicians and various forms of advertising are now used by both groups.[13]

Self-Regulation by Businesses

A number of self-regulatory mechanisms have been established by the business community in an effort to control advertising practices.[14] The largest and best known is the **Better Business Bureau (BBB)**, which promotes fair advertising and selling practices across all industries. The BBB was established in 1916 to handle consumer complaints about local business practices and particularly advertising. Local BBBs are located in most large cities throughout the United States and supported entirely by dues of the more than 100,000 member firms.

Local BBBs receive and investigate complaints from consumers and other companies regarding the advertising and selling tactics of businesses in their area. Each local office has its own operating procedures for handling complaints; generally, the office contacts the violator and, if the complaint proves true, requests that the practice be stopped or changed. If the violator does not respond, negative publicity may be used against the firm or the case may be referred to appropriate government agencies for further action.

While BBBs provide effective control over advertising practices at the local level, the parent organization, the **Council of Better Business Bureaus (CBBB)**, plays a major role at the national level as the third-party administrator of the advertising industry self-regulatory system. Policies and procedures for industry self-regulation are established by the Advertising Self-Regulatory Council (ASRC) and implemented through four programs—the National Advertising Division (NAD), the Children's Advertising Review Unit (CARU), the Electronic Retailing Self-Regulation Program (ERSP), and the Online Interest-Based Advertising Accountability Program. The ASRC also has an appellate unit, the **National Advertising Review Board (NARB)**. Staffed primarily by attorneys, the NAD, CARU, ERSP, and Accountability Program review advertising claims that are national in scope. CARU reviews advertising directed to children under the age of 12, and ERSP examines advertising claims in direct-response advertising, including infomercials and home shopping channels, while the Accountability Program regulates online behavioral advertising (OBA) across the Internet.

The Advertising Self-Regulatory Council and the NAD/NARB

In 1971 four associations—the American Advertising Federation (AAF), the American Association of Advertising Agencies (the 4A's), the Association of National Advertisers (ANA), and the Council of Better Business Bureaus—joined forces to establish the National Advertising Review Council (NARC). In 2009 the CEOs of three other major marketing organizations—the Direct Marketing Association (DMA), Electronic Retailing Association (ERA), and the Interactive Advertising Bureau (IAB)—joined the NARC Board of Directors, and in 2012 the organization changed its name to the **Advertising Self-Regulatory Council (ASRC)**.

The ASRC's mission is to sustain high standards of truth and accuracy in national advertising. The NAD has examined advertising for truth and accuracy since 1971 and has published more than 5,000 decisions, focusing on areas that include product

EXHIBIT 20–4

The ASRC partners with various advertising and marketing organizations to create an effective self-regulatory system

Source: The Advertising Self-Regulatory Council (ASRC)

performance claims, superiority claims against competitive products, and all kinds of scientific and technical claims. The ASRC has a process that it follows for self-regulation and follows a specific set of policies and procedures that can be found on its website (Exhibit 20–4).

Federal law requires that advertisers possess substantiation for their advertising claims before the claims are published. After initiating or receiving a complaint, the NAD requests the advertiser's substantiation, reviews the information, and reaches a determination. In cases where the substantiating evidence does not support the claim, the NAD recommends that the advertiser modify or discontinue the claim. When an advertiser or a challenger disagrees with the NAD's findings, its decision can be appealed to the NARB for additional review.

As can be seen in Figure 20–1, the vast majority of the complaints to the NAD come from marketers challenging claims made by their competitors, often in the context of a comparative advertising message.[15] For example, the online dating service eHarmony filed a complaint with the NAD over advertising used by competitor Chemistry.com, which claimed that it could use "the latest science of attraction to predict which single men and women [one] will have a relationship and dating chemistry with."[16] Chemistry.com's matchmaking system was developed by an anthropologist who studies mate selection and uses responses to an extensive survey to determine people who might be attracted to one another. The NAD concluded that the dating service could not substantiate many of the advertising claims and ruled that the company should discontinue them. Chemistry's parent company, Match.com, issued a statement saying that it disagreed with some of the NAD's findings, but agreed to discontinue the claims at issue.[17]

The NAD's advertising monitoring program is also the source of many of the cases it reviews (Figure 20–1). It also reviews complaints from consumers and consumer groups, trade associations, local BBBs, and competitors. For example, the NAD received a complaint from the Center for Science in the Public Interest, a consumer advocacy group, over an ad run by Campbell Soup for the company's V8 vegetable juice that suggested a link between the tomato-based product and a reduced risk of cancer. Though the NAD decided that Campbell provided competent and reliable evidence to support certain claims, it recommended that the company modify language stating "for prostate cancer, a lower risk is apparent when five or more servings (of tomato products) are consumed per week." Campbell agreed to change the wording of the ad.[18]

Lawyers at the NAD routinely scour magazines, newspapers, radio, television, and social media to find misleading advertisements. For example, the NAD staff recently challenged an ad for CoverGirl mascara featuring singer Taylor Swift, arguing that it was misleading because her eyelashes had been enhanced after the fact to look fuller.

FIGURE 20–1

Sources of NAD Cases and Decisions, 2015

Sources	Number	Percentage	Decisions	Number	Percentage
Competitor challenges	87	74%	Modified/discontinued	39	33%
NAD monitoring	21	18	Substantiated/modified/discontinued	35	30
Local BBB challenges	9	8	Administratively closed	4	4
Consumer challenges	0	0	Compliance	22	19
Total	117	100%	Substantiated	6	5
			Referred to government	5	4
			Compliance/referred to government	6	5
			Total	117	100%

The fine print under the photo of Swift read that her lashes had been "enhanced in post-production." However, the NAD considered the express claims made in the ad that indicated that the mascara would give eyelashes "2x more volume" and that the product was "20 percent lighter" than the most expensive mascara. The NAD attorneys argued that the photograph stood as a product demonstration and at issue was what one's lashes would look like when using the product. Procter & Gamble, the parent company of the CoverGirl brand, fully cooperated with the NAD and voluntarily discontinued making the challenged claims as well as the photograph.[19]

Advertisers that disagree with NAD's findings have an automatic right to appeal NAD's decision to the National Advertising Review Board. The NARB is made up of 70 professionals from three different categories: national advertisers (40 members), advertising agencies (20 members), and public members (10), which includes academics and former members of the public sector. Although the self-regulatory system has no power to order an advertiser to modify or stop running an ad and no sanctions it can impose, advertisers who participate in NAD/CARU/ERSP or NARB proceedings generally comply. When companies refuse to participate in a self-regulatory proceeding or do not comply with the terms of a decision, their disputed advertising may be referred to the most appropriate federal agency for further review. In 2015, of the 117 cases handled by the NAD, 39 were modified or discontinued; 35 were substantiated, modified, or discontinued; 22 complied with the NAD; 6 complied with the NAD and were referred to government; 5 were referred to government; 6 were substantiated; and 4 were administratively closed (Figure 20–1).[20]

CARU's activities include the review and evaluation of child-directed advertising in all media, as well as online privacy issues that affect children. The organization also provides a general advisory service for advertisers and agencies and has developed self-regulatory guidelines for children's advertising. CARU recognizes that the special nature and needs of a youthful audience require particular care and diligence on the part of advertisers. As such, CARU's Self-Regulatory Program for Children's Advertising goes beyond truthfulness and accuracy to address children's developing cognitive abilities.

The ASRC is also involved in the self-regulation of electronic retailing through the Electronic Retailing Self-Regulation Program (ERSP). The program is sponsored by the Electronic Retailing Association (ERA), although it works independently of the ERA to create an unbiased self-regulatory system. The mission of the ERSP is to enhance consumer confidence in electronic retailing, to discourage advertising and marketing in the electronic retailing industry that contains unsubstantiated claims, and to demonstrate a commitment to meaningful and effective self-regulation. The majority of claims reviewed under the ERSP program are for direct-response TV ads, including long- and short-form infomercials. Reviews apply to all aspects of a marketing campaign, including radio and Internet marketing. Spam e-mails along with Internet pop-up ads that lead to further e-commerce are in the ERSP's purview as well as advertising on TV shopping channels.[21]

In 2012 the ASRC became an independent U.S. enforcement mechanism for a new self-regulatory program, the Interest-Based Advertising Accountability Program, which was developed by the Digital Advertising Alliance (DAA) and applies consumer-friendly standards to online behavioral advertising (OBA) across the Internet. OBA uses information collected across multiple unaffiliated websites—and more recently mobile apps—to predict a user's preferences and display ads most likely to interest consumers. The new program was developed by the DAA at the urging of leading industry associations and its first product was the seven Self-Regulatory Principles for Online Behavioral Advertising, which are based on Fair Information Practices. The principles correspond with tenets supported by the Federal Trade Commission, and also address public education and industry accountability issues raised by the FTC. The OBA Self-Regulatory Principles, which are shown in Figure 20–2, are designed to address consumer concerns about the use of personal information for interest-based advertising and focus on transparency and

FIGURE 20–2

Self-Regulatory Principles
for Online Behavioral
Advertising

Source: Developed by American
Association of Advertising Agencies,
Association of National Advertisers,
Council of Better Business Bureaus,
Data & Marketing Association, Network
Advertising Initiative, and Interactive
Advertising Bureau. Reprinted with
permission from Digital Advertising
Alliance.

The Education Principle calls for organizations to participate in efforts to educate individuals and businesses about online behavioral advertising and the Principles.

The Transparency Principle calls for clearer and easily accessible disclosures to consumers about data collection and use practices associated with online behavioral advertising. It will result in new, enhanced notice on the page where data is collected through links embedded in or around advertisements, or on the web page itself.

The Consumer Control Principle provides consumers with an expanded ability to choose whether data is collected and used for online behavioral advertising purposes. This choice will be available through a link from the notice provided on the web page where data is collected.

The Consumer Control Principle requires "service providers," a term that includes Internet access service providers and providers of desktop applications software such as web browser "tool bars" to obtain the consent of users before engaging in online behavioral advertising, and take steps to de-identify the data used for such purposes.

The Data Security Principle calls for organizations to provide appropriate security for, and limited retention of, data collected and used for online behavioral advertising purposes.

The Material Changes Principle calls for obtaining consumer consent before a Material Change is made to an entity's Online Behavioral Advertising data collection and use policies unless that change will result in less collection or use of data.

The Sensitive Data Principle recognizes that data collected from children and used for online behavioral advertising merits heightened protection, and requires parental consent for behavioral advertising to consumers known to be under 13 on child-directed websites. This Principle also provides heightened protections to certain health and financial data when attributable to a specific individual.

The Accountability Principle calls for development of programs to further advance these Principles, including programs to monitor and report instances of uncorrected non-compliance with these Principles to appropriate government agencies. The CBBB and DMA have been asked and agreed to work cooperatively to establish accountability mechanisms under the Principles.

consumer-control issues. The OBA Principles are also the basis of additional guidance that applies self-regulatory principles developed by the DAA to mobile advertising as well as the practice of using multi-site data and cross-app data for interest-based advertising purposes. The ASRC's Online Interest-Based Advertising Accountability Program monitors companies engaged in OBA and provides objective, independent, and vigorous oversight and enforcement of the principles.

The Advertising Self-Regulatory Council, working through the NAD/CARU/ERSP and NARB, is a valuable and effective self-regulatory body. Cases brought to it are handled at a fraction of the cost (and with much less publicity) than those brought to court and are expedited more quickly than those reviewed by a government agency such as the FTC. The system also works because judgments are made by the advertiser's peers, and most companies feel compelled to comply. Firms may prefer self-regulation rather than government intervention in part because they can challenge competitors' unsubstantiated claims and achieve a more rapid resolution.[22]

Advertising Associations   Various groups in the advertising industry also favor self-regulation. The two major national organizations, the 4A's and the American Advertising Federation, actively monitor and police industrywide advertising practices. The 4A's, which is the major trade association of the ad agency business in the United States, has established standards of practice and its own creative code (Figure 20–3). The AAF consists of advertisers, agencies, media, and numerous advertising clubs. The association has standards for truthful and responsible

CHAPTER 20

FIGURE 20–3

Standards of Practice of the
4A's: Creative Code

CREATIVE CODE

We, the members of the American Association of Advertising Agencies, in addition to supporting and obeying the laws and legal regulations pertaining to advertising, undertake to extend and broaden the application of high ethical standards. Specifically, we will not knowingly create advertising that contains:

a) False or misleading statements or exaggerations, visual or verbal

b) Testimonials that do not reflect the real opinion of the individual(s) involved

c) Price claims that are misleading

d) Claims insufficiently supported or that distort the true meaning or practicable application of statements made by professional or scientific authority

e) Statements, suggestions, or pictures offensive to public decency or minority segments of the population

Source: Copyright © 2016. Reprinted with permission from 4A's.

advertising, is involved in advertising legislation, and actively influences agencies to abide by its code and principles.

Self-Regulation by Media

The media are another important self-regulatory mechanism in the advertising industry. Most media maintain some form of advertising review process and, except for political ads, may reject any they regard as objectionable. Some media exclude advertising for an entire product class; others ban individual ads they think offensive or objectionable. For example, *Reader's Digest* does not accept advertising for tobacco or liquor products. A number of magazines in the United States and other countries refused to run some of Benetton's shock ads on the grounds that their readers would find them offensive or disturbing (Exhibit 20–5).[23]

Newspapers and magazines have their own advertising requirements and restrictions, which often vary depending on the size and nature of the publication. Large, established publications, such as major newspapers or magazines, often have strict standards regarding the type of advertising they accept. Some magazines, such as *Parents* and *Good Housekeeping*, regularly test the products they advertise and offer a "seal of approval" and refunds if the products are later found to be defective. Such policies are designed to enhance the credibility of the publication and increase the reader's confidence in the products it advertises.

Advertising on television and radio has been regulated for years through codes developed by the industry trade association, the National Association of Broadcasters (NAB). Both the radio code (established in 1937) and the television code (1952) provided standards for broadcast advertising for many years. Both codes prohibited the advertising of certain products, such as hard liquor. They also affected the manner in which products could be advertised. However, in 1982 the NAB suspended all of its code provisions after the courts found that portions (dealing with time standards and required length of commercials in the TV code) were in restraint of trade. While the NAB codes are no longer

EXHIBIT 20–5

A number of magazines refused to run this Benetton ad

© Ropi/ZUMAPRESS/Newscom

Each of the major TV networks has its own set of guidelines for children's advertising, although the basics are very similar. A few rules, such as the requirement of a static "island" shot at the end, are written in stone; others, however, can sometimes be negotiated. Many of the rules below apply specifically to toys. The networks also have special guidelines for kids' food commercials and for kids' commercials that offer premiums.

Must not overglamorize product

No exhortative language, such as "Ask Mom to buy . . ."

No realistic war settings

Generally no celebrity endorsements

Can't use "only" or "just" in regard to price

Show only two toys per child or maximum of six per commercial

Five-second "island" showing product against plain background at end of spot

Animation restricted to one-third of a commercial

Generally no comparative or superiority claims

No costumes or props not available with the toy

No child or toy can appear in animated segments

Three-second establishing shot of toy in relation to child

No shots under one second in length

Must show distance a toy can travel before stopping on its own

in force, many individual broadcasters, such as the major TV networks, have incorporated major portions of the code provisions into their own standards.[24]

The four major television networks have the most stringent review process of any media. All four networks maintain standards and practices divisions, which carefully review all commercials submitted to the network or individual affiliate stations. Advertisers must submit for review all commercials intended for airing on the network or an affiliate.

A commercial may be submitted for review in the form of a script, storyboard, animatic, or finished commercial (when the advertiser believes there is little chance of objection). A very frustrating, and often expensive, scenario for both an agency and its client occurs when a commercial is approved at the storyboard stage but then is rejected after it is produced. Commercials are rejected for a variety of reasons, including violence, morbid humor, sex, politics, and religion. Network reviewers also consider whether the proposed commercial meets acceptable standards and is appropriate for certain audiences. For example, different standards are used for ads designated for prime-time versus late-night spots or for children's versus adults' programs (see Figure 20–4). Although most of these guidelines for children's advertising remain in effect, several networks have loosened their rules on celebrity endorsements.[25]

The four major networks receive nearly 50,000 commercials a year for review; nearly two-thirds are accepted, and only 3 percent are rejected. Most problems with the remaining 30 percent are resolved through negotiation, and the ads are revised and resubmitted.[26] Most commercials run after changes are made. For example, censors initially rejected a humorous "Got Milk?" spot that showed children watching an elderly neighbor push a wheelbarrow. Suddenly, the man's arms rip off, presumably because he doesn't drink milk. The spot was eventually approved after

it was modified so that the man appears unhurt after losing his limbs and there was no expression of pain (Exhibit 20–6).[27]

Some digital advertising platforms also have restrictions regarding the advertising of certain types of products and services. For example, in 2016 Facebook imposed a global ban on private gun sales on its social media platform as well as on Instagram, which it also owns. The policy does not apply to licensed retailers, which can market firearms on Facebook and Instagram while completing the transaction offline. The new policy is designed to stop "peer-to-peer" sales of firearms by prohibiting people from using Facebook and Instagram to offer and coordinate private sales of firearms on the sites.[28]

Appraising Self-Regulation

The three major participants in the advertising process—advertisers, agencies, and the media—work individually and collectively to encourage truthful, ethical, and responsible advertising. The advertising industry views self-regulation as an effective mechanism for controlling advertising abuses and avoiding the use of offensive, misleading, or deceptive practices, and it prefers this form of regulation to government intervention. Self-regulation of advertising has been effective and in many instances probably led to the development of more stringent standards and practices than those imposed by or beyond the scope of legislation. Moreover, over 90 percent of advertisers comply with NAD decisions since failure to do so can result in government action, which can be very expensive to companies and result in more punitive measures.[29]

A senior vice president and general counsel at Kraft Foods, while praising the NAD, summarized the feelings of many advertisers toward self-regulation. In his testimonial he stated: "NAD is superior to its competition, which is regulation by the government or regulation by the courts. Accurate, prompt, and inexpensive decisions year in and year out have earned NAD its well-deserved credibility with the industry and with regulators." C. Lee Peeler, president-CEO of the Advertising Self-Regulatory Council, wrote: "With more than four decades of experience, the self-regulatory system built by the advertising industry and administered by the Council of Better Business Bureaus is the gold standard against which other self-regulation is judged."[30] He notes that the self-regulatory system protects consumers from misleading advertising by acting quickly and decisively against misleading advertising claims; it points the way on new media issues, providing advertisers with guidance that helps avoid missteps; it provides a fast, efficient, and expert forum that levels the playing field for all advertisers by holding them to high standards of truthfulness and requiring claim substantiation; and it provides the intellectual capital for the development of strong, new self-regulation programs. Exhibit 20–7 shows a page from the ASRC website summarizing the value of the NAD.

EXHIBIT 20–7

The NAD is an effective alternative to government intervention and/or litigation

Source: The Advertising Self-Regulatory Council (ASRC)

There are, however, limitations to self-regulation, and the process has been criticized in a number of areas. For example, the NAD may take three or four months to a year to resolve a complaint, during which time a company often stops using the commercial anyway. Budgeting and staffing constraints may limit the number of cases the NAD/NARB system investigates and the speed with which it resolves them. Financial support remains an important challenge for the ASCR as its programs are supported by about 200 national companies through partnership with the Council of Better Business Bureaus. Support for self-regulatory programs is much smaller in the United States than many other countries despite the fact that the advertising market in the United States is much larger.[31] And some critics believe that self-regulation is self-serving to the advertisers and advertising industry because it lacks the power or authority to be a viable alternative to federal or state regulation. However, while state and federal agencies do not always pursue the cases referred by the NAD, the threat of referral serves as an important deterrent.[32]

An American Bar Association (ABA) working group consisting of attorneys who practice before the NAD released a report in 2015 that reviewed and suggested improvements to the advertising industry's self-regulatory system.[33] The ABA report concluded that the current system of advertising self-regulation administered by the NAD works well but did find areas for improvement. Among the recommendations were that the NAD issue its decisions in a timelier manner, as well as permitting advertisers to reach settlement agreements without the issuance of a press release and instead release only case abstracts or summaries taken from the NAD decision. However, press releases would continue to be used in cases where an advertiser has refused to participate or accept the NAD's recommendations and the case has been referred to federal regulatory agencies or law enforcement. One of the most important recommendations from the report was the need for additional funding for the NAD since implementation of the recommendations would require more staff.[34]

Many do not believe advertising can or should be controlled solely by self-regulation. They argue that regulation by government agencies is necessary to ensure that consumers get accurate information and are not misled or deceived. Moreover, since advertisers do not have to comply with the decisions and recommendations of self-regulatory groups, it is sometimes necessary to turn to the federal and/or state government.

FEDERAL REGULATION OF ADVERTISING

Advertising is controlled and regulated through federal, state, and local laws and regulations enforced by various government agencies. The federal government is the most important source of external regulation since many advertising practices come under the jurisdiction of the **Federal Trade Commission (FTC)**. In addition, depending on the advertiser's industry and product or service, other federal agencies such as the Federal Communications Commission, the Food and Drug Administration, the U.S. Postal Service, and the Bureau of Alcohol, Tobacco, Firearms and Explosives may have regulations that affect advertising. We will begin our discussion of federal regulation of advertising by considering the basic rights of marketers to advertise their products and services under the First Amendment.

Advertising and the First Amendment

Freedom of speech or expression, as defined by the First Amendment to the U.S. Constitution, is the most basic federal law governing advertising in the United States.

For many years, freedom of speech protection did not include advertising and other forms of speech that promote a commercial transaction. However, the courts have extended First Amendment protection to **commercial speech**, which is speech that promotes a commercial transaction. There have been a number of landmark cases over the past three decades where the federal courts have issued rulings supporting the coverage of commercial speech by the First Amendment.

In a 1976 case, *Virginia State Board of Pharmacy v. Virginia Citizens Consumer Council*, the U.S. Supreme Court ruled that states cannot prohibit pharmacists from advertising the prices of prescription drugs, because such advertising contains information that helps the consumer choose between products and because the free flow of information is indispensable.[35] As noted earlier, in 1977 the Supreme Court ruled that state bar associations' restrictions on advertising are unconstitutional and attorneys have a First Amendment right to advertise their services and prices.[36] In another landmark case in 1980, *Central Hudson Gas & Electric Corp. v. New York Public Service Commission*, the Supreme Court ruled that commercial speech was entitled to First Amendment protection in some cases. However, the Court ruled that the U.S. Constitution affords less protection to commercial speech than to other constitutionally guaranteed forms of expression. In this case the Court established a four-part test, known as the **Central Hudson Test**, for determining restrictions on commercial speech.[37] In another important case, the Supreme Court's 1996 decision in *44 Liquormart, Inc. v. Rhode Island* struck down two state statutes designed to support the state's interest in temperance. The first prohibited the advertising of alcoholic beverage prices in Rhode Island except on signs within a store, while the second prohibited the publication or broadcast of alcohol price ads. The Court ruled that the Rhode Island statutes were unlawful because they restricted the constitutional guarantee of freedom of speech, and the decision signaled strong protection for advertisers under the First Amendment.[38]

In the cases regarding advertising, the U.S. Supreme Court has ruled that freedom of expression must be balanced against competing interests. For example, the courts have upheld bans on the advertising of products that are considered harmful, such as tobacco. The Court has also ruled that only truthful commercial speech is protected, not advertising or other forms of promotion that are false, misleading, or deceptive.

In an important case involving Nike, the California Supreme Court issued a ruling that is likely to impact the way companies engage in public debate regarding issues that affect them. Nike was sued for false advertising under California consumer protection laws for allegedly making misleading statements regarding labor practices and working conditions in its foreign factories. Nike argued that statements the company made to defend itself against the charges should be considered political speech, which is protected by the First Amendment, rather than commercial speech, which is subject to advertising regulations. However, the California high court ruled that statements made by the company to defend itself against the allegations were commercial in nature and thus subject to the state's consumer protection regulations. Nike appealed the case to the U.S. Supreme Court, which sent it back to California for trial to determine if the company's statements were deceptive and misleading. However, Nike settled the case rather than risking a long and costly court battle. While the ruling in this case applies to only California, it is important as the courts ruled that speech in the form of press releases or public statements by company representatives can be considered commercial and subject to consumer protection laws.[39]

The job of regulating advertising at the federal level and determining whether advertising is truthful or deceptive is a major focus of the Federal Trade Commission. We now turn our attention to federal regulation of advertising and the FTC.

Background on Federal Regulation of Advertising

Federal regulation of advertising originated in 1914 with the passage of the **Federal Trade Commission Act**, which created the FTC, the agency that is today the most active in, and has primary responsibility for, controlling and regulating advertising. The FTC Act was originally intended to help enforce antitrust laws, such as the Sherman and Clayton Acts, by helping restrain unfair methods of competition. The main focus of the first five-member commission was to protect competitors from one another; the issue of false or misleading advertising was not even mentioned. In 1922, the Supreme Court upheld an FTC interpretation that false advertising was an unfair method of competition, but in the 1931 case *FTC v. Raladam Co.*, the Court ruled the commission could not prohibit false advertising unless there was evidence of injury to a competitor.[40] This ruling limited the power of the FTC to protect consumers from false or deceptive advertising and led to a consumer movement that resulted in an important amendment to the FTC Act.

In 1938, Congress passed the **Wheeler-Lea Amendment**. It amended section 5 of the FTC Act to read: "Unfair methods of competition in commerce and unfair or deceptive acts or practices in commerce are hereby declared to be unlawful." The amendment empowered the FTC to act if there was evidence of injury to the public; proof of injury to a competitor was not necessary. The Wheeler-Lea Amendment also gave the FTC the power to issue cease-and-desist orders and levy fines on violators. It extended the FTC's jurisdiction over false advertising of foods, drugs, cosmetics, and therapeutic devices. And it gave the FTC access to the injunctive power of the federal courts, initially only for food and drug products but expanded in 1972 to include all products in the event of a threat to the public's health and safety.

In addition to the FTC, numerous other federal agencies are responsible for, or involved in, advertising regulation. The authority of these agencies is limited, however, to a particular product area or service, and they often rely on the FTC to assist in handling false or deceptive advertising cases.

The Federal Trade Commission

The FTC is responsible for protecting both consumers and businesses from anticompetitive behavior and unfair and deceptive practices. The major divisions of the FTC include the bureaus of competition, economics, and consumer protection. The Bureau of Competition seeks to prevent business practices that restrain competition and is responsible for enforcing antitrust laws. The Bureau of Economics helps the FTC evaluate the impact of its actions and provides economic analysis and support to antitrust and consumer protection investigations and rule makings. It also analyzes the impact of government regulation on competition and consumers. The Bureau of Consumer Protection's mandate is to protect consumers against unfair, deceptive, or fraudulent practices. This bureau also investigates and litigates cases involving acts or practices alleged to be deceptive or unfair to consumers. The Division of Advertising Practices protects consumers from deceptive and unsubstantiated advertising and enforces the provisions of the FTC Act that forbid misrepresentation, unfairness, and deception in general advertising at the national and regional level (Exhibit 20–8). The Division of Marketing Practices engages in activities that are related to various marketing and warranty practices such as fraudulent telemarketing schemes, 900-number programs, and disclosures relating to franchise and business opportunities.

Since the 1970s, the FTC made enforcement of laws regarding false and misleading advertising a top priority. Several new programs were instituted, budgets were increased, and the commission became a very powerful regulatory agency. However, many of these programs, as well as the expanded powers of the FTC to develop regulations on the basis of "unfairness," became controversial. At the root of this controversy is the fundamental issue of what constitutes unfair advertising.

EXHIBIT 20–8

The Division of Advertising Practices protects consumers from deceptive and unsubstantiated advertising claims

Source: Federal Trade Commission

CHAPTER 20

The Concept of Unfairness

Under section 5 of the FTC Act, the Federal Trade Commission has a mandate to act against unfair or deceptive advertising practices. However, this statute does not define the terms *unfair* and *deceptive*, and the FTC has been criticized for not doing so itself. While the FTC has taken steps to clarify the meaning of *deception*, people have been concerned for years about the vagueness of the term *unfair*.

The FTC responded to these criticisms in 1980 by sending Congress a statement containing an interpretation of unfairness. According to FTC policy, the basis for determining **unfairness** is that a trade practice (1) causes substantial physical or economic injury to consumers, (2) could not reasonably be avoided by consumers, and (3) must not be outweighed by countervailing benefits to consumers or competition. The agency also stated that a violation of public policy (such as other government statutes) could, by itself, constitute an unfair practice or could be used to prove substantial consumer injury. Practices considered unfair are claims made without prior substantiation, claims that might exploit such vulnerable groups as children and older adults, and instances where consumers cannot make a valid choice because the advertiser omits important information about the product or competing products mentioned in the ad.[41]

The FTC does have specific regulatory authority in cases involving deceptive, misleading, or untruthful advertising. The vast majority of advertising cases that the FTC handles concern deception and advertising fraud, which usually involve knowledge of a false claim.

Deceptive Advertising

In most economies, advertising provides consumers with information they can use to make consumption decisions. However, if this information is untrue or misleads the consumer, advertising is not fulfilling its basic function. Moreover, a study by Peter Drake and Robin Ritchie found that deceptive advertising engenders mistrust, which negatively affects consumers' responses to subsequent advertising from the same source as well as second-party sources. They note that deceptive advertising can seriously undermine the effectiveness and credibility of advertising and marketing in general by making consumers defensive toward future advertising and should be of concern to all marketers.[42] But what constitutes an untruthful or deceptive ad? Deceptive advertising can take a number of forms, ranging from intentionally false or misleading claims to ads that, although true, leave some consumers with a false or misleading impression.

The issue of deception, including its definition and measurement, receives considerable attention from the FTC and other regulatory agencies. One of the problems regulatory agencies deal with in determining deception is distinguishing between false or misleading messages and those that, rather than relying on verifiable or substantiated objective information about a product, make subjective claims or statements, a practice known as puffery. **Puffery** has been legally defined as "advertising or other sales presentations which praise the item to be sold with subjective opinions, superlatives, or exaggerations, vaguely and generally, stating no specific facts."[43] The use of puffery in advertising is common. For example, Bayer aspirin calls itself the "wonder drug that works wonders," Nestlé claims "Nestlé makes the very best chocolate," Snapple advertises that its beverages are "made from the best stuff on Earth," and POM Wonderful refers to its juices as "Crazy Healthy." Superlatives such as *greatest, best,* and *finest* are puffs that are often used.

Puffery has generally been viewed as a form of poetic license or allowable exaggeration. The FTC takes the position that because consumers expect exaggeration or inflated claims in advertising, they recognize puffery and don't believe it. But some studies show that consumers may believe puffery and perceive such claims as true.[44] One study found that consumers could not distinguish between a verifiable fact-based claim and puffery and were just as likely to believe both types

EXHIBIT 20–9

Domino's poked fun at Papa John's puffery defense in a clever TV commercial

© Domino's Pizza LLC

of claims.[45] It has also been argued that puffery has a detrimental effect on consumers' purchase decisions by burdening them with untrue beliefs and refers to it as "soft-core deception" that should be illegal.[46]

Advertisers' battle to retain the right to use puffery was supported in the latest revision of the Uniform Commercial Code in 1996. The revision switches the burden of proof to consumers from advertisers in cases pertaining to whether certain claims were meant to be taken as promises. The revision states that the buyer must prove that an affirmation of fact (as opposed to puffery) was made, that the buyer was aware of the advertisement, and that the affirmation of fact became part of the agreement with the seller.[47]

One of the most intense battles regarding the use of puffery was fought by Papa John's and Pizza Hut and went all the way to the United States Supreme Court.[48] The central issue in the case was Papa John's use of the tagline "Better Ingredients. Better Pizza." Pizza Hut filed a lawsuit against Papa John's claiming that the latter's ads were false and misleading because it had failed to prove its sauce and dough were superior. Following a long-drawn-out legal battle that lasted nearly five years and cost the two companies millions of dollars, the U.S. Supreme Court issued a decision in support of the use of puffery as the basis for a comparative advertising claim. The advertising industry was relieved that the Supreme Court ruled in favor of Papa John's because a ruling against the puffery defense could have opened the door for other challenges and a redrawing of the blurry line between so-called puffery and outright false advertising.[49]

As an interesting by-product of the case, Domino's Pizza decided to take advantage of the appellate court ruling that Papa John's slogan was considered puffery and ran TV commercials showing the company's head chef, Brian Solano, standing outside a federal court of appeals building in New Orleans talking about Papa John's and its slogan. In the spot Solano says: "For years Papa John's has been telling us they have better ingredients and better pizza. But when challenged in this court, they stated their slogan is puffery." He then turns to a lawyer standing next to him and asks him: "What's puffery?" Reading from a law book, the lawyer says: "Puffery. An exaggerated statement based on opinion. Not fact" (Exhibit 20–9). Solano then says, "Here's what's not puffery" and goes on to explain how Domino's beat Papa John's in a national taste test. The spot ends with Solano stating, "Our pizza tastes better and that's not puffery, that's proven.[50]

Since unfair and deceptive acts or practices have never been precisely defined, the FTC is continually developing and refining a working definition in its attempts to regulate advertising. The traditional standard used to determine deception was whether a claim had the "tendency or capacity to deceive." However, this standard was criticized for being vague and all-encompassing.

In 1983, the FTC, under chair James Miller III, put forth a new working definition of **deception**: "The commission will find deception if there is a misrepresentation, omission, or practice that is likely to mislead the consumer acting reasonably in the circumstances to the consumer's detriment."[51] There are three essential elements to this definition of deception.[52] The first element is that the representation, omission, or practice must be *likely to mislead* the consumer. The FTC defines *misrepresentation* as an express or implied statement contrary to fact, whereas a *misleading omission* occurs when qualifying information necessary to prevent a practice, claim, representation, or reasonable belief from being misleading is not disclosed.

The second element is that the act or practice must be considered from the perspective of *the reasonable consumer.* In determining reasonableness, the FTC considers the group to which the advertising is targeted and whether their interpretation of or reaction to the message is reasonable in light of the circumstances. The standard is flexible and allows the FTC to consider factors such as the age, education level, intellectual capacity, and frame of mind of the particular group to which the message or practice is targeted. For example, advertisements targeted to a particular group, such as children or older adults, are evaluated with respect to their effect on a reasonable member of that group.

The third key element to the FTC's definition of deception is *materiality*. According to the FTC a "material" misrepresentation or practice is one that is likely to affect a consumer's choice or conduct with regard to a product or service. What this means is that the information, claim, or practice in question is important to consumers and, if acted upon, would be likely to influence their purchase decisions. In some cases the information or claims made in an ad may be false or misleading but would not be regarded as material since reasonable consumers would not make a purchase decision on the basis of this information.

Miller's goal was to help the commission determine which cases were worth pursuing and which were trivial. Miller argued that for an ad to be considered worthy of FTC challenge, it should be seen by a substantial number of consumers, it should lead to significant injury, and the problem should be one that market forces are not likely to remedy. However, the revised definition may put a greater burden on the FTC to prove that deception occurred and that the deception influenced the consumers' decision-making process in a detrimental way.

Determining what constitutes deception is still a gray area. Two of the factors the FTC considers in evaluating an ad for deception are (1) whether there are significant omissions of important information and (2) whether advertisers can substantiate the claims made for the product or service. The FTC has developed several programs to address these issues.

Affirmative Disclosure   An ad can be literally true yet leave the consumer with a false or misleading impression if the claim is true only under certain conditions or circumstances or if there are limitations to what the product can or cannot do. Thus, under its **affirmative disclosure** requirement, the FTC may require advertisers to include certain types of information in their ads so that consumers will be aware of all the consequences, conditions, and limitations associated with the use of a product or service. The goal of affirmative disclosure is to give consumers sufficient information to make an informed decision. An ad may be required to define the testing situation, conditions, or criteria used in making a claim. For example, fuel mileage claims in car ads are based on Environmental Protection Agency (EPA) ratings since they offer a uniform standard for making comparisons. Cigarette ads must contain a warning about the health risks associated with smoking.

An example of an affirmative disclosure ruling is the FTC's case against Campbell Soup for making deceptive and unsubstantiated claims. Campbell's ads, run as part of its "Soup is good food" campaign, linked the low-fat and low-cholesterol content of its soup with a reduced risk of heart disease. However, the advertising failed to disclose that the soups are high in sodium, which may increase the risk of heart disease. In a consent agreement, Campbell agreed that, for any soup containing more than 500 milligrams of sodium in an 8-ounce serving, it will disclose the sodium content in any advertising that directly or by implication mentions heart disease in connection with the soup. Campbell also agreed it would not imply a connection between soup and a reduction in heart disease in future advertising.[53]

Another area where the Federal Trade Commission is seeking more specificity from advertisers is in regard to country-of-origin claims. The FTC has been working with marketers and trade associations to develop a better definition of what the "Made in USA" label means. The 50-year-old definition used until 1998 required full manufacturing in the United States, using U.S. labor and parts, with only raw materials from overseas.[54] Many companies argue that in an increasingly global economy, it is becoming very difficult to have 100 percent U.S. content and remain price-competitive. However, the FTC argues that advertising or labeling a product as "Made in USA" can provide a company with a competitive advantage. For many

EXHIBIT 20–10

New Balance promotes its commitment to U.S. manufacturing

Source: New Balance

EXHIBIT 20–11

The U.S. Champagne Bureau is running ads calling for clarification of the region of origin on wine labels

Source: The U.S. Champagne Bureau

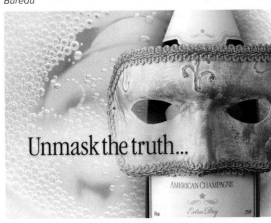

Unmask the truth...

AMERICAN CHAMPAGNE

No more cover-ups.

It's not just subprime mortgages and derivative insurance that bury honesty in legal mumbo jumbo. A legal loophole allows some U.S. wines to masquerade as something they're not.

There are many fine sparkling wines, but only those from **Champagne** can use that region's name. Names of American wine regions like Napa Valley and Willamette are also misused.

Consumer groups agree: deceptive wine labeling must stop. Tell Congress to protect consumers. Sign the petition at **www.champagne.us.**

Champagne *only* comes from Champagne, France.

products some consumers do respond to the claim, as they trust the quality of domestic-made products and/or feel patriotic when they buy American. For example, athletic shoemaker New Balance is a company that promotes its commitment to domestic manufacturing and the fact that it is the only major company that assembles many of its shoes in the United States (Exhibit 20–10).

In December 1998, the FTC issued new guidelines for American-made products. The guidelines spell out what it means by "all or virtually all" in mandating how much U.S. content a product must have to wear a "Made in USA" label or be advertised as such. According to the new FTC guidelines, all significant parts and processing that go into the product must be of U.S. origin and the product should have no or very little foreign content. Companies do not have to receive the approval of the FTC before making a "Made in USA" claim. However, the commission does have the authority to take action against false and unsubstantiated "Made in USA" claims just as it does with other advertising claims.[55] As a result of the FTC ruling, marketers must be careful in using "Made in USA" claims. For example, New Balance now qualifies its claims by noting that it labels its shoes as "Made in the USA" only where the domestic value is at least 70 percent, as shown in Exhibit 20–10.

Another interesting example of a case involving product origin claims is in the wine industry. The U.S. Champagne Bureau launched its "Unmask the Truth" ad campaign which has the goals of rallying consumers and demanding lawmakers protect place-of-origin names on wine sold in the United States. The ad, which is shown in Exhibit 20–11, features a mask over a sparkling wine bottle mislabeled "American Champagne" and asks consumers to voice their support for truthful labeling regarding where wine comes from. The campaign is designed to address a loophole in federal law that allows some U.S. sparkling wine producers to mislead consumers by labeling their products "Champagne" even though they do not come from the Champagne region of France. The trade association argues that names of American wine regions such as Napa Valley and Williamette also risk being misused.[56]

Advertising Substantiation A major area of concern to regulatory agencies is whether advertisers can support or substantiate their claims. For many years, there were no formal requirements concerning substantiation of advertising claims. Many companies made claims without any documentation or support such as laboratory tests or clinical studies. In 1971, the FTC's **advertising substantiation** program required advertisers to have supporting documentation for their claims and to prove the claims are truthful.[57] Broadened in 1972, this program now requires advertisers to substantiate their claims before an ad appears. Substantiation is required for all express or implied claims involving safety, performance, efficacy, quality, or comparative price.

The FTC's substantiation program has had a major effect on the advertising industry, because it shifted the burden of proof from the commission to the advertiser. Before the substantiation program, the FTC had to prove that an advertiser's claims were unfair or deceptive. However, ad substantiation seeks to provide

CHAPTER 20

EXHIBIT 20–12

This advertisement for The Atkins Diet gives an example of how weight-loss program marketers substantiate their claims

Source: Atkins Nutritionals, Inc.

a basis for believing advertising claims so consumers can make rational and informed decisions and companies are deterred from making claims they cannot adequately support. The FTC takes the perspective that it is illegal and unfair to consumers for a firm to make a claim for a product without having a "reasonable basis" for the claim. In their decision to require advertising substantiation, the commissioners made the following statement:

> Given the imbalance of knowledge and resources between a business enterprise and each of its customers, economically it is more rational and imposes far less cost on society, to require a manufacturer to confirm his affirmative product claims rather than impose a burden on each individual consumer to test, investigate, or experiment for himself. The manufacturer has the ability, the know-how, the equipment, the time and resources to undertake such information, by testing or otherwise, . . . the consumer usually does not.[58]

Many advertisers respond negatively to the FTC's advertising substantiation program. They argue it is too expensive to document all their claims and most consumers either won't understand or aren't interested in the technical data. Some advertisers threaten to avoid the substantiation issue by using puffery claims, which do not require substantiation. Generally, advertisers making claims covered by the substantiation program must have available prior substantiation of all claims. However, in 1984, the FTC issued a new policy statement that suggested after-the-fact substantiation might be acceptable in some cases and it would solicit documentation of claims only from advertisers that are under investigation for deceptive practices.

In a number of cases, the FTC has ordered advertisers to cease making inadequately substantiated claims. In 1990s, the FTC took on the weight-loss industry when it filed a complaint charging that none of five large, well-known diet program marketers had sufficient evidence to back up claims that their customers achieved their weight-loss goals or maintained the loss. Three of the companies agreed to publicize the fact that most weight loss is temporary and to disclose how long their customers kept off the weight they lost. The agreement required the companies to substantiate their weight-loss claims with scientific data and to document claims that their customers keep off the weight by monitoring a group of them for two years[59] (Exhibit 20–12).

The FTC has continued to take actions against companies that cannot adequately substantiate their advertising claims. IMC Perspective 20–1 discusses how athletic shoe companies Reebok and Skechers agreed to pay large amounts of money to settle charges that they deceived consumers by making unsubstantiated claims regarding their toning shoes. The FTC has also stepped up its action against false and unsubstantiated claims in ads and infomercials. A few years ago, the commission fined the Home Shopping Network $1.1 million for making unsubstantiated advertising claims for two weight-loss products, an acne treatment, and a dietary supplement for menopause and premenstrual syndrome. Under the settlement, Home Shopping is enjoined from making product claims about curing and treating diseases without "reliable scientific evidence."

In another high-profile case the FTC issued a very important ruling against POM Wonderful LLC—the maker of juices, teas, and fruit—upholding an initial finding by an administrative law judge that the company had made a number of unsubstantiated claims for its pomegranate juice. One of the ads run by the company showed a bottle with a noose around its neck and the headline "Cheat Death" while the ad copy claimed that the juice "can help prevent premature aging, heart disease stroke, Alzheimer's, even cancer. Eight ounces a day is all you need." The ruling by FTC commissioners stated that POM's claims must be backed by randomized, controlled clinical trials, which is the same type of evidence the FDA requires when approving new drugs.[60] POM appealed the ruling, arguing that the FTC was taking an unprecedented step in holding food companies to the same standard as pharmaceuticals. However, the FTC countered that its standards for food health claims are not nearly as stringent as those of the FDA for drugs.

In 2016 the US. Supreme Court rejected POM Wonderful's challenge to the FTC findings, leaving in place the agency's determination that the juice maker's advertising was misleading. FTC chair Edith Ramirez issued a statement noting that "The outcome of this case makes clear that companies like POM making serious health claims about food and nutritional supplement products must have rigorous scientific evidence to back them up." The FTC ruling in the case suggests that the commission plans to continue to take a more aggressive approach toward health claims made by food companies and marketers of natural products and may require more substantiation to support any health-related claims they make.[61]

In another major case involving inadequate advertising substantiation the FTC also took action against Volkswagen Group of America in 2016 charging that the company's "clean diesel" advertising campaign was deceptive. The U.S. Environmental Protection Agency discovered that special software installed in Volkswagen diesel-powered vehicles was designed to defeat emissions testing, making the cars seem far cleaner and safer for the environment than they actually were as the cars were emitting up to 40 times more toxic fumes than permitted. In its complaint the FTC alleges that during a seven-year period Volkswagen deceived consumers by selling or leasing more than 550,000 diesel cars based on false claims that the cars were low-emission, environmentally friendly, met emissions standards, and would maintain a high resale value. The FTC is seeking a court order requiring Volkswagen to compensate consumers who bought or leased any of the affected vehicles between late 2008 and late 2015, as well as an injunction to prevent Volkswagen from engaging in this type of conduct again. While it may take years to settle the case, it is possible that it will cost the German automotive company billions of dollars to settle the claims as well as the fine that may be imposed by the FTC.[62]

The FTC's Handling of Deceptive Advertising Cases

Consent and Cease-and-Desist Orders Allegations of unfair or deceptive advertising come to the FTC's attention from a variety of sources, including competitors, consumers, other government agencies, or the commission's own monitoring and investigations. Once the FTC decides a complaint is justified and warrants further action, it notifies the offender, who then has 30 days to respond. The advertiser can agree to negotiate a settlement with the FTC by signing a **consent order**, which is an agreement to stop the practice or advertising in question. This agreement is for settlement purposes only and does not constitute an admission of guilt by the advertiser. Most FTC inquiries are settled by consent orders because they save the advertiser the cost and possible adverse publicity that might result if the case went further.

If the advertiser chooses not to sign the consent decree and contests the complaint, a hearing can be requested before an administrative law judge employed by the FTC but not under its influence. The judge's decision may be appealed to the full five-member commission by either side. The commission either affirms or modifies the order or dismisses the case. If the complaint has been upheld by the administrative law judge and the commission, the advertiser can appeal the case to the federal courts.

The appeal process may take some time, during which the FTC may want to stop the advertiser from engaging in the deceptive practice. The Wheeler-Lea Amendment empowers the FTC to issue a **cease-and-desist order**, which requires that the advertiser stop the specified advertising claim within 30 days and prohibits the

Marketers of Toning Shoes Pay for Deceptive Ads

For years Nike dominated the $1.7 billion women's athletic footwear market; by 2009 its market share in the category reached 37 percent. However, within a year Nike's share dropped to just under 30 percent as its sales declined by 7 percent even though the women's athletic shoe market was experiencing double-digit sales growth. It was no mystery where all of the women abandoning Nike were going to purchase their athletic shoes—most were switching to Skechers and Reebok. Skechers tripled its market share during the same period, from 5.5 to 16.5 percent, and Reebok nearly did the same, jumping from 3.3 to 8 percent.

The reason women were moving to Skechers and Reebok was because both companies were investing heavily in product development and advertising for a new type of athletic footwear called toning shoes that promised women they could get in shape and firm up their leg muscles and butts simply by walking in them. However, Nike refused to enter the toning shoe market because it was skeptical about the claims being made for the products and said the shoes did not fit with the company's performance-focused brand image. And as it turns out, Nike made a wise decision; the Federal Trade Commission charged both Skechers and Reebok with deceptive advertising based on the claims they were making for their shoes.

The toning shoe market was in its infancy in 2009; there were a few brands that had achieved a cult-like following such as MBT, Ryn, and FitFlop before Reebok and Skechers entered the market. The idea behind the oddly shaped shoes was that they could simulate walking on a soft surface, causing the wearer to use muscles not normally used when walking on hard surfaces. They created instability, which would force the wearer to engage certain muscles to maintain balance. The benefits resulting from the shoes were purported to include weight loss, greater muscle tone, reduced cellulite, and firmer butts. Skechers put a spotlight on the toning shoe category by running an ad on the 2010 Super Bowl that featured testimonials by NFL Hall of Fame quarterback Joe Montana as well as consumers. The company ran another Super Bowl spot in 2011 featuring celebrity Kim Kardashian and was also running ads with Brooke Burke, who was endorsing its Shape Up shoes. Skechers's ads included claims such

as "Shape up while you walk" and "Get in shape without setting foot in a gym." The ads also told women that wearing the shoes would help tone their butt, leg, and abdominal muscles; burn calories; fight cellulite; improve posture and circulation; and reduce joint stress. By early 2011 the toning shoe category reached $1.1 billion in sales, with Skechers controlling nearly 60 percent of the market.

Reebok also invested heavily in what became known as the "derriere-enhancing" shoes as the sales for the category skyrocketed. Reebok was a leading brand in the women's athletic shoe category during the 1980s, when it dominated the aerobics shoe market. Reebok saw the toning shoe category as a way to once again focus on the female market and reconnect with women who still had favorable feelings about the company. The company put its energy behind its EasyTone line that was marketed with claims such as "Get a better butt" and "EasyTone shoes help tone your butt and legs with every step." Reebok's ads and website claimed that its shoes generated more muscle activity in the gluteus maximus as well as users' hamstrings and calves. Reebok spent over $30 million in advertising for EasyTone in the United States alone in 2010 and also launched a global campaign that included the introduction of the EasyTone apparel line. By the end of 2010 Reebok had a 33 percent share of the toning shoe market and claimed to have sold 5 million pairs of the shoes in the United States and double that globally. The CEO of Reebok's parent company adidas said: "The explosion of growth in this space in such a short period of time eclipses nearly everything I have witnessed in the industry over the last 25 years."

Skechers and Reebok continued to invest heavily in advertising while other athletic shoe companies such as Avia and New Balance also introduced their brands of toning shoes. Although the market continued to grow, many in the medical profession were skeptical about the efficacy claims being made for toning shoes, arguing that they were "far-fetched" and "utter nonsense" and could not be supported. Some doctors also expressed concern that the shoes could be dangerous and lead to injuries resulting from their instability. Based on these concerns, the Federal Trade Commission (FTC), along with attorneys general from nearly all 50 states,

advertiser from engaging in the objectionable practice until after the hearing is held. Violation of a cease-and-desist order is punishable by a fine of up to $10,000 a day. Figure 20–5 summarizes the FTC complaint procedure.

Corrective Advertising By using consent and cease-and-desist orders, the FTC can usually stop a particular advertising practice it believes is unfair or deceptive. However, even if an advertiser ceases using a deceptive ad, consumers may still remember some or all of the claim. To address the problem of residual effects, in the 1970s, the FTC developed a program known as **corrective advertising**. An advertiser

© Kevan Brooks/AdMedia/Newscom

related to its Shape Up shoes and other toning products. The FTC charged that specific muscle activation results related to the use of the shoes that were used as the basis of advertising claims made by Skechers were "cherry-picked" from a study and the company failed to substantiate its advertising claims. The FTC also noted that Skechers's ads included an endorsement from a chiropractor who was married to a marketing executive in the company and that the independent clinical study conducted by the chiropractor did not produce the results claimed. The $40 million settlement was one of the largest ever agreed to with the FTC and barred Skechers from making any claims about strengthening, weight loss, or any other health or fitness-related benefits from its toning shoes, unless they are true and backed by scientific evidence.

Both Reebok and Skechers were required to put most of the $65 million into a fund intended to return money to consumers who bought their toning products. The funds were to be made available to consumers either directly from the FTC or through a court-approved class action lawsuit. In May 2013 a federal judge approved a $40 million class action settlement between Skechers and consumers who bought the company's toning shoes whereby approved claims would result in repayment of up to $84 a pair, depending on the price of the shoes. Under the terms of the FTC settlement, the funds were distributed through a court-approved settlement administrator and in July 2013 checks were mailed to eligible consumers who submitted a valid claim for a refund.

Sales of toning shoes in the U.S. market declined by 50 percent following the negative publicity resulting from the deceptive advertising claims and settlements. However, Reebok has not given up on the toning shoe category; the company claims there is still a market for the shoes and announced that it was enhancing its testing protocol and tweaking its advertising claims. While the company rolled out a new campaign in Europe and Asia using the tagline "A beautiful way to reduce body fat," it has not run the ads in the United States—yet.

Sources: "FTC Mails Refund Checks to Consumers Who Bought Skecher's Shape-Ups and Other 'Toning' Shoes," Federal Trade Commission press release, July 11, 2013; Natalie Zmuda, "Reebok Bounces Back in Toning Category after FTC Settlement," *Advertising Age*, April 22, 2012, http://adage.com/article/news/reebok-toning-body-fat-reduction-claim/234272/; Natalie Zmuda, "Skechers Pays $40 Million to Settle Toning Claims FTC: Settlement May Be Largest Payout Ever to Consumers," *Advertising Age*, May 16, 2012, http://adage.com/article/news/skechers-pays-40-million-settle-toning-claims/234799/; Natalie Zmuda, "Reebok Agrees to $25M Settlement over Butt-Shaping Shoes," *Advertising Age*, September 28, 2011, http://adage.com/article/news/ftc-calls-butt-shaping-shoes-bogus-reebok-stands-claims/230082/.

launched an investigation of the toning shoe category and the advertising claims being made by Reebok and Skechers.

Following an investigation, the FTC alleged that the testing conducted by Reebok did not substantiate certain claims used in the advertising of its EasyTone line of toning shoes. In the fall of 2011 the FTC announced that Reebok had agreed to a $25 million settlement to resolve charges that it deceptively advertised its toning shoe and apparel. Reebok issued a statement saying that it was standing behind its shoes and agreed to the settlement only to avoid a protracted legal battle. As part of the settlement, Reebok is barred from making claims that toning shoes or apparel strengthen muscles or that using the products will result in a specific percentage or amount of muscle toning or strengthening, unless the claims can be supported by scientific evidence.

A few months later, in May 2012, the FTC announced that Skechers had agreed to pay $40 million to settle charges that it deceived consumers with weight-loss and toning claims

found guilty of deceptive advertising can be required to run additional advertising designed to remedy the deception or misinformation contained in previous ads.

The impetus for corrective advertising was another case involving Campbell Soup, which when making a photo for an ad placed marbles in the bottom of a bowl of vegetable soup to force the solid ingredients to the surface, creating a false impression that the soup contained more vegetables than it really did. (Campbell Soup argued that if the marbles were not used, all the ingredients would settle to the bottom, leaving an impression of fewer ingredients than actually existed!) While Campbell Soup agreed to stop the practice, a group of law students calling themselves SOUP

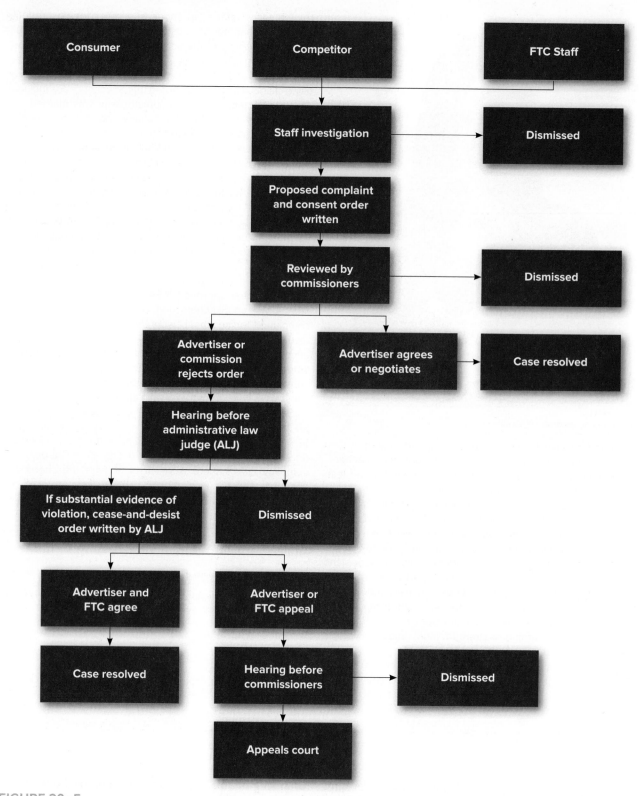

FIGURE 20–5

FTC Complaint Procedure

(Students Opposed to Unfair Practices) argued to the FTC that this would not remedy false impressions created by prior advertising and contended Campbell Soup should be required to run advertising to rectify the problem.[63]

Although the FTC did not order corrective advertising in the Campbell case, it has done so in many cases since then. Profile Bread ran an ad stating each slice contained fewer calories than other brands, but the ad did not mention that slices of

Profile bread were thinner than those of other brands. Ocean Spray cranberry juice was found guilty of deceptive advertising because it claimed to have more "food energy" than orange or tomato juice but failed to note it was referring to the technical definition of food energy, which is calories. In each case, the advertisers were ordered to spend 25 percent of their annual media budgets to run corrective ads. The STP Corporation was required to run corrective advertising for claims regarding the ability of its oil additive to reduce oil consumption. Many of the corrective ads run in the STP case appeared in business publications to serve notice to other advertisers that the FTC was enforcing the corrective advertising program.

Corrective advertising is probably the most controversial of all the FTC programs.[64] Advertisers argue that corrective advertising infringes on First Amendment rights of freedom of speech. In one of the most publicized corrective advertising cases ever, involving Listerine mouthwash, Warner-Lambert tested the FTC's legal power to order corrective messages.[65] For more than 50 years Warner-Lambert had advertised that gargling with Listerine helped prevent colds and sore throats or lessened their severity because it killed the germs that caused these illnesses. In 1975, the FTC ruled these claims could not be substantiated and ordered Warner-Lambert to stop making them. In addition, the FTC argued that corrective advertising was needed to rectify the erroneous beliefs that had been created by Warner-Lambert as a result of the large amount of advertising it had run for Listerine over the prior 50 years.

Warner-Lambert argued that the advertising was not misleading and, further, that the FTC did not have the power to order corrective advertising. Warner-Lambert appealed the FTC decision all the way to the Supreme Court, which rejected the argument that corrective advertising violates advertisers' First Amendment rights. The powers of the FTC in the areas of both claim substantiation and corrective advertising were upheld. Warner-Lambert was required to run $10 million worth of corrective ads over a 16-month period stating, "Listerine does not help prevent colds or sore throats or lessen their severity." Since the Supreme Court ruling in the Listerine case, there have been several other situations where the FTC has ordered corrective advertising on the basis of the "Warner-Lambert test," which considers whether consumers are left with a latent impression that would continue to affect buying decisions and whether corrective ads are needed to remedy the situation. While the FTC's authority to order corrective advertising has been challenged in several cases, its right to do so has been upheld by appellate courts.[66]

Advertisers have expressed concern that the FTC might increase its use of the remedy for deceptive advertising cases, but the agency has not substantially changed its request for corrective ads. However, in 2009 another federal agency, the FDA, ordered Bayer to run a six-month, $20 million corrective advertising campaign for Yaz, the company's birth-control product. The FDA ruled that Bayer's marketing and advertising for Yaz, which is the leading nongeneric in the birth-control market, was deceptive and made false claims regarding its efficacy for acne and premenstrual syndrome. Bayer was ordered to spend nearly a third of the $66.7 million it spent in measured media the prior year on corrective ads and was also required to submit all of its advertising for Yaz to the FDA for approval for the next six years.[67]

Developments in Federal Regulation by the FTC

Over the past decade the FTC has focused its attention on the enforcement of existing regulations, particularly in areas such as telemarketing and Internet privacy.[68] The FTC also has focused on eliminating false e-mail advertising and has stepped up its enforcement against senders of deceptive or misleading claims via e-mail. The commission also scrutinized the use of testimonial ads more carefully, particularly with respect to the use of a "results not typical" disclosure in situations where the outcomes are more likely to vary substantially than be typical for most consumers.[69] The FTC has been active in bringing enforcement action against deceptive health claims and companies and principals in the mortgage lending industry

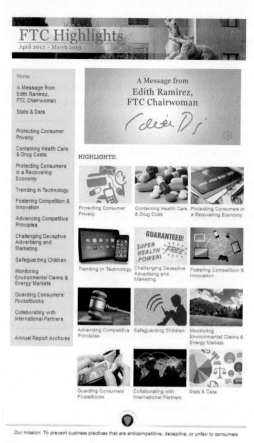

EXHIBIT 20–13

The FTC issues an annual highlights report on its activities and initiatives

Source: Federal Trade Commission

for deceptive and unfair practices in servicing mortgage loans. The FTC has also become more involved in the area of environmental marketing and the use of "green" claims for carbon offset, landfill reduction, and sustainable packaging.[70]

Under the Obama administration, the FTC was very active in the regulation of advertising as well as of other marketing practices. The administration asked Congress to grant the agency increased powers to protect consumers from deceptive practices by unscrupulous providers of financial services and products. The FTC has noted that it intends to step up its efforts to stop fraud that targets financially distressed consumers. It has joined forces with a number of states and other federal agencies to take action against mortgage modification and foreclosure rescue scams; phony debt reduction and credit repair operations; and payday lenders, get-rich-quick schemes, and bogus government grants. To better protect consumers, the FTC is also seeking to streamline its rule-making procedures, asking for power to bring charges directly against aiders and abettors of financial fraud and expanding the commission's remedial powers.

The FTC is focusing attention on protecting consumers' online privacy and the collection of sensitive information, particularly for those using social media such as Facebook and Twitter. As noted in the chapter opener, in 2009 it passed a new set of guidelines for online endorsements that requires bloggers to disclose any "material connection" to an advertiser.[71] The FTC also released its Self-Regulatory Principles for Online Behavioral Advertising in 2009 which were discussed earlier in the chapter and shown in Figure 20–2. In its 2015 Annual Highlights report the commission outlined its major initiatives and achievements, which included protecting consumers' interests in areas that have the greatest impact on them including health care and the digital economy, and ensuring that consumers' personal information is handled responsibly and securely, both online and offline. The FTC also continues to challenge deceptive advertising and marketing practices such as claims made by for-profit universities regarding the likelihood students would find jobs after graduation in their field of study (Exhibit 20–13). Over the next several years the FTC is expected to increase its efforts to enforce federal privacy laws, particularly in the expanding world of smartphones and mobile apps.[72] The commission will continue to be the primary regulator of advertising and marketing practices in the United States, although the direction of the FTC is likely to be influenced by the political party of the presidential administration.

While the FTC is the major regulator of advertising for products sold in interstate commerce, several other federal agencies and departments also regulate advertising and promotion.

Additional Federal Regulatory Agencies

The Federal Communications Commission   The Federal Communications Commission (FCC), founded in 1934 to regulate broadcast communication, has jurisdiction over the radio, television, telephone, and telegraph industries. The FCC has the authority to license broadcast stations as well as to remove a license or deny renewal to stations not operating in the public's interest. The commission's authority over the airways gives it the power to control advertising content and to restrict what products and services can be advertised on radio and TV. The FCC can eliminate obscene and profane programs and/or messages and those it finds in poor taste. While the FCC can purge ads that are deceptive or misleading, it generally works closely with the FTC in the regulation of advertising.

Many of the FCC's rules and regulations for TV and radio stations have been eliminated or modified. The FCC no longer limits the amount of television time that

EXHIBIT 20–14

Janet Jackson's "wardrobe malfunction" during the 2004 Super Bowl halftime show led to greater enforcement of obscenity laws by the FCC

© Frank Micelotta/Getty Images

can be devoted to commercials. (But in 1991, the Children's Television Act went into effect. The act limits advertising during children's programming to 10.5 minutes an hour on weekends and 12 minutes an hour on weekdays.)

Under the Reagan administration, the controversial Fairness Doctrine, which required broadcasters to provide time for opposing viewpoints on important issues, was repealed on the grounds that it was counterproductive. It was argued that the Fairness Doctrine actually reduced discussion of important issues because a broadcaster might be afraid to take on a paid controversial message in case it might be required to provide equal free exposure for opposing viewpoints. It was under this doctrine that the FCC required stations to run commercials about the harmful effects of smoking before passage of the Public Health Cigarette Smoking Act of 1970, which banned broadcast advertising of cigarettes. Many stations still provide time for opposing viewpoints on controversial issues as part of their public service requirement, not necessarily directly related to fairness.

The FCC has become very active in enforcing laws governing the airing of obscene, indecent, and profane material. For example, in 2004 the commission fined "shock jock" Howard Stern $495,000 for broadcasting indecent content and also levied fines against Clear Channel Communications (now iHeart-Communications, Inc.), the nation's largest owner of radio stations, which carried his syndicated show. Concern over Stern's constant battling with the FCC led to a decision by Clear Channel to drop his daily radio show.[73] Stern subsequently signed a contract with SiriusXM Satellite radio, the subscription-based radio service, where his show is not subject to FCC regulations. The FCC also stepped up its enforcement of obscenity in the wake of the controversy following the baring of Janet Jackson's breast during the halftime show of the 2004 Super Bowl (Exhibit 20–14).[74] These incidents resulted in federal legislation dramatically increasing the amount both radio and television networks and stations can be fined for broadcast obscenity violations.

The FCC has also become involved in issues affecting the area of publicity and public relations. In 2005, the commission issued a missive insisting that broadcasters screen video news releases to ensure that they clearly disclose "the nature, source and sponsorship" of the material. The crackdown was designed to address a marketing practice whereby prepackaged promotional videos sent to TV stations by companies, organizations, and government agencies are represented as news stories.[75]

The FCC is also currently considering the regulation of the use of product placements in television shows. Unlike some countries, the United States does not prohibit product placements in the broadcast or motion picture industries. However, the use of undisclosed commercial messages in broadcasting has been regulated by section 317 of the Communications Act of 1934, which requires broadcasters to disclose "any money, service or valuable consideration" that is paid to, or promised to, or charged by the broadcaster in exchange for product placements. However, broadcasters do not have to disclose product placements when they are offered without charge or for a nominal fee. The FCC has basically interpreted the purpose of section 317 to be that the viewers in the TV audience must be clearly informed that what they are viewing has been paid for and that the entity paying for the broadcast must be clearly identifiable.

Critics are concerned not just by the prevalence of products appearing in shows but also by the various forms of integration whereby brands are actually written into TV plots. Some are calling on the FCC to require the TV networks to disclose product placements by using some form of onscreen notification system. Proposals range from requiring programs to run text along the bottom of the screen when a product appears in a scene, to using a flashing red light to alert viewers that a marketer is promoting a product in a TV show.[76]

The Food and Drug Administration Now under the jurisdiction of the Department of Health and Human Services, the FDA has authority over the

EXHIBIT 20–15

The Nutritional Labeling and Education Act requires that labels be easy for consumers to understand

© Dennis MacDonald/Alamy RF

labeling, packaging, branding, ingredient listing, and advertising of packaged foods and drug products, as well as cosmetics. The FDA is authorized to require caution and warning labels on potentially hazardous products and also has limited authority over nutritional claims made in food advertising. This agency has the authority to set rules for promoting these products and the power to seize food and drugs on charges of false and misleading advertising.

Like the FTC, the Food and Drug Administration has become a very aggressive regulatory agency in recent years. The FDA has cracked down on a number of commonly used descriptive terms it believes are often abused in the labeling and advertising of food products—for example, *natural, light, no cholesterol, fat free,* and *organic*. The FDA has also become tougher on nutritional claims implied by brand names that might send a misleading message to consumers. For example, Great Foods of America was not permitted to continue using the HeartBeat trademark under which it sold most of its foods. The FDA argued the trademark went too far in implying the foods have special advantages for the heart and overall health.

Many changes in food labeling are a result of the Nutritional Labeling and Education Act, which Congress passed in 1990. Under this law the FDA established legal definitions for a wide range of terms (such as *low fat, light,* and *reduced calories*) and required straightforward labels for all foods beginning in early 1994 (Exhibit 20–15). In its current form the act applies only to food labels, but it may soon affect food advertising as well. The FTC would be asked to ensure that food ads comply with the new FDA standards.

The FDA has also become increasing active in policing health-related claims for food products. General Mills received a warning letter from the FDA for violations stemming from claims the company has been making that eating Cheerios cereal can reduce cholesterol by 4 to 6 percent in six weeks. The FDA charged that the claims made for the product based on clinical studies would make it a drug, not a food, because it is intended for use in the prevention, mitigation, and treatment of disease. General Mills worked with the FDA to resolve the issue as the cholesterol-reduction claims are an important part of the brand's positioning and used as the basis for much of its advertising.[77] However, the company did remove the specific cholesterol reduction claim and replaced it with a more general statement that the toasted oats "can help reduce cholesterol" and "along with a diet low in saturated fat and cholesterol may reduce the risk of heart disease."[78]

Another regulatory area where the FDA has been heavily involved is the advertising and promotion of tobacco products. In 1996, President Clinton signed an executive order declaring that nicotine is an addictive drug and giving the FDA broad jurisdiction to regulate cigarettes and smokeless tobacco. Many of the regulations resulting from this order were designed to keep teenagers from smoking.[79] However, the tobacco industry immediately appealed the order. While continuing to fight its legal battle with the federal government over the FDA regulations, the tobacco makers did agree to settle lawsuits brought by 46 states against the industry in late 1998 by signing the Master Settlement Agreement. This settlement was considered a better deal for the tobacco industry, as many of the onerous cigarette marketing restrictions contained in the original FDA proposal settlement were missing. The agreement allows large outdoor signs at retailers, whereas the original proposal banned all outdoor ads. The original deal banned all use of humans and cartoons in ads, while the current settlement bans only cartoons and even permits their use on cigarette packs. And while the original proposal eliminated sports sponsorships, the current agreement allows each company to continue one national sponsorship.[80]

In 2000, the United States Supreme Court ruled that the Food and Drug Administration did not have the authority to regulate tobacco as a drug and that Congress would have to specifically enact legislation to allow the FDA to regulate tobacco. As a result, all FDA tobacco regulations were dropped. However, in June 2009 Congress passed a tobacco-control bill giving the FDA sweeping new powers over the packaging, manufacturing, and marketing of tobacco products, and it was signed into law by President Obama shortly thereafter. The Family Smoking Prevention and Tobacco Control Act calls for restrictions on marketing and sales to youths, including a ban on all outdoor tobacco advertising within 1,000 feet of schools and playgrounds; a ban on all remaining tobacco-brand sponsorships of sports and entertainment events; a ban on free giveaways of nontobacco products with the purchase of a tobacco product; a limit on advertising in publications with significant teen readership as well as limiting outdoor and point-of-sale advertising, except in adult-only facilities, to black-and-white ads only; and a restriction on ads on vending machines and self-service displays to adult-only facilities.[81]

A number of consumer advocacy groups as well as health departments in many states run ads warning consumers against the dangers of smoking and tobacco-related diseases. For example, the American Legacy Foundation (ALF), which was established as part of the 1998 tobacco settlement and is dedicated to reducing tobacco use, has run a number of hard-hitting ads warning consumers of the risk of smoking. One of the most successful programs developed by the ALF has been truth®, which was launched in 2000 and is the largest national youth smoking prevention campaign. truth® exposes the tactics of the tobacco industry, the truth about addiction, the health effects and consequences of smoking, and is designed to allow teens to make informed choices about tobacco use by giving them the facts about the industry and its products. truth® is a fully integrated campaign that includes advertising in media that are popular with youth, a summer travel tour that allows teens to engage firsthand with the campaign, and a website (www.thetruth.com) that contains a number of distinctive interactive elements (Exhibit 20–16).

In 2016 the Food and Drug Administration was given the authority to regulate electronic cigarettes (e-cigarettes) as well as other tobacco products.[82] The new regulations cover products including hookah, cigar and pipe tobacco, vape pens, and refillable vaporizers. The rules prohibit sales to minors, ban free samples, require package warning labels, and call for makers of products released after 2007 to seek FDA permission to remain on store shelves. While the tobacco industry has claimed that e-cigarettes help people trying to quit smoking, health experts argue that it is important for lawmakers to control their use as users of the product can still become hooked on nicotine and e-cigarette use has been rising steadily, especially among youth. According to the U.S. Centers for Disease Control and Prevention, e-cigarette use among high school students rose from 1.5 percent in 2011 to 16 percent in 2015.[83]

Another area where the Food and Drug Administration has become more involved is the advertising of prescription drugs. Tremendous growth in direct-to-consumer (DTC) drug advertising has occurred since the FDA issued new guidelines making it easier for pharmaceutical companies to advertise prescription drugs to consumers. In 2007, Congress passed legislation giving the FDA more power to regulate DTC drug advertising. The bill gives the FDA the power to require drug companies to submit TV ads for review before they run, but it can only recommend changes, not require them. The bill also granted the FDA the power to impose fines on a drug company if its ads are found to be false and misleading. The fines can amount to $250,000 a day for the first violation in any three-year period and up to $5,000 for any subsequent violation.[84]

The DTC advertising of prescription drugs is very controversial. Ethical Perspective 20–1 discusses the reasons why many oppose the practice and why groups such as the American Medical Association as well as some members of Congress are calling for a ban on DTC drug ads.

EXHIBIT 20–16

truth® has been a very effective youth smoking prevention campaign by the American Legacy Foundation, which was created and funded by the four largest tobacco companies

Source: truth initiative, www.thetruth.com

Should Direct-to-Consumer Drug Advertising Be Banned?

The advertising of prescription drugs directly to consumers has always been a very controversial issue; the United States and New Zealand are the only two countries in the world where the practice is permitted. The Food and Drug Administration (FDA) oversees the advertising of prescription drugs while the Federal Trade Commission regulates the advertising of over-the-counter (OTC) drugs. For years, pharmaceutical companies in the United States marketed most of their prescription drug products directly to physicians, either through their sales force or by advertising in medical journals. However, in 1997 the FDA issued new guidelines making it easier for pharmaceutical companies to advertise prescription drugs on television as well as in print media. Consumers are still required to have the explicit permission of a physician to buy a prescription medication, so pharmaceutical companies face the challenge of motivating consumers to see their doctor while touting their brand as a remedy to the problem. With the change in the FDA guidelines, direct-to-consumer (DTC) drug advertising has exploded over the past two decades and pharmaceutical companies have some of the largest advertisers in the United States.

Direct-to-consumer drug advertising spending increased from $859 million in 1997 to $5.2 billion in 2015, with most of the money being spent for ads on television ($3 billion) and in magazines ($1.4 billion), although online DTC advertising is growing rapidly as well. Brand-name prescription drugs such as Eliquis, Celebrex, Humira, Viagra, and Cialis have become as well known to consumers as brands of soft drinks. It is hard to make it through a television show without seeing a commercial hawking prescription drugs for a variety of medical problems and conditions including allergies, heartburn, arthritis, depression, and erectile dysfunction. Drug companies use celebrities and athletes to pitch their products almost as frequently and effectively as other marketers. Actress Sally Field is a spokesperson for the bone-building drug Boniva, while one of the most heavily advertised products is the blood-thinning drug Xarelto which runs commercials featuring a group of celebrities that includes NBA star Chris Bosh, actor/comedian Kevin Nealon, and NASCAR driver Brian Vickers.

The pharmaceutical companies contend that the increased spending on drug advertising helps inform and educate consumers about diseases and treatment options, encourages people to seek medical advice, and helps remove stigmas associated with medical conditions. They also note that the advertising helps generate sales revenue needed to fund costly research and development of new drugs. However, opponents argue that DTC drug advertising misinforms patients, promotes the use of drugs before long-term safety profiles can be known, medicalizes and stigmatizes normal conditions and bodily functions such as aging and low testosterone, and has led to society's overuse of prescription drugs. They also argue that drug advertising leads patients to ask their doctors to prescribe specific drugs when other treatments or lifestyle changes might be better for them.

The FDA is charged with the responsibility of ensuring that drug advertising is fair, balanced, and truthful. In 2007 Congress passed legislation giving the FDA more power to regulate DTC drug advertising such as requiring pharmaceutical companies to submit TV ads for review no later than 45 days before they run. While the FDA can only recommend changes and not require them, it does have the power to impose fines on a pharmaceutical company if its ads are found to be false and misleading. In 2009 the FDA published new advertising guidelines cautioning companies not to downplay a drug's risks and/or side effects by using tactics such as loud music or distracting visuals or typeface smaller than that used to describe a drug's benefits. The FDA can also require that DTC drug ads disclose specific safety risks as well as clear, conspicuous, and neutral statements about any side effects.

While the FDA's power to regulate DTC drug advertising is increasing, it has become very difficult for the agency to do so since the number of ads submitted annually for FDA scrutiny, including TV spots, magazine and newspaper ads, online ads and websites, and even pamphlets used by sales continues to increase. The FDA approved 41 new medications in 2014, more than in any year since the 1990s. Many of these are expected to be billion-dollar blockbusters that address new unmet needs with years of patent protection for their manufacturers because drugs have a patent life of 20 years from the initial filing date of the application. Pharmaceutical companies are likely to spend heavily to promote these new products to recoup their investment. In 2015 the FDA made changes to its drug advertising review process, making it easier for pharmaceutical companies to submit their materials for review by regulators; ads and documents can now be submitted electronically rather than by the old paper process.

The U.S. Postal Service Many marketers use the U.S. mail to deliver advertising and promotional messages. The U.S. Postal Service has control over advertising involving the use of the mail and ads that involve lotteries, obscenity, or fraud. The regulation against fraudulent use of the mail has been used to control deceptive advertising by numerous direct-response advertisers. These firms advertise on TV or radio or in magazines and newspapers and use the U.S. mail to receive orders and payment. Many have been prosecuted by the Post Office Department for use of the mail in conjunction with a fraudulent or deceptive offer.

© RosaBetancourt 0 people images/Alamy

While DTC drug advertising continues to increase, many consumer and medical groups have been renewing their efforts to reign it in or ban it all together. In late 2015 the American Medical Association called for a ban on DTC drug advertising, arguing that it inflates demands for new and more expensive drugs that may not be appropriate for patients' conditions and blaming escalating drugs prices squarely on marketing and advertising costs.

Public sentiment against drug companies escalated in February 2016, when the former CEO of Turing Pharmaceuticals, Martin Shkreli, testified before Congress and refused to answer questions about how Turing purchased a drug called Daraprim, which is used to treat cancer and AIDS, and immediately raised its price by more than 5,000 percent. Shkreli repeatedly exercised his Fifth Amendment right to avoid self-incrimination, and smirked several times and even appeared on the verge of laughter at one point, infuriating members of the House Committee on Oversight and Government Reform. After the hearings Shkreli tweeted out a message

stating: "Hard to accept that these imbeciles represent the people in our government."

Martin Shkreli's testimony stoked the general public's ire against the pharmaceutical industry as well as that of many lawmakers. A few weeks later Rep. Rosa DeLauro (D-CT) introduced her Responsibility in Drug Advertising Act which would impose a three-year moratorium on the advertising of newly approved prescription drugs directly to consumers. The legislation would also prohibit advertising after the three-year moratorium if it is determined that a new drug has significant side effects. Supporters of the bill argue that it would help hold down health care costs and prevent consumers from receiving inaccurate information. Opponents of the bill argue that it would actually hurt consumers by eliminating the advantages of DTC drug advertising and also note that even if Congress were to enact legislation restricting DTC drug advertising, it would be lost in the courts since it would violate the First Amendment which protects commercial speech.

The pharmaceutical industry recognizes that it must address the concerns over DTC drug advertising, and has been taking steps to restore its reputation. Following Shkreli's testimony, the Pharmaceutical Research and Manufacturers of America (PhRMA), the industry's trade association, launched an ad campaign called "Hopes to Cures" which is designed to highlight the value that pharmaceutical innovation brings to patients' lives by telling the stories of patients and researchers. Pfizer also launched a campaign titled "Before It Became a Medicine" which included print and digital ads and videos featuring the company's scientists and doctors discussing the long R&D process involved with developing new drugs.

While the battle over drug advertising is likely to continue, many argue that DTC in traditional media such as television and print is likely to fade away in the coming years as consumers go online to get information about drug products. The CEO of InterbrandHealth notes that 60 percent of consumers already get their first piece of health information by going online, e-mailing their friends, or checking social media. Thus, banning DTC drug advertising will not really matter because the activity is happening in areas that companies cannot control and the government really cannot regulate.

Sources: Christine Birkner, "With the Threat of an Ad Ban Looming, Pharma Is Fighting to Repair Its Reputation," Adweek, March 27, 2016, www.adweek.com/news/advertising-branding/threat-ad-ban-looming-pharma-fighting-repair-its-reputation-170409; Ana Radelat, "Lawmaker Introduces Bill That Would Curb Drug Advertising," Advertising Age, February 22, 2016, http://adage.com/article/cmo-strategy/lawmaker-introduces-bill-curb-drug-advertising/302797/; Andrew Pollack and Emmarie Huettman, "Martin Shkreli Invokes the Fifth Amendment during Grilling by Congress," The New York Times, February 4, 2016, www.nytimes.com/2016/02/05/business/drug-prices-valeant-martin-shkreli-congress.html?_r=0.

Bureau of Alcohol, Tobacco, Firearms and Explosives The Bureau of Alcohol, Tobacco, Firearms and Explosives (ATF) is an agency within the Treasury Department that enforces laws, develops regulations, and is responsible for tax collection for the liquor industry. ATF regulates and controls the advertising of alcoholic beverages. The agency determines what information can be provided in ads as well as what constitutes false and misleading advertising. It is also responsible for including warning labels on alcohol advertising and banning the use of active athletes in beer commercials. ATF can impose strong sanctions for violators.

The advertising of alcoholic beverages has become a very controversial issue, with many consumer and public interest groups calling for a total ban on the advertising of beer, wine, and liquor.

The Lanham Act

While most advertisers rely on self-regulatory mechanisms and the FTC to deal with deceptive or misleading advertising by their competitors, many companies are filing lawsuits against competitors they believe are making false claims. One piece of federal legislation that has become increasingly important in this regard is the Lanham Act. This act was originally written in 1947 as the Lanham Trade-Mark Act to protect words, names, symbols, or other devices adopted to identify and distinguish a manufacturer's products. The **Lanham Act** was amended to encompass false advertising by prohibiting "any false description or representation including words or other symbols tending falsely to describe or represent the same." While the FTC Act did not give individual advertisers the opportunity to sue a competitor for deceptive advertising, civil suits are permitted under the Lanham Act.

Suing competitors for false claims was made even easier with passage of the TradeMark Law Revision Act of 1988. According to this law, anyone is vulnerable to civil action who "misrepresents the nature, characteristics, qualities, or geographical origin of his or her or another person's goods, services, or commercial activities." This wording closed a loophole in the Lanham Act, which prohibited only false claims about one's own goods or services. While many disputes over comparative claims are never contested or are resolved through the NAD, more companies are turning to lawsuits for several reasons: the broad information discovery powers available under federal civil procedure rules, the speed with which a competitor can stop the offending ad through a preliminary injunction, and the possibility of collecting damages.[85] However, companies do not always win their lawsuits. Under the Lanham Act you are required to prove five elements to win a false advertising lawsuit containing a comparative claim.[86] You must prove that:

- False statements have been made about the advertiser's product or your product.
- The ads actually deceived or had the tendency to deceive a substantial segment of the audience.
- The deception was "material" or meaningful and is likely to influence purchasing decisions.
- The falsely advertised products or services are sold in interstate commerce.
- You have been or likely will be injured as a result of the false statements, by either loss of sales or loss of goodwill.

Marketers using comparative ads have to carefully consider whether their messages have the potential to mislead consumers or may overstate their brand's performance relative to that of competitors. In some cases, a competitor may run an ad challenging a rival's claim if they feel that it misleading or is not based on accurate information. For example, Exhibit 20–17 shows an ad run by the TaylorMade Golf Company challenging rival Callaway's claim of its driver being the number 1 driver used on the Professional Golf Association tour. The ad provides information to substantiate TaylorMade's claim that it is the number 1 driver on tour. A study by Michael J. Barone and his colleagues provides a framework for developing measures to assess the misleading effects that may arise from various types of comparative advertising.[87]

EXHIBIT 20–17

TaylorMade ran this ad to challenge rival Callaway's claim of having the number 1 driver on the PGA Tour

Source: TaylorMade Golf Company, Inc.

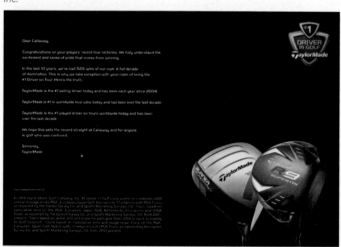

STATE REGULATION

In addition to the various federal rules and regulations, advertisers must also concern themselves with numerous state and local controls. An important early development in state regulation of advertising was the adoption in 44 states of the *Printers Ink* model statutes as a basis for advertising regulation. These statutes were drawn up in 1911 by *Printers Ink*, for many years the major trade publication of the advertising industry. Many states have since modified the original statutes and adopted laws similar to those of the Federal Trade Commission Act for dealing with false and misleading advertising.

In addition to recognizing decisions by the federal courts regarding false or deceptive practices, many states have special controls and regulations governing the advertising of specific industries or practices. As the federal government became less involved in the regulation of national advertising during the 1980s, many state attorneys general (AGs) began to enforce state laws regarding false or deceptive advertising.

The **National Association of Attorneys General (NAAG)** moved against a number of national advertisers as a result of inactivity by the FTC during the Reagan administration. In 1987, the NAAG developed enforcement guidelines on airfare advertising that were adopted by more than 40 states. The NAAG has also been involved in other regulatory areas, including car-rental price advertising as well as advertising dealing with nutrition and health claims in food ads. The NAAG's foray into regulating national advertising raises the issue of whether the states working together can create and implement uniform national advertising standards that will, in effect, supersede federal authority. However, an American Bar Association panel concluded that the Federal Trade Commission is the proper regulator of national advertising and recommended the state AGs focus on practices that harm consumers within a single state.[88] This report also called for cooperation between the FTC and the state attorneys general.

In recent years state attorneys general have been working with the FTC and other federal government agencies on false advertising cases. For example, 27 state attorneys general worked with the FDA in the deceptive advertising case for Bayer's Yaz birth-control pill that resulted in corrective advertising. A group of state attorneys general also worked with the FTC in a recent case against the makers of Airborne, a multivitamin and herbal supplement whose labels and ads falsely claimed that the product cures and prevents colds. Airborne had been making the false claims since 1999 and agreed to refund the money to consumers who had bought the product, as part of a $23.3 million class action settlement.[89]

Advertisers are concerned about the trend toward increased regulation of advertising at the state and local levels because it could mean that national advertising campaigns would have to be modified for every state or municipality. Yet the FTC takes the position that businesses that advertise and sell nationwide need a national advertising policy. While the FTC recognizes the need for greater cooperation with the states, the agency believes regulation of national advertising should be its responsibility.[90] Just in case, the advertising industry is still keeping a watchful eye on changes in advertising rules, regulations, and policies at the state and local levels.

REGULATION OF OTHER PROMOTIONAL AREAS

So far we've focused on the regulation of advertising. However, other elements of the promotional mix also come under the surveillance of federal, state, and local laws and various self-regulatory bodies. This section examines some of the rules, regulations, and guidelines that affect sales promotion, direct marketing, and marketing on the Internet.

Sales Promotion

Both consumer- and trade-oriented promotions are subject to various regulations. The Federal Trade Commission regulates many areas of sales promotion through the Marketing Practices Division of the Bureau of Consumer Protection. Many promotional practices are also policed by state attorneys general and local regulatory agencies. Various aspects of trade promotion, such as allowances, are regulated by the Robinson-Patman Act, which gives the FTC broad powers to control discriminatory pricing practices.

Contest and Sweepstakes   As noted in Chapter 16, numerous legal considerations affect the design and administration of contests and sweepstakes, and these promotions are regulated by a number of federal and state agencies. There are two important considerations in developing contests (including games) and sweepstakes. First, marketers must be careful to ensure their contest or sweepstakes is not classified as a *lottery*, which is considered a form of gambling and violates the Federal Trade Commission Act and many state and local laws. A promotion is considered a lottery if a prize is offered, if winning a prize depends on chance and not skill, and if the participant is required to give up something of value in order to participate. The latter requirement is referred to as *consideration* and is the basis on which most contests, games, and sweepstakes avoid being considered lotteries. Generally, as long as consumers are not required to make a purchase to enter a contest or sweepstakes, consideration is not considered to be present and the promotion is not considered a lottery.

The second important requirement in the use of contests and sweepstakes is that the marketer provide full disclosure of the promotion. Regulations of the FTC, as well as many state and local governments, require marketers using contests, games, and sweepstakes to make certain all of the details are given clearly and to follow prescribed rules to ensure the fairness of the game.[91] Disclosure requirements include the exact number of prizes to be awarded and the odds of winning, the duration and termination dates of the promotion, and the availability of lists of winners of various prizes (Exhibit 20–18). The FTC also has specific rules governing the way games and contests are conducted, such as requirements that game pieces be randomly distributed, that a game not be terminated before the distribution of all game pieces, and that additional pieces not be added during the course of a game.

A number of states have responded to concerns over fraud on the part of some contest and sweepstakes operators and have either passed or tightened prize notification laws, requiring fuller disclosure of rules, odds, and the retail value of prizes. Some of the most ambitious legal actions are taking place in individual states, where prosecutors are taking sweepstakes and contest companies to court for misleading and deceptive practices.[92]

Many marketers are now using the Internet and social media sites such as Facebook, YouTube, and Twitter to run their contests and sweepstakes. This is creating additional issues that marketers must consider such as whether automated or repetitive electronic submissions will be accepted, how the contest website will detect violations, and restrictions on length, size, or format of content submitted. If the contest or sweepstakes is being marketed using e-mail, marketers must comply with online data privacy laws as well as the CAN-SPAM Act, which is discussed later in the chapter. If the online entry form collects personal information from persons under the age of 13 (including e-mail addresses), marketers must comply with the Children's Online Privacy Protection Act.[93]

EXHIBIT 20–18

Marketers are required to provide consumers with full details of a contest or sweepstakes

Source: Scion by Toyota Motor Sales USA, Inc.

Marketers that post audiovisual entries on YouTube or feature a contest on Facebook or Twitter must comply with each site's guidelines for on-site promotions. For contests that involve user-generated content, such as photos, videos, or short stories, the rules must contain specific language granting the company the necessary rights and licenses to use the content. Marketers that want to use the content for marketing purposes should obtain a liability and publicity release from every individual who appears in the photos or videos that are displayed on their website.[94] The Internet and social media provide marketers with a greater opportunity to promote their contests and sweepstakes to specific target audiences and make the administration of these promotions more efficient and cost-effective. However, they also bring a host of additional legal factors that must be considered by companies.

Some social media sites are also imposing their own restrictions on how marketers can conduct contests and sweepstakes using their platforms. For example, in 2014 Facebook changed its policy to prohibit marketers from "like-gating" a page to gain access to content or enter a contest. Facebook said the change was made to make sure people are liking pages because they truly want to connect with a business or brand, not because they were enticed by artificial incentives such as promotional offers.[95]

Premiums   Another sales promotion area subject to various regulations is the use of premiums. A common problem associated with premiums is misrepresentation of their value. Marketers that make a premium offer should list its value as the price at which the merchandise is usually sold on its own. Marketers must also be careful in making premium offers to special audiences such as children. While premium offers for children are legal, their use is controversial; many critics argue that they encourage children to request a product for the premium rather than for its value. The Children's Advertising Review Unit has voluntary guidelines concerning the use of premium offers. These guidelines note that children have difficulty distinguishing a product from a premium. If product advertising contains a premium message, care should be taken that the child's attention is focused primarily on the product. The premium message should be clearly secondary. Conditions of a premium offer should be stated simply and clearly. "Mandatory" statements and disclosures should be stated in terms that can be understood by the child audience.[96]

Trade Allowances   Marketers using various types of trade allowances must be careful not to violate any stipulations of the Robinson-Patman Act, which prohibits price discrimination. Certain sections of the act prohibit a manufacturer from granting wholesalers and retailers various types of promotional allowances and/or payments unless they are made available to all customers on proportionally equal terms.[97] Another form of trade promotion regulated by the Robinson-Patman Act is vertical cooperative advertising. The FTC monitors cooperative advertising programs to ensure that co-op funds are made available to retailers on a proportionally equal basis and that the payments are not used as a disguised form of price discrimination.

Direct Marketing   As we saw in Chapter 14, direct marketing is growing rapidly. Many consumers now purchase products directly from companies in response to TV and print advertising or direct selling. The Federal Trade Commission enforces laws related to direct marketing, including mail-order offers, the use of 900 telephone numbers, and direct-response TV advertising. The U.S. Postal Service enforces laws dealing with the use of the mail to deliver advertising and promotional messages or receive payments and orders for items advertised in print or broadcast media.

A number of laws govern the use of mail-order selling. The FTC and the Postal Service police direct-response advertising closely to ensure the ads are not deceptive or misleading and do not misrepresent the product or service being offered. Laws also forbid mailing unordered merchandise to consumers, and rules govern the use of "negative option" plans whereby a company proposes to send merchandise to consumers and expects payment unless the consumer sends a notice of rejection

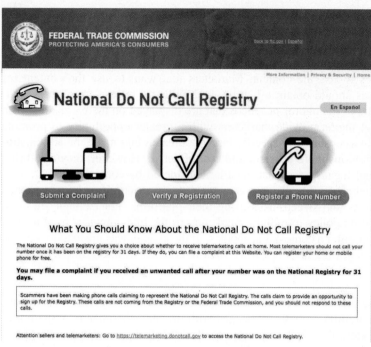

EXHIBIT 20–19

The National Do Not Call Registry protects consumers from calls by telemarketers

Source: Federal Trade Commission

or cancellation.[98] FTC rules also encourage direct marketers to ship ordered merchandise promptly. Companies that cannot ship merchandise within the time period stated in the solicitation (or 30 days if no time is stated) must give buyers the option to cancel the order and receive a full refund.[99]

Another area of direct marketing facing increased regulation is telemarketing. With the passage of the Telephone Consumer Protection Act of 1991, marketers who use telephones to contact consumers must follow a complex set of rules developed by the Federal Communications Commission. These rules require telemarketers to maintain an in-house list of residential telephone subscribers who do not want to be called. Consumers who continue to receive unwanted calls can take the telemarketer to state court for damages of up to $500. The rules also ban telemarketing calls to homes before 8:00 A.M. and after 9:00 P.M.; automatic dialer calls; and recorded messages to emergency phones, health care facilities, and numbers for which the call recipient may be charged. They also ban unsolicited junk fax ads and require that fax transmissions clearly indicate the sender's name and fax number.[100]

In 2003, Congress approved a Federal Trade Commission proposal for the formation of a National Do Not Call Registry allowing consumers to opt out of most commercial telemarketing.[101] Consumers can place their home phone numbers, as well as personal cell phone numbers, on the National Do Not Call Registry (Exhibit 20–19). Commercial telemarketers must pay a fee to access the registry and generally are prohibited from calling the listed numbers. Telemarketers have three months to comply once a number goes on the list, and a consumer's registration lasts five years. Political and charitable solicitation calls are not affected by the regulation, and telemarketers can call consumers with whom they have an established relationship. Marketers face penalties of $11,000 per incident for calling someone on the list. The Federal Trade Commission, the Federal Communications Commission, and individual states are enforcing the National Do Not Call Registry, which contains nearly 220 million phone numbers.[102]

The National Do Not Call Registry affects the direct-marketing industry because it greatly reduces the number of households that telemarketers can call. As might be expected, the direct-marketing industry is strongly opposed to the registry, arguing that it violates their First Amendment rights and, further, that such a program is not needed. The Direct Marketing Association (DMA), which is the primary trade group for the direct-marketing industry, has argued that consumers already have a number of do-not-call options. They can ask to be excluded from an individual company's telemarketing list; at the same time they can sign up with state lists or pay $5 to sign up on the voluntary national list maintained by the Direct Marketing Association. The DMA argues that the national registry imposes more bureaucracy on the direct-marketing industry and that the same goal can be achieved by the industry itself with better education and enforcement.

The Direct Marketers Association and the American Teleservices Association, which represent callers, challenged the legality of the registry on the grounds that it took away their rights to First Amendment–protected speech and that it was excessive and poorly drafted, with competitive marketers forced to abide by different rules. However, in 2004 the U.S. Court of Appeals upheld the registry's validity, ruling that it is a valid commercial speech regulation. The appellate court said that because the registry doesn't affect political or charitable calls and because there is a danger of abusive telemarketing and invasion of consumer privacy from telemarketers, the government has a right to regulate its use.[103]

Direct marketers have been adjusting their telemarketing strategies to deal with the restrictions imposed by the Do Not Call Registry. They are focusing more attention on generating leads through promotional efforts such as sweepstakes and direct-mail programs, prompting consumers to opt in and agree to receive calls from direct marketers.[104] Some industry experts as well as academics argue that the Do Not Call Registry may actually improve telemarketing practice and the general efficiency of the business because direct marketers must focus more attention on consumers who are receptive to receiving their telemarketing calls.[105] However, there is also concern that some companies are finding loopholes in the rules governing the Do Not Call Registry. For example, one technique that has emerged is the use of a marketing tool called a "lead card," which invites a recipient to mail a reply card for free information. However, the cards often fail to warn consumers that by sending a reply, they are giving up their right to avoid telephone solicitations from the sender—even if their phone numbers are listed on the Do Not Call list.[106]

Another tactic being used by some companies to avoid the Do Not Call Registry is to use sweepstakes entry forms as a way to harvest consumers' telephone numbers for telemarketing purposes. When done correctly, this may be a legitimate direct-marketing tool; however, the FTC has cracked down on some companies that have violated Do Not Call regulations by calling phone numbers obtained via sweepstakes entry forms. Companies that want to collect telemarketing leads through a sweepstakes entry form must clearly and conspicuously disclose that their entry-form information will be used for telemarketing purposes and include a statement to be signed by consumers expressing agreement under the Do Not Call provision.[107]

The direct-marketing industry is also scrutinized by various self-regulatory groups, such as the Direct Marketing Association and the Direct Selling Association, that have specific guidelines and standards member firms are expected to adhere to and abide by. But some critics argue that these self-regulatory groups are not doing enough to keep consumers from receiving unwanted marketing messages, such as calls from telemarketers and direct-mail offers and solicitations. Thus, it is likely that they will continue to call for more government intervention and regulations.

Direct mail is also area that has been under attack as many consumers are tired of seeing their mailboxes bulging with catalogs as well other forms of direct mail and want to take action. Some states have considered legislation that would create state-run do-not-mail registries that would allow consumers to keep unsolicited direct mail out of their mailboxes. However, none of the proposed do-not-mail bills have made it beyond the hearing stage and it may take years before any type of legislation is enacted. A number of advocacy groups are not waiting for the government to address the problem, though, and are taking steps to help consumers reduce the amount of unwanted direct mail they are receiving. Several of these initiatives have been started by groups that are interested in reducing the environmental impact created by the direct-mail industry.

One initiative having a significant impact in terms of reducing the amount of direct mail is Catalog Choice, which was launched in 2007 with the mission of reducing the number of repeat and unsolicited catalog mailings, and promoting the adoption of sustainable industry best practices (Exhibit 20–20).[108] The company offers an online service that allows people to compile a list of catalogs, coupons, credit-card offers, and other types of direct mail they do not want to receive. The company then contacts the retailers with a request to take the person's name off their mailing list or makes a downloadable file available that merchants can then feed into their direct-mail database. Several thousand merchants and marketers have agreed to abide by the site's opt-out requests, including major companies such as Lands' End, Office Depot, and REI. In 2012 Catalog Choice was acquired by TrustedID, a company that delivers privacy, security, and reputation management services to proactively help protect against credit and identity theft—safeguarding individuals,

EXHIBIT 20–20

Catalog Choice offers consumers a way to opt out of receiving unwanted direct mail

Source: Catalog Choice

EXHIBIT 20–21

The Network Advertising Initiative website provides consumers with information about online advertising practices

Source: Network Advertising Initiative

families, and businesses. In 2013 TrustedID was acquired by Equifax which is one of the major credit monitoring and consumer data analytics companies. Catalog Choice now operates as a nonprofit organization in partnership with TrustedID.

Marketing on the Internet

The rapid growth of the Internet as a marketing tool has created a new area of concern for regulators. The same consumer protection laws that apply to commercial activities in other media apply to online as well. The Federal Trade Commission Act, which prohibits "unfair or deceptive acts or practices," encompasses Internet advertising, marketing, and sales. Claims made in Internet ads or on websites must be substantiated, especially when they concern health, safety, or performance, and disclosures are required to prevent ads from being misleading and to ensure that consumers receive material information about the terms of a transaction. There are a number of regulatory areas companies must now adhere to when marketing on the Internet. These include privacy issues, data security, online marketing to children, endorsements made through social media or blogs, native advertising, and the use of spam or unsolicited e-mails for commercial purposes.

Privacy and Security   Consumer privacy and security have become major issues among government regulators as a result of high-profile data breaches and concerns over the collection and use of consumer data for marketing purposes. Marketers must ensure that their online marketing programs are in compliance with consumer privacy and data security guidelines; failure to do so can lead to government enforcement actions, expensive litigation, and negative publicity that can be very damaging to their reputations and have long-term effects.

The major privacy issue regarding the Internet that has emerged involves undisclosed profiling whereby online marketers can profile a user on the basis of name, address, demographics, and online/offline purchasing data. Marketers argue that profiling offers them an opportunity to target specific niches and reach consumers with custom-tailored messages. However, the FTC has stated that Internet sites that claim they don't collect information but permit advertisers to surreptitiously profile viewer sites are violating consumer protection laws and are open to a charge of deception.[109] In 1999, DoubleClick, the company that is the leader in selling and managing online advertising as well as tracking web users and is now owned by Google, set off a controversy by connecting consumers' names, addresses, and other personal information with information it collects about where consumers go online. The controversy resulted in the company being investigated by the Federal Trade Commission and lawsuits being filed in some states.[110]

In response to the profiling controversy, companies that collect Internet usage data and information joined together under the banner of the Network Advertising Initiative (NAI) to develop a self-regulatory code.[111] The NAI has developed a set of privacy principles in conjunction with the Federal Trade Commission that provides consumers with explanations of Internet advertising practices and how they affect both consumers. The NAI has also launched a website (www.networkadvertising.org) that provides consumers with information about online advertising practices and gives them the choice to opt out of targeted advertising delivered by NAI member companies (Exhibit 20–21).

Consumer privacy and security have become major issues with the FTC in recent years.[112] The agency has requested that marketers voluntarily step up the disclosures they make about data they collect and seek permission from consumers before tracking their Internet surfing behavior.[113] Many marketers now adhere to the Digital Alliance Ad Choices program, which is a self-regulatory initiative that was implemented by the Advertising Self-Regulatory Council as part of its Interest-Based Advertising Accountability Program discussed earlier in the chapter. However, critics have argued that the program only blocks behavioral ad targeting rather than actually stopping behavioral data collection. There continues to be calls for the FTC to oversee the development of a Do-Not-Track program that would prohibit websites or mobile app operators from compiling or disclosing personal data to third parties for targeted marketing purposes. The FTC began work as far back as 2010 on a Do Not Track initiative that would let consumers opt out of having any of their online data shared with third parties.[114] Although many digital advertising companies agreed to the idea in principle, it has been difficult to reach agreement over the definition, scope, and application of the program, and little progress has been made over the past six years in finalizing a standard.[115]

Concerns over privacy and security have also increased with the explosion in the popularity of social media sites such as Facebook, Twitter, and others. For example, the FTC settled a complaint against Twitter charging it deceived consumers and put their privacy at risk by failing to safeguard their personal information, marking the agency's first such case against a social networking service. The FTC ordered Twitter to establish a security program subject to government monitoring for the next 10 years. Twitter agreed to the terms in exchange for the FTC not pursuing a civil lawsuit against the company.[116] Facebook has also announced significant changes to its privacy policies giving users more control over their content, reducing the amount of their information that is available to others, and also making it easier to control whether applications and websites can access their information.[117]

Privacy and data security are likely to remain the top of the enforcement lists for the FTC as well as state attorneys general and other regulatory groups. In 2015 the FTC won an important case against Wyndham Hotels and Resorts when an appeals court affirmed its authority to require companies to securely store customer data and punish them for failing to do so. The FTC charged that the company's security practices unfairly exposed the payment card information of hundreds of thousands of consumers to hackers in three separate data breaches. Wyndham challenged the scope of the FTC's authority to regulate data security arguing that the agency had no clear standards for what constitutes reasonable cyber security. However, the appellate court ruled in favor of the FTC, which was seen as a victory for consumer privacy, especially as companies collect increasing amounts of data and information about their customers. Many legal experts view this as a pivotal case that could lead to more scrutiny of companies' data security in the future.[118]

Online Marketing to Children   While various proposals are aimed at protecting the privacy rights of adults, one of the biggest concerns is over restricting marketers whose activities or websites are targeted at children. These concerns over online marketing to children led to the passage of the **Children's Online Privacy Protection Act (COPPA) of 1998**, which the FTC began enforcing in April 2000.[119] This act places tight restrictions on collecting information from children via the Internet and requires that websites directed at children and young teens have a privacy policy posted on their home page and areas of the site where information is collected. The law also requires websites aimed at children under age 13 to obtain parental permission to collect most types of personal information and to monitor chat rooms and bulletin boards to make sure children do not disclose personal information there. When the law was enacted in 2000, it was left to the FTC to determine how to obtain the required permission, and the FTC temporarily allowed websites to let parents simply return an e-mail to approve certain information. Since then no other solution to the permission issue has surfaced, and the FTC has made the solution permanent.[120] However, the issue continues to be an area of concern since many marketers close their websites to children under the age of 13, but children under this age will often lie about their ages to gain access to the sites. The prevalence of social media is adding to the problem; many young people want access to fan clubs, blogs, and other websites that allow online interaction.[121]

As of July 1, 2013, the FTC began enforcing updates to COPPA that are designed to bring the law in line with changes that have occurred in the market, including the explosive growth of mobile device usage among kids and the data collection that goes along with it. The changes include the categorization of geolocation information, photos, and videos as personal information, requiring parental consent before such data are collected on children under age 13. The changes also extended COPPA to cover persistent device identifiers such as IP addresses and mobile device IDs that allow companies to track a user across various personal devices but do not cover mobile app stores.[122]

Online Endorsements and Native Ads   As discussed in the chapter opener, the FTC has also taken action to address the issue of endorsements made through social media sites and blogs and ensure that the same rules apply in this context as they do in traditional advertising and infomercials. In 2009 the agency passed a new set of guidelines for online endorsements that require online endorsers and bloggers to disclose any "material connection" to an advertiser.[123] Under the new guidelines, bloggers as well as paid endorsers who post on social media sites such as Facebook, Instagram, or Twitter or post product reviews on sites such as Amazon can be held liable if they do not identify themselves as having a material connection to a company or brand. The FTC rules also apply to third-party ad networks, which are paid by advertisers and then turn around and pay bloggers or Twitterers on behalf of the ad client.

Another aspect of online marketing where the FTC has become involved is native advertising, which refers to online ads that are similar in format and topic to content on the publishers website. As was discussed in Chapter 15, in late 2015 the FTC published its long-awaited guidelines for native advertising, which has become a very common practice as marketers shift more of their ad spending to digital media. A major goal of the FTC guidelines is to ensure that there is no misleading representations or omissions about an online advertisement's true nature or source. According to the policy statement: "In evaluating whether an ad's format is misleading, the Commission will scrutinize the entire ad, examining such factors as its overall appearance, the similarity of its written, spoken, or visual style to non-advertising content offered on a publisher's site, and the degree to which it is distinguishable from such other content."[124]

While the FTC has made it clear that it does not consider native ads inherently deceptive, the agency is very prescriptive about where and how disclosures should be made and what language is required. The guidelines state that when labels such as "advertisement" are necessary, they need to be prominent on first contact with consumers, and disclosures should appear near a native ad. They also emphasize the need to disclose that native content is an ad before the consumer clicks on it and note that labels such as "sponsored content" or "presented by" may not may be sufficient to avoid misleading consumers regarding the intention of the content. Many of these requirements are at odds with industry practices, which will mean that marketers and online publishers must reexamine their policies and procedures. It also means that the FTC is likely to take enforcement actions against marketers whose use of native advertising violates the new guidelines.[125]

Spamming   Another Internet-related marketing area receiving regulatory attention is **spamming**, which is the sending of unsolicited multiple commercial electronic messages. Spamming has become a major problem; studies show that the typical Internet user spends the equivalent of 10 working days a year dealing with incoming spam.[126] Spam also costs businesses billions of dollars every year in terms of lost worker productivity and network maintenance. Moreover, many of these messages are fraudulent or deceptive in one or more respects. A number of states have enacted antispamming legislation, and a comprehensive federal antispam bill, the Controlling the Assault of Non-Solicited Pornography and Marketing Act of 2003 (CAN-SPAM Act), went into effect on January 1, 2004. The act's general requirements for commercial e-mails include the following requirements:

- A prohibition against false or misleading transmission information.
- Conspicuous notice of the right to opt out and a functioning Internet-based mechanism that a recipient may use to request to not receive future commercial e-mail messages from the sender.
- Clear and conspicuous identification that the message is an advertisement.
- A valid physical postal address for the sender.

Violations of the CAN-SPAM law include both civil and criminal penalties, including a fine of $250 (calculated on a per e-mail basis) up to a maximum of $2 million. While the CAN-SPAM Act carries severe penalties for violators, thus far it has done little to stop unsolicited e-mail messages. Spammers have been able to stay one step ahead of law enforcement officials by operating offshore and by constantly moving the Internet hosting source.[127]

As marketers expend more of their IMC efforts online, they are facing many challenges as regulation of digital, social, and mobile advertising is becoming increasingly restrictive. They must understand and follow legal requirements in areas such as privacy and data security as well as guidelines regarding the use of endorsers and the types of online advertising formats they can use. Many companies work closely with law firms specializing in these areas to ensure that their digital marketing programs comply with rules and regulations governing online marketing. Marketers are recognizing that it is very important to embed privacy and data security considerations into their digital marketing campaigns and programs.[128] They must also understand rules and regulations regarding endorser disclosures as well as monitor what is being said and posted about their companies and brands online.

Summary

Regulation and control of advertising stem from internal regulation or self-regulation as well as from external control by federal, state, and local regulatory agencies. For many years the advertising industry has promoted the use of voluntary self-regulation to regulate advertising and limit government interference with and control over advertising. Self-regulation of advertising emanates from all segments of the advertising industry, including advertisers and their agencies, business and advertising associations, and the media.

The Advertising Self-Regulatory Council, the primary self-regulatory mechanism for national advertising, has been very effective in achieving its goal of voluntary regulation of advertising and other forms of marketing communication. Various media also have their own advertising guidelines. The major television networks maintain the most stringent review process and restrictions.

Advertising is viewed as commercial speech, which is speech promoting a commercial transaction, and is protected under the First Amendment. The federal government is the most important source of external regulation, with the Federal Trade Commission serving as the major watchdog of advertising in the United States. The FTC protects both consumers and businesses from unfair and deceptive practices and anticompetitive behavior. The FTC is very active in the regulation of advertising and other marketing practices and has authority in cases involving deceptive, misleading, or

untruthful advertising. The agency has a number of tools and programs that are used to regulate advertising including affirmative disclosure, advertising substantiation, cease-and-desist orders, and corrective advertising. A number of other federal agencies regulate advertising and promotion including the Federal Communications Commission, the Food and Drug Administration, the U.S. Postal Service, and the Bureau of Alcohol, Tobacco, Firearms and Explosives. The FDA regulates the advertising and promotion of cigarettes and other tobacco-related products, as well as direct-to-consumer drug advertising.

While most advertisers rely on self-regulatory mechanisms and the FTC to deal with deceptive or misleading advertising by their competitors, many are filing lawsuits against competitors under the Lanham Act for making false or misleading claims through comparative advertising. Many states, as well as the National Association of Attorneys General, are also active in exercising their jurisdiction over false and misleading advertising.

A number of laws also govern the use of other promotional-mix elements, such as sales promotion and direct marketing. The Federal Trade Commission regulates many areas of IMC including sales promotion as well as direct marketing. Various consumer-oriented sales promotion tools such as contests, games, sweepstakes, and premiums are subject to regulation. Trade promotion practices, such as the use of promotional allowances and vertical cooperative advertising, are regulated by the Federal Trade Commission under the Robinson-Patman Act. The FTC also enforces laws in a variety of areas that relate to direct marketing and mail-order selling as well as the Internet, while the FCC has rules governing telemarketing companies.

The rapid growth of the Internet as a marketing tool has created a new area of concern for regulators. The same consumer protection laws that apply to commercial activities in other media apply online as well. Major areas of concern with regard to advertising and marketing on the Internet are privacy and security, online marketing to children, and spamming or the sending of unsolicited commercial e-mail messages. Concerns over online marketing to children have led to the passage of the Children's Online Privacy Protection Act, which the FTC began enforcing in early 2000 and updated in 2013.

The federal government passed the CAN-SPAM Act, which went into effect on January 1, 2004, and was updated in 2013. This legislation sets stringent requirements for commercial e-mail messages.

The Federal Trade Commission has become increasingly concerned over privacy issues related to the popularity of social media and is requiring various sites to protect the privacy of users. The FTC also has issued new guidelines covering online endorsements that require endorsers and bloggers to disclose any material connection to an advertiser. In 2015 the FTC published guidelines for native advertising, which has become a very common practice as marketers shift more of their ad spending to digital media. A major goal of the FTC guidelines is to ensure that there are no misleading representations or omissions about an online advertisement's true nature or source.

Key Terms

self-regulation 692
Better Business Bureau (BBB) 694
Council of Better Business Bureaus (CBBB) 694
National Advertising Review Board (NARB) 694
Advertising Self-Regulatory Council (ASRC) 694
Federal Trade Commission (FTC) 701

commercial speech 702
Central Hudson Test 702
Federal Trade Commission Act 702
Wheeler-Lea Amendment 703
unfairness 704
puffery 704
deception 705
affirmative disclosure 706
advertising substantiation 707

consent order 709
cease-and-desist order 709
corrective advertising 710
Lanham Act 720
National Association of Attorneys General (NAAG) 721
Children's Online Privacy Protection Act (COPPA) of 1998 727
spamming 728

Discussion Questions

1. The chapter opener discusses the rules and regulations the Federal Trade Commission (FTC) uses for online endorsements. Do you agree with the new guidelines from the FTC requiring bloggers and endorsers to disclose any material connection to a company whose product or service they are endorsing? How might this impact companies that use social media in their IMC programs? (LO 20-1, 20-3)

2. Discuss the need for regulation of advertising and other IMC tools. Do you advocate more or less regulation of advertising and other forms of promotion by governmental agencies such as the Federal Trade Commission and the Food and Drug Administration? (LO 20-1, 20-3, 20-4)

3. Discuss the role the Advertising Self-Regulatory Council plays in the self-regulation of advertising. Discuss the arguments for and against self-regulation as an effective way of protecting consumers from misleading or deceptive advertising as well as companies competing against one another. (LO 20-2)

4. Do you agree with the DISCUS argument that advertising for hard liquor should be treated the same as advertising for beer and wine? Should advertising for spirits be confined to late-night programs on the

networks or should the ads be permitted to run earlier in the evening as well? (LO 20-2)

5. IMC Perspective 20–1 discusses how Skechers and Reebok were fined for making advertising claims for their toning shoes that the Federal Trade Commission argues were false, misleading, and unsubstantiated. Evaluate the claims made by these companies in their toning shoe ads from a deceptive advertising perspective. Why do you think they agreed to settle their cases rather than appeal them? (LO 20-1, 20-3)

6. Find several examples of advertising claims or slogans that are based on puffery rather than substantiated claims. Discuss whether you feel these advertising claims can be defended on the basis of puffery. (LO 20-3)

7. Evaluate the charges the Federal Trade Commission brought against Volkswagen Group of America for deceptive advertising. How might this issue affect consumer perceptions of Volkswagen and how should the company handle this controversy? (LO 20-1, 20-3)

8. Ethical Perspective 20–1 discusses the controversy surrounding the direct-to-consumer (DTC) advertising of prescription drugs. Evaluate the arguments both for and against pharmaceutical companies being allowed

to advertise their drug products directly to consumers. (LO 20-3)

9. Do you think the U.S. Food and Drug Administration should consider adopting the type of cigarette packaging being used in Australia that requires graphic images and removes all branding elements? How effective do you think this type of packaging would be in reducing cigarette smoking? (LO 20-3)

10. Discuss how the Do Not Call Registry developed by the Federal Trade Commission is impacting the direct-marketing industry. What arguments might direct marketers make in their efforts to have this program rescinded? (LO 20-4)

11. What are some of the regulatory issues marketers must take into consideration in developing contest, sweepstakes, and other types of promotions that will be offered online or through social media? (LO 20-4)

12. Discuss how regulatory agencies such as the FTC are responding to the increased use of digital and social media by marketers. What are the key areas that are requiring regulation to protect consumers from online marketing practices of companies? (LO 20-4)

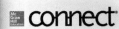

Digital users can access their personalized and adaptive SmartBook, Ad Forum Video Cases, and interactive exercises to review chapter concepts.

21

Evaluating the Social, Ethical, and Economic Aspects of Advertising and Promotion

Source: Lane Bryant, Inc.

LEARNING OBJECTIVES

LO1 Discuss various ethical perspectives on advertising and promotion.

LO2 Discuss various social perspectives on advertising and promotion.

LO3 Evaluate the social criticisms of advertising.

LO4 Discuss the effect of advertising on consumer choice, competition, and prices.

ADVERTISING THAT EMPOWERS WOMEN—BREAKING STEREOTYPES AND MAKING AN IMPACT

In the lead-in to Chapter 5 you read about the very effective "Like a Girl" campaign. As noted, that campaign has been acclaimed for its empowerment of young women, as well as its positive effects on young men. While "Like a Girl" has been the most acclaimed, a number of companies have developed ads to empower women. So many, in fact, that there is now a category of such ads referred to as femvertising, and an annual #Femvertising Awards program has just launched. The first #Femvertising Awards, sponsored by an 80-million-strong women's lifestyle network of digital media called SheKnows Media, took place in 2016. The awards honored brands in categories including Humor (Hello Flo, for "First Moon Party"); Social Impact (Dove, for "Speak Beautiful"); Inspiration (Ram Trucks, for "Courage Inside"); Next Generation (Always, for "Like a Girl"); Wildfire (L'Oréal Paris, for "Women of Worth"); and Hatch (Sport England, for "This Girl Can"). Samantha Skey, SheKnows Media's chief revenue and marketing officer, said the awards were developed because "We decided it was a good moment to reward the companies that were making a special effort to inspire and motivate positive behaviors among women and girls." Over 60 campaigns were submitted. Skey made it clear that the campaigns were not public service announcements but were meant to drive product sales while empowering women at the same time.

Perhaps the first female empowerment campaign to gain notable attention was the "Dove Campaign for Real Beauty," sponsored by Dove in 2004 and then followed by "The Dove Movement for Self-Esteem" in 2010. The highly successful campaign is often considered the impetus for those that followed. Now there are a number of such campaigns and awards programs, including Pantene's #ShineStrong and "Not Sorry," Goldie-Blox's "The Princess Machine," Nike's #BetterForIt, and many more. They seem to work for everyone.

Consider these numbers: Ads Leaderboard—*Adweek's* monthly tracker of the most watched ads on YouTube—showed that from 2015 to 2016 the number of watched empowerment ads more than doubled. The ads were 2.5 times less likely to be skipped than other ads. Women ages 18 to 34 were twice as likely to think highly of a brand that aired an empowering ad and nearly 80 percent more likely to like, share, comment, and subscribe to one. They also showed some of the highest recall of all ads on the site. Other studies have also shown that the empowerment ads work for the cause as well as the marketer. A study conducted by SheKnows indicated that (1) over 50 percent of women polled said they bought a product because they liked how the brand and its advertising portrayed women; (2) 81 percent of women said that ads that positively portray women are important for the younger generation to see; (3) 51 percent of women say that they like the ads because they believe they break down gender equality barriers; and (4) 71 percent of respondents think brands should be responsible for using advertising to promote positive messages to women and girls. Based on these results, it seems clear that the use of these female empowerment ads are a win–win for all involved.

But, of course, not everyone sees things the same. Ask Lane Bryant, the marketer of plus-size clothing for women. Lane Bryant is not a newcomer to #Femvertising, having previously launched the #ImNoAngel and #Plus Is Equal campaigns—both of which were focused on body acceptance. However, in its latest venture titled "ThisBody" the company was accused of going too far. According to CEO and president Linda Heasley, the new campaign featured top plus models and was positioned as a "declaration (and an invitation) to let the world know how plus-size women feel about their bodies, as demonstrated on the handwritten shirts worn in the campaign." The goal of the campaign was to have the world know that all women are beautiful, and to consider Lane Bryant as "an inspiring brand for empowered, beautiful, and confident women." To communicate this, a TV commercial was developed in which the models wear everything from "killer" outfits to nothing at all. And that is where the trouble started. ABC and NBC refused to air the "ThisBody" ads, with a spokesperson for NBC saying that they didn't comply with broadcast indecency guidelines (ABC would not comment) potentially because of the nudity and/or breastfeeding that was shown. Lane Bryant had a different perspective, however, claiming the models were no more nude than other models seen on TV. The company implies that the ads were rejected only because the women were of plus size, and sent a series of tweets that stated they were "definitely made for prime-time." While ABC refused to comment, NBC contends that it did not reject the ads, but only asked for edits to be compliant with FTC guidelines. Lane Bryant said it would not edit the ads, but would air them on social media sites.

In the end, Lane Bryant still got a lot of attention for its "banned" ads. Within one day of posting on Facebook, the ads received 800,000 views and 20,000 shares and 600 comments. Most of the comments were supportive of Lane Bryant. Is it possible that Lane Bryant is using the "ban" to gain attention? Some may think so given that a Lane Bryant commercial featuring Ashley Graham was also banned in 2014. Others asked why Lane Bryant didn't consider the edits? Or is it that the TV networks are still not ready to accept plus-size sexy models? Seems like the start of a good debate!

Sources: Susan Wojcicki, "Ads That Empower Women Don't Just Break Stereotype—They're Also Effective," April 24, 2016, www.adweek.com; Jordan Valinsky, "Lane Bryant's 'Banned' Television Ad Is Raking in Viewers Online," March 11, 2016, www.digiday.com; Ahiza Garcia, "Lane Bryant Slams Networks for Refusing to Air 'ThisBody' Ad," March 11, 2016, www.money.cnn.com; Kandia Johnson, "Fem-Advertising: 3 Campaigns Empowering and Inspiring Women," June 6, 2016, www.blackenterprise.com; Lindsey Lanquist, "This Body-Positive Lane Bryant Ad Was 'Too Sexy' for TV," March 10, 2016, www.self.com; Liz Black, "Lane Bryant's Latest Campaign Is All about Body Inclusivity," February 9, 2016, www.refinery29.com; Kristina Monllos, "These Empowering Ads Were Named the Best of #Femvertising," July 17, 2015, www.adweek.com.

> If I were to name the deadliest subversive force within capitalism, the single greatest source of its waning morality—I would without hesitation name advertising. How else should one identify a force that debases language, drains thought, and undoes dignity?[1]

The increase in the number of campaigns that support empowerment of women can have both positive and negative results. As shown in the opening vignette to this chapter, while both sponsors of these campaigns and the subjects of the campaigns—in this case women and girls—may benefit from their exposure, at the same time there will be skeptics of the motivations of the companies behind them, as well as those who just don't like the fact that they are being shown. The same holds true of ads that may feature interracial and/or LGBT (lesbian, gay, bisexual, transgender) relationships. When advertisers choose to use these forms of advertising they must be aware of the impact they may have on viewers and society as a whole—as well as on themselves.

The primary focus of this text has been on the role of advertising and promotion as marketing activities used to convey information to, and influence the behavior of, consumers. We have been concerned with examining the advertising and promotion function in the context of a business and marketing environment and from a perspective that assumes these activities are appropriate. However, as you can see in the lead-in, not everyone shares the viewpoints and/or perspectives. Advertising and promotion are the most visible of all business activities and are prone to scrutiny by those who are concerned about the methods that marketers use to sell their products and services.

Proponents of advertising argue that it is the lifeblood of business—it provides consumers with information about products and services and encourages them to improve their standard of living. They say advertising produces jobs and helps new firms enter the marketplace. Companies employ people who make the products and provide the services that advertising sells. Free-market economic systems are based on competition, which revolves around information, and nothing delivers information better and at less cost than advertising.

Not everyone, however, is sold on the value of advertising. Critics argue that most advertising is more propaganda than information; it creates needs and faults consumers never knew they had. Ads suggest that children need cell phones, that our bodies should be leaner, our faces younger, and our houses cleaner. They point to the sultry, scantily clad bodies used in ads to sell everything from perfume to beer to power tools and argue that advertising promotes materialism, insecurity, and greed.

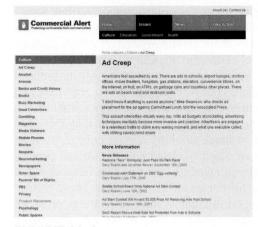

EXHIBIT 21–1

Commercial Alert, a project of Public Citizen, is concerned with the excessive amount of marketing messages consumers receive

© Commercial Alert, a project of Public Citizen

One of the reasons advertising and other forms of integrated marketing communications are becoming increasingly criticized is that they are so prevalent. Not only are there more ads than ever, but there are more places where these ads appear. Advertising professor David Helm notes: "Between the stickered bananas and the ads over the urinals and the ones on the floor of the supermarkets, we're exposed to 3,000 commercial messages a day. That's one every 15 seconds, assuming we sleep for 8 hours, and I'd guess right now there's someone figuring out how to get us while our eyes are closed."[2]

As marketers intensify their efforts to get the attention of consumers, resentment against their integrated marketing communications efforts is likely to increase. Concern is growing that there may be a consumer backlash as integrated marketing efforts move to new heights and marketers become increasingly aggressive. The growing practice of placing ads and logos everywhere seems a desperate last attempt to make branding work according to the old rules. As telemarketing, advertising in the digital and social media, in movie theaters, in classrooms, and seemingly everywhere else continues at a frenzied pace, the value of the messages decreases. The system seems headed for a large implosion. Groups such as Commercial Alert are concerned about intrusion of advertising and other types of marketing messages into all aspects of consumers' lives. In addition to their concerns about the pervasiveness of commercially related messages, the organization is also concerned with other ad-related issues, as can be seen in Exhibit 21–1. Consumer advocacy groups also argue that many companies are obliterating the line between marketing communications and entertainment by creating and delivering ads and other messages that appear to be part of popular culture but have a persuasive intent.[3] (You may recall our earlier discussion on native ads.)

Advertising is a very powerful force, and this text would not be complete without a look at the criticisms regarding its social and economic effects as well as some defenses against these charges. We consider the various criticisms of advertising and promotion from an ethical and social perspective and then appraise the economic effects of advertising.

ADVERTISING AND PROMOTION ETHICS

In the previous chapter, we examined the regulatory environment in which advertising and promotion operate. While many laws and regulations determine what advertisers can and cannot do, not every issue is covered by a rule. Marketers must often make decisions regarding appropriate and responsible actions on the basis of ethical considerations rather than on what is legal or within industry guidelines. **Ethics** are moral principles and values that govern the actions and decisions of an individual or group.[4]

A particular action may be within the law and still not be ethical. A good example of this involves target marketing. No laws restrict tobacco companies from targeting advertising and promotion for new brands to African Americans. However, given the high levels of lung cancer and smoking-related illnesses among the black population, many people would consider this an unethical business practice. The same holds true for ads targeting children.

Throughout this text we have presented a number of ethical perspectives to show how various aspects of advertising and promotion often involve ethical considerations. Ethical issues must be considered in integrated marketing communications decisions. And advertising and promotion are areas where a lapse in ethical standards or judgment can result in actions that are highly visible and often very damaging to a company.

EXHIBIT 21–2

This ad is part of a campaign to drink responsibly by the Alberta Gaming and Liquor Commission

© Alberta Gaming and Liquor Commission

EXHIBIT 21–3

After receiving criticism, Anheuser-Busch issued an apology for the tagline on this label. To read the full statement, visit http://newsroom. anheuser-busch.com/ statement-on-bud-light-bottle/

Source: Bud Light, Anheuser Busch

The role of advertising in society is controversial and has sometimes resulted in attempts to restrict or ban advertising and other forms of promotion to certain groups or for certain products. College students are one such group. The level of alcohol consumption and binge drinking by college students has become a serious problem. Alcohol-related problems have proliferated on college campuses in recent years and have resulted in many negative consequences including sexual abuse, assault, and even death.[5] Several studies have shown that there has been a significant increase in binge drinking among college students and have advocated a ban on alcohol-related advertising and promotion to this segment.[6] Many colleges and universities have imposed restrictions on the marketing of alcoholic beverages to their students. These restrictions include banning sponsorships or support of athletic, musical, cultural, or social events by alcoholic-beverage companies and limiting college newspaper advertising to price and product information ads.

A great deal of attention is being focused on the issue of whether alcoholic-beverage companies target not only college students but underage drinkers as well. As noted in Chapter 20, the actions of beer, wine, and liquor marketers are being closely scrutinized in the wake of the distilled-spirits industry's decisions to reverse its long-standing ban on television and radio advertising. Many people believe the industry's push to join beer and wine advertisers on television is testing the public's attitudes and may lead to support for more government restrictions and regulations on alcohol advertising.[7] The U.S. surgeon general has issued a report stating that alcohol is the most widely used substance of abuse among America's youth and urged marketers of alcoholic beverages to cut back on outdoor advertising and end any remaining college newspaper advertising as well as event sponsorships.[8] The report also called on the media, alcohol marketers, and colleges and universities to work to address the problem by not glamorizing underage alcohol use in movies and TV shows and minimizing youth exposure to alcohol advertising through the media as well as on the Internet.

Companies marketing alcoholic beverages such as beer and liquor recognize the need to reduce alcohol abuse and drunken driving, particularly among young people, as do government agencies. Many of these companies have developed programs and ads designed to address this problem. The same is true in Canada, where the Alberta Gaming and Liquor Commission (Alberta, Canada) has been running an advertising campaign that uses ads such as the one shown in Exhibit 21–2 to encourage drinkers to consume responsibly. The campaign also includes an age-verification splash page, a Facebook page, and images on Pinterest, Instagram, and Twitter. The Beer Institute and Distilled Spirits Council of the United States marketing codes also ban college newspaper ads, prohibit rite-of-passage ad appeals, and limit some outdoor ads. Both groups also require that ads be placed in media where 70 percent of the audience is 21 or older.

Criticism often focuses on the actions of specific advertisers. Groups like the National Organization for Women and Women Against Pornography have been critical of advertisers for promoting sexual permissiveness and objectifying women in their ads. These groups have now been joined by the general public. You may recall from Chapter 17 the incidence where Bud Light's "Up for Whatever" campaign was criticized for the tagline "The perfect beer for removing 'no' from your vocabulary for the night," which some people took as an endorsement of date rape. The company soon apologized and stopped printing the slogan on its labels. Nevertheless, the negative publicity that resulted was certainly not in Bud's best interest[9] (Exhibit 21–3). On the positive side, some beer companies are now thinking more about how their ads will be perceived by women. Coors Light's "Climb On" campaign depicts men *and women* participating in rugged sports like mountain climbing, white water rafting, and so on while Heineken introduced a campaign that suggests that women are more

EXHIBIT 21–4

This Heineken TV spot uses targeted marketing to say that women are more attracted to men who drink less

Source: Heineken

attracted to men who drink less. The campaign features women singing the Bonnie Tyler song "I Need a Hero" as they walk away from ostensibly inebriated men (Exhibit 21–4). NOW posts ads it considers offensive to women such as this on the Love Your Body: Offensive Ads section of its website.

As you read this chapter, remember that the various perspectives presented reflect judgments of people with different backgrounds, values, and interests. You may see nothing wrong with the ads for cigarettes or beer or sexually suggestive ads. Others, however, may oppose these actions on moral and ethical grounds. While we attempt to present the arguments on both sides of these controversial issues, you will have to draw your own conclusions as to who is right or wrong.

SOCIAL AND ETHICAL CRITICISMS OF ADVERTISING

Much of the controversy over advertising stems from the ways many companies use it as a selling tool and from its impact on society's tastes, values, and lifestyles. Specific techniques used by advertisers are criticized as deceptive or untruthful, offensive or in bad taste, and exploitative of certain groups, such as women or children. We discuss each of these criticisms, along with advertisers' responses. We then turn our attention to criticisms concerning the influence of advertising on values and lifestyles, as well as charges that it perpetuates stereotyping and that advertisers exert control over the media.

Advertising as Untruthful or Deceptive

One of the major complaints against advertising is that many ads are misleading or untruthful and deceive consumers. A number of studies have shown a general mistrust of advertising among consumers. These studies have shown that consumers don't find most commercials to be honest and do not trust them. In an *Adweek* Media/Harris Poll, 65 percent of those surveyed said they trust advertising only sometimes, 18 percent most of the time, and 13 percent never.[10] A more specific analysis is carried out by the Nielsen Company that conducts an annual survey examining consumers trust in advertising based on earned versus owned media. The results, shown in Figure 21–1, indicate that there is little change in perceptions of trust over the past few years, and that these levels vary depending on the source of the ads.

What these studies seem to indicate is that although consumers may not completely trust advertising in general, when it comes to owned media these levels of trust have remained about the same over the years. Earned media, in general, are considered more trustworthy, but have experienced a slight drop more recently.

Attempts by industry and government to regulate and control deceptive advertising were discussed in Chapter 20. We noted that advertisers should have a reasonable basis for making a claim about product performance and may be required to

FIGURE 21–1

Global Trust in Advertising

Source: Nielsen, 2015.

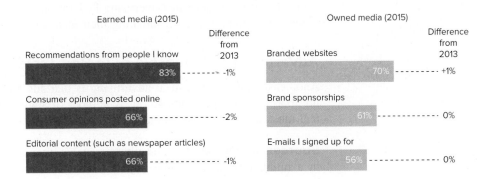

Earned media (2015)	Difference from 2013
Recommendations from people I know	
83%	-1%
Consumer opinions posted online	
66%	-2%
Editorial content (such as newspaper articles)	
66%	-1%

Owned media (2015)	Difference from 2013
Branded websites	
70%	+1%
Brand sponsorships	
61%	0%
E-mails I signed up for	
56%	0%

provide evidence to support their claims. However, deception can occur more subtly as a result of how consumers perceive the ad and its impact on their beliefs.[11] The difficulty of determining just what constitutes deception, along with the fact that advertisers have the right to use puffery and make subjective claims about their products, tends to complicate the issue. But a concern of many critics is the extent to which advertisers are *deliberately* untruthful or misleading.

Sometimes advertisers have made false or misleading claims or failed to award prizes promoted in a contest or sweepstakes. However, these cases usually involved smaller companies and only a tiny portion of the hundreds of billions of dollars spent on advertising and promotion each year. Most advertisers do not design their messages with the intention to mislead or deceive consumers or run sweepstakes with no intention of awarding prizes. Not only are such practices unethical, but the culprits would damage their reputation and risk prosecution by regulatory groups or government agencies. National advertisers invest large sums of money to develop loyalty to, and enhance the image of, their brands. These companies are not likely to risk hard-won consumer trust and confidence by intentionally deceiving consumers.

The problem of untruthful or fraudulent advertising and promotion exists more at the local level and in specific areas such as Internet fraud, telemarketing, and other forms of direct marketing. Yet there have been many cases where large companies were accused of misleading consumers with their ads or promotions. For example, automobile companies Kia and Hyundai were the targets of U.S. government and class action suits when the Environmental Protection Agency found both manufacturers guilty of posting inflated fuel-economy estimates on their vehicles.[12] Hyundai and Kia agreed to pay a $100 million fine, give up $200 million in emission credits, spend $50 million setting up independent tests to certify mileage claims to settle with the U.S. government, and settle the class actions. In another case, Ford was required to lower mileage ratings for a second time in a year on its hybrids and compensated more than 200,000 owners of models such as the C-Max and Fusion hybrid.[13] In 2016, Mitsubishi admitted that it had manipulated fuel-economy tests, and as you read in Chapter 20, Volkswagen was caught manipulating emissions tests. Some companies test the limits of industry and government rules and regulations to make claims in an attempt to give their brands an advantage in highly competitive markets. This seems to be the case in the auto industry.

Many critics of advertising would probably agree that most advertisers are not out to deceive consumers deliberately, but they are still concerned that consumers may not be receiving enough information to make an informed choice. They say advertisers usually present only information that is favorable to their position and do not always tell consumers the whole truth about a product or service.

Some critics believe advertising should be primarily informative in nature and should not be permitted to use puffery or embellished messages. Others argue that advertisers have the right to present the most favorable case for their products and services and should not be restricted to just objective, verifiable information.[14] They note that consumers can protect themselves from being persuaded against their will and that the various industry and government regulations suffice to keep advertisers from misleading consumers. Figure 21–2 shows the advertising ethics and principles of the American Advertising Federation, which many advertisers use as a guideline in preparing and evaluating their ads.

Advertising as Offensive or in Bad Taste

Another common criticism of advertising is that ads are offensive, tasteless, irritating, boring, obnoxious, and so on. A number of studies have found that consumers feel most advertising insults their intelligence and that many ads are in poor taste.[15]

Sources of Distaste   Consumers can be offended or irritated by advertising in a number of ways. Some object when certain products or services such as

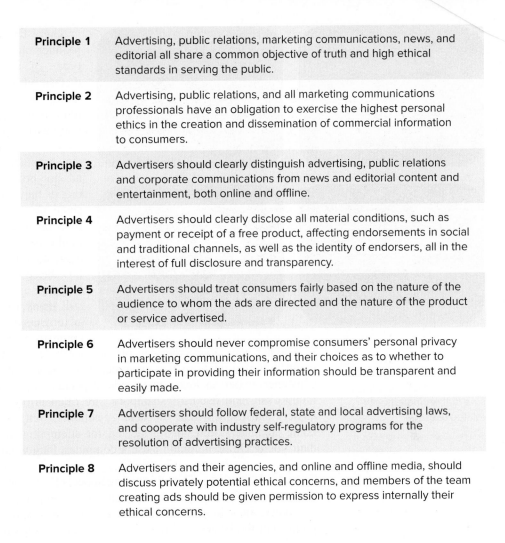

FIGURE 21–2

The American Advertising Federation Principles and Practices for Advertising Ethics

Principle 1	Advertising, public relations, marketing communications, news, and editorial all share a common objective of truth and high ethical standards in serving the public.
Principle 2	Advertising, public relations, and all marketing communications professionals have an obligation to exercise the highest personal ethics in the creation and dissemination of commercial information to consumers.
Principle 3	Advertisers should clearly distinguish advertising, public relations and corporate communications from news and editorial content and entertainment, both online and offline.
Principle 4	Advertisers should clearly disclose all material conditions, such as payment or receipt of a free product, affecting endorsements in social and traditional channels, as well as the identity of endorsers, all in the interest of full disclosure and transparency.
Principle 5	Advertisers should treat consumers fairly based on the nature of the audience to whom the ads are directed and the nature of the product or service advertised.
Principle 6	Advertisers should never compromise consumers' personal privacy in marketing communications, and their choices as to whether to participate in providing their information should be transparent and easily made.
Principle 7	Advertisers should follow federal, state and local advertising laws, and cooperate with industry self-regulatory programs for the resolution of advertising practices.
Principle 8	Advertisers and their agencies, and online and offline media, should discuss privately potential ethical concerns, and members of the team creating ads should be given permission to express internally their ethical concerns.

contraceptives or personal hygiene products are advertised at all. Most media did not accept ads for condoms until the AIDS crisis forced them to reconsider their restrictions. The major TV networks gave their affiliates permission to accept condom advertising in 1987, but the first condom ad did not appear on network TV until 1991.

In 1994, the U.S. Department of Health's Centers for Disease Control and Prevention (CDC) began a new HIV prevention campaign that included radio and TV commercials urging sexually active people to use latex condoms. The commercials prompted strong protests from conservative and religious groups, which argued that the government should stress abstinence in preventing the spread of AIDS among young people. NBC and ABC agreed to broadcast all the commercials, while CBS said it would air certain spots.[16]

Advertising for condoms has now been appearing on TV for over 20 years, but only in late-night time slots or on cable networks. However, in 2005 the broadcast networks agreed to accept commercials for condoms during prime time by agreeing to run heath-oriented ads for the Trojan brand.[17] The tone of the Trojan advertising was informational and provided facts and figures designed to raise viewers' consciousness and awareness about the potential consequences of unprotected sex among those who are sexually active (Exhibit 21–5). In 2007 both CBS and Fox rejected a commercial for Trojan condoms because of concerns about the creative content of the ad. Fox indicated that it rejected the ad because contraceptive advertising must stress health-related uses rather than the prevention of pregnancy.[18]

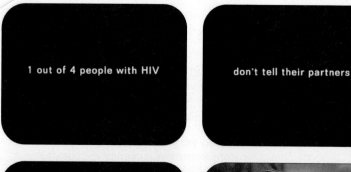

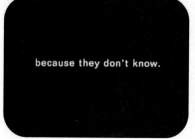

EXHIBIT 21–5

Many of the broadcast networks now accept ads for condoms during prime time that promote health-related uses

Source: Church & Dwight Co., Inc.

There has been found to be a strong product class effect with respect to the types of ads consumers perceived as distasteful or irritating. The most irritating commercials tend to be for feminine hygiene products; ads for women's undergarments and hemorrhoid products were close behind. Another study found that consumers are more likely to dislike ads for products they do not use and for brands they would not buy.[19] Ads for personal products have become more common on television and in print, and the public is more accepting of them. However, advertisers must still be careful of how these products are presented and the language and terminology used. There are still many rules, regulations, and taboos advertisers must deal with to have their TV commercials approved by the networks.[20]

Another way advertising can offend consumers is by the type of appeal or the manner of presentation. For example, many people object to appeals that exploit consumer anxieties. Fear appeal ads, especially for products such as deodorants, mouthwash, and dandruff shampoos, are often criticized for attempting to create anxiety and using a fear of social rejection to sell these products. Some ads for home computers were also criticized for attempting to make parents think that if their young children couldn't use a computer, they would fail in school.

Sexual Appeals The advertising appeals that have received the most criticism for being in poor taste are those using sexual appeals such as suggestiveness and/or nudity. In a longitudinal study of TV viewers in Australia, Michael Ewing found that the issue resulting in the most complaints to the country's advertising Standards Bureau involved sex, sexuality, and/or nudity—almost three times more than any other issue.[21] Similar attitudes have been demonstrated in other countries as well. These techniques are often used to gain consumers' attention and may not even be appropriate to the product being advertised. Even if the sexual appeal relates to the product, people may be offended by it.

As you have seen earlier in this text, a common criticism of sexual appeals is that they can demean women (or men) by depicting them as sex objects. Ads for cosmetics and lingerie are among the most criticized for their portrayal of women as sex objects and for being implicitly suggestive, though many other products also make use of this appeal, including a number of clothing companies. One of the reasons for using sexy ads is the attention they get as well as the free exposure that often results from the ads through publicity and/or word of mouth. For example, sexy ad campaigns using actor Megan Fox, Beyoncé, and David Beckham have each gathered over 12 million views in ads that have appeared in for Armani, H&M, and H&M, respectively.[22]

A company that has used sexy ads in a direct attempt to garner publicity (and has done so quite successfully!) is Calvin Klein. Since the first controversial Brooke Shields ad in 1981, the company has released very sexy ads that push the limits of compliance and have been debated in a variety of media, from both pro and against perspectives—all the while gaining even more exposure for the ads (Exhibit 21–6).

EXHIBIT 21–6

Calvin Klein started pushing the limits with this ad in 1981

© The Advertising Archives/Alamy

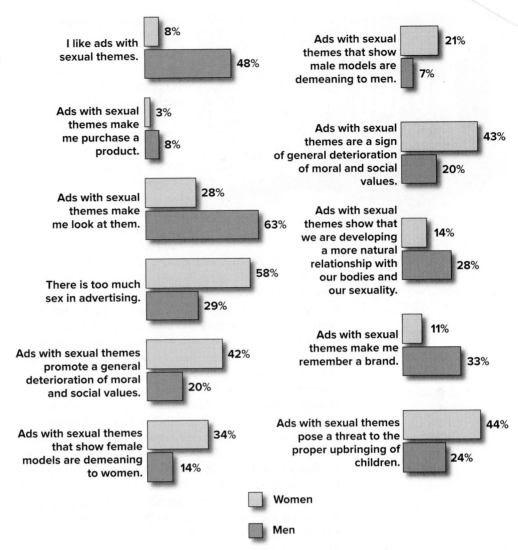

No doubt viewers will continue to hold different perspectives of the use of sex in advertising. Advertisers, however, are not likely to discontinue the practice. As noted by one company spokesperson responding to the criticisms, "Style is a matter of interpretation and like with all art we appreciate all points of view."[23]

Attitudes toward the use of sex in advertising is a polarizing issue because opinions regarding its use vary depending on the individual's values and religious orientation, as well as by age, education, and gender. One study found major differences between men and women in their attitudes toward sex in advertising.[24] As you can see in Figure 21–3, while almost half of men said they liked sexual ads, only 8 percent of women felt the same way. Most men (63 percent) indicated that sexual ads have high stopping power and get their attention, but fewer women thought the same (28 percent). Also, most women (58 percent) said there is too much sex in advertising versus only 29 percent of the men. Women were also much more likely than men to say that sexual ads promote a deterioration of moral and social values and that they are demeaning of the models used in them.

Shock Advertising With the increasing clutter in the advertising environment, advertisers continue to use sexual appeals and other techniques that offend some people but catch the attention of consumers and may even generate publicity for their companies. In recent years, there has been an increase in what is often referred

EXHIBIT 21-7

Tecate's billboard gained attention and criticism

© Jose Ybarra

to as **shock advertising**, in which marketers use nudity, sexual suggestiveness, or other startling images to get consumers' attention. As discussed earlier in the chapter, shock advertising is nothing new; companies such as American Apparel and Calvin Klein have been using this tactic in their ads for quite a while. However, a number of other marketers have been criticized for using shock techniques in their ads as well as in other promotional materials. Mexican beer brand Tecate recently shocked people passing by its billboard in Los Angeles and San Francisco when the advertisement displayed a tree with the word *baño* (Spanish for "bathroom") overlaying the image (Exhibit 21–7). The tongue-in-cheek message was meant to imply that it is easier for guys to go to the bathroom. While Tecate said the ad was not intended for the U.S. market, and took it down, one still wonders what it was meant to accomplish. Clothing retailer Abercrombie & Fitch has been criticized numerous times for the content and images used in its quarterly catalogs, which have included sex tips from porn star Jenna Jameson, a spoof interview with a shopping mall Santa portrayed as a pedophile, and nude photos. A few years ago the retailer promoted its Christmas catalog with an advertisement across the plastic covering stating, "Two-hundred and eighty pages of sex and Xmas fun" (Exhibit 21–8) Officials in four states threatened or pursued legal action against the company, which responded by implementing a policy of carding would-be buyers of the catalog to ensure they are at least 18 years old.[25] Abercrombie seems to now have taken on a different way to shock consumers, as can be seen in Ethical Perspective 21–1.

Many advertising experts argue that what underlies the increase in the use of shock advertising is the pressure on marketers and their agencies to do whatever it takes to get their ads noticed—we have seen this in earlier chapters. However, critics argue that the more advertisers use the tactic, the more shocking the ads have to be to get attention. How far advertisers can go with these appeals will probably depend on the public's reaction. When consumers think the advertisers have gone too far, they are likely to pressure the advertisers to change their ads and the media to stop accepting them.

EXHIBIT 21-8

Abercrombie & Fitch's catalogs were criticized over the use of sex and nudity

© Splash News/Newscom

While marketers and ad agencies often acknowledge that their ads push the limits with regard to taste, they also complain about a double standard that exists for advertising versus editorial television program content. The creative director for Abercrombie & Fitch's agency argued that there is a double standard and hypocrisy in the shock advertising debate: "When advertising uses sex, everybody complains—when editorial does it, nobody cares."[26] Advertisers and agency creative directors argue that even the most suggestive commercials are bland compared with the content of many television programs.

Advertising and Children

Another controversial topic advertisers must deal with is the issue of advertising to children. TV and the Internet are two vehicles through which advertisers can reach children easily. Estimates are that children between the ages of 7 and 16 in the United States spend approximately 3.0 hours a week online on the average, with those 15 to 16 spending 4.8.[27] Young people 16 to 24 spend more than 27 hours a week on the Internet in the UK.[28] Many other countries children spend even more time there[29] (Figure 21–4). A study conducted by the *Campaign for a Commercial-Free Childhood*

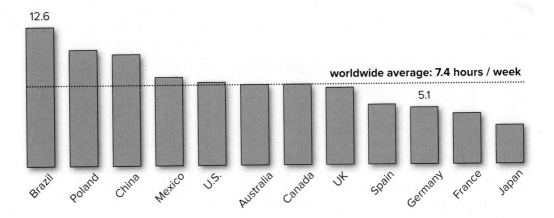

worldwide average: 7.4 hours / week

12.6

5.1

Brazil Poland China Mexico U.S. Australia Canada UK Spain Germany France Japan

FIGURE 21–4

Children's Time Spent on the Internet

Source: The Marketing Store, "The New Definition of Childhood."

estimated that children ages 2 to 11 see more than 25,000 commercials a year on TV alone, not to mention the ones they may see on the Internet, cell phones, video games, and so on.[30] Companies spend approximately $17 billion a year advertising to children, with most of this advertising falling into four categories: toys, food, clothing, and accessories.[31] Children are targeted because the ads influence their purchases as well as influencing other family members' purchases. In addition, if the child continues to use the product into adulthood, his or her lifetime value as a customer increases significantly. Perhaps this is why Camel cigarettes has often come under fire for marketing to youth. Interestingly, but not surprisingly, the most popular brand of cigarettes among teens just happens to be Camel.[32] Concern has also been expressed about marketers' use of other promotional vehicles and techniques such as radio ads, point-of-purchase displays, premiums in packages, product placements, and commercial characters as the basis for TV shows. A number of advocacy groups have petitioned the FTC to investigate a YouTube app that offers kids the opportunity to watch hundreds of channels of entertainment and educational programs. But, according to the watchdog groups, there are numerous branded content programs from McDonald's, Mattel, and Hasbro mixed in. In assisting the groups to draft the FTC complaint, University of Arizona professor Dale Kunkel said, "this is the most hyper-commercialized media for kids I have ever seen." A spokesperson for YouTube claimed that the company consulted with numerous child advocacy and privacy groups in the development of the app, and were always open to feedback on ways to improve the app.[33]

Critics argue that children, particularly young ones, are especially vulnerable to advertising because they lack the experience and knowledge to understand and critically evaluate the purpose of persuasive advertising appeals. Research has shown that preschool children cannot differentiate between commercials and programs, do not perceive the selling intent of commercials, and cannot distinguish between reality and fantasy.[34] The study also concluded that children must understand how advertising works in order to use their cognitive defenses against it effectively. Because of children's limited ability to interpret the selling intent of a message or identify a commercial, critics charge that advertising to them is inherently unfair and deceptive and should be banned or severely restricted.

At the other extreme are those who argue that advertising is a part of life and children must learn to deal with it in the **consumer socialization process** of acquiring the skills needed to function in the marketplace. They say existing restrictions are adequate for controlling children's advertising and that marketplace knowledge plays an important role in adolescents' skepticism toward advertising. They contend that greater knowledge of the marketplace appears to give teens a basis by which to evaluate ads and enables them to recognize the persuasion techniques used by advertisers.[35]

CHAPTER 21

Ethical Perspective 21-1 > > >

Abercrombie and American Apparel (NSFW) Shock Consumers into Their Ads—but Apparently Not into Their Stores

Perhaps the two most consistent users of shock advertising to gain consumers' attention are these two clothing companies whose ads almost always push the envelope regarding sexy and raunchy. Both brands at one time enjoyed famous brand images, and both now are considered by many to be infamous. Both had controversial CEOs, and both have been forced out. Both companies are on the skids.

In an age when brand image is everything, a company's leadership should take every measure possible toward making sure that nothing compromises the brand's image. That hasn't exactly been the case for Abercrombie & Fitch (A&F) CEO Mike Jeffries, who according to retail industry expert Barbara Farfan noted, "During his tenure as CEO, his business philosophies and views about sexualizing the Abercrombie & Fitch brand shocked its customers, the parents of its customers, investors, fellow retailers, advocacy groups, and just about anybody else who was paying attention." In early 2013 Jeffries found himself in the middle of a unique controversy that left both fans and critics of A&F scratching their heads as to whether or not Jeffries and his company possessed any sort of ethical decency. A&F is not new to controversy and in the past may have actually gained from the publicity it generated. However, this time was different, as Jeffries was asked to resign as the head of the company after 22 years in December 2014.

Abercrombie has pushed the envelope for decades, primarily with sexual content in its ads and catalogs, resulting in criticism from a variety of sources. For a while, the company seemingly laid low, still using the sexy positioning, but in a less shocking manner. But it seems shock may have just taken a different set of clothes. The controversy actually goes back to 2006, when Jeffries was quoted as stating the following in an interview with *Salon* magazine:

"In every school there are the cool and popular kids, and then there are the not-so-cool kids. . . . Candidly, we go after the cool kids . . . the attractive all-American kid with a great attitude and a lot of friends. . . . Are we exclusionary? Absolutely."

But he didn't stop there.

"Those companies that are in trouble are trying to target everybody: young, old, fat, skinny. But then you become totally vanilla. . . . You don't alienate anybody, but you don't excite anybody, either."

Nor there.

"We hire good-looking people in our stores . . . because good-looking people attract other good-looking people, and we want to market to cool, good-looking people. We don't market to anyone other than that."

Interestingly enough, Jeffries's comments didn't receive a fraction of the attention in 2006 that his new remarks did in 2013. That's when, amid discussion of A&F's declining stock price, Abercrombie said that the company did not wish to sell clothing to women with a physical stature beyond size "large." The old quotes were dug up from the pages of an "old-school" magazine interview and put on full display in the "new-school" social world. Not surprisingly, given the polarizing nature of the comments, Jeffries's words went viral.

But they actually went viral in two different ways. The first criticisms came from social activists who found Jeffries and his company to be insensitive and discriminatory. The individuals who made up this group created digital petitions, wrote letters, and made YouTube videos boycotting A&F's clothing. The second group? Wall Street, as analysts questioned whether Jeffries's refusal to manufacture and sell clothing to plus-size women was a sound business decision given that the plus-size women's apparel market generated over $13 billion in retail sales between March 2012 and March 2013. In addition, A&F had been losing share to brands like American Eagle, H&M, and Old Navy—the latter two both carrying plus-size clothes.

Children are also protected from the potential influences of commercials by network censors and industry self-regulatory groups such as the Council of Better Business Bureaus's Children's Advertising Review Unit (CARU). CARU has strict self-regulatory guidelines regarding the type of appeals, product presentation and claims, and disclosures and disclaimers, and the use of premiums, safety, and techniques such as special effects and animation. Commercial Alert's Parents' Bill of Rights is shown in Figure 21–5.

As we saw in Chapter 20, the major networks also have strict guidelines for ads targeted to children. For example, in network TV ads, only 10 seconds can be devoted to animation and special effects; the final 5 seconds are reserved for

© Craig Warga/Bloomberg/Getty Images

Perhaps the worst part about Jeffries's words, however, wasn't necessarily *what* he said seven years before (as insensitive as it may have been perceived), but that he did nothing toward retracting the comments. His refusal to comment on the matter likely meant that nothing would change.

But for anyone who truly knows the A&F brand, none of this should come as a surprise. After all, this is a company that for years produced a quarterly fashion catalog (called *Quarterly*) that often featured nude young adult models in sexually explicit poses along with numerous accompanying articles about sex. It reluctantly stopped producing the catalog in 2003 in response to protests and potential boycotts of Abercrombie products. In 2011 the company offered to pay MTV show *Jersey Shore* to stop putting its characters in Abercrombie apparel—particularly Mike "The Situation" Sorrentino—as his wearing the clothing could cause the brand "significant damage." (Mike's only response was to tweet "Looks like Abercrombie got themselves into a situation.") In 2012, *Bloomberg News* published a story about Jeffries's 40-page "Aircraft Standards" manual that detailed how he wished to be served aboard the company's G550 corporate jet. In case you're wondering, the CEO requested that "clean shaven males [wear] a uniform of Abercrombie polo shirts, boxer briefs, flip-flops, and a 'spritz' of A&F cologne," among many other practices.

Clearly, both Jeffries and his company have not lacked for head-scratching, controversial actions over the past two decades, some feel as a strategy to gain free publicity. But what Jeffries may not realize is that

times have changed since the controversy surrounding *Quarterly* in 2003 and his comments in 2006, and even 2011. *Quarterly*, at its peak, sold roughly 200,000 copies of each issue before suspending production. Compare that to Abercrombie's 400,000-plus Twitter followers and 7.6 million Facebook fans (as of this writing), and it's clear that in today's world nothing goes unnoticed. One incensed male created a video in which he is shown giving A&F clothing to the homeless (among others who might be perceived by Jeffries as "uncool"). The video quickly received over a million views. Numerous celebrities including Ellen, Kirstie Alley, and Miley Cyrus threatened boycotts or said they would burn their A&F clothes. After the publicity, attitudes toward the brand among Abercrombie's core market of 18- to 34-year-olds took a hit, while H&M received a boost. By 2016, when the American Customer Satisfaction Index was released, Abercrombie & Fitch received the lowest customer satisfaction ratings in the history of that measurement system, and sales continued to decline. Maybe Jeffries would have been wiser to think a little harder about his actions and business decisions, or the brand known for pushing the envelope just may have pushed it too far.

And then there is American Apparel. Without going into great lengths about its advertising, suffice it to say that it pretty much mirrored that of A&F in regard to sexuality and controversy. Many of American Apparel's ads were banned in a variety of countries, and seemingly all were controversial. A Google search will reveal just how many. Unfortunately, American Apparel image and sales also mirrored those of A&F, as in 2013 American Apparel reported a net loss of $106.3 million, after a 2012 loss of $106 million. By December 2014, CEO Dov Charney was gone—fired. Maybe the old phrase "sex sells" isn't right after all. Or maybe they just both went too far.

Sources: Barbara Farfan, "Brand Image vs Brand Reality in Mike Jeffries Led Abercrombie & Fitch," June 4, 2016, www.retailindustryabout.com; Jessica Goldstein, "American Apparel Fires Controversial CEO Accused of Sexual Harrassment, Hires Woman Instead," December 17, 2014, www.thinkprogress.org; Nico Amarca, "20 Controversial Ads That Defined American Apparel (NSFW)," October 7, 2015, www.highsnobiety.com; Barbara Thau, "Why Floundering Abercrombie Should Reconsider Snubbing the Full-Figure Set," May 10, 2013, www.forbes.com; Barbara Thau, "Embattled Abercrombie CEO Backpedals on Exclusionary Comments," May 17, 2013, www.adweek.com; Barbara Thau, "Man Strikes Back at Abercrombie & Fitch by Giving Its Clothes to the Homeless," May 15, 2013, www.adweek.com; Ann Oldenburg, "*Jersey Shore* Boys Fire Back at Abercrombie," August 18, 2011, www.usatoday.com.

displaying all the toys shown in the ad and disclosing whether they are sold separately and whether accessories such as batteries are included.[36]

Concerns over advertising and other forms of promotion directed at children diminished somewhat during the late 1990s and the early part of the new decade. However, the issue has once again begun receiving a considerable amount of attention as various groups are calling for restrictions on advertising targeted to children. The American Psychological Association (APA), the nation's largest organization of psychologists, issued a report criticizing the increasing commercialization of childhood and calling for new curbs on marketing aimed at children.[37] The APA report faulted marketers for taking advantage of an ever-fragmenting media landscape of

Commercial Alert's
PARENTS' BILL OF RIGHTS

WHEREAS, the nurturing of character and strong values in children is one of the most important functions of any society;

WHEREAS, the primary responsibility for the upbringing of children resides in their parents;

WHEREAS, an aggressive commercial culture has invaded the relationship between parents and children, and has impeded the ability of parents to guide the upbringing of their own children;

WHEREAS, corporate marketers have sought increasingly to bypass parents, and speak directly to children in order to tempt them with the most sophisticated tools that advertising executives, market researchers and psychologists can devise;

WHEREAS, these marketers tend to glorify materialism, addiction, hedonism, violence and anti-social behavior, all of which are abhorrent to most parents;

WHEREAS, parents find themselves locked in constant battle with this pervasive influence, and are hard pressed to keep the commercial culture and its degraded values out of their children's lives;

WHEREAS, the aim of this corporate marketing is to turn children into agents of corporations in the home, so that they will nag their parents for the things they see advertised, thus sowing strife, stress and misery in the family;

WHEREAS, the products advertised generally are ones parents themselves would not choose for their children: violent and sexually suggestive entertainment, video games, alcohol, tobacco, gambling and junk food;

WHEREAS, this aggressive commercial influence has contributed to an epidemic of marketing-related diseases in children, such as obesity, type 2 diabetes, alcoholism, anorexia and bulimia, while millions will eventually die from the marketing of tobacco;

WHEREAS, corporations have latched onto the schools and compulsory school laws as a way to bypass parents and market their products and values to a captive audience of impressionable and trusting children;

WHEREAS, these corporations ultimately are creatures of state law, and it is intolerable that they should use the rights and powers so granted for the purpose of undermining the authority of parents in these ways;

- -

THEREFORE, BE IT RESOLVED, that the U.S. Congress and the fifty state legislatures should right the balance between parents and corporations and restore to parents some measure of control over the commercial influences on their children, by enacting this Parents' Bill of Rights, including,

- -

Leave Children Alone Act. This act bans television advertising aimed at children under 12 years of age. (federal)

Child Privacy Act. This act restores to parents the ability to safeguard the privacy of their own children. It gives parents the right to control any commercial use of personal information concerning their children, and the right to know precisely how such information is used. (federal, state)

Advertising to Children Accountability Act. This act helps parents affix individual responsibility for attempts to subject their children to commercial influence. It requires corporations to disclose who created each of their advertisements, and who did the market research for each ad directed at children under 12 years of age. (federal)

Commercial-Free Schools Act. Corporations have turned the public schools into advertising free-fire zones. This act prohibits corporations from using the schools and compulsory school laws to bypass parents and pitch their products to impressionable schoolchildren. (federal, state)

Fairness Doctrine for Parents. This act provides parents with the opportunity to talk back to the media and the advertisers. It makes the Fairness Doctrine apply to all advertising to children under 12 years of age, providing parents and community with response time on broadcast TV and radio for advertising to children. (federal)

Product Placement Disclosure Act. This law gives parents more information with which to monitor the influences that prey upon their children through the media. Specifically, it requires corporations to disclose, on packaging and at the outset, any and all product placements on television and videos, and in movies, video games and books. This prevents advertisers from sneaking ads into media that parents assume to be ad-free. (federal)

Child Harm Disclosure Act. Parents have a right to know of any significant health effects of products they might purchase for their children. This act creates a legal duty for corporations to publicly disclose all information suggesting that their product(s) could substantially harm the health of children. (federal)

Children's Food Labeling Act. Parents have a right to information about the food that corporations push upon their children. This act requires fast food restaurant chains to label contents of food, and provide basic nutritional information about it. (federal, state)

Children's Advertising Subsidy Revocation Act. It is intolerable that the federal government actually rewards corporations with a big tax write-off for the money they spend on psychologists, market researchers, ad agencies, media and the like in their campaigns to instill their values in our children. This act eliminates all federal subsidies, deductions and preferences for advertising aimed at children under 12 years of age. (federal)

- -

Please make copies of the Parents' Bill of Rights, and give or mail them to your members of Congress, state legislators and candidates. Ask them to turn the provisions into law. Distribute this at day care centers, schools, churches, synagogues, coffee shops, grocery stores and other places where parents gather. Call 503.235.8012 to volunteer or to find out how you can help enact the Parents' Bill of Rights into law.

Commercial Alert • www.commercialalert.org • 4110 SE Hawthorne Blvd. #123, Portland, OR 97214-5246 • 503.235.8012

cable channels and the Internet to target children. The report noted that marketing activities focused on America's youth have reached unprecedented levels and called for restrictions on advertising in TV programming that appeals primarily to children under the age of eight and a total ban on advertising in programs aimed at very young children in this group. The report also found that the Internet is a particularly effective, and thus potentially harmful, means of sending advertising messages to children as websites often blur or even ignore the boundaries between commercial and noncommercial content. Marketing and advertising trade groups have been critical of the report and continue to defend their right to advertise on the basis that parents of younger children, rather than the children themselves, make purchase decisions.[38]

In addition to concerns over the increasing amount of advertising targeted to children, there are a number of other issues that consumer groups and regulatory agencies have raised with respect to young people. These include an increase in the number of ads encouraging children to call 900 numbers, and general concerns over the content of children's programming, particularly with regard to violence. The marketing of violent entertainment to minors and the advertising practices and rating systems of the film, music, and electronic game industries are also being monitored very carefully. The issue of what young consumers are watching, listening to, communicating, and playing and how much violence that entertainment contains became an area of great concern following a flurry of shootings at schools.

As discussed in the previous chapter, there is also growing concern over how marketers are using the Internet and social media to communicate with and sell to children. Studies have claimed that advertisers avoid many of the regulations designed to protect children by advertising on the Internet and mobile instead of traditional media. Noting that the Internet is less regulated, one study claims that advertising regulators are failing to protect children who are the targets of aggressive marketing through ads as well as in Internet video games.[39] Another study demonstrated that children and youth can be reached through games, ads, brand pages, and social networking sites, and as a result, marketers have increased their efforts to reach these groups.[40] The study argues that these efforts may be even more fruitful than TV given the stronger attraction to online activities.

Advertising to children will remain a controversial topic. Some groups feel that the government is responsible for protecting children from the potentially harmful effects of advertising and other forms of promotion, while others argue that parents are ultimately responsible for doing so.

It is important to many companies to communicate directly with children. However, only by being sensitive to the naiveté of children as consumers will they be able to do so freely and avoid potential conflict with those who believe children should be protected from advertising and other forms of promotion.

Social and Cultural Consequences

Concern is often expressed over the impact of advertising on society, particularly on values and lifestyles. While a number of factors influence the cultural values, lifestyles, and behavior of a society, the overwhelming amount of advertising and its prevalence in the mass media lead many critics to argue that advertising plays a major role in influencing and transmitting social values. In his book *Advertising and Social Change*, Ronald Berman says:

> The institutions of family, religion, and education have grown noticeably weaker over each of the past three generations. The world itself seems to have grown more complex. In the absence of traditional authority, advertising has become a kind of social guide. It depicts us in all the myriad situations possible to a life of free choice. It provides ideas about style, morality, behavior.[41]

Mike Hughes, president and creative director of the Martin Agency, notes that advertising has a major impact on society: "Ads help establish what is cool in

CHAPTER 21

society; their messages contribute to the public dialogue. Gap ads show white, black, and Hispanic kids dancing together. Hilfiger ads showed it's cool for people to get along. IKEA showed a gay couple." He argues that advertising agencies have a social and ethical responsibility to consider the impact of the advertising messages they create for their clients.[42] Gap, JCPenney, McDonald's, Levis, and Amazon Kindle have all produced ads that are lesbian, gay, bisexual, and transgender friendly.[43]

While there is general agreement that advertising is an important social influence agent, opinions as to the value of its contribution are often negative. Advertising is criticized for encouraging materialism, manipulating consumers to buy things they do not really need, perpetuating stereotypes, and controlling the media.

Advertising Encourages Materialism   Many critics claim advertising has an adverse effect on consumer values by encouraging **materialism**, a preoccupation with material things rather than intellectual or spiritual concerns. They argue that a major contributor to materialism is advertising that

- Seeks to create needs rather than merely showing how a product or service fulfills them.
- Surrounds consumers with images of the good life and suggests the acquisition of material possessions leads to contentment and happiness and adds to the joy of living.
- Suggests material possessions are symbols of status, success, and accomplishment and/or will lead to greater social acceptance, popularity, sex appeal, and so on.

Advertising for products such as expensive automobiles and luxury goods like clothing, jewelry, and alcoholic beverages is often criticized for promoting materialistic values (Exhibit 21–9).

This criticism of advertising assumes that materialism is undesirable and is sought at the expense of other goals. But many believe materialism is an acceptable part of the **Protestant ethic**, which stresses hard work and individual effort and initiative and views the accumulation of material possessions as evidence of success. Others argue that the acquisition of material possessions has positive economic impact by encouraging consumers to keep consuming after their basic needs are met. Many Americans believe economic growth is essential and materialism is both a necessity and an inevitable part of this progress.

It has also been argued that an emphasis on material possessions does not rule out interest in intellectual, spiritual, or cultural values. Defenders of advertising say consumers can be more interested in higher-order goals when basic needs have been met and point out that consumers may purchase material things in the pursuit of nonmaterial goals. For example, a person may buy an expensive stereo system to enjoy music rather than simply to impress someone or acquire a material possession.

Even if we assume materialism is undesirable, there is still the question of whether advertising is responsible for creating and encouraging it. While many critics argue that advertising is a major contributing force to materialistic values, others say advertising merely reflects the values of society rather than shaping them.[44] They argue that consumers' values are defined by the society in which they live and are the results of extensive, long-term socialization or acculturation.

The argument that advertising is responsible for creating a materialistic and hedonistic society is addressed by Stephen Fox in his book *The Mirror Makers: A History of American Advertising and Its Creators.* Fox concludes advertising has become

EXHIBIT 21–9

Critics argue that advertising contributes to materialistic values

© Rolls-Royce Motor Cars NA, LLC

Rolls-Royce
Like nothing else on earth

Some people say that advertising determines America's tastes.
Which is another way of saying that advertising determines *your* tastes.
Which is, in turn, another way of saying that you don't have a mind of your own.
Well, time and time again the advertising industry has found that you do have a mind of your own. If a product doesn't interest you, you simply don't buy it.
And if the product's advertising doesn't interest you, you don't buy that either.
Think of it as a sort of natural selection.

Good products and good advertising survive. Bad products and bad advertising perish. All according to the decisions you make in the marketplace.
So we've concluded that advertising is a mirror of society's tastes. Not vice versa.
Our conclusion is based on a great deal of thought. And many years of reflection.

ADVERTISING.
ANOTHER WORD FOR FREEDOM OF CHOICE.
American Association of Advertising Agencies

EXHIBIT 21–10

The advertising industry argues that advertising reflects society

Source: American Association of Advertising Agencies

a prime scapegoat for our times and merely reflects society. Regarding the effect of advertising on cultural values, he says:

> To blame advertising now for those most basic tendencies in American history is to miss the point. It is too obvious, too easy, a matter of killing the messenger instead of dealing with the bad news. The people who have created modern advertising are not hidden persuaders pushing our buttons in the service of some malevolent purpose. They are just producing an especially visible manifestation, good and bad, of the American way of life.[45]

The ad shown in Exhibit 21–10 was developed by the American Association of Advertising Agencies (4As) and suggests that advertising is a reflection of society's tastes and values, not vice versa. The ad was part of a campaign that addressed criticisms of advertising.

Individuals from a variety of backgrounds are concerned over the values they see driving our society. They believe that materialism, greed, and selfishness increasingly dominate American life and that advertising is a major reason for these undesirable values. The extent to which advertising is responsible for materialism and the desirability of such values are deep philosophical issues that will continue to be part of the debate over the societal value and consequences of advertising.

Advertising Makes People Buy Things They Don't Need   A common criticism of advertising is that it manipulates consumers into buying things they do not need. Many critics say advertising should just provide information useful in making purchase decisions and should not attempt to persuade. They view information advertising (which reports price, performance, and other objective criteria) as desirable but persuasive advertising (which plays on consumers' emotions, anxieties, and psychological needs and desires such as status, self-esteem, and attractiveness) as unacceptable. Persuasive advertising is criticized for fostering discontent among consumers and encouraging them to purchase products and services to solve deeper problems.

Defenders of advertising offer a number of rebuttals to these criticisms. First, they point out that a substantial amount of advertising is essentially informational in nature. Also, it is difficult to separate desirable informational advertising from undesirable persuasive advertising. Shelby Hunt, in examining the *information-persuasion dichotomy*, points out that even advertising that most observers would categorize as very informative is often very persuasive. He says, "If advertising critics really believe that persuasive advertising should not be permitted, they are actually proposing that no advertising be allowed, since the purpose of all advertising is to persuade."[46]

Defenders of advertising also take issue with the argument that it should be limited to dealing with basic functional needs. In our society, most lower-level needs recognized in Maslow's hierarchy, such as the need for food, clothing, and shelter, are satisfied for most people. It is natural to move from basic needs to higher-order ones such as self-esteem and status or self-actualization. Consumers are free to choose the degree to which they attempt to satisfy their desires, and wise advertisers associate their products and services with the satisfaction of higher-order needs.

Proponents of advertising offer two other defenses against the charge that advertising makes people buy things they do not really need. First, this criticism attributes too much power to advertising and assumes consumers have no ability to defend themselves against it. Second, it ignores the fact that consumers have the freedom to make their own choices when confronted with persuasive advertising. While they readily admit the persuasive intent of their business, advertisers are quick to note it is extremely difficult to make consumers purchase a product they do not want or for which they do not see a personal benefit. If advertising were as powerful as the critics claim, we would not see products with multimillion-dollar advertising budgets

DESPITE WHAT SOME PEOPLE THINK, ADVERTISING CAN'T MAKE YOU BUY SOMETHING YOU DON'T NEED.

Some people would have you believe that you are putty in the hands of every advertiser in the country.

They think that when advertising is put under your nose, your mind turns to oatmeal.

It's mass hypnosis. Subliminal seduction. Brain washing. Mind control. It's advertising.

And you are a pushover for it.

It explains why your kitchen cupboard is full of food you never eat.

Why your garage is full of cars you never drive.

Why your house is full of books you don't read, TV's you don't watch, beds you don't use, and clothes you don't wear.

You don't have a choice. You are forced to buy.

That's why this message is a cleverly disguised advertisement to get you to buy land in the tropics.

Got you again, didn't we? Send in your money.

ADVERTISING

ANOTHER WORD FOR FREEDOM OF CHOICE.

American Association of Advertising Agencies

EXHIBIT 21–11

The 4As responds to the claim that advertising makes consumers buy things they do not need

Source: American Association of Advertising Agencies

failing in the marketplace. The reality is that consumers do have a choice and they are not being forced to buy. Consumers ignore ads for products and services they do not really need or that fail to interest them (see Exhibit 21–11).

Advertising and Stereotyping Advertising is often accused of creating and perpetuating stereotypes through its portrayal of women, ethnic minorities, and other groups.

Women As you have read, the portrayal of women in advertising is an issue that has received a great deal of attention through the years. In addition to the sexual portrayals discussed, advertising has received much criticism for stereotyping women and failing to recognize the changing role of women in our society. Critics have argued that advertising often depicts women as preoccupied with beauty, household duties, and motherhood or shows them as decorative objects or sexually provocative figures. Various research studies conducted through the years show a consistent picture of gender stereotyping that has varied little over time. Portrayals of adult women in American television and print advertising have emphasized passivity, deference, lack of intelligence and credibility, and punishment for high levels of effort. In contrast, men have been portrayed as constructive, powerful, autonomous, and achieving.[47]

Research on gender stereotyping in advertising targeted to children has found a pattern of results similar to that reported for adults. A study found sex-role stereotyping in television advertising targeted at children in the United States as well as in Australia.[48] Boys are generally shown as being more knowledgeable, active, aggressive, and instrumental than girls. Nonverbal behaviors involving dominance and control are associated more with boys than girls. Advertising directed toward children has also been shown to feature more boys than girls, to position boys in more dominant, active roles, and to use male voiceovers more frequently than female ones.[49] A study examining race and gender stereotyping of children's advertising on the Turner Cartoon Network found that the primary target for most of the commercials was active, white boys. Girls were portrayed in traditional roles and shown performing limited passive, indoor activities, while boys were shown in the outdoor world engaging in more exciting and active things.[50]

Feminist groups such as the National Organization for Women (NOW) and the Sexual Assault Prevention and Awareness Center argue that advertising that portrays women as sex objects contributes to violence against women. These groups often protest to advertisers and their agencies about ads they find insulting to women and have even called for boycotts against offending advertisers. NOW has also been critical of advertisers for the way they portray women in advertising for clothing, cosmetics, and other products. The organization feels that many of these ads contribute to the epidemic of eating disorders and smoking among women and girls who hope such means will help them control their weight.[51]

As seen, while sexism and stereotyping still exist, advertising's portrayal of women is improving in many areas. Many advertisers have begun to recognize the importance of portraying women realistically. The increase in the number of working women has resulted not only in women having more influence in family decision making but also in more single-female households, which means more independent purchasers.

Researchers Steven Kates and Glenda Shaw-Garlock argue that the transformed social positioning of women in North American society is perhaps the most important social development of this century.[52] They note that as women have crossed the boundary from the domestic sphere to the professional arena, expectations

and representations of women have changed as well. For example, a number of magazines, such as *Ms.* and *Working Mother*, now incorporate and appeal to the sociocultural shifts in women's lives. Many advertisers are now depicting women in a diversity of roles that reflect their changing place in society. In many ads, the stereotypic character traits attributed to women have shifted from weak and dependent to strong and autonomous. The ad for Network Solutions shown in Exhibit 21–12 is an example of how advertisers are changing the way they portray women in their ads. One reason for these changes is the emergence of females in key agency roles. Women advertising executives are likely to be more sensitive to the portrayal of their own gender and to strengthen the role of women beyond stereotypical housewives or a position of subservience to men.[53]

African Americans and Hispanics African Americans and Hispanics have also been the target of stereotyping in advertising. For many years, advertisers virtually ignored all nonwhite ethnic groups as identifiable subcultures and viable markets. Ads were rarely targeted to these ethnic groups, and the use of blacks and Hispanics as spokespeople, communicators, models, or actors in ads was very limited.

One study of minorities in magazine print ads showed that 83.8 percent of all models used were Caucasian, 9.5 percent African American, and 6.6 percent Asian American. While this study concluded that Asian Americans were overrepresented relative to the percentage of this ethnicity in the United States, it also showed that the variety of roles in which they were depicted and the variety of magazines were restricted. Asians were more likely to appear in science, business, and technology media and typically in nonworking decorative roles.[54] The study was consistent with a previous study conducted by Taylor et al. five years earlier.[55] A study conducted in the UK indicated that black, Asian, or other ethnic minority groups appeared in only 5 percent of 35,000 commercials aired, even though these groups constituted 13 percent of the UK population.

EXHIBIT 21–12

Many advertisers now portray women in powerful roles

Source: Network Solutions LLC

EXHIBIT 21–13

Many marketers are creating ads specifically for the African American market

Source: Levi Strauss & Co.

Ads are increasingly likely to be racially integrated. As seen in Digital and Social Media Perspective 21–1, advertisers have begun breaking the taboo against suggesting interracial attraction. A number of companies now run interracial ads—but not without risk. Advertisers are also finding that advertising developed specifically for the African American market, such as the Levi's ad shown in Exhibit 21–13, is an effective way of reaching this ethnic market. A study by Corliss L. Green found that ads targeting African Americans through racially targeted media, especially with race-based products, benefit from featuring African American models with a dominant presence in the ad.[56]

There is little question that advertising has been guilty of stereotyping women and ethnic groups in the past and, in some cases, still does

Digital and Social Media Perspective 21–1 > > >

HOW FAR HAVE WE COME ON RACIAL EQUALITY?

"The times, they are a changing." These famous song lyrics were written by singer Bob Dylan over 40 years ago to reflect that events were taking place in America that would change the future of the country. At the time, Dylan probably hoped—but never realized—that these words would become prophetic. Well, for many of us, but not all.

A relatively unassuming commercial called "Just Checking" featuring an interracial family with a little girl expressing concern for her father's health was aired in 2013—almost exactly 40 years to the day of Dylan's song release—by Cheerios. Yes, Cheerios, the cereal, not some edgy brand trying to get attention. (The iconic Cheerios brand has been around since 1945!) And, even though the United States has had a black president for two terms, there are still many out there who apparently haven't gotten Dylan's message. The response to the commercial, which was viewed over 2 million times on YouTube, received such racist and vitriolic feedback that General Mills had to disable the comments section of the posting. As noted by media and pop culture columnist Barbara Lippert, "A progressive-looking commercial collides with the ugliness of the Internet." At the same time, it should be reported that while comments referring to Nazis, "troglodytes," and even "racial genocide" were way too frequent, there were also many positive reactions to the commercial commending the brand for being progressive, timely, and considerate. Within a few days, Cheerio's Facebook page was flooded with positive comments praising the ad, with more than a million "likes," and YouTube ratings reflected over 21,000 "thumbs up" compared to less than 1,500 "thumbs down."

Three years later Old Navy received a similar reaction to its ad. The ad was simply supposed to promote a sale—30 percent off an entire Old Navy purchase. But some took the ad, which featured an interracial family, to promote a larger message on race. Social media users took to Twitter, calling the ad "absolutely disgusting" and supportive of "the genocide of the white race" and threatened to boycott the store. Old Navy was not backing down and gave this response: "We are a brand with a proud history of championing diversity and inclusion. At Old Navy, everyone is welcome." Even Senator John McCain's son—a Navy helicopter pilot whose wife is African American—responded to the racial accusations of "miscegenation," "anti-white propaganda," and "white genocide" being levied against Old Navy, calling them "ignorant racists." Later, Swift McCain tweeted a photo of herself and her husband with the caption: "I was just in @OldNavy this weekend! Bought something for me and my husband. #LoveWins." As with the Cheerios ad, the number of positive responses far outnumbered the negative ones—with many posting pictures of their interracial families online.

So what do you do if you are Old Navy or General Mills? Well—according to most marketing experts—the right thing. Other than disabling the comments section on the YouTube video, Cheerios stood by the spot, keeping it on the air, as well as on YouTube. As noted by Camille Gibson, vice president of marketing for Cheerios, in an e-mail comment, "There are many kinds of families, and Cheerios celebrates them all." Gibson explained that the comments section on the YouTube video was disabled because Cheerios is a family brand and not all of the comments were family-friendly. Navy stuck by its position stating that it was proud of the ad, calling it a message of diversity and inclusion.

Praise from the marketing community was overwhelmingly positive. (While some skeptics wondered if "Just

---

so. But as the role of women changes, advertisers are changing their portrayals to remain accurate and appeal to their target audience. Advertisers are also trying to increase the incidence of minority groups in ads while avoiding stereotypes and negative role portrayals. They are being careful to avoid ethnic stereotyping and striving to develop advertising that has specific appeals to various ethnic groups. Increases in the size and purchasing power of ethnic minorities are leading companies to give more attention to multicultural marketing.

Other Groups While the focus here has been on women and ethnic minorities, some other groups feel they are victims of stereotyping by advertisers. Many groups in our society are battling against stereotyping and discrimination, and companies must consider whether their ads might offend them. Creative personnel in agencies sometimes feel restricted as their ideas are squelched out of concern that they might offend someone or be misinterpreted. However, advertisers must be sensitive to the portrayal of specific types of people in their ads, for both ethical and commercial reasons. For example, both Volkswagen and General Motors received protests from mental health groups over commercials considered insensitive to the problem of suicide. The Volkswagen spot showed a young man about to commit

Old Navy Official ✓
@OldNavy

Oh, happy day! Our #ThankYouEvent is finally here. Take 30% off your entire purchase: oldnvy.me/1LUMNBd

Source: Old Navy

Checking" was an attempt to get attention, they were few and far between.) Allen Adamson, managing director of Landor Associates, told *CBS News* that he applauded General Mills for standing by the ad, noting that "the traditional approach depicting the old 'Leave It to Beaver' family, while offending no one, is not very realistic." Meagan

Hatcher-Mays, a celebrity fashion columnist, in a post on Jezebel commented, "this commercial is a huge step for interracial families like mine who want to be seen in public together and maybe eat some heart-healthy snacks." Numerous others took the same position, commending and cheering on Cheerios marketers for their actions. Old Navy received similar acclaim.

But in marketing, we also have to look at the bottom line. How did the commercials impact the brands? Besides the millions of exposures the brands received on social media, the publicity surrounding the ads and the brands was enormous. In many cases those posting said the ads made them want to shop in the stores even more than before. But cultural strategist Denitria Lewis seemed to imply that the ads can cut both ways. Lewis notes that for some "It's frightening to see a couple that is antithesis of what you think a wholesome family would be. I don't know if the general public is prepared to have their brands tell them how to live." Lewis also stated that there are many people who believe we live in a post racism society, but "If you pay only a modest bit of the attention to the news, you know we don't." And for those who still don't like the idea of being interracial, those who portray themselves as supporting this position are likely to lose their support.

So while all of the negativity generated by the commercials actually resulted in many good things for both Old Navy and Cheerios, the fact remains that all is not well that ends well. As noted by Charles Malik Whitfield, the father in the Cheerios ad, "Let's not pretend racism doesn't exist. Let's not pretend that we've come so far." We wonder what Bob Dylan would think.

Sources: Christopher Heine, "Cheerios' Interracial Ad Spiked Its Online Branding by 77%," www.adweek.com, June 7, 2013; Bruce Horovitz, "Hate Talk Won't Derail Mixed-Race Cheerios Ad," www.USAtoday.com, June 3, 2013; Morgan Whitaker, "Interracial Family in Cheerios Ad Sparks Online Backlash," www.morganwinn.com, June 3, 2013; Sheila Shayon, "General Mills Cheered for Defying Racial Backlash over Cheerios Ad," www.brandchannel.com, June 6, 2013; Stacy Lambe, "An Internet High-Five to Cheerios for Showcasing Diverse Families," www.qeerty.com, June 2, 2013.

suicide by jumping off a roof after he is seen expressing his unhappiness with the state of the world, but ultimately opts not to do so after he learns that there are three VW models available for under $17,000. Volkswagen ended up pulling the spot after receiving protests from a number of suicide prevention groups.[57] The General Motors ad, which premiered on the Super Bowl, created a controversy by showing a robot that gets fired for dropping a bolt on the assembly line, takes a succession of lesser jobs, and eventually jumps off a bridge in despair. GM agreed to change the ad, which was designed to show the company's obsession with product quality, after discussing concerns about it with the American Foundation for Suicide Prevention.[58]

One area where significant changes have taken place recently is in advertising targeted to gay and LGBT consumers. In 1995 IKEA broke new ground with a TV commercial featuring a gay couple shopping for furniture. Target and Subaru have also aired gay-friendly ads, as have Kohl's, Tylenol, and Campbell's Soup, among many others. For years, beer companies targeted this market by placing ads in local gay media to support or sponsor AIDS awareness, Gay Pride festivals, and the Gay Games. A number of beer companies, including Anheuser-Busch and MillerCoors, now run gay-specific, brand-specific ads in national gay publications.

More advertisers are turning to gay themes in their mainstream commercials, though often subtly. (Interestingly, sometimes ads are perceived as targeting gays when that was not the intention, resulting in very positive feedback from this segment nevertheless.) However, few run these ads on network television; they limit them to spot TV and local stations in more gay-friendly cities such as New York, Los Angeles, and San Francisco. The Miller Brewing Co. took a bold step by airing one of the first gay-themed commercials on network television. One ad was for Miller Lite beer and showed a gay couple holding hands in a straight bar to the dismay of two women who are interested in them. Levi Strauss created a spot with alternative endings, one of which was designed to appeal to the gay market. The spot featured a young, attractive male in his second-floor apartment slipping on his Levi's. The motion of yanking up his jeans inexplicably causes the street below his apartment to get pulled up as well, crashing through his floor and bringing with it an attractive female in a telephone booth who he walks away with. In a version of the ad that aired on Logo, MTV's gay cable network seen in more than 27 million homes, an attractive man is in the phone booth and the two men run off together in the same manner as their heterosexual counterparts.[59]

Like the interracial discussion earlier in this chapter, not everyone approves of gay and LGBT ads, however. An emotional 90-second McDonald's video for McCafe that was posted on the company's Facebook page in Taiwan that depicted a young man coming out to his father video was viewed more than 3.6 million times, with the original post gaining more than 92,000 likes and 11,800 shares. However, an anti-gay religious group called for a boycott of the video saying it was inappropriate since many children eat at McDonald's (Exhibit 21–14).

Advertising and the Media   The fact that advertising plays such an important role in financing the media has led to concern that advertisers may influence or even control the media. It is well documented that *economic censorship* occurs, whereby the media avoid certain topics or even present biased news coverage, in acquiescence to advertiser demands.[60] In fact, Professors Lawrence Soley and Robert Craig say, "The assertion that advertisers attempt to influence what the public sees, hears, and reads in the mass media is perhaps the most damning of all criticisms of advertising, but this criticism isn't acknowledged in most advertising textbooks."[61] We will address this important issue in this book by considering arguments on both sides.

Arguments Supporting Advertiser Control Advertising is the primary source of revenue for nearly all the news and entertainment media in the United States. Some critics charge that the media's dependence on advertisers' support makes them susceptible to various forms of influence, including exerting control over the editorial content of magazines and newspapers; biasing editorial opinions to favor the position of an advertiser; limiting coverage of a controversial story that might reflect negatively on a company; and influencing the news and program content of television.

Newspapers and magazines receive nearly 70 percent of their revenue from advertising; commercial TV and radio derive virtually all their income from advertisers. Advertising in digital media is increasing at a rapid rate. Small, financially insecure newspapers, magazines, or broadcast stations are the most susceptible to pressure from advertisers, particularly companies that account for a large amount of the media outlet's advertising revenue. In some local markets, automobile and furniture advertisers may constitute as much as 80 percent of the TV stations' ad revenues. As you might imagine, the stations may tread lightly when reporting news that does not portray these industries positively. A local newspaper may be reluctant to print an unfavorable story about a car dealer or supermarket chain on whose advertising it depends. For example, a number of years ago more than 40 car dealers canceled their ads in the *San Jose Mercury News* when the paper printed an article titled "A Car Buyer's Guide to Sanity." The dealers objected to the tone of the article, which they felt implied consumers should consider car dealers unethical adversaries in the negotiation process.[62] A study by Soontae An and Lori Bergen surveyed advertising directors at 219 daily newspapers in the United States and found frequent conflicts between the business side and editorial side of the newspaper operations. Advertising directors at small newspapers or chain-owned newspapers were more likely to endorse scenarios where editorial integrity was compromised to please, or refrain from offending, their advertisers.[63]

Individual TV stations and even the major networks also can be influenced by advertisers. Programming decisions are made largely on the basis of what shows will attract the most viewers and thus be most desirable to advertisers. Critics say this often results in lower-quality television as educational, cultural, and informative programming is usually sacrificed for shows that get high ratings and appeal to the mass markets. It is well recognized that advertisers often avoid TV shows that deal with controversial issues. Most advertisers also have contract stipulations allowing them to cancel a media buy if, after prescreening a show, they are uncomfortable with its content or feel sponsorship of it may reflect poorly on their company.

Advertisers have also been accused of pressuring the networks to change their programming. Many advertisers have withdrawn commercials from programs that contain too much sex or violence, often in response to threatened boycotts of their products by consumers if they advertise on these shows. For example, groups such as the American Family Association have been fighting sex and violence in TV programs by calling for boycotts. A number of companies, including Procter & Gamble, Mars Inc., and Kraft Foods, pulled their advertising from certain shows while others have not responded to their actions.

Arguments against Advertiser Control The commercial media's dependence on advertising means advertisers can exert influence on their character, content, and coverage of certain issues. However, media executives offer several reasons why advertisers do not exert undue influence over the media.

First, they point out it is in the best interest of the media not to be influenced too much by advertisers. To retain public confidence, they must report the news fairly and accurately without showing bias or attempting to avoid controversial issues. Media executives point to the vast array of topics they cover and the investigative reporting they often do as evidence of their objectivity. They want to build a large audience for their publications or stations so that they can charge more for advertising space and time.

Media executives also note that an advertiser needs the media more than they need any individual advertiser, particularly when the medium has a large audience or does a good job of reaching a specific market segment. Many publications and stations have a broad base of advertising support and can afford to lose an advertiser that attempts to exert too much influence. This is particularly true for the larger, more established, financially secure media. For example, a consumer-product company would find it difficult to reach its target audience without network TV and could not afford to boycott a network if it disagreed with a station's editorial policy or program content. Even the local advertiser in a small community may be dependent on the local newspaper, since it may be the most cost-effective media option available.

Most magazine and newspaper publishers insist they do not allow advertiser pressure to influence their editorial content. They argue that they have long regarded the formal separation of their news and business departments as essential to their independence and credibility. This separation is often referred to as "The Wall" and is often spoken of with a mixture of reverence and trepidation.[64] Many magazines and newspapers have traditionally discouraged employees on the publishing side—including advertising, circulation, and other business departments—from interacting with those on the editorial side, who write and edit the articles. This is done by separating editorial and advertising offices, barring the sales force from reading articles before they are printed, and prohibiting editorial employees from participating in advertising sales calls.

Most print media are very concerned over maintaining the concept of The Wall and ensuring that decisions on the writing, editing, and publishing of stories are made on journalistic merit rather than on whether they will attract or repel advertisers. However, the new economics of the publishing industry is making it difficult to maintain the separation: Competition from TV, direct media, and the Internet is increasing, and newspaper and magazine readership and revenues continue to decline. There have been several well-publicized situations in the past where major magazines and newspapers were found to have given favorable editorial consideration to an advertiser.[65] However, the media usually hold their ground when challenged by companies that threaten to pull their advertising, or even do so, when they find editorial coverage objectionable. For example, in April 2005 General Motors canceled all of its advertising in the *Los Angeles Times* after a series of articles in the newspaper were unflattering to the automaker. GM, which was spending an estimated $21 million in the *Times* each year, claimed that "factual errors and misrepresentations" in various articles led it to withdraw its advertising in the paper. The paper had run several articles that were critical of certain GM vehicles, and also suggested that some senior GM executives should be dismissed because of the company's sales and profit woes. GM's advertising boycott of the *Los Angeles Times* lasted four months and was finally ended after executives from the two sides met to resolve their differences.[66] At the same time, more recent negative reports regarding the false mileage claims of Kia and Hyundai and other autos resulted in no backlash against the media.

The media in the United States are basically supported by advertising; this means we can enjoy them for free or for a fraction of what they would cost without advertising. The alternative to an advertiser-supported media system is support by users through higher subscription costs for print media and increased rates for cable and satellite TV access. Note that the decrease in newspaper subscriptions has led some papers to reduce their publication schedules and begin charging or increasing rates for online subscriptions. The ad in Exhibit 21–15, part of a campaign by the International Advertising Association, explains how advertising lowers the cost of print media for consumers. Another alternative is government-supported media like those in many other countries, but this runs counter to most people's desire for freedom of the press. Although not perfect, our system of advertising-supported media provides the best option for receiving information and entertainment.

EXHIBIT 21–15

This ad points out how advertising lowers the cost of newspapers for consumers

Source: International Advertising Association

WITHOUT ADVERTISING, YOUR NEWSPAPER WOULD COST YOU A BUNDLE.

Did you know that every ad in your newspaper helps pay for the rest of the essential pages? The fact is, your paper would cost you about $5.00 a day without advertisements. A price that would make news indeed.

Advertising. That's the way it works.

The global partnership of advertisers, agencies and media

Summarizing Social Effects

We have examined a number of issues and have attempted to analyze the arguments for and against them. Many people have reservations about the impact of advertising and promotion on society. The numerous rules, regulations, policies, and guidelines marketers comply with do not cover every advertising and promotional situation. Moreover, what one individual views as distasteful or unethical may be acceptable to another.

Negative opinions regarding advertising and other forms of promotion have been around almost as long as the field itself, and it is unlikely they will ever disappear. However, the industry must address the various concerns about the effects of advertising and other forms of promotion on society. Advertising is a very powerful institution, but it will remain so only as long as consumers have faith in the ads they see and hear every day. Many of the problems discussed here can be avoided if individual decision makers make ethics an important element of the IMC planning process.

The primary focus of this discussion of social effects has been on the way advertising is used (or abused) in the marketing of products and services. It is important to note that advertising and other IMC tools are also used to promote worthy causes and to deal with problems facing society (drunk driving, drug abuse, and the obesity crisis, among others). For

EXHIBIT 21–16

In this commercial "Phases," a teen is shown stealing money from his mother's purse; The Partnership at Drugfree.org helps families address teen drug abuse

Source: Partnership for Drug-Free Kids

EXHIBIT 21–17

This Recycle Across America ad is an example of the pro bono space donated by an outdoor media company

Source: Recycle Across America and Lamar Advertising

example, the Partnership at Drugfree.org (formerly the Partnership for a Drug Free America) has created a website and uses social media, as well as print and TV ads to drive awareness and action around teen substance abuse (Exhibit 21–16). The Partnership is funded primarily by donations from individuals, corporations, foundations, and the public sector. The organization has also partnered with the U.S. Office of National Drug Control Policy (ONDCP), and the joint campaign "Above the influence.com." Above the Influence (ATI) won an Effie Award given for sustainability for its long-term effectiveness. Youth who are aware of ATI advertising are consistently more likely to have stronger anti-drug beliefs compared to those unaware of campaign advertising. However, concern with the misuse and abuse of prescription drugs is increasing and The Partnership created The Medicine Abuse Project, using ads to address this problem. As an example, when the organizations discovered that Urban Outfitters, the national retail store popular with teens, was selling products made to look like prescription pill bottles that made light of prescription drug misuse and abuse, they launched an advocacy effort and petition to ask the company to remove these products from their stores and website. The successful effort led Urban Outfitters to halt sales of the products. Campaigns for nonprofit organizations and worthy causes are often developed pro bono by advertising agencies, and free advertising time and space are donated by the media. Exhibit 21–17 shows an outdoor ad from a successful public service campaign for recycling. The board was provided pro bono from Lamar Advertising to nonprofit Recycle Across America.

ECONOMIC EFFECTS OF ADVERTISING

Advertising plays an important role in a free-market system like ours by making consumers aware of products and services and providing them with information for decision making. Advertising's economic role goes beyond this basic function, however. It is a powerful force that can affect the functioning of our entire economic system (Exhibit 21–18).

Advertising can encourage consumption and foster economic growth. It not only informs customers of available goods and services but also facilitates entry into markets for a firm or a new product or brand; leads to economies of scale in production, marketing, and distribution, which in turn lead to lower prices; and hastens the acceptance of new products and the rejection of inferior products.

Critics of advertising view it as a detrimental force that not only fails to perform its basic function of information provision adequately but also adds to the cost of

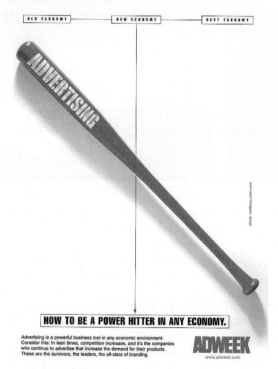

EXHIBIT 21–18

This ad from *ADWeek* promotes the economic value of advertising by comparing the companies that continue to advertise as the all-stars of branding

Source: Adweek

EXHIBIT 21–19

Virgin Atlantic Airways chair Richard Branson acknowledges the importance of advertising

Source: Virgin Atlantic Airways

products and services and discourages competition and market entry, leading to industrial concentration and higher prices for consumers.

In their analysis of advertising, economists generally take a macroeconomic perspective: They consider the economic impact of advertising on an entire industry or on the economy as a whole rather than its effect on an individual company or brand. Our examination of the economic impact of advertising focuses on these broader macro-level issues. We consider its effects on consumer choice, competition, and product costs and prices.

Effects on Consumer Choice

Some critics say advertising hampers consumer choice, as large advertisers use their power to limit our options to a few well-advertised brands. Economists argue that advertising is used to achieve (1) **differentiation**, whereby the products or services of large advertisers are perceived as unique or better than competitors', and (2) brand loyalty, which enables large national advertisers to gain control of the market, usually at the expense of smaller brands.

Larger companies often end up charging higher prices and achieve a more dominant position in the market than smaller firms that cannot compete against them and their large advertising budgets. When this occurs, advertising not only restricts the choice alternatives to a few well-known, heavily advertised brands but also becomes a substitute for competition based on price or product improvements.

Heavily advertised brands dominate the market in certain product categories, such as soft drinks, beer, and cereals. But advertising generally does not create brand monopolies and reduce the opportunities for new products to be introduced to consumers. In most product categories, a number of different brands are on the store shelves and thousands of new products are introduced every year. In 2015, there was over $15 billion worth of bottled water (11 billion gallons) sold in the United States—an average of 34 gallons per person—up from 1.6 gallons per person in 1976. There were over 170 bottled water brands.[67] The opportunity to advertise gives companies the incentive to develop new brands and improve their existing ones. When a successful new product such as a smartphone or tablet is introduced, competitors quickly follow and use advertising to inform consumers about their brand and attempt to convince them it is superior to the original. Companies like Virgin Atlantic Airways recognize that advertising has been an important part of their success (Exhibit 21–19).

Effects on Competition

One of the most common criticisms economists have about advertising concerns its effects on competition. They argue that power in the hands of large firms with huge advertising budgets creates a **barrier to entry**, which makes it difficult for other firms to enter the market. This results in less competition and higher prices. Economists note that smaller firms already in the market find it difficult to compete against the large advertising budgets of the industry leaders and are often driven out of business. Take the U.S. wireless market as an example. While there are a number of wireless providers, the market is dominated by seven major providers. Verizon and AT&T hold the major share of the market, with an estimated 264 million subscribers between them. These companies are also two of the largest advertisers, spending over $2 billion a year each. As you might imagine, to try to break into this market would be extremely difficult, if not impossible.

Large advertisers clearly enjoy certain competitive advantages. First, there are **economies of scale** in advertising, particularly with respect to factors such as media costs. Firms such as Procter & Gamble and PepsiCo, which spend several billion dollars a year on advertising and promotion, are able to make large media buys at a reduced rate and allocate them to their various products.

Large advertisers usually sell more of a product or service, which means they may have lower production costs and can allocate more monies to advertising, so they can afford the costly but more efficient media like network television. Their large advertising outlays also give them more opportunity to differentiate their products and develop brand loyalty. To the extent that these factors occur, smaller competitors are at a disadvantage and new competitors are deterred from entering the market.

While advertising may have an anticompetitive effect on a market, there is no clear evidence that advertising alone reduces competition, creates barriers to entry, and thus increases market concentration. High levels of advertising are not always found in industries where firms have a large market share. These findings run contrary to many economists' belief that industries controlled by a few firms have high advertising expenditures, resulting in stable brand shares for market leaders.

Defenders of advertising say it is unrealistic to attribute a firm's market dominance and barriers to entry solely to advertising. There are a number of other factors, such as price, product quality, distribution effectiveness, production efficiencies, competitive strategies, and even government legislation. For many years, products such as Coors beer and Hershey's chocolate bars were dominant brands even though these companies spent little on advertising. Hershey did not advertise at all until 1970. For 66 years, the company relied on the quality of its products, its favorable reputation and image among consumers, and its extensive channels of distribution to market its brands. Industry leaders often tend to dominate markets because they have superior product quality and the best management and competitive strategies, not simply the biggest advertising budgets.[68] SPANX is another good example. The billion-dollar company was started without a single cent being spent on advertising— primarily because founder Sara Blakely didn't have any money to buy it. Starting the company with only $5,000, Blakely relied on word of mouth and endorsements from celebrities like Oprah, Brooke Shields, Julia Roberts, and Gwyneth Paltrow, and other marketing factors like packaging and product benefits. Even today, SPANX does not advertise[69] (Exhibit 21–20).

While market entry against large, established competitors is difficult, companies with a quality product at a reasonable price often find a way to break in. Moreover, they usually find that advertising actually facilitates their market entry by making it possible to communicate the benefits and features of their new product or brand to consumers.

EXHIBIT 21–20

SPANX has been successful even with no advertising

© Rebecca Sapp/Wire Image for Kari Feinstein PR/Getty Images

Effects on Product Costs and Prices

A major area of debate among economists, advertisers, consumer advocates, and policymakers concerns the effects of advertising on product costs and prices. Critics argue that advertising increases the prices consumers pay for products and services. First, they say the large sums of money spent on advertising a brand constitute an expense that must be covered and the consumer ends up paying for it through higher prices. As discussed in the previous chapter, concern has been expressed that the tremendous increase in direct-to-consumer drug advertising by pharmaceutical companies is driving up the cost of prescription drugs. Critics argue that the millions of dollars spent on advertising and other forms of promotion are an expense that must be covered by charging higher prices.[70]

A second way advertising can result in higher prices is by increasing product differentiation and adding to the perceived value of the product in consumers' minds. The fundamental premise is that advertising increases the perceived differences between physically homogeneous products and enables advertised brands to command a premium price without an increase in quality.

Critics of advertising generally point to the differences in prices between national brands and private-label brands that are physically similar, such as aspirin or tea bags, as evidence of the added value created by advertising. They see consumers' willingness to pay more for heavily advertised national brands rather than purchasing the lower-priced, nonadvertised brand as wasteful and irrational. The prescription drug industry is again a very good example of this, as critics argue that the increase in advertising is encouraging consumers to request brand-name drugs and steering them away from lower-priced generics.[71] (As we write this chapter, there is pressure being brought to reinstate the ban on pharmaceutical advertising.) However, consumers do not always buy for rational, functional reasons. The emotional, psychological, and social benefits derived from purchasing a national brand are important to many people. Moreover, say researchers Farris and Albion,

> Unfortunately there seems to be no single way to measure product differentiation, let alone determine how much is excessive or attributable to the effects of advertising. . . . Both price insensitivity and brand loyalty could be created by a number of factors such as higher product quality, better packaging, favorable use experience and market position. They are probably related to each other but need not be the result of advertising.[72]

Proponents of advertising offer several other counterarguments to the claim that advertising increases prices. They acknowledge that advertising costs are at least partly paid for by consumers. But advertising may help lower the overall cost of a product more than enough to offset them. For example, advertising may help firms achieve economies of scale in production and distribution by providing information to and stimulating demand among mass markets. These economies of scale help cut the cost of producing and marketing the product, which can lead to lower prices—if the advertiser chooses to pass the cost savings on to the consumer. The ad in Exhibit 21–21, from a campaign sponsored by the American Association of Advertising Agencies, emphasizes this point.

Advertising can also lower prices by making a market more competitive, which usually leads to greater price competition. It has been shown that for some products, advertising has helped to keep the costs down. Finally, advertising is a means to market entry rather than a deterrent and helps stimulate product innovation, which makes markets more competitive and helps keep prices down.

Overall, it is difficult to reach any firm conclusions regarding the relationship between advertising and prices. After an extensive review of this area, Farris and Albion concluded, "The evidence connecting manufacturer advertising to prices is neither complete nor definitive . . . consequently, we cannot say whether advertising is a tool of market efficiency or market power without further research."[73]

Summarizing Economic Effects

Economists' perspectives can be divided into two principal schools of thought that make different assumptions regarding the influence of advertising on the economy.[74] Figure 21–6 summarizes the main points of the "advertising equals market power" and "advertising equals information" perspectives.

Advertising Equals Market Power The belief that advertising equals market power reflects traditional economic thinking and views

EXHIBIT 21–21

This ad refutes the argument that reducing advertising expenditures will lead to lower prices

© The American Association of Advertising Agencies

ADVERTISING MAKES THINGS COST MORE, RIGHT?

We admit it. Advertising has a tremendous impact on prices. But you may be surprised by what *kind* of impact.

In addition to being informative, educational and sometimes entertaining, advertising can actually lower prices.

It works like this: Advertising spurs competition which holds down prices. And since advertising also creates a mass market for products, it can bring down the cost of producing each product, a savings that can be passed on to consumers.

Moreover, competition created by advertising provides an incentive for manufacturers to produce new and better products.

Which means advertising can not only reduce prices, but it can also help you avoid lemons.

ADVERTISING ANOTHER WORD FOR FREEDOM OF CHOICE.
American Association of Advertising Agencies

Advertising = Market Power		Advertising = Information
Advertising affects consumer preferences and tastes, changes product attributes, and differentiates the product from competitive offerings.	Advertising	Advertising informs consumers about product attributes but does not change the way they value those attributes.
Consumers become brand-loyal and less price-sensitive and perceive fewer substitutes for advertised brands.	Consumer buying behavior	Consumers become more price-sensitive and buy best "value." Only the relationship between price and quality affects elasticity for a given product.
Potential entrants must overcome established brand loyalty and spend relatively more on advertising.	Barriers to entry	Advertising makes entry possible for new brands because it can communicate product attributes to consumers.
Firms are insulated from market competition and potential rivals; concentration increases, leaving firms with more discretionary power.	Industry structure and market power	Consumers can compare competitive offerings easily and competitive rivalry increases. Efficient firms remain, and as the inefficient leave, new entrants appear; the effect on concentration is ambiguous.
Firms can change higher prices and are not as likely to compare on quality or price dimensions. Innovation may be reduced.	Market conduct	More informed consumers pressure firms to lower prices and improve quality; new entrants facilitate innovation.
High prices and excessive profits accrue to advertisers and give them even more incentive to advertise their products. Output is restricted compared with conditions of perfect competition.	Market performance	Industry prices decrease. The effect on profits due to increased competition and increased efficiency is ambiguous.

FIGURE 21–6

Two Schools of Thought on Advertising's Role in the Economy

advertising as a way to change consumers' tastes, lower their sensitivity to price, and build brand loyalty among buyers of advertised brands. This results in higher profits and market power for large advertisers, reduces competition in the market, and leads to higher prices and fewer choices for consumers. Proponents of this viewpoint generally have negative attitudes regarding the economic impact of advertising.

Advertising Equals Information   The belief that advertising equals information takes a more positive view of advertising's economic effects. This model sees advertising as providing consumers with useful information, increasing their price sensitivity (which moves them toward lower-priced products), and increasing competition in the market. Advertising is viewed as a way to communicate with consumers and tell them about a product and its major features and attributes. More informed and knowledgeable consumers pressure companies to provide high-quality products at lower prices. Efficient firms remain in the market, whereas inefficient firms leave as new entrants appear. Proponents of this model believe the economic effects of advertising are favorable and think it contributes to more efficient and competitive markets.

There is considerable evidence that advertising does provide the information consumers need to make purchase decisions. Avery Abernethy and George Franke performed a meta-analysis of studies examining the information content of advertising and found that more than 84 percent of 91,000 ads analyzed in these studies contain at least one information cue. The most commonly provided types of information included performance, availability, components, price, and quality, all of which are important to consumers in making an informed choice.[75]

It is unlikely the debate over the economic effects and value of advertising will be resolved soon. Many economists will continue to take a negative view of advertising and its effects on the functioning of the economy, while advertisers will continue to view it as an efficient way for companies to communicate with their customers and an essential component of our economic system. The International

Advertising Association has been running a campaign for several years to convince consumers around the world of the economic value of advertising. Ads like the one shown in Exhibit 21–22 are used in countries where consumers may be less familiar with the concept of advertising. The goal of the campaign is to get consumers in these countries to recognize the role advertising plays in contributing to their economic well-being.

The advertising industry in the United States continually promotes the value of advertising. Major advertising associations, such as the 4As, the American Advertising Federation (AAF), along with trade associations for various media, often run campaigns reminding the general public of advertising's contributions to the economy as well as to consumers' social well-being. However, sometimes the industry must also remind advertisers themselves of the value of advertising. Recently the AAF, which is the advertising industry's primary trade organization, decided to take action to change the way advertising is viewed by companies. It decided that the best way to get marketers to recognize the value of advertising was to practice what it preaches, and thus an integrated marketing communications campaign was developed to redefine advertising in the eyes of corporate executives.

The campaign was targeted at corporate executives who were responsible for establishing and maintaining budget levels for advertising. The theme of the campaign, "Advertising. The way great brands get to be great brands," cautions corporate executives not to neglect their brand development. The great brands campaign promoted the economic power of advertising by featuring companies synonymous with quality advertising and for whom advertising has played a critical role in building brand equity. Exhibit 21–23 shows one of the ads from the campaign featuring Intel, the market leader for computer chips and microprocessors.

EXHIBIT 21–22

This ad is part of a global campaign by the International Advertising Association to educate consumers about the economic value of advertising

© The American Association of Advertising Agencies

WHEN ADVERTISING DOES ITS JOB, MILLIONS OF PEOPLE KEEP THEIRS.

Good advertising doesn't just inform. It sells. It helps move product and keep businesses in business. Every time an ad arouses a consumer's interest enough to result in a purchase, it keeps a company going strong. And it helps secure the jobs of the people who work there.

Advertising. That's the way it works.

INTERNATIONAL ADVERTISING ASSOCIATION

The global partnership of advertisers, agencies and media

EXHIBIT 21–23

The AAF promotes the value of advertising in building strong brands

Source: American Advertising Federation

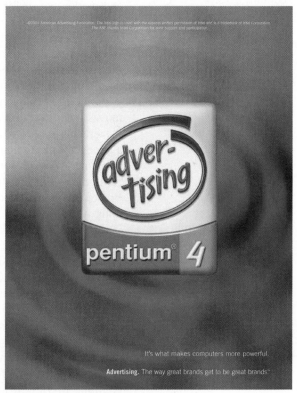

To me it means that if we believe to any degree whatsoever in the economic system under which we live, in a high standard of living and in high employment, advertising is the most efficient known way of moving goods in practically every product class.

My proof is that millions of businessmen have chosen advertising over and over again in the operations of their business. Some of their decisions may have been wrong, but they must have thought they were right or they wouldn't go back to be stung twice by the same kind of bee.

It's a pretty safe bet that in the next 10 years many Americans will be using products and devices that no one in this room has even heard of. Judging purely by past performance, American advertising can be relied on to make them known and accepted overnight at the lowest possible prices.

Advertising, of course, makes possible our unparalleled variety of magazines, newspapers, business publications, and radio and television stations.

It must be said that without advertising we would have a far different nation, and one that would be much the poorer—not merely in material commodities, but in the life of the spirit.

Leo Burnett

Source: Excerpts from a speech given by Leo Burnett on the American Association of Advertising Agencies's 50th anniversary, April 20, 1967.

Figure 21–7, excerpts from a speech given by famous ad executive Leo Burnett, summarizes the perspective of most advertising people on the economic effects of advertising. Advertising and marketing experts agree that advertising and promotion play an important role in helping to expand consumer demand for new products and services and in helping marketers differentiate their existing brands.

Summary

Advertising is a powerful institution and has been the target of considerable criticism regarding its social and economic impact. The criticism of advertising concerns the specific techniques and methods used as well as its effect on societal values, tastes, lifestyles, and behavior. Critics argue that advertising is deceptive and untruthful; that it can be offensive, irritating, or in poor taste; and that it exploits certain groups, such as children. Many people believe advertising should be informative only and advertisers should not use subjective claims, puffery, embellishment, or persuasive techniques.

Advertising often offends consumers by the type of appeal or manner of presentation used; sexually suggestive ads and nudity receive the most criticism. Advertisers say their ads are consistent with contemporary values and lifestyles and are appropriate for the target audiences they are attempting to reach. Advertising to children is an area of particular concern, since critics argue that children lack the experience, knowledge, and ability to process and evaluate persuasive advertising messages rationally. Although an FTC proposal to severely restrict advertising to children was defeated, it remains an issue.

The pervasiveness of advertising and its prevalence in virtually all media have led critics to argue that it plays a major role in influencing and transmitting social values. Advertising has been charged with encouraging materialism; manipulating consumers to buy things they do not really want or need; perpetuating stereotypes through its portrayal of certain groups such as women, minorities, and older adults; and controlling the media.

Advertising has also been scrutinized with regard to its economic effects. The basic economic role of advertising is to give consumers information that helps them make consumption decisions. Some people view advertising as a detrimental force that has a negative effect on competition, product costs, and consumer prices. Economists' perspectives regarding the effects of advertising follow two basic schools of thought: the advertising equals market power model and the advertising equals information model. Arguments consistent with each perspective were considered in analyzing the economic effects of advertising.

ethics 735
shock advertising 742
consumer socialization process 743

materialism 748
Protestant ethic 748
differentiation 758

barrier to entry 758
economies of scale 759

Discussion Questions

1. What are some of the different ways companies use shock ads? Do you think they are designed to create sales, or to bring attention to specific issues? Do they work? Give examples. (LO 21-2)

2. The chapter discussed the empowerment of females in advertising. Give examples of some of the companies that have used this form of advertising. Why do you think they have done this? Is it for altruism or financial gain? (LO 21-1)

3. The chapter discusses how many marketers are struggling with their multicultural marketing efforts and suggests that one reason may be the lack of diversity in advertising agencies. What are some of the reasons for the low number of minorities, such as African Americans, working in advertising? How can the industry address this problem? (LO 21-2)

4. The CEOs of Abercrombie & Fitch and American Apparel have both been variously characterized as either manipulators of the media for their ability to generate publicity for their companies or petulant. Both have lost their jobs in the face of declining sales. Are they geniuses or just sexist? Support your argument. (LO 21-1)

5. Companies like Old Navy and General Mills have employed the use of interracial ads, and have stirred up both controversy and support. Comments have been made that while some believe that we are in a postracism era, others disagree. Provide arguments for both sides and explain the potential impact on the brands. (LO 21-3)

6. The use of ads that use interracial and gay and lesbian themes appear to be on the increase. There seems to be a relaxed atmosphere regarding the use of these groups in advertising. Explain the benefits and pitfalls inherent in this strategy. (LO 21-2)

7. There are conflicting positions as to whether the government should get involved in issues regarding issues such as obesity, cigarette smoking, and vaping by passing regulations, restrictions, and/or taxes. Present both sides of the argument and take a position, providing support for your opinion. (LO 21-3)

8. Groups such as Commercial Alert are concerned about the intrusion of advertising and other types of marketing messages into all aspects of consumers' lives. Discuss some of the reasons consumer watchdog groups are critical of advertising and other types of marketing practices. (LO 21-2)

9. Discuss how attitudes toward the use of sex in advertising differ between men and women. Discuss the implications of these attitudinal differences for marketers who are developing ads for each sex. (LO 21-1)

10. Economists argue that advertising can be a barrier to entry for many companies that simply cannot come up with the money required to initiate an effective advertising campaign. At the same time, SPANX has succeeded without spending any money to promote the product. Explain how a company like SPANX can be successful with little or no advertising. (LO 21-4)

connect Digital users can access their personalized and adaptive SmartBook, Ad Forum Video Cases, and interactive exercises to review chapter concepts.

22 Personal Selling

LEARNING OBJECTIVES

LO1 Describe the role of personal selling in the IMC program.

LO2 Compare the advantages and disadvantages of personal selling as a promotional tool.

LO3 Explain how to combine personal selling with other elements in an IMC program.

LO4 Discuss how to measure the effectiveness of the personal-selling effort.

CHAPTER 22 IS AVAILABLE ONLINE THROUGH THE CONNECT PLATFORM.

GLOSSARY OF ADVERTISING AND PROMOTION TERMS

A/B testing A process that involves the testing of two versions of an advertisement or homepage to see which will be the more effective prior to launch.

absolute cost The actual total cost of placing an ad in a particular media vehicle.

account executive The individual who serves as the liaison between the advertising agency and the client. The account executive is responsible for managing all of the services the agency provides to the client and representing the agency's point of view to the client.

account planner The individual who gathers information that is relevant to a client's product or service and can be used in the development of the creative strategy as well as other aspects of an IMC campaign.

account planning The process of conducting research and gathering all relevant information about a client's product, service, brand, and consumers in the target audience for use in the development of creative strategy as well as other aspects of an IMC campaign.

account-specific marketing Development of customized promotional programs for individual retail accounts by marketers.

ad execution–related thoughts A type of thought or cognitive response a message recipient has concerning factors related to the execution of the ad, such as creativity, visual effects, color, and style.

adjacencies Commercial spots purchased from local television stations that generally appear during the time periods adjacent to network programs.

advergame Online game designed to promote a product and/or brand.

advertainment Media combining the use of advertising and entertainment (for example, in-game advertising, advergaming).

advertising Any paid form of nonpersonal communication about an organization, product, service, or idea by an identified sponsor.

advertising agency A firm that specializes in the creation, production, and placement of advertising messages and may provide other services that facilitate the marketing communications process.

advertising appeal The basis or approach used in an advertising message to attract the attention or interest of consumers and/or influence their feelings toward the product, service, or cause.

advertising campaign A comprehensive advertising plan that consists of a series of messages in a variety of media that center on a single theme or idea.

advertising creativity The ability to generate fresh, unique, and appropriate ideas that can be used as solutions to communication problems.

advertising manager The individual in an organization who is responsible for the planning, coordinating, budgeting, and implementing of the advertising program.

Advertising Self-Regulatory Council (ASRC) An organization founded by the Council of Better Business Bureaus and various advertising industry groups to promote high standards of truth, accuracy, morality, and social responsibility in national advertising.

advertising substantiation A Federal Trade Commission regulatory program that requires advertisers to have documentation to support the claims made in their advertisements.

advocacy advertising Advertising that is concerned with the propagation of ideas and elucidation of social issues of public importance in a manner that supports the position and interest of the sponsor.

aerial advertising A form of outdoor advertising where messages appear in the sky in the form of banners pulled by airplanes, skywriting, and on blimps.

affect referral decision rule A type of decision rule where selections are made on the basis of an overall impression or affective summary evaluation of the various alternatives under consideration.

affiliates Local television stations that are associated with a major network. Affiliates agree to preempt time during specified hours for programming provided by the network and carry the advertising contained in the program.

affirmative disclosure A Federal Trade Commission program whereby advertisers may be required to include certain types of information in their advertisements so consumers will be aware of all the consequences, conditions, and limitations associated with the use of the product or service.

affordable method A method of determining the budget for advertising and promotion where all other budget areas are covered and remaining monies are available for allocation.

AIDA model A model that depicts the successive stages a buyer passes through in the personal-selling process, including attention, interest, desire, and action.

alpha activity A measure of the degree of brain activity that can be used to assess an individual's reactions to an advertisement.

alternative media A term commonly used in advertising to describe support media.

animatic A preliminary version of a commercial whereby video of the frames of a storyboard is produced along with an audio soundtrack.

arbitrary allocation A method for determining the budget for advertising and promotion based on arbitrary decisions of executives.

attitude toward the ad A message recipient's affective feelings of favorability or unfavorability toward an advertisement.

attractiveness A source characteristic that makes him or her appealing to a message recipient. Source attractiveness can be based on similarity, familiarity, or likability.

average frequency The number of times the average household reached by a media schedule is exposed to a media vehicle over a specified period.

average quarter-hour (AQH) figure The average number of persons listening to a particular station for at least 5 minutes during a 15-minute period. Used by Arbitron in measuring the size of radio audiences.

average quarter-hour rating (AQH RTG) The average quarter-hour figure estimate expresses the estimated number of listeners as a percentage of the survey area population. Used by Nielsen in measuring the size of radio audiences

average quarter-hour share (AQH SHR) The percentage of the total listening audience tuned to each station.

balance-of-trade deficit A situation where the monetary value of a country's imports exceeds its exports.

banner ad An ad on a web page that may be "hot-linked" to the advertiser's site.

barrier to entry Conditions that make it difficult for a firm to enter the market in a particular industry, such as high advertising budgets.

behavioral targeting A basis for target marketing based on consumers' website surfing behaviors.

behavioristic segmentation A method of segmenting a market by dividing customers into groups based on their usage, loyalties, or buying responses to a product or service.

below-the-line media A term used to refer to support media whose costs are not assigned directly to advertising and/or promotional budgets.

benchmark measures Measures of a target audience's status concerning response hierarchy variables such as awareness, knowledge, image, attitudes, preferences, intentions, or behavior. These measures are taken at the beginning of an advertising or promotional campaign to determine the degree to which a target audience must be changed or moved by a promotional campaign.

benefit segmentation A method of segmenting markets on the basis of the major benefits consumers seek in a product or service.

Better Business Bureau (BBB) An organization established and funded by businesses that operate primarily at the local level to monitor activities of companies and promote fair advertising and selling practices.

billings The amount of client money agencies spend on media purchases and other equivalent activities. Billings are often used as a way of measuring the size of advertising agencies.

bleed page Magazine advertisement where the printed area extends to the edge of the page, eliminating any white margin or border around the ad.

blog Also known as a weblog, a blog is a Web-based publication consisting primarily of periodic articles written and provided in reverse chronological order. Blogs may reflect the writings of an individual, community political organization, or corporation.

body copy The main text portion of a print ad. Also often referred to as copy.

bonus pack Special packaging that provides consumers with extra quantity of merchandise at no extra charge over the regular price.

brand development index (BDI) An index that is calculated by taking the percentage of a brand's total sales that occur in a given market as compared to the percentage of the total population in the market.

brand equity The intangible asset of added value or goodwill that results from the favorable image, impressions of differentiation, and/or the strength of consumer attachment of a company name, brand name, or trademark.

brand identity The combination of the name, logo, symbols, design, packaging, image, and associations held by consumers toward a brand.

brand loyalty Preference by a consumer for a particular brand that results in continual purchase of it.

brand manager The person responsible for the planning, implementation, and control of the marketing program for an individual brand.

branded entertainment The combined use of an audio-visual program (such as TV, radio, podcast, or videocast) and a brand to market a product or service. The purpose of a branded entertainment program is to entertain, while at the same time provide the opportunity for brands or products to be promoted.

buildup approach A method of determining the budget for advertising and promotion by determining the specific tasks that have to be performed and estimating the costs of performing them. See also *objective and task method.*

buzz marketing The use of various activities that generate conversations and word-of-mouth communication about a particular topic such as a company, brand, or marketing activity.

cable television A form of television where signals are carried to households by wire rather than through the airways.

campaign theme The central message or idea that is communicated in all advertising and other promotional activities.

carryover effect A delayed or lagged effect whereby the impact of advertising on sales can occur during a subsequent time period.

category development index (CDI) An index that is calculated by taking the percentage of a product category's total sales that occur in a given market area as compared to the percentage of the total population in the market.

category management system An organizational system whereby managers have responsibility for the marketing programs for a particular category or line of products.

cause-related marketing Image-related advertising in which companies link with charities or nonprofit organizations as contributing sponsors.

cease-and-desist order An action by the Federal Trade Commission that orders a company to stop engaging in a practice that is considered deceptive or misleading until a hearing is held.

Central Hudson Test A four-part test used by the courts for determining restrictions on commercial speech.

central route to persuasion One of two routes to persuasion recognized by the elaboration likelihood model. The central route to persuasion views a message recipient as very active and involved in the communications process and as having the ability and motivation to attend to and process a message.

centralized system An organizational system whereby advertising along with other marketing activities such as sales, marketing research, and planning are divided along functional lines and are run from one central marketing department.

channel The method or medium by which communication travels from a source or sender to a receiver.

Children's Online Privacy Protection Act (COPPA) of 1998 Federal legislation that places restrictions on information collected from children via the Internet and requires that websites directed at children have a privacy policy posted on their home page and areas of the site where information is collected.

city zone A category used for newspaper circulation figures that refers to a market area composed of the city where the paper is published and contiguous areas similar in character to the city.

classical conditioning A learning process whereby a conditioned stimulus that elicits a response is paired with a neutral stimulus that does not elicit any particular response. Through repeated exposure, the neutral stimulus comes to elicit the same response as the conditioned stimulus.

classified advertising Advertising that runs in newspapers and magazines that generally contains text only and is arranged under subheadings according to the product, service, or offering. Employment, real estate, and automotive ads are the major forms of classified advertising.

clients The organizations with the products, services, or causes to be marketed and for which advertising agencies and other marketing promotional firms provide services.

clipping service A service that clips competitors' advertising from local print media, allowing the company to monitor the types of advertising that are running or to estimate their advertising expenditures.

close Obtaining the commitment of the prospect in a personal-selling transaction.

clutter The nonprogram material that appears in a broadcast environment, including commercials, promotional messages for shows, public service announcements, and the like.

cognitive dissonance A state of psychological tension or post-purchase doubt that a consumer may experience after making a purchase decision. This tension often leads the consumer to try to reduce it by seeking supportive information.

cognitive responses Thoughts that occur to a message recipient while reading, viewing, and/or hearing a communication.

collateral services Agencies that provide companies with specialized services such as package design, advertising production, and marketing research.

combination rate A special space rate or discount offered for advertising in two or more periodicals. Combination rates are often offered by publishers who own both morning and evening editions of a newspaper in the same market.

commercial ratings Measures of the average viewership of a television commercial both live and up to three days after the ads are played back on a digital video recorder (DVR).

commercial speech Speech that promotes a commercial transaction.

commission system A method of compensating advertising agencies whereby the agency receives a specified commission (traditionally 15 percent) from the media on any advertising time or space it purchases.

communication The passing of information, exchange of ideas, or process of establishing shared meaning between a sender and a receiver.

communication objectives Goals that an organization seeks to achieve through its promotional program in terms of communication effects such as creating awareness, knowledge, image, attitudes, preferences, or purchase intentions.

communications task Under the DAGMAR approach to setting advertising goals and objectives, something that can be performed by and attributed to advertising such as awareness, comprehension, conviction, and action.

comparative advertising The practice of either directly or indirectly naming one or more competitors in an advertising message and usually making a comparison on one or more specific attributes or characteristics.

competitive advantage Something unique or special that a firm does or possesses that provides an advantage over its competitors.

competitive parity method A method of setting the advertising and promotion budget based on matching the absolute level of percentage of sales expenditures of the competition.

compliance A type of influence process where a receiver accepts the position advocated by a source to obtain favorable outcomes or to avoid punishment.

comprehension and reaction tests Advertising testing to ensure receivers comprehend the message and to gauge their reaction to the same.

computer simulation models Quantitative-based models that are used to determine the relative contribution of advertising expenditures on sales response.

concave-downward function model An advertising/sales response function that views the incremental effects of advertising on sales as decreasing.

concentrated marketing A type of marketing strategy whereby a firm chooses to focus its marketing efforts on one particular market segment.

concept testing A method of pretesting alternative ideas for an advertisement or campaign by having consumers provide their responses and/or reactions to the creative concept.

conditioned response In classical conditioning, a response that occurs as a result of exposure to a conditioned stimulus.

conditioned stimulus In classical conditioning, a stimulus that becomes associated with an unconditioned stimulus and capable of evoking the same response or reaction as the unconditioned stimulus.

consent order A settlement between a company and the Federal Trade Commission whereby an advertiser agrees to stop the advertising or practice in question. A consent order is for settlement purposes only and does not constitute an admission of guilt.

consumer behavior The process and activities that people engage in when searching for, selecting, purchasing, using, evaluating, and disposing of products and services to satisfy their needs and desires.

consumer franchise-building (CFB) promotions Sales promotion activities that communicate distinctive brand attributes and contribute to the development and reinforcement of brand identity.

consumer juries A method of pretesting advertisements by using a panel of consumers who are representative of the target audience and provide ratings, rankings, and/or evaluations of advertisements.

consumer socialization process The process by which an individual acquires the skills needed to function in the marketplace as a consumer.

consumer-oriented sales promotion Sales promotion techniques that are targeted to the ultimate consumer such as coupons, samples, contests, rebates, sweepstakes, and premium offers.

content sponsorship The sponsor not only provides dollars in return for name association on the Internet but also participates in the provision of content itself.

contest A promotion whereby consumers compete for prizes or money on the basis of skills or ability, and winners are determined by judging the entries or ascertaining which entry comes closest to some predetermined criteria.

contextual advertising Internet advertising placed on the basis of the content of the web page.

continuity A media scheduling strategy where a continuous pattern of advertising is used over the time span of the advertising campaign.

contribution margin The difference between the total revenue generated by a product or brand and its total variable costs.

controlled-circulation basis Distribution of a publication free to individuals a publisher believes are of importance and responsible for making purchase decisions or are prescreened for qualification on some other basis.

cooperative advertising Advertising program in which a manufacturer pays a certain percentage of the expenses a retailer or distributor incurs for advertising the manufacturer's product in a local market area.

copywriter Individual who helps conceive the ideas for ads and commercials and writes the words or copy for them.

corporate advertising Advertising designed to promote overall awareness of a company or enhance its image among a target audience.

corrective advertising An action by the Federal Trade Commission whereby an advertiser can be required to run advertising messages designed to remedy the deception or misleading impression created by its previous advertising.

cost per order (CPO) A measure used in direct marketing to determine the number of orders generated relative to the cost of running the advertisement.

cost per ratings point (CPRP) A computation used by media buyers to compare the cost-efficiency of broadcast programs that divides the cost of commercial time on a program by the audience rating.

cost per thousand (CPM) A computation used in evaluating the relative cost of various media vehicles that represents the cost of exposing 1,000 members of a target audience to an advertising message.

cost-plus system A method of compensating advertising agencies whereby the agency receives a fee based on the cost of the work it performs plus an agreed-on amount for profit.

Council of Better Business Bureaus (CBBB) The parent office of local offices of the Better Business Bureau. The council assists in the development of codes and standards for ethical and responsible business and advertising practices.

counterargument A type of thought or cognitive response a receiver has that is counter or opposed to the position advocated in a message.

country-of-origin effect The impact on consumers' perceptions of products and/or brands that results from where the products are manufactured.

coverage A measure of the potential audience that might receive an advertising message through a media vehicle.

creative boutique An advertising agency that specializes in and provides only services related to the creative aspects of advertising.

creative brief A document that specifies the basic elements of the creative strategy such as the basic problem or issue the advertising must address, the advertising and communications objectives, target audience, major selling idea or key benefits to communicate, campaign theme or appeal, and supportive information or requirements.

creative execution style The manner or way in which a particular advertising appeal is transformed into a message.

creative selling A type of sales position where the primary emphasis is on generating new business.

creative strategy A determination of what an advertising message will say or communicate to a target audience.

creative tactics A determination of how an advertising message will be implemented to execute the creative strategy.

credibility The extent to which a source is perceived as having knowledge, skill, or experience relevant to a communication topic and can be trusted to give an unbiased opinion or present objective information on the issue.

cross sell A term used in personal selling that refers to the sale of additional products and/or services to the same customer.

Cross-Platform Campaign Ratings An audience measurement from the Nielsen Co. that measures the number of people who watch an ad only on television, the number who view it online, and the overlap between the two.

cultural values Refers to beliefs and goals shared by members of a society regarding ideal end states of life and modes of conduct.

culture The complexity of learned meanings, values, norms, and customs shared by members of a society.

cume A term used for cumulative audience, which is the estimated total number of different people who listened to a radio station for a minimum of five minutes during a particular daypart.

Customer Lifetime Value (CLTV) An estimate of the total lifetime profit that can be generated from a specific customer.

customer relationship management (CRM) Programs that involve the systematic tracking of consumers' preferences and behaviors and modifying the product or service offers as much as possible to meet individual needs and wants.

DAGMAR An acronym that stands for defining advertising goals for measured advertising results. An approach to setting advertising goals and objectives developed by Russell Colley.

daily inch rate A cost figure used in periodicals based on an advertisement placed one inch deep and one column wide (whatever the column inch).

dayparts The time segments into which a day is divided by radio and television networks and stations for selling advertising time.

decentralized system An organizational system whereby planning and decision-making responsibility for marketing, advertising, and promotion lies with a product/brand manager or management team rather than a centralized department.

deception According to the Federal Trade Commission, a misrepresentation, omission, or practice that is likely to mislead the consumer acting reasonably in the circumstances to the consumer's detriment.

decoding The process by which a message recipient transforms and interprets a message.

demographic segmentation A method of segmenting a market based on the demographic characteristics of consumers.

departmental system The organization of an advertising agency into departments based on functions such as account services, creative, media, marketing services, and administration.

designated market areas (DMAs) The geographic areas used by the Nielsen Station Index in measuring audience size. DMAs are nonoverlapping areas consisting of groups of counties from which stations attract their viewers.

differentiated marketing A type of marketing strategy whereby a firm offers products or services to a number of market segments and develops separate marketing strategies for each.

differentiation A situation where a particular company or brand is perceived as unique or better than its competitors.

digital out of home (DOOH) media Traditional out of home media (billboards, transit ads, etc.), now presented in a digital format.

digital/interactive agency Agencies that specialize in the development and strategic use of various digital and interactive marketing tools such as websites for the Internet, banner ads, search engine optimization, mobile marketing, and social media campaigns.

direct broadcast by satellite (DBS) A television signal delivery system whereby programming is beamed from satellites to special receiving dishes mounted in the home or yard.

direct channel A marketing channel where a producer and ultimate consumer interact directly with one another.

direct headline A headline that is very straightforward and informative in terms of the message it is presenting and the target audience it is directed toward. Direct headlines often include a specific benefit, promise, or reason for a consumer to be interested in a product or service.

direct marketing A system of marketing by which an organization communicates directly with customers to generate a response and/or a transaction.

direct selling The direct personal presentation, demonstration, and sale of products and services to consumers usually in their homes or at their jobs.

direct-marketing agency A company that provides a variety of direct-marketing services to its clients, including database management, direct mail, research, media service, creative, and production.

direct-response advertising A form of advertising for a product or service that elicits a sales response directly from the advertiser.

direct-response media Media used to seek a direct response from the consumer, including direct mail, telemarketing, interactive TV, print, the Internet, and other media.

directional medium Advertising media that are not used to create awareness or demand for products or services but rather to inform customers as to where purchases can be made once they have decided to buy. The Yellow Pages are an example of a directional medium.

display advertising Advertising in newspapers and magazines that uses illustrations, photos, headlines, and other visual elements in addition to copy text.

dissonance/attribution model A type of response hierarchy where consumers first behave, then develop attitudes or feelings as a result of that behavior, and then learn or process information that supports the attitude and behavior.

divergence The extent to which an advertisement contains certain creative elements that are novel, different, or unusual.

duplicated reach Individuals exposed to the same commercial on two or more media vehicles.

dyadic communication A process of direct communication between two persons or groups such as a salesperson and a customer.

e-commerce Direct selling of goods and services through the Internet.

e-mail Messages sent electronically over the Internet.

earned media Exposure for a company or brand that it did not have to pay for and is generated by entities outside the firms such as media coverage or through others sharing information via social media.

economic infrastructure A country's communications, transportation, financial, and distribution networks.

economies of scale A decline in costs with accumulated sales or production. In advertising, economies of scale often occur in media purchases as the relative costs of advertising time and/or space may decline as the size of the media budget increases.

effective reach A measure of the percentage of a media vehicle's audience reached at each effective frequency increment.

80–20 rule The principle that 80 percent of sales volume for a product or service is generated by 20 percent of the customers.

elaboration likelihood model (ELM) A model that identifies two processes by which communications can lead to persuasion—central and peripheral routes.

electrodermal response (EDR) A measure of the resistance the skin offers to a small amount of current passed between two electrodes. Used as a measure of consumers' reaction level to an advertisement.

electroencephalographic (EEG) measures Measures of the electrical impulses in the brain that are sometimes used as a measure of reactions to advertising.

emotional appeals Advertising messages that appeal to consumers' feelings and emotions.

encoding The process of putting thoughts, ideas, or information into a symbolic form.

ethics Moral principles and values that govern the actions and decisions of an individual or group.

ethnographic research A research technique that involves observing or studying consumers in their natural environment.

evaluative criteria The dimensions or attributes of a product or service that are used to compare different alternatives.

event marketing A type of promotion where a company or brand is linked to an event, or where a themed activity is developed for the purpose of creating experiences for consumers and promoting a product or service.

event sponsorship A type of promotion whereby a company develops sponsorship relations with a particular event such as a concert, sporting event, or other activity.

exchange Trade of something of value between two parties such as a product or service for money. The core phenomenon or domain for study in marketing.

exclusive A public relations tactic whereby one particular medium is offered exclusive rights to a story.

external analysis The phase of the promotional planning process that focuses on factors such as the characteristics of an organization's customers, market segments, positioning strategies, competitors, and marketing environment.

external audiences In public relations, a term used in reference to individuals who are outside or not closely connected to the organization such as the general public.

external search The search process whereby consumers seek and acquire information from external sources such as advertising, other people, or public sources.

eye tracking A method for following the movement of a person's eyes as he or she views an ad or commercial. Eye tracking is used for determining which portions or sections of an ad attract a viewer's attention and/or interest.

failure fee A trade promotion arrangement whereby a marketer agrees to pay a penalty fee if a product stocked by a retailer does not meet agreed-upon sales levels.

fear appeal An advertising message that creates anxiety in a receiver by showing negative consequences that can result from engaging in (or not engaging in) a particular behavior.

Federal Trade Commission (FTC) The federal agency that has the primary responsibility for protecting consumers and businesses from anticompetitive behavior and unfair and deceptive practices. The FTC regulates advertising and promotion at the federal level.

Federal Trade Commission Act Federal legislation passed in 1914 that created the Federal Trade Commission and gave it the responsibility to monitor deceptive or misleading advertising and unfair business practices.

fee–commission combination A type of compensation system whereby an advertising agency establishes a fixed monthly fee for its services to a client and media commissions received by the agency are credited against the fee.

feedback Part of the message recipient's response that is communicated back to the sender. Feedback can take a variety of forms and provides a sender with a way of monitoring how an intended message is decoded and received.

field of experience The experiences, perceptions, attitudes, and values that senders and receivers of a message bring to a communication situation.

field tests Tests of consumer reactions to an advertisement that are taken under natural viewing situations rather than in a laboratory.

financial audit An aspect of the advertising agency evaluation process that focuses on how the agency conducts financial affairs related to serving a client.

first cover The outside front cover of a magazine

fixed-fee method A method of agency compensation whereby the agency and client agree on the work to be done and the amount of money the agency will be paid for its services.

flat rate A standard newspaper advertising rate where no discounts are offered for large-quantity or repeated space buys.

Flesch formula A test used to assess the difficulty level of writing based on the number of syllables and sentences per 100 words.

flighting A media scheduling pattern in which periods of advertising are alternated with periods of no advertising.

focus groups A qualitative marketing research method whereby a group of 10 to 12 consumers from the target market is led through a discussion regarding a particular topic such as a product, service, or advertising campaign.

fourth cover The outside back cover position of a magazine where an ad can be placed

freestanding insert (FSI) A four-color multipage printed advertising booklet that contains consumer-packaged-goods coupon offers delivered with newspapers (usually in Sunday editions). FSIs can also be delivered in direct-mail packages along with local retailer ads or can be cooperative booklets such as RedPlum or SmartSource as well as solo books done by companies.

frequency The number of times a target audience is exposed to a media vehicle(s) in a specified period.

full-service agency An advertising agency that offers clients a full range of marketing and communications services, including the planning, creating, producing, and placing of advertising messages and other forms of promotion.

functional consequences Outcomes of product or service usage that are tangible and can be directly experienced by a consumer.

game A promotion that is a form of sweepstakes because it has a chance element or odds of winning associated with it. Games usually involve game card devices that can be rubbed or opened to unveil a winning number or prize description.

gatefold An oversize magazine page or cover that is extended and folded over to fit into the publication. Gatefolds are used to extend the size of a magazine advertisement and are always sold at a premium.

general advertising rates Rates charged by newspapers to display advertisers outside the paper's designated market areas and to any classification deemed by the publisher to be general in nature.

general preplanning input Information gathering and/or market research studies on trends, developments, and happenings in the marketplace that can be used to assist in the initial stages of the creative process of advertising.

geographic segmentation A method of segmenting a market on the basis of different geographic units or areas.

global advertising The use of the same basic advertising message in all international markets.

global marketing A strategy of using a common marketing plan and program for all countries in which a company operates, thus selling the product or services the same way everywhere in the world.

gross ratings points (GRPs) A measure that represents the total delivery or weight of a media schedule during a specified time period. GRPs are calculated by multiplying the reach of the media schedule by the average frequency.

group system The organization of an advertising agency by dividing it into groups consisting of specialists from various departments such as creative, media, marketing services, and other areas. These groups work together to service particular accounts.

halo effect The tendency for evaluations of one attribute or aspect of a stimulus to distort reactions to its other attributes or properties.

headline Words in the leading position of the advertisement; the words that will be read first or are positioned to draw the most attention.

hemispheric lateralization The notion that the human brain has two relatively distinct halves or hemispheres with each being responsible for a specific type of function. The right side is responsible for visual processing while the left side conducts verbal processing.

heuristics Simplified or basic decision rules that can be used by a consumer to make a purchase choice, such as buy the cheapest brand.

hierarchy of effects model A model of the process by which advertising works that assumes a consumer must pass through a sequence of steps from initial awareness to eventual action. The stages include awareness, interest, evaluation, trial, and adoption.

hierarchy of needs Abraham Maslow's theory that human needs are arranged in an order or hierarchy based on their importance. The need hierarchy includes physiological, safety, social/love and belonging, esteem, and self-actualization needs.

horizontal cooperative advertising A cooperative advertising arrangement where advertising is sponsored in common by a group of retailers or other organizations providing products or services to a market.

households using television (HUT) The percentage of homes in a given area that are watching television during a specific time period.

identification The process by which an attractive source influences a message recipient. Identification occurs when the receiver is motivated to seek some type of relationship with the source and adopt a similar position in terms of beliefs, attitudes, preferences, or behavior.

image advertising Advertising that creates an identity for a product or service by emphasizing psychological meaning or symbolic association with certain values, lifestyles, and the like.

image transfer A radio advertising technique whereby the images of a television commercial are implanted into a radio spot.

in-house agency An advertising agency set up, owned, and operated by an advertiser that is responsible for planning and executing the company's advertising program.

in-store media Advertising and promotional media that are used inside of a retail store such as point-of-purchase displays, ads on shopping carts, coupon dispensers, and display boards.

incentive-based system A form of compensation whereby an advertising agency's compensation level depends on how well it meets predetermined performance goals such as sales or market share.

index number A ratio used to describe the potential of a market. The index number is derived by dividing the percentage of users in a market segment by the percentage of population in the same segment and multiplying by 100.

indirect channel A marketing channel where intermediaries such as wholesalers and retailers are utilized to make a product available to the customer.

indirect headline Headline that is not straightforward with respect to identifying a product or service or providing information regarding the point of an advertising message.

infomercial Television commercial that is very long, ranging from several minutes to an hour. Infomercials are designed to provide consumers with detailed information about a product or service.

information processing model A model of advertising effects developed by William McGuire that views the receiver of a message as an information processor and problem solver. The model views the receiver as passing through a response hierarchy that includes a series of stages including message presentation, attention, comprehension, acceptance or yielding, retention, and behavior.

informational/rational appeals Advertising appeals that focus on the practical, functional, or utilitarian need for a product or service and emphasize features, benefits, or reasons for owning or using the brand.

ingredient-sponsored cooperative advertising Advertising supported by raw material manufacturers with the objective being to help establish end products that include materials and/or ingredients supplied by the company.

inherent drama An approach to advertising that focuses on the benefits or characteristics that lead a consumer to purchase a product or service and uses dramatic elements to emphasize them.

ink-jet imaging A printing process where a message is reproduced by projecting ink onto paper rather than mechanical plates. Ink-jet imaging is being offered by many magazines to allow advertisers to personalize their messages.

innovation adoption model A model that represents the stages a consumer passes through in the adoption process for an innovation such as a new product. The series of steps includes awareness, interest, evaluation, trial, and adoption.

inquiry tests Tests designed to measure advertising effectiveness on the basis of inquiries or responses generated from the ad such as requests for information, number of phone calls, or number of coupons redeemed.

inside cards A form of transit advertising where messages appear on cards or boards inside of vehicles such as buses, subways, or trolleys.

integrated marketing communications (IMC) A strategic business process used to develop, execute, and evaluate coordinated, measurable, persuasive brand communications programs over time with consumers, customers, prospects, employees, associates, and other targeted relevant external and internal audiences. The goal is to both generate short-term financial returns and build long-term brand and shareholder value.

integrated marketing communications management The process of planning, executing, evaluating, and controlling the use of various promotional-mix elements to effectively communicate with a target audience.

integrated marketing communications objectives Statements of what various aspects of the integrated marketing communications program will accomplish with respect to factors such as communication tasks, sales, market share, and the like.

integrated marketing communications plan A document that provides the framework for developing, implementing, and controlling an organization's integrated marketing communications program.

integration processes The way information such as product knowledge, meanings, and beliefs is combined to evaluate two or more alternatives.

interactive media A variety of media that allow the consumer to interact with the source of the message, actively receiving information and altering images, responding to questions, and so on.

interconnects Groups of cable systems joined together for advertising purposes.

internal analysis The phase of the promotional planning process that focuses on the product/service offering and the firm itself, including the capabilities of the firm and its ability to develop and implement a successful integrated marketing communications program.

internal audiences In public relations, a term used to refer to individuals or groups inside the organization or with a close connection to it.

internal search The process by which a consumer acquires information by accessing past experiences or knowledge stored in memory.

internalization The process by which a credible source influences a message recipient. Internalization occurs when the receiver is motivated to have an objectively correct position on an issue and the receiver will adopt the opinion or attitude of the credible communicator if he or she believes the information from this source represents an accurate position on the issue.

interstitial An advertisement that appears in a window on your computer screen while you are waiting for a web page to load.

issue advertising (issue ad) A form of advocacy advertising in which the advertiser wishes to bring attention to what it considers to be an important issue.

jingle Song about a brand or company that usually carries the advertising theme and a simple message.

laboratory tests Tests of consumer reactions to advertising under controlled conditions.

Lanham Act A federal law that permits a company to register a trademark for its exclusive use. The Lanham Act was amended to encompass false advertising and prohibits any false description or representation including words or other symbols tending falsely to describe or represent the same.

layout The physical arrangement of the various parts of an advertisement including the headline, subheads, illustrations, body copy, and any identifying marks.

lead A name given to a personal sales agent as a possible consumer.

linear TV Television service where the viewer has to watch a scheduled TV program at the particular time it's offered, and on the particular channel it's presented on.

local advertising Advertising done by companies within the limited geographic area where they do business.

localized advertising strategy Developing an advertising campaign specifically for a particular country or market rather than using a global approach.

low-involvement hierarchy A response hierarchy whereby a message recipient is viewed as passing from cognition to behavior to attitude change.

loyalty program Program designed to encourage repeat purchase or patronage of a specific brand of a product or service.

magazine network A group of magazines owned by one publisher or assembled by an independent network that offers advertisers the opportunity to buy space in a variety of publications through a package deal.

mailing list The database from which names are generated, and the ability to segment markets and, of course the offer.

major selling idea The basis for the central theme or message idea in an advertising campaign.

marginal analysis A principle of resource allocation that balances incremental revenues against incremental costs.

market opportunities Areas where a company believes there are favorable demand trends, needs, and/or wants that are not being satisfied, and where it can compete effectively.

market segmentation The process of dividing a market into distinct groups that have common needs and will respond similarly to a marketing action.

market segments Identifiable groups of customers sharing similar needs, wants, or other characteristics that make them likely to respond in a similar fashion to a marketing program.

marketing The activity, set of institutions, and processes for creating, communicating, delivering, and exchanging offerings that have value for customers, clients, partners, and society at large.

marketing channels The set of interdependent organizations involved in the process of making a product or service available to customers.

marketing mix The controllable elements of a marketing program including product, price, place (distribution), and promotion.

marketing objectives Goals to be accomplished by an organization's overall marketing program such as sales, market share, or profitability.

marketing plan A written document that describes the overall marketing strategy and programs developed for an organization, a particular product line, or a brand.

marketing public relations (MPR) Public relations activities designed to support marketing objectives and programs.

mass media Nonpersonal channels of communication that allow a message to be sent to many individuals at one time.

materialism A preoccupation with material things rather than intellectual or spiritual concerns.

media objectives The specific goals an advertiser has for the media portion of the advertising program.

media organizations One of the four major participants in the integrated marketing communications process whose function is to provide information or entertainment to subscribers, viewers, or readers while offering marketers an environment for reaching audiences with print and broadcast messages.

media planning The series of decisions involved in the delivery of an advertising message to prospective purchasers and/or users of a product or service.

media specialist companies Companies that specialize in the buying of advertising media time and space, particularly for television and digital advertising.

media strategies Plans of action for achieving stated media objectives such as which media will be used for reaching a target audience, how the media budget will be allocated, and how advertisements will be scheduled.

media vehicle The specific program, publication, or promotional piece used to carry an advertising message.

medium The general category of communication vehicles that are available for communicating with a target audience such as broadcast, print, direct mail, outdoor, and other support media.

message A communication containing information or meaning that a source wants to convey to a receiver.

missionary sales A type of sales position where the emphasis is on performing supporting activities and services rather than generating or taking orders.

mnemonics Basic cues such as symbols, rhymes, and associations that facilitate the learning and memory process.

mobile Type of services accessed through a portable communications device.

mobile billboard An out of home medium in which advertisements are able to be transported to different locations (signs painted on automobiles, trailers pulling billboards, and the like).

mobile marketing Promotional activity designed for delivery to cell phones, smartphones, tablets, and other handheld devices that includes apps, messaging, commerce, and customer relationship management.

mock magazine test Test in which an ad is placed in an actual magazine and a similar methodology is employed.

motivation research Qualitative research designed to probe the consumer's subconscious and discover deeply rooted motives for purchasing a product.

motive Something that compels or drives a consumer to take a particular action.

multiattribute attitude model A model of attitudes that views an individual's evaluation of an object as being a function of the beliefs that he or she has toward the object on various attributes and the importance of these attributes.

multiplexing An arrangement where multiple channels are transmitted by one cable network.

narrowcasting The reaching of a very specialized market through programming aimed at particular target audiences. Cable television networks offer excellent opportunities for narrowcasting.

National Advertising Review Board (NARB) A part of the National Advertising Division of the Council of Better Business Bureaus. The NARB is the advertising industry's primary self-regulatory body.

National Association of Attorneys General (NAAG) An organization consisting of state attorneys general that is involved in the regulation of advertising and other business practices.

national spot advertising All nonnetwork advertising done by a national advertiser in local markets.

native advertising Web advertising in which the advertiser attempts to gain attention by providing content in the context of the user's experience.

needledrop A term used in the advertising industry to refer to music that is prefabricated, multipurpose, and conventional and can be used in a commercial when a particular normative effect is desired.

negotiated commission A method of compensating advertising agencies whereby the client and agency negotiate the commission structure rather than relying on the traditional 15 percent media commission.

new media A term used to describe the proliferation of media resulting from the advent of Web 2.0.

Nielsen Television Index A service that provides daily and weekly estimates of the size and composition of national television viewing audiences for the network shows.

noise Extraneous factors that create unplanned distortion or interference in the communications process.

nonfranchise-building (non-FB) promotions Sales promotion activities that are designed to accelerate the purchase decision process and generate an immediate increase in sales but do little or nothing to communicate information about a brand and contribute to its identity and image.

nonmeasured media A term commonly used in the advertising industry to describe support media.

nonorganic (paid) search results Internet search results that are impacted by advertisements paid for by marketers.

nontraditional media Newer media, including various forms of support media such as entertainment marketing, guerrilla marketing, product placements, and the like, as well as Internet and interactive media, such as blogs, podcasts, and more.

objective and task method A buildup approach to budget setting involving a three-step process: (1) determining objectives, (2) determining the strategies and tasks required to attain these objectives, and (3) estimating the costs associated with these strategies and tasks.

off-invoice allowance A promotional discount offered to retailers or wholesalers whereby a certain per-case amount or percentage is deducted from the invoice.

omnichannel retailing A strategy whereby companies sell their products through multiple distribution channels including retail stores, online, catalogs, and mobile apps.

on-air tests Testing the effectiveness of television commercials by inserting test ads into actual TV programs in certain test markets.

one-sided message Communications in which only positive attributes or benefits of a product or service are presented.

one-step approach A direct-marketing strategy in which the medium is used directly to obtain an order (for example, television direct-response ads).

online commercial The equivalent of a traditional television commercial that appears on the Net.

open-rate structure A rate charged by newspapers in which discounts are available based on frequency or bulk purchases of space.

operant conditioning (instrumental conditioning) A learning theory that views the probability of a behavior as being dependent on the outcomes or consequences associated with it.

order taking A personal selling responsibility in which the salesperson's primary responsibility is taking the order.

organic search results Search results that appear due to the relevance of the search terms, not advertisements.

out of home (OOH) advertising The variety of advertising forms including outdoor, transit, skywriting, and other media viewed outside the home.

outside posters Outdoor transit posters appearing on buses, taxis, trains, subways, and trolley cars.

owned media Channels of marketing communication that a company controls, such as its websites, blogs, and mobile apps as well as social media channels.

paid media Channels of communication a marketer pays for including traditional advertising media such as television, radio, print, outdoor, and direct mail as well as various forms of digital advertising such as paid search and online display and video ads

participations The situation where several advertisers buy commercial time or spots on network television.

pass-along rate An estimate of the number of readers of a magazine in addition to the original subscriber or purchaser.

pass-along readership The audience that results when the primary subscriber or purchaser of a magazine gives the publication to another person to read, or when the magazine is read in places such as waiting rooms in doctors' offices.

pattern advertising Advertisements that follow a basic global approach although themes, copy, and sometimes even visual elements may be adjusted.

pay-per-click Advertisement payment method in which advertisers' costs are based on the number of times the ad is clicked on during a search.

payout plan A budgeting plan that determines the investment value of the advertising and promotion appropriation.

people meter An electronic device that automatically records a household's television viewing, including channels watched, number of minutes of viewing, and members of the household who are watching.

percentage charges The markups charged by advertising agencies for services provided to clients.

percentage-of-sales method A budget method in which the advertising and/or promotions budget is set based on a percentage of sales of the product.

perception The process by which an individual receives, selects, organizes, and interprets information to create a meaningful picture of the world.

peripheral route to persuasion In the elaboration likelihood model, one of two routes to persuasion in which the receiver is viewed as lacking the ability or motivation to process information and is not likely to be engaging in detailed cognitive processing.

personal selling Person-to-person communication in which the seller attempts to assist and/or persuade prospective buyers to purchase the company's product or service or to act on an idea.

persuader stage A role of personal selling that attempts to persuade market members to buy the supplier's offerings.

persuasion matrix A communication planning model in which the stages of the response process (dependent variables) and the communication components (independent variables) are combined to demonstrate the likely effect that the independent variables will have on the dependent variables.

planogram A planning configuration of products that occupy a shelf section in a store that is used to provide more efficient shelf space utilization.

podcasting A medium using the Internet to distribute files for downloading into iPods and other MP3 players.

pop-under Ad that pops up as the user is leaving the website.

pop-up Advertisement window on the Internet usually larger than a banner ad and smaller than a full screen.

Portable People Meter (PPM) A wearable pager-sized device that electronically traces what consumers listen to on the radio by detecting inaudible identification codes that are embedded in the programming.

portfolio test A laboratory methodology designed to expose a group of respondents to a portfolio consisting of both control and test print ads.

positioning The art and science of fitting the product or service to one or more segments of the market in such a way as to set it meaningfully apart from competition.

Positioning Advertising Copy Testing (PACT) A set of principles endorsed by 21 of the largest U.S. ad agencies aimed at improving the research used in preparing and testing ads, providing a better creative product for clients, and controlling the cost of TV commercials.

posttests Ad effectiveness measures that are taken after the ad has appeared in the marketplace.

pre-roll Video display advertisement that plays on an Internet site before the video requested appears.

preferred position rate A rate charged by newspapers that ensures the advertiser the ad will appear in the position required and/or in a specific section of the newspaper.

premium An offer of an item of merchandise or service either free or at a low price that is used as an extra incentive for purchasers.

preprinted insert Advertising distributed through newspapers that is not part of the newspaper itself, but is printed by the advertiser and then taken to the newspaper to be inserted.

press conference The calling together of the press to announce significant news and/or events.

press release Factual and interesting information released to the press.

pretests Advertising effectiveness measures that are taken before the implementation of the advertising campaign.

price-off deal A promotional strategy in which the consumer receives a reduction in the regular price of the brand.

primacy effect A theory that the first information presented in the message will be the most likely to be remembered.

problem detection A creative research approach in which consumers familiar with a product (or service) are asked to generate an exhaustive list of problems encountered in its use.

problem recognition The first stage in the consumer decision-making process in which the consumer perceives a need and becomes motivated to satisfy it.

problem-solver stage A stage of personal selling in which the seller obtains the participation of buyers in identifying their problems, translates these problems into needs, and then presents a selection from the supplier's offerings that can solve those problems.

procreator stage A stage of personal selling in which the seller defines the buyer's problems or needs and the solutions to those problems through active buyer–seller collaboration, thus creating a market offering tailored to the customer.

product integration The act of integrating the product into television program content.

product placement A form of advertising and promotion in which products are placed in television shows and/or movies to gain exposure.

product symbolism The meaning that a product or brand has to consumers.

product- or service-specific preplanning input Specific studies provided to the creative department on the product or service, the target audience, or a combination of the two.

program rating The percentage of TV households in an area that are tuned to a program during a specific time period.

programmatic buying A wide range of technologies that have begun automating the buying, placement, and optimization of advertising media time and space.

promotion The coordination of all seller-initiated efforts to set up channels of information and persuasion to sell goods and services or to promote an idea.

promotional mix The tools used to accomplish an organization's communications objective. The promotional mix includes advertising, direct marketing, digital/Internet marketing, sales promotion, publicity/public relations, and personal selling.

promotional products marketing The advertising or promotional medium or method that uses promotional products such as ad specialties, premiums, business gifts, awards, prizes, or commemoratives.

promotional pull strategy A strategy in which advertising and promotion efforts are targeted at the ultimate consumers to encourage them to purchase the manufacturer's brand.

promotional push strategy A strategy in which advertising and promotional efforts are targeted to the trade to attempt to get them to promote and sell the product to the ultimate consumer.

Prospecting The process of seeking out prospective customers.

prospector stage A selling stage in which activities include seeking out selected buyers who are perceived to have a need for the offering as well as the resources to buy it.

prospects Prospective customers.

Protestant ethic A perspective of life that stresses hard work and individual effort and initiative and views the accumulation of material possessions as evidence of success.

provider stage A stage of personal selling in which activities are limited to accepting orders for the supplier's available offering and conveying it to the buyer.

psychoanalytic theory An approach to the study of human motivations and behaviors pioneered by Sigmund Freud.

psychographic segmentation Dividing the product on the basis of personality and/or lifestyles.

psychosocial consequences Purchase decision consequences that are intangible, subjective, and personal.

public relations (PR) The management function that evaluates public attitudes, identifies the policies and procedures of an individual or organization with the public interest, and executes a program to earn public understanding and acceptance.

public relations firm An organization that develops and implements programs to manage a company's publicity, image, and affairs with consumers and other relevant publics.

publicity Communications regarding an organization, product, service, or idea that are not directly paid for or run under identified sponsorship.

puffery Advertising or other sales presentations that praise the item to be sold using subjective opinions, superlatives, or exaggerations, vaguely and generally, stating no specific facts.

pulsing A media scheduling method that combines flighting and continuous scheduling.

pupillometrics An advertising effectiveness methodology designed to measure dilation and constriction of the pupils of the eye in response to stimuli.

purchase intention The predisposition to buy a certain brand or product.

push money (pm) Cash payments made directly to the retailers' or wholesalers' sales force to encourage them to promote and sell a manufacturer's product.

QR code Short for quick response code; an optically machine-readable label attached to an item or advertisement that records information, which can be revealed to the viewer through an imaging device, which translates the code into content.

qualified prospects Those prospects that are able to make the buying decision.

qualitative audit An audit of the advertising agency's efforts in planning, developing, and implementing the client's communications programs.

qualitative media effect The positive or negative influence the medium may contribute to the message.

ratings point A measurement used to determine television viewing audiences in which one ratings point is the equivalent of 1 percent of all of the television households in a particular area tuned to a specific program.

reach The number of different audience members exposed at least once to a media vehicle (or vehicles) in a given period.

readers per copy A cost comparison figure used for magazines that estimates audience size based on pass-along readership.

Really Simple Syndication (RSS) A specification that uses XML to organize and format Web-based content in a standard way to provide RSS feeds, which consist of titles and brief descriptions of other online articles.

recall An advertising effectiveness score indicating the number of persons who remember an ad.

recall tests Advertising effectiveness tests designed to measure advertising recall.

receiver The person or persons with whom the sender of a message shares thoughts or information.

recency The idea that advertising will have the most effect on someone who is in the market for the product and that planners should attempt to reach that consumer as close as possible to their purchase decision.

recency effect The theory that arguments presented at the end of the message are considered to be stronger and therefore are more likely to be remembered.

recency planning Media planning that attempts to reach the consumer in the period of time just before their purchase decision.

recognition method An advertising effectiveness measure of print ads that allows the advertiser to assess the impact of an ad in a single issue of a magazine over time and/or across alternative magazines.

reference group A group whose perspectives, values, or behavior is used by an individual as the basis for his or her judgments, opinions, and actions.

refund An offer by a manufacturer to return a portion of a product's purchase price, usually after the consumer supplies a proof of purchase.

refutational appeal A type of message in which both sides of the issue are presented in the communication, with arguments offered to refute the opposing viewpoint.

reinforcement The rewards or favorable consequences associated with a particular response.

relationship marketing An organization's effort to develop a long-term cost-effective link with individual customers for mutual benefit.

relative cost The relationship between the price paid for advertising time or space and the size of the audience delivered; it is used to compare the prices of various media vehicles.

relevance The degree to which the various elements of an advertisement are meaningful, useful, or valuable to the consumer.

reminder advertising Advertising designed to keep the name of the product or brand in the mind of the receiver.

repositioning The changing of a product or brand's positioning.

response The set of reactions the receiver has after seeing, hearing, or reading a message.

retail or local advertising rates Rates newspapers charge to advertisers that conduct business or sell goods and services within the paper's designated market area.

retail trading zone The market outside the city zone whose residents regularly trade with merchants within the city zone.

retargeting Resending an ad to a website visitor who previously visited the site seeking information but did not purchase, in an attempt to make a sale.

RFM analysis A marketing technique used to determine quantitatively which customers are the most profitable by examining how recently a customer has purchased (recency), how often he or she purchases (frequency), and how much the customer spends (monetary).

rich media A term for advanced technology used in Internet ads, such as a streaming video, which allows interaction and special effects.

ROI budgeting method (return on investment) A budgeting method in which advertising and promotions are considered investments, and thus measurements are made in an attempt to determine the returns achieved by these investments.

run of paper (ROP) A rate quoted by newspapers that allows the ad to appear on any page or in any position desired by the medium.

S-shaped response curve A sales response model that attempts to show sales responses to various levels of advertising and promotional expenditures.

sales promotion Marketing activities that provide extra value or incentives to the sales force, distributors, or the ultimate consumer and can stimulate immediate sales.

sales promotion agency An organization that specializes in the planning and implementation of promotional programs such as contests, sweepstakes, sampling, premiums, and incentive offers for its clients.

sales promotion trap A spiral that results when a number of competitors extensively use promotions. One firm uses sales promotions to differentiate its product or service and other competitors copy the strategy, resulting in no differential advantage and a loss of profit margins to all.

salient attributes Attributes considered important to consumers in the purchase decision process.

salient beliefs Beliefs concerning specific attributes or consequences that are activated and form the basis of an attitude.

sampling A variety of procedures whereby consumers are given some quantity of a product for no charge to induce trial.

scatter market A period for purchasing television advertising time that runs throughout the TV season.

schedules of reinforcement Schedules by which a behavioral response is rewarded.

script A written version of the commercial that provides a detailed description of its video and audio content.

search engine optimization (SEO) The process of improving ranking in search engine results.

search Looking for a term, company, and so forth on the Internet.

second cover The inside front cover position of a magazine where a print ad can be placed.

seeding The process of identifying and choosing the initial group of consumers who will be used to start the diffusion or spreading of a message.

selective attention A perceptual process in which consumers choose to attend to some stimuli and not others.

selective binding A computerized production process that allows the creation of hundreds of copies of a magazine in one continuous sequence.

selective comprehension The perceptual process whereby consumers interpret information based on their own attitudes, beliefs, motives, and experiences.

selective exposure A process whereby consumers choose whether or not to make themselves available to media and message information.

selective perception The perceptual process involving the filtering or screening of exposure, attention, comprehension, and retention.

selective retention The perceptual process whereby consumers remember some information but not all.

selectivity The ability of a medium to reach a specific target audience.

self-liquidating premium Premium that requires the consumer to pay some or all of the cost of the premium plus handling and mailing costs.

self-regulation The practice by the advertising industry of regulating and controlling advertising to avoid interference by outside agencies such as the government.

sensation The immediate and direct response of the senses (taste, smell, sight, touch, and hearing) to a stimulus such as an advertisement, package, brand name, or point-of-purchase display.

shaping The reinforcement of successive acts that lead to a desired behavior pattern or response.

share of audience The percentage of households watching television in a special time period that are tuned to a specific program.

shock advertising Advertising in which marketers use nudity, sexual suggestiveness, or other startling images to get consumers' attention.

single-source tracking method A research method designed to track the behaviors of consumers from the television set to the supermarket checkout counter.

situational determinants Influences originating from the specific situation in which consumers are to use the product or brand.

sleeper effect A phenomenon in which the persuasiveness of a message increases over time.

slogan (tagline) A statement or phrase consisting of a few words that succinctly expresses the company image, identity, and/or positioning a company or brand wants to communicate.

slotting allowance Fees that must be paid to retailers to provide a "slot" or position to accommodate a new product on the store shelves.

social class Relatively homogeneous divisions of society into which people are grouped based on similar lifestyles, values, norms, interests, and behaviors.

social media Online means of communication and interactions among people that are used to create, share, and exchange content such as information, insights, experiences, perspectives, and even media themselves.

social networking sites Online platforms for networks or social relations among people who share interests, activities, backgrounds, or real-life connections.

source The sender—person, group, or organization—of the message.

source bolsters Favorable cognitive thoughts generated toward the source of a message.

source derogations Negative thoughts generated about the source of a communication.

source power The power of a source as a result of his or her ability to administer rewards and/or punishments to the receiver.

spam Unsolicited commercial e-mail.

spamming The sending of unsolicited multiple commercial electronic messages.

specialized marketing communication services Organizations that provide marketing communication services in their areas of expertise including direct marketing, public relations, and sales promotion firms.

specialty advertising An advertising, sales promotion, and motivational communications medium that employs useful articles of merchandise imprinted with an advertiser's name, message, or logo.

split runs Two or more versions of a print ad are printed in alternative copies of a particular issue of a magazine.

split-run test An advertising effectiveness measure in which different versions of an ad are run in alternate copies of the same newspaper and/or magazine.

sponsorship When the advertiser assumes responsibility for the production and usually the content of a television program as well as the advertising that appears within it.

sponsorship When an advertiser sponsors content on a website, it is considered a sponsorship.

spot advertising Commercials shown on local television stations, with the negotiation and purchase of time being made directly from the individual stations.

standard advertising unit (SAU) A standard developed in the newspaper industry to make newspaper purchasing rates more comparable to other media that sell space and time in standard units.

standard learning model Progression by the consumers through a learn-feel-do hierarchical response.

station reps Individuals who act as sales representatives for a number of local stations and represent them in dealings with national advertisers.

storyboard A series of drawings used to present the visual plan or layout of a proposed commercial.

strategic marketing plan The planning framework for specific marketing activities.

subcultures Smaller groups within a culture that possess similar beliefs, values, norms, and patterns of behavior that differentiate them from the larger cultural mainstream.

subhead Secondary headline in a print ad.

subliminal perception The ability of an individual to perceive a stimulus below the level of conscious awareness.

superagencies Large external agencies that offer integrated marketing communications on a worldwide basis.

superstations Independent local stations that send their signals via satellite to cable operators that, in turn, make them available to subscribers (e.g., WWOR, WPIX, WGN, WSBK, WTBS).

support advertising A form of direct marketing in which the ad is designed to support other forms of advertising appearing in other media.

support argument Consumers' thoughts that support or affirm the claims being made by a message.

support media Those media used to support or reinforce messages sent to target markets through other more "dominant" and/or more traditional media.

survey of buying power index An index that provides information regarding population, effective buying income, and total retail sales in an area.

sustainability Development that meets the needs of the current generation without compromising the ability of future generations to meet their needs.

sweeps periods The times of year in which television audience measures are taken (February, May, July, and November).

sweepstakes A promotion whereby consumers submit their names for consideration in the drawing or selection of prizes and winners are determined purely by chance. Sweepstakes cannot require a proof of purchase as a condition for entry.

syndicated programs Shows sold or distributed to local stations.

target CPM (TCPM) A relative cost comparison that calculates CPMs based on the target audience as opposed to the overall audience.

target marketing The process of identifying the specific needs of segments, selecting one or more of these segments as a target, and developing marketing programs directed to each.

target ratings points (TRPs) The number of persons in the primary target audience that the media buy will reach—and the number of times.

teaser advertising An ad designed to create curiosity and build excitement and interest in a product or brand without showing it.

telemarketing Selling products and services by using the telephone to contact prospective customers.

television household Defined by Nielsen as a home with at least one operable TV/monitor with the ability to deliver video via traditional means of antennae, cable set-top-box or satellite receiver and/or with a broadband connection.

television network The provider of news and programming to a series of affiliated local television stations.

terminal posters Floor displays, island showcases, electronic signs, and other forms of advertisements that appear in train or subway stations, airline terminals, and the like.

testing bias A bias that occurs in advertising effectiveness measures because respondents know they are being tested and thus alter their responses.

theater test An advertising effectiveness pretest in which consumers view ads in a theater setting and evaluate these ads on a variety of dimensions.

third cover The inside back cover position of a magazine where a print ad can be placed

top-down approaches Budgeting approaches in which the budgetary amount is established at the executive level and monies are passed down to the various departments.

total audience (television) The total number of homes viewing any five-minute part of a television program.

total audience/readership A combination of the total number of primary and pass-along readers multiplied by the circulation of an average issue of a magazine.

touch point Each and every opportunity a consumer has to see or hear about a company and/or its brands or have an encounter or experience with it.

tracking studies Advertising effectiveness measures designed to assess the effects of advertising on awareness, recall, interest, and attitudes toward the ad as well as purchase intentions.

trade advertising Advertising targeted to wholesalers and retailers.

trade allowance A discount or deal offered to retailers or wholesalers to encourage them to stock, promote, or display a manufacturer's product.

trade show A type of exhibition or forum where manufacturers can display their products to current as well as prospective buyers.

trade-oriented sales promotion A sales promotion designed to motivate distributors and retailers to carry a product and make an extra effort to promote or "push" it to their customers.

transformational ad An ad that associates the experience of using the advertised brand with a unique set of psychological characteristics that would not typically be associated with the brand experience to the same degree without exposure to the advertisement.

transit advertising Advertising targeted to target audiences exposed to commercial transportation facilities, including buses, taxis, trains, elevators, trolleys, airplanes, and subways.

two-sided message A message in which both good and bad points about a product or claim are presented.

two-step approach A direct-marketing strategy in which the first effort is designed to screen or qualify potential buyers, while the second effort has the responsibility of generating the response.

undifferentiated marketing A strategy in which market segment differences are ignored and one product or service is offered to the entire market.

unduplicated reach The number of persons reached once with a media exposure.

unfairness A concept used by the Federal Trade Commission to determine unfair or deceptive advertising practices. Unfairness occurs when a trade practice causes substantial physical or economic injury to consumers, could not be avoided by consumers, and must not be outweighed by countervailing benefits to consumers or competition.

unique selling proposition (USP) An advertising strategy that focuses on a product or service attribute that is distinctive to a particular brand and offers an important benefit to the customer.

up-front market A buying period that takes place prior to the upcoming television season when the networks sell a large part of their commercial time.

user-generated content (UGC) Advertising and/or other forms of content provided by consumers or other nonprofessional sources.

value The customer's perception of all the benefits of a product or service weighed against the costs of acquiring and consuming it.

vehicle option source effect The differential impact the advertising exposure will have on the same audience member if the exposure occurs in one media option rather than another.

vertical cooperative advertising A cooperative arrangement under which a manufacturer pays for a portion of the advertising a retailer runs to promote the manufacturer's product and its availability in the retailer's place of business.

video news release (VNR) News story produced by publicists so that television stations may air it as news.

video on demand (VOD) Video clips of various entertainment activities, which include ads or are sponsored, are also available through the Internet.

viral marketing The act of propagating marketing-relevant messages through the help and cooperation of individual consumers.

virtual and augmented reality View of the real-world environment supplemented by computer-generated sensory input.

voiceover A message or action on the screen in a commercial that is narrated or described by a narrator who is not visible.

want A felt need shaped by a person's knowledge, culture, and personality.

waste coverage A situation where the coverage of the media exceeds the target audience.

wearout The tendency for a television or radio commercial to lose its effectiveness when it is seen and/or heard repeatedly.

Web 2.0 Web applications that facilitate interactive information sharing, interoperability, user-centered design, and interactivity.

webisode Short featured film created by the advertiser.

Wheeler-Lea Amendment An act of Congress passed in 1938 that amended section 5 of the FTC Act to read that unfair methods of competition in commerce and unfair or deceptive acts or practices in commerce are declared unlawful.

word-of-mouth (WOM) communications Social channels of communication such as friends, neighbors, associates, co-workers, or family members.

Yellow Pages A telephone directory providing names of companies that provide specific products and/or services.

zapping The use of a remote control device to change channels and switch away from commercials.

zero-based communications planning An approach to planning the integrated marketing communications program that involves determining what tasks need to be done and what marketing communication functions should be used to accomplish them and to what extent.

zipping Fast-forwarding through commercials during the playback of a program previously recorded on DVR.

ENDNOTES

Chapter 1

1. Jack Neff, "The Big Agenda: What Lies Ahead for Marketing in an Increasingly Ad-Free Future," *Advertising Age*, January 11, 2016, http://adage.com/article/print-edition/big-agenda-ad-industry-2016/302067/; Bob Garfield, *The Chaos Scenario* (Nashville, TN: Stielstra Publishing, 2009).
2. "2016 Will Be a Growth Year in Marketing Spending," *Direct Marketing News*, February 1, 2016, http://www.dmnews.com/marketing-strategy/2016-will-be-a-growth-year-in-marketing-spending/article/469545/; Sponsorship Spending Report, IEG, http://www.sponsorship.com/IEG/files/4e/4e525456-b2b1-4049-bd51-03d9c35ac507.pdf.
3. "Digital Ad Spending to Surpass TV Next Year," *eMarketer*, March 8, 2016, http://www.emarketer.com/Article/Digital-Ad-Spending-Surpass-TV-Next-Year/1013671.
4. "Growth of Time Spent on Mobile Devices Slows," *eMarketer*, October 7, 2015, http://www.emarketer.com/Article/Growth-of-Time-Spent-on-Mobile-Devices-Slows/1013072.
5. "Worldwide Ad Spending Growth Revised Downward," April 21, 2016, *eMarketer*, http://www.emarketer.com/Article/Worldwide-Ad-Spending-Growth-Revised-Downward/1013858.
6. "Total Media Ad Spending Growth Slows Worldwide," *eMarketer*, September 15, 2015, www.emarketer.com/Article/Total-Media-Ad-Spending-Growth-Slows-Worldwide/1012981 .
7. "AMA Approves New Marketing Definition," *Marketing News*, March 1, 1985, p. 1.
8. Richard P. Bagozzi, "Marketing as Exchange," *Journal of Marketing* 39 (October 1975), pp. 32–39.
9. Lisa M. Keefe, "Marketing Defined," *Marketing News*, January 15, 2008, pp. 28–29.
10. Frederick E. Webster Jr., "Defining the New Marketing Concept," *Marketing Management* 3, no. 4 (1993), pp. 22–31.
11. Adrienne Ward Fawcett, "Integrated Marketing—Marketers Convinced: Its Time Has Arrived," *Advertising Age*, November 6, 1993, pp. S1–S2.
12. "Do Your Ads Need a SuperAgency?" *Fortune*, April 27, 1991, pp. 81–85; Faye Rice, "A Cure for What Ails Advertising?" *Fortune*, December 16, 1991, pp. 119–22.
13. Scott Hume, "Campus Adopts 'New' Advertising," *Advertising Age*, September 23, 1991, p. 17.
14. Don E. Schultz, "Integrated Marketing Communications: Maybe Definition Is in the Point of View," *Marketing News*, January 18, 1993, p. 17.
15. Ibid.
16. Joep P. Cornelissen and Andrew R. Lock, "Theoretical Concept or Management Fashion? Examining the Significance of IMC," *Journal of Advertising Research*, September/October 2000, pp. 7–15.
17. Philip J. Kitchen, Joanne Brignell, Tao Li, and Graham Spickett Jones, "The Emergence of IMC: A Theoretical Perspective," *Journal of Advertising Research*, March 2004, pp. 19–30.
18. Don E. Schultz, "IMC Receives More Appropriate Definition," *Marketing News*, September 15, 2004, pp. 8–9.
19. Cornelissen and Lock, "Theoretical Concept or Management Fashion?"
20. Harlan E. Spotts, David R. Lambert, and Mary L. Joyce, "Marketing Déjà Vu: The Discovery of Integrated Marketing Communications," *Journal of Marketing Education* 20, no. 3 (December 1998), pp. 210–18.
21. Tom Duncan and Sandra E. Moriarty, "A Communication-Based Model for Managing Relationships," *Journal of Marketing* 62, no. 2 (April 1998), pp. 1–13.
22. Anthony J. Tortorici, "Maximizing Marketing Communications through Horizontal and Vertical Orchestration," *Public Relations Quarterly* 36, no. 1 (1991), pp. 20–22.
23. Emily Steel, "Advertising's Brave New World: Different Lineup of Players Emerges with Online's Rise," *The Wall Street Journal*, May 25, 2007, p. B1.
24. W. Glynn Mangold and David J. Faulds, "Social Media: The New Hybrid Element of the Promotion Mix," *Business Horizons* 52, no. 4 (July/August 2009), pp. 52, 357–65.
25. "Digital Ad Spending to Surpass TV Next Year," March 8, 2016, www.emarketer.com/Article/Digital-Ad-Spending-Surpass-TV-Next-Year/1013671.
26. Nat Ives, "Consumers Bugged by Many Ads," *Advertising Age*, December 1, 2008, http://adage.com/article/media/consumers-bugged-ads/132867/.
27. Mike Ayers, "'Back to the Future' Brands: How Pepsi and Nike Hit Product Placement Gold," *The Wall Street Journal*, October 20, 2015, http://blogs.wsj.com/speakeasy/2015/10/20/back-to-the-future-pepsi-perfect-nike/.
28. Jack Neff, "The Big Agenda," *Advertising Age*, January 11, 2016, pp. 11–13.
29. Bob Garfield, "The Chaos Scenario 2.0: The Post Advertising Age," *Advertising Age* March 26, 2007, pp. 1, 12–14; Sergio Zyman, *The End of Marketing as We Know It* (New York: HarperBusiness, 1999); Joe Cappo, "Agencies: Change or Die," *Advertising Age*, December 7, 1992, p. 26.
30. Kevin Lane Keller, "The Brand Report Card," *Harvard Business Review* 78, no. 1 (January/February 2000), pp. 3–10.
31. Kevin Lane Keller, "Conceptualizing, Measuring, and Managing Customer-Based Brand Equity," *Journal of Marketing* 57 (January 1993), pp. 1–22.
32. Doug Levy and Bob Garfield, "The Dawn of the Relationship Era," *Advertising Age*, January 2, 2013, pp. 1, 8–11.
33. Andrea Prothero, Susan Dobscha, Jim Freund, William E. Kilbourne, Michael G. Luchs, Lucie K. Ozanne, and John Thøgersen, "Sustainable Consumption: Opportunities for Consumer Research and Public Policy," *Journal of Public Policy & Marketing* 30, no. 1 (2011), pp. 31–38.
34. Michael L. Ray, *Advertising and Communication Management* (Englewood Cliffs, NJ: Prentice Hall, 1982).
35. Ralph S. Alexander, ed., *Marketing Definitions* (Chicago: American Marketing Association, 1965), p. 9.
36. "TV Costs & CPM Trends," Television Bureau of Advertising, 2016,

http://www.tvb.org/Public/Home.aspx.

37. Anthony Crupi, "Forget Ad Avoidance, Growth of Digital—TV Advertising Holding Its Own," *Advertising Age*, June 9, 2015, http://adage.com/article/media/study/298943/.

38. Rance Crain, "Why Business-to-Business Advertising Is Increasingly Also Aimed at Consumers," *Advertising Age*, June 17, 2012, http://adage.com/article/rance-crain/b-b-advertising-increasingly-aimed-consumers/235413/.

39. Kate Maddox, "BtoB 100," *Advertising Age,* August 24, 2015, pp. 15–16.

40. Daniel Newman, "What You Need to Know About Omni-channel Marketing," September 21, 2015, *Entrepreneur*, www.entrepreneur.com/article/250833.

41. Barbara Conners, "Use CRM Data to Build Relevance—and Avoid Message Overload," *Advertising Age*, August 13, 2013, http://adage.com/article/datadriven-marketing/making-crm-data-work-avoiding-offer-overload/243441/.

42. *Internet World Stats: Usage and Population Statistics*—June 2016, http://www.internetworldstats.com/stats.htm.

43. Andrew Perrin, "Social Media Usage: 2005–2015," Pew Research Center, October 8, 2015, www.pewinternet.org/2015/10/08/social-networking-usage-2005-2015/.

44. Todd Powers, Dorothy Advincula, Manila S. Austin, Stacy Graiko, and Jasper Snyder, "Digital and Social Media in the Purchase Decision Process: A Special Report from the Advertising Research Foundation," *Journal of Advertising Research* 52, no. 4 (December 2012), pp. 479–89.

45. Rita Chang, "Marketers Say Hello to Long-Awaited Mobile Technology," *Advertising Age*, March 16, 2009, http://adage.com/article/digital/long-awaited-mobile-technology-2-d-barcodes/135248/; Alice Z. Cuneo, "Mobile Marketing Based on Place Is Finally Making Strides," *Advertising Age*, March 31, 2008, p. 24; Alice Z. Cuneo, "Wireless Giants Leap into Third-Screen Marketing," September 11, 2006, http://adage.com/article/digital/wireless-giants-leap-screen-marketing/111748/.

46. "Digital Ad Spending to Surpass TV Next Year," *eMarketer*, March 8, 2016, http://www.emarketer.com/Article/Digital-Ad-Spending-Surpass-TV-Next-Year/1013671.

47. Jennifer Valentino-Devries and Jeremy Singer-Vine, "They Know What You're Shopping For," *The Wall Street Journal*, December 7, 2012, pp. C1, C2.

48. Jennifer Valentino-Devries, Jeremy Singer-Vine, and Ashkan Soltani, "Websites Vary Prices, Deals Based on Users' Information," *The Wall Street Journal*, December 24, 2012, pp. A1, A10.

49. "2009 Promo Industry Trends Report," *Promo*, http://promomagazine.com/09-industry-trends-report/.

50. Natalie Zmuda, "Coca-Cola Addresses Obesity Head On in New Ads," *Advertising Age*, January 14, 2013, http://adage.com/article/news/coca-cola-addresses-obesity-ads/239163/.

51. Susan Berfield, "Can Chipotle Get Over Food Poisoning?" *Bloomberg Businessweek,* December 26, 2015, pp. 44–49.

52. Jessica Wohl, "Chipolte's Comeback Plan Includes Free Burritos," *Advertising Age*, February 8, 2016,

53. "About Public Relations," Publication Relations Society of America, https://www.prsa.org/aboutprsa/publicrelationsdefined/#.V5-nz4MrJaQ.

54. Jooyoung Kim, Hye Jin Yoon, and Sun Young Lee, "Integrating Advertising and Publicity," *Journal of Advertising* 39, no. 1 (Spring 2010), pp. 97–114; Paul Holmes, "Marketers See a Greater Role for Public Relations in the Marketing Mix," *Advertising Age*, January 24, 2005, pp. C4–C10; Jack Neff, "Ries' Thesis: Ads Don't Build Brands, PR Does," *Advertising Age*, July 15, 2002, pp. 14–15.

55. Tom Duncan, *Principles of Advertising & IMC*, 2nd ed. (New York: McGraw-Hill/Irwin, 2005).

56. Ibid.

57. Daniel Newman, "The Role of Paid, Owned and Owned Media in Your Marketing Strategy," *Forbes*, December 3, 2014, www.forbes.com/sites/danielnewman/2014/12/03/the-role-of-paid-owned-and-earned-media-in-your-marketing-strategy/#112ddfd411d3.

Chapter 2

1. Stuart Elliott, "It's a Fine Broth of a Campaign," November 2, 2009, www.nytimes.com/2009/11/02/business/media/02adnewsletter1.html?_r=0.

2. Julia Kollewe, "Global Luxury Goods Market Exceeds *Eltn,*" October 29, 2015, www.theguardian.com.

3. Ben Bouckley, "Beverages Show More 'Brand Momentum' Than Soup for Campbell's," May 22, 2012, www.beveragedaily.com.

4. Meghan Casserly, "Dells Revamped 'Della' Site for Women," *Forbes,* May 22, 2009, www.forbes.com.

5. Linda Lowen, "Beating the Odds—Verizon Grants Help Domestic Violence Survivors Gain Independence," March 1, 2012, www.about.com.

6. Thomas A. Hargett, "Former Wachovia Reps Preyed on Elderly, SEC Says," December 20, 2010, www.istockanalyst.com.

7. "AARP's Audience," www.advertise.AARP.org. 2016.

8. Jamie Beckland, "The End of Demographics: How Marketers Are Going Deeper with Personal Data," June 30, 2011, www.mashable.com.

9. Edward M. Tauber, "Research on Food Consumption Values Finds Four Market Segments: Good Taste Still Tops," *Marketing News,* May 15, 1981, p. 17; Rebecca C. Quarles, "Shopping Centers Use Fashion Lifestyle Research to Make Marketing Decisions," *Marketing News,* January 22, 1982, p. 18; "Our Auto, Ourselves," *Consumer Reports,* June 1985, p. 375.

10. Judith Graham, "New VALS2 Takes Psychological Route," *Advertising Age,* February 13, 1989, p. 24.

11. Beckland, "The End of Demographics."

12. Andrew M. Carlo, "The Comfort Zone," *Home Channel News,* May 24, 2004, pp. 3, 29; Davis A. Aaker and John G. Myers, *Advertising Management,* 3rd ed. (Englewood Cliffs, NJ: Prentice Hall, 1987), p. 125.

13. Jack Trout and Al Ries, "Positioning Cuts through Chaos in the Marketplace," *Advertising Age,* May 1, 1972, pp. 51–53.

14. Jack Trout, "Branding Can't Exist without Positioning," *Advertising Age,* March 14, 2005, p. 28.

15. *Ayer's Dictionary of Advertising Terms* (Philadelphia: Ayer Press, 1976).

16. David A. Aaker and J. Gary Shansby, "Positioning Your Product," *Business Horizons,* May/June 1982, pp. 56–62.

17. Aaker and Myers, *Advertising Management*.

18. J. Paul Peter and Jerry C. Olson, *Consumer Behavior* (Burr Ridge, IL: Irwin, 1987), p. 505.

19. Michael R. Solomon, "The Role of Products as Social Stimuli: A Symbolic Interactionism Perspective," *Journal of Consumer Research*, December 10, 1983, pp. 319–29.

20. Don E. Schultz, Stanley I. Tannenbaum, and Robert F. Lauterborn, *Integrated Marketing Communications* (Lincolnwood, IL: NTC Publishing Group, 1993), p. 72.

21. Samantha Bomkamp, "Wrigley Wants Gum to Stick Out in Checkout Line," *San Diego Union Tribune*, Jan 18, 2016, pp. C1,3.

22. Peter and Olson, *Consumer Behavior*, p. 571.

23. Jack Neff, "Study: TV Spots Reduce Consumers' Sensitivity to Price Change," *Advertising Age*, October 10, 2007.

24. Roger A. Kerin, Steven W. Hartley, Eric N. Berkowitz, and William Rudelius, *Marketing,* 8th ed. (Burr Ridge, IL: Irwin/McGraw-Hill, 2006).

25. David W. Stewart, Gary L. Frazier, and Ingrid Martin, "Integrated Channel Management: Merging the Communication and Distribution Functions of the Firm," in *Integrated Communication: Synergy of Persuasive Voices*, Esther Thorson and Jeri Moore, eds. (Mahwah, NJ: Erlbaum, 1996), pp. 185–215.

Chapter 3

1. Jack Neff, "P&G Redefines the Brand Manager," *Advertising Age*, October 13, 1997, pp. 1, 18, 20.

2. Thomas J. Cosse and John E. Swan, "Strategic Marketing Planning by Product Managers—Room for Improvement?" *Journal of Marketing* 47 (Summer 1983), pp. 92–102.

3. "Behind the Tumult at P&G," *Fortune*, March 7, 1994, pp. 74–82; "Category Management: New Tools Changing Life for Manufacturers, Retailers," *Marketing News*, September 25, 1989, pp. 2, 19.

4. Timothy Dewhirst and Brad Davis, "Brand Strategy and Integrated Marketing Communications," *Journal of Advertising* 34, no. 4 (Winter 2005), pp. 81–92.

5. Cosse and Swan, "Strategic Marketing Planning by Product Managers."

6. Victor P. Buell, *Organizing for Marketing/Advertising Success* (New York: Association of National Advertisers, 1982).

7. Jean Halliday, "GM Puts Final Nail in Coffin of Brand-Management Effort," *Advertising Age*, April 5, 2004, p. 8.

8. Jack Neff, "Why It's Time to Do Away with the Brand Manager," *Advertising Age*, October 12, 2009, http://adage.com/print?article_id=139593; Tom Hinkes, "Our Biggest Brands Can No Longer Be Managed by Nerds," *Advertising Age*, March 17, 2010, http://adage.com/article/cmo-strategy/biggest-brands-longer-managed-nerds/142841/.

9. Jenna Schnuer, "How to Manage Your Brand's Social Life," *Advertising Age*, April 23, 2012, http://adage.com/article/digital/manage-brand-s-social-life/234309/; Chris Perry, "What's Your Brand's Social ID? Lost Amid the Tweets Posts, Streams and Feeds Is Your Brand's Social Identity," *Advertising Age*, September 8, 2010, https://adage.com/print/145795.

10. Rupal Parekh, "Thinking of Pulling a CareerBuilder? Pros and Cons of Bringing an Account In-House," *Advertising Age*, May 18, 2009, http://adage.com/article/agency-news/pros-cons-house-careerbuilder/136701/.

11. Ibid.

12. Bruce Horovitz, "Some Companies Say the Best Ad Agency Is No Ad Agency at All," *Los Angeles Times*, July 19, 1989, sec. IV, p. 5.

13. Suzanne Vranica, "Google, Expanding Its Reach, Taps into Madison Avenue," *The Wall Street Journal*, September 19, 2007, p. B3.

14. Shareen Pathak, "72andSunny Picks Up Google Chrome Assignment: A Look Back at the Brand's Recent Messaging Via BBH," *Advertising Age*, February 22, 2013, http://adage.com/article/agency-news/72andsunny-picks-google-chrome-assignment/239983/.

15. Joan Voight, "The Outsiders," *Adweek*, October 4, 2004, pp. 32–35.

16. Jeff Beer, "How Under Armour Uses a Scrappy Outsider Will to Get What It Wants," *FastCoCreate*, August 31, 2015, www.fastcocreate.com/3050420/behind-the-brand/how-under-armour-uses-a-scrappy-outsider-will-to-get-what-it-wants.

17. Anne-Christine Diaz, "Under Armour's 'I Will What I Want' Takes Sole Cyber Grand Prix," *Advertising Age*, June 24, 2015, http://adage.com/article/special-report-cannes-lions/armour-s-i-i-campaign-starring-gisele-bundchen-takes-sole-cyber-grand-prix-cannes/299195/.

18. Aaron Baar and Noreen O'Leary, "Second City, Second Thoughts," *Adweek*, May 14, 2007, pp. 8–9.

19. Alice Z. Cuneo, "Not So Golden Anymore," *Advertising Age*, January 24, 2005, pp. 1, 53; Kate MacArthur, "Chicago Blues," *Advertising Age*, September 10, 2001, pp. 1, 12; Anthony Vagnoni, "Gotham Regains Some Lost Luster as Center of U.S. Agency Creativity," *Advertising Age*, April 12, 1999, pp. 1, 10.

20. Sally Goll Beatty, "Global Needs Challenge Midsize Agencies," *The Wall Street Journal*, December 14, 1995, p. B9.

21. Bradley Johnson, "What's Up at Agencies? Revenue, Stocks—and Digital," *Advertising Age*, May 1, 2016, http://adage.com/article/agency-news/agency-report-web-mainbar/303704/.

22. Bradley Johnson, "What's Up at Agencies? Revenue, Stocks—and Digital," *Advertising Age*, May 1, 2016, http://adage.com/article/agency-news/agency-report-web-mainbar/303704/.

23. Bob Lammons, "A Good Account Exec Makes a Big Difference," *Marketing News*, June 3, 1996, p. 12.

24. Maureen Morrison, "Wanted: Not Your Dad's Account Man," *Advertising Age*, May 2, 2016, pp. 36–37; Matthew Creamer, "The Demise of the Suit," *Advertising Age*, March 13, 2006, pp. 1, 41.

25. Phil Johnson, "A Vision for the Future of Account Management," *Advertising Age*, March 24, 2010, http://adage.com/article/small-agency-diary/account-management-entrepreneurs-suits/142947.

26. Jon Steel, *Truth, Lies & Advertising: The Art of Account Planning* (New York: Wiley, 1998).

27. Quote in Alice Z. Cuneo, "Account Planners at a Crossroads," *Advertising Age*, July 30, 2007, http://adage.com/article/news/account-planners-a-crossroads/119558/.

28. Jay Chiat Awards, http://stratfest.aaaa.org/jaychiats/.

29. Ann-Christine Diaz, "Droga5 Is the Ad Age and Creativity Agency of hte Year," *Advertising Age*, January

25, 2016, http://adage.com/article/special-report-agency-alist-2016/droga5-ad-age-s-agency-year/302235/.

30. Mike Shields, "Programmatic for Dummies," *Adweek,* November 4, 2013, pp. 20–25.

31. Alexandra Bruell, "Programmatic Buys to Account for $10B of TV Budgets by 2019," *Advertising Age,* June 1, 2015, p. 10.

32. David Beals, *Trends in Agency Compensation*, 14th ed. (New York: Association of National Advertisers, 2007).

33. Alexandra Bruell, "It's Not Just Cyclical: Industry Change Is Driving Marketing Giants to Review Media Agencies," *Advertising Age,* May 12, 2015, http://adage.com/article/agency-news/industry-change-drives-massive-media-agency-reviews/298579/.

34. David Beals, *Global Agency Compensation: Key Findings Report* (New York: Association of National Advertisers, 2012).

35. Kate Maddox, "Fee-Based Model Dominant in Global Agency Compensation," *BtoB Magazine,* September 17, 2012, www.btobonline.com/article/20120917/AGENCIES/309179973/fee-based-model-dominant-in-global-agency-compensation.

36. Chris Kuenne, "Why Ad Agencies Need to Embrace Value-Based Compensation," *Advertising Age,* March 22, 2010, http://adage.com/article/agency-news/ad-agencies-embrace-based-compensation/142915/.

37. Beals, *Global Agency Compensation.*

38. Rupal Parekh, "ANA Survey: 52% of Marketers Will Ask Agencies to Lower Internal Costs," *Advertising Age,* April 2, 2012, http://adage.com/article/cmo-strategy/survey-majority-marketers-shops-lower-costs/233880/.

39. Ibid.

40. Jack Neff, "ANA Survey: Agency-Performance Reviews Are Now Business as Usual, *Advertising Age,* September 14, 2009, http://adage.com/article/agency-news/ana-surveyagency-performance-reviews-business-usual/138983/.

41. *Report on the Agency-Advertiser Value Survey*, American Association of Advertising Agencies and Association of National Advertisers, August 2007.

42. Tim Williams and Ronald Baker, "New Value-Based Comp Model Needed," *Advertising Age,* June 11, 2007, http://adage.com/article/cmo-strategy/based-comp-model-needed/117143/.

43. Lindsay Stein, "Love Me Tender: Why Agencies and Clients Stay—and Why They Stray," *Advertising Age*, February 12, 2016, http://adage.com/article/agency-news/longstanding-agency-client-relationships-highs-lows/302674/.

44. Teressa Iezzi, "What's to Become of Long-Term Marketer, Agency Relationships?," *Advertising Age*, March 26, 2007, p. 17; Joanne Lipman, "Study Shows Clients Jump Ship Quickly," *The Wall Street Journal*, May 21, 1992, p. B6.

45. Alexandra Bruell and Maureen Morrison, "Exxon Consolidates Global Ad Duties with Omnicom and Interpublic," *Advertising Age*, November 3, 2011, http://adage.com/article/agency-news/exxon-consolidates-global-duties-omnicom-interpublic/230804/.

46. Rupal Parekh, "Why the Client–Agency Bond Just Isn't What It Used to Be," *Advertising Age*, February 14, 2011, http://adage.com/article/agency-news/long-term-ad-agency-client-bonds-a-rarity/148787/.

47. David Kiley, "Innocean Strives to Be Known as More Than Hyundai Agency," *Advertising Age,* April 25, 2011, pp. 8, 9.

48. Maureen Morrison, "Marketing Executives Reveal What They Want from Strong Client–Agency Relationship," *Advertising Age,* July 18, 2012, http://adage.com/article/cmo-strategy/marketers-ad-agency-relationships/236100/; "How to Be a Better Agency Client," *Advertising Age,* January 9, 2012, pp. 8, 9; Kathleen Sampley, "Love's Labors Lost: Behind the Breakups," *Adweek,* August 1, 2005, p. 8; Fred Beard, "Marketing Client Role Ambiguity as a Source of Dissatisfaction in Client–Ad Agency Relationships," *Journal of Advertising Research*, September/October 1996, pp. 9–20; Paul Michell, Harold Cataquet, and Stephen Hague, "Establishing the Causes of Disaffection in Agency–Client Relations," *Journal of Advertising Research* 32, no. 2 (1992), pp. 41–48; Peter Doyle, Marcel Corstiens, and Paul Michell, "Signals of Vulnerability in Agency–Client Relations," *Journal of Marketing* 44 (Fall 1980), pp. 18–23; Daniel B. Wackman, Charles Salmon, and Caryn C. Salmon, "Developing an Advertising Agency–Client Relationship," *Journal of Advertising Research* 26, no. 6 (December 1986–January 1987), pp. 21–29.

49. E. J. Schultz, "Can Wieden & Kennedy Save Bud Light?," *Advertising Age,* October 30, 2015, http://adage.com/article/cmo-strategy/wieden-kennedy-save-bud-light/301157/; E.J. Schultz, "Big Beer Churns Through Agencies," *Advertising Age*, August 24, 2015, p. 6.

50. Joan Voight and Wendy Melillo, "Study: Clients Want Multiple Partners," *Adweek,* May 14, 2007, pp. 20–21.

51. Alvin J. Silk, "Conflict Policy and Advertising Agency–Client Relations: The Problem of Competing Clients Sharing a Common Agency," *Working Knowledge, Harvard Business School Working Paper Number 12–104*, May 31, 2012, http://hbswk.hbs.edu/item/7021.html.

52. Suzanne Vranica, "Pinched Firms Woo Rivals' Happy Clients," *The Wall Street Journal*, March 4, 2002, p. B8.

53. Jack Neff, "Why Spec Creative Should Go Away but Won't," *Advertising Age*, January 9, 2012, pp. 10, 11.

54. Jennifer Comiteau, "What Agencies Think of Search Consultants," *Adweek*, August 4, 2003, pp. 14–16.

55. Fred K. Beard, "Exploring the Use of Advertising Agency Review Consultants," *Journal of Advertising Research* 42, no. 1 (January/February) 2002, pp. 39–50.

56. "Introducing the Ad Age A-List and Creativity Awards," *Advertising Age*, April 5, 2016, http://adage.com/article/advertising/introducing-ad-age-a-list-creativity-awards/303353/; Patrick Coffee, "U.S. Agency of the Year: BBDO Was 2015's Unstoppable Creative Juggernaut," *ADWEEK*, December 6, 2015, http://www.adweek.com/news/advertising-branding/us-agency-year-bbdo-was-2015s-unstoppable-creative-juggernaut-168435.

57. Jack Neff, "Ries' Thesis: Ads Don't Build Brands, PR Does," *Advertising Age*, July 15, 2002, pp. 14–15; Prema Nakra, "The Changing Role of Public Relations in Marketing Communications," *Public Relations Quarterly* 1 (1991), pp. 42–45.

58. "The New VW.com Takes a Page from Online Dating to Help You Find a Car," *Fastcocreate,* May 4, 2014, www.fastcocreate.com/3030032/the-new-vwcom-takes-a-page-from-online-dating-to-help-you-find-a-car.

59. Betsy Spathmann, "Sudden Impact," *Promo,* April 1999, pp. 42–48.

60. Quoted in Laura Q. Hughes and Kate MacArthur, "Soft Boiled," *Advertising Age,* May 28, 2001, pp. 3, 54.

61. Study cited in Michael Bush, "Memo to Marketers: It's Your Fault If Your Shops Flounder," *Advertising Age,* March 29, 2010, http://adage.com/article/cmo-strategy/marketers-fault-ad-agencies-flounder/143010/.

62. Kunur Patel, "Adland's Identity Crisis Leaves Clients' Heads Spinning," *Advertising Age,* April 25, 2011, p. 4.

63. William N. Swain, "Perceptions of IMC after a Decade of Development: Who's at the Wheel and How Can We Measure Success?" *Journal of Advertising Research,* March 2004, pp. 46–67; Philip J. Kitchen and Don E. Schultz, "A Multi-Country Comparison of the Drive for IMC," *Journal of Advertising Research* 39, no. 1 (January 1999), pp. 21–38.

64. David N. McArthur and Tom Griffin, "A Marketing Management View of Integrated Marketing Communications," *Journal of Advertising Research* 37, no. 5 (September/October) 1997, pp. 19–26; Adrienne Ward Fawcett, "Integrated Marketing—Marketers Convinced: Its Time Has Arrived," *Advertising Age,* November 6, 1993, pp. S1–S2.

65. Voight and Melillo, "Study: Clients Want Multiple Partners."

66. Quoted in Michael Bush, "Memo to Marketers: It's Your Fault If Your Shops Flounder," *Advertising Age,* March 2, 2010.

67. Tim Williams, "A Mind Map of the 2020 Agency," Ignition Consulting Group, May 27, 2015, http://www.ignitiongroup.com/propulsion-blog-post/mind-map-foundations-of-the-2020-agency.

Chapter 4

1. Dirk Zeims, "The Morphological Approach for Unconscious Consumer Motivation Research," *Journal of Advertising Research* 44, no. 2 (June 2004), pp. 210–15.

2. Jeffrey Ball, "But How Does It Make You Feel?" *The Wall Street Journal,* May 3, 1999, p. B1.

3. Jagdish N. Sheth, "The Role of Motivation Research in Consumer Psychology" (Faculty Working Paper, University of Illinois, Champaign, 1974); Bill Abrams, "Charles of the Ritz Discovers What Women Want," *The Wall Street Journal,* August 20, 1981, p. 29; Ernest Dichter, *Getting Motivated* (New York: Pergamon Press, 1979).

4. Ball, "But How Does It Make You Feel?"

5. Gary Strauss, "TV Sex: Uncut, Unavoidable," *USA Today,* January 20, 2010, p. 1.

6. Joanne Lipman, "Leaders Turning Up Their Noses at 'Scent Strips' Ads in Magazines," *The Wall Street Journal,* December 6, 1989, p. 1.

7. Gord Hotchkiss, "4,000 Ads a Day, and Counting," November 14, 2007, www.mediapost.com/publications/article/68986/.

8. David Raab, "How Many Ads Do You See Each Day? Fewer Than It Seems (I think)," www.customerexperiencematrix.blogspot.com, September 29, 2015.

9. Gordon W. Allport, "Attitudes," in *Handbook of Social Psychology,* C. M. Murchison, ed. (Winchester, MA: Clark University Press, 1935), p. 810.

10. Robert B. Zajonc and Hazel Markus, "Affective and Cognitive Factors in Preferences," *Journal of Consumer Research* 9, no. 2 (June 1982), pp. 123–31.

11. Joel B. Cohen, Paul W. Minniard, and Peter R. Dickson, "Information Integration: An Information Processing Perspective," in *Advances in Consumer Research* (vol. 7), Jerry C. Olson, ed. (Ann Arbor, MI: Association for Consumer Research, 1980), pp. 161–70.

12. James F. Engel, "The Psychological Consequences of a Major Purchase Decision," in *Marketing in Transition,* William S. Decker, ed. (Chicago: American Marketing Association, 1963), pp. 462–75.

13. Leon G. Schiffman and Leslie Lazar Kannuk, *Consumer Behavior,* 4th ed. (Englewood Cliffs, NJ: Prentice Hall, 1991), p. 192.

14. Gerald J. Gorn, "The Effects of Music in Advertising on Choice: A Classical Conditioning Approach," *Journal of Marketing* 46 (Winter 1982), pp. 94–101.

15. James J. Kellaris, Anthony D. Cox, and Dena Cox, "The Effect of Background Music on Ad Processing: A Contingency Explanation," *Journal of Marketing* 57, no. 4 (Fall 1993), p. 114.

16. Brian C. Deslauries and Peter B. Everett, "The Effects of Intermittent and Continuous Token Reinforcement on Bus Ridership," *Journal of Applied Psychology* 62 (August 1977), pp. 369–75.

17. Lyman E. Ostlund, "Role Theory and Group Dynamics," in *Consumer Behavior: Theoretical Sources,* Scott Ward and Thomas S. Robertson, eds. (Englewood Cliffs, NJ: Prentice Hall, 1973), pp. 230–75.

Chapter 5

1. Wilbur Schram, *The Process and Effects of Mass Communications* (Urbana: University of Illinois Press, 1955).

2. Ibid.

3. Maureen Morrison, "Starbucks' New Logo Signals Intent to 'Think Beyond Coffee,'" *Advertising Age,* January 5, 2011, http://adage.com/article/news/starbucks-logo-signals-intent-coffee/148020/.

4. Andrew Hampp and Rupal Parekh, "Gap to Scrap New Logo, Return to Old Design Plans to Announce Change of Company Facebook Page," *Advertising Age,* October 11, 2010, http://adage.com/article/news/gap-scrap-logo-return-design/146417/.

5. Adrienne Pasquarelli, "Coach Invests in New Campaign to Help Revive Ailing Brand," *Advertising Age,* January 11, 2016, http://adage.com/article/cmo-strategy/coach-hopes-cute-english-bulldog-sell-clothes/302087/.

6. Joseph T. Plummer, "Word-of-Mouth—a New Advertising Discipline?" *Journal of Advertising Research* 47, no. 4 (December 2007), pp. 385–86; Dee T. Allsop, Bryce R. Bassett, and James A. Hoskins, "Word-of-Mouth Research: Principles and Applications," *Journal of Advertising Research* 47, no. 4 (December 2007), pp. 398–411; Robert E. Smith and Christine A. Vogt, "The Effects of Integrating Advertising and Negative Word-of-Mouth

Communications on Message Processing and Response," *Journal of Consumer Psychology* 4, no. 2 (1995), pp. 133–51; Barry L. Bayus, "Word of Mouth: The Indirect Effect of Marketing Efforts," *Journal of Advertising Research* 25, no. 3 (June/July 1985), pp. 31–39.

7. Kate Niederhoffer, Rob Mooth, David Wiesenfeld, and Jonathon Gordon, "The Origin and Impact of CPG New-Product Buzz: Emerging Trends and Implications," *Journal of Advertising Research*, December 2007, pp. 420–26; Catharine P. Taylor, "Pssst! How Do You Measure Buzz?" *Adweek*, October 24, 2005, pp. 26–28; Robert Brenner, "I Sold It through the Grapevine," *BusinessWeek*, May 26, 2006, pp. 32–34; Garry Khermouch and Jeff Green, "Buzz Marketing," *BusinessWeek*, July 30, 2001, pp. 50–56.

8. E. J. Schultz, "Why 'Crash the Super Bowl' Hasn't Burned Out for Doritos," *Advertising Age*, January 24, 2013, http://adage.com/article/special-report-super-bowl/crash-super-bowl-burned-doritos/239373/; Michael Learmoth, "Doritos, Google, Super Bowl Ads Storm Chart," *Advertising Age*, February 18, 2010, http://adage.com/article/the-viral-video-chart/doritos-google-super-bowl-ads-storm-viral-video-chart/142151/.

9. Kristina Monllos, "Doritos Is Ending Its 'Crash the Super Bowl' Contest, but Not Before One Last Hurrah," *Adweek*, September 9, 2015, www.adweek.com/news/advertising-branding/doritos-ending-its-crash-super-bowl-contest-not-one-last-hurrah-166784; Christopher Heine, "Frito-Lay Likes the Data from Doritos' 'Crash the Super Bowl,'" *Adweek*, February 7, 2013, www.adweek.com/news/technology/frito-lay-likes-data-doritos-crash-super-bowl-147127.

10. Yuping Liu-Thompkins, "Seeding Viral Content," *Journal of Advertising Research* 52, no. 4 (December 2012), pp. 465–78.

11. Ibid.

12. Tim Nudd, "The 20 Most Viral Ads of 2015," *Adweek*, November 19, 2015, www.adweek.com/news-gallery/advertising-branding/20-most-viral-ads-2015-168213.

13. H. C. Chiu, Y. C. Hsieh, Y. H. Kao, and M. Lee, "The Determinants of

Email Receivers' Disseminating Behaviors on the Internet," *Journal of Advertising Research* 47, no. 4 (December 2007), pp. 524–34; T. Sun, S. Y. G. Wu, and M. Kuntaraporn, "Online Word-of-Mouth (or Mouse): An Exploration of Its Antecedents and Consequences," *Journal of Computer-Mediated Communication* 11, no. 4 (2006).

14. J. Y. C. Ho and M. Dempsey, "Viral Marketing Motivations to Forward Online Content," *Journal of Business Research* 63, no. 9/10 (2010), pp. 1000–06; Z. Katona, P. Zubcsek, and M. Sarvary, "Network Effect and Personal Influences: Diffusion of an Online Social Network," *Journal of Marketing Research* 48, no. 3 (2011), pp. 425–43; M. Trusov, A. V. Bodpati, and R. E. Bucklin, "Determining Influential Users in Internet Social Networks," *Journal of Marketing Research* 47, no. 4 (2010), pp. 643–58.

15. "Why Some Videos Go Viral," *Harvard Business Review*, September 2015, pp. 34–35.

16. Liu-Thompkins, "Seeding Viral Content."

17. Eric Tegler, "Ford Is Counting on Army of 1,000 Bloggers to Launch Ford Fiesta," *Advertising Age*, April 20, 2009, p. 17.

18. Ed Keller and Brad Fay, "The Role of Advertising in Word of Mouth," *Journal of Advertising Research* 49, no. 2 (June 2009), pp. 154–58; Ed Keller and Jon Berry, "Word-of-Mouth: The Real Action Is Offline," *Advertising Age*, December 4, 2006, p. 20.

19. Ed Keller and Brad Fay, "Word-of-Mouth Advocacy," *Journal of Advertising Research*, December 2012, pp. 459–64.

20. Ibid.

21. Ed Keller and Brad Fay, *The Face-to-Face Book: Why Real Relationships Rule in a Digital Marketplace* (New York: Free Press, 2012), pp. 103–06.

22. Larry Yu, "How Companies Turn Buzz into Sales," *MIT Sloan Management Review*," Winter 2005, pp. 5–6.

23. Suzanne Vranica, "Getting Buzz Marketers to Fess Up," *The Wall Street Journal*, February 9, 2005, p. B9.

24. Ibid.

25. Keller and Fay, "Word-of-Mouth Advocacy."

26. Quote by Gordon S. Bower in *Fortune*, October 14, 1985, p. 11.

27. Meg James, "Over 50 and out of Favor," *The Los Angeles Times*, May 10, 2005, pp. A1, A10.

28. "Most Digital Viewers Multitask While Watching Live TV," *eMarketer.com*, November 30, 2015, www.emarketer.com/Article/Most-Digital-Viewers-Multitask-While-Watching-Live-TV/1013281.

29. Thomas V. Bonoma and Leonard C. Felder, "Nonverbal Communication in Marketing: Toward Communicational Analysis," *Journal of Marketing Research*, May 1977, pp. 169–80.

30. Jacob Jacoby and Wayne D. Hoyer, "Viewer Miscomprehension of Televised Communication: Selected Findings," *Journal of Marketing* 46, no. 4 (Fall 1982), pp. 12–26; Jacob Jacoby and Wayne D. Hoyer, "The Comprehension and Miscomprehension of Print Communications: An Investigation of Mass Media Magazines," *Advertising Education Foundation Study*, New York, 1987.

31. E. K. Strong, *The Psychology of Selling* (New York: McGraw-Hill, 1925), p. 9.

32. Brent Adamason, Matthew Dixon, and Nicholas Toman, "The End of Solution Sales," *Harvard Business Review* 90, no. 7/8 (July/August 2012), pp. 60–68.

33. Robert J. Lavidge and Gary A. Steiner, "A Model for Predictive Measurements of Advertising Effectiveness," *Journal of Marketing* 24 (October 1961), pp. 59–62.

34. Thomas Barry, "The Development of the Hierarchy of Effects: An Historical Perspective," *Current Issues & Research in Advertising* 10, no. 2 (1987), pp. 251–95.

35. Everett M. Rogers, *Diffusion of Innovations* (New York: Free Press, 1962), pp. 79–86.

36. "Shiny New Things: What Digital Adopters Want, How to Reach Them, and Why Every Marketer Should Pay Attention," *Advertising Age Insights White Paper*, March 15, 2010.

37. Ibid.

38. William J. McGuire, "An Information Processing Model of Advertising Effectiveness," in *Behavioral and Management Science in Marketing*, Harry J. Davis and Alvin J. Silk, eds. (New York: Ronald Press, 1978), pp. 156–80.

39. Michael L. Ray, "Communication and the Hierarchy of Effects," in

New Models for Mass Communication Research, P. Clarke, ed. (Beverly Hills, CA: Sage, 1973), pp. 147–75.

40. Herbert E. Krugman, "The Impact of Television Advertising: Learning without Involvement," *Public Opinion Quarterly* 29 (Fall 1965), pp. 349–56.

41. Scott A. Hawkins and Stephen J. Hoch, "Low-Involvement Learning: Memory without Evaluation," *Journal of Consumer Research* 19, no. 2 (September 1992), pp. 212–25.

42. Harry W. McMahan, "Do Your Ads Have VIP?" *Advertising Age*, July 14, 1980, pp. 50–51.

43. Robert E. Smith, "Integrating Information from Advertising and Trial: Processes and Effects on Consumer Response to Product Information," *Journal of Marketing Research* 30 (May 1993), pp. 204–19.

44. DeAnna S. Kempf and Russell N. Laczniak, "Advertising's Influence on Subsequent Product Trial Processing," *Journal of Advertising* 30, no. 3 (Fall 2001), pp. 27–38.

45. Judith L. Zaichkowsky, "Conceptualizing Involvement," *Journal of Advertising* 15, no. 2 (1986), pp. 4–14; Anthony G. Greenwald and Clark Leavitt, "Audience Involvement in Advertising: Four Levels," *Journal of Consumer Research* 11, no. 1 (June 1984), pp. 581–92; Richard Vaughn, "How Advertising Works: A Planning Model," *Journal of Advertising Research* 20, no. 5 (October 1980), pp. 27–33; Richard Vaughn, "How Advertising Works: A Planning Model Revisited," *Journal of Advertising Research* 26, no. 1 (February/March 1986), pp. 57–66.

46. Todd Powers, Dorothy Advincula, Manila S. Austin, Stacy Graiko, and Jasper Snyder, "Digital and Social Media in the Purchase Decision Process," *Journal of Advertising Research*, December 2012, pp. 479–89.

47. Roxane Divol, David Edelman, and Hugo Sarrazin, "Demystifying Social Media," *McKinsey Quarterly*, April 2012, www.mckinsey.com/insights/marketing_sales/demystifying_social_media.

48. Ibid.

49. David Court, Dave Elzinga, Susan Mulder, and Ole Jorgen Vetvik, "The Consumer Decision Journey," *McKinsey Quarterly*, June 2009, www.mckinsey.com/insights/marketing_sales/the_consumer_decision_journey.

50. Ibid.

51. Jerry C. Olson, Daniel R. Toy, and Phillip A. Dover, "Mediating Effects of Cognitive Responses to Advertising on Cognitive Structure," in *Advances in Consumer Research* (vol. 5), H. Keith Hunt, ed. (Ann Arbor, MI: Association for Consumer Research, 1978), pp. 72–78.

52. Anthony A. Greenwald, "Cognitive Learning, Cognitive Response to Persuasion and Attitude Change," in *Psychological Foundations of Attitudes*, A. G. Greenwald, T. C. Brock, and T. W. Ostrom, eds. (New York: Academic Press, 1968); Peter L. Wright, "The Cognitive Processes Mediating Acceptance of Advertising," *Journal of Marketing Research* 10 (February 1973), pp. 53–62; Brian Wansink, Michael L. Ray, and Rajeev Batra, "Increasing Cognitive Response Sensitivity," *Journal of Advertising* 23, no. 2 (June 1994), pp. 65–76.

53. Peter Wright, "Message Evoked Thoughts, Persuasion Research Using Thought Verbalizations," *Journal of Consumer Research* 7, no. 2 (September 1980), pp. 151–75.

54. Scott B. Mackenzie, Richard J. Lutz, and George E. Belch, "The Role of Attitude toward the Ad as a Mediator of Advertising Effectiveness: A Test of Competing Explanations," *Journal of Marketing Research* 23 (May 1986), pp. 130–43; Rajeev Batra and Michael L. Ray, "Affective Responses Mediating Acceptance of Advertising," *Journal of Consumer Research* 13 (September 1986), pp. 234–49; Tim Ambler and Tom Burne, "The Impact of Affect on Memory of Advertising," *Journal of Advertising Research* 29, no. 3 (March/April 1999), pp. 25–34.

55. Ronald Alsop, "TV Ads That Are Likeable Get Plus Rating for Persuasiveness," *The Wall Street Journal*, February 20, 1986, p. 23.

56. David J. Moore and William D. Harris, "Affect Intensity and the Consumer's Attitude toward High Impact Emotional Advertising Appeals," *Journal of Advertising* 25, no. 2 (Summer 1996), pp. 37–50; Andrew A. Mitchell and Jerry C. Olson, "Are Product Attribute Beliefs the Only Mediator of Advertising Effects on Brand Attitude?" *Journal of Marketing Research* 18 (August 1981), pp. 318–32.

57. David J. Moore, William D. Harris, and Hong C. Chen, "Affect Intensity: An Individual Difference Response to Advertising Appeals," *Journal of Consumer Research* 22 (September 1995), pp. 154–64; Julie Edell and Marian C. Burke, "The Power of Feelings in Understanding Advertising Effects," *Journal of Consumer Research* 14 (December 1987), pp. 421–33.

58. Richard E. Petty and John T. Cacioppo, "Central and Peripheral Routes to Persuasion: Application to Advertising," in *Advertising and Consumer Psychology*, Larry Percy and Arch Woodside, eds. (Lexington, MA: Lexington Books, 1983), pp. 3–23.

59. Ibid.

60. Richard E. Petty, John T. Cacioppo, and David Schumann, "Central and Peripheral Routes to Advertising Effectiveness: The Moderating Role of Involvement," *Journal of Consumer Research* 10 (September 1983), pp. 135–46.

61. Fred K. Beard, "Peer Evaluation and Readership of Influential Contributions to the Advertising Literature," *Journal of Advertising* 31, no. 4 (2002), pp. 65–75.

62. Philip J. Kitchen, Gayle Kerr, Don E. Schultz, Rod McColl, and Heather Pals, "The Elaboration Likelihood Model: Review, Critique and Research Agenda," *European Journal of Marketing* 48, no. 11/12 (2014), pp. 2033–50; Catherine Cole, Richard Ettenson, Suzanne Reinke, and Tracy Schrader, "The Elaboration Likelihood Model (ELM): Replication, Extensions, and Some Conflicting Findings," *Advances in Consumer Research* 17 (1990), pp. 231–236.

63. Gayle Kerr, Don E. Schultz, Philip J. Kitchen, Frank J. Mulhern, and Park Beede, "Does Traditional Advertising Theory Apply to the Digital World?" *Journal of Advertising Research* 55, no. 1 (2015), pp. 1–11.

64. Demetrios Vakratsas and Tim Ambler, "How Advertising Works: What Do We Really Know?" *Journal of Marketing* 63 (January 1999), pp. 26–43.

65. Bruce F. Hall, "A New Model for Measuring Advertising Effects," *Journal of Advertising Research* 42, no. 2 (March/April 2002), pp. 23–31.

66. Thomas E. Barry, "In Defense of the Hierarchy of Effects: A Rejoinder to Weilbacher," *Journal of Advertising Research*, May/June 2002, pp. 44–47.

67. William M. Weilbacher, "Point of View: Does Advertising Cause a 'Hierarchy of Effects?,'" *Journal of Advertising Research* 41, no. 6 (November/December 2001), pp. 19–26.

Chapter 6

1. William J. McGuire, "An Information Processing Model of Advertising Effectiveness," in *Behavioral and Management Science in Marketing*, Harry J. Davis and Alvin J. Silk, eds. (New York: Ronald Press, 1978), pp. 156–80.

2. Dennis Thompsett, "Kardashians Know How to Attract Their Target Audience," *Owen Sound Sun Times,* May 2, 2012, www.owensoundsuntimes.com/2012/05/02/kardashians-know-how-to-attract-their-target-audience.

3. Kate Niedeerhoffer, Rob Mooth, David Wiesenfeld, and Jonathon Gordon, "The Origin and Impact of CPG New-Product Buzz: Emerging Trends and Implications," *Journal of Advertising Research* 47, no. 4 (December 2007), pp. 420–26.

4. Herbert C. Kelman, "Processes of Opinion Change," *Public Opinion Quarterly* 25 (Spring 1961), pp. 57–78.

5. William J. McGuire, "The Nature of Attitudes and Attitude Change," in *Handbook of Social Psychology* (2nd ed.), G. Lindzey and E. Aronson, eds. (Cambridge, MA: Addison-Wesley, 1969), pp. 135–214; Daniel J. O'Keefe, "The Persuasive Effects of Delaying Identification of High- and Low-Credibility Communicators: A Meta-Analytic Review," *Central States Speech Journal* 38 (1987), pp. 63–72.

6. Roobina Ohanian, "The Impact of Celebrity Spokespersons' Image on Consumers' Intention to Purchase," *Journal of Advertising Research* 21 (February/March 1991), pp. 46–54.

7. Clinton Amos, Gary Holmes, and David Strutton, "Exploring the Relationship between Celebrity Endorser Effects and Advertising Effectiveness," *International Journal of Advertising* 27, no. 2 (2008), pp. 209–34.

8. "E-Score Celebrity Special Report–Year End 2012," E-Poll Market Research, www.epollresearch.com/marketing/E-score%20Celebrity%20YE%202012%202013-03-19-01-sl.pdf.

9. David P. Hamilton, "Celebrities Help 'Educate' Public on New Drugs," *The Wall Street Journal*, April 22, 2002, p. B1.

10. James Bandler, "How Companies Pay TV Experts for On-Air Product Mentions," *The Wall Street Journal*, April 19, 2005, pp. A1, A12.

11. Michael Learmonth, "FTC Cracks Down on Blogger Payola, Celebrity Tweets," *Advertising Age*, October 5, 2009, http://adage.com/article/digital/ftc-regulates-social-media-endorsements-blogger-payola/139457/.

12. Karlene Lukovitz, "Ads Starring CEOs: What Makes Winners, Losers?" *Marketing Daily*, March 13, 2012, www.mediapost.com/publications/article/170057/?print#axzz2i1DzzuMl.

13. Frank Green, "Masters of the Pitch," *San Diego Union-Tribune*, January 30, 2000, pp. 1, 6.

14. Barbara Lippert, "A Winner out of the Gates," *Adweek*, September 22, 2008, p. 28.

15. Bruce Horovitz and Theresa Howard, "Wendy's Loses Its Legend," *USA Today*, January 9, 2002, pp. 1B, 2B.

16. Emily Bryson York and Brooke Capps, "Dave Disciples Flip Wigs over Trendy Wendy," *Advertising Age*, September 3, 2007, pp. 1, 22; Kate MacArthur, "Wendy's Unveils New Brand Spokesperson," *Advertising Age*, February 18, 2004, http://adage.com/article/news/wendy-s-unveils-brand-spokesman/39467/.

17. Rupal Parekh and Kunur Patel, "Ten Things to Think Hard about before Featuring the Chairman in Advertising," *Advertising Age*, September 14, 2009, http://adage.com/print?article_id=138984.

18. Erick Reidenback and Robert Pitts, "Not All CEOs Are Created Equal as Advertising Spokespersons: Evaluating the Effective CEO Spokesperson," *Journal of Advertising* 20, no. 3 (1986), pp. 35–50; Roger Kerin and Thomas E. Barry, "The CEO Spokesperson in Consumer Advertising: An Experimental Investigation," in *Current Issues in Research in Advertising*, J. H. Leigh and C. R. Martin, eds.

(Ann Arbor: University of Michigan, 1981), pp. 135–48; J. Poindexter, "Voices of Authority," *Psychology Today*, August 1983.

19. Green, "Masters of the Pitch."

20. A. Eagly and S. Chaiken, "An Attribution Analysis of the Effect of Communicator Characteristics on Opinion Change," *Journal of Personality and Social Psychology* 32 (1975), pp. 136–44.

21. For a review of these studies, see Brian Sternthal, Lynn Philips, and Ruby Dholakia, "The Persuasive Effect of Source Credibility: A Situational Analysis," *Public Opinion Quarterly* 42 (Fall 1978), pp. 285–314.

22. Brian Sternthal, Ruby Dholakia, and Clark Leavitt, "The Persuasive Effects of Source Credibility: Tests of Cognitive Response," *Journal of Consumer Research* 4, no. 4 (March 1978), pp. 252–60; Robert R. Harmon and Kenneth A. Coney, "The Persuasive Effects of Source Credibility in Buy and Lease Situations," *Journal of Marketing Research* 19 (May 1982), pp. 255–60.

23. For a review, see Noel Capon and James Hulbert, "The Sleeper Effect: An Awakening," *Public Opinion Quarterly* 37 (1973), pp. 333–58.

24. Darlene B. Hannah and Brian Sternthal, "Detecting and Explaining the Sleeper Effect," *Journal of Consumer Research* 11, no. 2 (September 1984), pp. 632–42.

25. H. C. Triandis, *Attitudes and Attitude Change* (New York: Wiley, 1971).

26. J. Mills and J. Jellison, "Effect on Opinion Change Similarity between the Communicator and the Audience He Addresses," *Journal of Personality and Social Psychology* 9, no. 2 (1969), pp. 153–56.

27. Arch G. Woodside and J. William Davenport Jr., "The Effect of Salesman Similarity and Expertise on Consumer Purchasing Behavior," *Journal of Marketing Research* 11 (May 1974), pp. 198–202; Paul Busch and David T. Wilson, "An Experimental Analysis of a Salesman's Expert and Referent Bases of Social Power in the Buyer–Seller Dyad," *Journal of Marketing Research* 13 (February 1976), pp. 3–11.

28. Tim Nudd, "How Milan Vayntrub Became Advertising's New 'It' Girl," *Adweek*, January 13,

2015, www.adweek.com/news/ advertising-branding/how-milana-vayntrub-became-advertisings-new-it-girl-162297.

29. Marshall McLuhan, "Top Ad Campaigns of the 21st Century," *Advertising Age*, January 12, 2015, pp. 14–22; Jeff Graham, "Whassup with All Those Award Wins?" *Advertising Age*, August 21, 2000, http://adage. com/article/cracks-in-the-foundation/ defense-whassup/56775/.

30. Louise Story, "Seeing Stars," *The New York Times*, October 12, 2006, p. C1; Rich Thomaselli, "Searching for Michael Jordan," *Advertising Age*, September 5, 2005, p. 12.

31. George E. Belch and Michael A. Belch, "A Content Analysis Study of the Use of Celebrities in Magazine Advertising," *International Journal of Advertising* 32, no. 3 (2013), pp. 369–89.

32. Utpal Dhokakia, "Can a Celebrity Endorsement Hurt the Brand?," *Psychology Today*, November 3, 2015, www.psychologytoday. com/blog/the-science-behind-behavior/201511/can-celebrity-endorsement-hurt-the-brand.

33. Sejung Marina Choi, Wei-Na Lee, and Hee-Jung Kim, "Lessons from the Rich and Famous: A Cross-Cultural Comparison of Celebrity Endorsement in Advertising," *Journal of Advertising* 34, no. 2 (Summer 2005), pp. 85–99.

34. Kurt Badenhausen, "The World's Highest-Paid Athletes," *Forbes*, June 18, 2012, www.forbes.com/ sites/kurtbadenhausen/2012/06/18/ mayweather-tops-list-of-the-worlds-100-highest-paid-athletes/.

35. Carsten Erfgen, Sebastian Zenker, and Henrik Sattler, "The Vampire Effect: When Do Celebrity Endorsers Harm Brand Recall?," *International Journal of Research in Marketing* 32 (January 2015), pp. 155–163; Utpal Dhokakia, "Can a Celebrity Endorsement Hurt the Brand?," *Psychology Today*, November 3, 2015, www.psychologytoday. com/blog/the-science-behind-behavior/201511/can-celebrity-endorsement-hurt-the-brand.

36. Elena Gorgan, "Angelina Jolie Dumped by St. John for Overshadowing the Brand," *Softpedia*, January 9, 2010, http://news.softpedia.com/ news/Angelina-Jolie-Dumped-by-St-John-for-Overshadowing-the-Brand-131636.shtml.

37. Jasmina Elicic and Cynthia M. Webster, "Eclipsing: When Celebrities Overshadow the Brand," *Psychology & Marketing* 31, no. 11 (November 2014), pp. 1040–50.

38. Valerie Folkes, "Recent Attribution Research in Consumer Behavior: A Review and New Directions," *Journal of Consumer Research* 14 (March 1988), pp. 548–65; John C. Mowen and Stephen W. Brown, "On Explaining and Predicting the Effectiveness of Celebrity Endorsers," in *Advances in Consumer Research* (vol. 8), K. B. Monroe, ed. (Ann Arbor, MI: Association for Consumer Research, 1981), pp. 437–41.

39. Bruce Horovitz, "Armstrong Rolls to Market Gold," *USA Today*, May 4, 2000, pp. 1, 2B.

40. Stephen Rae, "How Celebrities Make Killings on Commercials," *Cosmopolitan*, January 1997, pp. 164–67.

41. Jessica Wohl, "Done with McDonald's, James Takes His Endorsing Talents to Pizza Chain," *Advertising Age*, October 8, 2015, http://adage. com/article/cmo-strategy/lebron-james-mcdonald-s-end-endorsement-deal/300826/; Lee Hawkins and Suzanne Vranica, "McDonald's Bets LeBron James Won't Be a Tiger," *The Wall Street Journal*, February 1, 2010, http://online.wsj.com/news/articles/ SB100014240527487043431045750 3378169040057.

42. Charles Atkin and M. Block, "Effectiveness of Celebrity Endorsers," *Journal of Advertising Research* 23, no. 1 (February/March 1983), pp. 57–61.

43. Kurt Badenhausen, "New Balance Challenges Nike and adidas with Entry into Global Soccer Market," *Forbes*, February 4, 2015, www. forbes.com/sites/kurtbadenhausen/ 2015/02/04/new-balance-enters-global-soccer-market/#390b46733f4f.

44. Brian D. Till and Terence A. Shimp, "Endorsers in Advertising: The Case of Negative Celebrity Information," *Journal of Advertising* 27, no. 1 (Spring 1998), pp. 67–82.

45. Rich Thomaselli, "Kobe Kept on the Marketing Bench," *Advertising Age*, September 13, 2004, p. 16; Mallory Russell, "Kobe Bryant and Lionel Messi Go Head-to-Head for Turkish Airlines," *Advertising Age*, December 11, 2012, http:// adage.com/article/the-viral-video-chart/kobe-bryant-lionel-messi-head-head-turkish-airlines/238716/; "Vitamin Water Planning Full Marketing Campaign around Kobe Bryant," *Sports Business Daily*, May 13, 2008, www.sportsbusinessdaily. com/article/120800.

46. Elizabeth Lazarowitz, "Paula Deen Has Lost as Much as $12.5 Million in Earnings over N-Word Controversy: Experts," *New York Daily News*, June 28 2013, www.nydailynews.com/ entertainment/tv-movies/deen-lost-12-5-million-experts-article-1.1385469.

47. Maureen Morrision, "Subway Officially Cuts Ties with Jared," *Advertising Age*, August 8 , 2015, http://adage. com/article/cmo-strategy/subway-officially-cuts-ties-jared/300012/.

48. Stephanie Thompson, "Heroin Chic OK, Cocaine Use Not," *Advertising Age*, September 26, 2005, pp. 3, 80.

49. Cathy Yingling, "Beware the Lure of Celebrity Endorsers," *Advertising Age*, September 24, 2007, http://adage. com/article/cmo-strategy/beware-lure-celebrity-endorsers/120560/; James Tenser, "Endorser Qualities Count More Than Ever," *Advertising Age*, November 8, 2004, pp. S2, S4.

50. Anita Elberse and Jeroen Verleun, "The Economic Value of Celebrity Endorsements," *Journal of Advertising Research* 52, no. 2 (June 2012), pp. 149–65.

51. E. J. Schultz, "Justin Timberlake Leaves A-B InBev, Joins Beam," *Advertising Age*, January 9, 2014, http://adage.com/article/news/ justin-timberlake-leaves-a-b-inbev-joins-beam/291005/.

52. E. J. Schultz and Rupal Parekh, "Justin Timberlake Is the New Face of Bud Light Platinum," *Advertising Age*, February 7, 2013, http://adage.com/ article/news/justin-timberlake-face-bud-light-platinum/239672/.

53. Shareen Pathak, "Beyonce Just Latest to Become Brand Ambassador, but Do These Deals Actually Work?," *Advertising Age*, December 17, 2012, http://adage.com/article/news/ beyonce-latest-brand-ambassador-deals-work/238795/.

54. Natalie Zmuda, "Beverage Brand Swaps Equity for Met's Endorsements," *Advertising Age*, April 20, 2009, http:// adage.com/article/news/

beverage-brand-sonu-swaps-equity-mets-endorsements/136085/.

55. Dean Crutchfield, "Celebrity Endorsements Still Push Product," *Advertising Age*, September 22, 2010, http://adage.com/article/cmo-strategy/marketing-celebrity-endorsements-push-product/146023/.

56. Kevin Plank, "Under Armour's Founder on Learning to Leverage Celebrity Endorsements," *Harvard Business Review*, May 2012, pp. 45–48.

57. Dave McCaughan, "The Fine Art of Matching a Celebrity with a Brand," *Advertising Age*, April 16, 2007, p. 34; Betsy Cummings, "Star Power," *Sales and Marketing Management*, April 2001, pp. 52–59; Michael A. Kamins, "An Investigation into the 'Match-Up' Hypothesis in Celebrity Advertising," *Journal of Advertising* 19, no. 1 (1990), pp. 4–13.

58. Grant McCracken, "Who Is the Celebrity Endorser? Cultural Foundations of the Endorsement Process," *Journal of Consumer Research* 16, no. 3 (December 1989), pp. 310–21.

59. Ibid., p. 315.

60. Stephen Williams, "Fiat Enlists Ultimate Bad Boy for Its Ads: Charlie Sheen," *Advertising Age*, March 1, 2012, http://adage.com/article/adages/fiat-enlists-ultimate-bad-boy-ads-charlie-sheen/233045/.

61. Srivdya Kalganavaman, "American Express Taps Tina Fey to Introduce New Credit Card," *Advertising Age*, March 2, 2014, http://adage.com/article/cmo-strategy/american-express-taps-tina-fey-introduce-credit-card/291924/.

62. B. Zafer Erdogan, Michael J. Baker, and Stephen Tagg, "Selecting Celebrity Endorsers: The Practitioner's Perspective," *Journal of Advertising Research* 41, no. 43 (May/June 2001), pp. 39–48.

63. For an excellent review of these studies, see Marilyn Y. Jones, Andrea J. S. Stanaland, and Betsy D. Gelb, "Beefcake and Cheesecake: Insights for Advertisers," *Journal of Advertising* 27, no. 2 (Summer 1998), pp. 32–51; W. B. Joseph, "The Credibility of Physically Attractive Communicators," *Journal of Advertising* 11, no. 3 (1982), pp. 13–23.

64. Michael Solomon, Richard Ashmore, and Laura Longo, "The Beauty Match-Up Hypothesis: Congruence between Types of Beauty and Product Images in Advertising," *Journal of Advertising* 21, no. 4, pp. 23–34; M. J. Baker and Gilbert A. Churchill Jr., "The Impact of Physically Attractive Models on Advertising Evaluations," *Journal of Marketing Research* 14 (November 1977), pp. 538–55.

65. Robert W. Chestnut, C. C. La Chance, and A. Lubitz, "The Decorative Female Model: Sexual Stimuli and the Recognition of the Advertisements," *Journal of Advertising* 6 (Fall 1977), pp. 11–14; Leonard N. Reid and Lawrence C. Soley, "Decorative Models and Readership of Magazine Ads," *Journal of Advertising Research* 23, no. 2 (April/May 1983), pp. 27–32.

66. Amanda B. Bower, "Highly Attractive Models in Advertising and the Women Who Loathe Them: The Implications of Negative Affect for Spokesperson Effectiveness," *Journal of Advertising* 30, no. 3 (Fall 2001), pp. 51–63; Amanda B. Bower and Stacy Landreth, "Is Beauty Best? Highly versus Normally Attractive Models in Advertising," *Journal of Advertising* 30, no. 1 (2001), pp. 1–12.

67. Jack Neff, "In Dove Ads, Normal Is the New Beautiful," *Advertising Age*, September 27, 2004, pp. 1, 80.

68. Michelle Jeffers, "Behind Dove's 'Real Beauty,'" *Adweek*, September 12, 2005, pp. 34–35.

69. Herbert E. Krugman, "On Application of Learning Theory to TV Copy Testing," *Public Opinion Quarterly* 26 (1962), pp. 626–39.

70. C. I. Hovland and W. Mandell, "An Experimental Comparison of Conclusion Drawing by the Communicator and by the Audience," *Journal of Abnormal and Social Psychology* 47 (July 1952), pp. 581–88.

71. Alan G. Sawyer and Daniel J. Howard, "Effect of Omitting Conclusions in Advertisements to Involved and Uninvolved Audiences," *Journal of Marketing Research* 28 (November 1991), pp. 467–74.

72. Paul Chance, "Ads without Answers Make Brain Itch," *Psychology Today* 9 (1975), p. 78.

73. Connie Pechmann, "Predicting When Two-Sided Ads Will Be More Effective Than One-Sided Ads," *Journal of Marketing Research* 24 (November 1992), pp. 441–53; George E. Belch, "The Effects of Message Modality on One- and Two-Sided Advertising Messages," in *Advances in Consumer Research* (vol. 10), Richard P. Bagozzi and Alice M. Tybout, eds. (Ann Arbor, MI: Association for Consumer Research, 1983), pp. 21–26.

74. Robert E. Settle and Linda L. Golden, "Attribution Theory and Advertiser Credibility," *Journal of Marketing Research* 11 (May 1974), pp. 181–85; Edmund J. Faison, "Effectiveness of One-Sided and Two-Sided Mass Communications in Advertising," *Public Opinion Quarterly* 25 (Fall 1961), pp. 468–69.

75. Martin Eisend, "Two-Sided Advertising: A Meta-Analysis," *International Journal of Research in Marketing* 23 (June 2006), pp. 187–98.

76. Paul Farhi, "Behind Domino's Mea Culpa Ad Campaign," *The Washington Post*, January 12, 2010, p. C7.

77. Alan G. Sawyer, "The Effects of Repetition of Refutational and Supportive Advertising Appeals," *Journal of Marketing Research* 10 (February 1973), pp. 23–37; George J. Szybillo and Richard Heslin, "Resistance to Persuasion: Inoculation Theory in a Marketing Context," *Journal of Marketing Research* 10 (November 1973), pp. 396–403.

78. Andrew A. Mitchell, "The Effect of Verbal and Visual Components of Advertisements on Brand Attitudes and Attitude toward the Advertisement," *Journal of Consumer Research* 13 (June 1986), pp. 12–24; Julie A. Edell and Richard Staelin, "The Information Processing of Pictures in Advertisements," *Journal of Consumer Research* 10, no. 1 (June 1983), pp. 45–60; Elizabeth C. Hirschmann, "The Effects of Verbal and Pictorial Advertising Stimuli on Aesthetic, Utilitarian and Familiarity Perceptions," *Journal of Advertising* 15, no. 2 (1986), pp. 27–34.

79. Jolita Kisielius and Brian Sternthal, "Detecting and Explaining Vividness Effects in Attitudinal Judgments," *Journal of Marketing Research* 21, no. 1 (1984), pp. 54–64.

80. H. Rao Unnava and Robert E. Burnkrant, "An Imagery-Processing View of the Role of Pictures in Print Advertisements," *Journal of Marketing Research* 28 (May 1991), pp. 226–31.

81. Susan E. Heckler and Terry L. Childers, "The Role of Expectancy and Relevancy in Memory for Verbal

and Visual Information: What Is Incongruency?" *Journal of Consumer Research* 18, no. 4 (March 1992), pp. 475–92.

82. Michael J. Houston, Terry L. Childers, and Susan E. Heckler, "Picture-Word Consistency and the Elaborative Processing of Advertisements," *Journal of Marketing Research* 24 (November 1987), pp. 359–69.

83. William L. Wilkie and Paul W. Farris, "Comparative Advertising: Problems and Potential," *Journal of Marketing* 39 (1975), pp. 7–15.

84. For a review of comparative advertising studies, see Fred K. Beard, "Practitioner View of Comparative Advertising," *Journal of Advertising Research* 53, no. 3 (September 2013), pp. 313–23; Cornelia Pechmann and David W. Stewart, "The Psychology of Comparative Advertising," in *Attention, Attitude and Affect in Response to Advertising*, E.M. Clark, T.C. Brock, and D.W. Stewart, eds. (Hillsdale, NJ: Erlbaum, 1994), pp. 79–96; Thomas S. Barry, "Comparative Advertising: What Have We Learned in Two Decades?" *Journal of Advertising Research* 33, no. 2 (1993), pp. 19–29.

85. Emily Bryson York, "Brand vs. Brand: Attack Ads on the Rise," *Advertising Age*, October 27, 2008, http://adage.com/article/news/brand-brand-attack-ads-rise/132028/.

86. Amir Nasr, "What's Up with Those Wireless Attack Ads?," *Morning Consult*, January 25, 2016, https://morningconsult.com/2016/01/25/whats-up-with-those-wireless-attack-ads/.

87. Beth Snyder Bulik, "Marketer of the Decade: Apple," *Advertising Age*, October 18, 2010, http://adage.com/article/special-report-marketer-of-the-year-2010/marketer-decade-apple/146492/.

88. Fred Beard, "The Effectiveness of Comparative versus Non-Comparative Advertising," *Journal of Advertising Research* 55, no. 3 (September 2015), pp. 296–306.

89. Patrick Meirick, "Cognitive Responses to Negative and Comparative Political Advertising," *Journal of Advertising* 31, no. 1 (Spring 2002), pp. 49–59.

90. Bruce E. Pinkleton, Nam-Hyun Um, and Erica Weintraub Austin, "An Exploration of the Effects of Negative Political Advertising on Political

Decision Making," *Journal of Advertising* 31, no. 1 (Spring 2002), pp. 13–25.

91. Bruce E. Pinkleton, "The Effects of Negative Comparative Political Advertising on Candidate Evaluations and Advertising Evaluations: An Exploration," *Journal of Advertising* 26, no. 1 (1997), pp. 19–29.

92. Michael L. Ray and William L. Wilkie, "Fear: The Potential of an Appeal Neglected by Marketing," *Journal of Marketing* 34 (January 1970), pp. 54–62.

93. Brian Sternthal and C. Samuel Craig, "Fear Appeals Revisited and Revised," *Journal of Consumer Research* 1 (December 1974), pp. 22–34.

94. Punam Anand Keller and Lauren Goldberg Block, "Increasing the Persuasiveness of Fear Appeals: The Effect of Arousal and Elaboration," *Journal of Consumer Research* 22, no. 4 (March 1996), pp. 448–60.

95. John F. Tanner Jr., James B. Hunt, and David R. Eppright, "The Protection Motivation Model: A Normative Mode of Fear Appeals," *Journal of Marketing* 55 (July 1991), pp. 36–45.

96. Ibid.

97. Sternthal and Craig, "Fear Appeals Revisited and Revised."

98. Herbert Jack Rotfeld, "The Textbook Effect: Conventional Wisdom, Myth and Error in Marketing," *Journal of Marketing* 64 (April 2000), pp. 122–27.

99. The Meth Project, http://foundation.methproject.org/About-Us/index.php.

100. Andrea C. Morales, Eugenia C. Wu, and Gavan J. Fitzsimons, "How Disgust Enhances the Effectiveness of Fear Appeals," *Journal of Marketing Research*, June 2012, pp. 383–93.

101. Fred K. Beard, "One Hundred Years of Humor in American Advertising," *Journal of Macromarketing,* 25, no. 2 (June 2005), pp. 54–65; C. Samuel Craig and Brian Sternthal, "Humor in Advertising," *Journal of Marketing,* 37, October 1973, pp. 12–18.

102. Eisend, "Two-Sided Advertising: A Meta-Analysis."

103. Bobby J. Calder and Brian Sternthal, "A Television Commercial Wearout: An Information Processing View," *Journal of Marketing Research* 17 (May 1980), pp. 173–87.

104. Dottie Enroco, "Humorous Touch Resonates with Consumers," *USA Today*, May 13, 1996, p. 3B.

105. Yong Zhang, "Response to Humorous Advertising: The Moderating Effect of Need for Cognition," *Journal of Advertising* 25, no. 1 (Spring 1996), pp. 15–32; Marc G. Weinberger and Charles S. Gulas, "The Impact of Humor in Advertising: A Review," *Journal of Advertising* 21 (December 1992), pp. 35–59.

106. Marc G. Weinberger and Leland Campbell, "The Use of Humor in Radio Advertising," *Journal of Advertising Research* 31 (December/January 1990–91), pp. 44–52.

107. Yong Zhang and George M. Zinkhan, "Responses to Humorous Ads," *Journal of Advertising*, Winter 2006, pp. 113–27.

108. Harold C. Cash and W.J.E. Crissy, "Comparison of Advertising and Selling: The Salesman's Role in Marketing," *Psychology of Selling* 12 (1965), pp. 56–75.

109. Marshall McLuhan, *Understanding Media: The Extensions of Man* (New York: McGraw-Hill, 1966).

110. Marvin E. Goldberg and Gerald J. Gorn, "Happy and Sad TV Programs: How They Affect Reactions to Commercials," *Journal of Consumer Research* 14, no. 3 (December 1987), pp. 387–403.

111. Andrew B. Aylesworth and Scott B. MacKenzie, "Context Is Key: The Effect of Program-Induced Mood on Thoughts about the Ad," *Journal of Advertising* 27, no. 2 (Summer 1998), pp. 17–32.

112. Michael T. Elliott and Paul Surgi Speck, "Consumer Perceptions of Advertising Clutter and Its Impact across Various Media," *Journal of Advertising Research* 38, no. 1 (January/February 1998), pp. 29–41; Peter H. Webb, "Consumer Initial Processing in a Difficult Media Environment," *Journal of Consumer Research* 6, no. 3 (December 1979), pp. 225–36.

113. Sam Thielman, "You Endure More Commercials When Watching Cable Networks," *Adweek*, June 23, 2013, www.adweek.com/news/television/you-endure-more-commercials-when-watching-cable-networks-150575.

114. "How Many Minutes of Commercials Are Shown in an Average TV Hour? The Number Has Been Steadily Climbing," May 13, 2014, www.tvweek.com/tvbizwire/2014/05/how-many-minutes-of-commercial/.

115. Katy Bachman, "Clutter Makes TV Ads Less Effective," *Adweek*, February 9, 2010, www.adweek.com/aw/content_display/news/media/e3i4fe3d67e44c8b3ad4c3fcbfe797fc862.

116. Joe Flint, "Cable TV Shows Are Sped Up to Squeeze in More Ads," *The Wall Street Journal*, February 18, 2015, www.wsj.com/articles/cable-tv-shows-are-sped-up-to-squeeze-in-more-ads-1424301320.

117. Steve McClellan, "Buyers, Now Try to Skirt Clutter with Sponsor Deals," *Adweek*, October 31, 2005, p. 9.

Chapter 7

1. "Do Marketers Rely on Instinct over ROI?" www.eMarketer.com, February 24, 2015.

2. Mya Frazier, "GEICO's Big Spending Pays Off, Study Says," *Advertising Age*, June 26, 2007, http://adage.com/article/news/geico-s-big-spending-pays-study/118844/.

3. Mark Miller, "Coca-Cola Sees Pay-Off from Increased Marketing Spend," www.brandchannel.com, July 30, 2015.

4. Donald S. Tull, "The Carry-Over Effect of Advertising," *Journal of Marketing*, April 1965, pp. 46–53.

5. Darral G. Clarke, "Econometric Measurement of the Duration of Advertising Effect on Sales," *Journal of Marketing Research* 23 (November 1976), pp. 345–57.

6. Philip Kotler, *Marketing Decision Making: A Model Building Approach* (New York: Holt, Rinehart & Winston, 1971), Ch. 5.

7. Becky Ebencamp, "You Can Teach an Old Hot Dog Brand Some New Design Tricks," www.brandweek.com, September 28, 2009.

8. Stephanie Thompson, "Kellogg's Roars Back with Out of Box Ads," *Advertising Age*, May 3, 2004, pp. 4–5.

9. Adam Tschorn, "How Vans Tapped Southern California Skate Culture and Became a Billion-Dollar Shoe Brand," www.latimes.com, March 12, 2016.

10. Russell H. Colley, *Defining Advertising Goals for Measured Advertising Results* (New York: Association of National Advertisers, 1961).

11. Don E. Schultz, Dennis Martin, and William Brown, *Strategic Advertising Campaigns*, 2nd ed. (Lincolnwood, IL: Crain Books, 1984).

12. Michael L. Ray, "Consumer Initial Processing: Definitions, Issues, Applications," in *Buyer/Consumer Information Processing*, G. David Hughes, ed. (Chapel Hill: University of North Carolina Press, 1974); David A. Aaker and John G. Myers, *Advertising Management*, 2nd ed. (Englewood Cliffs, NJ: Prentice Hall, 1982), pp. 122–23.

13. Aaker and Myers, *Advertising Management*.

14. Steven W. Hartley and Charles H. Patti, "Evaluating Business to Business Advertising: A Comparison of Objectives and Results," *Journal of Advertising Research*, 28 (April/May 1988), pp. 21–27.

15. Jerry Thomas, "Advertising Effectiveness, 2008, www.decisionanalyst.com.

16. Don E. Schultz, "Integration Helps You Plan Communications from Outside-In," *Marketing News*, March 15, 1993, p. 12.

17. Thomas R. Duncan, "To Fathom Integrated Marketing, Dive!," *Advertising Age*, October 11, 1993, p. 18.

18. G. Tellis and K Tellis, "Research on Advertising in a Recession," *Journal of Advertising Research* 49, no. 3 (2009), 304–27. Retrieved from Communication & Mass Media Complete database.

19. Robert L. Steiner, "The Paradox of Increasing Returns to Advertising," *Journal of Advertising Research*, February/March 1987, pp. 45–53.

20. David A. Aaker and James M. Carman, "Are You Overadvertising?" *Journal of Advertising Research* 22, no. 4 (August/September 1982), pp. 57–70.

21. Julian A. Simon and Johan Arndt, "The Shape of the Advertising Response Function," *Journal of Advertising Research* 20, no. 4 (1980), pp. 11–28.

22. Melvin E. Salveson, "Management's Criteria for Advertising Effectiveness," in *Proceedings to the 5th Annual Conference, Advertising Research Foundation*, New York, 1959, p. 25.

23. Boonghee Yoo and Rujirutana Mandhachitara, "Estimating Advertising Effects on Sales in a Competitive Setting," *Journal of Advertising Research* 43, no. 3 (2003), pp. 310–20.

24. Dan Lippe, "Media Scorecard: How ROI Adds Up," *Advertising Age*, June 20, 2005, pp. S-6, S-42.

25. Mike Beirne and Kenneth Hein, "Marketers' Mantra: It's ROI, or I'm Fired!," *Brandweek*, October 18, 2004, pp. 14–15.

26. Joe Mandese, "Half of Media Buys Driven by ROI, TV, Online Dominate," April 20, 2005, www.mediapost.com/publications/article/29392/half-of-media-buys-driven-by-roi-tv-online-domin.html.

27. Wayne Friedman, "ROI Measurement Still Falls Short," *TelevisionWeek*, January 31, 2005, p. 19.

28. Hillary Chura, "Advertising ROI Still Elusive Metric," *Advertising Age*, July 26, 2004, p. 8.

29. James O. Peckham, "Can We Relate Advertising Dollars to Market Share Objectives?" in *How Much to Spend for Advertising*, M. A. McNiven, ed. (New York: Association of National Advertisers, 1969), p. 30.

30. George S. Low and Jakki Mohr, "Setting Advertising and Promotion Budgets in Multi-Brand Companies," *Journal of Advertising Research* 39, no. 1 (January/February 1999), pp. 667–78.

31. John P. Jones, "Ad Spending: Maintaining Market Share," *Harvard Business Review* 68, no. 1 (January/February 1990), pp. 38–42; James C. Schroer, "Ad Spending: Growing Market Share," *Harvard Business Review* 68, no. 1 (January/February 1990), pp. 44–48.

32. Randall S. Brown, "Estimating Advantages to Large-Scale Advertising," *Review of Economics and Statistics* 60 (August 1978), pp. 428–37.

33. Kent M. Lancaster, "Are There Scale Economies in Advertising?" *Journal of Business* 59, no. 3 (1986), pp. 509–26.

34. Johan Arndt and Julian Simon, "Advertising and Economics of Scale: Critical Comments on the Evidence," *Journal of Industrial Economics* 32, no. 2 (December 1983), pp. 229–41; Aaker and Carman, "Are You Overadvertising?"

35. George S. Low and Jakki J. Mohr, "The Budget Allocation between Advertising and Sales Promotion: Understanding the Decision Process," *AMA Educators' Proceedings, Summer 1991* (Chicago: American Marketing Association 1991), pp. 448–57.

Chapter 8

1. Quoted in Werner Reinartz and Peter Saffert, "Creativity in Advertising: When It Works and When It Doesn't," *Harvard Business Review,* June 2013, pp. 4–8.

2. Keith Reinhard, "After 60 Years in Advertising, I Believe True Creativity Is More Powerful Than Ever," *ADWEEK*, May 22, 2016, http://www.adweek.com/news/advertising-branding/after-60-years-advertising-i-believe-true-creativity-more-powerful-ever-171542; Jeremy Mullman and Stephanie Thompson, "Burnett's Stumble Continues as Altoids Slips Away," *Advertising Age*, January 5, 2007, http://adage.com/article/agency-news/burnett-s-stumble-continues-altoids-slips/114094/.

3. Maureen Morrison, "DDB Cut from Bud Light Review, Move Ends 30 Year Relationship with Brand in U.S.," *Advertising Age*, October 11, 2011, p. 3.

4. Tripp Mickle, "Can Advertising Revive Light Beer?," *The Wall Street Journal*, October 12, 2015, pp. B1, 4.

5. E. J. Schultz, "New Coors Light Campaign Has Women Drinkers in Mind," *Advertising Age,* January 25, 2016, http://adage.com/article/cmo-strategy/coors-light-campaign-women-drinkers-mind/302334/.

6. Douglas West, Albert Caruana, and Kannika Leelapanyalert, "What Makes Win, Place, or Show: Judging Creativity in Advertising at Award Shows," *Journal of Advertising Research* 53, no. 3 (2013), pp. 324–38; Bob Garfield, "Award Winners' Edge: That's Entertainment," *Advertising Age*, August 3, 2004, pp. 16–17; Brent Bouchez, "Trophies Are Meaningless," *Advertising Age*, July 30, 2001, p. 16; Vanessa O'Connell, "Ad Slump Deflates Awards Show," *The Wall Street Journal*, May 21, 2002, p. B2; Jennifer Pendleton, "Awards-Creatives Defend Pursuit of Prizes," *Advertising Age*, April 25, 1988, pp. 1, 7.

7. Elizabeth C. Hirschman, "Role-Based Models of Advertising Creation and Production," *Journal of Advertising* 18, no. (1989), pp. 42–53.

8. Ibid., p. 51.

9. Cyndee Miller, "Study Says 'Likability' Surfaces as Measure of TV Ad Success," *Marketing News*, January 7, 1991, pp. 6, 14; Ronald Alsop, "TV Ads That Are Likeable Get Plus Rating for Persuasiveness," *The Wall Street Journal*, February 20, 1986, p. 23.

10. Sheila L. Sasser and Scott Kaslow, "Desperately Seeking Advertising Creativity: Engaging an Imaginative 3 P's Research Agenda," *Journal of Advertising* 37, no. 4 (2008), pp. 5–19.

11. Scott Koslow, "I Love Creative Advertising," *Journal of Advertising Research* 55, no. 1 (March 2015), pp. 5–8.

12. Brian D. Till and Daniel W. Baack, "Recall and Persuasion: Does Creativity Matter?" *Journal of Advertising* 34, no. 3 (2005), pp. 47–57.

13. Robert E. Smith, Scott B. MacKenzie, Xiaojing Yang, Laura Buchholz, William K. Darley, and Xiaojing Yang, "Modeling the Determinants and Effects of Creativity in Advertising*,*" *Marketing Science* 26, no. 6 (2007), pp. 819–33; Robert E. Smith and Xiaojing Yang, "Toward a General Theory of Creativity in Advertising: Examining the Role of Divergence," *Marketing Theory* 4, no. 1/2 (2004), pp. 29–55.

14. Deborah J. MacInnis and Bernard J. Jaworski, "Information Processing from Advertisement: Toward an Integrative Framework," *Journal of Marketing* 53, no. 4 (October 1989), pp. 1–23.

15. Personal correspondence with Douglas Van Praet.

16. Robert E. Smith, Jiemiao Chen, and Xiaojing Yang*,* "The Impact of Advertising Creativity on the Hierarchy of Effects*,*" *Journal of Advertising* 37, no. 4 (Winter 2008), pp. 47–61.

17. Smith et al., "Modeling the Determinants and Effects of Creativity in Advertising."

18. Swee Hoon Ang, Yih Hwai Lee, and Siew Meng Leong, "The Ad Creativity Cube: Conceptualization and Initial Validation," *Journal of the Academy of Marketing Science* 35, no. 23 (2007), pp. 220–32; Arthur J. Kover, Stephen M. Goldenberg, and William L. James, "Creativity vs. Effectiveness? An Integrative Classification for Advertising," *Journal of Advertising Research* 35 (November/December 1995), pp. 29–38.

19. Reinartz and Saffert, "Creativity in Advertising: When It Works and When It Doesn't," *Harvard Business Review,* June 2013, pp. 4–8.

20. Smith et al., "Modeling the Determinants and Effects of Creativity in Advertising."

21. For an interesting discussion on the embellishment of advertising messages, see William M. Weilbacher, *Advertising*, 2nd ed. (New York: Macmillan, 1984), pp. 180–82.

22. David Ogilvy, *Confessions of an Advertising Man* (New York: Atheneum, 1963); Hanley Norins, *The Compleat Copywriter* (New York: McGraw-Hill, 1966).

23. Hank Sneiden, *Advertising Pure and Simple* (New York: ANACOM, 1977).

24. Quoted in Valerie H. Free, "Absolut Original," *Marketing Insights*, Summer 1991, p. 65.

25. Scott Koslow, Sheila L. Sasser, and Edward A. Riordan, "Do Marketers Get the Advertising They Need or the Advertising They Deserve?" *Journal of Advertising* 35, no. 3 (Fall 2006), pp. 81–101.

26. Jeff Jensen, "Marketer of the Year," *Advertising Age*, December 16, 1996, pp. 1, 16.

27. Ann Christine Diaz, "Creativity's Agency of the Year," *Advertising Age*, January 28, 2013, p. 24; Cathy Taylor, "Risk Takers: Wieden & Kennedy," *Adweek's Marketing Week*, March 23, 1992, pp. 26, 27.

28. Anthony Vagnoni, "Creative Differences," *Advertising Age*, November 17, 1997, pp. 1, 28, 30.

29. Jonathon Cranin, "Has Advertising Gone the Way of the Costra Nostra?" *Advertising Age*, June 6, 2005.

30. Vagnoni, "Creative Differences."

31. Cranin, "Has Advertising Gone the Way of the Costra Nostra?"

32. Arthur J. Kover, "Copywriters' Implicit Theories of Communication: An Exploration," *Journal of Consumer Research* 21, no. 4 (March 1995), pp. 596–611.

33. Sheila L. Sasser and Scott Koslow, "Desparately Seeking Advertising Creativity," *Journal of Advertising* 37, no. 4 (Winter 2008), pp. 5–19.

34. James Webb Young, *A Technique for Producing Ideas*, 3rd ed. (Chicago: Crain Books, 1975), p. 42.

35. Graham Wallas, *The Art of Thought* (New York: Harcourt Brace, 1926).

36. Debra Goldman, "Origin of the Species: Has the Planner Finally Evolved into the Agency's Most Potent Creature?" *Adweek*, April 10, 1995, pp. 28–38.

37. Jon Steel, *Truth, Lies & Advertising: The Art of Account Planning* (New York: Wiley, 1998).

38. Sandra E. Moriarty, *Creative Advertising: Theory and Practice* (Englewood Cliffs, NJ: Prentice Hall, 1986).

39. E. E. Norris, "Seek Out the Consumer's Problem," *Advertising Age*, March 17, 1975, pp. 43–44.

40. Thomas L. Greenbaum, "Focus Groups Can Play a Part in Evaluating Ad Copy," *Marketing News*, September 13, 1993, pp. 24–25.

41. Emily Steel, "The New Focus Groups: Online Networks, Proprietary Panels Help Consumer Companies Shape Product Ads," *The Wall Street Journal*, January 14, 2008, p. B6.

42. Jennifer Comiteau, "Why the Traditional Focus Group Is Dying," *ADWEEK*, October 31, 2005, pp. 24–25, 32; Stephanie Thompson, "'Tipping Point' Guru Takes on Focus Groups," *Advertising Age*, January 24, 2005, pp. 4, 54; Malcolm Gladwell, *Blink: The Power of Thinking without Thinking* (New York: Little, Brown, 2004).

43. David Kiley, "Shoot the Focus Group," *BusinessWeek*, November 14, 2005, pp. 120–21.

44. Thompson, "'Tipping Point' Guru Takes on Focus Groups."

45. Eric J. Arnould and Melanie Wallendorf, "Market-Oriented Ethnography: Interpretation Building and Marketing Strategy Formulation," *Journal of Marketing Research* 31 (November 1994), pp. 388–96.

46. "360i & Lean Cuisine Awarded Grand Ogilvy in the ARF David Ogilvy Awards," *360i Blog*, March 21, 2016, http://blog.360i.com/360i-news/360i-lean-cuisine-awarded-grand-ogilvy-arf-david-ogilvy-awards.

47. Stephen Winzenburg, "Your Advertising Slogans Are Crummy. Can't You Do Better?" *Advertising Age*, January 14, 2008, p. 15; John Mathes, "Taglines That Stick; Here's How to Create an Effective Brand Summation Line. How Long Should It Be? Is It the Same as Your Brand Positioning? How Often Do You Need to Refresh It?" *ABA Bank Marketing*, December 1, 2008, pp. 22–25.

48. Chiranjeev Kohli, Lance Leuthesser, and Rajneesh Suri, "Got Slogan? Guidelines for Creating Effective Slogans," *Business Horizons* 50 (2007), pp. 415–22.

49. Ibid.

50. John Sutherland, Lisa Duke, and Avery Abernethy, "A Model of Marketing Information Flow," *Journal of Advertising* 22, no. 4 (Winter 2004), pp. 39–52.

51. A. Jerome Jeweler, *Creative Strategy in Advertising* (Belmont, CA: Wadsworth, 1981).

52. John O'Toole, *The Trouble with Advertising*, 2nd ed. (New York: Random House, 1985), p. 131.

53. David Ogilvy, *Ogilvy on Advertising* (New York: Crown, 1983), p. 16.

54. Julie Halpet, "Chrysler Group Is Ad Age's Marketer of the Year," *Advertising Age,* November 26, 2012, http://adage.com/article/special-report-marketer-alist-2012/chrysler-group-ad-age-s-marketer-year/238443/.

55. E. J. Schultz, "Dos Equis Will Swap Actor Who Plays Most Interesting Role," *Advertising Age*, March 9, 2016, http://adage.com/article/cmo-strategy/dos-equis-swap-actor-plays-interesting-man/303026/.

56. Christine Birkner, "Success by Association," *Marketing News*, April 30, 2012, pp. 14–18.

57. Kate Maddox, "Siemens Launches U.S. Brand Campaign 'Ingenuity for Life,' " *Advertising Age*, February 23, 2016, http://adage.com/article/btob/siemens-launches-u-s-brand-campaign-ingenuity-life/302786/.

58. Arthur J. Kover, "Copywriters' Implicit Theories of Communication: An Exploration," *Journal of Consumer Research* 21, no. 4 (March 1995), pp. 596–611.

59. John R. Rossiter, "Defining the Necessary Components of Creative, Effective Ads," *Journal of Advertising Research* 37, no. 4 (Winter 2008), pp. 139–44.

60. Rosser Reeves, *Reality in Advertising* (New York: Knopf, 1961), pp. 47, 48.

61. Shelly Branch and Frances A. McMorris, "Irate Firms Take Comparisons to Court," *The Wall Street Journal*, December 22, 1999, p. B8.

62. Jeremy Mullman, "Hey, Those A-B Brands Look Like Miller Beers," *Advertising Age*, June 11, 2009, http://adage.com/article/news/beer-marketing-a-b-brands-miller-beers/137260/; Jeremy Mullman, "Miller Lightens Its Load: Will Go National with MGD 64 by Fall," *Advertising Age*, http://adage.com/article/news/miller-lightens-load-national-mgd-64-fall/127945/.

63. Ogilvy, *Confessions of an Advertising Man*.

64. Martin Mayer, *Madison Avenue, U.S.A.* (New York: Pocket Books, 1958).

65. "Hallmark's Mother's Day Ads Are Shockingly Edgy. Just Kidding, They're Really, Really Sappy," *Adweek*, April 24, 2015, www.adweek.com/adfreak/hallmarks-mothers-day-ads-are-shockingly-edgy-just-kidding-theyre-really-really-edgy-164275.

66. Al Ries and Jack Trout, *Positioning: The Battle for Your Mind* (New York: McGraw-Hill, 1985); Jack Trout and Al Ries, "The Positioning Era Cometh," *Advertising Age*, April 24, 1972, pp. 35–38; May 1, 1972, pp. 51–54; May 8, 1972, pp. 114–16.

67. Jack Trout, "Brands Can't Exist without Positioning," *Advertising Age*, March 14, 2005, p. 28.

68. Jessica Wohl, "Special K Recipe for 2016: New Cereal Promoted by New Agency," *Advertising Age,* December 29, 2015, http://adage.com/article/see-the-spot/special-k-recipe-2016-cereal-promoted-agency/301946/.

69. Jean Halliday, "Sometimes Oil and Oil Don't Mix," *Advertising Age*, March 4, 2002, pp. 4, 62.

70. Rajeev Batra, John G. Myers, and David A. Aaker, *Advertising Management*, 5th ed. (Upper Saddle River, NJ: Prentice Hall, 1996).

71. Anthony Vagnoni, "They Might Be Giants," *Advertising Age*, April 27, 1998, pp. 1, 20, 24.

72. Anthony Vagnoni, "Goodby, Silverstein Do 'Intelligent Work' with a Sales Pitch," *Advertising Age*, April 27, 1998, pp. 20, 24.

73. Anthony Vagnoni, "Having Ad Bosses Focus on the Work Key to Cult of Clow," *Advertising Age*, April 27, 1998, pp. 22, 24.

74. Jean Lin, "Liberating Creativity: The Old Agency Model Doesn't Work Anymore," *Advertising Age*, February 9, 2015, http://adage.com/article/agency-viewpoint/liberating-creativity-agency-model-work/296965/.

75. Rupal Parkeh, "Lee Clow on Advertising, Then and Now," *Advertising Age*, June 11, 2013, http://adage.com/article/agency-news/lee-clow-advertising/241987/.

Chapter 9

1. Sandra E. Moriarty, *Creative Advertising: Theory and Practice*, 2nd ed. (Englewood Cliffs, NJ: Prentice Hall, 1991), p. 76.

2. William M. Weilbacher, *Advertising*, 2nd ed. (New York: Macmillan, 1984), p. 197.

3. William Wells, John Burnett, and Sandra Moriarty, *Advertising* (Englewood Cliffs, NJ: Prentice Hall, 1989), p. 330.

4. Hamish Pringle and Peter Field, "Why Emotional Messages Beat Rational Ones," *Advertising Age*, March 2, 2009, http://adage.com/article/cmo-strategy/emotional-messages-beat-rational/134920/; Stuart J. Agres, "Emotion in Advertising: An Agency Point of View," in *Emotion in Advertising: Theoretical and Practical Explanations*, Stuart J. Agres, Julie A. Edell, and Tony M. Dubitsky, eds. (Westport, CT: Quorom Books, 1991).

5. Edward Kamp and Deborah J. Macinnis, "Characteristics of Portrayed Emotions in Commercials: When Does What Is Shown in Ads Affect Viewers?" *Journal of Advertising Research* 22, no. 4 (November/December 1995), pp. 19–28.

6. For a review of research on the effect of mood states on consumer behavior, see Meryl Paula Gardner, "Mood States and Consumer Behavior: A Critical Review," *Journal of Consumer Research* 12, no. 3 (December 1985), pp. 281–300.

7. Cathy Madison, "Researchers Work Advertising into an Emotional State," *Adweek*, November 5, 1990, p. 30.

8. Hamish Pringle and Peter Field, *Brand Immortality: How Brands Can Live Long and Prosper* (London: Kogan Page Limited, 2009).

9. Pringle and Field, "Why Emotional Messages Beat Rational Ones."

10. Tim Baysinger, "How the Ad Council and R/GA Created the Powerful 'Love Has No Labels' PSA," *Advertising Age*, August 17, 2015, www.adweek.com/news/advertising-branding/how-ad-council-and-rga-created-powerful-love-has-no-labels-psa-166412.

11. Christopher P. Puto and William D. Wells, "Informational and Transformational Advertising: The Different Effects of Time," in *Advances in Consumer Research* (vol. 11), Thomas C. Kinnear, ed. (Ann Arbor, MI: Association for Consumer Research, 1984), p. 638.

12. Ibid.

13. E. J. Schultz, "Corona Light Ditches the Beach in New Spot," *Advertising Age*, April 11, 2011, http://adage.com/article/news/corona-light-ditches-beach-commercial/226928/.

14. David Ogilvy and Joel Raphaelson, "Research on Advertising Techniques That Work and Don't Work," *Harvard Business Review*, July/August 1982, p. 18.

15. Xiang Fang, Surendra Singh, and Rohini Ahluwalia, "An Examination of Different Explanations for the Mere Exposure Effect," *Journal of Consumer Research* 34 (June 2007), pp. 97–103.

16. Robert Zajonc, "Attitudinal Effects of Mere Exposure," *Journal of Personality and Social Psychology Monographs*, no. 2 (Pt. 2), pp. 1–27.

17. John Young, "Making Online Ad Suck Less in 8 Easy Steps," *Advertising Age*, April 10, 2010, http://adage.com/article/digitalnext/making-online-ads-suck-8-easy-steps/143368/.

18. Helge Thorbjornsen, Paul Ketelaar, Jonathan Van'T Riet, and Micael Dahlen, "How Do Teaser Advertisements Boost Word of Mouth about New Products?" *Journal of Advertising Research* 55, no. 1, (March 2015), pp. 73–80.

19. Quote by Irwin Warren, cited in Enrico, "Teaser Ads Grab Spotlight," *USA Today*, July 6, 1995, pp. 1B, 2B.

20. Colin Campbell, Leyland F. Pitt, Michael Parent, and Pierre R. Berthhon, "Understanding Consumer Conversations around Ads in a Web 2.0 World," *Journal of Advertising* 40, no. 1 (Spring 2011), pp. 87–102; E. J. Schultz, "Why 'Crash the Super Bowl' Hasn't Burned Out for Doritos," *Advertising Age*, January 24, 2013, http://adage.com/article/special-report-super-bowl/crash-super-bowl-burned-doritos/239373/.

21. Christopher Heine, "New Ford Fiesta Campaign Will Be Entirely User-Generated," *Adweek*, February 19, 2013, www.adweek.com/news/advertising-branding/ford-campaign-will-be-all-user-generated-147384.

22. Eric Siu, "10 User Generated Content Campaigns That Actually Worked," *Hubspot*, March 22, 2015, http://blog.hubspot.com/marketing/examples-of-user-generated-content#sm.00015wzjc5qxeez3x5j2knoyrw5ir.

23. Martin Mayer, *Madison Avenue, U.S.A.* (New York: Pocket Books, 1958), p. 64.

24. Chris Reidy, "Gillette Rolls Out Shaving Products Designed for Men with Sensitive Skin," *Boston Globe,* February 14, 2013, www.boston.com/businessupdates/2013/02/14/gillette-rolls-out-shaving-products-designed-for-men-with-sensitive-skin/va3MCX5AoS9ueUx9NvqinO/story.html.

25. Sally Beatty, "P&G to Ad Agencies: Please Rewrite Our Old Formulas," *The Wall Street Journal*, November 5, 1998, pp. B1, B10; Alecia Swasy, "P&G Tries Bolder Ads—with Caution," *The Wall Street Journal*, May 7, 1990, pp. B1, B7.

26. Lynn Coleman, "Advertisers Put Fear into the Hearts of Their Prospects," *Marketing News*, August 15, 1988, p. 1.

27. Ibid.

28. Stuart Elliott, "Look Who's Talking for Mr. Peanut Now," *The New York Times,* July 1, 2013, www.nytimes.com/2013/07/01/business/media/look-whos-talking-for-mr-peanut-now.html.

29. Ann Christine Diaz, "Chipotle and CAA Add a Film Grand Prix to Collection of Top Honors," *Advertising Age*, June 23, 2012, http://adage.com/article/special-report-cannes-2012/chipotle-caa-add-a-film-grand-prix-collection-top-honors/235603/.

30. Candice Choi, "Channeling Colonel Sanders," *The San Diego Union-Tribune*, February 18, 2016, p. C3.

31. Theresa Howard, "Aflac Duck Gives Wings to Insurer's Name Recognition," *USA Today*, May 17, 2001, p. B9.

32. Barbara B. Stern, "Classical and Vignette Television Advertising: Structural Models, Formal Analysis, and Consumer Effects," *Journal of Consumer Research* 20, no. 4 (March 1994), pp. 601–15; John Deighton, Daniel Romer, and Josh McQueen, "Using Drama to Persuade," *Journal of Consumer Research* 15, no. 3 (December 1989), pp. 335–43.

33. Moriarty, *Creative Advertising*, p. 77.

34. Mario Pricken, *Creative Advertising* (New York: Thames & Hudson, 2009).

35. W. Keith Hafer and Gordon E. White, *Advertising Writing*, 3rd ed. (St. Paul, MN: West Publishing, 1989), p. 98.

36. Kate Maddox, "UPS Launches 'United Problem Solvers' Campaign," *Advertising Age*, March 8, 2015, http://adage.com/article/btob/ups-launches-united-problem-solvers-campaign/297486/.

37. Carol Marie Cooper, "Who Says Talk Is Cheap?" *The New York Times*, October 22, 1998, pp. C1, C5; Wendy Brandes, "Star Power Leaves Some Voice-Over Artists Speechless," *The Wall Street Journal*, June 2, 1995, p. B6.

38. Siddarth Vodnala, "Voice-Over Actors Are Talking Up the Apps That Help Them Get Work," *The Los Angeles Times*, September 8, 2015, http://www.latimes.com/entertainment/envelope/cotown/la-et-ct-voiceover-tech-20150909-story.html.

39. David Allan, "A Content Analysis of Music Placement in Prime-Time Advertising," *Journal of Advertising Research*, September 2008, pp. 404–14.

40. Linda M. Scott, "Understanding Jingles and Needledrop: A Rhetorical Approach to Music in Advertising," *Journal of Consumer Research* 17, no. 2 (September 1990), pp. 223–36.

41. Kineta Hung, "Framing Meaning Perceptions with Music: The Case of Teaser Ads," *Journal of Advertising* 30, no. 3 (Fall 2001), pp. 39–49; Russell I. Haley, Jack Richardson, and Beth Baldwin, "The Effects of Nonverbal Communications in Television Advertising," *Journal of Advertising Research* 24, no. 4 (July/August 1984), pp. 11–18.

42. Maureen Morrison, "Kia to Bring Back Hamsters for New Campaign," *Advertising Age*, July 26, 2012, http://adage.com/article/special-report-small-agency-awards-2012/kia-bring-back-hamsters-campaign/236351/.

43. Steve Oakes, "Evaluating Empirical Research into Music in Advertising: A Congruity Perspective," *Journal of Advertising Research*, March 2007, pp. 38–50.

44. Gerald J. Gorn, "The Effects of Music in Advertising on Choice Behavior: A Classical Conditioning Approach," *Journal of Marketing* 46 (Winter 1982), pp. 94–100.

45. Donna DeMarco, "TV Ads Go Pop: Advertisers Marry Modern Music with Their Products," *The Washington Times*, May 12, 2002, p. A1.

46. Christine Birkner, "Striking a Chord," *Marketing News,* October 2015, pp. 18–19.

47. Matthew Boyle, "The Accidental Hero," *BusinessWeek*, November 5, 2009, www.businessweekcom/print/magazine/content/09_46/b4155058815908.htm.

48. Jessica Wohl, "Armour Updates Famous Kids Jingle, Now Sung for Moms," *Advertising Age*, February 1, 2016, http://adage.com/article/cmo-strategy/armour-updates-famous-kids-jingle-sung-moms/302437/.

49. Quote from Suzanne Vranica, "P&G Dusts Off a Familiar Tune," *The Wall Street Journal*, March 3, 2005, p. B2.

50. Andrew Hampp, "A Reprise for Jingles on Madison Avenue, Brands, Agencies Rediscovering Power of Original Tunes in Ad Campaigns," *Advertising Age*, September 6, 2010, http://adage.com/article/madisonvine-news/a-reprise-jingles-madison-avenue/145744/.

51. Ken Wheaton, "Stop the Presses: Cee Lo Green, Purrfect Remix Meow Mix Jinge," *Advertising Age*, May 4, 2012, http://adage.com/article/adages/cee-lo-green-remix-a-song-a-rented-cat/234574/.

52. Vranica, "P&G Dusts Off a Familiar Tune."

53. "Results of 4A's 2011 Television Production Costs Survey," American Association of Advertising Agencies, Bulletin #7480, January 22, 2013.

54. Reed Smith, "SAG-AFTRA and the Joint Policy Committee Reach Tentative Agreement on Successor Commercials Contracts," *Lexology*, April 4, 2016, www.lexology.com/library/detail.aspx?g=094ab5d3-eade-40e6-b28e-be2e478603cf; Jack Neff, "Industry Explores New Compensation Model for Talent," *Advertising Age*, May 3, 2010, http://adage.com/article/news/industry-explores-compensation-model-talent-fees/143638/.

55. Dave Chaffey, "Display advertising clickthrough rates," *Smart Insights*, April 16, 2016, http://www.smartinsights.com/internet-advertising/internet-advertising-analytics/display-advertising-clickthrough-rates/.

56. Kunar Pattel, "Online Ads Not Working for You? Blame the Creative," *Advertising Age*, October 20, 2009, http://adage.com/article/digital/digital-online-ads-working-blame-creative/139795/.

57. Hernan Lopez, "Why Interactive Advertising Needs a Creative Revolution," *Advertising Age*, June 15, 2009, http://adage.com/article/digital/interactive-advertising-a-creative-revolution/137246/.

58. Kendall Goodrich, Shu Z. Schiller, and Dennis Galletta, "Consumer Reactions to Intrusiveness of Online-Video Advertisements," *Journal of Advertising Research*, 55, no. 1, (March 2015), pp. 37–50.

59. Michael Learmonth, "He Thought Different," *Advertising Age*, October 10, 2011, pp. 1–3; Steve Hayden, "'1984': As Good As It Gets," *Adweek Media*, January 31, 2011, pp. 14, 15.

60. Meg James, "Over 50 and out of Flavor," *Los Angeles Times*, May 10, 2005, pp. A1, A10.

61. Rupel Parekh, "Brand Awareness Was Only Half the Battle for Aflac," *Advertising Age*, June 22, 2009, http://adage.com/article/cmo-strategy/aflac-s-jeff-charney-insurance-brand-awareness/137392/; Suzanne Vranica, "Aflac Partly Muzzles Iconic Duck," *The Wall Street Journal*, December 2, 2004, p. B8.

62. David Kiefaber, "Bloomingdale's Apologizes for This Weird, Vaguely Date-Rapey Holiday Ad," *Adweek*, November 16, 2015, www.adweek.com/adfreak/bloomingdales-apologizes-weird-vaguely-date-rapey-holiday-ad-168146.

Chapter 10

1. Jamie Turner, "Top 52 Social Media Platforms Every Marketer Should Know," April 9, 2010, www.60secondmarketer.com.

2. Ronald D. Geskey, *Media Planning & Buying in the 21st Century,* 2nd ed. (Rochester, MI: 2020 Marketing Communications, LLC, 2014).

3. Matthew Creamer, "Ad Groups Back Switch from 'Frequency' to 'Engagement,'" *Advertising Age,* July 21, 2005, http://adage.com/article/news/ad-groups-back-switch-frequency-engagement/46348/.

4. Mindi Chahal, "Is 'Brand Engagement' a Meaningless Metric?" *Marketing Week*, August 10, 2016.

5. "Marketers Shaky about Right Media Mix," eMarketer.com, July 1, 2015.

6. Chuck Ross, "Study Finds for Continuity vs. Flights," *Advertising Age*, April 19, 1999, p. 2.

7. Joseph W. Ostrow, "Setting Frequency Levels: An Art of a Science?" *Journal of Advertising Research* 24, (August/September 1984), pp. 9–11.

8. David Crane, "Arnold vs Calbuzz, eMeg's Ad Buy; Memo to Media," March 10, 2010, www.calbluzz.com.

9. Scott Walker, "Ratings and TV Advertising Sales," April 2, 2008, www.tvadvertising.suite101.com.

10. David Berger, "How Much to Spend," *Foote, Cone & Belding Internal Report*, in *Advertising,* Michael L. Rothschild (Lexington, MA: Heath, 1987), p. 468.

11. David W. Olson, "Real World Measures of Advertising Effectiveness for New Products," *Speech to the 26th Annual Conference of the Advertising Research Foundation*, New York, March 18, 1980.

12. Joseph W. Ostrow, "What Level Frequency?" *Advertising Age*, November 1981, pp. 13–18.

13. Jack Myers, "More is Indeed Better," *MediaWeek*, September 6, 1993, pp. 14–18.

14. Jim Surmanek, "One-Hit or Miss: Is a Frequency of One Frequently Wrong?" *Advertising Age*, November 27, 1995, p. 46.

15. Erwin Ephron, "Back to the Future," April 14, 2010, www.ephrononmedia.com.

16. Sheree Johnson, "New Research Sheds Light on daily Ad Exposures," www.sjinsights.com, September 29, 2014.

17. Ostrow, "What Level Frequency?"

18. Susanne Schmidt and Martin Eisend, "Advertising Repetition: A Meta-Analysis on Effective Frequency in Advertising," *Journal of Advertising*, 44, no. 4 (2015), pp. 415–428.

19. Erwin Ephron, "Recency Planning," March 18, 1998, www.ephrononmedia.com.

20. Erwin Ephron, "Sitting on the Shelf," www.ephronmedia.com, October 1, 2009.

21. Susan Krashinsky, "Mood Mismatch Between TV Shows and Ads May Hurt advertisers:study," www.theglobeandmail.com, March 29, 2015.

Chapter 11

1. Radio Advertising Bureau, "Why Radio," 2016, www.rab.com/whyradio/.

2. "Subaru of America, Inc. Announces December 2015 Sales as Best Sales Month Ever; Sets Seventh Consecutive Yearly Sales Record," January 5, 2016, *U.S. Media Center*, www.media.subaru.com/pressrelease/909/120/subaru-america-inc-announces-december-2015-sales-best; Tim Nudd, "How Subaru Fell in Love and Never Looked Back," *Adweek*, April 13, 2013, www.adweek.com/news/advertising-branding/how-subaru-fell-love-and-never-looked-back-148475.

3. "Network Television Cost and CPM Trends," *Trends in Media,* Television Bureau of Advertising, www.tvb.org/rcentral.

4. Rebecca Dana and Stephane King, "Answer to Vexing Question: Who's Not Watching Ads," *The Wall Street Journal*, October 17, 2009, p. B2; Lex van Meurs, "Zapp! A Study on Switching Behavior during Commercial Breaks," *Journal of Advertising Research*, January/February 1998, pp. 43–53; John J. Cronin, "In-Home Observations of Commercial Zapping Behavior," *Journal of Current Issues and Research in Advertising* 17, no. 2 (Fall 1995), pp. 69–75.

5. "Results of 4A's 2011 Television Production Costs Survey," American Association of Advertising Agencies, Bulletin #7480, January 22, 2013.

6. Laurel Wentz, "Behind the Five Most Creative U.S. Hispanic Ideas," *Advertising Age*, May 1, 2013, http://adage.com/article/hispanic-marketing/creative-u-s-hispanic-ideas/241197/; Brian Grow, "Hispanic Nation," *BusinessWeek*, March 15, 2004, pp. 58–70.

7. "TV Activity by Commercial Length," TVB, www.tvb.org/research/95487.

8. Jeanine Poggi, "Cable Strives to Keep Marketers Invested amid Ratings Fall," *Advertising Age*, September 15, 2015, pp. 36–38.

9. Joe Flint, "Cable TV Shows Are Sped Up to Squeeze in More Ads," *The Wall Street Journal,* February 18, 2015, www.wsj.com/articles/cable-tv-shows-are-sped-up-to-squeeze-in-more-ads-1424301320.

10. Jon Lafayette, "Nielsen: Live TV Viewing Drops, More Homes Get SVOD," *Broadcasting & Cable*, December 10, 2015, www.broadcastingcable.com/news/currency/nielsen-live-tv-viewing-drops-more-homes-get-svod/146304.

11. Suzanne Vranica, "TiVo Serves Up Portrait of the Ad-Zappers," *The Wall Street Journal*, November 8, 2007, p. B5.

12. Cronin, "In-Home Observations of Commercial Zapping Behavior."

13. Carrie Heeter and Bradley S. Greenberg, "Profiling the Zappers," *Journal of Advertising Research* 25, no. 2 (April/May 1985), pp. 9–12; Fred S. Zufryden, James H. Pedrick, and Avu Sandaralingham, "Zapping and Its Impact on Brand Purchase Behavior," *Journal of Advertising Research* 33, no. 1 (January/February 1993), pp. 58–66; Patricia Orsini, "Zapping: A Man's World," Spring Television Report, *Adweek's Marketing Week*, April 8, 1991, p. 3.

14. van Meurs, "Zapp! A Study on Switching Behavior during Commercial Breaks."

15. Alan Ching Biu Tse and Rub P. W. Lee, "Zapping Behavior during Commercial Breaks," *Journal of Advertising Research* 41, no. 3 (May/June 2001), pp. 25–29.

16. Keach Hagey, "CBS Quashes Award for DVR," *The Wall Street Journal*, January 15, 2013, p. B3.

17. Brian Steinberg, "ABC Tests Ad Packages including 'On-Demand' Viewers," *Advertising Age*, March 22, 2012, http://adage.com/article/media/abc-tests-ad-packages-including-demand-viewers/233462/; Brooks Barnes, "ABC, Cox Bar Ad Skipping in Video on Demand," *The Wall Street Journal*, May 8, 2007, p. B8.

18. Linda F. Alwitt and Paul R. Prabhaker, "Identifying Who Dislikes Television Advertising: Not by Demographics Alone," *Journal of Advertising Research* 34, no. 6 (November/December 1994), pp. 30–42.

19. Banwari Mittal, "Public Assessment of TV Advertising: Faint Praise and Harsh Criticism," *Journal of Advertising Research* 34, no. 1 (1994), pp. 35–53.

20. Lucy L. Henke, "Young Children's Perceptions of Cigarette Brand Advertising Symbols: Awareness, Affect, and Target Market Identification," *Journal of Advertising* 24, no. 4 (Winter 1995), pp. 13–28.

21. "Recommendations from Friends Remain Most Credible Form of Advertising among Consumers; Branded Websites Are the Second-Highest-Rated Form," *Nielsen Press Room*, September 28, 2015, www.nielsen.com/us/en/press-room/2015/recommendations-from-friends-remain-most-credible-form-of-advertising.html.

22. Brian Steinberg, "How Fox Went from Small Outcast to Broadcast Powerhouse," *Advertising Age*, April 18, 2011, pp. 2–3.

23. Bill Mann, "What's with CW? Result of Merger between WB and UPN Targets 18-and-Ups," *The Press Democrat*, December 16, 2007, p. D8.

24. Brooks Barnes and Miram Jordan, "Big Four TV Networks Get a Wake-Up Call—in Spanish," *The Wall Street Journal*, May 2, 2005, pp. B1, B6.

25. Fernando Rodriguez, "Six Things Advertisers Need to Know about the Growing Hispanic Market," *Advertising Age*, July 26, 2012, http://adage.com/article/the-big-tent/advertisers-reach-growing-u-s-hispanic-market/236336/.

26. Anthony Crupi, "NFL Ad Rates Soar as Marketers Clamor for Time in TV's Last Great Reach Vehicle," *Advertising Age*, September 9, 2016, http://adage.com/article/media/nfl/305791/.

27. Brian Steinberg, "TV Nets Notice Uptick in 'Just in Time' Ad Buying," *Advertising Age*, September 7, 2009, http://adage.com/article/media/tv-networks-notice-uptick-scatter-advertising-buying/138856/.

28. Jeanine Poggi, "Why Cable Has Become More Like Broadcast TV," *Advertising Age*, May 14, 2012, p. 16; Brian Steinberg, "Broadcast TV or Cable, It's All the Same to Consumers," *Advertising Age,* March 23, 2009, http://adage.com/print?article_id=135246.

29. A. J. Frutkin, "Do Sweeps Still Matter?" Mediaweek.com, April 30, 2007.

30. "Measuring TV Audience," *Broadcast Engineering*, October 1, 2007, p. 26.

31. Brian Steinberg and Andrew Hampp, "Commercial Ratings? Nets Talk TiVo Instead," *Advertising Age*, June 4, 2007, pp. 1, 60.

32. Antony Young, "Shifting to C7 Ratings Would Be Good for TV and Advertisers," *Advertising Age,* May 12, 2014, p. 29.

33. Jason Lynch, "A First Look at Nielsen's Total Audience Measurement and How It Will Change the Industry," *Adweek,* October 20, 2015, www.adweek.com/news/television/first-look-nielsen-s-total-audience-measurement-and-how-it-will-change-industry-167661.

34. Jason Lynch, "With Its Total Audience Measurement Rollout Delayed, Nielsen Will Share More Connected TV Data," *Adweek*, March 23, 2016, www.adweek.com/news/television/its-total-audience-measurement-delayed-nielsen-will-share-more-connected-tv-data-170381.

35. Ibid.

36. Steinberg, "Marketers Demanding Ratings for Each TV Ad."

37. Andrew Hampp, "Nielsen Adds Ratings for Away-from-Home TV Networks," *Advertising Age*, April 14, 2010, http://adage.com/article/media/nielsen-adds-ratings-home-tv-networks/143308/.

38. Kate Fitzgerald, "Campus Viewing Stirs a Romp," *Advertising Age*, April 9, 2007, http://adage.com/article/special-report-upfront07/campus-viewing-stirs-a-rumpus/115950/.

39. Nancy Vogt, "Audio Fact Sheet," *State of the News Media 2015: Pew Research Center*, April 29, 2015, www.journalism.org/2015/04/29/audio-fact-sheet/.

40. *Radio Marketing Guide* (New York: Radio Advertising Bureau, 2010), www.rab.com.

41. "Jacobs Media Unveils Tech Survey 11 at Worldwide Radio Summit 2015," Allaccess.com, April 23, 2015, www.allaccess.com/net-news/archive/story/140769/jacobs-media-unveils-techsurvey-11-at-worldwide-ra.

42. Verne Gay, "Image Transfer: Radio Ads Make Aural History," *Advertising Age*, January 24, 1985, p. 1.

43. *The Benefits of Synergy: Moving Money into Radio* (New York: Radio Ad Effectiveness Lab, Inc., December 2004), www.radioadlal.com.

44. Avery Abernethy, "Differences between Advertising and Program Exposure for Car Radio Listening," *Journal of Advertising Research* 31, no. 2 (April/May 1991), pp. 33–42.

45. *Radio Marketing Guide*.

46. Martin Peers, "Radio Produces Both Gains and Skeptics," *The Wall Street Journal*, January 1, 1999, p. B6.

47. Andrew Hampp, "Liberty Media Rides in to Rescue Sirius XM," *Advertising Age*, February 17, 2009, http://adage.com/article/media/liberty-media-rides-rescue-sirius-xm/134661/.

48. Heather Green, Tom Lowry, Catherine Young, and David Kiley, "The New Radio Revolution," *BusinessWeek*, March 14, 2005, pp. 32–35.

49. Andrew Hampp, "Contextual Radio Ads: Clear Channel's New Pitch to National Marketers," *Advertising Age*, January 15, 2010, http://adage.com/article/media/radio-clear-channel-rolls-contextual-radio-advertising/141533/.

50. David McLaughlin, "Nielsen's $1.26 Billion Arbitron Purchase Cleared by U.S.," *Bloomberg Businessweek*, September 20, 2013, www.bloomberg.com/news/2013-09-20/nielsen-s-1-26-billion-arbitron-purchase-cleared-by-u-s-.html.

51. Jon Fine, "A Better Measure of Old Media," *BusinessWeek,* July 9, 2007, p. 20.

52. "Media Rating Council Grants Accreditation to Four Additional Arbitron Portable People Meter Markets," *PR Newswire*, February 5, 2013, www.prnewswire.com/news-releases/media-rating-council-grants-accreditation-to-four-additional-arbitron-portable-people-meter-markets-189901731.html; Steve Carney, "Don't Touch That Radio Dial—Arbitron Is Listening," *Los Angeles Times*, August 24, 2011, http://articles.latimes.com/2011/aug/24/entertainment/la-et-radio-ratings-20110824.

Chapter 12

1. An excellent resource on the role of magazines as advertising media vehicles is the Association of Magazine Media website at www.magazine.org/ and the News Media Alliance at www.newsmediaalliance.org/.

2. Herbert E. Krugman, "The Measurement of Advertising Involvement," *Public Opinion Quarterly* 30 (Winter 1966–67), pp. 583–96.

3. *Magazine Media Factbook 2016/2017* (New York: MPA—The Association of Magazine Media), http://www.magazine.org/insights-resources/magazine-media-factbook.

4. Ibid.

5. *Mr. Magazine: Launch Monitor*, 2015, www.mrmagazine.com/.

6. Tim Nudd, "Lexus Print Ad Roars to Life, with a Little Help from an iPad," *Adweek*, October 10, 2012, www.adweek.com/adfreak/lexus-print-ad-roars-life-little-help-ipad-144349.

7. David Gianatasio, "The CW Embeds a Live Twitter Feed Inside Its 'EW' Print Ad," *Adweek*, September 28, 2012, www.adweek.com/adfreak/cw-embeds-live-twitter-feed-inside-its-ew-print-ad-144048.

8. Brian Steinberg, "Gimmicky Magazine Inserts Aim to Grab Page Flippers," *The Wall Street Journal*, August 8, 2005, pp. B1, 2.

9. *Magazine Media Factbook 2016/2017.*

10. Ibid.

11. Sarah Ellison, "Good Housekeeping Touts Its Test Lab to Seek New Readers' Seal of Approval," *The Wall Street Journal*, October 11, 2006, pp. B1, B4.

12. Sara Rosengren and Micael Dahlén, "Judging a Magazine by Its Advertising," *Journal of Advertising Research* 53, no. 1 (March 2013), pp. 61–70.

13. Steve Fajen, "Numbers Aren't Everything," *Media Decisions* 10 (June 1975), pp. 65–69.

14. *Magazine Media Factbook, 2016/2017.*

15. *Magazine Media: MPA Factbook 2013/2014.*

16. Sally Goll Beatty, "Philip Morris Starts Lifestyle Magazine," *The Wall Street Journal*, September 16, 1996, pp. B1, B8.

17. Jack Neff, "P&G Extends Online Custom Publishing," *Advertising Age*, March 22, 2004, pp. 24–25.

18. Jon Fine, "Audit Bureau to Change How It Counts Circulation," *Advertising Age*, July 17, 2001, http://adage.com/article/news/audit-bureau-change-counts-circulation/30030/.

19. "ASME Guidelines for Editors and Publishers Updated September 2013," *American Society of Magazine Editors*, www.magazine.org/asme/editorial-guidelines.

20. Study cited in Jim Surmanek, *Media Planning: A Practical Guide* (Lincolnwood, IL: Crain Books, 1985).

21. "How Advertising Readership Is Influenced by Ad Size," Report no. 110.1, *Cahners Advertising Research*, Newton, MA; "Larger Advertisements Get Higher Readership," *LAP Report no. 3102*, McGraw-Hill Research, New York; "Effect of Size, Color and Position on Number of Responses to Recruitment Advertising," *LAP Report no. 3116*, McGraw-Hill Research, New York.

22. "Almost Everything You Want to Know about Positioning in Magazines," study by Roper Starch Worldwide, Inc. 1999.

23. "Readership by Advertising Unit Type," *Magazine Dimensions*, 2001, Media Dynamics, Inc., www.magazine.org/resources/fact_sheets/adv.

24. Nat Ives, "Why Ad Pages Won't Ever Fully Return to Mags," *Advertising Age*, July 27, 2009, http://adage.com/article/media/magazines-ad-pages-fully-return/138131/.

25. Nat Ives, "Sporting News Ends Print Edition after 126 Years," *Advertising Age,* December 11, 2012, http://adage.com/article/media/sporting-news-ends-print-edition-126-years/238719/; Michael Learmonth, "Newsweek to End Print Edition in Quest to Cut Losses," *Advertising Age,* October 18, 2012, http://adage.com/article/media/newsweek-end-print-edition/237833/.

26. Katy Bachman, "Magazines, Newspaper Brace for Exigent Postal Rate Hike," *Adweek*, August 29, 2013, www.adweek.com/news/press/magazines-newspapers-brace-exigent-postal-rate-hike-152010.

27. "Ad Age's Magazine A-List: Marie Claire Is Magazine of the Year," *Advertising Age*, October 14, 2012, http://adage.com/article/media/ad-ages-magazine-a-list-marie-claire-magazine-year/237716/; Emma Bazilian, "Advertisers Keep It Real with Marie Claire Pub," *Adweek*, April 2, 2012, p. 14.

28. "Don't Be Mislead by Publishers Clearing House," *Consumer Reports*, April 23, 2014, www.consumerreports.org/cro/news/2014/04/don-t-be-mislead-by-publishers-clearing-house/index.htm#.

29. Nat Ives, "Mags March Calmly into Face of Chaos," *Advertising Age*, April 23, 2007, http://adage.com/article/media/mags-march-calmly-face-chaos/116231/.

30. Nat Ives, "Magazines to Sell Subscriptions within Facebook's News Feed," *Advertising Age*, May 12, 2010, http://adage.com/article/media/magazines-sell-subscriptions-facebook-news-feed/143813/.

31. Rupal Parekh, "Daily-Deal Sites Offer Dose of Growth for Magazine Circulation," *Advertising Age*, February 27, 2012, p. 17; Nat Ives, "Many Magazines That Cut Subscription Prices Lose Subscribers Anyway," *Advertising Age*, February 5, 2010, http://adage.com/article/media/magazines-cheaper-subscriptions-win-subscribers/141945/.

32. Seb Joseph, "Magazine Circulation Growth Fueled by Digital Subscriptions," *The Drum*, August 13, 2015, http://www.thedrum.com/news/2015/08/13/magazine-circulation-growth-fueled-digital-subscriptions.

33. Mitch Joel, "We Need a Better Definition of 'Native Advertising,'" *Harvard Business Review Blog Network*, February 13, 2013, http://blogs.hbr.org/cs/2013/02/we_need_a_better_definition_of.html.

34. Lucia Moses, "Who Killed the Magazine App?" *Adweek*, October 20, 2013, www.adweek.com/news/press/who-killed-magazine-app-153253.

35. "State of the News Media 2016," Pew Research Center, http://www.journalism.org/media-indicators/newspapers-daily-readership-by-age/.

36. Michael Barthel, "Around Half of Newspaper Readers Rely Only on Print Edition," Pew Research Center, January 6, 2016, www.pewresearch.org/fact-tank/2016/01/06/around-half-of-newspaper-readers-rely-only-on-print-edition/.

37. Amy Mitchell and Jesse Holcomb, "The State of the News Media 2016," Pew Research Center, June 15, 2016, http://www.journalism.org/2016/06/15/state-of-the-news-media-2016/.

38. Nat Ives, "Newspaper Subscribers Stick around Longer, Pay More," *Advertising Age*, September 30, 2009, http://adage.com/article/media/media-news-newspaper-subscribers-cancel-pay/139346/.

39. "The State of the News Media 2016."

40. "Up against the Paywall," *The Economist*, November 21, 2015, p. 62.

41. "State of the News Media 2016," PewResearchCenter, http://www.journalism.org/media-indicators/newspapers-daily-readership-by-age/

42. "Smart Is the New Sexy," Newspaper Association of America, www.naa.org/smart-is-the-new-sexy-ads.aspx.

43. Jim Conaghan, "Newspaper Digital Audience Grew Twice as Fast as the Internet in Past 12 Months," Newspaper Association of America,

October 8, 2015, www.naa.org/~/media/NAACorp/Public%20Files/TrendsAndNumbers/Newspaper-Websites/Final_Aug-2015_DigitalAudience.pdf.

44. Julia Angwin, "Newspapers Set to Jointly Sell Ads on Web Sites," *The Wall Street Journal*, January 10, 2007, pp. A1, A8.

45. Rebecca McPheters, "Magazines and Newspapers Need to Build Better Apps," *Advertising Age*, January 13, 2012, http://adage.com/article/media/viewpoint-magazines-newspapers-build-apps/232085/.

Chapter 13

1. Outdoor Advertising Association of America, 2016.
2. A. Jay, "Is There a Future for Traditional Sign Shops in the Face of Digital Signage?" April 8, 2016, www.digitalsignagetoday.com.
3. Product Acceptance & Research, 2007.
4. David Kaplan, "Agency Offers In-Store Insight: End-Aisles, Print Surpass TV," June 23, 2005, www.mediapost.com.
5. Point of Purchase Advertising International, 2016.
6. Outdoor Advertising Association of America, 2013.
7. Ibid.
8. Mukesh Bhargava and Naveen Donthu, "Sales Response to Outdoor Advertising," *Journal of Advertising Research* 39, no. 3 (July/August 1999).
9. American Public Transportation Association, *2015 Public Transportation Fact Book*, November 2015.
10. Andrew Hampp, "Outdoor Ad Industry Finally Gets Its Improved Metrics," *Advertising Age*, March 30, 2010, http://adage.com/article/media/outdoor-ad-industry-finally-improved-metrics/143049/.
11. Promotional Products Association International, 2016.
12. Ibid.
13. Ibid.
14. Ibid.
15. Ibid.
16. Gene Marks, "Do People Still Use the Yellow Pages? The Answer May Surprise You," www.inc.com, January 28, 2015.
17. Yellow Pages Association, 2013.
18. Kristina Knight, "Study: Yellow Pages Still Working for Many Consumers, Businesses," www.bizreport.com, March 19, 2014.

19. "Domestic Movie Theatrical Market Summary 1995 to 2016," www.thenumbers, March 12, 2016.
20. "Catch a Commercial at the Movies," October 29, 2007, www.mediapost.com.
21. Cinema Advertising Council, 2015.
22. Erik Sass, "Movie Metrics: Cinema Ads Click with Viewers," April 13, 2010, www.mediapost.com.
23. Cinema Advertising council, 2015.
24. Hank Kim, "Regal Pre-Movie Package Boosts Recall," *Advertising Age*, June 7, 2004, p. 21.
25. Joe Mandese, "And the Winner Is . . . Cinema Ads: Brain Research Shows They're More Emotionally Engaging Than TV Spots," February 27, 2012, www.mediapost.com.
26. Sarah McBride, "Cinema Surpassed DVD Sales in 2009," January 4, 2010, http://online.wsj.com/news/articles/SB100014240527487047894045746531903626624.
27. Katy Bachman, "Taco Bell Goes Cinematic with Ad Campaign," June 28, 2009, www.mediaweek.com.
28. "Online Viewers Are More Likely Than the Typical Adult to Go to the Movies," *Adweek*, February 20, 2012, p. 17.
29. Simon Hudson, "From Product Placement to Branded Entertainment," June 2010. http://hotelexecutive.com/business_review/4127/from-product-placement-to-branded-entertainment.
30. Mindi Chahal, "Is Product Placement Out of Control?" www.marketingweek.com, June 23, 2015.
31. Shahnaz Mahmud, "Branded Content, Mobile to Grow," *Adweek*, August 8, 2007.
32. Michael Belch and Cristel A. Russell, "A Managerial Investigation into the Product Placement Industry," *Journal of Advertising Research*, March 2005, pp. 73–92.
33. Emma Hall, "UK Gives Product Placement Go-Ahead for February—with Conditions," *Advertising Age*, December 21, 2010, http://adage.com/article/global-news/product-placement-uk-start-date-official-rules/147786/.
34. Marc Graser, "Movie Placement Creates Demand for Nonexistent Show," www.adage.com, January 31, 2005.
35. Brian Steinberg, "'Modern Family' Featured an iPad, but ABC Didn't Collect," *Advertising Age*, April 1, 2010, http://adage.com/article/media/modern-family-ipad-abc-collect/143105/.

36. Abe Sauer, "Product Placements (Including Seoul) Abound in *Avengers: Age of Ultron*," www.brandchannel.com, May 5, 2015.
37. Lauren Maffeo, "The Legal Loophole of Advergames: How Ads Disguised as Video Games Are Impacting Today's Youth," www.thenextweb.com, June 29, 2014.
38. "VOD Ads Can Complement TV," April 26, 2016, www.warc.com.
39. Kennedy, "Coming of Age in Consumerdom."
40. Kaplan, "Product Placement: Well-Placed among Consumers," March 25, 2005, www.mediapost.com/publications/article/28530/.
41. Abe Sauer, "Marlboro Washes Up in *Jersey Shore*: Best Anti-Smoking Ad Ever?" July 19, 2011, www.brandchannel.com.
42. Gail Schiller, "Tie-ins Often Sobering for Liquor Firms," *Hollywood Reporter*, August 1, 2005, pp. 1–3; MarinInstitute.org, 2006.
43. Katy Bachman, "Study: Industry's Found Sneaky Way to Keep Advertising Junk Food to Kids," August 2, 2011, www.adweek.com.
44. John Consoli, "80% TV Viewers Approve Product Placement," March 28, 2005, www.insidebrandedentertainment.com.
45. Kennedy, "Coming of Age in Consumerdom."
46. Harris Interactive, "Attitudes of US Children and Teens toward Advertising Tactics, by Age," *eMarketer*, May 2006.
47. Steve McClellan, "Branded Entertainment Finding Its Place(ment)," March 28, 2005, www.insidebrandedentertainment.com.
48. Belch and Russell, "A Managerial Investigation into the Product Placement Industry."
49. David Gianatasio, "Prankvertising: Are Outrageous Marketing Stunts Worth the Risks?" April 1, 2013, www.adweek.com.
50. PRN.com.
51. Joe Liebkind, "Shoppers Take to In-Store Video Ads," www.venturebeat.com, April 17, 2016.

Chapter 14

1. Direct Marketing Association, 2016.
2. *Direct Marketing Association Statistical Fact Book* (New York: Direct Marketing Association, 2015).
3. Ibid.

4. "Average Credit Card Debt in America: 2016 Facts and Figures," www.valuepenguin.com.

5. Bureau of Labor Statistics, 2016.

6. Abby Callard, "When Manufacturers Sell Directly to Consumers Online, Retailers Benefit," June 10, 2014, www.internetretailer.com.

7. Erik Sass, "Survey Results Make a Case for Direct Mail," *MediaPost,* June 12, 2007.

8. *Direct Marketing Association Statistical Fact Book, 2015.*

9. *Direct Marketing Association Statistical Fact Book* (New York: Direct Marketing Association, 2015).

10. Ibid.

11. Ibid.

12. Juliette Kopecky, "An Investigation into the ROI of Direct Mail versus E-mail Marketing," January 10, 2013, www.hubspot.com.

13. Elaine Underwood, "Is There a Future for the TV Mall?" *Brandweek,* March 25, 1996, pp. 24–26.

14. www.responsemagazine.com, April 2013.

15. *Direct Marketing Association Statistical Fact Book* (New York: Direct Marketing Association, 2015).

16. Marianna Morello, "Print Media + DRTV = Retail Success," *Response,* September 2002, p. 6.

17. Sheila Shayon, "QVC Acquires Zulily for $2.4 Billion to Attract a Younger Demographic," www.brandchannel.com, August 18, 2015.

18. Direct Selling Association, 2016.

19. *Direct Marketing Association Statistical Fact Book* (New York: Direct Marketing Association, 2015).

Chapter 15

1. "Dove Real Beauty Sketches," www.dove.com.

2. Terry Flew, *New Media: An Introduction*, 3rd ed. (Melbourne: Oxford University Press., 2008), p. 19.

3. www.wikipedia.com, 2016.

4. Brian Morrissey, "15 Alarming Stats about Banner Ads," March 21, 2013, www.digiday.com.

5. Dave Chaffey, "Display Advertising Clickthrough Rates," April 26, 2016, www.smartinsights.com.

6. Xiang Fang, Surendra Singh, and Rohini Ahluwalia, "An Examination of Different Explanations for the Mere Exposure Effect," *Journal of Consumer Research,* June 2007.

7. "Consumers Unhappy with Web Site Simply Go Away," August 23, 2005, www.mediapost.com/publications/article/33195/.

8. Barry Schwartz," Google Warns It Will Crack Down on "Intrusive Interstitials," www.searchengineland.com, August 23, 2016.

9. "US Digital Display Ad Spending to Surpass Search Ad Spending in 2016," January 11, 2016, www.emarketer.com.

10. "Google Still Dominates the World Ad Search Market," July 26, 2016, www.emarketer.com, July 26, 2016.

11. "State of the Industry 2016," www.adroll.com, January 2016.

12. www.Wikipedia.com, 2016.

13. Ian Schafer, "What Is Rich Media, Really?" September 23, 2005, www.clickz.com/clickz/column/1692953/what-is-rich-media-really.

14. Wikipedia.org, 2013.

15. "Dictionary and Thesaurus | Merriam-Webster".*www.merriam-webster.com.* August 10, 2016.

16. "Number of Social Media Users Worldwide, 2010 to 2020," www.statista.com, 2016.

17. "China Internet Watch," 2015, www.chinainternetwatch.com.

18. Daniel Muntinga, "Catching COBRAS," The Foundation for Scientific Research on Commercial Communication, Amsterdam, The Netherlands, 2013.

19. Andrew Perrin, "Social Media Usage: 2005–2015," August 8, 2015, www.pewinternet.org.

20. Michael Steizner, "2014 Social Media Marketing Industry Report," May 2014, www.socialmediaexaminer.com.

21. "Time Spent on Social Networking by Internet Users Worldwidr from 2012 to 2016," www.statista.com, 2016.

22. Andrew Meola, "Social Ad Revenue Set to Double by 2021," www.businessinside.com, May 11, 2016.

23. "By the Numbers: 170+ Amazing Twitter Statistics," April 30, 2016, www.dmrstats.com.

24. Ibid.

25. Garette Sloane, "Twitter's Tailored Audiences Program Gets More Targeted," January 14, 2014, www.adweek.com.

26. Sheila Shayon, "Twitter Scores Touchdown to Live-Stream Thursday Night Football," www.brandchannel.com, April 5, 2016.

27. Dave Chaffey, "Global Social Media Research Summary 2016," www.smartinsights.com, August 8, 2016.

28. Shareen Pathak, "Luxury Brands on Snapchat? Why Michael Kors Is Taking the Plunge," www.digiday.com, February 19, 2015.

29. Ivonne Teoh, "Pinterest: 2016 Statistics: 110 Million Monthly Users,"www.linkedin.com, March 5, 2016.

30. Ibid.

31. Craig Smith, "By the Numbers: 125+ Amazing LinkedIn Statistics," May 1, 2016, www.expandedramblings.com.

32. "Could YouTube Become as Big as CBS or Viacom?" May 3, 2013, www.variety.com.

33. Lauren Johnson, "After 11 Years in Digital Video, YouTube Wants to Take on TV-Sized Budgets," www.adweek.com, May 1, 2016.

34. Lauren Johnson, "How YouTube Beauty Star Rachel Levin Keeps 7 Million Subscribers Tuned In," www.adweek.colm May. 1, 2016; Smosh YouTube Stats. www.socialblade.com, September 9, 2016.

35. David Pierson, "Stars' Ads Don't Upset Youth," *Los Angeles Times,* April 1, 2016, p. C3.

36. Stephen Perlberg, "Podcasts Face Advertising Hurdle," February 18, 2016, www.wsj.com.

37. www.statista.com, May 2016.

38. "Marketers Boost Efforts to Reach Coupon Clippers via Mobile," May 15, 2015, www.emarketer.com.

39. "comScore Reports February 2016 U.S. Smartphone Subscriber Market Share," www.comscore.com, April 6, 2016.

40. "Together, TV and Tablets Drive Brand Searches," December 6, 2012, www.emarketer.com.

41. E. J. Schultz, "Mobile Becomes Engine for Auto Marketing," www.adage.com, February 23, 2016.

42. Ibid.

43. "Study Claims 99 Percent of Users Ignore Sharing Buttons on Mobile," June 11, 2015, www.zdnet.com.

44. "Baby Boomers Not Fans of Mobile Ads," September 21, 2015, www.eMarketer.com.

45. "Measurement Guidelines and Measurement Certification," 2006, www.iab.net.

46. Jack Neff, "Study: ROI May Be Measurable in Facebook, MySpace After All," *Advertising Age,* April 13, 2009, http://adage.com/article/digital/study-cpg-roi-measurable-facebook-myspace/135940/.

47. "Measurement Guidelines and Measurement Certification."

48. Steve Latham, "Why Marketers Are Not Investing Online," *MediaPost,* February 13, 2008.

49. "Brands Failing to Measure Social Results," August 12, 2012, www.warc.com.

50. Gavin O'Malley, "Excessive Online Ads Curbed by Metric Standard," August 16, 2012, www.mediapost.com.

Chapter 16

1. Louis J. Haugh, "Defining and Redefining," *Advertising Age,* February 14, 1983, p. M44.

2. Wendy Goldman Getzier, "McDonald's, General Mills among *Despicable Me 2* Marketing Minions," *kidscreen,* May 21, 2013, http://kidscreen.com/2013/05/21/mcdonalds-general-mills-among-despicable-me-2-marketing-minions/.

3. Scott A. Nielsen, John Quelch, and Caroline Henderson, "Consumer Promotions and the Acceleration of Product Purchases," in *Research on Sales Promotion: Collected Papers,* Katherine E. Jocz, ed. (Cambridge, MA: Marketing Science Institute, 1984).

4. J. Jeffrey Inman and Leigh McAlister, "Do Coupon Expiration Dates Affect Consumer Behavior?" *Journal of Marketing Research* 31 (August 1994), pp. 423–28.

5. "2016 Will Be a Growth Year in Marketing Spending," *Direct Marketing News,* February 1, 2016, http://www.dmnews.com/marketing-strategy/2016-will-be-a-growth-year-in-marketing-spending/article/469545/.

6. "2009 Promo Industry Trends Report," *Promo,* December 1, 2009, http://promomagazine.com/09-industry-trends-report/index.html.

7. Betsy Spethman, "Is Promotion a Dirty Word?" *Promo,* March 2001, pp. 64–72.

8. "Clutter: Extras, Extras!," August 1, 2001, www.promomagazine.com.

9. Ibid.

10. Ellen Byron and Suzanne Vranica, "Scanners Check Out Who's Browsing," *The Wall Street Journal,* September 27, 2006, p. B2.

11. "Private Label and National Brands: Dialing in on Core Shoppers," The Food Institute, January 2015, www.foodinstitute.com/images/media/iri/TTJan2015.pdf.

12. Hank Schultz, "Private Label Sales Hit $98 Billion on 6% Growth, Report Says," October 30, 2012, FoodNavigator–USA, www.foodnavigator-usa.com/Markets/Private-label-sales-hit-98-billion-on-6-growth-report-says.

13. http://beta.fortune.com/fortune500/walmart-1.

14. Andy Serwer, "Bruised in Bentonville," *Fortune,* April 18, 2005, pp. 84–89.

15. IRI Market Pulse Survey, Q3 2014 cited in "Private Label and National Brands."

16. Betsy Spethman, "Tuning in at the Shelf," *Promo 13th Annual Source Book,* 2006, pp. 22, 24.

17. *Coupon Trends–2012 Year-End Report* (Winston-Salem, NC: 2013).

18. Joan Schneider and Julie Hall, "Why Most Product Launches Fail," *Harvard Business Review,* April 2011, http://hbr.org/2011/04/why-most-product-launches-fail/.

19. Leonard M. Lodish and Carl F. Mela, "If Brands Are Built over Years, Why Are They Managed over Quarters?" *Harvard Business Review* 85, no. 7/8 (July/August 2007), pp. 104–12.

20. "Special 'Made in the U.S.A.' WD-40 Smart Straw Cans Celebrate Hard Work, Heritage," *WD-40 Product News and Information,* http://wd40.com/news/in-the-news/JUN0313/.

21. Liva LaMontagne, "MarketingSherpa Consumer Purchase Preference Survey: Why Customers Follow Brands' Social Accounts," *MarketingSherpa,* November 17, 2015, www.marketingsherpa.com/article/chart/why-customers-follow-brands-social-accounts.

22. Lodish and Mela, "If Brands Are Built over Years, Why Are They Managed over Quarters?"

23. Michael Barbaro, Karen Ann Cullotta, and Christopher Maag, "Given Fewer Coupons to Clip, Bargain Hunters Snub Macy's," *The New York Times,* September 29, 2007, www.nytimes.com/2007/09/29/business/29coupons.html?_r=0p.

24. Lodish and Mela, "If Brands Are Built over Years, Why Are They Managed over Quarters?"

25. R. M. Prentice, "How to Split Your Marketing Funds between Advertising and Promotion Dollars," *Advertising Age,* January 10, 1977, pp. 41–42, 44.

26. Betsy Spethman, "Money and Power," *Brandweek,* March 15, 1993, p. 21.

27. "Miller Taste Challenge," 2005 Reggie Awards, Promotion Marketing Association, www.baalink.org/.

28. "Con Kleenex Expresa tu Hispanidad Art Contest," 2010 Reggie Awards Multi-Cultural/Ethnic, www.baalink.org/?reggieawards.

29. "Trial and Conversion VI: Consumers' Reactions to Samples and Demonstrations," Promotional Marketing Association, Inc., 2002.

30. Natalie Zmuda, "Facebook Turns Focus Group with Splenda Product-Sampling App," *Advertising Age,* July 13, 2009, http://adage.com/article?article_id=137851.

31. *Annual Topline View CPG Coupon Facts* (Deerfield, IL: NCH Marketing Services, 2015).

32. Inman and McAlister, "Do Coupon Expiration Dates Affect Consumer Behavior?"

33. *Annual Topline View CPG Coupon Facts.*

34. Richard Sale, "Serving Up Sweeps," *Promo,* August 1999, pp. 70–78; "Sweepstakes Fever," *Forbes,* October 3, 1988, pp. 164–66.

35. Douglas Karr, "What Are the Most Popular Prizes for Your Promotion Giveaways?," *Marketing Tech Blog,* May 5, 2016, https://marketingtechblog.com/popular-prizes-promotion-giveaways/.

36. David Kiefaber, "Lay's Crowdsourced Potato-Chip Finalists: Cheesy Garlic Bread, Chicken & Waffles, Sriracha," *Adweek,* February 11, 2013, www.adweek.com/adfreak/lays-crowdsourced-potato-chip-finalists-cheesy-garlic-bread-chicken-waffles-sriracha-147197; David Kiefaber, "Sam Adams Crowdsourcing Its Next Beer," *Adweek,* January 20, 2012, www.adweek.com/adfreak/sam-adams-crowdsourcing-its-next-beer-137619.

37. Bob Woods, "Picking a Winner," *Promo,* August 1998, pp. 57–62; Richard Sale, "Sweeping the Courts," *Promo,* May 1998, pp. 148–52, 422–45; Maxine S. Lans, "Legal Hurdles Big Part of Promotions Game," *Marketing News,* October 24, 1994, pp. 15–16.

38. Normandy Madden, "KFC Gets Burned by Digital Coupon Promotion," *Advertising Age,* April 14, 2010, http://adage.com/print?article_id5143283; Kate McArthur, "McSwindle," *Advertising Age,* August 27, 2002, pp. 1, 22;

Betsy Spethmann, "Harrah's Coupon Error to Cost $2.8 Billion," promomagazine.com, November 23, 2005; "User-Generated Content: The Good, the Bad and the Ugly," Yahoo! Advertising Solutions, December 19, 2011, http://advertising.yahoo.com/blogs/advertising/user-generated-content-good-bad-ugly-193505793.html.

39. Melanie Trottman and Ron Lieber, "Contest Winner Declines 'Free' Airline Tickets," *The Wall Street Journal,* July 6, 2005.

40. Kimberly Palmer, "Why Shoppers Love to Hate Rebates," January 18, 2008, www.usnews.com.

41. Peter Tat, William A. Cunningham III, and Emin Babakus, "Consumer Perceptions of Rebates," *Journal of Advertising Research* 28, no. 4 (August/September 1988), pp. 45–50.

42. "Rebates: Get What You Deserve," *Consumer Reports,* September 2009, p. 7; Brian Grow, "The Great Rebate Runaround," *BusinessWeek,* December 5, 2005, pp. 34–37.

43. Grow, "The Great Rebate Runaround."

44. Edward A. Blair and E. Lair Landon, "The Effects of Reference Prices in Retail Advertisements," *Journal of Marketing* 45, no. 2 (Spring 1981), pp. 61–69.

45. "U.S. Customer Loyalty Program Memberships Top 3 Billion for First Time, 2015 Colloquy Census Shows," February 9, 2015, COLLOQUY, www.colloquy.com/latest-news/2015-colloquy-loyalty-census/.

46. Suzette Parmley, "Loyalty Draws a Card," *San Diego Union-Tribune,* February 9, 2016, pp. C1, C4.

47. "U.S. Customer Loyalty Program Memberships Top 3 Billion For First Time, 2015 Colloquy Census Shows," February 9, 2015, COLLOQUY, https://www.colloquy.com/latest-news/2015-colloquy-loyalty-census/

48. Betsy Spethman, "Switching Loyalty," *Promo,* July 2002, pp. 40–45.

49. Kathleen M. Joyce, "Keeping the Faith," *Promo's 12th Annual Source Book 2005,* p. 24.

50. Kate Taylor, "Starbucks' Controversial New Rewards Program Launches Today—Here Are the Major Changes You Should Know About," *Business Insider,* April 12, 2016, www.businessinsider.com/starbucks-rewards-makes-major-change-2016-4.

51. Adapted from Terrence A. Shimp, *Advertising, Promotion, and Supplemental Aspects of Integrated Marketing Communication,* 6th ed. (Mason, OH: South-Western, 2003), p. 524.

52. William L. Wilkie, Debra M. Desrochers, and Gregory T. Gundlach, "Marketing Research and Public Policy: The Case of Slotting Fees," *Journal of Marketing & Public Policy* 21, no. 2 (Fall 2002), pp. 275–88; Frank Green, "Battling for Shelf Control," *San Diego Union-Tribune,* November 19, 1996, pp. C1, C6, C7.

53. Warren Thayer, "When Are Slotting Fees Warranted?" *RetailWire,* May 12, 2015, www.retailwire.com/discussion/when-are-slotting-fees-warranted/.

54. "Want Shelf Space at the Supermarket? Ante Up," *BusinessWeek,* August 7, 1989, pp. 60–61.

55. Ira Teinowitz, "Senators Berate Industry Abuse of Slotting Fees," *Advertising Age,* September 20, 1999, pp. 3, 66.

56. Paul N. Bloom, Gregory T. Gundlach, and Joseph P. Cannon, "Slotting Allowances and Fees: Schools of Thought and Views of Practicing Managers," *Journal of Marketing* 64, April 2000, pp. 92–108.

57. Brian Stoffel, "The Hidden Profit Machine for Grocery Stores," *The Motley Fool,* August 26, 2013, www.fool.com/investing/general/2013/08/26/the-hidden-profit-machine-for-grocery-stores.aspx.

58. "Crunching the Numbers," *Promo,* May 1, 2001, pp. 49–50.

59. Matthew Kinsman, "No Pain, No Gain," *Promo,* January 2002, pp. 26–28.

60. Tom Steinhagen, "Space Management Shapes Up with Planograms," *Marketing News,* November 12, 1990, p. 7.

61. Srinath Gopalakrishna, Gary L. Lilien, Jerome D. Williams, and Ian K. Sequeria, "Do Trade Shows Pay Off?" *Journal of Marketing* 59 (July 1995), pp. 75–83.

62. Beth Snyder Bulik, "Inside the 'Intel Inside' Campaign," *Advertising Age,* September 21, 2009, http://adage.com/article/news/advertising-inside-inside-intel-campaign/139128/.

63. Stuart Elliott, "'Intel Inside' Ad Campaign Shifts Focus to the Web," *International Herald Tribune,* October 11, 2007, www.iht.com.

64. Rebecca Lieb, "Co-op Advertising: Digital's Lost Opportunity?" IAB, October 13, 2012, www.iab.com/insights/co-op-advertising-digitals-lost-opportunity-a-new-study-by-iab-local-search-association/.

65. Jack Neff, "As Retailer Digital Exchanges Proliferate, Will They Become The New Trade Promotion?" *Advertising Age,* October 26, 2015, p. 26.

66. Edwin L. Artzt, "The Lifeblood of Brands," *Advertising Age,* November 4, 1991, p. 32.

67. Lodish and Mela, "If Brands Are Built over Years, Why Are They Managed over Quarters?"; Jack Neff, "The New Brand Management," *Advertising Age,* November 8, 1999, pp. S2, S18; Benson P. Shapiro, "Improved Distribution with Your Promotional Mix," *Harvard Business Review,* March/April 1977, p. 116; Roger A. Strang, "Sales Promotion—Fast Growth, Faulty Management," *Harvard Business Review,* July/August 1976, p. 119.

68. Quote by Thomas E. Hamilton, director of sales promotion service, William Esty Advertising, cited in Felix Kessler, "The Costly Couponing Craze," *Fortune,* June 9, 1986, p. 84.

69. Priya Raghubir and Kim Corfman, "When Do Price Promotions Affect Pretrial Brand Evaluations?" *Journal of Marketing Research* 36 (May 1999), pp. 211–22.

70. Alan G. Sawyer and Peter H. Dickson, "Psychological Perspectives on Consumer Response to Sales Promotion," in *Research on Sales Promotion: Collected Papers,* Katherine E. Jocz, ed. (Cambridge, MA: Marketing Science Institute, 1984).

71. William E. Myers, "Trying to Get Out of the Discounting Box," *Adweek,* November 11, 1985, p. 2.

72. Leigh McAlister, "Managing the Dynamics of Promotional Change," in *Looking at the Retail Kaleidoscope, Forum IX* (Stamford, CT: Donnelley Marketing, April 1988).

73. "Promotions Blemish Cosmetic Industry," *Advertising Age,* May 10, 1984, pp. 22–23, 26; Cliff Edwards, "Everyone Loves a Freebie—except Dell's Rivals," *BusinessWeek,* July 22, 2002, p. 41.

74. Lauren Shepherd, "Customers Getting More Burger for the Buck," *San Diego Union-Tribune,* February 13, 2008, pp. C1, C3.

75. "Taco Bell '$1 Cravings' Value Menu to Likely Go National," *The Huffington Post,* May 2, 2013, www.huffingtonpost.com/2013/05/02/taco-bell-1-cravings_n_3203491.html.

76. Jessica Wohl, "McDonald's Dollar Menu & More Is No More: Now There's McPick," *Advertising Age,* November 16, 2015, http://adage.com/article/cmo-strategy/mcdonald-s-play-called-mcpick/301385/.

77. Priya Raghubir, J. Jeffrey Inman, and Hans Grande, "The Three Faces of Consumer Promotions," *California Management Review,* Summer 2004, pp. 23–42.

Chapter 17

1. www.publicrelationsnewspr.com.
2. Scott M. Cutlip, Allen H. Center, and Glen M. Broom, *Effective Public Relations,* 11th ed. (Upper Saddle River, NJ: Prentice Hall, 2012).
3. Jonah Bloom, "The Cultural Gulf That Separates Marketing and PR," *Advertising Age,* March 11, 2007.
4. "PR News/PRSA Survey," *PR News,* May 25, 2005, p. 1.
5. William N. Curry, "PR Isn't Marketing," *Advertising Age,* December 18, 1991, p. 18.
6. Martha M. Lauzen, "Imperialism and Encroachment in Public Relations," *Public Relations Review* 17, no. 3 (Fall 1991), pp. 245–55.
7. Cutlip, Center, and Broom, *Effective Public Relations.*
8. Thomas L. Harris, "How MPR Adds Value to Integrated Marketing Communications," *Public Relations Quarterly,* Summer 1993, pp. 13–18.
9. Thomas L. Harris, "Marketing PR—The Second Century, Reputation Management," January/February 1999, www.prcentral.com.
10. Jennifer Kay and Mike Schneider, " SeaWorld Has Realized That Its Shamu Image Is No Longer Viable for the Company's Future," March 19, 2016, www.usnews.com.
11. Cutlip, Center, and Broom, *Effective Public Relations.*
12. John E. Marston, *Modern Public Relations* (New York: McGraw-Hill, 1979).
13. Joyce Freiden, "AMA Wants Ban on DTC Advertising," www.medpagetoday.com, November 18, 2015.
14. Stephen Sprayberry, "Measuring the Effectiveness of Your Public Relations Efforts," *PR Insights,* April 2, 2015, www.williammills.com.
15. Jim Macnamara, "PR Metrics: How to Measure Public Relations and Corporate Communication," www.researchgate.net, September 8, 2015.

16. Amit Jain, " Emerging Models of PR Measurement," www.prweek.com, July 16, 2014.
17. Mark Weiner, "Marketing PR Revolution," *Communication World,* January/February 2005, pp. 1–5.
18. Rebekah Iliff, "Why PR Is Embracing the PESO Model," December 4, 2014, www.themediabuy.com.
19. Jaye S. Niefeld, "Corporate Advertising," *Industrial Marketing,* July 1980, pp. 64–74.
20. "Naming Rights, Naming Wrongs," October 2013, www.performanceresearch.com.
21. Mark J. Miller, "NASCAR Sponsors: Hertz Backs Penske as Teams Look to Get Back on Track," January 24, 2013, www.brandchannel.com.
22. Wayne Friedman, "Supreme Court OKs Corporate-Sponsored Issue Ads," *MediaPost,* June 27, 2007.
23. "Statistics Every Cause Marketer Should Know," 2016, www.causemarketingforum.com.
24. Matt Petronzio, "90% of Americans More Likely to Trust Brands That Back Social Causes," January 11, 2015, www.mashable.com.
25. "Statistics Every Cause Marketer Should Know," 2016, www.causemarketingforum.com.
26. Janas Sinclair and Tracy Irani, "Advocacy Advertising for Biotechnology," *Journal of Advertising,* Fall 2005, pp. 59–74.

Chapter 18

1. Lara O'Reilly, "These Are the 10 Companies That Spend the Most on Advertising," July 6, 2015, www.businessinsider.com.
2. Laurie Sullivan, "Marketing Budgets Rise, Determining Multichannel ROI, Metrics Remain a Challenge," www.mediapost.com, February 5, 2013.
3. Ibid.
4. Fournaise Marketing Group, "Marketers Use 'Shocking' Metrics," September 22, 2015, www.warc.com.
5. Peter Minnium, "It's the Creative, Stupid: 3 Reasons Why Ad Creative Trumps Technology Every Time," February 4, 2015, www.marketingland.com.
6. Tim Nudd, "Does Sex Really Sell?" *Adweek,* October 17, 2005, pp. 14–17.
7. David A. Aaker and John G. Myers, *Advertising Management*, 3rd ed. (Englewood Cliffs, NJ: Prentice Hall, 1987), p. 474.

8. Spike Cramphorn, "What Advertising Testing Might Have Been, If We Had Only Known," *Journal of Advertising Research* 44, no. 2 (June 2004), pp. 170–80.
9. "21 Ad Agencies Endorse Copy-Testing Principles," *Marketing News* 15 (February 19, 1982), p. 1.
10. Ibid.
11. http://measurementnow.net/principles-solution, 2016.
12. Molly Soat, "The Case for Earlier Insights," *Marketing News,* July 2015, pp. 16–17.
13. Ye Hu, Leonard Lodish, Abba Krieger, and Babak Hayati, "An Update of Real-World TV Advertising Tests," *Journal of Advertising Research*, June 2009, pp. 201–06.
14. Steve Outing and Laura Ruel, "The Best of Eyetrack III: What We Saw When When We Looked through Their Eyes," 2004, www.poynterextra.org.
15. Hubert A. Zielske, "Does Day-After-Recall Penalize 'Feeling Ads'?" *Journal of Advertising Research* 22, no. 1 (1982), pp. 19–22.
16. Arthur J. Kover, "Why Copywriters Don't Like Advertising Research—and What Kind of Research Might They Accept," *Journal of Advertising Research* 36 (March/April 1996), pp. RC8–RC10; Gary Levin, "Emotion Guides BBDO's Ad Tests," *Advertising Age*, January 29, 1990, p. 12.
17. Terry Haller, "Day-after Recall to Persist Despite JWT Study; Other Criteria Looming," *Marketing News*, May 18, 1979, p. 4.
18. Joel Dubow, "Recall Revisited: Recall Redux," *Journal of Advertising Research* 34, no. 3 (May/June 1994), p. 92.
19. Ravi Chandiramani, "Reckitt Launches Debut iTV Campaign for Finish," *Marketing*, January 10, 2002, p. 9.
20. Gary Levin, "Tracing Ads' Impact," *Advertising Age*, November 12, 1990, p. 49.
21. Jeffrey L. Seglin, "The New Era of Ad Measurement," *Adweek's Marketing Week*, January 23, 1988, p. 24.
22. "Yankelovich Study Shows Advertising's Effects Vary, Depending on Category and Purchase Funnel Stage," April 16, 2009, www.tvb.org.
23. Russell I. Haley and Allan L. Baldinger, "The ARF Copy Research Validity Project," *Journal of Advertising Research*, April/May 1991, pp. 11–32.

24. Glenn Heitsmith, "Something for Nothing," *Promo*, September 1993, pp. 30, 31, 93.

25. "Applying Customer Analytics to Promotion Decisions," 2012, www.sas.com.

26. ShopperTrak.com, 2016.

27. David W. Schumann, Jennifer Grayson, Johanna Ault, Kerri Hargrove, Lois Hollingsworth, Russell Ruelle, and Sharon Seguin, "The Effectiveness of Shopping Cart Signage: Perceptual Measures Tell a Different Story," *Journal of Advertising Research* 31 (February/March 1991), pp. 17–22.

28. Steve McClellan, "New Software to Track In-Store Radio," *Adweek*, October 10, 2005, p. 10.

29. Michel Tuan Pham, "The Evaluation of Sponsorship Effectiveness: A Model and Some Methodological Considerations," Gestion 2000, pp. 47–65.

30. Ibid.

31. John Nardone and Ed See, "Measure Sponsorship to Drive Sales-Shift Gears: Move beyond Perceiving Them as Mere Brand Builders and Instead Assess ROI," *Advertising Age*, March 5, 2007.

32. Teresa F. Lindeman, "Good Wal-Mart, Bad Wal-Mart; Retail Giant Hopes to Combat Negative Publicity," *Knight Ridder Tribune Business News*, April 10, 2005, pp. 1–6.

33. "Advertisers Demand More Accountability for Digital Media," *Center for Media Research*, February 22, 2007, pp. 1–2.

34. Isaac M. Dinner, Harald J. Van Heerde, and Scott A. Neslin, "Driving Online and Offline Sales: The Cross-Channel Effects of Traditional, Online Display, and Paid Search Advertising," *Journal of Marketing Research*, Volume 51, October 2015, pp. 527–545.

35. John M. McGrath, "An Experimental Approach to Testing IMC Effects on Consumer Attitudes, Behavioral Intentions and Recall," *Journal of Applied Marketing Theory* 2, no. 2 (November 2011), pp. 25–44.

36. Marek Winearz, "The Market Contact Audit," 2010, www.integration-imc.com.

Chapter 19

1. Richard S. Post and Penelope N. Post, *Global Brand Integrity Management* (New York: McGraw-Hill, 2008); David A. Aaker and Erich Joachimsthaler, "The Lure of Global Branding," *Harvard Business Review*, November/December 1999, pp. 137–44.

2. David Kiley and Burt Helm, "The Great Trust Offensive," *BusinessWeek*, September 28, 2009, pp. 38–42.

3. Emma Hall, "As Regulation Increases, WFA Must Decide What's Worth Protecting," *Advertising Age*, March 12, 2013, http://adage.com/article/cmo-interviews/pernod-ricard-cmo-riley-leads-wfa-amid-regulation-concerns/240222/.

4. Geoff Colvin, "Indra Nooyi's Challenge," *Fortune*, June 11, 2012, pp. 149–56; Mutsa Chironga, Acha Leke, Susan Lund, and Arend van Wamelen, "Cracking the Next Growth Market: Africa," *Harvard Business Review*, May 2011, pp. 117–22.

5. "Australia Launches New International Tourism Campaign," Tourism Australia, January 26, 2016, www.tourism.australia.com/news/Media-Releases-17782.aspx.

6. Joan Voight, "The Great Brand of China," *Adweek*, October 29, 2012, p. 22; Christine Birkner, "Eastern Influence," *Marketing News*, September 15, 2012, pp. 10–15; Normandy Madden, "China Ad Opportunities to Grow with WTO Deal," *Advertising Age International*, January 2000, p. 6.

7. Thomas L. H. Friedman, *The World Is Flat* (New York: Farrar, Straus and Giroux, 2005).

8. "Global Ad Market Is Growing, Powered by Digital," *Advertising Age*, December 7, 2015, p. 22.

9. "Global Ad Market Is Growing, Powered By Digital," *Advertising Age*, December 7, 2015. p. 22.

10. Vern Terpstra, *International Marketing*, 4th ed. (New York: Holt, Rinehart & Winston/Dryden Press, 1987), p. 427.

11. Rana Foroohar, "Why the Mighty BRIC Nations Have Finally Broken," *Time*, November 10, 2015, http://time.com/4106094/goldman-sachs-brics/.

12. Claudia Penteado, "Emerging Lower Middle Class Fires Up Marketers in Brazil," *Advertising Age*, June 14, 2010, p. 12.

13. Angela Doland, "The Race to Reach India's Next Billion Internet Users," *Advertising Age*, June 15, 2016, http://adage.com/article/digital/race-reach-india-s-billion-internet-users/304467/; "Marketers Remain Bullish on China Despite Potential for Slower Growth," *Advertising Age*, July 13, 2015, p. 8.

14. Manuela Mesco, "Unfashionably Late to China," *The Wall Street Journal*, March 26, 2013, http://search.proquest.com/docview/1319502349?accountid=13758.

15. "Have the BRICs Hit a Wall? The Next Emerging Markets," KNOWLEDGE@WHARTON, January 12, 2016, http://knowledge.wharton.upenn.edu/article/98411/.

16. Noreen O'Leary, "The Rise of BRIC," *Adweek*, February 4–11, 2008, pp. 32–37, 65; Noreen O'Leary, "Bright Lights, Big Challenges," *Adweek*, January 15, 2007, 22–33.

17. Mark Lasswell, "Lost in Translation," *Business 2.0*, August 2004, pp. 68–70.

18. George E. Belch and Michael A. Belch, "Toward Development of a Model and Scale for Assessing Consumer Receptivity to Foreign Products and Global Advertising," in *European Advances in Consumer Research* (vol. 1), Gary J. Bamossy and W. Fred van Raaij, eds. (Provo, UT: Association for Consumer Research, 1993), pp. 52–57.

19. Subhash Sharma, Terrence Shimp, and Jeongshin Shin, "Consumer Ethnocentrism: A Test of Antecedents and Moderators," *Journal of the Academy of Marketing Science*, Winter 1995, pp. 26–37.

20. Steve Hamm, "Borders Are So 20th Century," *BusinessWeek*, September 22, 2003, pp. 68–73.

21. For an excellent discussion of various elements of Japanese culture such as language and its implications for promotion, see John F. Sherry Jr. and Eduardo G. Camargo, "May Your Life Be Marvelous: English Language Labelling and the Semiotics of Japanese Promotion," *Journal of Consumer Research* 14, no. 2 (September 1987), pp. 174–88.

22. Barbara Mueller, "Reflections on Culture: An Analysis of Japanese and American Advertising Appeals," *Journal of Advertising Research*, June/July 1987, pp. 51–59.

23. Barbara Mueller, "Standardization vs. Specialization: An Examination of Westernization in Japanese Advertising," *Journal of Advertising Research* 31, no. 1 (January/February 1992), pp. 15–24; Johny K. Johansson, "The Sense of Nonsense: Japanese TV Advertising," *Journal of Advertising* 23, no. 1 (March 1994), pp. 17–26.

24. Michael L. Maynard and Charles R. Taylor, "Girlish Images across Cultures: Analyzing Japanese versus U.S. Seventeen Magazine Ads," *Journal of Advertising* 28, no. 1 (Spring 1999), pp. 39–49.

25. Shintaro Okazaki and Barbara Mueller, "The Impact of the Lost Decade on Advertising in Japan: A Grounded Theory Approach," *International Journal of Advertising* 30, no. 2 (December 2010), pp. 205–32.

26. Francis Hsu, *Americans and Chinese: Passage to Differences* (Honolulu: University Press of Hawaii, 1981).

27. Geoffrey A. Fowler, "China Bans Nike's LeBron Ad as Offensive to Nation's Dignity," *The Wall Street Journal,* December 7, 2004, p. B4.

28. Gerard Prendergast, Wah-Leung Cheung, and Douglas West, "How Far Is Too Far? The Antecedents of Offensive Advertising in Modern China," *Journal of Advertising Research* 48, no. 4 (December 2008), pp. 484–95.

29. Rich Thomaselli, "Will Australia's Cigarette Branding Ban Spread beyond Borders, Tobacco?" *Advertising Age,* August 19, 2012, http://adage.com/article/news/australia-s-cigarette-brand-ban-prompt-domino-effect/236761/.

30. "Malaysia Bans 'Sly' Tobacco Ads," *Marketing News,* September 1, 2002, p. 7.

31. Vanessa Fuhrmans, "In Europe, Prescription-Drug Ads Are Banned—and Health Costs Lower," *The Wall Street Journal,* March 15, 2002, pp. B1, B4.

32. Pritha Mitra Dasgupta, "In Absence of Any Clear Ad Rules, Liquor Companies Using Social Media to Promote Their Brands," *The Economic Times,* July 31, 2014, http://articles.economictimes.indiatimes.com/2014-07-31/news/52285216_1_social-media-liquor-companies-liquor-products; Niraj Sheth, "India Liquor, Tobacco Firms Shift Tack," *The Wall Street Journal,* May 6, 2008, p. B8.

33. Jeremy Slate, "EC Lets Stand Toy Ad Ban," *Advertising Age International,* August 1999, pp. 1, 11.

34. Sam Loewenberg, "Effort in EU to Ban TV Ads Aimed at Kids Gains Steam," *Los Angeles Times,* July 9, 2001, p. C3.

35. Safran S. Al-Makaty, G. Norman van Tubergen, S. Scott Whitlow, and Douglas S. Boyd, "Attitudes toward Advertising in Islam," *Journal of Advertising Research* 36, no. 3 (May/June 1996), pp. 16–26; Marian Katz, "No Women, No Alcohol: Learn Saudi Taboos before Placing Ads," *International Advertiser,* February 1986, pp. 11–12.

36. "Misleading Advertising," *European Commission,* http://ec.europa.eu/justice/consumer-marketing/unfair-trade/false-advertising/; Naveen Donthu, "A Cross-Country Investigation of Recall of and Attitude toward Comparative Advertising," *Journal of Advertising* 27, no. 2 (Summer 1998), pp. 111–22.

37. Dannemann Siemsen Advogados, "Comparative Advertising and Ambush Marketing on the Rise in Brazil," *World Trademark Review,* December/January 2010, www.worldtrademarkreview.com.

38. J. Craig Andrews, Steven Lysonski, and Srinivas Durvasula, "Understanding Cross-Cultural Student Perceptions of Advertising in General: Implications for Advertising Educators and Practitioners," *Journal of Advertising* 20, no. 2 (June 1991), pp. 15–28.

39. Jonathan Cheng, "China Demands Concrete Proof of Ad Claims," *The Wall Street Journal,* July 8, 2005, pp. B1, B4.

40. Stephanie Thompson, "Europe Slams Icons as Food Fights Back," *Advertising Age,* January 31, 2005, pp. 1, 38.

41. Robert D. Buzzell, "Can You Standardize Multinational Marketing?" *Harvard Business Review,* November/December 1968, pp. 102–13; Ralph Z. Sorenson and Ulrich E. Wiechmann, "How Multinationals View Marketing," *Harvard Business Review,* May/June 1975, p. 38.

42. Theodore Levitt, "The Globalization of Markets," *Harvard Business Review,* May/June 1983, pp. 92–102; Theodore Levitt, *The Marketing Imagination* (New York: Free Press, 1986).

43. Melissa Akaka and Dana A. Alden, "Global Brand Positioning and Perceptions: International Advertising and Global Consumer Culture," *International Journal of Advertising* 29, no. 1 (2010), pp. 37–56.

44. Charles R. Taylor and Shintaro Okazaki, "Do Global Brands Use Similar Executional Styles across Cultures?: A Comparison of U.S. and Japanese Television Advertising," *Journal of Advertising* 44, no. 3 (2015), pp. 276–88.

45. Maduh Agrawal, "Review of a 40-Year Debate in International Advertising," *International Marketing Review* 12, no. 1 (1995), pp. 26–48; William L. James and John S. Hill, "International Advertising Messages, to Adapt or Not to Adapt (That Is the Question)," *Journal of Advertising Research* 31 (June/July 1991), pp. 65–71; Keith Reinhard and W. E. Phillips, "Global Marketing: Experts Look at Both Sides," *Advertising Age,* April 15, 1988, p. 47; Anthony Rutigliano, "The Debate Goes On: Global vs. Local Advertising," *Management Review,* June 1986, pp. 27–31.

46. Jack Neff, "Gillette Signs Three Sports Giants for Global Effort," *Advertising Age,* February 5, 2007, http://adage.com/article/news/gillette-signs-sports-giants-global-effort/114822/; Bernhard Warner, "IQ News: Gillette's Mach 3 Media Heft Hits Web: Eureopean Sites Next?" *Adweek Online,* August 24, 1998.

47. E. J. Schultz, "Doritos Launches First Global Campaign," *Advertising Age,* March 6, 2013, http://adage.com/article/news/doritos-launches-global-campaign/240173/.

48. Kevin Goldman, "Professor Who Started Debate on Global Ads Still Backs Theory," *The Wall Street Journal,* October 13, 1992, p. B8.

49. Anita Chang Beattie, "In Japan, Pizza Is Recast as a Meal for Special Occasions," *Advertising Age,* April 2, 2012, p. 16.

50. Eric White and Jeffrey A. Trachtenberg, "One Size Doesn't Fit All," *The Wall Street Journal,* October 1, 2003, pp. B1, B2.

51. Criteria cited by Edward Meyer, CEO, Grey Advertising, in Rebecca Fannin, "What Agencies Really Think of Global Theory," *Marketing & Media Decisions,* December 1984, p. 74.

52. George Slefo, "Fitbit's Latest Global Campaign Is All about 'Sweat and Swagger,'" *Advertising Age,* January 7, 2016, http://adage.com/article/cmo-strategy/fitbit-s-latest-campaign-sweat-swagger/302032/.

53. Kunur Patel, "HTC Goes All-In on 'One' Phone in Battle with Apple, Samsung," *Advertising Age,* March 30, 2012, http://adage.com/article/digital/htc-phone-battle-apple-samsung/233843/.

54. Durairaj Maheswaran, "Country of Origin as a Stereotype: Effects on Product Evaluations," *Journal of Consumer Research,* September 1994, pp. 354–65.

55. Daniel Gross, "Yes We Can Still Market: Why U.S. Brands Remain World's Most Valuable," *The Daily Beast,* June 1, 2014, www.thedailybeast.com/articles/2014/06/01/yes-we-can-still-market-why-u-s-brands-remain-world-s-most-valuable.html.

56. Paul Chao, "The Moderating Effects of Country of Assembly, Country of Parts, and Country of Design on Hybrid Product Evaluations," *Journal of Advertising* 20, no. 4 (Winter 2001), pp. 67–82.

57. Beth Snyder Bulik, "Ditch the Flags, Kids Don't Care Where You Come From," *Advertising Age,* June 4, 2007, pp. 1, 59.

58. Ibid.

59. Salah S. Hassan and Lea P. Katsansis, "Identification of Global Consumer Segments: A Behavioral Framework," *Journal of International Consumer Marketing* 3, no. 2 (1991), pp. 11–28.

60. Arundhati Parmar, "Global Youth United," *Marketing News,* October 28, 2002, pp. 1, 49; "Ready to Shop until They Drop," *BusinessWeek,* June 22, 1998, pp. 104–10; "Teens Seen as the First Truly Global Consumers," *Marketing News,* March 27, 1995, p. 9; Shawn Tully, "Teens: The Most Global Market of All," *Fortune,* May 16, 1994, pp. 90–97.

61. Jerry Wind, Stan Sthanunathan, and Rob Malcolm, "Great Advertising Is Both Local and Global," *Harvard Business Review,* March 29, 2013, https://hbr.org/2013/03/great-advertising-is-both-loca/.

62. Ibid.

63. Nigel Hollis, *The Global Brand* (New York: Palgrave Macmillan, 2008).

64. Nigel Hollis, "Global Brands, Local Cultures," *Research World,* July/August 2009, pp. 20–24; Piet Levy, "10 Minutes with Nigel Hollis," *Marketing News,* August 30, 2009, pp. 18–19.

65. Penelope Rowlands, "Global Approach Doesn't Always Make Scents," *Advertising Age International,* January 17, 1994, pp. i1, 38.

66. Natalie Zmuda, "Levi's Names Jaime Szulc Its First Global CMO," *Advertising Age,* August 26, 2009, http://adage.com/article/cmo-strategy/levi-s-names-jaime-szulc-global-cmo/138659/.

67. Normandy Madden, "Shanghai Rises as Asia's Newest Marketing Capital," *Advertising Age,* October 14, 2002, pp. 1, 13.

68. Kevin Goldman, "Global Companies Hone Agency Rosters," *The Wall Street Journal,* July 25, 1995, p. B8.

69. Goldman, "Global Companies Hone Agency Rosters."

70. "Advertising Is Indeed Going Global," *Market Europe,* October 1997, pp. 8–10.

71. Anne-Marie Crawford, "Clients and Agencies Split over Ad Superstars," *Ad Age Global* 1, no. 9 (May 2001), p. 16.

72. Katie Richards, "Put Away the Selfie Stick and Live Like a Local, Urges Airbnb's New Campaign," *Adweek,* April 19, 2016, www.adweek.com/news/advertising-branding/put-away-selfie-stick-and-live-local-urges-airbnbs-new-campaign-170920.

73. Joan Voight, "Exporting Las Vegas," *Adweek,* September 3, 2007, pp. 14–15.

74. Erin White, "German Ads Get More Daring, but Some Firms Aren't Pleased," *The Wall Street Journal,* November 22, 2002, p. B6.

75. Larry Speer, "French Government Attacks 'Sexist' Ads," *Ad Age Global,* May 2001, p. 7.

76. Normandy Madden, "Looking for the Next Brazil? Try Thailand," *Advertising Age,* April 11, 2005, p. 22.

77. Stephanie King, "Indian Ads Come into Their Own," *The Wall Street Journal,* December 12, 2007, p. B4.

78. Normandy Madden, "Two Chinas," *Advertising Age,* August 16, 2004, pp. 1, 22.

79. Derek Thompson, "How the World Consumes Media," *Atlantic,* May 28, 2014, www.theatlantic.com/business/archive/2014/05/global-mobile-media-smartphones-tv-maps/371760/.

80. Matthew Holehouse, "More Adverts in Prime Time Whows under EU Rules Change, after Broadcasters Lose Viewers to Netflix," *The Telegraph,* May 26, 2016, www.telegraph.co.uk/news/2016/05/25/more-adverts-in-prime-time-shows-under-eu-rules-change-after-bro/.

81. Rochell Burbury, "Australia Ends Ban on Cable TV Spots," *Advertising Age International,* March 1997, p. i22.

82. Leslie Chang, "Cracking China's Huge TV Market," *The Wall Street Journal,* August 1, 2000, pp. B1, B4.

83. "To Cope with New Rules, China TV Station Holds Ad Auction Do-Over," *Advertising Age,* December 9, 2011, http://adage.com/article/global-news/china-tv-station-holds-ad-auction-cope-rules/231492/.

84. Jane Lanhee Lee, "TV Marketers Aim to Reap Rural China's Fertile Land," *The Wall Street Journal,* July 30, 2007, p. B2.

85. Hearst International Magazines, www.hearst.com/magazines/hearst-magazines-international.php.

86. Noreen O'Leary, "The Lay of the Land," *Adweek,* February 5, 2007, pp. 14–21.

87. Kamran Kashani and John A. Quelch, "Can Sales Promotion Go Global?" *Business Horizons,* May/June 1990, pp. 37–43.

88. Lenard C. Huff and Dana L. Alden, "An Investigation of Consumer Response to Sales Promotion in Developing Markets: A Three Country Analysis," *Journal of Advertising Research* 26, no. 1 (May/June 1998), pp. 47–56.

89. "Global Consumers Go Sale Searching and Coupon Clipping," *Nielsen,* October 12, 2011, www.nielsen.com/us/en/newswire/2011/global-consumers-go-sale-searching-and-coupon-clipping.html.

90. Douglas J. Wood and Linda A. Goldstein, "A Lawyer's Guide to Going Global," *Promo Magazine,* Special Report, August 1998, p. S11.

91. "Foreign Ads Go Further with PR," *International Advertiser,* December 1986, p. 30.

92. Loewenberg, "Effort in EU to Ban TV Ads Aimed at Kids Gains Steam."

93. Laurie Burkitt, "KFC Apologizes amid Probe," *The Wall Street Journal,* January 11, 2013, p. B7.

94. Laurie Burkitt and Julie Jargon, "China Woes Put Dent in Yum Brand," *The Wall Street Journal,* January 9, 2013, p. B3.

95. *Internet World Stats: Usage and Population Statistics: 2016,* www.internetworldstats.com/stats.htm.

96. Kaveh Waddell, "Why Google Quit China—and Why It's Heading Back," *The Atlantic,* January 19, 2016, www.theatlantic.com/technology/archive/2016/01/why-google-quit-china-and-why-its-heading-back/424482/.

97. Leo Barraclough, "Global Advertising Spend to Rise 4.6% to $579 Billion in 2016," *Variety,* March 21, 2016, http://variety.com/2016/digital/global/global-advertising-spend-rise-2016-1201735023/.

98. Jonathan Espinosa, "Facebook Overtakes Japanese Social Network Mixi in Japan," *Inside Facebook,* September 13, 2012, www.insidefacebook.com/2012/09/13/facebook-overtakes-japanese-social-network-mixi-in-japan/.

99. Jessica Guynn, "Twitter Growth Grinds to a Halt," *USA TODAY,* February 11, 2016, http://www.usatoday.com/story/tech/news/2016/02/10/twitter-fourth-quarter-earnings-user-decline/80178140/.

Chapter 20

1. Fred W. Morgan and Jeffrey J. Stoltman, "Advertising and Product Liability Litigation," *Journal of Advertising* 26, no. 2 (Summer 1997), pp. 63–75.

2. Ira Teinowitz, "Curb Proposal Raises Tobacco Marketers' Ire," *Advertising Age,* March 18, 2002, p. 70; Myron Levin, "U.S. to Pursue Lawsuit to Curb Cigarette Marketing," *Los Angeles Times,* March 12, 2002, pp. C1, C15.

3. Christine Birkner, "With the Threat of an Ad Ban Looming, Pharma Is Fighting to Repair Its Reputation, *Adweek,* March 27, 2016, www.adweek.com/news/advertising-branding/threat-ad-ban-looming-pharma-fighting-repair-its-reputation-170409.

4. Alice Z. Cuneo, "Of Contracts and Claims; Agencies Face Liability Issues," *Advertising Age,* January 31, 2000, p. 25.

5. Alice Z. Cuneo, "Can an Agency Be Guilty of Malpractice?" *Advertising Age,* January 31, 2000, pp. 24–25; Steven W. Colford and Raymond Serafin, "Scali Pays for Volvo Ad: FTC," *Advertising Age,* August 26, 1991, p. 4.

6. Priscilla A. LaBarbera, "Analyzing and Advancing the State of the Art of Advertising Self-Regulation," *Journal of Advertising* 9, no. 4 (1980), pp. 27–38.

7. Ian P. Murphy, "Competitive Spirits: Liquor Industry Turns to TV Ads," *Marketing News,* December 2, 1996, pp. 1, 17.

8. Stuart Elliott, "Facing Outcry, NBC Ends Plan to Run Liquor Ads," *The New York Times,* March 21, 2002, p. C1.9.

9. E. J. Schultz, "Hard Time: Liquor Advertising Pours into TV," *Advertising Age,* May 14, 2012, pp. 1, 41; Mike Esterl, "Liquor Ads Win Airtime," *The Wall Street Journal,* August 2, 2012, p. B6.

10. John F. Archer, "Advertising of Professional Fees: Does the Consumer Have a Right to Know?" *South Dakota Law Review* 21 (Spring 1976), p. 330.

11. Bates v. State Bar of Arizona, 97 S. Ct. 2691. 45, *U.S. Law Week* 4895 (1977).

12. Charles Laughlin, "Ads on Trial," *Link,* May 1994, pp. 18–22; "Lawyers Learn the Hard Sell—and Companies Shudder," *BusinessWeek,* June 10, 1985, p. 70.

13. Bruce H. Allen, Richard A. Wright, and Louis E. Raho, "Physicians and Advertising," *Journal of Health Care Marketing* 5 (Fall 1985), pp. 39–49.

14. LaBarbera, "Analyzing and Advancing the State of the Art of Advertising Self-Regulation."

15. Jack Neff, "Household Brands Counterpunch," *Advertising Age,* November 1, 1999, p. 26.

16. Jessica E. Vascellaro, "Regulators Say Love Ain't 'Chemistry' After All," *The Wall Street Journal,* September 17, 2007, p. B5.

17. Ibid.

18. Shelly Branch, "Campbell Is in the Soup on V8 Ad," *The Wall Street Journal,* April 26, 2002, p. B4.

19. Tanzina Vega, "CoverGirl Withdraws 'Enhanced' Taylor Swift Ad," *The New York Times,* December 21, 2011, http://mediadecoder.blogs.nytimes.com/2011/12/21/covergirl-withdraws-enhanced-taylor-swift-ad/?_r=0.

20. *NAD/CARU Case Reports, Summary of NAD/CARU/NARB/ERSP Case Work,* (National Advertising Division, Council of Better Business Bureaus), January 2016, p. 2.

21. "The Electronic Retailing Self-Regulation Program: Policy and Procedures," National Advertising Review Council, www.narcpartners.org/ersp.

22. Dorothy Cohen, "The FTC's Advertising Substantiation Program," *Journal of Marketing* 44, no. 1 (Winter 1980), pp. 26–35.

23. Rupal Parekh, "Netanyahu, Abbas Smooch in Benetton Ad," *Advertising Age,* November 16, 2011, http://adage.com/article/agency-news/netanyahu-abbas-smooch-latest-benetton-ad-campaign/231037/; Eric J. Lyman, "The True Colors of Toscani," adageglobal.com, August 2001, www.ericjlyman.com/adageglobal.html.

24. Lynda M. Maddox and Eric J. Zanot, "The Suspension of the National Association of Broadcasters' Code and Its Effects on the Regulation of Advertising," *Journalism Quarterly* 61 (Summer 1984), pp. 125–30, 156.

25. Joe Mandese, "ABC Loosens Rules," *Advertising Age,* September 9, 1991, pp. 2, 8.

26. Avery M. Abernethy and Jan LeBlanc Wicks, "Self-Regulation and Television Advertising: A Replication and Extension," *Journal of Advertising Research* 41, no. 3 (May/June 2001), pp. 31–37; Eric Zanot, "Unseen but Effective Advertising Regulation: The Clearance Process," *Journal of Advertising* 14, no. 4 (1985), p. 48.

27. Joanne Voight and Wendy Melillo, "To See or Not to See?" *Adweek,* March 11, 2002, p. 30.

28. Christoper Heine, "New Facebook Policy Bans Private Gun Sales from Its Platform and Instagram," *Adweek,* January 29, 2016, www.adweek.com/news/technology/facebook-no-longer-allowing-private-gun-sales-its-platform-169312.

29. Irina Slutsky, "Nine Things You Can't Do in Advertising If You Want to Stay on Right Side of the Law," *Advertising Age,* March 6, 2011, http://adage.com/article/news/advertising-regulation-nad-case-rulings-remember/149226/.

30. C. Lee Peeler, "Four Decades Later, Ad Industry's Self-Regulation Remains the Gold Standard," *Advertising Age,* March 13, 2013, http://adage.com/article/guest-columnists/40-years-adland-s-regulation-remains-gold-standard/240245/.

31. Steven W. Colford, "Speed Up the NAD, Industry Unit Told," *Advertising Age,* May 1, 1989, p. 3.

32. Linda Goldstein, "The NAD Sets Precedent for Others in Media, Marketing," *Advertising Age,* March 6, 2011, http://adage.com/article/guest-columnists/nad-sets-precedent-media-marketing/149217/.

33. "Self-Regulation of Advertising in the United States: An Assessment of the National Advertising Division," April 2015, www.olshanlaw.com/resources-publications-Self-Regulation-Advertising-US-NAD.html.

34. Ana Radelat, "Lawyers Recommend Slew of Changes to Advertising Self-Regulation," *Advertising Age,* April 15, 2015, http://adage.com/article/cmo-strategy/lawyers-recommend-slew-ad-regulation/298068/.

35. Virginia State Board of Pharmacy v. Virginia Citizens Consumer Council, 425 U.S. 748, 96 S. Ct. 1817, 48 L. Ed. 2d 346 (1976).

36. Bates v. State Bar of Arizona.

37. Central Hudson Gas & Electric v. Public Service Commission, 447 U.S. 557, 100 S. Ct. 2343, 65 L. Ed. 2d 341 (1980).

38. Liquormart, Inc. v. Rhode Island, 517 U.S. 484 (1996).

39. Erik L. Collins, Lynn Zoch, and Christopher S. McDonald, "When Professional Worlds Collide: Implications of Kasky v. Nike for Corporate Reputation Management," *Public Relations Review* 30, no. 4 (November 2004), pp. 411–18; Anne Gearan, "High Court Passes Up Decision on Nike Case," *San Diego Union-Tribune,* June 27, 2003, p. C1.

40. FTC v. Raladam Co., 258 U.S. 643 (1931).

41. Federal Trade Commission Improvement Act of 1980, Pub. L. No. 96–252.

42. Peter R. Darke and Robin J. Ritchie, "The Defensive Consumer: Advertising Deception, Defensive Processing, and Distrust," *Journal of Marketing Research* 44 (February 2007), 114–27.

43. Ivan L. Preston, *The Great American Blow-Up: Puffery in Advertising and Selling* (Madison: University of Wisconsin Press, 1975), p. 3.

44. Isabella C. M. Cunningham and William H. Cunningham, "Standards for Advertising Regulation," *Journal of Marketing* 41 (October 1977), pp. 91–97; Herbert J. Rotfeld and Kim B. Rotzell, "Is Advertising Puffery Believed?" *Journal of Advertising* 9, no. 3 (1980), pp. 16–20.

45. Herbert J. Rotfeld and Kim B. Rotzell, "Puffery vs. Fact Claims—Really Different?" in *Current Issues and Research in Advertising,* James H. Leigh and Claude R. Martin Jr., eds. (Ann Arbor: University of Michigan, 1981), pp. 85–104.

46. Preston, *The Great American Blow-Up.*

47. Chuck Ross, "Marketers Fend Off Shift in Rules for Ad Puffery," *Advertising Age,* February 19, 1996, p. 41.

48. Louise Kramer, "Jury Finds Papa John's Ads Misled," *Advertising Age,* November 22, 1999, http://adage.com/article/news/jury-finds-papa-john-s-ads-misled/60251/.

49. Apryl Duncan, "Better Pizza? Bigger Lawsuit," *About Advertising,* http://advertising.about.com/od/foodrelatedadnews/a/papajohns.htm.

50. Emily Bryson York, "Domino's Claims Victory with Pizza Makeover Strategy," *Advertising Age,* May 20, 2010, http://advertising.about.com/od/foodrelatedadnews/a/papajohns.htm.

51. Federal Trade Commission, "Policy Statement on Deception," 45 ATRR 689 (October 27, 1983), at p. 690.

52. For an excellent discussion and analysis of these three elements of deception, see Gary T. Ford and John E. Calfee, "Recent Developments in FTC Policy on Deception," *Journal of Marketing* 50, no. 3 (July 1986), pp. 86–87.

53. Ray O. Werner, ed., "Legal Developments in Marketing," *Journal of Marketing* 56 (January 1992), p. 102.

54. Ira Teinowitz, "FTC Strives to Clarify 'Made in USA' Rules," *Advertising Age,* April 29, 1996, p. 12.

55. Kalpana Srinivasan, "FTC Spells Out Tough Standards for 'Made in USA,'" *Marketing News,* January 18, 1999, p. 18.

56. "Champagne Bureau; Ad Campaign Urges Consumers to 'Unmask the Truth' about Champagne & Wine Place Names," *Marketing Weekly News,* December 26, 2009, p. 41.

57. Cohen, "The FTC's Advertising Substantiation Program."

58. *Trade Regulation Reporter,* Par. 20,056 at 22,033, 1970–1973 Transfer Binder, Federal Trade Commission, July 1972.

59. John E. Califee, "FTC's Hidden Weight-Loss Ad Agenda," *Advertising Age,* October 25, 1993, p. 29; Chester S. Galloway, Herbert Jack Rotfeld, and Jeff I. Richards, "Holding Media Responsible for Deceptive Weight-Loss Advertising," *West Virginia Law Review* 107, no. 2 (Winter 2005), pp. 353–84; Herbert Jack Rotfeld, "Desires versus the Reality of Self-Regulation," *The Journal of Consumer Affairs* 27, no. 2 (Winter 2003), pp. 424–27.

60. Alicia Mundy, "FTC Bars Pom Juice's Health Claims," *The Wall Street Journal,* January 16, 2013, http://online.wsj.com/article/SB10001424127887323468604578245740405648024.html.

61. Lawrence Hurley, "U.S. Top Court Rejects POM Wonderful Appeal Over Ads," *Reuters,* May 3, 2016. www.reuters.com/article/us-usa-court-pom-idUSKCN0XT14K.

62. E.J. Schultz, "FTC Charges Volkswagen With Deceptive Advertising," *Advertising Age,* March 29, 2016, http://adage.com/article/cmo-strategy/ftc-charges-volkswagen-deceptive-advertising/303306/

63. For an excellent description of the Campbell Soup corrective advertising case, see Dick Mercer, "Tempest in a Soup Can," *Advertising Age,* October 17, 1994, pp 25, 28–29.

64. William L. Wilkie, Dennis L. McNeill, and Michael B. Mazis, "Marketing's 'Scarlet Letter': The Theory and Practice of Corrective Advertising," *Journal of Marketing* 48 (Spring 1984), pp. 11–31.

65. Warner-Lambert Co. v. Federal Trade Commission, CCH P61, 563A-D.C., August 1977 and CCH P61, 646 CA-D.C., September 1977.

66. Ira Teinowitz, "Doan's Decision Sets Precedent for Corrective Ads," *Advertising Age,* September 4, 2000, http://adage.com/article/news/doan-s-decision-sets-precedent-corrective-ads/57074/.

67. Rich Thomaselli, "What Bayer Campaign Means for Pharma Ads," *Advertising Age,* February 16, 2009, http://adage.com/article/news/bayer-campaign-means-pharma-ads/134624/.

68. "Brill Tells DMA That FTC Is 'Ramping Up Enforcement,'" *Advertising Age,* March 13, 2013, http://adage.com/article/digital/brill-tells-dma-ftc-ramping-enforcement/240330/.

69. Ira Teinowitz, "Beales Makes Regulation Academic as FTC Director," *Advertising Age,* December 10, 2001, p. 66.

70. Laurie Sullivan, "FTC Pushes up Hearings on Environmental Marketing Guides," November 29, 2007, www.mediapost.com/publications/article/71725/?print.

71. Michael Bush, "Blogger Be Warned: FTC May Monitor What You Say," *Advertising Age,* April 13, 2009, http://adage.com/article/news/bloggers-warned-ftc-monitor/135938/.

72. Ira Teinowitz, "FTC to Marketers: Self-Regulate Behavioral Targeting," *Advertising Age,* February 12, 2009, http://adage.com/article/digital/ftc-marketers-regulate-targeting-online-ads/134587/.

73. Ira Teinowitz, "Howard Stern to Abandon FM Radio," *Advertising Age,* October 6, 2004, http://adage.com/article/media/

howard-stern-abandon-fm-radio-move-sirius/41266/; Ira Teinowitz, "Clear Channel Drops Howard Stern," *Advertising Age,* February 26, 2004, http://adage.com/article/media/clear-channel-drops-howard-stern-fcc-indecency-fine/39530/.

74. Ira Teinowitz, "FCC to Probe Super Bowl Halftime Breast Incident," *Advertising Age,* February 2, 2004, http://adage.com/article/media/fcc-probe-super-bowl-halftime-show-wardrobe-malfunction/39341/.

75. Ira Teinowitz and Matthew Creamer, "Fake News Videos Unmasked in FCC Crackdown," *Advertising Age,* April 18, 2005, http://adage.com/article/news/fake-news-videos-unmasked-fcc-crackdown/102925/.

76. Daniel Hertzberg, "Blasting Away at Product Placement," *Bloomberg Businessweek,* October 26, 2010, p. 60.

77. Rich Thomaselli, "Cheerios First in FDA Firing Line. Who's Next?," *Advertising Age,* May 18, 2009, http://adage.com/print?article_id=136704.

78. E. J. Schultz, "Did FDA Cross the Line in Its 2009 Cheerios-Case Finding?" *Advertising Age,* March 6, 2011, http://adage.com/article/news/fda-cross-line-2009-cheerios-case-finding/149236/.

79. Sheryl Stolberg, "Clinton Imposes Wide Crackdown on Tobacco Firms," *Los Angeles Times,* August 24, 1996, pp. A1, A10.

80. Joy Johnson Wilson, Summary of the Attorneys General Master Tobacco Settlement Agreement, National Conference of State Legislators, www.academic.udayton.edu/health/syllabi/tobacco/summary.

81. Rich Thomaselli, "FDA Set to Take Control of Tobacco Regulation," *Advertising Age,* June 11, 2009, http://adage.com/article/news/marketing-curbs-expected-fda-controls-tobacco/137253/.

82. "E-Cigarettes, Vapor Devices to Come under FDA Oversight," *Advertising Age,* May 5, 2016, http://adage.com/article/media/e-cigarettes-vapor-devices-fda-oversight/303899/.

83. Jayne O'Donnell and Laura Ungar, "Feds Announce Much Tougher E-Cigarette, Cigar Rule," *USA Today,* May 5, 2016, www.usatoday.com/story/news/politics/2016/05/05/feds-expected-announce-final-e-cigarette-rule-could-nearly-ban-them/83951786/.

84. Jisu Huh and Rita Langteau, "Presumed Influence of Direct-to-Consumer (DTC) Prescription Drug Advertising on Patients: The Physician's Perspective," *Journal of Advertising* 36, no. 3 (Fall 2007), pp. 151–72; Sejung Marina Choi and Wei-Na Lee, "Understanding the Impact of Direct-to-Consumer (DTC) Pharmaceutical Advertising on Patient–Physician Interaction," *Journal of Advertising* 36, no. 3 (Fall 2007), pp. 137–49.

85. Bruce Buchanan and Doron Goldman, "Us vs. Them: The Minefield of Comparative Ads," *Harvard Business Review,* May/June 1989, pp. 38–50.

86. Maxine Lans Retsky, "Lanham Have It: Law and Comparative Ads," *Marketing News,* November 8, 1999, p. 16.

87. Michael J. Barone, Randall L. Rose, Paul W. Minniard, and Kenneth C. Manning, "Enhancing the Detection of Misleading Comparative Advertising," *Journal of Advertising Research* 39, no. 5 (September/October 1999), pp. 43–50.

88. Steven Colford, "ABA Panel Backs FTC over States," *Advertising Age,* April 10, 1994, p. 1.

89. "Airborne to Pay $23.3 Million for False Advertising," *Natural Standard Blog,* March 21, 2008, http://blog.naturalstandard.com/natural-standard-blog/2008/03/airborne.

90. S. J. Diamond, "New Director Putting Vigor Back into FTC," *Los Angeles Times,* March 29, 1991, pp. D1, D4.

91. Federal Trade Commission, "Trade Regulation Rule: Games of Chance in the Food Retailing and Gasoline Industries," 16 CFR, Part 419 (1982).

92. Richard Sale, "Sweeping the Courts," *Promo,* May 1998, pp. 42–45, 148–52; Ira Teinowitz and Carol Krol, "Multiple States Scrutinize Sweepstakes Mailings," *Advertising Age,* February 9, 1998, p. 41; Mark Pawlosky, "States Rein in Sweepstakes, Game Operators," *The Wall Street Journal,* July 3, 1995, pp. B1, B3.

93. Steven Winters and Joann Kohl, "Keep Your Online Sweepstakes and Contests on the Right Side of the Law," *Advertising Age,* March 6, 2011, http://adage.com/article/guest-columnists/online-sweepstakes-legal/149206/.

94. Ibid.

95. Martin Beck, "Facebook Is Tearing Down the Like Gate: Are You Ready?" *Marketing Land,* November 4, 2014, http://marketingland.com/facebook-tearing-like-gate-ready-106611.

96. *Children Advertising Review Unit Self Regulatory Guidelines for Children's Advertising,* Council of Better Business Bureaus, 2003, www.caru.org/guidelines/index.

97. Federal Trade Commission, "Guides for Advertising Allowances and Other Merchandising Payments and Services," 16 CFR, Part 240 (1983).

98. Federal Trade Commission, "Trade Regulation Rule: Use of Negative Option Plans by Sellers in Commerce," 16 CFR, Part 42 (1982).

99. For a more thorough discussion of legal aspects of sales promotion and mail-order practices, see Dean K. Fueroghne, *Law & Advertising* (Chicago: Copy Workshop, 1995).

100. Mary Lu Carnevale, "FTC Adopts Rules to Curb Telemarketing," *The Wall Street Journal,* September 18, 1992, pp. B1, B10.

101. Ira Teinowitz, "Congress Approves National 'Do Not Call,'" *Advertising Age,* February 13, 2003, http://adage.com/article/news/congress-approves-national-call/36837/.

102. Maggie Shader, "National Do-Not-Call List Hits 217 Million Phone Numbers, FTC Wants to Stop Illegal Robocalls," *Consumer Reports,* October 18, 2012, www.consumerreports.org/cro/news/2012/10/national-do-not-call-list-hits-217-million-phone-numbers-ftc-wants-to-stop-illegal-robocalls/index.htm.

103. Ira Teinowitz, "'Do Not Call' Law Upheld as Constitutional," *Advertising Age,* February 17, 2004, http://adage.com/article/news/call-law-upheld-constitutional/39453/.

104. Ira Teinowitz, "'Do Not Call' Does Not Hurt Direct Marketers," *Advertising Age,* April 11, 2005, pp. 3, 95.

105. Herbert Jack Rotfeld, "Do-Not-Call as the US Government's Improvement to Telemarketing Efficiency," *Journal of Consumer Marketing* 21, no. 4 (2004), pp. 242–44.

106. Jennifer Levitz and Kelly Greene, "Marketers Use Trickery to Evade No-Call Lists," *The Wall Street Journal,* October 26, 2007, p. A1, A8.

107. Natasha Shabani, "Are You Using Sweepstakes to Skirt the Do-Not-Call List?," *Advertising*

Age, April 12, 2010, http://adage.com/article/guest-columnists/sweepstakes-skirt-call-list/143190/.

108. Jenny Rough, "Saving Trees and Your Sanity by Managing Junk Mail," *The Examiner,* February 14, 2010, p. 31; Steven Swanson, "Up to Here in Catalogs?," There Is a Solution Online," *Tribune Business News,* November 4, 2007.

109. Ira Teinowitz and Jennifer Gilbert, "FTC Chairman: Stop Undisclosed Profiling on Net," *Advertising Age,* November 8, 1999, p. 2.

110. Andrea Petersen, "DoubleClick Reverses Course after Privacy Outcry," *The Wall Street Journal,* March 3, 2000, pp. B1, B6; Jennifer Gilbert and Ira Teinowitz, "Privacy Debate Continues to Rage," *Advertising Age,* February 7, 2000, pp. 44, 46.

111. "NAI Launches Privacy-Awareness Web Site," *Advertising Age,* May 28, 2001, http://adage.com/article/news/nai-launches-privacy-awareness-website/11226/; "Online Advertisers Launch Two Consumer Privacy Tools," *Network Advertising Initiative,* May 23, 2001, www.networkadvertising.org/aboutnai.

112. Cotton Delo, "FTC Privacy Report Urges Congress to Pass Data-Security Legislation," *Advertising Age,* March 26, 2012, http://adage.com/article/digital/ftc-urges-congress-pass-data-security-legislation/233719/; Larry Dobrow, "Privacy Issues Loom for Marketers," *Advertising Age,* March 13, 2006, http://adage.com/article/100-leading-media-companies/privacy-issues-loom-companies-marketing-kids-online/107066/.

113. Ira Teinowitz, "Why Ignoring New Voluntary FTC Privacy Guidelines Could Be Perilous," *Advertising Age,* December 28, 2007, http://adage.com/article/digital/ignoring-voluntary-ftc-privacy-guidelines-perilous/122814/; Betsy Spethmann,"Private Eyes," *Promo,* January 2002, pp. 37–43; "Protecting Consumers' Privacy: 2002 and Beyond," Remarks of FTC chair Timothy J. Muris at the Privacy 2001 Conference, Cleveland, Ohio, October 4, 2001, www.ftc.gov/speeches/muris/privisp1002.

114. Kate Kaye, "Do-Not-Track Show Will Go on at W3C—for Now Group Names Two New Co-Chairs," *Advertising Age,* September 20, 2013, http://adage.com/article/privacy-and-regulation/track-show-w3c/244285/;

Ira Teinowitz, "Consumer Groups Push Obama for 'Do Not Track' List," *Advertising Age,* December 16, 2008, http://adage.com/article/news/consumer-groups-push-obama-track-list/133329/.

115. Dawn Chmielewski, "How 'Do Not Track' Ended Up Going Nowhere," *recode,* January 4, 2016, http://www.recode.net/2016/1/4/11588418/how-do-not-track-ended-up-going-nowhere; Fred B. Campbell, "The Slow Death of 'Do Not Track,'" *The New York Times,* December 26, 2014, www.nytimes.com/2014/12/27/opinion/the-slow-death-of-do-not-track.html.

116. Bryon Acohido, "FTC Tells Twitter to Protect the Private Data of Its Users," *USA Today,* June 25, 2010, p. 3B.

117. Vindu Goel, "Facebook to Update Privacy Policy, but Adjusting Settings Is No Easier," *The New York Times: Bits,* August 29, 2013, http://bits.blogs.nytimes.com/2013/08/29/facebook-to-update-privacy-policy-but-adjusting-settings-is-no-easier/; Bryon Acohido, "FTC Tells Twitter to Protect the Private Data of Its Users," *USA Today,* June 25, 2010, p. 3B; Mark Zuckerberg, "Making Control Simple," *The Facebook Blog,* May 26, 2010, http://blog.facebook.com/blog.php?post=391922327130.

118. Stacey Higginbotham, "The FTC's Wyndham Victory Is Good for Privacy but Confusing for Business," *Fortune,* August 28, 2015, http://fortune.com/2015/08/28/ftc-wyndham-privacy-courts/.

119. James Heckman, "COPPA to Bring No Surprises, Hefty Violation Fines in April," *Marketing News,* January 31, 2000, p. 6.

120. Ira Teinowitz, "FTC Proposal on Kids' Privacy Raises Ire of Watchdog Groups," *Advertising Age,* March 14, 2005, http://adage.com/article/digital/ftc-proposal-kids-privacy-raises-ire-watchdog-groups/102494/.

121. Kate Kaye, "In Wake of Privacy Laws, Kids' Site See Ad Revenue Plummet," *Advertising Age,* August 23, 2013, http://adage.com/article/privacy-and-regulation/kids-sites-freaking-privacy-laws/243795/.

122. Kate Kaye, "FTC Aims to Bring Child Privacy Law into 21st Century," *Advertising Age,* December 19, 2012, http://adage.com/article/digital/ftc-aims-bring-child-privacy-law-21st-century/238842/.

123. Abbey Klassen and Michael Learmonth, "What You Need to Know about the New FTC Endorsement Rules and Why," *Advertising Age,* October 12, 2009, http://adage.com/article/digital/ftc-endorsement-rules/139595/.

124. "FTC Issues Enforcement Policy Statement Addressing 'Native' Advertising and Deceptively Formatted Advertisements," Federal Trade Commission, December 22, 2015, https://www.ftc.gov/public-statements/2015/12/commission-enforcement-policy-statement-deceptively-formatted.

125. Jeremy Barr, "FTC Spells Out Its Guidelines for Native Ads," *Advertising Age,* December 22, 2015, http://adage.com/article/media/federal-trade-commission-releases-native-ad-guidelines/301921/.

126. Ira Teinowitz, "U.S. House Passes Anti-Spam Measure in Dawn Session," *Advertising Age,* November 23, 2003, http://adage.com/article/digital/u-s-house-passes-anti-spam-measure-dawn-session/38896/; Lisa Takeuchi Cullen, "Some More Spam, Please," *Time,* November 11, 2002, pp. 58–62.

127. Tom Zeller Jr., "Federal Law Hasn't Curbed Junk E-mail," *San Diego Union-Tribune,* February, 1, 2005, pp. C1, C5.

128. Jesse Brody, "Terms and Conditions," *Marketing News,* November 2014, pp. 34–41.

Chapter 21

1. Robert L. Heilbroner, "Demand for the Supply Side," *New York Review of Books* 38 (June 11, 1981), p. 40.

2. David Helm, "Advertising's Overdue Revolution," speech given to the Adweek Creative Conference, October 1, 1999.

3. Claire Atkinson, "FTC and FCC Nearing Product-Placement Decisions," *Advertising Age,* October 29, 2004, http://adage.com/article/news/ftc-fcc-nearing-product-placement-decisions/41433/; Daniel Eisenberg, "Its an Ad, Ad, Ad World," *Time,* September 2, 2002, pp. 38–41.

4. Eric N. Berkowitz, Roger A. Kerin, Steven W. Hartley, and William Rudelius, *Marketing,* 7th ed. (Burr Ridge, IL: Irwin/McGraw-Hill, 2003), p. 21.

5. "College Drinking," National Institute on Alcohol Abuse and Alcoholism, June 2016.

6. Editorial Board, "Dartmouth College Tackles Campus Drinking with a Ban on Hard Alcohol," January 31, 2015, www.washingtonpost.com; Vivian B. Faden and Marcy L. Baskin, "Evaluation of College Alcohol Policies," 2014, www.collegedrinkingprevention.gov.

7. N. Siegfried, D. C. Pienaar, J. E. Ataguba, J. Volmink, T. Kredo, M. Jere, and C. D. Parry, "Restricting or Banning Alcohol Advertising to Reduce Alcohol Consumption in Adults and Adolescents," November 4, 2014, www.ncbi.nim.nih.gov.

8. Ira Teinowitz, "Underage-Drinking Report Calls for Voluntary Alcohol Cutbacks," *Advertising Age,* March 6, 2007, http://adage.com/article/news/underage-drinking-report-calls-voluntary-alcohol-ad-cutbacks/115414/.

9. E. J. Schultz, "Bud Light Apologizes for Message on Its Bottle That Critics Linked to Rape Culture," April 28, 2015, www.adage.com.

10. Samantha Braverman, "Young Adults More Trusting of Advertising," November 5, 2010, www.harrisinteractive.com.

11. Gita Venkataramini Johar, "Consumer Involvement and Deception from Implied Advertising Claims," *Journal of Marketing Research* 32 (August 1995), pp. 267–79; J. Edward Russo, Barbara L. Metcalf, and Debra Stephens, "Identifying Misleading Advertising," *Journal of Consumer Research* 8 (September 1981), pp. 119–31.

12. Zach Bowman, "Hyundai, Kia Admit Exageratged Mileage Claims, Will Compensate Owners," November 2, 2012, www.autoblog.com.

13. Danielle Ivory, "Ford Lowers Gas Mileage on 6 Models, All 2013–14s," www.nytimes.com, June 12, 2014.

14. Shelby D. Hunt, "Informational vs. Persuasive Advertising: An Appraisal," *Journal of Advertising,* Summer 1976, pp. 5–8.

15. "The Take on You," *Adweek,* September 24, 2007, pp. 14–15; Banwari Mittal, "Public Assessment of TV Advertising: Faint Praise and Harsh Criticism," *Journal of Advertising Research* 34, no. 1 (January/February 1994), pp. 35–53; J. C. Andrews, "The Dimensionality of Beliefs toward Advertising in General," *Journal of Advertising* 18, no. 1 (1989), pp. 26–35.

16. Helen Cooper, "CDC Advocates Use of Condoms in Blunt AIDS-Prevention Spots," *The Wall Street Journal,* January 5, 1994, p. B1.

17. Jack Neff, "Trojan Ads Ready for Prime Time: NBC," *Advertising Age,* May 16, 2005, p. 3.

18. Claude Brodesser-Akner, "Sex on TV Is OK as Long as It's Not Safe," *Advertising Age,* September 17, 2007, http://adage.com/article/news/sex-tv-long-safe/120489/.

19. Stephen A. Greyser, "Irritation in Advertising," *Journal of Advertising Research* 13 (February 1973), pp. 3–10.

20. Joan Voight and Wendy Melillo, "Rough Cut," *Adweek,* March 11, 2002, pp. 27–29; Joanne Lipman, "Censored Scenes: Why You Rarely See Some Things in Television Ads," *The Wall Street Journal,* August 17, 1987, p. 17.

21. Michael T. Ewing, "The Good News about Television: Attitudes Aren't Getting Worse," *Journal of Advertising Research,* March 2013, p. 89.

22. Visible Measures, "The Most Successful Sexy Ads," https://adsoftheworld.com/blog/the_most_successful_sexy_ads.

23. James B. Arndorfer, "Skyy Hit the Limit with Racy Ad: Critics," *Advertising Age,* February 7, 2005, p. 6.

24. Tim Nudd, "Does Sex Really Sell?," *Adweek,* October 17, 2005, pp. 14–17.

25. Leanne Potts, "Retailers, Ads Bare Flesh for Bottom Line," *Albuquerque Journal,* December 20, 2002, p. D1.

26. Rebecca Quick, "Is Ever-So-Hip Abercrombie & Fitch Losing Its Edge with Teens?" *The Wall Street Journal,* February 22, 2000, pp. B1, B4.

27. "Young People Online," Childhood Monitor Report 2016.

28. Elizabeth Anderson, "Teenagers Spend 27 Hours a Week Online: How Internet Use Has ballooned in the Last Decade," www.telegraph.co.uk, April 11, 2016.

29. The Marketing Store, "The New Definition of Childhood," March 2012, www.themarketingstore.com.

30. Marketing to Children Overview, 2016, www.commercialfreechildhood.org.

31. Ibid.

32. Mark J. Miller, "Camel Cigarettes under Fire for Targeting Kids—Again," May 31, 2013, www.brandchannel.com.

33. Saba Hamedy, "Ad Overload?," *Los Angeles Times,* April 7, 2015, pp. C1, C3.

34. Merrie Brucks, Gary M. Armstrong, and Marvin E. Goldberg, "Children's Use of Cognitive Defenses against Television Advertising: A Cognitive Response Approach," *Journal of Consumer Research* 14, no. 4 (March 1988), pp. 471–82.

35. Tamara F. Mangleburg and Terry Bristol, "Socialization and Adolescents' Skepticism toward Advertising," *Journal of Advertising* 27, no. 3 (Fall 1998), pp. 11–21.

36. Ronald Alsop, "Watchdogs Zealously Censor Advertising Targeted to Kids," *The Wall Street Journal,* September 5, 1985, p. 35.

37. *Report of the APA Task Force on Advertising and Children,* February 20, 2004, www.apa.org.

38. Tiffany Meyers, "Marketing to Kids Comes under Fresh Attack," *Advertising Age,* February 21, 2005, pp. S2, S8.

39. Robert Booth, "Junk Foods Avoid Ad Ban by Targeting Children Online," April 28, 2013, www.guardian.co.uk.

40. Betsy McKay, "Soda Marketers Will Cut Back Sales to Schools," *The Wall Street Journal,* August 17, 2005, pp. B1, B3.

41. Ronald Berman, *Advertising and Social Change* (Beverly Hills, CA: Sage, 1981), p. 13.

42. Quoted in Voight, "The Consumer Rebellion."

43. Glennisha Morgan, "Amazon Kindle Backs Gay Marriage with New Commercial," February 21, 2013, www.huffingtonpost.com.

44. Morris B. Holbrook, "Mirror Mirror on the Wall, What's Unfair in the Reflections on Advertising," *Journal of Marketing* 5 (July 1987), pp. 95–103; Theodore Levitt, "The Morality of Advertising," *Harvard Business Review,* July/August 1970, pp. 84–92.

45. Stephen Fox, *The Mirror Makers: A History of American Advertising and Its Creators* (New York: Morrow, 1984), p. 330.

46. Hunt, "Informational vs. Persuasive Advertising."

47. Daniel J. Brett and Joanne Cantor, "The Portrayal of Men and Women in U.S. Television Commercials: A Recent Content Analysis and Trends of 15 Years," *Sex Roles* 18, no. 9/10 (1998), pp. 595–608; John B. Ford and Michael La Tour, "Contemporary Perspectives of Female Role Portrayals in Advertising," *Journal of Current Issues and Research in Advertising* 28, no. 1 (1996), pp. 81–93.

48. Beverly A. Browne, "Gender Stereotypes in Advertising on Children's Television in the 1990s: A Cross-National Analysis," *Journal of Advertising* 27 no. 1 (Spring 1998), pp. 83–96.

49. Richard H. Kolbe, "Gender Roles in Children's Advertising: A Longitudinal Content Analysis," in *Current Issues and Research in Advertising,* James H. Leigh and Claude R. Martin Jr., eds. (Ann Arbor: University of Michigan, 1990), pp. 197–206.

50. Debra Merskin, "Boys Will Be Boys: A Content Analysis of Gender and Race in Children's Advertisements on the Turner Cartoon Network," *Journal of Current Issues and Research in Advertising* 24, no. 1 (Spring 2002), pp. 51–60.

51. Cate Terwilliger, "'Love Your Body Day' Auraria Event Takes Aim at 'Offensive' Images, Ads," *Denver Post,* September 23, 1999, p. E3.

52. Steven M. Kates and Glenda Shaw-Garlock, "The Ever Entangling Web: A Study of Ideologies and Discourses in Advertising to Women," *Journal of Advertising* 28, no. 2 (Summer 1999), pp. 33–49.

53. Suzanne Vranica, "Stereotypes of Women Persist in Ads," *The Wall Street Journal,* October 17, 2003, p. B4.

54. Thomas H. Stevenson, "How Are Blacks Portrayed in Business Ads?" *Industrial Marketing Management* 20 (1991), pp. 193–99; Helen Czepic and J. Steven Kelly, "Analyzing Hispanic Roles in Advertising," in *Current Issues and Research in Advertising,* James H. Leigh and Claude R. Martin Jr., eds. (Ann Arbor: University of Michigan, 1983), pp. 219–40; R. F. Busch, Allan S. Resnik, and Bruce L. Stern, "A Content Analysis of the Portrayal of Black Models in Magazine Advertising," in *American Marketing Association Proceedings: Marketing in the 1980s,* Richard P. Bagozzi, ed. (Chicago: American Marketing Association, 1980); R. F. Busch, Allan S. Resnik, and Bruce L. Stern, "There Are More Blacks in TV Commercials," *Journal of Advertising Research* 17 (1977), pp. 21–25.

55. Malgorzata Kolling (Skorek), "Portrayal of Asian Americans in U.S. Magazines," in *One World Periphery Reads the Other: Knowing the "Oriental" in the Americas and the Iberian Peninsula,* I. Lopez-Calvo, ed. (Newcastle, England: Cambridge Scholars Publishing, 2010), pp. 330–45.

56. Corliss L. Green "Ethnic Evaluations of Advertising: An Examination of the Interaction Effects of Strength of Ethnic Identification, Media Placement, and Degree of Racial Composition," *Developments in Marketing Science: Proceedings of the Academy of Marketing Science,* 1998, pp. 392–93.

57. Bruce Horovitz, "Mental Health Groups Slam Volkswagen Ad," *USA Today,* February 15, 2007, p. B1.

58. Brooke Capps, "Suicide Prevention Group Tells GM to Yank Robot Spot," *Advertising Age,* February 7, 2007, http://adage.com/article/news/suicide-prevention-group-tells-gm-yank-robot-spot/114866/.

59. Andrew Hampp, "An Ad in Which Boy Gets Girl . . . or Boy," *Advertising Age,* August 6, 2007, http://adage.com/article/news/ad-boy-girl-boy/119705/.

60. Jef I. Richards and John H. Murphy, II, "Economic Censorship and Free Speech: The Circle of Communication between Advertisers, Media and Consumers," *Journal of Current Issues and Research in Advertising* 18, no. 1 (Spring 1996), pp. 21–33.

61. Lawrence C. Soley and Robert L. Craig, "Advertising Pressure on Newspapers: A Survey," *Journal of Advertising,* December 1992, pp. 1–10.

62. Mark Simon, "Mercury News Ad Dispute Cooling Off: Advertisers Return While Reporters Stew," *San Francisco Business Chronicle,* July 15, 1994, p. B1.

63. Soontae An and Lori Bergen, "Advertiser Pressure on Daily Newspapers," *Journal of Advertising* 36, no. 2 (Summer 2007), pp 111–21.

64. David Shaw, "An Uneasy Alliance of News and Ads," *Los Angeles Times,* March 29, 1998, pp. A1, A28.

65. Steven T. Goldberg, "Do the Ads Tempt the Editors?" *Kiplingers Personal Finance,* May 1996, pp. 45–49.

66. Nat Ives, "GM Ends 'L.A.Times' Boycott, Resumes Advertising," *Advertising Age,* August 2, 2005, http://adage.com/article/media/gm-ends-l-a-times-boycott-resumes-advertising/46441/.

67. "Bottled Water," IBWA Member Brands & Water Quality Information, www.bottledwater.org, April 11, 2016.

68. Robert D. Buzzell, Bradley T. Gale, and Ralph G. M. Sultan, "Market Share—a Key to Profitability," *Harvard Business Review,* January/February 1975, pp. 97–106.

69. Clare O'Connor, "How Spanx Became a Billion-Dollar Business without Advertising," *Forbes,* March 12, 2012, www.forbes.com.

70. Paul W. Farris and Mark S. Albion, "The Impact of Advertising on the Price of Consumer Products," *Journal of Marketing* 44, no. 3 (Summer 1980), pp. 17–35.

71. Buron, "Reining in Drug Advertising."

72. Farris and Albion, "The Impact of Advertising on the Price of Consumer Products."

73. Ibid., p. 30.

74. Ibid.

75. Avery M. Abernethy and George R. Franke, "The Information Content of Advertising: A Meta-Analysis," *Journal of Advertising* 25, no. 2 (Summer 1996), pp. 1–17.

NAME AND COMPANY INDEX

In this index *f* indicates figure and *n* indicates note.

A

Aaker, David, 58, 58n, 59, 59n, 61, 62n, 234n, 235n, 242, 242n, 260n, 296n, 619n, 652n
Aaker, Jennifer, 111
AARP, The Magazine, 54, 55, 422, 428
AARP Bulletin, 428
ABC, 378, 387, 393, 733, 734, 739
Abercrombie & Fitch, 742, 744–745
Abernethy, Avery, 288–289, 288n, 410n, 699n, 761, 761n
Abramovich, Giselle, 25
Abrams, Bill, 118n
Acohido, Bryon, 727n
Absolut vodka, 275
Academy Awards, 188
Accenture, 69, 197
AC/DC, 411
Ace Hardware, 57
Ace Metrix, 190, 283, 302
Acura, 485
Acxiom, 514
Adamason, Brent, 161n
Ad Age, 88, 611
Adams, Scott, 159
Adamson, Allen, 753
Ad Council, 210, 211, 306
Adidas, 111, 183, 194, 459, 470
Adlink Digital Interconnect, 396
Adobe, 278, 479
Advertising Age, 13, 49, 69, 88, 101, 138, 159, 193, 252, 268, 277, 279, 296, 316, 321, 333, 334, 439, 582, 589, 614, 617, 651
Advertising Digital Identification (Ad-Id), 526
Advertising Education Foundation (AEF), 589
Advertising Research Foundation (ARF), 100, 138, 169, 170, 171, 231, 281, 282, 283, 345, 568, 611–612, 643
Advertising Self-Regulatory Council (ASRC), 694–695, 697, 700, 727

Advincula, Dorothy, 22n, 169n, 231
Advocare, 65
Adweek, 88, 101, 209, 277, 333, 339, 370, 733, 737
AdWords, 11
A&E, 397
Aegis Group, 252
Afar Collection, 507
Afar magazine, 507
Affectiva, 615
Aflac, 281, 316, 335, 383
AGB Nielsen Media Research, 677
Agrawal, Maduh, 666n
Agres, Stuart J., 305n
Ahluwalia, Rohini, 310n, 505n
Airbnb, 48, 674
Airborne, 721
Air Products & Chemicals, 495
Akaka, Melissa, 666n
AKQA agency, 103, 104
Alberstadt, Ben, 491
Alberta Gaming and Liquor Commission, 736
Albion, Mark. S., 760
Alcon, 313
Alden, Dana A. , 666n, 680, 680n
Alexander, Ralph S., 17n
Alibaba, 682
Allan, David, 324n
Allen, Bruce H., 694n
Alley, Kirstie, 745
Alleyne, Richard, 123
Alliance for Audited Media (AAM), 430–431, 443
Allianz, 222
Allport, Gordon W., 125n
Allsop, Dee T., 150n
Allstate Insurance, 49, 127, 283, 286, 383, 468, 518
Allure magazine, 120, 421, 436
Ally Bank, 129
Al-Makaty, Safran S., 665n
Almond Board of California, 310
Alsop, Ronald, 174n, 271n, 745n
Alt, Susanne, 201
Alwitt, Linda F., 387n
Amazing Discoveries, 491
Amazon.com, 15, 18, 377, 385, 386, 388, 398, 483, 490, 501, 514, 515, 517, 528, 533, 682, 689, 728, 746
Amazon Prime, 11

Ambler, Tim, 174n, 177–178, 177n
AMC (cable network), 69, 389, 397
American Advertising Federation (AAF), 18, 19, 279, 694, 697–698, 738, 739, 762
American Airlines, 74, 555, 561, 562, 600
American Apparel, 742, 744–745
American Association of Advertising Agencies (4As), 9, 96, 100, 121, 279, 327, 345, 526, 694, 749
American Ballet Theater, 184
American Bar Association (ABA), 693, 701, 721
American Cancer Society, 62
American Council on Dental Therapeutics, 313
American Dental Association (ADA), 597
American Eagle, 744
American Eurocopter, 136, 340
American Express Co., 18, 81, 186, 199, 200, 398, 483, 518, 562, 666
American Family Association, 755
American Football League, 489
American Heart Association, 603–604
American Honda Motor Co., 26
American Indian College Fund, 322
American Legacy Foundation (ALF), 269, 717
American Life Project, 351
American Marketing Association (AMA), 7
American Medical Association (AMA), 589, 693, 717, 719
American Psychological Association (APA), 745, 747
American Public Transportation Association (APTA), 464
American Red Cross, 7
American Society of Magazine Editors, 433
American Stroke Association, 603–604
American Teleservices Association, 724
America's Auction Network, 492

America's Next Top Model, 388
Ameritrade, 130, 356
Amnesty International, 475
Amos, Clinton, 188n
Amtrak, 60
Amway, 19, 493
An, Soontae, 755, 755n
Anand-Keller, Punam, 211
Anchor, Shawn, 43
Anderson, Elizabeth, 742n
Anderson, Pamela, 434
Anderson Direct Marketing, 101
Andrews, J. C., 665n, 738n
Android, 151
Angels in Waiting, 4
Anger Management, 199
Angie's List, 119
Angwin, Julia, 449n
Anheuser-Busch InBev, 18, 98, 197, 198, 210, 214, 215, 268–270, 283, 292, 454, 470, 473, 505, 597, 602, 753
Anholt, Simon, 147
Anniston, Jennifer, 200
Ann Taylor, 503
Anthropologie, 420
Any Given Sunday (movie), 183
AOL, 24
Apple Inc., 12, 15, 24–25, 47, 48, 59, 115, 128*f,* 138, 199, 209, 210, 267, 287, 290, 296, 327, 333, 377, 386, 388, 398, 410, 434, 453, 456, 471, 473, 491, 492, 501, 503, 508, 542, 582, 583, 602, 605, 606, 653, 668
Aquafina, 301
Arbitron Inc., 410, 412, 413
Arc, 103
Archer, John F., 693n
Architectural Digest, 366, 426
Architectural Forum, 421
Armani, 194, 740
Arm & Hammer, 60, 547
Armour hot dogs, 326
Armstrong, Gary M., 743n
Armstrong, Lance, 194, 197, 593
Armstrong Partnership, 572
Arndorfer, James B., 741n
Arndt, Johan, 244, 244n, 260n
Arnould, Eric J., 282n
Arrow, 388
Arrowhead Mountain Spring Water, 208, 301, 579

McArthur, Kate, 559n
McBride, Sarah, 469n
McCain, John, 752
McCain, Swift, 752
McCann advertising, 80f
McCann Erickson, 97, 118
McCarthy, Jenny, 410
McCarthy, Michael, 381
McCaughan, Dave, 198n
McClellan, Steve, 217n, 473n, 644n
McColl, Rod, 177n
McConaughey, Matthew, 87, 188
McCracken, Grant, 198–199, 198n
McDermott, John, 499, 500
McDonald, Christopher S., 702n
McDonald's, 15, 47, 61, 65, 81, 97, 138, 148, 194, 195, 267, 268, 290, 291, 293, 306, 321, 339, 456, 458, 460, 524, 555, 575, 579, 601, 653, 681, 743, 746, 754
McFarland, John, 48
McGrath, John M., 647, 647n
McGraw-Hill Corp., 781–782
McGuire, William J., 163, 163n, 185n, 187n
MCI, 603
McIlroy, Rory, 183
McKay, Betsy, 302, 747n
McKee, Steve, 773
McKinsey, 69, 529
McKinsey & Company Global Digital Marketing Strategy practice group, 169–170
McLaughlin, David, 412n
McLuhan, Marshall, 193n, 216, 216n, 269, 434
McMahan, Harry W., 168, 168n
McMorris, Frances A., 292n
McNeill, Dennis L., 713n
McNiven, M. A., 255n
McPheters, Rebecca, 449n
McQueen, Josh, 318n
McQuivey, James, 773
Mean Girls, 199
MEC Sensor, 459
Media Analysis Plus, 363
Media Dynamics, Inc., 363–364
Media Harris Poll, 737
Media Markt, 371
Media Metrix, 526
Media Plan of the Year Award, 370
Media Radar, 507
Medicine Abuse Project, 757
Meirick, Patrick, 210n
Mela, Carl F., 540, 540n, 543n, 544, 544n, 574n

Melia Hotels International, 339
Melillo, Wendy, 106n, 700n, 740n, 99n
Men's Health, 436
Men's Journal, 436
Meow Mix, 327
Mercedes-Benz, 46, 54, 59, 159, 324, 441, 453, 514
Mercer, Dick, 712n
Meredith Corp., 417–418
Merkle Digital Bowl, 266, 514
Merriam-Webster dictionary, 509
Merskin, Debra, 750n
Mesco, Manuela, 657n
Messi, Lionel, 183, 193
MetaVision, 611
Metcalf, Barbara L., 738n
MetLife Insurance, 603
MetroCards, 476
Metropolitan magazine, 435
Meyer, Edward, 668n
Meyers, Tiffany, 747
Miami Dolphins (NFL), 183
Michael Kors, 515
Michelin Tires, 47, 62, 126
Michell, Paul, 97n
Michelson, Phil, 193, 441
Mickle, Tripp, 270n
Microsoft, 15, 19, 97, 163, 164, 191, 209, 210, 268, 476, 491, 506, 605, 689–690
Middle, The, 367
Milk Processor Education Program, 186
Miller, Cyndee, 271n
Miller, James, 705, 706
Miller, Mark, 602
Miller, Mark J., 243, 602, 743n
Miller Brewing Co., 99, 210, 754
MillerCoors, 51, 270, 282, 292, 547, 753
Mills, J., 192n
Millward Brown, 193, 283, 418, 475, 615, 618, 628, 636, 637, 646, 670
Mindset Media, 351
Minniard, Paul W., 126n, 720n
Minnium, Peter, 330, Peter, 617n
Missing, 474
Mitchell, Amy, 448n
Mitchell, Andrew A., 175n, 208n
Mitra Dasgupta, Pritha, 664n
Mitsubishi, 738
Mittal, Banwari, 387n, 738n
Mixi social network, 683
Mlodinow, Leonard, 123
M&M's candy, 286, 468

Moat, 630
Modern Family, 55, 391, 392, 471, 473
Modern Healthcare, 421
Moeller, Joe, 242
Mohan, Geoffrey, 351
Mohr, Jakki J., 257, 258n, 260, 260n
Mole, Jay, 652
Mondelēz International, 172, 512
Monllos, Kristina, 150n, 734
Monroe, K. B., 194n
Monroe, Marilyn, 434
Monster, 446
Montague, Travis, 112
Montana Farmer Stockman, 421
Montana, Joe, 710
Montana Meth Project (MMP), 206, 213, 214
Montblanc, 9
Montgomery Ward catalog, 479
Moore, David J., 175n
Moore, Jeri, 64n
Moore, Timothy, 123
Mooth, Rob, 150n, 186n
MoPub, 507
Morales, Andrea C., 214, 214n
Morello, Marianna, 492n
Morgan, Fred W., 691n
Morgan, Glennisha, 748n
Moriarty, Sandra E., 10n, 279, 279n, 303n, 318, 318n
Morrill, John, 781
Morris the Cat, 168, 316
Morrison, Denise, 173
Morrison, Maureen, 13, 84n, 97n, 149n, 195n, 270n, 321, 325n
Morrissey, Brian, 504n
Moses, Lucia, 437n
Moss, Kate, 195, 434
Mota, Bethany, 517
Motion Picture Association of America, 693
Motor Trend, 592
Motorola, 495, 597
Mountain Dew, 512, 562, 563
Mountain High yogurt, 60
Moveable Ink, 488
Movie Channel, 394, 472
Movies Unlimited, 339
Mowen, John C., 194n
Moxie, 53
MPA, 49
Mr. Clean, 168
Mr. Peanut, 315
Mr. Whipple, 316
Ms. magazine, 751
MSN, 24
MSW-ARS Research, 628, 629
MTV, 11, 62, 159, 397, 398–399, 472, 693, 745, 754

MTV Music Awards, 389
MTV News, 399
MTV Unplugged, 399
Mueller, Barbara, 660n, 661n
Mulder, Susan, 170n
Mulhern, Frank J., 177n
Mullman, Jeremy, 197, 269n, 292n
Mundy, Alicia, 708n
Muntinga, Daniel, 509–510, 509n
Murchison, C. M., 125n
Muris, Timothy J., 727n
Murphy, John H., II, 754n
Murphy, Ian P., 693n
Mustafa, Isaiah, 269
Muzak, 476
Myers Report, 363
Myers, Jack, 363n
Myers, John, 58, 61, 363
Myers, John G., 58n, 59n, 234n, 235n, 296n, 619n
Myers, William E., 575n
MySpace, 24, 526

N

Nadal, Rafael, 193
Nakra, Prema, 103n
Nam-Hyun Um, 210n
Nardone, John, 646, 646n
NASCAR, 283, 351, 410, 603, 604
Nasr, Amir, 209n
National Advertising Division of the Council of Better Business Bureaus, 691, 694, 700, 701
National Advertising Review Board (NARB), 691, 694, 696
National Advertising Review Council (NARC), 694, 695
National Aeronautics and Space Administration (NASA), 558
National Association of Advertisers, 473
National Association of Attorneys General (NAAG), 721
National Association of Broadcasters (NAB), 693, 698
National Basketball Association (NBA), 194, 381
National Enquirer, 366
National Football League (NFL), 13, 183, 184, 381, 383, 387, 488–489, 514, 537, 600
National Geographic Channel, 397, 600
National Geographic magazine, 72, 677

SUBJECT INDEX

In this index *f* indicates figure.

A

Ability, 175
Absolute cost, 367
Absolute Zero service, 266
A/B testing, 282, 625–626
Abuse, sales promotion, 574–576
Acceleration tool, 535
Acceptance
    of branded entertainment, 473
    of newspaper ads, 441
Accountability, 540
Accountability principle, of self-regulation, 697*f*
Account executives, 83–84
Account planners, 85
Account planning, 278
Account services, 83–85
Account-specific marketing, 540–541
Accuracy
    direct marketing, 495
    publicity and, 598
Action, DAGMAR and, 233
Active shopping, 169
Actual state, consumer, 114
Ad-blocking software, 12–14
Ad execution–related thoughts, 174–175
Adjacencies, 393
Adoption model, 162–163
Adoption rate
    Internet, 500–501
    mobile devices, 522–523
Ad recall, engagement and, 345*f*
Ads Leaderboard, 733
Ad-supported video on demand (VOD), 472
Ad-to-consumer relevance, 272
Advanced delivery systems (ADS), 394
AD*VANTAGE Pulse surveys, 628*f*
Advergame, 471
Advertainment, 471
Advertiser/controller
    cons, 755–756
    pros, 754–755
Advertisers
    IMC process and, 71
    leading in U.S. 2015, 18*f*

risks of celebrity endorsements, 195–196
    self-regulation, 692
Advertiser-supported syndication, 391
Advertising
    ageism, digital media and, 158–159
    awards for, 611–612
    carryover effect, 226
    centralized system of, 73–74
    classifications of, 20*f*
    client's role in, 72–79
    comparative, 209–210
    decentralized system of, 74–77
    direct marketing and, 483
    effectiveness of, belief in, 242–243
    ethics, 735–737
    feel-good placement and, 216–217
    framework for studying operation of, 178*f*
    future of television and, 377–378
    global trust in, 737*f*
    growth of promotion and, 5–6
    as information, 761–763
    in-house agencies and, 77–79
    market power and, 760–761
    message recall, 205*f*
    mobile, 522–525
    personal selling and, 781–782
    political attack ads, 212–213
    price and, 64
    promotion mix and, 17–19
    recessions and, 241*f*
    response process and, 177–178
    ROI on various types of, 253*f*
    role of, 66
    spending, 6
    subliminal, 123
    See also Digital advertising;
        Global advertising;
        International advertising;
        Internet advertising
Advertising agency, 71
    account services, 83–85
    client retention/loss evaluating, 95–101
    collateral services, 104
    compensation, 90–95. *See also* Agency compensation systems

consolidation of, 82
    creative boutiques, 88–89
    creative services, 86–87
    departmental/group system, 87–88
    digital/interactive, 103–104
    direct-marketing, 101–102
    full-service type, 83
    future foundations of, 107*f*
    geographic locations of, 81
    integrated services, pros/cons, 106–107
    international advertising and, 672–674
    management/finance, 87
    marketing services, 85–86
    media specialist companies, 90
    organizational systems comparison, 79*f*
    public relations firms, 102–103
    reasons to use, 83
    sales promotion, 102
    self-regulation and, 692
    top U.S., 80*f*
Advertising and Social Change (Berman), 747
Advertising appeals
    defined, 303
    emotional, 304–307
    global advertising and, 668–669
    informational/rational, 303–304. *See also* Informational/rational appeals
    international advertising and, 675
    rational/emotional, combining, 308–309
    reminder advertising, 309–310
    teaser advertising, 310–311
    user-generated content (UGC), 311
Advertising associations, self-regulation and, 697, 698*f*
Advertising campaigns, 285–286
Advertising creativity, 270, 271. *See also* Creativity, advertising
Advertising execution. *See* Creative execution

Advertising manager, 73, 76
Advertising media, ROI ratings of various, 253*f*. *See also* Media *entries*
Advertising Pure and Simple (Sneiden), 274
Advertising sales relationship, share of, 256*f*
Advertising scheduling, 356–358
Advertising Self-Regulatory Council (ASRC), 694–697
Advertising substantiation, 707–709
Advertising-to-sales ratio, by industry, 248*f*–249*f*
Advocacy advertising, corporate, 603–605
Aerial advertising, 457–458
Affective stage, 162*f*, 164
Affect referral decision rule, 127
Affiliates, 387
Affirmative disclosure, 706–707
Affordable method, of budgeting, 246–247
African Americans, stereotypes, 751–753
Age
    ageism, digital media and, 158–159
    advertising messages and, 156
    celebrity endorsement receptivity and, 194–195
    digital media use and, 221
    marketing campaigns and, 202
    media choices and, 351
    radio formats by group, 407*f*
    teenagers, global marketing and, 669–670
    YouTube stars, and, 200–201
    See also Demographics
Agency compensation systems
    commission system, 91–92
    cost-plus agreement, 93
    fee arrangement, 92
    future of, 94–95
    incentive-based, 93
    percentage charges, 93
Age segmentation, 53–54
AIDA model of response, 161, 162*f*
Alcohol advertising, 691, 693, 702, 719–720, 736

Allocation, budget. *See* Promotional budget

Alpha activity, physiological testing and, 632–633

Alternative delivery systems (ADS), 377–378

Alternative evaluation
criteria/consequences, 124–125
evoked set, 122, 124

Alternative media, 455, 475–476

American Advertising Federation Principles and Practices for Advertising Ethics, 739*f*

Analysis
communication process, 36–37
competitive, 46–48
external, 35–36
internal, 34–35
internal/external, 36*f*
opportunity, 45–46

Android operation system, 23, 25

Animatic, 285

Animation, advertising and, 315–316

Appeals. *See* Advertising appeals

Application, positioning and, 59–60

Apps
Bazaarvoice, 23
Fashim, 23
Google Play store, 78
Groupon, 555
interstitial, 505
live streaming, Periscope, 517
magazine readers, 417
mobile marketing and, 22–23, 522
online behavioral advertising and, 696
Purchx, 23
RedLaser, 23
regulation and, 714
Shazam (QR codes), 519
ShopSavvy, 23
SitOrSquat, 4, 5
Taco Bell Mobile Ordering and Payment, 321
uses of, 25
virtual/augmented reality, 519
WeChat, 659, 685
YouTube for kids, 743

Arbitrary allocation, budget setting, 247

Arguments, consumer communications, 173–174

Art department, ad agency, 86

Artistic value, in advertising, 272

Art of Thought, The (Wallas), 277–278

Aspirational reference groups, 136

"As Seen on TV," 492

Associations, for self-regulatory advertising, 694–697

Association tests, 117*f*, 620*f*

Associative process, 130

Athletes, celebrity endorsements and, 193. *See also* Celebrity endorsements

Attack advertising, political, 210, 212–213

Attainable objectives, 224

Attention
movie theater advertising, 469
nontraditional media, 476
television advertising and, 380, 384–386

Attitudes
attitude change strategies, 126
ELM and, 175
multiattribute attitude models, 125–126
public, evaluate/determine, PR and, 585–586

Attitude surveys, corporate advertising, 607

Attitude toward the ad, 174–175

Attorneys, advertising and, 702

Attractiveness, of spokespeople, 192–201, 203

Attributes, positioning and, 59

Attribution theory, 574–575

Audience
celebrity endorsement receptivity, 194–195
DAGMAR and target, 233
development in measures of, 403–404
identify target, 160–161
identify target, media planning, 347–349
international advertising, measures of, 677
levels of aggregation, 160*f*
local, information on, 402
magazine, total/pass-along, 432
magazine ad planning, research data, 432–433
measures of, 400–401

narrowcasting, cable television and, 396
national, information on, 401–402
Nielsen Audio, radio and, 412–413
RADAR (radio audience measure), 414
radio, limited attention, 409, 410
selectivity, television advertising and, 384
share of, 401
See also Target audience

Audience, for PR
civic/business organizations, 589
community members, 588
educators, 589
employees, 587
external, 587
financial groups, 589–590
government, 589
internal, 587
media, 589
stakeholders/investors, 587–588
suppliers/customers, 588–589

Audience contacts, IMC and, 27–31
company-created, 28
customer-initiated, 29
intrinsic touch points, 28
paid/owned/earned media, 30*f*
unexpected touch points, 28–29

Audio elements, of commercials, 324–327

Augmented reality, 519

Average frequency, 363–364

Average quarter-hour (AQH) figure, 412–413

Average quarter-hour rating (AQH RTG), 413

Average quarter-hour share (AQH SHR), 413

Awards, advertising, 611–612

Awareness
DAGMAR and, 233
Internet advertising creates, 501
nontraditional media, 476
trade shows and, 569

B

Baby boomers, 525
age segment, 53–54
brand image and, 43, 44

Background research, creative process, 278–279

Balance-of-trade deficit, 654

Banner ads, online, 330–331, 504

Banner blindness, 330

Barrier to entry, competition, 758–759

Barter syndication, 391

Bazaarvoice (app), 23

Behavior, consumer. *See* Consumer behavior

Behavioral targeting, Internet advertising and, 506

Behavioristic segmentation, 56

Behavior learning theory
application of shaping procedures, 133*f*
classical conditioning, 130–132
cognitive learning theory, 133–134
operant conditioning, 132–133

BehaviorScan, 639

Below-the-line media, 455

Benchmark measures, 234

Benefits, positioning and, 59

Benefit segmentation, 56

Better Business Bureau (BBB), 694

Bias
interviewers and, 636
in source/spokespeople, 187
spokesperson product promotion, 190
testing, 621

Big data, programmatic advertising and, 339. *See also* Data *entries*

Big idea, 267, 289, 296–297

Billboards, digital, 458–459. *See also* Outdoor advertising

Billings, 79

Bleed pages, in magazine ads, 424

Blended compensation plans, 92

Blimps, advertising and, 458

Blogs, 152, 153, 190
advertising and, 518
as earned media, 30
endorsements and, 689–690, 728
influence marketing and, 520
personal selling, Internet and, 785
Pinterest and, 516
PR and, 591
product consideration/evaluation, 503

clutter, 217
context/environment, effects
of, 216–217
information processing rates,
216
personal v. nonpersonal, 215
Channel/presentation,
persuasion matrix,
185–186
Channels of communication,
149–150
Chat rooms, 153
Chief executive officer, 78,
190–191
Chief financial officers (CFOs),
94
Chief marketing officer (CMO),
78
Children
advertising to, 664–665,
699f, 715, 742–747
Internet, time spent on, 743f
online marketing to,
regulations, 727–728
Parents' Bill of Rights
(Commercial Alert), 744,
746f
Children's Advertising Review
Unit, 723
Children's Online Privacy
Protection Act, 722,
727–728
Children's Television Act, 715
Cinema, ROI advertising and,
253f
Circulation
magazine, primary/
guaranteed, 430
newspaper, 438, 443–444, 448
verification services, 430–432
City zone, 443
Civic organizations, as PR
audience, 589
Classical conditioning
applying, 131–132
defining, 130
instrumental conditioning, 132f
music in advertising and,
325–326
process, 131f
Classified advertising, 440, 447f
Clayton Act, 703
Click-through rates (CTRs),
329, 504, 507
Client–agent policies, budget
allocation and, 258–259
Client evaluation/approval, of
creative output, 332–336
Clients
agencies add value to, 96f
agency relationships and, 97

how agencies gain, 99
IMC process and, 71
role, advertising/promotion,
72–79
why agencies lose, 98–99
Clipping service, 251
Close, 776
Clutter
in branded entertainment,
474
couponing and, 553
Internet/digital/social media
advertising, 529
magazine advertising and,
429–430
message channel and, 217
movie theater advertising,
468
music in commercials and,
325
newspaper advertising and,
443
PR, avoidance and, 593
radio advertising and,
410–411
spot advertising and, 391
television advertising and,
384–385
Cognitive/behavioral stage,
162f, 165
Cognitive dissonance, 129
Cognitive learning theory,
133–134
Cognitive orientation, 130
Cognitive response approach,
communications, 171–172,
174f
Cognitive stage, 162f, 164
Collateral services
advertising agencies and, 104
IMC and, 71f, 72
Collectivism, 660
College football, broadcast
rights and, 382–383
College newspapers, 439
Color
branding and, 111–112
magazine advertising and,
424, 433–434
newspaper advertising and,
445
perception and, 122
Comarketing, 540–541
Combination rates, 445
Combination style advertising,
319
Commerce ads, online, 330
Commercial ratings (C3), 403
Commercials. See Television
advertising
Commercial speech, 702

Commission system
ad agency compensation,
91–92
payment, 91f
Common ground,
communications and,
155, 157
Communication
ad execution thoughts, 174–175
cognitive response approach,
171–172, 174f
defining, 145
effectiveness, determine,
163–164
elaboration likelihood model
(ELM), 175–177
flow of marketing
information, to creative
staff, 289f
IMC objectives, 223
international marketing,
issues and, 146–147
language as barrier to, 145
mass, 161
product/message thoughts,
172–174
source-oriented thoughts, 174
See also Information
Communication Effects
Pyramid, 229f
Communication model, 146, 147f
channel, 149–150
message, 149
noise, message distortion,
156–157
receiver/decoding, 155–156
response/feedback, 157–158
source encoding, 147–149
viral marketing, 150–153
Communication objectives, 37
DAGMAR goals and, 232–
233. See also DAGMAR,
objective setting and
effects pyramid, 229–230
IMC program, setting for,
236–238
issues in setting, 235–238
issues with, 230–232
marketing v., 224–225
promotional planners and,
235–236
purchase funnel, 232f
sales, 225–228
social consumer decision
making, 237f
traditional advertising-based
view of marketing, 236f
Communication process,
analysis of, 36–37
Communications Act of 1934,
715

Communications management,
IMC, 31
Communications program
develop, IMC and, 37–38
Communications situation, 137
Communications task, 232–233.
See also DAGMAR,
objective setting and
Community antenna television
(CATV), 394
Community members, as PR
audience, 588
Company-created touch points,
28
Comparative advertising, 209–
210, 313, 665
Comparison
brand, 189
media costs and, 367–369
Competition
advertising effects on,
758–759
in branded entertainment,
474
in magazine advertising,
429–430
sales promotion growth and,
540–541
Competitive advantage appeals,
304
Competitive analysis, 46–48
Competitive parity method, of
budget setting
competitor outlay, 252f
defining, 251
return on investment (ROI)
method, 252
top-down budgeting methods,
252
Competitor, positioning by, 61
Competitor advertising
spending, 252f
Compliance, 204
Comprehension
DAGMAR and, 233
reaction tests and, 620f, 624
Comprehensive measures,
broadcast commercials
and, 637–638
Computer simulation models,
of budget setting,
256–257
Concave-downward function
model, 244
Concentrated marketing, 58
Concept tests, 620f, 622–623
Conclusion drawing, message
structure, 206
Conditioned response, 131
Conditioned stimulus, 131
Condoms, 739–740

Coverage, of advertising, 343, 380

Creative Advertising (Pricken), 318

Creative aspects, of media strategy, 365

Creative boutiques, 88–89

Creative brief, 85, 286–290

Creative execution style, 303
  animation, 315–316
  combination advertising, 319
  comparison, 313
  defining, 311–312
  demonstration, 313
  dramatization, 317–318
  humor, 318
  imagery, 316–317
  personality symbols, 316
  scientific/technical evidence, 313
  slice of life, 314–315
  straight-sell/factual message, 312
  testimonial, 313–314

Creative factors, in frequency, 365*f*

Creative output, evaluation/ approval of, 332–336

Creative process
  account planning, 278
  background research, 278–279
  inputs, verification/revision, 284–285
  models of, 277–278
  product- or service-specific preplanning input, 279–280
  qualitative research input, 280–284

Creative selling, personal selling and, 774, 775*f*

Creative services, ad agency, 86–87

Creative space buys, in magazines, 425

Creative strategy, 37, 266
  advertising campaigns, 285–286
  big idea, 296–297
  brand image, create, 292–294
  challenges, 274
  creative brief, 286–290
  hard-sell *v*. creative, 275–276
  inherent drama, 294–295
  major selling idea, 290–292
  marketing information flow, 289*f*
  personnel, 276–277
  positioning, 294–295
  risk taking, 275

slogans/taglines, creating, 285, 286–287
  unique selling position (USP), 292

Creative Strategy in Advertising (Jeweler), 290

Creative tactics, 266
  client evaluation/approval of output, 332–336
  online advertising, 329–332
  in print advertising, 319–323
  for television advertising, 323–329
  See also specific media

Creativity
  DAGMAR and, 235
  importance of, 267–270

Creativity, advertising and
  defining, 270
  determinants of, 271–274
  effectiveness measures and, 616–617
  international, 674–676
  Internet/digital/social media, 528
  mobile, 524
  perspectives on, 270–271
  sales, impact on, 274*f*
  television, 379–380

Credibility
  PR and, 592–593
  source factor, 187

Credit cards, direct marketing and, 482–483

CRM. *See* Customer relationship management

Cross sell, 776

Crowdsource ideas, 514

Cultural consequences, advertising, 747–748
  African Americans/ Hispanics, 751–752
  LGBT, 753–754
  mental health, 752–753
  persuasion dichotomy, 749–750
  racial equality, 752–753
  women, stereotyping, 750–751

Cultural meaning, celebrity endorsements, 199

Cultural symbols, positioning and, 61

Cultural values, 660

Culture
  consumer behavior and, 134–135
  international marketing and, 658–659

Cume (cumulative audience), 413

Customer analysis, 36*f*

Customer engagement, advertising and, 320–321

Customer-initiated touch points, 29

Customer Lifetime Value (CLTV), 494

Customer/organization interactions, on Internet, 504*f*

Customer relationship management (CRM), 21, 768
  software for, 772
  technology and, 773

Customers, as PR audience, 588–589

Cyberattacks, 682

D

DAGMAR, objective setting and
  assessing, 234
  concrete measurable tests, 233
  criticisms of, 234–235
  goals of, 232–233
  specified time period, 234
  target audience, 233

Daily inch rate, newspaper advertising, 368*f*

Daily newspapers, 438

Data
  audience information and, 400–402
  local audience information, 402
  magazine ad planning, 432–433
  national audience information, 401–402
  newspaper circulation, 443–444
  Nielsen Audio audience information, 412–413
  out of home media, measures, 465
  radio advertising, limited, 409
  real-time, 540
  ROI and, 612

Databases
  customer information and, 21
  loyalty programs and, 561–562
  programmatic advertising and, 339

Data collection, eye tracking, mouse-hovering, 630–631

Data security principle, of self-regulation, 697*f*

Day-after recall (DAR) testing, 637, 638*f*

Dayparts, 393

Dealer incentives, 536*f*

Decentralization, international advertising and, 671

Decentralized system, of advertising, 74–77, 79*f*

Deception, 705

Deceptive advertising
  corrective advertising and, 710–713
  ethics and, 737–738
  FTC and, 704–706
  on Internet, 529, 703
  toning shoes, 711–712

Decision makers, 137

Decision rules, 126–127

Decoding, communications and, 155–156

Defining Advertising Goals for Measured Advertising Results (DAGMAR), 232–233

Demographic market, sales promotion targets, 547–548

Demographics
  age, advertising and, 156
  ageism, digital media and, 158–159
  Facebook advertising and, 512, 513*f*
  Hispanic market, growth of, 54–55
  international marketing and, 657–658
  lifestyle, advertising and, 350–351
  LinkedIn, 516
  media usage, sample, 357*f*
  mobile device use and, 554
  Pinterest use, 516
  race/ethnicities, subcultures and, 135
  radio format by age group, 407*f*
  sample data, 348*f*, 349*f*
  social media use and, 22
  Spanish-language programming, 388
  where to promote?, 349–350
  See also Age; Baby boomers; Generation Y; Millennials

Demographic segmentation, 52*f*, 53–54

Demographic selectivity, magazines and, 422

Demonstration, ad execution, 313

Departmental system, ad agency, 87–88

Federal Trade Commission Act, 702–703, 721, 726
Federal Trade Commission (FTC), 703
    advertising substantiation, 707–709
    affirmative disclosure, 706–707
    complaint procedure, 712*f*
    consent/cease-and-desist orders, 709–710
    corrective advertising, 710–713
    deceptive advertising, 704–706, 710–711
    developments, 713–714
    Internet advertising, 726–729
    online endorsements and, 689–690
    sales promotions regulations, 722–726
    unfairness, 704
    See also Federal advertising regulations; Organization index
Fee–commission combination, 92
Feedback
    apps and, 23
    audience, 161
    concept testing and, 623
    direct marketing, 495
    direct network for, 777
    focus groups and, 280–282
    message receiver, 157–158
    methods of obtaining, 164*f*
    reviews, Yelp, 29
    sampling and, 550
    See also Effectiveness, measuring; Measures
Feel-good programming, 216–217
Field of experience, communications and, 155–156
Field tests, 620*f*, 621
Fifth Amendment, 719
Financial audit, 96
Financial groups, as PR audience, 589–590
Financial support, corporate advertising and, 601
Firearms, advertising and, 700, 719–720
Fire starting, personal selling and, 772
First Amendment, advertising and, 210, 460, 693–694, 701–702, 713, 723
First cover, magazine ad, 433
First-run syndicated programs, 391

Fitness industry, advertising substantiation and, 708
Fixed-fee method, of compensation, 92
Fixed transaction, 503
Flat rates, 445
Fleeting message, television advertising and, 384
Flesch formula, 627
Flesch Kincaid Reading Ease Score, 627
Flexibility
    in advertising, 272
    factors in media strategy, 366
    geographic, outdoor advertising and, 462
    in magazine advertising options, 424–425
    newspaper advertising, 440–441
    promotional products, 465
    of radio advertising, 408
    spot and local advertising, 390–392
    television advertising, 380–382
Flighting, advertising scheduling, 356, 358*f*
fMRI, neuromarketing and, 138, 630, 633
Focus groups, 117*f*, 138, 280–282, 607
    weakness of, 623*f*
Food and Drug Administration
    advertising regulations and, 715–719
    direct-to-consumer drug advertising and, 718–719
Food industry, FDA, advertising restrictions and, 716–719
Foreign-language newspapers, 439
Four Ps of marketing, 8
44 Liquormart, Inc. v. Rhode Island, 702
Fragmentation, radio advertising and, 409
Freedom of speech. *See* First Amendment
Free goods, 567
Freestanding insert (FSI), 553*f*, 546, 551, 552, 554, 643*f*
Frequency
    of association, 131
    branded entertainment, 472
    direct marketing, 494
    promotional products, 465
    transit advertising, 463
Frequency, of advertising, 359–360, 359*f*
    average, 363–364

effects of reach and, 362*f*
factors in determining levels of, 365*f*
limited, magazine ads, 428
outdoor, 462
Frequency, of exposure, media vehicles, 343
Frequency program, 561–562
Fry Graph Readability, 627
FSI. *See* Freestanding insert
FTC v. Raladam Co., 703
Full-service agency, 83, 84*f*
    account services, 83–84
    departmental/group system of, 87–88
    management/finance, 87
    marketing services, 85–86
    organizational chart, 84*f*
Functional consequences, 124
Fundraising, nonprofits, Internet and, 522

G

Gallup and Robinson's Impact System, 626*f*
Galvanic skin response (GSR), physiological testing and, 630–631
Game, 557
Gas station pump ads, 475
Gatefold ads, in magazines, 424
Gender
    ethics, advertising and, 736–339
    sex in advertising, attitudes by, 741*f*
    stereotypes, 749–750
General advertising, 440
General advertising rates, 444
General preplanning input, 279
Generation Benchmark Survey, 777*f*
Generation X, 159, 525
Generation Y, 48–49
Generation Z, 321
Geographic coverage
    cable television and, 397
    Facebook advertising and, 512, 513*f*
    media planning, 356
    MTV, 398
    radio/digital media, 410
    sweeps periods, 402
Geographic flexibility, outdoor advertising and, 462
Geographic locations, advertising agencies, 81
Geographic markets, sales promotions target, 547–548

Geographic segmentation, 51–53
Geographic selectivity
    magazine advertising and, 422
    newspapers, 438–439, 441
    television advertising and, 383
GfK International purchase funnel, 231, 232*f*
Gift-with-purchase promotions, 575
Global advertising
    advantages of, 666–667
    localized *v.*, 665–670
    problems with, 667–668
Global brands, best, 15*f*
Global consumer culture theory (GCCT), 666
Global economy, 654, 656
Globalization, when appropriate?, 668–669
Global marketing
    advantages of, 666–667
    celebrity endorsements, 193
    similarity, source, 192
    spending, 6
Global Perspective
    celebrity endorsements, abroad, 188–189
    FIFA World Cup, Qatar, 662–663
    international marketing, communication issues and, 146–147
    marketing, China, growth of, 658–659
Global positioning satellite (GPS), 461
Global products, local message, 670
Global Responsibility Annual Report, 35
Global Technology Adoption Index (GTAI), 595
Global Trust in Advertising, 737*f*
Goodwill, promotional products, 466
Government regulations, international advertising, 663–664
Gratitude Passion Index, 645*f*
Great Depression, 533
Great Recession, 15, 320, 533
Gross domestic product (GDP), 658
Gross ratings points (GPRs), reach and, 361–362
Group, as audience, 160

effectiveness measures and, 616

eye movement, 632*f*

magazine ad planning data, 432–433

qualitative input, creative process, 280–284

radio advertising, limited data on, 409

sabotage, competitor, 621

Research, message effectiveness and

budgeting decisions, 619

current methods issues, 641–642

field tests, 620*f*, 621

five guiding principles of digital measurement, 622*f*

how to, 621–622

laboratory tests, 620–621

media strategies, 619

message variables, 618–619

positioning advertising copy testing (PACT), 621*f*, 641–642, 642–642

posttesting, 619, 620

pretesting, 619–620

source factors, 618

testing methods, classification, 620*f*

testing process. *See* Testing process

what to test, 618–619

when to test, 619–620

where to test, 620–621

Research department, of ad agency, 85–86

Reseller, sales promotions and, 566*f*

Residuals, 328

Response, message receiver, 157–158

Response advertisement, 597

Response functions, advertising/ sales, 244*f*

Response hierarchy models

AIDA model, 161, 162*f*

alternative models, 165*f*

dissonance/attribution, 165*f*, 166–167

evaluating traditional, 164–165

hierarchy of effects, 162

implications, 163–164, 168–169

information processing, 163

innovation adoption model, 162–163

issues with, DAGMAR and, 234–235

low-involvement, 165*f*, 167–168

response process, 162*f*

social consumer decision-making, 169–171

standard learning, 165–166

Response process, advertising effects and, 177–178

Results-Oriented-Integration, 474

Retail advertising, 227

physiological testing and, 630–631

rates, newspaper, 444

Retailers

brand displays and, 565

growth/power of, 537–538

Retail/local advertising, 20*f*

Retail Promotion Effectiveness solution, 643

Retail trading zones, 443

Retargeting, Internet advertising, 506

Retention, Internet metric, 526

Return on investment (ROI)

budgeting method, 252

celebrity endorsements and, 196–198

competitive parity method, 252

data and, 612

e-mail marketing and, 489

Internet metrics, 526

marketing PR and, 583

programmatic advertising and, 339

types of, 253*f*

Revision, creative input, 284–285

RFM analysis, direct marketing, 494

Rich media

defined, 508

online commercials, 508

other forms of, 508

video on demand, 508

webisodes, 508

Risks, in creative strategy, 275

Risk-takers, 351

Robinson-Patman Act, 723

ROI budgeting method, 252

Rough tests, 620*f*, 624*f*

Run-of-book ad, 433

Run of paper (ROP), 445

S

Safari mobile browser, 12

Sales

creativity impact on, 274*f*

factors influencing, 226*f*

Internet metrics, 526

Sales force evaluation criteria, 787*f*

Sales objectives, 225

DAGMAR and, 235

issues with, 225–226

when to use, 227–228

Salespeople

buyers likes/dislikes about, 779*f*

traits of successful, 778*f*

Salespeople, as personal channels, 150

Sales potential, Internet/digital/ social media, 528

Sales promotion

abuse, 574–576

accountability and, 540

agencies of, shifting roles, 574*f*

attribution theory and, 574–575

bonus packs, 560

brand loyalty, declining, 538

brand proliferation, 539

budget allocation, 572

competition and, 540–541

consumer franchise-building (CFB), 544–545

consumer love of, 542–543

consumer-oriented, 548–550, 563*f*

contests/sweepstakes, 557–559

cooperative advertising, 570–571

criticism of, 542–544

defining, 23–25,

digital marketing, 541–542

direct marketing and, 484

displays/point-of-purchase, 568–569

economic development, 680

effectiveness measures, 643–644

event marketing, 562–563

growth of, 536–537

IMC tools/advertising coordination, 571–573

increase in, reasons for, 537

international advertising and, 654–655

international marketing and, 677–681

on Internet, 519, 521

loyalty programs, 561–562

market maturity and, 680

media support, timing and, 573

nonfranchise-building (non-FB), 545

personal selling and, 783–784

premiums, free/self-liquidating, 555–557

price-off deals, 560–561

promotional sensitivity, 539

refunds/rebates, 559–560

regulations and, 681, 722–726

resellers and, 566*f*

retailers, growth/power of, 537–538

sales training programs, 569

scope/role of, 535–536

short-term focus, 539–540

social media, reasons to connect on, 542*f*

themes/ads, coordination of, 572–573

trade shows, 569, 570

trade structure and, 680

trap, 575*f*

types of activities, 536*f*

See also Consumer–oriented sales promotion; Trade-oriented sales promotion

Sales promotion agency, 102

Sales/response advertising functions, 244*f*

Sales response models, budget and, 243–244

Sales review process, 786*f*

Sales training programs, 569

Salient attributes, 59

Salient beliefs, 125–126

Samples, 536*f*

Sampling

benefits/limitations/methods, 548–550

demonstration program, 162–163

SAP software, 772

SAS software, 772

Satellite broadcast, 377–378, 677

Satisfaction, 128

Saturation, promotional products, 466

ScanTrack, 644

Scatter market, 390

Schedules of reinforcement, 132–133

Scheduling, media planning, 356–358*f*

Scientific evidence, ad execution, 313

Scratch-and-sniff ads, in magazines, 424

Script, television commercial, 328

Seamless communication, 9

Search, 505

Search engine optimization (SEO), 506